AF512056

Digital Signal Processing

(*for* Computer Science & Information Technology)

Digital Signal Processing

(*for* Computer Science & Information Technology)

Dr. S.Palani

Dean and Professor,
Department of Electronics and Communication Engineering,
Sudharsan Engineering College,
Pudukkottai

Former Professor and Head,
National Institute of Technology
Tiruchirappali

☆

D. Kalaiyarasi

Assistant Professor in Department of ECE,
Panimalar Engineering College,
Chennai

Ane Books Pvt. Ltd.

New Delhi ♦ Chennai

Digital Signal Processing: for Computer Science & Information Technology

Dr. S. Palani & D. Kalaiyarasi

© Authors

First Edition : 2022

Price: ₹795/-

Pages: 825 (PB)

Size : (7.25" × 9.50")

Paper Quality (GSM) : 80

Published by

Ane Books Pvt. Ltd.
4821, Parwana Bhawan, 1st Floor, 24 Ansari Road,
Darya Ganj, **New Delhi** - 110 002, India
Tel.: +91(011) 23276843-44, Fax: +91(011) 23276863
e-mail: kapoor@anebooks.com, Website: www.anebooks.com

Branch Office:

- Avantika Niwas, 1st Floor, 19 Doraiswamy Road, T. Nagar, **Chennai** - 600 017, Tel.: +91(044) 28141554, 28141209
  e-mail: anebooks_tn@airtelmail.in

Disclaimer: Please be informed that the author and the publisher have put in their best efforts in producing this book. Every care has been taken to ensure the accuracy of the contents. However, we make no warranties for the same and therefore shall not be responsible or liable for any loss or any commercial damages accruing thereof. Neither the publisher nor the author is engaged in providing services of any professional nature and shall therefore not be responsible for any incidental, consequential, special or any other damages. Please do consult a professional where appropriate.

ISBN : 978-93-8061-838-8

All rights reserved. No part of this book may be reproduced in any form including photocopying, microfilms, photoprints, storage in any retrieval system, transmission in any permanent or temporary form, without the prior written consent of the publisher.

Printed at : R.K. Offset Process, New Delhi.

PINGALA *(200BC) in India invented that any number can merely be represented by binary system using* **1s** *and* **0s**. *A spiritual significance of this is that* **1** *represented a symbol for* **GOD** *while* **0** *represented nothingness. God created the universe out of nothing. This book is dedicated to the father of the Universe, THE GOD.*

Preface

Signal processing is all about taking a signal, applying some changes to it and then getting a new signal out. The change might be amplification or filtration or something else, but nearly all electronic circuits can be considered as signal processors. Thus, the signal processor might be composed of discrete components like capacitors and resistors, or it could be a complex integrated circuits, or it could be a digital system which accepts a signal on its input and outputs the changed signal. Digital Signal Processing (DSP) is the processing of signals by digital means. The term 'digital' comes from 'digit', meaning a number and so 'digital' literally means numerical. A signal carries a stream of information representing anything from stock prices to data from a remote sensing satellite. If they are represented in the form of stream of numbers, they are called digital signals. The processing of a digital signal is done by Digital Signal Processor (DSP) by performing numerical calculations. Digital signal processors require several things to work properly. The processor should be fast enough with enough precision to support the required mathematics it needs to implement. It requires memory to store programming, samples, intermediate results and final results. It also requires A/D and D/A converters to bring real signals into and out of the digital domain. Further, it requires programming to do the job.

The main application of DSP are audio signal processing, audio compression, digital image processing, video compression, speech processing, speech recognition, digital communications, Radar, Sonar, Seismology and biomedicine. Specific examples include speech compression and transmission in digital mobile phones, room matching equalization of sound, analysis and control of industrial process, seismic data processing, medical imaging such as CAT scans and MRI, MP3 compression, image manipulation, computer-generated animations in movies, high fidelity loud speaker cross overs and equalization, audio effects *etc.* Digital signal processing is often implemented using specialized microprocessors such as the DSP 56000, the TMS320 or the SHARC. Multi-core implementations of DSPs have started to emerge from companies including Free scale and stream processors.

The book is divided into six chapters. Chapter 1 deals with the representations of discrete signals and systems. It motivates the reader as to what signals and systems are and how they are related to other areas such as communication systems, signal processing, computer science and engineering, electrical engineering, information technology, data compression *etc.* Further, in this chapter various terminologies related to signals and systems are defined. Further more mathematical descriptions representations and classifications of signals and systems are explained.

The discrete time sequence $x[n]$ can be transformed as $X(j\omega)$ by Fourier transform and can be analyzed using digital computer. However, $X(j\omega)$ is a continuous function of frequency ω and computationally difficulties are encountered while analyzing $X(j\omega)$ using DSP. In Chapter 2, we convert $X(j\omega)$ into equally spaced samples. Such a sequence is called discrete Fourier transform (DFT) which is a powerful computational tool for the frequency analysis of discrete time signals. Several methods are available for computing DFT. However fast Fourier transform (FFT) algorithms eliminate redundant calculations and offer rapid frequency domain analysis. In Chapter 2 the properties of DFT, FFT algorithms, decimation in time and decimation in frequency, linear filtering and correlation are discussed.

The digital filters are classified as Infinite Impulse Response (IIR) and Finite Impulse Response (FIR) filters. Digital IIR filter design procedure is the extension of analog filter design. In Chapter 3, designs of IIR filter using impulse invariant method and bilinear transformation are described. IIR filter is also designed using system function $H(s)$. Low pass IIR Butterworth Chebyshev digital filter designs are also described in this chapter.

Design techniques for finite impulse response digital filter are discussed in Chapter 4. These filters are designed using windows such as rectangular window, Hamming window, Kaiser window and Hanning window. FIR filters are designed using frequency sampling method.

The linear time invariant discrete time system is described by linear differential equation with constant coefficients. These coefficients and the signal variables are assumed, when implemented in digital hardware to take a specified range and stored in finite length in a digital machine. During discritization and quantization processes errors occur in different form. They are discussed in Chapter 5. Quantization noise, over flow error, limit cycle oscillations, signal scaling and sampling and hold operations are also discussed in this chapter.

Modern digital systems require to process data at more than one sampling rate. This is called multi-rate processing which has two primary operations namely decimation and interpolation which alter the data rate in an efficient manner. While decimation reduces the sampling rate, interpolation increases the sampling rate. In Chapter 6, multi-rate digital signal processing is discussed in detail and presented. Sampling rate reduction (down sampling) sampling rate increase (up sampling), sampling rate conversion, polyphase implementation of interpolation are discussed in this chapter.

The notable features of this book include the following:

1. The syllabus content of Digital Signal Processing of undergraduate level of most of the Indian Universities has been well covered.
2. The organization of the chapters is sequential in nature.
3. Large number of numerical examples have been worked out.
4. Learning objectives and summary are given in each chapter.
5. For the students to practice, short and long questions with answers are given at the end of each chapter.

The authors take this opportunity to thank Shri Sunil Saxena, Managing Director, Ane Books Pvt. Ltd, India, for coming forward to publish this book. We would like to express our sincere thanks to Shri A. Rathinam, General Manager (South), Ane Books Pvt. Ltd., who took the initiatives to publish the book in a short span of time. We would like to express our sincere thanks to Mr. V. Ashok who has done a wonderful job to key the voluminous book like this in a very short time and beautifully too. Suggestions and constructive criticisms are welcome from staff and students.

THE AUTHORS

About the Authors

Dr. Sankaran Palani obtained his B.E. degree in Electrical Engineering in the year 1966 from University of Madras, M.Tech. in Control Systems Engineering from IIT Kharagpur in 1968 and Ph.D in Control Systems Engineering from University of Madras in 1982 with academic excellence. He has wide teaching experience of over four decades. He started his teaching career in the year 1968 at the erstwhile Regional Engineering College (Now National Institute of Technology), Tiruchirapalli in the department of EEE and occupied various positions. As Professor and Head, he took the initiatives to start the Instrumentation and Control Engineering Department. After a meritorious service of more than three decades in REC, Tiruchirapalli, he joined Sudharsan Engineering College, Pudukkottai as the founder Principal. He established various departments with massive infrastructure. Since 2006, he is the Dean and Professor of ECE department in the same college.

He has published more than fifty research papers in reputed national and international journals and conferences and has won many cash awards. His notable research work includes the first paper, at the international level, on stepper motor non-linear model published in IEEE Transaction on Automatic Control in the year 1969. Under his guidance four scholars were awarded Ph.D and 14 scholars are pursuing Ph.D. He has carried out several research projects funded by Government of India and other agencies. As the theme leader of the Indo - UK, REC Project on energy, he has visited many Universities and industries in United Kingdom. He is the author of the books titled Control Systems Engineering and Signals and Systems. His areas of research include design of Intelligent Controllers for Dynamic systems, Digital Signal Processing and Image Processing.

D. Kalaiyarasi received B.E. Degree in Electronics and Communication Engineering from the University of Madras in 2000 and M.E. Degree in Power Electronics and Drives from the Anna University in 2006. She has about 10 years of teaching experience. Presently, she is working as Assistant Professor in Department of ECE, Panimalar Engineering College, Chennai. Her area of interest includes Digital Signal Processing and Power Electronics.

Contents

1 Representation of Discrete Signals and Systems

Learning Objectives

After completing this chapter, you should be able to:

- define various terminologies related to signals and systems.
- classify signals and systems.
- give mathematical description and representation of signals and systems.
- perform basic operations on DT signals.
- classify DT signals as periodic and non-periodic, odd and even and power and energy signals.
- classify DT systems.
- find the convolution of DT signals.
- obtain the step response, causality and stability of DT systems.
- describe sampling techniques, quantization, Nyquist rate and aliasing effect.

1.1 Introduction

Most of the signals encountered in science and engineering are analog in nature. That is, the signals are functions of a continuous variable, such as time or space, and usually take on values in a continuous range. Such signals may be processed directly by appropriate analog systems (such as filter or frequency analyzers or frequency multipliers) for the purpose of changing their characteristics or extracting some desired information. In such a case, the signal has been processed directly in its analog form. Both the input signal and the output signal are in analog form and is shown in Figure 1.1(a).

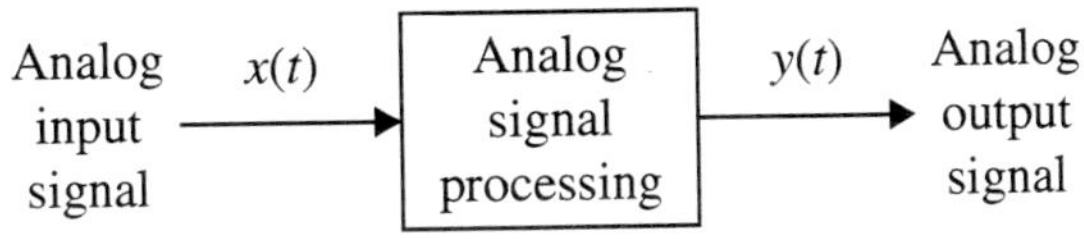

Figure 1.1 (a) Analog signal processing.

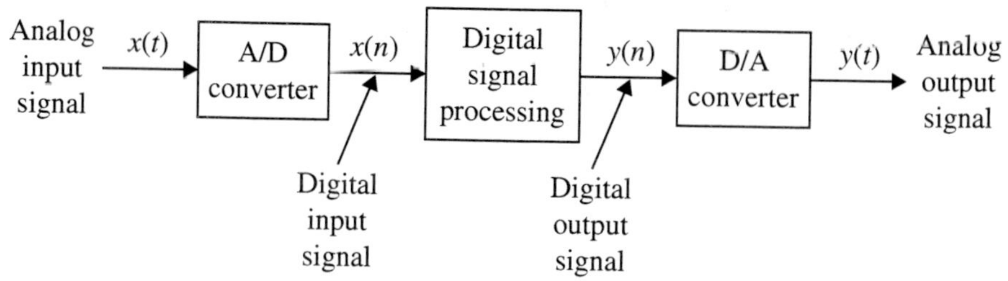

Figure 1.1 (*b*) Digital signal processing.

Digital signal processing provides an alternative method for processing the analog signal and is shown in Figure 1.1(*b*). To perform processing digitally, there is a need for an interface between the analog signal and the digital processor. This interface is called an analog to digital (A/D) converter. The output of A/D converter is a digital signal that is applied as an input to the digital processor.

The digital signal processor may be a large programmable digital computer or a small microprocessor programmed to perform the desired operations on the input signal. Programmable machines provide the flexibility to change the signal processing operation through a change in the software, whereas hardwired machines are difficult to reconfigure. In application where the digital output from the digital signal processor is to be given to the user in analog form we must provide interface and this is called digital to analog (D/A) converter. Thus the signal is provided to the user in analog form.

Digital signal processing has developed very rapidly over the past five decades mainly due to the advances in digital computer technology and very large scale integrated electronic circuits. These inexpensive smaller but faster and more powerful digital computers are capable of performing very complex signal processing functions which are usually too difficult to perform by analog circuitry. The following are the advantages of digital signal processing (DSP) over analog processing.

1. Flexibility : Digital programmable systems allow flexibility in reconfiguring the DSP operations by simply changing the program.
2. Accuracy : DSP provides better control of accuracy requirements, while tolerance limits has to be met in the analog counterpart.
3. Easy storage : Digital signals can be easily stored in magnetic media without deterioation or loss of signal fidelity. They can also be easily transportable and can be processed off-time in remote laboratories.
4. Processing : DSP allows for the implementation of more sophisticated signal processing than its analog counterpart.
5. cost effective : With advancement in VLSI technology digital implementation of the signal process system is cheaper.

The limitation of DSP is that the conversion speed of ADC and the process speed of signal processors should be very high to perform real time processing. Signals of high bandwidth require fast sampling rate ADCs and fast processors.

Some of the applications of digital signal processor are: Speech processing, signal transmission on telephone channels, image processing, biomedical, seismology, consumer electronics.

Speech processing	:	Speech compression and decompression for voice storage system and for transmission and reception of voice signals.
Communication	:	Elimination of noise by filtering and echo cancellation by adaptive filtering in transmission channels.
Biomedical	:	Spectrum analysis of ECG signals to identify various disorders in heart. Spectrum analysis of EEG signals to study the malfunction or disorders in the brain.
Consumer electronics	:	Music synthesis, digital audio and video.
Seismology	:	Spectrum analysis of seismic signals can be used to predict the earthquake, nuclear explosions and earth movement.
Image processing	:	Two dimensional filtering on images for image enhancement, finger print matching, identifying hidden images in the signals received by radars, *etc.*,

The concepts of signals and systems play a very important role in many areas of science and technology. These concepts are very extensively applied in the field of circuit analysis and design, long distance communication, power system generation and distribution, electron devices, electrical machines, biomedical engineering, aeronautics, process control, speech and image processing to mention a few. **Signals represent some independent variables which contain some information about the behavior of some natural phenomenon.** Voltages and currents in electrical and electronic circuits, electromagnetic radio waves, human speech and sounds produced by animals are some of the examples of signals. **When these signals are operated on some objects, they give out signals in the same or modified form. These objects are called systems.** A system is, therefore, defined as the interconnection of objects with a definite relationship between objects and attributes. Signals appearing at various stages of the system are attributes. R, L, C components, spring, dash-pots, mass *etc.* are the objects. The electrical and electronic circuits comprising of R, L, C components and amplifiers, the transmitter and receiver in a communication system, the petrol and diesel engines in an automobile, chemical plants, nuclear reactor, human beings, animals, a government establishment *etc.* are all examples of systems. **In this book, we deal with only discrete signals and systems.**

1.2 Terminologies Related to Signals and Systems

Before we give mathematical descriptions and representations of various terminologies related to signals and systems, the following terminologies which are very frequently used are defined as follows.

1.2.1 Signal

A signal is defined as a physical phenomenon which carries some information or data. The signals are usually functions of independent variable time. There are some cases where the signals are not functions of time. The electrical charge distributed in a body is a signal which is a function of space and not time.

1.2.2 System

A system is defined as the set of interconnected objects with a definite relationship between objects and attributes. The inter-connected components provide desired function.

Objects are parts or components of a system. For example, switches, springs, masses, dash-pots *etc.* in a mechanical systems and inductors, capacitors, resistors in an electrical system are the objects. The displacement of mass, spring and dash pot and the current flow and the voltage across the inductor, capacitor and resistor are the attributes. There is a definite relationship between the objects and attributes. The voltages across R, L, C series components can be expressed as $v_R = iR$; $V_L = L\frac{di}{dt}$ and $V_C = \frac{1}{C}\int idt$. If this series circuit is excited by the voltage source $e_i(t)$, the $e_i(t)$ is the input attribute or the input signal. If the voltage across any of the objects R, L and C is taken then such an attribute is called the output signal. The block diagram representation of input and output (voltage across the resistor) signals and the system is shown in Figure 1.1(c).

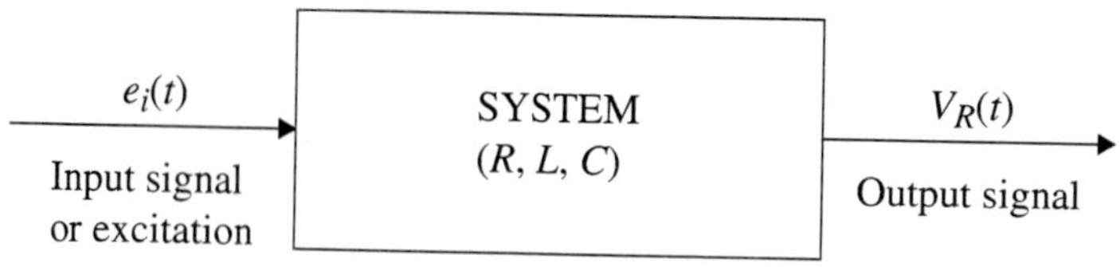

Figure 1.1 (c) Block diagram representation of signals and systems.

1.3 Continuous and Discrete Time Signals

Signals are broadly classified as:

1. Continuous time signal (CT signal).
2. Discrete time signal (DT signal).
3. Digital signal.

The signal that is specified for every value of time t is called continuous time signal and is denoted by $x(t)$. On the other hand, the signal that is specified at discrete value of time is called discrete time signal. The discrete time signal is represented as a sequence of numbers and is denoted by $x[n]$ where n is an integer. Here, time t is divided into n discrete time intervals. The continuous time signal (CT) and discrete time signal (DT) are represented in Figures 1.2 and 1.3 respectively.

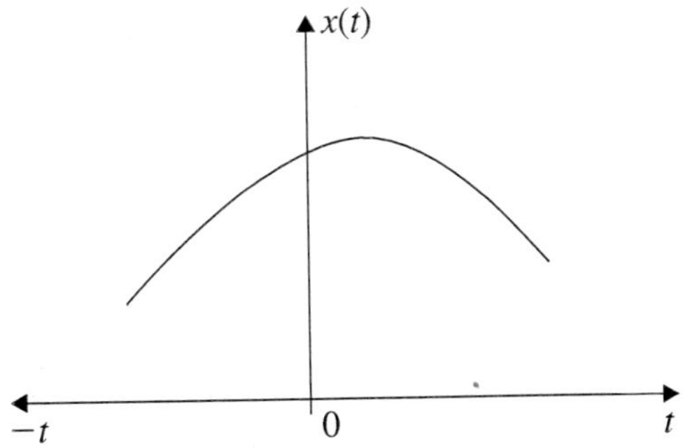

Figure 1.2 CT signal.

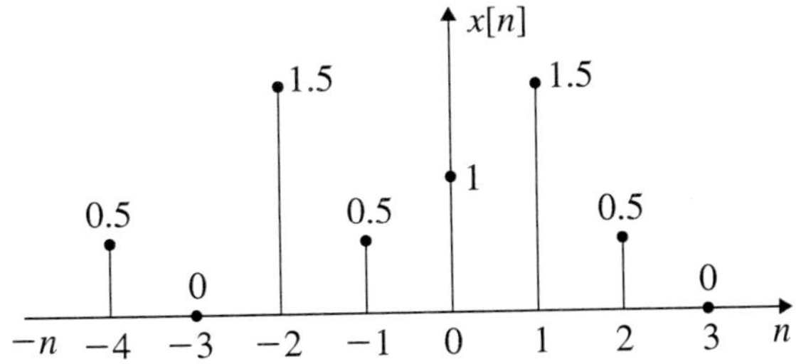

Figure 1.3 (*a*) Discrete time (DT) signal.

It is to be noted that in continuous time signal representation the independent variable t which has unit as sec. is put in the parenthesis $(\cdot)$ and in discrete time signal the independent variable n which is an integer is put inside the square parenthesis $[\cdot]$. Accordingly, the dependent variables of the continuous time signal/system are denoted as $x(t)$, $g(t)$, $u(t)$ etc. Similarly the dependent variables of discrete time signals/systems are denoted as $x[n]$, $g[n]$, $u[n]$ *etc.*

A discrete time signal $x[n]$ is represented by the following two methods:

1.

$$x[n] = \begin{cases} \left(\frac{1}{a}\right)^n & n \geq 0 \\ 0 & n < 0 \end{cases} \tag{1.1}$$

Substituting various values of n where $n \geq 0$ in Equation (1.1) the sequence for $x[n]$ which is denoted by $x\{n\}$ is written as follows:

$$x\{n\} = \left\{1, \frac{1}{a}, \frac{1}{a^2}, \ldots, \frac{1}{a^n}\right\}$$

2. The sequence is also represented as given below.

$$x\{n\} = \{3,\ 2, \underset{\uparrow}{5},\ 4,\ 6,\ 8,\ 2\}$$

The arrow indicates the value of $x[n]$ at $n = 0$ which is 5 in this case. The numbers to the left of the arrow indicates to the negative sequence $n = -1, -2$ *etc.* The numbers to the right of the arrow corresponds to $n = 1, 2, 3, 4,$ *etc.* Thus, for the above sequence $x[-1] = 2$; $x[-2] = 3$; $x[0] = 5$; $x[1] = 4$;

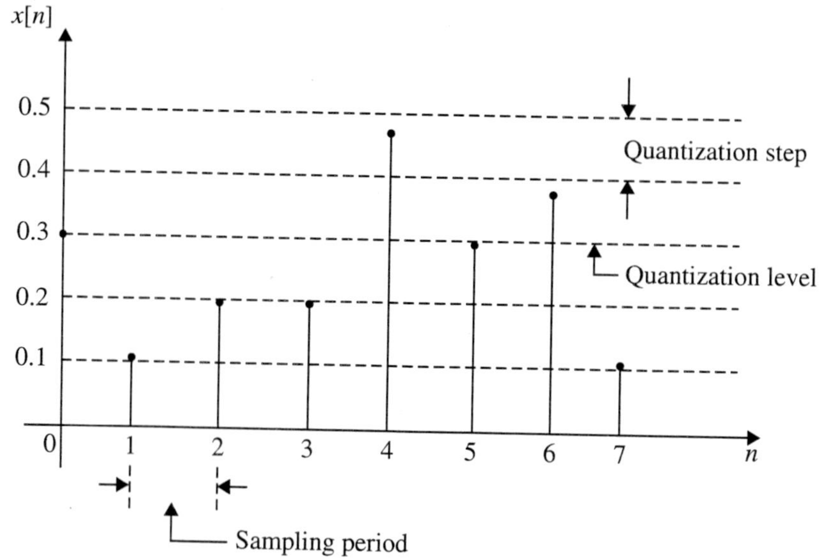

Figure 1.3 (*b*) Digital signal.

$x[2] = 6$; $x[3] = 8$ and $x[4] = 2$. If no arrow is marked for a sequence, the sequence starts from the first term in the extreme left. Consider the sequence

$$x\{n\} = \{5, 3, 4, 2\}.$$

Here, $x[0] = 5$; $x[1] = 3$; $x[2] = 4$ and $x[3] = 2$. There is no negative sequence here.

A digital signal is not very much different from a discrete signal except that a digital signal amplitude is quantized at certain specific level. This is because a digital computer can accept only sequences of numbers which are expressed in terms of bits. The representation of digital signal is shown in Figure 1.3(*b*). The amplitude at any discrete time interval can be only one of quantization levels. If the amplitude is chosen from a finite set of numbers, the amplitude is said to be discritized. The quantization level is equidistance and is called quantization step. An analog signal can be converted into a digital signal by means of sampling and quantizing. It is then digitized by rounding off its value to the closest permissible level. Thus error exists when an analog signal is discritized and quantized. This is called quantization error. The digital signal is therefore discritzed in time and quantized in amplitude.

Example 1.1

Graphically represent the following sequence:

$$x\{n\} = \{1, 0, -1, 1\}$$

Solution The graphical representation $x\{n\} = \{1, 0, -1, 1\}$ is shown in Figure 1.4.

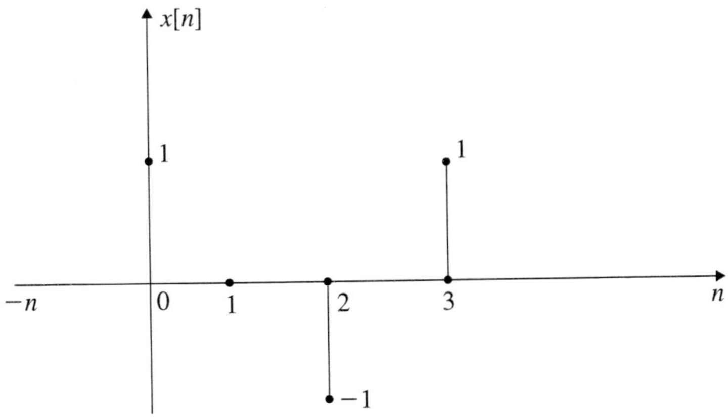

Figure 1.4 Graphical representation of $x[n]$.

Example 1.2

Graphically represent the following sequence:

$$x\{n\} = \{-2,\ 1,\ 0,\ \underset{\uparrow}{1},\ 2,\ 0,\ 1\}$$

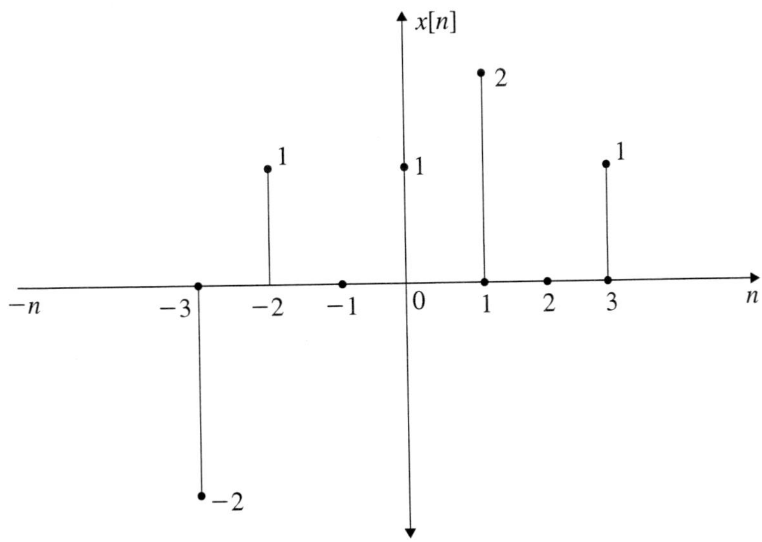

Figure 1.5 Graphical representation of $x[n]$.

Solution The sequence

$$x\{n\} = \{-2,\ 1,\ 0,\ \underset{\uparrow}{1},\ 2,\ 0,\ 1\}$$

is represented in Figure 1.5.

1.4 Basic Discrete Time Signals

Similar to continuous time signals, basic discrete signals are available. However, these signals are represented at discrete interval of time 'n' where n is an integer. Representation of basic discrete time signals are discussed below.

1.4.1 The Unit Impulse Sequence

The basic impulse sequence is shown in Figure 1.6. The unit impulse sequence also called sample is defined as

$$\delta[n] = \begin{cases} 1 & n = 0 \\ 0 & n \neq 0 \end{cases} \tag{1.2}$$

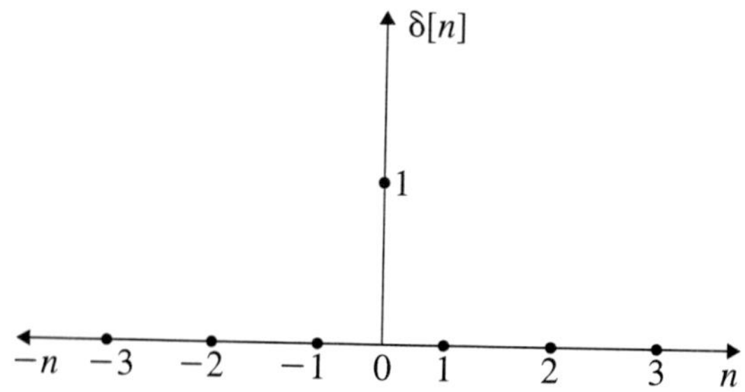

Figure 1.6 Basic unit impulse sequence.

1.4.2 The Basic Unit Step Sequence

The basic unit step sequence is represented in Figure 1.7. It is denoted by $u(n)$. It is defined as

$$u[n] = \begin{cases} 1 & n \geq 0 \\ 0 & n < 0 \end{cases} \tag{1.3}$$

Any discrete sequences $x[n]$ for $n \geq 0$ is expressed as $x[n]u[n]$. For $n < 0$, it is expressed as $x[n]u[-n]$. It is be noted that at $n = 0$, the value of $u[n] = 1$.

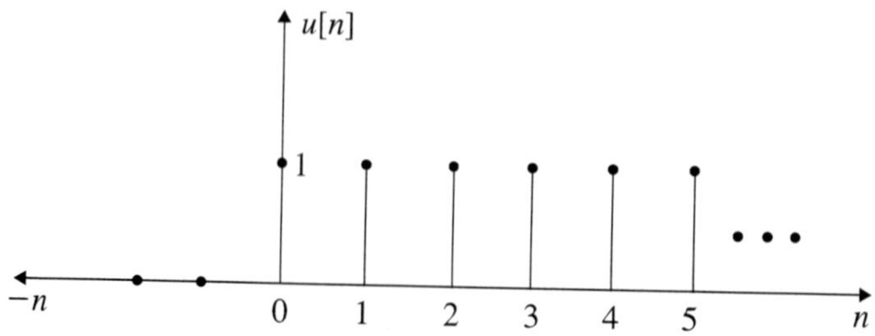

Figure 1.7 Basic unit step sequence.

1.4.3 The Basic Unit Ramp Sequence

The basic unit ramp sequence which is denoted by $r[n]$ is represented in Figure 1.8. It is defined as

$$r[n] = \begin{cases} n & n \geq 0 \\ 0 & n < 0 \end{cases} \tag{1.4}$$

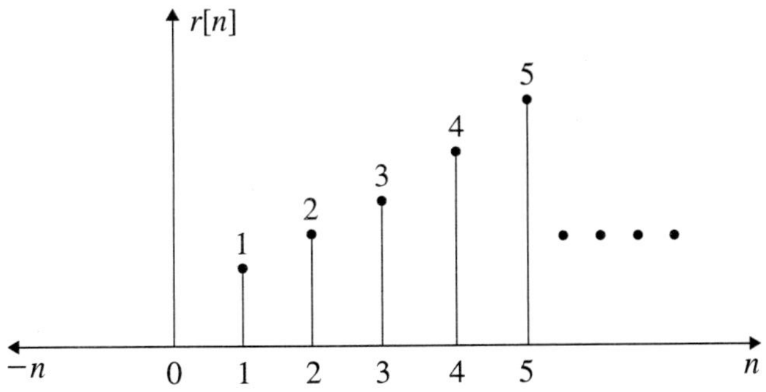

Figure 1.8 Basic unit ramp sequence.

1.4.4 Unit Rectangular Sequence

The discrete time unit rectangular sequence is shown in Figure 1.9. It is defined as

$$\text{rect}[n] = \begin{cases} 1 & |n| \leq N \\ 0 & |n| > N \end{cases} \tag{1.5}$$

The above equation can also be expressed as

$$\text{rect}[n] = 1 \qquad -N \leq n \leq N.$$

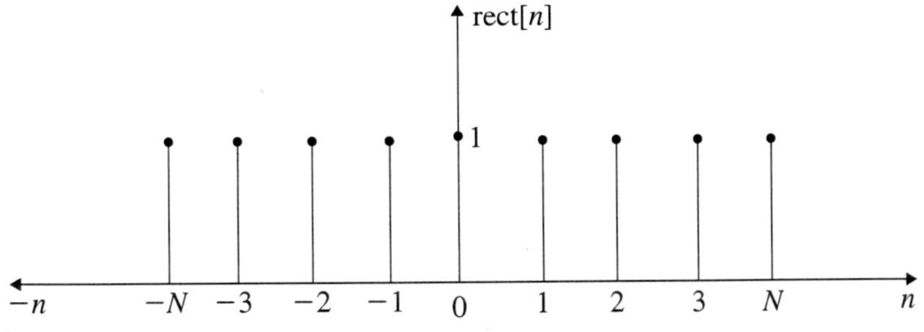

Figure 1.9 Unit rectangular sequence.

1.4.5 Sinusoidal Sequence

The discrete time sinusoidal signal is defined by the following mathematical expression:

$$x[n] = Ae^{-\alpha n}\sin(\omega_0 n + \phi) \tag{1.6}$$

where A and α are real numbers and ϕ is the phase shift. Depending on the value of α, the sinusoidal sequence is divided into the following categories:

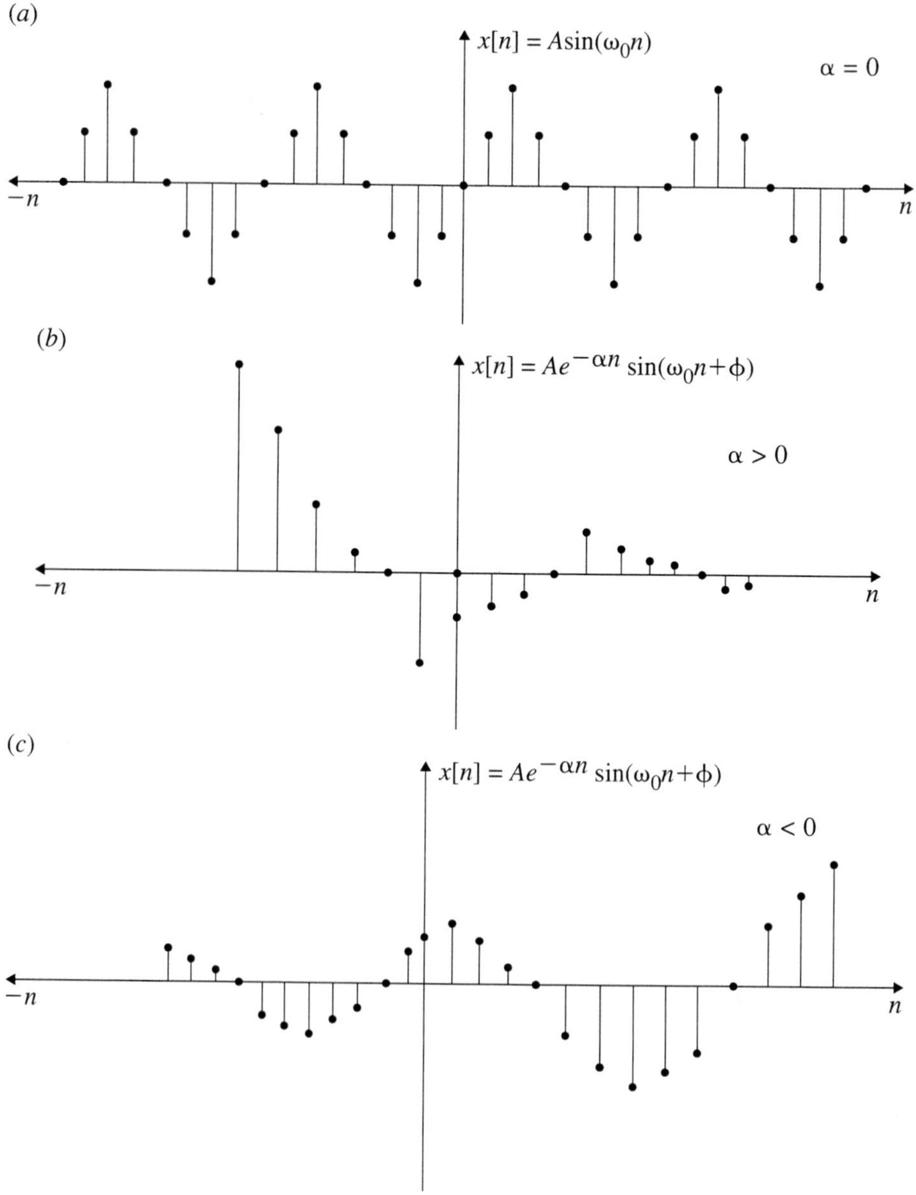

Figure 1.10 Discrete time sinusoidal signal. (*a*) Purely sinusoidal; (*b*) Decaying sinusoidal; (*c*) Growing sinusoidal.

- A purely sinusoidal sequence ($\alpha = 0$).
- Decaying sinusoidal sequence ($\alpha > 0$).
- Growing sinusoidal sequence ($\alpha < 0$).

The above sinusoidal sequences are illustrated in Figures 1.10(*a*), (*b*) and (*c*) respectively.

1.4.6 Discrete Time Real Exponential Sequence

The general complex exponential sequence is defined as

$$x[n] = A\alpha^n \tag{1.7}$$

where A and α are in general complex numbers.

In Equation (1.7) if A and α are real, the sequence is called real exponential. These sequences for various values of α are shown in Figure 1.11. Depending on the value of α, the sequence is classified as:

1. Exponentially growing signal ($\alpha > 1$, Figure 1.11(*a*)).
2. Exponentially decaying signal ($0 < \alpha < 1$, Figure 1.11(*b*)).
3. Exponentially growing for alternate value of n ($\alpha < -1$, Figure 1.11(*c*)).
4. Exponentially decaying for alternate value of n ($-1 < \alpha < 0$, Figure 1.11(*d*)).

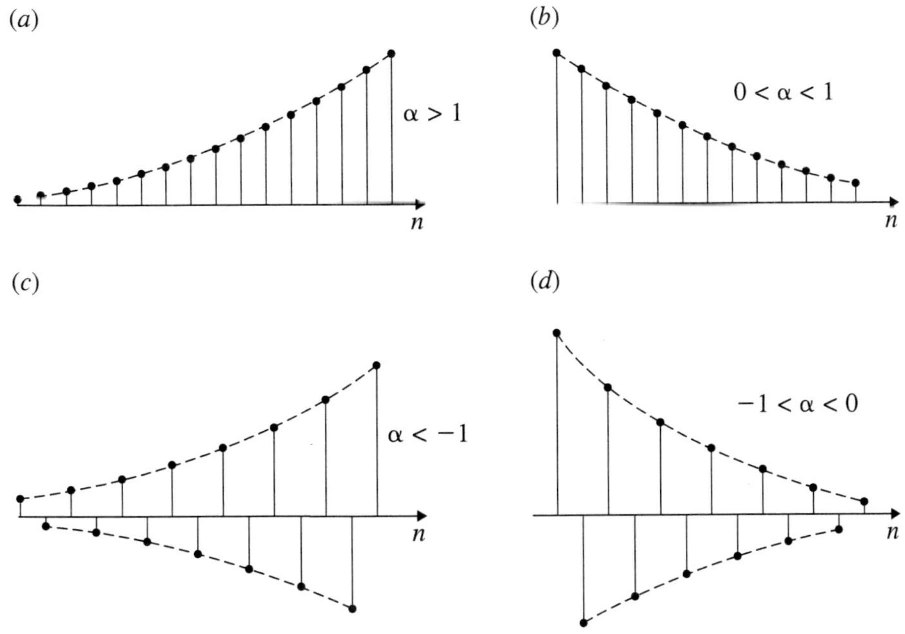

Figure 1.11 Discrete time real exponential sequences. (*a*) $\alpha > 1$; (*b*) $0 < \alpha < 1$; (*c*) $\alpha < -1$; (*d*) $-1 < \alpha < 0$.

1.5 Basic Operations on Discrete Time Signals

The basic operations that are applied to continuous time signals are also applicable to discrete time signals. The time t in CT signal is replaced by n in DT signals. The basic operations as applied to DT signals are explained below.

1.5.1 Addition of Discrete Time Sequence

Addition of discrete time sequence is done by adding the signals at every instant of time. Consider the signals $x_1[n]$ and $x_2[n]$ shown in Figures 1.12(a) and (b) respectively. The addition of these signals at every n is done and represented as $y[n] = x_1[n] + x_2[n]$. This is shown in Figure 1.12(c).

1.5.2 Multiplication of DT Signals

The multiplication of two DT signals $x_1[n]$ and $x_2[n]$ is obtained by multiplying the signal values at each instant of time n. Consider the signal $x_1[n]$ and $x_2[n]$ represented in Figures 1.13(a) and (b). At each instant of time n, the samples of $x_1[n]$ and $x_2[n]$ are multiplied and represented as shown in Figure 1.13(c).

1.5.3 Amplitude Scaling of DT Signal

Let $x[n]$ be a discrete time signal. The signal $Ax[n]$ is represented by multiplying the amplitude of the sequence by A at each instant of time n. Consider the signal $x[n]$ shown in Figure 1.14(a). The signal $2x[n]$ is represented and shown in Figure 1.14(b).

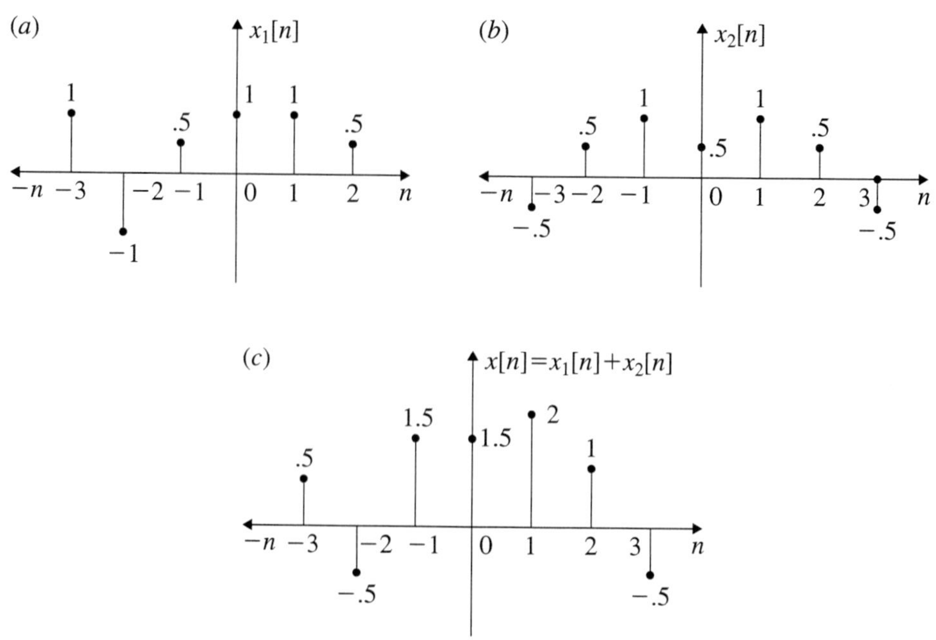

Figure 1.12 Addition of DT signals.

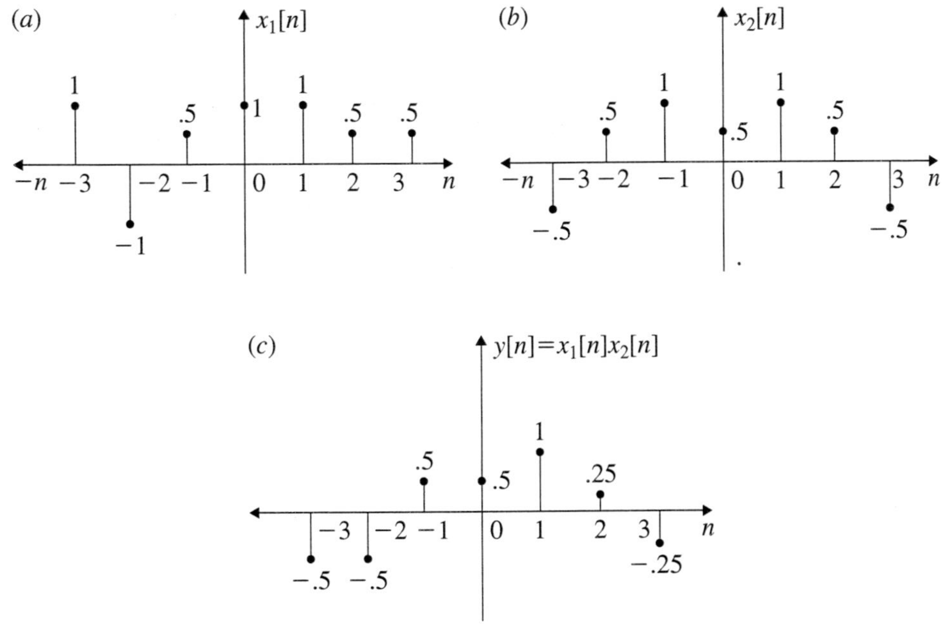

Figure 1.13 Multiplications of two DT signals.

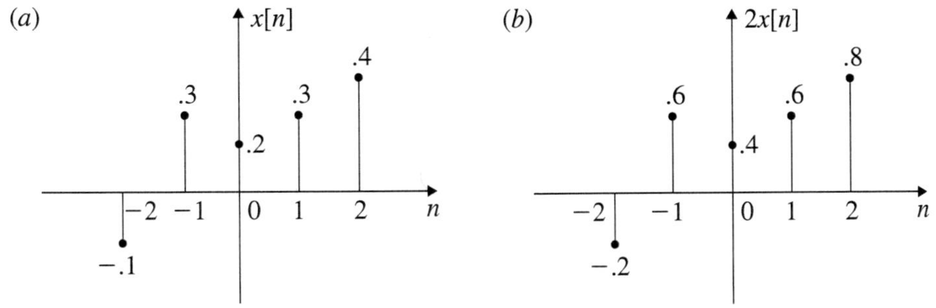

Figure 1.14 Amplitude scaling of DT signals.

1.5.4 Time Scaling of DT Signal

The time compression or expansion of a DT signal in time is known as time scaling. Consider the signal $x[n]$ shown in Figure 1.15(a). The time compressed signal $x[2n]$ and time expanded signal $x[\frac{n}{2}]$ are shown in Figures 1.15(b) and (c) respectively. One should note that while doing compression and expansion of DT signal, **only for integer value of n the samples exist. For non-integer value of n, the samples do not exist**.

Time Compression

Let

$$y[n] = x[2n]$$

$$y[-2] = x[-4] = -0.5$$

$$y[-1] = x[-2] = 0.5$$

$$y[0] = x[0] = 0.5$$

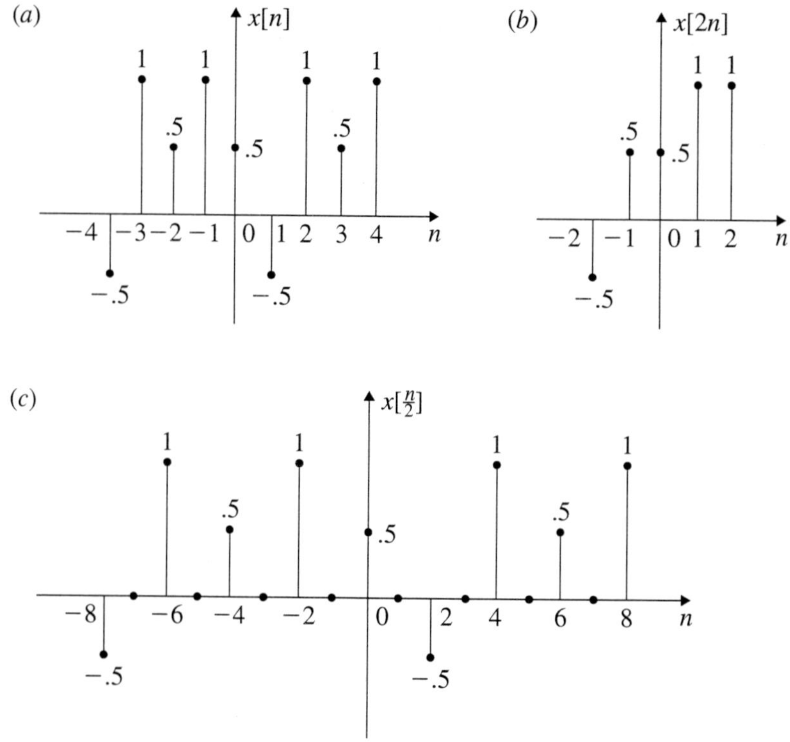

Figure 1.15 Time scaling of DT signal.

$$y[1] = x[2] = 1$$

$$y[2] = x[4] = 1.$$

The plot of $x[2n]$ is shown in Figure 1.15(*b*).

Time Expansion

Let

$$y[n] = x\left[\frac{n}{2}\right]$$

$$y[-8] = x[-4] = -0.5$$

$$y[-6] = x[-3] = 1$$

$$y[-4] = x[-2] = 0.5$$

$$y[-2] = x[-1] = 1$$

$$y[0] = x[0] = 0.5$$

$$y[2] = x[1] = -0.5$$

$$y[4] = x[2] = 1$$

$$y[6] = x[3] = 0.5$$

$$y[8] = x[4] = 1.$$

The plot of $x[\frac{n}{2}]$ is shown in Figure 1.15(*c*).

1.5.5 Time Shifting of DT Signal

As in the case of CT signal, time shifting property is applied to DT signal also. Let $x[n]$ be the DT signal. Let n_0 be the time by which $x[n]$ is time shifted. Since n is an integer, n_0 is also an integer. The following points are applicable while DT signal is time shifted.

- For the DT signals $x[-n-n_0]$ and $x[n+n_0]$, the signals $x[-n]$ and $x[n]$ are to be left shifted by n_0.
- For the DT signals $x[n-n_0]$ and $x[-n+n_0]$, the signals $x[n]$ and $x[-n]$ are to be right shifted by n_0.

Figure 1.16 shows time shifting of DT signal.

In Figure 1.16(a) the sequence $x[n]$ is shown. The sequence $x[n-2]$ which is right shifted by 2 samples is shown in Figure 1.16(b). $x[-n]$ which is the folded signal is shown in Figure 1.16(c). $x[-n+2]$ which is left shifted of $x[-n]$ is shown in Figure 1.16(d). $x[n+2]$ which is right shifted of $x[n]$ is shown in Figure 1.16(e). $x[-n-2]$ which is left shifted of $x[-n]$ is shown in Figure 1.16(f).

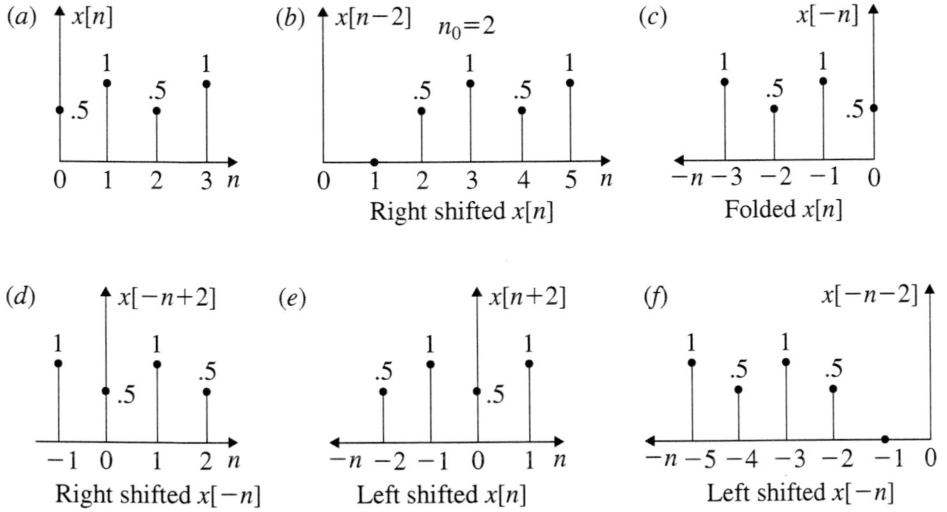

Figure 1.16 Time shifting of DT signal.

1.5.6 Multiple Transformation

The transformations namely amplitude scaling, time reversal, time shifting, time scaling *etc.* are applied to represent DT sequence. The sequence of operation of these transformations is important and followed as described below.

Consider the following DT signal:

$$y[n] = Ax\left[-\frac{n}{a} + n_0\right]$$

1. Plot $x[n]$ sequence and obtain $Ax[n]$ by amplitude scaling.
2. Using time reversal (folding), plot $Ax[-n]$.

3. Using time shifting, plot $Ax[-n+n_0]$ where $n_0 > 0$. The time shift is to be right of $x[-n]$ by n_0 samples.
4. Using time scaling, plot $Ax[-\frac{n}{a}+n_0]$ where a is in integer. In the above case, keeping amplitude constant, time is expanded by a.

The following examples illustrate the above operations:

Example 1.3

Let $x[n]$ and $y[n]$ be as given in Figures 1.17(a) and (b) respectively. Plot

(a) $x[2n]$

(b) $x[3n-1]$

(c) $x[n-2]+y[n-2]$

(d) $y[1-n]$

(*Anna University, December, 2006*)

Solution

(a) **To plot $x[2n]$**
Here, the DT sequence is time compressed by a factor 2. Hence, the samples only with even numbers are divided by a factor 2 and the corresponding

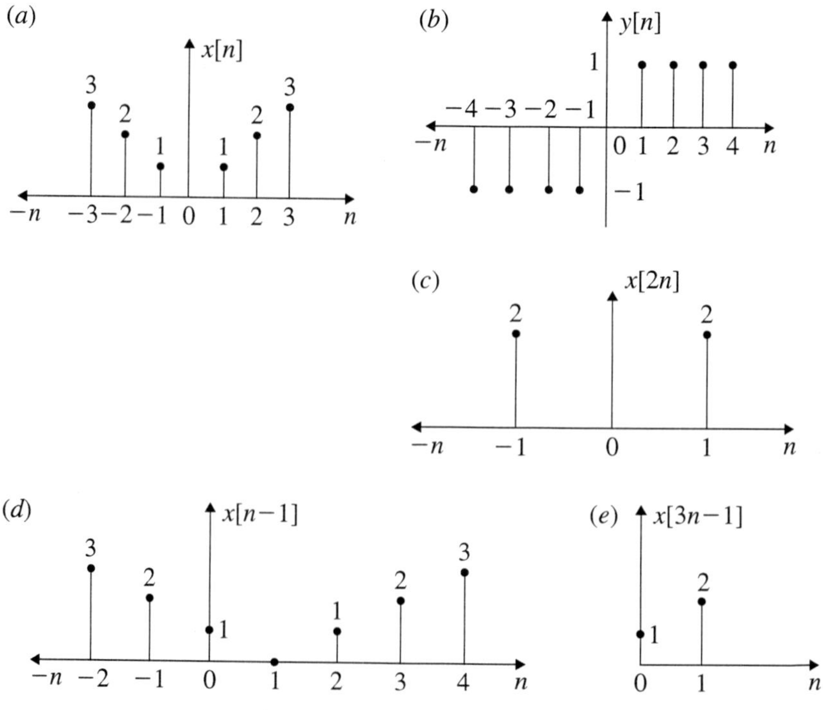

Figure 1.17 Two discrete sequences.

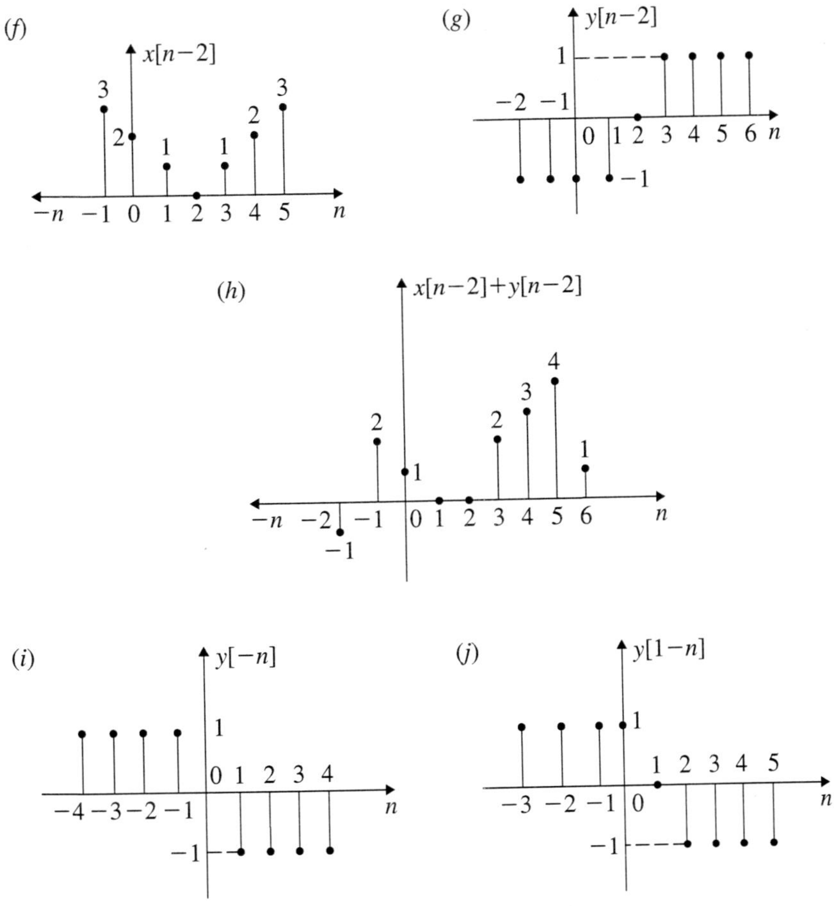

Figure 1.17

amplitudes marked and shown in Figure 1.17(*c*). When odd values of n are divided by the factor 2, it becomes a fraction and they are skipped.

(*b*) **To plot $x[3n-1]$**

The plot of $x[n-1]$ is obtained by right shifting of $x[n]$ by $n_0 = 1$. This is shown in Figure 1.17(*d*). When $x[n-1]$ is time compressed by a factor 3, $x[3n-1]$ is obtained. Only integers which are divisible by 3 in the sequence $x[n-1]$ are to be taken to plot $x[3n-1]$. Thus samples for $n = 0$ and $n = 3$, will be plotted as shown in Figure 1.17(*e*).

(*c*) **To plot $x[n-2] + y[n-2]$**

The sequence $x[n-2]$ is obtained by right shifting of $x[n]$ by 2 and is shown in Figure 1.17(*f*). Similarly, the sequence $y[n-2]$ is obtained by right shifting of $y[n]$ by 2 and is shown in Figure 1.17(*g*). The sequence $x[n-2] + y[n-2]$ is obtained by summing up the sequences in Figures 1.17(*f*) and (*g*) for all n and is shown in Figure 1.17(*h*).

(*d*) **To plot $y[1-n]$**

The sequence $y[-n]$ is obtained by folding $y[n]$ and is shown in Figure 1.17(*i*). $y[-n]$ is right shifted by 1 sample to get the sequence $y[1-n]$. This is shown in Figure 1.17(*j*).

Example 1.4

Consider the sequence shown in Figure 1.18(a). Express the sequence in terms of step function.

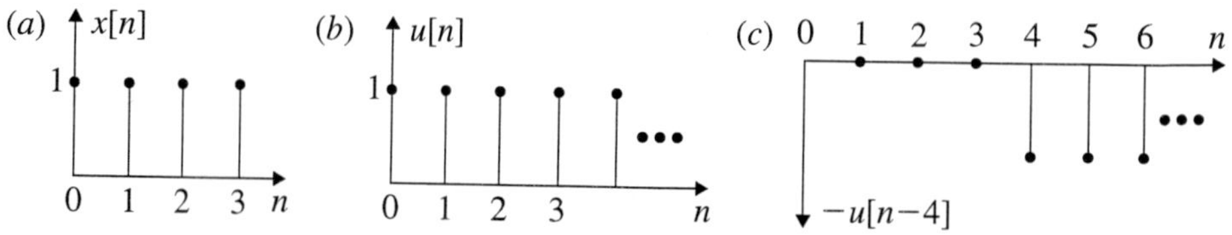

Figure 1.18 Sequences expressed in terms of step sequences.

Solution The unit step sequence $u[n]$ is shown in Figure 1.18(b). The unit negative step sequence with a time delay of $n_0 = 4$ is shown in Figure 1.18(b). It is evident form Figure 1.18 that $\{u[n] - u[n-4]\}$ gives the required $x[n]$ sequence which is represented in Figure 1.18(a). Thus, $x[n] = \{u[n] - u[n-4]\}$.

Example 1.5

Consider the sequence shown in Figure 1.19(a). Express the sequence in terms of step function.

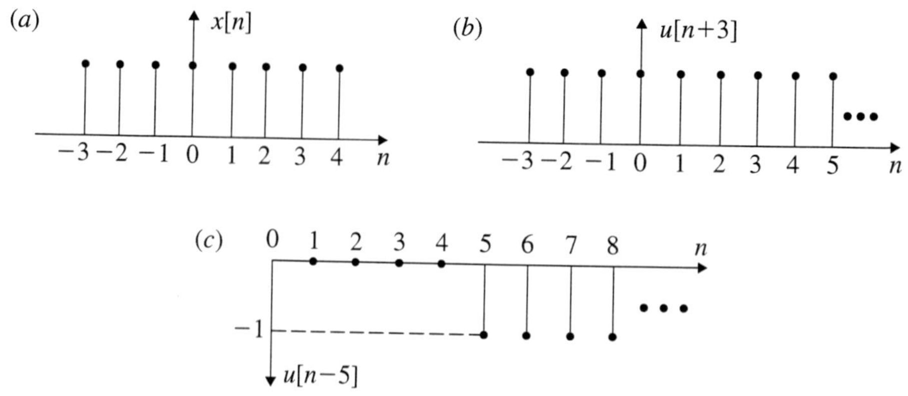

Figure 1.19 DT sequences expressed in terms of step sequences.

Solution

1. Figure 1.19(a) represents the sequence $x[n]$ in the interval $-3 \leq n \leq 4$.
2. Consider $u[n+3]$ which is represented in Figure 1.19(b). The sequence interval is $-3 \leq n < \infty$.
3. Consider the step sequence with a time delay of $n_0 = 5$ and inverted. This can be written as $-u[n-5]$ for the interval $5 \leq n < \infty$. This is represented in Figure 1.19(c).

4. Now consider the sum of the sequences $u[n+3]$ and $-u[n-5]$. This is nothing but $x[n]$. Thus

$$\boxed{x[n] = u[n+3] - u[n-5]}$$

Example 1.6

A discrete time sequence $x[n]$ is shown in Figure 1.20(*a*). Find

$$x[n]\{u[n+1] - u[n-3]\}$$

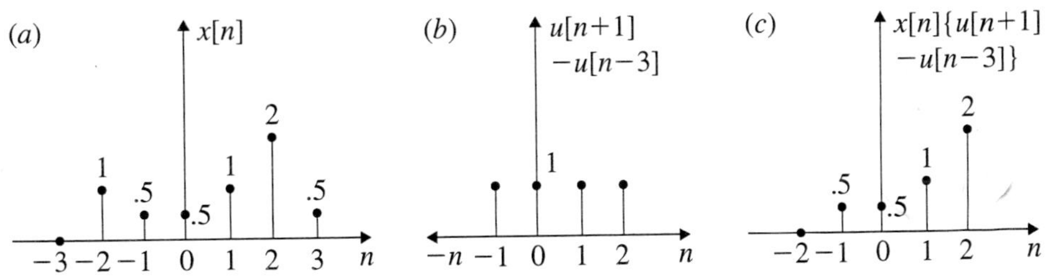

Figure 1.20 Multiplication of DT sequences.

Solution

1. $x[n]$ sequence is represented in Figure 1.20(*a*).
2. $\{u[n+1]-u[n-3]\}$ sequence is nothing but the time delayed unit step sequence with $n_0 = 3$, being subtracted from the time advanced unit step sequence with $n_0 = 1$. This sequence is represented in Figure 1.20(*b*).
3. Multiplying, sample wise of Figures 1.20(*a*) and (*b*), the required sequence $x[n]\{u[n+1] - u[n-3]\}$ is obtained and represented in Figure 1.20(*c*).

Example 1.7

Sketch $x[n] = a^n$ where $-2 \leq n \leq 2$ for the two cases shown below:

$$(1) \quad a = \left(-\frac{1}{4}\right)$$

$$(2) \quad a = -4$$

(Anna University, May, 2007)

Solution For $x[n] = (-\frac{1}{4})^n$ and $x[n] = (-4)^n$ where $-2 \leq n \leq 2$, $x[n]$ is found and tabulated below:

n	-2	-1	0	1	2
$x[n] = (-\frac{1}{4})^n$	16	-4	1	$-\frac{1}{4}$	$\frac{1}{16}$
$x[n] = (-4)^n$	$\frac{1}{16}$	$-\frac{1}{4}$	1	-4	16

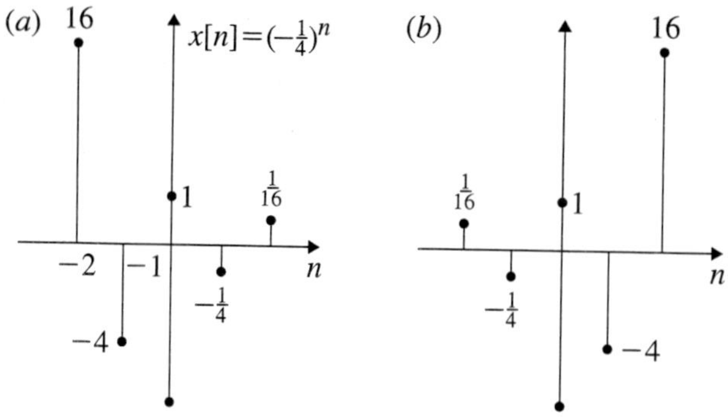

Figure 1.21 DT sequences of Example 1.7.

The samples of $x[n]$ are plotted and shown in Figure 1.21. $x[n] = (-\frac{1}{4})^n$ is represented in Figure 1.21(a) and $x[n] = (-4)^n$ is represented in Figure 1.21(b).

Example 1.8

Express

$$x[n] = (-1)^n \qquad -2 \leq n \leq 2$$

as a sum of scaled and shifted step function.

(*Anna University, May, 2007*)

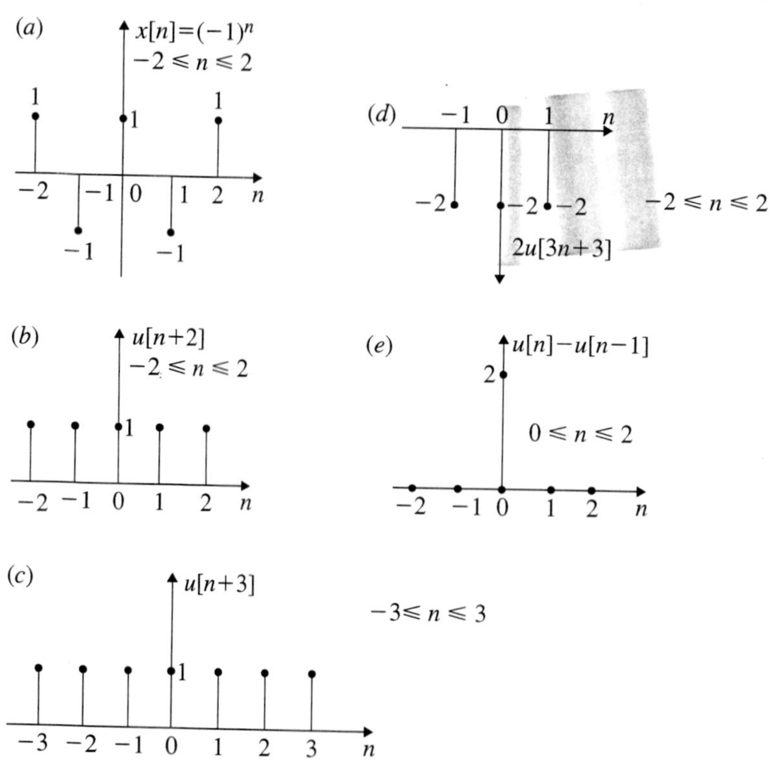

Figure 1.22 DT sequences of Example 1.8.

Solution

(1) $x[n] = (-1)^n$ is tabulated for $-2 \le n \le 2$.

n	-2	-1	0	1	2
$x[n]$	1	-1	1	-1	1

The samples corresponding to the above table are sketched and shown as $x[n]$ in Figure 1.22(*a*).

(2) Consider the step sequence $u[n+2]$ for $-2 \le n \le 2$. The samples are shown in Figure 1.22(*b*).

(3) Consider unit step sequence $u[n+3]$ for $-3 \le n \le 3$. This is represented in Figure 1.22(*c*). From Figure 1.22(*c*), $-2u[3n+3]$ is obtained by amplitude inversion and multiplication and time scaling (compression). This is represented in Figure 1.22(*d*) for $-2 \le n \le 2$.

(4) Consider the step sequence $2\{u[n] - u[n-1]\}$ for $n \ge 0$. This is represented in Figure 1.22(*e*). This is nothing but the sample of strength 2 at $n = 0$.

(5) Now, by adding the samples in Figure 1.22(*b*), Figures 1.22(*d*) and (*e*), it can be easily verified that

$$\boxed{x[n] = u[n+2] - 2u[3n+3] + 2[u[n] - u[n-1]]} \quad -2 \le n \le 2$$

Example 1.9

Given

$$x[n] = \{1, 2, \underset{\uparrow}{3}, -4, 6\}$$

Plot the signal $x[-n-1]$.

(*Anna University, May, 2007*)

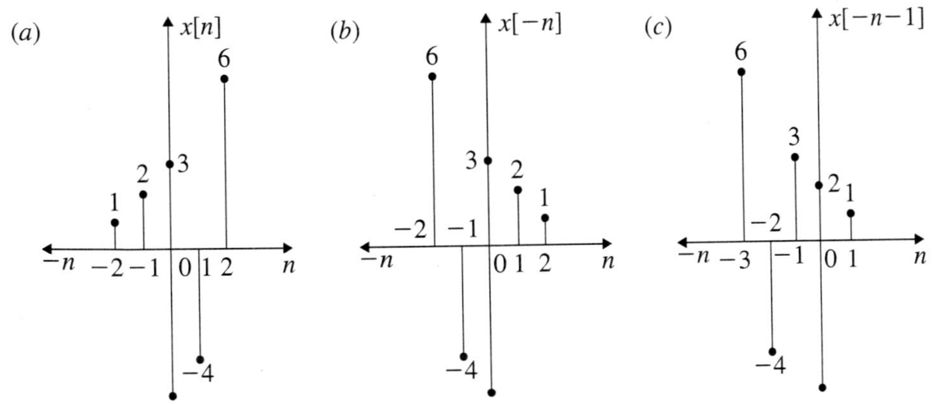

Figure 1.23 DT sequences of Example 1.9.

Solution

1. The sequence $x[n]$ is represented in Figure 1.23(a).
2. By folding $x[n]$, $x[-n]$ is obtained and represented in Figure 1.23(b).
3. $x[-n]$ is shifted to the left by one sample and $x[-n-1]$ is obtained. This is represented in Figure 1.23(c).

1.6 Classification of Discrete Time Signals

Discrete time signals are classified as

1. Periodic and non-periodic signals.
2. Odd and even signals.
3. Power and energy signals.

They are discussed below with suitable examples.

1.6.1 Periodic and Non-Periodic DT Signals

A discrete time signal (sequence) $x[n]$ is said to be periodic with period N which is a positive integer if

$$x[n+N] = x[n] \quad \text{for all } n \tag{1.8}$$

Consider the DT sequence shown in Figure 1.24. The signal gets repeated for every N. For Figure 1.24, the following equation is written:

$$x[n+mN] = x[n] \quad \text{for all } n \tag{1.9}$$

where m is any integer. The smallest positive integer N in Equation (1.9) is called the fundamental period N_0. Any sequence which is not periodic is said to be non-periodic or aperiodic.

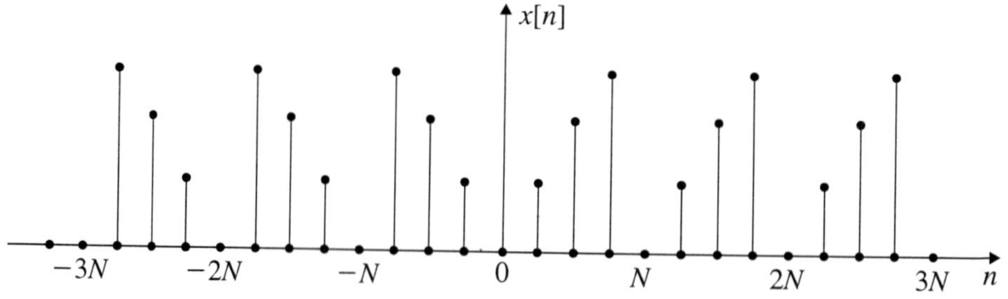

Figure 1.24 Periodic sequence.

Example 1.10

Show that complex exponential sequence $x[n] = e^{j\omega_0 n}$ is periodic and find the fundamental period.

Solution

$$
\begin{aligned}
x[n] &= e^{j\omega_0 n} \\
x[n+N] &= e^{j\omega_0(n+N)} \\
&= e^{j\omega_0 n}e^{j\omega_0 N} \\
&= e^{j\omega_0 n} \quad \text{if } e^{j\omega_0 N} = 1 \\
\omega_0 N &= m2\pi \quad \text{where } m \text{ is any integer.}
\end{aligned}
$$

$$\boxed{N = m\frac{2\pi}{\omega_0}}$$

or

$$\frac{\omega_0}{2\pi} = \frac{m}{N} = \text{rational number.}$$

Thus, $e^{j\omega_0 n}$ is periodic if $\frac{m}{N}$ is rational. For $m = 1$, $N = N_0$. The corresponding frequency $F_0 = \frac{1}{N_0}$ is the fundamental frequency. F_0 is expressed in cycles and not Hz. Similarly ω_0 is expressed in radians and not in radians per second.

Example 1.11

Consider the following DT Signal.

$$x[n] = \sin(\omega_0 n + \phi)$$

Under what condition, the above signal is periodic.

Solution

$$
\begin{aligned}
x[n] &= \sin(\omega_0 n + \phi) \\
x[n+N] &= \sin(\omega_0(n+N) + \phi) \\
&= \sin(\omega_0 n + \omega_0 N + \phi) \\
&= \sin(\omega_0 n + \phi) \quad \text{if } \omega_0 N = 2\pi m \qquad \text{where } m \text{ is an integer} \\
&= x[n]
\end{aligned}
$$

$$\boxed{\frac{\omega_0}{2\pi} = \frac{m}{N} = \text{rational}}$$

Example 1.12

If $x_1[n]$ and $x_2[n]$ are periodic then show that the sum of the composite signal $x[n] = x_1[n] + x_2[n]$ is also periodic with the least common multiple (LCM) of the fundamental period of individual signal.

Solution Let N_1 and N_2 be the fundamental periods of $x_1[n]$ and $x_2[n]$ respectively. Since both $x_1[n]$ and $x_2[n]$ are periodic,

$$\begin{aligned} x_1[n] &= x_1[n + mN_1] \\ x_2[n] &= x_2[n + kN_2] \\ x[n] &= x_1[n] + x_2[n] \\ &= x_1[n + mN_1] + x_2[n + kN_2] \end{aligned}$$

For $x[n]$ to be periodic with period N,

$$\begin{aligned} x[n+N] &= x_1[n+N] + x_2[n+N] \\ x[n] &= x[n+N] \\ x_1[n + mN_1] + x_2[n + kN_2] &= x_1[n+N] + x_2[n+N] \end{aligned}$$

The above equation is satisfied if

$$mN_1 = kN_2 = N$$

m and k which are integers are chosen to satisfy the above equation. It implies that N is the LCM of N_1 and N_2.

On similar line it can be proved that if $x_1[n]$ and $x_2[n]$ are periodic signals with fundamental period N_1 and N_2 respectively, then $x[n] = x_1[n]x_2[n]$ is periodic if

$$mN_1 = kN_2 = N$$

Example 1.13

Find whether the following signals are periodic. If periodic, determine the fundamental period

$$(a) \qquad x[n] = e^{j\pi n}$$

$$(b) \qquad x[n] = \cos\left[\frac{n}{8} - \pi\right]$$

$$(c) \qquad x[n] = \sin^2 \frac{\pi}{4} n$$

Solution

(*a*) $\boldsymbol{x[n] = e^{j\pi n}}$

$$\begin{aligned} \omega_0 &= \pi \\ N &= \frac{2\pi}{\omega_0} m \end{aligned}$$

$$\boxed{N = \frac{2\pi}{\pi} = 2} \quad \text{if } m = 1$$

$x[n]$ is periodic with fundamental period 2.

(*b*) $\boldsymbol{x[n] = \cos\left[\frac{n}{8} - \pi\right]}$

$$\omega_0 = \frac{1}{8}$$

$$N = \frac{2\pi}{\omega_0}m = 16\pi m$$

For any integer value of m, N is not integer. Hence, $x[n]$ is not periodic.

$$\boxed{x[n] \text{ is not periodic}}$$

(*c*) $\boldsymbol{x[n] = \sin^2 \frac{\pi}{4} n}$

$$\begin{aligned}
x[n] &= \sin^2 \frac{\pi}{4} n \\
&= \frac{1}{2} - \frac{1}{2}\cos\frac{2\pi}{4}n \\
&= x_1[n] + x_2[n] \\
x_1[n] &= \frac{1}{2} = \frac{1}{2}(1)^n \text{ is periodic with } N_1 = 1 \\
x_2[n] &= -\frac{1}{2}\cos\frac{\pi}{2}n \\
\omega_0 &= \frac{\pi}{2} \\
N_2 &= \frac{2\pi}{\omega_0}m = 4m = 4 \qquad \text{for } m = 1 \\
\frac{N_1}{N_2} &= \frac{1}{4} \\
\text{or} \quad 4N_1 &= N_2 = N
\end{aligned}$$

$$\boxed{N = 4}$$

Example 1.14

Find the periodicity of the DT signal

$$x[n] = \sin\frac{2\pi}{3}n + \cos\frac{\pi}{2}n$$

(*Anna University, December, 2007*)

Solution

$$\begin{aligned}
x[n] &= \sin\frac{2\pi}{3}n + \cos\frac{\pi}{2}n \\
&= x_1[n] + x_2[n] \\
x_1[n] &= \sin\frac{2}{3}\pi n \\
\omega_1 &= \frac{2}{3}\pi \\
N_1 &= \frac{2\pi}{\omega_1}m_1 = \frac{2\pi}{2\pi}3m_1 = 3 \quad \text{for } m_1 = 1 \\
x_2[n] &= \cos\frac{\pi}{2}n \\
\omega_2 &= \frac{\pi}{2} \\
N_2 &= \frac{2\pi}{\omega_2}m_2 = \frac{2\pi}{\pi}2m_2 = 4 \quad \text{for } m_2 = 1 \\
\frac{N_1}{N_2} &= \frac{3}{4} \text{ or } 4N_1 = 3N_2 = N
\end{aligned}$$

$$\boxed{N = 12}$$

Example 1.15

Determine whether the following signal is periodic. If periodic find its fundamental period.

$$x[n] = \cos\left(\frac{n\pi}{2}\right)\cos\left(\frac{n\pi}{4}\right)$$

(Anna University, December, 2006)

Solution

$$\begin{aligned}
x[n] &= \cos\left(\frac{n\pi}{2}\right)\cos\left(\frac{n\pi}{4}\right) \\
&= x_1[n]x_2[n] \\
x_1[n] &= \cos\frac{n\pi}{2} \\
\omega_1 &= \frac{\pi}{2} \\
N_1 &= \frac{2\pi}{\omega_1}m_1 = \frac{2\pi}{\pi}2m_1 = 4 \quad \text{for } m_1 = 1
\end{aligned}$$

$$x_2[n] = \cos\frac{n\pi}{4}$$

$$\omega_2 = \frac{\pi}{4}$$

$$N_2 = \frac{2\pi}{\omega_2}m_2 = \frac{2\pi}{\pi}4m_2 = 8 \quad \text{for } m_2 = 1$$

$$\frac{N_1}{N_2} = \frac{4}{8} = \frac{1}{2} \quad \text{or}$$

$$2N_1 = N_2 = N$$

$$\boxed{N = 8}$$

The signal is periodic and the fundamental period $N = 8$.

Example 1.16

Test whether the following signals are periodic or not and if periodic, calculate the fundamental period.

$$(a) \qquad x[n] = \cos\left(\frac{\pi}{2}n\right) + \sin\left(\frac{\pi}{8}n\right) + 3\cos\left(\frac{\pi}{4}n + \frac{\pi}{3}\right)$$

$$(b) \qquad x[n] = e^{j\frac{2\pi}{3}n} + e^{j\frac{3\pi}{4}n}$$

(Anna University, December, 2007)

Solution

(*a*)

$$x[n] = \cos\left(\frac{\pi}{2}n\right) + \sin\left(\frac{\pi}{8}n\right) + 3\cos\left(\frac{\pi}{4}n + \frac{\pi}{3}\right)$$

$$= x_1[n] + x_2[n] + x_3[n]$$

$$x_1[n] = \cos\frac{\pi}{2}n$$

$$\omega_1 = \frac{\pi}{2}; \quad N_1 = \frac{2\pi}{\omega_1} = \frac{2\pi\, 2}{\pi} \quad \text{for } m_1 = 1$$

$$N_1 = 4$$

$$x_2[n] = \sin\left(\frac{\pi}{8}n\right)$$

$$\omega_2 = \frac{\pi}{8}; \quad N_2 = \frac{2\pi}{\omega_2}m_2 = \frac{2\pi\, 8}{\pi} \quad \text{for } m_2 = 1$$

$$N_2 = 16$$

$$x_3[n] = 3\cos\left(\frac{\pi}{4}n + \frac{\pi}{3}\right)$$

$$\omega_3 = \frac{\pi}{4}; \quad N_3 = \frac{2\pi}{\omega_3}m_3 = \frac{2\pi\,4}{\pi} \quad \text{for } m_3 = 1$$

$$N_3 = 8$$

To find the LCM of N_1, N_2 and N_3.

4	4,	8,	16
2	1,	2,	4
	1,	1,	2

$$\text{LCM} = 4 \times 2 \times 2 = 16$$

$$\boxed{N = 16}$$

The signal is periodic.

(*b*)

$$x[n] = e^{j\frac{2\pi}{3}n} + e^{j\frac{3\pi}{4}n}$$

$$= x_1[n] + x_2[n]$$

$$x_1[n] = e^{j\frac{2\pi}{3}n}$$

$$\omega_1 = \frac{2\pi}{3}; \; N_1 = \frac{2\pi}{\omega_1}m_1 = \frac{2\pi}{2\pi}3 \quad \text{for } m_1 = 1$$

$$N_1 = 3$$

$$x_2[n] = e^{j\frac{3\pi}{4}n}$$

$$\omega_2 = \frac{3\pi}{4}; \; N_2 = \frac{2\pi}{\omega_2}m_2 = \frac{2\pi}{3\pi}4m_2$$

$$N_2 = 8 \quad \text{for } m_2 = 3$$

$$\frac{N_1}{N_2} = \frac{3}{8}$$

$$8N_1 = 3N_2 = N = 24$$

$$\boxed{N = 24}$$

The signal is periodic with fundamental period $N = 24$.

1.6.2 Odd and Even DT Signals

DT signals are classified as odd and even signals. The relationships are analogous to CT signals.

A discrete time signal $x[n]$ is said to be an even signal if

$$x[-n] = x[n] \tag{1.10}$$

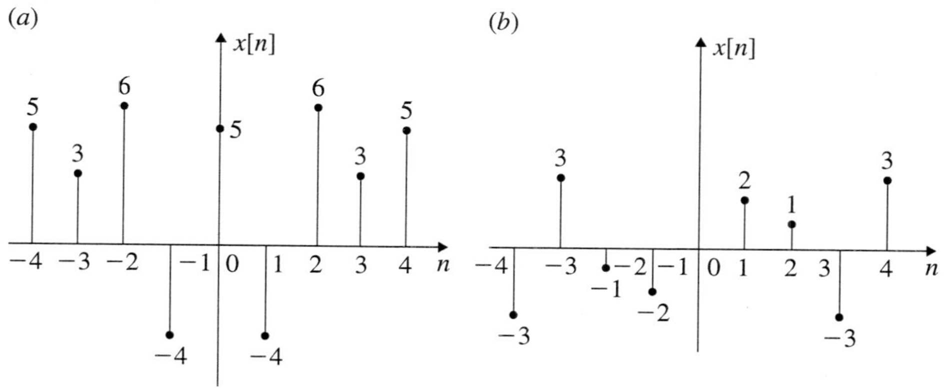

Figure 1.25 (*a*) Even Function and (*b*) Odd function.

A discrete time signal $x[n]$ is said to be an odd signal if

$$x[-n] = -x[n] \tag{1.11}$$

The signal $x[n]$ can be expressed as the sum of odd and even signals as

$$x[n] = x_e[n] + x_0[n] \tag{1.12}$$

The even and odd components of $x[n]$ can be expressed as

$$x_e[n] = \frac{1}{2}[x[n] + x[-n]] \tag{1.13}$$

$$x_0[n] = \frac{1}{2}[x[n] - x[-n]] \tag{1.14}$$

It is to be noted that

- An even function has an odd part which is zero.
- An odd function has an even part which is zero.
- The product of two even signals or of two odd signals is an even signal.
- The product of an odd and an even signal is an odd signal.
- At $n = 0$, the odd signal is zero.

The even and odd signals are represented in Figures 1.25(*a*) and (*b*) respectively.

Example 1.17

Determine whether the following functions are odd or even:

(*a*) $x[n] = \sin 2\pi n$

(*b*) $x[n] = \cos 2\pi n$

Solution

(*a*) $\boldsymbol{x[n] = \sin 2\pi n}$

$$x[-n] = \sin(-2\pi n) = -\sin 2\pi n$$
$$= -x[n]$$

$$\boxed{\text{This is an odd signal.}}$$

(*b*) $\boldsymbol{x[n] = \cos 2\pi n}$

$$x[-n] = \cos(-2\pi n) = \cos 2\pi n$$
$$= x[n]$$

$$\boxed{\text{This is an even signal.}}$$

Example 1.18

Find the even and odd components of DT signal given below. Verify the same by graphical method.

$$x[n] = \{-2,\ 1, \underset{\uparrow}{3},\ -5,\ 4\}$$

Solution $x[-n]$ is obtained by folding $x[n]$. Thus

$$x[-n] = \{4,\ -5,\ \underset{\uparrow}{3},\ 1,\ -2\}$$

$$-x[-n] = \{-4,\ 5,\ \underset{\uparrow}{-3},\ -1,\ 2\}$$

$$x_e[n] = \frac{1}{2}\left[x[n] + x[-n]\right]$$
$$= \frac{1}{2}\left[\{-2,\ 1,\ \underset{\uparrow}{3},\ -5,\ 4\} + \{4,\ -5,\ \underset{\uparrow}{3},\ 1,\ -2\}\right]$$
$$= \frac{1}{2}\left[(-2+4),\ (1-5),\ \underset{\uparrow}{(3+3)},\ (-5+1),\ (4-2)\right]$$

$$\boxed{x_e[n] = \{1,\ -2,\ \underset{\uparrow}{3},\ -2,\ 1\}}$$

$$
\begin{aligned}
x_0[n] &= \frac{1}{2}\,[x[n] - x[-n]] \\
&= \frac{1}{2}\,[\{-2,\ 1,\ \underset{\uparrow}{3},\ -5,\ 4\} + \{-4,\ 5,\ \underset{\uparrow}{-3},\ -1,\ 2\}] \\
&= \frac{1}{2}\,[(-2-4), (1+5), \underset{\uparrow}{(3-3)}, (-5-1), (4+2)]
\end{aligned}
$$

$$
\boxed{x_0[n] = \{-3,\ 3,\ \underset{\uparrow}{0},\ -3,\ 3\}}
$$

Odd and even components by graphical method.

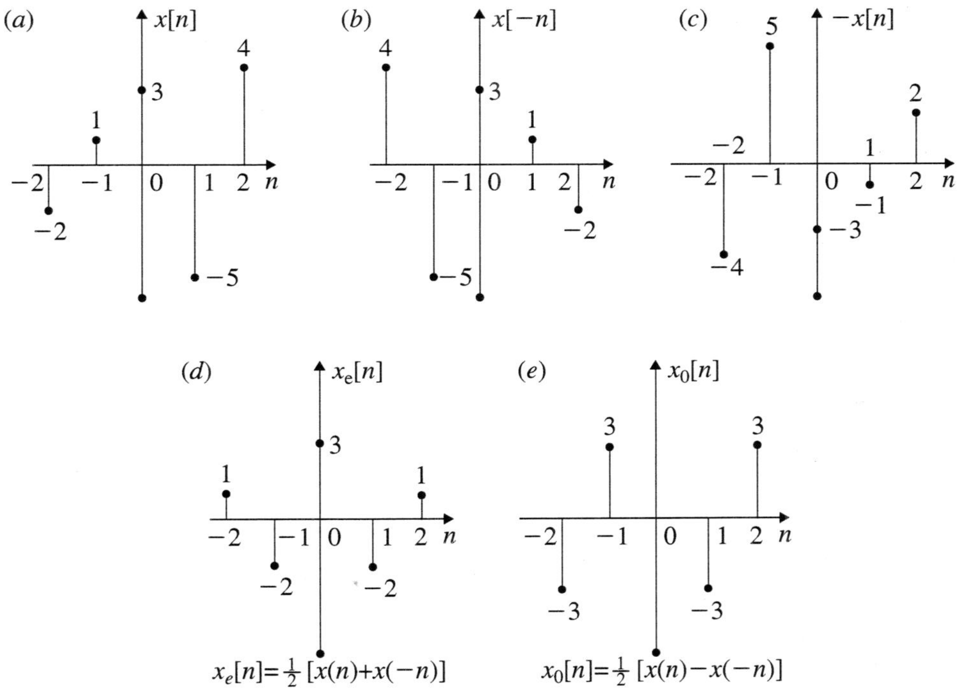

Figure 1.26 Graphical determination of even and odd function from $x[n]$.

Solution

1. $x[n]$ is represented in Figure 1.26(a).
2. $x[-n]$ is obtained by folding $x[n]$ which is represented in Figure 1.26(b).
3. $-x[n]$ is obtained by inverting $x[-n]$ of Figure 1.26(b). This is represented in Figure 1.26(c).
4. $x_e[n] = \frac{1}{2}\,[x[n] + x[-n]]$. Figures 1.26($a$) and ($b$) sample wise are added and their amplitudes are divided by the factor 2. This gives $x_e[n]$ and is represented in Figure 1.26(d).

5. $x_0[n] = \frac{1}{2}[x[n] - x[-n]]$. Figures 1.26($a$) and ($c$) sample wise are added and their amplitudes are divided by a factor 2 to get $x_0[n]$. This is represented in Figure 1.26(e).

Example 1.19

Find the even and odd components of the following DT signal and sketch the same.

$$x[n] = \{-2, 1, 2, -1, 3\}$$

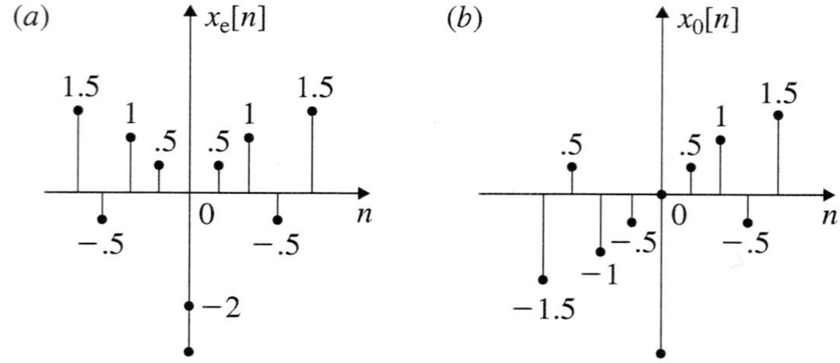

Figure 1.27 (a) Even Function and (b) Odd function.

(*Anna University, December, 2007*)

Solution

$$x[n] = \{-2, 1, 2, -1, 3\}$$

$$x[-n] = \{3, -1, 2, 1, \underset{\uparrow}{-2}\}$$

$$x_e[n] = \frac{1}{2}\{x[n] + x[-n]\}$$

$$= \frac{1}{2}[\{\underset{\uparrow}{-2}, 1, 2, -1, 3\} + \{3, -1, 2, 1, \underset{\uparrow}{-2}\}]$$

$$= \{1.5, -.5, 1, .5, \underset{\uparrow}{-2}, .5, 1, -.5, 1.5\}$$

$$x_0[n] = \frac{1}{2}[x[n] - x[-n]]$$

$$= \frac{1}{2}[\{\underset{\uparrow}{-2}, 1, 2, -1, 3\} - \{3, -1, 2, 1, \underset{\uparrow}{-2}\}]$$

$$x_0[n] = \{-1.5, .5, -1, -.5, \underset{\uparrow}{0}, .5, 1, -.5, 1.5\}$$

Even and odd components of $x[n]$ are represented in Figures 1.27(a) and (b) respectively.

1.6.3 Energy and Power of DT Signals

For a discrete time signal $x[n]$, the total energy is defined as

$$E = \sum_{n=-\infty}^{\infty} |x[n]|^2 \tag{1.15}$$

The average power is defined as

$$P = \underset{N\to\infty}{Lt} \frac{1}{(2N+1)} \sum_{n=-N}^{N} |x[n]|^2 \tag{1.16}$$

From the definitions of energy and power, the following inferences are derived:

1. $x[n]$ is an energy sequence iff $0 < E < \infty$. For finite energy signal, the average power $P = 0$.
2. $x[n]$ is a power sequence iff $0 < P < \infty$. For a sequence with average power P being finite, the total energy $E = \infty$.
3. Periodic signal is a power signal and *vice versa* is not true. Here, the energy of the signal per period is finite.
4. Signals which do not satisfy the definitions of total energy and average power, neither termed as power signal nor energy signal. The following summation formulae are very often used while evaluating the average power and total energy of DT sequence.

1.

$$\sum_{n=0}^{N-1} a^n = \frac{(1-a^n)}{(1-a)} \qquad a \neq 1 \tag{1.17}$$

$$= N \qquad a = 1$$

2.

$$\sum_{n=0}^{\infty} a^n = \frac{1}{(1-a)} \qquad a < 1 \tag{1.18}$$

3.

$$\sum_{n=m}^{\infty} a^n = \frac{a^m}{(1-a)} \qquad a < 1 \tag{1.19}$$

4.

$$\sum_{n=0}^{\infty} na^n = \frac{a}{(1-a)^2} \qquad a < 1 \tag{1.20}$$

Example 1.20

Determine whether the following signals are energy signals or power signals:

$$(a) \quad x[n] = A\delta[n]$$
$$(b) \quad x[n] = u[n]$$
$$(c) \quad x[n] = \text{ramp}\, n$$
$$(d) \quad x[n] = A$$
$$(e) \quad x[n] = 2e^{j(\pi n+\theta)}$$
$$(f) \quad x[n] = \cos\frac{\pi}{2}n$$

Solution

(*a*) $\boldsymbol{x[n] = A\delta[n]}$

$$\begin{aligned} x[n] &= A\delta[n] \\ &= A \qquad n = 0 \\ &= 0 \qquad n \neq 0 \end{aligned}$$

$$\text{Energy } E = \sum_{n=0}^{0}(A)^2$$

$$\boxed{E = A^2}$$

For unit impulse, $A = 1$ and $E = 1$.

(*b*) $\boldsymbol{x[n] = u[n];\ n \geq 0}$

$$\begin{aligned} P &= \underset{N\to\infty}{Lt} \frac{1}{(2N+1)} \sum_{n=0}^{N} |x(n)|^2 \\ &= \underset{N\to\infty}{Lt} \frac{1}{(2N+1)} \sum_{n=0}^{N} 1 \end{aligned}$$

But $\sum_{n=0}^{N} 1 = (N+1)$

$$\begin{aligned} P &= \underset{N\to\infty}{Lt} \frac{(N+1)}{(2N+1)} \\ &= \underset{N\to\infty}{Lt} \frac{N(1+\frac{1}{N})}{N(2+\frac{1}{N})} = \frac{1}{2} \end{aligned}$$

$$\boxed{\begin{aligned} P &= \frac{1}{2} \\ E &= \infty \end{aligned}}$$

(*c*) $\boldsymbol{x[n] = \text{ramp}\, n;\ n \geq 0}$

$$P = \underset{N\to\infty}{Lt} \frac{1}{(2N+1)} \sum_{n=0}^{N} |x[n]|^2$$

$$P = \underset{N\to\infty}{Lt} \frac{1}{(2N+1)} \sum_{n=0}^{N} n^2$$

But $\sum_{n=0}^{N} n^2 = \frac{N(N+1)(2N+1)}{6}$

$$P = \underset{N\to\infty}{Lt} \frac{N(N+1)(2N+1)}{(2N+1)6}$$

$$\boxed{P = \infty}$$

$$E = \underset{N\to\infty}{Lt} \sum_{n=0}^{N} n^2$$

$$= \underset{N\to\infty}{Lt} \frac{N(N+1)(2N+1)}{6} = \infty$$

$$\boxed{E = \infty}$$

The signal $x[n] = n$ is neither power signal nor energy signal.

(*d*) $\boldsymbol{x[n] = A}$

$$P = \underset{N\to\infty}{Lt} \frac{1}{(2N+1)} \sum_{n=-\infty}^{\infty} A^2$$

$$= \underset{N\to\infty}{Lt} \frac{A^2}{(2N+1)}(2N+1) \qquad \left[\sum_{n=-\infty}^{\infty} 1 = (2N+1)\right]$$

$$\boxed{\begin{aligned} P &= A^2 \\ E &= \infty \end{aligned}}$$

(*e*) $\boldsymbol{x[n] = 2e^{j(\pi n+\theta)}}$

$$P = \underset{N\to\infty}{Lt} \frac{1}{(2N+1)} \sum_{-N}^{N} |2e^{j(n\pi+\theta)}|^2$$

$$P = \underset{N\to\infty}{Lt} \frac{1}{2N+1} 4 \sum_{-N}^{N} |e^{j(n\pi+\theta)}|^2$$

But $|e^{j(n\pi+\theta)}| = 1$ and $\sum_{-N}^{N} 1 = (2N+1)$

$$P = \underset{N\to\infty}{Lt}\ 4\frac{(2N+1)}{(2N+1)} = 4$$

$$\boxed{\begin{array}{c} P = 4 \\ E = \infty \end{array}}$$

(*f*) $\boldsymbol{x[n] = \cos \frac{\pi}{2} n}$

$$P = \frac{1}{(2N+1)} \sum_{-N}^{N} \cos^2 \frac{\pi}{2} n$$

Since $\sum_{-N}^{N} \cos \pi n = 0$,

$$\begin{aligned} P &= \underset{N\to\infty}{Lt} \frac{1}{(2N+1)} \sum_{-N}^{N} \frac{(1+\cos \pi n)}{2} \\ &= \frac{1}{2} \underset{N\to\infty}{Lt} \frac{(2N+1)}{(2N+1)} \\ &= \frac{1}{2} \end{aligned}$$

$$\boxed{\begin{array}{c} P = \frac{1}{2} \\ E = \infty \end{array}}$$

Example 1.21

Determine the energy of the signal shown in Figure 1.28 whose

$$x[n] = \left(\frac{1}{3}\right)^n u[n]$$

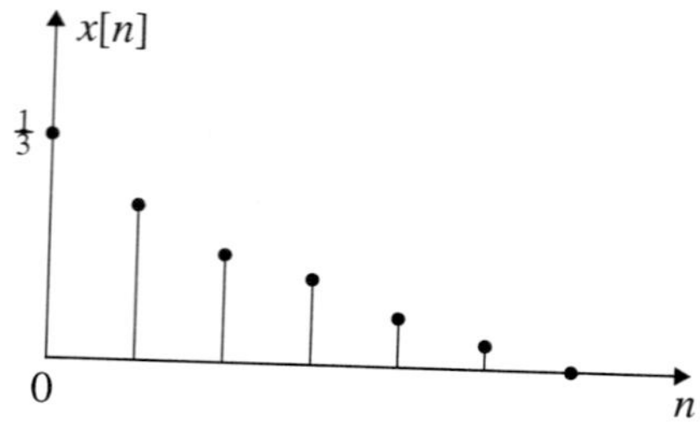

Figure 1.28 $x[n] = \left(\frac{1}{3}\right)^2 u[n]$.

(Anna University, December, 2007)

Solution

$$E = \underset{N\to\infty}{Lt} \sum_{n=0}^{N} \left(\frac{1}{3}\right)^{2n}$$

$$= \underset{N\to\infty}{Lt} \sum_{n=0}^{N} \left(\frac{1}{9}\right)^{n}$$

$$= 1 + \frac{1}{9} + \left(\frac{1}{9}\right)^2 + \ldots$$

$$= \frac{1}{1-\frac{1}{9}}$$

$$\boxed{\begin{array}{c} E = \dfrac{9}{8} \\ P = 0 \end{array}}$$

Example 1.22

Find the energy of the following sequence shown below:

$$x[n] = n \qquad 0 \le n \le 4$$

Solution

$$x[n] = n$$

$$= \{0,\ 1,\ 2,\ 3,\ 4\}$$

$$E = \sum_{n=0}^{4} n^2$$

$$= 0 + 1 + 4 + 9 + 16$$

$$\boxed{E = 30}$$

Example 1.23

Determine the average power and the energy per period of the sequence shown in Figure 1.29.

Solution The fundamental period N of the signal is 5. Hence, the average power per period is

$$P = \frac{1}{5}\sum_{n=0}^{4} n^2 = \frac{1}{5}[0 + 1 + 4 + 9 + 16]$$

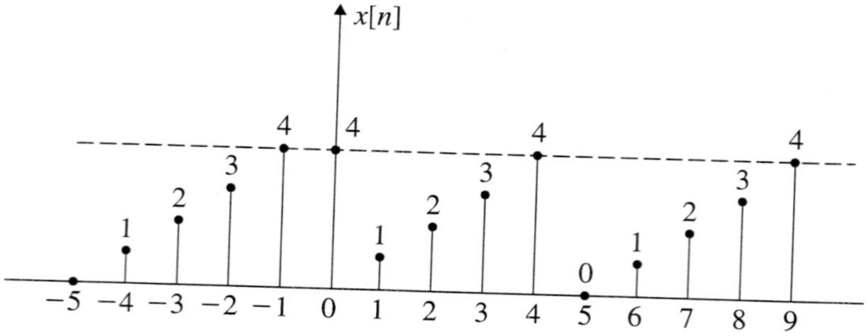

Figure 1.29 $x[n]$ of Example 1.23.

$$\boxed{P = 6}$$

Average energy per period is

$$E = \sum_{n=0}^{4} n^2$$

$$= [0 + 1 + 4 + 9 + 16]$$

$$\boxed{E = 30}$$

Example 1.24

Find the energy and power of the following signal:

$$x[n] = a^n u[n]$$

for the following cases:

(a) $|a| < 1$

(b) $|a| = 1$

(c) $|a| > 1$

Solution

(a) **$x[n] = a^n u[n]$ where $|a| < 1$ and $n \geq 0$**

$$E = \sum_{n=0}^{\infty} (a^n)^2$$

$$= 1 + a^2 + a^4 + \ldots$$

$$\boxed{E = \frac{1}{1 - |a|^2}}$$

$$P = 0$$

(*b*) $\mathbf{x[n] = a^n u[n]}$ **where** $\mathbf{|a| = 1}$

$$E = \underset{N\to\infty}{Lt} \sum_{0}^{N} 1^n = \underset{N\to\infty}{Lt} (N+1)$$

$$\boxed{E = \infty}$$

$$P = \underset{N\to\infty}{Lt} \frac{1}{(2N+1)} \sum_{0}^{N} (1)^n$$

$$P == \underset{N\to\infty}{Lt} \frac{(N+1)}{(2N+1)}$$

$$= \underset{N\to\infty}{Lt} \frac{N(1+\frac{1}{N})}{N(2+\frac{1}{N})}$$

$$\boxed{P = \frac{1}{2}}$$

(*c*) $\mathbf{x[n] = a^n u[n]}$ **where** $\mathbf{|a| > 1}$

$$E = \underset{N\to\infty}{Lt} \sum_{0}^{N} a^n$$

$$= 1 + a + a^2 + \cdots + a^N$$

$$\boxed{E = \infty}$$

$$P = \underset{N\to\infty}{Lt} \frac{1}{(2N+1)} \sum_{n=0}^{N} a^n$$

$$= \underset{N\to\infty}{Lt} \frac{1}{(N+1)} \frac{(1-a^{N+1})}{(1-a)}$$

$$\boxed{P = \infty}$$

The signal is neither energy nor power signal.

Example 1.25

Find the energy of the following signal:

$$x[n] = \text{ramp}[n] - 2\,\text{ramp}[n-4] + \text{ramp}[n-8]$$

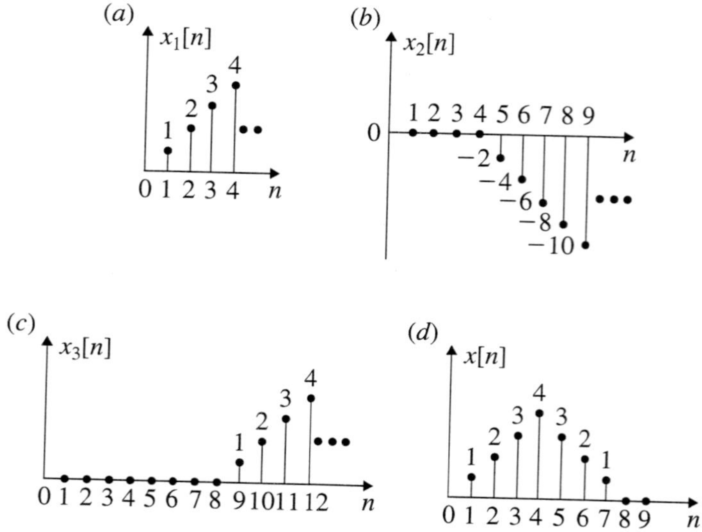

Figure 1.30 DT energy signal of Example 1.25.

Solution

$$x[n] = \text{ramp}[n] - 2\,\text{ramp}[n-4] + \text{ramp}[n-8]$$
$$= x_1[n] + x_2[n] + x_3[n]$$

$x_1[n]$, $x_2[n]$ and $x_3[n]$ are shown in Figures 1.30(*a*), (*b*) and (*c*) respectively. Figure 1.30(*d*) represents $x[n]$. From Figure 1.30(*d*), the energy of the signal $x[n]$ is obtained as

$$E = 1^2 + 2^2 + 3^2 + 4^2 + 3^2 + 2^2 + 1^2$$

$$\boxed{E = 44}$$

Example 1.26

Determine the value of power and energy of each of the following signals:

$$(a) \qquad x[n] = e^{j\left(\frac{\pi n}{2}+\frac{\pi}{8}\right)}$$

$$(b) \qquad x[n] = \left(\frac{1}{2}\right)^n u[n]$$

Solution

(Anna University, April, 2008)

(*a*) $\boldsymbol{x[n] = e^{j\left(\frac{\pi n}{2}+\frac{\pi}{8}\right)}}$

$$P = \underset{N\to\infty}{Lt} \frac{1}{2N+1} \sum_{-N}^{N} |e^{j\left(\frac{\pi n}{2}+\frac{\pi}{8}\right)}|^2$$

$$= \underset{N\to\infty}{Lt} \frac{1}{(2N+1)} \sum_{-N}^{N} 1$$

$$P = \frac{(2N+1)}{(2N+1)} = 1$$

$$\boxed{P = 1 \text{ and } E = \infty}$$

(*b*) $\boldsymbol{x[n] = \left[\frac{1}{2}\right]^n u[n]}$

$$E = \underset{N\to\infty}{Lt} \sum_0^N \left(\frac{1}{2}\right)^{2n}$$

$$= \underset{N\to\infty}{Lt} \sum_0^N \left(\frac{1}{4}\right)^{n} = \frac{1}{1-\frac{1}{4}} = \frac{4}{3}$$

$$\boxed{E = \frac{4}{3} \text{ and } P = 0}$$

Example 1.27

Find the energy of the following DT signal

$$x[n] = \left(\frac{1}{2}\right)^n \qquad n \geq 0$$
$$= 3^n \qquad n < 0$$

(*Anna University, April, 2005*)

Solution

$$E = \left[\sum_{-\infty}^{-1} (3)^{2n} + \sum_0^{\infty} \left(\frac{1}{2}\right)^{2n}\right]$$

$$= \left[\sum_{-\infty}^{-1} (9)^{n} + \sum_0^{\infty} \left(\frac{1}{4}\right)^{n}\right]$$

$$= \left[\sum_{1}^{\infty} (9)^{-n} + \frac{1}{(1-\frac{1}{4})}\right]$$

$$= \left[\sum_{1}^{\infty} \left(\frac{1}{9}\right)^{n} + \frac{4}{3}\right]$$

$$= \left[\frac{1}{9} + \frac{1}{9^2} + \frac{1}{9^3} + \cdots\right] + \frac{4}{3}$$

$$= \frac{1}{9}\left[1 + \frac{1}{9} + \frac{1}{9^2} + \frac{1}{9^3} + \cdots\right] + \frac{4}{3}$$

$$= \frac{1}{9}\frac{1}{[1-\frac{1}{9}]} + \frac{4}{3}$$

$$= \frac{1}{8} + \frac{4}{3}$$

$$\boxed{E = \frac{35}{24}}$$

1.7 Discrete Time System

The block diagram of a discrete time system is shown in Figure 1.31. $x[n]$ is the excitation (input) signal and $y[n]$ is the response (output) signal of the DT system. H represents the functional relationship between the input and output which is described by difference equation. The input-output signals appear at discrete interval of time n where $n = 0, 1, 2 \ldots$ which is an integer. n can also take negative value of an integer.

1.8 Properties of Discrete Time System

Like CT systems, DT systems also possesses similar properties which are given below:

1. Linearity and non-linearity
2. Time varying and time invariant
3. Causal and non-causal
4. Stable and unstable
5. Static (instantaneous) and dynamic (system without and with memory)
6. Invertibility and inverse.

1.8.1 Linear and Non-linear Systems

A linear discrete time system obeys the property of superposition. As discussed for CT system, the superposition property is composed of homogeneity and additivity. Let $x_1[n]$ excitation produce $y_1[n]$ response and $x_2[n]$ produce $y_2[n]$ response. According to additivity property of superposition theorem, if both $x_1[n]$ and $x_2[n]$ are applied simultaneously, then

$$x_1[n] + x_2[n] = y_1[n] + y_2[n]$$

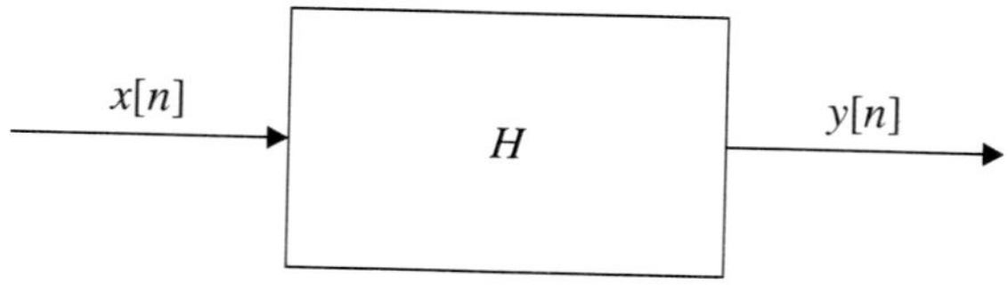

Figure 1.31 Block diagram representation of discrete time system.

Let $a_1x_1[n]$ and $a_2x_2[n]$ be the inputs. According the homogeneity (scaling) property, when these signals are separately applied,

$$a_1x_1[n] = a_1y_1[n]$$
$$a_2x_2[n] = a_2y_2[n]$$

If $a_1x_1[n] + a_2x_2[n]$ are simultaneously applied the output is obtained by applying superposition theorem as,

$$a_1x_1[n] + a_2x_2[n] = a_1y_1[n] + a_2y_2[n]$$

In the above equation, $a_1x_1[n] + a_2x_2[n]$ is called the weighted sum of input and $a_1y_1[n]+a_2y_2[n]$ is called the weighted sum of the output. Therefore, the following procedure is followed to test the linearity of a DT system.

1. Express

$$y_1[n] = f(x_1[n])$$
$$y_2[n] = f(x_2[n])$$

2. Find the weighted sum of the output as

$$y_3[n] = a_1y_1[n] + a_2y_2[n]$$

3. Find the output $y_4[n]$ due to the weighted sum of input as

$$y_4[n] = f(a_1x_1[n] + a_2x_2[n])$$

4. If $y_3[n] = y_4[n]$, then given DT system is linear. Otherwise it is non-linear.

The following examples illustrate the method of testing a DT system for its linearity.

Example 1.28

Test whether the following DT systems are linear or not:

$$(a) \quad y[n] = x^2[n]$$
$$(b) \quad y[n] = x[4n+1]$$
$$(c) \quad y[n] = x[n] + \frac{1}{x[n+1]}$$
$$(d) \quad y[n] = x[n^2]$$
$$(e) \quad y[n] = x[n] + nx[n+1]$$

Solution

(*a*) $\boldsymbol{y[n] = x^2[n]}$

$$y_1[n] = x_1^2[n]$$
$$y_2[n] = x_2^2[n]$$

1. The weighted sum of the output $y_3[n]$ is,

$$\begin{aligned} y_3[n] &= a_1 y_1[n] + a_2 y_2[n] \\ &= a_1 x_1^2[n] + a_2 x_2^2[n] \end{aligned}$$

2. The output due to the weighted sum of the input $y_4[n]$ is,

$$\begin{aligned} y_4[n] &= [a_1 x_1[n] + a_2 x_2[n]]^2 \\ &= a_1^2 x_1^2[n] + a_2^2 x_2^2[n] + 2a_1 a_2 x_1[n] x_2[n] \end{aligned}$$

3.

$$y_3[n] \neq y_4[n]$$

The system is Non-linear.

(*b*) $\boldsymbol{y[n] = x[4n + 1]}$

$$a_1 y_1[n] = a_1 x_1[4n + 1]$$
$$a_2 y_2[n] = a_2 x_2[4n + 1]$$
$$y_3[n] = a_1 y_1[n] + a_2 y_2[n]$$

1. The weighted sum of the output is,

$$\begin{aligned} y_3[n] &= a_1 y_1[n] + a_2 y_2[n] \\ &= a_1 x_1[4n + 1] + a_2 x_2[4n + 1] \end{aligned}$$

2. The output due to the weighted sum of the input is,

$$y_4[n] = a_1 x_1[4n + 1] + a_2 x_2[4n + 1]$$

3.

$$y_3[n] = y_4[n]$$

The system is Linear.

(*c*) $\mathbf{y[n] = x[n] + \frac{1}{x(n+1)}}$

$$a_1y_1[n] = a_1\left[x_1[n] + \frac{1}{x_1(n+1)}\right]$$

$$a_2y_2[n] = a_2\left[x_2[n] + \frac{1}{x_2(n+1)}\right]$$

1. The weighted sum of the output $y_3[n]$ is,

$$\begin{aligned} y_3[n] &= a_1y_1[n] + a_2y_2[n] \\ &= a_1\left[x_1[n] + \frac{1}{x_1(n+1)}\right] + a_2\left[x_2[n] + \frac{1}{x_2(n+1)}\right] \end{aligned}$$

2. The output due to the weighted sum of the input is,

$$\begin{aligned} y_4[n] &= f[a_1x_1[n] + a_2x_2[n]] \\ &= a_1[x_1[n] + a_2x_2[n]] + \left[\frac{1}{a_1x_1[n+1] + a_2x_2[n+1]}\right] \end{aligned}$$

3.

$$y_3[n] \neq y_4[n]$$

The system is Non-linear.

(*d*) $\mathbf{y[n] = x[n^2]}$

$$a_1y_1[n] = a_1x_1[n^2]$$

$$a_2y_2[n] = a_2x_2[n^2]$$

1. The weighted sum of the output $y_3[n]$ is,

$$\begin{aligned} y_3[n] &= a_1y_1[n] + a_2y_2[n] \\ &= a_1x_1[n^2] + a_2x_2[n^2] \end{aligned}$$

2. The output $y_4[n]$ due to the weighted sum of input is,

$$y_4[n] = a_1x_1[n^2] + a_2x_2[n^2]$$

3.

$$y_3[n] = y_4[n]$$

The system is Linear.

(*e*) $\mathbf{y[n] = x[n] + nx[n+1]}$

$$a_1 y_1[n] = a_1[x_1[n] + nx_1[n+1]]$$
$$a_2 y_2[n] = a_2[x_2[n] + nx_2[n+1]]$$

1. The weighted sum of the output is,

$$\begin{aligned} y_3[n] &= a_1 y_1[n] + a_2 y_2[n] \\ &= a_1[x_1[n] + nx_1[n+1]] + a_2[x_2[n] + nx_2[n+1]] \end{aligned}$$

2. The output due to the weighted sum of the input is,

$$y_4[n] = a_1 x_1[n] + a_2 x_2[n] + a_1 n x_1[n+1] + a_2 n x_2[n+1]$$

3.

$$y_3[n] = y_4[n]$$

The system is Linear.

1.8.2 Time Invariant and Time Varying DT Systems

Consider the discrete time system represented in block diagram of Figure 1.32(*a*). If the input is $x[n]$ then the output is $y[n]$. If the input is time delayed by n_0, which becomes $x[n-n_0]$, the output becomes $y[n-n_0]$. The signal representation and the delayed signals are shown in Figures 1.32(*b*) and (*c*) respectively. Such systems are called time invariant.

If an arbitrary excitation $x[n]$ of a system causes a response $y[n]$ and the delayed excitation $x[n-n_0]$ where n_0 is any arbitrary integer causes $y[n-n_0]$ then the system is said to be time invariant.

PROCEDURE TO CHECK TIME INVARIANCY OF DT SYSTEMS

1. For the delayed input $x[n-n_0]$ find the output $y[n, n_0]$.
2. Obtain the delayed output $y[n-n_0]$ by substituting $n = n - n_0$ in $y[n]$.
3. If $y[n, n_0] = y[n-n_0]$, the system is time invariant. Otherwise the system is time varying.

The following examples illustrate the method of testing the time invariancy of DT systems.

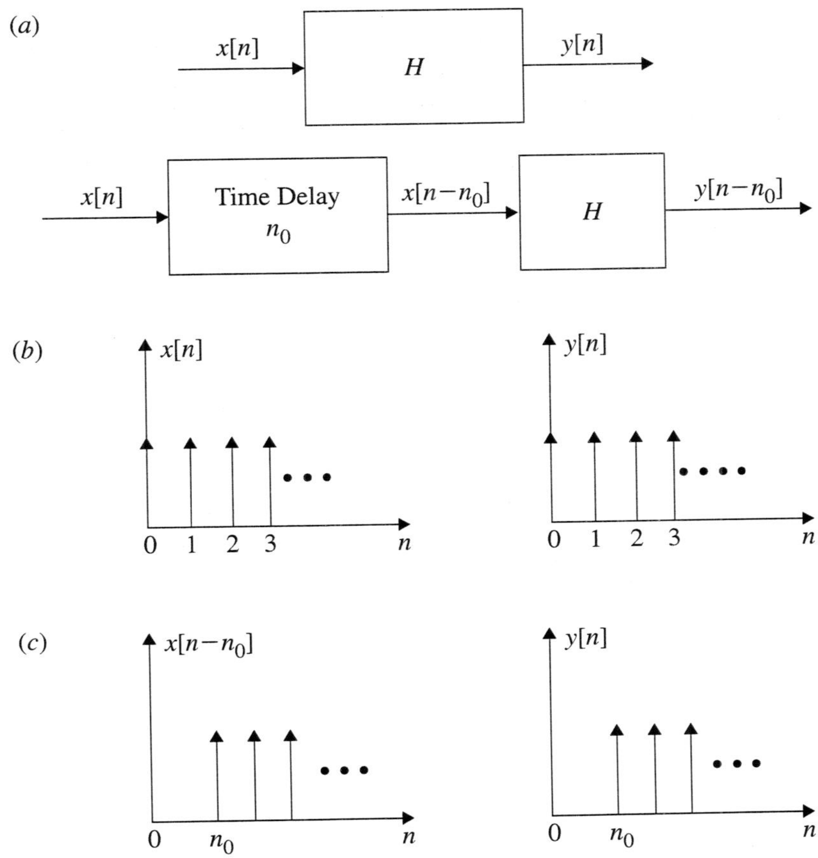

Figure 1.32 Block diagram and signal representation to illustrate time invariancy of DT system.

Example 1.29

Determine whether the following systems are time invariant or not:

$$(a) \quad y[n] = nx[n]$$
$$(b) \quad y[n] = x[2n]$$
$$(c) \quad y[n] = x[-n]$$
$$(d) \quad y[n] = \sin(x[n])$$
$$(e) \quad y[n] = x[n]x[n-1]$$

Solution

(*a*) $\boldsymbol{y[n] = nx[n]}$

1. The output for the delayed input $x[n - n_0]$ is,

$$y[n, n_0] = nx[n - n_0]$$

2. The delayed output for the input $x[n]$ is,

$$y[n - n_0] = (n - n_0)x[n - n_0]$$

3.

$$y[n, n_0] \neq y[n - n_0]$$

The system is Time Variant.

(*b*) $\boldsymbol{y[n] = x[2n]}$

$$\begin{aligned} y[n, n_0] &= x[2n - n_0] \\ y[n - n_0] &= x[2(n - n_0)] \\ &= x[2n - 2n_0] \\ y[n, n_0] &\neq y[n - n_0] \end{aligned}$$

The system is Time Varying.

(*c*) $\boldsymbol{y[n] = x[-n]}$

$$\begin{aligned} y[n, n_0] &= x[-n - n_0] \\ y[n - n_0] &= x[-(n - n_0)] \\ &= x[-n + n_0] \\ y[n, n_0] &\neq y[n - n_0] \end{aligned}$$

The system is Time Varying.

(*d*) $\boldsymbol{y[n] = \sin(x[n])}$

$$\begin{aligned} y[n, n_0] &= \sin(x[n - n_0]) \\ y[n - n_0] &= \sin(x[n - n_0]) \\ y[n, n_0] &= y[n - n_0] \end{aligned}$$

The system is Time Invariant.

(*e*) $\boldsymbol{y[n] = x[n]x[n-1]}$

$$y[n, n_0] = x[n - n_0]x[n - n_0 - 1]$$
$$y[n - n_0] = x[n - n_0]x[n - n_0 - 1]$$
$$y[n, n_0] = y[n - n_0]$$

The system is Time Invariant.

1.8.3 Causal and Non-causal DT Systems

A discrete time system is said to be causal if the response of the system depends on the present or the past inputs applied. The systems is non-causal if the output depends on the future input.

The following examples illustrate the method of identifying causal and non-causal systems.

Example 1.30

Determine whether the following systems are causal or not:

$$(a) \quad y[n] = x[n-1]$$
$$(b) \quad y[n] = x[n] + x[n-1]$$
$$(c) \quad y[n-1] = x[n]$$
$$(d) \quad y[n] = \sin(x[n])$$
$$(e) \quad y[n] = \sum_{k=-\infty}^{n+4} x(k)$$
$$(f) \quad y[n] = \sum_{k=0}^{-3} x(k)$$

Solution

(*a*) $\boldsymbol{y[n] = x[n-1]}$

$$y[0] = x[-1]$$
$$y[1] = x[0]$$

The output depends on the past value of $x[n]$. Hence

The system is Causal.

(*b*) $\mathbf{y[n] = x[n] + x[n-1]}$

$$y[0] = x[0] + x[-1]$$
$$y[1] = x[1] + x[0]$$

here $x[1]$ is present value and $x[0]$ is past value. The output depends on the present and past inputs. Hence

The system is Causal.

(*c*) $\mathbf{y[n-1] = x[n]}$

$$y[-1] = x[0] \qquad \text{(Future input)}$$
$$y[0] = x[1] \qquad \text{(Future input)}$$

The output depends on the future inputs. Hence

The system is Non-causal.

(*d*) $\mathbf{y[n] = \sin x[n]}$

$$y[0] = \sin x[0]$$
$$y[-1] = \sin x[-1]$$

The output depends on the present input. Hence

The system is Causal.

(*e*) $\mathbf{y[n] = \sum_{k=-\infty}^{n+4} x[k]}$

$$y[0] = \sum_{-\infty}^{4} x[k]$$
$$= x[-\infty] + x[-\infty + 1] + \cdots + x[-1] + x[0] + x[1] + x[2] + x[3] + x[4]$$

$$x[-\infty] + x[-\infty + 1], \ldots, x[-1] = \text{Past input}$$
$$x[0] = \text{Present input}$$
$$x[0],\ x[1],\ x[2],\ x[3] \text{ and } x[4] = \text{Future input}$$

The output depends on past, present and future input. Hence

The system is Non-causal.

(*f*) $\boldsymbol{y[n] = \sum_{k=0}^{n-3} x[k]}$

$$y[0] = \sum_{k=0}^{-3} x[k]$$

$$= x[0] + x[-1] + x[-2] + x[-3]$$

$$x[0] = \text{Present input}$$

$$x[-1] = \text{Past input}$$

The output depends on the present and past input. Hence

The system is Causal.

1.8.4 Stable and Unstable Systems

A discrete time system is said to be stable if for any bounded input, it produces a bounded output. This implies that the impulse response

$$\boldsymbol{y[n] = \sum_{-\infty}^{\infty} |h[n]| < \infty}$$

is absolutely summable.

For a bounded input,

$$|x[n]| \leq M_x < \infty$$

the output

$$|y[n]| \leq M_y < \infty$$

From the above two conditions, it can be obtained

$$y[n] = \sum_{-\infty}^{\infty} |h[n]| < \infty$$

The following examples illustrate the above procedure.

Example 1.31

Check whether the DT systems described by the following equations are stable or not.

$$(a) \qquad y[n] = \sin x[n]$$

$$(b) \qquad y[n] = \sum_{k=0}^{n+1} x[k]$$

$$(c) \qquad y[n] = e^{x[n]}$$

(d) $h[n] = 3^n u[n+3]$

(e) $y[n] = x[-n-3]$

(f) $y[n] = x[n-1] + x[n] + x[n+1]$

(g) $h[n] = e^{-|n|}$

(h) $h[n] = n\,u[n]$

(i) $h[n] = 3^n u[n-3]$

(j) $h[n] = 2^n u[-n]$

Solution

(a) $\boldsymbol{y[n] = \sin x[n]}$

If $x[n]$ is bounded, then $\sin x[n]$ is also bounded and so $y[n]$ is also bounded

The system is Stable.

(b) $\boldsymbol{y[n] = \sum_{k=0}^{n+1} x[k]}$

Here, as $n \to \infty$, $y[n] \to \infty$ and the output is unbounded. For bounded input n should be a finite number. In that case $y[n]$ is bounded and the system is stable.

The system is Stable.	for $n =$ finite
The system is Unstable.	for $n = \infty$

(c) $\boldsymbol{e^{x[n]}}$

For $|x[n]|$ bounded, $e^{|x[n]|}$ is bounded and the system is stable.

The system is Stable.

(d) $\boldsymbol{h[n] = 3^n u[n+3]}$

$$\begin{aligned}|y[n]| &= \sum_{n=-3}^{\infty} 3^n \\ &= (3)^{-3} + (3)^{-2} + (3)^{-1} + (3)^0 + (3)^1 + \cdots + (3)^{\infty} \\ &= \infty\end{aligned}$$

The output is unbounded.

The system is Unstable.

(e) $\boldsymbol{y[n] = x[-n-3]}$

$$\begin{aligned} y[n] &= x[-n-3] \\ &= 1 \qquad n = -3 \\ &= 0 \qquad \text{otherwise} \end{aligned}$$

The system is Stable.

(f) $\boldsymbol{y[n] = x[n-1] + x[n] + x[n+1]}$

$$\begin{aligned} y[0] &= \delta[-1] + \delta[0] + \delta[1] = 0 + 1 + 0 = 1 \\ y[1] &= \delta[0] + \delta[1] + \delta[2] = 1 + 0 + 0 = 1 \\ y[-1] &= \delta[-2] + \delta[-1] + \delta[0] = 0 + 0 + 1 = 1 \\ y[-2] &= \delta[1] + \delta[2] + \delta[3] = 0 + 0 + 0 = 0 \\ y[2] &= \delta[1] + \delta[2] + \delta[3] = 0 + 0 + 0 = 0 \\ y[n] &= \sum_{-\infty}^{\infty} |h[k]| = 1 + 1 + 1 = 3 < \infty \end{aligned}$$

The system is Stable.

(g) $\boldsymbol{h[n] = e^{-|n|}}$

$$\begin{aligned} y[n] &= \sum_{-\infty}^{\infty} e^{|n|} = \sum_{-\infty}^{-1} e^{|n|} + \sum_{0}^{\infty} e^{-|n|} \\ &= \sum_{1}^{\infty} e^{-n} + \sum_{0}^{\infty} e^{-n} \\ &= e^{-1} + e^{-2} + \cdots + 1 + e^{-1} + e^{-2} + \cdots \\ &= e^{-1}[1 + e^{-1} + e^{-2} + \cdots] + 1 + e^{-1} + e^{-2} + \cdots \\ &= e^{-1}\frac{1}{[1-e^{-1}]} + \frac{1}{[1-e^{-1}]} \\ &= \frac{e^{-1}}{(1-e^{-1})} + \frac{1}{(1-e^{-1})} \\ &= \frac{[1+e^{-1}]}{[1-e^{-1}]} < \infty \end{aligned}$$

The system is Stable.

(*h*) $\boldsymbol{h[n] = n\,u[n]}$

$$y[n] = \sum_{0}^{\infty} n = 1 + 2 + \cdots + \infty = \infty$$

The system is Unstable.

(*i*) $\boldsymbol{h[n] = 3^n u[n-3]}$

$$y[n] = \sum_{3}^{\infty} 3^n = 3^3 + 3^2 + \cdots + \infty = \infty$$

The system is Unstable.

(*j*) $\boldsymbol{h[n] = 2^n u[-n]}$

$$y[n] = \sum_{-\infty}^{-1} 2^n = \sum_{1}^{\infty} \left(\frac{1}{2}\right)^n$$

$$= \frac{1}{2} + \left(\frac{1}{2}\right)^2 + \cdots$$

$$= \frac{1}{2}\left[1 + \frac{1}{2} + \left(\frac{1}{2}\right)^2 + \cdots\right]$$

$$= \frac{1}{2}\left[\frac{1}{1-\frac{1}{2}}\right] = 1 < \infty$$

The system is Stable.

1.8.5 Static and Dynamic Systems

A discrete time system is said to be static (memoryless or instantaneous) if the output response depends on the present value only and not on the past and future values of excitation. Discrete systems described by difference equations require memory and hence they are dynamic systems.

The following examples illustrate the method identifying static and dynamic discrete systems.

Example 1.32

Identify whether the following systems are static or dynamic:

(*a*) $y[n] = x[3n]$

(*b*) $y[n] = \sin(x[n])$

(*c*) $y[n-1] + y[n] = x[n]$

(*d*) $y[n] = \text{sgn}|x[n]|$

Solution

(*a*) $\mathbf{y[n] = x[3n]}$

$$y[1] = x[3]$$
$$y[-1] = x[-3]$$

The output $y[1]$ and $y[-1]$ depends on the future value $x[3]$ and the past input $x[-3]$ respectively. Hence

The system is Dynamic.

(*b*) $\mathbf{y[n] = \sin(x[n])}$

$$y[0] = \sin(x[0])$$
$$y[1] = \sin(x[1])$$

The output depends on the present input at all time. Hence

The system is Static.

(*c*) $\mathbf{y[n-1] + y[n] = x[n]}$

The system is described by first order difference equation which require memory. Hence

The system is Dynamic.

(*d*) $\mathbf{y[n] = \mathrm{sgn}|x[n]|}$

$$\begin{aligned} \mathrm{sgn}|x[n]| &= 1 \qquad \text{for } n > 0 \\ &= -1 \qquad \text{for } n < 0 \end{aligned}$$

$$y[1] = x[1] = 1$$
$$y[-1] = x[-1] = -1$$

The output depends on the present value of the input. Hence

The system is Static.

1.8.6 Invertible and Inverse Discrete Time Systems

A discrete time system is said to be invertible if distinct input leads to distinct output. If a system is invertible then an inverse system exists.

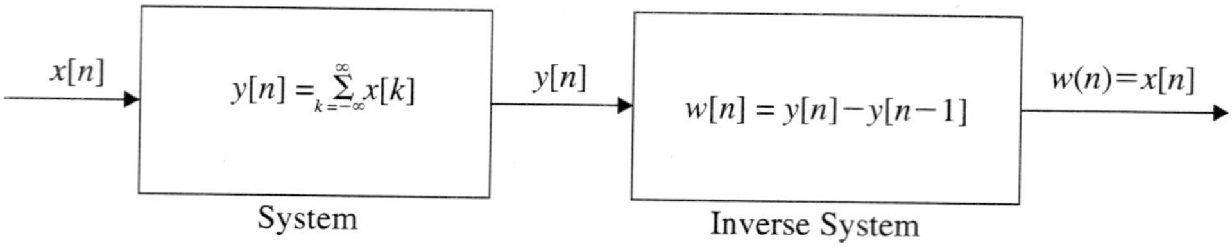

Figure 1.33 Inverse discrete time system.

Consider the system shown in Figure 1.33. The input $x[n]$ produces the output $y[n]$. This system is in cascade with its inverse system. The output of this system is nothing but the difference of the two successive inputs $y[n] - y[n-1]$. This is the input to the original system. Thus, by connecting an inverse system in cascade with the original system, the excitation signal $x[n]$ is re-established provided the original system is invertible. The concept of invertibility is very widely used in communications.

Example 1.33

Determine whether the following systems are static, causal, time invariant, linear and stable.

$$(a) \quad y[n] = x[4n+1]$$
$$(b) \quad y[n] = x[n] + n\,x[n+1]$$
$$(c) \quad y[n] = x[n]u[n]$$
$$(d) \quad y[n] = \log_{10} x[n]$$
$$(e) \quad y[n] = x^2[n]$$

(Anna University, 2007)

Solution

(*a*) $\boldsymbol{y[n] = x[4n+1]}$

1.

$$y[0] = x[1]$$

The output depends on future input. Hence

The system is Dynamic and Non-causal.

2. The output due to the delayed input is,

$$y[n, n_0] = x[4n - n_0 + 1]$$

The delayed output due to the input is,

$$y[n-n_0] = x[4(n-n_0)+1]$$
$$= x[4n-4n_0+1]$$
$$y[n,n_0] \neq y[n-n_0]$$

The system is Time Variant.

3.

$$a_1y_1[n] = a_1x_1[4n+1]$$
$$a_2y_2[n] = a_2x_2[4n+1]$$
$$y_3[n] = a_1y_1[n] + a_2y_2[n]$$
$$= a_1x_1[4n+1] + a_2x_2[4n+1]$$
$$y_4[n] = a_1x_1[4n+1] + a_2x_2[4n+1]$$
$$y_3[n] = y_4[n]$$

The system is Linear.

4. The input is time shifted and time compressed signal. As long as the input is bounded the output is also bounded.

The system is Stable.

The system is

(1) Dynamic, (2) Non-causal, (3) Time Variant, (4) Linear and (5) Stable.

(*b*) $\boldsymbol{y[n] = x[n] + n\,x[n+1]}$

1.

$$y[0] = x[0] + 0 \times x[1]$$

The output depends on present and future inputs.

The system is Dynamic and Non-causal.

2. The output due to the delayed input is,

$$y[n,n_0] = x[n-n_0] + nx[n-n_0+1]$$

The delayed output due to the input is,

$$y[n-n_0] = x[n-n_0] + (n-n_0)x[n-n_0+1]$$
$$y[n,n_0] \neq y[n-n_0]$$

The system is Time Variant.

3. The weighted sum of the output due to the input is,

$$y_3[n] = a_1 y_1[n] + a_2 y_2[n] = a_1 x_1[n] + a_1 n x_1[n+1] + a_2 x_2[n] + a_2 n x_2[n+1]$$

The output due to the weighted sum of the input is,

$$y_4[n] = a_1\{x_1[n] + n x_1[n+1]\} + a_2\{x_2[n] + a_2 n x_2[n+1]\}$$
$$y_3[n] = y_4[n]$$

The system is Linear.

4. As long as $x[n]$ is bounded, $y[n]$ is also bounded for $n =$ finite.

The system is Stable.

The system is

(1) Dynamic, (2) Non-causal, (3) Time Variant, (4) Linear and (5) Stable.

(c) $\boldsymbol{y[n] = x[n]u[n]}$

1.

$$y[0] = x[0]u[0]$$
$$y[1] = x[1]u[1]$$

The output depends on present input only.

The system is Static and Causal.

2. For a causal signal $n \geq 0$. The weighted sum of the output due to input is,

$$y_3[n] = a_1 y_1[n] + a_2 y_2[n]$$
$$= \{a_1 x_1[n] + a_2 x_2[n]\}u[n]$$

The output due to the weighted sum of input is,

$$y_4[n] = \{a_1 x_1[n] + a_2 x_2[n]\}u[n]$$
$$y_3[n] = y_4[n]$$

The system is Linear.

3. The output due to the delayed input is,

$$y[n, n_0] = x_1[n - n_0]u[n]$$

The delayed output due to the input is,

$$y[n - n_0] = x_1[n - n_0]u[n - n_0]$$
$$y[n, n_0] \neq y[n - n_0]$$

The system is Time Variant.

4. As long as $x[n]$ is bounded, $y[n]$ is also bounded.

The system is Stable.

The system is

(1) Static, (2) Causal, (3) Linear, (4) Time Variant and (5) Stable.

(*d*) $\mathbf{y[n] = \log_{10} x[n]}$

1.

$$y[0] = \log_{10} x[0]$$
$$y[1] = \log_{10} x[1]$$
$$y[-1] = \log_{10} x[-1]$$

The output depends on present input only.

The system is Static and Causal.

2. The weighted sum of the output due to input is,

$$y_3[n] = a_1 y_1[n] + a_2 y_2[n]$$
$$= a_1 \log_{10} x_1[n] + a_2 \log_{10} x_2[n]$$

The output due to the weighted sum of input is,

$$y_4[n] = \log_{10}(a_1 x_1[n] + a_2 x_2[n])$$
$$y_3[n] \neq y_4[n]$$

The system is Non-linear.

3. The output due to the delayed input is,

$$y[n, n_0] = \log_{10}[n - n_0]$$

The delayed output due to input is,

$$y[n - n_0] = \log_{10}[n - n_0]$$
$$y[n, n_0] = y[n - n_0]$$

The system is Time Invariant.

4. As long as $x[n]$ is bounded, $\log_{10} x[n]$ is bounded and $y[n]$ is also bounded.

The system is Stable.

The system is

(1) Static, (2) Causal, (3) Non-linear, (4) Time invariant and (5) Stable.

(*e*) $\boldsymbol{y[n] = x^2[n]}$

1.

$$y[0] = x^2[0]$$
$$y[1] = x^2[1]$$

The output depends on present input only.

The system is Static and Causal.

2. The weighted sum of the output due to input is,

$$\begin{aligned} y_3[n] &= a_1 y_1[n] + a_2 y_2[n] \\ &= a_1 x_1^2[n] + a_2 x_2^2[n] \end{aligned}$$

The output due to weighted sum of input is,

$$\begin{aligned} y_4[n] &= \{a_1 x_1[n] + a_2 x_2[n]\}^2 \\ &= a_1^2 x_1^2[n] + a_2^2 x_2^2[n] + 2a_1 a_2 x_1[n] x_2[n] \\ y_3[n] &\neq y_4[n] \end{aligned}$$

The system is Non-linear.

3. The output due to the delayed input is,

$$y[n, n_0] = x^2[n - n_0]$$

The delayed output due to the input is,

$$y[n - n_0] = x^2[n - n_0]$$
$$y[n, n_0] = y[n - n_0]$$

The system is Time Invariant.

4. If $x[n]$ is bounded, $x^2[n]$ is bounded and $y[n]$ is also bounded.

The system is Stable.

The system is

(1) Static, (2) Causal, (3) Non-linear, (4) Time invariant and (5) Stable.

1.9 The Discrete Time Unit Impulse Response

Let $\delta(n - k)$ be unit impulse which is shifted by k. It has value 1 corresponding to value k. Let $h_k(n)$ denote the response of the linear time invariant discrete time system. By superposition theorem the output response $y(n)$ to the input $x(n)$ is obtained as the weighted linear combination of these responses. Thus, the impulse response $y(n)$ can be expressed as

$$y(n) = \sum_{k=-\infty}^{\infty} x(k)h_k(n) \tag{1.21}$$

Thus, if we know the response of a linear system to the set of shifted unit impulses, it is possible to determine the response to any arbitrary input sequence. The block diagram of DT system is shown in Figure 1.34.

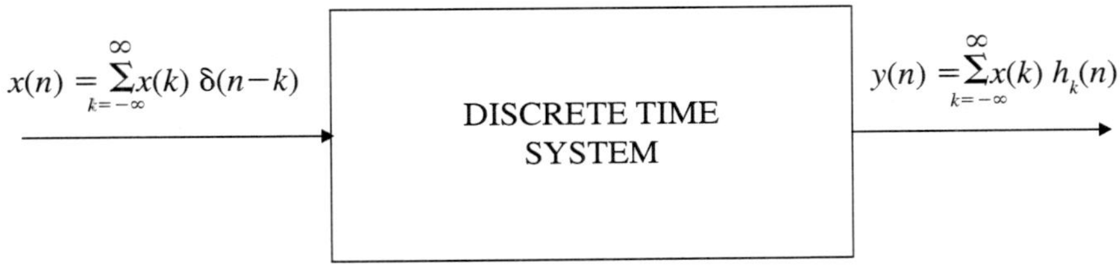

Figure 1.34 Input-output of DT system.

$$y(n) = \sum_{k=-\infty}^{\infty} x(k)h(n-k) \tag{1.22}$$

The above equation is referred to as the convolution sum or superposition sum. $h(n)$ is the impulse response of the LTID time system for the input $\delta(n)$. The convolution sum is symbolically represented as

$$y(n) = x(n) * h(n) \tag{1.23}$$

There are different methods available to get the solution of $y(n)$ by the convolution method, and they are described and illustrated below with examples. The properties of convolution which will be useful for solving convolution sum are discussed first as follows.

1.10 Step Response in Terms of Impulse Response of a LTDT System

The step response $s(n)$ is obtained from the impulse response as

$$s(n) = \sum_{k=0}^{n} h(k)$$

$$s(n) = \sum_{k=0}^{n} h(k) \tag{1.24}$$

The properties of LTID system convolution and the connected results are summarized below.

Important Points to Remember in Connection with Convolution Sum

1. The convolution sum is mathematically expressed as

$$y(n) = x(n) * h(n)$$

$$y(n) = \sum_{k=-\infty}^{\infty} x(k)h(n-k)$$

'$*$' denotes convolution operation.

2. The commutative property of convolution is

$$x(n) * h(n) = h(n) * x(n)$$

3. The distributive property of convolution is

$$y(n) = x(n) * h(n)$$

where

$$h(n) = h_1(n) + h_2(n)$$

4. The associative property of convolution is

$$[x(n) * h_1(n)] * h_2(n) = x(n) * [h_1(n) * h_2(n)]$$

5. The shifting property of convolution is

$$x(n-p) * h(n-q) = y(n-p-q)$$

6. The width property of convolution is

$$[x(n) * h(n)] = T_1 + T_2$$

where T_1=width of $x(n)$ sequence and T_2=width of $h(n)$ sequence.
7. The convolution with an impulse is

$$x(n) * \delta(n) = x(n)$$

8. The convolution with delayed impulse is

$$x(n) * \delta(n - n_0) = x(n - n_0)$$

9. Convolution with unit step is

$$x(n) * u(n) = \sum_{k=-\infty}^{\infty} x(k)$$

10. Convolution with a delayed step is

$$x(n) * u(n - n_0) = \sum_{k=-\infty}^{\infty} x(k - n - n_0)$$

11. System causality in terms of impulse response is

$$h(n) = 0 \qquad \text{for } n < 0$$

12. The necessary and sufficient BIBO stability condition is

$$\sum_{n=-\infty}^{\infty} |h(n)| < \infty$$

In other words $|h(n)|$ should be absolutely summable.

13. Step response $s(n)$ is obtained from impulse response using the following mathematical expression:

$$s(n) = \sum_{k=0}^{n} h(k)$$

1.11 Response Using Convolution Sum

If the impulse response $h(n)$ is known, the output response $y(n)$ can be obtained for any input sequence $x(n)$ by using the following methods:

- Analytical methods and
- Graphical method

In analytical method, $y(n)$ is obtained by

— Using mathematical expression for the convolution sum
— Multiplication method
— Tabulation method
— Matrix method.

1.11.1 Analytical Method Using Convolution Sum

Example 1.34

The impulse response $h(n)$ of a certain LTID system is given by $h(n) = a^n u(n)$ where $0 < a < 1$. The system is excited by $x(n) = u(n)$, a step sequence. Find $y(n)$ using convolution sum.

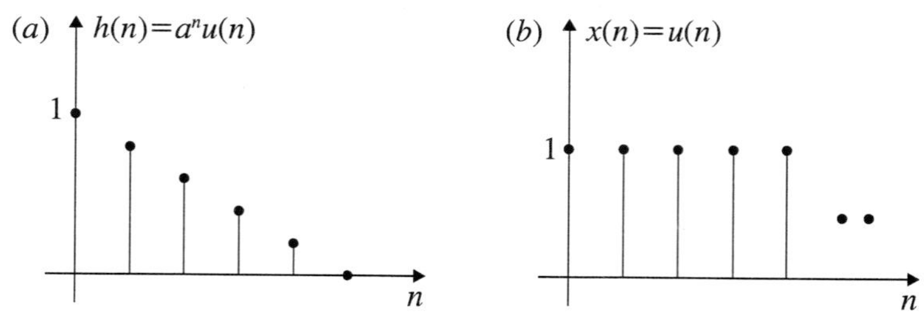

Figure 1.35 Representation of $h(n)$ and $x(n)$ sequences.

(Anna University, December, 2006)

Solution The impulse response and input sequences are represented in Figures 1.35(a) and (b) respectively. They are causal sequences. Hence, the convolution sum given in Equation (1.22) is written as follows:

$$x(n) = u(n)$$
$$x(k) = u(k) = 1$$
$$h(n) = a^n u(n)$$
$$h(n-k) = a^{n-k} u(n-k)$$
$$u(k) = 1$$
$$u(n-k) = 1$$

$$y(n) = \sum_{k=-0}^{n} x(k)h(n-k)$$
$$= \sum_{k=-0}^{n} (a^{n-k})$$
$$= a^n \sum_{k=-0}^{n} \left(\frac{1}{a}\right)^k$$

The above expression is simplified using the finite summation formula

$$\boxed{\sum_{k=-0}^{n} A^k = \frac{(1-A^{n+1})}{(1-A)}}$$

Therefore,

$$y(n) = \frac{a^n\left(1-\frac{1}{a^{n+1}}\right)}{\left(1-\frac{1}{a}\right)}$$

$$\boxed{y(n) = \frac{(1-a^{n+1})}{(1-a)} u(n)}$$

Example 1.35

$$x(n) = u(n)$$
$$h(n) = u(n)$$

Find

$$y(n) = x(n) * h(n)$$

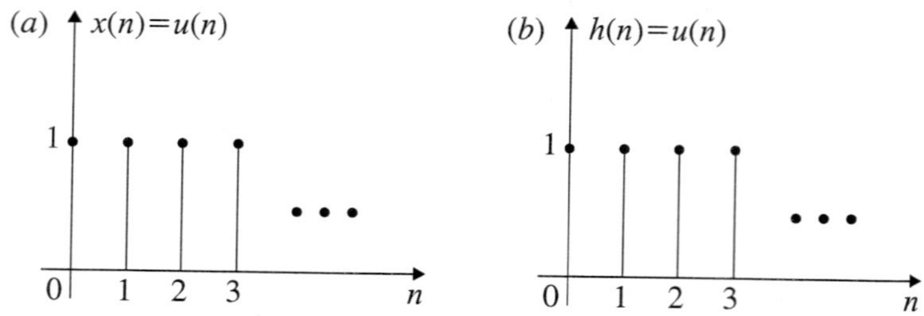

Figure 1.36 Representation of $x(n) = u(n)$ and $h(n) = u(n)$.

Solution The excitation sequence $x(n)$ and the impulse response sequence $h(n)$ are shown in Figures 1.36(*a*) and (*b*) respectively. Since these two signals are causal, the convolution sum can be written as follows:

$$y(n) = \sum_{k=0}^{n} (1)^k (1)^{n-k} = (1)^n \sum_{k=0}^{n} (1) = \sum_{k=0}^{n} 1$$

According to finite summation formula

$$\boxed{\sum_{k=0}^{n} 1 = (1+n)}$$

Therefore,

$$\boxed{y(n) = (1+n)u(n)}$$

Example 1.36

$$x(n) = u(n)$$
$$h(n) = (0.6)^n u(n)$$

Find

$$y(n) = x(n) * h(n)$$

Solution

$$x(n) = 1^n$$
$$x(k) = 1^k$$
$$h(n) = (0.6)^n u(n)$$
$$h(n-k) = (0.6)^{n-k} u(n-k)$$

$$y(n) = \sum_{k=-0}^{n} 1^k (0.6)^{n-k}$$

$$= (0.6)^n \sum_{k=0}^{n} 1^k (0.6)^{-k}$$

$$= (0.6)^n \sum_{k=0}^{n} \left(\frac{1}{0.6}\right)^k$$

$$= (0.6)^n \frac{\left[1 - \frac{1}{(0.6)^{n+1}}\right]}{\left[1 - \frac{1}{0.6}\right]}$$

[Using Finite Summation Formula]

$$= \frac{[(0.6)^{n+1} - 1]}{(0.6) - 1}$$

$$\boxed{y(n) = 2.5[1 - (0.6)^{n+1}]u(n)}$$

Example 1.37

$$x(n) = \left(\frac{1}{5}\right)^n u(n)$$

$$h(n) = 3^n u(n)$$

Find

$$y(n) = x(n) * h(n)$$

Solution

$$x(n) = \left(\frac{1}{5}\right)^n u(n)$$

$$x(k) = \left(\frac{1}{5}\right)^k u(k)$$

$$h(n) = 3^n u(n)$$

$$h(n-k) = 3^{n-k} u(n-k)$$

For causal $x(n) * h(n)$

$$y(n) = \sum_{k=0}^{n} x(k)h(n-k)$$

$$= \sum_{k=0}^{n} \left(\frac{1}{5}\right)^k 3^{n-k}$$

$$y(n) = 3^n \sum_{k=0}^{n} \left(\frac{1}{15}\right)^k$$

Using finite summation formula we get

$$y(n) = 3^n \frac{\left[1 - \frac{1}{15^{n+1}}\right]}{\left(1 - \frac{1}{15}\right)}$$

$$= 3^n \frac{[15^{n+1} - 1]}{(14)} \frac{15}{15^{n+1}}$$

$$\boxed{y(n) = \frac{1}{14(5)^n}[15^{n+1} - 1]u(n)}$$

Example 1.38

Determine the convolution of the signals

$$x(n) = \cos \pi n\, u(n)$$

$$h(n) = \left(\frac{1}{2}\right)^n u(n)$$

(*Anna University, May, 2007*)

Solution

$$x(n) = \cos \pi n\, u(n)$$

$$= (-1)^n u(n)$$

$$x(k) = (-1)^k u(k)$$

$$h(n) = \left(\frac{1}{2}\right)^n u(n)$$

$$h(n-k) = \left(\frac{1}{2}\right)^{n-k} u(n-k)$$

Both $x(n)$ and $h(n)$ are casual. Hence, the convolution sum takes the range of $0 < k < n$.

$$y(n) = \sum_{k=0}^{n} x(k)h(n-k)$$

$$y(n) = \sum_{k=0}^{n}(-1)^k\left(\frac{1}{2}\right)^{n-k}$$

$$= \left(\frac{1}{2}\right)^n \sum_{k=0}^{n}[(-1)(2)]^k$$

$$= \left(\frac{1}{2}\right)^n \sum_{k=0}^{n}(-2)^k$$

$$= \left(\frac{1}{2}\right)^n \frac{[1-(-2)^{n+1}]}{[1-(-2)]}$$

$$= \frac{1}{3}\left(\frac{1}{2}\right)^n [1-(-2)^{n+1}]$$

$$\boxed{y(n) = \frac{1}{3}\left(\frac{1}{2}\right)^n [1+2(-2)^n]u(n)}$$

Example 1.39

$$x(n) = (0.2)^n u(n)$$
$$h(n) = (0.2)^{-n} u(-n)$$

Find

$$y(n) = x(n) * h(n)$$

Solution The signal $x(n)$ is a casual signal and $h(n)$ is an anti-causal signal. $x(k)$ is shown in Figure 1.37(a) and $h(k)$ is shown in Figure 1.37(b) respectively. $h(-k)$ is shown in Figure 1.37(c) and $h(n-k)$ shifted to the extreme left for $n < 0$ and to the right for $n > 0$. They are shown in Figures 1.37(d) and (e) respectively.

$$y(n) = x(n) * h(n)$$

$$= \sum_{k=-\infty}^{\infty} x(k)h(n-k)$$

$$= \sum_{k=-\infty}^{\infty} (0.2)^k u(k)(0.2)^{-(n-k)}u(-(n-k))$$

$$= (0.2)^{-n} \sum_{k=-\infty}^{\infty} (0.2)^{2k}u(k)u(k-n)$$

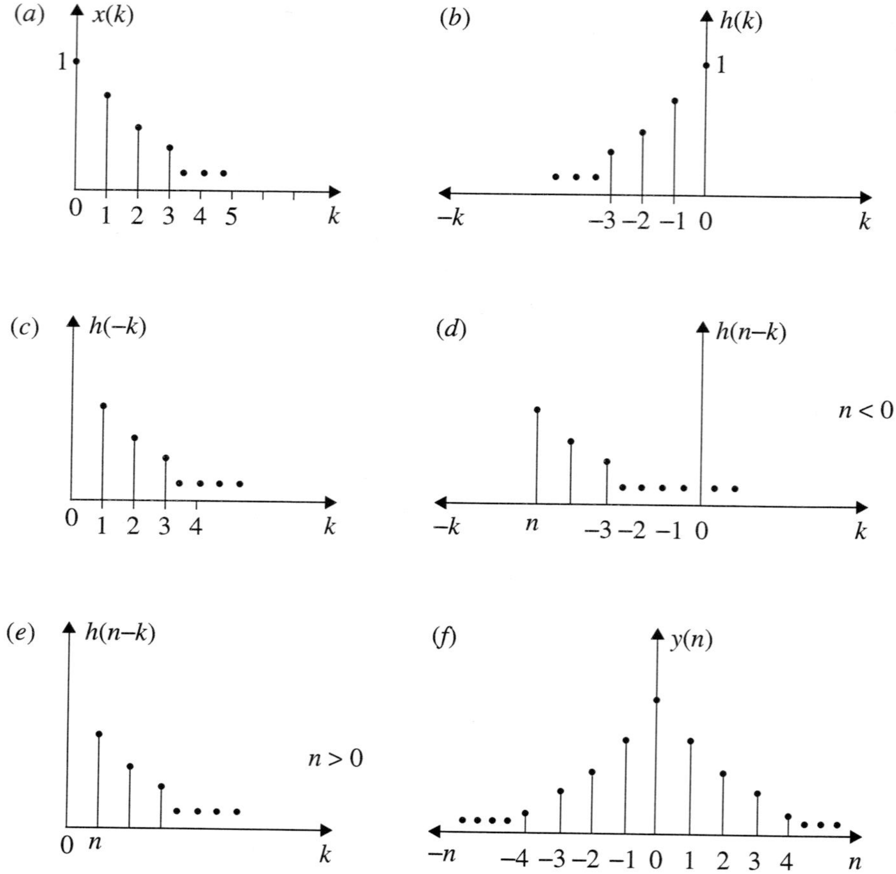

Figure 1.37 Convolution of casual and anti-causal signals.

When $h(n-k)$ is moved towards the right, it overlaps with $x(k)$ for $n<0$ and for $n>0$. For $n<0$

$$u(k)u(k-n)=\begin{cases}1 & k>0\\ 0 & \text{otherwise}\end{cases}$$

Now the limits of summation of $y(n)$ is $0<k<\infty$. Therefore

$$y(n)=(0.2)^{-n}\sum_{k=0}^{\infty}[(0.2)^2]^k$$

$$=(0.2)^{-n}\left[\frac{1}{1-(0.2)^2}\right]$$

$$y(n)=\frac{(0.2)^{-n}}{0.96}\qquad n<0$$

For $n > 0$

$$u(k)u(k-n) = \begin{cases} 1 & \text{for } k \geq n \\ 0 & \text{otherwise} \end{cases}$$

The limits of the summation of $y(n)$ is $n \leq k \leq \infty$

$$y(n) = \sum_{k=n}^{\infty} (0.2)^k u(k)(0.2)^{-(n-k)} u(-n+k)$$

$$= (0.2)^{-n} \sum_{k=n}^{\infty} [(0.2)^2]^k$$

Using the finite summation formula

$$\sum_{k=n}^{\infty} a^k = \frac{a^n}{1-a}$$

we get

$$y(n) = (0.2)^{-n} \left[\frac{(0.2)^{2n}}{(1-0.2^2)} \right]$$

$$= \frac{(0.2)^n}{0.96} \qquad n \geq 0.$$

In general

$$\boxed{y(n) = \frac{(0.2)^{|n|}}{0.96}} \qquad \text{for all } n$$

The response $y(n)$ is plotted and is shown in Figure 1.37(*f*).

Example 1.40

$$x(n) = \begin{cases} 0 & n < -6 \\ \left(\frac{1}{4}\right)^n & n \geq -6 \end{cases}$$

$$h(n) = \begin{cases} 0 & n < 4 \\ \left(\frac{1}{5}\right)^n & n \geq 4 \end{cases}$$

Find

$$y(n) = x(n) * h(n)$$

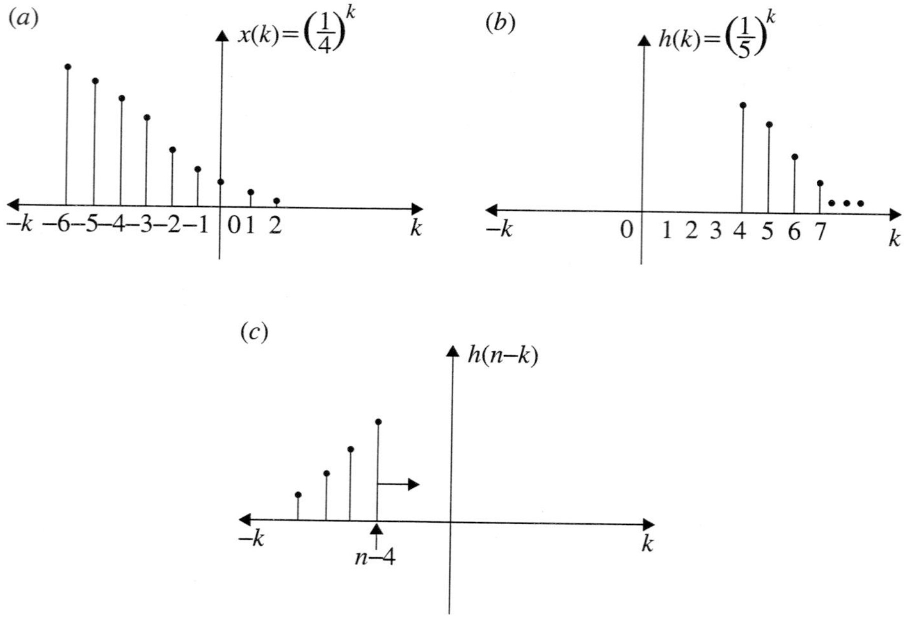

Figure 1.38 Representation of signals for Example 1.40.

Solution Figures 1.38(a), (b) and (c) show $x(h)$, $h(k)$ and $h(n-k)$ respectively.

$$y(n) = x(n) * h(n)$$

$$= \sum_{k=-6}^{n-4} x(k)h(n-k)$$

From Figure 1.38(a), the following equation is written.

$$x(k) = \begin{cases} 0 & k < -6 \\ \left(\frac{1}{4}\right)^k & k \geq -6 \end{cases}$$

From Figure 1.38(b), the following equation is written.

$$h(n-k) = \begin{cases} 0 & (n-k) < 4 \text{ or } k > n-4 \\ \left(\frac{1}{5}\right)^k & (n-k) > 4 \text{ or } k < n-4 \end{cases}$$

When $h(n-k)$ is moved towards the right, $h(n-k)$ overlaps with $x(k)$ at $n \geq -2$

$$y(n) = \begin{cases} 0 & n < -2 \\ \sum_{k=-6}^{n-4} \left(\frac{1}{4}\right)^k \left(\frac{1}{5}\right)^{n-k} & n \geq -2 \end{cases}$$

Put $p = k + 6$ for $n \geq -2$

$$y(n) = \sum_{p=0}^{n+2} \left(\frac{1}{4}\right)^{p-6} \left(\frac{1}{5}\right)^{n-p+6}$$

$$= \left(\frac{4}{5}\right)^6 \left(\frac{1}{5}\right)^n \sum_{p=0}^{n+2} \left(\frac{5}{4}\right)^p$$

$$= \left(\frac{4}{5}\right)^6 \left(\frac{1}{5}\right)^n \left[\frac{1-\left(\frac{5}{4}\right)^{n+3}}{\left(1-\frac{5}{4}\right)}\right]$$

$$\boxed{y(n) = 4^7 \left(\frac{1}{5}\right)^{n+6} \left[\left(\frac{5}{4}\right)^{n+3} - 1\right]} \quad n \geq -2$$

Example 1.41

A linear time invariant discrete time system has the following impulse response.

$$h(n) = \left(\frac{1}{2}\right)^n u(n)$$

The system is excited by the signal $x(n)$=$u(n)$ determine the output of the system at $n = -6$, $n = 6$ and $n = 12$.

Solution $x(k)$, $h(k)$ and $h(n-k)$ are shown in Figures 1.39(a), (b) and (c) respectively. At $n = -6$, $h(n-k) < 0$ and it does not overlap with $x(k)$ and hence

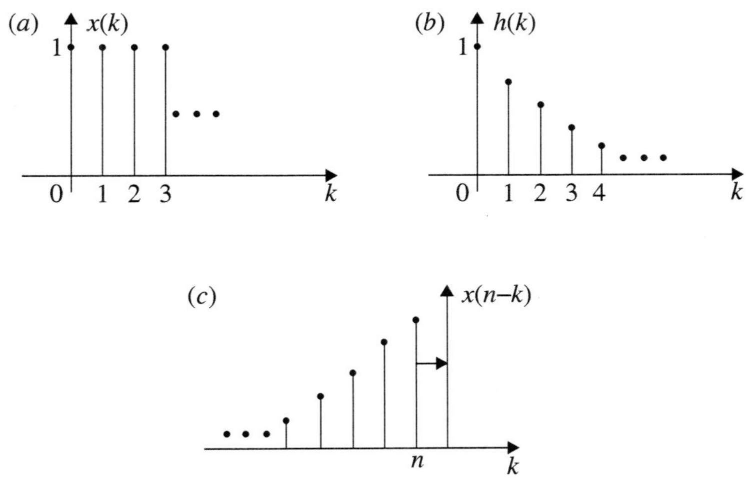

Figure 1.39 Representation of signals for Example 1.41.

$y(n) = 0$. For $n > 0$, the following equation is written:

$$y(n) = x(n) * h(n)$$
$$= \sum_{k=0}^{n} x(n)h(k)$$
$$= \sum_{k=0}^{n} \left(\frac{1}{2}\right)^{n-k}$$
$$= \left(\frac{1}{2}\right)^{n} \sum_{k=0}^{n} (2)^k$$
$$= \left(\frac{1}{2}\right)^{n} \frac{1-2^{n+1}}{(1-2)}$$
$$= \left(\frac{1}{2}\right)^{n} (2^{n+1}-1)u(n)$$

Substituting $n = 6$

$$y(6) = \left(\frac{1}{2}\right)^{6} [2^7 - 1]$$

$$\boxed{y(6) = \frac{127}{64}}$$

Substituting $n = 12$

$$y(12) = \left(\frac{1}{2}\right)^{12} [2^{13} - 1]$$

$$\boxed{y(12) = \frac{8191}{4096}}$$

$$\boxed{y(-6) = 0}$$

Example 1.42

A linear time invariant system has the following impulse response:

$$h(n) = [u(n) - u(n-6)]$$

The system is excited by

$$x(n) = [u(n-1) - u(n-5)]$$

Determine the output of the system.

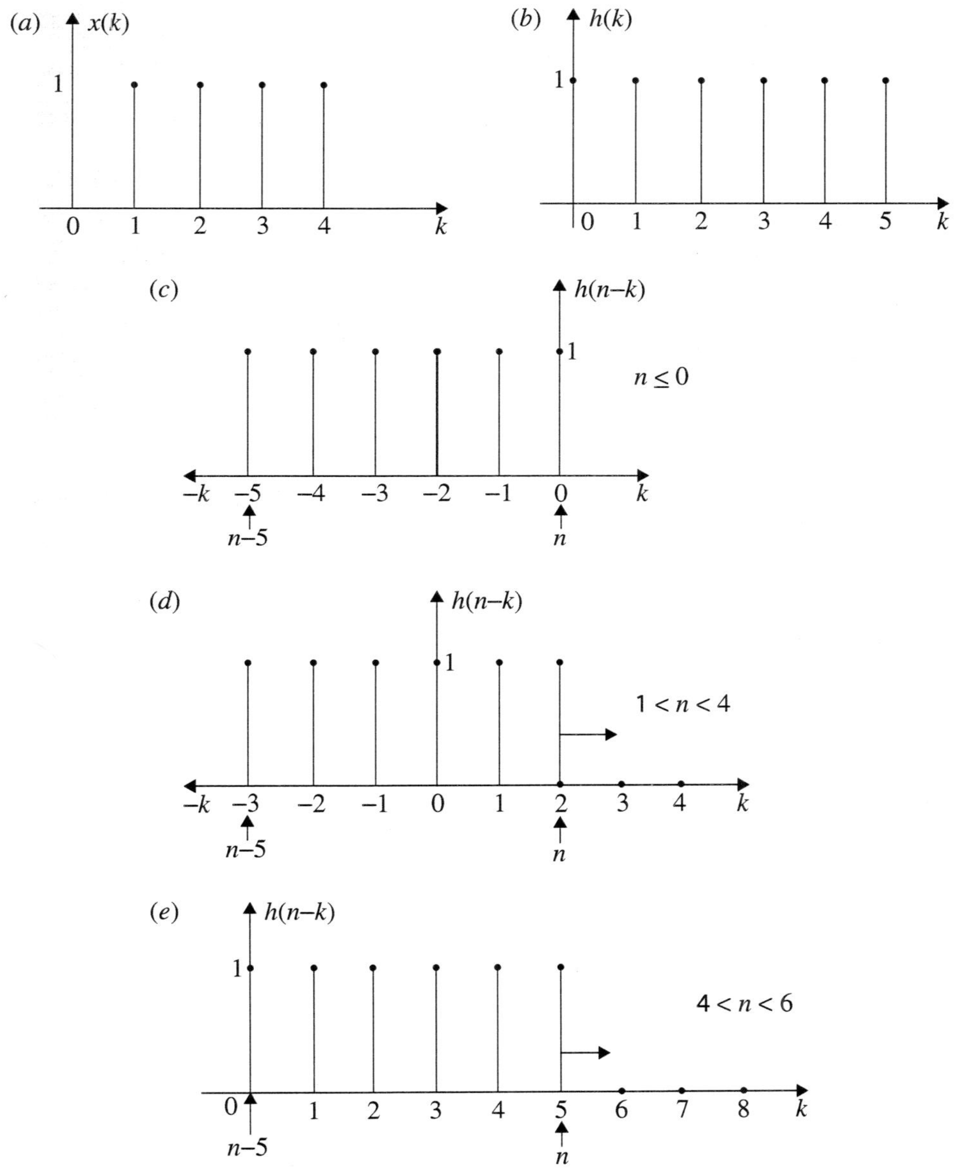

Figure 1.40 Convolution sum for Example 1.42.

Solution

1. $x(k)$, $h(k)$ and $h(n-k)$ are represented in Figures 1.40(a), (b) and (c) respectively. For $n = 0$, there is no overlapping and hence $y(n) = 0$.
2. **Overlapping interval 1:**
   $h(n-k)$ when moved towards right overlaps with $x(k)$ when the leading edge (right edge) of $h(n-k)$ crosses past the left edge $x(k)$. This happens when $n > 1$. This overlapping does not change until $n < 4$. Hence, the overlapping interval

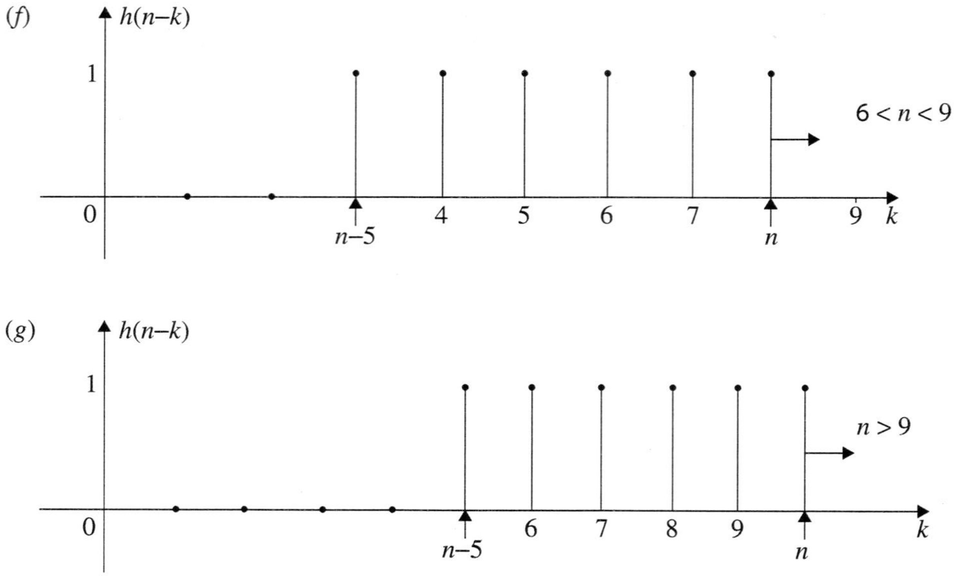

Figure 1.40 *Continued.*

is $1 \leq n \leq 4$. The summation interval is from $k = 1$ to $k = n$.

$$y_1(n) = \sum_{k=1}^{n} 1$$

The finite summation formula used is

$$\sum_{k=N_1}^{N_2} 1 = N_2 - N_1 + 1$$

Therefore,

$$y_1(n) = n - 1 + 1 = n \qquad 1 \leq n \leq 4$$

This is shown in Figure 1.40(*d*).

3. **Overlapping interval 2:**
   For $n > 4$, the right edge of $h(n-k)$ crosses past the right edge of $x(k)$. This change of overlapping occurs during the time interval $4 < n < 6$. The output during this interval is $y_2(n)$

$$y_2(n) = \sum_{k=1}^{4} 1 \qquad 4 \leq n \leq 6$$
$$= 4 - 1 + 1$$
$$= 4$$

This is shown in Figure 1.40(*e*).

4. **Overlapping interval 3:**
When the left edge of $h(n-k)$ crosses past the left edge of $x(k)$, there is overlapping and it continues until $n = 4$. The overlapping interval is therefore $6 \leq n < 9$. The output is $y_3(n)$. The limits of summation is from $k = n-5$ to $k = 4$

$$\begin{aligned} y_3(n) &= \sum_{k=n-5}^{4} 1 \\ &= -n+5+4+1 \\ &= 10-n \qquad 6 < n < 9 \end{aligned}$$

This is shown in Figure 1.40(*f*).
5. For $n > 9$, there is no overlapping and hence $y(n) = 0$. This is shown in Figure 1.40(*g*). Hence, the output response $y_1(n)$, $y_2(n)$ and $y_3(n)$ are summed up with their respective time interval to get the total response $y(n)$.
6.

$$\begin{aligned} y(n) &= n && 1 < n < 4 \\ y(n) &= 4 && 4 < n < 6 \\ y(n) &= 10-n && 6 < n < 9 \end{aligned}$$

The values of $y(n)$ for $1 \leq n \leq 10$ is shown in the following table. $y(n) = \{0, 1, 2, 3, 4, 4, 4, 3, 2, 1\}$

n	0	1	2	3	4	5	6	7	8	9	10
$y(n)$	0	1	2	3	4	4	4	3	2	1	0

7. The plot of $y(n)$ with respect to n is shown in Figure 1.40(*h*).

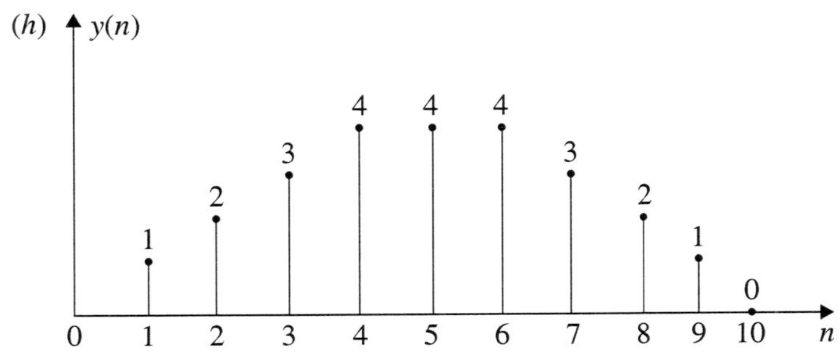

Figure 1.40 Response plot of Example 1.42.

8. To check the width property of convolution. The width property can be easily checked. The number of elements of $h(n)$ is $T_1 = 4$. The number of elements of $h(n)$ is $T_2 = 6$. The width property of $y(n)$ is $T = T_1 + T_2 - 1 = 6+4-1 = 9$. From Figure 1.40(*h*) it is seen that $y(n)$ has 9 elements.

Example 1.43

$$x(n) = [u(n) - u(n-6)]$$
$$h(n) = a^n[u(n) - u(n-3)] \quad \text{where} \quad 0 < a < 1$$

Find

$$y(n) = x(n) * h(n)$$

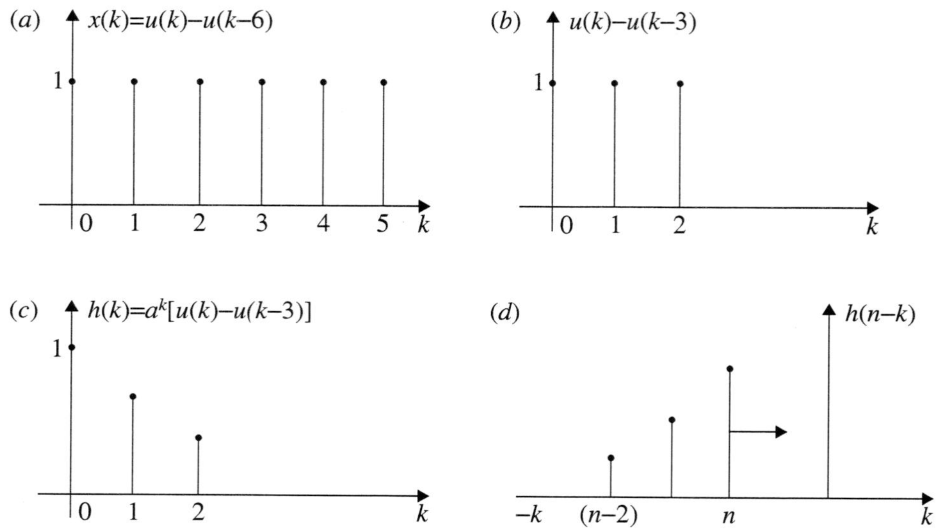

Figure 1.41 Representation of signals for Example 1.43.

Solution

1. For $n < 0$, $h(n-k)$ and $x(k)$ do not overlap. Hence

$$y(n) = 0 \text{ for } n < 0$$

2. When $h(n-k)$ is moved towards right $h(n-k)$ overlaps with $x(k)$ for the time interval $0 \le n \le 2$. Here, the limits of the convolution sum is $0 \le k \le 5$

$$x(k) = \begin{cases} 1 & 0 \le k \le 5 \\ 0 & \text{otherwise} \end{cases}$$

$$h(n-k) = \begin{cases} a^{(n-k)} & k \le n \\ 0 & \text{otherwise} \end{cases}$$

$$y(n) = \sum_{k=0}^{n} a^{n-k} \qquad 0 \le n \le 2$$

$$y(n) = a^n \left[\sum_{k=0}^{n} \left(\frac{1}{a}\right)^k \right]$$

$$= a^n \frac{\left[1 - \frac{1}{a^{n+1}}\right]}{\left(1 - \frac{1}{a}\right)}$$

$$\boxed{y(n) = \frac{(1 - a^{n+1})}{(1 - a)}} \qquad 0 \le n \le 2$$

3. For $n \ge 2$, the left edge of $h(n-k)$ slides over the left edge of $x(k)$. But the right edge of $h(n-k)$ is within the right edge of $x(k)$. For this the time duration is $2 \le n \le 5$. Here, the limit of the convolution sum is $(n-2) \le k \le n$

$$y(k) = \sum_{k=n-2}^{n} a^{n-k}$$

Put $p = k - n + 2$

$$= \sum_{p=0}^{2} a^{(2-p)}$$

$$= a^2 \left[\sum_{p=0}^{2} \left(\frac{1}{a}\right)^p \right]$$

$$= a^2 \frac{\left[1 - \frac{1}{a^3}\right]}{\left(1 - \frac{1}{a}\right)}$$

$$\boxed{y(n) = \frac{(1 - a^3)}{(1 - a)}} \qquad 2 \le n \le 5$$

4. For $n > 5$, the right edge of $h(n-k)$ slides past the right edge of $x(k)$. The left edge of $h(n-k)$ is within the right edge of $x(k)$ if $n < 7$. Hence, the time interval is $5 \le n \le 7$. The limits of the convolution sum is $(n-2) \le k \le 5$.

$$y(n) = \sum_{k=n-2}^{k=5} a^{n-k} \qquad 5 \le n \le 7$$

Put $p = k - n + 2$

$$n - k = 2 - p$$

For $k = 5, p = 7 - n$

$$y(n) = \sum_{p=0}^{7-n} a^{2-p}$$

$$= a^2 \sum_{p=0}^{7-n} \left(\frac{1}{a}\right)^p$$

$$= a^2 \frac{\left[1 - \frac{1}{a^{(7+1-n)}}\right]}{\left[1 - \frac{1}{a}\right]}$$

$$= a^3 \frac{[a^{8-n} - 1]}{(a-1)} \frac{1}{a^{8-n}}$$

$$\boxed{y(n) = a^{n-5} \frac{[1 - a^{8-n}]}{(1-a)}} \qquad 5 \le n \le 7$$

5. For $n > 7$, the left edge of $h(n-k)$ leaves the right edge of $x(k)$ and there is no overlapping between $x(k)$ and $h(n-k)$. Consequently $y(n) = 0$ for $n > 7$.

Example 1.44

$$x(n) = 2^n u(-n-2) \qquad \text{and} \qquad h(n) = u(n-1)$$

Find

$$y(n) = x(n) * h(n)$$

by analytical method.

Solution

$$\begin{aligned} x(k) &= 0 && \text{for } k > -2 \\ &= 2^k && \text{for } k \le -2 \\ h(n-k) &= 0 && \text{for } k > n-1 \\ &= 1 && \text{for } k \le n-1 \end{aligned}$$

1. **Time interval $-\infty < n < -1$.**
When $h(n-k)$ is moved from extreme left towards right, the right edge of $h(n-k)$ starts overlapping with the left edge of $x(k)$ during the interval $-\infty < k < n-1$. Hence, the summation interval is from $-\infty$ to $(n-1)$.

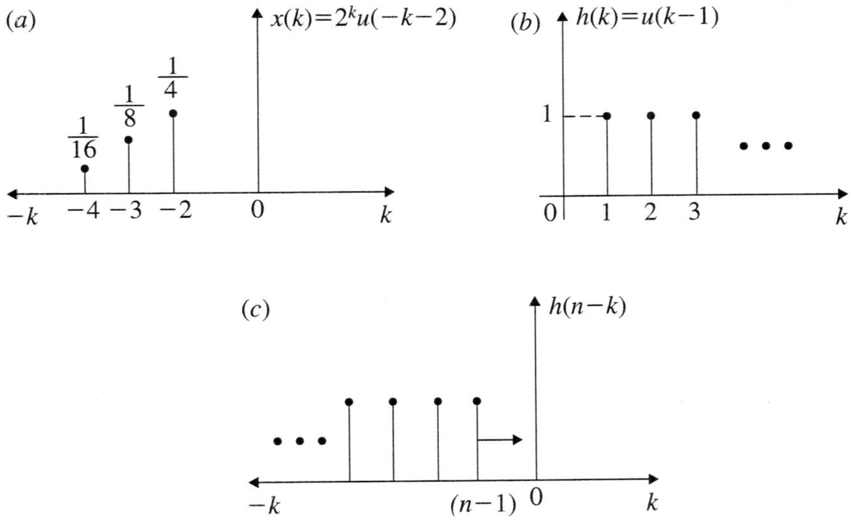

Figure 1.42 Signal representation of Example 1.44.

$$y(n) = \sum_{k=-\infty}^{n-1} 2^k \qquad -\infty < n < -1$$

$$= 2^{n-1} + 2^{n-2} + 2^{n-3} + \cdots$$

$$y(n) = 2^{n-1}\left[1 + \frac{1}{2} + \frac{1}{2^2} + \frac{1}{2^3} + \cdots\right]$$

$$= 2^{n-1}\left[\frac{1}{1-\frac{1}{2}}\right]$$

$$\boxed{y(n) = 2^n} \qquad -\infty < n < -1$$

2. **Time interval $n > -1$.**
For $n \geq -1$, the right edge of $h(n-k)$ slides past the right edge of $x(k)$ where there is transition. The limits of convolution sum is therefore $-\infty < k < -2$.

$$y(n) = \sum_{k=-\infty}^{-2} 2^k \qquad n > -1$$

$$= \sum_{2}^{\infty}\left(\frac{1}{2}\right)^k$$

Using the summation formula

$$\sum_{k=n}^{\infty}(a)^k = \frac{a^n}{(1-a)}$$

we get

$$y(n) = \left(\frac{1}{2}\right)^2 \frac{1}{1-\left(\frac{1}{2}\right)}$$

$$= 0.5 \qquad n > -1$$

$$\boxed{y(n) = 2^n} \qquad n < -1$$

$$\boxed{y(n) = 0.5} \qquad n > -1$$

Example 1.45

What is the response of an LTID system with impulse response $h(n) = \delta(n) + 2\delta(n-1)$ for the input $x(n) = \{1, 2, 3\}$?

(Anna University, April, 2005)

Solution

$$h(n) = \delta(n) + 2\delta(n-1)$$

$$x(n) = \{1, 2, 3\}$$

$$= \delta(n) + 2\delta(n-1) + 3\delta(n-2)$$

The output response $y(n)$ is obtained by the following convolution

$$y(n) = h(n) * x(n)$$

$$= h(n) * \delta(n) + h(n) * 2\delta(n-1) + h(n) * 3\delta(n-2)$$

$$= y_1(n) + y_2(n) + y_3(n)$$

where

$$y_1(n) = h(n) * \delta(n) = h(n)$$

$$y_2(n) = h(n) * 2\delta(n-1) = 2h(n-1)$$

$$y_3(n) = h(n) * 3\delta(n-2) = 3h(n-2)$$

$$y_1(n) = h(n) = \delta(n) + 2\delta(n-1)$$

$$y_2(n) = 2h(n-1) = 2\delta(n-1) + 4\delta(n-2)$$

$$y_3(n) = 3h(n-2) = 3\delta(n-2) + 6\delta(n-3)$$

$$\boxed{\therefore \quad y(n) = \delta(n) + 4\delta(n-1) + 7\delta(n-2) + 6\delta(n-3)}$$

The response is plotted and is shown in Figure 1.43.

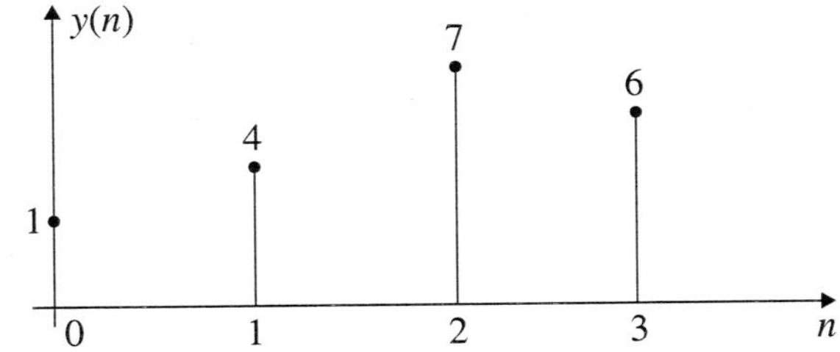

Figure 1.43 Response of Example 1.45.

1.11.2 Convolution Sum of Two Sequences by Multiplication Method

Let

$$x(n) = \{x_1,\ x_2, \underset{\uparrow}{x_3},\ x_4\}$$

$$h(n) = \{h_1,\ h_2, \underset{\uparrow}{h_3}\}$$

The convolution of these two sequences $x(n) * h(n)$ is obtained as given below:

1. Write down $x(n)$ and $h(n)$ one below the other

$$\begin{matrix} x_1 & x_2 & x_3 & x_4 \\ & h_1 & h_2 & h_3 \end{matrix}$$

2. Carry out the multiplication of the first row by the second row as given below:

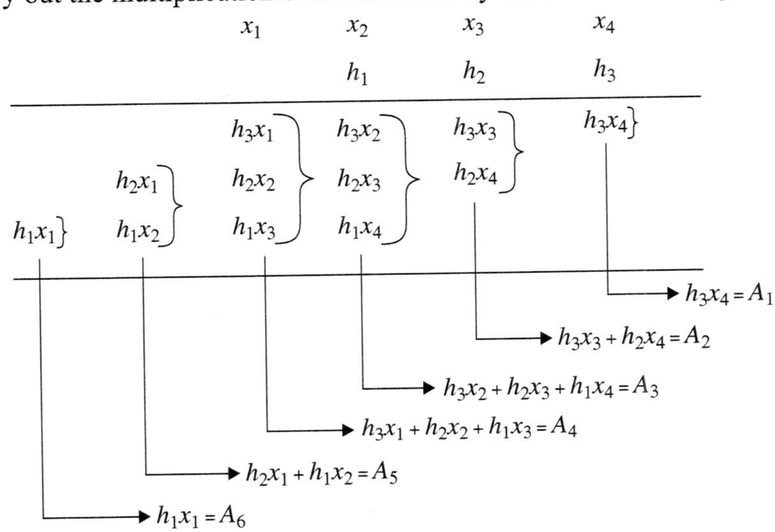

3. Arrange the sequences so obtained as given below:

$$y(n) = \{A_6,\ A_5,\ A_4,\ A_3, \underset{\uparrow}{A_2},\ A_1\}$$

4. Let N_1 = width of the $x(n)$ sequence to the left and N_2 = width of the $h(n)$ sequence to the left.

   The width of the output sequence $y(n)$ to the left is $N = N_1 + N_2$. In the example illustrated above $N_1 = 2$ and $N_2 = 2$. In the $y(n)$ sequence the arrow corresponding to $n = 0$ is marked such that to the left of the arrow $N = N_1 + N_2 = 4$ is marked which is at A_2. From $y(n)$ sequence $y(0) = A_2$; $y(1) = A_1$; $y(-1) = A_3$; $y(-2) = A_4$; $y(-3) = A_5$ and $y(-4) = A_6$.

   The width property can also be easily checked. For $x(n)$ the width $T_1 = 4$. For $h(n)$, the width $T_2 = 3$. The width of $y(n) = T = T_1+T_2-1 = 4+3-1 = 6$.

The following examples illustrate the above method.

Example 1.46

What is the response of an LTID system with impulse response $h(n) = \delta(n) + 2\delta(n-1)$ for the input $x(n) = \{1, 2, 3\}$.

Solution

$$h(n) = \delta(n) + 2\delta(n-1) = \{\underset{\uparrow}{1},\ 2\}$$

$$x(n) = \{\underset{\uparrow}{1},\ 2,\ 3\}$$

where $N_1 = 0$, $N_2 = 0$, $N = N_1 + N_2 = 0$ and $T_1 = 2$, $T_2 = 3$, $T = 3+2-1 = 4$

$$\begin{array}{cccc} & & 1 & 2 \\ & 1 & 2 & 3 \\ \hline & & 3 & 6 \\ & 2 & 4 & \\ 1 & 2 & & \\ \hline 1 & 4 & 7 & 6 \\ \hline \end{array}$$

$$\boxed{y(n) = \{\underset{\uparrow}{1},\ 4,\ 7,\ 6\}}$$

The same result as in Example 1.53 is obtained.

Example 1.47

Find the convolution of $x(n) = \{1, 2, 3, 4, 5\}$ with $h(n) = \{1, 2, 3, 3, 2, 1\}$.

(Anna University, May, 2005)

Solution When no arrow is marked in $x(n)$ or $h(n)$, the signals are to be taken as causal and therefore $N_1 = 0, N_2 = 0$ and $N = N_1 + N_2 = 0$; $T_1 = 6,\ T_2 = 5,\ T = 6 + 5 - 1 = 10$.

The following multiplication is done.

				1	2	3	3	2	1
					1	2	3	4	5
				5	10	15	15	10	5
			4	8	12	12	8	4	
		3	6	9	9	6	3		
	2	4	6	6	4	2			
1	2	3	3	2	1				
1	4	10	19	30	36	35	26	14	5

$$y(n) = \{\underset{\uparrow}{1},\ 4,\ 10,\ 19,\ 30,\ 36,\ 35,\ 26,\ 14,\ 5\}$$

Example 1.48

Find the convolution of the following

$$x(n) = u(n) - 3u(n-2) + 2u(n-4)$$

$$h(n) = u(n+1) - u(n-8)$$

Solution

1. $x(n)$ and $h(n)$ are represented in Figures 1.44(a) and (b) respectively.

   From Figure 1.44(a), $x(n)$ is written as

$$x(n) = \{\underset{\uparrow}{1},\ 1,\ -2,\ -2\} \qquad N_1 = 0;\ T_1 = 4$$

   From Figure 1.44(d), $h(n)$ is written as

$$h(n) = \{1, \underset{\uparrow}{1},\ 1,\ 1,\ 1,\ 1,\ 1,\ 1,\ 1\} \qquad N_2 = 1;\ T_2 = 9$$

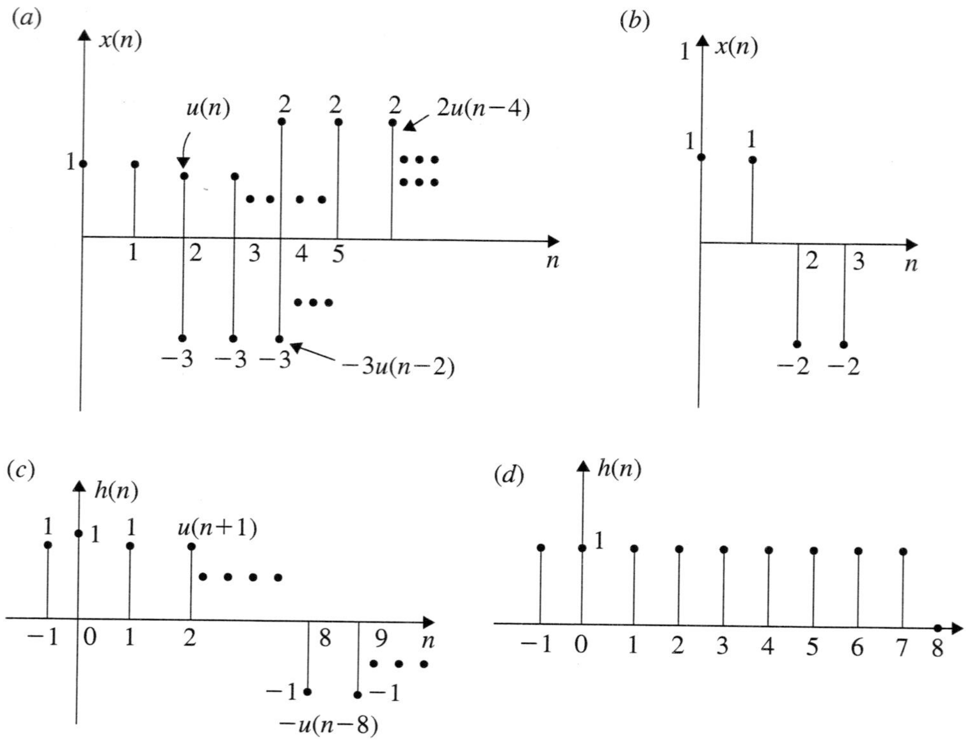

Figure 1.44 Representation of $x(n)$ and $h(n)$ of Example 1.48.

2. The following multiplication is carried out:

			1	1	1	1	1	1	1	1	1
								1	1	−2	−2
			−2	−2	−2	−2	−2	−2	−2	−2	−2
		−2	−2	−2	−2	−2	−2	−2	−2	−2	
	1	1	1	1	1	1	1	1	1		
1	1	1	1	1	1	1	1	1			
1	2	0	−2	−2	−2	−2	−2	−2	−3	−4	−2

$N = N_1 + N_2 = 0 + 1 = 1$ and $T = T_1 + T_2 - 1 = 4 + 9 - 1 = 12.$

$$y(n) = \{1, \underset{\uparrow}{2}, 0, -2, -2, -2, -2, -2, -2, -3, -4, -2\}$$

1.11.3 Convolution Sum by Tabulation Method

The convolution sum of two sequences $x(n)$ and $h(n)$ to obtain $y(n)$ by tabulation method is explained below:

1. Let
$$x(n) = \{x_1, x_2, \ldots, x_{(n)}\}$$
$$h(n) = \{h_1, h_2, \ldots, h_{(n)}\}$$
Mark $x_1, x_2, \ldots, x_n$ in columns and $h_1(n), h_2(n), \ldots, h(n)$ in rows.
2. The h_1 row is completed by multiplying the corresponding column. Thus when h_1 row crosses with x_1 column, the product becomes x_1h_1. Similarly, when h_1 row crosses with x_2 column, the product becomes h_1x_2. Thus all the elements row wise are determined and tabulated.
3. Draw the diagonal dotted lines as shown in Table 1.1.
4. By adding the elements in a particular diagonal gives $y(n)$.
5. The value of N and T of the sequence $y(n)$ are determined as explained in the previous examples.

From Table 1.1, $y(n)$ is obtained and is given below.

From diagonal 1, $y(0) = x_1h_1$

From diagonal 2, $y(1) = x_1h_2 + x_2h_1$

From diagonal 3, $y(2) = x_1h_3 + x_2h_2 + x_3h_1$

Table 1.1 Tabulation method of convolution.

	x_1 ↓ $y(0)$	x_2 ↓ $y(1)$	x_3 ↓ $y(2)$	x_4 ↓ $y(3)$	x_5 ↓ $y(4)$	
h_1	x_1h_1	x_2h_1	x_3h_1	x_4h_1	x_5h_1	
diagonal 1 →						← $y(5)$
h_2	x_1h_2	x_2h_2	x_3h_2	x_4h_2	x_5h_2	
diagonal 2 →						← $y(6)$
h_3	x_1h_3	x_2h_3	x_3h_3	x_4h_3	x_5h_3	
diagonal 3 →						← $y(7)$
h_4	x_1h_4	x_2h_4	x_3h_4	x_4h_4	x_5h_4	
diagonal 4 →						← $y(8)$
h_5	x_1h_5	x_2h_5	x_3h_5	x_4h_5	x_5h_5	
diagonal 5 →	diagonal 6 ↑	diagonal 7 ↑	diagonal 8 ↑	diagonal 9 ↑		

From diagonal 4, $y(3) = x_1h_4 + x_2h_3 + x_3h_2 + x_4h_1$

From diagonal 5, $y(4) = x_1h_5 + x_2h_4 + x_3h_3 + x_4h_2 + x_5h_1$

From diagonal 6, $y(5) = x_2h_5 + x_3h_4 + x_4h_3 + x_5h_2$

From diagonal 7, $y(6) = x_3h_5 + x_4h_4 + x_5h_3$

From diagonal 8, $y(7) = x_4h_5 + x_5h_4$

From diagonal 9, $y(8) = x_5h_5$

$$y(n) = \{y(0), y(1), y(2), y(3), y(4), y(5), y(6), y(7), y(8)\}$$

From the $y(n)$, the width property $T = T_1 + T_2$ can be easily checked. The arrow $\uparrow$ corresponding to $n = 0$ is decided by N_1 and N_2. The following examples illustrate the above method.

1.12 Convolution Sum by Graphical Method

The procedure for the determination of convolution sum by graphical method is similar to the convolution integral of continuous time system. The following steps are followed.

1. Represent $x(n)$ vs. n in a graph. Replace n by k and $x(k)$ vs. k is represented in a graph. One can straightaway plot $x(k)$ vs. k.
2. Similar to Step 1, plot $h(k)$ vs. k.
3. By folding $h(k)$, obtain $h(-k)$.
4. By adding 'n' to $h(-k)$, obtain $h(n-k)$. Shift $h(n-k)$ to the extreme left. Start moving $h(n-k)$ towards the right so that $x(k)$ and $h(n-k)$ overlap each other. It is to be noted that $x(k)$ should be kept fixed and $h(n-k)$ alone should be moved by one sample at an instant. Calculate $y(n)$ at that instant.
5. The procedure is repeated at other instants and at each time $y(n)$ is calculated. When there is no overlapping, the movement of $h(n-k)$ is stopped and here $y(n) = 0$.

The following examples illustrate this graphical procedure.

Example 1.49

Compute the convolution of the two sequences $x(n)$ and $h(n)$ shown in Figures 1.45(a) and (b) respectively and plot $y(n)$ vs. n. Use graphical method.

(Anna University, December, 2006)

Solution

1. Figure 1.45(a) shows the sequence of $x(n)$ and Figure 1.45(b) the sequence of $h(n)$

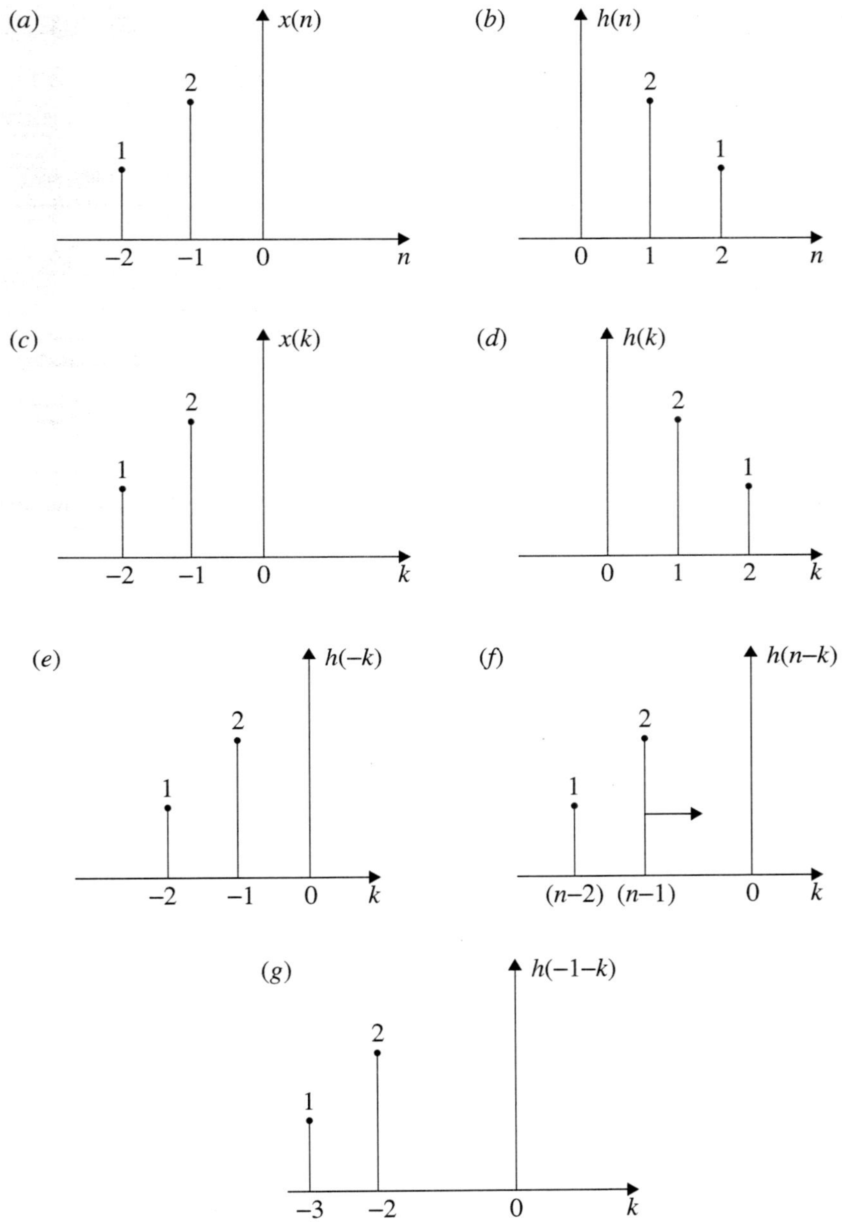

Figure 1.45 Signal representation of Example 1.49 (a) to (g).

2. n is replaced by k and $x(k)$ and $h(k)$ are represented in Figures 1.45(c) and (d) respectively.
3. $h(-k)$ is obtained from $h(k)$ by folding and is shown in Figure 1.45(e).
4. n is added in $h(-k)$ and $h(n-k)$ is obtained. $h(n-k)$ is moved to the extreme left so that there is no overlapping between $x(k)$ and $h(n-k)$ initially. This is shown in Figure 1.45(f).

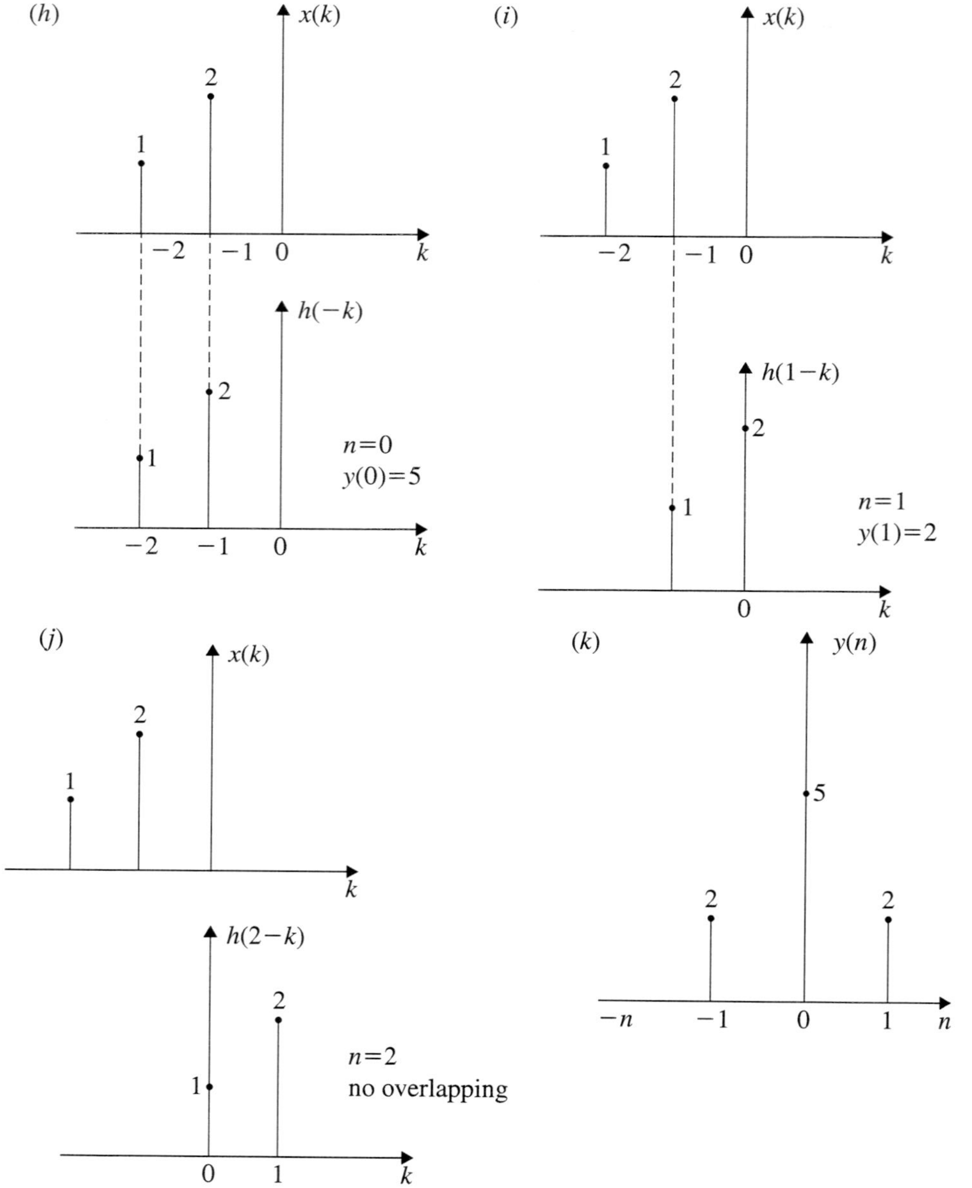

Figure 1.45 Signal representation of Example 1.45 (h) to k

5. $x(k)$ is fixed and $h(n-k)$ is moved towards right so that it overlaps with $x(k)$. At $n=-1$, the first overlapping occurs and $y(-1)=1\times 2=2$. This is shown in Figures 1.45(c) and (g).
6. When $h(n-k)$ is moved towards right by one more sample (now $n=0$), the plot of $x(k)$ and $h(n-k)$ are shown in Figure 1.45(h) and $y(n)=1\times 1+2\times 2=5$.
7. For $n=1$, the plot of $x(k)$ and $h(n-k)$ are shown in Figure 1.45(i) and the overlapping is shown in dotted line. $y(1)=1\times 2=2$.

8. For $n = 2$, the plot of $x(k)$ and $h(n-k)$ are shown in Figure 1.45(j). Here, there is no overlapping. Hence $y(2) = 0$.
9. $N_1 = 2$ and $N_2 = 0$. Therefore, $N = N_1 + N_2 = 2$, $T_1 = 3$ and $T_2 = 3$. Therefore, $T = T_1 + T_2 - 1 = 5$
10.

$$\begin{array}{c} \longleftarrow T = 5 \longrightarrow \\ y(n) = \{0,\ 2,\ 5,\ 2,\ 0\} \\ |N = 2|\ \uparrow \end{array}$$

The plot of $y(n)$ is shown in Figure 1.45(k).

The graphical procedure discussed above appears very complicated and discouraging at first reading. Indeed the "bark of convolution is worse than its bite".

1.13 Step Response of the System

Equation given below gives the step response of the discrete time system if the impulse response $h(n)$ is known

$$s(n) = \sum_{k=0}^{k=n} h(n)$$

The following examples illustrate how to find step response from impulse response.

Example 1.50

Find the step response of the system whose impulse response is

$$h(n) = a^n u(n) \qquad \text{where } 0 < a < 1$$

Solution

$$s(n) = \sum_{k=0}^{n} h(k)$$

$$s(n) = \sum_{k=0}^{n} a^k$$

Using the finite summation formula we get

$$\boxed{s(n) = \frac{(1-a^{n+1})}{(1-a)}}$$

Example 1.51

Find the step response whose impulse response is given by

$$h(n) = \delta(n-1) + \delta(n-5)$$

Solution

$$s(n) = h(n) * u(n) = [\delta(n-1) + \delta(n-5)] * u(n)$$
$$= \delta(n-1) * u(n) + \delta(n-5) * u(n)$$

By using the property $\delta(n-1) * u(n) = u(n-1)$ we get

$$\boxed{s(n) = u(n-1) + u(n-5)}$$

Example 1.52

Find the step response of the system whose impulse response is

$$h(n) = \left(\frac{1}{3}\right)^n.$$

Solution

$$s(n) = \sum_{k=0}^{n} \left(\frac{1}{3}\right)^k$$
$$= \frac{1-\frac{1}{3^{n+1}}}{1-\frac{1}{3}} = \frac{(3^{n+1}-1)}{(3-1)}\frac{1}{3^n}$$

$$\boxed{s(n) = \frac{1}{2}\left(\frac{1}{3}\right)^n (3^{n+1}-1)u(n)}$$

Example 1.53

Find the step response if the impulse response $h(n) = u(n)$

Solution

$$s(n) = \sum_{k=0}^{n} h(k) = \sum_{k=0}^{n} u(k)$$

$$= \sum_{k=0}^{n} 1$$

$$\boxed{s(n) = (n+1)}$$

1.14 Stability from Impulse Response

From Equation given below, for the discrete time system to be bounded input output stable, $M_y(n) = \sum_{n=-\infty}^{\infty} |h(n)| < \infty$. The following examples illustrate this.

Example 1.54

The impulse response of a certain system is

$$h(n) = a^n u(n) \qquad \text{where } 0 < a < 1$$

Find whether the system is BIBO stable.

Solution $h(n)$ is causal. Hence

$$M_y(n) = \sum_{n=0}^{\infty} a^n = \frac{1}{(1-a)} < \infty$$

Hence, the system is BIBO stable.

Example 1.55

$$h(n) = a^n u(-n)$$

Find whether the system is BIBO stable.

Solution

$$M_y(n) = \sum_{n=-\infty}^{\infty} a^n$$

For $n > 0$, $u(n) = 0$. Hence

$$M_y(n) = \sum_{n=-\infty}^{0} a^n$$
$$= \sum_{n=0}^{\infty} a^{-n} = \sum_{n=0}^{\infty} \left(\frac{1}{a}\right)^n = \frac{1}{1-\frac{1}{a}}$$
$$= \frac{a}{a-1} < \infty$$

Hence, the system is BIBO stable.

Example 1.56

$$h(n) = a^n u(n-1) \quad \text{where} \quad a > 1$$

Find whether the system is BIBO stable.

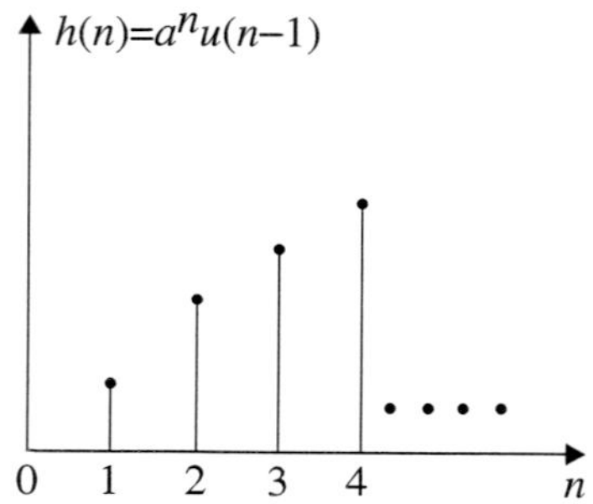

Figure 1.46 Impulse response plot of Example 1.56.

Solution The impulse response plot of $h(n) = a^n u(n-1)$ is shown in Figure 1.46 and it is noticed that the sequence is not summable. Hence, the system is unstable.

$$M_y(n) = \sum_{n=1}^{\infty} a^n = a + a^2 + a^3 + \dots$$

$$\boxed{M_y(n) = \infty}$$

The system is BIBO unstable.

Example 1.57

$$h(n) = 2^n u(5-n)$$

Find whether the system is BIBO stable

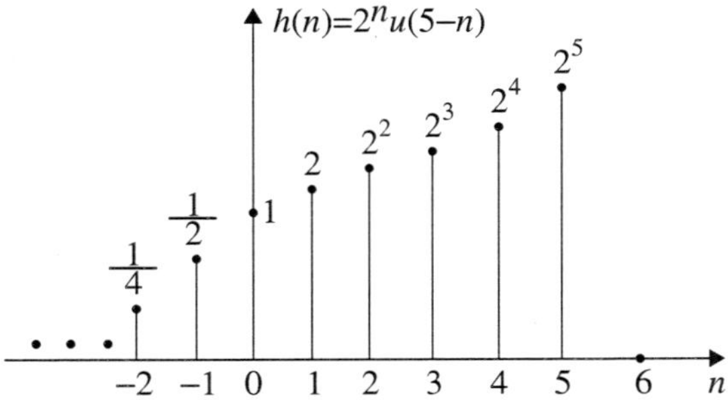

Figure 1.47 Impulse response plot of Example 1.57.

Solution The impulse response plot of $h(n) = 2^n u(5-n)$ is shown in Figure 1.47. $u(5-n) = 0$ for $n > 5$. For $-\infty \geq n \leq 5$, $h(n) = 2^n$

$$M_y(n) = \sum_{n=-\infty}^{5} 2^n$$

$$= \sum_{n=-\infty}^{0} 2^n + \sum_{1}^{5} 2^n$$

$$= \sum_{n=0}^{\infty} 2^{-n} + \sum_{1}^{5} 2^n$$

$$= \sum_{n=0}^{\infty} \left(\frac{1}{2}\right)^n + \sum_{1}^{5} 2^n$$

$$M_y(n) = \frac{1}{1-1/2} + \sum_{0}^{5} 2^n - 1$$

$$= 2 + \frac{(1-2^6)}{1-2} - 1$$

$$= 1 + 2^6 - 1 = 2^6$$

$$\boxed{M_y(n) = 2^6 < \infty}$$

The system is BIBO stable.

Example 1.58

$$h(n) = e^{-5|n|}$$

Find whether the system is BIBO stable.

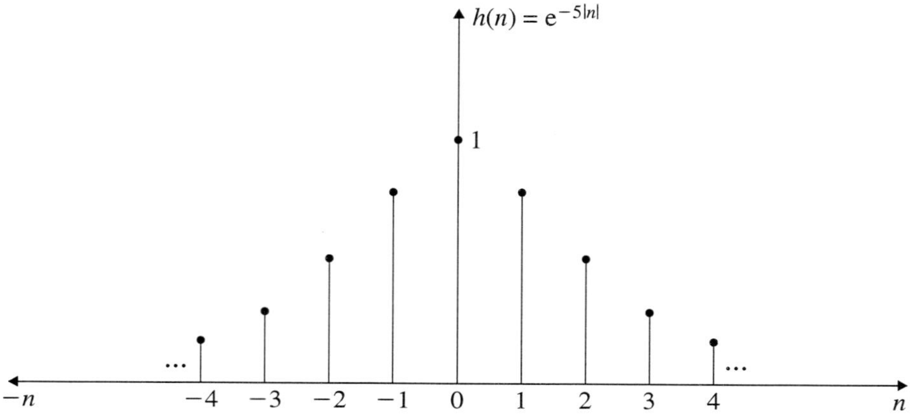

Figure 1.48 Impulse responses plot of Example 1.58.

Solution

$$M_y(n) = \sum_{n=-\infty}^{\infty} e^{-5|n|}$$

$$= \sum_{n=-\infty}^{-1} e^{5n} + \sum_{n=0}^{\infty} e^{-5n}$$

$$= \sum_{n=1}^{\infty} e^{-5n} + \sum_{n=0}^{\infty} e^{-5n}$$

$$M_y(n) = \frac{e^{-5}}{(1-e^{-5})} + \frac{1}{(1-e^{-5})}$$

$$= \frac{(1+e^{-5})}{(1-e^{-5})} = 1.0136 < \infty$$

$$\boxed{M_y(n) = 1.0136}$$

$M_y(n)$ is finite and hence the system is stable.

1.15 System Causality

From expression for the impulse response function $h(n) = 0$ for $n < 0$ for the system to be causal. This is illustrated in the following examples.

Example 1.59

$$h(n) = a^n u(-n)$$

Find whether the system is causal.

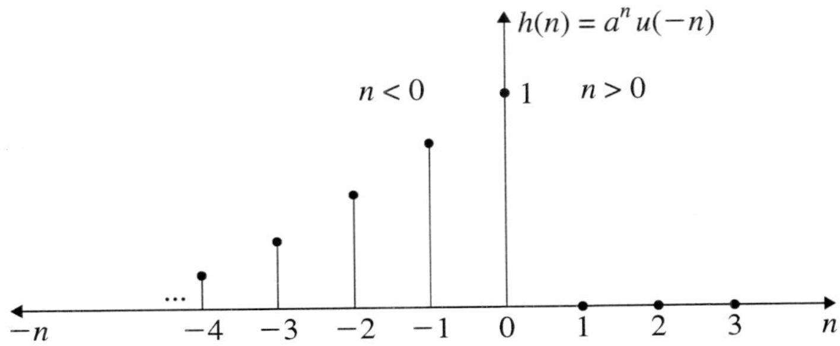

Figure 1.49 Impulse response of Example 1.59.

Solution The impulse response plot of $h(n)$ is shown in Figure 1.49. From Figure 1.49, it is evident that at $n = -1$, $h(-1) = \frac{1}{a}$ and is not zero. Hence, the system is non-causal.

Example 1.60

$$h(n) = a^n u(n-1) \qquad \text{where } a > 1$$

Find whether the system is causal.

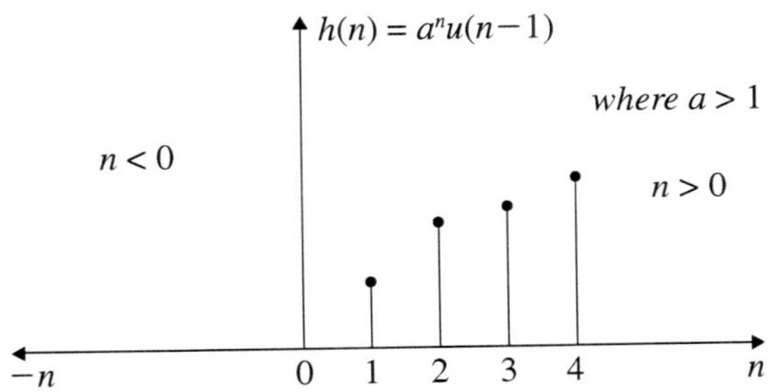

Figure 1.50 Impulse response of Example 1.60.

Solution The plot of $h(n) = a^n u(n-1)$ is shown in Figure 1.50. It is observed that for $n < 0$, $h(n) = 0$. Hence, the system is causal.

Example 1.61

$$h(n) = e^{-a|n|}$$

Find whether the system is causal.

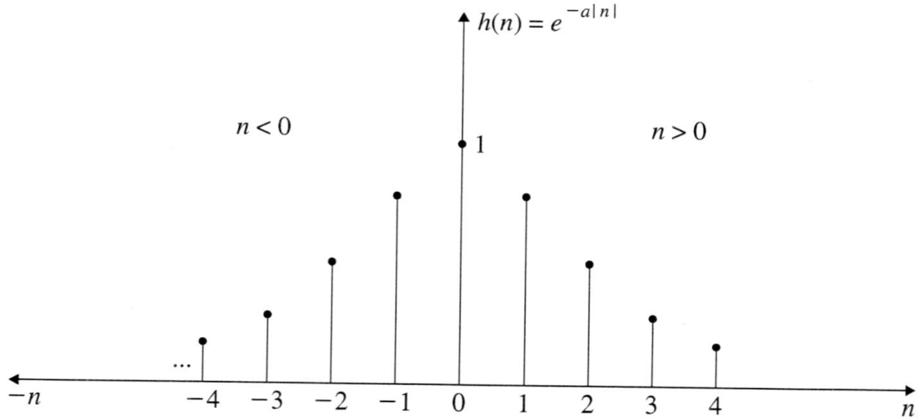

Figure 1.51 Impulse response of Example 1.61.

Solution The impulse response plot of $h(n)$ is shown in Figure 1.51.

$$h(n) = e^{-an} \qquad n \geq 0$$
$$= e^{an} \qquad n < 0$$
$$h(n) \neq 0 \qquad \text{for } n < 0.$$

Hence, the system is non-causal.

1.16 Sampling

1.16.1 Sampling Process

Sampling is a process of converting a continuous time signal into discrete-time signal. After sampling, the signal is defined at discrete instants of time and the time interval between two subsequent sampling instants is called sampling interval. In this process of sampling one of the important factors that we have to consider is that the sampling rate must be kept sufficiently high so that the original signal can be reconstructed from its samples.

The sampling operation can be represented by a switch as shown in Figure 1.52. The switch is closed for a very short interval of time τ, during which the signal is available at the out. Therefore, if the input is $x(t)$ then the output is $x(nT)$, $n = 0, \pm 1, \pm 2, \ldots$ and $x(nT)$ is called the sampled sequence of $x(t)$ where T is the time interval between successive samples and the sampling frequency is given by $f_s = \frac{1}{T}$ Hz. Therefore, the discrete time signal

$$x(nT) = x_s(t) = x(t)\delta_T(t) \tag{1.25}$$

where

$$\begin{aligned}\delta_T(t) &= \sum_{n=-\infty}^{\infty} \delta(t - nT)\\ &= \frac{1}{T}\sum_{m=-\infty}^{\infty} e^{jm\Omega_0 t}\end{aligned} \tag{1.26}$$

Equation (1.26) is Fourier series representation of impulse, $\left[c_k = \frac{1}{T}\right]$

$$x_s(t) = x(t)\left[\frac{1}{T}\sum_{m=-\infty}^{\infty} e^{jm\Omega_0 t}\right]$$

$$x_s(t) = \frac{1}{T}\sum_{m=-\infty}^{\infty} x(t)e^{jm\Omega_0 t} \tag{1.27}$$

$$F[x_s(t)] = \frac{1}{T}\sum_{m=-\infty}^{\infty} F[x(t)e^{jm\Omega_0 t}] \tag{1.28}$$

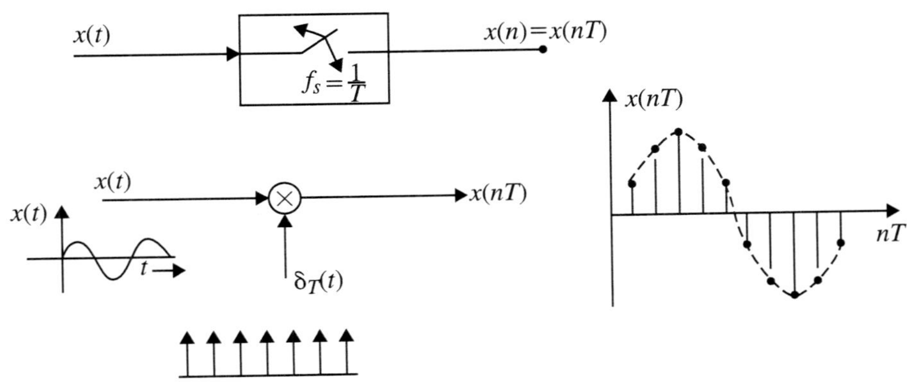

Figure 1.52 Sampling process.

If $F[x(t)] = X(i\Omega)$ then

$$F[x(t)e^{jm\Omega_0 t}] = X(j(\Omega - m\Omega_0)) \tag{1.29}$$

$$\therefore\ F[x_s(t)] = \frac{1}{T}\sum_{m=-\infty}^{\infty} X(j\Omega - m\Omega_0) \tag{1.30}$$

$$X_s(i\Omega) = F[x_s(t)] = \frac{1}{T}\sum_{m=-\infty}^{\infty} X\left[j\left(\Omega - \frac{2\pi}{T}m\right)\right] \tag{1.31}$$

Thus the Fourier transform of the sampled signal is given by an infinite sum of shifted replicas of the Fourier transform of the original signal.

Consider the signal $x(t)$ is band limited to f_m. *i.e.*, the highest frequency component of $x(t)$ is f_m. Then $X(j\Omega) = 0$ for $|\Omega| > \Omega_m$ is shown in Figure 1.53.

In equation (1.31), the term $X[j(\Omega - \frac{2\pi m}{T})]$ is the shifting of $X(j\Omega)$ from $\Omega = 0$ to $\Omega = \frac{2\pi m}{T}$ where $m = 0 \pm 1, \pm 2, \ldots$

Case (i) If $\frac{\pi}{T} = \Omega m$, the spectrum of sampled signal is shown in Figure 1.54. The replicas will not overlap.

As a result, the frequency spectrum of $TX_s(j\Omega)$ in the frequency range $\left(-\frac{\pi}{T}, \frac{\pi}{T}\right)$ is identical to $X(j\Omega)$. The frequency spectrum $X(j\Omega)$ can be recovered from $X_s(i\Omega)$, by using a low pass filter which has sharp cut off at $\Omega = \frac{\pi}{T}$.

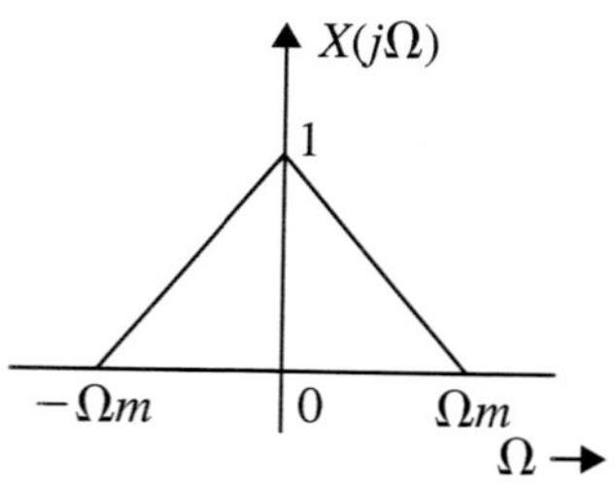

Figure 1.53 Spectrum of continuous time signal.

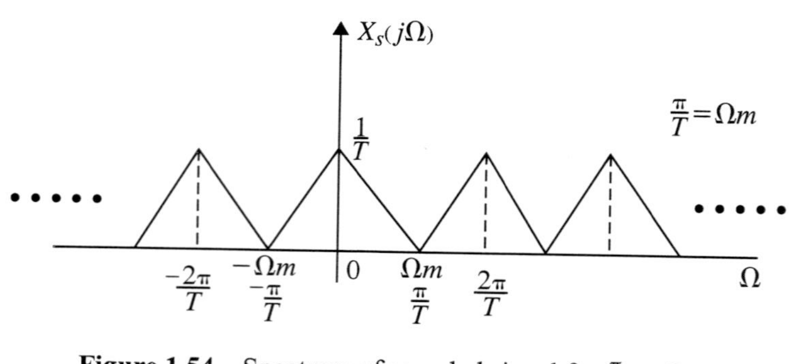

Figure 1.54 Spectrum of sampled signal for $\frac{\pi}{T} = \Omega m$.

Case (ii) If $\frac{\pi}{T} > \Omega m$, the spectrum of sampled signal is shown in Figure 1.55. The replicas will not overlap.

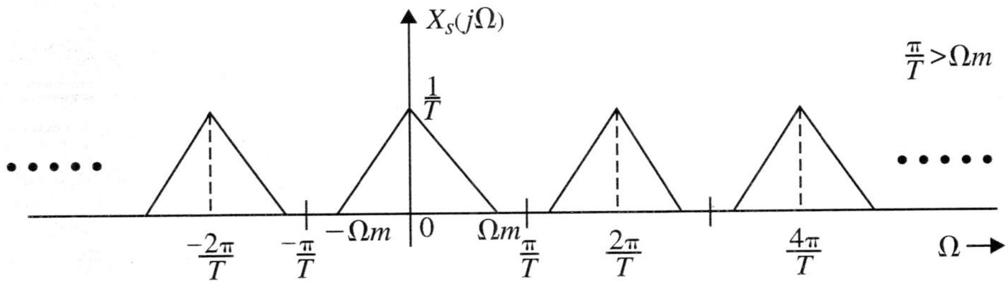

Figure 1.55 Spectrum of sampled signal for $\frac{\pi}{T} > \Omega m$.

The frequency spectrum $X(j\Omega)$ can be recovered from $X_s(j\Omega)$.

Case (iii) If $\frac{\pi}{T} < \Omega m$, the successive frequency replicas will overlap is shown in Figure 1.56.

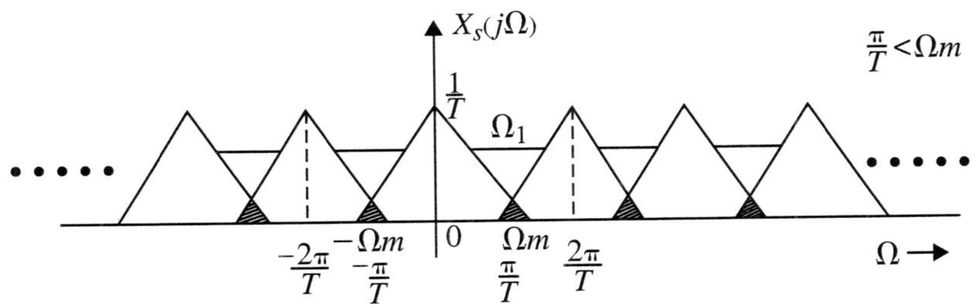

Figure 1.56 Spectrum of sampled signal for $\frac{\pi}{T} < \Omega m$.

As a result, the frequency spectrum $X(j\Omega)$ will not be recovered from the frequency spectrum of $TX(j\Omega)$.

For example, consider an arbitrary point at Ω_1, which falls in the region of the overlap. The frequency spectrum at $\Omega = \Omega_1$ is the sum of two components, one component is $X_s(j\Omega_1)$ and the other component is $X_s[j(\frac{2\pi}{T} - \Omega_1)]$. This high frequency component $(\frac{2\pi}{T} - \Omega_1)$ is folded in about the folding frequency $\frac{\pi}{T}$ and appears as a low frequency at Ω_1. The super imposition of high frequency component on the low frequency is known as "frequency aliasing". Because of aliasing, the spectrum $X(j\Omega)$ is no longer recoverable from the spectrum of $X_s(j\Omega)$. The aliasing error can be prevented if the highest frequency component Ωm in the signal $x(t)$ is less than or equal to $\frac{\pi}{T}$. That is

$$\frac{\pi}{T} \geq \Omega m \tag{1.32}$$

If $f_s = \frac{1}{T}$. Then

$$\pi f_s \geq \Omega m \quad (1.33)$$

$$\pi f_s \geq 2\pi f_m \quad (1.34)$$

$$\boxed{f_s \geq 2f_m} \quad (1.35)$$

To avoid aliasing the sampling frequency must be greater than twice the highest frequency present in the signal.

1.16.2 Sampling Theorem

A band limited signal $x(t)$ with $X(j\Omega) = 0$ for $|\Omega| > \Omega_m$ is uniquely determined from its sample $x(nT)$, if the sampling frequency $f_s \geq 2f_m$ *i.e.*, sampling frequency must be at least twice the highest frequency present in the signal.

1.16.3 Nyquist Rate

The minimum rate at which a signal can be sampled and still be reconstructed from its samples is called the Nyquist rate. It is always equal to $2f_m$, where f_m is the maximum frequency component present in the signal.

$$\boxed{\text{Nyquist rate} = 2f_m.} \quad (1.36)$$

A signal sampled at greater than Nyquist rate, is said to be over sampled and a signal sampled at less than Nyquist rate is said to be under sampled.

1.16.4 Anti-Aliasing Filter

Sampling theorem states that a signal can be perfectly reconstructed if it is band limited. In practice, communication signals have frequency spectra consisting of low frequency components as well as high frequency noise components. When a signal is sampled, with sampling frequency f_s, all signals with frequency range higher than f_s appear as signal frequency between 0 and $\frac{\Omega_s}{2}$ creating aliasing.

Therefore, to avoid aliasing errors caused by the undesired high frequency signals, an analog lowpass filter called an anti-aliasing filter is used prior to sampler.

A filter that is used to reject high frequency signals before it is sampled to reduce the aliasing is called an anti-alising filter and is shown in Figure 1.57.

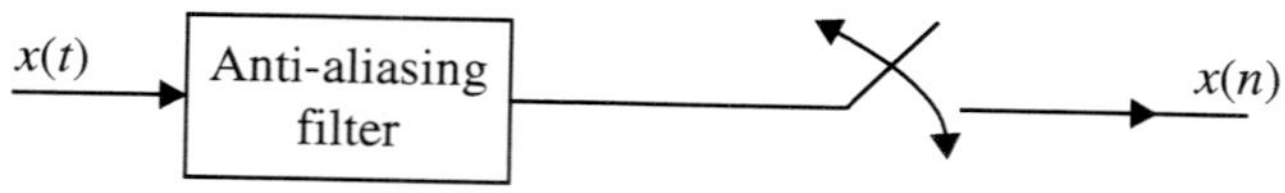

Figure 1.57 Anti-aliasing filter before the sampler.

1.16.5 Signal Reconstruction

The band limited signal $x(t)$ can be reconstructed from its samples if the sampling rate is above Nyquist rate.

Let the sampled signal be $x_s(t)$.

$$x_s(t) = \sum_{n=-\infty}^{\infty} x(nT)\delta(t - nT) \tag{1.37}$$

$$F[x_s(t)] = \sum_{n=-\infty}^{\infty} F[x(nT)\delta(t - nT)] \tag{1.38}$$

$$X(j\omega) = \frac{1}{T}\sum_{m=-\infty}^{\infty} X\left(j\left(\Omega - \frac{2\pi m}{T}\right)\right) \tag{1.39}$$

To get the original spectrum the signal $x_s(t)$ is to be passed thought a reconstruction (low-pass) filter with an impulse response $h(t)$.

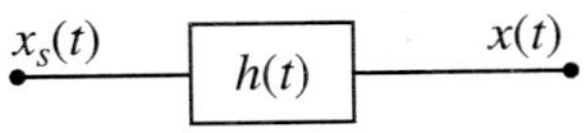

The original signal can be obtained by convolving the sampled signal $x_s(t)$ and the impulse response $h(t)$ of the filter

$$x(t) = x_s(t) * h(t) \tag{1.40}$$

$$= \left[\sum_{n=-\infty}^{\infty} x(nT)\delta(t - nT)\right] * h(t) \tag{1.41}$$

$$= \int_{-\infty}^{\infty} \sum_{n=-\infty}^{\infty} x(nT)\delta(\lambda - nT)h(t - \lambda)d\lambda \tag{1.42}$$

$$= \sum_{n=-\infty}^{\infty} x(nT) \int_{-\infty}^{\infty} \delta(\lambda - nT)h(t - \lambda)d\lambda \tag{1.43}$$

$$\therefore\ \delta(\lambda - nT) = \begin{cases} 1, & \lambda = nT \\ 0, & \lambda \neq nT \end{cases}$$

$$x(t) = \sum_{n=-\infty}^{\infty} x(nT)h(t - nT) \tag{1.44}$$

The frequency response of the lowpass filter can be expressed by

$$H(i\Omega) = \begin{cases} T, & \text{for } |\Omega| \leq \frac{\Omega_s}{2} \\ 0, & \text{for } |\Omega| > \frac{\Omega_s}{2} \end{cases} \tag{1.45}$$

The spectrum of ideal lowpass filter is shown in Figure 1.58.

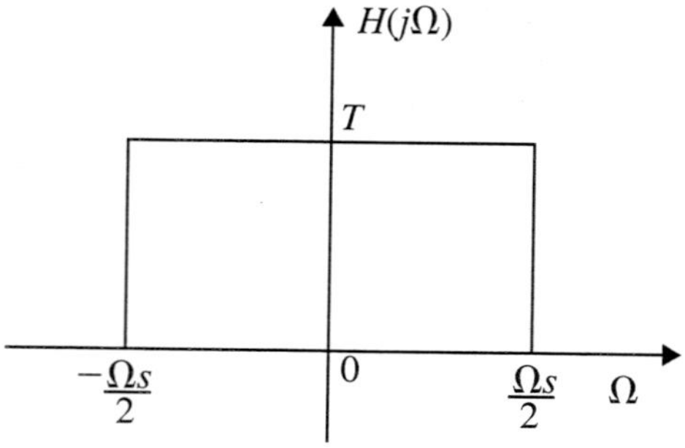

Figure 1.58 Spectrum of lowpass filter.

The impulse response of the lowpass filter is,

$$h(t) = F^{-1}[H(j\Omega)]$$

$$h(t) = \frac{1}{2\pi}\int_{\frac{-\Omega_s}{2}}^{\frac{\Omega_s}{2}} H(j\Omega)e^{j\Omega t}d\Omega \tag{1.46}$$

$$= \frac{T}{2\pi}\int_{\frac{-\Omega_s}{2}}^{\frac{\Omega_s}{2}} e^{j\Omega t}d\Omega = \frac{T}{\pi t}\sin\frac{\Omega_s t}{2}$$

$$= \frac{T}{\pi T}\sin\frac{2\pi f_s t}{2} = \frac{T}{\pi t}\sin\frac{\pi t}{T}$$

$$h(t) = \frac{T}{\pi}\frac{\sin\frac{\pi t}{T}}{t} \tag{1.47}$$

$$h(t-nT) = \frac{T}{\pi}\frac{\sin\frac{\pi}{T}(t-nT)}{t-nT} \tag{1.48}$$

Substitute equation (1.48) in equation (1.43)

$$x(t) = \sum_{n=-\infty}^{\infty} x(nT) \times \frac{\sin\frac{\pi}{T}(t-nT)}{\frac{\pi}{T}(t-nT)} \tag{1.49}$$

$$x(t) = \sum_{n=-\infty}^{\infty} x(nT)\sin c\frac{\pi}{T}(t-nT) \tag{1.50}$$

The response $x(t)$ given by the formula is suitable for practical implementation. The $\sin c$ function spreads over entire time axis. To reconstruct the signal at the time $t = t_0$, we must know all the samples values including those for $nT > t_0$.

That is, $x(t_0)$ requires the knowledge of future values of $x(nT)$ so it represents a non-casual system. Hence, this type of reconstruction is not suitable for real time applications. Therefore, we need a different approach to convert digital signal to analog signal which is shown in Figure 1.59.

The digital to analog converter produces an output voltage that is proportional to the value of the binary word. The output of DAC is applied to an interpolator

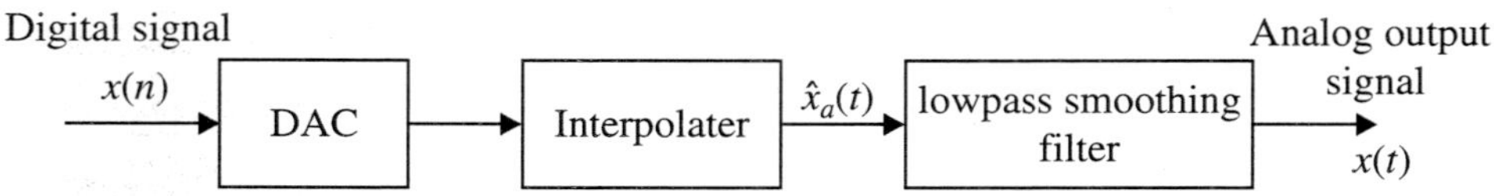

Figure 1.59 Digital to analog conversion.

which converts the output samples of DAC into an analog signal. There are several interpolators. One of the interpolators is zero-order hold.

1.16.6 Sampling with Zero Order Hold

One of the most widely used interpolators is zero order hold. The block diagram and input-output of zero order hold is shown in Figure 1.60. In this technique a given sample is held for an interval until the next sample is received.

$$\hat{x}_a(t) = x(n) \quad \text{for } nT \leq n \leq (n+1)T \quad n = 0, 1, 2, \ldots \tag{1.51}$$

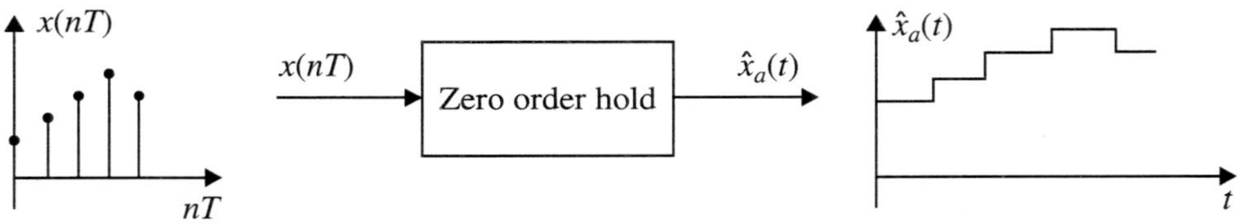

Figure 1.60 Input-output of zero-order hold.

$$\begin{aligned}\hat{x}_a(t) &= x(0) \quad \text{for } 0 \leq t < T \\ &= x(T) \quad \text{for } t \leq t < 2T \\ &= x(2T) \quad \text{for } 2T \leq t < 3T\end{aligned}$$

The impulse response of zero order hold in given by

$$h(t) = \begin{cases} 1, & 0 \leq t \leq T \\ 0, & \text{otherwise} \end{cases} \tag{1.52}$$

1.16.6.1 Transfer Function of a Zero Order Hold

The output of zero order hold is expressed in terms of $h(t)$. That is the output $\hat{x}_a(t)$ is the convolution of $x(nT)$ and $h(t)$

$$\hat{x}_a(t) = \sum_{n=-\infty}^{\infty} x(nT)h(t - nT) \tag{1.53}$$

$h(t)$ can be expressed as

$$h(t) = u(t) - u(t - T) \tag{1.54}$$

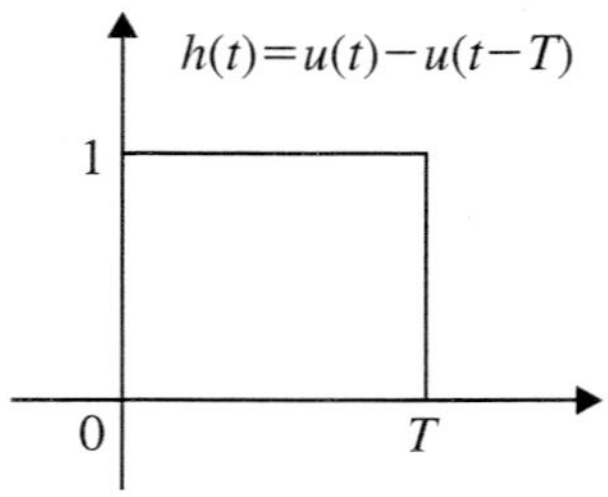

Figure 1.61 Output of a zero-order hold.

Taking Laplace transform on both sides we get

$$H(s) = U(s) - U(s)e^{-st}$$

$$\boxed{H(s) = \frac{1}{s}[1 - e^{-st}]} \qquad (1.55)$$

where $U(s) = \frac{1}{s}$.

The output of zero order hold consists of higher order harmonics. To remove these harmonics the output of zero order hold is applied to a lowpass filter. This filter is often called a smoothing filter because it tends to smooth the corners on the step approximations generated by ZOH.

Example 1.62

A signal having a spectrum ranging from DC to 10 kHz is to be sampled and converted into discrete form. What is the minimum number of samples per second that must be taken to ensure recovery?

Solution Given $f_m = 10\,\text{kHz}$. From Nyquist rate, the minimum number of samples per second that must be taken to ensure recovery is

$$f_s = 2f_m$$

$$f_s = 20,000 \text{ samples/sec.}$$

Example 1.63

Consider the following analog signal

$$x_a(t) = 3\cos 100\pi t$$

(*a*) Determine the minimum sampling rate required to avoid aliasing.

(*b*) Suppose that the signal is sampled at the rate $F_s = 200$ Hz, what is the discrete time signal obtained after sampling?

(*c*) Repeat (*b*) it $F_s = 75$ Hz.
(*d*) What is the frequency $0 < F < \frac{F_s}{2}$ of a sinusoid that yields samples identical to those obtained in part (*c*).

Solution

(*a*) Given

$$\Omega_m = 100\pi$$
$$2\pi f_m = 100\pi$$
$$f_m = 100/2$$

Hence, the minimum sampling rate required to avoid aliasing $f_s = 2f_m = 100$ Hz.

(*b*) If the signal is sampled at $f_s = 200$ Hz, the discrete time signal is $3\cos 100\pi nT$

$$x(n) = x(t)|_{t=nT}$$
$$x(n) = 3\cos\frac{100\pi}{200}n$$
$$x(n) = 3\cos\frac{n\pi}{2}$$

(*c*) If the signal is sampled at $F_s = 75$ Hz, the discrete-time signal is

$$\begin{aligned} x(n) &= x(t)\Big|_{t=nT} \\ &= 3\cos 100\pi nT \\ &= 3\cos\frac{100\pi}{75}n \\ &= 3\cos\left(\frac{4\pi}{3}\right)n \\ &= 3\cos\left(2\pi - \frac{2\pi}{3}\right)n \\ x(n) &= 3\cos\frac{4\pi}{3}n \end{aligned}$$

(*d*) For the sampling rate of $F_s = 75$ Hz, we have

$$F = \frac{F_0}{F_s}$$
$$F_0 = F \cdot F_s$$

Therefore, in general, the sampling of CT sinusoidal signal $x(t) = A\cos(2\pi F_0 t + \theta)$ with sampling rate $F_s = (1/T)$ results in a discrete time signal $x(n) = A\cos(2\pi f_0 n + \theta)$. Therefore, relative frequency $f_0 = (F_0/F_s)$.

The frequency of the sinusoidal in part (c) is,

$$F = \frac{1}{3}$$

$$\omega = \left(\frac{2\pi}{3}\right)$$

$$T = \left(\frac{2\pi}{\omega}\right) m$$

$$T = \left(\frac{2\pi}{2\pi/3}\right) m = 3m = 3$$

Hence

$$F_0 = \frac{1}{3} \cdot 75$$

$$F_0 = 25 \text{ Hz}$$

Clearly, the sinusoidal signal

$$y_a(t) = 3\cos 2\pi F_0 t$$

$$y_a(t) = 3\cos 50\pi t$$

Example 1.64

The signal $x(t) = 10\cos(10\pi t)$ is sampled at a rate of 8 samples per second. Plot the amplitude spectrum for $|\Omega| \leq 30\pi$. Can the original signal be recovered from samples? Explain.

Solution Given

$$x(t) = 10\cos(10\pi t)$$

$$\Omega m = 10\pi$$

$$F[x(t)] = X(j\Omega) = 10[\pi[\delta(\Omega + \Omega_0) + \delta(\Omega - \Omega_0)]]$$

$$X(j\Omega) = 10\pi[\delta(\Omega + 10\pi) + \delta(\Omega - 10\pi)]$$

The amplitude spectrum of $x(t)$ is shown in Figure 1.62.

$$\text{The sampling rate } f_s = 8 \text{ Hz} \quad \Rightarrow T = \frac{1}{8}$$

$$\Omega_s = 2\pi f_s = 16\pi$$

$$\Omega m = 10\pi = 2\pi f_m$$

$$f_m = 5 \text{ Hz}$$

$$\text{Nquist rate} = 2f_m = 10 \text{ Hz} \qquad (\text{Here } f_s < 2f_m)$$

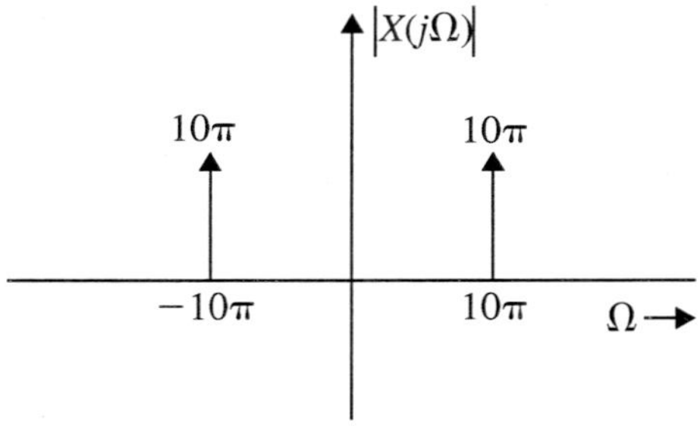

Figure 1.62 Amplitude spectrum of continuous time signal.

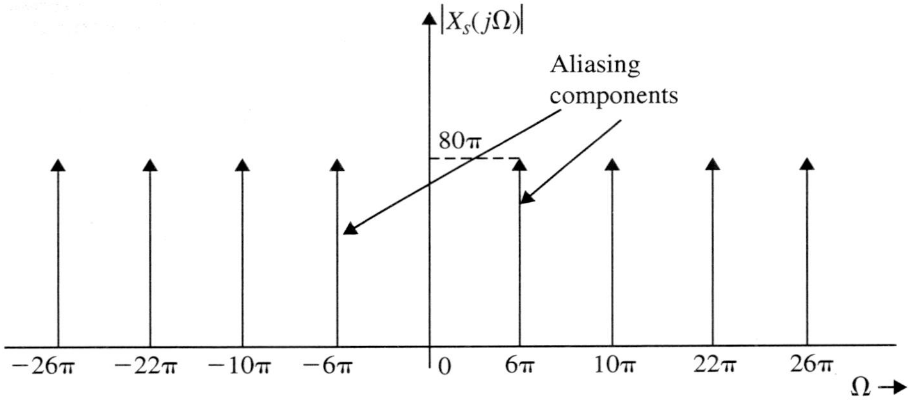

Figure 1.63 Amplitude spectrum of sampled signal.

Therefore, the original signal cannot be recovered from the samples. The frequency spectrum of sampled signal $x(t)$ is given by

$$X_s(j\Omega) = \frac{1}{T}\sum_{n-\infty}^{\infty} X\left[j\left(\Omega - \frac{2\pi n}{T}\right)\right]$$

$$= \frac{1}{T}\sum_{n=-\infty}^{\infty} 10\pi\left[\delta\left(\Omega + 10\pi - \frac{2\pi}{T}n\right) + \delta\left(\Omega - 10\pi - \frac{2\pi}{T}n\right)\right]$$

$$X_s(j\Omega) = 80\pi\sum_{n=-\infty}^{\infty}\left[\delta\left(\Omega + 10\pi - 16\pi n\right) + \delta\left(\Omega - 10\pi - 16\pi n\right)\right]$$

The plot of amplitude spectrum for $|\Omega| \leq 30\pi$ is shown in Figure 1.63.

Example 1.65

A signal $x(t) = \sin c(150\pi t)$ is sampled at a rate of

(a) 100 Hz;
(b) 200 Hz and
(c) 300 Hz.

For each of these three cases, can you recover the signal $x(t)$ from the sampled signal.

Solution Given

$$x(t) = \sin c(150\pi t)$$
$$\Omega_m = 150\pi$$
$$2\pi f_m = 150\pi$$
$$f_m = 75$$
$$f_s = 2f_m \Rightarrow f_s = 150, \quad T = \frac{1}{150}$$

The spectrum of the signal $x(t)$ is a rectangular pulse with a band width (maximum frequency components of 150π rad/sec. is shown in Figure 1.64.
(a) In the first case, the sampling rate is 100 Hz which is less than Nyquist rate. Therefore, $x(t)$ can be recovered from its samples.

$$f_s = 100, \quad 2f_m = 150 \Rightarrow f_s < 2f_m$$

For (b) and (c) cases the sampling rate is greater than Nyquist rate. Therefore, $x(t)$ can not be recovered from its samples. For $f_s = 200$ and $f_s = 300$

$$2fm = 150 \quad \text{and} \quad f_s > 2f_m$$

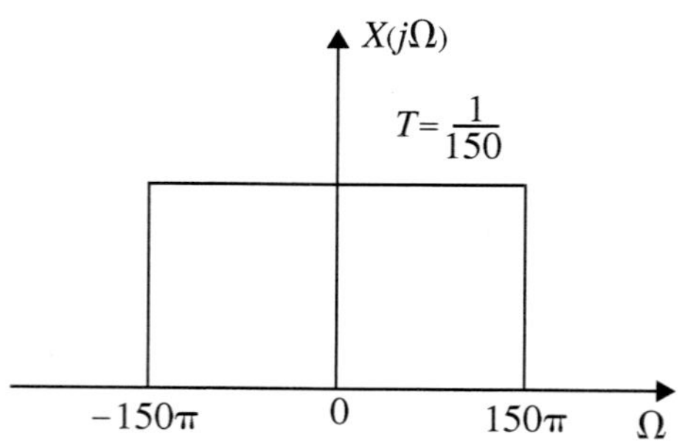

Figure 1.64 Spectrum of $x(t)$.

Example 1.66

Draw $|X_s(i\Omega)|$ for the following cases when $x_s(t) = x(t)\delta_T(t)$ with sampling period T, where

$$\delta_T(t) = \sum_{n=-\infty}^{\infty} \delta(t - nT)$$

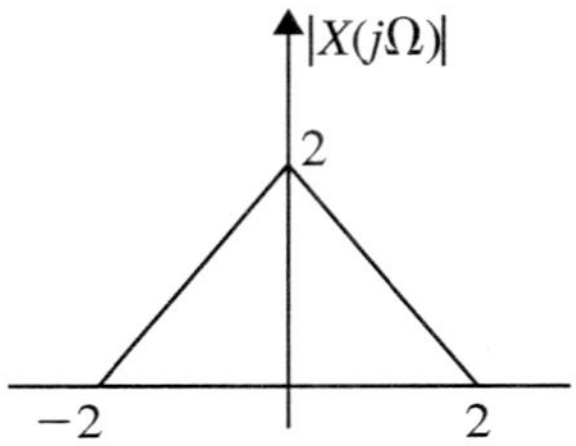

Figure 1.65 Spectrum of $x(t)$ for Example 1.66.

(*a*) $T = \frac{\pi}{3}$ sec.
(*b*) $T = \frac{\pi}{2}$
(*c*) $T = \frac{2\pi}{3}$

Solution In general for band limited signal the amplitude spectrum is shown in Figure 1.66.

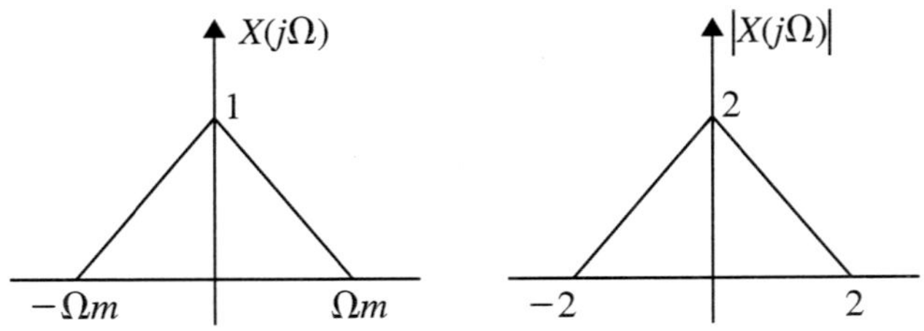

Figure 1.66 Spectrum of bandlimited signal.

$$\begin{aligned}
\therefore \; \Omega_m &= 2\text{rad/sec.} \\
2\pi f_m &= 2 \\
f_m &= \frac{1}{\pi}\text{ Hz} \\
\text{Nyquist rate} &= 2f_m \\
&= \frac{2}{\pi}\text{ Hz}
\end{aligned}$$

(*a*) Given

$$T = \frac{\pi}{3} \text{ sec.}$$

$$f_s = \frac{1}{T} = \frac{3}{\pi} \text{ Hz}$$

$$\Omega_s = 2\pi f_s = 6 \text{ rad/sec.}$$

$$f_s > 2f_m \quad \left[\therefore \text{ since } \frac{2}{\pi} > \frac{3}{\pi}\right]$$

Therefore, the spectrum $|X_s(j\Omega)|$ is free from aliasing and is shown in Figure 1.67.

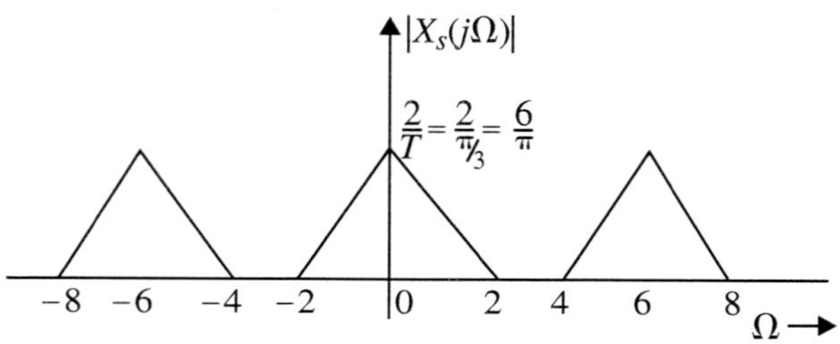

Figure 1.67 Spectrum of sampled signal for $T = \pi/3$ sec.

(*b*) Given

$$T = \frac{\pi}{2} \text{ sec.}$$

$$f_s = \frac{2}{\pi} \text{ Hz}$$

$$\Omega_s = 2\pi f_m = 4 \text{ rad/sec.}$$

$$2f_m = \frac{2}{\pi} \text{ Hz}$$

$$f_s = 2f_m.$$

Therefore, the spectrum $|X_s(i\Omega)|$ in free from aliasing and is shown in Figure 1.68.

(*c*) Given

$$T = \frac{2\pi}{3}, \quad f_s = \frac{3}{2\pi} \text{ sec.}, \quad \Omega_s = 3 \text{ rad/sec.}$$

$$f_s < 2f_m$$

The sampling frequency is less than the Nyquist rate. The spectra $X(j\Omega)$ repeats for every 3 rad/sec and the successive spectrum overlaps. Therefore, $x(t)$ cannot

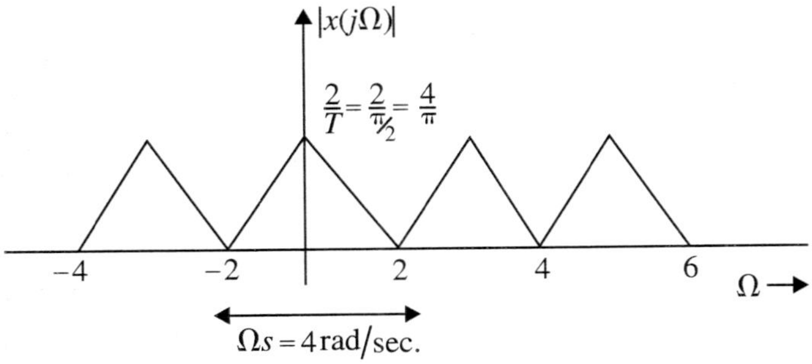

Figure 1.68 Spectrum of sampled signal for $T = \pi/2$ sec.

be recovered from its samples. The spectrum of sampled signal for $T = 2\pi/3$ is shown in Figure 1.69.

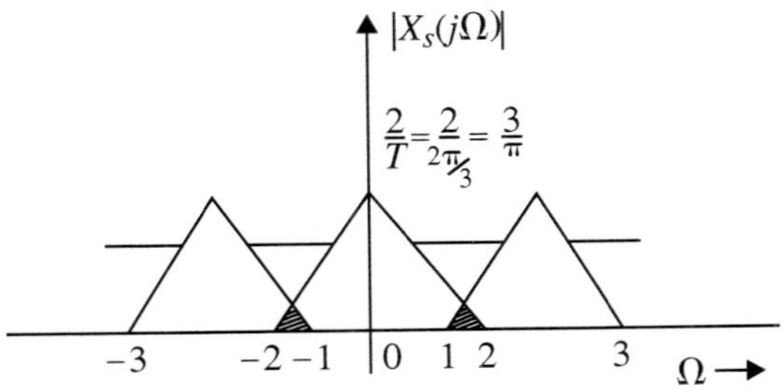

Figure 1.69 Spectrum of sampled signal for $T = \frac{2\pi}{3}$ sec.

Example 1.67

Consider the following sampling and reconstruction block as shown in Figure 1.70.

The output of the ideal reconstruction filter can be found by sending signal $x_s(t)$ through an ideal lowpass filter having characteristics as shown in Figure 1.71.

For the following signals draw the spectrum of $|X_s(j\Omega)|$, and find expression for $x(nT)$ and $y(t)$

(*i*) $x(t) = 2 + \cos(100\pi t)$ for $T = 0.0125$ sec.

(*ii*) $x(t) = 2 + \cos(100\pi t)$ for $T = \frac{1}{150}$ sec.

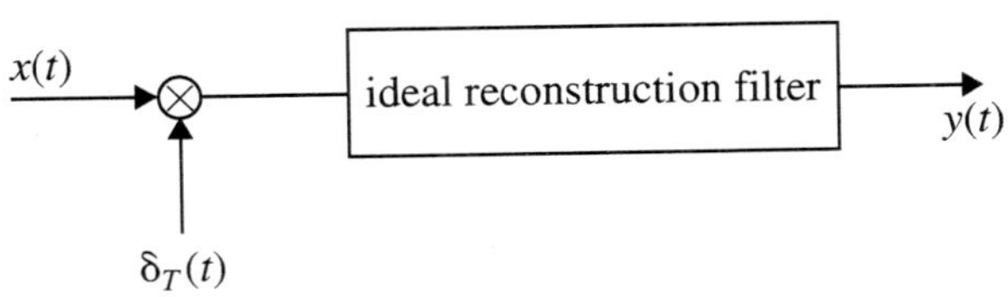

Figure 1.70 Sampling and reconstruction block.

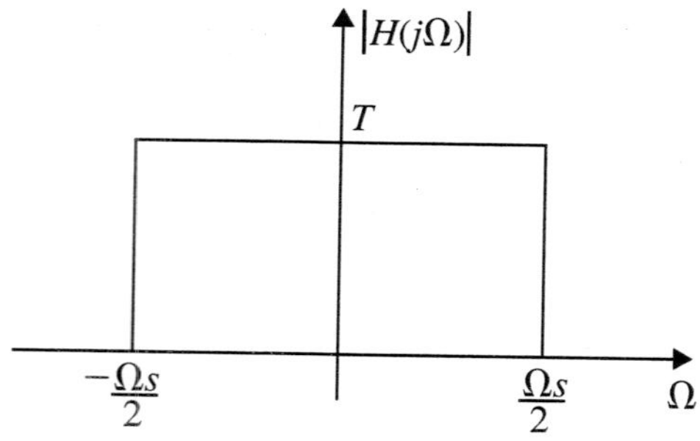

Figure 1.71 Frequency response of lowpass filter.

(*iii*) $x(t) = 1 + \cos(10\pi t) + \cos 30\pi t$ for $T = 0.04$ sec.
(*iv*) If $X(j\Omega) = \frac{1}{2+j\Omega}$ and $T = 2$ sec.

Draw $|X_s(j\Omega)|$. Test for aliasing.

Solution

(*i*) $x(t) = 2 + \cos(100\pi t)$ for $T = 0.0125$ sec.

$$
\begin{aligned}
x(t) &= 2 + \cos(100\pi t) \\
&= 2 + \frac{1}{2}\left[e^{j100\pi t} + e^{-j100\pi t}\right] \\
X(i\Omega) &= 4\pi\delta(\Omega) + \pi\left[\delta(\Omega + 100\pi) + \delta(\Omega - 100\pi)\right] \\
\because\ F[1] &= 2\pi\delta(\Omega) \\
F[e^{j\Omega_0 t}] &= 2\pi\delta(\Omega + \Omega_0)
\end{aligned}
$$

The sketch of amplitude spectrum of $x(t)$ is shown in Figure 1.72.
The sampling time

$$
\begin{aligned}
T &= 0.0125 \\
f_s &= \frac{1}{T} = \frac{1}{0.0125} = 80 \text{ Hz} \\
\Omega_s &= 2\pi f_s = 160 \text{ rad/sec} \\
\Omega_m &= 100\pi
\end{aligned}
$$

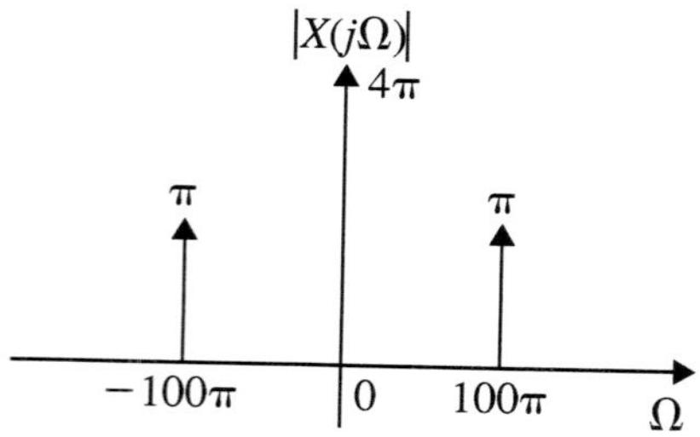

Figure 1.72 Spectrum of $x(t)$.

Given

$$f_m = 50 \text{ Hz}$$

Nyquist rate is $2f_m = 100$ Hz

$$f_s < 2fm$$

Therefore, the successive spectrum $X_s(j\Omega)$ overlap and the signal $x(t)$ cannot be recovered from its samples.

The spectrum $X_s(j\Omega)$ of the sampled signal $x(t)$ is periodic repetition of $X(j\Omega)$ for every 160π rad/sec. (80 Hz) is shown in Figure 1.73.

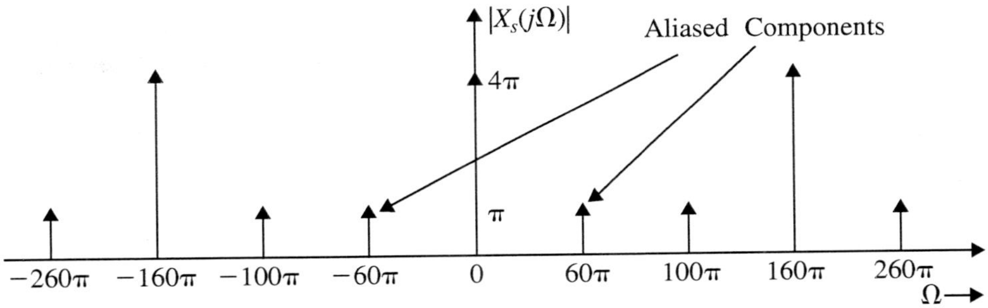

Figure 1.73 Spectrum of sampled signal.

The frequency characteristics of the reconstruction filter (LPF), is

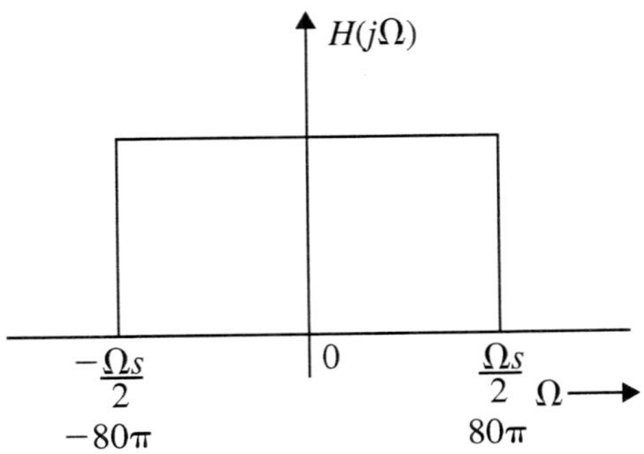

When the spectrum $|X_s(j\Omega)|$ is passed through the reconstruction filter (LPF) the output of the filter consists of the frequency components given by,

$$Y(j\Omega) = 4\pi 8(\Omega) + \pi[\delta(\Omega + 60\pi) + \delta(\Omega - 60\pi)]$$

The spectrum of output $y(t)$ is shown in Figure 1.74.

$$y(t) = 2 + \cos 60\pi t$$

$$x(nT) = x(t)|_{t=nT}$$

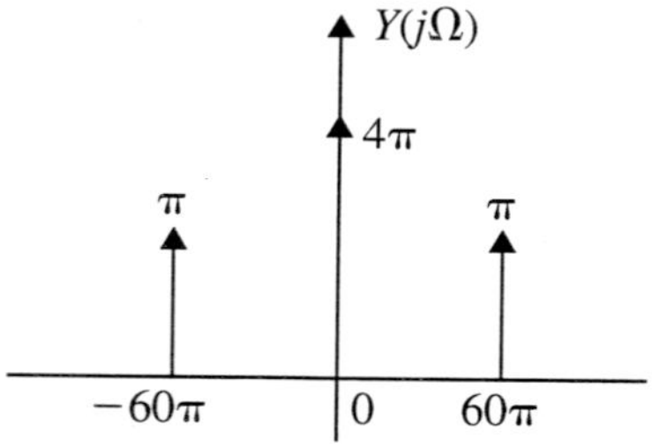

Figure 1.74 Spectrum of output $y(t)$.

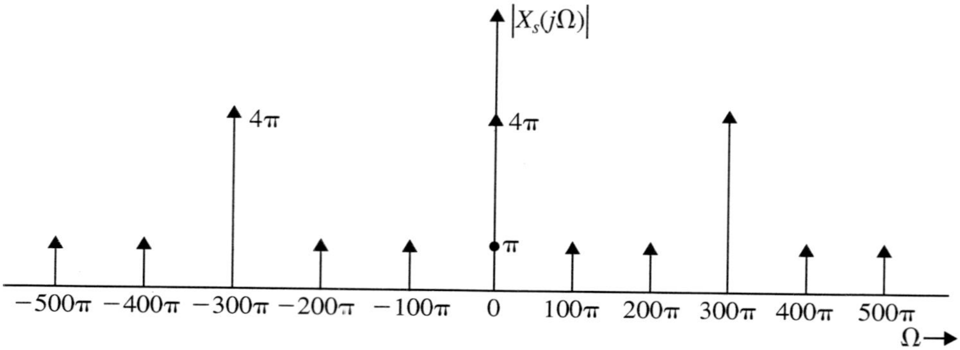

Figure 1.75 Spectrum of sampled signal.

$$x(nT) = 2 + \cos 100\pi t|_{t=0.0125n}$$
$$= 2 + \cos(1.25)n\pi$$
$$x(nT) = 2 + \cos(0.75n\pi)$$

(*ii*) Given $x(t) = 2 + \cos(100\pi t)$

$$T = \frac{1}{150} \text{ sec}$$
$$f_s = \frac{1}{T} = 150 \text{ Hz}$$
$$\Omega_s = 2\pi f_s = 300\pi \text{ rad/sec.}$$

The Amplitude spectrum ($|X(i\Omega)|$) of the signal is same as Figure 1.75. The spectrum of sampled signal of $x(t)$, is periodic extension of $X(j\Omega)$ for every 300π (rad/sec.) and is shown in Figure 1.76.

The frequency characteristics of a reconstruction filter is shown below.

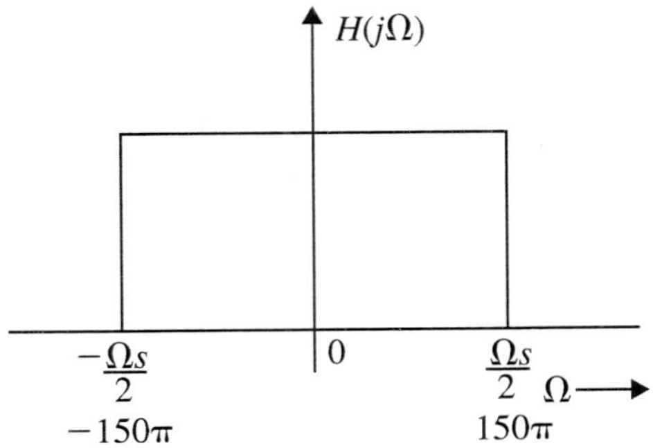

The resultant output spectrum is shown in Figure 1.76.

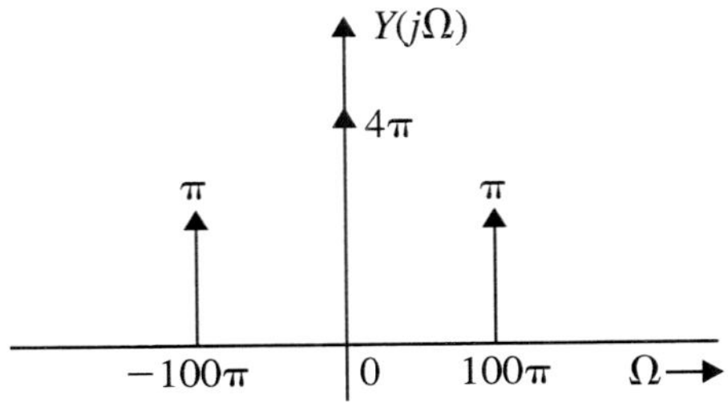

Figure 1.76 Spectrum of output $y(t)$.

$$Y(j\Omega) = 4\pi\delta(\Omega) + \pi[\delta(\Omega - 100\pi) + \delta(\Omega + 100\pi)]$$

$$y(t) = 2 + \cos 100\pi t$$

$$x(nT) = x(t)\Big|_{t=nT}$$

$$= 2 + \cos 100\pi t\Big|_{t=\frac{1}{150}n}$$

$$x(nT) = 2 + \cos(0.666n\pi)$$

(*iii*) Given

$$x(t) = 1 + (\cos 10\pi t) + (\cos 30\pi t); \qquad T = 0.04 \text{ sec}$$

$$x(nT) = x(t)\Big|_{t=nT} = 0.04n$$

$$x(nT) = 1 + (\cos 0.4\pi t) + (\cos 0.2\pi t)$$

$$x(nT) = 1 + (\cos 0.4n\pi) + (\cos 1.2n\pi)$$

$$f_s = \frac{1}{T} = 25 \text{ Hz}, \quad \Omega_s = 2\pi f_s = 50\pi \text{ rad/sec.}$$

$$\Omega_m = 2\pi f_m = 30\pi$$

$$f_m = 15 \text{ Hz}$$

$$2f_m = 30 \text{ Hz} \qquad (\therefore f_s < 2f_m)$$

Therefore, the successive spectrum of $X(j\Omega)$ in $X_s(j\Omega)$ overlaps and $x(t)$ cannot be recovered from $x(nT)$

$$X(j\Omega) = 2\pi\delta(\Omega) + \pi[\delta(\Omega + 10\pi) + \delta(\Omega - 10\pi)]$$
$$+ \pi[8(\Omega + 30\pi) + (\Omega - 30\pi)]$$

The sketch of spectrum of sampled signal is shown in Figure 1.77.

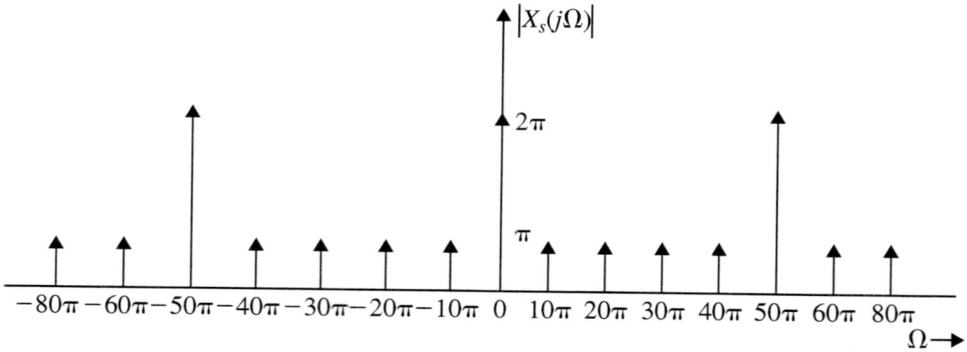

Figure 1.77 Spectrum of sampled signal.

The frequency spectrum of the lowpass filter is given below

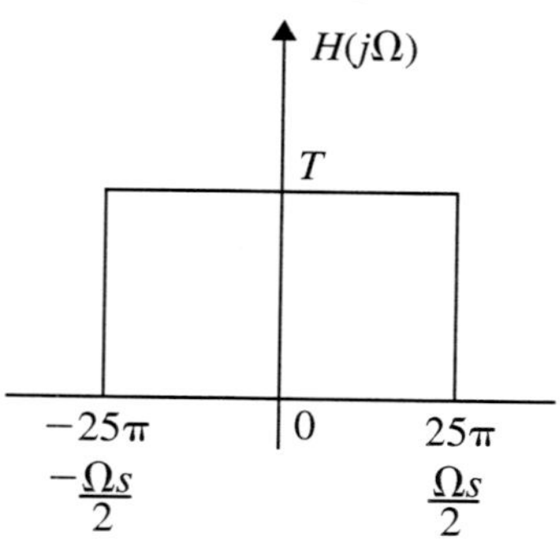

The output spectrum is shown in Figure 1.78. From that, we can obtain

$$Y(j\Omega) = 2\pi\delta(\Omega) + \pi[\delta(\Omega + 10\pi) + \delta(\Omega - 10\pi)]$$
$$+ \pi[\delta(\Omega + 20\pi) + \delta(\Omega - 20\pi)]$$
$$y(t) = 1 - \cos(10\pi t) + \cos(20\pi t)$$

(*iv*) Given $T = 2$ sec, $f_s = 0.5$ Hz

$$\Omega_s = \pi \text{ rad/sec}$$
$$X(j\Omega) = \frac{1}{2 + j\Omega}$$
$$|X(j\Omega)| = \frac{1}{\sqrt{4 + \Omega^2}}$$

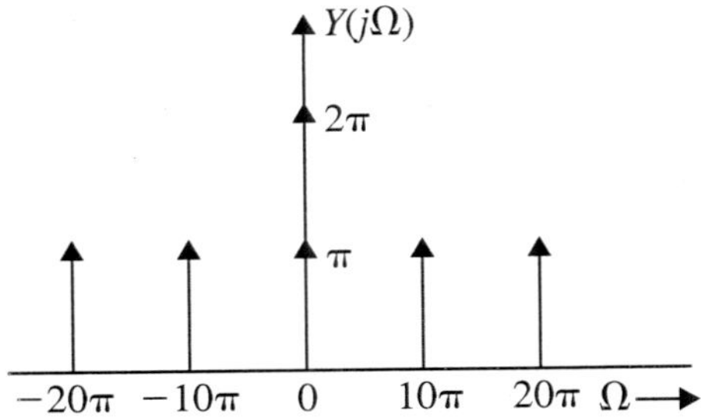

Figure 1.78 Spectrum of output $y(t)$.

The spectrum of $|X(j\Omega)|$ is not band limited. Therefore, aliasing of successive frequency components occurs even Ω is large. The spectra $|X_s(j\Omega)|$ is shown in Figure 1.79.

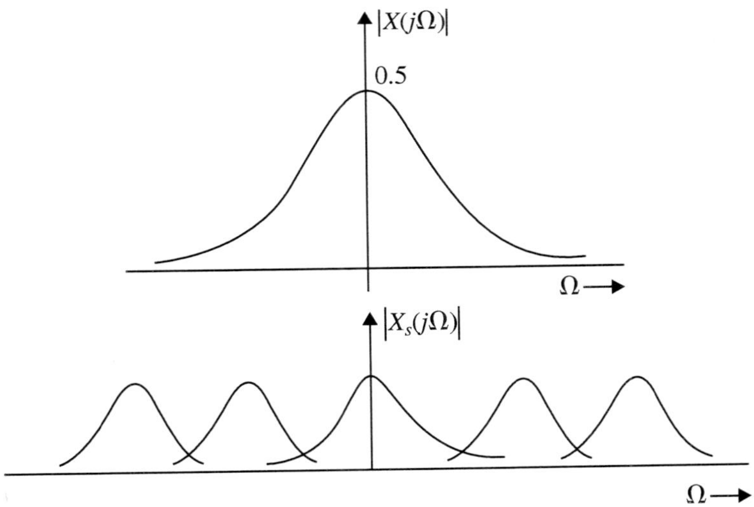

Figure 1.79 Spectrum of sampled signal.

Example 1.68

Determine the Nyquist sampling rate and Nyquist sampling intervals for the following signals.

(i) $\sin c^2(200\pi t)$

(ii) $0.5 \sin c^2(200\pi t)$

(iii) $\sin c(200\pi t) + 3\sin^2 c(120\pi t)$

(iv) $\sin c(100\pi t) \sin c(200\pi t)$

Solution The Fourier transform of triangular function is square of sin c function.

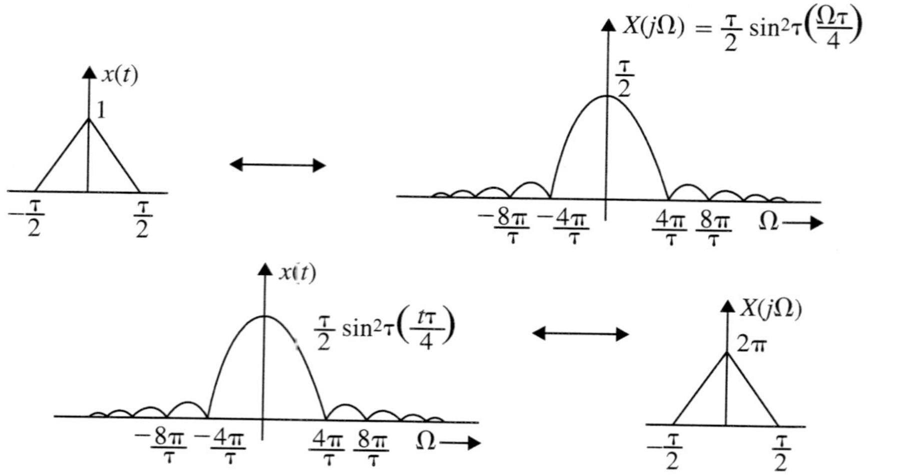

Figure 1.80 (a) Fourier transform of triangular function. (b) Dual property of figure (a).

Similarly Fourier transform of a rectangular pulse is a sin c function. This is shown in Figures 1.80 and 1.81 respectively.

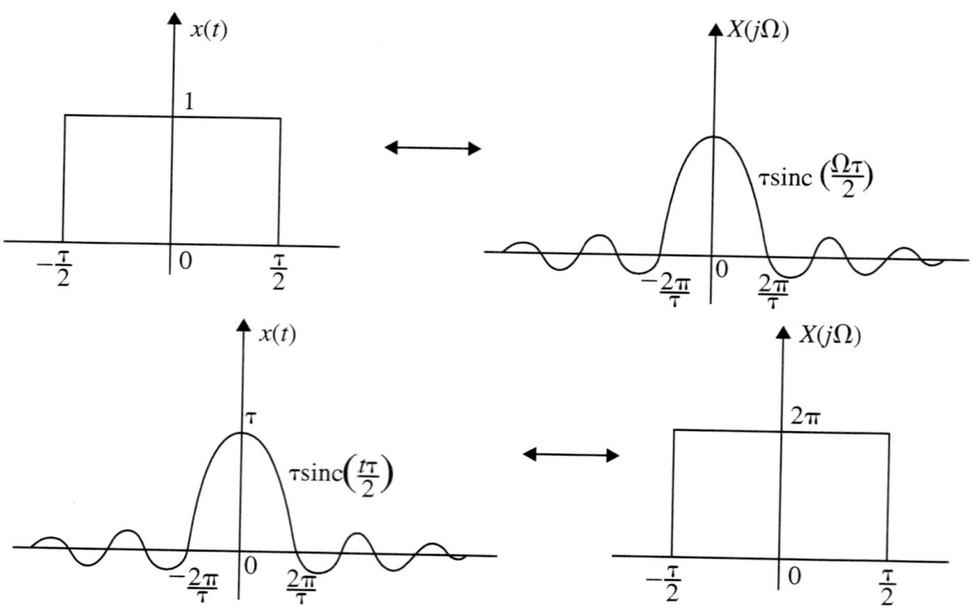

Figure 1.81 (a) Fourier transform of rectangular pulse. (b) Dual property of figure (a).

(*i*) Given,

$$x(t) = \sin c^2(200\pi t)$$

Comparing the signal $x(t)$ with the above signal we get

$$x(t) = \frac{\tau}{2} \sin c^2 \left(\frac{t\tau}{4}\right)$$

$$\frac{t\tau}{4} = 200\pi t$$

$$\tau = 800\pi$$

$$\frac{\tau}{2} = 400\pi$$

That is the maximum frequency component present in the signal is 400π rad/sec. (or) the signal is band limited to 400π rad/sec.

$$\Omega_m = 400\pi \quad \text{and} \quad f_m = 200 \text{ Hz}$$

$$\text{Nyquist rate } f_s = 2f_m = 400 \text{ Hz.}$$

Sampling interval $T = \frac{1}{f_s} = \frac{1}{400} = 2.5$ m sec.

(*ii*) Same values as above.

(*iii*) Given

$$x(t) = \sin c(200\pi t) + 3 \sin c^2(120\pi t)$$

Let

$$x_1(t) = \sin c(200\pi t)$$

$$x_2(t) = 3 \sin^2 c(120\pi t)$$

Compare the signal $x_1(t)$ with the signal $x(t) = \tau \sin c\left(\frac{\tau t}{2}\right)$

$$\frac{\tau t}{2} = 200\pi t$$

$$\frac{\tau}{2} = 200\pi \text{ rad/sec}$$

$$\therefore \Omega m_1 = 200 \text{ rad/sec}$$

$$fm_1 = 100 \text{ Hz}$$

Compare the signal $x_2(t)$ with the signal $x(t) = \frac{\tau}{2} \sin c^2 \left(\frac{\tau t}{4}\right)$,

$$\frac{\tau t}{4} = 120\pi t$$

$$\frac{\tau}{4} = 120\pi$$

$$\frac{\tau}{2} = 240\pi$$

$$\therefore \quad \Omega m_2 = 240\pi \text{ rad/sec.}$$

When both signals are added, the maximum frequency components is

$$\Omega_m = \Omega m_2 = 240\pi \text{ rad/sec}$$
$$fm = 120 \text{ Hz}$$
$$\text{Nyquist rate } f_s = 2fm = 240 \text{ Hz}$$
$$\text{Nyquist interval } = \frac{1}{f_s} = 4.167 \text{ m sec.}$$

(*iv*) $x(t) = \sin c(100\pi t) \sin c(200\pi t)$

Let

$$x_1(t) = \sin c(100\pi t); x_2(t) = \sin c(200\pi t)$$

The signal $x_1(t)$ is band limited to frequency 100π rad/sec and the signal $x_2(t)$ is bandlimited to frequency 200π rad/sec and are shown in Figure 1.82.

$$F[x_1(t) \cdot x_2(t)] = X_i(j\Omega) * X_2(j\Omega)$$

The convolution of $X_1(j\Omega)$ and $X_2(j\Omega)$ results is a triangular shape frequency spectra with $\Omega_m = 300\pi$ rad/sec and is shown in Figure 1.83.

$$fm = \frac{\Omega m}{2\pi}$$
$$fm = 150 \text{ Hz}$$

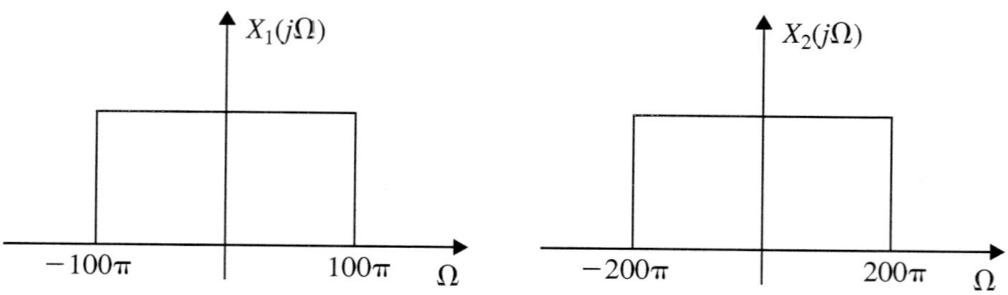

Figure 1.82 Spectrum of $x_1(t)$ and $x_2(t)$.

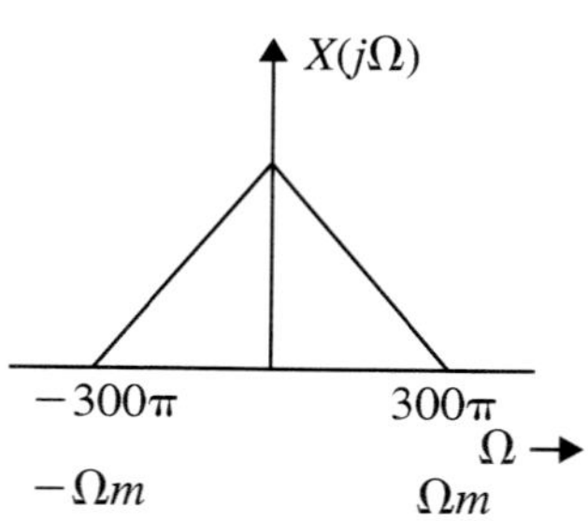

Figure 1.83 Spectrum of $x(t)$.

$$\text{Nyquist rate } = 2fm = 300 \text{ Hz}$$
$$\text{Nyquist interval } = \frac{1}{300} = 3.33 \text{ m sec.}$$

Example 1.69

A signal $x(t)$, whose spectrum is shown in Figure 1.84, is sampled at a rate of 300 samples/sec. What is the spectrum of the sampled discrete-time signal?

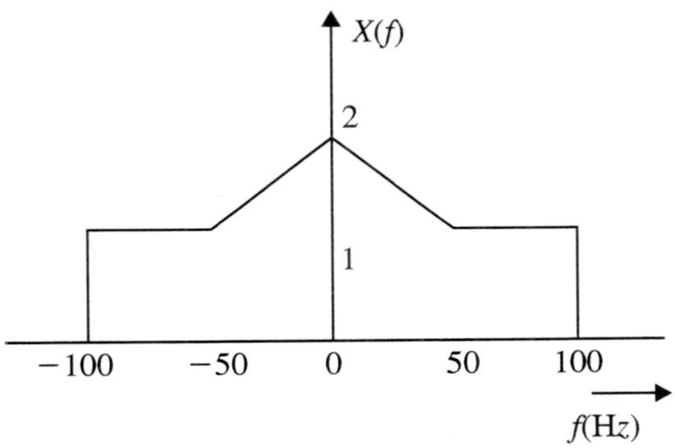

Figure 1.84 Spectrum of $x(t)$.

Solution

$$fm = 100 \text{ Hz}$$
$$\text{Nyquist rate} = 2fm = 200 \text{ Hz}$$
$$\text{Sampling frequency } (f_s) = 300 \text{ Hz}$$
$$f_s > 2fm.$$

Therefore, there is no aliasing. The sketch of spectrum of sampled signal is shown in Figure 1.85.

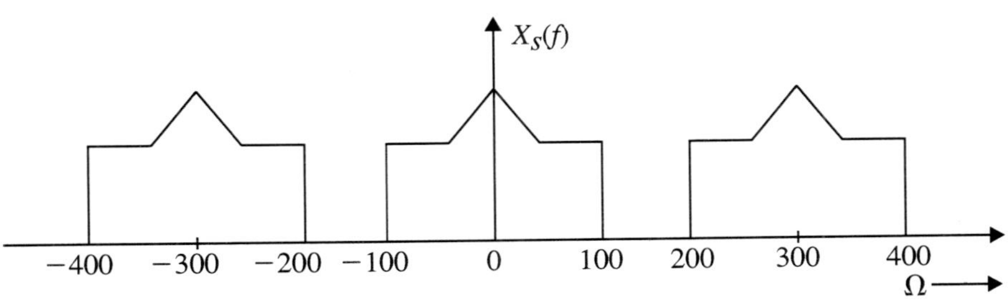

Figure 1.85 Spectrum of sampled signal.

1.17 Correlation of Two Sequences

Correlation is basically used to compare two signals. It occupies a significant place in signal processing. It has application in radar and sonar system where the location of target is measured by comparing the transmitted and reflected signals. Other applications of correlation include image processing and control engineering *etc.* Correlation is a measure of the degree to which two signals are similar. The correlation of two signals is divided into (*i*) Cross-correlation and (*ii*) Auto-correlation.

The computation of cross-correlation of two sequences has some similarities with convolution sum. In convolution, one of the sequences is folded, then shifted and finally the values of the product sequence are summed. In cross-correlation, the computation is similar to convolution except for the folding operation. In correlation, one of the sequences is shifted, the two sequences are multiplied and finally summed over all values of the product sequence.

1.17.1 Cross Correlation

The cross-correlation between a pair of signal $x(n)$ and $y(n)$ is given by

$$\gamma_{xy}(l) = \sum_{n=-\infty}^{\infty} x(n)y(n-l) \quad l = 0, 1, \pm 2, \pm 3, \ldots.$$

$$\gamma_{yx}(l) = \sum_{n=-\infty}^{\infty} y(n)x(n-l) \tag{1.56}$$

$$= \sum_{n=-\infty}^{\infty} y(n+l)x(n) \tag{1.57}$$

If the time shift $l = 0$, we get

$$\gamma_{xy}(0) = \gamma_{yx}(0) = \sum_{n=-\infty}^{\infty} x(n)y(n)$$

Comparing equations (1.56) and (1.57), we get

$$\gamma_{xy}(l) = \gamma_{xy}(-l) \tag{1.58}$$

$$\gamma_{xy}(l) = \sum_{n=-\infty}^{\infty} x(n)y(-(l-n))$$

$$= x(l) * y(-l) \tag{1.59}$$

Therefore, correlation process is essentially the convolution of two data sequences in which one of the sequences has been reversed.

1.17.2 Auto Correlation

The auto-correlation of a sequence is correlation of a sequence with itself.

$$\gamma_{xx}(l) = \sum_{n=-\infty}^{\infty} x(n)x(n-l) \tag{1.60}$$

or

$$\gamma_{xx}(l) = \sum_{n=-\infty}^{\infty} x(n+l) \cdot x(n) \tag{1.61}$$

1.17.3 Computation of Correlation

Step 1. Sketch $x(n)$ and $y(n)$

Step 2. Obtain the sequence $y(n-l)$ by shifting the sequence right by l if l is positive and left by l if l is negative

Step 3. Multiply the shifted sequence $y(n-l)$ with $x(n)$ and sum all the values to obtain $\gamma_{xy}(l)$.

Step 4. Repeat steps 2 and 3 for all values of l.

Like convolution, the following methods are used to compute cross-correlation and auto-correlation.

1. Graphical method.
2. Tabulation method.
3. Multiplication method.

The following numerical examples illustrate the method of determining cross-correlation and auto-correlation. The width, the number of samples to the left of auto-correlation and cross-correlation functions are defined as follows.

1. N_1 = Number of left sided samples of $x(n)$.
2. N_2 = Number of left sided samples of $y(-n)$.
3. T_1 = Width of $x(n)$.
4. T_2 = Width of $y(n)$.
5. T = Width of cross-correlation or auto-correlation function.
6. N = Number of left sided samples of cross-correlation or auto-correlation function.
7. $N = N_1 + N_2$.
8. $T = T_1 + T_2 - 1$.

Example 1.70

Find the cross-correlation of two finite length sequence

$$x(n) = \{1, 2, 1, 1\} \quad \text{and} \quad y(n) = \{1, 1, 2, 1\}$$

Solution

GRAPHICAL METHOD

The plots of $x(n)$ and $y(n-l)$ are shown in Figure 1.86.

$$x(l) = \{\underset{\uparrow}{1}, 2, 1, 1\},\ y(l) = \{\underset{\uparrow}{1}, 1, 2, 1\} \quad \text{and} \quad y(-l) = \{1, 2, 1, \underset{\uparrow}{1}\}$$

where $N_1 = 0$ and $N_2 = -3$ and so $N = N_1 + N_2 = 3$; $T_1 = 4$; $T_2 = 4$ and $T = T_1 + T_2 - 1 = 4 + 4 - 1 = 7$.

$$\gamma_{xy}(l) = \sum_{n=-\infty}^{\infty} x(n)y(n-l)$$

From Figure 1.86(a) & (b), $\gamma_{xy}(0) = \sum_{n=-\infty}^{\infty} x(n)y(n)$

$$= 1 \times 1 + 2 \times 1 + 1 \times 2 + 1 \times 1 = 6$$

From Figure 1.86(a) & (c), $\gamma_{xy}(-1) = \sum_{n=-\infty}^{\infty} x(n)y(n+1) = 1 + 4 + 1 = 6$

From Figure 1.86(a) & (d), $\gamma_{xy}(-2) = \sum_{n=-\infty}^{\infty} x(n)y(n+2) = 2 + 2 = 4$

From Figure 1.86(a) & (e), $\gamma_{xy}(-3) = \sum_{n=-\infty}^{\infty} x(n)y(n+3) = 1 \times 1 = 1$

From Figure 1.86(a) & (f), $\gamma_{xy}(1) = \sum_{n=-\infty}^{\infty} x(n)y(n-1) = 2 + 2 + 1 = 5$

From Figure 1.86(a) & (g), $\gamma_{xy}(2) = \sum_{n=-\infty}^{\infty} x(n)y(n-2) = 1 + 1 = 2$

From Figure 1.86(a) & (h), $\gamma_{xy}(3) = \sum_{n=-\infty}^{\infty} x(n)y(n-3) = 1 \times 1 = 1$

$$\boxed{\gamma_{xy}(l) = \{1, 4, 6, \underset{\uparrow}{6}, 5, 2, 1\}}$$

TABULATION METHOD

	$y(-l)$	1	2	1	1
$x(l)$	1	1	2	1	1
	2	2	4	2	2
	1	1	2	1	1
	1	1	2	1	1

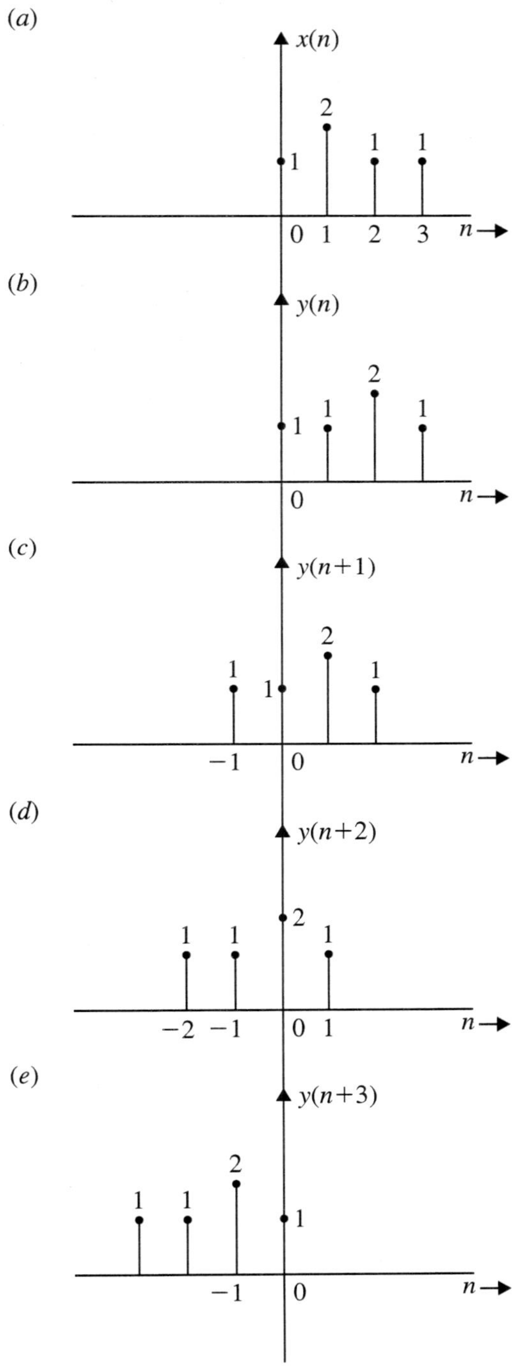

Figure 1.86 Cross correlation of Example 1.70.

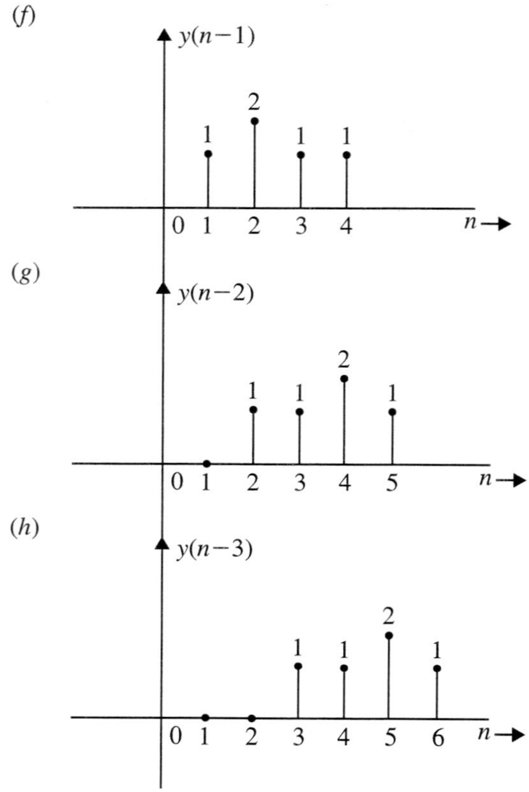

Figure 1.86 *Cross-correction of Example 1.70 (f) to (h)*

$$\gamma_{xy}(l) = \{\overbrace{1,4,6}^{}\!,6,5,2,1\}$$
$$N = 3 \uparrow$$
$$\leftarrow -T = 7- \rightarrow$$

MULTIPLICATION METHOD

			1	2	1	1
			1	2	1	1
			1	2	1	1
		1	2	1	1	
	2	4	2	2		
1	2	1	1			
1	4	6	6	5	2	1

$$\boxed{\gamma_{xy}(l) = \{1,4,6,\underset{\uparrow}{6},5,2,1\}}$$

Example 1.71

Find the convolution and correlation for

$$x(n) = \{\underset{\uparrow}{0}, 1, -2, 3, -4\} \quad \text{and} \quad h(n) = \{\underset{\uparrow}{0.5}, 1, 2, 1, 0.5\}$$

Solution Convolution of $x(n)$ and $y(n)$ is

$$y(n) = x(n) * h(n)$$

TABULATION METHOD

$x(n)$ \ $h(n)$	0.5	1	2	1	0.5
0	0	0	0	0	0
1	0.5	1	2	1	0.5
−2	−1	−2	−4	−2	−1
3	1.5	3	6	3	1.5
−4	−2	−4	−8	−4	−2

where $N_1 = 0$; $N_2 = 0$; $N = 0$ and $T_1 = 5$; $T_2 = 5$; $T = 9$.

$$\boxed{y(n) = \{\underset{\uparrow}{0}, 0.5, 0, 1.5, -2, 0.5, -6, -2.5, -2\}}$$

MULTIPLICATION METHOD

				0.5	1	2	1	0.5
				0	1	−2	3	−4
				−2	−4	−8	−4	−2
			1.5	3	6	3	1.5	
		−1	−2	−4	−2	−1		
	0.5	1	2	1	0.5			
0	0	0	0	0				
0	0.5	0	1.5	−2	0.5	−6	−2.5	−2

$$\boxed{y(n) = \{\underset{\uparrow}{0}, 0.5, 0, 1.5, -2, 0.5, -6, -2.5, -2\}}$$

Correlation of $x(n)$ and $y(n)$ is

$$\gamma_{xy}(l) = x(l) * h(-l)$$

$$x(l) = \{\underset{\uparrow}{0}, 1, -2, 3, -4\} \quad \text{and} \quad h(-l) = \{0.5, 1, 2, 1, \underset{\uparrow}{0.5}\}$$

TABULATION METHOD

$x(n)$ \ $h(n)$	0.5	1	2	1	0.5
0	0	0	0	0	0
1	0.5	1	2	1	0.5
−2	−1	−2	−4	−2	−1
3	1.5	3	6	3	1.5
−4	−2	−4	−8	−4	−2

where $N_1 = 0, N_2 = 4$ so $n = 0+(4) = 4$ and $T_1 = 5, T_2 = 5$ so $T = 5+5-1 = 9$.

$$\boxed{\gamma_{xy}(l) = \{0, 0.5, 0, 1.5, \underset{\uparrow}{-2}, 0.5, -6, -2.5, -2\}}$$

MULTIPLICATION METHOD

				0.5	1	2	1	0.5
				0	1	−2	3	−4
				−2	−4	−8	−4	−2
			1.5	3	6	3	1.5	
		−1	−2	−4	−2	−1		
	0.5	1	2	1	0.5			
0	0	0	0	0				
0	0.5	0	1.5	−2	0.5	−6	−2.5	−2

$$\boxed{\gamma_{xy}(l) = \{0, 0.5, 0, 1.5, -2, 0.5, -6, -2.5, -2\}}$$

Example 1.72

(*a*) Determine the cross-correlation values of the sequences.

$$x_1(n) = \{1, 2, 3, 4\} \quad \text{and} \quad x_2(n) = \{4, 3, 2, 1\}$$

(*b*) Determine the auto-correlation values of the sequences.

$$x(n) = \{1, 0, 1, 2, 3, 0, 1, 2\}$$

Solution

(*a*) TABULATION METHOD

$$x_1(l) = \{\underset{\uparrow}{1}, 2, 3, 4\}, \quad x_2(l) = \{\underset{\uparrow}{4}, 3, 2, 1\} \quad x_2(-l) = \{1, 2, 3, \underset{\uparrow}{4}\}$$

	1	2	3	4
1	1	2	3	4
2	2	4	6	8
3	3	6	9	12
4	4	8	12	16

where $N_1 = 0$; $N_2 = 3$, so $N = N_1 + N_2 = 3$ and $T_1 = 4$; $T_2 = 4$, so $T = T_1 + T_2 - 1 = 7$

$$\boxed{\gamma_{x_1x_2}(l) = \{1, 4, 10, \underset{\uparrow}{20}, 25, 24, 16\}}$$

MULTIPLICATION METHOD

$$\begin{array}{ccccccc}
 & & & 1 & 2 & 3 & 4 \\
 & & & 1 & 2 & 3 & 4 \\
\hline
 & & & 4 & 8 & 12 & 16 \\
 & & 3 & 6 & 9 & 12 & \\
 & 2 & 4 & 6 & 8 & & \\
1 & 2 & 3 & 4 & & & \\
\hline
1 & 4 & 10 & 20 & 25 & 24 & 16 \\
\hline
\end{array}$$

$$\boxed{\gamma_{x_1x_2}(l) = \{1, 4, 10, \underset{\uparrow}{20}, 25, 24, 16\}}$$

(b)

$$x(n) = \{1, 0, 1, 2, 3, 0, 1, 2\}$$

$$x(l) = \{\underset{\uparrow}{1}, 0, 1, 2, 3, 0, 1, 2\}$$

$$x(-l) = \{\underset{\uparrow}{2}, 1, 0, 3, 2, 1, 0, 1\}$$

where $N_1 = 0$; $N_2 = 7$, so $N = N_1 + N_2 = 7$ and $T_1 = 8$; $T_2 = 8$, so $T = T_1 + T_2 - 1 = 8 + 8 + 1 = 15$

							1	0	1	2	3	0	1	2
							2	1	0	3	2	1	0	1
							1	0	1	2	3	0	1	2
						0	0	0	0	0	0	0	0	
					1	0	1	2	3	0	1	2		
				2	0	2	4	6	0	2	4			
			3	0	3	6	9	0	3	6				
		0	0	0	0	0	0	0	0					
	1	0	1	2	3	0	1	2						
2	0	2	4	6	0	2	4							
2	1	2	8	10	7	10	20	10	7	10	8	2	1	2

$$\gamma_{xx} = \{2, 1, 2, 8, 10, 7, 10, \underset{\uparrow}{20}, 10, 7, 10, 8, 2, 1, 2\}$$

1.18 The Concept of Frequency in Continuous-Time and Discrete-Time Signals

1.18.1 Concept of Frequency in CT Signal

Consider the following CT sinusoids which are periodic

$$x_1(t) = \sin \omega_0 t \quad \text{and} \quad x_2(t) = \cos \omega_0 t$$

The signals have frequency ω_0 in radians per second or frequency $f = \omega_0/2\pi$ in Hz. They have the period $T = \frac{2\pi}{\omega_0} = \frac{1}{f}$. The above signals can be expressed as a function of complex exponential as

$$e^{j\omega_0 t} = \cos \omega_0 t + j \sin \omega_0 t$$

The function $e^{j\omega_0 t}$ can be plotted as a two dimensional vector rotating around a unit circle in the clockwise and anti-clock directions as represented in Figure 1.87(a). For $\omega_0 < 0$, it rotates in the counter clockwise direction and for $\omega_0 < 0$, in the clockwise direction. The same function $e^{j\omega_0 t}$ is plotted in three dimensional direction as shown in Figure 1.87(b) which is somewhat difficult to visualize. The negative frequency complex exponential rotates in the opposite direction of a positive frequency complex exponential.

1.18.2 Concept of Frequency in DT Signal

Consider the discrete time sequence $x[n]$. The sequence $x[n]$ is said to be periodic if there exists an integer N such that $x[n] = x[n + N]$. The sequence repeats itself

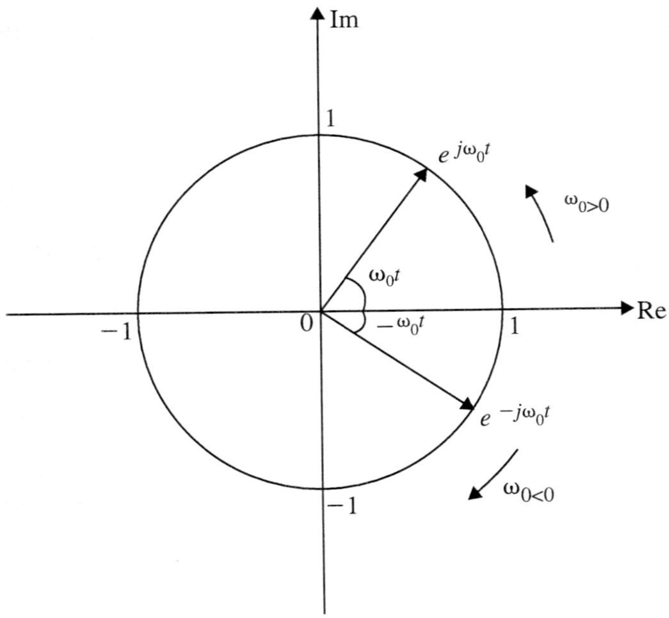

Figure 1.87 (*a*) Plot of $e^{j\omega_0 t}$ (2 dimensional).

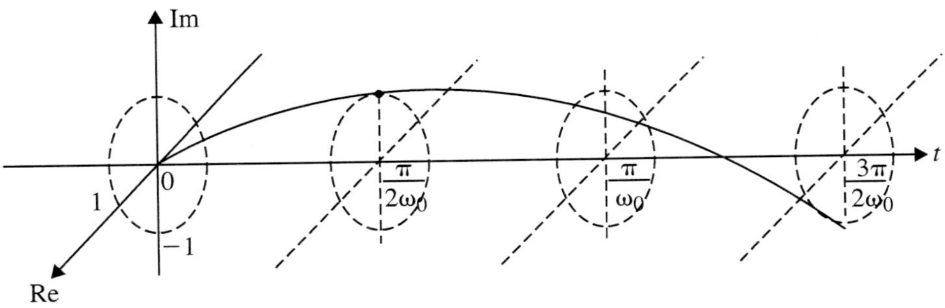

Figure 1.87 (*b*) Plot of $e^{j\omega_0 t}$ (3 dimensional).

every N samples or every NT seconds where T is the sampling period. If $x[n]$ is periodic with period N, it is also periodic with period $2N, 3N, \ldots$. The smallest such integer is called the fundamental period. Now consider the following sequence which is periodic.

$$\begin{aligned} x[n] &= \sin \omega_0 nT \\ &= \sin \omega_0 (n+N)T \\ &= \sin \omega_0 nT \cos \omega_0 NT + \cos \omega_0 nT \sin \omega_0 NT \end{aligned}$$

This holds good for every integer n iff

$$\cos \omega_0 NT = 1 \qquad \text{and} \qquad \sin \omega_0 NT = 0$$

This implies that

$$\omega_0 NT = 2\pi k$$
$$\omega_0 T = 2\pi \frac{k}{N}$$

where k is an integer and k/N is a rational number.

The sequence repeats itself every N samples. On similar line it can be shown that $\cos \omega_0 nt$ and $e^{j\omega_0 nt}$ are periodic iff $\omega_0 T$ is a rational number multiple of π. The periods of these sequences are

$$B = \frac{2\pi k}{\omega_0 T}, \qquad k = 0, \pm 1, \pm 2, \ldots$$

Consider the following sequences

$$x_1[n] = \sin 0.1\pi n$$
$$x_2[n] = \sin 0.3\pi n$$

The periodicity of $x_1[n]$ is (assuming $T = 1$ sec.)

$$N_1 = \frac{2\pi k}{0.1\pi}$$

and its fundamental period N_{01} is given by

$$N_{01} = 20 \qquad \text{for } k = 1$$

The periodicity of $x_2[n]$ is

$$N_2 = \frac{2\pi k}{0.3\pi}$$

and its fundamental period N_{02} is given by

$$N_{02} = 20 \qquad \text{for } k = 3$$

The fundamental period of these two sequences is the same and therefore it is erroneous to define the frequency of $\sin \omega_0 nT$, $\cos \omega_0 nT$ and $e^{j\omega_0 nT}$ as $f = \frac{1}{NT}$. Consider the envelops of $\sin 0.1\pi n$ and $\sin 0.3\pi n$ as shown in Figure 1.88. These two envelops have the same fundamental period $N = 20$. It can be shown that every DT sinusoid $\sin \omega_0 nT$ has infinitely many CT sinusoidal envelops. In order to determine the frequency, only the primary envelope has to be considered. The frequency of the primary envelope gives the frequency of the given DT sequence. Thus the frequency of $\sin 0.1\pi n$ and $\sin 0.3\pi n$ is same and is given by $f = \frac{1}{N} = \frac{1}{20}$ cycles. Thus it is concluded that a CT sinusoid $x(t) = \sin \omega_0 t$ is periodic for every ω_0. On the other hand a DT sinusoid $x[n] = \sin \omega_0 nT$ need not be periodic for every ω_0 and every T.

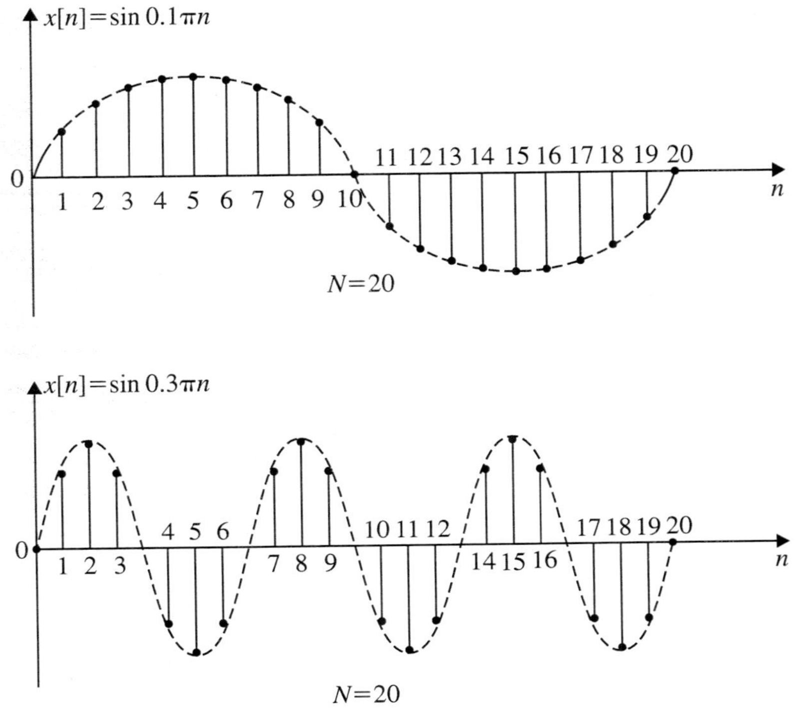

Figure 1.88 Envelopes of (*a*) sin $0.1\pi n$ and (*b*) sin $0.3\pi n$.

1.19 Analog to Digital Conversion

A signal that is specified for continuum of values of time is a continuous time signal and a signal that is specified only at discrete value of t is a discrete time signal. Continuous time signals are even though often referred to as analog signals, it is not strictly true. Similarly, discrete time signals are not the same as the digital signals. A signal whose amplitude can take on any value in a continuous range is an analog signal. This means an analog signal amplitude can take on an infinite number of values. On the other hand a digital signal is one whose amplitude can take on only a finite number of values. The signals which are associated with microprocessor or a digital signal processor or a digital computer are digital signals and they take on only two values (binary). The terms continuous time and discrete time indicate the nature of a signal along the time axis whereas the terms analog and digital indicates the nature of the amplitude of the signal which is represented in the vertical axis. Thus the signals are classified as analog continuous time, digital continuous time, analog discrete time and digital discrete time signal. The necessity of converting analog signal into a digital signal is explained as given below.

The block diagram of a typical DSP system in its simplest form is shown in Figure 1.89. The analog signal $x(t)$ is applied to ADC that converts into $x(n)$ which is in digital form. The digital signal $x(n)$ is processed by DSP and the output $y(n)$ is obtained. The ADC normally has built in sample and hold circuit. The DAC

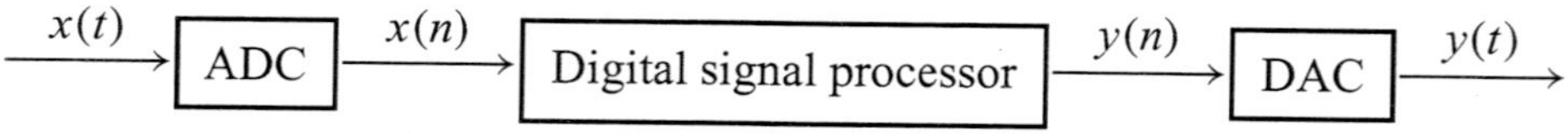

Figure 1.89 Block diagram of digital signal processing system.

converts the processed signal back into analog from as $y(t)$ which is applied to continuous time system. Signal processing using a digital processor implies that the input signal $x(n)$ must be in digital form before it can be processed. The analog to digital conversion requires that the signal is first sample and converted into discrete time continuous time amplitude signal. The amplitude of each sample is then quantized into one of 2^b levels where b is the number of bits used to represent a sample in ADC. The discrete amplitude levels are represented or encoded into distinct binary words each of length 'b' bits.

1.20 Quantization

Quantization is the process of converting analog signal to digital signal. The signal $x(t)$ is converted to a sampled signal at $t = nT$ where n is an integer and T is the sampling period. The sampling rate is at least twice the bandwidth of the signal which is called the Nyquist sampling rate or else analog signal recovery after it was processed by a digital computer or DSP is not possible without distortion. Figure 1.90 shows the continuous signal $x(t)$ which is to be digitized and quantized. The signal $x(t)$ is sampled at discrete time intervals $t = nT$ and held over the sampling interval by a device called zero order hold circuit (ZOH) that yields staircase approximation to the analog signal. The ZOH circuit keeps its output level equal to the magnitude of an input pulse and then resets itself when a new pulse arrives. On the arrival of the new pulse, the signal jumps to the new height of the continuous signal and holds the output at that level. After sampling and holding the analog to digital converter converts the sample to a digital number as explained below.

The analog voltage of $x(t)$ is divided into equal discrete levels and each level is assigned a digital number. These levels are called quantization levels. A 16 level discritization is shown in Figure 1.90. A four bit digital number can represent each of the 16 levels. If v is the maximum value of the analog signal, then each level will represent $\frac{v}{16}$ volts. In general the difference between any two quantization levels is $\frac{v}{2^b}$ volts where b is the binary bit used for analog to digital conversion. However, the quantization level has to be converted to binary bits because the digital computer or the digital signal processor will accept only binary bits as the input for processing the signal. Thus it necessiates that each sample amplitude is approximated to the nearest quantization level. Each sample can be represented by pulses. Dealing with large number of distinct pulses is difficult and therefore the use of smallest possible number of distinct pulses is preferrable, the number two being the best choice. Thus we need to assign a distinct electrical pulses to each

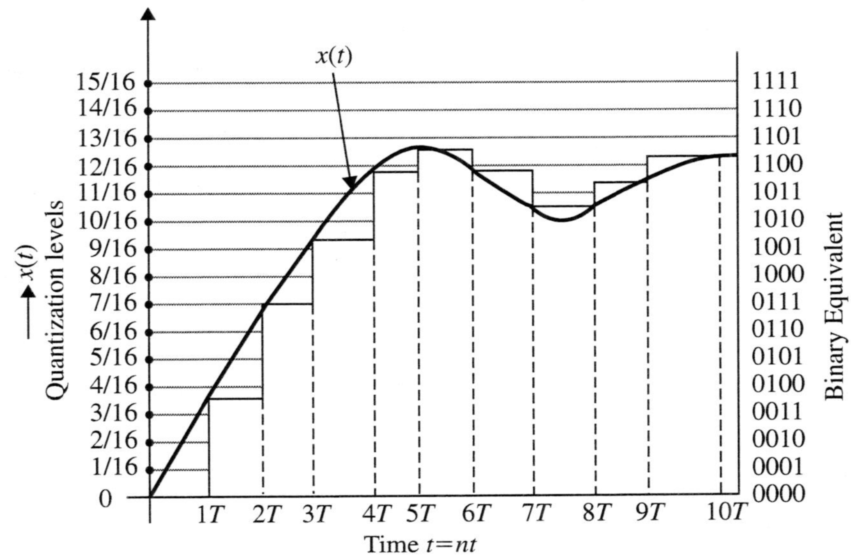

Figure 1.90 Quantizing analog signal $x(t)$.

of the two binary states. In practice a positive pulse is used to represent binary 1 and negative pulse to represent binary 0. Thus the sample is represented by a group of four binary pulses for 16 levels quantization thus the binary 0110 represents quantization six.

1.20.1 Quantization Error

The analog signal $x(t)$ is sampled at regular interval to get $x(n)$ at $t = nT$ where $n = 0, 1, 2, \ldots$. The amplitude of the sample should be assigned to the nearest quantization level to express it in terms of numeric equivalent $x_q(n)$. This is shown in Figure 1.91. The difference between $x(n)$, amplitude of the sampled signal and $x_q(n)$ the quantized value of $x(n)$ is expressed as

$$e(n) = x_q(n) - x(n)$$

$e(n)$ is called quantization error.

Let a sinusoidal signal amplitude vary from $+1$ to -1 volt. Let the ADC use $(b+1)$ bits which includes sign bit. The number of levels available for quantization of $x(n)$ is 2^{b+1}. Therefore, the interval between any quantization level is given by

$$q = \frac{2}{2^{b+1}} = 2^{-b}$$

For $b = 4$, $q = 0.0625$. The sampled signal $x(n)$ is quantized as $x_q(n)$ by the following methods.

(a) Truncation.
(b) Rounding.

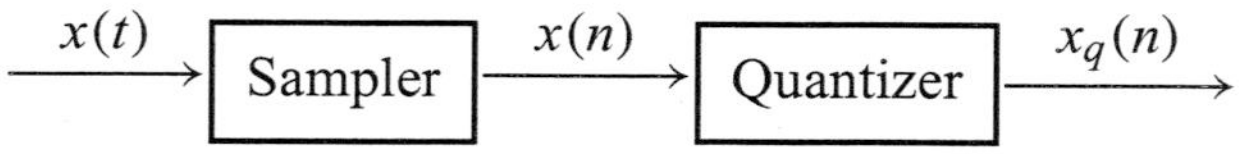

Figure 1.91 Block diagram of sampler and quantizer.

By truncation the sampled signal is approximated to the nearest higher quantization level. By rounding the b bit sampled signal is rounded to the original number unrounded.

1.21 The z-transform

Let z^n be an everlasting exponential. Let $h(n)$ be the impulse response of the discrete time system. The response of a linear, time invariant discrete time system to the everlasting exponential z^n is given as $H(z)z^n$. That is, it is the same exponential within a multiplicative constant. Thus, the system response to the excitation $x[n]$ is the sum of the system's responses to all these exponentials. The tool that is used to represent an arbitrary discrete signal $x[n]$ as a sum of everlasting exponential of the form z^n is called the z-transform.

Let $x[n] = z^n$ be the input signal applied to an LTI discrete time system whose impulse response is $h[n]$. The system output $y[n]$ is given by

$$\begin{aligned} y[n] &= x[n] * h[n] \\ &= \sum_{k=-\infty}^{\infty} h[k]x[n-k] \end{aligned}$$

Substitute $x[n] = z^n$

$$y[n] = \sum_{k=-\infty}^{\infty} h[k]z^{n-k} = z^n \left[\sum_{k=-\infty}^{\infty} h[k]z^{-k} \right]$$

Define the transfer function

$$H[z] = \sum_{k=-\infty}^{\infty} h[k]z^{-k} \tag{1.62}$$

Equation (1.62) may be written as

$$H[z^n] = H[z]z^n$$

To represent any arbitrary signals as a weighted superposition of the Eigen function z^n, let us substitute $z = re^{j\Omega}$ into Equation (1.62)

$$H[re^{j\Omega}] = \sum_{n=-\infty}^{\infty} h[n][re^{j\Omega}]^{-n}$$

$$= \sum_{n=-\infty}^{\infty} \left(h[n]r^{-n}\right) e^{-j\Omega n} \tag{1.63}$$

Equation (1.63) corresponds to the DTFT of the signal $h[n]r^{-n}$. The inverse of $H[re^{j\Omega}]$, by mathematical manipulation of Equation (1.63) can be obtained as

$$h[n] = \frac{1}{2\pi j} \oint H(z)z^{n-1}dz \tag{1.64}$$

More generally Equations (1.63) and (1.64) can be written as

$$X[z] = \sum_{n=-\infty}^{\infty} x[n]z^{-n} \tag{1.65}$$

$$x[n] = \frac{1}{2\pi j} \oint X(z)z^{n-1}dz \tag{1.66}$$

The above equations are called z-transform pair. Equation (1.65) is the z-transform of $x[n]$ and Equation (1.66) is called inverse z-transform. In Equation (1.65) the range of n is $-\infty < n < \infty$ and hence it is called bilateral z-transform. If $x[n] = 0$ for $n < 0$, Equation (1.65) can be written as

$$X[z] = \sum_{n=0}^{\infty} x[n]z^{-n} \tag{1.67}$$

Equation (1.67) is called unilateral or right-sided z-transform. Bilateral z-transform has limited practical applications. Unless otherwise it is specifically mentioned, z-transform means unilateral. z-transform and inverse z-transform are symbolically represented as given below.

$$\begin{aligned} Z[x[n]] &= X[z] \\ x[n] &\overset{Z}{\longleftrightarrow} X[z] \\ z^{-1}[X[z]] &= x[n] \\ X[z] &\overset{Z^{-1}}{\longleftrightarrow} x[n] \end{aligned} \tag{1.68}$$

1.22 Existence of the z-transform

Consider the unilateral z-transform given by Equation (1.68)

$$X[z] = \sum_{n=0}^{\infty} x[n]z^{-n} = \sum_{n=0}^{\infty} \frac{x[n]}{z^n}$$

For the existence of $X[z]$,

$$|X[z]| \leq \sum_{n=0}^{\infty} \frac{|x[n]|}{|z|^n} < \infty \tag{1.69}$$

If the signal $x[n]$ is expressed in terms of an exponential signal r^n, then if $x[n] \leq r^n$ for some r, then

$$|x[n]| \leq r^n \tag{1.70}$$

Substitute Equation (1.70) in Equation (1.69)

$$\begin{aligned} |X[z]| &\leq \sum_{n=0}^{\infty} \left(\frac{r}{z}\right)^n \\ &= \frac{1}{\left[1 - \frac{r}{|z|}\right]} \qquad \text{iff } |z| > r \end{aligned} \tag{1.71}$$

From Equation (1.71), it is evident that the z-transform of $x[n]$ which is $X(z)$ exists for $|z| > r$ and the signal is z-transformable. If the signal $x[n]$ grows faster than the exponential signal r^n for any r, Equation (1.71) is not convergence and $x[n]$ is not z-transformable.

1.23 Connection between Laplace Transform, z-transform and Fourier Transform

Consider the Laplace transform of $x(t)$ which is represented below

$$X(s) = \int_{-\infty}^{\infty} x(t)e^{-st}dt \tag{1.72}$$

When $s = j\omega$, Equation (1.72) becomes

$$X(j\omega) = \int_{-\infty}^{\infty} x(t)e^{-j\omega t}dt \tag{1.73}$$

Equation (1.73) represents the Fourier transform. **The Laplace transform reduces to the Fourier transform on the imaginary axis where $s = j\omega$.** The relationship

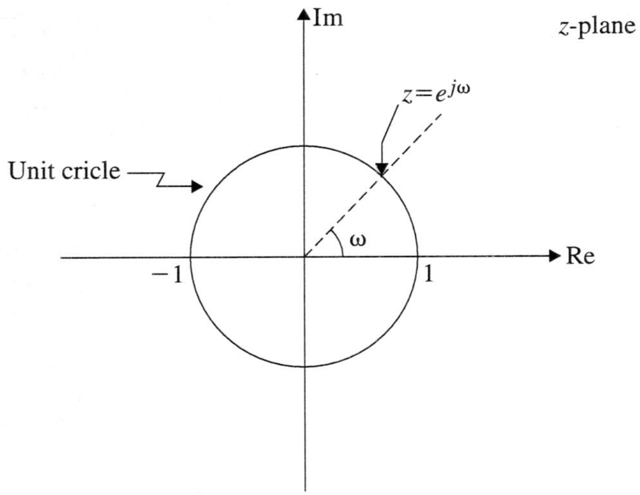

Figure 1.92 z-transform reduces to FT on the unit circle.

between these two transforms can also be interpreted as follows. The complex variable s can be written as $(\sigma + j\omega)$. Equation (1.72) is written as

$$X(\sigma + j\omega) = \int_{-\infty}^{\infty} x(t)e^{-(\sigma + j\omega)t}dt$$

$$= \int_{-\infty}^{\infty} \left[x(t)e^{-\sigma t}\right] e^{-j\omega t}dt \qquad (1.74)$$

Equation (1.74) can be recognized as the Fourier transform of $[x(t)e^{-\sigma t}]$. **Thus, the Laplace transform of $x(t)$ is the Fourier transform of $x(t)$ after multiplication by the real exponential $e^{-\sigma t}$ which may be growing or decay with respect to time.**

The complex variable z can be expressed in polar form as

$$z = re^{j\omega} \qquad (1.75)$$

where r is the magnitude of z and ω is the angle of z.

Substitute $z = re^{j\omega}$ in Equation (1.65)

$$X(re^{j\omega}) = \sum_{n=-\infty}^{\infty} x[n](re^{j\omega})^{-n}$$

$$= \sum_{n=-\infty}^{\infty} \{x[n]r^{-n}\}e^{-j\omega n}$$

$$= F[x[n]r^{-n}] \qquad (1.76)$$

Thus, $X(re^{j\omega})$ is the Fourier transform of the sequence $x[n]$ which is multiplied by a real exponential r^{-n} which may be growing or decaying with

increasing n depending on whether r is greater or less than unity. If $r = 1$, then $|z| = 1$ and equation becomes

$$X(e^{j\omega}) = \sum_{n=-\infty}^{\infty} x[n]e^{-j\omega n} = F[x[n]]$$

The z-transform reduces to Fourier transform in the complex z-plane on the contour of a circle with unit radius. The circle which is called unit circle plays the role in the z-transform similar to the role of the imaginary axis in the s-plane for Laplace transform. The unit circle in the z-plane is shown in Figure 1.92.

1.24 The Region of Convergence (ROC)

In Equation (1.65) which defines the z-transform $X(z)$ the sum may not converge for all values of z. The values of z in the complex z-plane for which the sum in the z-transform equation converges is called the region of convergence which is written in abbreviated form as ROC. The concept of ROC is illustrated in the following examples.

Example 1.73

Consider the following discrete time signals:

(a) $x[n] = a^n u[n] \qquad a < 1$

(b) $x[n] = -a^n u(-n-1) \qquad a < 1$

(c) $x[n] = a^n u[n] - b^n u(-n-1) \qquad b > a$ and $a > b$

Find the z-transform and the ROC in the z-plane.

Solution

(a) $\boldsymbol{x[n] = a^n u[n]}$

The signal $x[n]$ is shown in Figure 1.93(a) which is a right-sided signal.

$$\begin{aligned} X(z) &= \sum_{n=0}^{\infty} a^n u[n] z^{-n} \\ &= \sum_{n=0}^{\infty} a^n z^{-n} \qquad [\because\ u[n] = 1 \text{ all } n \geq 0] \\ &= \sum_{n=0}^{\infty} \left(\frac{a}{z}\right)^n \end{aligned}$$

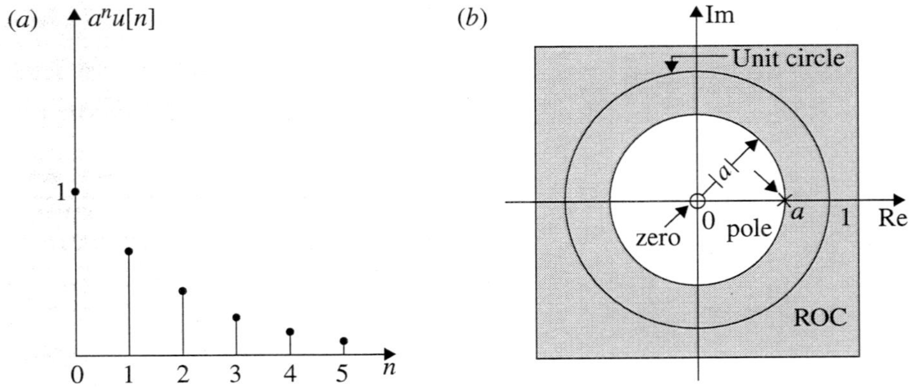

Figure 1.93 (a) $x[n] = a^n u[n]$ and (b) ROC: $0 < a < 1$.

Using the power series we get

$$X(z) = \frac{1}{\left[1 - \frac{a}{z}\right]}$$

where $\frac{a}{z} < 1$ or $|z| > |a|$.

$$X(z) = \frac{z}{(z-a)} \tag{1.77}$$

$$X(z) = \frac{1}{1 - az^{-1}} \tag{1.78}$$

Fourier transform is represented in the form as shown in Equation (1.78) to identify poles and zero and system transfer function. Equation (1.78) form is used when inverse z-transform is taken and also for structure realization. z^{-1} is used as time delay operation. z-transform for the causal real exponential converges if $|z| > |a|$. Thus, the ROC of $X(z)$ is to the exterior of the circle of radius a, which is shown in Figure 1.93(b) in shaded area. The ROC includes the unit circle for $|a| < 1$.

(b) $\boldsymbol{x[n] = -a^n[u[-n-1]]}$

The signal $x[n]$ is shown in Figure 1.94(a) which is a left-sided signal

$$Z[-a^n u[-n-1]] = \sum_{n=-\infty}^{-1} -a^n z^{-n} \qquad \because\ [u(-n-1)] = 1 \text{ for all } -n$$

$$= \sum_{n=-\infty}^{-1} -\left[\frac{a}{z}\right]^n = \sum_{n=1}^{\infty} -\left[\frac{z}{a}\right]^n$$

$$= -\left[\frac{z}{a} + \frac{z^2}{a^2} + \frac{z^3}{a^3} + \cdots\right]$$

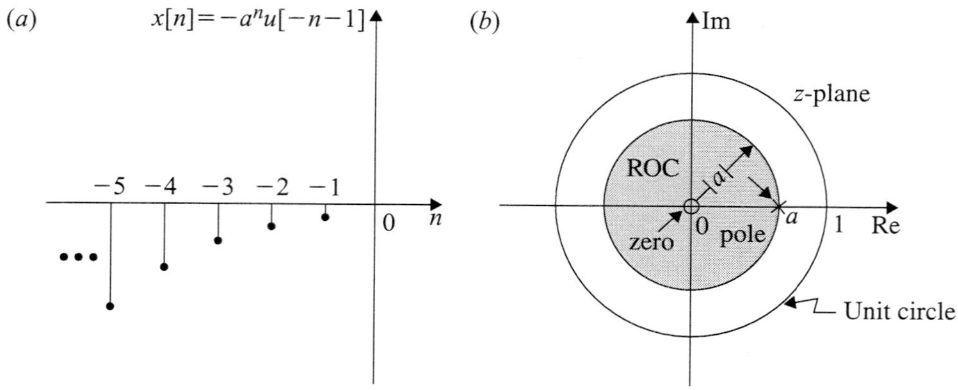

Figure 1.94 (*a*) $x[n] = -a^n u[-n-1]$ and (*b*) ROC: $0 < a < 1$.

$$Z[-a^n u[-n-1]] = 1 - \left[1 + \frac{z}{a} + \left(\frac{z}{a}\right)^2 + \left(\frac{z}{a}\right)^3 + \cdots\right]$$

$$= 1 - \frac{1}{1-\frac{z}{a}} \qquad \text{if } \left|\frac{z}{a}\right| < 1$$

$$\boxed{Z[-a^n u[-n-1]] = \frac{z}{(z-a)}} \quad \text{ROC } |z| < a \quad (1.79)$$

The z-transforms of $x[n] = a^n u[n]$ which is causal and that of $x[n] = -a^n u[-n-1]$ which is anti-causal are identical. In the former case the ROC is to the exterior of the circle passing through the outermost pole and in the latter case (anti-causal) the ROC is to the interior of the circle passing through the innermost pole. The ROC is shown in Figure 1.94(*b*).

(*c*) $\boldsymbol{x[n] = a^n u[n] - b^n u[-n-1]}$

From the results derived in Example 1.73(*a*) and (*b*), we can find the z-transform of $x[n]$ as

$$X(z) = \frac{z}{(z-a)} + \frac{z}{(z-b)}$$

The right-sided signal $a^n u[n]$ converges if $|z| > a$ and the left-sided signal $-b^n u[-n-1]$ converges if $|z| < b$. The ROC for $|a| > |b|$ and $|a| < |b|$ are shown in Figures 1.95(*a*) and (*b*) respectively. From Figure 1.95(*a*) it is observed that the two ROCs do not overlap and hence z-transform does not exist for this signal. Now consider Figure 1.95(*b*), it is observed that the two ROCs overlap and the overlapping area is shaded in the form of a ring. The z-transform exists in the case with ROC as $|a| < |z| < |b|$.

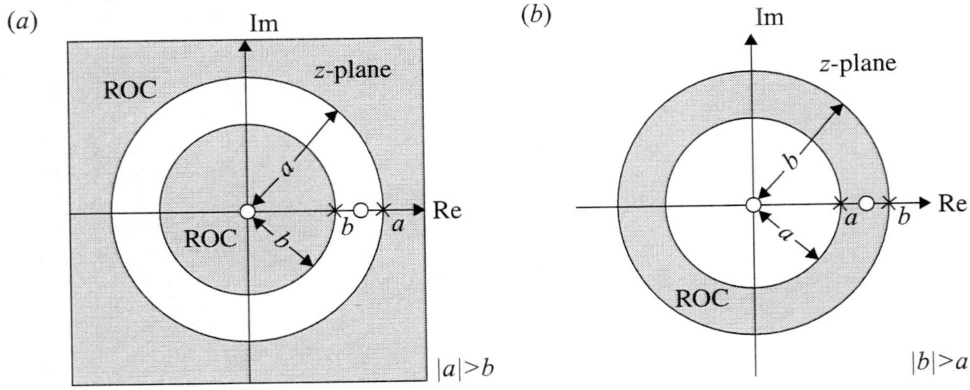

Figure 1.95 ROC of a two sided sequence.

1.25 Properties of the ROC

Assuming that $X(z)$ is the rational function of z the properties of the ROC are summed up and given below:

1. The ROC is a concentric ring in the z-plane.
2. The ROC does not contain any pole.
3. If $x[n]$ is a finite sequence in a finite interval $N_1 \leq n \leq N_2$, then the ROC is the entire z-plane except $z = 0$ and $z = \infty$.
4. If $x[n]$ is a right-sided sequence (causal), then the ROC is the exterior of the circle $|z| = r_{\max}$ where $r_{\max}$ is the radius of the outermost pole of $X(z)$.
5. If $x[n]$ is a left-sided sequence (non-causal), then the ROC is the interior of the circle $|z| = r_{\min}$ where $r_{\min}$ is the radius of the innermost pole of $X(z)$.
6. If $x[n]$ is a two sided sequence, then the ROC is given by $r_1 < |z| < r_2$ where r_1 and r_2 are the magnitudes of the two poles of $X(z)$. Here, ROC is an annular ring between the circle $|z| = r_1$ and $|z| = r_2$ which does not include any poles.

The following examples illustrate the method of finding z-transform $X(z)$ for the discrete time sequence $x[n]$.

Example 1.74

Find the z-transform and the ROC for the sequences $x[n]$ given below:

1. $x[n] = \{\underset{\uparrow}{2}, -1, 0, 3, 4\}$
2. $x[n] = \{1, -2, 3, -1, \underset{\uparrow}{2}\}$
3. $x[n] = \{5, 3, \underset{\uparrow}{-2}, 0, 4, -3\}$

4. $x[n] = \delta[n]$
5. $x[n] = u[n]$
6. $x[n] = u[-n]$
7. $x[n] = a^{-n}u[-n]$
8. $x[n] = a^{-n}u[-n-1]$
9. $x[n] = (-a)^n u[-n]$
10. $x[n] = a^{|n|}$ for $|a| < 1$ and $|a| > 1$
11. $x[n] = e^{j\omega_0 n}u[n]$
12. $x[n] = \cos \omega_0 n u[n]$
13. $x[n] = \sin \omega_0 n u[n]$
14. $x[n] = u[n] - u[n-6]$
15. $x[n] = \left[\cos\left(\frac{\pi n}{3} + \frac{\pi}{4}\right)\right] u[n]$

(Anna University, May, 2007)

Solution

1. $\boldsymbol{x[n] = \{2, -1, 0, 3, 4\}}$

$$X[z] = \sum_{n=0}^{4} x[n]z^{-n}$$

$$\boxed{X[z] = 2 - z^{-1} + 0 + 3z^{-3} + 4z^{-4}}$$

$X[z]$ will not converge if $|z| = 0$. Hence, ROC is $|z| > 0$.

2. $\boldsymbol{x[n] = \{1, -2, 3, -1, \underset{\uparrow}{2}\}}$

$$X[z] = \sum_{n=-4}^{0} x[n]z^{-n}$$

$$\boxed{X[z] = z^4 - 2z^3 + 3z^2 - z + 2}$$

$X[z]$ will not converge if $|z| = \infty$. Hence, ROC is $|z| < \infty$.

3. $\boldsymbol{x[n] = \{5, 3, \underset{\uparrow}{-2}, 0, 4, -3\}}$

$$X[z] = \sum_{n=-2}^{3} x[n]z^{-n}$$

$$X[z] = 5z^2 + 3z - 2 + 0 + 4z^{-2} - 3z^{-3}$$

For $|z| = 0$ and $|z| = \infty$, $X[z]$ is infinity. Hence, ROC is $0 < |z| < \infty$.

4. $\boldsymbol{x[n] = \delta[n]}$

$$X[z] = \sum_{n=-\infty}^{\infty} \delta[n]z^{-n}$$

$$\begin{aligned} \delta[n] &= 1 \qquad n = 0 \\ &= 0 \qquad n \neq 0 \end{aligned}$$

$$X[z] = 1 \qquad \text{ROC is entire } z\text{-plane.}$$

5. $\boldsymbol{x[n] = u[n]}$

$$\begin{aligned} X[z] &= \sum_{n=0}^{\infty} z^{-n} \\ &= 1 + \frac{1}{z} + \frac{1}{z^2} + \cdots \\ &= \frac{1}{1 - \frac{1}{z}} \qquad \text{[By using summation formula]} \end{aligned}$$

$$\begin{aligned} X[z] &= \frac{z}{(z-1)} \\ X[z] &= \frac{1}{(1 - z^{-1})} \end{aligned} \qquad \text{ROC: } |z| > 1 \tag{1.80}$$

6. $\boldsymbol{x[n] = u[-n]}$

$$\begin{aligned} X[z] &= \sum_{n=-\infty}^{0} z^{-n} \\ &= \sum_{n=0}^{\infty} z^{n} \\ &= 1 + z + z^2 + \cdots \end{aligned}$$

$$X[z] = \frac{1}{1 - z} \qquad \text{ROC: } |z| < 1 \tag{1.81}$$

7. $\boldsymbol{x[n] = a^{-n}u[-n]}$

$$\begin{aligned} X[z] &= \sum_{n=-\infty}^{0} a^{-n}z^{-n} \\ &= \sum_{n=-\infty}^{0} (az)^{-n} \\ &= \sum_{n=0}^{\infty}(az)^{n} \\ &= 1 + (az) + (az)^2 + \cdots \end{aligned}$$

$$\boxed{X[z] = \frac{1}{(1 - az)}} \qquad \text{ROC: } |z| < \frac{1}{a} \tag{1.82}$$

8. $\boldsymbol{x[n] = a^{-n}u[-n-1]}$

$$\begin{aligned} X[z] &= \sum_{n=-\infty}^{-1} a^{-n}z^{-n} \\ &= \sum_{n=-\infty}^{-1} (az)^{-n} \\ &= \sum_{n=1}^{\infty}(az)^{n} \\ &= az + (az)^2 + (az)^3 + \cdots \end{aligned}$$

$$\begin{aligned} X[z] &= az[1 + az + (az)^2 + \cdots] \\ &= \frac{az}{1 - az} \end{aligned}$$

$$\boxed{X[z] = \frac{-z}{\left(z - \frac{1}{a}\right)}} \qquad \text{ROC: } |z| < \frac{1}{a} \tag{1.83}$$

9. $\boldsymbol{x[n] = (-a)^n u[-n]}$

$$X[z] = \sum_{n=-\infty}^{0} (-a)^n z^{-n}$$
$$= \sum_{n=-\infty}^{0} \left(\frac{z}{-a}\right)^{-n}$$
$$= \sum_{n=0}^{\infty} \left(\frac{z}{-a}\right)^{n}$$
$$= 1 + \left(\frac{z}{-a}\right) + \left(\frac{z}{-a}\right)^2 + \left(\frac{z}{-a}\right)^3 + \cdots$$

$$\boxed{X[z] = \frac{a}{(z+a)}} \qquad \text{ROC: } |z| < |a| \qquad (1.84)$$

10. $\boldsymbol{x[n] = a^{|n|};\ a < 1}$

$$x[n] = a^n u[n] + a^{-n} u[-n-1]$$
$$Z[a^n u[n]] = \frac{z}{(z-a)} \qquad \text{ROC: } |z| > a$$
$$Z[a^{-n} u[-n-1]] = \frac{-z}{\left(z - \frac{1}{a}\right)} \qquad \text{ROC: } |z| < \frac{1}{a}$$
$$X[z] = \frac{z}{(z-a)} - \frac{z}{\left(z-\frac{1}{a}\right)}$$

$$\boxed{X[z] = \frac{(a^2-1)}{a}\frac{z}{(z-a)\left(z-\frac{1}{a}\right)}} \qquad (1.85)$$

ROC: $a < |z| < \frac{1}{a}$. The ROC is sketched and shown in Figure 1.96(a) for $a < 1$.

$$x[n] = a^{|n|} \qquad a > 1$$

The ROC is sketched and shown in Figure 1.96(*b*). In Figure 1.96(*b*) the two ROCs do not overlap and there is no common ROC. Hence, $x[n]$ does not have $X[z]$.

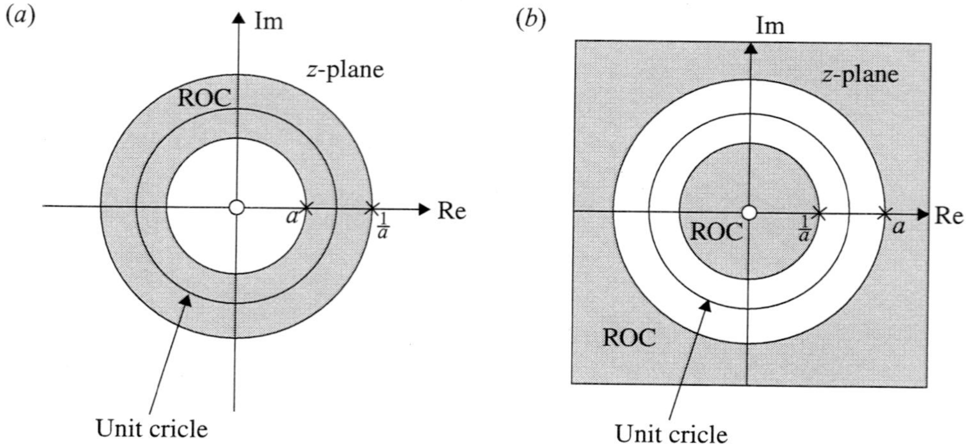

Figure 1.96 ROC of $x[n] = a^{|n|}$. (*a*) $a < 1$ and (*b*) $a > 1$.

11. $\boldsymbol{x[n] = e^{j\omega_0 n}u[n]}$

$$X[z] = \sum_{n=0}^{\infty} e^{j\omega_0 n} z^{-n}$$

$$= \sum_{n=0}^{\infty} \left(\frac{e^{j\omega_0}}{z}\right)^n$$

$$= \left(\frac{1}{1 - \frac{e^{j\omega_0}}{z}}\right)$$

$$\boxed{X[z] = \frac{z}{(z - e^{j\omega_0})} \qquad \text{ROC: } |z| > |e^{j\omega_0}| \text{ or } |z| > 1} \tag{1.86}$$

12. $\boldsymbol{x[n] = \cos\omega_0 n u[n]}$

$$x[n] = \frac{1}{2}[e^{j\omega_0 n} + e^{-j\omega_0 n}]$$

$$Z[e^{j\omega_0 n}] = \frac{z}{(z - e^{j\omega_0})}$$

$$Z[e^{-j\omega_0 n}] = \frac{z}{(z - e^{-j\omega_0})}$$

$$X[z] = \frac{1}{2}\left[\frac{z}{(z - e^{j\omega_0})} + \frac{z}{(z - e^{-j\omega_0})}\right]$$

$$= \frac{z}{2}\frac{\left[z - e^{-j\omega_0} + z - e^{j\omega_0}\right]}{\left[z^2 - z(e^{-j\omega_0} + e^{j\omega_0}) + 1\right]}$$

$$X[z] = \frac{z}{2}\frac{[2z - 2\cos\omega_0]}{\left[z^2 - 2z\cos\omega_0 + 1\right]}$$

$$X[z] = \frac{(1 - z^{-1}\cos\omega_0)}{(1 - z^{-1}2\cos\omega_0 + z^{-2})} \qquad \text{ROC: } |z| > 1 \tag{1.87}$$

13. $\boldsymbol{x[n] = \sin\omega_0 n u[n]}$

$$x[n] = \frac{1}{2j}[e^{j\omega_0 n} - e^{-j\omega_0 n}]$$

$$Z[e^{j\omega_0 n}u[n]] = \frac{z}{(z - e^{j\omega_0})}$$

$$Z[e^{-j\omega_0 n}u[n]] = \frac{z}{(z - e^{-j\omega_0})}$$

$$X[z] = \frac{z}{2j}\left[\frac{1}{(z - e^{j\omega_0})} - \frac{1}{(z - e^{-j\omega_0})}\right]$$

$$= \frac{z}{2j}\frac{\left[z - e^{-j\omega_0} - z + e^{j\omega_0}\right]}{\left[z^2 - 2z\cos\omega_0 + 1\right]}$$

$$= \frac{z\sin\omega_0}{(z^2 - 2z\cos\omega_0 + 1)}$$

$$X[z] = \frac{z^{-1}\sin\omega_0}{(1 - 2z^{-1}\cos\omega_0 + z^{-2})} \qquad \text{ROC: } |z| > 1 \tag{1.88}$$

14. $\boldsymbol{x[n] = u[n] - u[n-6]}$

$$x[n] = \{1,\ 1,\ 1,\ 1,\ 1,\ 1\}$$

$$X[z] = 1 + z^{-1} + z^{-2} + z^{-3} + z^{-4} + z^{-5}$$

$$= \left[1 + \frac{1}{z} + \frac{1}{z^2} + \frac{1}{z^3} + \frac{1}{z^4} + \frac{1}{z^5}\right]$$

$$X[z] = \frac{[z^5 + z^4 + z^3 + z^2 + z + 1]}{[z^5]} \qquad \text{ROC: all } z \text{ except } z \neq 0 \tag{1.89}$$

The above result can be represented is a compact form as

$$X[z] = \sum_{n=0}^{5} z^{-n}$$

$$= \sum_{n=0}^{5}\left(\frac{1}{z}\right)^n$$

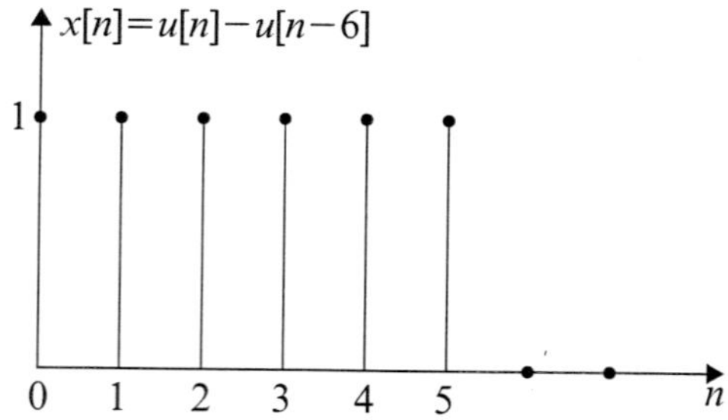

Figure 1.97 $x[n] = u[n] - u[n-6]$.

The following summation formula is used to simplify this

$$\sum_{k=m}^{n} a^k = \frac{a^{n+1} - a^m}{(a-1)}$$

where $a = \frac{1}{z}$; $k = 0$ and $n = 5$

$$X[z] = \frac{\left(\frac{1}{z}\right)^6 - \left(\frac{1}{z}\right)^0}{\left(\frac{1}{z} - 1\right)}$$

$$\boxed{X[z] = \frac{z}{(z-1)}(1 - z^{-6})}$$

15. $\boldsymbol{x[n] = \left[\cos\left(\frac{\pi n}{3} + \frac{\pi}{4}\right)\right] u[n]}$

$$x[n] = \frac{1}{2}\left[e^{j\left(\frac{\pi n}{3}+\frac{\pi}{4}\right)} + e^{-j\left(\frac{\pi n}{3}+\frac{\pi}{4}\right)}\right]$$

$$= \frac{1}{2}\left[e^{j\frac{\pi}{4}} e^{j\frac{\pi n}{3}} + e^{-j\frac{\pi}{4}} e^{-j\frac{\pi}{4}}\right]$$

$$X[z] = \frac{1}{2}\left[e^{j\frac{\pi}{4}} \frac{z}{(z - e^{j\frac{\pi}{3}})} + e^{-j\frac{\pi}{4}} \frac{z}{(z - e^{-j\frac{\pi}{3}})}\right]$$

$$X[z] = \frac{z}{2} \frac{\left[ze^{j\frac{\pi}{4}} - e^{-j\frac{\pi}{12}} + ze^{-j\frac{\pi}{4}} - e^{-j\frac{\pi}{12}}\right]}{z^2 - z(e^{j\frac{\pi}{3}} + e^{-j\frac{\pi}{3}}) + 1}$$

$$= \frac{z}{2} \frac{\left[2z\cos\frac{\pi}{4} - 2\cos\frac{\pi}{12}\right]}{\left(z^2 - 2z\cos\frac{\pi}{3} + 1\right)}$$

$$\boxed{X[z] = \frac{z[0.707z - 0.966]}{(z^2 - z + 1)} \qquad \text{ROC: } |z| > 1}$$

1.25.1 Final Value Theorem

If $Z[x[n]] = X[z]$ where $x[n]$ is a causal signal and the ROC of $X[z]$ has no poles on or outside the unit circle then

$$x[\infty] = \underset{z\to 1}{Lt}(z-1)X[z]$$

Proof:

$$Z[x[n+1]] - Z[x[n]] = \underset{k\to\infty}{Lt}\sum_{n=0}^{k}[x[n+1]-x[n]]z^{-n}$$

$$x[\infty] = \underset{k\to\infty}{Lt}\sum_{n=0}^{k}[x[n+1]-x[n]]z^{-n}$$

$$zX[z] - x[0] - X[z] = \underset{k\to\infty}{Lt}\sum_{n=0}^{k}[x[n+1]-x[n]]z^{-n}$$

$$(z-1)X[z] - x[0] = \underset{k\to\infty}{Lt}\sum_{n=0}^{k}[x[n+1]-x[n]]z^{-n}$$

Taking $\underset{z\to\infty}{Lt}$ on both sides we get

$$\underset{z\to\infty}{Lt}(z-1)X[z] - x[0]$$

$$= \underset{k\to\infty}{Lt}[x[1]-x[0]] + [x[2]-x[-1]] + [x[3]-x[2]] + \cdots + [x[k+1]-x[k]]$$

$$= x[\infty] - x[0]$$

$$\boxed{x[\infty] = \underset{z\to 1}{Lt}(z-1)X[z]} \quad (1.90)$$

Example 1.75

Find the z-transform of the following sequences and also ROC using the properties of z-transform:

1. $x[n] = \delta[n-n_0]$
2. $x[n] = u[n-n_0]$
3. $x[n] = a^{n+1}u[n+1]$
4. $x[n] = a^{n-1}u[n-1]$
5. $x[n] = \left(\frac{1}{2}\right)^n u[-n]$

(Anna University, December, 2007)

6. $x[n] = u[n-6] - u[n-10]$
7. $x[n] = nu[n]$

8. $x[n] = n[u[n] - u[n-8]]$
9. $x[n] = a^n \cos \omega_0 n u[n]$
10. $x[n] = a^n \sin \omega_0 n u[n]$
11. Show that $u[n] * u[n-1] = nu[n]$
12. $x[n] = n\left(-\frac{1}{4}\right)^n u[n] * \left(\frac{1}{6}\right)^{-n} u[-n]$
13. $x[n] = \left[\left(\frac{1}{2}\right)^n - \left(\frac{1}{4}\right)^n\right] u[n]$

Find $X[z]$ and plot the poles and zeros. *(Anna University, December, 2007)*

14. $x[n] = 1 \qquad n \geq 0$

$= z^n \qquad n < 0$

(Anna University, April, 2005)

15. (a) $x[n] = \left[\left(-\frac{1}{3}\right)^n + 3\left(\frac{1}{6}\right)^n\right] u[n]$

(b) $x[n] = \left[\left(-\frac{1}{3}\right)^n u[-n] + 3\left(\frac{1}{6}\right)^n\right] u[n]$

(c) $x[n] = \left[\left(-\frac{1}{3}\right)^n + 3\left(\frac{1}{6}\right)^n\right] u[-n]$

16. (a) $x[n] = \left[\left(\frac{1}{4}\right)^n + \left(\frac{1}{5}\right)^n\right] u[n]$

(b) $x[n] = \left[\left(\frac{1}{5}\right)^n u[n] + \left(\frac{1}{4}\right)^n u[-n-1]\right]$

(c) $x[n] = \left(\frac{1}{4}\right)^n u[n] + \left(\frac{1}{5}\right)^n u[-n-1]$

17. $x[n] = \delta[n] + \frac{1}{2}\delta(n+1) + \delta(n-3)$ *(Anna University, December, 2006)*

18. $x[n] = 4^n \cos\left[\frac{2\pi n}{6} + \frac{\pi}{4}\right] u[-n-1]$. Sketch the pole-zero plot and indicate the ROC. *(Anna University, April, 2008)*

19. $x[n] = nu[n-1]$ *(Anna University, December, 2006)*

20. $x[n] = (4)^n \qquad n < 0$

$= \left(\frac{1}{4}\right)^n \qquad n = 0, 2, 4, \ldots$

$= \left(\frac{1}{5}\right)^n \qquad n = 1, 3, 5, \ldots$

Solution

1. $\boldsymbol{x[n] = \delta[n - n_0]}$

$$\delta[n] \overset{Z}{\longleftrightarrow} 1 \qquad \text{ROC: } |z| > 0$$

By applying time shifting property we get

$$Z[\delta[n - n_0]] = z^{-n_0} \tag{1.91}$$

ROC: all z excluding $|z| = 0$.

2. $\boldsymbol{x[n] = u[n - n_0]}$

$$u[n] \overset{Z}{\longleftrightarrow} \frac{z}{(z-1)}$$

By applying time shifting (right shifted) property we get

$$Z[u[n - n_0]] = \frac{z^{-n_0} z}{(z-1)} = \frac{z^{-(n_0-1)}}{(z-1)}$$

$$\boxed{X[z] = \frac{z^{-(n_0-1)}}{(z-1)} \qquad \text{ROC: } 1 < |z| < \infty} \tag{1.92}$$

3. $\boldsymbol{x[n] = a^{n+1} u[n+1]}$

$$a^n u[n] \overset{Z}{\longleftrightarrow} \frac{z}{(z-a)}$$

By applying time shifting (left shifted) property we get

$$Z[a^{n+1} u[n+1]] = z\frac{z}{(z-a)}$$

$$\boxed{X[z] = \frac{z^2}{(z-a)} \qquad \text{ROC: } |a| < |z| < \infty} \tag{1.93}$$

4. $\boldsymbol{x[n] = a^{n-1} u[n-1]}$

$$a^n u[n] \overset{Z}{\longleftrightarrow} \frac{z}{(z-a)}$$

Applying time shifting (right shifted) property we get

$$Z[a^{n-1} u[n-1]] = \frac{z^{-1} z}{(z-a)}$$

$$\boxed{X[z] = \frac{1}{(z-a)} \qquad \text{ROC: } a < |z| < \infty} \tag{1.94}$$

5. $\boldsymbol{x[n] = \left(\frac{1}{2}\right)^n u[-n]}$

$$u[-n] \stackrel{Z}{\longleftrightarrow} \frac{1}{(1-z)}$$

$$x[n] = \left(\frac{1}{2}\right)^n u[-n]$$

By using multiplication property (replacing z by $(\frac{1}{2})^{-1}z$) we get

$$\boxed{X[z] = \frac{1}{(1-2z)}} \qquad \text{ROC: } |z| < \frac{1}{2}$$

6. $\boldsymbol{x[n] = u[n-6] - u[n-10]}$

The signal is represented in Figure 1.98.

$$X[z] = z^{-6} + z^{-7} + z^{-8} + z^{-9}$$
$$= \frac{1}{z^6} + \frac{1}{z^7} + \frac{1}{z^8} + \frac{1}{z^9}$$

$$\boxed{X[z] = \frac{z^8 + z^2 + z + 1}{z^9}}$$

ROC: all z except $z \neq 0$. The above result can be simplified using summation formula as

$$X[z] = \sum_{n=6}^{9} \left(\frac{1}{z}\right)^n$$
$$= \frac{\left(\frac{1}{z}\right)^{10} - \left(\frac{1}{z}\right)^6}{\left(\frac{1}{z} - 1\right)}$$

$$\boxed{X[z] = \frac{z}{(z-1)}[z^{-6} - z^{-10}]}$$

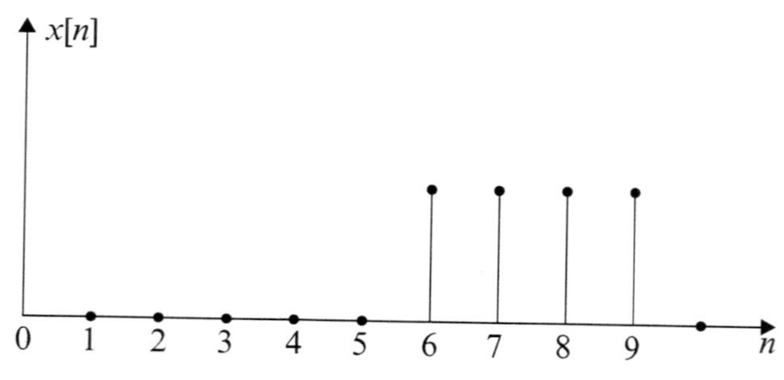

Figure 1.98 $x[n] = u[n-6] - u[n-10]$.

The above result can be obtained by time shifting property of unit step sequence.

$$Z[u[n-6]] = \frac{z}{(z-1)}z^{-6}$$

$$Z[u[n-10]] = \frac{z}{(z-1)}z^{-10}$$

$$X[z] = \frac{z}{(z-1)}[z^{-6} - z^{-10}]$$

$$\boxed{X[z] = \frac{(z^{-5} - z^{-9})}{(z-1)}}$$

7. $\boldsymbol{x[n] = nu[n]}$

$$Z[u[n]] = \frac{z}{(z-1)}$$

Applying the differentiation property in z

$$Z[nu[n]] = -z\frac{dX[z]}{dz}$$

$$Z[nu[n]] = -z\frac{d}{dz}\left[\frac{z}{(z-1)}\right]$$

$$\boxed{X[z] = \frac{z}{(z-1)^2}} \tag{1.95}$$

8. $\boldsymbol{x[n] = n[u[n] - u[n-8]]}$
By using shift theorem we get

$$Z[u[n] - u[n-8]] = \frac{z}{(z-1)}[1 - z^{-8}]$$

$$= \frac{(z - z^{-7})}{(z-1)}$$

$$Z[n[u[n] - u[n-8]]] = -z\frac{d}{dz}\frac{[z - z^{-7}]}{z-1}$$

$$X[z] = -z\frac{[(z-1)(1 + 7z^{-8}) - (z - z^{-7})]}{(z-1)^2}$$

$$X[z] = \frac{(-8z^{-6} + 7z^{-7} + z)}{(z-1)^2}$$

$$\boxed{X[z] = \frac{[z^8 - 8z + 7]}{z^7(z-1)^2}}$$

9. $\boldsymbol{x[n] = a^n \cos \omega_0 n u[n]}$
For Example 1.74.12 we get

$$Z[\cos \omega_0 n u[n]] = \frac{[1 - z^{-1} \cos \omega_0]}{[1 - 2\cos \omega_0 z^{-1} + z^{-2}]}$$

To apply multiplication property, replace z by $|\frac{z}{a}|$ or $z^{-1} = |\frac{z}{a}|^{-1} = az^{-1}$

$$\therefore\ Z[a^n \cos \omega_0 n u[n]] = \frac{[1 - az^{-1} \cos \omega_0]}{[1 - 2a\cos \omega_0 z^{-1} + a^2 z^{-2}]}$$

$$\boxed{X[z] = \frac{[1 - az^{-1} \cos \omega_0]}{[1 - 2a\cos \omega_0 z^{-1} + a^2 z^{-2}]}} \qquad (1.96)$$

10. $\boldsymbol{x[n] = a^n \sin \omega_0 n u[n]}$
For Example 1.74.13 we get

$$Z[\sin \omega_0 n u[n]] = \frac{z^{-1} \sin \omega_0}{[1 - 2\cos \omega_0 z^{-1} + z^{-2}]}$$

To apply multiplication property, as in the previous example, replace z^{-1} by a z^{-1} and $z^{-2} = a^2 z^{-2}$

$$Z[a^n \sin \omega_0 n u[n]] = \frac{az^{-1} \sin \omega_0}{[1 - 2a\cos \omega_0 z^{-1} + a^2 z^{-2}]}$$

$$\boxed{X[z] = \frac{[az^{-1} \sin \omega_0]}{[1 - 2a\cos \omega_0 z^{-1} + a^2 z^{-2}]}} \qquad (1.97)$$

11. **Show that $\boldsymbol{u[n] * u[n-1] = nu[n]}$**

$$\begin{aligned}
Z[u[n]] &= \frac{z}{(z-1)} \\
Z[u[n-1]] &= \frac{1}{(z-1)} \\
Z[u[n] * u[n-1]] &= Z[u[n]]Z[u[n-1]] \\
&= \frac{z}{(z-1)} \frac{1}{(z-1)} \\
&= \frac{z}{(z-1)^2}
\end{aligned}$$

Multiplying by Z^{-1} both sides we get

$$u[n] * u[n-1] = Z^{-1}\left[\frac{z}{(z-1)^2}\right]$$

$$\boxed{u[n] * u[n-1] = n[u[n]]}$$

12. $\boldsymbol{x[n] = n\left(-\frac{1}{4}\right)^n u[n] * \left(-\frac{1}{6}\right)^{-n} u[-n]}$

$$x_1[n] = \left(-\frac{1}{4}\right)^n u[n] \overset{Z}{\longleftrightarrow} \frac{z}{\left(z+\frac{1}{4}\right)}$$

$$n\left[\left(-\frac{1}{4}\right)^n u[n]\right] \overset{Z}{\longleftrightarrow} -z\frac{d}{dz}\frac{z}{\left(z+\frac{1}{4}\right)}$$

$$= -z\frac{\left[z+\frac{1}{4}-z\right]}{\left(z+\frac{1}{4}\right)^2}$$

$$= \frac{\left[-\frac{z}{4}\right]}{\left(z+\frac{1}{4}\right)^2} \qquad \text{ROC: } |z| > \frac{1}{4}$$

$$x_2[n] = \left(\frac{1}{6}\right)^n u[n] \overset{Z}{\longleftrightarrow} \frac{z}{\left(z-\frac{1}{6}\right)} \qquad \text{ROC: } |z| > \frac{1}{6}$$

If time reversal property is used. z is to be replaced by z^{-1}

$$\left(\frac{1}{6}\right)^{-n} u[-n] \overset{Z}{\longleftrightarrow} \frac{z^{-1}}{\left(z^{-1}-\frac{1}{6}\right)}$$

$$X_1[z] = -\frac{6}{z-6} \qquad \text{ROC: } |z| < 6$$

$$X[z] = X_1[z]X_2[z]$$

$$= \frac{\frac{z}{4}6}{\left(z+\frac{1}{4}\right)^2(z-6)}$$

$$\boxed{X[z] = \frac{1.5z}{\left(z+\frac{1}{4}\right)(z-6)}} \qquad \text{ROC: } \frac{1}{4} < |z| < 6$$

13. $\boldsymbol{x[n] = \left[\left(\frac{1}{2}\right)^n - \left(\frac{1}{4}\right)^n\right] u[n]}$

Find $X[z]$ and plot the poles and zeros. (*Anna University, December, 2007*)

$$x_1[n] = \left(\frac{1}{2}\right)^n u[n] \overset{Z}{\longleftrightarrow} \frac{z}{\left(z-\frac{1}{2}\right)}$$

$$x_2[n] = \left(\frac{1}{4}\right)^n u[n] \overset{Z}{\longleftrightarrow} \frac{z}{\left(z-\frac{1}{4}\right)}$$

$$x[n] = x_1[n] - x_2[n]$$

$$X[z] = X_1[z] - X_2[z]$$

$$= \frac{z}{(z-0.5)} - \frac{z}{(z-0.25)}$$

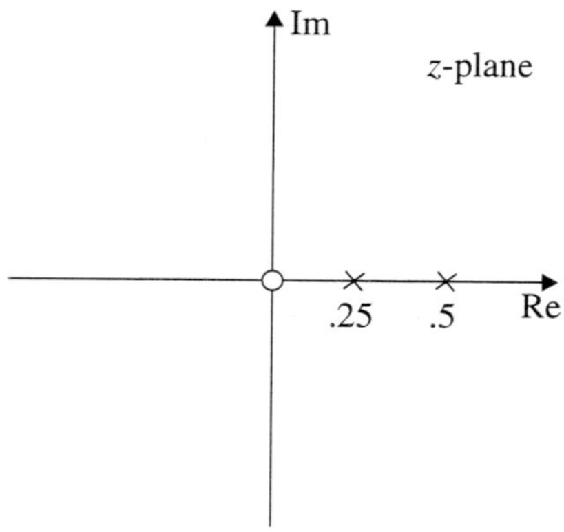

Figure 1.99 Pole-zero plot.

$$X[z] = \frac{z0.25}{(z-0.5)(z-0.25)}$$

The pole-zero plot is shown in Figure 1.99.

14.

$$\begin{aligned} \boldsymbol{x[n] = 1} & \quad \boldsymbol{n \geq 0} \\ \boldsymbol{= 3^n} & \quad \boldsymbol{n < 0} \end{aligned}$$

(*Anna University, April, 2005*)

$$\begin{aligned} x[n] &= u[n] + 3^n u[-n-1] \\ &= x_1[n] + x_2[n] \\ X_1[z] &= \frac{z}{(z-1)} \qquad \text{ROC: } |z| > 1 \\ X_2[z] &= (3)^n u[-n-1] \end{aligned}$$

Using time reversal and multiplication properties we get

$$\begin{aligned} X_2[z] &= -\frac{z}{(z-3)} \qquad \text{ROC: } |z| < 3 \\ X[z] &= X_1(z) + X_2(z) \\ &= \frac{z}{(z-1)} - \frac{z}{(z-3)} \end{aligned}$$

$$X[z] = \frac{-2z}{(z-1)(z-3)} \qquad \text{ROC: } 1 < z < 3$$

15.

$$(a)\quad \mathbf{x[n]=\left(-\frac{1}{3}\right)^{n}u[n]+3\left(\frac{1}{6}\right)^{n}u[n]}$$

$$(b)\quad \mathbf{x[n]=\left[\left(-\frac{1}{3}\right)^{n}u[-n]+3\left(\frac{1}{6}\right)^{n}\right]u[n]}$$

$$(c)\quad \mathbf{x[n]=\left[\left(-\frac{1}{3}\right)^{n}+3\left(\frac{1}{6}\right)^{n}\right]u[-n]}$$

(*a*)

$$x[n]=\left(-\frac{1}{3}\right)^{n}+3\left(\frac{1}{6}\right)^{n}u[n]$$

$$=x_1[n]+x_2[n]$$

$$X_1[z]=\frac{z}{\left(z+\frac{1}{3}\right)}\qquad \text{ROC: } |z|>-\frac{1}{3}$$

$$X_2[z]=3\frac{z}{\left(z-\frac{1}{6}\right)}\qquad \text{ROC: } |z|>\frac{1}{6}$$

$$X[z]=X_1[z]+X_2[z]$$

$$=z\left[\frac{1}{\left(z+\frac{1}{3}\right)}+\frac{3}{\left(z-\frac{1}{6}\right)}\right]\qquad \text{ROC: } |z|>\frac{1}{6}$$

(*b*)

$$x[n]=\left[\left(-\frac{1}{3}\right)^{n}u[-n]+3\left(\frac{1}{6}\right)^{n}\right]u[n]$$

$$=x_1[n]+x_2[n]$$

$$x_1[n]=\left(-\frac{1}{3}\right)^{n}u[-n]$$

Applying the properties of time reversal and multiplication we get

$$X_1[z]=\frac{1}{(1+3z)}\qquad \textit{See } \text{Example 1.75.12; ROC: } |z|<\frac{1}{3}$$

$$x_2[n]=3\left(\frac{1}{6}\right)^{n}u[n]$$

$$X_2[z]=\frac{3z}{\left(z-\frac{1}{6}\right)}\qquad \text{ROC: } |z|>\frac{1}{6}$$

$$X[z]=X_1[z]+X_2[z]$$

$$\boxed{X[z] = \left[\frac{1}{(1+3z)} + \frac{3z}{\left(z-\frac{1}{6}\right)}\right]} \quad \text{ROC: } \frac{1}{6} < |z| < \frac{1}{3}$$

(*c*)

$$x[n] = \left[\left(-\frac{1}{3}\right)^n + 3\left(\frac{1}{6}\right)^n\right] u[-n]$$

$$= x_1[n] + x_2[n]$$

$$X_1[z] = \frac{1}{(1+3z)} \qquad \text{ROC: } |z| < \frac{1}{3}$$

The derivation is given in Example 1.75.12(*b*)

$$x_2[n] = 3\left(\frac{1}{6}\right)^n u[-n]$$

$$u[-n] \overset{Z}{\longleftrightarrow} \frac{1}{(1-z)}$$

Applying multiplication property we get

$$Z\left(\frac{1}{6}\right)^n u[-n] \overset{Z}{\longleftrightarrow} \frac{1}{(1-6z)} \qquad \text{ROC: } |z| > \frac{1}{6}$$

$$\boxed{X[z] = \left[\frac{1}{(1+3z)} + \frac{3}{(1-6z)}\right]} \quad \text{ROC: } \frac{1}{6} < |z| < \frac{1}{3}$$

16. (*a*)

$$\mathbf{x[n] = \left[\left(\frac{1}{4}\right)^n + \left(\frac{1}{5}\right)^n\right] u[n]}$$

Applying results of Equation (1.77) we get

$$\boxed{X[z] = \left[\frac{z}{\left(z-\frac{1}{4}\right)} + \frac{z}{\left(z-\frac{1}{5}\right)}\right]} \qquad \text{ROC: } |z| > \frac{1}{4}$$

(*b*)

$$\mathbf{x[n] = \left[\left(\frac{1}{5}\right)^n u[n] + \left(\frac{1}{4}\right)^n u[-n-1]\right]}$$

$$\left(\frac{1}{5}\right)^n u[n] \overset{Z}{\longleftrightarrow} \frac{z}{\left(z-\frac{1}{5}\right)} \qquad \text{ROC: } |z| > \frac{1}{5}$$

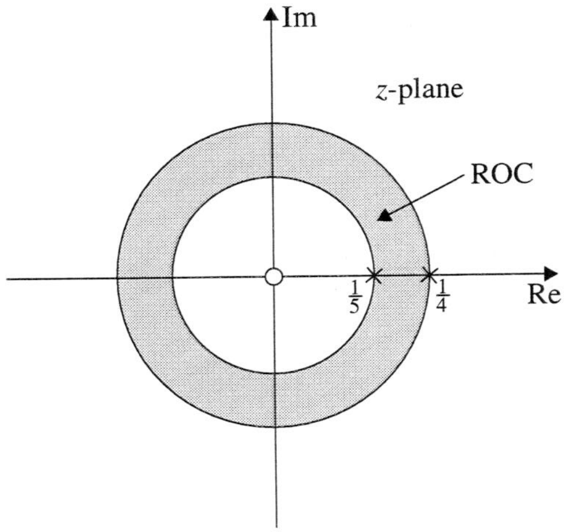

Figure 1.100 $X[z]$ and its ROC of Example 1.75(b).

$$\left(\frac{1}{4}\right)^n u[-n-1] \overset{Z}{\longleftrightarrow} \frac{-z}{\left(z-\frac{1}{4}\right)} \qquad \text{ROC: } |z| < \frac{1}{4}$$

$$\left(\frac{1}{5}\right)^n u[n] + \left(\frac{1}{4}\right)^n u[-n-1] \overset{Z}{\longleftrightarrow} \frac{z}{\left(z-\frac{1}{5}\right)} - \frac{z}{\left(z-\frac{1}{4}\right)}$$

$$\boxed{X[z] = \frac{-\frac{z}{20}}{\left(z-\frac{1}{5}\right)\left(z-\frac{1}{4}\right)}} \quad \text{ROC: } \frac{1}{5} < |z| < \frac{1}{4}$$

The poles and zero and the ROC are marked in Figure 1.100.

(c)

$$\mathbf{x[n] = \left[\left(\frac{1}{4}\right)^n u[n] + \left(\frac{1}{5}\right)^n\right] u[-n-1]}$$

$$\left(\frac{1}{4}\right)^n u[n] \overset{Z}{\longleftrightarrow} \frac{z}{\left(z-\frac{1}{4}\right)} \qquad \text{ROC: } |z| > \frac{1}{4}$$

$$\left(\frac{1}{5}\right)^n u[-n-1] \overset{Z}{\longleftrightarrow} \frac{-z}{\left(z-\frac{1}{5}\right)} \qquad \text{ROC: } |z| < \frac{1}{5}$$

The ROCs of the above two equations are shown in Figure 1.101 and it is seen that they do not overlap and thus the given $x[n]$ does not have $X[z]$.

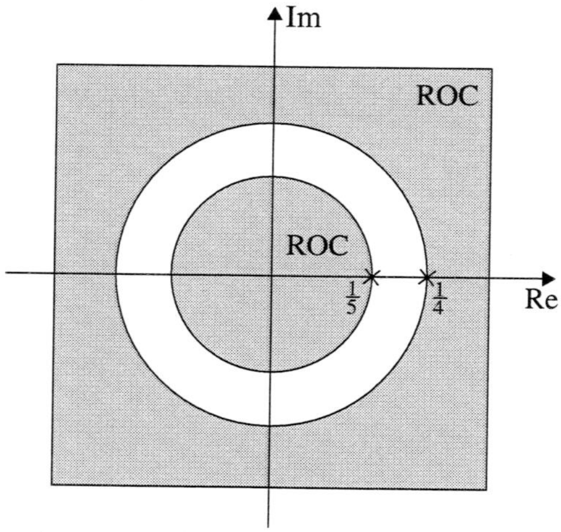

Figure 1.101 ROC of Example 1.75(*c*).

17. $\boldsymbol{x[n] = \delta[n] + \frac{1}{2}\delta(n+1) + \delta(n-3)}$

$$\delta[n] \overset{Z}{\longleftrightarrow} 1$$

$$\frac{1}{2}\delta[n+1] \overset{Z}{\longleftrightarrow} \frac{1}{2}z$$

$$\delta[n-3] \overset{Z}{\longleftrightarrow} z^{-3}$$

$$\boxed{X[z] = 1 + \frac{1}{2}z + z^{-3}}$$

18. $\boldsymbol{x[n] = 4^n \cos\left[\frac{2\pi n}{6} + \frac{\pi}{4}\right] u[-n-1]}$

$$\cos\left(\frac{2\pi n}{6}\right) = \cos\frac{\pi n}{3}$$

$$\cos\left(\frac{2\pi n}{6} + \frac{\pi}{4}\right) = \frac{e^{j\left(\frac{\pi}{4}+\frac{\pi n}{3}\right)} + e^{-j\left(\frac{\pi}{4}+\frac{\pi n}{3}\right)}}{2}$$

$$= \frac{1}{2}e^{j\left(\frac{\pi}{4}\right)}e^{j\left(\frac{\pi n}{3}\right)} + \frac{1}{2}e^{-j\left(\frac{\pi}{4}\right)}e^{-j\left(\frac{\pi n}{3}\right)}$$

$$4^n \cos\left(\frac{2\pi n}{6} + \frac{\pi}{n}\right) = \frac{1}{2}e^{j\left(\frac{\pi}{4}\right)}\left(4e^{j\frac{\pi}{3}}\right)^n + \frac{1}{2}e^{-j\frac{\pi}{4}}\left(4e^{-j\frac{\pi}{3}}\right)^n$$

From Equation (1.83)

$$\left(4e^{j\frac{\pi}{3}}\right)^n u[-n-1] \overset{Z}{\longleftrightarrow} \frac{-z}{(z-4e^{j\frac{\pi}{3}})} \qquad \text{ROC: } |z| < 4$$

$$\left(4e^{-j\frac{\pi}{3}}\right)^n u[-n-1] \overset{Z}{\longleftrightarrow} \frac{-z}{(z-4e^{-j\frac{\pi}{3}})} \qquad \text{ROC: } |z| < 4$$

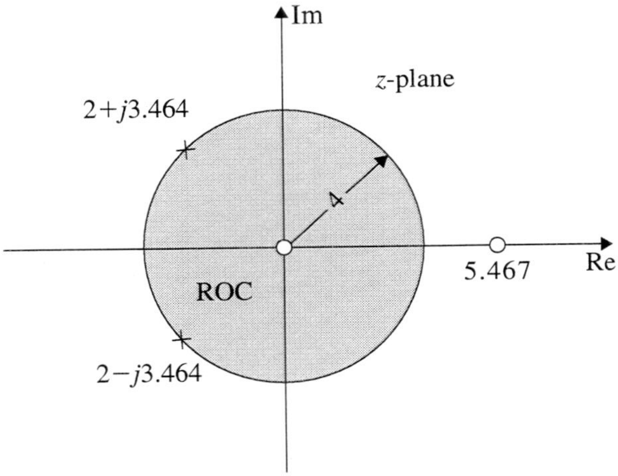

Figure 1.102 Poles and zeros and ROC of Example 1.75.18.

$$
\begin{aligned}
X[z] &= -\frac{1}{2}z\left[\frac{e^{j\frac{\pi}{4}}}{(z-4e^{j\frac{\pi}{3}})} + \frac{e^{-j\frac{\pi}{4}}}{(z-4e^{-j\frac{\pi}{3}})}\right] \\
&= -\frac{1}{2}z\left[\frac{ze^{j\frac{\pi}{4}} - 4e^{-j\frac{\pi}{12}} - 4e^{j\frac{\pi}{12}} + ze^{-j\frac{\pi}{4}}}{z^2 - z4(e^{j\frac{\pi}{3}} + e^{-j\frac{\pi}{3}}) + 16}\right] \\
&= \frac{-\frac{1}{2}z[\sqrt{2}z - 7.73]}{(z^2 - 4z + 16)}
\end{aligned}
$$

$$
\boxed{X[z] = \frac{-0.707z[z-5.467]}{(z-2+j3.464)(z-2-j3.464)}} \quad \text{ROC: } |z| < 4
$$

The pole zero diagram is shown in Figure 1.102. The ROC is the interior of the circle.

19. $\boldsymbol{x[n] = nu[n-1]}$

Method 1

$$
u[n-1] \overset{Z}{\longleftrightarrow} \frac{1}{(z-1)}
$$

Using differential property we get

$$
nu[n-1] \overset{Z}{\longleftrightarrow} -z\frac{d}{dz}\frac{1}{(z-1)}
$$

$$
\boxed{z[nu[n-1]] = \frac{z}{(z-1)^2}}
$$

Method 2

$$
nu[n-1] = (n-1)u[n-1] + u[n-1]
$$

$$
(n-1)u[n-1] \overset{Z}{\longleftrightarrow} \frac{zz^{-1}}{(z-1)^2} = \frac{1}{(z-1)^2}
$$

$$u[n-1] \overset{Z}{\longleftrightarrow} \frac{1}{(z-1)}$$

$$nu[n-1] \overset{Z}{\longleftrightarrow} \frac{1}{(z-1)^2} + \frac{1}{(z-1)}$$

$$\boxed{Z[nu[n-1]] = \frac{z}{(z-1)^2}}$$

20.

$$\boldsymbol{x[n] = \begin{cases} (4)^n & n < 0 \\ \left(\frac{1}{4}\right)^n & n = 0, 2, 4, \ldots \\ \left(\frac{1}{5}\right)^n & n = 1, 3, 5, \ldots \end{cases}}$$

$$\begin{aligned} X[z] &= \sum_{n=-\infty}^{-1} (4)^n z^{-n} + \sum_{n=0}^{\infty} \left(\frac{1}{4}\right)^n z^{-n} + \sum_{n=0}^{\infty} \left(\frac{1}{5}\right)^n z^{-n} \\ &= X_1[z] + X_2[z] + X_3[z] \end{aligned}$$

$$\begin{aligned} X_1[z] &= \sum_{n=-\infty}^{-1} (4)^n z^{-n} \\ &= \sum_{n=-\infty}^{-1} \left(\frac{z}{4}\right)^{-n} \\ &= \sum_{n=1}^{\infty} \left(\frac{z}{4}\right)^n \\ &= \frac{z}{4} + \left(\frac{z}{4}\right)^2 + \cdots \\ &= \frac{z}{4}\left[1 + \frac{z}{4} + \left(\frac{z}{4}\right)^2 + \cdots\right] \\ &= \frac{z}{4}\frac{1}{\left(1 - \frac{z}{4}\right)} \\ &= \frac{-z}{(z-4)} \qquad \text{ROC: } |z| < 4 \end{aligned}$$

$$\begin{aligned} X_2[z] &= \sum_{n=0}^{\infty} \left(\frac{1}{4}\right)^n z^{-n} \\ &= \sum_{n=0}^{\infty} (4z)^{-n} \\ &= \sum_{p=0}^{\infty} (4z)^{-2p} \qquad \text{where } n = 2p \text{ and } p = 0, 1, 2, \ldots \end{aligned}$$

$$X_2[z] = \sum_{p=0}^{\infty} \left(16z^2\right)^{-p}$$

$$= \frac{1}{\left(1 - \frac{1}{16z^2}\right)}$$

$$= \frac{z^2}{\left(z^2 - \frac{1}{16}\right)} \qquad \text{ROC: } |z| > \frac{1}{4}$$

$$X_3[z] = \sum_{n=0}^{\infty} \left(\frac{1}{5}\right)^n z^{-n}$$

$$= \sum_{n=0}^{\infty} (5z)^{-n}$$

$$= \sum_{q=0}^{\infty} (5z)^{-(2q+1)} \qquad \text{where } n = 2q + 1$$

$$= \frac{1}{5z} \sum_{q=0}^{\infty} \left(25z^2\right)^{-q}$$

$$= \frac{1}{5z} \frac{1}{\left(1 - \frac{1}{25z^2}\right)}$$

$$= \frac{z/5}{\left(z^2 - \frac{1}{25}\right)} \qquad \text{ROC: } |z| > \frac{1}{5}$$

$$\boxed{X[z] = \left[-\frac{z}{(z-4)} + \frac{z^2}{\left(z^2 - \frac{1}{16}\right)} + \frac{z/5}{\left(z^2 - \frac{1}{25}\right)}\right]}$$

ROC: $\frac{1}{4} < |z| < 4$.

Example 1.76

Find the initial and final values of the following functions:

(a) $$X[z] = \frac{z}{(4z^2 - 5z - 1)} \qquad \text{ROC: } |z| > 1$$

(b) $$x[z] = \frac{10z(z - 0.4)}{(z - 0.5)(z - 0.3)} \qquad \text{ROC: } |z| > 0.5$$

Solution

(*a*) $X[z] = \frac{z}{(4z^2-5z-1)}$

Initial Value

$$x[0] = \underset{z\to\infty}{Lt}\ X[z]$$

$$= \underset{z\to\infty}{Lt}\ \frac{z}{z^2\left(4-\frac{5}{z}-\frac{1}{z^2}\right)}$$

$$= \underset{z\to\infty}{Lt}\ \frac{1}{z\left(4-\frac{5}{z}-\frac{1}{z^2}\right)}$$

$$\boxed{x[0] = 0}$$

Final Value

$$x[\infty] = \underset{z\to 1}{Lt}\ \frac{(z-1)}{z}$$

Provided all the poles are inside the unit circle and possibly one pole on the unit circle.

$$(4z^2-5z+1) = 4(z-1)\left(z-\frac{1}{4}\right)$$

$$X[z] = \frac{z}{4(z-1)\left(z-\frac{1}{4}\right)}$$

The poles $(z-1)$ is on the unit circle and $z=\frac{1}{4}$ within unit circle. $X[z]$ is valid to apply final value theorem.

$$x[\infty] = \underset{z\to 1}{Lt}\ \frac{(z-1)}{z}\frac{z}{4(z-1)\left(z-\frac{1}{4}\right)}$$

$$\boxed{x[\infty] = \frac{1}{3}}$$

(*b*) $X[z] = \frac{10z(z-0.4)}{(z-0.5)(z-0.3)}$

$$x[0] = \underset{z\to\infty}{Lt}\ \frac{10z^2\left(1-\frac{0.4}{z}\right)}{z^2\left(1-\frac{0.5}{z}\right)\left(1-\frac{0.3}{z}\right)}$$

$$\boxed{x[0] = 10}$$

To find the final value $x[\infty]$, the poles of $X[z]$ are all inside the unit circle and hence is valid to apply final value theorem.

$$x[\infty] = \underset{z\to 1}{Lt}\ \frac{10z(z-1)(z-0.4)}{z(z-0.5)(z-0.3)}$$

$$\boxed{x[\infty] = 0}$$

Example 1.77

$$X[z] = \frac{\left[1-\frac{1}{4}z^{-2}\right]}{\left[1+\frac{1}{4}z^{-2}\right]\left[1+\frac{5}{4}z^{-1}+\frac{3}{8}z^{-2}\right]}$$

How many different regions of convergence could correspond to $X[z]$?

(Anna University, May, 2008)

Solution

$$X[z] = \frac{z^2\left[z^2-\frac{1}{4}\right]}{\left(z^2+\frac{1}{4}\right)\left(z^2+\frac{5}{4}z+\frac{3}{8}\right)}$$

$$= \frac{z^2\left(z+\frac{1}{2}\right)\left(z-\frac{1}{2}\right)}{\left(z-\frac{j}{2}\right)\left(z+\frac{j}{2}\right)\left(z+\frac{3}{4}\right)\left(z+\frac{1}{2}\right)}$$

$$X[z] = \frac{z^2\left[z-\frac{1}{2}\right]}{\left(z-\frac{j}{2}\right)\left(z+\frac{j}{2}\right)\left(z+\frac{3}{4}\right)}$$

The poles and zeros are located in Figure 1.103.

From Figure 1.103 circle passing through $|z| = \frac{3}{4}$ and $|z| = \frac{1}{2}$ are drawn. $X[z]$ exists from the following ROCs.

(*a*)

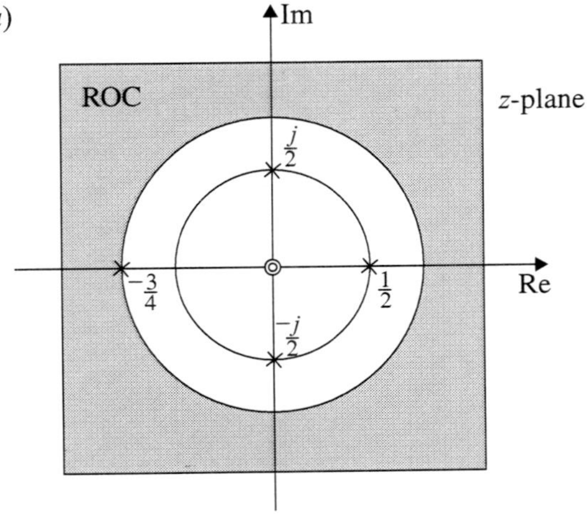

Figure 1.103 Pole zero diagram and ROC of $X[z]$.

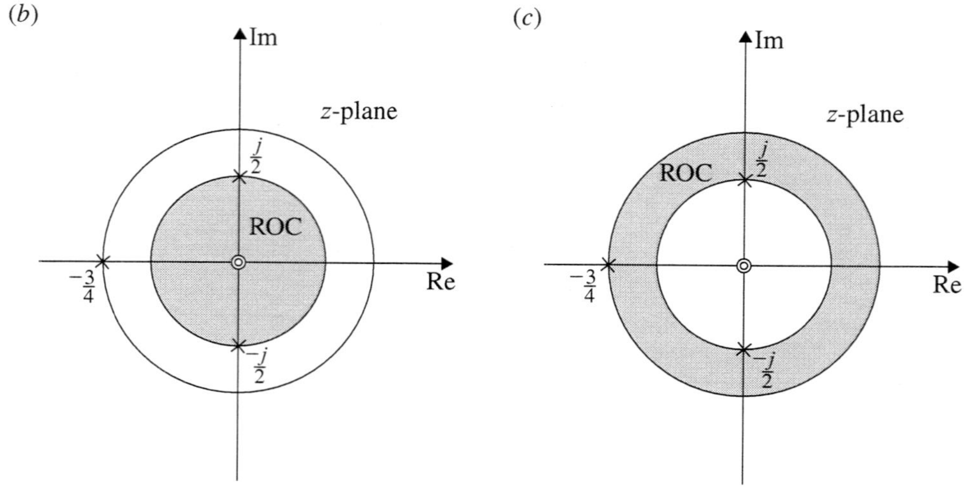

Figure 1.103 Pole zero diagram and ROC of $X[z]$.

Table 1.2 Unilateral z-transform pairs.

No	$x[n]$	$X[z]$
1	$\delta[n]$	1
2	$u[n]$	$\frac{z}{(z-1)}$
3	$nu[n]$	$\frac{z}{(z-1)^2}$
4	$n^2u[n]$	$\frac{z(z+1)}{(z-1)^3}$
5	$a^nu[n]$	$\frac{z}{(z-a)}$
6	$a^{n-1}u[n-1]$	$\frac{1}{(z-a)}$
7	$na^nu[n]$	$\frac{az}{(z-a)^2}$
8	$\cos\omega_0nu[n]$	$\frac{1-\cos\omega_0z^{-1}}{1-2\cos\omega_0z^{-1}+z^{-2}}$
9	$\sin\omega_0nu[n]$	$\frac{z^{-1}\sin\omega_0}{1-2\cos\omega_0z^{-1}+z^{-2}}$
10	$a^n\cos\omega_0nu[n]$	$\frac{1-az^{-1}\cos\omega_0}{1-2a\cos\omega_0z^{-1}+a^2z^{-2}}$
11	$a^n\sin\omega_0nu[n]$	$\frac{az^{-1}\sin\omega_0}{1-2a\cos\omega_0z^{-1}+a^2z^{-2}}$

Table 1.3 z-transform properties (operations).

Operation	$x[n]$	$X[z]$
Linearity	$a_1x_1[n] + a_2x_2[n]$	$a_1X_1[z] + a_2X_2[z]$
Multiplication by a^n	$a^n x[n]u[n]$	$X\left[\frac{z}{a}\right]$
Multiplication by n	$nx[n]u[n]$	$-z\frac{d}{dz}X[z]$
Time shifting	$x[n-n_0]$	$z^{-n_0}X[z]$
Multiplication by $e^{j\omega_0 n}$	$e^{j\omega_0 n}x[n]$	$X[e^{-j\omega_0}z]$
Time reversal	$x[-n]$	$X\left[\frac{1}{z}\right]$
Accumulation	$\sum_{k=-\infty}^{n} x[n]$	$\frac{z}{(z-1)}X[z]$
Convolution	$x_1[n] * x_2[n]$	$X_1[z]X_2[z]$
Initial value	$x[0]$	$\underset{z\to\infty}{Lt}\ X[z]$
Final value	$x[\infty]$	$\underset{z\to 1}{Lt}\ \frac{(z-1)}{z}X[z]$ poles of $(z-1)X[z]$ are inside the unit circle.
Right shifting	$x[n-m]u[n-m]$	$\frac{1}{z^m}X[z]$
	$x[n-m]u[n]$	$\frac{1}{z^m}X[z] + \frac{1}{z^m}\sum_{n=1}^{m} x(-m)z^n$
	$x[n-1]u[n]$	$\frac{1}{z}X[z] + x[-1]$
	$x[n-2]u[n]$	$\frac{1}{z^2}X[z] + \frac{1}{z}x[-1] + x[-2]$
Left shifting	$x[n+m]u[n]$	$z^m X[z] - z^m \sum_{n=0}^{m-1} x[n]z^{-n}$
	$x[n+1]u[n]$	$zX[z] - zx(0)$
	$x[n+2]u[n]$	$z^2X[z] - z^2x[0] - zx[1]$

1. $|z| > \frac{3}{4}$. ROC is the exterior of the outermost pole $z = -\frac{3}{4}$. The system is causal and $X[z]$ exits (Figure 1.103(a)).
2. $|z| < \frac{1}{2}$. ROC is the interior of the innermost pole $\pm\frac{j}{2}$. The system is anti-causal and $X[z]$ exits (Figure 1.103(b)).
3. $\frac{1}{2} < |z| < \frac{3}{4}$. The ROC is a ring between the two circles of radius $r_1 = \frac{3}{4}$ and $r_1 = \frac{1}{2}$. Here, $X[z]$ exits. The system is both causal and anti-causal (Figure 1.103(c)).

The unilateral z-transform pairs are given in Table 1.2, The properties of z-transform are given in Table 1.3.

1.26 Inverse z-transform

If $X[z]$ is given then the sequence $x[n]$ is determined. This is called inverse z-transform. As in the Laplace transform, in inverse z-transform also, the integration in the complex z-plane using Equation (1.97) is avoided since it is tedious. Instead the following methods are used. They are:

1. Partial fraction method;
2. Power series expansion;
3. Residue method.

Of these, the partial fraction method is very easy to apply as was done in determining inverse Laplace transform.

1.26.1 Partial Fraction Method

If $X[z]$ is a rational function of z then it can be expressed as follows:

$$X[z] = \frac{N[z]}{D[z]} = \frac{K(z-z_1)(z-z_2)\ldots(z-z_m)}{(z-p_1)(z-p_2)\ldots(z-p_n)} \tag{1.98}$$

where $n \geq m$ and all the poles are simple.

$$\begin{aligned}\frac{X[z]}{z} &= \frac{K(z-z_1)(z-z_2)\ldots(z-z_m)}{z(z-p_1)(z-p_2)\ldots(z-p_n)}\\ &= \frac{A_0}{z} + \frac{A_1}{z-p_1} + \frac{A_2}{z-p_2} + \ldots + \frac{A_n}{z-p_n}\end{aligned}$$

where

$$A_0 = X[z]|_{z=0}$$

$$A_1 = (z-p_1)\frac{X[z]}{z}\bigg|_{z=p_1}$$

$$X[z] = A_0 + A_1\frac{z}{z-p_1} + \cdots + \frac{A_n z}{z-p_n} \tag{1.99}$$

Table 1.4 z-transform pairs of repeated poles.

$X[z]$	$x[n]$ ROC: $\lvert z\rvert > \lvert a\rvert$
1. $\dfrac{z}{z-a}$	$a^n u[n]$
2. $\dfrac{z}{(z-a)^2}$	$na^{n-1}u[n]$
3. $\dfrac{z}{(z-a)^3}$	$\dfrac{n(n-1)a^{n-2}}{\angle 2}u[n]$
4. $\dfrac{z}{(z-a)^k}$	$\dfrac{n(n-1)(n-2)\ldots(n-(k-2))a^{n-k+1}}{\angle(k-1)}u[n]$

Using z-transform pair table, $x[n]$ can be determined. The following examples illustrate the above method. For repeated poles, the z-transform pairs given in Table 1.4 may be referred to.

Example 1.78

Find the inverse z-transform of

$$X[z] = \frac{1 - \frac{1}{3}z^{-1}}{(1 - z^{-1})(1 + 2z^{-1})} \qquad \text{ROC: } |z| > 2$$

(*Anna University, April, 2004*)

Solution

$$X[z] = \frac{1 - \frac{1}{3}z^{-1}}{(1 - z^{-1})(1 + 2z^{-1})}$$

$$= \frac{z\left(z - \frac{1}{3}\right)}{(z - 1)(z + 2)}$$

$$\frac{X[z]}{z} = \frac{A_1}{(z - 1)} + \frac{A_2}{(z + 2)}$$

$$\left(z - \frac{1}{3}\right) = A_1(z + 2) + A_2(z - 1)$$

Substitute $z = 1$

$$A_1 = \frac{2}{9}$$

Substitute $z = -2$

$$A_2 = \frac{7}{9}$$

$$X[z] = \frac{1}{9}\left[\frac{2z}{z - 1} + \frac{7z}{z + 2}\right]$$

$$\boxed{x[n] = \frac{1}{9}\left[2(1)^n + 7(-2)^n\right] u[n]}$$

Example 1.79

Find the inverse z-transform of

$$X[z] = \frac{1}{1024}\left[\frac{1024 - z^{-10}}{1 - \frac{1}{2}z^{-1}}\right] \qquad \text{ROC: } |z| > 0$$

(*Anna University, April, 2008*)

Solution

$$X[z] = \frac{1}{1024}\left[\frac{1024 - z^{-10}}{1 - \frac{1}{2}z^{-1}}\right]$$

$$= \frac{z}{\left(z - \frac{1}{2}\right)} - \frac{z}{\left(z - \frac{1}{2}\right)}\frac{z^{-10}}{1024}$$

Taking inverse z-transform we get

$$x[n] = \left(\frac{1}{2}\right)^n u[n] - \frac{1}{1024}\left(\frac{1}{2}\right)^{n-10} u[n-10]$$

$$= \left(\frac{1}{2}\right)^n u[n] - \frac{1}{1024}\left(\frac{1}{2}\right)^n\left(\frac{1}{2}\right)^{-10} u[n-10]$$

$$= \left(\frac{1}{2}\right)^n u[n] - \frac{1}{1024}\left(\frac{1}{2}\right)^n 1024u[n-10]$$

$$= \left(\frac{1}{2}\right)^n u[n] - \left(\frac{1}{2}\right)^n u[n-10]$$

$$x[n] = \left(\frac{1}{2}\right)^n - 0 \qquad 0 \le n \le 9$$

$$= \left(\frac{1}{2}\right)^n - \left(\frac{1}{2}\right)^n$$

$$= 0 \qquad n \ge 10$$

$$\boxed{\begin{aligned} x[n] &= \left(\frac{1}{2}\right)^n && 0 \le n \le 9 \\ &= 0 && \text{otherwise} \end{aligned}}$$

Example 1.80

Find the inverse z-transform of

$$X[z] = \frac{z^2}{(1 - az)(z - a)}$$

(Anna University, December, 2007)

Solution

$$X[z] = \frac{z^2}{(1 - az)(z - a)}$$

$$\frac{X[z]}{z} = \frac{-z}{a\left[z - \frac{1}{a}\right][z - a]}$$

$$\frac{X[z]}{z} = \frac{A_1}{\left(z - \frac{1}{a}\right)} + \frac{A_2}{(z-a)}$$

$$-\frac{z}{a} = A_1(z-a) + A_2\left(z - \frac{1}{a}\right)$$

Substitute $z = \frac{1}{a}$

$$-\frac{1}{a^2} = A_1\left(\frac{1}{a} - a\right)$$

$$A_1 = \frac{-1}{a(1-a^2)}$$

Substitute $z = a$

$$-1 = A_2\left(a - \frac{1}{a}\right)$$

$$A_2 = \frac{a}{(1-a^2)}$$

$$X[z] = \frac{1}{(1-a^2)}\left[\frac{-1}{a}\frac{z}{\left(z-\frac{1}{a}\right)} + \frac{az}{(z-a)}\right]$$

For $a > 1$, the ROC is shown in Figure 1.104(a). For $a < 1$, the ROC is shown in Figure 1.104(b).

For $a > 1$, the ROC is exterior of the outer most pole. Hence, the function is casual.

$$x[n] = \frac{1}{(1-a^2)}\left[\frac{-1}{a}\frac{1}{(a)^n} + a(a)^n\right]u[n]$$

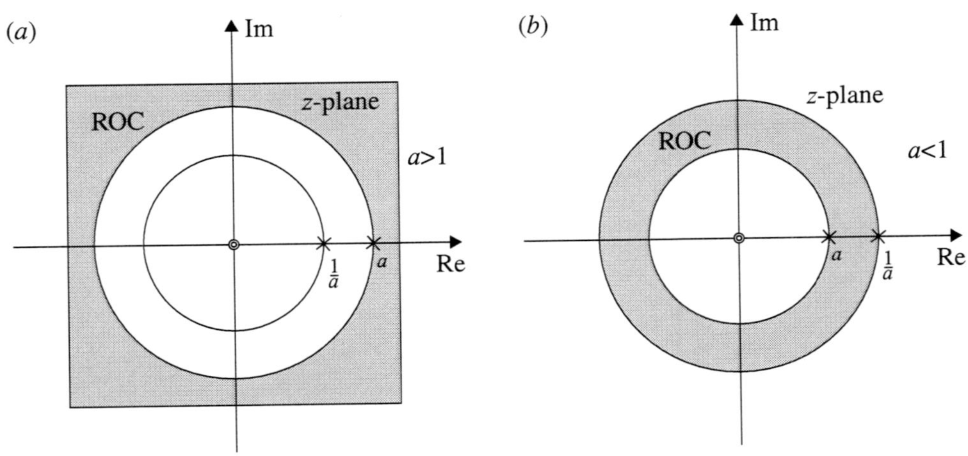

Figure 1.104 ROC of Example 1.80.

$$x[n] = \frac{1}{(1-a^2)}\left[-\left(\frac{1}{a}\right)^{n+1} + (a)^{n+1}\right]u[n]$$

For $a < 1$, the ROC is $a < |z| < \frac{1}{a}$ and it is a concentric strip. The pole at $|z| = \frac{1}{a}$ is anti-causal and $z = a$ is causal.

$$x[n] = \frac{1}{(1-a^2)}\left[\left(\frac{1}{a}\right)^{n+1} u[-n-1] + (a)^{n+1}u[n]\right]$$

Example 1.81

$$X[z] = \frac{z(z^2+z-30)}{(z-2)(z-4)^3} \qquad \text{ROC: } |z| > 4$$

Find $x[n]$ using partial fraction method.

Solution **This is the case with poles repeated thrice**

$$X[z] = \frac{z(z^2+z-30)}{(z-2)(z-4)^3}$$

$$\frac{X[z]}{z} = \frac{(z^2+z-30)}{(z-2)(z-4)^3} = \frac{(z-5)(z+6)}{(z-2)(z-4)^3}$$

$$= \frac{A_1}{(z-2)} + \frac{A_2}{(z-4)^3} + \frac{A_3}{(z-4)^2} + \frac{A_4}{(z-4)}$$

$$(z^2+z-30) = A_1(z-4)^3 + A_2(z-2) + A_3(z-2)(z-4) + A_4(z-2)(z-4)^2$$

Substitute $z = 2$

$$(-3)(8) = -8A_1; \qquad A_1 = 3$$

Substitute $z = 4$

$$(-1)(10) = 2A_2; \qquad A_2 = -5$$

$$(z^2+z-30) = 3(z^3-12z^2+48z-64) - 5(z-2) + A_3(z^2-6z+8) + A_4(z^3-10z^2+32z-32)$$

Compare the coefficients of z^2

$$1 = -36 + A_3 - 10A_4$$

$$A_3 - 10A_4 = 37$$

Compare the coefficients of z

$$1 = 144 - 5 - 6A_3 + 32A_4$$

$$6A_3 - 32A_4 = 138$$

Solving the above equation we get

$$A_3 = 7; \qquad A_4 = -3$$

$$X[z] = \frac{3z}{(z-2)} - \frac{5z}{(z-4)^3} + \frac{7z}{(z-4)^2} - \frac{3z}{(z-4)}$$

$$\frac{z}{(z-4)^3} \overset{Z^{-1}}{\longleftrightarrow} \frac{n(n-1)}{\angle 2}(4)^{n-2}u[n] = \frac{n(n-1)}{32}(4)^n u[n]$$

$$\frac{z}{(z-4)^2} \overset{Z^{-1}}{\longleftrightarrow} n(4)^{n-1}u[n] = \frac{1}{4}n(4)^n u[n]$$

$$\boxed{x[n] = \left[3(2)^n + \left\{-\frac{5}{32}n(n-1) + \frac{7}{4}n - 3\right\}(4)^n\right]u[n]}$$

The values of A_1, A_2 and A_3 determined are checked for their correctness as follows.

$$\frac{X[z]}{z} = \frac{(z-5)(z+6)}{(z-2)(z-4)^3}$$

Substitute $z = 0$

$$\left.\frac{X[z]}{z}\right|_{z=0} = \frac{(-5)(6)}{(-2)(-4)^3} = -\frac{15}{64}$$

$$\frac{X[z]}{z} = \frac{3}{z-2} - \frac{5}{(z-4)^3} + \frac{7}{(z-4)^2} - \frac{3}{(z-4)}$$

Substitute $z = 0$

$$\left.\frac{X[z]}{z}\right|_{z=0} = -\frac{3}{2} + \frac{5}{64} + \frac{7}{16} + \frac{3}{4} = -\frac{15}{64}$$

Hence, the values of A_1, A_2, A_3 and A_4 are found to be correct.

Example 1.82

$$X[z] = \frac{z(z+10)}{(z-1)(z^2-8z+20)}$$

Find $x[n]$ using partial fraction method.

Solution This is the case with complex poles

$$X[z] = \frac{z(z+10)}{(z-1)(z^2-8z+20)}$$

$$\frac{X[z]}{z} = \frac{(z+10)}{(z-1)(z-4+j2)(z-4-j2)}$$

$$= \frac{A_1}{(z-1)} + \frac{A_2}{(z-4+j2)} + \frac{A_3}{(z-4-j2)}$$

$$(z+10) = A_1(z^2-8z+20) + A_2(z-1)(z-4-j2) + A_3(z-1)(z-4+j2)$$

Substitute $z = 1$

$$11 = A_1(13); \qquad A_1 = \frac{11}{13}$$

Substitute $z = 4 + j2$

$$(14+j2) = A_3(4+j2-4+j2)(4+j2-1)$$

$$A_3 = \frac{(14+j2)}{j4(3+j2)} = \frac{14.142\angle 8.13^\circ}{4\sqrt{13}\angle 123.69^\circ}$$

$$= 0.98\angle -115.56^\circ = 0.98e^{-j115.56^\circ}$$

$$A_2 = \text{conjugate of } A_3$$

$$= 0.98\angle 115.56^\circ = 0.98e^{j115.56^\circ}$$

$$X[z] = \frac{11}{13}\frac{z}{(z-1)} + \frac{0.98e^{j115.56^\circ}}{(z-4+j2)} + \frac{0.98e^{-j115.56^\circ}}{(z-4-j2)}$$

Using z-transform pair we get the following inverse z-transform

$$x[n] = \frac{11}{13}u[n] + [0.98e^{j115.56^\circ}(4-j2)^n + 0.98e^{-j115.56^\circ}(4+j2)^n]u[n]$$

$115.56^\circ = 2$ radians

$$(4+j2)^n = (4.47)^n e^{j0.4636n}$$

$$(4-j2)^n = (4.47)^n e^{-j0.4636n}$$

$$x[n] = \frac{11}{13}u[n] + [0.98e^{j2}e^{-j0.4636n}(4.47)^n + 0.98(4.47)^n e^{-j2}e^{j0.4636n}]u[n]$$

$$= \frac{11}{13}u[n] + 0.98 * (4.47)^n[e^{j(2-.4636n)} + e^{-j(2-.4636n)}]u[n]$$

$$\boxed{x[n] = \left[\frac{11}{13} + 1.96(4.47)^n\cos(2-0.4636n)\right]u[n]}$$

Example 1.83

$$X[z] = \frac{(5z^3 - 29z^2 + 8z + 60)}{(z^2 - 7z + 10)}$$

Find $x[n]$ by partial fraction method.

Solution This is the case with irrational system function. The solution of $x[n]$ will have forward and backward shifts. Dividing the numerator polynomial by the denominator polynomial we get

$$\begin{array}{r|l} & 5z + 6 \\ z^2 - 7z + 10 & 5z^3 - 29z^2 + 8z + 60 \\ & 5z^3 - 35z^2 + 50z \\ \hline & 6z^2 - 42z + 60 \\ & 6z^2 - 42z + 60 \\ \hline \end{array}$$

$$(z^2 - 7z + 10) = (z-2)(z-5)$$

$$X[z] = (5z+6) + \frac{1}{(z-2)(z-5)}$$

$$= X_1[z] + X_2[z]$$

where

$$X_1[z] = (5z+6)$$

$$X_2[z] = \frac{1}{(z-2)(z-5)}$$

$$\frac{X_2[z]}{z} = \frac{1}{z(z-2)(z-5)}$$

$$= \frac{A_1}{z} + \frac{A_2}{z-2} + \frac{A_3}{z-5}$$

$$1 = A_1(z-2)(z-5) + A_2 z(z-5) + A_3 z(z-2)$$

Substitute $z = 0$

$$A_1 = \frac{1}{10}$$

Substitute $z = 2$

$$1 = A_2(2)(-3); \qquad A_2 = -\frac{1}{6}$$

Substitute $z = 5$

$$1 = A_3(5)(3); \qquad A_3 = \frac{1}{15}$$

$$X[z] = 5z + 6 + \frac{1}{10} - \frac{1}{6}\frac{z}{(z-2)} + \frac{1}{15}\frac{z}{(z-5)}$$

$$\boxed{x[n] = \left[\delta(n+1) + 6.1\delta[n] - \frac{1}{6}(2)^n + \frac{1}{15}(5)^n\right]u[n]}$$

Example 1.84

Find the inverse z-transform of

$$X[z] = \frac{(5 + z^{-2} + 4z^{-3})}{(z^2 + 7z + 10)}$$

Solution

$$\begin{aligned} X[z] &= \frac{(5 + z^{-2} + 4z^{-3})}{(z^2 + 7z + 10)} \\ &= \frac{(5 + z^{-2} + 4z^{-3})}{z}\frac{z}{(z+2)(z+5)} \\ &= [5z^{-1} + z^{-3} + 4z^{-4}]\frac{z}{(z+2)(z+5)} \end{aligned}$$

$$\frac{z}{(z+2)(z+5)} = \frac{1}{3}\left[\frac{z}{z+2} - \frac{z}{z+5}\right]$$

$$\frac{z}{(z+2)(z+5)} \xleftrightarrow{Z^{-1}} \frac{1}{3}\left[(-2)^n - (-5)^n\right]u[n]$$

Now

$$x[n] = [5z^{-1} + z^{-3} + 4z^{-4}]\frac{1}{3}[(-2)^n - (-5)^n]u[n]$$

Using the time shifting property we get

$$\boxed{\begin{aligned} x[n] = {} & \frac{5}{3}\left[(-2)^{n-1} - (-5)^{n-1}\right]u[n-1] + \frac{1}{3}\left[(-2)^{n-3} - (-5)^{n-3}\right]u[n-3] \\ & + \frac{4}{3}\left[(-2)^{n-4} - (-5)^{n-4}\right]u[n-4] \end{aligned}}$$

Example 1.85

Find the inverse z-transform for the following system functions:

(*a*) $\quad X[z] = \dfrac{4}{(z-5)} \qquad$ ROC: $|z| < 5$

(*b*) $\quad X[z] = z(1 - z^{-1})(1 + 2z^{-1}) \qquad$ ROC: $0 < |z| < \infty$

Solution

(*a*) $X[z] = \frac{4}{(z-5)}$

$$X[z] = \frac{4}{(z-5)} = 4z^{-1}\frac{z}{z-5}$$

$$x[n] = 4z^{-1}[(5)^n]u[n]]$$

$$\boxed{x[n] = 4(5)^{n-1}u[n-1]}$$

(*b*) $X[z] = z(1 - z^{-1})(1 + 2z^{-1})$

$$X[z] = z(1 - z^{-1})(1 + 2z^{-1})$$

$$X[z] = z[1 + 2z^{-1} - z^{-1} - 2z^{-2})$$

$$= [z + 1 - 2z^{-1}]$$

$$\boxed{x[n] = \{1, \underset{\uparrow}{1}, -2\}}$$

1.26.2 Inverse *z*-transform using Power Series Expansion

The *z*-transform Equation (1.65)

$$X[z] = \sum_{n=-\infty}^{\infty} x[n]z^{-n}$$

can be expressed in power series form and the coefficients of $z^{|n|}$ give the values of the sequence. Equation (1.65) can be expressed as,

$$X[z] = \cdots + x[-3]z^3 + x[-2]z^2 + x[-1]z + x[0] + x[1]z^{-1} + x[2]z^{-2} + x[3]z^{-3} + \cdots \tag{1.100}$$

Equation (1.100) does not give closed form. However if $X[z]$ is not in a simpler form other than the polynomial in z^{-1}, using power series method $x[n]$ is easily obtained. If $X[z]$ is rational, the power series is obtained by long division. The following examples illustrate the above method.

Example 1.86

Using power series expansion, find the inverse *z*-transform of the following $X[z]$:

(*a*) $X[z] = \frac{4z}{(z^2 - 3z + 2)}$ ROC: $|z| > 2$

(*b*) $X[z] = \frac{4z}{(z^2 - 3z + 2)}$ ROC: $|z| < 1$

(*c*) $X[z] = \frac{1}{(1 - az^{-1})}$ ROC: $|z| > |a|$ and ROC: $|z| < |a|$

(*Anna University, December, 2006*)

Solution

(*a*) $X[z] = \frac{4z}{(z^2-3z+2)}$; **ROC: $|z| > 2$**

$$X[z] = \frac{4z}{(z^2 - 3z + 2)} = \frac{4z}{(z-1)(z-2)}$$

For ROC: $|z| > 2$, $x[n]$ is a right-sided sequence where $n \geq 0$. Hence, the long division is done in such a way that $X[z]$ is expressed in power of z^{-1}.

$$\begin{array}{r l}
 & 4z^{-1} + 12z^{-2} + 28z^{-3} + \cdots \\
z^2 - 3z + 2 \,\big)\!\! & 4z \\
 & \underline{4z - 12 + 8z^{-1}} \\
 & \quad 12 - 8z^{-1} \\
 & \quad \underline{12 - 36z^{-1} + 24z^{-2}} \\
 & \qquad 28z^{-1} - 24z^{-2} \\
 & \qquad \underline{28z^{-1} - 84z^{-2} + 56z^{-3}}
\end{array}$$

$$X[z] = 4z^{-1} + 12z^{-2} + 28z^{-3} + \cdots$$

$$\boxed{x[n] = \{\underset{\uparrow}{0},\ 4,\ 12,\ 28, \ldots\}}$$

(*b*) $X[z] = \frac{4z}{(z^2-3z+2)}$; **ROC: $|z| < 1$**

For ROC: $|z| < 1$, $x[n]$ sequence is negative where $n \leq 0$. The long division is done in such a way that $X[z]$ is expressed in power of z.

$$\begin{array}{r l}
 & 2z + 3z^2 + \frac{7}{2}z^3 \\
2 - 3z + z^2 \,\big)\!\! & 4z \\
 & \underline{4z - 6z^2 + 2z^3} \\
 & \quad 6z^2 - 2z^3 \\
 & \quad \underline{6z^2 - 9z^3 + 3z^4} \\
 & \qquad 7z^3 - 3z^4 \\
 & \qquad \underline{7z^3 - \frac{21}{2}z^4 + \frac{7}{2}z^5}
\end{array}$$

$$X[z] = 2z + 3z^2 + \frac{7}{2}z^3 + \cdots$$

$$\boxed{x[n] = \left\{\cdots \frac{7}{2},\ 3,\ 2,\ \underset{\uparrow}{0}\right\}}$$

(c) $X[z] = \frac{1}{(1-az^{-1})}$; **ROC: $|z| > |a|$**

$$X[z] = \frac{z}{(z-a)}$$

The ROC: $|z| > a$, and it is exterior of the circle of radius $|a|$. Hence, $x[n]$ is a right-sided sequence where $n \geq 0$. The long division is done in such that $X[z]$ is expressed in terms of power of z^{-1} as shown below:

$$\begin{array}{r|l} & 1 + az^{-1} + a^2z^{-2} + a^3a^{-3} + \cdots \\ z - a & z \\ & \underline{z - a} \\ & a \\ & \underline{a - a^2z^{-1}} \\ & a^2z^{-1} \\ & \underline{a^2z^{-1} - a^3z^{-2}} \\ & a^3z^{-2} \\ & \underline{a^3z^{-2} - a^4z^{-3}} \end{array}$$

$$X[z] = 1 + az^{-1} + a^2z^{-2} + a^3z^{-3} + \cdots$$

$$x[n] = \{\underset{\uparrow}{1},\ a,\ a^2,\ a^3, \cdots\}$$

$$x[n] = a^n u[n]$$

For ROC: $|z| < |a|$, $x[n]$ sequence is left-sided

$$\begin{array}{r|l} & -a^{-1}z - a^{-2}z^2 - a^{-3}z^3 \cdots \\ -a + z & z \\ & \underline{z - a^{-1}z^2} \\ & a^{-1}z^2 \\ & \underline{a^{-1}z^2 - a^{-2}z^3} \\ & a^{-2}z^3 \\ & \underline{a^{-2}z^3 - a^{-3}z^4} \end{array}$$

$$X[z] = -a^{-1}z - a^{-2}z^2 - a^{-3}z^3 + \cdots$$

$$x[n] = \left\{\cdots,\ \frac{1}{a^3},\ -\frac{1}{a^2},\ -\frac{1}{a},\ \underset{\uparrow}{0}\right\}$$

$$x[n] = -a^n u[-n-1]$$

Example 1.87

The input to the causal LTI system is

$$x[n] = u[-n-1] + \left(\frac{1}{2}\right)^n u[n]$$

The z-transform of the output of the system is

$$Y[z] = \frac{-\frac{1}{2}z^{-1}}{\left(1-\frac{1}{2}z^{-1}\right)(1+z^{-1})}$$

Determine $H[z]$, the z-transform of the impulse response and also determine the output $y[n]$.

(*Anna University, December, 2007*)

Solution

$$X[z] = -\frac{z}{(z-1)} + \frac{z}{(z-0.5)}$$

$$= \frac{-0.5z}{(z-1)(z-0.5)}$$

$$Y[z] = \frac{-\frac{1}{2}z^{-1}}{\left(1-\frac{1}{2}z^{-1}\right)(1+z^{-1})}$$

$$= \frac{-\frac{1}{2}z}{(z-0.5)(z+1)}$$

$$H[z] = \frac{Y[z]}{X[z]}$$

$$= \frac{(-0.5)z(z-1)(z-0.5)}{(z-0.5)(z+1)(-0.5)z}$$

$$= \frac{(z-1)}{(z+1)}$$

$$\frac{H[z]}{z} = \frac{(z-1)}{z(z+1)}$$

$$= \frac{A_1}{z} + \frac{A_2}{z+1}$$

$$(z-1) = A_1(z+1) + A_2 z$$

Substitute $z = 0$

$$-1 = A_1$$

Substitute $z = -1$

$$-2 = -A_2; \qquad A_2 = 2$$

$$H[z] = -1 + \frac{2z}{(z+1)}$$

$$\boxed{h[n] = -\delta[n] + (-1)^n 2u[n]}$$

$$Y[z] = \frac{-\frac{1}{2}z}{(z-0.5)(z+1)}$$

$$\frac{Y[z]}{z} = \frac{-\frac{1}{2}}{(z-0.5)(z+1)}$$

$$= \frac{A_1}{z-0.5} + \frac{A_2}{z+1}$$

$$-\frac{1}{2} = A_1(z+1) + A_2(z-0.5)$$

Substitute $z = 0.5$

$$-\frac{1}{2} = \frac{3}{2}A_1; \qquad A_1 = -\frac{1}{3}$$

Substitute $z = -1$

$$-\frac{1}{2} = -\frac{3}{2}A_2; \qquad A_2 = \frac{1}{3}$$

$$Y[z] = \frac{1}{3}\left[-\frac{1}{(z-0.5)} + \frac{1}{(z+1)}\right]$$

$$\boxed{y[n] = \frac{1}{3}\left[-\left(\frac{1}{2}\right)^n + (-1)^n\right]u[n]}$$

Example 1.88

Given

$$y[n] = \left(\frac{1}{4}\right)^n u[n]$$

$$x[n] = \left(\frac{1}{2}\right)^n u[-n-1]$$

Find the system function and hence the system impulse response.

Solution

$$y[n] = \left(\frac{1}{4}\right)^n u[n]$$

$$Y[z] = \frac{z}{\left(z - \frac{1}{4}\right)} \qquad |z| > \frac{1}{4}$$

$$x[n] = \left(\frac{1}{2}\right)^n u[-n-1]$$

$$X[z] = -\frac{z}{\left(z - \frac{1}{2}\right)} \qquad |z| < \frac{1}{2}$$

$$H[z] = \frac{Y[z]}{X[z]}$$

$$\boxed{H[z] = \frac{-\left(z - \frac{1}{2}\right)}{\left(z - \frac{1}{4}\right)}}$$

$$\frac{H[z]}{z} = \frac{-\left(z - \frac{1}{2}\right)}{z\left(z - \frac{1}{4}\right)}$$

$$= \frac{A_1}{z} + \frac{A_2}{z\left(z - \frac{1}{4}\right)}$$

$$\frac{1}{2} - z = A_1\left(z - \frac{1}{4}\right) + A_2 z$$

Substitute $z = 0$

$$\frac{1}{2} = -\frac{1}{4}A_1; \qquad A_1 = -2$$

Substitute $z = \frac{1}{4}$

$$\frac{1}{2} = \frac{1}{4}A_2; \qquad A_2 = 2$$

$$H[z] = 2\left[-1 + \frac{z}{\left(z - \frac{1}{4}\right)}\right]$$

$$\boxed{h[n] = 2\left[-\delta[n] + \left(\frac{1}{4}\right)^n\right] u[n]}$$

Example 1.89

Consider the following system functions:

$$(a) \qquad H[z] = \frac{(1 + 4z^{-1} + z^{-2})}{(2z^{-1} + 5z^{-2} + z^{-3})}$$

$$(b) \qquad H[z] = \frac{(z-1)(z+2)}{\left(z - \frac{1}{2}\right)\left(z - \frac{3}{4}\right)} \qquad \text{ROC: } |z| > \frac{3}{4}$$

$$(c) \qquad H[z] = \frac{(z-1)(z+2)}{\left(z - \frac{1}{2}\right)\left(z - \frac{3}{4}\right)} \qquad \text{ROC: } |z| < \frac{1}{2}$$

Determine whether these systems are causal or not.

Solution

(*a*) $\boldsymbol{H[z] = \frac{(1+4z^{-1}+z^{-2})}{(2z^{-1}+5z^{-2}+z^{-3})}}$

$$H[z] = \frac{(z^3 + 4z^2 + z)}{(2z^2 + 5z + 1)}$$

$H[z]$ is irrational since the degree of the numerator polynomial is greater than the denominator polynomial.

The System is Non-causal.

(*b*) $\boldsymbol{H[z] = \frac{(z-1)(z+2)}{\left(z-\frac{1}{2}\right)\left(z-\frac{3}{4}\right)}}$; **ROC:** $\boldsymbol{|z| > \frac{3}{4}}$

The ROC is the exterior of the circle passing through the outermost pole of $H[z]$. Hence $h[n]$, the impulse response is right-sided.

The System is Causal.

(*c*) $\boldsymbol{H[z] = \frac{(z-1)(z+2)}{\left(z-\frac{1}{2}\right)\left(z-\frac{3}{4}\right)}}$ **ROC :** $\boldsymbol{|z| < \frac{1}{2}}$

The ROC is the interior of the circle passing through the innermost pole of $H[z]$. Hence $h[n]$, the impulse response is left-sided.

The System is Non-causal.

Example 1.90

Consider the following system function

$$H[z] = \frac{\left(2 - \frac{13}{4}z^{-1}\right)}{\left(1 - \frac{1}{4}z^{-1}\right)\left(1 - 3z^{-1}\right)}$$

Determine the causality and stability of the system for the following cases.

(*a*) ROC: $|z| > 3$;
(*b*) ROC: $|z| < \frac{1}{4}$;
(*c*) ROC: $\frac{1}{4} < |z| < 3$.

Solution

$$H[z] = \frac{\left(2 - \frac{13}{4}z^{-1}\right)}{\left(1 - \frac{1}{4}z^{-1}\right)\left(1 - 3z^{-1}\right)}$$

$$= \frac{z\left(2z - \frac{13}{4}\right)}{\left(z - \frac{1}{4}\right)(z - 3)}$$

(*a*) **ROC: $|z| > 3$**
The ROC is the exterior of the circle passing through the outermost pole of $H[z]$ which is rational (the denominator and numerator polynomials have same order). The impulse response $h[n]$ is a right-sided sequence. Hence, $H[z]$ is causal. The ROC does not contain unit circle. Hence, $h[n]$ is not summable. The system is unstable. Refer to Figure 1.105(*a*).

The System is Causal and Unstable.

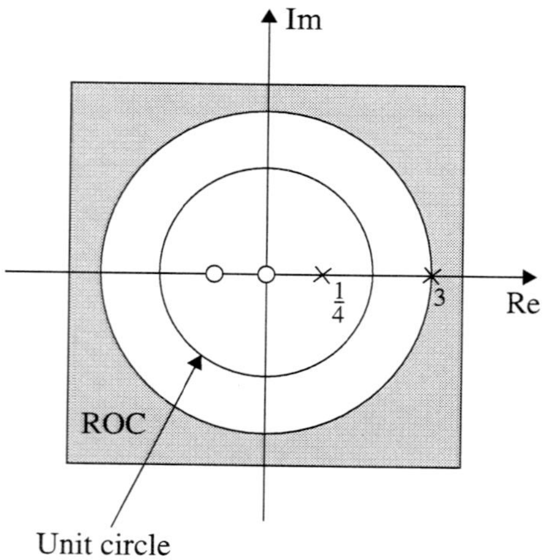

Figure 1.105 (*a*) Causal and stable system.

(*b*) **ROC: $|z| < \frac{1}{4}$**
The ROC is the interior of the circle passing through the innermost pole of $H[z]$. The impulse response is a left-sided sequence. $H[z]$ is therefore non-causal.

The ROC does not include the unit circle. The $h[n]$ is growing exponential negative sequence. The system is unstable. Refer to Figure 1.105(b).

The System is Non-causal and Unstable.

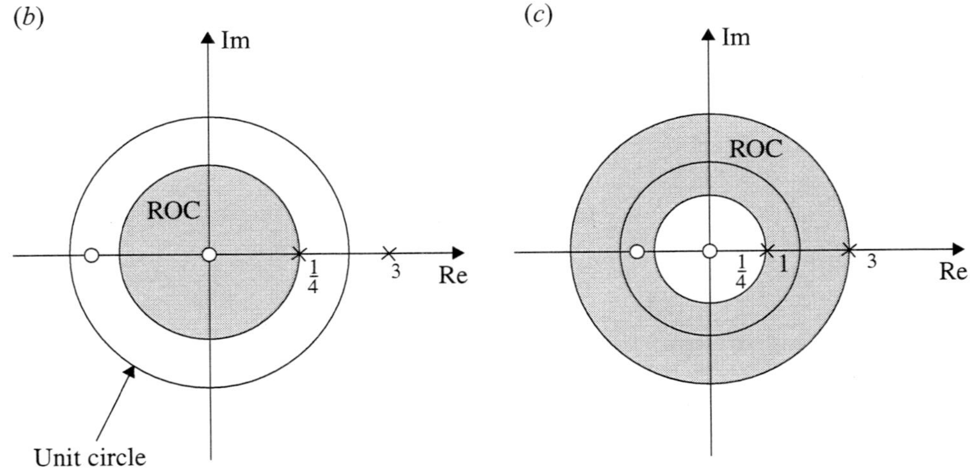

Figure 1.105 (b) Non-causal and unstable system and (c) Non-causal and stable system.

(c) **ROC: $\frac{1}{4} < |z| < 3$**
The ROC is to the left of the outermost pole and to the right innermost pole. Hence, $h[n]$ will have right and left-sided sequences, which is non-causal. The ROC includes unit circle, which means that the right and left side sequences of $h[n]$ will exponentially decay and the system is stable. Refer to Figure 1.105(c).

The System is Non-causal and Stable.

The system cannot be both Causal and Stable.

Example 1.91

Consider the following system function

$$H[z] = \frac{z}{\left(z - \frac{1}{4}\right)\left(z + \frac{1}{4}\right)\left(z - \frac{1}{2}\right)}$$

For different possible ROCs, determine the causality, stability and the impulse response of the system.

Solution

$$H[z] = \frac{z}{\left(z-\frac{1}{4}\right)\left(z+\frac{1}{4}\right)\left(z-\frac{1}{2}\right)}$$

The possible ROCs for $H[z]$ to exist are (*a*) ROC: $|z| > \frac{1}{2}$, (*b*) ROC: $|z| < \frac{1}{4}$ and (*c*) ROC: $\frac{1}{4} < |z| < \frac{1}{2}$.

$$\frac{H[z]}{z} = \frac{1}{\left(z-\frac{1}{4}\right)\left(z+\frac{1}{4}\right)\left(z-\frac{1}{2}\right)}$$

$$= \frac{A_1}{\left(z-\frac{1}{4}\right)} + \frac{A_2}{\left(z+\frac{1}{4}\right)} + \frac{A_3}{\left(z-\frac{1}{2}\right)}$$

$$1 = A_1\left(z+\frac{1}{4}\right)\left(z-\frac{1}{2}\right) + A_2\left(z-\frac{1}{4}\right)\left(z-\frac{1}{2}\right) + A_3\left(z-\frac{1}{4}\right)\left(z+\frac{1}{4}\right)$$

Substitute $z = \frac{1}{4}$

$$1 = A_1\left(\frac{1}{4}+\frac{1}{4}\right)\left(\frac{1}{4}-\frac{1}{2}\right); \qquad A_1 = -8$$

Substitute $z = -\frac{1}{4}$

$$1 = A_2\left(-\frac{1}{4}-\frac{1}{4}\right)\left(-\frac{1}{4}-\frac{1}{2}\right); \qquad A_2 = \frac{8}{3}$$

Substitute $z = \frac{1}{2}$

$$1 = A_3\left(\frac{1}{2}-\frac{1}{4}\right)\left(\frac{1}{2}+\frac{1}{4}\right); \qquad A_3 = \frac{16}{3}$$

$$H[z] = -\frac{8z}{\left(z-\frac{1}{4}\right)} + \frac{8}{3}\frac{z}{\left(z+\frac{1}{4}\right)} + \frac{16}{3}\frac{z}{\left(z-\frac{1}{2}\right)}$$

(*a*) **ROC: $|z| > \frac{1}{2}$**

The pole-zero diagram and the ROC are shown in Figure 1.106(*a*). From Figure 1.106(*a*) the ROC is the exterior of the outermost pole $z = \frac{1}{2}$. Further, ROC includes unit circle. Thus $h[n]$ is a right-sided sequence and hence $H[z]$ is causal. Since ROC includes unit circle and all the poles are within unit circle, the system is stable.

Now,

$$H[z] = -\frac{8z}{\left(z-\frac{1}{4}\right)} + \frac{8}{3}\frac{z}{\left(z+\frac{1}{4}\right)} + \frac{16}{3}\frac{z}{\left(z-\frac{1}{2}\right)}$$

$$h[n] = \left[-8\left(\frac{1}{4}\right)^n + \frac{8}{3}\left(-\frac{1}{4}\right)^n + \frac{16}{3}\left(\frac{1}{2}\right)^n\right]u[n]$$

The System is Causal and Stable.

(*b*) **ROC: $|z| < \frac{1}{4}$**

For ROC: $|z| < \frac{1}{4}$, the pole zero diagram is shown in Figure 1.106(*b*). The ROC is interior of the circle passing through the innermost pole. Hence, the system is non-causal. The condition that the ROC does not include unit circle implies that the system is unstable. The sequence $h[n]$ is left-sided. This is obtained as

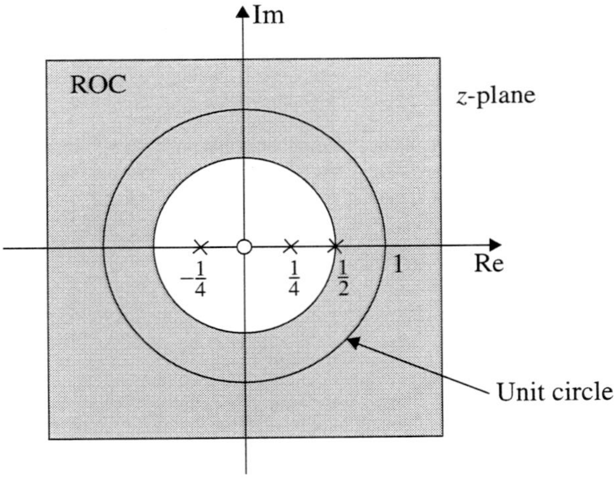

Figure 1.106 (*a*) Pole zero diagram and ROC: $|z| > \frac{1}{2}$ of Example 1.91.

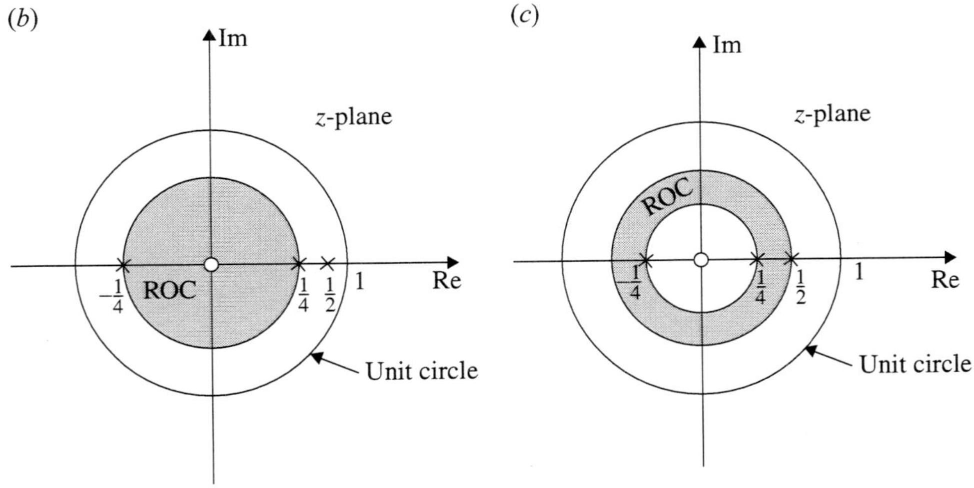

Figure 1.106 (*b*) Pole zero diagram and ROC: $|z| < \frac{1}{4}$ and (*c*) Pole-zero diagram and ROC: $\frac{1}{4} < |z| < \frac{1}{2}$.

follows.

$$H[z] = -\frac{8z}{\left(z-\frac{1}{4}\right)} + \frac{8}{3}\frac{z}{\left(z+\frac{1}{4}\right)} + \frac{16}{3}\frac{z}{\left(z-\frac{1}{2}\right)}$$

$$h[n] = \left[8\left(\frac{1}{4}\right)^n - \frac{8}{3}\left(-\frac{1}{4}\right)^n - \frac{16}{3}\left(\frac{1}{2}\right)^n\right]u[-n-1]$$

The left-sided sequence $u[-n-1]$ will exponentially increase for $n < 0$ and makes the system unstable.

The System is Non-causal and Unstable.

(c) **ROC:** $\frac{1}{4} < |z| < \frac{1}{2}$
The pole-zero diagram and ROC of $H[z]$ are shown in Figure 1.106(c). The ROC is concentric ring for $\frac{1}{4} < |z| < \frac{1}{2}$. The $h[n]$ sequences die to the poles at $z = \frac{1}{4}$ and $z = -\frac{1}{4}$ are right-sided and the sequence due to the pole $z = \frac{1}{2}$ is left-sided. Hence, the system is non-causal. The ROC does not include the unit circle and hence the system is unstable. The impulse response is obtained as follows.

$$H[z] = -\frac{8z}{\left(z-\frac{1}{4}\right)} + \frac{8}{3}\frac{z}{\left(z+\frac{1}{4}\right)} + \frac{16}{3}\frac{z}{\left(z-\frac{1}{2}\right)}$$

$$\boxed{h[n] = \left[-8\left(\frac{1}{4}\right)^n + \frac{8}{3}\left(-\frac{1}{4}\right)^n\right]u[n] - \frac{16}{3}\left(\frac{1}{2}\right)^n u[-n-1]}$$

The term $-\frac{16}{3}(1/2)^n u[-n-1]$ for $n < 0$ yields exponentially increasing sequence.

The System is Non-causal and Unstable.

1.27 z-transform Solution of Linear Difference Equations

As in the case of Laplace transform with differential equation, to get the solution in time domain z-transform is used to solve difference equation to get the output sequence as a function of n. By using the time shift property of z-transform, the difference equation is converted into algebraic equation, taking into account the initial conditions. by taking z-inverse transform, the time domain solution is obtained.

1.27.1 Right Shift (Delay)

If

$$x[n]u[n] \overset{Z}{\longleftrightarrow} X[z]$$

then

$$x[n-1]u[n-1] \overset{Z}{\longleftrightarrow} \frac{1}{z}X[z]$$

$$x[n-1]u[n] \overset{Z}{\longleftrightarrow} \frac{1}{z}X[z] + x[-1]$$

$$x[n-2]u[n] \overset{Z}{\longleftrightarrow} \frac{1}{z^2}X[z] + \frac{1}{z}x[-1] + x[-2]$$

In general,

$$\boxed{x[n-m]u[n] \overset{Z}{\longleftrightarrow} z^{-m}X[z] + z^{-m}\sum_{n=1}^{m} x[-n]z^{n}} \tag{1.101}$$

1.27.2 Left Shift (Advance)

If

$$x[n]u[n] \overset{Z}{\longleftrightarrow} X[z]$$

$$x[n+1]u[n] \overset{Z}{\longleftrightarrow} zX[z] - zx[0]$$

$$x[n+2]u[n] \overset{Z}{\longleftrightarrow} z^2X[z] - z^2x[0] - zx[1]$$

In general,

$$\boxed{x[n+m]u[n] \overset{Z}{\longleftrightarrow} z^{m}x[z] - z^{m}\sum_{n=0}^{m-1} x[n]z^{-n}} \tag{1.102}$$

Equations (1.101) and (1.102) are used to convert difference equations with initial conditions to algebraic equations in z. Application of Equation (1.102), the delay shift is more common. The following examples illustrate the above procedure.

Example 1.92

Consider the following linear constant coefficient difference equation

$$y[n] - \frac{3}{4}y[n-1] + \frac{1}{8}y[n-2] = 2x[n-1]$$

Determine $y[n]$ when $x[n] = \delta[n]$ and $y[n] = 0,\ n < 0$.

(Anna University, May and December, 2007)

Solution If $y[n] = 0,\ n = 0$ implies the initial conditions are zero. Taking z-transform on both sides of the given equation we get

$$\left[1 - \frac{3}{4}z^{-1} + \frac{1}{8}z^{-2}\right] Y[z] = 2z^{-1}X[z]$$

For $\delta[n]$, $X[z] = 1$

$$Y[z] = \frac{2z^{-1}}{1 - \frac{3}{4}z^{-1} + \frac{1}{8}z^{-2}}$$

$$= \frac{2z}{z^2 - \frac{3}{4}z + \frac{1}{8}}$$

$$\frac{Y[z]}{z} = \frac{2}{\left(z - \frac{1}{2}\right)\left(z - \frac{1}{4}\right)}$$

$$= \frac{A_1}{\left(z - \frac{1}{2}\right)} + \frac{A_2}{\left(z - \frac{1}{4}\right)}$$

$$2 = A_1\left(z - \frac{1}{4}\right) + A_2\left(z - \frac{1}{2}\right)$$

Substitute $z = \frac{1}{2}$

$$2 = A_1\frac{1}{4}; \qquad A_1 = 8$$

Substitute $z = \frac{1}{4}$

$$2 = A_2\left(-\frac{1}{4}\right); \qquad A_2 = -8$$

$$Y[z] = 8\left[\frac{z}{\left(z - \frac{1}{2}\right)} - \frac{z}{\left(z - \frac{1}{4}\right)}\right]$$

$$\boxed{y[n] = 8\left[\left(\frac{1}{2}\right)^n - \left(\frac{1}{4}\right)^n\right]u[n] \qquad \text{ROC: } |z| > \frac{1}{2}}$$

Example 1.93

$$y[n+2] + 1.1y[n+1] + 0.3y[n] = x[n+1] + x[n]$$

where $x[n] = (-4)^{-n}u[n]$. Find $y[n]$ if the initial conditions are zero.

Solution Taking z-transform using left shift property we get

$$[z^2 + 1.1z + 0.3]Y[z] = [z + 1]X[z]$$
$$x[n] = (-4)^{-n}u[n]$$

$$X[z] = \frac{z}{\left(z + \frac{1}{4}\right)}$$

$$Y[z] = \frac{z(z+1)}{\left(z + \frac{1}{4}\right)(z^2 + 1.1z + 0.3)}$$

$$= \frac{z(z+1)}{\left(z + \frac{1}{4}\right)(z + 0.5)(z + 0.6)}$$

$$\frac{Y[z]}{z} = \frac{(z+1)}{\left(z + \frac{1}{4}\right)(z + 0.5)(z + 0.6)}$$

$$= \frac{A_1}{\left(z + \frac{1}{4}\right)} + \frac{A_2}{(z + 0.5)} + \frac{A_3}{(z + 0.6)}$$

$$(z+1) = A_1(z + 0.5)(z + 0.6) + A_2\left(z + \frac{1}{4}\right)(z + 0.6)$$
$$+ A_3\left(z + \frac{1}{4}\right)(z + 0.5)$$

Substitute $z = -\frac{1}{4}$

$$\left(-\frac{1}{4} + 1\right) = A_1\left(-\frac{1}{4} + 0.5\right)\left(-\frac{1}{4} + 0.6\right); \qquad A_1 = 8.57$$

Substitute $z = -0.5$

$$(-0.5 + 1) = A_2\left(-0.5 + \frac{1}{4}\right)(-0.5 + 0.6); \qquad A_2 = -20$$

Substitute $z = -0.6$

$$(-0.6 + 1) = A_3\left(-0.6 + \frac{1}{4}\right)(-0.6 + 0.5); \qquad A_3 = 11.43$$

$$Y[z] = \frac{8.57z}{\left(z + \frac{1}{4}\right)} - \frac{20z}{(z + 0.5)} + \frac{11.43}{(z + 0.6)}$$

$$\boxed{y[n] = \left[8.57\left(-\frac{1}{4}\right)^n - 20\,(-0.5)^n + 11.43(-0.6)^n\right]u[n]}$$

Example 1.94

A causal LTI system is described by the difference equation

$$y[n] = y[n-1] + y[n-2] + x[n-1]$$

Find (*a*) System function for this system and (*b*) Unit impulse response of the system.

(*Anna University, April, 2008*)

Solution Taking z-transform on both sides of the equation and making use of right shift property we get

$$[1 - z^{-1} - z^{-2}]Y[z] = z^{-1}X[z]$$

(*a*)

$$H[z] = \frac{Y[z]}{X[z]}$$

$$\boxed{H[z] = \frac{z^{-1}}{(1 - z^{-1} - z^{-2})}}$$

(*b*)

$$H[z] = \frac{z}{(z^{-2} - z - 1)}$$

$$\frac{H[z]}{z} = \frac{1}{(z - 1.618)(z + 0.618)}$$

$$= \frac{A_1}{(z - 1.618)} + \frac{A_2}{(z + 1.618)}$$

$$1 = A_1(z + 0.618) + A_2(z - 1.618)$$

Substitute $z = 1.618$

$$1 = A_1\,(1.618 + 0.618)\,; \qquad A_1 = 0.447$$

Substitute $z = -0.618$

$$1 = A_2\,(-0.618 - 1.618)\,; \qquad A_2 = -0.447$$

$$H[z] = 0.447\left[\frac{z}{z - 1.618} - \frac{z}{z + 0.618}\right]$$

$$\boxed{h[n] = 0.447\left[(1.618)^n - (-0.618)^n\right]u[n]}$$

Example 1.95

Find the output response of the discrete time system described by the following difference equation

$$y[n] - \frac{3}{4}y[n-1] + \frac{1}{8}y[n-2] = x[n]$$

the initial conditions are $y[-1] = 0$ and $y = [-2] = 1$. The input $x[n] = \left(\frac{1}{5}\right)^n u[n]$.

Solution

Taking z-transform on both sides of the above equation we get

$$Y[z] - \frac{3}{4}[z^{-1}Y[z] + y[-1]] + \frac{1}{8}[z^{-2}Y[z] + z^{-1}y[-1] + y[-2]] = X[z]$$

$$\left[1 - \frac{3}{4}z^{-1} + \frac{1}{8}z^{-2}\right]Y[z] = -\frac{1}{8} + \frac{z}{\left(z - \frac{1}{5}\right)}$$

$$\frac{\left[z^2 - \frac{3}{4}z + \frac{1}{8}\right]}{z^2}Y[z] = -\frac{1}{8} + \frac{z}{\left(z - \frac{1}{5}\right)}$$

$$\frac{Y[z]}{z} = -\frac{z}{8\left(z - \frac{1}{4}\right)\left(z - \frac{1}{2}\right)} + \frac{z^2}{\left(z - \frac{1}{5}\right)\left(z - \frac{1}{4}\right)\left(z - \frac{1}{2}\right)}$$

$$= Y_1[z] + Y_2[z]$$

$$Y_1[z] = -\frac{z}{8\left(z - \frac{1}{4}\right)\left(z - \frac{1}{2}\right)}$$

$$= -\frac{A_1}{\left(z - \frac{1}{4}\right)} + \frac{A_2}{\left(z - \frac{1}{2}\right)}$$

$$-\frac{z}{8} = A_1\left(z - \frac{1}{2}\right) + A_2\left(z - \frac{1}{4}\right)$$

Substitute $z = \frac{1}{4}$

$$-\frac{1}{4}\frac{1}{8} = -A_1\frac{1}{4}; \qquad A_1 = \frac{1}{8}$$

Substitute $z = \frac{1}{2}$

$$-\frac{1}{2}\frac{1}{8} = A_2\frac{1}{4}; \qquad A_2 = -\frac{1}{4}$$

$$Y_1[z] = \frac{1}{8\left(z-\frac{1}{4}\right)} - \frac{1}{4\left(z-\frac{1}{2}\right)}$$

$$Y_2[z] = \frac{z^2}{\left(z-\frac{1}{5}\right)\left(z-\frac{1}{4}\right)\left(z-\frac{1}{2}\right)}$$

$$z^2 = A_1\left(z-\frac{1}{4}\right)\left(z-\frac{1}{2}\right) + A_2\left(z-\frac{1}{5}\right)\left(z-\frac{1}{2}\right) + A_3\left(z-\frac{1}{5}\right)\left(z-\frac{1}{4}\right)$$

Substitute $z = \frac{1}{5}$

$$\frac{1}{25} = A_1\left(\frac{1}{5}-\frac{1}{4}\right)\left(\frac{1}{5}-\frac{1}{2}\right); \qquad A_1 = \frac{8}{3}$$

Substitute $z = \frac{1}{4}$

$$\frac{1}{16} = A_2\left(\frac{1}{4}-\frac{1}{5}\right)\left(\frac{1}{4}-\frac{1}{2}\right); \qquad A_2 = -5$$

Substitute $z = \frac{1}{2}$

$$\frac{1}{4} = A_3\left(\frac{1}{2}-\frac{1}{5}\right)\left(\frac{1}{2}-\frac{1}{4}\right); \qquad A_3 = \frac{10}{3}$$

$$Y_2[z] = \frac{8}{3}\frac{1}{\left(z-\frac{1}{5}\right)} - \frac{5}{\left(z-\frac{1}{4}\right)} + \frac{10}{3}\frac{1}{\left(z-\frac{1}{2}\right)}$$

$$Y[z] = \frac{z}{8\left(z-\frac{1}{4}\right)} - \frac{z}{4\left(z-\frac{1}{2}\right)} + \frac{8}{3}\frac{z}{\left(z-\frac{1}{5}\right)} - \frac{5z}{\left(z-\frac{1}{4}\right)} + \frac{10}{3}\frac{z}{\left(z-\frac{1}{2}\right)}$$

$$= -\frac{39}{8}\frac{z}{\left(z-\frac{1}{4}\right)} + \frac{37}{12}\frac{z}{\left(z-\frac{1}{2}\right)} + \frac{8}{3}\frac{z}{\left(z-\frac{1}{5}\right)}$$

$$\boxed{y[n] = \left[-\frac{39}{8}\left(\frac{1}{4}\right)^n + \frac{37}{12}\left(\frac{1}{2}\right)^n + \frac{8}{3}\left(\frac{1}{5}\right)^n\right]u[n]}$$

Example 1.96

Find the response of the LTID system described by the following difference equation

$$y[n+2] + y[n+1] + 0.24y[n] = x[n+1] + 2x[n]$$

where $x[n] = (\frac{1}{2})^n u[n]$ and all the initial conditions are zero.

Solution

When the initial conditions are zero.

$$y[n+2] \overset{Z}{\longleftrightarrow} z^2 Y[z]$$

$$y[n+1] \overset{Z}{\longleftrightarrow} zY[z]$$

$$x[n+1] \overset{Z}{\longleftrightarrow} zX[z]$$

$$\left(\frac{1}{2}\right)^2 u[n] \overset{Z}{\longleftrightarrow} \frac{z}{(z-0.5)}$$

The given difference equation can be written in the following form after taking z-transform on both sides.

$$[z^2 + z + 0.24]Y[z] = [z+2]\frac{z}{(z-0.5)}$$

$$(z^2 + z + 0.24) = (z+0.6)(z+0.4)$$

$$\frac{Y[z]}{z} = \frac{(z+2)}{(z-0.5)(z+0.6)(z+0.4)}$$

$$= \frac{A_1}{(z-0.5)} + \frac{A_2}{(z+0.6)} + \frac{A_3}{(z+0.4)}$$

$$(z+2) = A_1(z+0.6)(z+0.4) + A_2(z-0.5)(z+0.4) + A_3(z-0.5)(z+0.6)$$

Substitute $z = 0.5$

$$2.5 = A_1(1.1)(0.9); \qquad A_1 = 2.525$$

Substitute $z = -0.6$

$$1.4 = A_2(-1.1)(-0.2); \qquad A_2 = 6.36$$

Substitute $z = -0.4$

$$1.6 = A_3(-0.9)(-0.2); \qquad A_3 = -8.89$$

$$Y[z] = 2.525\frac{z}{(z-0.5)} + 6.36\frac{z}{(z+0.6)} - 8.89\frac{z}{(z+0.4)}$$

$$\boxed{y[n] = \left[2.525(0.5)^n + 6.36(-0.6)^n - 8.89(-0.4)^n\right] u[n]}$$

Summary

- Signals are broadly classified as continuous time (CT) and discrete time (DT) signals. They are further classified as deterministic and stochastic, periodic and non-periodic, odd and even and energy and power signals.

- Basic DT signals include impulse, step, ramp, parabolic, rectangular pulse, triangular pulse, signum function, sinc function, sinusoid, real and complex exponentials.
- Basic operations on DT signals include addition, multiplication, amplitude scaling, time scaling , time shifting, reflection or folding and amplitude inverted signals.
- In time shifting of DT signal, for $x(n+n_0)$ and $x(-n-n_0)$ the time shift is made to the left of $x(n)$ and $x(-n)$ respectively by n_0. For $x(n-n_0)$ and $x(-n+n_0)$ the time shift is made to the right of the $x(n)$ and $x(-n)$ respectively by n_0.
- To plot DT signals, the operation performed is in the following sequence. The signal is folded (if necessary), time shifted, time scaled, amplitude scaled and inverted.
- Signals are classified as even signals and odd signals. Even signals are **symmetric** about the vertical axis whereas odd signals are **anti-symmetric** about the time origin. Odd signals pass through the origin. The product of two even signals or two odd signals is an even signal. The product of an even and an odd signal is an odd signal.
- A DT signal which repeats itself every N sequence is called a periodic signal. If the signal is not periodic it is called an aperiodic or non-periodic signal. The necessary condition for the composite of two or more signals to be periodic is that the individual signal should be periodic.
- A signal is an energy signal iff the total energy of the signal satisfies the condition $0 < E < \infty$. A signal is called a power signal iff the average power of the signal satisfies the condition $0 < P < \infty$. If the energy of a signal is finite, the average power is zero. If the power of the signal is finite, the signal has infinite energy. All periodic signals are power signals. However all power signals need not be periodic. Signals which are deterministic and non-periodic are usually energy signals. Some signals are neither energy signal nor power signal.
- The system is broadly classified as continuous and discrete time system.
- The DT systems are further classified based on the property of causality, linearity, time invariancy, invertibility, memory and stability.
- A discrete time system is said to be causal if the impulse response $h(n) = 0$ for $n < 0$.
- If the impulse response of a discrete time system is absolutely summable, then the system is said to be BIBO stable.
- Step response $s(n)$ is obtained from impulse response $h(n)$ using the mathematical expression

$$s(n) = \sum_{k=0}^{n} h(k)$$

- The z-transform for discrete time signals and systems have been developed. This resembles corresponding treatment of Laplace transform for continuous time system.
- A definite connection exists between Laplace transform, Fourier transform and z-transform. The Laplace transform reduces to Fourier transform on the

imaginary axis in the s-plane. Then z-transform reduces to Fourier transform on the unit circle in the complex z-plane.

- For the causal signals system (right-sided), the z-transform exists if the ROC is exterior of the circle which passes through the outermost pole of the system function. For the anti-causal signal and system (left-sided) the z-transform exists if the ROC is interior of the circle which passes through the innermost pole of the system. For the right and left-sided signals, the ROC is a ring which does not include any pole of system function.
- The application of the properties of z-transform very much simplifies the procedure to determine z-transform and inverse z-transform.
- For an LTID system to be causal, the system function should be rational and the ROC is the exterior of the circle which passes through the outermost pole of the system function $H[z]$.
- An LTID system is said to be stable if the ROC of the system function $H[z]$ includes the unit circle.
- An LTID system is said to be causal and stable if all the poles of the system function $H[z]$ lie inside the unit circle in the z-plane.
- Using the properties of z-transform, LTID systems described by constant coefficient difference equation can be converted into algebraic equations and easily analyzed. The solution obtained are classified as zero state response, zero input response, natural response and forced response.

Short Questions and Answers

1. **How are signals classified?**
   Signals are generally classified as CT and DT signal. They are further classified as deterministic and non-deterministic, odd and even, periodic and non-periodic and power and energy signals.
2. **What are odd and even signals?**
   A continuous CT signal is said to be an even signal if it satisfies the condition $x(-t) = x(t)$ for all t. It is said to be an odd signal if $x(-t) = -x(t)$ for all t. For a DT signal if $x[-n] = x[n]$ condition is satisfied, it is an even sequence (signal). If $x[-n] = -x[n]$, the sequence is called odd sequence.
3. **How even and odd components of a signal are mathematically expressed?**

$$x_e[n] = \frac{1}{2}\{x[n] + x[-n]\}$$

$$x_0[n] = \frac{1}{2}\{x[n] - x[-n]\}$$

4. **What are periodic and non-periodic signals?**
   A discrete time signal is said to be a period signal if it satisfies the condition $x[n] = x[n+N]$ for all n. A signal which is not periodic is said to be non-periodic.
5. **What is the fundamental period of a periodic signal? What is fundamental frequency?**

A DT signal is said to be periodic if it satisfies the condition $x(n) = x(n+N)$. If this condition is satisfied for $N = N_0$, it is also satisfied for $N = 2N_0, 3N_0, \ldots$. The smallest value of N that satisfies the above condition is called fundamental period. The fundamental frequency $f_0 = \frac{1}{N_0}$ Hz. It is also expressed as $\omega_0 = \frac{2\pi}{N_0}$ rad.

6. **What are power and energy signals?**
   For a DT signal $x[n]$, the total energy is defined as

$$E = \sum_{n=-\infty}^{\infty} x^2[n]$$

   The average power is defined as

$$P = \underset{T\to\infty}{Lt} \frac{1}{2N+1} \sum_{n=-N}^{N} x^2[n]$$

7. **Determine whether the signal $x[n] = \cos[0.1\pi n]$ is periodic?**
   The signal $x[n]$ is periodic with fundamental period $N_0 = 20$.
8. **Find whether the signal $x[n] = 5\cos[6\pi n]$ is periodic?**
   The signal is periodic with fundamental period $N_0 = 1$.
9. **Find the average power of the signal?**

$$x[n] = u[n] - u[n-N]$$

   The average power $P = 1$.
10. **Find the total energy of**

$$x[n] = \{1, \underset{\uparrow}{1}, 1\}$$

   The total energy $E = 3$.
11. **If the discrete time signal $x[n] = \{0, 0, 0, 3, 2, 1, -1, -7, 6\}$ then find $y[n] = x[2n-3]$?**

$$y[n] = \{0, 0, 0, 3, 1, -7\}$$

12. **What is the energy of the signal $x[n] = u[n] - u[n-6]$?**

$$E = 6$$

13. **What are the properties of systems?**
   Systems are generally classified as continuous and discrete time systems. Further classifications of these systems are done based on their properties which include (*a*) linear and non-linear, (*b*) time invariant and time variant, (*c*) static and dynamic, (*d*) causal and non-causal, (*e*) stable and unstable and (*f*) Invertible and non-invertible.

14. **Define system. What is linear system?**
A system is defined as the interconnection of objects with a definite relationship between objects and attributes.
A system is said to be linear if the weighted sum of several inputs produce weighted sum of outputs. In other words, the system should satisfy the homogeneity and additivity of super position theorem if it is to be linear. Otherwise it is a non-linear system.
15. **What is time invariant and time varying system?**
A system is said to be time invariant if the output due to the delayed input is same as the delayed output due to the input. If the continuous time system is described by the differential equation its coefficients should be time independent for the system to be time invariant. In the case of discrete time system, the coefficients of the difference equation describing the system should be time independent (constant) for the system to be time invariants. If the above conditions are not satisfied the system (CT as well as DT) is said to be time variant.
16. **What are static and dynamic systems?**
If the output of the system depends only on the present input, the system is said to be static or instantaneous. If the output of the system depends on the past and future input, the system is not static and it is called dynamic system. Static system does not require memory and so it is called memoryless system. Dynamic system requires memory and hence, it is called system with memory. System which are described by differential and difference equations are dynamic systems.
17. **What are causal and non-causal systems?**
If the system output depends on present and on past inputs, it is called causal system. If the system output depends on future input it is called non-causal system.
18. **What are stable and unstable systems?**
If the input is bounded and output is also bounded, the system is called BIBO stable system. If the input is bounded and the output is unbounded, the system is unstable. System whose impulse response curve has finite area is also called stable systems.
19. **What are invertible and non-invertible systems?**
A system is said to be invertible if the distinct inputs give distinct outputs.
20. **State the condition for a discrete time LTI system to be causal and stable.**
(Anna University, 2008)
A discrete time LTI system is said to be causal and stable if the poles of the transfer function all lie in the left half s-plane and the Region of Convergence (ROC) is to the right of the right most pole.
21. **A certain LTID time system has the following impulse response.**

$$h[n] = \left(\frac{1}{3}\right)^n u[n-2]$$

Is the system both causal and stable?

The response depends on the past input $u[n-2]$ and hence, it is causal.

$$h[n] = \sum_{n=2}^{\infty} \left(\frac{1}{3}\right)^n$$
$$= \frac{1}{6} < \infty$$

The system is stable. The system is both causal and stable.

22. **What is convolution sum?**
If $h(n)$ is the impulse response of a linear time invariant discrete time system and if $x(n)$ is input, then the output $y(n)$ is obtained from the following equation

$$y(n) = \sum_{k=-\infty}^{\infty} x(k)h(n-k)$$

The above equation is called convolution sum. Symbolically it is represented as

$$y(n) = x(n) * h(n)$$

23. **Evaluate $x(n) * \delta(n)$ and $x(n) * \delta(n-n_0)$?**

$$x(n) * \delta(n) = x(n)$$
$$x(n) * \delta(n-n_0) = x(n-n_0)$$

24. **If $x(n) = \delta(n) - 2\delta(n-1) + 3\delta(n-2) - \delta(n+1)$. Express $x(n-1)$ in terms of sequences?**

$$x(n-1) = \delta(n-1) - 2\delta(n-2) + 3\delta(n-3) - \delta(n)$$

25. **$h(n) = \left(\frac{1}{2}\right)^n u(n)$. Find A so that $h(n) - Ah(n-1) = \delta(n)$?**

$$h(n) - h(n-1) = \left(\frac{1}{2}\right)^n u(n) - A\left(\frac{1}{2}\right)^{n-1} u(n-1)$$

If $A = 1/2$

$$h(n) - h(n-1) = \left(\frac{1}{2}\right)^n u(n) - \left(\frac{1}{2}\right)^n u(n-1) = \delta(n)$$

26. **An LTID system has the following impulse response**

$$h(n) = \left(\frac{1}{2}\right)^n u(n+1)$$

Is the system causal and BIBO stable?

The system is non-zero for $n = -1$. Hence, it is non-causal.

$$\sum_{-\infty}^{\infty} h(n) = \sum_{-1}^{\infty} \left(\frac{1}{2}\right)^n$$

$$= \left(\frac{1}{2}\right)^{-1} + \sum_{0}^{\infty} \left(\frac{1}{2}\right)^n$$

$$= 2 + \frac{1}{1 - 1/2} = 4 < \infty$$

The system is BIBO stable.

27. **Define z-transform.**

The z-transform of a discrete time signal $x[n]$ is defined as

$$X[z] = \sum_{n=-\infty}^{\infty} x[n]z^{-n}$$

where z is a complex variable.

28. **Define z-transform pair.**

When the discrete time signal $x[n]$ is z-transformed it is expressed as

$$X[z] = \sum_{n=-\infty}^{\infty} x[n]z^{-n}$$

If we want to recover $x[n]$ form $X[z]$, it is obtained using the following integration

$$x[n] = \frac{1}{2\pi j} \oint X[z]z^{n-1} dz$$

This equation is called as inverse z-transform. The above two equations for z-transform and inverse z-transform are called z-transform pair.

29. **What do you understand by ROC of z-transform?**

The range of values of z for which the function $X[z]$ converges is called region of convergence which is expressed in abbreviated form as ROC.

30. **Mention the properties of ROC.**
    1. The ROC of $X[z]$ is in the form of a ring in the z-plane which is centred about the origin.
    2. The ROC does not include any poles.
    3. For the right-sided sequence $x[n]$, the ROC is the exterior of the outermost pole.
    4. For the left-sided sequence $x[n]$, the ROC is the interior of the innermost pole.
    5. If the sequence $x[n]$ is two sided, then the ROC consist of a ring in the z-plane.

31. **What is the scaling property of z-transform?**
If

$$x[n] \overset{Z}{\longleftrightarrow} X[z] \qquad \text{ROC: } R$$

then

$$a^n x[n] \longleftrightarrow X\left[\frac{z}{a}\right] \qquad \text{ROC: } aR$$

By using multiplication property, the z-transform is obtained by replacing z by $\frac{z}{a}$ with ROC R replaced by aR.

32. **What is the convolution property of z-transform?**
If

$$x_1[n] \overset{Z}{\longleftrightarrow} X_1[z] \qquad \text{ROC: } R_1$$
$$x_2[n] \overset{Z}{\longleftrightarrow} X_2[z] \qquad \text{ROC: } R_2$$

then

$$x_1[n] * x_2[n] \overset{Z}{\longleftrightarrow} X_1[z]X_2[z] \qquad \text{ROC: } R_1 \cap R_2$$

33. **What is difference property in the z-transform?**
If

$$x[n] \overset{Z}{\longleftrightarrow} X[z] \qquad \text{ROC: } R$$

then

$$nx[n] \overset{Z}{\longleftrightarrow} -z\frac{dx[z]}{dz} \qquad \text{ROC: } R$$

34. **What are initial and final value theorems?**
If $x[n] = 0$ for $n < 0$, then

$$x[0] = \underset{z\to\infty}{Lt}\, X[z]$$

is called initial value theorem. According to the finial value theorem if $X[z]$ is the z-transform $x[n]$ and if all the poles of $X[z]$ are inside the unit circle, then the final value of $x[n] = x[\infty]$ is obtained form

$$x[\infty] = \underset{z\to 1}{Lt}\, (z-1)X[z]$$

35. **What do you understand by the time reversal property of z-transform?**
If

$$x[n] \overset{Z}{\longleftrightarrow} X[z] \qquad \text{ROC: } R$$

then

$$x[-n] \overset{Z}{\longleftrightarrow} X\left[\frac{1}{z}\right] \qquad \text{ROC: } \frac{1}{R}$$

Thus, the z-transform of the time reversal signal is obtained by replacing z by its reciprocal and also its ROC by its reciprocal.

36. **What do you understand by causality of an LTID system?**
A linear time invariant discrete time system is said to be causal if the ROC of the system function $H[z]$ is the exterior of the circle containing all the poles of $H[z]$.

37. **What do you understand by stability of an LTID system?**
An LTID system is said to be stable if the ROC of the system function $H[z]$ includes the unit circle in the z-plane.

38. **When the system is said to be both causal and stable?**
An LTID system is said to be both causal and stable if all the poles of the system function $H[z]$ are inside the unit circle in the z-plane.

39. **Define system function.**
System function or transfer function $H[z]$ is defined as the ratio of the z-transform of output sequence $y[n]$ and the input sequence $x[n]$

$$H[z] = \frac{Y[z]}{X[z]}$$

40. **What is the z-transform of $\delta[n-2]$?**

$$\delta[n-2] \overset{Z}{\longleftrightarrow} z^{-2}$$

41. **What is the z-transform of $u[n]$ and $\delta[n]$?**

$$u[n] \overset{Z}{\longleftrightarrow} \frac{z}{(z-1)}$$

$$\delta[n] \overset{Z}{\longleftrightarrow} 1$$

42. **Find the z-transform of $x[n] = u[n] - u[n-5]$.**

$$X[z] = \frac{z}{(z-1)}[1 - z^{-5}]$$

43. **Write the relationship between z-transform and Fourier transform.**
The z-transform reduces to Fourier transform on the unit circle in the complex z-plane.

44. **Write the relationship between z-transform and Laplace transform.**
The Laplace transform and z-transform are related as

$$e^s = z$$

$$X[s] = X[z]\Big|_{z=e^s}$$

45. **What is the inverse z-transform of $X[\frac{z}{a}]$?**

$$X\left[\frac{z}{a}\right] \overset{Z^{-1}}{\longleftrightarrow} a^n x[n]$$

46. **Find the system function of the following first order difference equation $y[n] - 2y[n-1] = x[n] + x[n-1]$?**

$$H[z] = \frac{Y[z]}{X[z]} = \frac{[1+z^{-1}]}{[1-2z^{-1}]}$$
$$= \frac{[z+1]}{[z-2]}$$

Long Answer Type Questions

1. **For the following DT signal find even and odd components**

$$x[n] = \{1, -3, 2, 5, 4\}$$
$$x_e[n] = \{2, 2.5, 1, -1.5, \underset{\uparrow}{1}, -1.5, 1, 2.5, 2\}$$
$$x_0[n] = \{-2, -2.5, -1, 1.5, \underset{\uparrow}{0}, -1.5, 1, 2.5, 2\}$$

2. **Find whether the following signals are periodic. If periodic, find the fundamental period.** **(*a*)** $x[n] = \cos(\frac{n}{8} - \pi)$; **(*b*)** $x[n] = \cos(\frac{\pi}{8} + \frac{\pi}{2}) + \cos(\frac{\pi}{6} - \frac{\pi}{2})$; **(*c*)** $x[n] = \cos(\frac{5\pi N}{12} + \frac{\pi}{2}) + \sin\frac{10\pi n}{8}$; **(*d*)** $x[n] = e^{j3n} + e^{j4\pi n}$.

   (*a*) Not periodic. (*b*) Periodic with fundamental period $N_0 = 48$ samples/sec. (*c*) Periodic with fundamental period $N_0 = 24$ samples/sec. (*d*) Non-periodic.

3. **Given $x[n]$ and $y[n]$**

$$x[-1] = 2$$
$$x[n] = 1 \qquad 1 \le n \le 5$$
$$x[6] = \frac{1}{2}$$
$$= 0 \qquad \text{for other } n$$

Plot (*a*) $x[\frac{n}{2}]$ and (*b*) $E_v x[n]$. *(Anna University, 2007).*

(*a*)

$$x[n] = \{\underset{\uparrow}{2}, 1, 1, 1, 1, 1, 1, 0.5\}$$

$$x\left[\frac{n}{2}\right] = \{\underset{\uparrow}{2}, 0, 1, 0, 1, 0, 1, 0, 1, 0, 1, 0, 1, 0.5\}$$

(*b*)

$$x_e[n] = \{0.25, 0.5, 0.5, 0.5, 0.5, 0.5, \underset{\uparrow}{1}, 0.5, 0.5, 0.5, 0.5, 0.5, 0.25\}$$

4. **Find whether the following signal is periodic. If periodic, find the fundamental period.**

$$x[n] = \cos\left(2\pi n + \frac{\pi}{2}\right) \sin\left(5\pi n - \frac{\pi}{4}\right) \sin\left(8\pi n + \frac{\pi}{2}\right)$$

The signal is periodic. Their fundamental period $N_0 = 2$ samples/sec.

5. **For the systems given below determine whether each of them is (*a*) static, (*b*) causal, (*c*) time invariant, (*d*) linear and (*e*) stable.**

$$\mathbf{y[n] = x[5n]}$$

(*a*) The system response depends on present, past and future inputs. Hence, it is dynamic.
(*b*) Non-causal.
(*c*) The output due to the delayed input is not same as the delayed output. Hence, it is time variant.
(*d*) The weighted sum of the output is same as output due to the weighted sum of the input. The system is linear.
(*e*) If the input $x[5n]$ is bounded, the output $y[n]$ is also bounded. The system is stable.

6.

$$\mathbf{y[k+2] + 3y[k+1] + 4y[k] = x[k]}$$

(*a*) The system is dynamic.
(*b*) The system is causal.
(*c*) The system is time invariant.
(*d*) The system is linear.
(*e*) The system is stable.

7.

$$\mathbf{y[n] = 5x[3^n]}$$

(*a*) The system is dynamic.
(*b*) The system is non-causal.
(*c*) The system is time invariant.
(*d*) The system is linear.
(*e*) The system is stable.

8.

$$y[n] = \sin(2\pi x[n]) + x[n+1]$$

(*a*) The system is dynamic.
(*b*) The system is non-causal.
(*c*) The system is time invariant.
(*d*) The system is non-linear.
(*e*) The system is stable.

9. **$x[n] = u[n-4] - u[n-10]$ and $h[n] = u[n-5] - u[n-16]$. Find $y[n] = x[n] * h[n]$?**

$$\begin{aligned} y[n] &= (n-8) && 9 \le n \le 13 \\ &= 6 && 10 \le n \le 19 \\ &= (25-n) && 20 \le n \le 24 \\ &= 0 && n > 24 \end{aligned}$$

10. **$x[n] = 4^n u[-n-2]$ and $h[n] = u[n-2]$. Find $y[n] = x[n] * h[n]$?**

$$\begin{aligned} y[n] &= \frac{1}{3}\left[\frac{1}{4}\right]^{n-1} && n < 0 \\ &= \frac{1}{12} && n > 0 \end{aligned}$$

11. **Determine whether the following LTID time systems whose impulse response given below are stable. (*a*) $h[n] = n \sin 2\pi n\, u[n]$, (*b*) $h[n] = 5^n u[-n]$ and (*c*) $h[n] = 2^{-n} u[n-5]$?**

(*a*) $y[n] = \infty$ B.I.B.O. unstable.

(*b*) $y[n] = \frac{1}{4} < \infty$ B.I.B.O. stable.

(*c*) $y[n] = \frac{1}{6} < \infty$ B.I.B.O. stable.

12. **$x[n]$ and $y[n]$ are shown in Figures 1.107(*a*) and (*b*) respectively. Derive expression for $y[n] = x[n] * h[n]$ and hence obtain the sequence $y[n]$ by substituting numerical values. Verify the results by multiplication method?**

$$\begin{aligned} y[n] &= (n+1) && 0 \le n \le 2 \\ &= (6-n) && 3 \le n \le 5 \\ &= 0 && n > 5 \end{aligned}$$

$$y[n] = \{\underset{\uparrow}{1}, 2, 3, 3, 2, 1\}$$

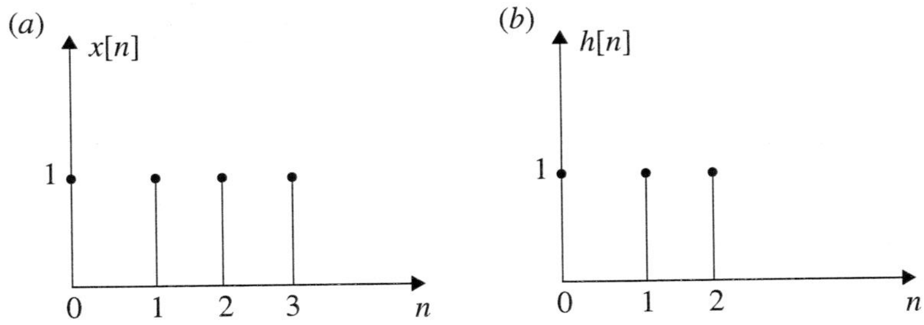

Figure 1.107 $x[n]$ and $h[n]$ for Problem 12.

The same answer is obtained by multiplication method.

13. $\boldsymbol{h[n] = u[n] - u[n-6]}$ **and** $\boldsymbol{x[n] = \delta[n-3] - \delta[n-5]}$**. Find** $\boldsymbol{y[n] = x[n] * h[n]}$ **and sketch the same?**

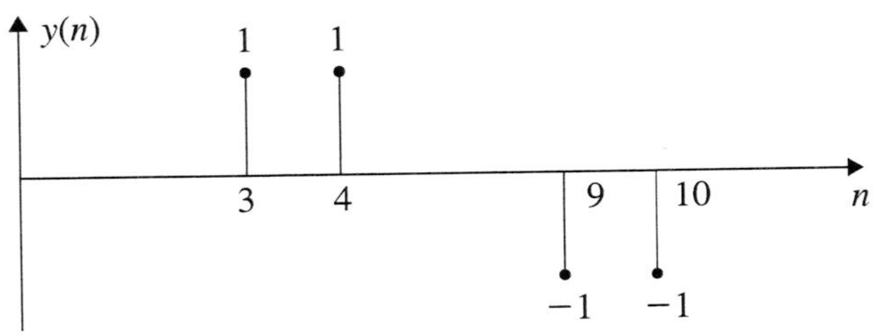

Figure 1.108 $y[n]$ of Problem 13.

14. $\boldsymbol{x[n] = e^{-2n}u[n]}$ **and** $\boldsymbol{h[n] = 3^{-n}u[n]}$**. Find** $\boldsymbol{y[n] = x[n] * h[n]}$**?**

$$y[n] = \frac{[3e^2 - (3e^2)^{-n}]u[n]}{[3e^2 - 1]}$$

15. $\boldsymbol{x[n] = (0.5)^n\ u[n]}$ **and** $\boldsymbol{h[n] = (0.9)^n u[n]}$**. Find** $\boldsymbol{y[n] = x[n] * h[n]}$**?**

$$y[n] = 2.5[0.9^{n+1} - 0.5^{n+1}]u[n]$$

16. **Determine the power and energy of the following signals?**

(a) $\quad x[n] = \left(\frac{1}{3}\right)^n$

(b) $\quad x[n] = e^{j\left(\frac{n\pi}{2} + \frac{\pi}{4}\right)}$

(c) $\quad x[n] = \sin\left(\frac{n\pi}{4}\right)$

(d) $\quad x[n] = e^{2n}u(n)$

Ans:

(a)	$E = \frac{9}{8}J;\ P = 0$
(b)	$E = \infty;\ P = 1W$
(c)	$E = \infty;\ P = \frac{1}{2}W$
(d)	$E = \infty;\ P = \infty$ (Neither power nor energy)

17. **Determine whether each of the following signal is periodic. Find the fundamental period.**

(a)	$x[n] = e^{j6\pi n}$
(b)	$x[n] = e^{j\frac{3}{5}\left(n+\frac{1}{2}\right)}$
(c)	$x[n] = \cos\left(\frac{2\pi}{3}\right)n$
(d)	$x[n] = \cos\frac{n\pi}{3} + \cos\frac{3n\pi}{4}$

Ans:

(a)	Periodic. $N = 1$ sample
(b)	Not Periodic.
(c)	Periodic. $N = 3$ samples
(d)	Periodic. $N = 24$ samples

18. **Find the odd and even components of the following sequence.**

$$x(n) = \{2, 3, \underset{\uparrow}{4}, 5, 6\}$$

Ans:

$$x_e(n) = \{4, 4, \underset{\uparrow}{4}, 4, 4\}$$

$$x_0(n) = \{-2, -1, 0, 1, 2\}$$

19. **Test whether the following systems are time variant or time invariant.**

(a) $y(n) = x(n) - x(n-1)$
(b) $y(n) = nx(n)$
(c) $y(n) = x(-n)$
(d) $y(n) = x(n)\cos\omega_0 n$
(e) $y(n) = x(n) - bx(n-1)$
(f) $y(n) = x(n) + c$

(*g*) $y(n) = e^{x(n)}$
(*h*) $y(n) = nx^2(n)$
(*i*) $y(n) = \sum_{k=0}^{m} a_k(n-k) - \sum_{k=1}^{m} b_k y(n-k)$

Ans:

(*a*) Time invariant.
(*b*) Time varying.
(*c*) Time varying.
(*d*) Time varying.
(*e*) Time varying.
(*f*) Time invariant.
(*g*) Time invariant.
(*h*) Time varying.
(*i*) Time invariant.

20. **Test the linearlity of the following systems.**

(*a*) $y(n) = nx(n)$
(*b*) $y(n) = x(n^2)$
(*c*) $y(n) = x^2(n)$
(*d*) $y(n) = Ax(n) + B$
(*e*) $y(n) = e^{x(n)}$

Ans: (*a*) Linear; (*b*) Linear; (*c*) Non-linear; (*d*) Non-linear and (*e*) Non-linear

21. **Test the causality of the following systems.**

(*a*) $y(n) = x(n) - x(n-1)$
(*b*) $y(n) = \sum_{k=\infty}^{n} x(k)$
(*c*) $y(n) = nx(n)$

Ans: (*a*) Causal; (*b*) Causal; and (*c*) Causal

22. **Test whether the following systems are stable or not.**

(*a*) $y(n) = x(-n-2)$
(*b*) $y(n) = x(n) + by(n-1)$
(*c*) $y(n) = \begin{cases} a^n & n \leq 0, \\ b^n & n < 0. \end{cases}$

Ans: (*a*) Stable; (*b*) Stable if $|b| < 1$; and (*c*) Stable if $|a| < 1$ and $|b| > 1$

23. **Determine the response of the relaxed system characterized by the impulse response $h(n) = (\frac{1}{2})^n u(n)$ to the input signal $x(n) = 2^n u(n)$.**

Ans:

$$y(n) = \left(\frac{1}{2}\right)^n \left(\frac{4^{n+1} - 1}{3}\right) u(n)$$

24. **Find the z-transform of the following sequence.**

$$\boldsymbol{x[n] = [3^{n-1} - (-3)^{n-1}]u[n]}$$

$$X[z] = \frac{2z^2}{3(z^2 - 9)} \qquad \text{ROC: } |z| > 3.$$

25. **Find the z-transform of**

$$\boldsymbol{x[n] = \sum_{n=0}^{\infty} \frac{1}{3} z^{-n} + \frac{1}{4}(-2)^n z^{-n}}$$

$$X[z] = \frac{1}{3}\frac{1}{(1 - z^{-1})} + \frac{1}{3}\frac{1}{(1 + 2z^{-1})} \qquad \text{ROC: } |z| > 2.$$

26. **Find the z-transform of**

$$\boldsymbol{x[n] = \sum_{n=-1}^{\infty} \left(\frac{1}{4}\right)^{n+1} z^{-n}}$$

$$X[z] = z + \frac{1}{4}\frac{1}{\left(1 - \frac{1}{4}z^{-1}\right)} \qquad \text{ROC: } |z| > \frac{1}{4}.$$

27. **Find the z-transform of**

$$\boldsymbol{x[n] = \sum_{n=1}^{\infty} \left(\frac{1}{4}\right)^{-n+1} z^{-n}}$$

$$X[z] = \frac{1}{4} + \frac{4}{(1 - 4z)} \qquad \text{ROC: } |z| < \frac{1}{4}.$$

28. **Find the z-transform of**

$$\boldsymbol{x[n] = \left(\frac{1}{10}\right)^{n} u[n-4]}$$

$$X[z] = 10^{-4}\frac{z^{-3}}{\left(z - \frac{1}{10}\right)} \qquad \text{ROC: } |z| > \frac{1}{10}.$$

29. **Find the z-transform of**

$$\begin{aligned} &(a) \qquad x[n] = 1 \qquad 0 \le n \le 9 \\ &\qquad\qquad\quad\; = 0 \qquad \text{otherwise} \\ &(b) \qquad y[n] = x[n] - x[n-1] \end{aligned}$$

$$(a) \qquad X[z] = \frac{(1 - z^{-10})}{(1 - z^{-1})} \qquad \text{ROC: } |z| > 0$$

$$(b) \qquad Y[z] = 1 - z^{-10} \qquad \text{ROC: } |z| > 0$$

30. **Find the unilateral z-transform and the ROC for the following sequences:**

$$(a) \quad x[n] = \left(\frac{1}{6}\right)^n u[n+6]$$

$$(b) \quad x[n] = 3\delta[n+4] + \delta[n] + (3)^n u[-n]$$

$$(c) \quad x[n] = \left(\frac{1}{4}\right)^{|n|}$$

$$(a) \quad X[z] = \frac{1}{(1-6z^{-1})} \qquad \text{ROC: } |z| > 6$$

$$(b) \quad X[z] = 4 \qquad \text{ROC: all } z$$

$$(c) \quad X[z] = \frac{1}{\left(1-\frac{1}{4}z^{-1}\right)} \qquad \text{ROC: } |z| > \frac{1}{4}$$

31. **By applying properties of z-transform find the z-transform of the following sequences given $x[n] \overset{Z}{\longleftrightarrow} \frac{z}{(z^2+2)}$**

$$(a) \quad y[n] = x[n-3]$$

$$(b) \quad y[n] = nx[n]$$

$$(c) \quad y[n] = x[n+1] + x[n-1]$$

$$(d) \quad x[n] = 2^n x[n]$$

$$(e) \quad x[n] = (n-2)x[n-1]$$

$$(f) \quad x[n] = x[-n]$$

$$(a) \quad Y[z] = \frac{z^{-2}}{(z^2+2)} \qquad \text{ROC: } |z| < 2 \text{ (Time shifting property)}$$

$$(b) \quad Y[z] = \frac{z[z^2-2]}{(z^2+2)^2} \qquad \text{(Differentiation property)}$$

$$(c) \quad Y[z] = \frac{(z^2+1)}{(z^2+2)} \qquad \text{(Time advancing and time delaying)}$$

$$(d) \quad Y[z] = \frac{2z}{(z^2+8)} \qquad \text{(Multiplying property)}$$

$$(e) \quad Y[z] = \frac{-4}{(z^2+2)^2} \qquad \text{(Time differentiation and time shifting)}$$

$$(f) \quad Y[z] = \frac{z}{(1+2z^2)} \qquad \text{(Time reversal)}$$

32. **Find the z-transform of**

$$(a) \quad x[n] = 2^n u[n-2]$$

$$(b) \quad x[n] = \left(\frac{1}{4}\right)^n u[-n]$$

$$(a) \qquad X[z] = \frac{4z^{-2}}{(1-2z^{-1})}$$

$$(b) \qquad X[z] = \frac{1}{(1-4z)}$$

33. **Find the z-transform of**

$$(a) \qquad x[n] = (n-4)u[n-4]$$

$$(b) \qquad x[n] = u[n] - u[n-4]$$

$$(c) \qquad x[n] = (n-4)u[n]$$

$$(d) \qquad x[n] = n[u[n] - u[n-4]]$$

$$(a) \qquad X[z] = \frac{z^{-3}}{(z-1)^2} \qquad \text{ROC: } |z| > 1$$

$$(b) \qquad X[z] = \frac{z}{(z-1)}[1 - z^{-4}] \qquad \text{ROC: } |z| > 1$$

$$(c) \qquad X[z] = \frac{(5z - 4z^2)}{(z-1)^2} \qquad \text{ROC: } |z| > 1$$

$$(d) \qquad X[z] = \frac{(z - 3z^{-2} + 2z^{-3})}{(z-1)^2} \qquad \text{ROC: } |z| > 1$$

34. **Find the z-transform of the following sequence**

$$x[n] = \left(\frac{1}{4}\right)^n u[n]$$

$$= \left(-\frac{1}{2}\right)^n u[-n-1]$$

$$X[z] = \frac{3}{4}\left[\frac{z}{\left(z-\frac{1}{4}\right)\left(z+\frac{1}{2}\right)}\right] \qquad \text{ROC: } \frac{1}{4} < |z| < \frac{1}{2}$$

35. **Using convolution find $y[n]$ given**

$$x[n] = \left(\frac{1}{2}\right)^n u[n]$$

$$h[n] = \left(\frac{1}{3}\right)^n u[n]$$

$$y[n] = x[n] * h[n]$$

$$y[n] = \left[3\left(\frac{1}{2}\right)^n - 2\left(\frac{1}{3}\right)^n\right] u[n] \qquad \text{ROC: } |z| < \frac{1}{2}$$

36. **Using partial function find the inverse z-transform**

$$H[z] = \frac{(1 - z^{-1} + z^{-2})}{(1 - z^{-1})(1 - 2z^{-1})(1 - 4z^{-1})} \qquad \text{ROC: } 2 < |z| < 4$$

$$h[n] = \left[\frac{1}{3} - \frac{3}{2}(2)^n\right]u[n] + \frac{3}{16}(4)^n u[-n-1]$$

37. **Find the inverse z-transform of**

$$H[z] = \frac{4z + 1}{z - \frac{1}{4}}$$

using power series expansion?

(*a*) ROC: $|z| > \frac{1}{4}$

(*b*) ROC: $|z| < \frac{1}{4}$

(*a*) $x[n] = \left\{\underset{\uparrow}{4}, 2, \frac{1}{2}, \frac{1}{8}, \frac{1}{32}, \ldots\right\}$

(*b*) $x[n] = \{\ldots, 2048, -512, -128, -32, \underset{\uparrow}{-4}\}$

38. **Consider the algebraic expression for the z-transform of $x[n]$**

$$x[n] = \frac{\left(1 - \frac{1}{4}z^{-2}\right)}{\left(1 + \frac{1}{4}z^{-1}\right)\left(1 - \frac{5}{6}z^{-1} + \frac{1}{6}z^{-2}\right)}$$

How many different ROCs could correspond the $X[z]$?

(*a*) ROC: $|z| > \frac{1}{2}$

(*b*) ROC: $0 < |z| < \frac{1}{4}$

(*c*) ROC: $\frac{1}{3} < |z| < \frac{1}{2}$

39. **Consider the algebraic expression for the z-transform of $x[n]$**

$$x[n] = \frac{\left(1 + z^{-1} + 4z^{-2}\right)}{\left(1 - \frac{1}{4}z^{-1}\right)\left(1 - \frac{7}{24}z^{-1} + \frac{1}{48}z^{-2}\right)}$$

ROC: $|z| > \frac{1}{4}$. Find whether the system is causal and stable.

$X[z]$ is rational and the poles are at $z = \frac{1}{4}$, $z = \frac{1}{6}$, and $z = \frac{1}{8}$. Since the ROC is exterior of the outermost pole the system is causal. The ROC includes unit circle and the poles are inside the unit circle. The system is stable. Therefore, the system is causal and stable.

40. **A system with impulse response $h[n] = 5(3)^n u[n-1]$ produces on output $y[n] = (-4)^n u[n-1]$. Determine the input $x[n]$.**

$$x[n] = \frac{1}{5}\left[(-4)^n u[n] - 3(-4)^{n-1} u[n-1]\right] \qquad \text{ROC: } |z| > 4$$

41. **Consider the following difference equation.**

$$y[n] - y[n-1] - 2y[n-2] = x[n] + 2x[n-1]$$

The initial conditions are $y[-1] = 1$ and $y[-2] = 2$. The input $x[n] = u[n]$. Find (*a*) Zero input response, (*b*) Zero state response, (*c*) Natural response, (*d*) Forced response and (*e*) Total response.

(*a*) $y_{0i}[n] = [(-1)^n + 4(2)^n]u[n]$

(*b*) $y_{0s}[n] = \left[-\frac{1}{6}(-1)^n + \frac{8}{3}(2)^n - \frac{3}{2}\right]u[n]$

(*c*) $y_n[n] = -\frac{3}{2}u[n]$

(*d*) $y_f[n] = \left[\frac{5}{6}(-1)^n + \frac{20}{3}(2)^n\right]u[n]$

(*e*) $y_{\text{total}}[n] = \left[-\frac{3}{2} + \frac{5}{6}(-1)^n + \frac{20}{3}(2)^n\right]u[n]$

42. **For each of the following difference equations determine the output response $y[n]$?**

(*a*) **$y[n] - 4y[n-1] = x[n]$ with $y[-1] = 2$ and $x[n] = \left(\frac{1}{3}\right)^n u[n]$**

(*b*) **$y[n] + \frac{1}{3}y[n-1] = x[n] - \frac{1}{3}x[n-1]$**
with $y[-1] = 1$ and $x[n] = u[n]$

(*a*) $y[n] = \left[\frac{100}{11}(4)^n - \frac{1}{11}\left(\frac{1}{3}\right)^n\right]u[n]$

(*b*) $y[n] = \left[\frac{3}{2} - \frac{5}{6}\left(-\frac{1}{3}\right)^n\right]u[n]$

43. **Find $x(\infty)$ if**

$$(a)\quad X(z) = \frac{(z+2)}{(z-0.8)^2}$$

$$(b)\quad X(z) = \frac{(3z+4)}{(z-1)(z+0.9)}$$

$$(a)\quad x(\infty) = 0; \qquad (b)\quad x(\infty) = \frac{7}{1.9}$$

44. **By using long direction, determine the inverse z-transform of**

$$(a)\quad X(z) = \frac{(1+2z^{-1})}{(1-2z^{-1}+z^{-2})}$$

$$(b)\quad X(z) = \frac{(z+1)}{(z^2+3z+2)}$$

for $x(n)$ being causal and non-causal.

$$(a)\quad x(n) = \{\underset{\uparrow}{1}, 4, 7, 10, 13, 16, 19, \ldots\} \text{ (causal)}$$

$$x(n) = \{\ldots, 17, 14, 11, 8, 5, 2, \underset{\uparrow}{0}\} \text{ (non-causal)}$$

$$(b)\quad x(n) = \{\underset{\uparrow}{0}, 1, 4, 10, 22, \ldots\} \text{ (causal)}$$

$$x(n) = \{\ldots, 1.8125, 1.625, 1.25, \underset{\uparrow}{0.5}\} \text{ (non-causal)}$$

45. **Find the inverse z-transform of the following**

$$(a)\quad X(z) = \frac{\frac{1}{4}z^{-1}}{\left(1-\frac{1}{2}z^{-1}\right)\left(1-\frac{1}{4}z^{-1}\right)} \qquad \text{ROC} : |z| > \frac{1}{2}$$

$$(b)\quad X(z) = \frac{z(z-1)}{(z+2)^3(z+1)}$$

$$(a)\quad x(n) = \left[\left(\frac{1}{2}\right)^n - \left(\frac{1}{4}\right)^n\right] u(n)$$

$$(b)\quad x(n) = \left[2(-2)^n + 2n(-2)^{n-1} + \frac{3n(n-1)}{\angle 2}(-2)^{n-2} - 2(-1)^n\right] u(n)$$

Discrete and Fast Fourier Transforms (DFT and FFT) 2

Learning Objectives

After completing this chapter, you should be able to:

- define Discrete Fourier Transform (DFT) and Inverse Discrete Fourier Transform (IDFT).
- establish the properties of DFT.
- study different methods of circular convolution and solve numerical problems.
- study different Fast Fourier Transform (FFT) algorithms and their applications.
- study the use of FFT algorithms in linear filtering and correlation.

2.1 Introduction

In the study of signals and systems, the discrete time periodic signals are represented by Discrete time Fourier Series (DFS) using a parallel development of continuous system. The fourier series representation in these cases was applicable only if the signals are periodic. If the signal is non-periodic, then applying a limiting process, the aperiodic discrete time signal $x[n]$ can be expressed as a sum of everlasting exponentials or sinusoids. The spectrum of $x(\omega)$ so obtained is called Discrete Time Fourier Transform (DTFT). If the spectrum obtained by DTFT is sampled for one period of the fourier transform, such a transformation is called Discrete Fourier Transform (DFT) which is a very powerful computational tool for the evaluation of fourier transform. DFT finds wide applications in linear filtering, correlation analysis and spectrum analysis. Some special algorithms are developed for the easy implementation of DFT which result in saving of considerable computation time. Such algorithms are called Fast Fourier Transform (FFT). By divide- and-conquer approach, the DFT which has a size N, where N is a composite number is reduced to the smaller DFTs and computation is performed. The computational algorithms are developed when the size of N is power of 2 and power of 4.

2.2 Discrete Fourier Transform (DFT)

By Fourier transform, the sequence $x[n]$ is transformed as $X(\omega)$ in the frequency domain. If the time sequence $x[n]$ is continuous and periodic, the transformation is called Discrete Time Fourier Transform (DTFT). For non-periodic signal $x[n]$, a slightly modified transform technique which is known as Discrete Fourier Transform (DFT) is used which transforms $x[n]$ to $X(\omega)$. DFT is a very powerful tool for the analysis and synthesis of discrete signals and systems. The method is ideally suited for use in digital computer or specially designed digital hardware. The DFT is obtained by sampling one period of DTFT only at a finite number of frequency points. It has the following features:

1. The original finite duration signal can be easily recovered from its DFT since there exists one to one correspondence between $x[n]$ and $X(\omega)$.
2. For the calculation of the DFT of finite duration sequences, a very efficient and fast technique called FFT has been developed.
3. As far as realization in digital computer is concerned, DFT is the appropriate representation since it is discrete and of finite length in both the time and frequency domains.
4. DFT is closely related to discrete Fourier series, the Fourier transform, convolution, correlation and filtering.

2.2.1 The Discrete Fourier Transform Pairs

Consider the sequence $x[n]$ of length N. The Fourier transform of $x[n]$ is given by

$$X(\Omega) = \sum_{n=-\infty}^{\infty} x[n]e^{-j\Omega n} \tag{2.1}$$

In Equation (2.1), $X(\Omega)$ is the continuous function of Ω. The range of Ω is from $-\pi$ to π or 0 to 2π. Hence, calculating $X(\Omega)$ on digital computer or DSP is impossible. It is, therefore, necessary to compute $X(\Omega)$ at discrete values of Ω. When Fourier transform $X(\Omega)$ is calculated at only discrete points k, it is called Discrete Fourier Transform (DFT). The DFT is denoted by $X(k)$. For finite discrete points N, Equation (2.1) is written as

$$X(k) = \sum_{n=0}^{N-1} x[n]e^{-j2\pi kn/N} \tag{2.2}$$

where $k = 0, 1, 2, \ldots, (N-1)$. $X(k)$ is computed at $k = 0, 1, 2, \ldots, (N-1)$ discrete points. $X(k)$ is the sequence of N samples. The sequence $x[n]$ is obtained back form

$$X[n] = \frac{1}{N}\sum_{k=0}^{N-1} X(k)e^{j2\pi kn/N} \tag{2.3}$$

Let us define $W_N = e^{-j2\pi/N}$, where W_N is called Twiddle factor. Equations (2.2) and (2.3) are called DFT and IDFT or simply discrete Fourier transform pair. They can be represented in terms of twiddle factor as given below

$$X(k) = \sum_{n=0}^{N-1} x[n] W_N^{kn} \tag{2.4}$$

$$x[n] = \frac{1}{N} \sum_{k=0}^{N-1} X(k) W_N^{-kn} \tag{2.5}$$

Let the sequence $x[n]$ be resentenced as a vector x_N of N samples as

$$x_N = \begin{matrix} n=0 \\ n=1 \\ \vdots \\ n=N-1 \end{matrix} \begin{bmatrix} x(0) \\ x(1) \\ \vdots \\ x(N-1) \end{bmatrix}_{N\times 1} \tag{2.6}$$

and $X(k)$ be represented as a vector X_N of N samples as

$$X_N = \begin{matrix} k=0 \\ k=1 \\ \vdots \\ k=N-1 \end{matrix} \begin{bmatrix} X(0) \\ X(1) \\ \vdots \\ X(N-1) \end{bmatrix}_{N\times 1} \tag{2.7}$$

The twiddle factor W_N^{kn} is represented as a matrix with k rows and N column as

$$W_N = \begin{matrix} k=0 \\ \\ \\ \\ k=N-1 \end{matrix} \begin{bmatrix} W_N^0 & W_N^0 & W_N^0 & \cdots & W_N^0 \\ W_N^0 & W_N^1 & W_N^2 & \cdots & W_N^{N-1} \\ W_N^0 & W_N^2 & W_N^4 & \cdots & W_N^{2(N-1)} \\ \vdots & \vdots & \vdots & \vdots & \vdots \\ W_N^0 & W_N^{N-1} & W_N^{2(N-1)} & \cdots & W_N^{(N-1)(N-1)} \end{bmatrix}_{N\times N} \tag{2.8}$$

Thus, Equations (2.4) and (2.5) can be written with matrix form as

$$X_N = [W_N] x_N \tag{2.9}$$

$$x_N = \frac{1}{N}[W_N^*] X_N \tag{2.10}$$

where $W_N^* = W_N^{-kn}$

$$\begin{aligned} W_N &= e^{-j\frac{2\pi}{N}} \\ &= 1\angle -2\pi/N \end{aligned} \tag{2.11}$$

From Equation (2.11), the magnitude of the twiddle factor is 1 and the phase angle is $-\frac{2\pi}{N}$. It lies on the unit circle in the complex plane from 0 to 2π angle and it gets repeated for every cycle.

2.2.2 Four Point, Six Point and Eight Point Twiddle Factors

As in Equation (2.11), the magnitude of the twiddle factor is 1 and the angle -2π is equally divided in the interval N. The most commonly used intervals are $N = 4$ and $N = 8$. For $N = 4$, the angle between any $N = 0$ and $N = 1$ is $\frac{\pi}{2}$.

2.2.2.1 *Four Point Twiddle Factor*

For $N = 4$

$$W_N = \begin{array}{c} \\ k=0 \\ 1 \\ 2 \\ 3 \end{array} \begin{array}{c} \begin{array}{cccc} n=0 & 1 & 2 & 3 \end{array} \\ \begin{bmatrix} W_4^0 & W_4^0 & W_4^0 & W_4^0 \\ W_4^0 & W_4^1 & W_4^2 & W_4^3 \\ W_4^0 & W_4^2 & W_4^4 & W_4^6 \\ W_4^0 & W_4^3 & W_4^6 & W_4^9 \end{bmatrix} \end{array} \tag{2.12}$$

Note: $W_4^4 = W_4^0$; $W_4^6 = W_4^2$ and $W_4^9 = W_4^1$. From Equation (2.11)

$$W_4^1 = 1\angle -\pi/2$$

For $N = 4$, the unit circle is divided into four equal segments in the clockwise sequence and labelled as W_4^0, W_4^1, W_4^2 and W_4^3. From Figure 2.1, the twiddle factors are obtained as

$$W_4^0 = 1; \quad W_4^1 = -j; \quad W_4^2 = -1; \quad W_4^3 = -j$$

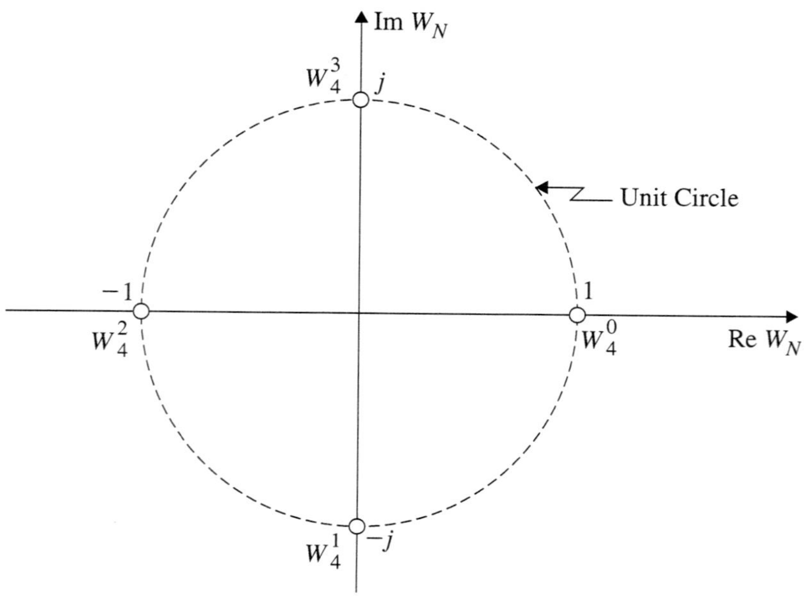

Figure 2.1 Representation of W_4^{-nk}.

Equation (2.12) is written as

$$W_N = \begin{bmatrix} 1 & 1 & 1 & 1 \\ 1 & -j & -1 & j \\ 1 & -1 & 1 & -1 \\ 1 & j & -1 & -j \end{bmatrix} \tag{2.13}$$

Equation (2.13) represents the twiddle factor to express DFT of any sequence $x[n]$. Twiddle factors for 6-points DFT and 8-points DFT are derived below.

2.2.2.2 *Six Point Twiddle Factor*

For $N = 6$, the unit circle is divided into six equal segments and in the clockwise sequence labelled as W_6^0, W_6^1, W_6^2, W_6^3, W_6^4 and W_6^5 noting that $W_6^6 = W_6^0$, $W_6^7 = W_6^1$ and so on. This is shown in Figure 2.2. Each segment is shifted by $-60°$ on the unit circle. For $N = 6$, W_6 is obtained by multiplying the rows and columns of W_6 and is given below.

$$W_N = \begin{bmatrix} W_6^0 & W_6^0 & W_6^0 & W_6^0 & W_6^0 & W_6^0 \\ W_6^0 & W_6^1 & W_6^2 & W_6^3 & W_6^4 & W_6^5 \\ W_6^0 & W_6^2 & W_6^4 & W_6^6 & W_6^8 & W_6^{10} \\ W_6^0 & W_6^3 & W_6^6 & W_6^9 & W_6^{12} & W_6^{15} \\ W_6^0 & W_6^4 & W_6^8 & W_6^{12} & W_6^{16} & W_6^{20} \\ W_6^0 & W_6^5 & W_6^{10} & W_6^{15} & W_6^{20} & W_6^{25} \end{bmatrix} \tag{2.14}$$

$$W_6^0 = W_6^6 = W_6^{12} = W_6^{18} = W_6^{24} = 1$$

$$W_6^1 = W_6^7 = W_6^{13} = W_6^{19} = W_6^{25} = 1e^{-j\frac{\pi}{3}} = 0.5 - j0.866$$

$$W_6^2 = W_6^8 = W_6^{14} = W_6^{20} = W_6^{26} = 1e^{-j\frac{2\pi}{3}} = -0.5 - j0.866$$

$$W_6^3 = W_6^9 = W_6^{15} = W_6^{21} = W_6^{27} = -1$$

$$W_6^4 = W_6^{10} = W_6^{16} = W_6^{22} = W_6^{28} = 1e^{j\frac{2\pi}{3}} = -0.5 + j0.866$$

$$W_6^5 = W_6^{11} = W_6^{17} = W_6^{23} = W_6^{29} = 1e^{j\frac{\pi}{3}} = 0.5 + j0.866$$

Substituting the values of the elements of the matrix W_6 we get

$$W_6 = \begin{bmatrix} 1 & 1 & 1 & 1 & 1 & 1 \\ 1 & 0.5 - j0.866 & -0.5 - j0.866 & -1 & -0.5 + j0.866 & 0.5 + j0.866 \\ 1 & -0.5 - j0.866 & -0.5 + j0.866 & 1 & -0.5 - j0.866 & -0.5 + j0.866 \\ 1 & -1 & 1 & -1 & 1 & -1 \\ 1 & -0.5 + j0.866 & -0.5 - j0.866 & 1 & -0.5 + j0.866 & -0.5 - j0.866 \\ 1 & 0.5 + j0.866 & -0.5 + j0.866 & -1 & -0.5 - j0.866 & 0.5 - j0.866 \end{bmatrix} \tag{2.15}$$

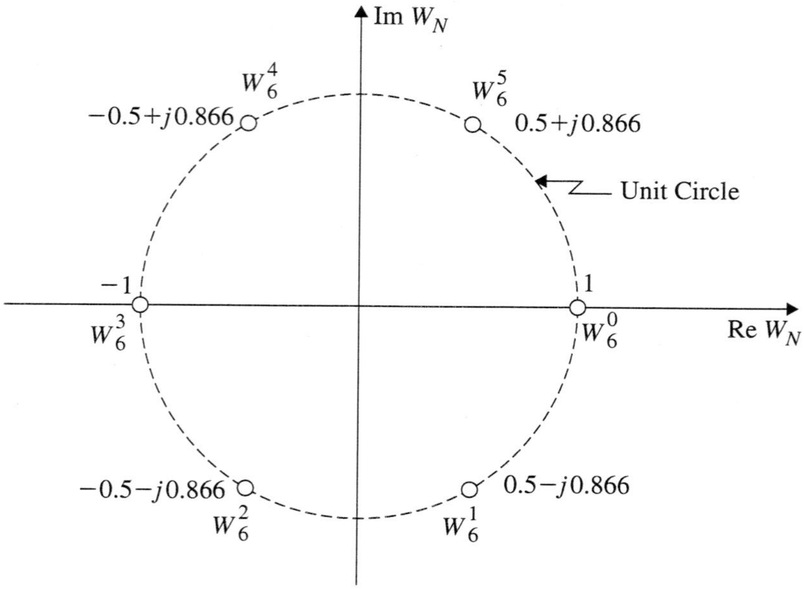

Figure 2.2 Representation of W_6^{-nk}.

2.2.2.3 *Eight Point Twiddle Factor*

The eight point twiddle factor is represented in Figure 2.3. The twiddle factor W_8 is obtained from Figure 2.3 and is shown below.

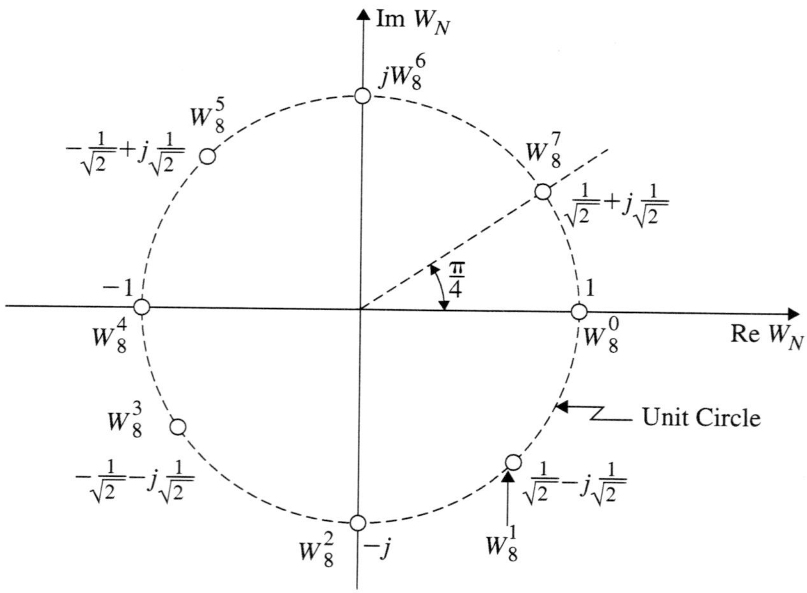

Figure 2.3 Representation of W_8^{-kn}.

$$W_8 = \begin{bmatrix} W_8^0 & W_8^0 & W_8^0 & W_8^0 & W_8^0 & W_8^0 & W_8^0 & W_8^0 \\ W_8^0 & W_8^1 & W_8^2 & W_8^3 & W_8^4 & W_8^5 & W_8^6 & W_8^7 \\ W_8^0 & W_8^2 & W_8^4 & W_8^6 & W_8^8 & W_8^{10} & W_8^{12} & W_8^{14} \\ W_8^0 & W_8^3 & W_8^6 & W_8^9 & W_8^{12} & W_8^{15} & W_8^{18} & W_8^{21} \\ W_8^0 & W_8^4 & W_8^8 & W_8^{12} & W_8^{16} & W_8^{20} & W_8^{24} & W_8^{28} \\ W_8^0 & W_8^5 & W_8^{10} & W_8^{15} & W_8^{20} & W_8^{25} & W_8^{30} & W_8^{35} \\ W_8^0 & W_8^6 & W_8^{12} & W_8^{18} & W_8^{24} & W_8^{30} & W_8^{36} & W_8^{42} \\ W_8^0 & W_8^7 & W_8^{14} & W_8^{21} & W_8^{28} & W_8^{35} & W_8^{42} & W_8^{49} \end{bmatrix} \tag{2.16}$$

$$W_8 = \begin{bmatrix} 1 & 1 & 1 & 1 & 1 & 1 & 1 & 1 \\ 1 & \frac{1}{\sqrt{2}} - j\frac{1}{\sqrt{2}} & -j & -\frac{1}{\sqrt{2}} - j\frac{1}{\sqrt{2}} & -1 & -\frac{1}{\sqrt{2}} + j\frac{1}{\sqrt{2}} & j & \frac{1}{\sqrt{2}} + j\frac{1}{\sqrt{2}} \\ 1 & -j & -1 & j & 1 & -j & -1 & j \\ 1 & -\frac{1}{\sqrt{2}} - j\frac{1}{\sqrt{2}} & j & \frac{1}{\sqrt{2}} - j\frac{1}{\sqrt{2}} & -1 & \frac{1}{\sqrt{2}} + j\frac{1}{\sqrt{2}} & -j & -\frac{1}{\sqrt{2}} + j\frac{1}{\sqrt{2}} \\ 1 & -1 & 1 & -1 & 1 & -1 & 1 & -1 \\ 1 & -\frac{1}{\sqrt{2}} + j\frac{1}{\sqrt{2}} & -j & \frac{1}{\sqrt{2}} + j\frac{1}{\sqrt{2}} & -1 & \frac{1}{\sqrt{2}} - j\frac{1}{\sqrt{2}} & j & -\frac{1}{\sqrt{2}} - j\frac{1}{\sqrt{2}} \\ 1 & j & -1 & -j & 1 & j & -1 & -j \\ 1 & \frac{1}{\sqrt{2}} + j\frac{1}{\sqrt{2}} & j & -\frac{1}{\sqrt{2}} + j\frac{1}{\sqrt{2}} & -1 & -\frac{1}{\sqrt{2}} - j\frac{1}{\sqrt{2}} & -j & \frac{1}{\sqrt{2}} - j\frac{1}{\sqrt{2}} \end{bmatrix} \tag{2.17}$$

Example 2.1

Compute the DFT of the sequence $x[n] = \{1, j, -1, -j\}$ for $N = 4$.

(Anna University, November, 2006)

Solution

Method 1

$$W_4 = \begin{bmatrix} 1 & 1 & 1 & 1 \\ 1 & -j & -1 & j \\ 1 & -1 & 1 & -1 \\ 1 & j & -1 & -j \end{bmatrix}; \qquad X_4 = \begin{bmatrix} 1 \\ j \\ -1 \\ -j \end{bmatrix}$$

From Equation (2.9)

$$X_4 = W_4 x_4$$

$$X_4 = \begin{bmatrix} 1 & 1 & 1 & 1 \\ 1 & -j & -1 & j \\ 1 & -1 & 1 & -1 \\ 1 & j & -1 & -j \end{bmatrix} \begin{bmatrix} 1 \\ j \\ -1 \\ -j \end{bmatrix}$$

$$= \begin{bmatrix} 1 + j - 1 - j \\ 1 + 1 + 1 + 1 \\ 1 - j - 1 + j \\ 1 - 1 + 1 - 1 \end{bmatrix} = \begin{bmatrix} 0 \\ 4 \\ 0 \\ 0 \end{bmatrix}$$

$$\boxed{\begin{aligned} X(0) &= 0 \\ X(1) &= 4 \\ X(2) &= 0 \\ X(3) &= 0 \end{aligned}}$$

Method 2

$$X(k) = \sum_{n=0}^{3} x[n] e^{-j\frac{2\pi kn}{4}}; \quad k = 0, 1, 2, 3, \ldots$$

For $k = 0$

$$\begin{aligned} X(0) &= \sum_{n=0}^{3} x[n] \\ &= x[0] + x[1] + x[2] + x[3] \\ &= 1 + j - 1 - j = 0 \end{aligned}$$

For $k = 1$

$$\begin{aligned} X(1) &= \sum_{n=0}^{3} x[n] e^{-j\frac{\pi n}{2}} \\ &= x[0] + x[1]e^{-j\frac{\pi}{2}} + x[2]e^{-j\pi} + x[3]e^{-j\frac{3\pi}{2}} \\ &= 1 + j(-j) + (-1)(-1) + (-j)(j) \\ &= 1 + 1 + 1 + 1 = 4 \end{aligned}$$

For $k = 2$

$$\begin{aligned} X(2) &= \sum_{n=0}^{3} x[n] e^{-j\pi n} \\ &= x[0] + x[1]e^{-j\pi} + x[2]e^{-j2\pi} + x[3]e^{-j3\pi} \\ &= 1 + j(-1) + (-1)(1) + (-j)(-1) \\ &= 1 - j - 1 + j = 0 \end{aligned}$$

For $k = 3$

$$
\begin{aligned}
X(3) &= \sum_{n=0}^{3} x[n]e^{-j\frac{3\pi n}{2}} \\
&= x[0] + x[1]e^{-\frac{3\pi}{2}} + x[2]e^{-j3\pi} + x[3]e^{-j\frac{9\pi}{2}} \\
&= 1 + j(j) + (-1)(-1) + (-j)(-j) \\
&= 1 - 1 + 1 - 1 = 0
\end{aligned}
$$

$$
\boxed{\begin{aligned} X(0) &= 0 \\ X(1) &= 4 \\ X(2) &= 0 \\ X(3) &= 0 \end{aligned}}
$$

Method 1 is simpler and quicker.

Example 2.2

Find 8-point DFT of $x[n] = \{1, -1, 1, -1, 1, -1, 1, -1\}$.

(*Anna University, April, 2004*)

Solution

$$
\begin{aligned}
X_N &= W_N x_N \\
&= W_8 x_8
\end{aligned} \tag{2.18}
$$

W_8 is given in Equation (2.17).

$$
x_8 = \begin{bmatrix} 1 \\ -1 \\ 1 \\ -1 \\ 1 \\ -1 \\ 1 \\ -1 \end{bmatrix}
$$

$X(0)$ is obtained by multiplying $x_8$with the first row of W_8. Thus

$$
\begin{aligned}
X(0) &= 1 - 1 + 1 - 1 + 1 - 1 + 1 - 1 = 0 \\
X(1) &= \text{2nd row of } W_8 \text{ to multiply } x_8 \\
&= 1 - \frac{1}{\sqrt{2}} + j\frac{1}{\sqrt{2}} - j + \frac{1}{\sqrt{2}} + j\frac{1}{\sqrt{2}} - 1 + \frac{1}{\sqrt{2}} - j\frac{1}{\sqrt{2}} + j = 0
\end{aligned}
$$

$$X(2) = \text{3rd row of } W_8 \text{ to multiply } x_8$$
$$= 1 + j - 1 - j + 1 + j - 1 - j = 0$$
$$X(3) = 1 + \frac{1}{\sqrt{2}} + j\frac{1}{\sqrt{2}} + j - \frac{1}{\sqrt{2}} + j\frac{1}{\sqrt{2}} - 1 - \frac{1}{\sqrt{2}} - j\frac{1}{\sqrt{2}} - j + \frac{1}{\sqrt{2}} - j\frac{1}{\sqrt{2}}$$
$$= 0$$
$$X(4) = \text{5th row of } W_8 \text{ to multiply } x_8$$
$$= 1 + 1 + 1 + 1 + 1 + 1 + 1 + 1 = 8$$
$$X(5) = \text{6th row of } W_8 \text{ to multiply } x_8$$
$$= 1 + \frac{1}{\sqrt{2}} - j\frac{1}{\sqrt{2}} - j - \frac{1}{\sqrt{2}} - j\frac{1}{\sqrt{2}} - 1 - \frac{1}{\sqrt{2}} + j\frac{1}{\sqrt{2}} + j + \frac{1}{\sqrt{2}} + j\frac{1}{\sqrt{2}}$$
$$= 0$$
$$X(6) = 1 - j - 1 + j + 1 - j - 1 + j = 0$$
$$X(7) = 1 - \frac{1}{\sqrt{2}} - j\frac{1}{\sqrt{2}} + j + \frac{1}{\sqrt{2}} - j\frac{1}{\sqrt{2}} - 1 + \frac{1}{\sqrt{2}} + j\frac{1}{\sqrt{2}} - j - \frac{1}{\sqrt{2}} + j\frac{1}{\sqrt{2}}$$
$$= 0$$
$$X_8 = \begin{bmatrix} 0 \\ 0 \\ 0 \\ 0 \\ 8 \\ 0 \\ 0 \\ 0 \end{bmatrix}$$

2.2.3 Zero Padding

In evaluating the DFT we assumed that the length of the DFT which is N is equal to the length L of the sequence $x[n]$. If $N < L$, time domain aliasing occurs due to under sampling and in the process we could miss out some important details and get misleading information. To avoid this N, the number of samples of $x[n]$ is increased by adding some dummy sample of 0 value. This addition of dummy samples is known as zero padding. The zero padding not only increases the number of samples but also helps in getting a better idea of the frequency spectrum of $X(\Omega)$.

Example 2.3

Compute the 4-point DFT of the sequence

$$x[n] = 1 \qquad 0 \leq n < 2$$

Solution For the given sequence $L = 3$ and $N = 4$. By adding a dummy sample of 0 values (zero padding), the given sequence becomes

$$x[n] = \{1,\ 1,\ 1,\ 0\}$$

$$x_N = \begin{bmatrix} 1 \\ 1 \\ 1 \\ 0 \end{bmatrix}$$

W_4 is given in Equation (2.13).

$$\begin{aligned} X_4 &= W_4 x_4 \\ &= \begin{bmatrix} 1 & 1 & 1 & 1 \\ 1 & -j & -1 & j \\ 1 & -1 & 1 & -1 \\ 1 & j & -1 & -j \end{bmatrix} \begin{bmatrix} 1 \\ 1 \\ 1 \\ 0 \end{bmatrix} \\ X(0) &= [1+1+1+0] = 3 \\ X(1) &= [1-j-1+0] = -j \\ X(2) &= [1-1+1+0] = 1 \\ X(3) &= [1+j-1+0] = j \\ X_4 &= \begin{bmatrix} 3 \\ -j \\ 1 \\ j \end{bmatrix} \end{aligned}$$

Example 2.4

Compute the 4-points DFT of the following sequences:

(1) $x[n] = \{1,\ 1,\ 1,\ 1\}$

(2) $x[n] = \{1,\ 1,\ 0,\ 0\}$

(3) $x[n] = \cos \pi n$

(4) $x[n] = \sin \dfrac{n\pi}{2}$

(Anna University, April, 2004; November, 2007)

Solution

(1) $\boldsymbol{x[n] = \{1, 1, 1, 1\}}$

$$x_4 = \begin{bmatrix} 1 \\ 1 \\ 1 \\ 1 \end{bmatrix}$$

$$X_4 = W_4 x_4$$

$$= \begin{bmatrix} 1 & 1 & 1 & 1 \\ 1 & -j & -1 & j \\ 1 & -1 & 1 & -1 \\ 1 & j & -1 & -j \end{bmatrix} \begin{bmatrix} 1 \\ 1 \\ 1 \\ 1 \end{bmatrix}$$

$$X(0) = 1 + 1 + 1 + 1$$
$$= 4$$
$$X(1) = 1 - j - 1 + j$$
$$= 0$$
$$X(2) = 1 - 1 + 1 - 1$$
$$= 0$$
$$X(3) = 1 + j - 1 - j$$
$$= 0$$

$$X_4 = \begin{bmatrix} 4 \\ 0 \\ 0 \\ 0 \end{bmatrix}$$

(2) $\boldsymbol{x[n] = \{1, 1, 0, 0\}}$

$$X_4 = W_4 x_4$$

$$X_4 = \begin{bmatrix} 1 & 1 & 1 & 1 \\ 1 & -j & -1 & j \\ 1 & -1 & 1 & -1 \\ 1 & j & -1 & -j \end{bmatrix} \begin{bmatrix} 1 \\ 1 \\ 0 \\ 0 \end{bmatrix}$$

$$X(0) = 1 + 1 + 0 + 0$$
$$= 2$$
$$X(1) = 1 - j + 0 + 0$$
$$= (1 - j)$$

$$X(2) = 1 - 1 + 0 + 0$$
$$= 0$$
$$X(3) = 1 + j + 0 + 0$$
$$= (1 + j)$$
$$X_4 = \begin{bmatrix} 2 \\ 1-j \\ 0 \\ 1+j \end{bmatrix}$$

(3) **$x[n] = \cos \pi n$; where $n = 0, 1, 2, 3, \ldots$**

$$x[n] = \{1,\ -1,\ 1,\ -1\}$$
$$X_4 = W_4 x_4$$
$$= \begin{bmatrix} 1 & 1 & 1 & 1 \\ 1 & -j & -1 & j \\ 1 & -1 & 1 & -1 \\ 1 & j & -1 & -j \end{bmatrix} \begin{bmatrix} 1 \\ -1 \\ 1 \\ -1 \end{bmatrix}$$
$$X(0) = 1 - 1 + 1 - 1$$
$$= 0$$
$$X(1) = 1 + j - 1 - j$$
$$= 0$$
$$X(2) = 1 + 1 + 1 + 1$$
$$= 4$$
$$X(3) = 1 - j - 1 + j$$
$$= 0$$
$$X_4 = \begin{bmatrix} 0 \\ 0 \\ 4 \\ 0 \end{bmatrix}$$

(4) **$x[n] = \sin \frac{n\pi}{2}$; where $n = 0, 1, 2, 3, \ldots$**

$$x[n] = \{0,\ 1,\ 0,\ -1\}$$
$$X_4 = W_4 x_4$$

$$X_4 = \begin{bmatrix} 1 & 1 & 1 & 1 \\ 1 & -j & -1 & j \\ 1 & -1 & 1 & -1 \\ 1 & j & -1 & -j \end{bmatrix} \begin{bmatrix} 0 \\ 1 \\ 0 \\ -1 \end{bmatrix}$$

$$X(0) = 0 + 1 + 0 - 1$$
$$= 0$$

$$X(1) = 0 - j + 0 - j$$
$$= -j2$$

$$X(2) = 0 - 1 + 0 + 1$$
$$= 0$$

$$X(3) = 0 + j + 0 + j$$
$$= j2$$

$$X_4 = \begin{bmatrix} 0 \\ -j2 \\ 0 \\ j2 \end{bmatrix}$$

Example 2.5

Find the N-point DFT of the following sequences for $0 \le n \le N-1$.

$$x[n] = \delta[n]$$

Solution

$\boldsymbol{x[n] = \delta[n]}$

$$X(k) = \sum_{n=0}^{N-1} x[n] e^{-j\frac{2\pi kn}{N}}$$

$$x[n] = \begin{cases} 1 & n = 0 \\ 0 & n \neq 0 \end{cases}$$

$$\boxed{X(k) = 1}$$

Example 2.6

Find the IDFT of the following functions with $N = 4$.

(1) $X(k) = \{1, 0, 1, 0\}$

(2) $X(k) = \{6, (-2 + j2), -2, (-2 - j2)\}$

Solution

(1) $\boldsymbol{X(k) = \{1, 0, 1, 0\}}$

From Equation (2.10)

$$x_N = \frac{1}{N}[W_N^*]X_N$$

$$X_N = \begin{bmatrix} 1 \\ 0 \\ 1 \\ 0 \end{bmatrix}$$

$$W_N^* = \begin{bmatrix} 1 & 1 & 1 & 1 \\ 1 & j & -1 & -j \\ 1 & -1 & 1 & -1 \\ 1 & -j & -1 & j \end{bmatrix}$$

For $N = 4$

$$x_N = \frac{1}{4}\begin{bmatrix} 1 & 1 & 1 & 1 \\ 1 & j & -1 & -j \\ 1 & -1 & 1 & -1 \\ 1 & -j & -1 & j \end{bmatrix}\begin{bmatrix} 1 \\ 0 \\ 1 \\ 0 \end{bmatrix}$$

$$x[0] = \frac{1}{4}[1 + 0 + 1 + 0] = 0.5$$

$$x[1] = \frac{1}{4}[1 + 0 - 1 + 0] = 0$$

$$x[2] = \frac{1}{4}[1 + 0 + 1 + 0] = 0.5$$

$$x[3] = \frac{1}{4}[1 + 0 - 1 + 0] = 0$$

$$\boxed{x[n] = \{0.5, 0, 0.5, 0\}}$$

(2) $\boldsymbol{x[n] = \{6, (-2+j2), -2, (-2-j2)\}}$

$$x_N = \frac{1}{4}\begin{bmatrix} 1 & 1 & 1 & 1 \\ 1 & j & -1 & -j \\ 1 & -1 & 1 & -1 \\ 1 & -j & -1 & j \end{bmatrix}\begin{bmatrix} 6 \\ -2+j2 \\ -2 \\ -2-j2 \end{bmatrix}$$

$$x[0] = \frac{1}{4}[6-2+j2-2-2-j2] = 0$$

$$x[1] = \frac{1}{4}[6-j2-2+2+j2-2] = 1$$

$$x[2] = \frac{1}{4}[6+2-j2-2+2+j2] = 2$$

$$x[3] = \frac{1}{4}[6+j2+2+2-j2+2] = 3$$

$$\boxed{x[n] = \{0,\ 1,\ 2,\ 3\}}$$

Example 2.7

Compute 4-point DFT of causal three sample sequence given by

$$x(n) = \begin{cases} \frac{1}{3}, & 0 \le n \le 2 \\ 0, & \text{else.} \end{cases}$$

Plot the magnitude and phase spectrum.

Solution N-point DFT of $x(n)$ is

$$X(k) = \sum_{n=0}^{N-1} x(n)e^{-j\frac{2\pi kn}{N}}; \qquad k = 0, \ldots, N-1$$

Here $N = 4$

$$X(k) = \sum_{n=0}^{3} x(n)e^{-j\frac{2\pi kn}{4}} = \sum_{n=0}^{3} x(n)e^{-j\frac{\pi kn}{2}}; \qquad k = 0, 1, 2, 3, \ldots$$

$$X(k) = x(0)e^{0} + x(1)e^{-\frac{j\pi k}{2}} + x(2)e^{-j\pi k} + x(3)e^{-\frac{j3\pi k}{2}}$$

$$= \frac{1}{3} + \frac{1}{3}e^{-\frac{j\pi k}{2}} + \frac{1}{3}e^{-j\pi k} + 0$$

$$= \frac{1}{3}\left[1 + e^{-\frac{j\pi k}{2}} + e^{-j\pi k}\right]$$

$$X(k) = \frac{1}{3}\left[1 + \cos\frac{\pi k}{2} - j\sin\frac{\pi k}{2} + \cos\pi k - j\sin\pi k\right]; \quad k = 0, 1, 2, 3, \ldots$$

For $k = 0$

$$X(0) = \frac{1}{3}[1 + \cos 0 - j\sin 0 + \cos 0 - j\sin 0]$$
$$= \frac{1}{3}[1 + 1 + 1] = 1\angle 0$$

For $k = 1$

$$X(1) = \frac{1}{3}\left[1 + \cos\frac{\pi}{2} - j\sin\frac{\pi}{2} + \cos\pi - j\sin\pi\right]$$
$$= \frac{1}{3}[1 - j - 1] = -\frac{1}{3}j = \frac{1}{3}\angle -\pi/2$$

For $k = 2$

$$X(2) = \frac{1}{3}[1 + \cos\pi - j\sin\pi + \cos 2\pi - j\sin 2\pi]$$
$$= \frac{1}{3}[1 - 1 + 1] = \frac{1}{3}\angle 0$$

For $k = 3$

$$X(3) = \frac{1}{3}\left[1 + \cos\frac{3\pi}{2} - j\sin\frac{3\pi}{2} + \cos 3\pi - j\sin 3\pi\right]$$
$$= \frac{1}{3}[1 + j - 1] = \frac{j}{3} = \frac{1}{3}\angle\pi/2$$

Therefore

$$X(k) = \left\{1\angle 0,\ \frac{1}{3}\angle -\pi/2,\ \frac{1}{3}\angle 0,\ \frac{1}{3}\angle\pi/2\right\}$$

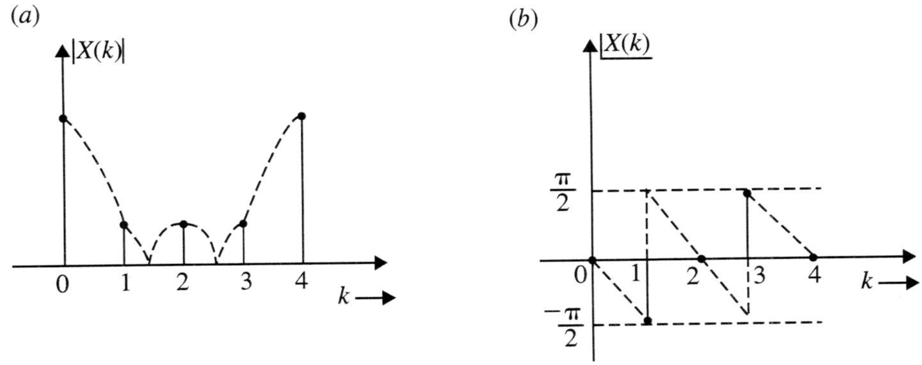

Figure 2.4 Magnitude and phase spectrum of Example 2.7.

$$\text{Magnitude function } |X(k)| = \left\{1,\ \frac{1}{3},\ \frac{1}{3},\ \frac{1}{3}\right\}$$

$$\text{Phase function } \angle X(k) = \left\{0,\ -\frac{\pi}{2},\ 0,\ \frac{\pi}{2}\right\}$$

The magnitude and phase spectrum shown in Figures 2.4(a) and (b) respectively.

Example 2.8

Compute the 4 point DFT of the sequence

$$x(n) = \{0,\ 1,\ 2,\ 3\}$$

Sketch the magnitude and phase spectrum.

Solution Given

$$x(n) = \{0, 1, 2, 3\}$$

Here the length of the sequence $L = 4$. Hence, we can compute 4-point DFT since $N \geq L$. The 4-point DFT of the sequence $x(n)$ is given by

$$X(k) = \sum_{n=0}^{3} x(n)e^{-j\frac{2\pi kn}{4}} = \sum_{n=0}^{3} x(n)e^{-j\frac{\pi kn}{2}}$$

$$= x(0)e^{0} + x(1)e^{-j\frac{\pi k}{2}} + x(2)e^{-j\pi k} + x(3)e^{-j\frac{3\pi k}{2}}$$

$$= 0 + e^{-j\frac{\pi k}{2}} + 2e^{-j\pi k} + 3e^{-j\frac{3\pi k}{2}}$$

$$X(4) = \left(\cos\frac{\pi k}{2} - j\sin\frac{\pi k}{2}\right) + 2\left(\cos\pi k - j\sin\pi k\right) + 3\left(\cos\frac{3\pi k}{2} - j\sin\frac{3\pi k}{2}\right)$$

For $k = 0$

$$X(0) = (\cos 0 - j\sin 0) + 2\,(\cos 0 - j\sin 0) + 3\,(\cos 0 - j\sin 0)$$

$$= 1 + 2 + 3 = 6 = 6\angle 0$$

For $k = 1$

$$X(1) = \left(\cos\frac{\pi}{2} - j\sin\frac{\pi}{2}\right) + 2(\cos\pi - j\sin\pi) + 3\left(\cos\frac{3\pi}{2} - j\sin\frac{3\pi}{2}\right)$$

$$= -j - 2 + 3j = -2 + 2j = 2.8\angle 135^\circ = 2.8\angle 135 \times \frac{\pi}{180}$$

$$= 2.8\angle 0.75\pi$$

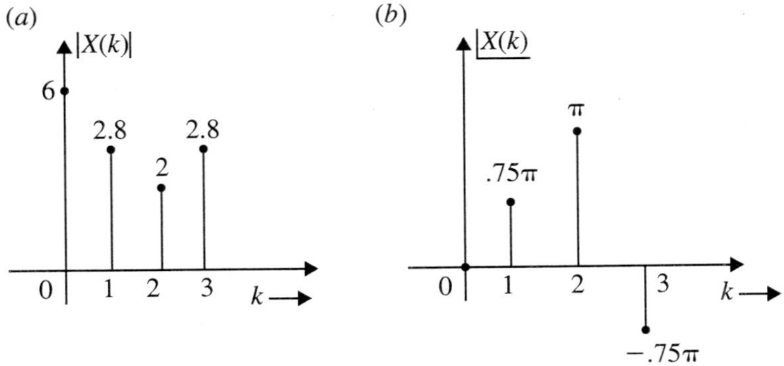

Figure 2.5 Magnitude and phase spectrum of Example 2.8.

For $k = 2$

$$
\begin{aligned}
X(2) &= (\cos\pi - j\sin\pi) + 2(\cos 2\pi - j\sin 2\pi) + 3(\cos 3\pi - j\sin 3\pi) \\
&= -1 + 2 - 3 = -2 = 2\angle 180 = 2\angle 180 \times \frac{\pi}{180} \\
&= 2\angle\pi
\end{aligned}
$$

For $k = 3$

$$
\begin{aligned}
X(3) &= \left(\cos\frac{3\pi}{2} - j\sin\frac{3\pi}{2}\right) + 2(\cos 3\pi - j\sin 3\pi) + 3\left(\cos\frac{9\pi}{2} - j\sin\frac{9\pi}{2}\right) \\
&= j - 2 - 3j = -2 - 2j = 2.8\angle{-135^\circ} = 2.8\angle{-135} \times \frac{\pi}{180} \\
&= 2.8\angle{-0.75\pi}
\end{aligned}
$$

Therefore,

$$X(k) = \{6\angle 0,\ 2.8\angle 0.75\pi,\ 2\angle\pi,\ 2.8\angle{-0.75\pi}\}$$

$$\text{Magnitude function } |X(k)| = \{6,\ 2.8,\ 2,\ 2.8\}$$
$$\text{Phase function } \angle X(k) = \{0,\ 0.75\pi,\ \pi,\ -0.75\pi\}$$

The magnitude and phase spectrum are shown in Figures 2.5(a) and (b) respectively.

Example 2.9

Find the DFT of a sequence $x(n) = \{1, 1, 0, 0\}$ and find the IDFT of $Y(k) = \{1, 0, 1, 0\}$

Solution Let us assume $L = N = 4$. The 4 point DFT of $x(n)$ is

$$X(k) = \sum_{n=0}^{N-1} x(n)e^{-j\frac{2\pi kn}{N}}, \quad k = 0, 1, \ldots, N-1$$

$$X(k) = \sum_{n=0}^{3} x(n)e^{-j\frac{2\pi kn}{N}} = \sum_{n=0}^{3} x(n)e^{-j\frac{\pi kn}{2}}$$

$$X(0) = \sum_{n=0}^{3} x(n) = x(0) + x(1) + x(2) + x(3)$$

$$= 1 + 1 + 0 + 0 = 2$$

$$X(1) = \sum_{n=0}^{3} x(n)e^{-j\frac{\pi n}{2}} = x(0) + x(1)e^{-j\frac{\pi}{2}} + x(2)e^{-j\pi} + x(3)e^{-j\frac{3\pi}{2}}$$

$$= 1 + \cos\frac{\pi}{2} - j\sin\frac{\pi}{2} = 1 - j$$

$$X(2) = \sum_{n=0}^{3} x(n)e^{-j\pi n} = x(0) + x(1)e^{-j\pi} + x(2)e^{-j2\pi} + x(3)e^{-j3\pi}$$

$$= 1 + \cos\pi - j\sin\pi = 1 - 1 = 0$$

$$X(3) = \sum_{n=0}^{3} x(n)e^{-j\frac{3\pi n}{2}} = x(0) + x(1)e^{-j\frac{3\pi}{2}} + x(2)e^{-j3\pi} + x(3)e^{-j\frac{9\pi}{2}}$$

$$= 1 + \cos\frac{3\pi}{2} - j\sin\frac{3\pi}{2} = 1 + j$$

Therefore

$$\boxed{X(k) = \{2,\ 1-j,\ 0,\ 1+j\}}$$

Given $Y(k) = \{1, 0, 1, 0\}$.

The 4 point IDFT of $Y(k)$ is

$$y(n) = \frac{1}{N}\sum_{k=0}^{N-1} Y(k)e^{j\frac{2\pi kn}{N}}, \qquad n = 0, 1, \ldots, N-1$$

$$y(n) = \frac{1}{4}\sum_{k=0}^{3} Y(k)e^{j\frac{2\pi kn}{3}}$$

$$y(0) = \frac{1}{4}\sum_{k=0}^{3} Y(k)$$

$$= \frac{1}{4}[Y(0) + Y(1) + Y(2) + Y(3)]$$

$$y(0) = \frac{1}{4}[1 + 0 + 1 + 0] = 0.5$$

$$y(1) = \frac{1}{4}\sum_{k=0}^{3} Y(k)e^{\frac{j\pi k}{2}}$$

$$= \frac{1}{4}\left[Y(0) + Y(1)e^{\frac{j\pi}{2}} + Y(2)e^{j\pi} + Y(3)e^{\frac{j3\pi}{2}}\right]$$

$$= \frac{1}{4}\left[Y(0) + Y(1)j\sin\frac{\pi}{2} + Y(2)\cos\pi + Y(3)j\sin\frac{3\pi}{2}\right]$$

$$= \frac{1}{4}[1 + 0 - 1 + 0] = 0$$

$$y(2) = \frac{1}{4}\sum_{k=0}^{3} Y(k)e^{\frac{j4\pi k}{4}}$$

$$= \frac{1}{4}\left[Y(0) + Y(1)e^{j\pi} + Y(2)e^{j2\pi} + Y(3)e^{j3\pi}\right]$$

$$= \frac{1}{4}[1 + 0 + \cos 2\pi + 0]$$

$$= \frac{1}{4}[1 + 0 + 1 + 0] = 0.5$$

$$y(3) = \frac{1}{4}\sum_{k=0}^{3} Y(k)e^{\frac{j3\pi k}{2}}$$

$$= \frac{1}{4}\left[Y(0) + Y(1)e^{j\frac{3\pi}{2}} + Y(2)e^{j3\pi} + Y(3)e^{j\frac{9\pi}{2}}\right]$$

$$= \frac{1}{4}[1 + 0 + \cos 3\pi + 0]$$

$$= \frac{1}{4}[1 + 0 - 1 + 0] = 0$$

Therefore,

$$\boxed{y(n) = \{0.5, 0, 0.5, 0\}}$$

Example 2.10

Find the DFT of a sequence

$$x(n) = \begin{cases} 1, & \text{for } 0 \le n \le 2 \\ 0, & \text{otherwise.} \end{cases}$$

for (*i*) $N = 4$ and (*ii*) $N = 8$. Plot $|X(k)|$ and $\angle X(k)$. Comment on the result.

Solution Given length of the sequence $L = 3$. $x[n]$ is represented in Figure 2.6(a).

(i) For $N = 4$ the periodic extension of the sequence is shown in Figure 2.6(b). Consider,

$$x[n] = \{1,\ 1,\ 1,\ 0\}$$

$$X(k) = \sum_{n=0}^{N-1} x(n)e^{-j\frac{2\pi kn}{N}}$$

$$= \sum_{n=0}^{3} x(n)e^{-j\frac{2\pi kn}{4}}$$

$$X(0) = \sum_{n=0}^{3} x(n) = x(0) + x(1) + x(2) + x(3)$$

$$= 3 = 3\angle 0$$

$$X(1) = \sum_{n=0}^{3} x(n)e^{-j\frac{\pi n}{2}}$$

$$= x(0) + x(1)e^{-j\frac{\pi}{2}} + x(2)e^{-j\pi} + x(3)e^{-j\frac{3\pi}{2}}$$

$$= 1 + (-j) + (-1)$$

$$= -j$$

$$= 1\angle \pi/2$$

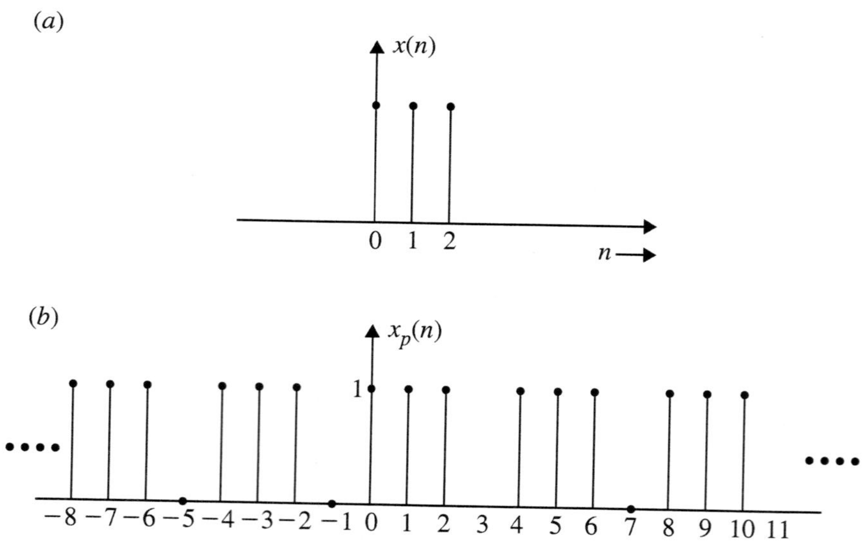

Figure 2.6 DT signal and its periodic extension.

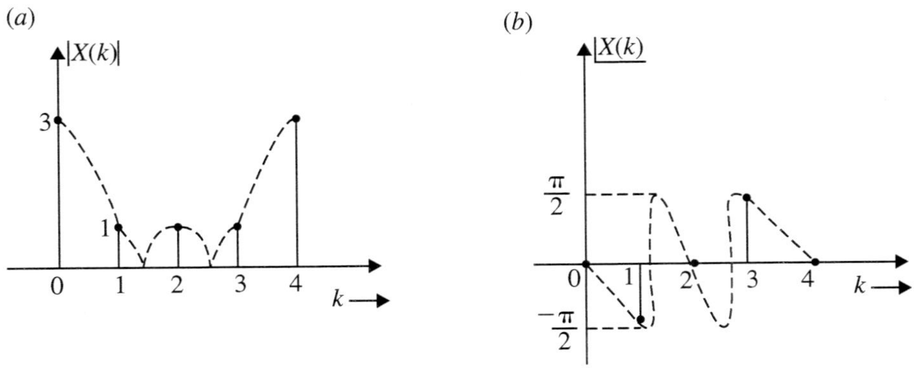

Figure 2.7 Magnitude and phase spectrum for $N = 4$.

$$X(2) = \sum_{n=0}^{3} x(n)e^{-j\pi n}$$

$$= x(0) + x(1)e^{-j\pi} + x(2)e^{-j2\pi} + x(3)e^{-j3\pi}$$

$$= 1 + (-1) + 1 = 1 = 1\angle 0$$

$$X(3) = \sum_{n=0}^{3} x(n)e^{-j\frac{3\pi n}{2}}$$

$$= x(0) + x(1)e^{-j\frac{3\pi}{2}} + x(2)e^{-j3\pi} + x(3)e^{-j\frac{9\pi}{2}}$$

$$= 1 + j - 1 = j = 1\angle \pi/2$$

Therefore,

$$X(k) = \{3\angle 0,\ 1\angle \pi/2,\ 1\angle 0,\ 1\angle \pi/2\}$$

$$|X(k)| = \{3, 1, 1, 1\}$$

$$\angle X(k) = \left\{0, -\frac{\pi}{2}, 0, \frac{\pi}{2}\right\}$$

Magnitude and phase spectrum are shown in Figures 2.7(a) and (b) respectively.

(ii) **For** $N = 8$

$$x(n) = \{1, 1, 1, 0, 0, 0, 0, 0\}$$

$$X(k) = \sum_{n=0}^{7} x(n)e^{-j\frac{2\pi kn}{8}}, \quad k = 0, \ldots, 7$$

$$X(0) = \sum_{n=i}^{7} x(n) = 1 + 1 + 1 + 0 + 0 + 0 + 0 + 0 = 3$$

$$= 3\angle 0$$

$$X(1)=\sum_{n=0}^{7}x(n)e^{-j\frac{\pi n}{4}}$$

$$=x(0)+x(1)e^{-j\frac{\pi}{4}}+x(2)e^{-j\frac{2\pi}{4}}+0+0$$

$$=1+\frac{1}{\sqrt{2}}-j\frac{1}{\sqrt{2}}-j=1.707-j1.707$$

$$X(1)=2.414\angle-\pi/4$$

$$X(2)=\sum_{n=0}^{7}x(n)e^{-j\frac{\pi n}{2}}$$

$$=x(0)+x(1)e^{-j\frac{\pi}{2}}+x(2)e^{-j\pi}+0+0$$

$$=1+\cos\frac{\pi}{2}-j\sin\frac{\pi}{2}+\cos\pi-j\sin\pi$$

$$=1-j-1=-j$$

$$=1\angle-\pi/2$$

$$X(3)=\sum_{n=0}^{7}x(n)e^{-j\frac{3\pi n}{4}}$$

$$=x(0)+x(1)e^{-j\frac{3\pi}{4}}+x(2)e^{-j\frac{3\pi}{2}}+0+0$$

$$=1+\cos\frac{3\pi}{4}-j\sin\frac{3\pi}{4}+\cos\frac{3\pi}{2}-j\sin\frac{3\pi}{2}$$

$$=1-0.707-j0.707+j=0.293+j0.293$$

$$=0.414\angle\pi/3$$

$$X(4)=\sum_{n=0}^{7}x(n)e^{-jn\pi}$$

$$=x(0)+x(1)e^{-j\pi}+x(2)e^{-j2\pi}+0+0$$

$$=1+\cos\pi-j\sin\pi+\cos2\pi-j\sin2\pi$$

$$=1-1+1=1\angle0$$

$$X(5)=\sum_{n=0}^{7}x(n)e^{-j\frac{5\pi n}{4}}$$

$$=x(0)+x(1)e^{-j\frac{5\pi}{4}}+x(2)e^{-j\frac{5\pi}{2}}$$

$$=1+\cos\frac{5\pi}{4}-j\sin\frac{5\pi}{7}+\cos\frac{5\pi}{2}-j\sin\frac{5\pi}{2}$$

$$=1-0.707+j0.707-j$$

$$=0.293-j0.293=0.414\angle-\pi/4$$

$$X(6) = \sum_{n=0}^{7} x(n)e^{-j\frac{3\pi n}{2}}$$

$$= x(0) + x(1)e^{-j\frac{3\pi}{2}} + x(2)e^{-j3\pi} + 0$$

$$= 1 + \cos\frac{3\pi}{2} - j\sin\frac{3\pi}{2} + \cos 3\pi - j\sin 3\pi$$

$$= 1 + j - 1 = j$$

$$= 1\angle\pi/2$$

$$X(7) = \sum_{n=0}^{7} x(n)e^{-j\frac{7\pi nk}{4}}$$

$$= 1 + e^{-j\frac{7\pi}{4}} + e^{-j\frac{7\pi}{2}} + 0$$

$$= 1 + \cos\frac{7\pi}{4} - j\sin\frac{7\pi}{4} + \cos\frac{7\pi}{2} - j\sin\frac{7\pi}{2} + 0$$

$$= 1 + 0.707 + j0.707 + j$$

$$= 1.707 + j1.707$$

$$= 2.414\angle\pi/4$$

Therefore

$$X(k) = \{3, 2.414, 1, 0.414, 1, 0.414, 1, 2.414\}$$

$$\angle X(k) = \left\{0, -\frac{\pi}{4}, -\frac{\pi}{2}, \frac{\pi}{4}, 0, -\frac{\pi}{4}, \frac{\pi}{2}, \frac{\pi}{4}\right\}$$

The magnitude and phase spectrum are shown in Figures 2.8(a) and (b) respectively.

Comments: It is very difficult to extrapolate the entire frequency spectrum with $N = 4$, *i.e.*, the resolution of the spectrum is very poor. In order to increase

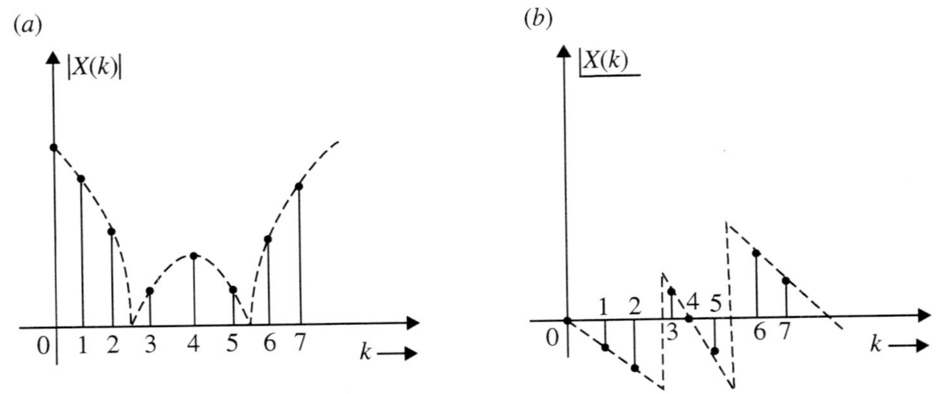

Figure 2.8 Magnitude and phase spectrum for $N = 8$.

the resolution, we must increase N. It is possible to extrapolate the frequency spectrum with $N = 8$. Thus, the zero padding gives us a high density spectrum and provides a better displayed magnitude and phase plots.

Example 2.11

Find IDFT of the sequence $X(k) = \{5, 0, 1 - j, 0, 1, 0, 1 + j, 0\}$

(Anna University, December, 2003)

Solution Given $N = 8$

$$x(n) = \frac{1}{N}\sum_{k=0}^{N-1} X(k)e^{j\frac{2\pi kn}{N}}, \quad n = 0, \ldots, N - 1$$

$$x(n) = \frac{1}{8}\sum_{k=0}^{7} X(k)e^{j\frac{\pi kn}{4}}, \quad n = 0, \ldots, 7$$

$$x(0) = \frac{1}{8}\sum_{k=0}^{7} X(k)$$

$$= \frac{1}{8}[5 + 0 + 1 - j + 0 + 1 + 0 + 1 + j + 0] = 1$$

$$x(1) = \frac{1}{8}\sum_{k=0}^{7} X(k)e^{j\frac{\pi k}{4}}$$

$$= \frac{1}{8}[5 + (1 - j)j + 1(-1) + (1 + j)(-j)]$$

$$= \frac{1}{8}[6] = 0.75$$

$$x(2) = \frac{1}{8}\sum_{k=0}^{7} X(k)e^{j\frac{\pi k}{2}}$$

$$= \frac{1}{8}[5 + (1 - j)(-1) + 1(1) + (1 + j)(-1)]$$

$$= \frac{1}{8}[4] = 0.5$$

$$x(3) = \frac{1}{8}\sum_{k=0}^{7} X(k)e^{j\frac{3\pi k}{4}}$$

$$= \frac{1}{8}[5 + (1 - j)(-j) + 1(-1) + (1 + j)(j)]$$

$$= \frac{1}{8}[2] = 0.25$$

$$x(4) = \frac{1}{8}\sum_{k=0}^{7} X(k)e^{j\pi k}$$

$$= \frac{1}{8}[5 + (1 - j)(1) + 1(1) + (1 + j)(1)] = 1$$

$$x(5) = \frac{1}{8}\sum_{k=0}^{7} X(k)e^{j\frac{5\pi k}{4}}$$

$$= \frac{1}{8}[5 + (1 - j)(j) + (1)(1) + (1 + j)(-j)]$$

$$= \frac{1}{8}[6] = 0.75$$

$$x(6) = \frac{1}{8}\sum_{k=0}^{7} X(k)e^{j\frac{3\pi k}{2}}$$

$$= \frac{1}{8}[5 + (1 - j)(-1) + 1(1) + (1 + j)(-1)]$$

$$= \frac{1}{8}[4] = 0.5$$

$$x(7) = \frac{1}{8}\sum_{k=0}^{7} X(k)e^{j\frac{7\pi k}{4}}$$

$$= \frac{1}{8}[5 + (1 - j)(-j) + 1(-1) + (1 + j)(j)]$$

$$= \frac{1}{8}[2] = 0.25$$

Therefore,

$$\boxed{x(n) = \{1, 0.75, 0.5, 0.25, 1, 0.75, 0.5, 0.25\}}$$

Example 2.12

Two finite duration sequences are given by

$$x[n] = \sin\left(\frac{n\pi}{2}\right) \qquad \text{for } n = 0, 1, 2, 3$$

$$h[n] = 2^n \qquad \text{for } n = 0, 1, 2, 3$$

(a) Calculate the 4 point DFT $X(k)$. (b) Calculate the 4 point DFT $H(k)$ and (c) If $Y(k) = X(k)H(k)$, determine the inverse DFT $y(n)$ of $Y(k)$ and sketch it.

(Anna University, December, 2007)

Solution

(*a*) To calculate the 4 point DFT $X(k)$

Given

$$x[n] = \sin\left(\frac{n\pi}{2}\right) \qquad \text{for } n = 0, 1, 2, 3$$

$$x[n] = \{0,\ 1,\ 0,\ -1\}$$

$$X_4 = W_4 x_4$$

$$= \begin{bmatrix} 1 & 1 & 1 & 1 \\ 1 & -j & -1 & j \\ 1 & -1 & 1 & -1 \\ 1 & j & -1 & -j \end{bmatrix} \begin{bmatrix} 0 \\ 1 \\ 0 \\ -1 \end{bmatrix}$$

$$X(0) = 0 + 1 + 0 - 1 = 0$$

$$X(1) = 0 - j + 0 - j = -j2$$

$$X(2) = 0 - 1 + 0 + 1 = 0$$

$$X(3) = 0 + j + 0 + j = j2$$

$$X_4 = \begin{bmatrix} 0 \\ -2j \\ 0 \\ 2j \end{bmatrix}$$

$$\boxed{X(k) = \{0,\ -2j,\ 0,\ 2j\}}$$

(*b*) Calculate the 4 point DFT $H(k)$

Given

$$h[n] = 2^n \qquad \text{for } n = 0, 1, 2, 3$$

$$h[n] = \{1,\ 2,\ 4,\ 8\}$$

$$H_4 = W_4 h_4$$

$$= \begin{bmatrix} 1 & 1 & 1 & 1 \\ 1 & -j & -1 & j \\ 1 & -1 & 1 & -1 \\ 1 & j & -1 & -j \end{bmatrix} \begin{bmatrix} 1 \\ 2 \\ 4 \\ 8 \end{bmatrix}$$

$$H(0) = 1 + 2 + 4 + 8 = 15$$

$$H(1) = 1 - 2j - 4 + 8j = -3 + 6j$$

$$H(2) = 1 - 2 + 4 - 8 = -5$$

$$H(3) = 1 + 2j - 4 - 8j = -3 - 6j$$

$$H_4 = \begin{bmatrix} 15 \\ -3+6j \\ -5 \\ -3-6j \end{bmatrix}$$

$$\boxed{H(k) = \{15,\ -3+6j,\ -5,\ -3-6j\}}$$

(c)
$$\begin{aligned} Y(k) &= X(k)H(k) \\ &= \{0,\ -j2,\ 0,\ j2\}\{15,\ -3+j6,\ -5,\ -3-j6\} \\ &= \{0 \times 15,\ (-j2)(-3+j6),\ 0 \times (-5), j2(-3-j6)\} \\ &= \{0,\ 6j+12,\ 0,\ -6j+12\} \\ Y(k) &= \{0,\ 12+6j,\ 0,\ 12-6j\} \end{aligned}$$

From Equation (2.10)

$$y_n = \frac{1}{N}[W_N^*]Y_N$$

$$Y_n = \begin{bmatrix} 0 \\ 12+6j \\ 0 \\ 12-6j \end{bmatrix}$$

$$W_N^* = \begin{bmatrix} 1 & 1 & 1 & 1 \\ 1 & j & -1 & -j \\ 1 & -1 & 1 & -1 \\ 1 & -j & -1 & j \end{bmatrix}$$

For $N = 4$

$$y_N = \frac{1}{4}\begin{bmatrix} 1 & 1 & 1 & 1 \\ 1 & j & -1 & -j \\ 1 & -1 & 1 & -1 \\ 1 & -j & -1 & j \end{bmatrix}\begin{bmatrix} 0 \\ 12+6j \\ 0 \\ 12-6j \end{bmatrix}$$

$$y[0] = \frac{1}{4}[0+12+6j+0+12-6j] = 6$$

$$y[1] = \frac{1}{4}[0+12j-6+0-12j-6] = -3$$

$$y[2] = \frac{1}{4}[0-12-6j+0-12+6j] = -6$$

$$y[3] = \frac{1}{4}[0-12j+6+0+12j+6] = 3$$

$$\boxed{y[n] = \{6,\ -3,\ -6,\ 3\}}$$

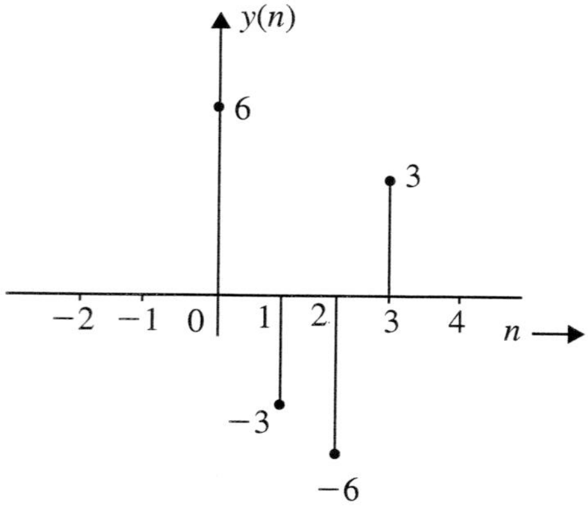

Example 2.13

Compute the DFT of

$$x[n] = e^{-0.5n}, \qquad 0 \le n \le 5$$

(Anna University, June, 2007)

Solution For the given sequence $L = 5$. In general $N \ge L$.

Let $N = 8$

$$X(k) = \sum_{n=0}^{N-1} x(n) e^{\frac{-j2\pi kn}{8}}$$

$$X(k) = \sum_{n=0}^{5} e^{-0.5n} e^{\frac{-j2\pi kn}{8}}$$

$$= \sum_{n=0}^{5} e^{-0.5n} e^{\frac{-j\pi kn}{4}}$$

$$= \sum_{n=0}^{5} \left(e^{-0.5} e^{\frac{-j\pi k}{4}}\right)^n$$

$$= \sum_{n=0}^{5} \left(0.607 e^{\frac{-j\pi k}{4}}\right)^n$$

$$= \frac{1 - \left(0.607 e^{\frac{-j\pi k}{4}}\right)^6}{1 - 0.607 e^{\frac{-j\pi k}{4}}}$$

$$\boxed{X(k) = \frac{1 - 0.05 e^{\frac{-j3\pi k}{2}}}{1 - 0.607 e^{\frac{-j\pi k}{4}}}}$$

The following summation formula is used above.

$$\sum_{n=0}^{N-1} x^n = \frac{1 - x^N}{1 - x}$$

Example 2.14

Calculate the DFT of the sequence

$$x[n] = \{1, 1, -2, -2\}$$

(Anna University, November, 2006)

Solution Given

$$x[n] = \{1, 1, -2, -2\}$$

$$x_4 = \begin{bmatrix} 1 \\ 1 \\ -2 \\ -2 \end{bmatrix}$$

W_4 is given in Equation (2.13)

$$X_4 = W_4 x_4$$

$$= \begin{bmatrix} 1 & 1 & 1 & 1 \\ 1 & -j & -1 & j \\ 1 & -1 & 1 & -1 \\ 1 & j & -1 & -j \end{bmatrix} \begin{bmatrix} 1 \\ 1 \\ -2 \\ -2 \end{bmatrix}$$

$$X(1) = 1 + 1 - 2 + 2 = 2$$

$$X(2) = 1 - j + 2 + 2j = 3 + j$$

$$X(3) = 1 - 1 - 2 - 2 = -4$$

$$X(4) = 1 + j + 2 - 2j = 3 - j$$

$$X_4 = \begin{bmatrix} 2 \\ 3 + j \\ -4 \\ 3 - j \end{bmatrix}$$

4 point DFT of $x(n)$ is

$$\boxed{X(k) = \{2, 3 + j, -4, 3 - j\}}$$

Example 2.15

A finite duration sequence of length L is given as

$$x(n) = \begin{cases} 1, & 0 \le n \le L-1, \\ 0, & \text{otherwise.} \end{cases}$$

Determine the N point DFT of the sequence for $N = L$.

(*Anna University, June, 2007*)

Solution For $N = L$. A finite duration $x(n)$ is

$$x(n) = \begin{cases} 1, & 0 \le n \le N-1, \\ 0, & \text{otherwise.} \end{cases}$$

N point DFT of $x(n)$ is

$$\begin{aligned} X(k) &= \sum_{n=0}^{N-1} x(n) e^{\frac{-j2\pi kn}{N}} \\ &= \sum_{n=0}^{N-1} 1 \cdot e^{\frac{-j2\pi kn}{N}} \\ &= \sum_{n=0}^{N-1} \left(e^{\frac{-j2\pi k}{N}}\right)^n \\ &= \frac{1 - e^{\frac{-j2\pi kN}{N}}}{1 - e^{\frac{-j2\pi k}{N}}} \qquad \because \quad e^{\frac{-j2\pi kN}{N}} = e^{-j2\pi k} = 1 \\ &= 0 \end{aligned}$$

Example 2.16

Compute DFT of $x[n]$

$$x(n) = \begin{cases} 0, & 0 \le n \le 4, \\ 1, & 5 \le n < 7. \end{cases}$$

(*Anna University, December, 2005*)

Solution Given

$$x(n) = \begin{cases} 0, & 0 \le n \le 4, \\ 1, & 5 \le n < 7. \end{cases}$$

$$x[n] = \{0, 0, 0, 0, 0, 1, 1\}$$

Let us assume $N = L = 8$. Therefore, $x[n] = \{0, 0, 0, 0, 0, 1, 1, 0\}$

$$X(k) = \sum_{n=0}^{N-1} x(n)e^{\frac{-j2\pi nk}{N}}, \quad k = 0, \ldots, N-1$$

$$X(k) = \sum_{n=0}^{7} x(n)e^{\frac{-j2\pi nk}{8}}, \quad k = 0, 1, \ldots, 7$$

$$X(k) = \sum_{n=0}^{7} x(n)e^{\frac{-j\pi nk}{4}}, \quad k = 0, 1, \ldots, 7$$

For $k = 0$

$$X(0) = \sum_{n=0}^{7} x(n)$$

$$X(0) = 0 + 0 + 0 + 0 + 0 + 1 + 1 + 0 = 2$$

For $k = 1$

$$\begin{aligned}
X(1) &= \sum_{n=0}^{7} x(n)e^{\frac{-j\pi n}{4}} \\
&= x(0) + x(1)e^{\frac{-j\pi}{4}} + x(2)e^{\frac{-j\pi}{2}} + x(3)e^{\frac{-j3\pi}{4}} + x(4)e^{-j\pi} \\
&\quad + x(5)e^{\frac{-j5\pi}{4}} + x(6)e^{\frac{-j3\pi}{2}} + x(7)e^{\frac{-j7\pi}{4}} \\
&= 0 + 0 + 0 + 0 + 0 + e^{\frac{-j5\pi}{4}} + e^{\frac{-j3\pi}{2}} + 0 \\
X(1) &= -0.707 + 0.707j + j \\
&= -0.707 + 1.707j
\end{aligned}$$

For $k = 2$

$$\begin{aligned}
X(2) &= \sum_{n=0}^{7} x(n)e^{\frac{-j\pi n}{2}} \\
&= x(5)e^{\frac{-j5\pi}{2}} + x(6)e^{-j3\pi} \\
&= -j - 1 = -1 - j
\end{aligned}$$

For $k = 3$

$$\begin{aligned}
X(3) &= \sum_{n=0}^{7} x(n)e^{\frac{-j3\pi n}{4}} \\
&= x(5)e^{\frac{-j15\pi}{4}} + x(6)e^{\frac{-j9\pi}{2}} \\
&= 0.707 + 0.707j - j \\
&= 0.707 - 0.293j
\end{aligned}$$

For $k = 4$

$$X(4) = \sum_{n=0}^{7} x(n)e^{-j\pi n}$$
$$= x(5)e^{-j5\pi} + x(6)e^{-j6\pi}$$
$$= -1 + 1 = 0$$

For $k = 5$

$$X(5) = \sum_{n=0}^{7} x(n)e^{\frac{-j5\pi n}{4}}$$
$$= x(5)e^{\frac{-j25\pi}{4}} + x(6)e^{\frac{-j15\pi}{2}}$$
$$= 0.707 - 0.707j + j$$
$$= 0.707 + 0.293j$$

For $k = 6$

$$X(6) = \sum_{n=0}^{7} x(n)e^{\frac{-j3\pi n}{2}}$$
$$= x(5)e^{\frac{-j15\pi}{2}} + x(6)e^{-j9\pi}$$
$$= j - 1 = -1 + j$$

For $k = 7$

$$X(7) = \sum_{n=0}^{7} x(n)e^{\frac{-j7\pi n}{4}}$$
$$= x(5)e^{\frac{-j35\pi}{2}} + x(6)e^{\frac{-j21\pi}{2}}$$
$$= -0.707 - 0.707j - j$$
$$= -0.707 - 1.707j$$

$$X(k) = \Big\{2,\ -0.707 + 1.707j,\ -1 - j,\ 0.707 - 0.293j,\ 0,\ 0.707 + 0.293j,\ -1 + j,\ -0.707 - 1.707j\Big\}$$

Example 2.17

Compute the DFT of the sequence $x[n] = e^{-n}$ where $0 \leq n \leq 4$.

(Anna University, December, 2004)

Solution Let $N = 8$, therefore

$$x(n) = \begin{cases} e^n, & 0 \le n \le 4, \\ 0, & 5 \le n \le 7. \end{cases}$$

$$\begin{aligned} X(k) &= \sum_{n=0}^{7} x(n) e^{\frac{-j2\pi nk}{8}} \\ &= \sum_{n=0}^{4} x(n) e^{\frac{-j2\pi nk}{8}} \\ &= \sum_{n=0}^{4} e^{-n} e^{\frac{-j2\pi nk}{8}} \\ &= \sum_{n=0}^{4} \left(e^{-1} \cdot e^{\frac{-j2\pi k}{8}}\right)^n \\ &= \sum_{n=0}^{4} \left(0.3679 e^{\frac{-j\pi k}{4}}\right)^n \end{aligned}$$

$$\boxed{X(k) = \frac{1 - \left(0.3679 e^{\frac{-j\pi k}{4}}\right)^5}{1 - 0.3679 e^{\frac{-j\pi k}{4}}}, \qquad k = 0, \ldots, N-1}$$

because

$$\sum_{n=0}^{N} x^n = \frac{1 - x^{N+1}}{1 - x}$$

Example 2.18

Determine the 8 point DFT of the sequence

$$x[n] = \{0,\ 0,\ 1,\ 1,\ 1,\ 0,\ 0,\ 0\}$$

(Anna University, May, 2004)

Solution Given

$$X_N = W_N x_N$$

$$X_8 = W_8 x_8$$

W_8 is given Equation (2.17)

$$x_8 = \begin{bmatrix} 0 \\ 0 \\ 1 \\ 1 \\ 1 \\ 0 \\ 0 \\ 0 \end{bmatrix}$$

$X(0)$ is obtained by multiplying x_8 with first row of W_8. Thus

$$\begin{aligned}
X(0) &= 0 + 0 + 1 + 1 + 1 + 0 + 0 + 0 = 3 \\
X(1) &= \text{2nd row of } W_8 \text{ to multiply } x_8 \\
&= -j - \frac{1}{\sqrt{2}} - \frac{j}{\sqrt{2}} - 1 = -1.707 - j1.707 \\
X(2) &= \text{3rd row of } W_8 \text{ to multiply } x_8 \\
&= -1 + j + 1 = j \\
X(3) &= \text{4th row of } W_8 \text{ to multiply } x_8 \\
&= j + \frac{1}{\sqrt{2}} - j\frac{1}{\sqrt{2}} - 1 = -0.293 + j0.293 \\
X(4) &= \text{5th row of } W_8 \text{ to multiply } x_8 \\
&= 1 - 1 + 1 = 1 \\
X(5) &= \text{6th row of } W_8 \text{ to multiply } x_8 \\
&= -j + \frac{1}{\sqrt{2}} + \frac{j}{\sqrt{2}} - 1 = -0.293 - j0.293 \\
X(6) &= \text{7th row of } W_8 \text{ to multiply } x_8 \\
&= -1 - j + 1 = -j \\
X(7) &= \text{8th row of } W_8 \text{ to multiply } x_8 \\
&= j - \frac{1}{\sqrt{2}} + \frac{j}{\sqrt{2}} - 1 = -1.707 + j1.707
\end{aligned}$$

Therefore,

$$\boxed{\begin{aligned} X(k) = \Big\{&3,\ -1.707 - j1.707,\ j,\ -0.293 + j0.293, \\ &1,\ -0.293 - j0.293,\ -j,\ -1.707 + j1.707\Big\} \end{aligned}}$$

Example 2.19

Find the N-point DFT of the following signals

$$(a) \qquad x[n] = \delta(n - n_0)$$

$$(b) \qquad x[n] = a^n$$

Solution

(a) $x[n] = \delta(n - n_0)$

$$X(k) = \sum_{n=0}^{N-1} x(n) e^{\frac{-j2\pi kn}{N}}$$

$$x[n] = \begin{cases} 1, & n = n_0, \\ 0, & n \neq n_0. \end{cases}$$

$$\boxed{X(k) = e^{\frac{-j2\pi kn_0}{N}}}$$

(b) $x[n] = a^n$

$$X(k) = \sum_{n=0}^{N-1} a^n e^{\frac{-j2\pi kn}{N}}$$

$$= \sum_{n=0}^{N-1} \left(ae^{\frac{-j2\pi k}{N}} \right)^n$$

using summation formula

$$\sum_{n=0}^{N} x^n = \frac{1 - x^{N+1}}{1 - x}$$

we get

$$X(k) = \frac{1 - \left(ae^{\frac{-j2\pi k}{N}} \right)^N}{1 - ae^{\frac{-j2\pi k}{N}}}$$

$$\boxed{X(k) = \frac{1 - a^N}{1 - ae^{\frac{-j2\pi k}{N}}}}$$

2.3 Relationship of the DFT to Other Transforms

2.3.1 Relationship to the Fourier Series Coefficients of a Periodic Sequence

Fourier series of the discrete time signal is written as

$$x(n) = \sum_{k=0}^{N-1} C_k e^{j\frac{2\pi nk}{N}} \qquad -\infty < n < \infty \tag{2.19}$$

where the Fourier series coefficients are represented as

$$C_k = \frac{1}{N}\sum_{n=0}^{N-1} x(n)e^{-j\frac{2\pi nk}{N}} \qquad k = 0, \ldots, N-1 \tag{2.20}$$

$$\text{DFT} \Longrightarrow \quad X(k) = \sum_{n=0}^{N-1} x(n)e^{-j\frac{2\pi nk}{N}} \tag{2.21}$$

Comparing Equations (2.20) and (2.21), we get

$$C_k = \frac{1}{N}X(k)$$

$$\boxed{X(k) = NC_k} \tag{2.22}$$

2.3.2 Relationship to the Fourier Transform of an Aperiodic Sequence

Fourier transform of $x(n)$ is

$$X(\omega) = \sum_{n=-\infty}^{\infty} x(n)e^{-j\omega n} \tag{2.23}$$

$$X(k) = X(\omega)\Big|_{\omega=\frac{2\pi k}{N}}, \qquad k = 0, \ldots, N-1 \tag{2.24}$$

The finite duration sequence

$$X(k) = \sum_{n=0}^{N-1} x(n)e^{-j\frac{2\pi kn}{N}}$$

2.3.3 Relationship to the z-transform

The z-transform of N-point sequence $x(n)$ is given by,

$$X(z) = \sum_{n=0}^{N-1} x(n)z^{-n} \tag{2.25}$$

Let us evaluate $X(z)$ at N equally spaced points on unit circle that is at $z = e^{j\frac{2\pi k}{N}}$

$$X(z)\Big|_{z=e^{j\frac{2\pi k}{N}}} = \sum_{n=0}^{N-1} x(n)e^{-j\frac{2\pi kn}{N}}$$
$$= X(k)$$
$$X(k) = X(z)\Big|_{z=e^{j\frac{2\pi k}{N}}} \quad (2.26)$$

From Equation (2.26), we can conclude that the N-point DFT of a finite duration sequence can be obtained from the z-transform of the sequence at N equally spaced points around the unit circle.

Example 2.20

Consider the finite length sequence $x(n)$ as represented below:

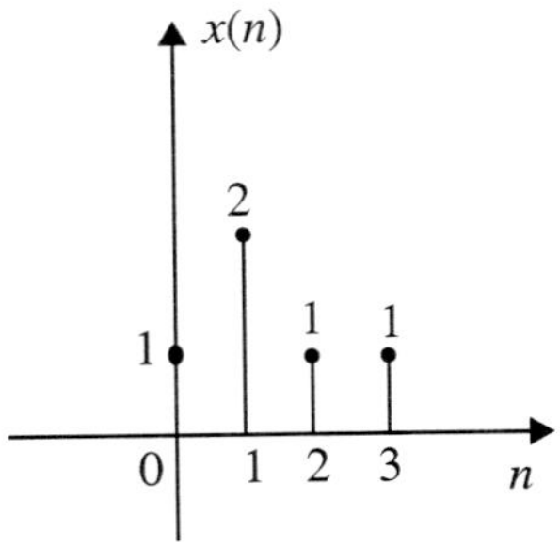

Representation of $x(n)$ sequence.

Let $X(z)$ be the z-transform of $x(n)$. If we sample $X(z)$ at

$$z = e^{j\left(\frac{2\pi}{4}\right)k}, \qquad k = 0, 1, 2, 3$$

Using the relation

$$X_1(k) = X(z)\Big|_{z=e^{j\left(\frac{2\pi}{4}\right)k}}$$

find the sequence $x_1(n)$.

Solution

$$X_1(k) = X(z)\Big|_{z=e^{j\left(\frac{2\pi}{4}\right)k}}$$

$$X(z) = \sum_{n=0}^{3} x(n)z^{-n} = x(0) + x(1)z^{-1} + x(2)z^{-2} + x(3)z^{-3}$$
$$= 1 + 2z^{-1} + z^{-2} + z^{-3}$$

$$X_1(k) = \left(1 + 2z^{-1} + z^{-2} + z^{-3}\right)\Big|_{z=e^{j\left(\frac{2\pi}{4}\right)k}}$$

$$X_1(k) = 1 + 2e^{\frac{-j2\pi k}{4}} + e^{\frac{-j2\pi k\cdot 2}{4}} + e^{\frac{-j2\pi k\cdot 3}{4}}$$

$$X_1(k) = x_1(0) + x_1(1)e^{\frac{-j2\pi k}{4}} + x_1(2)e^{\frac{-j2\pi k\cdot 2}{4}} + x_1(3)e^{\frac{-j2\pi k\cdot 3}{4}}$$

Therefore,

$$\boxed{x_1(n) = \{1,\ 2,\ 1,\ 1\}}$$

2.4 Properties of DFT

2.4.1 Periodicity

If a sequence $x(n)$ is periodic with periodicity of N samples, then N-point DFT of the sequence is also periodic with periodicity of N samples.

Hence, if $x(n)$ and $X(k)$ are an N point. DFT pair, then

$$x(n+N) = x(n) \qquad \text{for all } n$$

$$X(k+N) = X(k) \qquad \text{for all } k \tag{2.27}$$

Proof:

$$X(k) = \sum_{n=0}^{N-1} x(n)e^{-j\frac{2\pi kn}{N}}$$

$$X(k+N) = \sum_{n=0}^{N-1} x(n)e^{-j\frac{2\pi(k+N)n}{N}}$$

$$= \sum_{n=0}^{N-1} x(n)e^{-j\frac{2\pi kn}{N}}e^{-j2\pi n}$$

$$e^{-j2\pi n} = 1 \qquad \text{for all } n, \text{ (Here } n \text{ is an integer)}$$

$$X(k+N) = \sum_{n=0}^{N-1} x(n)e^{-j\frac{2\pi kn}{N}}$$

$$\boxed{X(k+N) = X(k)}$$

2.4.2 Linearity

If

$$x_1(n) \overset{\text{DFT}}{\underset{N}{\longleftrightarrow}} X_1(k) \quad \text{and} \quad x_2(n) \overset{\text{DFT}}{\underset{N}{\longleftrightarrow}} X_2(k)$$

then for any real-valued or complex valued constants a_1 and a_2

$$\boxed{a_1x_1(n) + a_2x_2(n) \overset{\text{DFT}}{\underset{N}{\longleftrightarrow}} a_1X_1(k) + a_2X_2(k)} \tag{2.28}$$

Proof:

$$\begin{aligned}
\text{DFT}\{a_1x_1(n) + a_2x_2(n)\} &= \sum_{n=0}^{N-1} (a_1x_1(n) + a_2x_2(n))e^{-j\frac{2\pi kn}{N}} \\
&= a_1 \sum_{n=0}^{N-1} x_1(n)e^{-j\frac{2\pi kn}{N}} + a_2 \sum_{n=0}^{N-1} x_2(n)e^{-j\frac{2\pi kn}{N}} \\
&= a_1X_1(k) + a_2X_2(k)
\end{aligned}$$

2.4.3 Circular Shift and Circular Symmetric of a Sequence

Consider a finite duration sequence $x(n)$ and its periodic extension $x_p(n)$. The periodic extension of $x(n)$ can be expressed as $x_p(n) = x(n + N)$ where N is the periodicity. For example, let

$$x(n) = \{\underset{\uparrow}{1}, 2, 3, 4\} \quad \text{and} \quad N = 4$$

The sequence and its periodic extension are shown in Figures 2.9(a) and (b) respectively. Let us shift the periodic sequence $x_p(n)$ by two units of time to the right.

Let us denote one period of this shifted sequence by $x'(n)$. The sequence $x'(n)$ can be represented by $x(n - 2, (\text{mod}4))$ where mod 4 indicates that the sequence repeats after 4 samples.

$$\begin{aligned}
x'(n) &= x(n-2,\ \text{mod } 4) \\
x'(0) &= x(-2,\ \text{mod } 4) = x(2) = 3 \\
x'(1) &= x(-1,\ \text{mod } 4) = x(3) = 4 \\
x'(2) &= x(0,\ \text{mod } 4) = x(0) = 1 \\
x'(3) &= x(1,\ \text{mod } 4) = x(1) = 2
\end{aligned}$$

Circular representation of $x(n)$ and $x'(n)$ are shown in Figure 2.10.

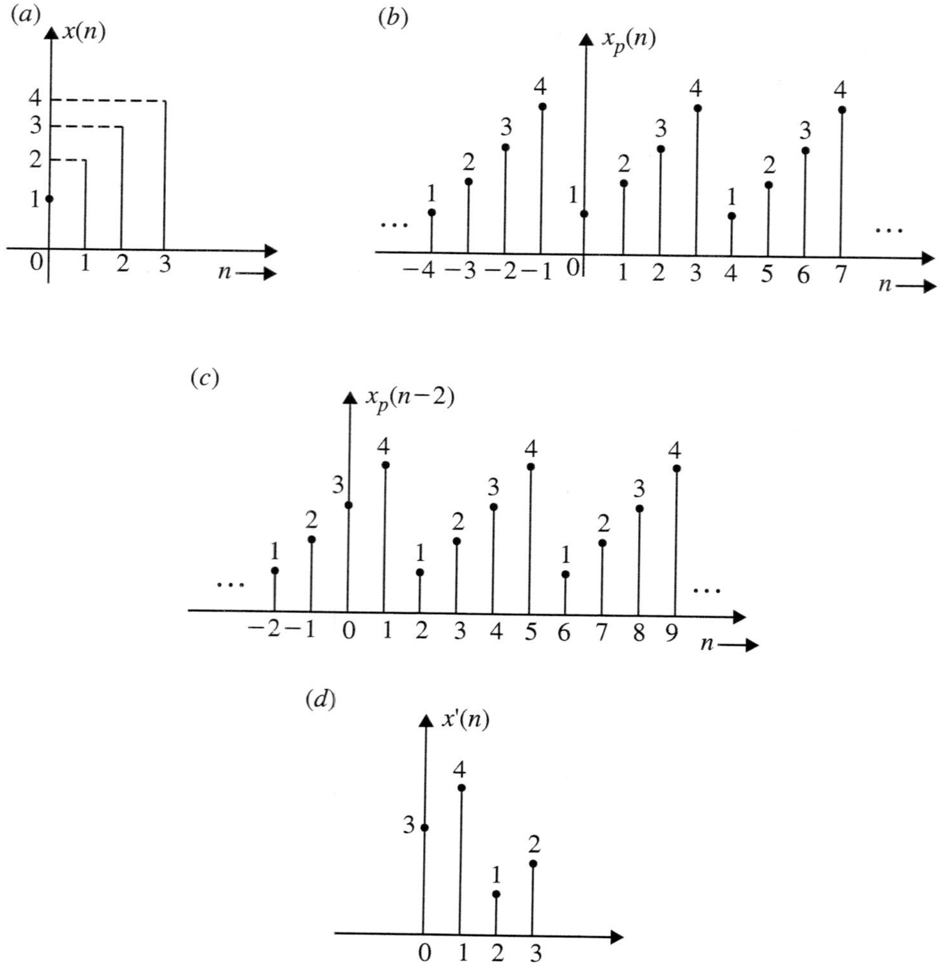

Figure 2.9 (*a*) Discrete time signal $x(n)$, (*b*) periodic extension of $x(n)$, (*c*) shifted periodic extension of $x(n)$ and (*d*) Discrete time signal $x'(n)$

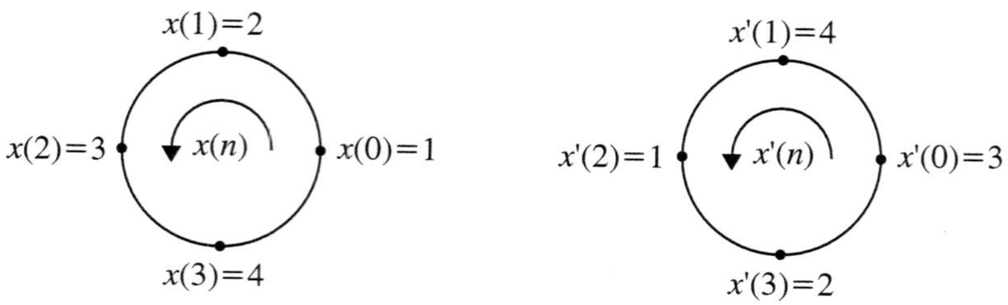

Figure 2.10 Circular representation.

From this, $x'(n)$ is simply $x(n)$ shifted circularly by two units in time where the counterclockwise direction has been arbitrarily selected as positive direction. From this we conclude that a circular shift of an N-point sequence is equivalent to linear shift of its periodic extension.

Let $x(n)$ be a N-point sequence represented on a circle and $x'(n)$ be its shifted sequence by k units of time

$$x'(n) = x(n-k, \bmod 4) = x(n-k)_N \tag{2.29}$$

Even Symmetry

An N-point sequence is called even, if it is symmetric about zero on the circle

$$x(N-n) = x(n) \quad \text{for} \quad 0 \le n \le N-1 \tag{2.30}$$

Odd Symmetry

An N-point sequence is called odd, if it is asymmetric about zero on the circle

$$x(N-n) = -x(n) \quad \text{for} \quad 0 \le n \le N-1 \tag{2.31}$$

Time Reversal

Time reversal of a N point sequence is obtained as

$$x(-n, \bmod N) = x(N-n) \tag{2.32}$$

$$x(-n)_N = x(N-n), \quad 0 \le n \le N-1 \tag{2.33}$$

Time reversal is equivalent to plotting $x(n)$ in a clockwise direction on a circle.

Even and odd sequences for a periodic sequence $x_p(n)$ is given as

$$\text{Even: } x_p(n) = x_p(-n) = x_p(N-n) \tag{2.34}$$

$$\text{Odd: } x_p(n) = -x_p(-n) = -x_p(N-n) \tag{2.35}$$

If the periodic sequence is complex valued, then

$$\text{Conjugate Even: } x_p(n) = x_p^*(N-n) \tag{2.36}$$

$$\text{Conjugate Odd: } x_p(n) = -x_p^*(N-n) \tag{2.37}$$

$$x_p(n) = x_{pe}(n) + x_{po}(n) \tag{2.38}$$

$$x_{pe}(n) = \frac{1}{2}[x_p(n) + x_p^*(N-n)] \tag{2.39}$$

$$x_{po}(n) = \frac{1}{2}[x_p(n) + x_p^*(N-n)] \tag{2.40}$$

2.4.4 Symmetry Properties of the DFT

Let us assume that N-point sequence $x(n)$ and its DFT are complex valued then,

$$x(n) = x_R(n) + jx_I(n) \qquad 0 \leq n \leq N-1$$

$$X(k) = X_R(k) + jX_I(k) \qquad 0 \leq k \leq N-1 \tag{2.41}$$

$$= \sum_{n=0}^{N-1} (x_R(n) + jx_I(n))e^{-j\frac{2\pi kn}{N}}$$

$$= \sum_{n=0}^{N-1} (x_R(n) + jx_I(n))\left(\cos\frac{2\pi kn}{N} - j\sin\frac{2\pi kn}{N}\right)$$

$$X(k) = \sum_{n=0}^{N-1}\left[x_R(n)\cos\frac{2\pi kn}{N} + x_I(n)\sin\frac{2\pi kn}{N}\right]$$

$$-j\sum_{n=0}^{N-1}\left[x_R(n)\sin\frac{2\pi kn}{N} - x_I(n)\cos\frac{2\pi kn}{N}\right]$$

$$= X_R(k) + jX_I(k)$$

where

$$X_R(k) = \sum_{n=0}^{N-1}\left[x_R(n)\cos\frac{2\pi kn}{N} + x_I(n)\sin\frac{2\pi kn}{N}\right]$$

$$X_I(k) = -\sum_{n=0}^{N-1}\left[x_R(n)\sin\frac{2\pi kn}{N} - x_I(n)\cos\frac{2\pi kn}{N}\right]$$

Similarly

$$x_R(n) = \frac{1}{N}\sum_{k=0}^{N-1}\left[X_R(k)\cos\frac{2\pi kn}{N} - X_I(k)\sin\frac{2\pi kn}{N}\right] \tag{2.42}$$

$$x_I(n) = \frac{1}{N}\sum_{k=0}^{N-1}\left[X_R(k)\sin\frac{2\pi kn}{N} + X_I(k)\cos\frac{2\pi kn}{N}\right] \tag{2.43}$$

Case (*i*) Real Value Sequence

If $x(n)$ is real,

$$X(N-k) = X^*(k) = X(-k)$$

$X(k) = X^*(N-k)$, $X(k)$ has complex conjugate symmetry

$$|X(N-k)| = |X(k)|$$

$$\angle X(N-k) = -\angle X(k) \tag{2.44}$$

Case (*ii*) Real and Even Value Sequence

If $x(n)$ is real and even that is,

$$x(n) = x(N-n), \quad 0 \le n \le N-1$$

$$X_I(k) = 0, \quad x_I(n) = 0$$

$$\text{DFT} \implies X(k) = X_R(k) = \sum_{n=0}^{N-1} x(n)\cos\frac{2\pi kn}{N}; \quad 0 \le n \le N-1 \quad (2.45)$$

$$\text{IDFT} \implies x(n) = \frac{1}{N}\sum_{k=0}^{N-1} X(k)\cos\frac{2\pi kn}{N}; \quad 0 \le n \le N-1 \quad (2.46)$$

Case (*iii*) Real and Odd Sequence

If $x(n)$ is real and odd that is,

$$x(n) = -x(N-n)$$

$$X_R(k) = 0, \quad x_I(n) = 0$$

$$\text{DFT} \implies X(k) = jX_I(k) = -j\sum_{n=0}^{N-1} x(n)\sin\frac{2\pi kn}{N}; \quad 0 \le n \le N-1 \quad (2.47)$$

$$\text{IDFT} \implies x(n) = j\frac{1}{N}\sum_{k=0}^{N-1} X(k)\sin\frac{2\pi kn}{N}; \quad 0 \le k \le N-1 \quad (2.48)$$

Case (*iv*) Purely Imaginary Sequence

$$x(n) = jx_I(n)$$

$$X_R(k) = \sum_{n=0}^{N-1} x_I(n)\sin\frac{2\pi kn}{N} \quad (2.49)$$

$$X_I(k) = \sum_{n=0}^{N-1} x_I(n)\cos\frac{2\pi kn}{N} \quad (2.50)$$

$$X(k) = X_R(k) + X_I(k) \quad (2.51)$$

Example 2.21

The first five points of the 8-point DFT of a real valued sequences are

$$\{28,\ -4+j9.565,\ -4+j4,\ -4+j1.656,\ -4\}$$

Determine the remaining three points.

Solution Give $N = 8$,

$$X(0) = 28 \qquad X(1) = -4 + j9.565$$
$$X(2) = -4 + j4 \qquad X(3) = -4 + j1.656$$
$$X(4) = -4$$

We have

$$X(k) = X^*(N-k)$$

The remaining three DFT points are,

$$X(5) = X^*(8-5) = X^*(3) = -4 - j1.656$$
$$X(6) = X^*(8-6) = X^*(2) = -4 - j4$$
$$X(7) = X^*(8-7) = X^*(1) = -4 - j9.565$$

2.4.5 Multiplication of Two DFTs and Circular Convolution

Let $x_1(n)$ and $x_2(n)$ are finite duration sequence of length N. Their respective N-point DFTs are

$$X_1(k) = \sum_{n=0}^{N-1} x_1(n) e^{-j\frac{2\pi nk}{N}}; \quad k = 0, 1, 2, \ldots, N-1 \tag{2.52}$$

$$X_2(k) = \sum_{n=0}^{N-1} x_2(l) e^{-j\frac{2\pi lk}{N}}; \quad k = 0, 1, 2, \ldots, N-1 \tag{2.53}$$

If we multiply the two DFTs together, the result is a DFT, say $X_3(k)$ of a sequence $x_3(n)$ of length N

$$X_3(k) = X_1(k) X_2(k); \quad k = 0, 1, 2, \ldots, N-1 \tag{2.54}$$

$$\text{IDFT}\{X_3(k)\} = x_3(m)$$

By the definition of IDFT

$$x_3(m) = \frac{1}{N} \sum_{k=0}^{N-1} X_3(k) e^{j\frac{2\pi km}{N}} \qquad m = 0, \ldots, (N-1) \tag{2.55}$$

$$= \frac{1}{N} \sum_{k=0}^{N-1} X_1(k) X_2(k) e^{j\frac{2\pi km}{N}}$$

$$= \frac{1}{N} \sum_{k=0}^{N-1} \left[\sum_{n=0}^{N-1} x_1(n) e^{-j\frac{2\pi nk}{N}} \right] \left[\sum_{l=0}^{N-1} x_2(l) e^{-j\frac{2\pi kl}{N}} \right] e^{j\frac{2\pi km}{N}}$$

$$x_3(m) = \frac{1}{N} \sum_{n=0}^{N-1} x_1(n) \sum_{l=0}^{N-1} x_2(l) \sum_{k=0}^{N-1} e^{j\frac{2\pi k[m-n-l]}{N}}$$

Let $(m-n-l) = PN$, where P is an integer.

$$\begin{aligned} e^{\frac{j2\pi k(m-n-l)}{N}} &= e^{\frac{j2\pi kPN}{N}} \\ &= e^{j2\pi kp} = (e^{j2\pi p})^k \end{aligned}$$

From finite geometric series sum formula

$$\sum_{n=0}^{N-1} a^n = \begin{cases} N, & \text{for } a = 1 \\ \frac{1-a^N}{1-a}, & \text{for } a \neq 1. \end{cases}$$

Therefore,

$$\sum_{k=0}^{N-1} e^{\frac{j2\pi k(m-n-l)}{N}} = \sum_{k=0}^{N-1} (e^{j2\pi p})^k = \sum_{k=0}^{N-1} 1^k = N$$

$$\begin{aligned} \therefore \quad x_3(m) &= \frac{1}{N} \sum_{n=0}^{N-1} x_1(n) \sum_{l=0}^{N-1} x_2(l) N \\ &= \sum_{n=0}^{N-1} x_1(n) \sum_{l=0}^{N-1} x_2(l) \end{aligned}$$

If $x_2(l)$ is a periodic sequence with periodicity of N samples then $x_2(l \pm PN) = x_2(l)$. Here $m-n-l = PN$, and therefore $l = m-n-PN$

$$\begin{aligned} x_2(l) &= x_2(m-n-PN) = x_2(m-n)_N \\ &= x_2((m-n), \quad \text{mod } N) \\ \therefore \; x_3(n) &= \sum_{n=0}^{N-1} x_1(n) \sum_{n=0}^{N-1} x_2(m-n)_N \\ &= \sum_{n=0}^{N-1} x_1(n) x_2(m-n)_N \end{aligned}$$

$$\begin{aligned} x_3(n) &= x_1(n) \; Ⓝ \; x_2(n) \\ \text{IDFT } [X_1(k)X_2(k)] &= x_1(n) \; Ⓝ \; x_2(n) \\ X_1(k)X_2(k) &= \text{DFT } [x_1(n) \; Ⓝ \; x_2(n)] \end{aligned} \tag{2.56}$$

Therefore,

$$\boxed{x_1(n) \; Ⓝ \; x_2(n) \overset{\text{DFT}}{\longleftrightarrow} X_1(k)X_2(k)} \tag{2.57}$$

Thus, we conclude that multiplication of the DFT's of two sequence is equivalent to the DFT of the circular convolution of the two sequences.

2.4.6 Time Reversal of a Sequence

If

$$x(n) \overset{\text{DFT}}{\underset{N}{\longleftrightarrow}} X(k)$$

then

$$x((-n))_N = x(N-n) \overset{\text{DFT}}{\underset{N}{\longleftrightarrow}} X((-k))_N = X(N-k) \tag{2.58}$$

Hence, reversing the N-point sequence in time is equivalent to reversing the DFT values (enter the sequence is clockwise direction in the circle).

Proof:

$$\text{DFT}\,\{x(n-N)\} = \sum_{n=0}^{N-1} x(N-m)e^{-j\frac{2\pi kn}{N}}$$

Let $m = N - n$

$$\text{DFT}\,\{x(n-N)\} = \sum_{n=0}^{N-1} x(m)e^{-j\frac{2\pi k(N-m)}{N}}$$

$$= \sum_{m=0}^{N-1} x(m)e^{j\frac{2\pi km}{N}} \cdot e^{-j\frac{2\pi kN}{N}}$$

$$= \sum_{m=0}^{N-1} x(m)e^{-j\frac{2\pi(N-k)m}{N}} = X(N-k)$$

$$X(N-k) = X((-k))_N, \quad 0 \le n \le N-1$$

2.4.7 Circular Time Shift of a Sequence

If

$$x(n) \overset{\text{DFT}}{\underset{N}{\longleftrightarrow}} X(k)$$

then

$$x(n-l)_N \overset{\text{DFT}}{\underset{N}{\longleftrightarrow}} X(k)e^{-j\frac{2\pi kl}{N}} \tag{2.59}$$

Proof:

$$\text{DFT}\,\{x((n-l))_N\} = \sum_{n=0}^{N-1} x((n-l))_N e^{-j\frac{2\pi kn}{N}}$$

$$\text{DFT}\,\{x((n-l))_N\} = \sum_{n=0}^{l-1} x((n-l))_N e^{-j\frac{2\pi kn}{N}} + \sum_{n=0}^{N-1} x(n-l)_N e^{-j\frac{2\pi kn}{N}}$$

let

$$\begin{aligned} x((n-l))_N &= x(N+(n-l)) \\ &= x(N+n-l) \\ m &= N+n-l \end{aligned}$$

$$\begin{aligned} \therefore \sum_{n=0}^{l-1} x((n-l))_N e^{-j\frac{2\pi kn}{N}} &= \sum_{m=N-l}^{N-1} x(N+n-l) e^{-j\frac{2\pi kn}{N}} \\ &= \sum_{m=N-l}^{N-1} x(m) e^{-j\frac{2\pi k(m+l-N)}{N}} \\ &= \sum_{m=N-l}^{N-1} x(m) e^{-j\frac{2\pi km}{N}} \cdot e^{-j\frac{2\pi kl}{N}} \\ \sum_{n=l}^{N-1} x(n-l) e^{-j\frac{2\pi kn}{N}} &= \sum_{m=0}^{N-1-l} x(m) e^{-j\frac{2\pi k(m+l)}{N}} \end{aligned}$$

Therefore,

$$\begin{aligned} \text{DFT}\,\{x(n-l)_N\} &= \sum_{m=N-l}^{N-1} x(m) e^{-j\frac{2\pi k(m+l)}{N}} + \sum_{m=0}^{N-1-l} x(m) e^{-j\frac{2\pi k(m+l)}{N}} \\ &= \sum_{m=0}^{N-1} x(m) e^{-j\frac{2\pi k(m+l)}{N}} \\ &= e^{-j\frac{2\pi kl}{N}} \sum_{m=0}^{N-1} x(m) e^{-j\frac{2\pi km}{N}} \\ &= e^{-j\frac{2\pi kl}{N}} \cdot X(k) \end{aligned}$$

2.4.8 Circular Frequency Shift

If

$$x(n) \overset{\text{DFT}}{\underset{N}{\longleftrightarrow}} X(k)$$

then

$$x(n) e^{j\frac{2\pi ln}{N}} \overset{\text{DFT}}{\underset{N}{\longleftrightarrow}} X((k-l))_N \tag{2.60}$$

Proof:

$$\text{DFT}\,\{X((k-l))_N\} = \frac{1}{N}\sum_{k=0}^{N-1} X((k-l))_N e^{j\frac{2\pi kn}{N}}$$

$$= \frac{1}{N}\sum_{k=0}^{l-1} X((k-l))_N e^{j\frac{2\pi kn}{N}} + \frac{1}{N}\sum_{k=l}^{N-1} X((k-l))_N e^{j\frac{2\pi kn}{N}}$$

Let $X((k-l))_N = X(N+k-l)$

$$N+k-l = m$$

$$\text{when } k = 0 \Longrightarrow \quad m = N-l$$

$$\text{when } k = l-1 \Longrightarrow \quad m = N-1$$

$$\frac{1}{N}\sum_{k=0}^{l-1} X((k-l))_N e^{j\frac{2\pi kn}{N}} = \frac{1}{N}\sum_{m=N-l}^{N-1} x(N+k-l) e^{j\frac{2\pi kn(m+l-N)}{N}}$$

$$= \frac{1}{N}\sum_{m=N-l}^{N-1} X(m) e^{j\frac{2\pi(m+l)n}{N}}$$

$$\frac{1}{N}\sum_{k=l}^{N-1} X((k-l)) e^{j\frac{2\pi kn}{N}} = \frac{1}{N}\sum_{m=0}^{N-1-l} X(m) e^{j\frac{2\pi(m+l)n}{N}}$$

$$\therefore\ \text{DFT}\,\{X((k-l))_N\} = \frac{1}{N}\sum_{m=0}^{N-1} X(m) e^{j\frac{2\pi(m+l)n}{N}}$$

$$= e^{j\frac{2\pi ln}{N}} \frac{1}{N}\sum_{m=0}^{N-1} X(m) e^{j\frac{2\pi mn}{N}}$$

$$= e^{j\frac{2\pi ln}{N}} x(n)$$

$$X((k-l))_N = \text{DFT}\left\{x(n) e^{j\frac{2\pi ln}{N}}\right\}$$

2.4.9 Complex–Conjugate Properties

If

$$x(n) \underset{N}{\overset{\text{DFT}}{\longleftrightarrow}} X(k)$$

then

$$x^*(n) \underset{N}{\overset{\text{DFT}}{\longleftrightarrow}} X^*((-k))_N = X^*(n-k) \tag{2.61}$$

Proof:

$$\text{DFT}\,\{X^*(n)\} = \sum_{n=0}^{N-1} x^*(n)e^{-j\frac{2\pi kn}{N}}$$

$$= \left[\sum_{n=0}^{N-1} x(n)e^{j\frac{2\pi kn}{N}}\right]^*$$

$$\text{DFT}\,\{X^*(n)\} = \left[\sum_{n=0}^{N-1} x(n)e^{-j\frac{2\pi(N-k)n}{N}}\right]^*$$

$$= X^*(n-k)$$

2.4.10 Circular Correlation

2.4.10.1 Circular Cross Correlation

In general, for complex-valued sequence $x(n)$ and $y(n)$ if

$$x(n) \underset{N}{\overset{\text{DFT}}{\longleftrightarrow}} X(k) \quad \text{and} \quad y(n) \underset{N}{\overset{\text{DFT}}{\longleftrightarrow}} Y(k)$$

then

$$\gamma_{xy}(l) \underset{N}{\overset{\text{DFT}}{\longleftrightarrow}} R_{xy}(k) = X(k)Y^*(k) \tag{2.62}$$

2.4.10.2 Circular Auto Correlation

If $x(n) = y(n)$

$$\gamma_{xx} \underset{N}{\overset{\text{DFT}}{\longleftrightarrow}} R_{xx}(k) = |X(k)|^2 \tag{2.63}$$

2.4.11 Multiplication of Two Sequences

If

$$x_1(n) \underset{N}{\overset{\text{DFT}}{\longleftrightarrow}} X_1(k) \quad \text{and} \quad x_2(n) \underset{N}{\overset{\text{DFT}}{\longleftrightarrow}} X_2(k)$$

then

$$x_1(n)x_2(n) \underset{N}{\overset{\text{DFT}}{\longleftrightarrow}} \frac{1}{N}\sum_{k=0}^{N-1} X_1(k) \circledN X_2(k) \tag{2.64}$$

2.4.12 Parseval's Theorem

For complex-valued sequences $x(n)$ and $y(n)$. If

$$x(n) \underset{N}{\overset{\text{DFT}}{\longleftrightarrow}} X(k) \quad \text{and} \quad y(n) \underset{N}{\overset{\text{DFT}}{\longleftrightarrow}} Y(k)$$

then

$$\sum_{n=0}^{N-1} x(n)y^*(n) = \frac{1}{N}\sum_{k=0}^{N-1} X(k)Y^*(k) \tag{2.65}$$

If $x(n) = y(n)$

$$\sum_{n=0}^{N-1} |x(n)|^2 = \frac{1}{N}\sum_{k=0}^{N-1} |X(k)|^2$$

Proof:

$$\begin{aligned} \text{IDFT}\{R_{xy}(k)\} &= \gamma_{xy}(l) \\ &= \frac{1}{N}\sum_{k=0}^{N-1} R_{xy}(k)e^{j\frac{2\pi kl}{N}} \end{aligned}$$

using cross correlation

$$\begin{aligned} \sum_{n=0}^{N-1} x(n)y^*(n-l) &= \frac{1}{N}\sum_{k=0}^{N-1} R_{xy}(k)e^{j\frac{2\pi kl}{N}} \\ \sum_{n=0}^{N-1} x(n)y^*(n) &= \frac{1}{N}\sum_{k=0}^{N-1} R_{xy}(k) \quad [\text{when } l = 0] \end{aligned}$$

If $x(n) = y(n)$

$$\sum_{n=0}^{N-1} |x(n)|^2 = \frac{1}{N}\sum_{k=0}^{N-1} R_{xy}(k)$$

Now

$$\begin{aligned} R_{xy}(k) &= X(k)Y^*(k) \\ X(k) &= Y(k) \\ R_{xy}(k) &= X(k)X^*(k) = |X(k)|^2 \end{aligned}$$

Therefore,

$$\boxed{\sum_{n=0}^{N-1} |x(n)|^2 = \frac{1}{N}\sum_{k=0}^{N-1} |X(k)|^2}$$

Table 2.1 Summary of Properties of the Discrete Fourier Transform.

No.	Finite-length sequence (length N)	N point DFT (length N)
1.	$x(n)$	$X(k)$
2.	$x_1(n), x_2(n)$	$X_1(k), X_2(k)$
3.	$ax_1(n) + bx_2(n)$	$aX_1(k) + bX_2(k)$
4.	$X[n]$	$Nx[((-k))_N]$
5.	$x[((n-m))_N]$	$e^{\frac{-j2\pi km}{N}} X[k]$
6.	$e^{\frac{-j2\pi ln}{N}} Nx(n)$	$X[((k-l))_N]$
7.	$\sum_{m=0}^{N-1} x_1(m)x_2((n-m))_N$	$X_1[k]X_2[k]$
8.	$x_1(n)x_2(n)$	$\frac{1}{2}\sum_{l=0}^{N-1} X_1(l)X_2((k-l))_N$
9.	$x^*(n)$	$X^*((-k))_N$
10.	$x^*((-n))_N$	$X^*(k)$
11.	$\text{Re}\{x(n)\}$	$X_e(k) = \frac{1}{2}\{X((k))_N + X^*((-k))_N\}$
12.	$j\text{Im}\{x(n)\}$	$X_o(k) = \frac{1}{2}\{X((k))_N - X^*((-k))_N\}$
13.	$x_e = \frac{1}{2}\{x(n) + x^*((-n))_N\}$	$\text{Re}\{X(k)\}$
14.	$x_o = \frac{1}{2}\{x(n) - x^*((-n))_N\}$	$j\text{Im}\{X(k)\}$
15.	Symmetric properties	$X(k) = X^*((-k))_N$ $\text{Re}\{X(k)\} = \text{Re}\{X((-k))_N\}$ $\text{Im}\{X(k)\} = -\text{Im}\{X((-k))_N\}$ $\|X(k)\| = \|X((-k))_N\|$ $\angle X(k) = -\angle X((-k))_N$
16.	$x_e(n) = \frac{1}{2}\{x(n) + x((-n))_N\}$	$\text{Re}\{X(k)\}$
17.	$x_o(n) = \frac{1}{2}\{x(n) - x((-n))_N\}$	$j\text{Im}\{X(k)\}$

2.5 Circular Convolution

The circular convolution of two sequences requires that, one of the sequences should be periodic. If both the sequences are non-periodic, then periodically extend one of the sequences and then perform circular convolution.

The circular convolution can be performed only if both the sequences consist of same number of samples. If the sequences have different number of samples, then convert the smaller size sequences to the size of larger size sequence by appending zero padding. The circular convolution has length same as the length of input sequences whereas in linear convolution the length is $N_1 + N_2 - 1$. That is,

$$\text{Linear convolution} \Rightarrow \text{output length} = N_1 + N_2 - 1 \tag{2.66}$$

$$\text{Circular convolution} \Rightarrow \text{output length} = \max(N_1, N_2) \tag{2.67}$$

2.5.1 Method of Performing Circular Convolution

2.5.1.1 *Graphical Method (Concentric Circle Method) (Method 1)*

Let $x_3(m)$ be the sequence obtained by circular convolution of $x_1(n)$ and $x_2(n)$

$$x_3(m) = \sum_{n=0}^{N-1} x_1(n)x_2(m-n) = x_1(n) \circledN x_2(n) \tag{2.68}$$

Procedure

1. Graph N samples of $x_1(n)$ at equally spaced points around the outer circle in counter clockwise direction.
2. Start at the same point as was done for $x_1(n)$. Graph N samples of $x_2(n)$ at equally spaced points around an inner circle in clockwise direction.
3. Multiply corresponding samples on the two circles and sum the products to produce the output.
4. Rotate the inner circle keeping the outer circle fixed by one sample in the counter clockwise direction and repeat step 3 to obtain the next value of output.
5. Repeat step 4 until the inner circle first sample coincides with the first sample of the exterior circle once again. This completes one complete rotation.

Example 2.22

Perform circular convolution of two sequences

$$x_1(n) = \{\underset{\uparrow}{2}, 1, 2, 1\} \quad \text{and} \quad x_2(n) = \{\underset{\uparrow}{1}, 2, 3, 4\}$$

Solution Given

$$x_1(n) = \{\underset{\uparrow}{2}, 1, 2, 1\} \quad \text{and} \quad x_2(n) = \{\underset{\uparrow}{1}, 2, 3, 4\}$$

$m=0$

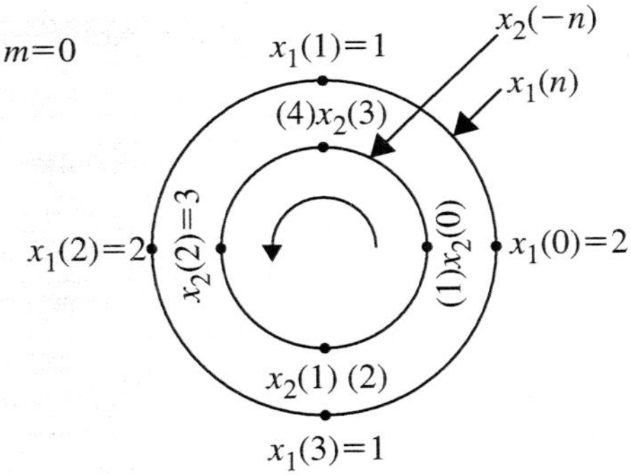

$x_3(0)=2\times1+1\times4+2\times3+1\times2=14$

$m=1$

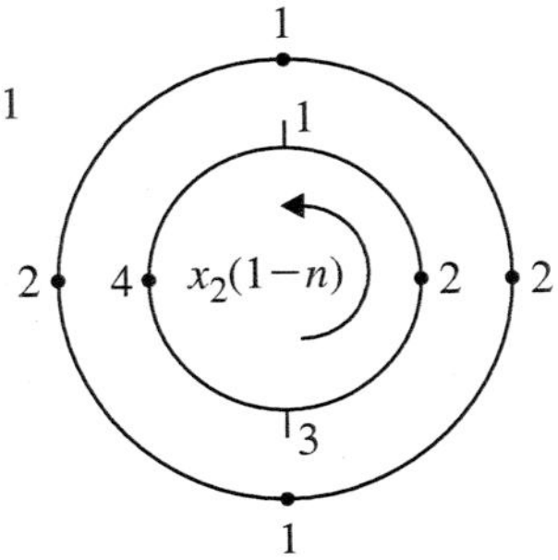

$x_3(1)=2\times2+1\times1+2\times4+1\times3=16$

$m=2$

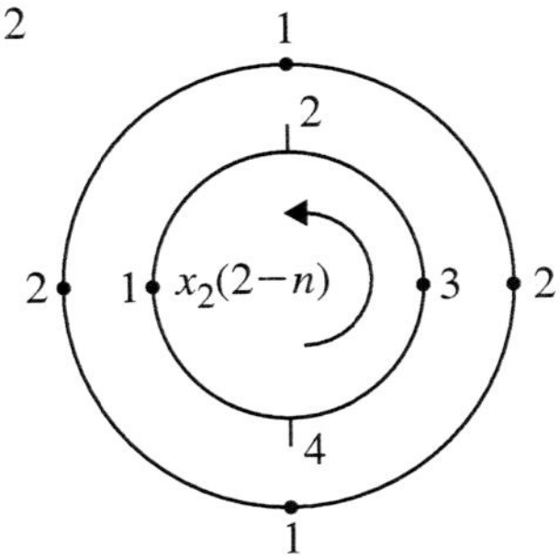

$x_3(2)=2\times3+1\times2+2\times1+1\times4=14$

$m=3$

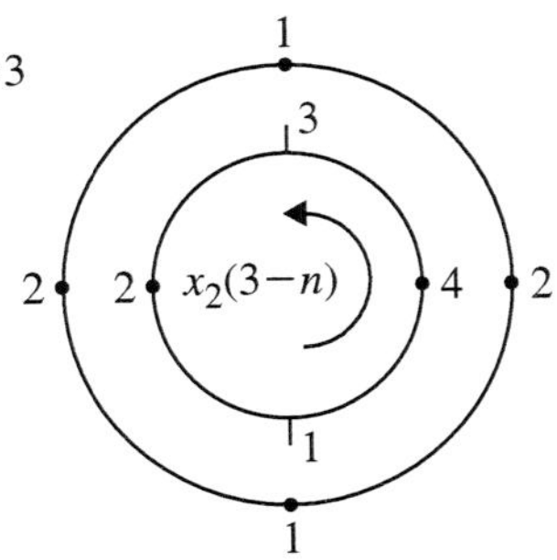

$x_3(3)=2\times4+1\times3+2\times2+1\times1=16$

Figure 2.11 Circular convolution of Example 2.22.

$$\therefore\ x_3(m) = \{\underset{\uparrow}{14}, 16, 14, 16\}$$

2.5.1.2 Circular Convolution Using DFT and IDFT (Method 2)

Procedure

1. Take N point DFT $x_1(n)$ and $x_2(n)$.

$$X_1(k) = \text{DFT}(x_1(n)) \quad \text{and} \quad X_2(k) = \text{DFT}[x_2(n)]$$

2. Determine product of $X_1(k)$ and $X_2(k)$. Let

$$X_3(k) = X_1(k)X_2(k)$$

3.

$$\begin{aligned} x_3(m) &= \text{IDFT}[X_3(k)] \\ &= \text{IDFT}[X_1(k)X_2(k)] \end{aligned}$$

Example 2.23

Find $x_3(m)$ using DFT and IDFT method.

$$x_1(n) = \{2, 1, 2, 1\} \quad \text{and} \quad x_2(n) = \{1, 2, 3, 4\}$$

Solution

$$X_1(k) = \sum_{n=0}^{3} x_1(n)e^{-j\frac{2\pi kn}{4}}, \quad k = 0, 1, 2, 3 \ldots$$

$$X_1(k) = x_1(0) + x_1(1)e^{-j\frac{\pi kn}{2}} + x_1(2)e^{-j\pi k} + x_1(3)e^{-j\frac{3\pi kn}{2}}$$

For $k = 0$

$$X_1(0) = 2 + 1 + 2 + 1 = 6$$

For $k = 1$

$$X_1(1) = 2 + e^{-j\frac{\pi}{2}} + 2e^{-j\pi} + e^{\frac{-j3\pi}{2}} = 2 - j - 2 + j = 0$$

For $k = 2$

$$X_1(2) = 2 + e^{-j\pi} + 2e^{-j2\pi} + e^{-j3\pi} = 2 - 1 + 2 - 1 = 2$$

For $k = 3$

$$X_1(3) = 2 + e^{-j\frac{3\pi}{2}} + 2e^{-j3\pi} + e^{-j\frac{9\pi}{2}} = 2 + j - 2 - j = 0$$

$$X_1(k) = \{\underset{\uparrow}{6}, 0, 2, 0\}$$

$$X_2(k) = \sum_{n=0}^{3} X_2(n)e^{-j\frac{2\pi nk}{4}}, \quad k = 0, 1, 2, 3 \ldots$$

$$X_2(k) = x_2(0) + x_2(1)e^{-j\frac{\pi k}{2}} + x_2(2)e^{-j\pi k} + x_3(3)e^{\frac{-j3\pi k}{2}}$$

For $k = 0$

$$X_2(0) = 1 + 2 + 3 + 4 = 10$$

For $k = 1$

$$X_2(1) = 1 + 2e^{-j\frac{\pi}{2}} + 3e^{-j\pi} + 4e^{-j\frac{3\pi n}{2}} = 1 - 2j - 3 + 4j = -2 + j2$$

For $k = 2$

$$X_2(3) = 1 + 2e^{-j\pi} + 3e^{-j2\pi} + 4e^{-j3\pi} = 1 - 2 + 3 - 4 = -2$$

For $k = 3$

$$X_2(3) = 1 + 2e^{-j\frac{3\pi}{2}} + 3e^{-j3\pi} + 4e^{-j\frac{9\pi}{2}} = 1 + 2j - 3 - 4j = -2 - 2j$$

$$\therefore X_2(k) = \{\underset{\uparrow}{10}, -2 + 2j, -2, -2 - 2j\}$$

$$\begin{aligned} X_3(k) &= X_1(k)X_2(k) \\ &= [6,\ 0,\ 2,\ 0][10,\ -2 + j2,\ -2,\ -2 - j2] \\ &= [6 \times 10,\ 0 \times (-2 + j2),\ 2 \times (-2),\ 0(-2 - j2)] \\ &= \{\underset{\uparrow}{60}, 0, -4, 0\} \end{aligned}$$

$$\begin{aligned} x_3(m) &= \text{IDFT}\ [X_3(k)] \\ &= \frac{1}{N}\sum_{k=0}^{N-1} X_3(k)e^{j\frac{2\pi mk}{N}}, \quad m = 0, 1, 2, 3, \ldots \\ &= \frac{1}{4}\sum_{k=0}^{3} X_3(k)e^{j\frac{2\pi mk}{4}} \\ &= \frac{1}{4}[X_3(0) + X_3(2)e^{j\pi m}] \\ x_3(m) &= \frac{1}{4}[60 - 4e^{j\pi m}] \end{aligned}$$

For $m = 0$

$$X_3(0) = \frac{1}{4}[60 - 4] = \frac{56}{4} = 14$$

For $m = 1$

$$X_3(1) = \frac{1}{4}[60 - 4e^{j\pi}] = \frac{64}{4} = 16$$

For $m = 2$

$$X_3(2) = \frac{1}{4}[60 - 4e^{2j\pi}] = \frac{56}{4} = 14$$

For $m = 3$

$$X_3(3) = \frac{1}{4}[60 - 4e^{3j\pi}] = \frac{64}{4} = 16$$

$$x_3(m) = x_1(n) \circledN x_2(n) = \{\underset{\uparrow}{14}, 16, 14, 16\}$$

2.5.1.3 Circular Convolution Using Matrices (Method 3)

Circular convolution of $x_1(n)$ and $x_2(n)$ is

$$x(m) = x_1(n) \circledN x_2(n)$$

$$= \begin{bmatrix} x_2(0) & x_2(N-1) & x_2(N-2) & \cdots & x(1) \\ x_2(1) & x(0) & x_2(N-1) & \cdots & x(2) \\ \vdots & \vdots & \vdots & \vdots & \vdots \\ x_2(N-1) & x_2(N-2) & x_2(N-3) & \cdots & x(0) \end{bmatrix} \begin{bmatrix} x_1(0) \\ x_1(1) \\ \vdots \\ x_1(N-1) \end{bmatrix}$$

$$= \begin{bmatrix} x_3(0) \\ x_3(1) \\ \vdots \\ x_3(m-1) \end{bmatrix}$$

Example 2.24

Perform the circular convolution using matrices method

$$x_1(n) = \{2, 1, 2, 1\} \quad \text{and} \quad x_2(n) = \{1, 2, 3, 4\}$$

(Anna University, May, 2007)

Solution

$$\overset{x_2(n-k)_N}{\begin{bmatrix} x_2(0) & x_2(3) & x_2(2) & x_2(1) \\ x_2(1) & x_2(0) & x_2(3) & x_2(2) \\ x_2(2) & x_2(1) & x_2(0) & x_2(3) \\ x_2(3) & x_2(2) & x_2(1) & x_2(0) \end{bmatrix}} \overset{x_1(n)}{\begin{bmatrix} x_1(0) \\ x_1(1) \\ x_1(2) \\ x_1(3) \end{bmatrix}} = \overset{x_3(m)}{\begin{bmatrix} x_3(0) \\ x_3(1) \\ x_3(2) \\ x_3(3) \end{bmatrix}}$$

$$\begin{bmatrix} 1 & 4 & 3 & 2 \\ 2 & 1 & 4 & 3 \\ 3 & 2 & 1 & 4 \\ 4 & 3 & 2 & 1 \end{bmatrix} \begin{bmatrix} 2 \\ 1 \\ 2 \\ 1 \end{bmatrix} = \begin{bmatrix} 14 \\ 16 \\ 14 \\ 16 \end{bmatrix}$$

Therefore,

$$\boxed{x_3(m) = x_1(n) \circledN x_2(n) = \{14, 16, 14, 16\}}$$

2.5.2 Performing Linear Convolution Using DFT

To perform linear convolution using DFT both the sequences should be converted into $N_1 + N_2 - 1$ point sequences by padding with zeros. Then take $N_1 + N_2 - 1$ point DFT of both the sequences and determine the product of their DFTs. The resultant sequence is obtained by taking inverse DFT of the product of the DFTs.

Example 2.25

Find the response (linear convolution) of the system whose impulse response and input sequence are

$$h(n) = \{\underset{\uparrow}{0.5}, 1\} \quad \text{and} \quad x(n) = \{\underset{\uparrow}{1}, 0.5\}$$

using DFT-IDFT.

Solution Here $N_1 = 2$ and $N_2 = 2$

$$N = N_1 + N_2 - 1 = 2 + 2 - 1 = 3$$

$$\therefore\ x(n) = \{\underset{\uparrow}{1}, 0.5, 0\} \quad \text{and} \quad h(n) = \{\underset{\uparrow}{0.5}, 1, 0\}$$

$$X(k) = \sum_{n=0}^{2} x(n) e^{\frac{-j2\pi kn}{3}}, \qquad k = 0, \ldots, 2$$

$$X(0) = 1 + 0.5 = 1.5$$

$$X(1) = \sum_{n=0}^{2} x(n) e^{\frac{-j2\pi n}{3}} = 1 + 0.5e^{\frac{-j2\pi}{3}} = 0.75 - j0.433$$

$$X(2) = \sum_{n=0}^{3} x(n) e^{\frac{-j2\pi n2}{3}} = \sum_{n=0}^{3} x(n) e^{\frac{-j4\pi n}{3}}$$

$$= 1 + 0.5e^{\frac{-j4\pi}{3}} + 0 = 0.75 + j0.433$$

Therefore,

$$X(k) = \{1.5, 0.75 - j0.433, 0.75 + j0.433\}$$

$$H(k) = \sum_{n=0}^{2} h(n)e^{\frac{-j2\pi kn}{3}}, \qquad k = 0, \ldots, 2$$

$$H(0) = h(0) + h(1) + h(3) = 0.5 + 1 + 0 = 1.5$$

$$H(1) = \sum_{n=0}^{2} h(n)e^{\frac{-j2\pi n}{3}}$$

$$H(1) = 0.5 + e^{\frac{-j2\pi}{3}} + 0 = 0.5 - 0.5 - j0.866$$

$$= -j0.866$$

$$H(2) = \sum_{n=0}^{2} h(n)e^{\frac{-j4\pi n}{3}}$$

$$= 0.5 + e^{\frac{-j4\pi}{3}} + 0 = j0.866$$

$$H(k) = \{1.5,\ -j0.866,\ j.866\}$$

Let

$$Y(k) = X(k)H(k)$$

$$= \{2.25, -0.375 - j0.6495, -0.375 + j0.6495\}$$

The sequence $y(n)$ is obtained by taking IDFT of $Y(k)$

$$y(n) = \frac{1}{N}\sum_{k=0}^{N-1} Y(k)e^{\frac{j2\pi kn}{N}}, \qquad n = 0, \ldots, N-1$$

$$y(n) = \frac{1}{3}\sum_{k=0}^{2} Y(k)e^{\frac{j2\pi kn}{3}}, \qquad n = 0, \ldots, 2$$

For $n = 0$,

$$y(0) = \frac{1}{3}[y(0) + y(1) + y(2)] = \frac{1}{3}[1.5] = 0.5$$

For $n = 1$,

$$y(1) = \frac{1}{3}\sum_{k=0}^{2} Y(k)e^{\frac{j2\pi k}{3}}$$

$$= \frac{1}{3}\left[y(0) + y(1)e^{\frac{j2\pi}{3}} + y(2)e^{\frac{j4\pi}{3}}\right]$$

$$= \frac{1}{3}[2.25 + 0.75 + j0 + 0.75 + j0] = 1.25$$

For $n = 2$,

$$y(2) = \frac{1}{3}\left[y(0) + y(1)e^{\frac{j4\pi}{3}} + y(2)e^{\frac{j8\pi}{3}}\right]$$
$$= \frac{1}{3}[2.25 - 0.375 + j.6495 - 0.375 - j0.6495]$$
$$= 0.5$$

$$\therefore \quad \boxed{y(n) = \{\underset{\uparrow}{0.5},\ 1.25,\ 0.5\}}$$

Example 2.26

Determine the output response $y(n)$ if

$$h(n) = \{1, 1, 1\} \quad \text{and} \quad x(n) = \{1, 2, 3, 1\}$$

by using (*i*) Linear convolution and (*ii*) Circular convolution.

Solution

(*i*) Linear Convolution

$$N_1 = 4 \quad \text{and} \quad N_2 = 3$$
$$N = N_1 + N_2 - 1 = 4 + 3 - 1 = 6$$

The linear convolution obtained by graphical method is shown in Figure 2.12.

(*ii*) Circular Convolution With Zero Padding

To get the result of linear convolution with circular convolution we have to add appropriate number of zeros to both sequence.

$$N = N_1 + N_2 - 1 = 4 + 3 - 1 = 6$$
$$\therefore\ x(n) = \{1,\ 2,\ 3,\ 1,\ 0,\ 0\}$$
$$h(n) = \{1,\ 1,\ 1,\ 0,\ 0,\ 0\}$$

$$\begin{bmatrix} 1 & 0 & 0 & 0 & 1 & 1 \\ 1 & 1 & 0 & 0 & 0 & 1 \\ 1 & 1 & 1 & 0 & 0 & 0 \\ 0 & 1 & 1 & 1 & 0 & 0 \\ 0 & 0 & 1 & 1 & 1 & 0 \\ 0 & 0 & 0 & 1 & 1 & 1 \end{bmatrix} \begin{bmatrix} 1 \\ 2 \\ 3 \\ 1 \\ 0 \\ 0 \end{bmatrix} = \begin{bmatrix} 1 \\ 3 \\ 6 \\ 6 \\ 4 \\ 1 \end{bmatrix}$$

$$\therefore\ y(n) = \{\underset{\uparrow}{1},\ 3,\ 6,\ 6,\ 4,\ 1\}$$

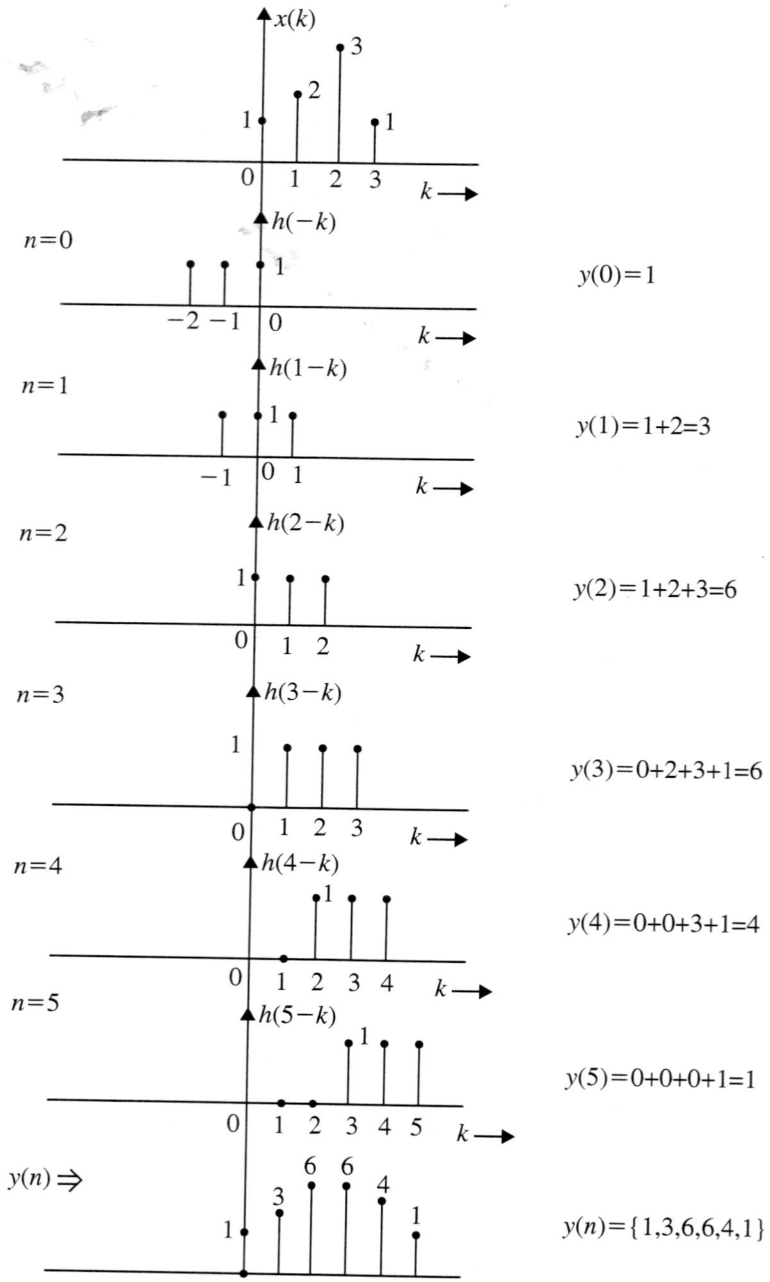

Figure 2.12 Linear convolution of two sequences for Example 2.26.

Example 2.27

For the $x_1(n)$, $x_2(n)$ and N given compute $x_1(n)$ Ⓝ $x_2(n)$

$$(a) \quad x_1(n) = \delta(n) + \delta(n-1) + \delta(n-2)$$

$$x_2(n) = 2\delta(n) - \delta(n-1) + 2\delta(n-2) \qquad (N = 3)$$

$$(b) \quad x_1(n) = \delta(n) + \delta(n-1) - \delta(n-2) + \delta(n-3)$$

$$x_2(n) = \delta(n) - \delta(n-2) + \delta(n-4) \qquad (N = 5)$$

Solution

(*a*) Given

$$x_1(n) = \{\underset{\uparrow}{1}, 1, 1\} \quad \text{and} \quad x_2(n) = \{\underset{\uparrow}{2}, -1, 2\}$$

$$N = 3$$

$$\begin{bmatrix} 2 & 2 & -1 \\ -1 & 2 & 2 \\ 2 & -1 & 2 \end{bmatrix} \begin{bmatrix} 1 \\ 1 \\ 1 \end{bmatrix} = \begin{bmatrix} 3 \\ 3 \\ 3 \end{bmatrix}$$

$$y(n) = x_1(n) \text{ Ⓝ } x_2(n) = \{\underset{\uparrow}{3}, 3, 3\}$$

(*b*) Given

$$x_1(n) = \{\underset{\uparrow}{1}, 1, -1, 1\} \quad \text{and} \quad x_2(n) = \{\underset{\uparrow}{1}, 0, -1, 0, 1\}$$

$$N = 5$$

Add one zero to the sequence $x_1(n)$

$$x_1(n) = \{\underset{\uparrow}{1}, 1, -1, 1, 0\} \quad \text{and} \quad x_2(n) = \{\underset{\uparrow}{1}, 0, -1, 0, 1\}$$

Using matrix method, we get,

$$\begin{bmatrix} 1 & 1 & 0 & -1 & 0 \\ 0 & 1 & 1 & 0 & -1 \\ -1 & 0 & 1 & 1 & 0 \\ 0 & -1 & 0 & 1 & 1 \\ 1 & 0 & -1 & 0 & 1 \end{bmatrix} \begin{bmatrix} 1 \\ 1 \\ -1 \\ 1 \\ 0 \end{bmatrix} = \begin{bmatrix} 3 \\ 0 \\ -1 \\ 0 \\ 2 \end{bmatrix}$$

$$\boxed{y(n) = \{\underset{\uparrow}{3}, 0, -1, 0, 2\}}$$

Example 2.28

Find the circular convolution of $x(n)$ Ⓝ $h(n)$

$$x(n) = 1, \qquad 0 \le n \le 10$$

$$h(n) = \left(\frac{1}{2}\right)^n, \qquad 0 \le n \le 10$$

(Anna University, December, 2005)

Solution

$$x(n) = 1, \qquad 0 \le n \le 10$$

$$x(n) = \{1,\ 1,\ 1,\ 1,\ 1,\ 1\ 1,\ 1,\ 1,\ 1,\ 1\}$$

$$h(n) = \left(\frac{1}{2}\right)^n, \qquad 0 \le n \le 10$$

$$= \{1,\ 0.5,\ 0.25,\ 0.125,\ 0.0625,\ 0.03125\ 0.0156,\ 0.008,\ 0.004,\ 0.002,\ 0.001\}$$

$$h((N-k))_N$$

$$\begin{bmatrix}
1 & 0.001 & 0.002 & 0.004 & 0.008 & 0.0156 & 0.03125 & 0.0625 & 0.125 & 0.25 & 0.5 \\
0.5 & 1 & 0.001 & 0.002 & 0.004 & 0.008 & 0.0156 & 0.03125 & 0.0625 & 0.125 & 0.25 \\
0.25 & 0.5 & 1 & 0.001 & 0.002 & 0.004 & 0.008 & 0.0156 & 0.03125 & 0.0625 & 0.125 \\
0.125 & 0.25 & 0.5 & 1 & 0.001 & 0.002 & 0.004 & 0.008 & 0.0156 & 0.03125 & 0.0625 \\
0.0625 & 0.125 & 0.25 & 0.5 & 1 & 0.001 & 0.002 & 0.004 & 0.008 & 0.0156 & 0.03125 \\
0.03125 & 0.0625 & 0.125 & 0.25 & 0.5 & 1 & 0.001 & 0.002 & 0.004 & 0.008 & 0.0156 \\
0.0156 & 0.03125 & 0.0625 & 0.125 & 0.25 & 0.5 & 1 & 0.001 & 0.002 & 0.004 & 0.008 \\
0.008 & 0.0156 & 0.03125 & 0.0625 & 0.125 & 0.25 & 0.5 & 1 & 0.001 & 0.002 & 0.004 \\
0.004 & 0.008 & 0.0156 & 0.03125 & 0.0625 & 0.125 & 0.25 & 0.5 & 1 & 0.001 & 0.002 \\
0.002 & 0.004 & 0.008 & 0.0156 & 0.03125 & 0.0625 & 0.125 & 0.25 & 0.5 & 1 & 0.001 \\
0.001 & 0.002 & 0.004 & 0.008 & 0.0156 & 0.03125 & 0.0625 & 0.125 & 0.25 & 0.5 & 1
\end{bmatrix}$$

$$\times \overset{x(n)}{\begin{bmatrix} 1 \\ 1 \\ 1 \\ 1 \\ 1 \\ 1 \\ 1 \\ 1 \\ 1 \\ 1 \\ 1 \end{bmatrix}} = \overset{x(n) \circledast h(n)}{\begin{bmatrix} 1.999 \approx 2 \\ 1.999 \approx 2 \\ 1.999 \approx 2 \\ 1.999 \approx 2 \\ 1.999 \approx 2 \\ 1.999 \approx 2 \\ 1.999 \approx 2 \\ 1.999 \approx 2 \\ 1.999 \approx 2 \\ 1.999 \approx 2 \\ 1.999 \approx 2 \end{bmatrix}}$$

$$\boxed{x(n) \circledast h(n) = \{2,\ 2,\ 2,\ 2,\ 2,\ 2,\ 2,\ 2,\ 2,\ 2,\ 2\}}$$

Example 2.29

Find the output sequence $y(n)$ if

$$h(n) = \{1,\ 1,\ 1\} \quad \text{and} \quad x(n) = \{1,\ 2,\ 3\ 1\}$$

using circular convolution.

((Anna University, May, 2004)

Solution

$$\text{Length of output sequence} = N_1 + N_2 - 1$$
$$= 3 + 4 - 1 = 6$$

Therefore

$$h(n) = \{1,\ 1,\ 1,\ 0,\ 0,\ 0\} \quad \text{and} \quad x(n) = \{1,\ 2,\ 3,\ 1,\ 0,\ 0\}$$

using circular convolution

$$y(n) = \overset{h((N-k))_N}{\begin{bmatrix} 1 & 0 & 0 & 0 & 1 & 1 \\ 1 & 1 & 0 & 0 & 0 & 1 \\ 1 & 1 & 1 & 0 & 0 & 0 \\ 0 & 1 & 1 & 1 & 0 & 0 \\ 0 & 0 & 1 & 1 & 1 & 0 \\ 0 & 0 & 0 & 1 & 1 & 1 \end{bmatrix}} \overset{x(n)}{\begin{bmatrix} 1 \\ 2 \\ 3 \\ 1 \\ 0 \\ 0 \end{bmatrix}}$$

$$= \begin{bmatrix} 1+0+0+0+0+0 \\ 1+2+0+0+0+0 \\ 1+2+3+0+0+0 \\ 0+2+3+1+0+0 \\ 0+0+3+1+0+0 \\ 0+0+0+1+0+0 \end{bmatrix} = \begin{bmatrix} 1 \\ 3 \\ 6 \\ 6 \\ 4 \\ 1 \end{bmatrix}$$

Example 2.30

Find the convolution sum of

$$x(n) = \begin{cases} 1, & n = -2, 0, 1 \\ 2, & n = -1 \\ 0, & \text{otherwise.} \end{cases}$$

$$h(n) = \delta(n) - \delta(n-1) + \delta(n-2) - \delta(n-3)$$

(Anna University, December, 2003)

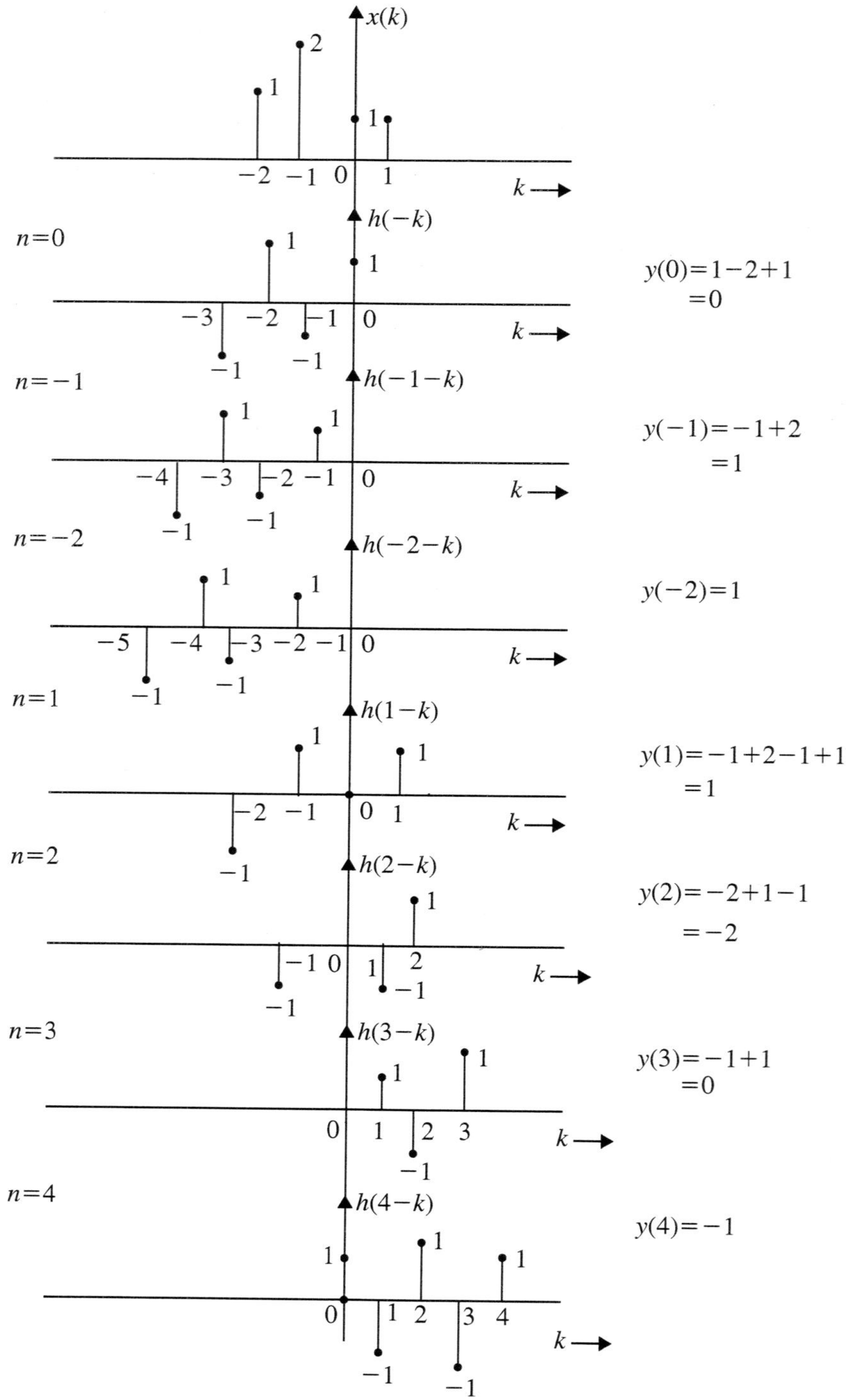

Figure 2.13 Linear convolution of two sequences for Example 2.30.

Solution $x(k)$ and $h(n-k)$ are represented as shown in Figure 2.13. $x(n-k)$ is moved such that it overlaps with $x(k)$ and $y(n)$ is obtained as shown in Figure 2.13.

$$x(n) = \{1, \underset{\uparrow}{2}, 1, 1\} \quad \text{and} \quad h(n) = \{\underset{\uparrow}{1}, -1, 1, -1\}$$

convolution sum

$$\begin{aligned} y(n) &= x(n) * h(n) \\ &= \sum_{n=0}^{N-1} x(k)h(n-k) \end{aligned}$$

Output sequence starts at

$$n = n_1 + n_2 = -2 + 0 = -2$$

Length of output (convolution sum) sequence

$$N = N_1 + N_2 - 1 = 4 + 4 - 1 = 7$$

$$\boxed{y(n) = \{1,\ 1,\ \underset{\uparrow}{0},\ 1,\ -2,\ 0,\ -1\}}$$

2.6 Fast Fourier Transform (FFT)

For spectral analysis of discrete signals, DFT approach is a very straight forward one. For larger values of N, DFT becomes tedious because of the huge number of mathematical operations required to perform. Consider the following DFT where $N = 8$

$$X(k) = \sum_{k=0}^{7} x(n)e^{\frac{-jk2\pi n}{8}}, \qquad k = 0, 1, \ldots, 7 \tag{2.69}$$

Substituting $(k2\pi/8) = K$ in the above equation we get,

$$\begin{aligned} X(k) = x(0)e^{-jK0} &+ x(1)e^{-jK} + x(2)e^{-jK2} + x(3)e^{-jK3} + x(4)e^{-jK4} \\ &+ x(5)e^{-jK5} + x(6)e^{-jK6} + x(7)e^{-jK7} \qquad k = 0, 1, \ldots, 7 \end{aligned} \tag{2.70}$$

Equation (2.70) has eight terms in the right hand side in which each term contains multiplication of a real term with complex exponential. Thus, for example $x(1)e^{-jk} = x(1)[\cos K - j\sin K]$ requires two multiplications and one addition for each value of K where $K = \frac{2\pi k}{8}$, $k = 0, 1, 2, \ldots, 7$. Thus, in Equation (2.70) each term in the right hand side requires eight complex multiplications and seven additions. The 8 point DFT therefore requires $8 \times 8 = 8^2 = 64$ complex multiplications $8 \times 7 = 8(8-1) = 56$ additions.

In general, for an N point DFT, N^2 multiplications and $N(N-1)$ additions are required. For $N = 1024$, about 10^8 multiplications and equal number of additions are required which results in computational burden. Further such a huge number of mathematical operations limit the bandwidth of digital signal processors. Several algorithms have been developed to reduce the computation burden and ease the implementation of DFT. The algorithm developed by Cooley and Tukey in 1965 is the most efficient one and is called Fast Fourier Transform (FFT). The application FFT algorithms are discussed below with illustrated examples.

2.6.1 Radix-2 FFT Algorithm

For efficient computation of DFT several algorithms have been developed based on divide and conquer methods. However, the method is applicable for N not being a prime number. Consider the case when $N = r_1 r_2 r_3 \ldots r_\nu$ where the $\{r_j\}$ are prime. If $r_1 = r_2 = r_3 = \ldots = r$, then $N = r^\nu$. In such a case the DFTs are of size r. The number r is called the radix of the FFT algorithm. The most widely used FFT algorithms are radix-2 and radix-4 algorithms and are discussed in the following sections.

For performing radix-2 FFT, the value of N should be such that, $N = 2^m$. Here the decimation can be performed m times, where $m = \log_2^N$.

In direct computation of N-point DFT, the total number of complex addition are $N(N-1)$ and total number of complex multiplications are N^2. In radix-2 FFT, the total number of complex additions are reduced to $N \log_2^N$ and total number of complex multiplications are $\left(\frac{N}{2}\right) \log_2^N$. Comparison of number of computations by DFT and FFT is shown in Table 2.2.

2.6.1.1 *Decimation in Time (DIT) Radix-2 FFT*

Consider Equations (2.71) and (2.72) which are given below.

$$X(k) = \sum_{n=0}^{N-1} x(n) e^{(-j2\pi kn)/N} \tag{2.71}$$

Table 2.2 Comparison of number of computations by DFT and FFT.

	Direct Computation		Radix-2 FFT	
Number of points N	Addition $N(N-1)$	Multiplication N^2	Addition $N \log_2^N$	Multiplication $\left(\frac{N}{2}\right) \log_2^N$
4	12	16	8	4
8	56	64	24	12
16	240	256	64	32
32	992	1,024	160	80
64	4,032	4,096	384	192
128	16,256	16,384	896	448

$$x(n) = \frac{1}{N}\sum_{k=0}^{N-1} X(k)e^{(j2\pi kn)/N} \tag{2.72}$$

In direct evaluation of spectral components, the number of complex multiplications and additions required are N^2 and $N(N-1)$ respectively as stated in Section 2.6. Such a huge number of mathematical operations limit the BW of digital signal processors. Classical DFT approach does not use the two important properties of twiddle factor namely symmetry and periodicity properties which are given below:

$$W_N^{k+N/2} = -W_N^k$$
$$W_N^{k+N} = W_N^k$$

Radix-2 FFT algorithm exploits these two properties thereby removing redundant mathematical operations. However the results obtained using FFT algorithms is exactly the same as that of DFT. Further, the efficiency of FFT algorithm increases as N is increased. For example, if $N = 512$, DFT requires nearly 110 times more multiplications than FFT algorithm. The basic principle of FFT algorithm is therefore to decompose DFT into successively smaller DFTs. The manner in which this decomposition is done leads to different FFT algorithms. The two basic classes of algorithms are:

1. Decimation in Time (DIT)
2. Decimation in Frequency (DIF)

In the algorithm developed by DIT, the sequence $x(n)$ is decomposed into successively smaller subsequences. In DIF algorithm, the sequence of DFT coefficients $x(k)$ is decomposed into smaller subsequences. DIT Radix-2 FFT algorithm is discussed in this section.

In decimation in Time (DIT) algorithm, the time domain sequence $x(n)$ is decimated and smaller point DFTs are performed. The results of smaller point DFTs are combined to get the result of N-point DFT.

In DIT radix-2 FFT, the time domain sequence is decimated into 2-point sequences. For each two point sequence, the two point DFT is computed. The results of 2-point DFTs are used to compute 4-point DFTs. Two numbers of 4 point DFTs are combined to get an 8-point DFT. This process is continued until we get N-point DFT. In general we can say that, in decimation in time algorithm, the N-point DFT can be realized from two numbers of $\frac{N}{2}$-point DFTs, and the $\frac{N}{2}$-point DFT can be realized from two numbers of $\frac{N}{4}$-point DFTs, and so on. This is explained as given below.

Let us consider N-point DFT of $x(n)$ which is written as,

$$X(k) = \sum_{n=0}^{N-1} x(n)e^{\frac{-j2\pi kn}{N}}, \qquad k = 0, 1, 2, \ldots, (N-1)$$

Let

$$W_N = e^{\frac{-j2\pi k}{N}},$$

where W_N = twiddle factor (or) phase factor. Therefore

$$e^{\frac{-j2\pi kn}{N}} = (e^{-j2\pi})^{\frac{n\pi}{N}} = W_N^{nk}$$

$$X(k) = \sum_{n=0}^{N-1} x(n) W_N^{nk}, \qquad k = 0, 1, 2, \ldots, (N-1) \tag{2.73}$$

Let $x(n)$ be N-sample sequence. Decimate $x(n)$ into two sequences of $\frac{N}{2}$ samples. Let the two sequences be $f_1(n)$ and $f_2(n)$. Let $f_1(n)$ be of even numbered samples of $x(n)$ and $f_2(n)$ that of odd numbered samples of $x(n)$. Thus

$$\therefore\ f_1(n) = x(2n), \qquad n = 0, 1, \ldots, \left(\frac{N}{2} - 1\right)$$

$$f_2(n) = x(2n+1) \qquad n = 0, 1, 2, \ldots, \left(\frac{N}{2} - 1\right)$$

Equation (2.73) can be written as

$$X(k) = \sum_{n=0}^{N-1} x(n) W_N^{kn}$$

$$X(k) = \sum_{n\,=\text{even}} x(n) W_N^{kn} + \sum_{n\,=\text{odd}} x(n) W_N^{kn}, \quad k = 0, 1, 2, \ldots, N-1 \tag{2.74}$$

$$X(k) = \sum_{n=0}^{\frac{N}{2}-1} x(2n) W_N^{k(2n)} + \sum_{n=0}^{\frac{N}{2}-1} x(2n+1) W_N^{k(2n+1)}$$

$$W_N^{k(2n)} = (e^{-j2\pi})^{\frac{k2n}{N}} = (e^{-j2\pi})^{\frac{kn}{\frac{N}{2}}} = W_{\frac{N}{2}}^{kn}$$

$$W_N^{k(2n+1)} = (e^{-j2\pi})^{\frac{k(2n+1)}{N}} = (e^{-j2\pi})^{\frac{k2n}{N}} \cdot (e^{-j2\pi})^{\frac{k}{N}}$$

$$= (e^{-j2\pi})^{\frac{kn}{\frac{N}{2}}} \cdot (e^{-j2\pi})^{\frac{k}{N}}$$

$$= W_{\frac{N}{2}}^{kn} \cdot W_N^k$$

Therefore

$$X(k) = \sum_{n=0}^{\frac{N}{2}-1} f_1(n) W_{\frac{N}{2}}^{kn} + \sum_{n=0}^{\frac{N}{2}-1} f_2(n) W_{\frac{N}{2}}^{kn} W_N^k \tag{2.75}$$

$$X(k) = F_1(k) + W_N^k F_2(k) \tag{2.76}$$

where $F_1(k)$ and $F_2(k)$ are $\frac{N}{2}$ point DFT of $f_1(n)$ and $f_2(n)$ respectively.

$$F_1(k) = \sum_{n=0}^{\frac{N}{2}-1} f_1(n) W_{\frac{N}{2}}^{kn}, \qquad F_2(k) = \sum_{n=0}^{\frac{N}{2}-1} f_2(n) W_{\frac{N}{2}}^{kn} \tag{2.77}$$

$f_1(n)$ would result in the two $\frac{N}{4}$ point sequences and $f_2(n)$ would result in another $\frac{N}{4}$ point sequences.

Let the decimated $\frac{N}{4}$ point sequences of $f_1(n)$ be $V_{11}(n)$ and $f_2(n)$ be $V_{12}(n)$. That is,

$$V_{11}(n) = f_1(2n), \qquad n = 0, 1, 2, \ldots, \left(\frac{N}{4} - 1\right)$$

$$V_{12}(n) = f_1(2n+1), \qquad n = 0, 1, 2, \ldots, \left(\frac{N}{4} - 1\right)$$

$$V_{21}(n) = f_2(2n), \qquad n = 0, 1, 2, \ldots, \left(\frac{N}{4} - 1\right)$$

$$V_{22}(n) = f_2(2n+1), \qquad n = 0, 1, 2, \ldots, \left(\frac{N}{4} - 1\right)$$

Let

$$V_{11}(k) = \frac{N}{4} \text{ point DFT of } V_{11}(n)$$

$$V_{12}(k) = \frac{N}{4} \text{ point DFT of } V_{12}(n)$$

$$V_{21}(k) = \frac{N}{4} \text{ point DFT of } V_{21}(n)$$

$$V_{22}(k) = \frac{N}{4} \text{ point DFT of } V_{22}(n)$$

Therefore

$$F_1(k) = V_{11}(k) + W_{\frac{N}{2}}^{k} V_{12}(k), \qquad k = 0, 1, 2, \ldots, \left(\frac{N}{2} - 1\right) \tag{2.78}$$

$$F_1\left(k + \frac{N}{4}\right) = V_{11}(k) - W_{\frac{N}{2}}^{k} V_{12}(k), \qquad k = 0, 1, 2, \ldots, \left(\frac{N}{2} - 1\right)$$

$$F_2(k) = V_{21}(k) + W_{\frac{N}{2}}^{k} V_{22}(k), \qquad k = 0, 1, 2, \ldots, \left(\frac{N}{2} - 1\right) \tag{2.79}$$

$$F_2\left(k + \frac{N}{4}\right) = V_{21}(k) - W_{\frac{N}{2}}^{k} V_{22}(k), \qquad k = 0, 1, 2, \ldots, \left(\frac{N}{2} - 1\right)$$

The decimation of the data sequence can be repeated again and again until the resulting sequences are reduced to two-point sequence.

8-point DFT Using Radix-2 DIT FFT

Let us consider the computation of an $N = 8$ point DFT. Here $N = 8 = 2^3$, and therefore the number of stages of computation is equal to 3. The given 8-point sequence is decimated to 2-point sequences. For each 2-point sequence, the 2-point

DFT is computed. From the result of 2-point DFT, 4-point DFT can be computed. From the result of 4-point DFT, 8-point DFT can be computed. The block diagram of radix-2 DIT FFT for $N = 8$ is shown in Figure 2.14(a).

Step 1: Before Decimation the Sequences are Arranged in Bit Reversed Order

Let us consider $N = 8$ sequence. In the first level decimation we have the sequence $x(0), x(2), x(4), x(6), x(1), x(3), x(5), x(7)$ and in the second level decimation, the

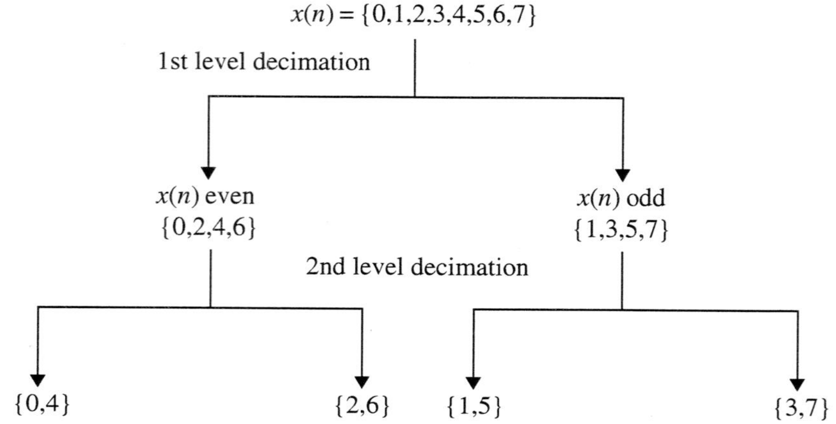

Figure 2.14 (a) Data sequence decimation by Radix-2.

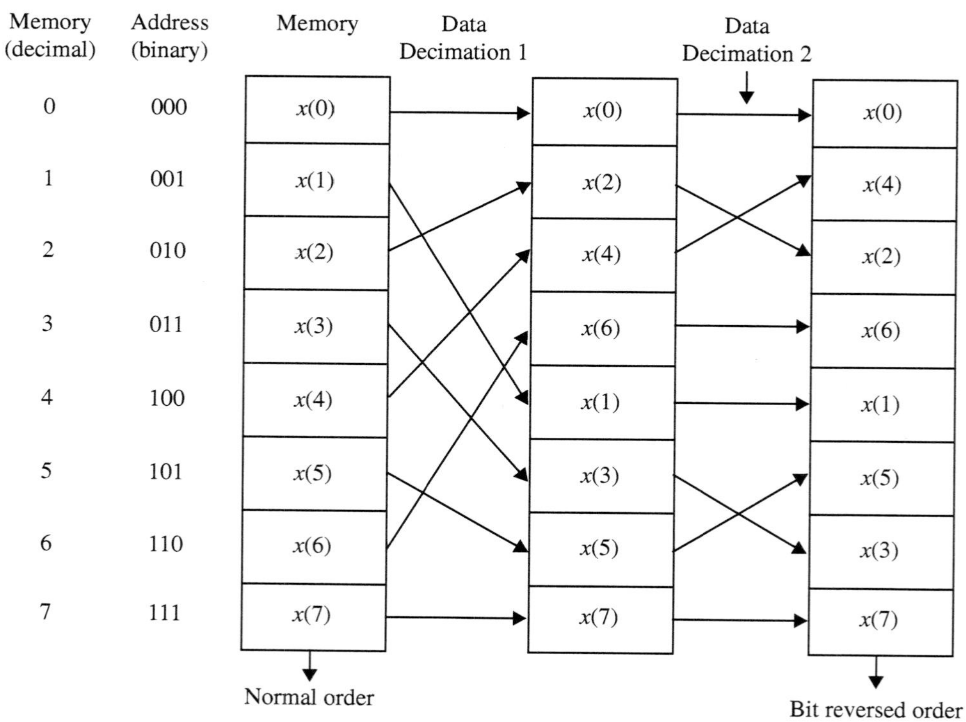

Figure 2.14 (b) Shifting of data and bit reversal.

sequence is $x(0), x(4), x(2), x(6), x(1), x(5), x(3)$ and $x(7)$. This is represented in Figure 2.14(a).

The shifting of the input data sequences is to be arranged in a well-defined order. The index n of $x(n)$ is expressed in binary form. The data point $x(4)$ is expressed in binary form as $x(100)$ and is placed in position $m = 001$ or $m = 1$ in the decimal array. Now the data $x(n)$ after decimation is stored in bit reversed order as shown in Figure 2.14(b).

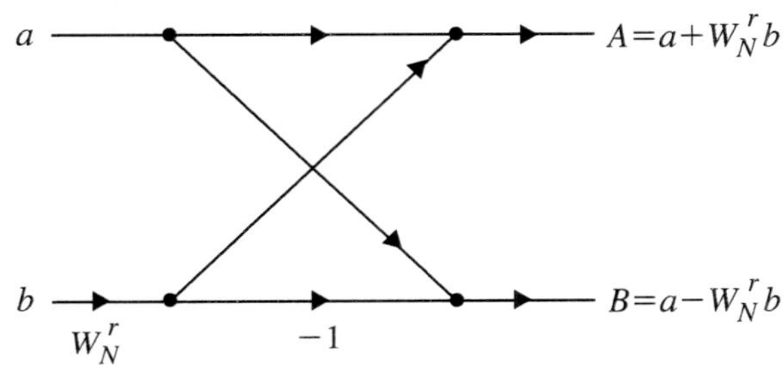

Figure 2.15 Basic butterfly computation in the DIT-FFT algorithm.

The basic computation in the above Figure 2.14(b) involves butterfly operation which is illustrated in Figure 2.15. Consider number a and b. The number b is multiplied by W_N^r and then added and the product subtracted form a to form a new complex numbers (A, B). This basic computation is called butterfly because the flow graph resembles a butterfly. In each butterfly one complex multiplication and two complex additions are performed.

Natural Order		**Bit Reversed Order**	
$x(0)$	$x(000)$	$x(000)$	$x(0)$
$x(1)$	$x(001)$	$x(100)$	$x(4)$
$x(2)$	$x(010)$	$x(010)$	$x(2)$
$x(3)$	$x(011)$	$x(110)$	$x(6)$
$x(4)$	$x(100)$	$x(001)$	$x(1)$
$x(5)$	$x(101)$	$x(101)$	$x(5)$
$x(6)$	$x(110)$	$x(011)$	$x(3)$
$x(7)$	$x(111)$	$x(111)$	$x(7)$

Let

$$x(n) = \text{8-point sequence}$$
$$f_1(n),\ f_2(n) = \text{4-point sequences obtained from } x(n)$$
$$V_{11}(n),\ V_{12}(n) = \text{2-point sequences obtained from } f_1(n)$$
$$V_{21}(n),\ V_{22}(n) = \text{2-point sequences obtained from } f_2(n)$$

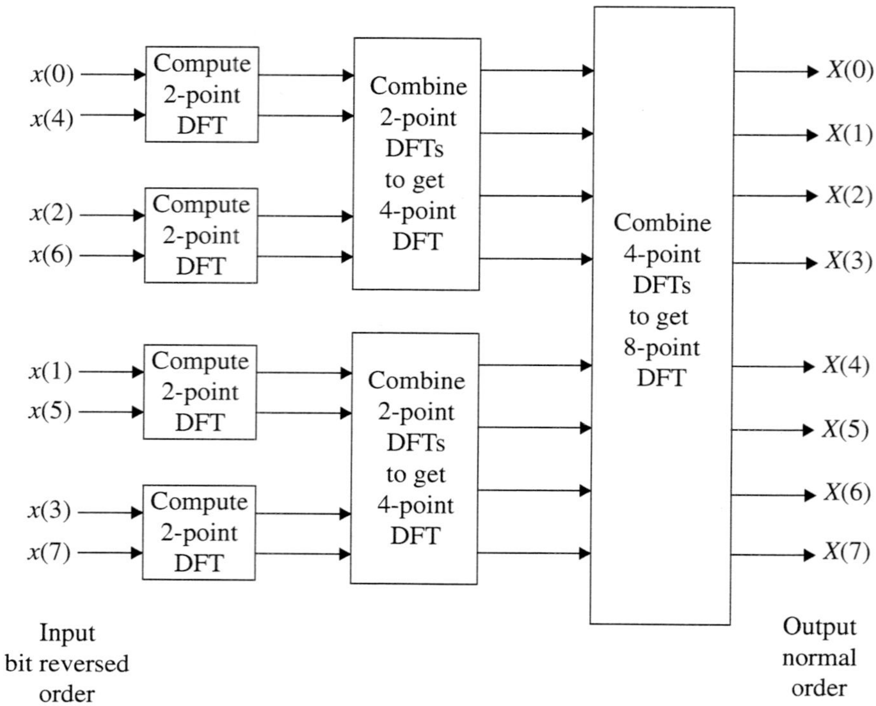

Figure 2.16 Block diagram of radix-2 DIT-FFT.

First Stage (2-point DFT Computation)

2-point DFT of $V_{11}(n)$ is

$$V_{11}(k) = \sum_{n=0,1} V_{11}(n) W_{\frac{N}{4}}^{nk} \quad \text{for } k = 0, 1 \tag{2.80}$$

$$V_{11}(0) = \sum_{n=0,1} V_{11}(n) = V_{11}(0) + V_{11}(1) = x(0) + x(4)$$

$$V_{11}(1) = \sum_{n=0,1} V_{11}(n) W_{\frac{N}{4}}^{n} = V_{11}(0) W_{\frac{N}{4}}^{0} + V_{11}(1) W_{\frac{N}{4}}^{1}$$

$$= V_{11}(0) - V_{11}(1) W_{\frac{N}{4}}^{0} = x(0) - x(4)$$

Similarly,

$$V_{12}(k) = \sum_{n=0,1} V_{12}(n) W_{\frac{N}{4}}^{nk}, \qquad k = 0, 1 \tag{2.81}$$

$$V_{12}(0) = \sum_{n=0,1} V_{12}(n) = V_{12}(0) + V_{12}(1) = x(2) + x(6)$$

$$
\begin{aligned}
V_{12}(1) &= \sum_{n=0,1} V_{12}(n)W_{\frac{N}{4}}^{n} = V_{12}(0)W_{\frac{N}{4}}^{0} + V_{12}(1)W_{\frac{N}{4}}^{1} \\
&= V_{12}(0) - V_{12}(1) \\
&= x(2) - x(6)
\end{aligned}
$$

$$
V_{21}(k) = \sum_{n=0,1} V_{21}(n)W_{\frac{N}{4}}^{nk}, \qquad k = 0, 1 \tag{2.82}
$$

$$
V_{21}(0) = \sum_{n=0,1} V_{21}(n) = V_{21}(0) + V_{21}(1) = x(1) + x(5)
$$

$$
\begin{aligned}
V_{21}(1) &= \sum_{n=0,1} V_{21}(n)W_{\frac{N}{4}}^{n} = V_{21}(0) + V_{21}(1)W_{\frac{N}{4}}^{1} \\
&= V_{21}(0) - V_{21}(1) \\
&= x(1) - x(5)
\end{aligned}
$$

$$
V_{22}(k) = \sum_{n=0,1} V_{22}(n)W_{\frac{N}{4}}^{nk}, \qquad k = 0, 1 \tag{2.83}
$$

$$
V_{22}(0) = \sum_{n=0,1} V_{22}(n) = V_{22}(0) + V_{22}(1) = x(3) + x(7)
$$

$$
\begin{aligned}
V_{22}(1) &= \sum_{n=0,1} V_{22}(n)W_{\frac{N}{7}}^{n} = V_{22}(0) + V_{22}(1)W_{\frac{N}{4}}^{1} \\
&= V_{22}(0) - V_{22}(1)
\end{aligned}
$$

The Second Stage Computation (4-point DFT)

Let

$$
F_1(k) = \text{DFT}\,[f_1(n)] \quad \text{and} \quad F_2(k) = \text{DFT}\,[f_2(n)]
$$

From the Equation (2.81) we get,

$$
\begin{aligned}
F_1(k) &= V_{11}(k) + W_{\frac{N}{2}}^{k}V_{12}(k) \quad \text{for } k = 0, 1, 2, 3 \\
F_1(0) &= V_{11}(0) + W_{\frac{N}{2}}^{0}V_{12}(0) \\
F_1(1) &= V_{11}(1) + W_{\frac{N}{2}}^{1}V_{12}(1) \\
F_1(2) &= V_{11}(2) + W_{\frac{N}{2}}^{2}V_{12}(2) \\
&= V_{11}(0) - W_{\frac{N}{2}}^{0}V_{12}(0) \\
F_1(3) &= V_{11}(3) + W_{\frac{N}{2}}^{3}V_{12}(3) \\
&= V_{11}(1) - W_{\frac{N}{2}}^{1}V_{12}(1)
\end{aligned}
$$

Here $V_{11}(k)$ and $V_{12}(k)$ are periodic with periodicity 2. Therefore,

$$V_{11}(k+2) = V_{11}(k) \quad \text{and} \quad V_{12}(k+2) = V_{12}(k)$$

Similarly, from the Equation (2.82) we get,

$$F_2(k) = V_{21}(k) + W_{\frac{N}{2}}^{k} V_{22}(k) \quad \text{for } k = 0, 1, 2, 3$$

$$F_2(0) = V_{21}(0) + W_{\frac{N}{2}}^{0} V_{22}(0)$$

$$F_2(1) = V_{21}(1) + W_{\frac{N}{2}}^{1} V_{22}(1)$$

$$F_2(2) = V_{21}(2) + W_{\frac{N}{2}}^{2} V_{22}(2)$$

$$= V_{21}(0) - W_{\frac{N}{2}}^{0} V_{22}(0)$$

$$F_2(3) = V_{21}(3) + W_{\frac{N}{2}}^{3} V_{22}(3)$$

$$= V_{21}(1) - W_{\frac{N}{2}}^{1} V_{22}(1)$$

The Third Stage of Computation (8-point DFT)

Let

$$X(k) = \text{DFT } x(n)$$

$$\therefore X(k) = F_1(k) + W_N^k F_2(k), \quad \text{for } k = 0, 1, 2, 3, 4, 5, 6, 7$$

$$X(0) = F_1(0) + W_N^0 F_2(0)$$

$$X(1) = F_1(1) + W_N^1 F_2(1)$$

$$X(2) = F_1(2) + W_N^2 F_2(2)$$

$$X(3) = F_1(3) + W_N^3 F_2(3)$$

$$X(4) = F_1(4) + W_N^4 F_2(4)$$

$$= F_1(0) - W_N^0 F_2(0)$$

$$X(5) = F_1(5) + W_N^5 F_2(5)$$

$$= F_1(1) - W_N^1 F_2(1)$$

$$X(6) = F_1(6) + W_N^6 F_2(6)$$

$$= F_1(2) - W_N^2 F_2(2)$$

$$X(7) = F_1(7) + W_N^7 F_2(7)$$

$$= F_1(3) - W_N^3 F_2(3)$$

$F_1(k)$ and $F_2(k)$ are periodic with period is 4. Therefore,

$$F_1(k+4) = F_1(k) \quad \text{and} \quad F_2(k+4) = F_2(k)$$

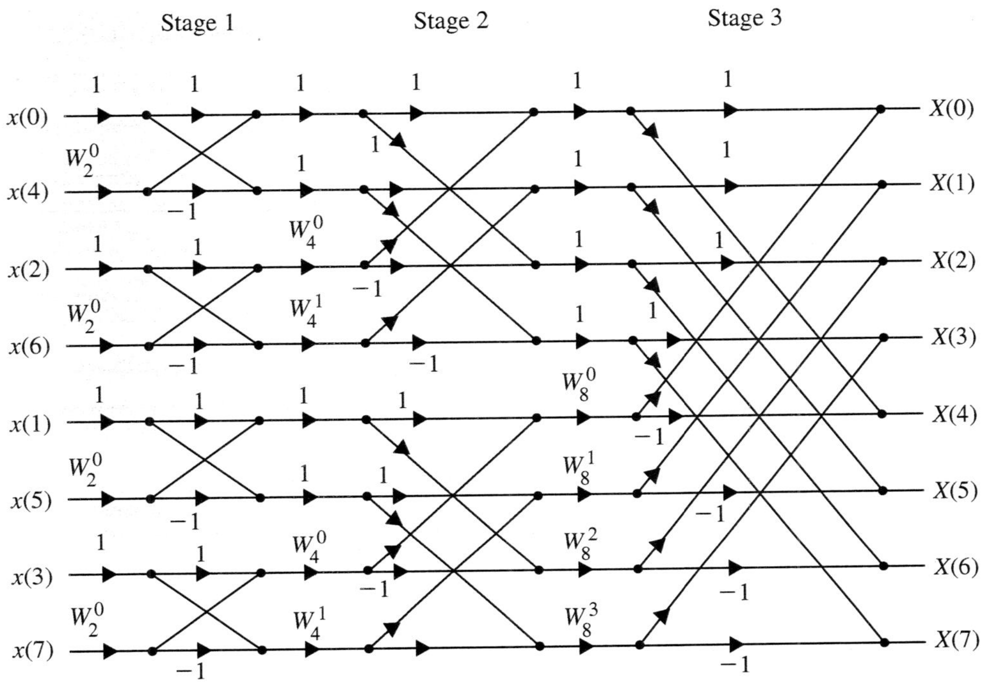

Figure 2.17 8 point radix-2 DIT-FFT Butterfly diagram.

The flow graph or butterfly diagram for 8-point DIT-FFT is shown in Figure 2.17.

The phase factor values are,

$$W_2^0 = 1$$

$$W_4^0 = e^{-j2\pi \times \frac{0}{4}} = 1$$

$$W_4^1 = e^{-j2\pi \times \frac{1}{4}} = e^{-j\frac{\pi}{2}} = -j$$

$$W_8^0 = 1$$

$$W_8^1 = e^{-j\frac{2\pi}{8}} = e^{\frac{-j\pi}{4}} = \frac{1}{\sqrt{2}} - j\frac{1}{\sqrt{2}}$$

$$W_8^2 = e^{-j2\pi \times \frac{2}{8}} = e^{\frac{-j\pi}{2}} = -j$$

$$W_8^3 = e^{-j2\pi \times \frac{3}{8}} = e^{-j\frac{3\pi}{4}} = \frac{-1}{\sqrt{2}} - j\frac{1}{\sqrt{2}}$$

Summary of steps of radix-2 DIT-FFT algorithm

1. The number of input samples $N = 2^M$, where M is an integer.
2. The input sequence is shuffled through bit-reversal.
3. The number of stages in the flow graph is given by $M = \log_2^N$.
4. Each stage consists of $N/2$ butterflies.

5. Input/output for each butterfly are separated by 2^{m-1} samples, where m represents the stage index, *i.e.*, for first stage $m = 1$ and for second stage $m = 2$ and so on.
6. The number of complex multiplications is given by $\frac{N}{2}\log_2^N$.
7. The number of complex additions is given by $N \log_2^N$.
8. The twiddle factor exponents are a function of the stage index m and is given by

$$k = \frac{Nt}{2^m}, \quad t = 0, 1, 2, \ldots, 2^{m-1} - 1.$$

9. The number of sets or sections of butterflies in each stage is given by the formula 2^{M-m}.
10. The exponent repeat factor (ERF), which is the number of times the exponent sequence associated with m is repeated is given by 2^{M-m}.

2.6.1.2 *Decimation in Frequency (DIF) Radix-2 FFT*

In decimation in frequency algorithm the frequency domain sequence $X(k)$ is decimated. In this algorithm the N-point time domain sequence is converted to two numbers of $\frac{N}{2}$ point sequences. Then each $\frac{N}{2}$ point sequence is converted to two numbers of $\frac{N}{4}$ point sequences. This process is continued until to get $\frac{N}{2}$ numbers of 2-point sequences. Finally the 2-point DFT of each 2-point sequence is computed. The 2-point DFTs of $\frac{N}{2}$ numbers of 2-point sequences will give N-samples, which is the N-point DFT of the time domain sequence.

Consider a N-point sequence $x(n)$. The N-point DFT of $x(n)$ is given by,

$$X(k) = \sum_{n=0}^{N-1} x(n) W_N^{kn} = \sum_{n=0}^{\frac{N}{2}-1} x(n) W_N^{kn} + \sum_{n=\frac{N}{2}}^{N-1} x(n) W_N^{kn} \tag{2.84}$$

$$= \sum_{n=0}^{\frac{N}{2}-1} x(n) W_N^{kn} + \sum_{n=0}^{\frac{N}{2}-1} x\left(n + \frac{N}{2}\right) W_N^{k\left(n+\frac{N}{2}\right)}$$

$$= \sum_{n=0}^{\frac{N}{2}-1} x(n) W_N^{kn} + \sum_{n=0}^{\frac{N}{2}-1} x\left(n + \frac{N}{2}\right) W_N^{kn} \cdot W_N^{\frac{kN}{2}}$$

$$= \sum_{n=0}^{\frac{N}{2}-1} \left[x(n) W_N^{kn} + (-1)^k x\left(n + \frac{N}{2}\right) W_N^{kn}\right] \qquad \left(\because\ W_N^{\frac{kN}{2}} = (-1)^k\right)$$

$$X(k) = \sum_{n=0}^{\frac{N}{2}-1} \left[x(n) + (-1)^k x\left(n + \frac{N}{2}\right)\right] W_N^{kn} \tag{2.85}$$

Let us split $X(k)$ into even and odd number sequences as follows.

$$X(2k)\ (\text{even}) = \sum_{n=0}^{\frac{N}{2}-1} \left[x(n) + (-1)^{2k} x\left(n + \frac{N}{2}\right)\right] W_N^{2kn} \tag{2.86}$$

$$= \sum_{n=0}^{\frac{N}{2}-1} \left[x(n) + x\left(n + \frac{N}{2}\right)\right] W_{\frac{N}{2}}^{kn}, \qquad k = 0, 1, \ldots, \left(\frac{N}{2} - 1\right)$$

$$X(2k+1)(\text{odd}) = \sum_{n=0}^{\frac{N}{2}-1} \left[x(n) + (-1)x\left(n + \frac{N}{2}\right)\right] W_N^{(2k+1)^n} \tag{2.87}$$

$$= \sum_{n=0}^{\frac{N}{2}-1} \left[x(n) - x\left(n + \frac{N}{2}\right)\right] W_N^{2kn} W_N^n$$

$$= \sum_{n=0}^{\frac{N}{2}-1} \left[x(n) - x\left(n + \frac{N}{2}\right)\right] W_N^n W_{\frac{N}{2}}^{kn}, k = 0, 1, 2, \ldots, \left(\frac{N}{2} - 1\right)$$

Let

$$g_1(n) = x(n) + x\left(n + \frac{N}{2}\right), \qquad n = 0, 1, 2 \ldots, \left(\frac{N}{2} - 1\right)$$

$$g_2(n) = \left[x(n) - x\left(n + \frac{N}{2}\right)\right] W_N^n, \qquad n = 0, 1, 2, \ldots, \left(\frac{N}{2} - 1\right)$$

where $g_1(n)$ and $g_2(n)$ are $\frac{N}{2}$ point time domain sequences. Therefore

$$X(2k) = \sum_{n=0}^{\frac{N}{2}-1} g_1(n) W_{\frac{N}{2}}^{kn}, \qquad k = 0, 1, 2, \ldots, \left(\frac{N}{2} - 1\right) \tag{2.88}$$

$$X(2k+1) = \sum_{n=0}^{\frac{N}{2}-1} g_2(n) W_{\frac{N}{2}}^{kn}, \qquad k = 0, 1, 2, \ldots, \left(\frac{N}{2} - 1\right) \tag{2.89}$$

$X(2k)$ is $\frac{N}{2}$ point DFT of $g_1(n)$ and $X(2k+1)$ is $\frac{N}{2}$ point DFT of $g_2(n)$

$$\therefore\ G_1(k) = \sum_{n=0}^{\frac{N}{2}-1} g_1(n) W_{\frac{N}{2}}^{kn}, \qquad k = 0, 1, 2, \ldots, \left(\frac{N}{2} - 1\right) \tag{2.90}$$

$$G_2(k) = \sum_{n=0}^{\frac{N}{2}-1} g_2(n) W_{\frac{N}{2}}^{kn}, \qquad k = 0, 1, 2, \ldots, \left(\frac{N}{2} - 1\right) \tag{2.91}$$

The $g_1(n)$ is $\frac{N}{2}$ point sequence and it can be decimated into two numbers of $\frac{N}{4}$ point sequences.

$$\begin{aligned}\therefore\ G_1(k) &= \sum_{n=0}^{\frac{N}{2}-1} g_1(n) W_{\frac{N}{2}}^{kn} \\ &= \sum_{n=0}^{\frac{N}{4}-1} g_1(n) W_{\frac{N}{2}}^{kn} + \sum_{n=0}^{\frac{N}{4}-1} g_1\left(n+\frac{N}{4}\right) W_{\frac{N}{2}}^{k\left(n+\frac{N}{4}\right)} \\ &= \sum_{n=0}^{\frac{N}{4}-1} \left[g_1(n) + g_1\left(n+\frac{N}{4}\right) W_{\frac{N}{2}}^{k\frac{N}{4}}\right] W_{\frac{N}{2}}^{kn}\end{aligned}$$

Therefore,

$$G_1(2k) = \sum_{n=0}^{\frac{N}{4}-1} d_{11}(n) W_{\frac{N}{4}}^{kn} = D_{11}(k) \tag{2.92}$$

$$G_1(2k+1) = \sum_{n=0}^{\frac{N}{4}-1} d_{12}(n) W_{\frac{N}{4}}^{kn} = D_{12}(k) \tag{2.93}$$

$$G_2(2k) = \sum_{n=0}^{\frac{N}{4}-1} d_{21}(n) W_{\frac{N}{4}}^{kn} = D_{21}(k) \tag{2.94}$$

$$G_2(2k+1) = \sum_{n=0}^{\frac{N}{4}-1} d_{22}(n) W_{\frac{N}{4}}^{kn} = D_{22}(k) \tag{2.95}$$

where $D_{11}(k)$, $D_{12}(k)$, $D_{21}(k)$ and $D_{22}(k)$ are $\frac{N}{4}$ point DFTs of $d_{11}(n)$, $d_{12}(n)$, $d_{21}(n)$ and $d_{22}(n)$ respectively.

The decimation of the frequency domain sequence can be continued until the resulting sequence are reduced to two-point sequences.

The 8-point DFT Using Radix-2 DIF FFT

Let $x(n)$ be an 8-point sequence where $N = 8$

First Stage of Computation

In the first stage of computation, two numbers of 4-point sequences $g_1(n)$ and $g_2(n)$ are obtained.

$$g_1(n) = x(n) + x\left(n+\frac{N}{2}\right)$$

$$g_1(n) = x(n) + x(n+4), \quad n = 0, 1, 2, 3$$

$$g_1(0) = x(0) + x(4)$$
$$g_1(1) = x(1) + x(5)$$
$$g_1(2) = x(2) + x(6)$$
$$g_1(3) = x(3) + x(7)$$

and

$$g_2(n) = \left[x(n) - x\left(n + \frac{N}{2}\right)\right] W_N^n$$
$$g_2(n) = [x(n) - x(n+4)]\, W_8^n, \quad n = 0, 1, 2, 3$$
$$g_2(0) = [x(0) - x(4)]\, W_8^0$$
$$g_2(1) = [x(1) - x(5)]\, W_8^1$$
$$g_2(2) = [x(2) - x(6)]\, W_8^2$$
$$g_2(3) = [x(3) - x(7)]\, W_8^3$$

Second Stage of Computation

In the second stage, 4 numbers of 2-point sequence is obtained.

$$d_{11}(n) = g_1(n) + g_1\left(n + \frac{N}{4}\right)$$
$$d_{11}(n) = g_1(n) + g_1(n+2), \qquad n = 0, 1$$
$$d_{11}(0) = g_1(0) + g_1(2)$$
$$d_{11}(1) = g_1(1) + g_1(3)$$
$$d_{12}(n) = \left[g_1(n) - g_1\left(n + \frac{N}{4}\right)\right] W_{\frac{N}{2}}^n$$
$$= [g_1(n) - g_1(n+2)]\, W_4^n, \qquad n = 0, 1$$
$$d_{12}(0) = [g_1(0) - g_1(2)]\, W_4^0$$
$$d_{12}(1) = [g_1(1) - g_1(3)]\, W_4^1$$
$$d_{21}(n) = g_2(n) + g_2\left(n + \frac{N}{4}\right)$$
$$= g_2(n) + g_2(2), \qquad n = 0, 1$$
$$d_{21}(n) = g_2(0) + g_2(2)$$
$$d_{21}(1) = g_2(1) + g_2(3)$$
$$d_{22}(n) = \left[g_2(n) - g_2\left(n + \frac{N}{4}\right)\right] W_{\frac{N}{2}}^n$$
$$= [g_2(n) - g_2(n+2)]\, W_4^n, \qquad n = 0, 1$$

$$d_{22}(0) = [g_2(0) - g_2(2)]\, W_4^0$$
$$d_{22}(1) = [g_2(1) - g_2(3)]\, W_4^1$$

Third Stage Computation

In the third stage, 2-point DFTs are calculated.

$$D_{11}(k) = \sum_{n=0,1} d_{11}(n) W_2^{kn}, \qquad k = 0, 1$$

$$D_{11}(0) = \sum_{n=0,1} d_{11}(n) = d_{11}(0) + d_{11}(1)$$

$$D_{11}(1) = \sum_{n=0,1} d_{11}(n) W_2^n = [d_{11}(0) - d_{11}(1)]\, W_2^0$$

Similarly

$$D_{12}(0) = d_{12}(0) + d_{12}(1)$$
$$D_{12}(1) = [d_{12}(0) - d_{12}(1)]\, W_2^0$$
$$D_{21}(0) = d_{21}(0) + d_{21}(1)$$
$$D_{21}(1) = [d_{21}(0) - d_{21}(1)]\, W_2^0$$
$$D_{22}(0) = d_{22}(0) + d_{22}(1)$$
$$D_{22}(1) = [d_{22}(0) - d_{22}(1)]\, W_2^0$$

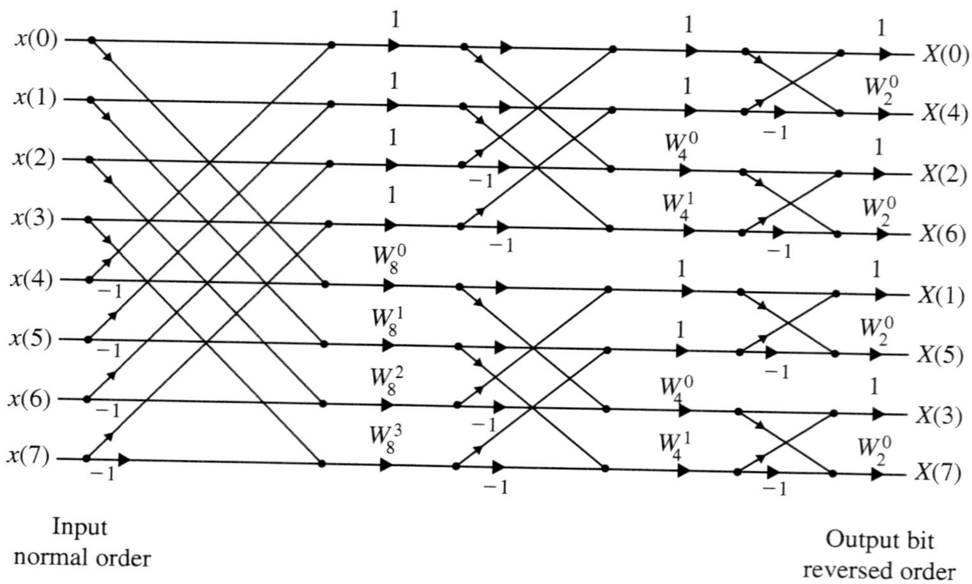

Figure 2.18 8-point radix-2 DIF-FFT Butterfly diagram.

The signal flow graph or butterfly diagram of all three stages is shown in Figure 2.18.

Summary of Steps of Radix-2 DIF-FFT Algorithm

1. The number of input samples $N = 2^M$, where M is an integer.
2. The input sequence is in normal order.
3. The number of stages in the flow graph is given by $M = \log_2^N$.
4. Each stage consists of $N/2$ butterflies.
5. Input/output for each butterfly are separated by 2^{m-1} samples, where m represents the stage index, *i.e.*, for first stage $m = 1$ and for second stage $m = 2$ and so on.
6. The number of complex multiplications is given by $\frac{N}{2}\log_2^N$.
7. The number of complex addition is given by $N\log_2^N$.
8. The twiddle factor exponents are a function of the stage index m and is given by

$$k = \frac{Nt}{2^{M-m+1}}, \qquad t = 0, 1, 2, \ldots, 2^{m-1} - 1.$$

9. The number of sets or sections of butterflies in each stage is given by the formula 2^{m-1}.
10. The exponent repeat factor (ERF), which is the number of times the exponent sequence associated with m is repeated is given by 2^{m-1}.

2.6.1.3 *Comparison of DIF and DIT*

Difference Between DIF and DIT

(*i*) In DIT, the input is bit-reversed while the output is in normal order. For DIF, the input is normal order, while output is in bit reversed order.
(*ii*) Considering the butterfly diagram, in DIF, the complex multiplication takes place after the add-subtract operation.

Similarities

(*i*) Both algorithms require same number of operations to compute DFT.
(*ii*) Both algorithms require bit-reversal at some place during computation.

2.6.2 Radix-4 FFT Algorithms

The decimation-in-time (DIT) radix-4 FFT recursively partitions a DFT into four quarter-length DFTs of groups of every fourth time sample. The outputs of these shorter FFT's are reused to compute many outputs, thus greatly reducing the total computation cost. In the decimation in frequency radix-4 FFT groups, every fourth output sample is decimated into shorter length DFTs to save computations.

2.6.2.1 Radix-4 DIT FFT Algorithms

Radix-4 DIT rearranges the DFT equation into four parts: sums over all groups of every fourth discrete-time index $n = [0, 4, 8, \ldots, N-4]$, $n = [15, 9, \ldots, N-3]$, $n = [2, 6, 10, \ldots, N-2]$ and $n = [3, 7, 11, \ldots, N-1]$, *i.e.*,

$$
\begin{aligned}
X(k) &= \sum_{n=0}^{N-1} x(n) e^{-j\frac{2\pi nk}{N}} \\
&= \sum_{n=0}^{\frac{N}{4}-1} x(4n) e^{-j\frac{2\pi k(4n)}{N}} + \sum_{n=0}^{\frac{N}{4}-1} x(4n+1) e^{-j\frac{2\pi k(4n+1)}{N}} \\
&\quad + \sum_{n=0}^{\frac{N}{4}-1} x(4n+2) e^{-j\frac{2\pi k(4n+2)}{N}} + \sum_{n=0}^{\frac{N}{4}-1} x(4n+3) e^{-j\frac{2\pi k(4n+3)}{N}}
\end{aligned} \tag{2.96}
$$

$$
\begin{aligned}
&= \sum_{n=0}^{\frac{N}{4}-1} x(4n) e^{-j\frac{2\pi k4n}{N}} + \sum_{n=0}^{\frac{N}{4}-1} x(4n+1) e^{-j\frac{2\pi k4N}{N}} \cdot e^{-j\frac{2\pi k}{N}} \\
&\quad + \sum_{n=0}^{\frac{N}{4}-1} x(4n+2) e^{-j\frac{2\pi 4n}{N}} \cdot e^{-j\frac{2\pi k \cdot 2}{N}} + \sum_{n=0}^{\frac{N}{4}-1} x(4n+3) e^{-j\frac{2\pi 4n}{N}} \cdot e^{-j\frac{2\pi k \cdot 3}{N}}
\end{aligned} \tag{2.97}
$$

$$
= X_1(k) + W_N^k X_2(k) + W_N^{2k} X_3(k) + W_N^{3k} X_4(k)
$$

where

$$
X_1(k) = \sum_{n=0}^{\frac{N}{4}-1} x(4n) W_N^{4nk} \tag{2.98}
$$

$$
X_2(k) = \sum_{n=0}^{\frac{N}{4}-1} x(4n+1) W_N^{4nk} \tag{2.99}
$$

$$
X_3(k) = \sum_{n=0}^{\frac{N}{4}-1} x(4n+2) W_N^{4nk} \tag{2.100}
$$

$$
X_4(k) = \sum_{n=0}^{\frac{N}{4}-1} x(4n+3) W_N^{4nk} \tag{2.101}
$$

16 Point Radix-4 DIT FFT

Here $N = 16 = 4^2$, and the number of stages are two.

$$
X(k) = X_1(k) + W_{16}^k X_2(k) + W_{16}^{2k} X_3(k) + W_{16}^{3k} X_4(k) \tag{2.102}
$$

Stage I

$$X_1(k) = \sum_{n=0}^{3} x(4n) W_{16}^{4nk}, \quad k = 0, 1, 2, 3$$

$$= x(0) + x(4)W_{16}^{4k} + x(8)W_{16}^{8k} + x(12)W_{16}^{12k} \tag{2.103}$$

$$X_2(k) = \sum_{n=0}^{3} x(4n+1) W_{16}^{4nk}$$

$$= x(1) + x(5)W_{16}^{4k} + x(9)W_{16}^{8k} + x(13)W_{16}^{12k} \tag{2.104}$$

$$X_3(k) = \sum_{n=0}^{3} x(4n+2) W_{16}^{4nk}$$

$$= x(2) + x(6)W_{16}^{4k} + x(10)W_{16}^{8k} + x(14)W_{16}^{12k} \tag{2.105}$$

$$X_4(k) = \sum_{n=0}^{3} x(4n+3) W_{16}^{4nk}$$

$$= x(3) + x(7)W_{16}^{4k} + x(11)W_{16}^{8k} + x(15)W_{16}^{12k} \tag{2.106}$$

Stage II

$$[X_i(k+4) = X_i(k)]$$

$$X(k) = X_1(k) + W_{16}^{k}X_2(k) + W_{16}^{2k}X_3(k) + W_{16}^{3k}X_4(k)$$

$$X(0) = X_1(0) + X_2(0) + X_3(0) + X_4(0)$$

$$X(1) = X_1(1) + W_{16}^{1}X_2(1) + W_{16}^{2}X_3(1) + W_{16}^{3}X_4(1)$$

$$X(2) = X_1(2) + W_{16}^{2}X_2(2) + W_{16}^{4}X_3(2) + W_{16}^{6}X_4(2)$$

$$X(3) = X_1(3) + W_{16}^{3}X_2(3) + W_{16}^{6}X_3(3) + W_{16}^{9}X_4(3)$$

$$X(4) = X_1(0) + W_{16}^{4}X_2(0) + W_{16}^{8}X_3(0) + W_{16}^{12}X_4(0)$$

$$X(5) = X_1(1) + W_{16}^{5}X_2(1) + W_{16}^{10}X_3(1) + W_{16}^{15}X_4(1)$$

$$X(6) = X_1(2) + W_{16}^{6}X_2(2) + W_{16}^{12}X_3(2) + W_{16}^{18}X_4(2)$$

$$X(7) = X_1(3) + W_{16}^{7}X_2(3) + W_{16}^{14}X_3(3) + W_{16}^{21}X_4(3)$$

$$X(8) = X_1(0) + W_{16}^{8}X_2(0) + W_{16}^{16}X_3(0) + W_{16}^{24}X_4(0)$$

$$X(9) = X_1(1) + W_{16}^{9}X_2(1) + W_{16}^{18}X_3(1) + W_{16}^{27}X_4(1)$$

$$X(10) = X_1(2) + W_{16}^{10}X_2(2) + W_{16}^{20}X_3(2) + W_{16}^{30}X_4(2)$$

$$X(11) = X_1(3) + W_{16}^{11}X_2(3) + W_{16}^{22}X_3(3) + W_{16}^{33}X_4(3)$$

$$X(12) = X_1(0) + W_{16}^{12}X_2(0) + W_{16}^{24}X_3(0) + W_{16}^{36}X_4(0)$$

$$X(13) = X_1(1) + W_{16}^{13}X_2(1) + W_{16}^{26}X_3(1) + W_{16}^{39}X_4(1)$$

$$X(14) = X_1(2) + W_{16}^{14}X_2(2) + W_{16}^{28}X_3(2) + W_{16}^{42}X_4(2)$$

$$X(15) = X_1(3) + W_{16}^{15}X_2(3) + W_{16}^{30}X_3(3) + W_{16}^{45}X_4(3)$$

16-point radix-4 DIT FFT butterfly diagram is shown in Figure 2.19.

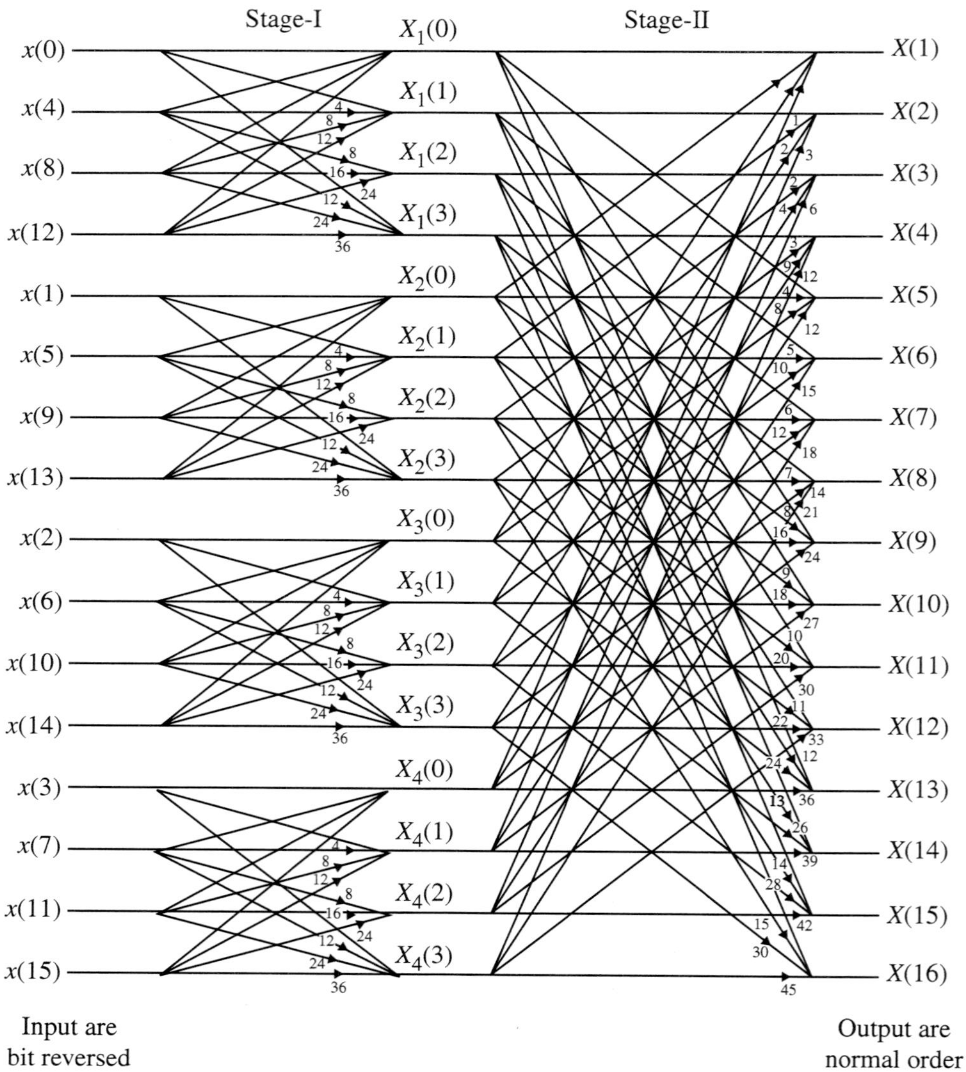

Figure 2.19 16-Point radix-4 DIT FFT butterfly diagram.

In Radix-4 FFT

$$N = 4^m$$
$$M = \log_4^N = \frac{\log_2^N}{2}$$

where $N/4$ butterflies per stage.

Number of complex multiplications

$$3\frac{N}{4}\frac{\log_N^2}{2} = \frac{3}{8}N\log_2^N \quad \text{(75\% of radix-2 FFT)}$$

Number of complex additions

$$8\frac{N}{4}\frac{\log_2^N}{2} = N\log_2^N \quad \text{(same as a radix-2 FFT)}$$

2.6.2.2 Radix-4 Decimation in Frequency FFT

N-point DFT formula breaking into four smaller DFTs is given by,

$$\begin{aligned}X(k) &= \sum_{n=0}^{N-1} x(n)W_N^{kn}\\
&= \sum_{n=0}^{\frac{N}{4}-1} x(n)W_N^{kn} + \sum_{n=\left(\frac{N}{4}\right)}^{\frac{N}{2}-1} x(n)W_N^{kn} + \sum_{n=\left(\frac{N}{2}\right)}^{3\left(\frac{N}{4}\right)-1} x(n)W_N^{kn}\\
&\quad + \sum_{n=\left(\frac{3N}{4}\right)}^{N-1} x(n)W_N^{kn}\end{aligned} \tag{2.107}$$

$$\begin{aligned}&= \sum_{n=0}^{\frac{N}{4}-1} x(n)W_N^{kn} + \sum_{n=0}^{\frac{N}{2}-1} x\left(n+\frac{N}{4}\right)W_N^{k\left(n+\frac{N}{4}\right)}\\
&\quad + \sum_{n=0}^{\frac{N}{4}-1} x\left(n+\frac{N}{2}\right)W_N^{k\left(n+\frac{N}{2}\right)} + \sum_{n=0}^{\frac{N}{4}-1} x\left(n+\frac{3N}{4}\right)W_N^{k\left(n+\frac{3N}{4}\right)}\end{aligned} \tag{2.108}$$

$$\begin{aligned}&= \sum_{n=0}^{\frac{N}{4}-1} x(n)W_N^{kn} + W_N^{kn/4}\sum_{n=0}^{\frac{N}{4}-1} x\left(n+\frac{N}{4}\right)W_N^{kn} + W_N^{kn/2}\\
&\quad + \sum_{n=0}^{\frac{N}{4}-1} x\left(n+\frac{N}{2}\right)W_N^{nk} + W_N^{3Nk/4}\sum_{n=0}^{\frac{N}{4}-1} x\left(n+\frac{3N}{4}\right)W_N^{kn}\end{aligned} \tag{2.109}$$

$$W_N^{kN/4} = e^{-j\frac{2\pi kN}{4N}} = \left(e^{-j\frac{\pi}{2}}\right)^k = (-j)^k$$

$$W_N^{kN/2} = (-1)^k$$

$$W_N^{3kN/4} = j^k$$

Substituting these twiddle factors in Equation (2.92) we get,

$$X(k) = \sum_{n=0}^{\frac{N}{4}-1}\left[x(n)+(-j)^k x\left(n+\frac{N}{4}\right)+(-1)^k x\left(n+\frac{N}{4}\right)+(j)^k x\left(n+\frac{3N}{4}\right)\right] W_N^{kn}$$

The four $N/4$ point DFTs are written as,

$$X(4k) = \sum_{n=0}^{\frac{N}{4}-1}\left[x(n)+x\left(n+\frac{N}{4}\right)+x\left(n+\frac{N}{2}\right)+x\left(n+\frac{3N}{4}\right)\right] W_N^{4kn}$$

$$X(4k) = \sum_{n=0}^{\frac{N}{4}-1}\left[x(n)+x\left(n+\frac{N}{4}\right)+x\left(n+\frac{N}{2}\right)+x\left(n+\frac{3N}{4}\right)\right] W_N^{0}\cdot W_{\frac{N}{4}}^{kn} \tag{2.110}$$

$$X(4k+1) = \sum_{n=0}^{\frac{N}{4}-1}\left[x(n)-jx\left(n+\frac{N}{4}\right)-x\left(n+\frac{N}{2}\right)+jx\left(n+\frac{3N}{4}\right)\right] W_N^{n}\cdot W_{\frac{N}{4}}^{kn} \tag{2.111}$$

$$X(4k+2) = \sum_{n=0}^{\frac{N}{4}-1}\left[x(n)-x\left(n+\frac{N}{4}\right)+x\left(n+\frac{N}{2}\right)-x\left(n+\frac{3N}{4}\right)\right] W_N^{2n}\cdot W_{\frac{N}{4}}^{kn} \tag{2.112}$$

$$X(4k+3) = \sum_{n=0}^{\frac{N}{4}-1}\left[x(n)+jx\left(n+\frac{N}{4}\right)-x\left(n+\frac{N}{2}\right)-jx\left(n+\frac{3N}{4}\right)\right] W_N^{3n}\cdot W_{\frac{N}{4}}^{kn} \tag{2.113}$$

16 Point DFT Using Radix-4 DIF FFT

Let $x(n)$ be an 16 point sequence. The samples of $x(n)$ are $x(0)$, $x(1)$, $x(2),\ldots,x(15)$. Here $N = 16$.

Stage I

In the first stage four numbers of 4-point sequences $g_1(n), g_2(n), g_3(n)$ and $g_4(n)$ are obtained from Equations (2.93)–(2.96) respectively. Thus,

$$g_1(n) = \left[x(n)+x\left(n+\frac{N}{4}\right)+x\left(n+\frac{N}{2}\right)+x\left(n+\frac{3N}{4}\right)\right] W_N^{0}$$

$n = 0, 1, 2, 3$ and $N = 16$.

$$g_1(0) = [x(0) + x(4) + x(8) + x(12)]\, W_{16}^0$$
$$g_1(1) = [x(1) + x(5) + x(9) + x(13)]\, W_{16}^0$$
$$g_1(2) = [x(2) + x(6) + x(10) + x(14)]\, W_{16}^0$$
$$g_1(3) = [x(3) + x(7) + x(11) + x(15)]\, W_{16}^0$$

$$g_2(n) = \left[x(n) - jx\left(n + \frac{N}{4}\right) - x\left(n + \frac{N}{2}\right) + jx\left(n + \frac{3N}{4}\right)\right] W_N^n$$

$$g_2(0) = [x(0) - jx(4) - x(8) + jx(12)]\, W_{16}^0$$
$$g_2(1) = [x(1) - jx(5) - x(9) + jx(13)]\, W_{16}^1$$
$$g_2(2) = [x(2) - jx(6) - x(10) + jx(14)]\, W_{16}^2$$
$$g_2(3) = [x(3) - jx(7) - x(11) + jx(15)]\, W_{16}^3$$

$$g_3(n) = \left[x(n) - x\left(n + \frac{N}{4}\right) + x\left(n + \frac{N}{2}\right) - x\left(n + \frac{3N}{4}\right)\right] W_N^{2n}$$

$$g_3(0) = [x(0) - x(4) + x(8) - x(12)]\, W_{16}^0$$
$$g_3(1) = [x(1) - x(5) + x(9) - x(13)]\, W_{16}^2$$
$$g_3(2) = [x(2) - x(6) + x(10) - x(14)]\, W_{16}^4$$
$$g_3(3) = [x(3) - x(7) + x(11) - x(15)]\, W_{16}^6$$

$$g_4(n) = \left[x(n) + jx\left(n + \frac{N}{4}\right) - x\left(n + \frac{N}{2}\right) - jx\left(n + \frac{3N}{4}\right)\right] W_N^{3n}$$

$$g_4(0) = [x(0) - jx(4) - x(8) - jx(12)]\, W_{16}^0$$
$$g_4(1) = [x(1) - jx(5) - x(9) - jx(13)]\, W_{16}^3$$
$$g_4(2) = [x(2) - jx(6) - x(10) - jx(14)]\, W_{16}^6$$
$$g_4(3) = [x(3) - jx(7) - x(11) - jx(15)]\, W_{16}^9$$

Stage II

The four 4-point DFTs are

$$G_1(k) = \sum_{n=0}^{\frac{N}{4}-1} g_1(n) W_{N/4}^{kn} \qquad k = 0, 1, \ldots, 3$$

$$G_1(k) = \sum_{n=0}^{3} g_1(n) W_4^{kn}$$

$$G_1(0) = \sum_{n=0}^{3} g_1(n) = g_1(0) + g_1(1) + g_1(2) + g_1(3)$$

$$G_1(1) = \sum_{n=0}^{3} g_1(n) W_4^{n}$$

$$= g_1(0) W_4^0 + g_1(1) W_4^1 + g_1(2) W_4^2 + g_1(3) W_4^3$$

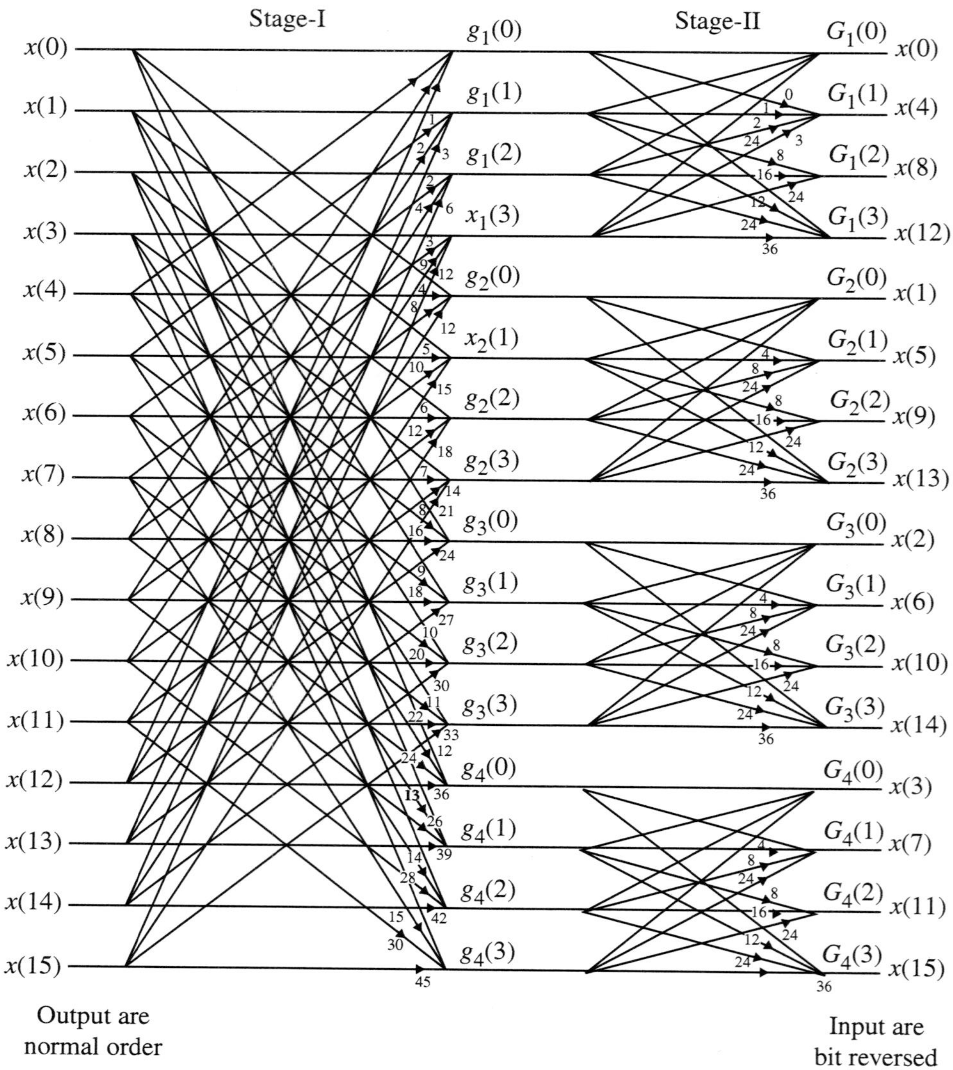

Figure 2.20 16-Point radix-4 DIF FFT butterfly diagram.

$$G_1(2) = \sum_{n=0}^{3} g_1(n)W_4^{2n}$$
$$= g_1(0)W_4^0 + g_1(1)W_4^2 + g_1(2)W_4^0 + g_1(3)W_4^2$$
$$G_1(3) = \sum_{n=0}^{3} g_1(n)W_4^{3n}$$
$$= g_1(0)W_4^0 + g_1(1)W_4^3 + g_1(2)W_4^2 + g_1(3)W_4^1$$

Similarly

$$G_2(k) = \sum_{n=0}^{\frac{N}{4}-1} g_2(n)W_{N/4}^{kn} \qquad k = 0, 1, \ldots, 3$$
$$G_3(k) = \sum_{n=0}^{\frac{N}{4}-1} g_3(n)W_{N/4}^{kn} \qquad k = 0, 1, \ldots, 3$$
$$G_4(k) = \sum_{n=0}^{\frac{N}{4}-1} g_4(n)W_{N/4}^{kn} \qquad k = 0, 1, \ldots, 3$$

16-point radix-4 DIF FFT butterfly diagram is shown in Figure 2.20.

$$\text{Number of complex multiplications} = \frac{3}{8}N\log_2^N \tag{2.114}$$

$$\text{Number of complex additions} = N\log_2^N \quad \text{(same as DIT algorithm)}$$

2.6.2.3 4 Point DFT Using Radix-4 FFT Algorithm

$$X(k) = \sum_{n=0}^{3} x(n)W_N^{kn} \qquad k = 0, \ldots, 3$$

$$X(0) = \sum_{n=0}^{3} x(n)W_N^0 = x(0) + x(1) + x(2) + x(3) \tag{2.115}$$

$$X(1) = \sum_{n=0}^{3} x(n)W_N^n = x(0)W_4^0 - jx(1)W_4^0 - x(2)W_4^0 + jx(3)W_4^0 \tag{2.116}$$

$$X(2) = \sum_{n=0}^{3} x(n)W_N^{2n} = x(0)W_4^0 - x(1)W_4^0 + x(2)W_4^0 - x(3)W_4^0 \tag{2.117}$$

$$X(3) = \sum_{n=0}^{3} x(n)W_N^{3n} = x(0)W_4^0 + jx(1)W_4^0 - x(2)W_4^0 - jx(3)W_4^0 \tag{2.118}$$

4-point radix-4 FFT butterfly diagram is shown in Figure 2.21.

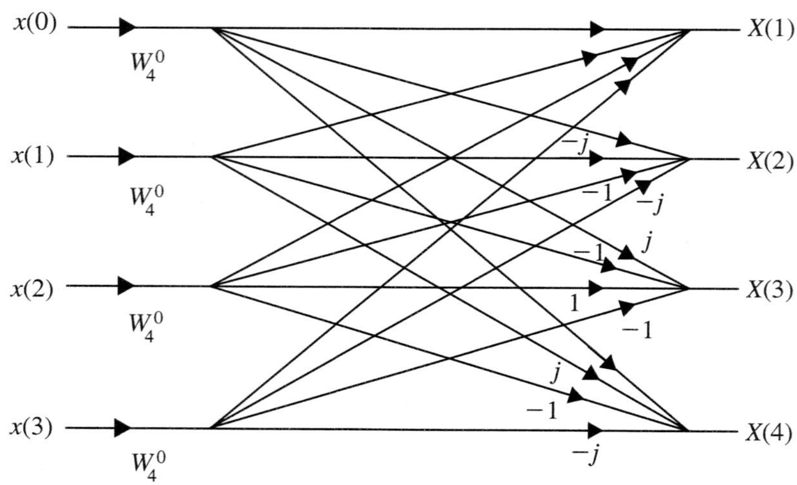

Figure 2.21 4-Point radix-4 FFT butterfly diagram.

In matrix form, the 4 point DFT is written as

$$\begin{bmatrix} X(0) \\ X(1) \\ X(2) \\ X(3) \end{bmatrix} = \begin{bmatrix} 1 & 1 & 1 & 1 \\ 1 & W_4^1 & W_4^2 & W_4^3 \\ 1 & W_4^2 & W_4^4 & W_4^6 \\ 1 & W_4^3 & W_4^6 & W_4^9 \end{bmatrix} \begin{bmatrix} x(0) \\ x(1) \\ x(2) \\ x(3) \end{bmatrix} \tag{2.119}$$

or

$$\begin{bmatrix} X(0) \\ X(1) \\ X(2) \\ X(3) \end{bmatrix} = \begin{bmatrix} 1 & 1 & 1 & 1 \\ 1 & -j & -1 & j \\ 1 & -1 & 1 & -1 \\ 1 & j & -1 & -j \end{bmatrix} \begin{bmatrix} W_4^0 x(0) \\ W_4^0 x(1) \\ W_4^0 x(2) \\ W_4^0 x(3) \end{bmatrix} \tag{2.120}$$

Therefore in general, the four $N/4$ point DFT of $X(k)$ in matrix form is

$$\begin{bmatrix} X(0,q) \\ X(1,q) \\ X(2,q) \\ X(3,q) \end{bmatrix} = \begin{bmatrix} 1 & 1 & 1 & 1 \\ 1 & -j & -1 & j \\ 1 & -1 & 1 & -1 \\ 1 & j & -1 & -j \end{bmatrix} \begin{bmatrix} W_N^0 F(0,q) \\ W_N^q F(1,q) \\ W_N^{2q} F(2,q) \\ W_N^{3q} F(3,q) \end{bmatrix} \tag{2.121}$$

The basic butterfly computation in radix-4 FFT algorithm is shown in Figure 2.22.

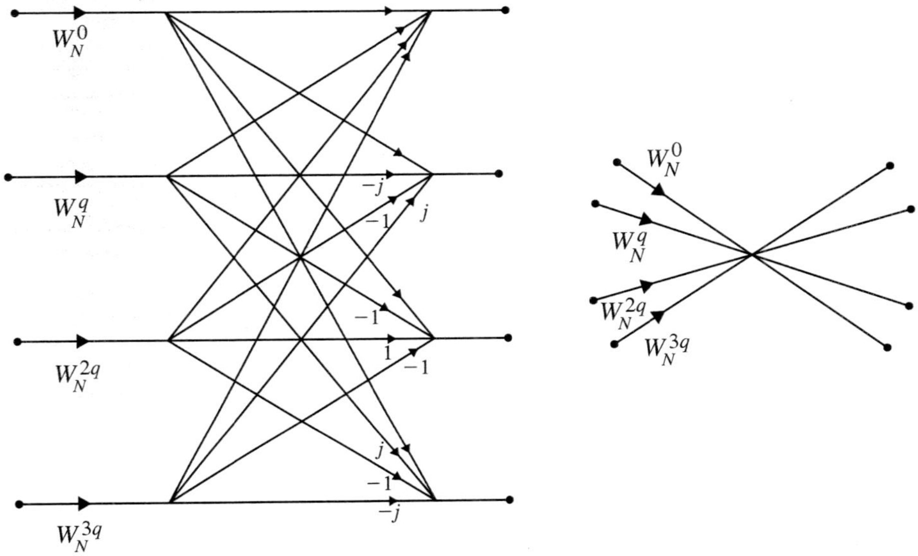

Figure 2.22 Basic butterfly in a radix-4 FFT algorithm.

2.6.3 Computation of IDFT through FFT

The IDFT of an N-point sequence $X(k)$ is defined as

$$x(n) = \frac{1}{N}\sum_{k=0}^{N-1} X(k) e^{j\frac{2\pi kn}{N}}$$

$$= \frac{1}{N}\sum_{k=0}^{N-1} X(k) W_N^{-nk} \qquad \left[\because\ W_N = e^{-j\frac{2\pi}{N}}\right]$$

Taking the conjugate and multiplying by N, we get

$$Nx^*(n) = \sum_{k=0}^{N-1} X^*(k) W_N^{nk}$$

$$x^*(n) = \frac{1}{N}\sum_{k=0}^{N-1} X^*(k) W_N^{nk}$$

$$x(n) = \frac{1}{N}\left[\sum_{k=0}^{N-1} X^*(k) W_N^{nk}\right]^* \tag{2.122}$$

where $\sum_{k=0}^{N-1} X^*(k) W_N^{nk}$ is N point DFT of $X^*(k)$.

Hence, in order to compute IDFT of $X(k)$ the following procedure is be followed:

1. Take conjugate of $X(k)$ [*i.e.*, determine $X^*(k)$].
2. Compute the N-point DFT of $X^*(k)$ using radix-2 FFT.
3. Take conjugate of the output sequence of FFT.
4. Divide the sequence obtained in step 3 by N. The resultant sequence is $x(n)$.

Example 2.31

An 8-point sequence is given by $x(n) = \{2, 2, 2, 2, 1, 1, 1, 1\}$. Compute 8-point DFT of $x(n)$ by (*i*) radix-2 DIT-FFT and (*ii*) radix-2 DIF-FFT. Also sketch the magnitude and phase spectrum.

(Madras University, October, 2002)
(Anna University, December, 2002)

Solution Given

$$x(n) = \{\underset{x(0)}{2}, \underset{x(1)}{2}, \underset{x(2)}{2}, \underset{x(3)}{2}, \underset{x(4)}{1}, \underset{x(5)}{1}, \underset{x(6)}{1}, \underset{x(7)}{1}\}$$

$$W_2^0 = 1$$
$$W_4^0 = 1$$
$$W_4^1 = e^{\frac{-j2\pi}{4}} = -j$$
$$W_8^0 = 1$$
$$W_8^1 = e^{\frac{-j2\pi}{8}} = \frac{1}{\sqrt{2}} - j\frac{1}{\sqrt{2}}$$
$$W_8^2 = e^{\frac{-j2\pi\times 2}{8}} = -j$$
$$W_8^3 = e^{\frac{-j2\pi\times 3}{8}} = -\frac{1}{\sqrt{2}} - j\frac{1}{\sqrt{2}}$$

(*i*) **DIT-FFT**

$$X(k) = \{12, -j2.414, 0, 1 - j0.414, 0, 1 + j0.414, 0, 1 + j2.414\}$$

Input	Stage-I	Stage-II	Stage-III	Output
2	$2+1=3$	$3+3=6$	$6+6=12$	$X(0)$
1	$2-1=1$	$1+(-j)=1-j$	$1-j+(\frac{1}{\sqrt{2}}-j\frac{1}{\sqrt{2}})(1-j)=1-j2.414$	$X(1)$
2	$2+1=3$	$3-3=0$	$0+0=0$	$X(2)$
1	$2-1=1$	$1+(-1)(-j)=1+j$	$1+j+(\frac{1}{\sqrt{2}}-\frac{j}{\sqrt{2}})(1+j)=1-j0.414$	$X(3)$
2	$2+1=3$	$3+3=6$	$6-6=0$	$X(4)$
1	$2-1=1$	$1+(-j)=1-j$	$1-j-(\frac{1}{\sqrt{2}}-\frac{j}{\sqrt{2}})(1-j)=1-j0.414$	$X(5)$
2	$2+1=3$	$3-3=0$	$0-0=0$	$X(6)$
1	$2-1=1$	$1+(-1)(-j)=1+j$	$1+j-(\frac{1}{\sqrt{2}}-\frac{j}{\sqrt{2}})(1+j)=1+j2.414$	$X(7)$

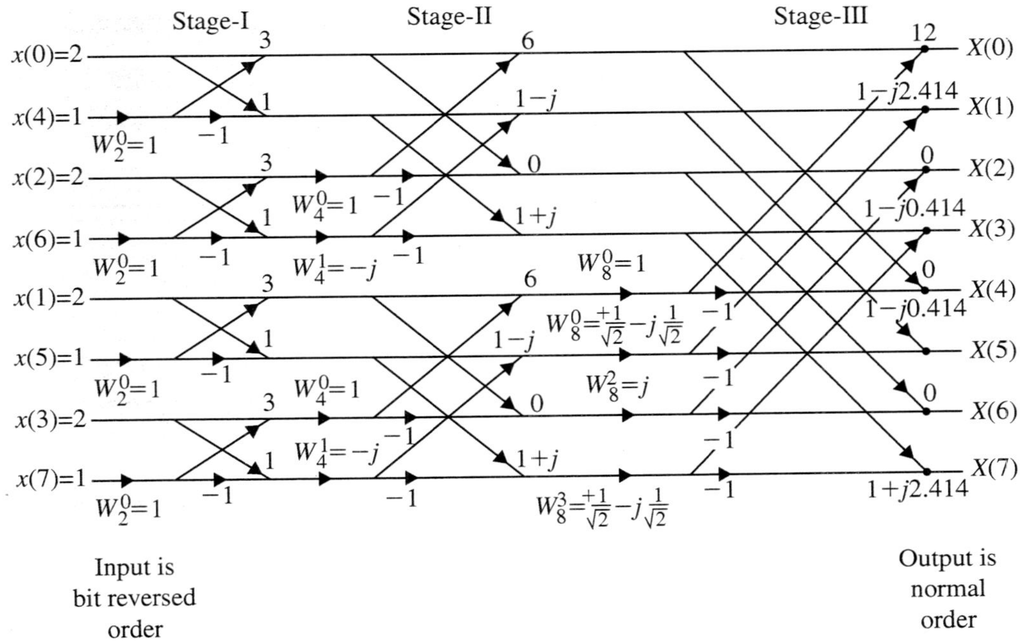

Figure 2.23 Butterfly diagram of Example 2.31(i).

(ii) DIF-FFT

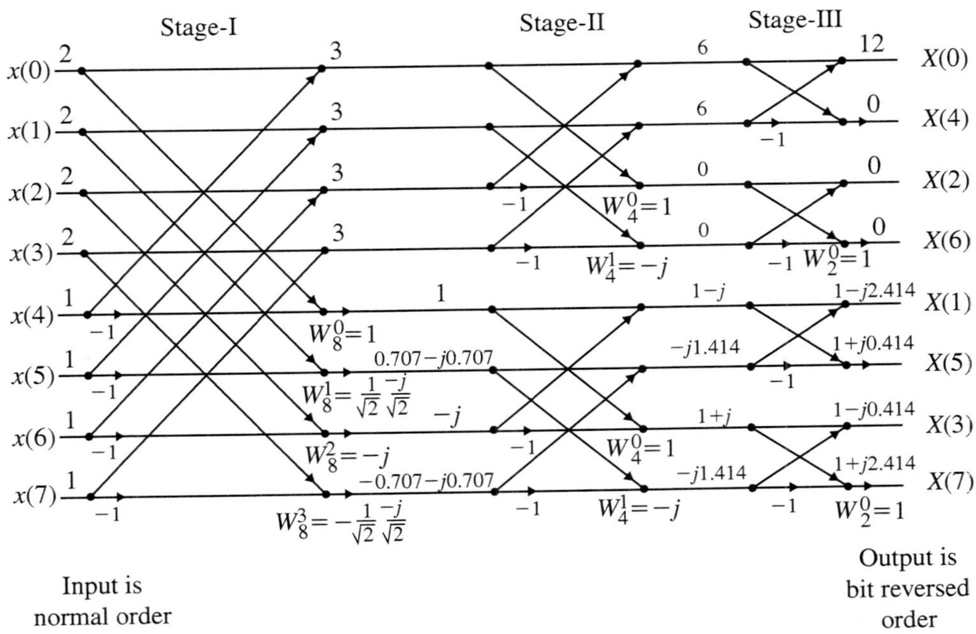

Figure 2.24 Butterfly diagram of Example 2.31(ii).

$$X(k) = \{12, 1 - j2.414, 0, 1 - j0.414, 0, 1 + j0.414, 0, 1 + j2.414\}$$
$$|X(k)| = \{12, 2.61, 0, 1.08, 0, 1.08, 0, 2.61\}$$
$$\angle X(k) = \{0, -0.37\pi, 0, -0.12\pi, 0, 0.12\pi, 0, 0.37\pi\}$$

Input	Stage-I	Stage-II	Stage-III	Output
2	$2+1=3$	$3+3=6$	$6+6=12$	$X(0)$
2	$2+1=3$	$3+3=6$	$6-6=0$	$X(4)$
2	$2+1=3$	$(3-3)(j)=0$	$0+0=0$	$X(2)$
2	$2+1=3$	$(3-3)(-j)=0$	$0-0=0$	$X(6)$
1	$(2-1)1=1$	$1-j$	$1-j-j1.414 =$ $1-j2.414$	$X(1)$
1	$(2-1)(\frac{1}{\sqrt{2}}-\frac{j}{\sqrt{2}}) =$ $\frac{1}{\sqrt{2}}-\frac{j}{\sqrt{2}}$	$\frac{1}{\sqrt{2}}-\frac{j}{\sqrt{2}}-\frac{1}{\sqrt{2}}-\frac{j}{\sqrt{2}} =$ $-j1.414$	$1-j+j1.414 =$ $1+j0.414$	$X(5)$
1	$(2-1)(-j)=-j$	$1-(-j)=1+j$	$1+j-j1.414 =$ $1-j0.414j$	$X(3)$
1	$(2-1)(\frac{-1}{\sqrt{2}}-\frac{-j}{\sqrt{2}}) =$ $\frac{-1}{\sqrt{2}}-\frac{j}{\sqrt{2}}$	$(\frac{1}{\sqrt{2}}-\frac{j}{\sqrt{2}}+\frac{1}{\sqrt{2}}+\frac{j}{\sqrt{2}})-j$ $=-j1.414$	$1+j+j1.414 =$ $1+j2.414$	$X(7)$

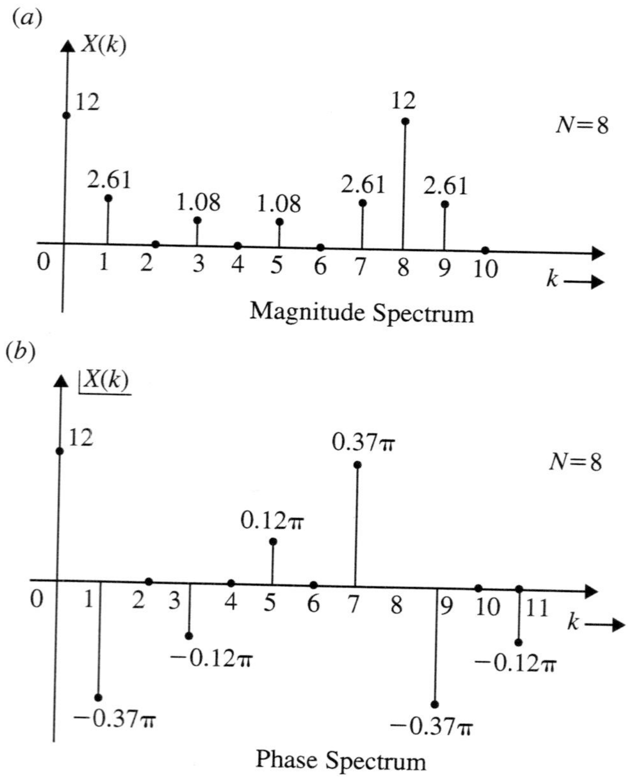

Figure 2.25 Magnitude and phase spectrum of Example 2.31.

Example 2.32

In an LTI system the input $x(n) = \{1, 1, 1\}$ and the impulse response $h(n) = \{-1, -1\}$. Determine the response of LTI system by radix-2 DIT FFT.

Solution The response of LTI system is given by linear convolution of input $x(n)$ and impulse response $h(n)$. That is

$$y(n) = x(n) * h(n)$$

where $N_1 = 3$ and $N_2 = 2$. The length of output sequence $y(n)$ is $N = N_1 + N_2 - 1 = 3 + 2 - 1 = 4$. Therefore, the given sequence $x(n)$ and $h(n)$ are converted into 4 point sequences by appending zeros.

$$x(n) = \{1, 1, 1, 0\} \quad \text{and} \quad h(n) = \{-1, -1, 0, 0\}$$
$$y(n) = x(n) * h(n)$$
$$Y(k) = X(k) * H(k)$$
$$y(n) = \text{IDFT}\,\{Y(k)\}$$
$$y(n) = \text{IDFT}\,\{X(k)H(k)\}$$

Step 1: To Determine $X(k)$

$$x(n) = \{1, 1, 1, 0\}$$

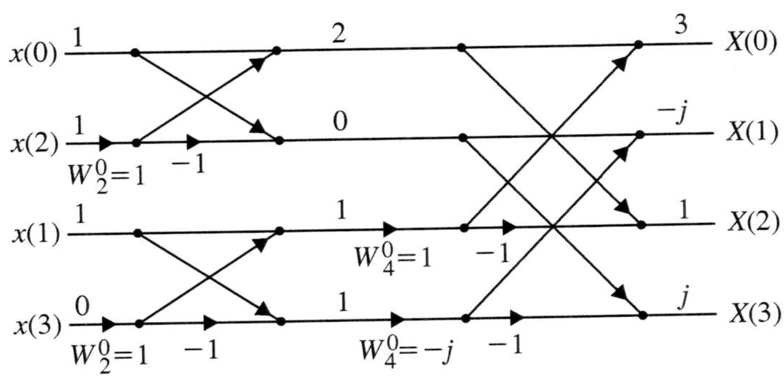

Figure 2.26 Butterfly diagram of $X(k)$.

Therefore, by referring to butterfly diagram we get

$$X(k) = \{3, -j, 1, j\}$$

Step 2: To Determine $H(k)$

$$h(n) = \{-1, -1, 0, 0\}$$

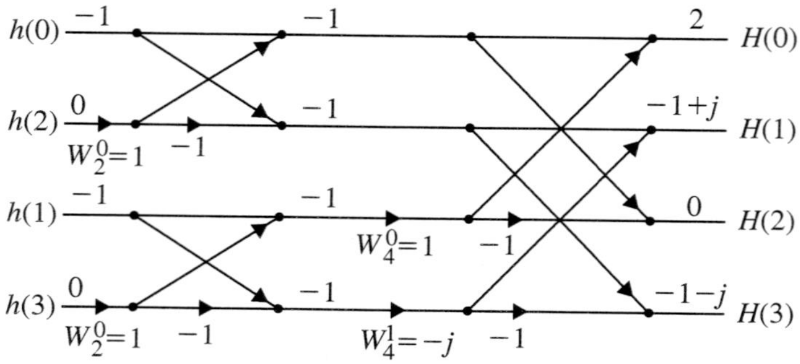

Figure 2.27 Butterfly diagram of $H(k)$.

Therefore, by referring to Figure 2.27 we get,

$$H(k) = \{2, -1+j, 0, -1-j\}$$

Step 3: To Determine the Product $X(k)H(k)$

Let

$$Y(k) = X(k)H(k)$$

where

$$\begin{aligned}
k &= 0, \quad Y(0) = X(0)H(0) = -6 \\
k &= 1, \quad Y(1) = X(1)H(1) = 1+j \\
k &= 2, \quad Y(2) = X(2)H(2) = 0 \\
k &= 3, \quad Y(3) = X(3)H(3) = 1-j
\end{aligned}$$

Therefore,

$$Y(k) = \{-6, 1+j, 0, 1-j\}$$

Step 4: To Determine IDFT of $Y(k)$

The IDFT of $Y(k)$ is given by

$$y(n) = \frac{1}{N}\left[\sum_{k=0}^{N-1} Y^*(k)W_N^{nk}\right]^*$$

$$\therefore \; Y^*(k) = \{-6, 1-j, 0, 1+j\}$$

The 4 point DFT of $Y^*(k)$ is,

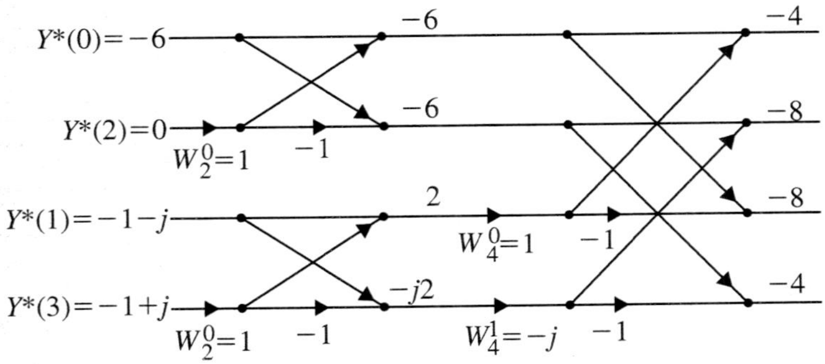

Figure 2.28 Butterfly diagram of $Y^*(k)$.

Therefore, by referring to Figure 2.28 we get,

$$\begin{aligned} y(n) &= \frac{1}{4}\{4 \text{ point DFT } Y^*(k)\}^* \\ &= \frac{1}{4}\{-4, -8, -8, -4\}^* \\ &= \frac{1}{4}\{-4, -8, -8, -4\} \\ y(n) &= \{-1, -2, -2, -1\} \end{aligned}$$

Example 2.33

Find the DFT of sequence

$$x(n) = \{1, 2, 3, 4, 4, 3, 2, 1\}$$

using DIT and DIF algorithm.

Solution The twiddle factors are

$$W_2^0 = 1, \quad W_4^0 = 1, \quad W_4^1 = -j$$

$$W_8^0 = 0, \quad W_8^1 = e^{-j\frac{2\pi}{8}} = \frac{1}{\sqrt{2}} - \frac{j}{\sqrt{2}}$$

$$W_8^2 = e^{-j\frac{2\pi\times 2}{8}} = -j$$

$$\begin{aligned} W_8^3 &= e^{-j\frac{2\pi\times 3}{8}} \\ &= -\frac{1}{\sqrt{2}} - \frac{j}{\sqrt{2}} \end{aligned}$$

The butterfly diagram is shown in Figure 2.29.

(*i*) Using DIT Algorithm

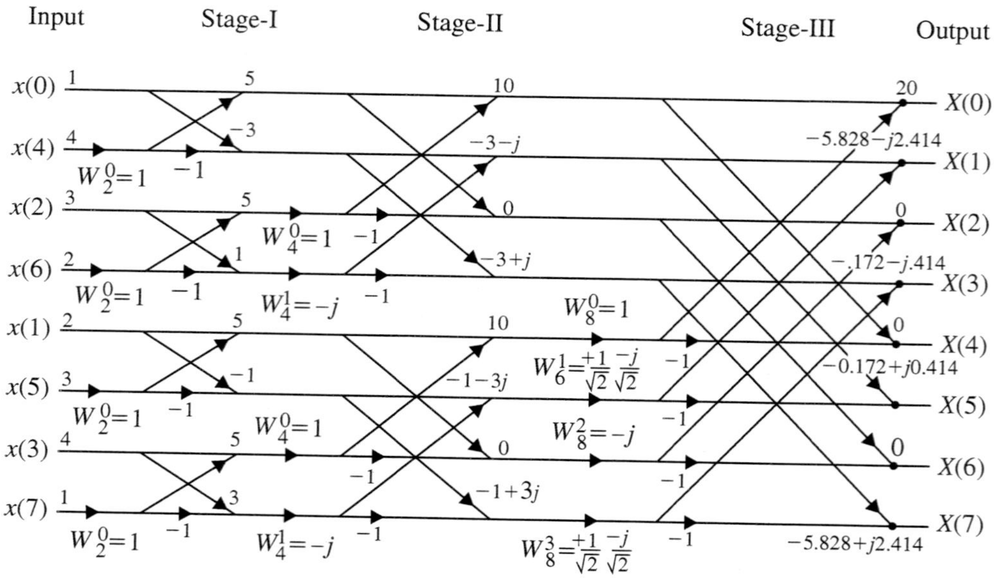

Figure 2.29 Butterfly diagram of Example 2.33(*i*).

Input	Stage-I	Stage-II	Output
1	$1+4=5$	$5+5=10$	$10+10=20$
4	$1-4=-3$	$-3-j$	$-3-j+(-1-3j)(\frac{1}{\sqrt{2}}-\frac{j}{\sqrt{2}})$ $=-5.828-j2.414$
3	$3+2=5$	$5-5=0$	$0+0=0$
2	$3-2=1$	$-3+j$	$-3+j+(-1+3j)(\frac{-1}{\sqrt{2}}-\frac{j}{\sqrt{2}})=$ $-0.172-j0.414$
2	$2+3=5$	$5+5=10$	$10-10=0$
3	$2-3=-1$	$-1+(3)(-j)=-1-3j$	$-3-j-(-1-3j)(\frac{1}{\sqrt{2}}-\frac{j}{\sqrt{2}})=$ $-0.172+j0.414$
4	$4+1=5$	$5-5=0$	$0+0=0$
1	$4-1=3$	$-1+(3)(-j)(-1)=-1+3j$	$-3+j-(-1+3j)(\frac{-1}{\sqrt{2}}-\frac{j}{\sqrt{2}})=$ $-5.828+j2.414$

$X(k)=$

$\{20,\ -5.828-j2.414,\ 0,\ -0.172-j0.414,\ 0,\ -0.172+j0.414,\ 0,\ -5.828+j2.414\}$

(*ii*) Using DIT Algorithm

$X(k)=$

$\{20,\ -5.828-j2.414,\ 0,\ -0.172vj0.414,\ 0,\ -0.172+j0.414,\ 0,\ -5.828+j2.414\}$

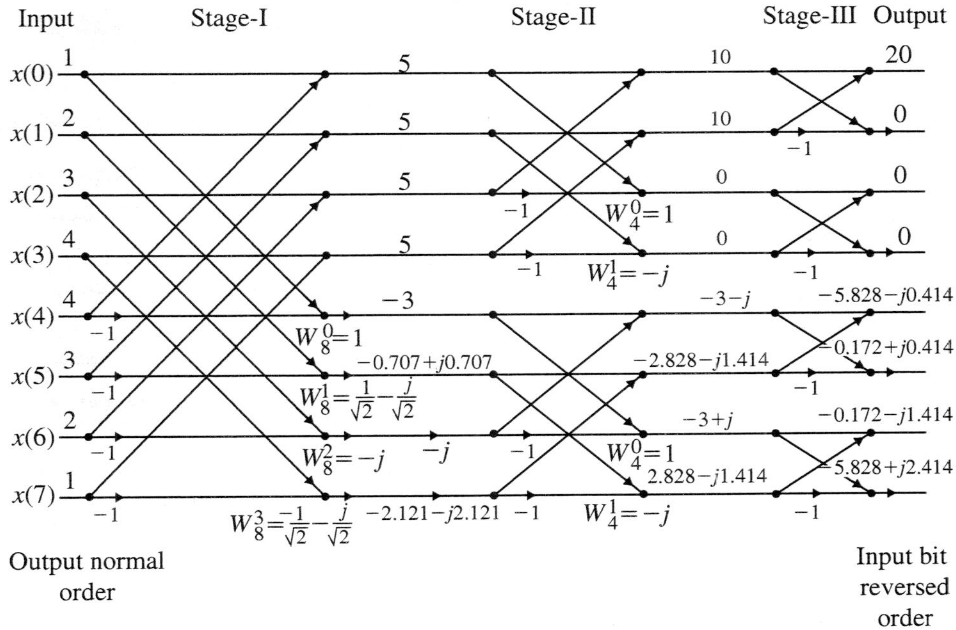

Figure 2.30 Butterfly diagram of Example 2.33(*ii*).

Input	Stage-I	Stage-II	Output
1	$1+4=5$	$5+5=10$	$10+10=20$
2	$2+3=5$	$5+5=10$	$10-10=0$
3	$3+2=5$	$(5-5)(1)=0$	$0+0=0$
4	$4+1=5$	$(5-5)(-j)=0$	$0-0=0$
4	$(1-4)1=-3$	$-3-j$	$-3-j-2.828-j1.414$ $=-5.828-j0.414$
3	$(2-3)(\frac{1}{\sqrt{2}}-\frac{j}{\sqrt{2}})$ $=-0.707+j0.707$	$-0.707+j0.707-2.121-j2.121$ $=-2.828-j1.414$	$-3-j+2.828+j1.414$ $=-0.172+j0.414$
2	$(3-2)(-j)=-j$	$-3+j$	$-3+j+2.828-j1.414$ $=-0.172-j0.414$
1	$(4-1)(\frac{-1}{\sqrt{2}}-\frac{j}{\sqrt{2}})$ $=-2.121-j2.121$	$-0.707+j0.707-(-2.121-j2.121)$ $(-j)=2.828-j1.414$	$-3+j-2.828+j1.414$ $=-5.828+j2.414$

Example 2.34

Compute 4 point of sequence

$$x(n)=\{0,\ 1,\ 2,\ 3\}$$

using DIT algorithm.

Solution The twiddle factors are

$$W_2^0 = 1, \quad W_4^0 = 1, \quad W_4^1 = -j$$

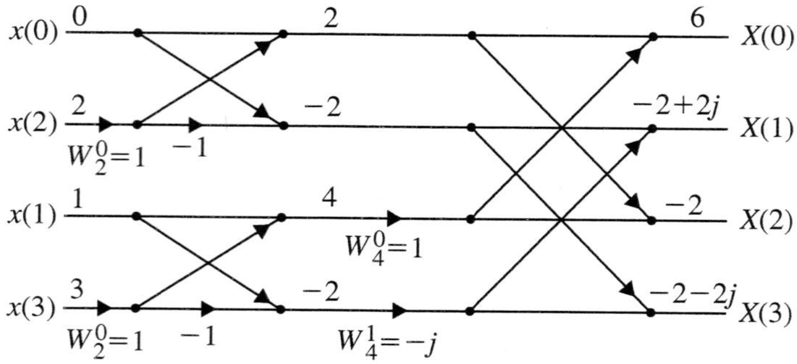

Figure 2.31 Butterfly diagram of $X(k)$ for Example 2.34.

$$\boxed{X(k) = \{6,\ -2+2j,\ -2,\ -2-2j\}}$$

Example 2.35

Find the IDFT of the sequence

$$X(k) = \{4,\ 1-j2.414,\ 0,\ 1-j0.414,\ 0,\ 1+j0.414,\ 0,\ 1+j2.414\}$$

using DIT algorithm.

Solution

$$X^*(k) = \{4,\ 1+j2.414,\ 0,\ 1+j0.414,\ 0,\ 1-j0.414,\ 0,\ 1-j2.414\}$$

The 8-point butterfly diagram of $X^*(k)$ is shown in Figure 2.32.

Input	**Stage-I**	**Stage-II**	**Output**
4	$4+0=4$	$4+0=4$	$4+4=8$
$1+j2.414$	$1+j2.414+1-j0.414=2+j2$	$2+j2+2-j2=4$	$4-4=0$
0	$0+0=0$	$4-0=4$	$4+4=8$
$1+j0.414$	$1+j0.414+1-j2.414=2-j2$	$2+j2-(2-j2)(-j)=4$	$4-4=0$
0	$4-0=4$	$4+0=4$	$4+4=8$
$1-j0.414$	$1+j2.414-(1-j0.414)\left(\frac{1}{\sqrt{2}}-\frac{j}{\sqrt{2}}\right)$ $=2+j2$	$2+j2+2-j2=4$	$4-4=0$
0	$0-0=0$	$4-0=4$	$4+4=8$
$1-j2.414$	$1-j0.414-(1-j2.414)\left(\frac{-1}{\sqrt{2}}-\frac{j}{\sqrt{2}}\right)$ $=2-j2$	$2+j2+2-(2-j2)(-j)=4$	$4-4=0$

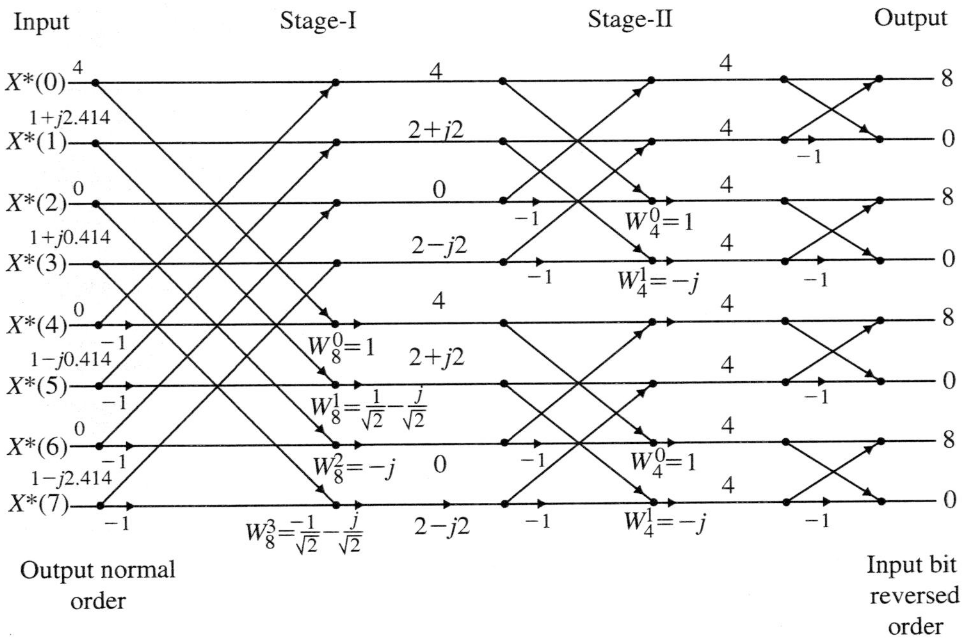

Figure 2.32 Butterfly diagram of $X^*(k)$.

8 point DFT of $X^*(k)$ is

$$x(n) = \frac{1}{8}\{8 \text{ point DFT of } X^*(k)\}^*$$
$$= \frac{1}{8}\{8,\ 8,\ 8,\ 8,\ 0,\ 0,\ 0,\ 0\}^*$$

$$\boxed{x(n) = \{1,\ 1,\ 1,\ 1,\ 0,\ 0,\ 0,\ 0\}}$$

Example 2.36

Find the IDFT of the sequence

$$X(k) = \{10,\ -2+j2,\ -2,\ -2-j2\}$$

using DIT algorithm.

Solution Given

$$X(k) = \{10,\ -2+j2,\ -2,\ -2-j2\}$$
$$X^*(k) = \{10,\ -2-j2,\ -2,\ -2+j2\}$$

The butterfly diagram of $X^*(k)$ is shown in Figure 2.33.

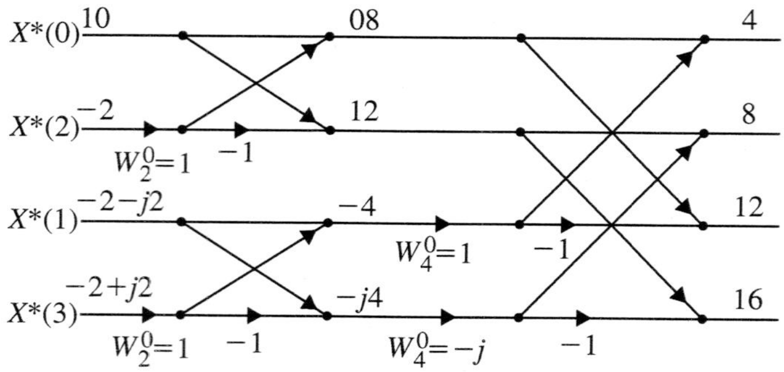

Figure 2.33 Butterfly diagram of $X^*(k)$.

4 point DFT of $X^*(k) = \{4,\ 12,\ 8,\ 16\}$

$$x(n) = \frac{1}{4}\{4 \text{ point DFT of } X^*(k)\}^*$$
$$= \frac{1}{4}\{4,\ 8,\ 12,\ 16\}^*$$

$$\boxed{x(n) = \{1,\ 2,\ 3,\ 4\}}$$

Example 2.37

Compute the DFT of the sequence

$$x(n) = \cos\left(\frac{n\pi}{2}\right)$$

where $N = 4$, using DIF FFT algorithm.

Solution Given

$$x(n) = \cos\left(\frac{n\pi}{2}\right), \qquad N = 4$$
$$x(0) = 1$$
$$x(1) = 0$$
$$x(2) = -1$$
$$x(3) = 0$$

Therefore,

$$x(n) = \{1,\ 0,\ -1,\ 0\}$$

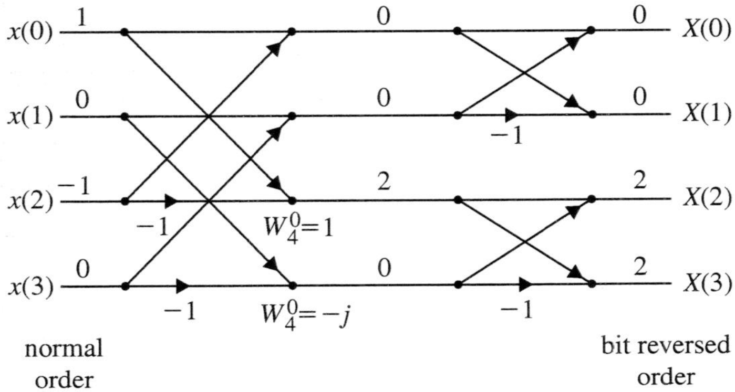

Figure 2.34 Butterfly diagram of $X(k)$ for Example 2.37.

Therefore,

$$\boxed{X(k) = \{0,\ 2,\ 0,\ 2\}}$$

Example 2.38

Using the decimation in frequency FFT flow graph compute DFT of

$$x[n] = \cos\left(\frac{n\pi}{4}\right) \qquad \text{for} \qquad 0 \le n \le 7$$

(Anna University, December, 2007)

Solution Given

$$x[n] = \cos\left(\frac{n\pi}{4}\right) \qquad \text{for} \qquad 0 \le n \le 7$$

$$x[n] = \{1,\ 0.707,\ 0,\ -0.707,\ -1,\ -0.07,\ 0,\ 0.707\}$$

The butterfly diagram is shown in Figure 2.35. From Figure 2.35, $X(k)$ is obtained as,

$$\boxed{X(k) = \{0,\ 4,\ 0,\ 0,\ 0,\ 0,\ 0,\ 4\}}$$

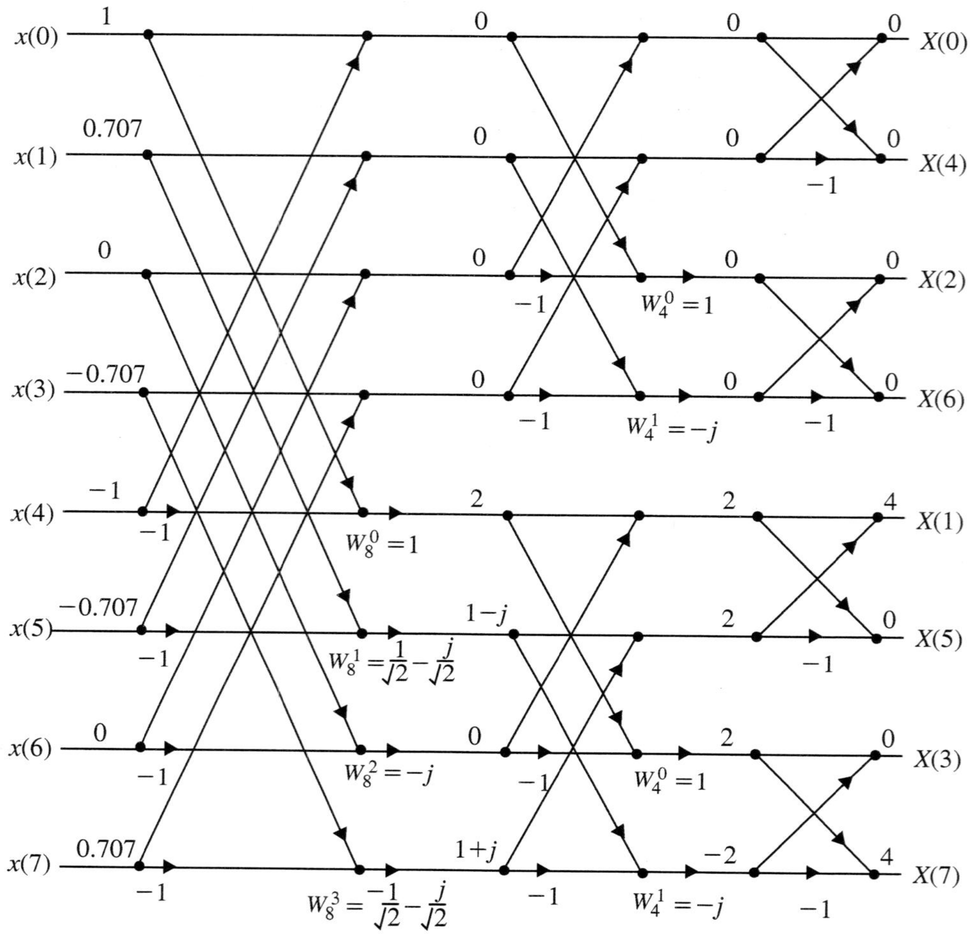

Figure 2.35 Butterfly diagram for Example 2.38.

Example 2.39

Draw the butterfly diagram using 8 point DIT-FFT for the following sequence

$$x[n] = \{1, 0, 0, 0, 0, 0, 0, 0\}$$

((Anna University, June, 2007)

Solution The butterfly diagram for Example 2.39 is shown in Figure 2.36.

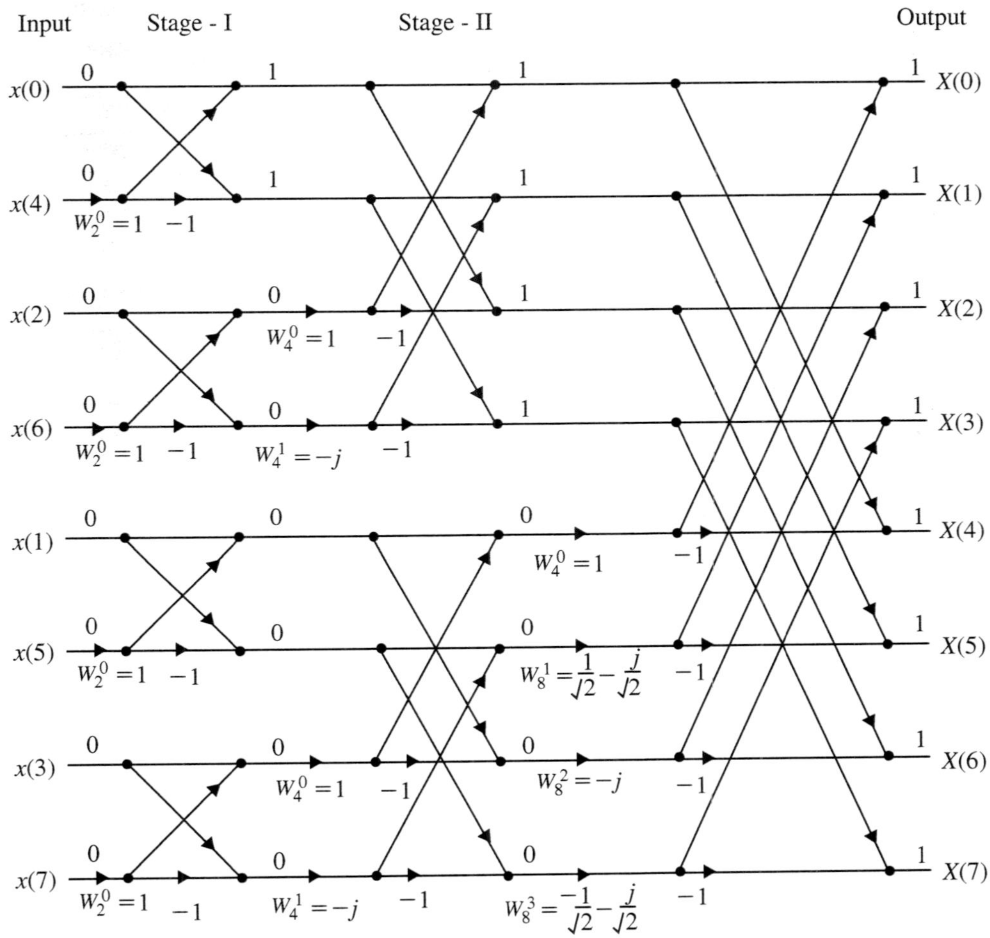

Figure 2.36 Butterfly diagram for Example 2.39.

Input	Stage-I	Stage-II	Output
1	$1+0=1$	$1+0=1$	$1+0=1$
0	$0+1=1$	$1+0=1$	$1+0=1$
0	$0+0=0$	$0+1=1$	$1+0=1$
0	$0+0=0$	$0+1=1$	$1+0=1$
0	$0+0=0$	$0+0=0$	$0+1=1$
0	$0+0=0$	$0+0=0$	$0+1=1$
0	$0+0=0$	$0+0=0$	$0+1=1$
0	$0+0=0$	$0+0=0$	$0+1=1$

$$X(k) = \{1, 1, 1, 1, 1, 1, 1, 1\}$$

Example 2.40

Compute the 8-point DFT of the sequence

$$x[n] = \{0.5, 0.5, 0.5, 0.5, 0, 0, 0, 0\}$$

using the in place radix-2 DIF-FFT algorithm.

Solution

The twiddle factors are

$$W_8^0 = 1,$$
$$W_8^1 = \frac{1}{\sqrt{2}} - \frac{j}{\sqrt{2}}$$
$$W_8^2 = -j$$
$$W_8^3 = -\frac{-1}{\sqrt{2}} - \frac{j}{\sqrt{2}}$$
$$W_4^0 = 1$$
$$W_4^1 = -j$$
$$W_2^0 = 1$$

The butterfly diagram is shown in Figure 2.37.

Input	Stage-I	Stage-II	Output
0.5	$0.5 + 0 = 0.5$	$0.5 + 0.5 = 1$	$1 + 1 = 2$
0.5	$0.5 + 0 = 0.5$	$0.5 + 0.5 = 1$	$1 - 1 = 0$
0.5	$0.5 + 0 = 0.5$	$(0.5 - 0.5)1 = 0$	$0 + 0 = 0$
0.5	$0.5 + 0 = 0.5$	$(0.5 - 0.5)(-j) = 0$	$0 - 0 = 0$
0	$(0.5 + 0)1 = 0.5$	$0.5 - 0.5j$	$0.5 - 0.5j - 0.707j$ $= 0.5 - 1.207j$
0	$(0.5 + 0)\left(\frac{1}{\sqrt{2}} - \frac{j}{\sqrt{2}}\right)$ $= 0.3535 - j0.3525$	$(0.3525 - j0.3525)$ $+(-0.3525 - j0.3525) = -0.707j$	$0.5 - 0.5j + 0.707j$ $= 0.5 + 0.207j$
0	$(0.5 + 0)(-j) = -0.5j$	$0.5 + 0.5j$	$0.5 + 0.5j - 0.707j$ $= 0.5 - 0.207j$
0	$(0.5 + 0)\left(\frac{-1}{\sqrt{2}} - \frac{j}{\sqrt{2}}\right)$ $= -0.3535 - j0.3525$	$[(0.3525 - j0.3525)$ $-(-0.3525 - j0.3525)](-j)$ $= -0.707j$	$0.5 + 0.5j + 0.707j$ $= 0.5 + 1.207j$

$$X(k) = \{2,\ 0.5 - 1.207j,\ 0,\ 0.5 - 0.207j,\ 0,\ 0.5 + 0.207j,\ 0,\ 0.5 + 1.207j\}$$

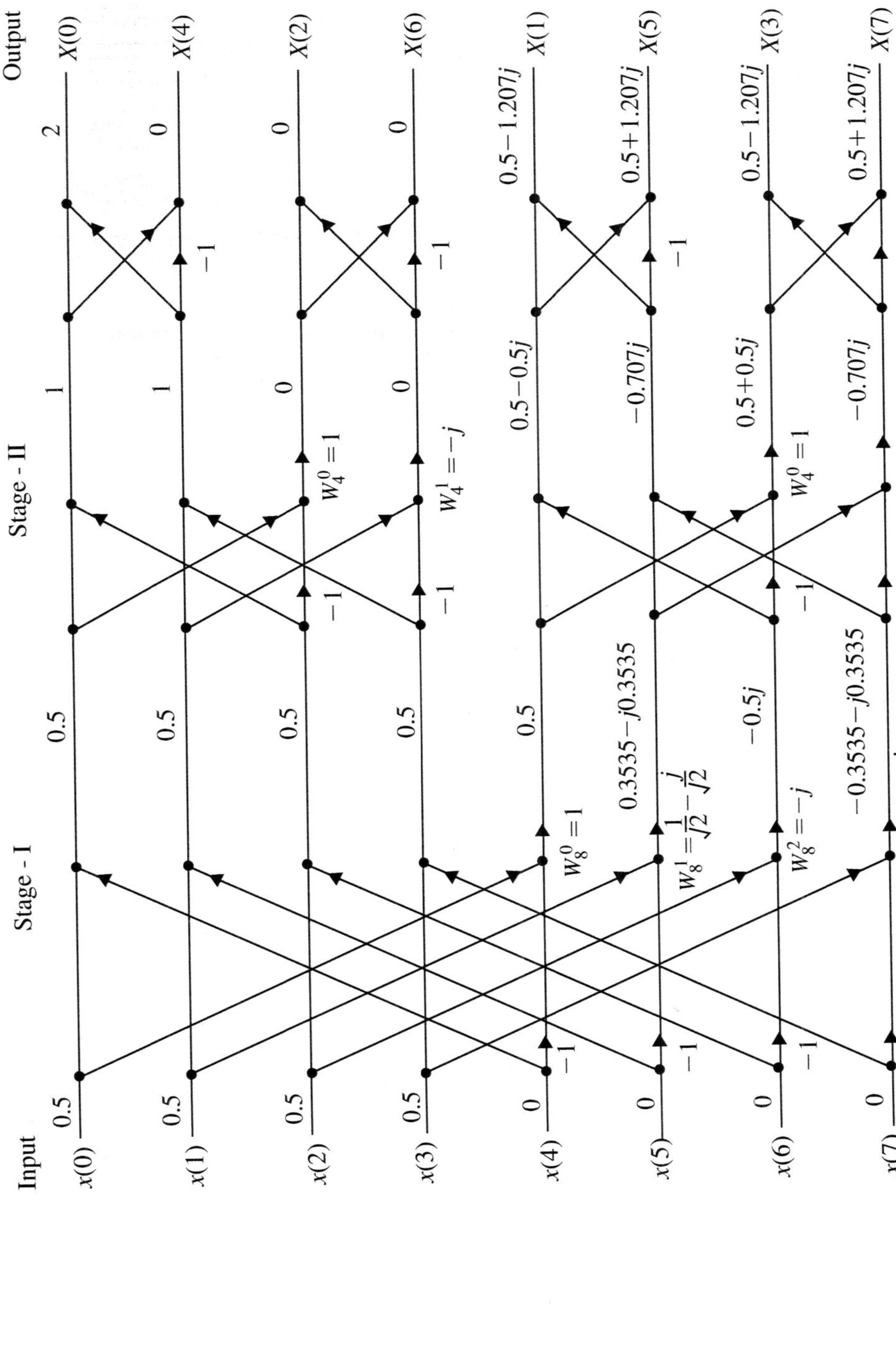

Figure 2.37 Butterfly diagram for Example 2.40.

Example 2.41

Find the 8 point DFT of the given sequence

$$x[n] = \{0, 1, 2, 3, 4, 5, 6, 7\}$$

using DIF radix-2 FFT algorithm.

(*Anna University, May, 2005*)

Solution

Input	Stage-I	Stage-II	Output
0	$0+4=4$	$8+4=12$	$12+16=28$
1	$1+5=6$	$6+10=16$	$12-16=-4$
2	$2+6=8$	$4-8=-4$	$-4+4j$
3	$3+7=10$	$(6-10)-j=4j$	$-4-4j$
4	$0-4=-4$	$-4+4j$	$-4+4j+\frac{8j}{\sqrt{2}}$ $=-4+9.656j$
5	$(1-5)\left(\frac{1}{\sqrt{2}}-\frac{j}{\sqrt{2}}\right)$ $=\frac{-4}{\sqrt{2}}+\frac{4j}{\sqrt{2}}$	$\frac{-4}{\sqrt{2}}+\frac{4j}{\sqrt{2}}+\frac{4}{\sqrt{2}}+\frac{4j}{\sqrt{2}}=\frac{8j}{\sqrt{2}}$	$-4+4j-\frac{8j}{\sqrt{2}}$ $=-4-1.656j$
6	$(2-6)(-j)=4j$	$-4-4j$	$-4+4j+\frac{8j}{\sqrt{2}}$ $=-4+1.656j$
7	$(3-7)\left(-\frac{1}{\sqrt{2}}-\frac{j}{\sqrt{2}}\right)$ $=\frac{4}{\sqrt{2}}+\frac{4j}{\sqrt{2}}$	$\left(-\frac{4}{\sqrt{2}}+\frac{4j}{\sqrt{2}}-\frac{4}{\sqrt{2}}-\frac{4j}{\sqrt{2}}\right)$ $-j=\frac{8j}{\sqrt{2}}$	$-4-4j-\frac{8j}{\sqrt{2}}$ $=-4-9.656j$

$$X(k) = \Big\{28, -4+9.656j, -4+4j, -4+1.656j, -4, -4-1.656j, -4-4j, -4-9.656j\Big\}$$

The butterfly diagram is shown in Figure 2.38.

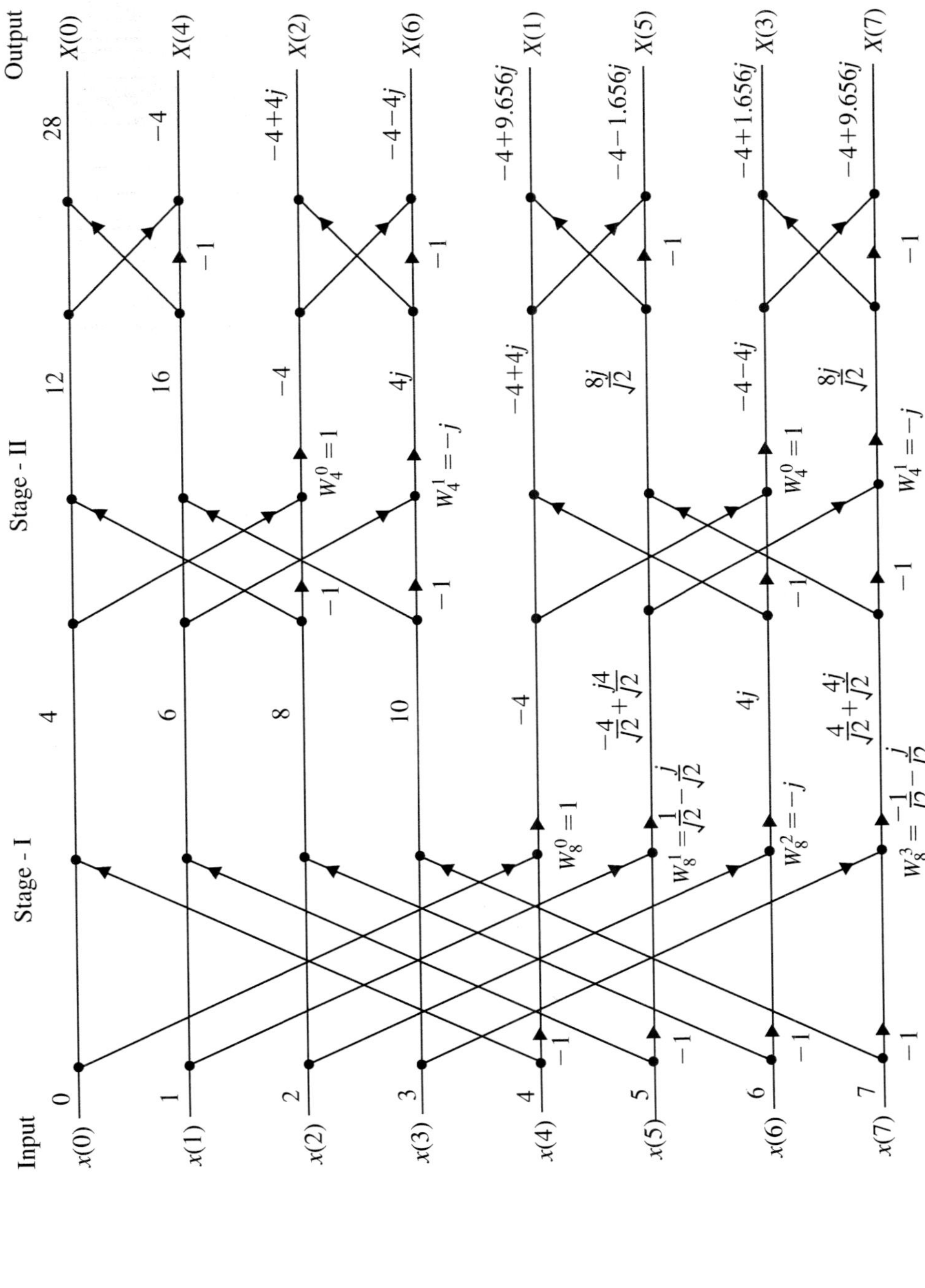

Figure 2.38 Butterfly diagram for Example 2.41.

Example 2.42

Find the response of an LTI system with impulse response $h(n) = \{2, 1, 3\}$ for the input $x(n) = \{1, 2\}$ using DIT radix-2 FFT algorithm.

(Anna University, December, 2007)

Solution The response of LTI system is given by linear convolution of input $x(n)$ and impulse $h(n)$ *i.e.*,

$$y(n) = x(n) * h(n)$$

$N_1 = 2$ and $N_2 = 3$. The length of output sequence $y(n)$ is $N = N_1 + N_2 - 1 = 2 + 3 - 1 = 4$. Therefore, the given sequence $x(n)$ and $h(n)$ are converted into 4 point sequence by appending zeros.

$$x(n) = \{1, 2, 0, 0\} \quad \text{and} \quad h(n) = \{2, 1, 3, 0\}$$

$$y(n) = \text{IDFT}\{X(k)H(k)\}$$

Step 1: To determine $X(k)$ (Refer Figure 2.39(a))

$$x(n) = \{1, 2, 0, 0\}$$

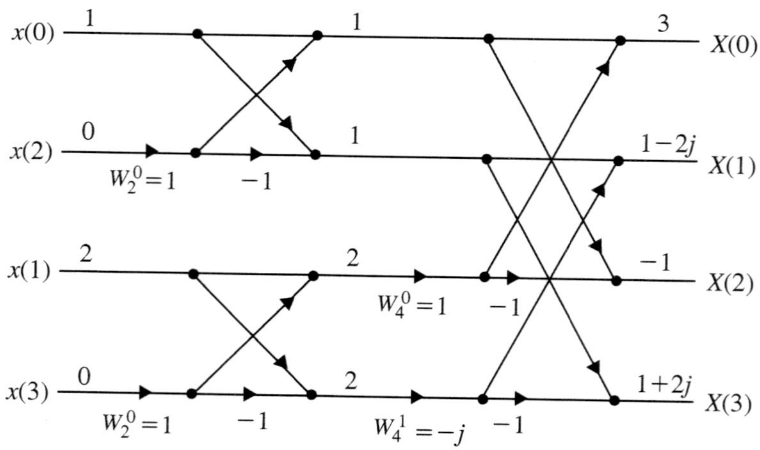

Figure 2.39 (a) Butterfly diagram for Example 2.42.

$$X(k) = \{3, 1 - 2j, -1, 1 + 2j\}$$

Step 2: To determine $H(k)$ (Refer Figure 2.39(b))

$$h(n) = \{2, 1, 3, 0\}$$

$$H(k) = \{6, -1 - j, 4, -1 + j\}$$

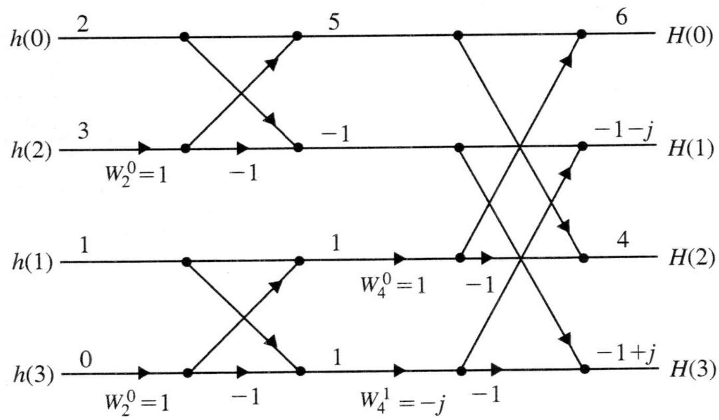

Figure 2.39 (*b*) Butterfly diagram for Example 2.42.

Step 3:

$$Y(k) = X(k)H(k)$$
$$= \{3,\ (1-2j),\ -1,\ (1+2j)\}\{6,\ (-1-j),\ 4,\ (-1+j)\}$$
$$= \{3\times 6,\ (1-2j)(-1-j),\ -1\times 4,\ (1+2j)(-1+j)\}$$
$$Y(k) = \{18, -3+j, -4, -3-j\}$$

Step 4: To determine IDFT of $Y(k)$ (Refer Figure 2.39(*c*))

The IDFT of $Y(k)$ is given by

$$y(n) = \frac{1}{N}\left[\sum_{k=0}^{N-1} Y^*(k)W_N^{nk}\right]^*$$
$$= \frac{1}{N}\left[N \text{ point DFT of } Y^*(k)\right]^*$$
$$Y^*(k) = \{18, -3-j, -4, -3+j\}$$

The 4 point DFT of $Y^*(k)$ is

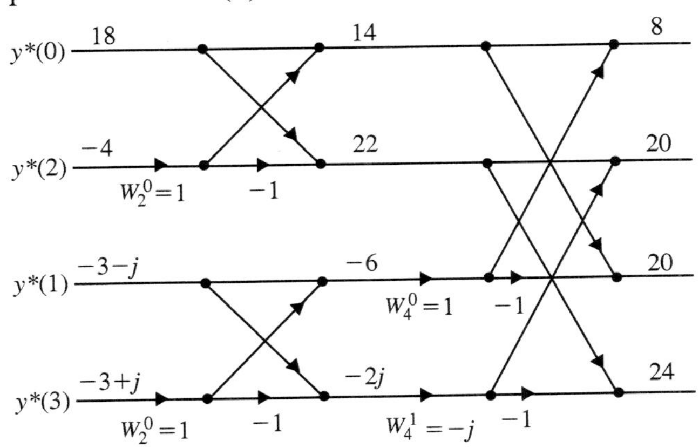

Figure 2.39 (*c*) Butterfly diagram for Example 2.42.

Therefore,

$$y(n) = \frac{1}{N}\left[4 \text{ point DFT of } Y^*(k)\right]^*$$
$$= \frac{1}{4}\{8, 20, 20, 24\}^*$$
$$= \frac{1}{4}\{8, 20, 20, 24\}$$

$$\boxed{y(n) = \{2, 5, 5, 6\}}$$

Example 2.43

Develop a radix-3 DIF-FFT algorithm for evaluating the DFT for $N = 9$.

Solution For $N = 9 = 3 \cdot 3$

$$X(k) = \sum_{n=0}^{2} x(3n)W_9^{3nk} + \sum_{n=0}^{2} x(3n+1)W_9^{(3n+1)k} + \sum_{n=0}^{2} x(3n+2)W_9^{(3n+2)k}$$

$$X(k) = X_1(k) + W_9^k X_2(k) + W_9^{2k} X_3(k)$$

where

$$X_1(k) = \sum_{n=0}^{2} x(3n)W_9^{3nk} = x(0) + x(3)W_9^{3k} + x(6)W_9^{6k} \qquad k = 0, \ldots, 2$$

$$X_2(k) = \sum_{n=0}^{2} x(3n+1)W_9^{3nk} = x(1) + x(4)W_9^{3k} + x(7)W_9^{6k} \qquad k = 0, \ldots, 2$$

$$X_3(k) = \sum_{n=0}^{2} x(3n+2)W_9^{3nk} = x(2) + x(5)W_9^{3k} + x(8)W_9^{6k} \qquad k = 0, \ldots, 2$$

The butterfly diagram is shown in Figure 2.40.

Stage-I: Computation

$$X_1(k) = \sum_{n=0}^{2} x(3n)W_9^{3nk}$$
$$= x(0) + x(3)W_9^{3k} + x(6)W_9^{6k} \qquad k = 0, \ldots, 2$$

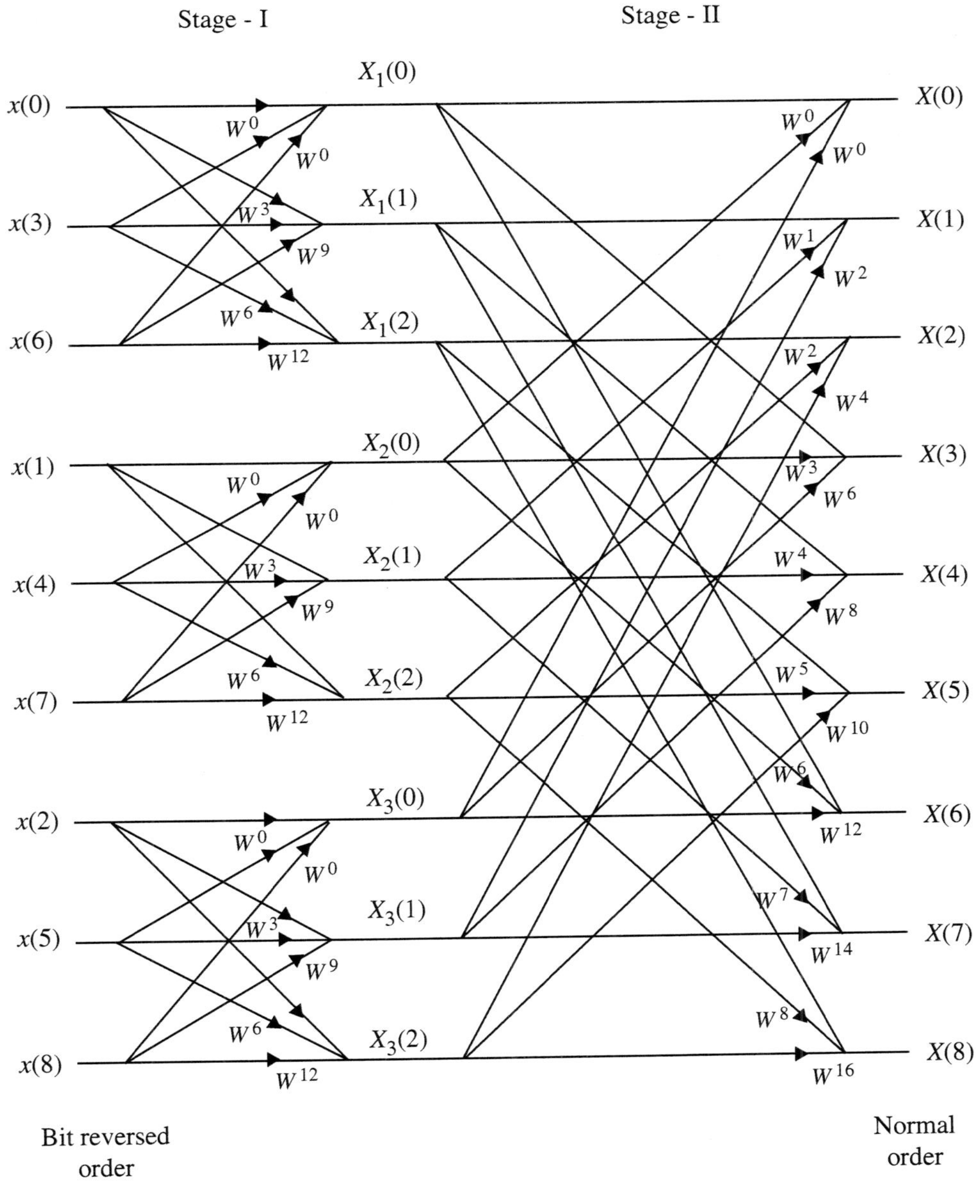

Figure 2.40 Radix-3 DIT FFT flow diagram for $N = 9$.

$$X_1(0) = x(0) + x(3)W_9^0 + x(6)W_9^0$$

$$X_1(1) = x(0) + x(3)W_9^3 + x(6)W_9^6$$

$$X_1(2) = x(1) + x(3)W_9^6 + x(6)W_9^{12}$$

$$X_2(k) = x(1) + x(4)W_9^{3k} + x(7)W_9^{6k}, \qquad k = 0, \ldots, 2$$

$$X_2(0) = x(1) + x(3)W_9^0 + x(7)W_9^0$$

$$X_2(1) = x(1) + x(3)W_9^3 + x(7)W_9^6$$

$$X_2(2) = x(1) + x(3)W_9^6 + x(7)W_9^{12}$$

$$X_3(k) = x(2) + x(5)W_9^{3k} + x(8)W_9^{6k}, \qquad k = 0, \dots, 2$$

$$X_3(0) = x(2) + x(5)W_9^0 + x(8)W_9^0$$

$$X_3(1) = x(2) + x(5)W_9^3 + x(8)W_9^6$$

$$X_3(2) = x(2) + x(5)W_9^6 + x(8)W_9^{12}$$

Stage-II: Computation

$$X(k) = X_1(k) + W_9^k X_2(k) + W_9^{2k} X_3(k) \qquad k = 0, \dots, 8$$

$$X(0) = X_1(0) + W_9^0 X_2(0) + W_9^0 X_3(0)$$

$$X(1) = X_1(1) + W_9^1 X_2(1) + W_9^2 X_3(1)$$

$$X(2) = X_1(2) + W_9^2 X_2(2) + W_9^4 X_3(2)$$

$$X(3) = X_1(0) + W_9^3 X_2(0) + W_9^6 X_3(0)$$

$$X(4) = X_1(1) + W_9^4 X_2(1) + W_9^8 X_3(1)$$

$$X(5) = X_1(2) + W_9^5 X_2(2) + W_9^{10} X_3(2)$$

$$X(6) = X_1(0) + W_9^6 X_2(0) + W_9^{12} X_3(0)$$

$$X(7) = X_1(1) + W_9^7 X_2(1) + W_9^{14} X_3(1)$$

$$X(8) = X_1(2) + W_9^8 X_2(2) + W_9^{16} X_3(2)$$

Example 2.44

Develop DIT FTT algorithm for decomposing the DFT for $N = 6$ and draw the flow diagrams for

(a) $N = 2 \cdot 3$

(b) $N = 3 \cdot 2$

(c) Also, by using the FFT algorithm developed in part (b); evaluate the DFT values for $x(n) = \{1, 2, 3, 4, 5, 6\}$.

Solution

(a) For $N = 6 = 2 \cdot 3$, where number of sequence ($m_1 = 2$), number of elements in each subsequences ($N_1 = 3$).

$$X(k) = \sum_{n=0}^{2} x(2n)W_6^{2nk} + \sum_{n=0}^{2} x(2n+1)W_6^{(2n+1)k} + \sum_{n=0}^{2} x(2)W_6^{2nk}$$

$$+ W_6^k \sum_{n=0}^{2} x(2n+1)W_6^{2nk}$$

Also, $X_i(k+3) = X_i(k)$

$$X(k) = X_1(k) + W_6^k X_2(k), \quad k = 0, \dots, 5$$

where

$$X_1(k) = \sum_{n=0}^{2} x(2n) W_6^{2nk} \qquad k = 0, \dots, 2$$

$$X_2(k) = \sum_{n=0}^{2} x(2n+1) W_6^{2nk} \qquad k = 0, \dots, 2$$

The butterfly diagram is shown in Figure 2.41.

Stage-I: Computation

$$X_1(k) = \sum_{n=0}^{2} x(2n) W_6^{2nk} \qquad k = 0, \dots, 2$$

$$X_1(k) = x(0) + x(2) W_6^{2k} + x(4) W_6^{4k} \qquad k = 0, \dots, 2$$

$$X_1(0) = x(0) + x(2) W_6^0 + x(4) W_6^0$$

$$X_1(1) = x(0) + x(3) W_6^2 + x(4) W_6^4$$

$$X_1(2) = x(1) + x(3) W_9^4 + x(4) W_6^8$$

$$X_1(2) = x(0) + x(3) W_9^4 + x(4) W_6^2$$

$$X_2(k) = \sum_{n=0}^{2} x(2n+1) W_6^{2nk} \qquad k = 0, \dots, 2$$

$$X_2(k) = x(1) + x(3) W_6^{2k} + x(5) W_6^{4k} \qquad k = 0, \dots, 2$$

$$X_2(0) = x(1) + x(3) W_6^0 + x(5) W_6^0$$

$$X_2(1) = x(1) + x(3) W_6^2 + x(5) W_6^4$$

$$X_2(2) = x(1) + x(3) W_6^4 + x(5) W_6^8$$

$$X_2(2) = x(1) + x(3) W_6^4 + x(5) W_6^2$$

Stage-II: Computation

$$X(k) = X_1(k) + W_6^k X_2(k), \qquad k = 0, \dots 5$$

$$X(0) = X_1(0) + W_6^0 X_2(0)$$

$$X(1) = X_1(1) + W_6^1 X_2(1)$$

$$X(2) = X_1(2) + W_6^2 X_2(2)$$

$$X(3) = X_1(3) + W_6^3 X_2(3) = X_1(0) + W_6^3 X_2(0)$$

$$X(4) = X_1(4) + W_6^4 X_2(4) = X_1(1) + W_6^4 X_2(1)$$

$$X(5) = X_1(5) + W_6^5 X_2(5) = X_1(2) + W_6^5 X_2(2)$$

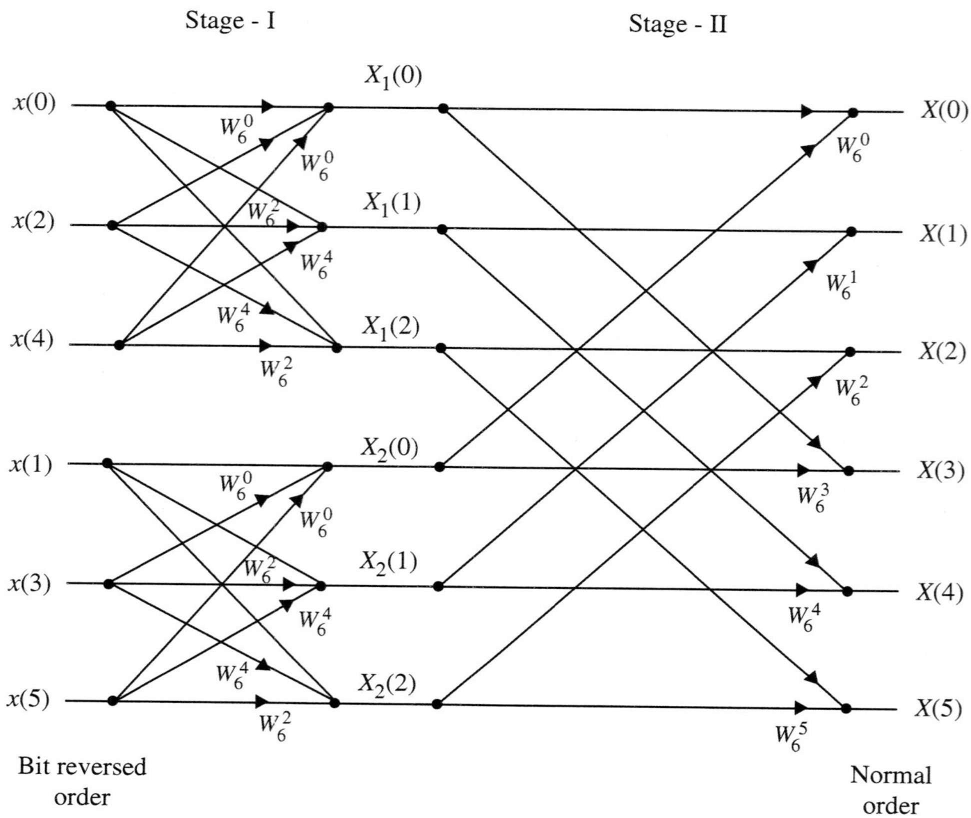

Figure 2.41 DIT FFT flow diagram for $N = 6 = 2 \cdot 3$.

(*b*) For $N = 6 = 2 \cdot 3$, where number of sequence ($m_1 = 3$), number of elements in each subsequences ($N_1 = 2$).

$$X(k) = \sum_{n=0}^{1} x(3n)W_6^{3nk} + \sum_{n=0}^{1} x(3n+1)W_6^{(3n+1)k} + \sum_{n=0}^{1} x(3n+2)W_6^{(3n+2)k}$$

$$= \sum_{n=0}^{1} x(3n)W_6^{3nk} + W_6^k \sum_{n=0}^{1} x(3n+1)W_6^{3nk} + W_6^{2k} \sum_{n=0}^{1} x(3n+2)W_6^{3nk}$$

$$X(k) = X_1(k) + W_6^k X_2(k) + W_6^{2k} X_3(k)$$

where

$$X_1(k) = \sum_{n=0}^{1} x(3n)W_6^{3nk} = x(0) + x(3)W_6^{3k}$$

$$X_2(k) = \sum_{n=0}^{1} x(3n+1)W_6^{3nk} = x(1) + x(4)W_6^{3k}$$

$$X_3(k) = \sum_{n=0}^{1} x(3n+2) W_6^{3nk} = x(2) + x(5) W_6^{3k}$$

Also, $X_i(k+2) = X_i(k)$.

Stage-I: Computation

$$\begin{aligned}
X_1(k) &= x(0) + x(3) W_6^{3k} \qquad k = 0, 1 \\
X_1(0) &= x(0) + x(3) W_6^{0} \\
X_1(1) &= x(0) + x(3) W_6^{3} \\
X_2(k) &= x(1) + x(4) W_6^{3k} \qquad k = 0, 1 \\
X_2(0) &= x(1) + x(4) W_6^{0} \\
X_2(1) &= x(1) + x(4) W_6^{3} \\
X_3(k) &= x(2) + x(5) W_6^{3k} \qquad k = 0, 1 \\
X_3(0) &= x(2) + x(5) W_6^{0} \\
X_3(1) &= x(2) + x(5) W_6^{3}
\end{aligned}$$

The butterfly diagram is shown in Figure 2.42.

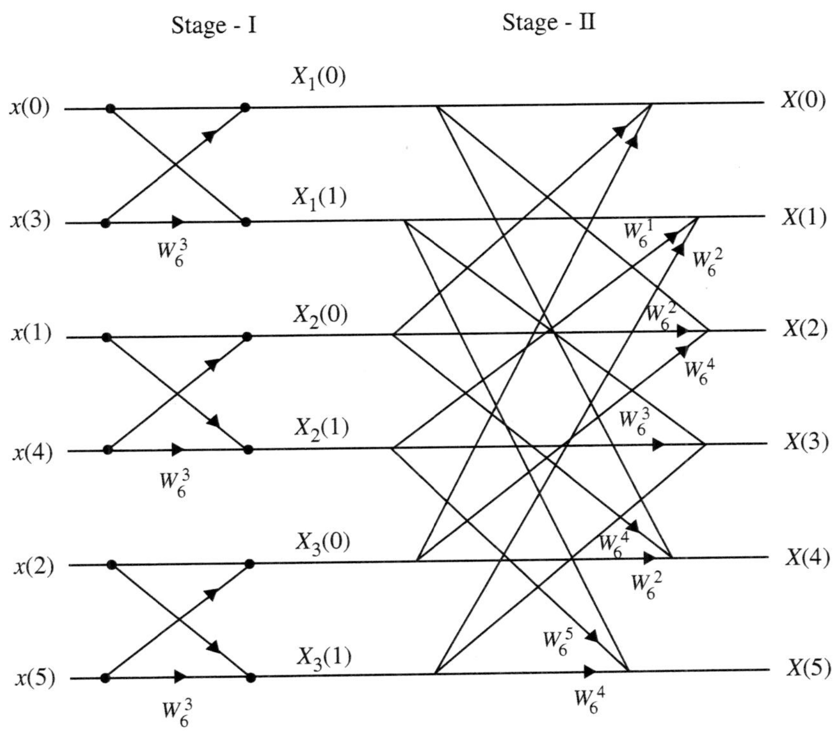

Figure 2.42 DIT FFT flow diagram for $N = 6 = 3 \cdot 2$.

Stage-II: Computation

$$
\begin{aligned}
X(k) &= X_1(k) + W_6^k X_2(k) + W_6^{2k} X_3(k), \qquad k = 0, \dots, 5 \\
X(0) &= X_1(0) + W_6^0 X_2(0) + W_6^0 X_3(0) \\
X(1) &= X_1(1) + W_6^1 X_2(1) + W_6^2 X_3(1) \\
X(2) &= X_1(2) + W_6^2 X_2(2) + W_6^4 X_3(2) \\
&= X_1(0) + W_6^2 X_2(0) + W_6^4 X_3(0) \\
X(3) &= X_1(3) + W_6^3 X_2(3) + W_6^6 X_3(3) \\
&= X_1(0) + W_6^3 X_2(1) + W_6^0 X_3(0) \\
X(4) &= X_1(4) + W_6^4 X_2(4) + W_6^8 X_3(4) \\
&= X_1(0) + W_6^4 X_2(0) + W_6^2 X_3(0) \\
X(5) &= X_1(5) + W_6^5 X_2(5) + W_6^{10} X_3(5) \\
&= X_1(1) + W_6^5 X_2(1) + W_6^4 X_3(1)
\end{aligned}
$$

(*c*) To evaluate the DFT values for $x(n)$ (Refer Figure 2.43)

$$x(n) = \{1, 2, 3, 4, 5, 6\}$$

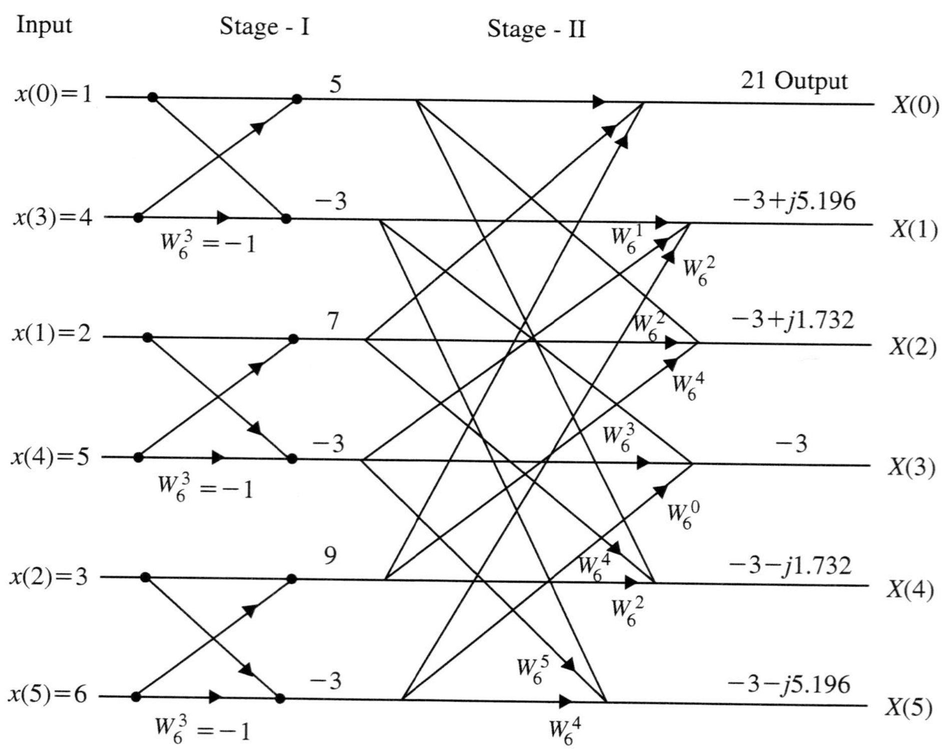

Figure 2.43 Butterfly diagram for Example 2.44(*c*).

by using the FFT algorithm developed in part (*b*) twiddle factors are,

$$W_6^0 = 1$$
$$W_6^1 = e^{-\frac{j2\pi}{6}} = 0.5 - j0.866$$
$$W_6^2 = e^{-\frac{j2\pi\cdot 2}{6}} = -0.5 - j0.866$$
$$W_6^3 = e^{-\frac{j2\pi\cdot 3}{6}} = -1$$
$$W_6^4 = e^{-\frac{j2\pi\cdot 4}{6}} = -0.5 + j0.866$$
$$W_6^5 = e^{-\frac{j2\pi\cdot 5}{6}} = 0.5 + j0.866$$

Input	Stage-I	Stage-II (or) Output
0	$1+4=5$	$5+7+9=21=X(0)$
4	$1-4=-3$	$-3+(0.5-j0.866)(-3)+(-0.5-j0.866)(-3)$ $=-3+j5.196=X(1)$
2	$2+5=7$	$5+(0.5-j0.866)(7)+(-0.5+j0.866)(9)$ $=-3+j1.732=X(2)$
5	$2-5=-3$	$-3+(-1)(-3)+(1)(-3)=-3=X(3)$
3	$3+6=9$	$5+(0.5+j0.866)(7)+(-0.5-j0.866)(9)$ $=-3-j1.732=X(4)$
6	$3-6=-3$	$-3+(0.5+j0.866)(-3)+(-0.5+j0.866)(-3)$ $=-3-j5.196=X(5)$

$$X(k) = \{21, -3+j5.196, -3+j1.732, -3, -3-j1.732, -3-j5.196\}$$

Example 2.45

Develop the DIT FFT algorithm for decomposing the DFT for $N = 12$ and draw the flow diagrams.

Solution For $N = 12 = 3\cdot 4$ where $m_1 = 3$ and $N_1 = 4$

$$X(k) = \sum_{n=0}^{3} x(3n)W_{12}^{3nk} + \sum_{n=0}^{3} x(3n+1)W_{12}^{(3n+1)k} + \sum_{n=0}^{3} x(3n+2)W_{12}^{(3n+2)k}$$

$$= \sum_{n=0}^{3} x(3n)W_{12}^{3nk} + W_{12}^{k}\sum_{n=0}^{3} x(3n+1)W_{12}^{3nk} + W_{12}^{2k}\sum_{n=0}^{3} x(3n+2)W_{12}^{3nk}$$

$$X(k) = X_1(k) + W_{12}^{k}X_2(k) + W_{12}^{2k}X_3(k)$$

where

$$X_1(k) = \sum_{n=0}^{3} x(3n)W_{12}^{3nk} \qquad k = 0, \ldots, 3$$

$$= x(0) + W_{12}^{3k}x(3) + W_{12}^{6k}x(6) + W_{12}^{9k}x(9)$$

$$X_2(k) = \sum_{n=0}^{3} x(3n+1)W_{12}^{3nk}$$

$$= x(1) + x(4)W_{12}^{3k} + x(7) + W_{12}^{6k} + x(0)W_{12}^{7k}$$

$$X_3(k) = \sum_{n=0}^{3} x(3n+2)W_{12}^{3nk}$$

$$= x(2) + W_{12}^{3k}x(5) + W_{12}^{6k}x(8) + W_{11}^{9k}$$

The butterfly diagram is shown in Figure 2.44.

Stage-I: Computation

$$X_1(k) = x(0) + W_{12}^{3k}x(3) + W_{12}^{6k}x(6) + W_{12}^{9k}x(9) \qquad k = 0, \ldots, 3$$

$$X_1(0) = x(0) + x(3) + x(6) + x(9)$$

$$X_1(1) = x(0) + W_{12}^{3}x(3) + W_{12}^{6}x(6) + W_{12}^{9}x(9)$$

$$X_1(2) = x(0) + W_{12}^{6}x(3) + W_{12}^{0}x(6) + W_{12}^{6}x(9)$$

$$X_1(3) = x(0) + W_{12}^{9}x(3) + W_{12}^{6}x(6) + W_{12}^{3}x(9)$$

$$X_2(k) = x(1) + x(4)W_{12}^{3k} + x(7)W_{12}^{6k} + x(10)W_{12}^{9k} \qquad k = 0, \ldots, 5$$

$$X_2(0) = x(1) + x(4) + x(7) + x(10)$$

$$X_2(1) = x(1) + x(4)W_{12}^{3} + x(7)W_{12}^{6} + x(10)W_{12}^{9}$$

$$X_2(2) = x(1) + x(4)W_{12}^{6} + x(7)W_{12}^{0} + x(10)W_{12}^{6}$$

$$X_2(3) = x(1) + x(4)W_{12}^{9} + x(7) + W_{12}^{6} + x(10)W_{12}^{3}$$

$$X_3(k) = x(2) + x(5)W_{12}^{3k} + x(8)W_{12}^{6k} + x(11)W_{12}^{9k} \qquad k = 0, \ldots, 5$$

$$X_3(0) = x(2) + x(5) + x(8) + x(11)$$

$$X_3(1) = x(2) + x(5)W_{12}^{3} + x(8)W_{12}^{6} + x(11)W_{12}^{9}$$

$$X_3(2) = x(2) + x(5)W_{12}^{6} + x(8)W_{12}^{0} + x(11)W_{12}^{6}$$

$$X_3(3) = x(2) + x(5)W_{12}^{9} + x(8)W_{12}^{6} + x(11)W_{12}^{3}$$

Stage-II: Computation

$$X(k) = X_1(k) + W_{12}^{k}X_2(k) + W_{12}^{2k}X_3(k), \qquad k = 0, \ldots, 11$$

$$X(0) = X_1(0) + X_2(0) + X_3(0)$$

$$X(1) = X_1(1) + W_{12}^{1}X_2(1) + W_{12}^{2}X_3(1)$$

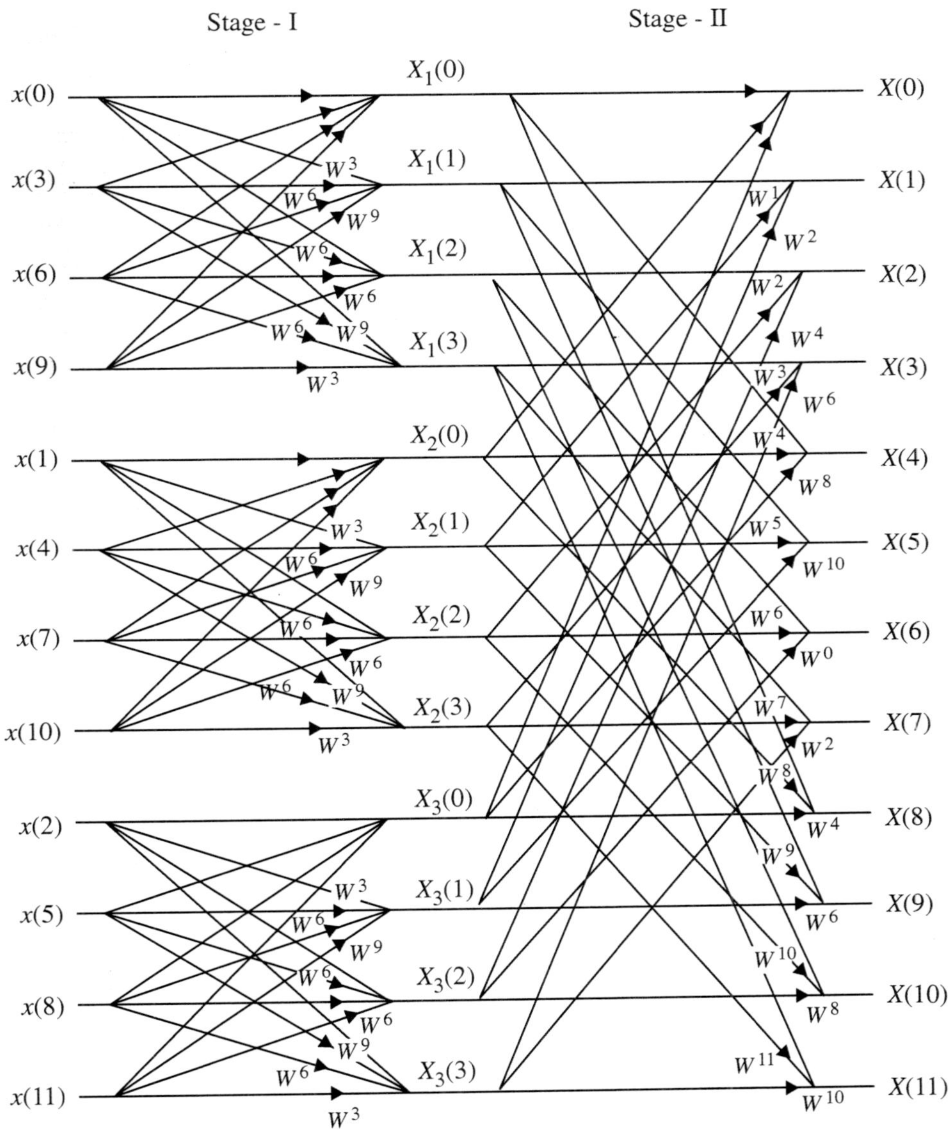

Figure 2.44 Flow diagram of 12-point composite radix-FFT.

$$X(2) = X_1(2) + W_{12}^{2}X_2(2) + W_{12}^{4}X_3(2)$$
$$X(3) = X_1(3) + W_{12}^{3}X_2(3) + W_{12}^{6}X_3(3)$$
$$X(4) = X_1(0) + W_{12}^{4}X_2(0) + W_{12}^{8}X_3(0)$$
$$X(5) = X_1(1) + W_{12}^{5}X_2(1) + W_{12}^{10}X_3(1)$$
$$X(6) = X_1(2) + W_{12}^{6}X_2(2) + W_{12}^{0}X_3(2)$$
$$X(7) = X_1(3) + W_{12}^{7}X_2(3) + W_{12}^{2}X_3(3)$$

$$X(8) = X_1(0) + W_{12}^{8}X_2(0) + W_{12}^{4}X_3(0)$$
$$X(9) = X_1(1) + W_{12}^{9}X_2(1) + W_{12}^{6}X_3(1)$$
$$X(10) = X_1(2) + W_{12}^{10}X_2(2) + W_{12}^{8}X_3(2)$$
$$X(11) = X_1(3) + W_{12}^{11}X_2(3) + W_{12}^{10}X_3(3)$$

Example 2.46

Develop a radix-4 DIT FFT algorithm for evaluating the DFT for $N = 16$ and hence determine the 16 point DFT of the sequence

$$x(n) = \{0, 1, 0, 1, 0, 1, 0, 1, 0, 1, 0, 1, 0, 1, 0, 1\}$$

Solution

For $N = 16 = 4 \cdot 4$ where $m_1 = 4$ and $N_1 = 4$

$$X(k) = \sum_{n=0}^{3} x(4n)W_{16}^{4nk} + \sum_{n=0}^{3} x(4n+1)W_{16}^{(4n+1)k}$$
$$+ \sum_{n=0}^{3} x(4n+2)W_{16}^{(4n+2)k} + \sum_{n=0}^{3} x(4n+3)W_{16}^{(4n+3)k}$$

$$X_1(k) = \sum_{n=0}^{3} x(4n)W_{16}^{4nk} + W_{16}^{k}\sum_{n=0}^{3} x(4n+1)W_{16}^{4nk}$$
$$+ W_{16}^{2k}\sum_{n=0}^{3} x(4n+2)W_{16}^{4nk} + W_{16}^{3k}\sum_{n=0}^{3} x(4n+3)W_{16}^{4nk}$$
$$= X_1(k) + W_{16}^{k}X_2(k) + W_{16}^{2k}X_3(k) + W_{16}^{3k}X_4(k)$$

The twiddle factors are,

$$W_{16}^{0} = 1$$
$$W_{16}^{1} = e^{-\frac{j2\pi}{16}} = (0.923 - j0.382)$$
$$W_{16}^{2} = e^{-\frac{j2\pi \cdot 2}{16}} = 0.707 - j0.707$$
$$W_{16}^{3} = e^{-\frac{j2\pi \cdot 3}{16}} = 0.3826 - j0.923$$
$$W_{16}^{4} = e^{-\frac{j2\pi \cdot 4}{16}} = -j$$
$$W_{16}^{5} = -0.3826 - j0.9238$$
$$W_{16}^{6} = e^{-\frac{j2\pi \cdot 6}{16}} = -0.707 - j0.707$$
$$W_{16}^{7} = e^{-\frac{j2\pi \cdot 7}{16}} = 0.9238 - j0.382$$

The radix-4 DIT-FFT algorithm is shown in Figure 2.45.

$$W_{16}^{8} = e^{-\frac{j2\pi\cdot 8}{16}} = -1$$

$$W_{16}^{9} = e^{-\frac{j2\pi\cdot 9}{16}} = -0.923 + j0.3826$$

$$W_{16}^{10} = -0.707 + j0.707$$

$$W_{16}^{11} = -0.3826 + j0.923$$

$$W_{16}^{12} = -j$$

$$W_{16}^{13} = 0.3826 + j0.923$$

$$W_{16}^{14} = 0.707 + j0.707$$

$$W_{16}^{15} = 0.9238 + j0.382$$

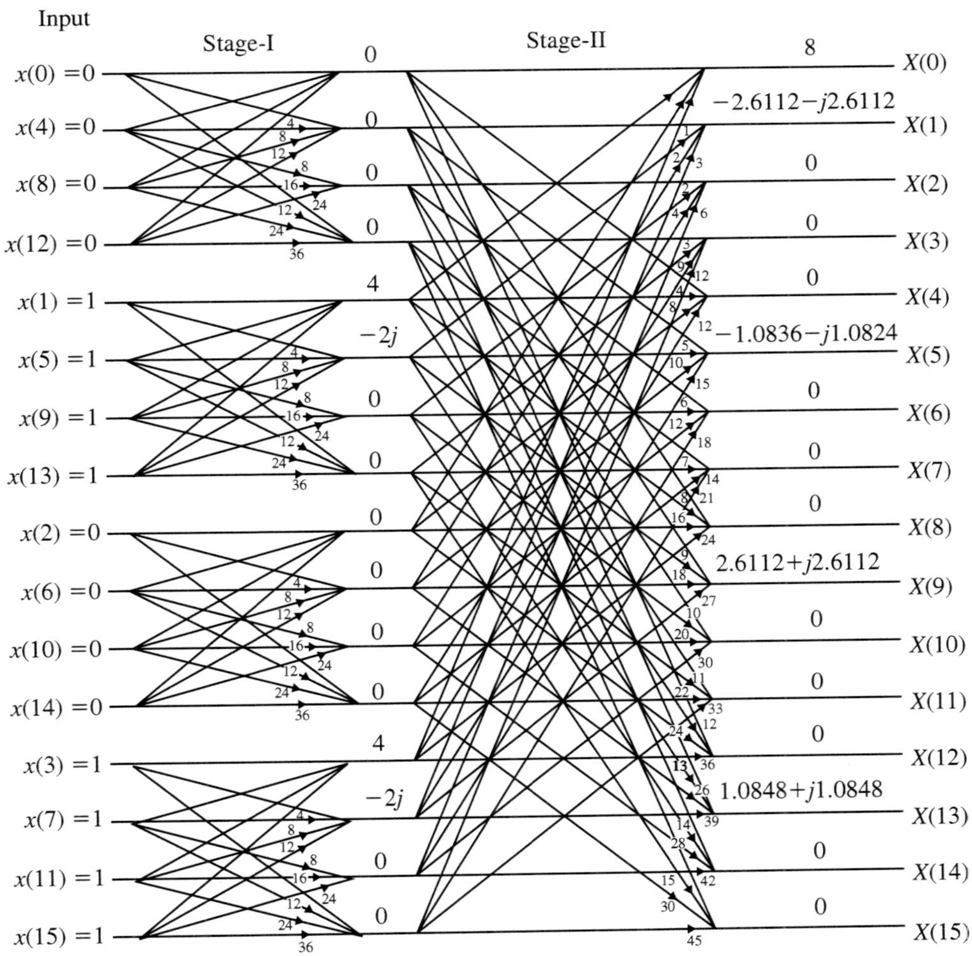

Figure 2.45 Radix-4 DIT-FFT algorithm for Example 2.46.

Input	Stage-I	Stage-II (or) Output
0	$0+0+0+0=0$	$0+4+0+4=8=X(1)$
0	$0+0+0+0=0$	$0+(0.923-j0.382)(-j2)+(0.707-j0.707)(0)+(0.3826-j0.923)(-j2)$ $=-2.61-j2.61=X(1)$
0	$0+0+0+0=0$	$0+0+0+0=0=X(2)$
0	$0+0+0+0=0$	$0+0+0+0=0=X(3)$
1	$1+1+1+1=4$	$0+(-j)4+(-1)(0)+(j)4=0=X(4)$
1	$1-j-1-j=-2j$	$0+(-j2)(-0.3826-j0.9238)+0+(-j2)(0.9038+j0.382)=-j1.0824-1.0836$ $=X(5)$
1	$1+1(-1)+1(1)+1(-1)=0$	$0+0+0+0=0=X(6)$
1	$1+1(-j)+1(-1)+1(j)=0$	$0+0+0+0=0=X(7)$
0	0	$0+4(-1)+0+4(1)=0=X(8)$
0	0	$0+(-j2)(-0.923+j0.9826)+0+(-j2)(-0.382+j0.923)=2.6112+j2.6112$ $=X(9)$
0	0	$0+0+0+0=0=X(10)$
0	0	$0+0+0+0=0=X(11)$
1	$1+1+1+1=4$	$0+4(-j)+0+j4=0=X(12)$
1	$1+1(-j)+1(-1)+1(-1)=-j2$	$0+(-j2)(0.3826+j0.923)+0+(-j2)(-0.9238-j0.382)=1.0818+j1.0848$ $=X(13)$
1	$1+1(-1)+1(1)+1(-1)=0$	$0+0+0+0=0=X(14)$
1	$1+1(-j)+1(-1)+1(j)=0$	$0+0+0+0=0=X(15)$

Example 2.47

Develop a DIF FFT algorithm for decomposing the DFT for $N = 6$ and draw the flow diagram for (*a*) $N = 3 \cdot 2$ and (*b*) $N = 2 \cdot 3$.

Solution

(*a*) To develop DIF FFT algorithm for $N = 3 \cdot 2$

$$X(k) = \sum_{n=0}^{5} x(n) W_6^{nk} = \sum_{n=0}^{2} x(n) W_6^{nk} + \sum_{n=3}^{5} x(n) W_6^{nk}$$

$$= \sum_{n=0}^{2} x(n) W_6^{nk} + \sum_{n=0}^{2} x(n+3) W_6^{(n+3)k}$$

$$X(k) = \sum_{n=0}^{2} [x(n) + x(n+3) W_6^{3k}] W_6^{nk}$$

$$X(2k) = \sum_{n=0}^{2} [x(n) + x(n+3) W_6^{6k}] + W_6^{2nk}$$

$$= \sum_{n=0}^{2} [x(n) + x(n+3)] W_6^{2nk}$$

$$X(2k+1) = \sum_{n=0}^{2} [x(n) + x(n+3) W_6^{3(2k+1)}] W_6^{(2k+1)n}$$

$$= \sum_{n=0}^{2} [x(n) - x(n+3)] W_6^{n} W_6^{2nk}$$

Let $g(n) = x(n) + x(n+3)$, $h(n) = x(n) - x(n+3)$

$$X(2k) = \sum_{n=0}^{2} g(n) W_6^{2nk}$$

$$X(2k+1) = \sum_{n=0}^{2} h(n) W_6^{n} W_6^{2nk}$$

The butterfly diagram is shown in Figure 2.46.

Stage I

$$g(0) = x(0) + x(3) \qquad h(0) = x(0) - x(3)$$

$$g(1) = x(1) + x(4) \qquad h(1) = x(1) - x(4)$$

$$g(2) = x(2) + x(5) \qquad h(2) = x(2) - x(5)$$

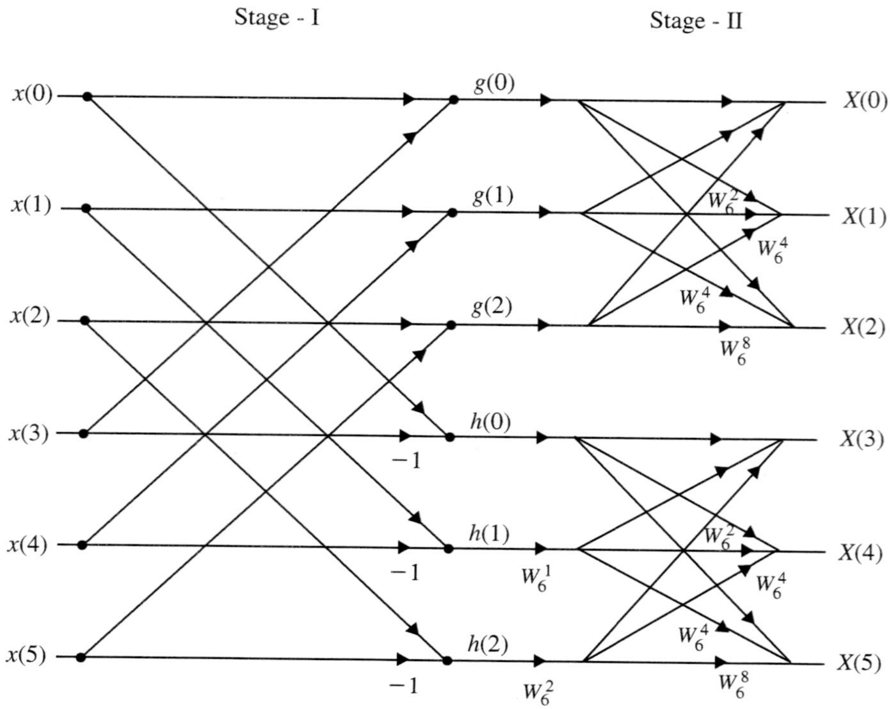

Figure 2.46 DIF FFT flow diagram for decomposing the DFT for $N = 6 = 3 \cdot 2$.

Stage II

$$X(0) = g(0) + g(1) + g(2)$$
$$X(2) = g(0) + g(1)W_6^2 + g(2)W_6^4$$
$$X(4) = g(0) + g(1)W_6^4 + g(2)W_6^8$$
$$X(1) = h(0) + h(1)W_6^1 + h(2)W_6^2$$
$$X(3) = h(0) + h(1)W_6^1 W_6^2 + h(2)W_6^2 W_6^4$$
$$X(5) = h(0) + h(1)W_6^1 W_6^4 + h(2)W_6^2 W_6^8$$

The DIF FFT flow diagram for decomposing the DFT is shown in Figure 2.47 for $N = 6 = 3 \times 2$.

(*b*) To develop DIF FFT algorithm for $N = 2 \cdot 3$

$$X(k) = \sum_{n=0}^{5} x(n)W_6^{nk} = \sum_{n=0}^{1} x(n)W^{nk} + \sum_{n=2}^{3} x(n)W_6^{nk} + \sum_{n=4}^{5} x(n)W_6^{nk}$$
$$= \sum_{n=0}^{1} [x(n) + x(n+2)W_6^{2k} + x(n+4)W_6^{4k}]W_6^{nk}$$
$$X(3k) = \sum_{n=0}^{1} [x(n) + x(n+2) + x(n+4)]W_6^{3nk}$$

$$X(3k+1) = \sum_{n=0}^{1}[x(n) + x(n+2)W_6^2 + x(n+4)W_6^4]W_6^n W_6^{3nk}$$

$$X(3k+2) = \sum_{n=0}^{1}[x(n) + x(n+2)W_6^4 + x(n+4)W_6^2]W_6^{2n} W_6^{3nk}$$

Let

$$f(n) = x(n) + x(n+2) + x(n+4), \qquad n = 0, 1, \ldots$$
$$g(n) = x(n) + x(n+2) + W_6^2 + x(n+4)W_6^4, \qquad n = 0, 1, \ldots$$
$$h(n) = x(n) + x(n+2)W_6^4 + x(n+4)W_6^2, \qquad n = 0, 1, \ldots$$

Stage I

$$f(0) = x(0) + x(2) + x(4)$$
$$f(1) = x(1) + x(3) + x(5)$$
$$g(0) = x(0) + x(2)W_6^2 + x(4)W_6^4$$
$$g(1) = x(1) + x(3)W_6^2 + x(5)W_6^4$$

The DIF FFT flow diagram for decomposing the DFT for $N = 6 = 2 \times 3$ is shown in Figure 2.47.

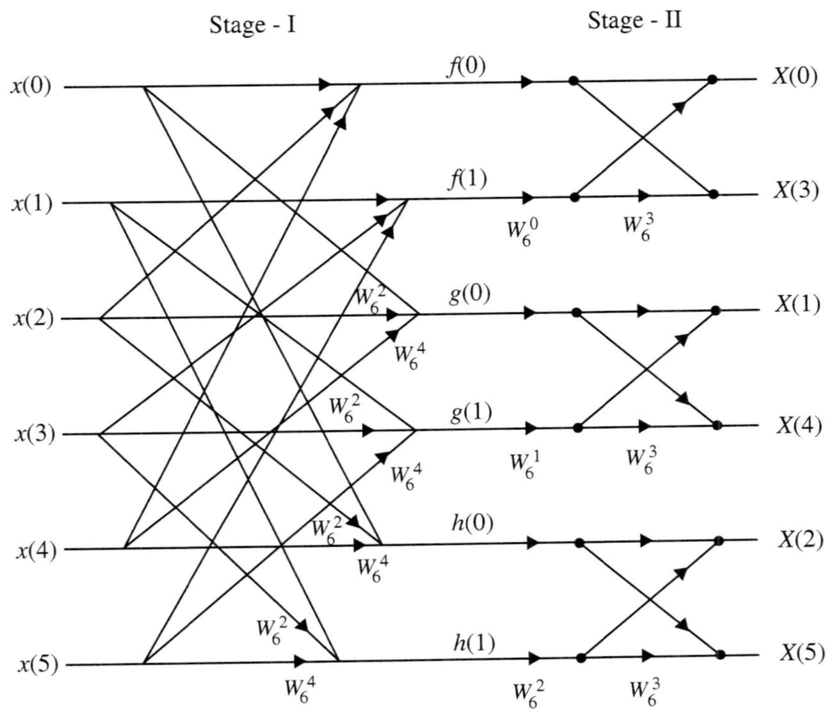

Figure 2.47 DIF FFT flow diagram for decomposing the DFT for $N = 6 = 2 \cdot 3$.

$$h(0) = x(0) + x(2)W_6^4 + x(4)W_6^2$$
$$h(1) = x(1) + x(3)W_6^4 + x(5)W_6^2$$

Stage II

$$X(0) = f(0) + f(1)W_6^0$$
$$X(1) = g(0) + g(1)W_6^1$$
$$X(2) = h(0) + h(1)W_6^2$$
$$X(3) = f(0) + f(1)W_6^0W_6^3$$
$$X(4) = g(0) + g(1)W_6^1W_6^3$$
$$X(5) = h(0) + h(1)W_6^2W_6^3$$

Example 2.48

Develop a radix-3 DIF FFT algorithm for evaluating the DFT for $N = 9$.

Solution To develop a radix-3 DIF FFT algorithm for $N = 9 = 3 \cdot 3$

$$X(k) = \sum_{n=0}^{2} x(n)W_9^{nk} + \sum_{n=0}^{2} x(n+3)W_9^{(n+3)k} + \sum_{n=0}^{2} x(n+6)W_9^{(n+6)k}$$

$$X(k) = \sum_{n=0}^{2} [x(n) + x(n+3)W_9^{3k} + x(n+6)W_9^{6k}]W_9^{nk}$$

$$X(3k) = \sum_{n=0}^{2} [x(n) + x(n+3) + x(n+6)]W_9^{3nk}]$$

$$= \sum_{n=0}^{2} f(n)W_9^{3nk}$$

$$X(3k+1) = \sum_{n=0}^{2} [x(n) + x(n+3)W_9^3 + x(n+6)W_9^6]W_9^nW_9^{3nk}$$

$$= \sum_{n=0}^{2} g(n)W_9^nW_9^{3nk}$$

$$X(3k+2) = \sum_{n=0}^{2} [x(n) + x(n+3)W_9^6 + x(n+6)W_9^3]W_9^{2n}W_9^{3nk}$$

$$= \sum_{n=0}^{2} h(n)W_9^{2n}W_9^{3nk}$$

The butterfly diagram is shown in Figure 2.48.

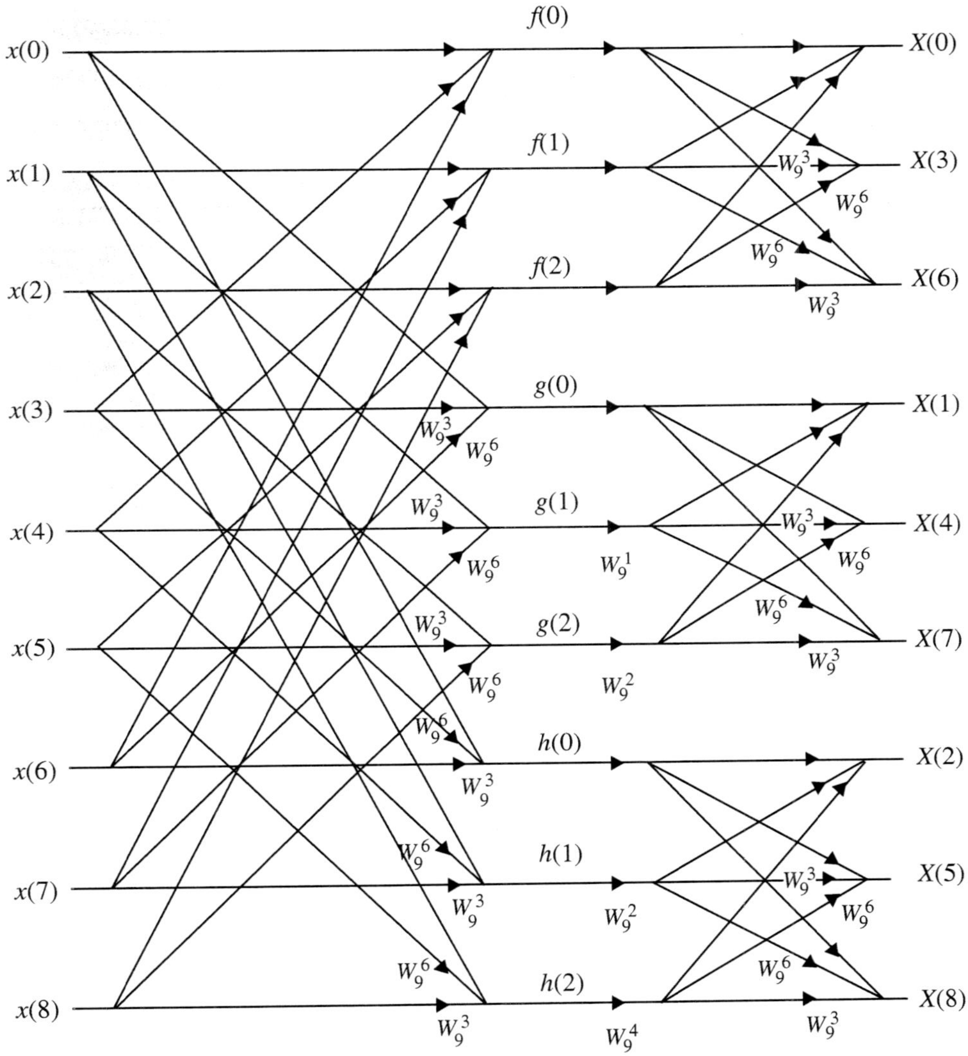

Figure 2.48 A radix-3 DIF FFT flow diagram for decomposing the DFT for $N = 9 = 3\cdot 3$.

Stage I

$$f(0) = x(0) + x(3) + x(6)$$
$$f(1) = x(1) + x(4) + x(7)$$
$$f(2) = x(2) + x(5) + x(8)$$
$$g(0) = x(0) + x(3)W_9^3 + x(6)W_9^6$$
$$g(1) = x(1) + x(4)W_9^3 + x(7)W_9^6$$
$$g(2) = x(2) + x(5)W_9^3 + x(8)W_9^6$$
$$h(0) = x(0) + x(3)W_9^6 + x(6)W_9^3$$

$$h(1) = x(1) + x(4)W_9^6 + x(7)W_9^3$$
$$h(2) = x(2) + x(5)W_9^6 + x(8)W_9^3$$

Stage II

$$X(0) = f(0) + f(1) + f(2)$$
$$X(3) = f(0) + f(1)W_9^3 + f(2)W_9^6$$
$$X(6) = f(0) + f(1)W_6^0 + f(2)W_9^3$$
$$X(1) = g(0) + g(1)W_9^1 + g(2)W_9^2$$
$$X(4) = g(0) + g(1)W_9^1W_9^3 + g(2)W_9^2W_9^6$$
$$X(7) = g(0) + g(1)W_9^1W_9^6 + g(2)W_9^2W_9^3$$
$$X(2) = h(0) + h(1)W_9^2 + h(2)W_9^4$$
$$X(5) = h(0) + h(1)W_9^2W_9^3 + h(2)W_9^4W_9^6$$
$$X(8) = h(0) + h(1)W_9^2W_9^6 + h(2)W_9^4W_9^3$$

2.6.4 Use of the FFT Algorithm in Linear Filtering and Correlation

An important application of the FFT algorithm is in FIR linear filtering of long data sequences. The response of an LTI system for any arbitrary input is given by linear convolution of the input and the impulse response of the system. If one of the sequences (either the input sequence or impulse response sequence) is very much larger than the other, then it is very difficult to compute the linear convolution using DFT for the following reasons:

1. The entire sequence should be available before convolution can be carried out. This makes long delay in getting the output.
2. Large amounts of memory is required to store the sequences.

The above problems can be overcome by linear filtering of longer sequence into the size of smaller sequences. Then the linear convolution of each section of longer sequences and the smaller sequence is performed. The output sequences obtained from the convolutions of the sections are combined to get the overall output sequences. There are two methods to perform the linear filtering. They are,

1. Overlap add method.
2. Overlap save method.

2.6.4.1 Overlap Add Method

Let N_1 be the length of longer sequence and N_2, the length of smaller sequence. Let the longer sequence be divided into sections of size N_3 samples. (*Note:* Normally the longer sequence is divided into sections of size same as that of smaller sequence.).

The linear convolution of each section with smaller sequence will produce an output sequence of size $N_3 + N_2 - 1$ samples. In this method last $N_2 - 1$ samples of each output sequence overlaps with the first $N_2 - 1$ samples of next section. While combining the output sequences of the various sectioned convolutions, the corresponding samples of overlapped regions are added and the samples of non-over lapped regions are retained as such.

2.6.4.2 Overlap Save Method

Let N_1 be the length of longer sequence and N_2, the length of smaller sequence. Let the longer sequence be divided into sections of size N_3 samples.

In overlap save method, the result of linear convolution are obtained by circular convolution. Hence, each section of longer sequence and the smaller sequence are converted to the size of the output sequence of size $N_3 + N_2 - 1$ samples. The smaller sequence is converted to size of $N_3 + N_2 - 1$ samples by appending with zeros. The conversion of each section of longer sequence to the size $N_3 + N_2 - 1$ samples can be performed in two different methods.

Method I

In this method the first $N_2 - 1$ samples of a section is appended as last $N_2 - 1$ samples of the previous section. The circular convolution of each section will produce an output sequence of size $N_3 + N_2 - 1$ samples. In this output the first $N_2 - 1$ samples are discarded and the remaining samples of the output of sectioned convolution are saved as the overall output sequence.

Method II

In this method the last $N_2 - 1$ samples of a section is appended as last $N_2 - 1$ samples of the next section. (*i.e.*, the overlapping samples are placed at the beginning of the section). The circular convolution of each section will produce an output sequence of size $N_3 + N_2 - 1$ samples. In this output the last $N_2 - 1$ samples are discarded and the remaining samples of the output of sectioned convolution are saved as the overall output sequence.

Example 2.49

Perform the linear convolution of the following sequence by (*i*) overlap add method and (*ii*) overlap save method.

$$x(n) = \{1, -1, 2, -2, 3, -3, 4, -4\} \quad \text{and} \quad h(n) = \{-1, 1\}$$

Solution

Overlap Add Method

Here $x(n)$ is a longer sequence when compared to $h(n)$. Hence, $x(n)$ is sectioned into sequences of size equal to $h(n)$.

Let $x(n)$ be sectioned into three sequences, each consisting of two samples of $x(n)$ as

$$x_1(n) = 1; \quad n = 0 \qquad x_2(n) = -2; \quad n = 3 \qquad x_3(n) = 4; \quad n = 6$$
$$-1; \quad n = 1 \qquad +3; \quad n = 4 \qquad -4; \quad n = 7$$
$$2; \quad n = 2 \qquad -3; \quad n = 5 \qquad 0; \quad n = 8$$

Let $y_1(n), y_2(n), y_3(n)$ and $y_4(n)$ be the output of linear convolution of $x_1(n), x_2(n)$, $x_3(n)$ and $x_4(n)$ with $h(n)$ respectively.

Convolution of Section I

$$y_1(n) = x_1(n) * h(n)$$
$$Y_1(k) = X_1(k)H(k)$$
$$y_1(n) = IDFT\,[X_1(k)H(k)]$$

$$X_1(k) \Rightarrow x_1(n) = \{1, -1, 2\}$$

and

$$h(n) = \{-1, 1\}$$

Length of $y_1(n) = 3 + 2 - 1 = 4$;

$$n_1 = 0 \quad \text{and} \quad n_2 = 0$$

so

$$n = n_1 + n_2 = 0.$$

Therefore,

$$x_1(n) = \{1, -1, 2, 0\}$$

and

$$h(n) = \{-1, 1, 0, 0\}$$

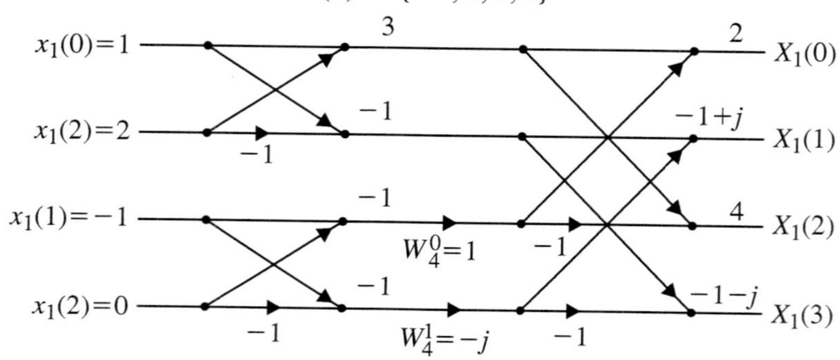

Figure 2.49 Butterfly diagram of $X(k)$.

Therefore

$$X_1(k) = \{2, -1+j, 4, -1-j\}$$

$H(k) \Rightarrow$

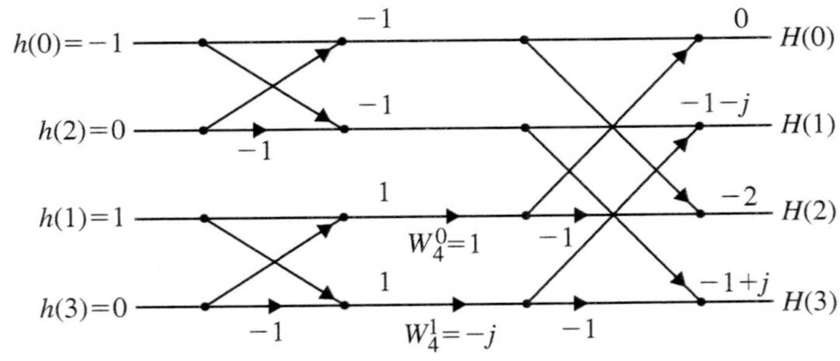

Figure 2.50 Butterfly diagram of $H(k)$.

$$\therefore\ H(k) = \{0, -1-j, -2, -1+j\}$$

$$X_1(k)H(k) = \{0, (-1+j)(-1-j), -8, (-1-j)(-1+j)\}$$

$$= \{0, 2, -8, 2\}$$

IDFT $[X_1(k)H(k)] \Rightarrow$

$$\{X_1(k)H(k)\}^* = \{0, 2, -8, 2\}$$

DFT of $[X_1(k)H(k)]^*$ is

$$\{-4, 8, -12, 8\}$$

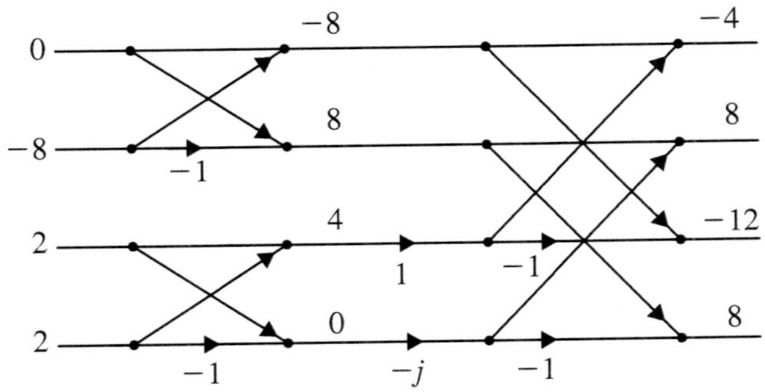

Figure 2.51 Butterfly diagram of $[X_1(k)H(k)]^*$.

$$\therefore\ y_1(n) = \frac{1}{n}\{-4, 8, -12, 8\}$$

$$= \frac{1}{4}\{-4, 8, -12, 8\} = \{-1, 2, -3, 2\}$$

$$\uparrow$$

Convolution of Section II

$$x_2(n) = \{-2, 3, -3\} \quad \text{and} \quad h(n) = \{-1, 1\}$$

$N = 3 + 2 - 1 = 4$

$$x_2(n) = \{-2, 3, -3, 0\} \quad \text{and} \quad h(n) = \{-1, 1, 0, 0\}$$

$n_1 = 3$, $n_2 = 0$ and $n = n_1 + n_2 = 3$.

$X_2(k) \Rightarrow$

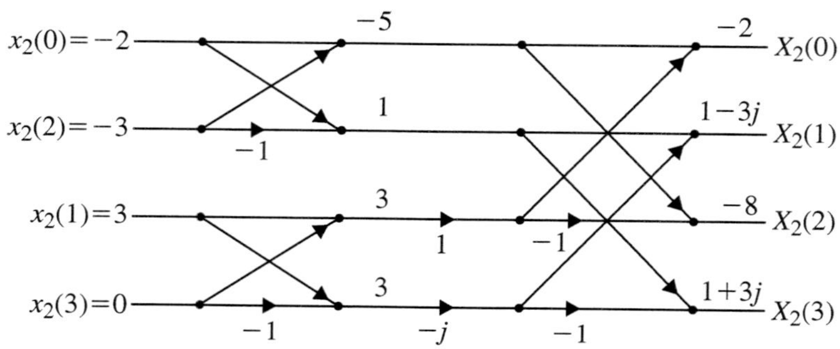

Figure 2.52 Butterfly diagram of $X_2(k)$.

$$\begin{aligned}
X_2(k) &= \{-2, 1-3j, -8, 1+3j\} \\
X_2(k)H(k) &= \{0, (-1-j)(1-3j), (-2)(-8), (-1+j)(1+3i)\} \\
&= \{0, -4+2j, 16, -4-2j\}
\end{aligned}$$

IDFT $[X_2(k)H(k)] \Rightarrow$

$$\{X_2(k)H(k)\}^* = \{0, -4-2j, 16, -4+2j\}$$

DFT $\{X_2(k)H(k)\}^*$ is

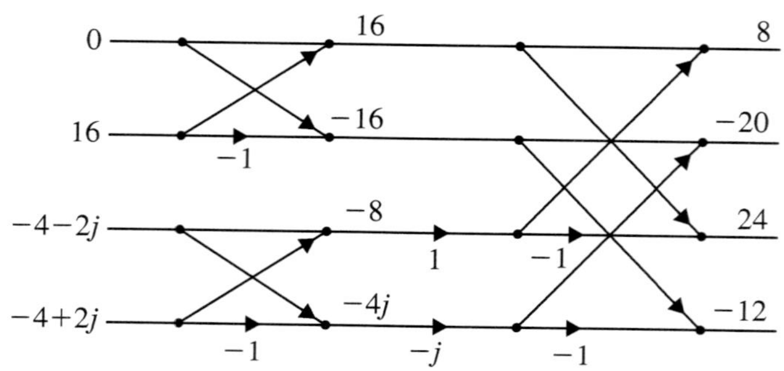

Figure 2.53 Butterfly diagram of $[X_2(k)H(k)]^*$.

Therefore,

$$y_2(n) = \frac{1}{N}\left\{DFT\left[X_2(k)H(k)\right]^*\right\}^* = \frac{1}{4}\{8, -20, 24, -12\}$$
$$= \{2, -5, 6, -3\}$$
$$\uparrow$$
$$n = 3$$

Convolution of Section III

$$x_3(n) = \{4, -4, 0\} \quad \text{and} \quad h(n) = \{-1, 1\}$$

$N = 3 + 2 - 1 = 4$, $n_1 = 6$, $n_2 = 0$ so $n = n_1 + n_2 = 6$. Therefore

$$x_3(n) = \{4, -4, 0, 0\} \quad \text{and} \quad h(n) = \{-1, 1, 0, 0\}$$

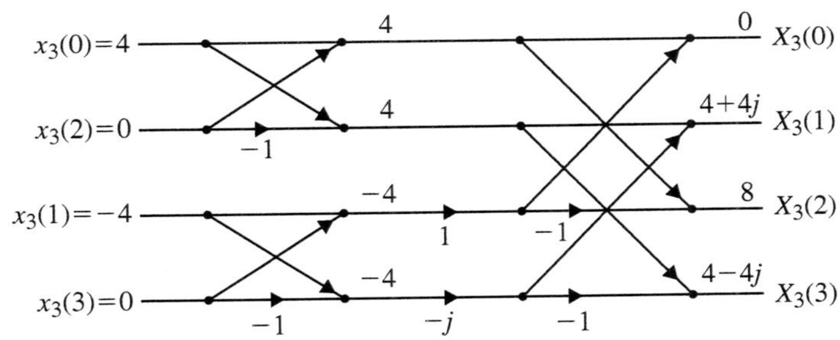

Figure 2.54 Butterfly diagram of $X_3(k)$.

$$X_3(k) = \{0, 4 + 4j, 8, 4 - 4j\}$$
$$X_3(k)H(k) = \{0, (-1 - j)(4 + 4j), -2(8), (-1 + j)(4 - 4j)\}$$
$$= \{0, -8j, -16, 8j\}$$

IDFT $[X_2(k)H(k)] \Rightarrow$

$$[x_3(k)H(k)]^* = \{0, 8j, -16, -8j\}$$

DFT $\left[\{x_3(k)H(k)\}^*\right]$ is

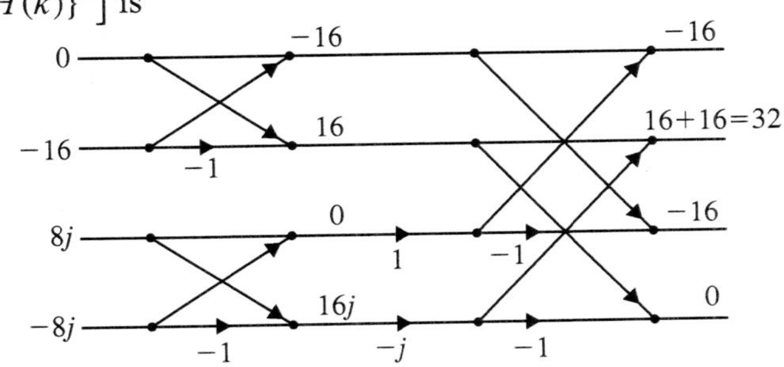

Figure 2.55 Butterfly diagram of $[x_3(k)H(k)]^*$.

$$\begin{aligned}
y_3(n) &= \frac{1}{N}\left[1DFT\left[x_3(k)H(k)\right]\right] \\
&= \frac{1}{N}\left[DFT\left[\left[x_3(k)H(k)\right]^*\right]\right]^* \\
&= \frac{1}{4}\{-16, 32, -16, 0\}^* \\
&= \{-4, 8, -4, 0\} \\
&\quad\; \uparrow \\
&\quad\; n = 6
\end{aligned}$$

To combine the output of the convolution of each section $N_2 - 1$ samples are overlapped. The overlapped portion (or samples) are added while combining the output.

Table 2.3 Combined output of each convolution section.

n	**0**	**1**	**2**	**3**	**4**	**5**	**6**	**7**	**8**
$y_1(n)$	-1	2	-3	2					
$y_2(n)$				2	-5	6	-3		
$y_3(n)$							-4	8	-4
$y(n)$	-1	2	-3	4	-5	6	-7	8	-4

where $N_2 - 1$ is samples are overlapped, here $N_2 = 2$ and $N_2 - 1 = 1$. Samples are overlapped that are added.

$$\boxed{\therefore\ y(n) = \{-1, 2, -3, 4, -5, 6, -7, 8, -4\}}$$

The above result can be verified as follows:

$$\begin{array}{rrrrrrrrr}
 & 1 & -1 & 2 & -2 & 3 & -3 & 4 & -4 \\
 & & & & & & & -1 & 1 \\
\hline
 & 1 & -1 & 2 & -2 & 3 & -3 & 4 & -4 \\
-1 & 1 & -2 & 2 & -3 & 3 & -4 & 4 & \\
\hline
-1 & 2 & -3 & 4 & -5 & 6 & -7 & 8 & -4 \\
\hline
\end{array}$$

$$\boxed{\begin{array}{l} y(n) = \{-1,\ 2,\ -3,\ 4,\ -5,\ 6,\ -7,\ 8,\ -4\} \\ \qquad\quad\ \uparrow \end{array}}$$

II Overlap Save Method

Method I

In this the $N_2 - 1$ overlapping samples are placed at the beginning of the section. Number of overlapping samples are $N_2 - 1 = 2 - 1 = 1$ sample.

$$
\begin{array}{llllll}
x_1(n) = 1; & n = 0 & x_2(n) = -2; & n = 3 & x_3(n) = 4; & n = 6 \\
\quad -1; & n = 1 & \quad +3; & n = 4 & \quad -4; & n = 7 \\
\quad 2; & n = 2 & \quad -3; & n = 5 & \quad 0; & n = 8 \\
\quad -2; & n = 2 & \quad 4; & n = 6 & \quad 0; & n = 9
\end{array}
$$

Convolution of Section-I

$$x_1(n) = \{\underset{\uparrow}{1}, -1, 2, -2\} \quad \text{and} \quad h(n) = \{\underset{\uparrow}{-1}, 1, 0, 0\}$$

at $n = 0$.

$X_1(k) \Rightarrow$

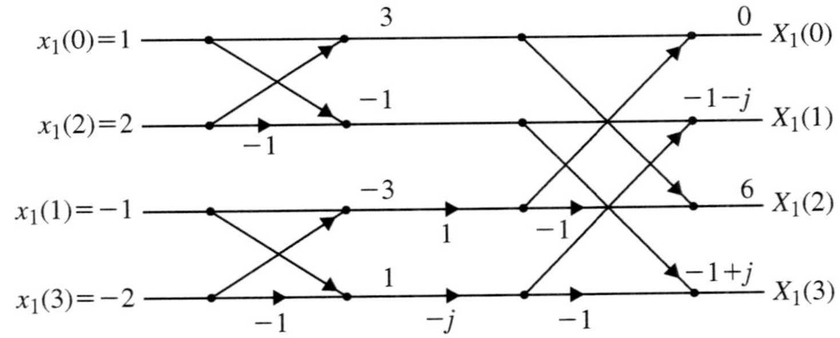

Figure 2.56 Butterfly diagram of $X_1(k)$.

$$X_1(k) = \{0, -1 - j, 6, -1 + j\}$$

$H(k) \Rightarrow$

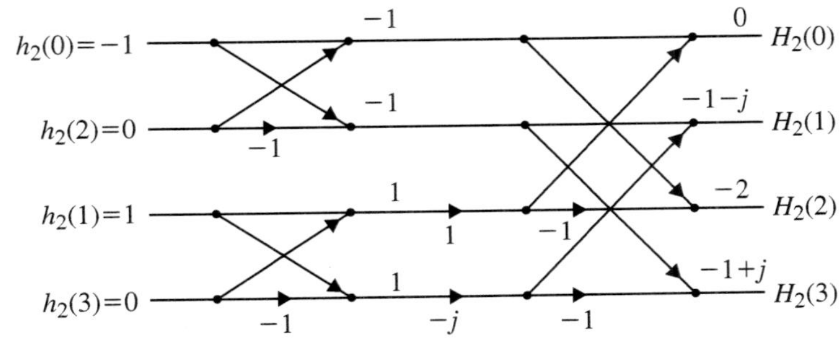

Figure 2.57 Butterfly diagram of $H(k)$.

$$H(k) = \{0, -1 - j, -2, -1 + j\}$$

$$X_1(k)H(k) = \{0, (-1-j)(-1-j), (-2)(6), (-1+j)(-1+j)\}$$
$$= \{0, 2j, -12, -2j\}$$
$$\{X_1(k)H(k)\}^* = \{0, -2j, -12, 2j\}$$

DFT $\left[[X_1(k)H(k)]^*\right]$ is

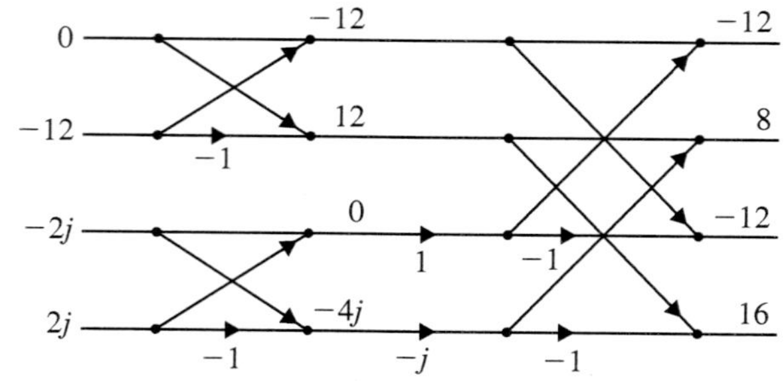

Figure 2.58 Butterfly diagram of $[X_1(k)H(k)]^*$.

$$\{-12, 8, -12, 16\}$$

$$y_1(n) = \frac{1}{N}\left\{DFT\left[[x(k)H(k)]^*\right]\right\}^* = \frac{1}{4}\{-12, 8, -12, 16\}^*$$
$$y_1(n) = \{\underset{\substack{\uparrow \\ n=0}}{-3}, 2, -3, 4\}$$

Convolution of Section-II

$$x_2(n) = \{\underset{\substack{\uparrow \\ n=3}}{-2}, 3, -3, 4\} \quad \text{and} \quad h(n) = \{\underset{\uparrow}{-1}, 1, 0, 0\}$$

$X_2(k) \Rightarrow$

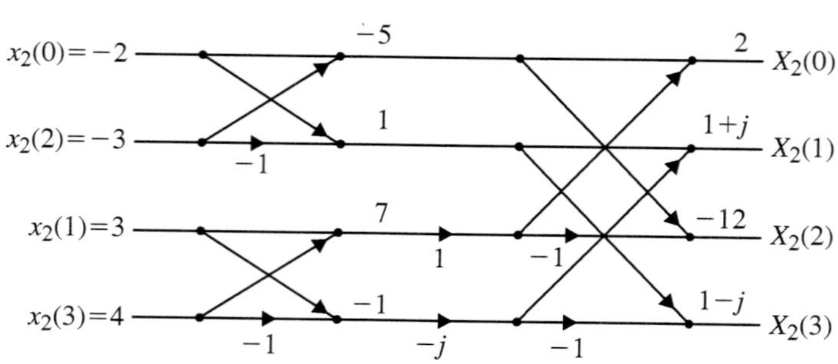

Figure 2.59 DFT Computation of $X_2(k)$.

$$X_2(k) = \{2, 1+j, -12, 1-j\}$$

$$X_2(k)H(k) = \{0, (1+j)(-1-j), (-12)(-2), (-1+j)(1-j)\}$$
$$= \{0, -2j, 24, 2j\}$$
$$[X_2(k)H(k)] = \{0, 2j, 24, -2j\}$$

DFT $\left[[X_2(k)H(k)]^*\right]$ is

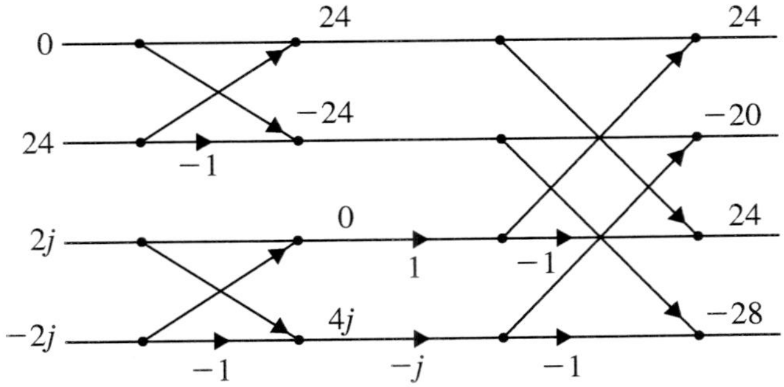

Figure 2.60 DFT computation of $[X_2(k)H(k)]^*$.

$$\{24, -20, 24, -28\}$$
$$y_2(n) = \frac{1}{4}\{24, -20, 24, -28\}$$
$$= \{6, -5, 6, -7\}$$
$$\uparrow$$
$$n = 3$$

Convolution of Section-III

$$x_3(n) = \{4, -4, 0, 0\} \quad \text{and} \quad h(n) = \{-1, 1, 0, 0\}$$
$$\uparrow \qquad\qquad\qquad\qquad \uparrow$$
$$n = 6$$

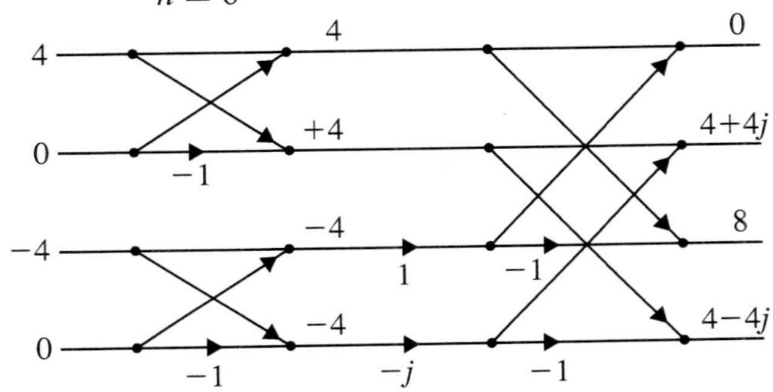

Figure 2.61 DFT Computation of $x_3(k)$.

$$X_3(k) = \{0, 4+4j, 8, 4-4j\}$$

$$
\begin{aligned}
X_3(k)H(k) &= \{0, (4+4j)(-1-j), 8(-2), (4-4j)(-1+j)\} \\
&= \{0, -8j, -16, 8j\} \\
\{X_3(k)H(k)\} &= \{0, 8j, -16, -8j\}
\end{aligned}
$$

DFT $\left[\{X_3(k)H(k)\}^*\right]$ is

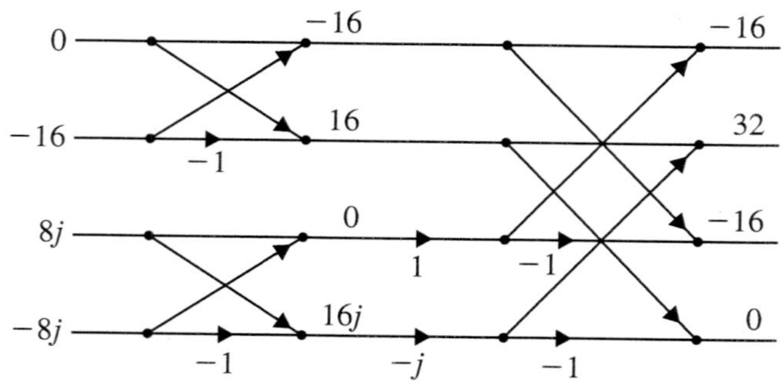

Figure 2.62 DFT Computation of $[X_3(k)H(k)]^*$.

$$
\begin{aligned}
y_3(n) &= \frac{1}{4}\{-16, 32, -16, 0\}^* \\
&= \{-4, 8, -4, 0\} \\
&\quad \uparrow \\
&\quad n = 6
\end{aligned}
$$

To combine the output of the convolution of each section, the first $N_2 - 1$ samples are overlapped that are discarded.

Table 2.4 Combined output of each convolution Section in Method I.

n	**0**	**1**	**2**	**3**	**4**	**5**	**6**	**7**	**8**	**9**
$y_1(n)$	~~−3~~	2	−3	4						
$y_2(n)$				~~6~~	−5	6	−7			
$y_3(n)$	3						~~−4~~	8	−4	0
$y(n)$	3	2	−3	4	−5	6	−7	8	−4	0

Here $y(n)$ is linear convolution of $x(n)$ and $h(n)$. It can be observed that the results of both the methods are same, except the first $N_2 - 1$ samples.

Method II

$$
\begin{aligned}
x_1(n) &= 1; \quad n = 0 & x_2(n) &= -2; \quad n = 3 & x_3(n) &= 4; \quad n = 7 \\
&\quad -1; \quad n = 1 & &\quad +3; \quad n = 4 & &\quad -4; \quad n = 8 \\
&\quad 2; \quad n = 2 & &\quad -3; \quad n = 5 & &\quad 0; \quad n = 9 \\
&\quad 0; \quad n = 2 & &\quad 4; \quad n = 6 & &\quad 0; \quad n = 10
\end{aligned}
$$

$h(n) = \{-1, 1, 0, 0\}$. Find $y_1(n), y_2(n)$ and $y_3(n)$ using FFT algorithm. Same above method. Result is shown in Table 2.5.

Table 2.5 Combined output of each convolution in method II.

n	0	1	2	3	4	5	6	7	8	9
$y_1(n)$	−1	2	−3	X						
$y_2(n)$				4	−5	6	X			
$y_3(n)$							−7	8	−4	X
$y(n)$	−1	2	−3	4	−5	6	−7	8	−4	×

2.7 In-Plane Computation

The flow graph of Figure 2.63 describes an algorithm for the computation of the DFT. In the flow graph the branches connecting the nodes and the transmittance of each of these branches. No matter how the nodes in the flow graph are rearranged, it will always represent the same computation provided that the connection between the nodes and the transmittance of the connection are maintained. The particular form for the flow graph in Figure 2.63 arose out of deriving the algorithm by separating the original sequences into the even numbered and odd numbered points and then continuing to create smaller and smaller subsequences in the same way. An interesting by-product of this derivation is that this flow graph, in addition to describing an efficient procedure for computing the discrete Fourier transform, also suggests a useful way of storing the original data and storing the results of the computation in intermediate arrays.

When implementing the computation depicting in Figure 2.63 we can imagine the use of two arrays of (complex) storage registers, one for the arrays being computed and one for the data being used in the computation. For example, in computing the first array in Figure 2.63, one set of storage registers would contain the input data and the second set would contain the computed results for the first stage. We denote the sequence of complex numbers resulting from the nth stage of computation as $X_m(l)$ where $l = 0, 1, \ldots N-1$, and $m = 1, 2, \ldots, v[v = \log_2^N]$. Furthermore, for convenience we define the set of input samples of $X_0[l]$. We can think of $X_{m-1}[l]$ as the input array and $X_m(l)$ as the output array for the mth stage computation. Thus, for the case $N = 8$ as in Figure 2.63, we get

$$X_0[0] = x[0] \qquad X_0[4] = x[1]$$
$$X_0[1] = x[4] \qquad X_0[5] = x[5]$$
$$X_0[2] = x[2] \qquad X_0[6] = x[3]$$
$$X_0[3] = x[6] \qquad X_0[7] = x[7]$$

Using this notation, the basic butterfly diagram is drawn as shown in Figure 2.63.

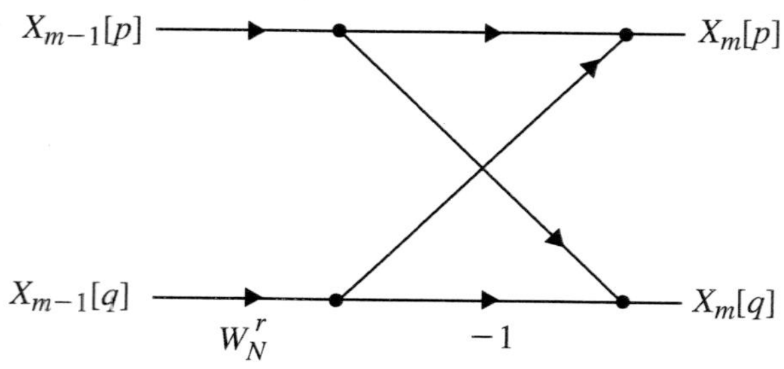

Figure 2.63 Flow graph.

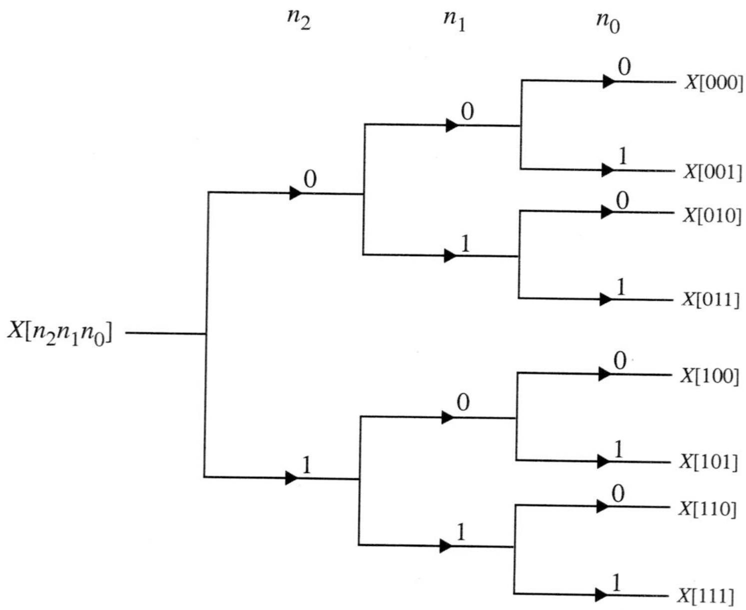

Figure 2.64 Tree diagram depicting normal-order sorting.

with the associated equation as,

$$X_m[p] = X_{m-1}[p] + W_N^r X_{m-1}[q]$$
$$X_m[q] = X_{m-1}[p] - W_N^r X_{m-1}[q]$$

In above equations p, q and r vary form stage to stage in a manner that is readily inferred from Figure 2.15. It is clear from Figure 2.15 and Figure 2.63 that only the complex numbers in locations p and q of the $(m-1)$st array are required to compute the elements p and q of the mth array. Thus only one complex array of N storage registers is physically necessary to implement the complete computation. That is $X_m[p]$ and $X_m[q]$ are stored in the same storage registers as $X_{m-1}[p]$ and $X_{m-1}[q]$ respectively. This kind of computation is commonly referred to as an "in-plane computation".

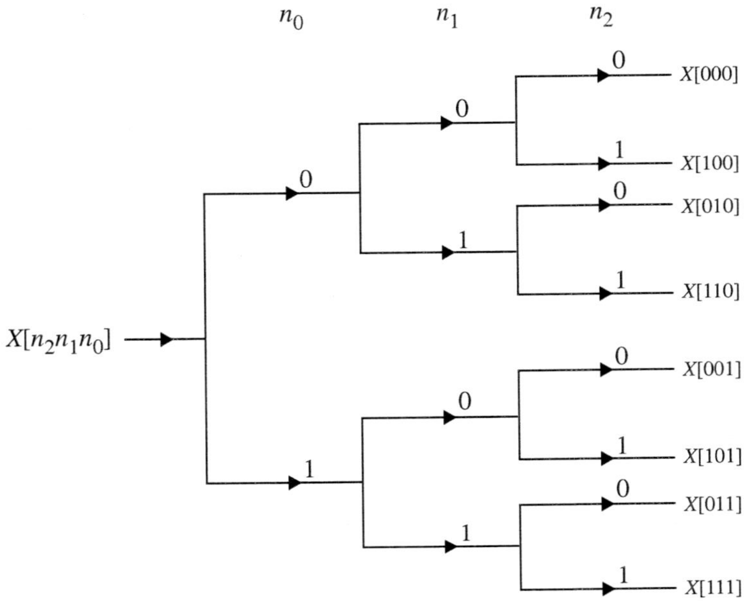

Figure 2.65 Tree diagram depicting bit-reversed-order sorting.

If (n_2, n_1, n_0) is the binary representation of the index of the sequence $x[n]$, then the sequence value $x[n_2, n_1, n_0]$ is stored in the array position $X_0[n_0, n_1, n_2]$. That is, in determining the position of $x[n_2, n_1, n_0]$ in the input array we must reverse the order of the bits of the index n. Let us first consider the process depicted in Figure 2.64 for sorting a data sequence in normal order by successive examination of the bits representing the data index. If the most significant bit of the data index is zero, $x[n]$ belongs to the top half of the sorted array, otherwise it belongs to the bottom half. Next the top half and bottom half subsequences can be sorted by examining the second most significant bit, and so on.

Let us now consider the process depicted in Figure 2.63 for sorting a data sequence in bit reversed order. If the least significant bit is 0, the sequence value corresponds to an even-numbered sample and therefore will appear in the top half and if the least significant bit is 1, the sequence value corresponds to an odd-numbered sample and consequently will appear in the bottom half of the array $X_0[l]$. Next the even and odd indexed subsequences are sorted into their even and odd indexed parts and this can be done by examining the second least significant bit in the index. This process is repeated until N subsequences is depicted by the tree diagram Figure 2.65.

Summary

- For spectral analysis of discrete signals, DFT approach is a very straight forward one. However, for larger values of N, DFT becomes tedious because of the huge number of mathematical operations required to perform. Such huge number of mathematical operations limit the bandwidth of the Digital Signal Processors.
- Several algorithms have been developed to reduce the computational burden and ease the implementation of DFT. The algorithm developed by Cooley and Tukey is the most efficient one and is called Fast Fourier Transform (FFT).
- The most widely used FFT algorithms are radix-2 and radix-4.
- Radix-2 FFT algorithm exploits the two important properties of twiddle factors namely symmetry and periodicity thereby removing redundant mathematical operations.
- The basic principle of FFT algorithm is to decompose DFT into successively smaller DFTs. The manner in which this decomposition is done leads to different FFT algorithms. Decimation in Time (DIT) and Decimation in Frequency (DIF) are the two basic classes of algorithm.
- In the algorithm in DIT, the sequence $x(n)$ is decomposed into successively smaller subsequences. Similarly in DIF algorithm, the sequence of DFT coefficients $X(k)$ is decomposed in smaller subsequences.

Short Questions and Answers

1. Define DFT of a discrete time sequence (or) analysis equation of DFT. *(Nov./Dec. 2003)*

Ans: The DFT is used to convert a finite discrete time sequence $x(n)$ to an N-point frequency domain sequence denoted by $X(k)$. The N-point DFT of a finite duration sequence $x(n)$ of length L, where $L \leq N$ is defined as

$$X(k) = \sum_{n=0}^{N-1} x(n)e^{-j\frac{2\pi kn}{N}} \quad \text{for} \quad k = 0, 1, 2, \ldots, (N-1)$$

2. Define IDFT (or) synthesis equation of DFT. *(Nov./Dec. 2003)*

Ans: The IDFT is used to convert the N-point frequency domain sequence $X(k)$ to an N-point time domain sequence. The IDFT of the sequence $X(k)$ of length N is defined as

$$x(n) = \frac{1}{N}\sum_{n=0}^{N-1} X(k)e^{j\frac{2\pi kn}{N}} \quad \text{for} \quad k = 0, 1, 2, \ldots, (N-1)$$

3. What is the drawback in Fourier transform and how it is overcome?

Ans: The drawback in Fourier transform is that it is a continuous function of ω and so it cannot be processed by digital system. This drawback is overcome by using Discrete Fourier transform. The DFT converts the continuous function of ω to a discrete function of ω.

4. Give any two applications of DFT (or the importance of DFT).

Ans:

(*i*) The DFT is used for spectral analysis of signals using a digital computer.

(*ii*) The DFT is used to perform filtering operation on signals using digital computer.

5. What is the relationship between z-transform and DFT?

Ans: Let N-point DFT of $x(n)$ be $X(k)$ and the z-transform of $x(n)$ be $X(z)$. The N-point sequence $X(k)$ can be obtained from $X(z)$ by evaluating $X(z)$ at N equally spaced points around the unit circle. That is

$$X(k) = X(z)\Big|_{Z=e^{j\frac{2\pi kn}{N}}} \quad \text{for} \quad k = 0, 1, 2, \ldots, (N-1)$$

6. Why linear convolution is important in DSP?

Ans: The response or output of LTI discrete time system for any input $x(n)$ is given by linear convolution of the input $x(n)$ and the impulse response $h(n)$ of the system. (This means that if the impulse response of a system is known, then the response of the system for any input can be determined by convolution operation).

7. Write the properties of linear convolution.

Ans: The linear convolution has the following properties:

1. Commutative property: $x(n) * h(n) = h(n) * x(n)$.
2. Associative property: $[x(n) * h_1(n)] * h_2(n) = x(n) * [h_1(n) * h_2(n)]$.
3. Distributive property: $x(n) * (h_1(n) + h_2(n)) = x(n) * h_1(n) + x(n) * h_2(n)$.

8. What is circular convolution?

Ans: The convolution of two periodic sequences with periodicity N is called circular convolution. If $x_1(n)$ and $x_2(n)$ are two periodic sequences with N samples in a period, then the circular convolution of $x_1(n)$ and $x_2(n)$ is defined as,

$$x_1(n) * x_2(n) = \sum_{n=0}^{N-1} x_1(n)x_2(m-n)$$

9. What is zero padding? Why it is needed? *(Nov./Dec. 2003)*

Ans: Appending zeros to a sequence in order to increase the size or length of the sequence is called zero padding. In circular convolution, when the two input sequences are of different size, then they are converted to equal size by zero padding.

10. List the difference between linear convolution and circular convolution.
Ans:

	Linear Convolution	Circular Convolution
1.	The length of the input sequences can be different.	The length of the input sequences should be same.
2.	Zero padding is not required.	If the length of the input sequences are different, then zero padding is required.
3.	The input sequences need not be periodic.	At least one of the input sequences should be periodic or should periodically be extended.
4.	The output sequence is non-periodic.	The output sequence is periodic. The periodicity is same as that of input sequence.
5.	The length of the output sequence will be greater than the length of input sequences.	The length of the input and output sequences are same.

11. Why circular convolution is important in DSP?
Ans: The Discrete Fourier Transform is used for the analysis and design of discrete time systems using digital computers. The DFT supports only circular convolution. Hence, when DFT techniques are employed, the results of linear convolution are obtained only via circular convolution.

12. How will you perform linear convolution via circular convolution?
(Anna University, May/June 2006)
Ans: The linear convolution of two sequences of length N_1 and N_2 produces an output sequence of length N_1+N_2-1. To perform linear convolution via circular convolution, convert the input sequences to N_1+N_2-1 point sequences by padding with zeros. Now the circular convolution of the N_1+N_2-1 point sequences will give an output sequence, which is same as that of linear convolution of the original two sequences of length N_1 and N_2.

13. What is sectioned convolution?
Ans: In linear convolution of two sequences, if one of the sequences is very much larger than the other, then it is very difficult to compute the linear convolution using DFT. In such cases, the longer sequence is sectioned into size of smaller sequence. Then the linear convolution of each section of longer sequence and the smaller sequence is performed. The output sequence obtained from the convolution of all the sections are combined to get the overall output sequence. This technique of convolution is called sectioned convolution.

14. Why sectioned convolution is performed?
Ans: In linear convolution of two sequences, if one of the sequences is very much larger than the other, then it is very difficult to compute the linear convolution using DFT for the following reasons:

(*i*) The entire sequence should be available before convolution can be carried out. This makes long delay in getting the output,
(*ii*) Large amount of memory is required to store the sequences.

15. Compare the overlap add and overlap save method of sectioned convolutions.

	Overlap Add Method	Overlap Save Method
1.	Linear convolution of each section of longer sequence with smaller sequence is performed.	Circular convolution of each section of longer sequence with smaller sequence is performed. (after converting them to the size of output sequence).
2.	Zero padding is not required.	Zero padding is required to convert the input sequence to the size of output sequence.
3.	Overlapping of samples of input sections are not required.	The $N_2 - 1$ samples of an input section of longer sequence is overlapped with next input section.
4.	The overlapped samples in the output of sectioned convolutions are added to get the overall output.	Depending on the method of overlapping the input samples, either the last $N_2 - 1$ samples or the first $N_2 - 1$ samples of the output sequence of each sectioned convolution are discarded.

16. In what way zero padding is implemented in overlap save method?

Ans: In overlap save method, the zero padding is employed to convert the small input sequence to the size of the output sequence of each sectioned convolution. The zero padding is also employed to convert either the last section or the first section of the longer input sequence to the size of the output sequence of each sectioned convolution.

17. What is FFT? *(Anna University, Nov./Dec. 2006)*

Ans: The FFT is a method for computing the DFT with reduced number of calculations. The computational efficiency is achieved by employing divide and conquer approach. This is based on the decomposition of an N point DFT into successively smaller DFTs.

In an N point sequence, if N can be expressed as $N = r^m$, then the sequence can be decimated into r-point sequence, and r-point DFTs are computed. From the results of r-point DFTs, the r^2-point DFTs are computed. From the results of r^2-point DFT, the r^3-point DFTs are computed and so on, until we get r^m point DFT. Hence, the number of stages of computation is m. The number r is called the radix of the FFT algorithm.

18. What is radix-2 FFT?

Ans: The radix-2 FFT is an efficient algorithm for computing N-point DFT of an N-point sequence. In radix-2 FFT the N-point sequence is decimated into 2-point sequences and 2-point DFT for each decimated sequence is computed. From the results of 2-point DFTs, the 4-point DFTs are computed. From the results of 4-point DFTs, the 8-point DFTs are computed and so on until we get N-point DFT.

19. How many multiplications and additions are involved in radix-2 FFT?

Ans: For performing radix-2 FFT, the value of N should be such that, $N = 2^m$. The total number of complex additions are $N \log_2 N$ and the total number of complex multiplications are $(N/2) \log_2 N$.

20. Calculate the percentage saving in calculations in a 512-point radix-2 FFT, when compared to direct DFT.

Ans: Direct computation of DFT:

$$\text{Number of complex additions} = N(N-1) = 512 \times (512 - 1) = 2,61,632$$

$$\text{Number of complex multiplications} = N^2 = 512 \times 512 = 2,61,144$$

Radix-2 FFT:

$$\text{Number of complex additions} = N \log_2 N = 4,608$$

$$\text{Number of complex multiplications} = (N/2) \log_2 N = 2,304$$

Percentage saving in additions

$$= 100 - \frac{\text{Number of additions in radix-2 FFT}}{\text{Number of additions in direct DFT}} \times 100$$

$$= 100 - \frac{(4,608)}{(2,61,632)} \times 100 = 98\%$$

Percentage saving in multiplications

$$= 100 - \frac{\text{Number of multiplications in radix-2 FFT}}{\text{Number of multiplications in direct DFT}} \times 100$$

$$= 100 - \frac{(2,304)}{(2,61,144)} \times 100 = 99.1\%$$

21. Draw and explain the basic butterfly diagram or flow graph of DIT radix-2 FFT.

Ans:

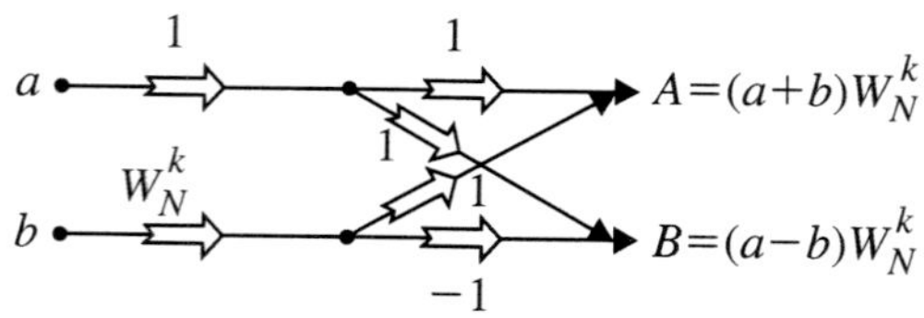

Figure 2.66

The basic butterfly diagram of DIT radix-2 FFT is shown in Figure 2.66. It performs the following operations. Here a and b are input complex numbers and A and B are output complex numbers.

(*i*) Input complex number b is multiplied by the phase factor W_N^k.

(*ii*) The product bW_N^k is added to the input complex number a to form a new complex number A.

(*iii*) The product bW_N^k is subtracted from the input complex number a to form a new complex number B.

22. What is DIF radix-2 FFT?

Ans: The DIF radix-2 FFT is an efficient algorithm for computing DFT. In this algorithm the N-point time domain sequence is converted to two numbers of $N/2$ point sequences. Then each $N/2$ point sequence is converted to two numbers of $N/4$ point sequences. This process is continued until we get $N/2$ numbers of 2-point sequences. Now the 2-point DFTs of $N/2$ numbers of 2-point sequences will give N samples, which is the N-point DFT of the time domain sequence. Here the equations for forming $N/2$ point sequences, $N/4$ point sequences, *etc.*, are obtained by decimation of frequency domain sequences. Hence, this method is called DIF.

23. Compare the DIT and DIF radix-2 FFT.

Ans:

	DIT Radix-2 FFT	**DIF Radix-2 FFT**
1.	The time domain sequence is decimated.	The frequency domain sequence is decimated.
2.	When the input is in bit reversed order, the output will be in normal order and *vice versa*.	When the input is in normal order, the output will be in bit reversed order and *vice versa*.
3.	In each stage of computation, the phase factor are multiplied before add and subtract operation.	In each stage of computation, the phase factor are multiplied after add and subtract operation.
4.	The value of N should be expressed such that $N-2m$ and this algorithm consists of m stages of computations.	The value of N should be expressed such that $N = 2m$ and this algorithm consists of m stages of computations.
5.	Total number of arithmetic operations are $N\log_2 N$ complex additions and $(N/2)\log_2 N$ complex multiplications.	Total number of arithmetic operations are $N\log_2 N$ complex additions and $(N/2)\log_2 N$ complex multiplications

24. How will you compute IDFT using radix-2 FFT algorithm?

Ans: Let $x(n)$ be an N-point sequence and $X(k)$ be the N-point DFT of $x(n)$. The sequence $x(n)$ can be computed from the sequence,

$$x(n) = \frac{1}{N}\left(\sum_{k=0}^{N-1} X^*(k)W_N^{nk}\right)^*$$

The following procedure can be used to determine $x(n)$ using radix-2 FFT algorithm.

(*i*) Take conjugate of $X(k)$ (*i.e.*, determine $X^*(k)$).
(*ii*) Compute N-point DFT of $X^*(k)$ using radix-2 FFT.
(*iii*) Take conjugate of the output sequence from FFT.
(*iv*) Divide the sequence obtained in Step (*iii*) by N. The resultant sequence is $x(n)$.

25. What is direct or slow convolution and fast convolution?

Ans: The response of an LTI system is given by convolution of input and impulse response. The computation of the response of LTI system by convolution sum formula is called slow convolution because it involves very large number of calculations. The number of calculations in DFT computation of the response of LTI system by FFT algorithm is called fast convolution.

26. Why FFT is needed?

Ans: The FFT is needed to compute DFT with reduced number of calculations. The DFT is required for spectrum analysis and filtering operations on the signals using digital computers.

27. How FFT is faster?

Ans: FFT algorithm exploits the two important properties if twiddle factors namely symmetry and periodicity thereby removing redundant mathematical operation. It requires $N/2\log_2^N$ complex multiplication and $N\log_2^N$ complex addition for computing Npoint DFT. FFT reduces the computation time required to compute a discrete Fourier transform and improves the performance by a factor 100 or more over direct evaluation of the DFT.

28. Compute DFT of the sequence $x(n) = e^{-n},\ 0 \le n \le 4$

Ans:

$$X(k) = \sum_{n=0}^{N-1} x(n)e^{-\frac{j2\pi kn}{N}}$$

$$= \sum_{n=0}^{4} e^{-n}e^{-\frac{j2\pi kn}{5}} = \sum_{n=0}^{4}\left[e^{-1-\frac{j2\pi k}{5}}\right]^n$$

$$X(k) = \frac{1-e^{-\left(1+\frac{j2\pi k}{5}\right)^5}}{1-e^{-\left(1+\frac{j2\pi k}{5}\right)}}$$

29. Calculate the number if complex multiplication for direct evaluation of 8-point DFT.

Ans: The number of complex multiplication required using direct computation is

$$N^2 = 8^2 = 64$$

30. Distinguish between DFT and DTFT.

Ans: DFT:

- Obtained by performing sampling operation in both the time and frequency domains.
- Discrete frequency spectrum (Discrete function of ω).

DTFT:

- Sampling is performed only in time domain.
- Continuous frequency spectrum (continuous function of ω).

31. Give computation efficiency of 1024 point FFT over 1024 point DFT.

Ans: The number of complex multiplication required using direct computation is

$$N^2 = (1024)^2 = 1048576$$

The number of complex multiplication required using FFT is

$$\begin{aligned}\frac{N}{2}\log_2^N &= \frac{1024}{2}\log_2^{1024}\\ &= 512\log_2^{2^{10}}\\ &= 5120\end{aligned}$$

Computation efficiency in multiplication

$$\begin{aligned}&= 100 - \frac{5120}{1048576}\times 100\\ &= 99.5\%\end{aligned}$$

The number of complex multiplication required using direct computation is

$$N(N-1) = 1024(1024-1) = 1047552$$

The number of complex multiplication required using FFT is

$$\begin{aligned}N\log_2^N &= 1024\log_2^{1024}\\ &= 1024\log_2^{2^{10}}\\ &= 10240\end{aligned}$$

Computation efficiency in addition

$$\begin{aligned}&= 100 - \frac{10240}{1048576}\times 100\\ &= 99\%\end{aligned}$$

32. Write the analysis and synthesis equation of DFT.

Ans: Analysis equation of DFT is

$$X(k) = \sum_{n=0}^{N-1} x(n)e^{\frac{-j2\pi kn}{N}}, \quad n = 0, 1, 2, \ldots, N-1$$

Synthesis equation of DFT is

$$x(n) = \frac{1}{N}\sum_{k=0}^{N-1} X(k)e^{\frac{j2\pi kn}{N}j}, \quad n = 0, 1, 2, \ldots, N-1$$

33. Determine the response of the system with $y(n) = x(n-1)$ for the input signal.

$$x(n) = \begin{cases} |n|, & -3 \le n \le 3 \\ 0, & \text{otherwise} \end{cases}$$

Ans:

$$x(n) = \begin{cases} |n|, & -3 \le n \le 3 \\ 0, & \text{otherwise} \end{cases}$$

$$x(n) = \{3, 2, 1, \underset{\uparrow}{0}, 1, 2, 3\}$$

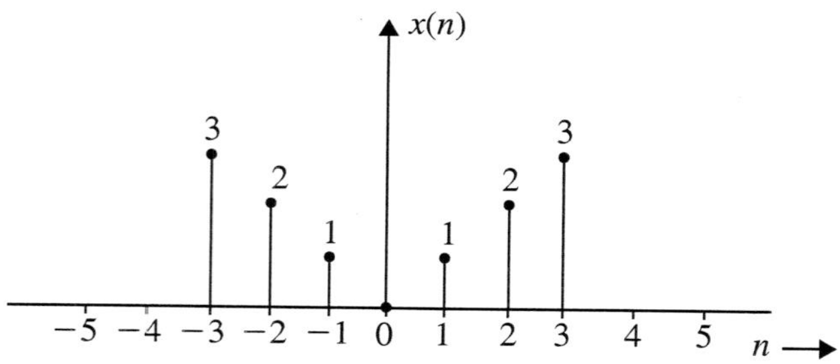

Figure 2.67

$$y(n) = x(n-1)$$

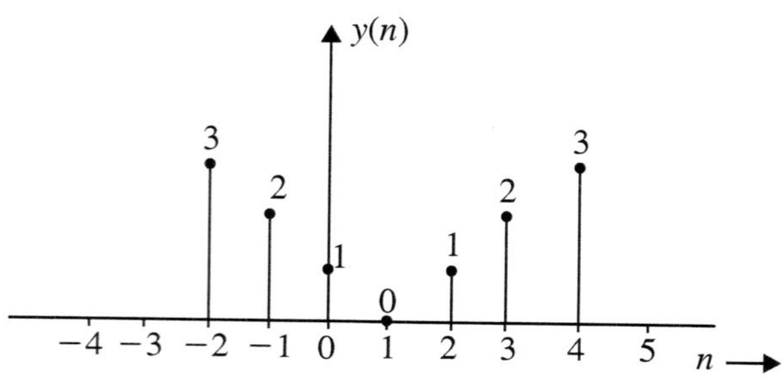

Figure 2.68

34. Calculate the multiplication reduction factor α in computing 1024 point DFT in a radix-2 FFT algorithm.

Ans: The number of complex multiplication required using direct computation is

$$N^2 = (1024)^2 = 1048576$$

The number of complex multiplication required using FFT is

$$\begin{aligned}\frac{N}{2}\log_2^N &= \frac{1024}{2}\log_2^{1024} \\ &= 512\log_2^{2^{10}} \\ &= 5120\end{aligned}$$

Multiplication reduction factor

$$\alpha = \frac{1048576}{5120} = 204.8$$

35. Find the values of W_N^k when $N = 8$ and $k = 2$ and also for $k = 3$.

$$W_N^k = e^{-\frac{j2\pi k}{N}}$$

Ans: For $N = 8$ and $k = 2$,

$$W_N^k = W_8^2 = e^{-\frac{j2\pi 2}{8}} = -j$$

For $N = 8$ and $k = 3$,

$$W_N^k = W_8^3 = e^{-\frac{j2\pi 3}{8}} = -0.707 - j0.707$$

36. State and prove Parsevals' relation DFT.

Ans: For complex-valued sequence $x(n)$ and $y(n)$, if

$$x(n) \xleftrightarrow[N]{\text{DFT}} X(k) \qquad \text{and} \qquad y(n) \xleftrightarrow[N]{\text{DFT}} Y(k)$$

then

$$\sum_{n=0}^{N-1} x(n)y^*(n) = \frac{1}{N}\sum_{k=0}^{N-1} X(k)Y^*(k)$$

Proof

$$\begin{aligned}\text{IDFT}\{R_{xy}(k)\} &= \Gamma_{xy}(l) \\ &= \frac{1}{N}\sum_{k=0}^{N-1} R_{xy}(k)e^{\frac{j2\pi kl}{N}}\end{aligned}$$

using cross correlation

$$\sum_{k=0}^{N-1} x(n)Y^*(n-l) = \frac{1}{N}\sum_{k=0}^{N-1} R_{xy}(k)e^{\frac{j2\pi kl}{N}}$$

$$\sum_{k=0}^{N-1} x(n)Y^*(n) = \frac{1}{N}\sum_{k=0}^{N-1} R_{xy}(k) \qquad [\text{when } l = 0]$$

$$\sum_{k=0}^{N-1} x(n)Y^*(n) = \frac{1}{N}\sum_{k=0}^{N-1} X(k)Y^*(k)$$

If $x(n) - y(n)$

$$\sum_{k=0}^{N-1} x(n)x^*(n-l) = \frac{1}{N}\sum_{k=0}^{N-1} X(k)X^*(k)$$

$$\sum_{k=0}^{N-1} |x(n)|^2 = \frac{1}{N}\sum_{k=0}^{N-1} |X(k)|^2$$

37. What do you mean by the term "bit reversal" as applied to FFT?

Ans: In FFT, before decimation the sequences are arranged in bit reversed order. Bit-reversal process for $N = 8$ is

Normal order		Bit reversal order	
Input sample	**Binary representation**	**Bit reversal binary**	**Bit reversed sample input**
$x(0)$	000	000	$x(0)$
$x(1)$	001	100	$x(4)$
$x(2)$	010	010	$x(2)$
$x(3)$	011	110	$x(6)$
$x(4)$	100	001	$x(1)$
$x(5)$	101	101	$x(5)$
$x(6)$	110	011	$x(3)$
$x(7)$	111	111	$x(7)$

38. The first five DFT coefficients of a sequence $x(n)$ are $X(0) = 20, X(1) = 5+j2, X(2) = 20, X(3) = 0.2+j0.4$ and $X(4) = 0$. Determine the remaining DFT coefficients.

Ans: Let $N = 8$. We have $X(k) = X^*(N-k)$. The first five DFT coefficients are given, and the remaining DFT coefficients are obtained as,

$$X(5) = X^*(8-5) = X^*(3) = 0.2 - j0.4$$

$$X(6) = X^*(8-6) = X^*(2) = 20$$

$$X(7) = X^*(8-7) = X^*(1) = 5 - j2$$

39. What are the advances of FFT algorithm over direct computation of DFT?
Ans:

1. FFT algorithm reduces the number of complex multiplication and complex addition operation.
2. It reduces the computation time required to compute DFT.

Long Answer Type Questions

1. Find 8 point DFT of the sequence $x(n) = a^n$ where $a = 3$.
2. Compute the DFTs of the following sequences where $N = 4$ suing DIT algorithm.

   (*a*) $x(n) = 2^n$
   (*b*) $x(n) = 2^{-n}$
   (*c*) $x(n) = \sin\left(\frac{n\pi}{2}\right)$
   (*d*) $x(n) = \cos\left(\frac{n\pi}{2}\right)$

3. Compute the 16 point DFTs of the following sequences:

$$x(n) = \cos\left(\frac{\pi}{2}\right), \quad 0 \leq n \leq 15$$

   using DIT algorithm.
4. Compute the FFT for the sequence $x(n) = n^2 + 1$ where $N = 8$ using DIT algorithm..
5. Compute the DFT coefficients of a finite duration sequence {0,1,2,3,0,0,0,0}.
6. Compute the IDFT of the following sequences using (*a*) DIT algorithm and (*b*) DIF algorithm.

$$(i) \quad \{5, 0, 1 - j, 0, 1, 0, 1 + j, 0\}$$

$$(ii) \quad \{1, 1 + j, 1 - j2, 1, 0, 1 + j2, 1 + j\}$$

7. Derive the equation for radix 4 FFT for $N = 4$ and draw the butterfly diagram.
8. Derive the DFT of the sample data sequence $x(n) = \{1, 1, 1, 0\}$ and compute the corresponding amplitude and phase spectrum.
9. Compute the DFT for the sequence $\{1, 2, 0, 0, 0, 2, 1, 1\}$ using radix-2 DIF-FFT algorithm.
10. Prove that multiplication of the DFT's of two sequences is equivalent to the DFT of the circular convolution of the two sequences in time domain.
11. Using DFT-IDFT method, perform circular convolution of the two sequences $x(n) = \{1, 2, 0, 1\}$ and $h(n) = \{2, 2, 1, 1\}$.
12. By means of DFT and IDFT, determine the response of an FIR filter with impulse response $h(n) = \{1, 2, 3\}$ to the input sequence $x(n) = \{1, 2, 2, 1\}$.
13. Develop a DIT FFT algorithm for $N = 12 = 3 \cdot 2 \cdot 2$ and draw the signal flow diagram.

14. The first five DFT coefficient are $\{22, -7.5353 - j3.1213, 1 + j, -0.4645 - j1.1213, 0\}$. Determine the remaining DFT coefficients for $N = 16$.
15. Determine the 8-point DFT of the sequence

$$x(n) = \begin{cases} 1, & -3 \le n \le 3 \\ 0, & \text{otherwise} \end{cases}$$

16. Convolve the following sequences using (*i*) overlap-add method and (*ii*) overlap save method.

$$x(n) = \{1, -1, 2, 1, 2, -1, 1, 3, 1\} \qquad \text{and} \qquad h(n) = \{1, 2, 1\}$$

17. An input sequence $x(n) = \{2, 1, 0, 1, 2\}$ is applied to a DSP system having an impulse sequence $h(n) = \{5, 3, 2, 1\}$. Determine the output sequence produced by (*i*) linear convolution and (*ii*) verify the same through circular convolution.
18. Determine the DFT of the sequence

$$x(n) = \begin{cases} 1, & 2 \le n \le 6 \\ 0, & \text{otherwise} \end{cases}$$

Assume that $N = 10$.
19. Derive and draw the radix-4 DIT and DFT algorithm for FFT of 8 points.
20. Discuss in detail the use of FFT algorithm in linear filtering.

MATLAB PROGRAM

Linear Convolution

Write a program to get the output sequence $y(n)$ by linear convolution of the sequence $x(n) = \{1, 2\}$ and $h(n) = \{1, 2, 4\}$.

```
%Linear convolution
clc;clear all;close all;
x=input('enter the first sequence');
h=input('enter the second sequence');
y=conv(x,h);
subplot(3,1,1);
stem(x);
xlabel('first sequence n→');
ylabel('amplitude→');
subplot(3,1,2);
stem(h);
xlabel('second sequence n→');
ylabel('amplitude→');
subplot(3,1,3);
stem(y);
xlabel('output sequence n→');
ylabel('amplitude→');
disp('the resultant signal is');y
```

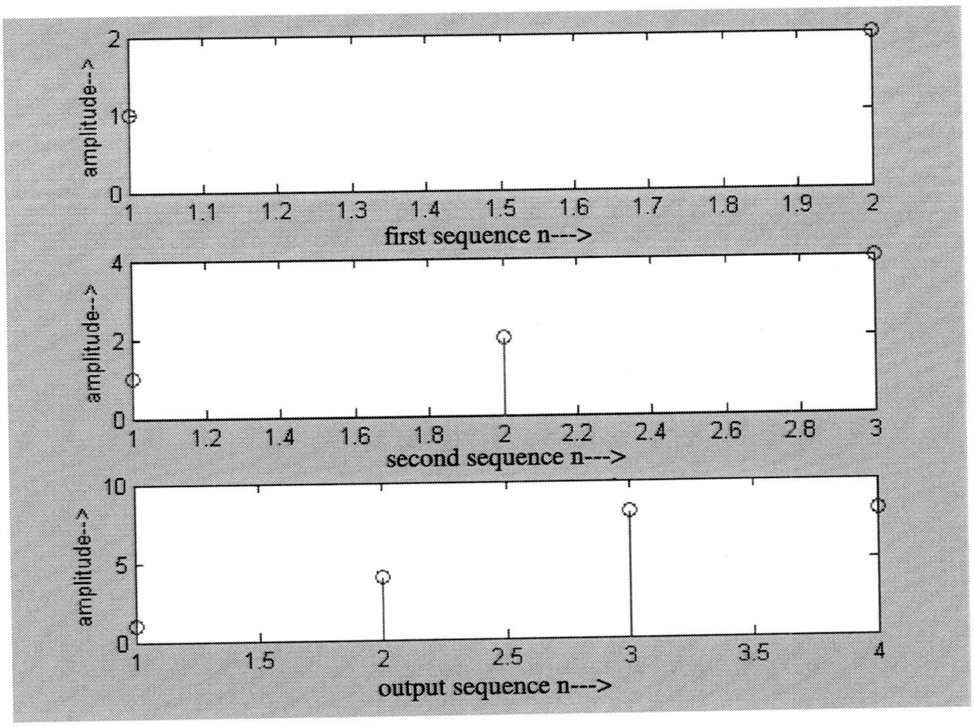

```
enter the first sequence[1 2]
enter the second sequence[1 2 4]
the resultant signal is
y = 1   4   8   8
```

Circular Convolution

Write a program to get the output sequence $y(n)$ by circular convolution of the sequence $x(n) = \{1, 2\}$ and $h(n) = \{1, 2, 4\}$.

```
%Circular convolution
clc;close all;clear all;
g=input('enter the first sequence');
h=input('enter the second sequence');
N1=length(g);
N2=length(h);
N=max(N1,N2);
N3=N1-N2;
%Loop for getting equal length sequence
if(N3 =0)
   if(N3<0)
     g=[g,zeros(1,-N3)];
   else
     h=[h,zeros(1,N3)];
     end
   end
   N4=N1+N2-1;
   g=[g,zeros(1,N4-N)];
   h=[h,zeros(1,N4-N)];
   disp('the input sequence');g,h
% Computation of circular convolution
for n=1:N4;
   y(n) =0;
   for i=1:N4;
     j=n-i+1;
     if(j<=0)
       j=N4+j;
     end
     y(n) = y(n)+ h(j)*g(i);
   end
end
subplot(3,1,1);
stem(g);
xlabel('first sequence n→');
ylabel('amplitude→');
```

```
subplot(3,1,2);
stem(h);
xlabel('second sequence n→');
ylabel('amplitude→');
subplot(3,1,3);
stem(y);
xlabel('output sequence   n→');
ylabel('amplitude→');
disp('the resultant signal is');y
```

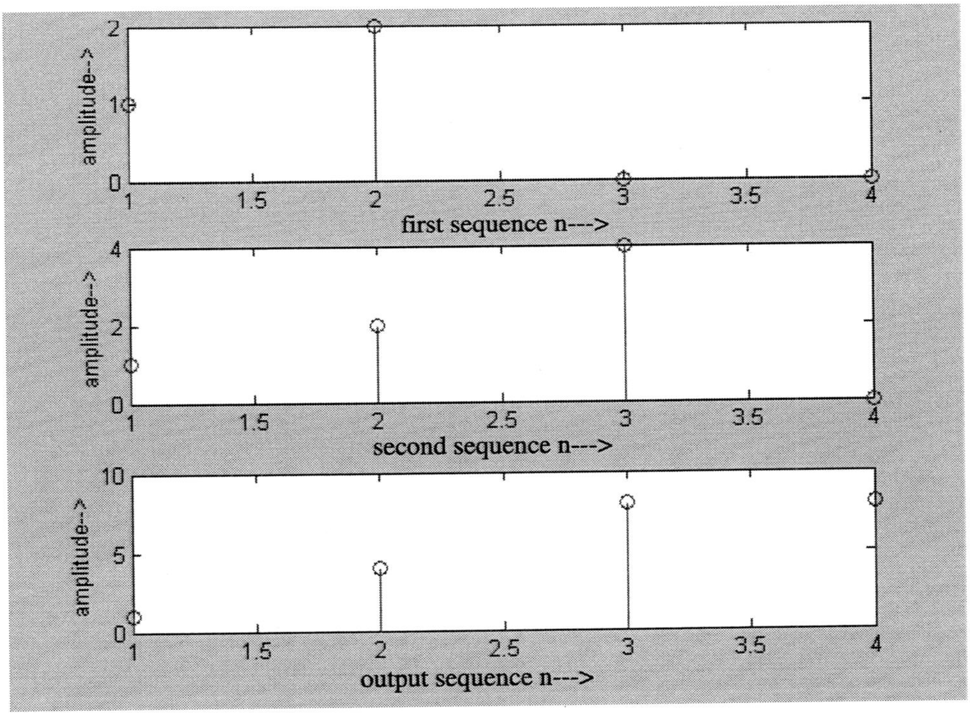


```
enter the first sequence[1 2]
enter the second sequence[1 2 4]
the input sequence
g =   1   2   0   0

h =   1   2   4   0

the resultant signal is
y =   1   4   8   8
```

FFT Computation

Write a program to find FFT of a given sequence.

```
clc;close all;clear all;
x=input('enter the sequence');
n=input('enter the length of fft');
y=fft(x,n);
stem(y);
xlabel('real axis→');
ylabel('imaginary axis→');
disp('the fft sequence is');y
```

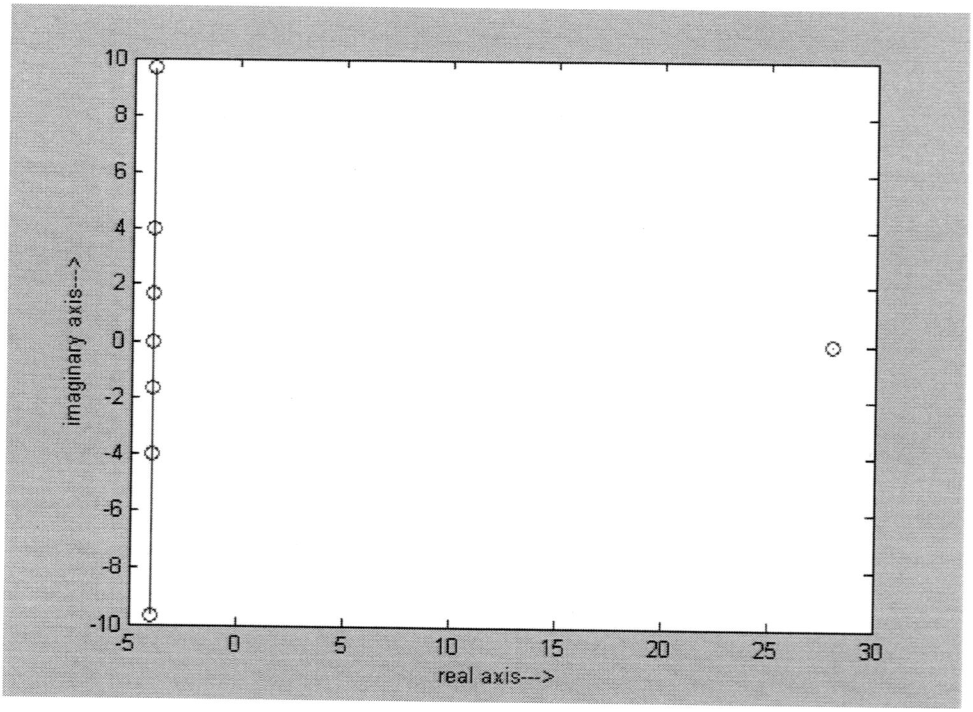


```
enter the sequence[0 1 2 3 4 5 6 7]
enter the length of fft8
the fft sequence is
y =Columns 1 through 3
    28.0000   -4.0000 + 9.6569i -4.0000 + 4.0000i
   Columns 4 through 6
    -4.0000 + 1.6569i -4.0000    -4.0000 - 1.6569i
   Columns 7 through 8
    -4.0000 - 4.0000i -4.0000 - 9.6569i
```

DFT Computation

Write a program to find n-point DFT of a given sequence.

```
clc;close all;clear all;
f1=1/128;
f2=5/128;fc=50/128;n=0:255;
x=cos(2*pi*f1*n)+cos(2*pi*f2*n);
xc=cos(2*pi*fc*n);
xamp=x.*xc;
subplot(2,2,1);
plot(n,x);
title('x(n)');
xlabel('n→');
ylabel('Amplitude→');
subplot(2,2,2);
plot(n,xc);
title('xc(n)');
xlabel('n→');
ylabel('Amplitude→');
subplot(2,2,3);
plot(n,xamp);
title('xamp(n)');
xlabel('n→');
ylabel('Amplitude→');
n=0:127;n1=128;
f1=1/128;
f2=5/128;fc=50/128;
x=cos(2*pi*f1*n)+cos(2*pi*f2*n);
xc=cos(2*pi*fc*n);
xamp=x.*xc;
xam=fft(xamp,n1);
figure(2);
subplot(2,1,1);
stem(n,xam);
title('xam(n)');
xlabel('n→');
ylabel('Amplitude→');
n=0:99;figure(2);n1=128;
f1=1/128;
f2=5/128;fc=50/128;
x=cos(2*pi*f1*n)+cos(2*pi*f2*n);
xc=cos(2*pi*fc*n);
xamp=x.*xc;
xam=fft(xamp,n1);n=0:127;
subplot(2,1,2);
```

```
stem(n,xam);
title('xam(n)');
xlabel('n→');
ylabel('Amplitude→');
```

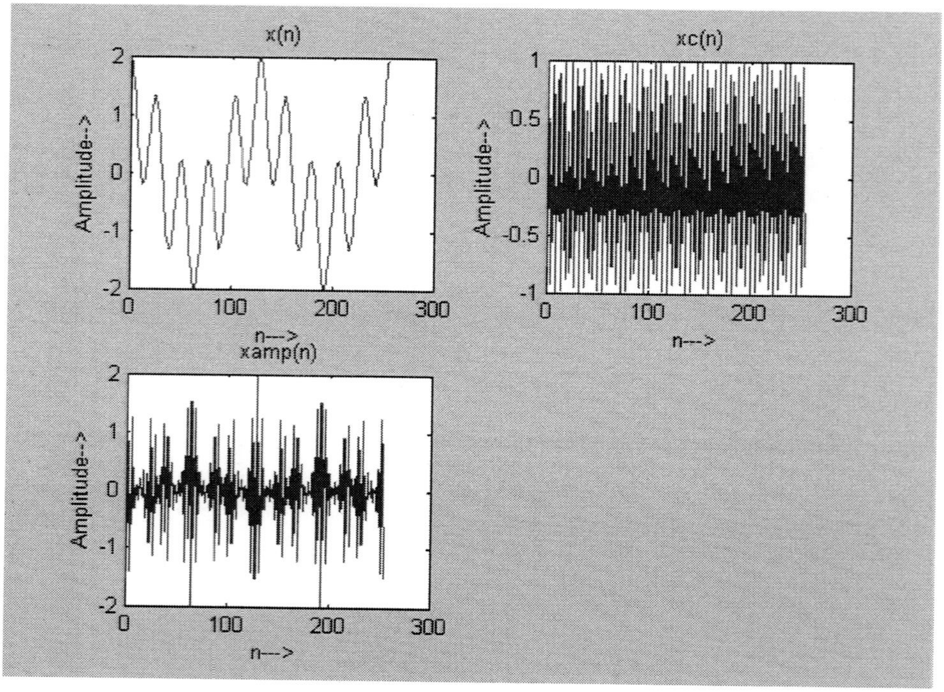

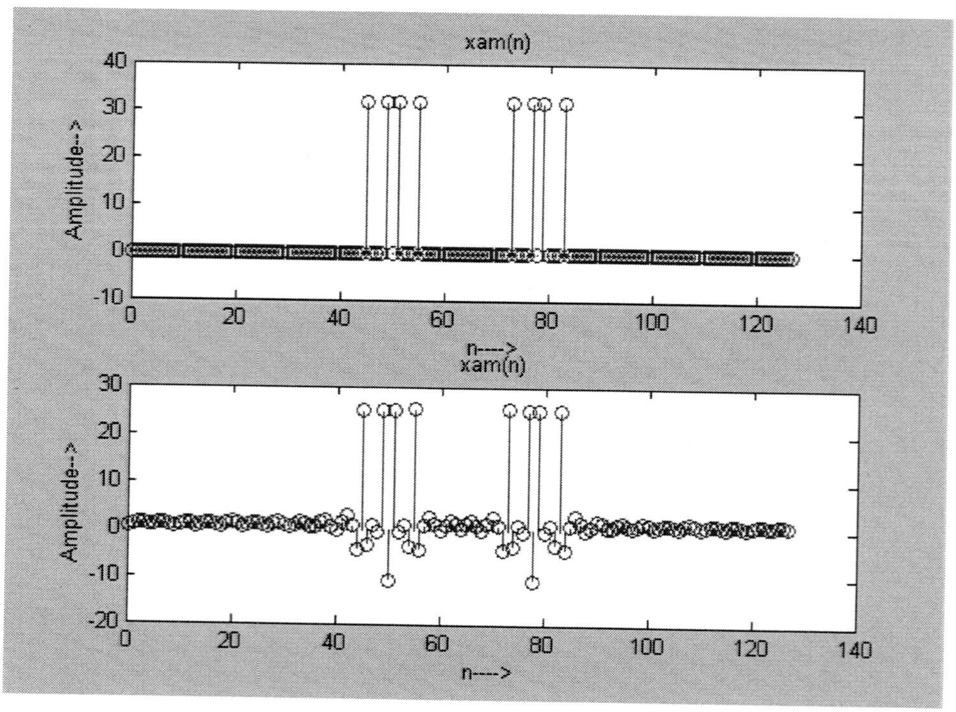

Design of IIR Digital Filters 3

Learning Objectives

After completing this chapter, you should be able to:

- study the characteristics and classify digital filters.
- establish the causality and stability conditions necessary when analog filters are converted into digital filters.
- design digital filters from analog filters using impulse invariance and bilinear transformation methods.
- design digital low-pass filters by Butterworth, Chebyshev approximations and approximation of derivatives.
- study analog and digital frequency transformations and design filters of different types.
- draw frequency response of digital filters from the system function.
- realize the structure of digital filters in different forms.

3.1 Introduction

A filter, is a network or system that changes the frequency response (amplitude *versus* frequency and phase *versus* frequency) characteristics of a signal in a desired manner. The filter extracts information from the signal by removing noise. It is also used to separate two or more signals which can make use of the available communication channel very efficiently. Filters are broadly classified as analog filters and digital filters. Analog filters operate on analog signals. They are governed by differential equations. They consist of electric components like resistors, capacitors and inductors. On the other hand, digital filters operate on digital samples of the signal. They are governed by linear difference equation. They consist of adders, multipliers and delay implemented in logic.

Digital filters play very important role in Digital Signal Processing. They are extensively used in data transmission, data compression, echo cancellation, image processing, speech processing, telephone, digital audio, biomedical signal processing *etc.* Digital filters have the following advantages over analog filters.

3.1.1 Advantages

1. Digital filters are used in low frequency devices used in biomedical applications where analog filters cannot be used.
2. They have linear phase response characteristic.
3. The performance of digital filters do not vary with environmental changes.
4. Filtered and unfiltered data can be saved for future use.
5. They are cheap and consume low power. Precision is high compared to analog filters.
6. The frequency response can be automatically adjusted using programmable processor.

3.1.2 Disadvantages

The disadvantages of digital filters include the following:

1. The time taken for the design and hardware development is longer compared to analog filters.
2. The maximum bandwidth of signals that can be handled by digital filters is lower compared to analog filters.
3. Digital filters are subject to ADC noise due to quantization and round off noise produced during computation.

3.2 IIR and FIR Filters

Digital filters are broadly classified as Infinite Impulse Response (IIR) and Finite Impulse Response (FIR) filters. The impulse response of the filters can be represented by the sequence $h(k)$, $(k = 0, 1, 2, \ldots)$ as in Figure 3.1.

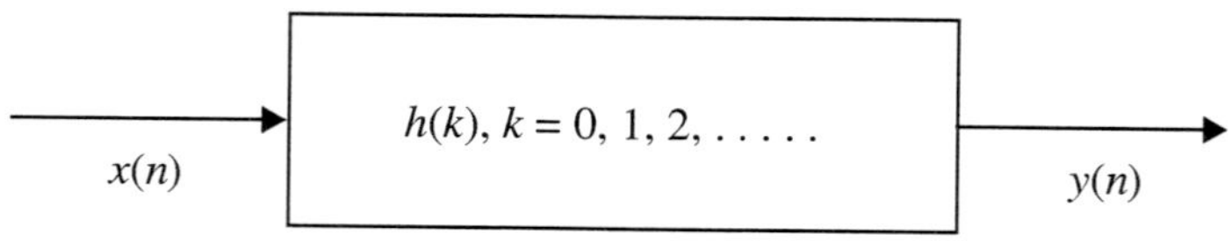

Figure 3.1 A digital filter.

From Figure 3.1, the following equations are written for the convolution sum.

$$y(n) = \sum_{R=0}^{\infty} h(k)x(n-k) \tag{3.1}$$

$$y(n) = \sum_{R=0}^{N-1} h(k)x(n-k) \tag{3.2}$$

Equation (3.1) gives the output of an IIR filter while equation (3.2) gives the output of an FIR filter, where the response is of infinite and finite duration respectively. The output of IIR filter using equation (3.1) cannot be computed in practice because the length of the impulse is too long. Equation (3.1) is therefore modified and expressed in recursive form as given below:

$$y(n) = \sum_{R=0}^{N} b_k x(n-k) - \sum_{k=1}^{M} a_k y(n-k) \tag{3.3}$$

In equation (3.3) a_k and b_k are the coefficients of IIR filter. Equations (3.2) and (3.3) are used to design FIR and IIR filters respectively. It is to be noted that, the output of the IIR filter (recursive filter) as seen from equation (3.3), depends on past outputs as well as present and past input samples. Further, equation (3.3) shows the inherent feedback present in the IIR filter. On the other hand, the output of the FIR filter (non-recursive filter) as seen from equation (3.2), depends on the past and present values of the input samples. Equations (3.2) and (3.3) can also be represented in terms of the transfer function as given below:

$$H(z) = \sum_{k=0}^{N-1} h(k) z^{-k} \tag{3.4}$$

$$H(z) = \frac{\sum_{k=0}^{N} b_k z^{-k}}{\left[1 + \sum_{k=1}^{M} a_k z^{-k}\right]} \tag{3.5}$$

Equation (3.4) and equation (3.5) respectively are the transfer functions of FIR and IIR filters.

3.3 Basic Features of IIR Filters

The transfer function of IIR filter is given in equation (3.5). For the IIR filter design, it is necessary to find suitable values for the coefficients a_k and b_k so that the desired frequency response is obtained. The design stages for digital IIR filters is as follows:

1. Filter specification: The function of the filter (lowpass, highpass, bandpass, band rejected filter) and the desired performance are given.
2. Calculation of coefficients a_k and b_k.
3. Structure realization.
4. Finite word length effects analysis and solutions.
5. Hardware and software implementation.

3.4 Performance Specifications

For the design of IIR filters, the following specifications are normally followed.

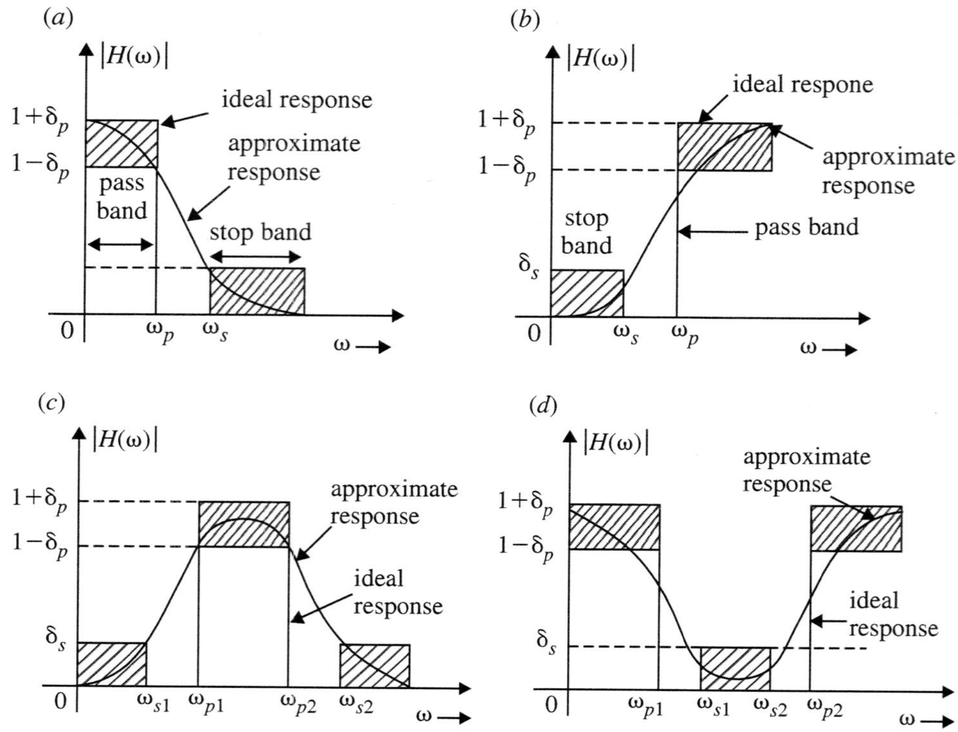

Figure 3.2 Magnitude response. (*a*) Lowpass, (*b*) Highpass, (*c*) Bandpass and (*d*) Band stop filter.

1. Signal characteristics.
2. The frequency response characteristics of the filter.
3. Cost constraints.
4. Mode of implementation.

The frequency response specifications of frequency selective filters such as lowpass, highpass, bandpass and band stop filters are expressed in the form of tolerance scheme as shown in Figure 3.2.

Analog filter design is a well-established one. Several techniques have been developed to design digital filters which are all based on converting an analog filter into a digital filter. The digital filter is therefore first designed in the analog domain and then the design is converted into the digital domain. For an analog filter, the system function can be represented by the following equation:

$$H_a(s) = \frac{B(s)}{A(s)} = \frac{\sum_{k=0}^{M} \beta_k s^k}{\sum_{k=0}^{N} \alpha_k s^k} \tag{3.6}$$

where $[\alpha_k]$ and $[\beta_k]$ are the coefficients of the filter. The system function $H_a(s)$ can also be written by its impulse response as given below:

$$H_a(s) = \int_{-\infty}^{\infty} h(t)e^{-st}dt \tag{3.7}$$

The analog filter input and output equation can also be represented by the following equations:

$$\sum_{k=0}^{N} \alpha_k \frac{d^k y(t)}{dt^k} = \sum_{k=0}^{M} \beta_k \frac{d^k x(t)}{dt^k} \tag{3.8}$$

where $x(t)$ is input signal and $y(t)$ is the output response. The above equations which represent the characteristics of analog filter in three different forms, are converted to their equivalent forms in digital domain while designing a digital filter. It is to be noted that the conversion becomes valid and effective if the following conditions are satisfied. If $H_a(s)$ is the system function of a linear time invariant stable system, then all its poles should fall in left half of the s-plane (LHP). On that basis, when analog filter is converted to digital filter, then it should satisfy the following stability conditions:

1. The j axis in the s-plane should map into unit circle in the z-plane. This results in a direct relationship between the two frequency variables in s-domain and z-domain.
2. The LHP of the s-plane should map into the interior of the unit circle in the z-plane. This guarantees the stability of the digital filter when converted from analog filter.
3. The T.F.s $H_a(s)$ and $H(z)$ should be rational, so that the filter is causal.

The following methods of digital filter design by converting analog filter are described:

1. Impulse invariance transform method.
2. Bilinear transformation method.

3.5 Impulse Invariance Transform Method

The impulse response of the digital filter is obtained by uniformly sampling the impulse response of the analog filter.

$$h(n) = h_a(t)\Big|_{t=nt} = h_a(nT) \tag{3.9}$$

$$H_a(s) = L[h_a(t)]$$

When $H_a(s)$ has distinct poles, it can be expressed by partial fraction expression as

$$H_a(s) = \sum_{i=1}^{N} \frac{A_i}{s-p_i} = \frac{A_1}{s-p_1} + \frac{A_2}{s-p_2} + \cdots + \frac{A_N}{s-p_N} \tag{3.10}$$

$$h_a(t) = A_1 e^{p_1 t} u_a(t) + A_2 e^{p_2 t} u_a(t) + \cdots + A_N e^{p_N t} u_a(t)$$

$$\therefore\ h(n) = h_a(t)\Big|_{t=nT}$$

$$h(n) = A_1 e^{p_1 nT} u_a(nT) + A_2 e^{p_2 nT} u_a(nT) + \cdots + A_N e^{p_N nT} u_a(nT) \tag{3.11}$$

$$H(z) = Z[h(n)]$$

$$= A_1 \frac{1}{1-e^{p_1 T} z^{-1}} + A_2 \frac{1}{1-e^{p_2 T} z^{-1}} + \cdots + A_N \frac{1}{1-e^{p_N T} z^{-2}}$$

$$= \sum_{i=1}^{N} \frac{A_i}{1-e^{p_i T} z^{-1}} \tag{3.12}$$

Therefore, by impulse invariant transformation

$$\boxed{\frac{1}{s-p_i} \xrightarrow[\text{is transformed to}]{} \frac{1}{1-e^{p_i T} z^{-1}}} \tag{3.13}$$

3.5.1 Relation between Analog and Digital Filter Poles

Let the analog poles be at $s = p_i$ where $i = 1, 2, \ldots, N$. The digital poles are given by roots of term $(1 - e^{p_i T} z^{-1})$, *i.e.*,

$$z = e^{p_i T}, \qquad i = 1, 2, \ldots, N \tag{3.14}$$

Any point in the s-plane, can be expressed as

$$s = \sigma_1 + j\Omega_1 \tag{3.15}$$

$$z = e^{p_i T}$$

$$z = e^{sT}$$

i.e., analog pole at $s = p_i$ is transformed to digital pole at $z = e^{p_i t}$

$$z = e^{(\sigma_1 + j\Omega_1)T}$$

$$z = e^{\sigma_1 T} \cdot e^{j\Omega_1 T}$$

$$|z|\angle z = e^{\sigma_1 T} \cdot e^{j\Omega_1 T}$$

$$|z| = e^{\sigma_1 T} \quad \text{and} \quad \angle z = \Omega_1 T \tag{3.16}$$

(*i*) If $\sigma_1 < 0$, then the analog pole s lies on left half of s-plane. In this case, $|z| < 1$, and hence the corresponding digital pole z will lie inside the unit circle in the z-plane.

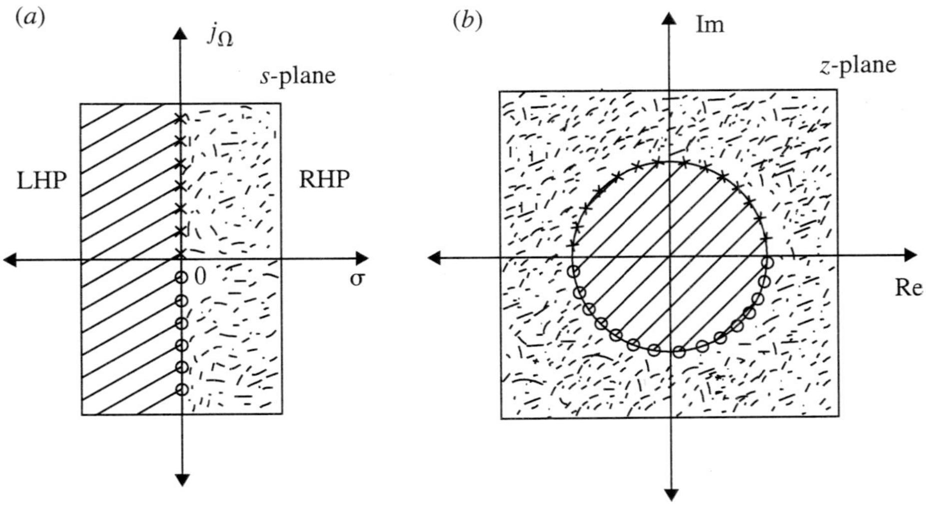

Figure 3.3 s-plane to z-plane mapping.

(*ii*) If $\sigma_1 = 0$, then the analog pole s lies on imaginary axis of s-plane. Therefore, $|z| = 1$, and hence the corresponding digital pole z will lie on the unit circle in the z-plane.

(*iii*) If $\sigma_1 > 0$, then the analog pole s lies on right half of s-plane. In this case, $|z| = 1$, and hence the corresponding digital pole z will lie outside the unit circle in z-plane as shown in Figure 3.3.

The stability of a filter is related to the location of the poles. For a stable analog filter the poles should lie on the left half of the s-plane. Since the left half of s-plane maps inside the unit circle in z-plane we can say that, for a stable digital filter the poles should lie inside the unit circle in z-plane.

3.5.2 Relation between Analog and Digital Frequency

Let Ω be the analog frequency in rad/sec., and ω is digital frequency in rad/sec.

$$z = re^{j\omega}$$

$$s = \sigma + j\Omega \tag{3.17}$$

By impulse invariant transformation, the following equations are written

$$z = e^{sT}$$

$$re^{j\omega} = e^{(\sigma + j\Omega)T}$$

$$re^{j\omega} = e^{\sigma T} \cdot e^{j\Omega T}$$

$$\boxed{\omega = \Omega T \quad \text{or} \quad \Omega = \frac{\omega}{T}} \tag{3.18}$$

The mapping of analog to digital frequency is not one to one. Since ω is unique over the range $(-\pi, \pi)$, *i.e.*, $\omega = \Omega T$ implies that the interval $-\pi/T \leq \Omega \leq (\pi/T)$ maps into the corresponding values of $-\pi \leq \omega \leq \pi$. This reflects the effects of aliasing in sampling.

The following impulse invariant transformations from s-plane to z-plane are used for different pole locations:

1. For distinct poles

$$\frac{1}{s - p_i} \longrightarrow \frac{1}{1 - e^{p_i T} z^{-1}} \tag{3.19}$$

2. For multiples poles

$$\frac{1}{(s + p_i)^m} \longrightarrow \frac{(-1)^{m-1}}{(m-1)!} \frac{d^{m-1}}{dp_i^{m-1}} \left(\frac{1}{1 - e^{-p_i T} z^{-1}} \right) \tag{3.20}$$

3. For complex poles

$$\frac{s + a}{(s + a)^2 + b^2} \longrightarrow \frac{1 - e^{-aT} (\cos bT) z^{-1}}{1 - 2e^{-aT} (\cos bT) z^{-1} + e^{-2aT} z^{-2}} \tag{3.21}$$

$$\frac{b}{(s + a)^2 + b^2} \longrightarrow \frac{1 - e^{-aT} (\sin bT) z^{-1}}{1 - 2e^{-aT} (\cos bT) z^{-1} + e^{-2aT} z^{-2}} \tag{3.22}$$

3.6 Bilinear Transformation Method

IIR filter design by means of impulse invariance method has a serve limitation in that it can be applied only for lowpass filters and a few limited bandpass filters. This serious limitation is overcome by bilinear transformation which is described below.

The bilinear transformation is a conformal mapping that transforms the imaginary axis of s-plane into the unit circle in the z-plane only once, thus avoiding aliasing of frequency components. In this mapping all points in the left half of s-plane are mapped inside the unit circle in the z-plane and all points in the right half of s-plane are mapped outside the unit circle in the z-plane.

Consider an analog filter with the following system function

$$H_a(s) = \frac{Y(s)}{X(s)} = \frac{b}{(s + a)} \tag{3.23}$$

Equation (3.23) is written in differential equation form as

$$\frac{dy(t)}{dt} + ay(t) = bx(t) \tag{3.24}$$

$y(t)$ can be expressed in terms of its derivative $y'(t)$ with the initial condition $y(t_0)$ as given below.

$$y(t) = \int_{t_0}^{t} y'(\tau)d\tau + y(t_0). \tag{3.25}$$

By using the trapezoidal formula at $t = nT$ and $t_0 = nT - T$, the above integral is approximated as

$$y(nT) = \frac{T}{2}[y'(nT) + y'(nT - T)] + y(nT - T) \tag{3.26}$$

Now equation (3.24) is written as follows.

$$y'(nT) = -ay(nT) + bx(nT) \tag{3.27}$$

Substituting equation (3.26) in equation (3.27), the following difference equation for the discrete system is obtained.

$$\left(1 + \frac{aT}{2}\right)y(n) - \left(1 - \frac{aT}{2}\right)y(n-1) = \frac{bT}{2}[x(n) + x(n-1)] \tag{3.28}$$

Taking z-transform on both sides of the above equation we get,

$$\left(1 + \frac{aT}{2}\right)Y(z) - \left(1 - \frac{aT}{2}\right)z^{-1}Y(z) = \frac{bT}{2}[1 + z^{-1}]X(z) \tag{3.29}$$

Rearranging the terms, the discrete system function is written as follows.

$$H(z) = \frac{Y(z)}{X(z)} = \frac{\left(\frac{bT}{2}\right)(1 + z^{-1})}{\left(1 + \frac{aT}{2}\right) - \left(1 - \frac{aT}{2}\right)z^{-1}}$$

$$= \frac{b}{\left[\frac{2}{T}\left(\frac{1 - z^{-1}}{1 + z^{-1}}\right) + a\right]} \tag{3.30}$$

Comparing equation (3.23) with equation (3.30), the following relationship becomes valid while mapping from s-plane to z-plane.

$$\boxed{s = \frac{2}{T}\left(\frac{1 - z^{-1}}{1 + z^{-1}}\right)} \tag{3.31}$$

Equation (3.31) is called the bilinear transformation. This holds good for any N^{th} order system. The following examples illustrate the method of transforming $H_a(s)$ to digital system function $H(z)$.

Example 3.1

All pole analog filters have transfer function

$$H(s) = \frac{1}{(s^2 + 5s + 6)}$$

Find $H(z)$ by impulse invariant technique. Assume $T = 1$ sec.

(Anna university, April, 2005)

Solution

$$(s^2 + 5s + 6) = (s + 2)(s + 3)$$

$$H(s) = \frac{1}{(s + 2)(s + 3)}$$

$$= \frac{A}{(s + 2)} + \frac{B}{(s + 3)}$$

$$H(s) = \frac{1}{(s + 2)} - \frac{1}{(s + 3)}$$

By applying impulse invariant transformation we get

$$H(z) = \frac{1}{(1 - e^{-2T}z^{-1})} - \frac{1}{(1 - e^{-3T}z^{-1})}$$

Substituting $T = 1$, we get

$$H(z) = \frac{1}{(1 - 0.135z^{-1})} - \frac{1}{(1 - 0.05z^{-1})}$$

$$\boxed{H(z) = \frac{0.085z^{-1}}{(1 - 0.135z^{-1})(1 - 0.05z^{-1})}}$$

Example 3.2

Design a digital filter using

$$H(s) = \frac{1}{s^2 + 9s + 18}$$

with $T = 0.2$ sec.

(Anna University, May, 2007)

Solution

$$(s^2 + 9s + 18) = (s+3)(s+6)$$

$$H(s) = \frac{1}{(s+3)(s+6)}$$

$$= \frac{1}{3}\left[\frac{1}{s+3} - \frac{1}{s+6}\right]$$

$$H(z) = \frac{1}{3}\left[\frac{1}{(1-e^{-3T}z^{-1})} - \frac{1}{(1-e^{-6T}z^{-1})}\right]$$

Substituting $T = 0.2$ sec. we get

$$H(z) = \frac{1}{3}\left[\frac{1}{(1-0.55z^{-1})} - \frac{1}{(1-0.3z^{-1})}\right]$$

$$\boxed{H(z) = \frac{0.083z^{-1}}{(1-0.55z^{-1})(1-0.3z^{-1})}}$$

Example 3.3

Consider the following TF of an analog filter

$$H(s) = \frac{(s+1)}{(s+1)^2 + 1}$$

Convert the analog filter into a digital IIR filter by impulse invariance method for $T = 1$.

Solution **Method 1**

$$H(s) = \frac{(s+1)}{(s+1)^2 + 1}$$

$$= \frac{(s+1)}{s^2 + 2s + 2}$$

$$= \frac{(s+1)}{(s+1+j)(s+1-j)}$$

$$= \frac{A_1}{(s+1+j)} + \frac{A_1^*}{(s+1-j)}$$

$$A_1 = \left.\frac{A(s+1)}{(s+1+j)}\right|_{s=-1+j} = \frac{1}{2}$$

$$A_1^* = \frac{1}{2}$$

By impulse invariant transformation the TF of digital IIR filter is obtained as follows:

$$H(z) = \frac{1}{2}\left[\frac{1}{1 - e^{-(1+j)T}z^{-1}}\right] + \frac{1}{2}\left[\frac{1}{1 - e^{(-1+j)T}z^{-1}}\right]$$

Substituting $T = 1$, we get

$$\begin{aligned} H(z) &= \frac{1}{2}\left[\frac{1}{1 - 0.3678e^{-j}z^{-1}}\right] + \frac{1}{2}\left[\frac{1}{1 - 0.3678e^{j}z^{-1}}\right] \\ &= \frac{1 - 0.3678e^{j}z^{-1} + 1 - 0.3678e^{-j}z^{-1}}{2(1 - 0.3678e^{-j}z^{-1})(1 - 0.3678e^{j}z^{-1})} \\ &= \frac{1 - 0.3678\cos 1z^{-1}}{1 - 0.3678z^{-1}(e^{j} + e^{-j}) + 0.1353z^{-2}} \end{aligned}$$

$$\boxed{H(z) = \frac{(1 - 0.2z^{-1})}{(1 - 0.4z^{-1} + 0.1353z^{-2})}}$$

Method 2: Using Equation (3.21), we get

$$\frac{(s+a)}{(s+a)^2 + b^2} = \frac{1 - e^{-aT}\cos bTz^{-1}}{1 - 2e^{-aT}\cos bTz^{-1} + 2e^{-2aT}z^{-2}}.$$

Here, $a = 1$; $b = 1$; $T = 1$.

$$\boxed{H(z) = \frac{(1 - 0.2z^{-1})}{(1 - 0.4z^{-1} + 0.1353z^{-2})}}$$

Example 3.4

Using impulse invariant method find $H(z)$ at $T = 1$ sec.

$$H(z) = \frac{2}{(s^2 + 8s + 15)}$$

(Anna University, December, 2003)

Solution

$$\begin{aligned} (s^2 + 8s + 15) &= (s+3)(s+5) \\ H(s) &= \frac{2}{(s+3)(s+5)} \\ &= \frac{1}{s+3} - \frac{1}{s+5} \end{aligned}$$

$$H(z) = \frac{1}{(1 - e^{-3T}z^{-1})} - \frac{1}{(1 - e^{-5T}z^{-1})}$$

$$= \frac{1}{(1 - 0.05z^{-1})} - \frac{1}{(1 - 6.73 \times 10^{-3}z^{-1})}$$

$$\boxed{H(z) = \frac{0.04326z^{-1}}{(1 - 0.05z^{-1})(1 - 6.73 \times 10^{-3}z^{-1})}}$$

Hence, in the s-domain transfer function, if s is substituted by the term $\frac{2}{T}\frac{1-z^{-1}}{1+z^{-1}}$, then the resulting transfer function will be z-domain transfer function.

3.6.1 Relation between Analog and Digital Filter Poles

The mapping of s-domain function to z-domain function by bilinear transformation is a one to one mapping *i.e.*, for every point in s-plane, there is exactly a corresponding point in z-plane and *vice versa*.

$$s = \frac{2}{T}\frac{1 - z^{-1}}{1 + z^{-1}} \tag{3.32}$$

$$\frac{Ts}{2} = \frac{1 - \frac{1}{z}}{1 + \frac{1}{z}}$$

$$\frac{Ts}{2} = \frac{z - 1}{z + 1}$$

$$\frac{Ts}{2}(z + 1) = z - 1$$

$$\frac{Ts}{2}z - z = -1 - \frac{Ts}{2}$$

$$-z\left(1 - \frac{Ts}{2}\right) = -\left(1 + \frac{Ts}{2}\right)$$

$$\boxed{z = \frac{1 + \frac{Ts}{2}}{1 - \frac{Ts}{2}}} \tag{3.33}$$

Let $s = \sigma_1 + j\Omega_1$

$$z = \frac{1 + \frac{T}{2}(\sigma_1 + j\Omega_1)}{1 - \frac{T}{2}(\sigma_1 + j\Omega_1)} = \frac{\left(1 + \frac{T}{2}\sigma_1\right) + j\frac{T}{2}\Omega_1}{\left(1 - \frac{T}{2}\sigma_1\right) + j\frac{T}{2}\Omega_1} \tag{3.34}$$

$$|z| = \sqrt{\frac{\left(1 + \frac{T}{2}\sigma_1\right)^2 + \left(\frac{T}{2}\Omega_1\right)^2}{\left(1 - \frac{T}{2}\sigma_1\right)^2 + \left(\frac{T}{2}\Omega_1\right)^2}} \tag{3.35}$$

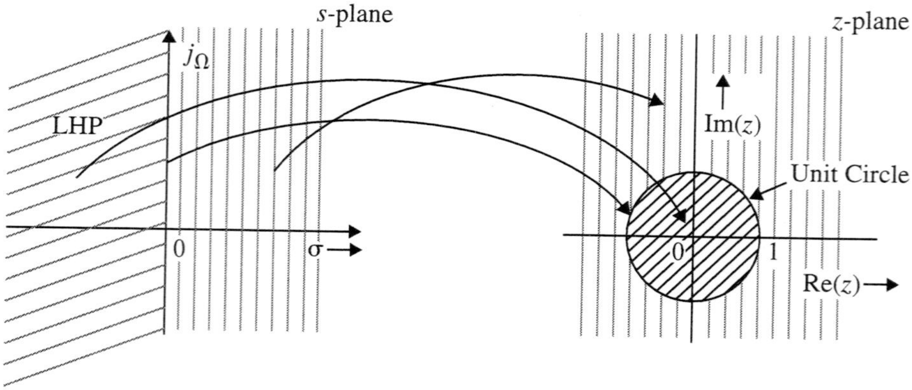

Figure 3.4 Mapping of s-plane into z-plane in Bilinear transformation.

1. If $\sigma_1 < 0$ (*i.e.*, σ_1 is negative), then the point $s = \sigma_1 + j\Omega_1$, lies on the left half of s-plane. In this case, $|z| < 1$, and hence the corresponding point in z-plane will lie inside the unit circle in z-plane.
2. If $\sigma_1 = 0$ (*i.e.*, real part is zero), then the point $s = \sigma_1 + j\Omega_1$, lies on the imaginary axis in the s-plane. In this case, $|z| = 1$, and hence the corresponding point in z-plane will lie on the unit circle in z-plane.
3. If $\sigma_1 > 0$ (*i.e.*, σ_1 is positive), then the point $s = \sigma_1 + j\Omega_1$, lies on the right half of s-plane. In this case, $|z| > 1$, and hence the corresponding point in z-plane will lie outside the unit circle in z-plane.

The above three transformations are represented in Figure 3.4.

3.6.2 Relation between Analog and Digital Frequency

Let $s = j\Omega$ be points on imaginary axis and the corresponding points on the z-plane on unit circle are given by $z = e^{j\omega}$ where Ω is the analog frequency and ω is the digital frequency. Using bilinear transformation

$$s = \frac{2}{T}\frac{1 - z^{-1}}{1 + z^{-1}}$$

and substituting $s = j\Omega$ and $z = e^{j\omega}$, we get

$$j\Omega = \frac{2}{T}\frac{1 - e^{-j\omega}}{1 + e^{-j\omega}} = \frac{2}{T}\left[\frac{e^{(j\omega)/2} \cdot e^{-(j\omega)/2} - e^{-j\omega}}{e^{(j\omega)/2} \cdot e^{-(j\omega)/2} + e^{-j\omega}}\right]$$

$$= \frac{2}{T}\frac{e^{-(j\omega)/2}(e^{(j\omega)/2} - e^{-(j\omega)/2})}{e^{-(j\omega)/2}(e^{(j\omega)/2} + e^{-(j\omega)/2})}$$

$$= \frac{2}{T}\frac{(e^{(j\omega)/2} - e^{-(j\omega)/2})/2}{(e^{(j\omega)/2} + e^{-(j\omega)/2})/2}$$

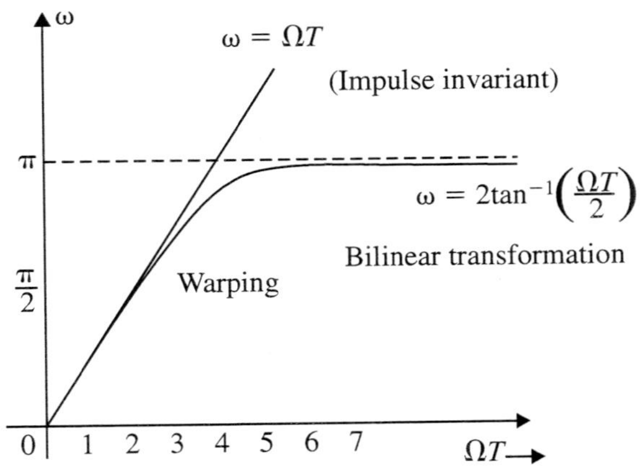

Figure 3.5 Correspondence between analog and digital frequencies.

$$\Omega = \frac{2}{T}\frac{(e^{(j\omega)/2} - e^{-(j\omega)/2})/2j}{\cos(\omega/2)}$$

$$= \frac{2}{T}\frac{\sin(\omega/2)}{\cos(\omega/2)} = \frac{2}{T}\tan\frac{\omega}{2}$$

Analog frequency

$$\boxed{\Omega = \frac{2}{T}\tan\frac{\omega}{2}} \tag{3.36}$$

Digital frequency

$$\boxed{\omega = 2\tan^{-1}\frac{\Omega T}{2}} \tag{3.37}$$

The analog frequency Ω and digital frequency ω have a non-linear relationship and is shown is Figure 3.5 because the entire negative imaginary axis in the s-plane ($\Omega = -\infty$ to 0) is mapped into the lower half of unit circle in z-plane ($\omega = -\pi$ to 0) and the entire positive imaginary axis in the s-plane ($\Omega = 0$ to ∞) is mapped into upper half of unit circle in z-plane ($\omega = 0$ to π). This non-linear mapping introduces a distortion in the frequency axis which is called frequency warping.

3.6.3 Effect of Warping on the Magnitude Response

Consider an analog filter with a number of passbands. The corresponding digital filter will have same number of passbands, but with disproportionate bandwidth as shown in Figure 3.6. The passband in the analog filter are of constant width with regular intervals. However, the passbands for the digital equivalent is somewhat pushed together.

The effect of warping on amplitude responses can be eliminated by pre-warping the analog filter. In this method, the specified digital frequencies are converted to analog equivalent ($\Omega = \frac{2}{T}\tan(\omega/2)$). These analog frequencies are called

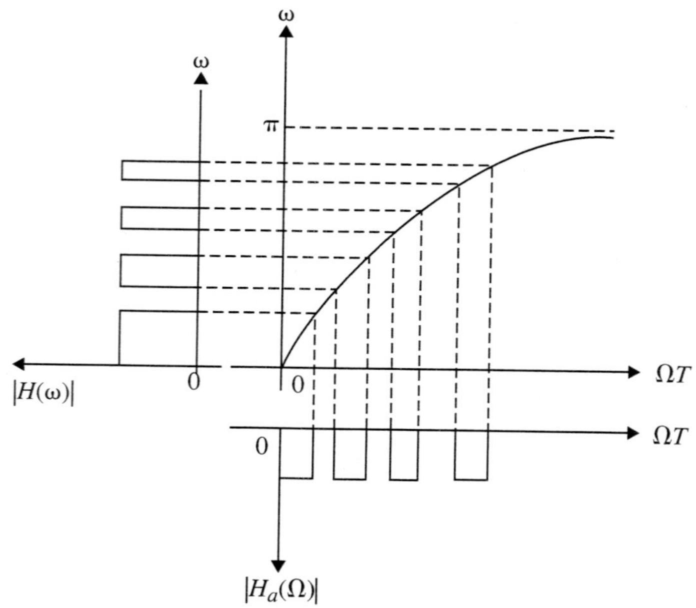

Figure 3.6 Effect of warping on the magnitude response. (Equally spaced analog passbands are pushed together at high frequency in the digital domain.)

pre-warps frequencies. Using the pre-warp frequencies, the analog filter transfer function is designed and then it is transformed to digital filter transfer function.

3.6.4 Effect of Warping on the Phase Response

Consider an analog filter with linear phase. The phase response of corresponding digital filter will be non-linear as shown in Figure 3.7.

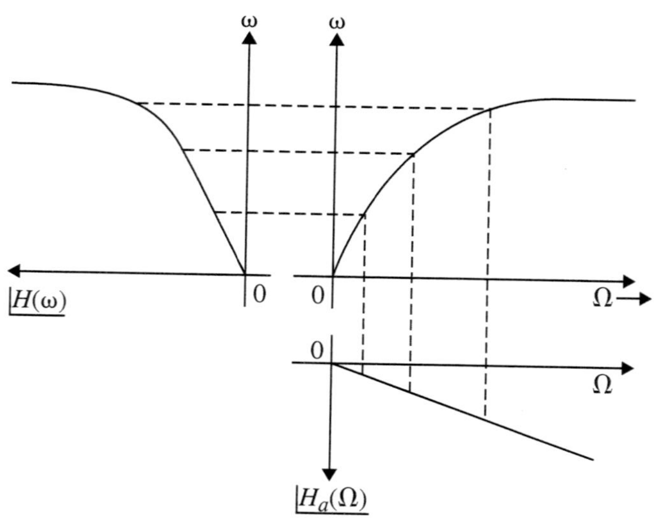

Figure 3.7 Effect of warping on the phase response.

From the above, it can be state that, the bilinear transformation preserves the magnitude response of an analog filter only if the specification requires piecewise constant magnitude, but the phase response of the analog filter is not preserved. Therefore, the bilinear transformation can be used only to design digital filters with prescribed magnitude response with piecewise constant values. A linear phase analog filter cannot be transformed to a linear phase digital filter using bilinear transformation.

Example 3.5

Convert the analog filter with system transfer function

$$H_a(s) = \frac{2}{(s+1)(s+2)}$$

into a digital IIR filter by impulse invariance method, when (*i*) $T = 1$ sec. and (*ii*) $T = 0.1$ sec.

(Anna University, December, 2004)

Solution Given

$$H_a(s) = \frac{2}{(s+1)(s+2)} = \frac{A}{s+1} + \frac{B}{s+2}$$

$$A = \left.\frac{2}{s+2}\right|_{s=-1} = 2$$

$$B = \left.\frac{2}{s+1}\right|_{s=-2} = -2$$

$$H_a(s) = \frac{2}{(s+1)} - \frac{2}{(s+2)} = \frac{2}{s-(-1)} - \frac{2}{s-(-2)}$$

By impulse invariant transformation, we know that

$$\frac{A_p}{s-p_i} \xrightarrow{\text{transformed to}} \frac{A_i}{1-e^{p_iT}z^{-1}}$$

$$H(z) = \frac{2}{1-e^{p_1T}z^{-1}} - \frac{2}{1-e^{p_2T}z^{-1}} \qquad (\text{where } p_1 = -1, p_2 = -2)$$

$$H(z) = \frac{2}{1-e^{-T}z^{-1}} - \frac{2}{1-e^{-2T}z^{-1}}$$

(*i*) When $T = 1$ sec.

$$H(z) = \frac{2}{1-e^{-1}z^{-1}} - \frac{2}{1-e^{-2}z^{-1}}$$

$$= \frac{2}{1-0.3678z^{-1}} - \frac{2}{1-0.1353z^{-1}}$$

$$\boxed{H(z) = \frac{0.465z^{-1}}{(1-0.3678z^{-1})(1-0.1353z^{-1})}}$$

(*ii*) When $T = 0.1$ sec.

$$H(z) = \frac{2}{1-e^{-0.1}z^{-1}} - \frac{2}{1-e^{-0.2}z^{-1}}$$

$$= \frac{2}{1-0.9048z^{-1}} - \frac{2}{1-0.8187z^{-1}}$$

$$\boxed{H(z) = \frac{0.1722z^{-1}}{(1-0.9048z^{-1})(1-0.8187z^{-1})}}$$

Example 3.6

Convert the analog filter with system transfer function

$$H_a(s) = \frac{(s+0.1)}{(s+0.1)^2+9}$$

into a digital IIR filter by using the impulse invariant method, when $T = 1$ sec.

(*Anna University, May, 2006*)

Solution Given

$$H(s) = \frac{(s+0.1)}{(s+0.1)^2+9}$$

$$= \frac{s+0.1}{s^2+0.2s+9.01}$$

$$= \frac{s+0.1}{[s-(-0.1+j3)][s-(-0.1-j3)]}$$

$$= \frac{A_1}{s-(-0.1+j3)} + \frac{A_1^*}{s-(-0.1-j3)}$$

$$A_1 = \left.\frac{s+0.1}{s-(-0.1-j3)}\right|_{s=-0.1+j3} = \frac{1}{2}$$

$$A_1^* = \frac{1}{2}$$

$$H(s) = \frac{1/2}{s-(-0.1+j3)} + \frac{1/2}{s-(-0.1-j3)}$$

By impulse invariant transformation we get,

$$
\begin{aligned}
H(z) &= \frac{1/2}{1-e^{(-0.1+j3)T}z^{-1}} + \frac{1/2}{1-e^{(-0.1-j3)T}z^{-1}} \\
&= \frac{0.5-0.5e^{-0.1T}e^{-j3T}z^{-1}+0.5-0.5e^{-0.1T}e^{j3T}z^{-1}}{(1-e^{(-0.1+j3)T}z^{-1})(1-e^{(-0.1-j3)T}z^{-1})} \\
&= \frac{1-0.5e^{-0.1T}z^{-1}(e^{j3T}+e^{-j3T})}{1-e^{-0.1T}-e^{-j3T}z^{-1}e^{-0.1T}e^{j3T}z^{-1}+e^{-0.1T}e^{j3T}e^{-0.1T}e^{-j3T}z^{-2}} \\
&= \frac{1-0.5e^{-0.1T}z^{-1}2\cos 3T}{1-e^{-0.1T}z^{-1}(e^{j3T}+e^{-j3T})+e^{-0.2T}z^{-2}} \\
&= \frac{1-\cos(3T)e^{-0.1T}z^{-1}}{1-2\cos(3T)e^{-0.1T}z^{-1}+e^{-0.2T}z^{-2}}
\end{aligned}
$$

For $T = 1$ sec.

$$H(z) = \frac{1-\cos(3)e^{-0.1}z^{-1}}{1-2\cos(z)e^{-0.1}z^{-1}+e^{-0.2}z^{-2}}$$

where 3 is in radian

$$\boxed{H(z) = \frac{1+0.8959z^{-1}}{1+1.7915z^{-1}+0.8187z^{-2}}}$$

Example 3.7

Apply the bilinear transformation to

$$H_a(s) = \frac{2}{(s+1)(s+2)}$$

with $T = 1$ sec. and find $H(z)$.

Solution Given

$$H_a(s) = \frac{2}{(s+1)(s+2)}$$

put $s = \frac{2}{T}\frac{1-z^{-1}}{1+z^{-1}}$ in $H_a(s)$ to get $H(z)$

$$
\begin{aligned}
H(z) &= \frac{2}{\left(\frac{2}{T}\frac{1-z^{-1}}{1+z^{-1}}+1\right)\left(\frac{2}{T}\frac{1-z^{-1}}{1+z^{-1}}+2\right)} \\
&= \frac{2}{\left(\frac{2-2z^{-1}+1+z^{-1}}{1+z^{-1}}\right)\left(\frac{2-2z^{-1}+2+2z^{-1}}{1+z^{-1}}\right)}
\end{aligned}
$$

$$H(z) = \frac{2(1+z^{-1})^2}{(3-z^{-1})4}$$

$$= \frac{0.5(1+z^{-1})^2}{3-z^{-1}}$$

$$\boxed{H(z) = \frac{-0.5(z^{-1}+1)^2}{(z^{-1}-3)}}$$

Example 3.8

The normalized transfer function of an analog filter is given by

$$Ha(s_n) = \frac{1}{s_n^2 + 1.414s_n + 1}$$

convert the analog filter to a digital filter with a cut off frequency of 0.4π, using bilinear transformation.

(Anna University, April, 2006)

Solution To preserve the magnitude response the pre-warping of analog filter has to be performed. For this analog cut-off frequency is determined. The analog transfer function is un-normalized by replacing $s_n = s/\Omega_c$ using this analog cut-off frequency. Then the analog transfer function is converted to digital filter transfer function using bilinear transformation.

Given $\omega_c = 0.4\pi$ rad/sec. Let $T = 1$ sec.

$$\Omega_c = \frac{2}{T}\tan\left(\frac{0.4\pi}{2}\right)$$

$$= 2\tan\left(\frac{0.4\pi}{2}\right) = 1.453 \text{ rad/sec.}$$

Normalized analog transfer function is,

$$H_a(s_n) = \frac{1}{s_n^2 + 1.414s_n + 1}$$

The analog transfer function is un-normalized by replacing s_n by s/Ω_c

$$H_a(s) = \frac{1}{\left(\frac{s}{\Omega_c}\right)^2 + 1.414\left(\frac{s}{\Omega_c}\right) + 1}$$

$$= \frac{\Omega_c^2}{s^2 + 1.414\Omega_c s + \Omega_c^2}$$

$$= \frac{2.11}{s^2 + 2.05s + 2.11}$$

$$H(z) = H_a(s)\Big|_{s=\frac{2}{T}\frac{1-z^{-1}}{1+z^{-1}}}$$

$$= \frac{2.11}{\left[\frac{2(1-z^{-1})}{1+z^{-1}}\right]^2 + 2.05\left[\frac{2(1-z^{-1})}{1+z^{-1}}\right] + 2.11}$$

$$= \frac{2.11(1+z^{-1})^2}{4(1-z^{-1})^2 + 4.1(1-z^{-1})(1+z^{-1}) + 2.11(1+z^{-1})^2}$$

$$H(z) = \frac{2.11(1+2z^{-1}+z^{-2})}{10.21 - 3.78z^{-1} + 2.01z^{-2}}$$

$$= \frac{2.11(1+2z^{-1}+z^{-2})}{10.21(1-0.37z^{-1}+0.197z^{-2})}$$

$$\boxed{H(z) = \frac{0.207(1+2z^{-1}+z^{-2})}{1-0.37z^{-1}+0.197z^{-2}}}$$

3.7 Specifications of the Lowpass Filter

Let ω_p be passband digital frequency in rad/sec. and ω_s be the stopband digital frequency in rad/sec. Let

$$A_p = |H(\omega)|_{\omega=\omega_p} \quad \text{and} \quad A_s = |H(\omega)|_{\omega=\omega_s} \tag{3.38}$$

where A_p is the gain at the passband frequency and A_s is the gain at the stopband frequency. Let

$$\alpha_1 = \frac{1}{A_p} \quad \text{and} \quad \alpha_2 = \frac{1}{A_s} \tag{3.39}$$

where α_1 is attenuation at the passband frequency and α_2 is attenuation at the stopband frequency.

The maximum values of normalized gain is unity and so A_p, A_s are less than 1 and α_1, α_2 are greater than 1. The magnitude response of lowpass filter in terms of gain and attenuation are shown in Figure 3.8.

The magnitude response in dB, is shown in Figure 3.9. Let k_1 be gain in dB at passband frequency and k_2 the gain in dB at stopband frequency.

$$k_1 = 20\log A_p \quad \text{and} \quad k_2 = 20\log A_s \tag{3.40}$$

$$A_p = 10^{k_1/20} \quad \text{and} \quad A_s = 10^{k_2/20} \tag{3.41}$$

Let α_1 be attenuation in dB at ω_1, α_2 be attenuation in dB at ω_2

$$\alpha_p = 20\log\left(\frac{1}{A_p}\right) \quad \text{and} \quad \alpha_s = 20\log\left(\frac{1}{A_s}\right)$$

$$\alpha_p = -20\log A_p \quad \text{and} \quad \alpha_s = -20\log A_s \tag{3.42}$$

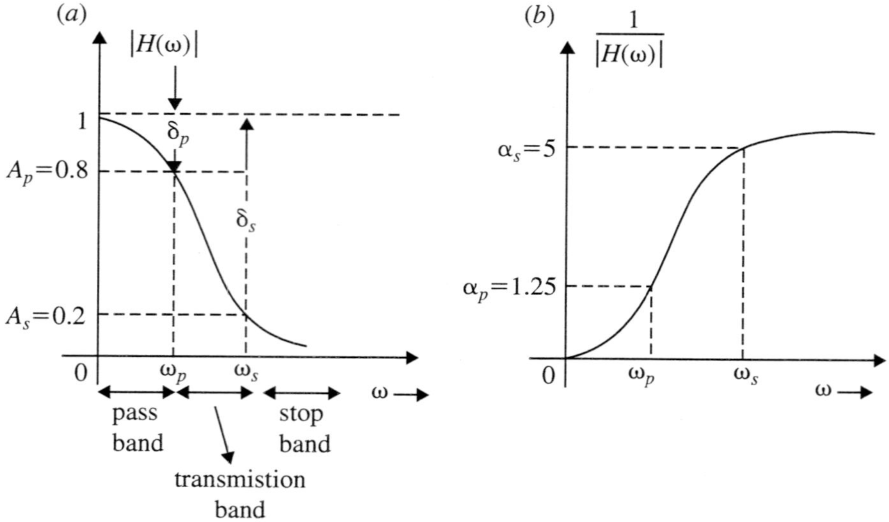

Figure 3.8 Gain $V_s\omega$ and attenuation $V_s\omega$.

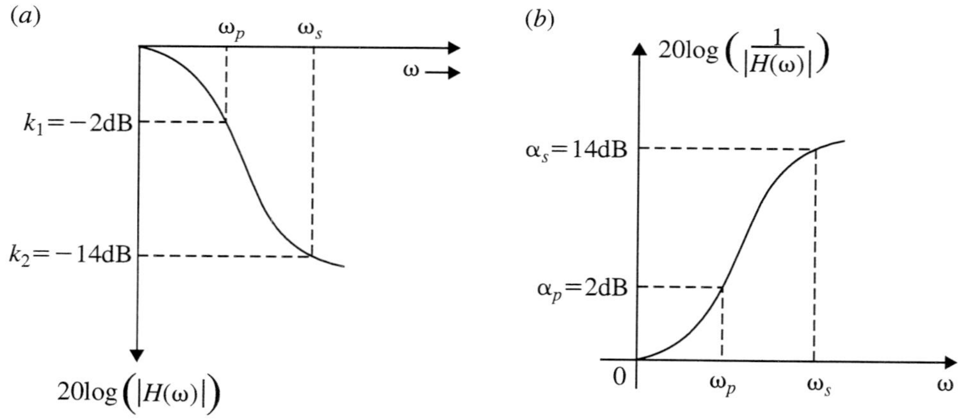

Figure 3.9 Gain and attenuation $V_s\omega$ in dB.

Sometimes the specifications are given in terms of passband ripple δ_p and stopband ripple δ_s. In this case dB gain and attenuation can be estimated as

$$k_1 = 20\log(1-\delta_p) \quad \text{and} \quad \alpha_p = -20\log(1-\delta_p)$$
$$k_2 = 20\log\delta_s \quad \text{and} \quad \alpha_s = -20\log\delta_s \tag{3.43}$$

3.8 Design of Lowpass Digital Butterworth Filter

On many practical applications, realization of $H(z)$ from analog transfer function $H(z)$ may not be available and it has to be determined from the specifications of

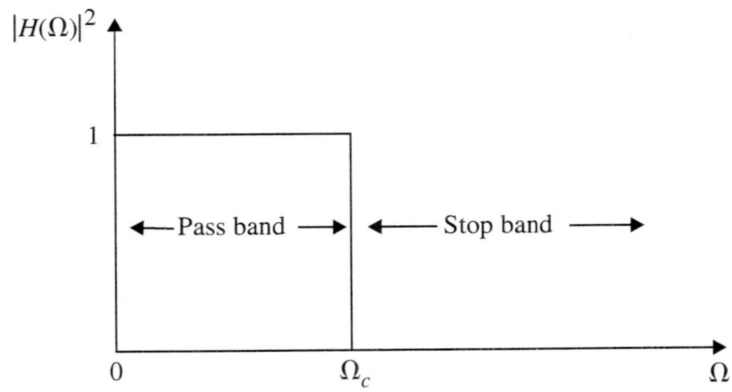

Figure 3.10 Magnitude square frequency response of an ideal lowpass filter.

the desired digital filters. Normally the cut off frequency Ω_c, of the filter, the passband attenuation and stopband attenuation are given. The system function $H(s)$ is obtained to satisfy the above specifications. For realization the filter response characteristics have to be approximated. There are several approximation techniques available for the filter design. The most widely used approximation techniques are:

1. Butterworth filter.
2. Chebyshev filter.
3. Approximation of derivatives.

The analog filter transfer function $H(s)$ obtained using any of these methods is converted to digital filter transfer function by using either impulse invariant transformation or bilinear transformation described earlier. The characteristics of Butterworth and Chebyshev filters are ideally suited to design lowpass filter. The design procedure for Butterworth filter is described below.

Let us consider the squared magnitude response of an ideal lowpass filter shown in Figure 3.10. Ω_c is the cut off frequency of the filter. This ideal lowpass filter characteristics is however not physically realizable.

3.8.1 Analog Butterworth Filter

The analog butterworth filter is designed by approximating the ideal frequency response using an error function. The error function is selected such that magnitude is maximally flat in the passband and monotonically decreasing in the stopband.

The magnitude response of lowpass filter obtained by the approximation is given by

$$|H_a(\Omega)|^2 = \frac{1}{1 + \left(\frac{\Omega}{\Omega_c}\right)^{2N}} \tag{3.44}$$

We know that $s = j\Omega$. Substituting Ω by s/j in equation (3.44)

$$H_a(s)H_a(-s) = \frac{1}{1+\left(\frac{s/j}{\Omega_c}\right)^{2N}} = \frac{1}{1+\left(-\frac{s^2}{\Omega_c^2}\right)^{N}} \tag{3.45}$$

Let $s/\Omega_c = s_n$ is the normalized function. Therefore, the normalized transfer function is

$$H_a(s_n)H_a(-s_n) = \frac{1}{1+\left(-s_n^2\right)^N} \tag{3.46}$$

The normalized transfer function has $2N$ poles. For a stable and causal filter, the poles should lie on the left half of s-plane. when N is even, all poles are complex and exit as conjugate pair. When N is odd, one of the poles is real and all other poles are complex and exit as conjugate pair.

From equation (3.46), it is possible to locate the poles of the analog filter in the s-plane. For odd number of N,

$$1 + (-s^2)^N = 0$$
$$s^{2N} = 1$$

For $N = 1$,

$$s^2 = 1$$
$$s_1 = 1$$
$$s_2 = -1$$

The poles are located as shown in Figure 3.11.

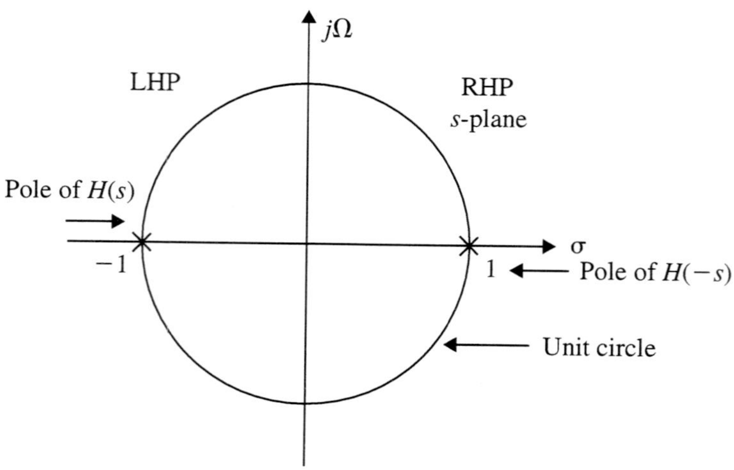

Figure 3.11 Pole location of first order filter.

For a stable filter, only LHP poles along are taken and the denominator of the TF is written as

$$\boxed{H(s) = \frac{1}{(s+1)}}$$

For $N = 3$,

$$s^6 = 1$$

The magnitude of the six poles are 1 and their phase angle is given as

$$\phi_k = \frac{(2k)\pi}{2N}, \quad k = 0, 1, 2, 3, 4, 5$$

Thus,

$$s_1 = 1\angle 0°;\ s_2 = 1\angle 60°;\ s_3 = 1\angle 120°;\ s_4 = 1\angle 180°;\ s_5 = 1\angle 240°;\ s_6 = 1\angle 300°$$

The pole locations are shown in Figure 3.12.

Considering only LHP poles, the LF of the filter is obtained as

$$H(s) = \frac{1}{(s+1)(s+0.5+j0.866)(s+5-j0.866)}$$

$$\boxed{H(s) = \frac{1}{(s+1)(s^2+s+1)}}$$

Now let us consider N being even. The following numerator polynomial for $H(s)$ is written.

$$\begin{aligned} 1 + (-s^2)^N &= 0 \\ s^{2N} &= 1 \\ s_k &= 1\angle(2k+1)\pi/2N; \quad k = 0, 1, \ldots, 2N \end{aligned}$$

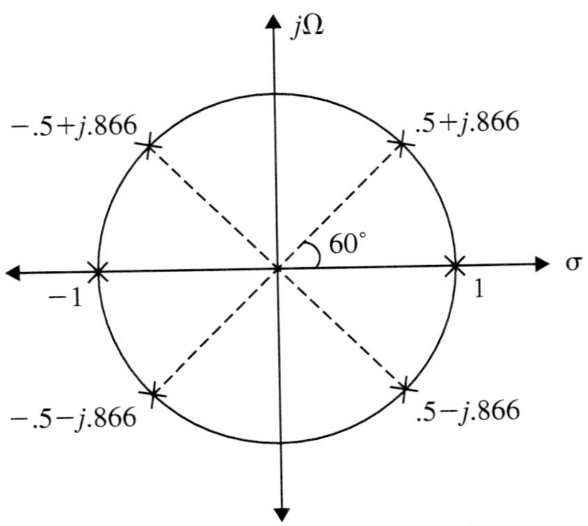

Figure 3.12 Pole location of third order filter.

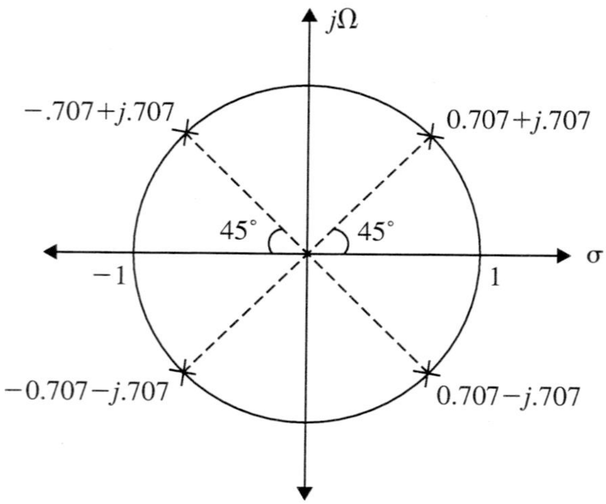

Figure 3.13 Pole location of a second order filter.

For a second order filter $N = 2$. The poles of $H(s)$ are located as follows:

$$s_1 = 1\angle 45°; \quad s_2 = 1\angle 135°; \quad s_3 = 1\angle 225°; \quad s_4 = 1\angle 315°;$$

The pole locations are shown in Figure 3.13.

Considering only the LHP poles, the TF of the filter is obtained as given below

$$H(s) = \frac{1}{(s + 0.707 + j0.707)(s + 0.707 - j.707)}$$

$$\boxed{H(s) = \frac{1}{(s^2 + \sqrt{2}s + 1)}}$$

Now consider $N = 4$,

$$s_k = 1\angle(2k + 1)\pi/2N; \qquad k = 0, 1, 2, 3, 4, 5, 6, 7$$

$$s_1 = 1\angle 22.5°; \quad s_2 = 1\angle 67.5°; \quad s_3 = 1\angle 112.5°; \quad s_4 = 1\angle 157.5°;$$

$$s_5 = 1\angle 202.5°; \quad s_6 = 1\angle 247.5°; \quad s_7 = 292.5°; \quad s_8 = 1\angle 337.5°$$

$$s_1 = 1\angle 22.5° = \cos 22.5° + j \sin 22.5° = 0.9239 + j.3827$$

$$s_2 = \cos 67.5° + j \sin 67.5° = -0.3827 + j.9239$$

$$s_3 = \cos 112.5° + j \sin 112.5° = -0.3827 + j.9239$$

$$s_4 = \cos 157.5° + j \sin 157.5° = -0.9239 + j.3827$$

$$s_5 = \cos 202.5° + j \sin 202.5° = -0.9239 - j.7071$$

$$s_6 = \cos 247.5° + j \sin 247.5° = -0.3827 - j.9239$$

$$s_7 = \cos 292.5° + j \sin 292.5° = 0.3227 - j.9239$$

$$s_8 = \cos 337.5° + j \sin 337.5° = 0.9239 - j.3827$$

The pole locations are given in Figure 3.14.

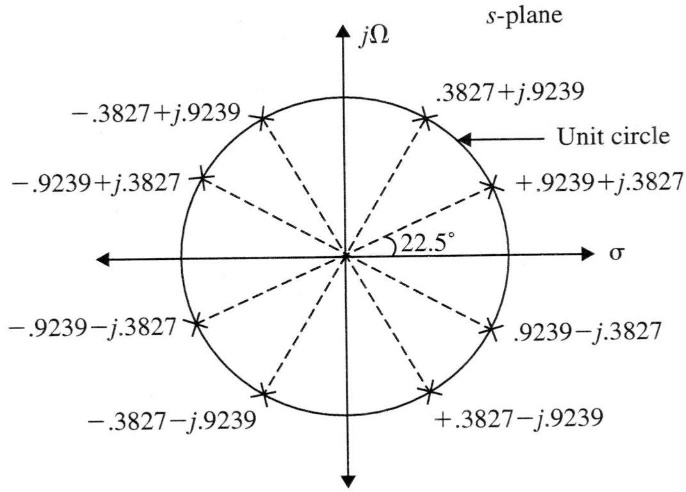

Figure 3.14 Pole location of fourth order filter.

Considering the LHP poles only, the TF of the filter is obtained as

$$H(s) = \frac{1}{\left[\begin{array}{l}(s + 0.3827 + j.9239)(s + 0.3827 - j.9239) \\ \times\ (s + 0.9239 + j.3827)(s + 0.9239 - j.3827)\end{array}\right]}$$

$$\boxed{H(s) = \frac{1}{(s + 0.7654s + 1)(s + 1.8478s + 1)}}$$

The Butterworth polynomial for various values of N for $\Omega_c = 1$ rad/sec is given in Table 3.1.

The Butterworth polynomials given in Table 3.1 are called **Normalized polynomials and the corresponding poles are normalized poles**. Here $\Omega_c = 1$ rad/sec. If $\Omega_c \neq 1$, the polynomial is called un-normalized polynomial and s is replaced by s/Ω_c in $H(s)$.

Table 3.1 Butterworth polynomial for different N.

N	**Denominator of $H(s)$**
1	$(s + 1)$
2	$(s^2 + \sqrt{2}s + 1)$
3	$(s + 1)(s^2 + s + 1)$
4	$(s^2 + 0.7654s + 1)(s + 1.8478s + 1)$
5	$(s + 1)(s^2 + 0.6180s + 1)(s^2 + 1.6180s + 1)$
6	$(s^2 + 1.9319s + 1)(s^2 + \sqrt{2}s + 1)(s^2 + 0.517s + s + 1)$
7	$(s + 1)(s^2 + 1.8019s + 1)(s^2 + 1.247s + 1)(s^2 + 0.44s + 1)$

3.8.1.1 Determination of Order N and Cut-Off Frequency 'Ω_c' of Butterworth Filter

Determination of order N and cut-off frequency Ω_c is very important in the design of Butterworth filter. Let the following specifications be considered.

$$A_p \leq |H_a(\Omega)| \leq 1 \qquad 0 \leq \Omega \leq \Omega_p$$
$$|H_a(\Omega)| \leq A_s \qquad \Omega_s \leq \Omega$$

Consider the squared magnitude response of Butterworth filter which is given below:

$$|H_a(\Omega)|^2 = \frac{1}{1 + \left(\frac{\Omega}{\Omega_c}\right)^{2N}}$$

Since $1 + \left(\frac{\Omega}{\Omega_c}\right)^{2N} \gg 1$, the above equation is written as

$$|H_a(\Omega)|^2 = \frac{1}{\left(\frac{\Omega}{\Omega_c}\right)^{2N}}$$

According to the given specifications, the following equations are written:

$$\frac{1}{\left(1 + \frac{\Omega_p}{\Omega_c}\right)^{2N}} \geq A_p^2$$

$$\frac{1}{\left(1 + \frac{\Omega_s}{\Omega_c}\right)^{2N}} \leq A_s^2$$

The above equations are rearranged and written as follows:

$$\left(\frac{\Omega_p}{\Omega_c}\right)^{2N} \leq \frac{1}{A_p^2} - 1$$

$$\left(\frac{\Omega_s}{\Omega_c}\right)^{2N} \geq \frac{1}{A_s^2} - 1$$

Dividing the equation one by the other after considering the equalities at Ω_c we get

$$\left(\frac{\Omega_s}{\Omega_p}\right)^{2N} = \frac{\left(\frac{1}{A_s^2} - 1\right)}{\left(\frac{1}{A_p^2} - 1\right)}$$

After taking logarithms on both sides, we solve for N as,

$$\boxed{N = \frac{1}{2}\frac{\log\left[\left(\frac{1}{A_s^2} - 1\right) \Big/ \left(\frac{1}{A_p^2} - 1\right)\right]}{\log\left(\frac{\Omega_s}{\Omega_p}\right)}}$$

Note: If the alternations A_p and A_s are given in dB, then A_p and A_s are determined as follows:

$$20 \log A_p = -\text{dB of passband attenuation}$$
$$20 \log A_s = -\text{dB of stopband attenuation}$$

Now to determine Ω_c, any of the equation for passband or stopband attenuation is considered.

$$\left(\frac{\Omega_p}{\Omega_c}\right)^{2N} = \frac{1}{A_p^2} - 1$$

$$\left(\frac{\Omega_p}{\Omega_c}\right) = \left(\frac{1}{A_p^2} - 1\right)^{\frac{1}{2N}}$$

$$\boxed{\Omega_c = \frac{\Omega_p}{\left(\frac{1}{A_p^2} - 1\right)^{1/2N}} \quad \text{or} \quad \Omega_c = \frac{\Omega_s}{\left(\frac{1}{A_s^2} - 1\right)^{1/2N}}}$$

The above equations may not give identical values for Ω_c. Sometimes, the average of these two frequencies are taken to determine Ω_c which is given below:

$$\Omega_c = \frac{1}{2}\left[\frac{\Omega_p}{\left(\frac{1}{A_p^2 - 1}\right)^{1/2N}} + \frac{\Omega_s}{\left(\frac{1}{A_s^2 - 1}\right)^{1/2N}}\right]$$

Therefore, the transfer function of the Butterworth filters will be product of second order factors. The analog filter transfer function of normalized and un-normalized Butterworth lowpass filter is also expressed as given below.

Normalized Butterworth Lowpass Filter Transfer Function

Let N be the order of the filter. When N is even

$$H_a(s) = \prod_{k=1}^{N/2} \frac{1}{s_n^2 + b_k s_n + 1} \tag{3.47}$$

When N is odd

$$H_a(s) = \frac{1}{s_n + 1} \prod_{k=1}^{(N-1)/2} \frac{1}{s_n^2 + b_k s_n + 1} \tag{3.48}$$

where

$$b_k = 2 \sin\left(\frac{(2k-1)\pi}{2N}\right) \tag{3.49}$$

Un-normalized Butterworth Lowpass Filter Transfer Function

The un-normalized transfer function is obtained by replacing s_n by s/Ω_c, where $\Omega_c = 3$ dB cutoff frequency. When N is even

$$H_a(s) = \prod_{k=1}^{N/2} \frac{\Omega_c^2}{s^2 + b_k\Omega_c s + \Omega_c^2} \tag{3.50}$$

When N is odd

$$H_a(s) = \frac{\Omega_c}{s + \Omega_c} \prod_{k=1}^{(N-1)/2} \frac{\Omega_c^2}{s^2 + b_k\Omega_c s + \Omega_c^2} \tag{3.51}$$

where

$$b_k = 2\sin\left(\frac{(2k-1)\pi}{2N}\right) \tag{3.52}$$

3.8.2 Frequency Response of Butterworth Filter

The frequency response of Butterworth filter depends on the order N. The approximated magnitude response approaches the ideal response as the value of N increases.

A_p is gain at the passband frequency ω_p and A_s is the stopband frequency ω_s. The order of the filter is given by

$$N \geq \frac{1}{2} \frac{\log\left[\left(\frac{1}{A_s^2} - 1\right) \Big/ \left(\frac{1}{A_p^2} - 1\right)\right]}{\log\left(\frac{\Omega_s}{\Omega_p}\right)} \tag{3.53}$$

The frequency response of Butterworth filter is shown in Figure 3.15.

3.8.3 Properties of Butterworth Filters

1. The butterworth filters are all poles designs (*i.e.*, the zeros of the filter exist at infinity).
2. At the cut off frequency Ω_c, the magnitude is $1/\sqrt{2}$ or -3 dB.
3. The filter order N completely specifies the filter.
4. The magnitude is flat at the origin.
5. The magnitude is monotonically decreasing function of Ω.
6. The magnitude response approaches the ideal response as the value of N increases.

3.8.4 Design Procedure for Lowpass Digital Butterworth Filters

Let A_p be gain at passband frequency ω_p and A_s be gain at stopband frequency ω_s. Let Ω_p is analog frequency corresponding to ω_p and Ω_s is analog frequency corresponding to ω_s.

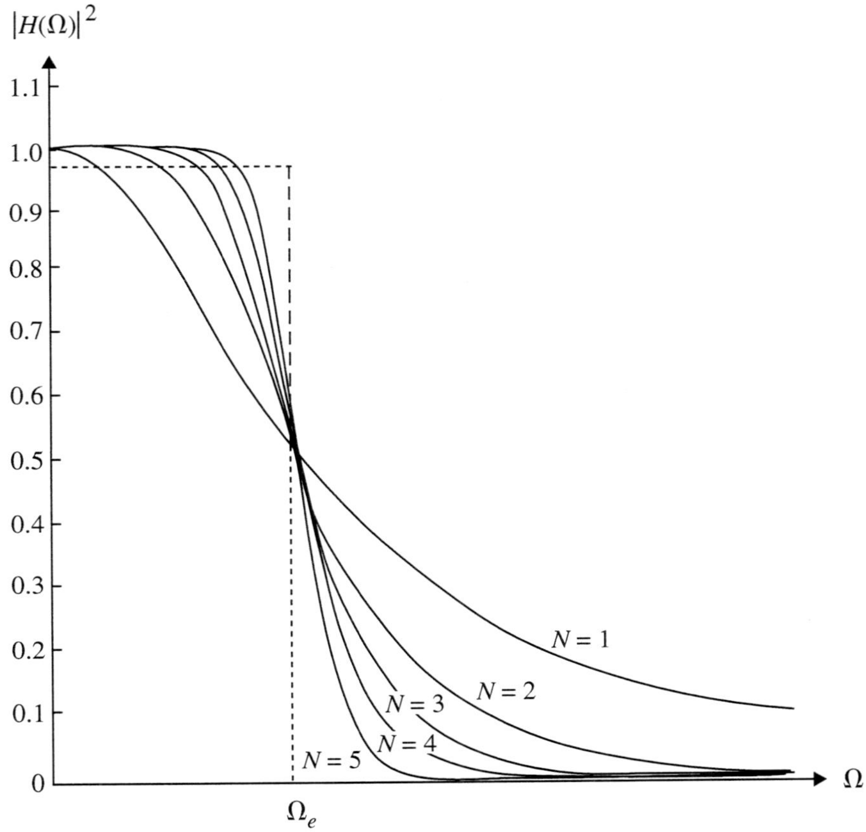

Figure 3.15 Frequency response of Butterworth filter.

Step 1. Choose either bilinear or impulse invariant transformation.
Step 2. Calculate the ratio Ω_s/Ω_p. For bilinear transformation,

$$\frac{\Omega_s}{\Omega_p} = \frac{\tan(\omega_s/2)}{\tan(\omega_p/2)}$$

For impulse invariant,

$$\frac{\Omega_s}{\Omega_p} = \frac{\omega_s}{\omega_p}$$

Step 3. Determine the order N of the filter using the following equation:

$$N \geq \frac{1}{2}\frac{\log\left[\left(\frac{1}{A_s^2}-1\right)\Big/\left(\frac{1}{A_p^2}-1\right)\right]}{\log\left(\frac{\Omega_s}{\Omega_p}\right)}$$

Step 4. Calculate the analog cut off frequency Ω_c.

For bilinear transformation,

$$\Omega_c = \frac{2}{T}\frac{\tan(\omega_p/2)}{\left[\frac{1}{A_p^2} - 1\right]^{1/2N}}$$

For impulse invariant,

$$\Omega_c = \frac{\omega_p/T}{\left[\frac{1}{A_p^2} - 1\right]^{1/2N}}$$

Step 5. Determine the analog transfer function of the filter.
When N is even

$$H_a(s) = \prod_{k=1}^{N/2} \frac{\Omega_c^2}{s^2 + b_k\Omega_c s + \Omega_c^2}$$

When N is odd

$$H_a(s) = \frac{\Omega_c}{s+\Omega_c} \prod_{k=1}^{(N-1)/2} \frac{\Omega_c^2}{s^2 + b_k\Omega_c s + \Omega_c^2}$$

where

$$b_k = 2\sin\left(\frac{(2k-1)\pi}{2N}\right)$$

Note: For normalized case take $\Omega_c = 1$ rad/sec.

Step 6. Using the chosen transformation determine $H(z)$.

Step 7. Realize the digital filter transfer function $H(z)$ by a suitable structure.

Example 3.9

The specification of the desired lowpass filter is

$$0.8 \le |H(\omega)| \le 1.0; \quad 0 \le \omega \le 0.2\pi$$
$$|H(\omega)| \le 0.2; \quad 0.32\pi \le \omega \le \pi$$

Design Butterworth digital filter using impulse invariant transformation.

(Anna University, April, 2006)

Solution Given $A_p = 0.8$ at $\omega_p = 0.2\pi$ rad/sec. and $A_s = 0.2$ at $\omega_s = 0.32\pi$

$$\frac{\Omega_s}{\Omega_p} = \frac{\omega_s}{\omega_p} = \frac{0.32\pi}{0.2\pi} = 1.6$$

$$N \geq \frac{1}{2} \frac{\log\left(\frac{1}{A_s^2} - 1\right) \Big/ \left(\frac{1}{A_p^2} - 1\right)}{\log\left(\frac{\Omega_s}{\Omega_p}\right)}$$

$$\geq \frac{1}{2} \frac{\log\left[\left(\frac{1}{(0.2)^2} - 1\right) \Big/ \left(\frac{1}{(0.8)^2} - 1\right)\right]}{\log 1.6}$$

$$N \geq 3.9931$$

Choose the order of the filter $N = 4$. The analog cut off frequency is,

$$\Omega_c = \frac{\omega_p/T}{\left(\frac{1}{A_p^2} - 1\right)^{1/2N}}$$

Let $T = 1$ sec.

$$\Omega_c = \frac{\omega_p}{\left(\frac{1}{A_p^2} - 1\right)^{1/2N}} = \frac{0.2\pi}{\left(\frac{1}{(0.8)^2} - 1\right)^{1/8}} = 0.675 \text{ rad/sec.}$$

For N is even, the analog transfer function is

$$H_a(s) = \prod_{k=1}^{N/2} \frac{\Omega_c^2}{s^2 + b_k\Omega_c s + \Omega_c^2}$$

where

$$b_k = 2\sin\left(\frac{(2k-1)\pi}{2N}\right)$$

$b_1 = 2\sin\left(\frac{\pi}{8}\right) = 0.765$ and $b_2 = 2\sin\left(\frac{3\pi}{8}\right) = 1.848$

$$H_a(s) = \prod_{k=1}^{2} \frac{\Omega_c^2}{s^2 + b_k\Omega_c s + \Omega_c^2}$$

$$= \frac{\Omega_c^2}{s^2 + b_1\Omega_c s + \Omega_c^2} \times \frac{\Omega_c^2}{s^2 + b_2\Omega_c s + \Omega_c^2}$$

$$= \frac{(0.675)^2}{s^2 + (0.765 \times 0.675)s + (0.675)^2} \times \frac{(0.675)^2}{s^2 + (1.848)(.675)s + (0.675)^2}$$

$$H_a(s) = \frac{0.2076}{s^2 + 0.516s + 0.456)(s^2 + 1.247s + 0.456)}$$

$$= 0.2076 \Big/ [s - (-0.26 + j0.62)][s - (-0.26 - j0.62)] \times [s - (-0.62 + j0.26)][s - (-0.6 - j0.26)]$$

Putting into partial fraction we get,

$$H_a(s) = \frac{A_1}{s - (-0.26 + j0.62)} + \frac{A_1^*}{s - (-0.26 - j0.62)} + \frac{A_2}{s - (-0.62 + j0.26)} + \frac{A_2^*}{s - (-0.62 - j0.26)}$$

$$A_1 = \left.\frac{0.2076}{[s-(-0.26-j0.62)][s-(-0.62+j0.26)][s-(-0.62-j0.26)]}\right|_{s=-0.26+j0.62}$$

$$A_1 = -0.32 + j0.13$$

$$A_1^* = -0.32 - j0.13$$

Similarly

$$A_2 = 0.32 + j0.76 \quad \text{and} \quad A_2^* = 0.32 - j0.76$$

The residues A_1, A_1^*, A_2 and A_2^* may be calculated by graphical method. The poles are located in the s-plane as shown in Figure 3.16.

$$A_1 = \frac{0.2076}{1.24\angle 90^\circ \times 0.51\angle 45^\circ 0.95\angle 68^\circ} = 0.3455\angle - 203$$

$$= 0.3455(\cos 203^\circ - j \sin 203^\circ) = -0.32 + j0.13$$

$$A_1^* = -0.32 - j0.13$$

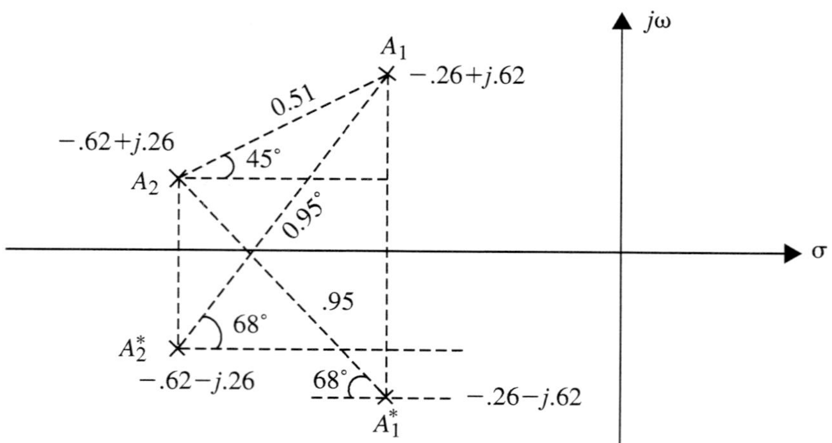

Figure 3.16 Determination of residues by graphical method.

$$A_2 = \frac{0.2076}{0.52\angle 90^\circ 0.51\angle 225^\circ 0.95\angle 112^\circ} = 0.824\angle -67^\circ$$
$$= 0.824(\cos 67^\circ - j\sin 67^\circ)$$
$$A_2 = 0.32 + j0.76$$
$$A_2^* = 0.32 - j0.76$$

$$H_a(s) = \frac{-0.32 + j0.13}{s - (-0.26 + j0.62)} + \frac{-0.32 - j0.13}{s - (-0.26 - j0.62)} + \frac{0.32 + j0.76}{s - (-0.62 + j0.26)} + \frac{0.32 - j0.76}{s - (-0.62 - j0.26)}$$

$$H(z) = H_a(s)\Big|_{\frac{A_i}{s-p_i} \longrightarrow \frac{A_i}{1-e^{p_i T}z^{-1}}}$$

Let $T = 1$ sec.

$$H(z) = \frac{-0.32 + j0.13}{1 - e^{-0.26+j0.62}z^{-1}} + \frac{-0.32 - j0.13}{1 - e^{-0.26-j0.62}z^{-1}} + \frac{0.32 + j0.76}{1 - e^{-0.62+j0.26}z^{-1}} + \frac{0.32 - j0.76}{1 - e^{-0.62-j0.26}z^{-1}}$$

The above equation is simplified as

$$H(z) = \frac{-0.64 + 0.28z^{-1}}{1 - 1.26z^{-1} + 0.59z^{-2}} + \frac{0.64 - 0.12z^{-1}}{1 - 1.04z^{-1} + 0.29z^{-2}}$$

The above system function is realized in direct form II and is shown in Figure 3.17.

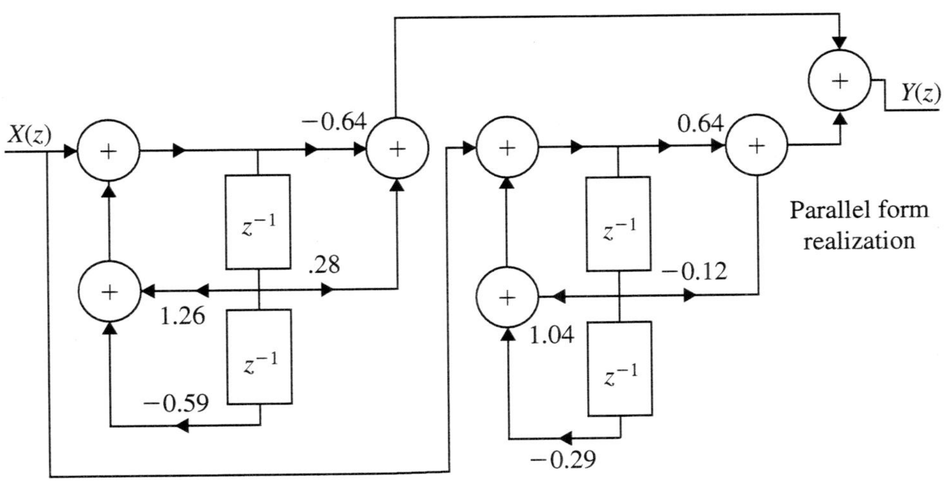

Figure 3.17 Parallel form realization of $H(z)$ for Example 3.9.

Note: For structure realization refer Section 3.

$$H(z) = \frac{-0.64 + 0.28z^{-1}}{1 - 1.26z^{-1} + 0.59z^{-2}} + \frac{0.64 - 0.12z^{-1}}{1 - 1.04z^{-1} + 0.29z^{-2}}$$

Example 3.10

Design a digital Butterworth filter satisfying the following constraints

$$0.707 \le |H(e^{j\omega})| \le 1 \qquad \text{for} \quad 0 \le \omega \le \frac{\pi}{2}$$

$$|H(e^{j\omega})| \le 0.2 \qquad \text{for} \quad \frac{3\pi}{4} \le \omega \le \pi$$

with $T = 1$ sec. using (*a*) the bilinear transformation; (*b*) impulse invariant method. Realize the filter in each case using the most convenient realization form.

(*Anna University, May, 2007*)

Solution

(*a*) **Bilinear Transformation**

Given $A_p = 0.707$ at $\omega_p = (\pi/2)$ and $A_s = 0.2$ at $\omega_s = (3\pi/4)$

$$\frac{\Omega_p}{\Omega_s} = \frac{\tan\frac{\omega_s}{2}}{\tan\frac{\omega_p}{2}} = \frac{\tan\frac{3\pi}{8}}{\tan\frac{\pi}{4}} = 2.414$$

The order of the filter

$$N \ge \frac{1}{2}\frac{\log\left[\left(\frac{1}{A_s^2} - 1\right) \Big/ \left(\frac{1}{A_p^2} - 1\right)\right]}{\log\left(\frac{\Omega_s}{\Omega_p}\right)}$$

$$= \frac{1}{2}\frac{\log\left[\left(\frac{1}{0.2^2} - 1\right) \Big/ \left(\frac{1}{0.707^2} - 1\right)\right]}{\log 2.414}$$

$$N \ge 1.803$$

Let $N = 2$. The analog cut off frequency

$$\Omega_c = \frac{2}{T}\frac{\tan(\omega_p/2)}{\left(\frac{1}{A_p^2} - 1\right)^{1/2N}}$$

$$= 2\frac{\tan(\pi/4)}{\left(\frac{1}{(0.707)^2} - 1\right)^{1/4}} = 2 \text{ rad/sec.}$$

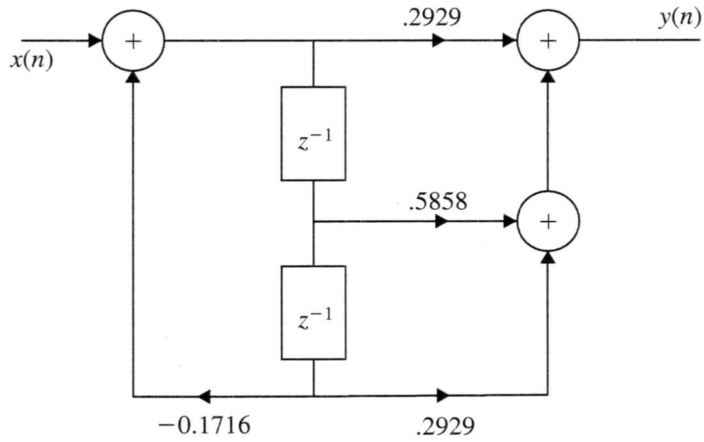

Figure 3.18 Direct form II realization of $H(z)$ for the Example 3.10(a).

The analog transfer function when N = even is

$$H_a(s) = \frac{\Omega_c^2}{s^2 + b_k\Omega_c s + \Omega_c^2} \qquad b_k = 2\sin\left[\frac{(2k-1)\pi}{2N}\right] = 2\sin\left(\frac{\pi}{4}\right) = 1.414$$

$$= \frac{4}{s^2 + 2.828s + 4}$$

By using bilinear transformation $H(z)$ is obtained as

$$H(z) = H_a(s)\Big|_{s=\frac{2}{T}\left(\frac{1-z^{-1}}{1+z^{-1}}\right)}$$

$$= \frac{4}{\left[2\left(\frac{1-z^{-1}}{1+z^{-1}}\right)\right]^2 + 2.828 \times 2\left(\frac{1-z^{-1}}{1+z^{-1}}\right) + 4}$$

$$= \frac{4(1+z^{-1})^2}{4(1-z^{-1})^2 + 5.656(1-z^{-2}) + 4(1+z^{-1})^2}$$

$$= \frac{0.2929(1+z^{-1})^2}{1+0.1716z^{-2}}$$

$$\boxed{H(z) = \frac{0.2929(1+2z^{-1}+z^{-2})}{1+0.1716z^{-2}}}$$

The above system is realized in direct form II and is shown in Figure 3.18(a).

(b) **Impulse Invariant Method**

Given $A_p = 0.707$ at $\omega_p = (\pi/2)$ and $A_s = 0.2$ at $\omega_s = (3\pi/4)$

$$\frac{\omega_s}{\omega_p} = \frac{3\pi/4}{\pi/2} = \frac{3}{2}$$

$$N \geq \frac{1}{2}\frac{\log\left[\left(\frac{1}{(0.2)^2}-1\right)\Big/\left(\frac{1}{(0.707)^2}-1\right)\right]}{\log\left(\frac{3}{2}\right)}$$

$$N \geq 3.924$$

$$N = 4$$

$$\Omega_c = \left(\frac{1}{A_p^2 - 1}\right)^{\frac{1}{2N}} \cdot \Omega_p$$

$$= \left(\frac{1}{0.707^2 - 1}\right)^{\frac{1}{8}} \cdot \frac{\pi}{2}$$

$$= 1.57$$

The transfer function of analog filter for N being even is,

$$H_a(s) = \prod_{k=1}^{2} \frac{\Omega_c^2}{s^2 + b_k\Omega_c s + \Omega_c^2}$$

where $b_1 = 0.7654$ and $b_2 = 1.8478$

$$H_a(s) = \frac{(1.57)^4}{(s^2+1.202s+2.465)(s^2+2.902s+2.465)}$$

$$= \frac{A}{s+1.45+j0.6} + \frac{A^*}{s+1.45-j0.6} + \frac{B}{s+0.6+j1.45} + \frac{B^*}{s+0.6-j1.45}$$

$$A = \left.\frac{(1.57)^4}{(s+1.45-j0.6)(s+0.6+j1.45)(s+0.6-j1.45)}\right|_{s=-1.45-j0.6}$$

$$= 0.7253 + j1.754$$

$$B = \left.\frac{(1.57)^4}{(s+1.45+j0.6)(s+1.45-j0.6)(s+0.6-j1.45)}\right|_{s=-0.6-j1.45}$$

$$= -0.7253 - j0.3$$

$$H_a(s) = \frac{0.7253+j1.754}{s+1.45+j0.6} + \frac{0.7253-j1.754}{s+1.45-j0.6} + \frac{-0.7253-0.3j}{s+0.6+j1.45} + \frac{-0.7253+0.3j}{s+0.6-j1.45}$$

Impulse invariant transformation is

$$\frac{1}{s-p_i} \Longrightarrow \frac{1}{1-e^{p_iT}z^{-1}}$$

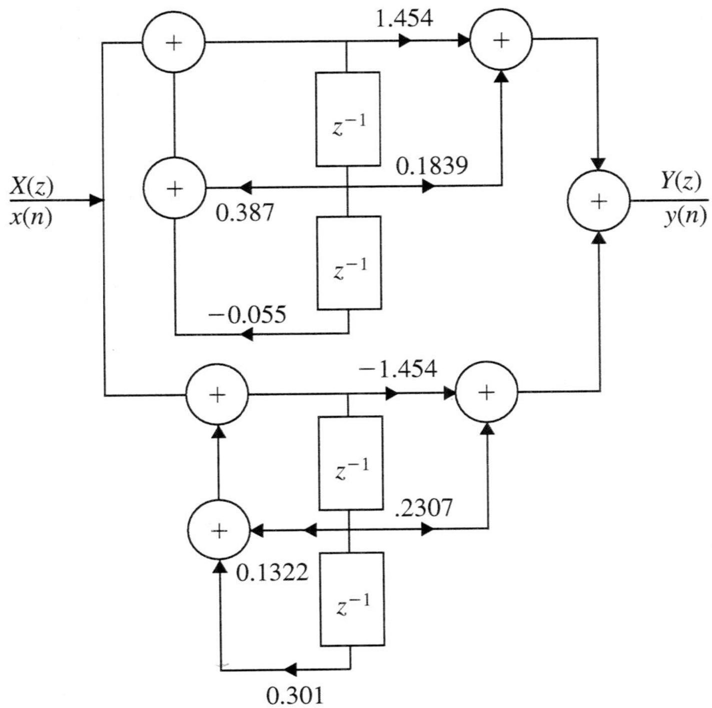

Figure 3.19 Parallel form realization of $H(z)$ for Example 3.10.

let $T = 1$ sec.

$$H(z) = \frac{0.7253 + j1.754}{1 - e^{-1.45} \cdot e^{-j0.6} z^{-1}} + \frac{0.7253 - j1.754}{1 - e^{-1.45} \cdot e^{+j0.6} z^{-1}} + \frac{-0.7253 - 0.3j}{1 - e^{-0.6} \cdot e^{-j1.45} z^{-1}} + \frac{-0.7253 + 0.3j}{1 - e^{-0.6} \cdot e^{j1.45} z^{-1}}$$

$$\boxed{H(z) = \frac{1.454 + 0.1839z^{-1}}{1 - 0.387z^{-1} + 0.055z^{-2}} + \frac{-1.454 + 0.2307z^{-1}}{1 - 0.1322z^{-1} + 0.301z^{-2}}}$$

This can be realized using parallel form as shown in Figure 3.19.

Example 3.11

For the given specification design an analog Butterworth filter

$$0.9 \leq |H(j\Omega)| \leq 1 \qquad \text{for} \quad 0 \leq \Omega \leq 0.2\pi$$
$$|H(j\Omega)| \leq 0.2 \qquad \text{for} \quad 0.4\pi \leq \Omega < \pi$$

Solution Given $\Omega_p = 0.2\pi$, $\Omega_s = 0.4\pi$, $A_p = 0.9$, $A_s = 0.2$.

$$N \geq \frac{1}{2}\frac{\log\left[\left(\frac{1}{A_s^2}-1\right)\Big/\left(\frac{1}{A_p^2}-1\right)\right]}{\log\left(\frac{\Omega_s}{\Omega_p}\right)}$$

$$N \geq \frac{1}{2}\frac{\log\left[\left(\frac{1}{(0.2)^2}-1\right)\Big/\left(\frac{1}{(0.9)^2}-1\right)\right]}{\log\left(\frac{0.4\pi}{0.2\pi}\right)}$$

$$N \geq 3.34$$

$$N = 4$$

$$\Omega_c = \frac{\Omega_p}{(10^{0.1}-1)^{1/2N}} \quad \text{or} \quad \Omega_c = \frac{\Omega_p}{\left(\frac{1}{A_p^2}-1\right)^{1/2N}}$$

$$= \frac{0.2\pi}{(0.484)^{1/4}} = 0.24\pi$$

The analog transfer function

$$H_a(s) = \prod_{k=1}^{2}\frac{\Omega_c^2}{s^2 + b_k\Omega_c s + \Omega_c^2}$$

$$= \frac{\Omega_c^2}{s^2 + b_1\Omega_c s + \Omega_c^2}\cdot\frac{\Omega_c^2}{s^2 + b_2\Omega_c s + \Omega_c^2}$$

$$b_k = 2\sin\left(\frac{(2k-1)\pi}{2N}\right), \qquad k = 1, 2,$$

where $b_1 = 0.7653$ and $b_2 = 1.8477$

$$H_a(s) = \frac{0.323}{(s^2 + 0.577s + 0.0576\pi^2)(s^2 + 1.393s + 0.0576\pi^2)}$$

Example 3.12

Determine the order and the poles of lowpass Butterworth analog filter that has a 3dB attenuation at 500 Hz and an attenuation of 40 dB at 1000 Hz.

Solution Given $-20\log A_p = 3\text{dB}$, $\Omega_p = 2\pi \times 500 = 1000\pi$ rad/sec and $-20\log A_s = 40\text{dB}$ $\Omega_s = 2\pi \times 1000 = 2000\pi$ rad/sec.

$$20\log A_p = -3$$
$$A_p = 0.707$$
$$20\log A_s = -40$$
$$A_s = 0.01$$

$$N \geq \frac{1}{2}\frac{\log\left[\left(\frac{1}{A_s^2}-1\right)\Big/\left(\frac{1}{A_p^2}-1\right)\right]}{\log\left(\frac{\Omega_s}{\Omega_p}\right)}$$

$$N \geq \frac{1}{2}\frac{\log\left[\left(\frac{1}{(0.01)^2}-1\right)\Big/\left(\frac{1}{(0.707)^2}-1\right)\right]}{\log\left(\frac{2000\pi}{1000\pi}\right)}$$

$$N \geq 6.64319$$

$$N = 7$$

The poles of Butterworth filter is given by $s_k = \Omega_c e^{j\Phi_k}$

$$\Omega_c = \frac{\Omega_p}{\left(\frac{1}{A_1^2}-1\right)^{1/2N}} = \frac{1000\pi}{\left(\frac{1}{(0.707)^2}-1\right)^{1/14}} = 1000\pi$$

$$s_k = 1000\pi e^{j\Phi_k}, \quad k = 1, \ldots, 7$$

where

$$\phi_k = \frac{\pi}{2} + \frac{(2k-1)\pi}{2N}, \quad k = 1, \ldots, 7$$

The normalized poles of analog Butterworth filter are obtained as follows. (This can be taken from Table 3.1 also).

$$\text{For } k = 1, \quad \phi_1 = \frac{\pi}{2} + \frac{\pi}{14} = 102.865^\circ$$
$$\text{For } k = 2, \quad \phi_2 = 128.57^\circ$$
$$\text{For } k = 3, \quad \phi_3 = 154^\circ$$
$$\text{For } k = 4, \quad \phi_4 = 180^\circ$$

The normalized LHP poles are,

$$s_1 = 1e^{j102.865^\circ} = -0.2265 + j0.9749$$
$$s_2 = e^{j128.57^\circ} = -0.6235 + j0.7818$$
$$s_3 = e^{j154^\circ} = -0.8987 + j0.4384$$

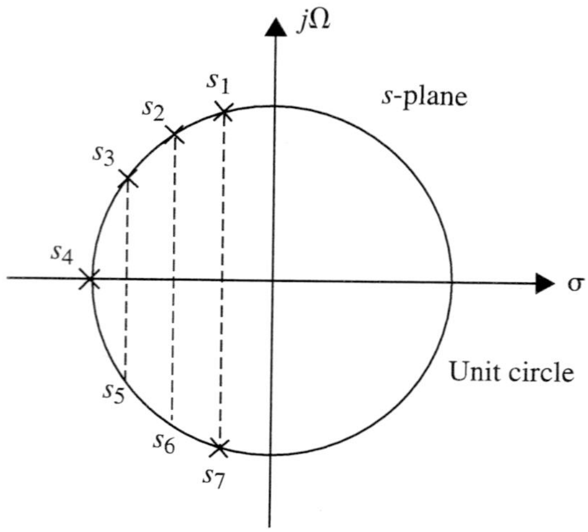

Figure 3.20 Location of normalized poles.

$$s_4 = e^{j180^\circ} = -1$$
$$s_5 = s_3^* = -0.8987 - j0.4384$$
$$s_6 = s_2^* = -0.6235 - j0.7818$$
$$s_7 = s_1^* = -0.2265 - j0.9749$$

These poles in LHP of the s-plane are shown in Figure 3.20.

The transfer function of analog Butterworth normalized filter is given as

$$H_a(s) = \frac{1}{(s+s_4)(s+s_1)(s+s_7)(s+s_2)(s+s_6)(s+s_3)(s+s_5)}$$
$$= \frac{1}{[(s+1)(s^2+1.8019s+1)(s^2+1.247s+1)(s^2+0.44s+1)]}$$

The transfer function of the un-normalized filter is obtained by replaced s by

$$\frac{s}{\Omega_c} = \frac{s}{1000\pi}.$$

Therefore

$$H_a(s) = \frac{(\Omega_c)^7}{[(s+\Omega_c)(s^2+1.8019\Omega_c s+\Omega_c^2)(s^2+1.247\Omega_c s+\Omega_c^2)(s^2+0.44\Omega_c s+\Omega_c^2)]}$$

$$H_a(s) = 3\times 10^{24} \Big/ \Big[(s+3140)(s^2+5658s+9.87\times 10^6)(s^2+3893.6s+9.87\times 10^6)(s^2+1381.6s+9.87\times 10^6)\Big]$$

Example 3.13

If $H(s) = \frac{1}{(s+1)(s+2)}$, find $H(z)$ using impulse invariance method for sampling frequency of 5 samples/sec.

(Anna University, May, 2007)

Solution

$$H(s) = \frac{1}{(s+1)(s+2)}$$

The above function can be put into partial fraction as,

$$H(s) = \frac{1}{(s+1)} - \frac{1}{(s+2)}$$

The sampling frequency is given as $F_s = 5$

$$T = \frac{1}{F_s} = \frac{1}{5} = 0.2 \text{ sec.}$$

Using impulse invariance we get,

$$\begin{aligned} H(z) &= \frac{1}{1 - e^{-T}z^{-1}} - \frac{1}{(1 - e^{2T}z^{-1})} \\ &= \frac{1}{1 - e^{-0.2}z^{-1}} - \frac{1}{(1 - e^{-0.4}z^{-1})} \\ &= \frac{1}{1 - 0.8187z^{-1}} - \frac{1}{(1 - 0.6703z^{-1})} \end{aligned}$$

$$\boxed{H(z) = \frac{0.1484z^{-1}}{(1 - 1.489z^{-1} + 0.5488z^{-2})}}$$

Example 3.14

Convert the analog filter with system function $H_a(s)$ into digital filter using bilinear transformation.

$$H_a(s) = \frac{(s+0.3)}{(s+0.3)^2 + 16}$$

(Anna University, November, 2006)

Solution

$$H_a(s) = \frac{(s+0.3)}{(s+0.3)^2 + 16} = \frac{(s+0.3)}{(s+0.3)^2 + 16}$$

The bilinear transformation is given by

$$s = \frac{2}{T}\frac{(1-z^{-1})}{(1+z^{-1})} = \frac{2}{T}\frac{(z-1)}{(z+1)}$$

Assuming $T = 1$ and substituting for s in $H_a(s)$ we get

$$H(z) = \frac{2\frac{(z-1)}{(z+1)} + 0.3}{\left(2\frac{(z-1)}{(z+1)}\right)^2 + 0.6 + \frac{(z-1)}{(z+1)} + 16.09}$$

$$= \frac{[2(z-1) + 0.3(z+1)](z+1)}{4(z-1)^2 + 0.6(z-1)(z+1) + 16.09(z+1)}$$

$$= \frac{(2.3z^2 + 0.6z - 1.7)}{(4.6z^2 + 8.09z + 19.49)}$$

$$\boxed{H(z) = \frac{(-1.7z^{-2} + 0.6z^{-1} + 2.3)}{(19.4z^{-2} + 8.09z^{-1} + 4.6)}}$$

Example 3.15

Find the analog T.F. for a digital Butterworth filter satisfying the following specifications.

$$0.7 \le |H(e^{j\omega})| \le 1, \quad 0 \le \omega \le 0.2\pi$$

$$|H(e^{j\omega})| \le 0.004, \quad 0.6\pi \le \omega \le \pi$$

Assume $T = 1$ sec. Apply impulse-invariant transformation.

(Anna University, December, 2007)

Solution Given $A_p = 0.7$; $\omega_p = 0.2\pi$ and $A_s = 0.004$; $\omega_s = 0.6\pi$

$$\frac{\Omega_s}{\Omega_p} = \frac{0.6\pi}{0.2\pi} = 3$$

$$N \ge \frac{1}{2}\frac{\log\left[\left(\frac{1}{A_s^2} - 1\right) \Big/ \left(\frac{1}{A_p^2} - 1\right)\right]}{\log\frac{\Omega_s}{\Omega_p}}$$

$$\le \frac{\frac{1}{2}\log\left[\left(\frac{1}{(0.004)^2} - 1\right) \Big/ \left(\frac{1}{(0.7)^2} - 1\right)\right]}{\log 3} = 5$$

$$\Omega_c = \frac{1}{T}\frac{\omega_p}{\left(\frac{1}{A_p^2}-1\right)^{1/2N}}$$

$$= \frac{0.2\pi}{\left(\frac{1}{0.49}-1\right)^{0.1}} = 0.2\pi \text{ rad/sec.}$$

$$\Omega_c = 0.6283$$

For $N = 5$ which is odd, the analog Butterworth filter is expressed by the following system function

$$H_a(s) = \frac{(\Omega_c)^5}{(s+\Omega_c)(s^2+b_1\Omega_c s+\Omega_c^2)(s^2+b_2\Omega_c s+\Omega_c^2)}$$

Since $b_1 = 0.618$ and $b_2 = 1.618$

$$\boxed{H_a(s) = \frac{(0.6283)^5}{(s+0.6283)(s^2+0.3883s+0.395)(s^2+s+0.395)}}$$

Example 3.16

Design a third order Butterworth digital filter using impulse invariant technique. Assume the sampling period $T = 1$ sec.

Solution Given $N = 3$. If N is odd, the analog transfer function is

$$H_a(s) = \frac{\Omega_c}{s+\Omega_c}\prod_{k=1}^{(N-1)/2}\frac{\Omega_c^2}{s^2+b_k\Omega_c s+\Omega_c^2}$$

$$= \frac{\Omega_c}{s+\Omega_c}\cdot\frac{\Omega_c^2}{s^2+b_k\Omega_c s+\Omega_c^2} \qquad \text{(Let } \Omega_c = 1 \text{ for normalized filter).}$$

$$= \frac{1}{(s+1)(s^2+b_1 s+1)} \qquad \left(b_k = 2\sin\left[\frac{(2k-1)\pi}{2N}\right]\right)$$

$$H_a(s) = \frac{1}{(s+1)(s^2+s+1)} \qquad (b_1 = 1)$$

$$= \frac{1}{(s+1)(s+0.5+j0.866)(s+0.5-j0.866)}$$

$$= \frac{A}{s+1}+\frac{B}{s+0.5+j0.866}+\frac{C}{s+0.5-j0.866}$$

$$A = \left.\frac{1}{s^2+s+1}\right|_{s=-1} = 1$$

$$B = \left.\frac{1}{(s+1)(s+0.5-j0.866)}\right|_{s=0.5-j0.866} = -0.5+j0.288$$

$$C = B^* = -0.5-j0.288$$

$$H(z) = \frac{1}{s+1} + \frac{-0.5+0.288j}{s+0.5+j0.866} + \frac{-0.5-0.288j}{s+0.5-j0.866}$$

By impulse invariant transformation, the transfer function of the digital filter is,

$$H(z) = \frac{1}{1-e^{-1}z^{-1}} + \frac{-0.5+0.288j}{1-e^{-0.5}\cdot e^{-j0.866}z^{-1}} + \frac{-0.5-0.288j}{1-e^{-0.5}e^{j0.866}z^{-1}}$$

$$\boxed{H(z) = \frac{1}{1-0.368z^{-1}} + \frac{-1+0.66z^{-1}}{1-0.786z^{-1}+0.368z^{-2}}}$$

Example 3.17

Apply impulse invariant method and find $H(z)$ for

$$H(s) = \frac{s+a}{(s+a)^2+b^2}$$

Solution The inverse Laplace transform of given function is

$$h(t) = \begin{cases} e^{-at}\cos bt, & t \geq 0 \\ 0, & \text{otherwise} \end{cases}$$

$$h(n) = h(t)\Big|_{t=nT}$$

$$h(n) = \begin{cases} e^{-anT}\cos(bnT), & t \geq 0 \\ 0, & \text{otherwise} \end{cases}$$

The digital transfer function is

$$H(z) = \sum_{n=0}^{\infty} e^{-anT}\cos bnT z^{-n}$$

$$= \sum_{n=0}^{\infty} e^{-anT}\left(\frac{e^{jbnT}+e^{-jbnT}}{2}\right)z^{-n}$$

$$H(z) = \frac{1}{2}\sum_{n=0}^{\infty}[(e^{-(a-jb)T}z^{-1})^n + (e^{-(a+jb)T}z^{-1})^n]$$

$$= \frac{1}{2}\left[\frac{1}{1-e^{-(a-jb)T}z^{-1}} + \frac{1}{1-e^{-(a+jb)T}z^{-1}}\right]$$

$$= \frac{1}{2}\left[\frac{1-e^{-(a+jb)T}z^{-1} + 1 - e^{-(a-jb)T}z^{-1}}{(1-e^{-(a-jb)T}z^{-1})(1-e^{-(a+jb)T}z^{-1})}\right]$$

$$\boxed{H(z) = \frac{1-e^{-aT}\cos(bT)z^{-1}}{1-2e^{-aT}\cos(bT)z^{-1} + e^{-2aT}z^{-2}}}$$

Example 3.18

An analog filter has a transfer function

$$H(s) = \frac{10}{s^2+7s+10}$$

Design a digital filter equivalent to this using impulse invariant method for $T = 0.2$ sec.

Solution Given

$$H(s) = \frac{10}{s^2+7s+10} \quad \text{and} \quad T = 0.2 \text{ sec.}$$

$$H(s) = \frac{10}{(s+5)(s+2)} = \frac{A}{(s+5)} + \frac{B}{(s+2)}$$

$$A = \left.\frac{10}{(s+2)}\right|_{s=-5} = -3.33$$

$$B = \left.\frac{10}{(s+5)}\right|_{s=-2} = 3.33$$

$$H(s) = \frac{-3.33}{(s+5)} + \frac{3.33}{(s+2)}$$

$$H(z) = \frac{-3.33}{1-e^{-5T}z^{-1}} + \frac{3.33}{1-e^{-2T}z^{-1}}$$

$$= \frac{-3.33}{1-e^{-1}z^{-1}} + \frac{3.33}{1-e^{-0.4}z^{-1}}$$

$$= \frac{-3.33}{1-0.3678z^{-1}} + \frac{3.33}{1-0.67z^{-1}}$$

$$H(z) = \frac{1.006z^{-1}}{1 - 1.0378z^{-1} + 0.247z^{-2}}$$

Example 3.19

Use bilinear transform to design a first order Butterworth LPF with 3 dB cut off frequency of 0.2π.

(Anna University, April, 2004)

Solution Given 3 dB cut off frequency $\omega_c = 0.2\pi = \omega_p$.

The analog transfer function for first order Butterworth filter is

$$H_a(s) = \frac{\Omega_c}{s + \Omega_c}$$

$$\Omega_c = \frac{2}{T}\tan\left(\frac{\omega_p}{2}\right) = 2\tan\left(\frac{0.2\pi}{2}\right) = 0.6498$$

$$H_a(s) = \frac{0.6498}{s + 0.6498}$$

Using bilinear transformation,

$$H(z) = H_a(s)\Big|_{s=\frac{2}{T}\frac{1-z^{-1}}{1+z^{-1}}}$$

Assume $T = 1$ sec.

$$H(z) = \frac{0.6498}{s + 0.6498}\Big|_{s=2\left(\frac{1-z^{-1}}{1+z^{-1}}\right)} \qquad [\because T = 1 \text{ sec.}]$$

$$= \frac{0.6498}{\frac{2(1-z^{-1})}{(1+z^{-1})} + 0.6498}$$

$$= \frac{0.6498(1 + z^{-1})}{2(1 - z^{-1}) + 0.6498(1 + z^{-1})}$$

$$= \frac{0.6498(1 + z^{-1})}{2 - 2z^{-1} + 0.6498 + 0.6498z^{-1}}$$

$$= \frac{0.6498(1 + z^{-1})}{2.6498 - 1.3502z^{-1}}$$

$$= \frac{0.6498(1 + z^{-1})}{2.6498(1 - 0.5095z^{-1})}$$

$$H(z) = \frac{0.2452(1 + z^{-1})}{1 - 0.5095z^{-1}}$$

Example 3.20

Using bilinear transformation design a digital bandpass Butterworth filter with the following specifications:

Sampling frequency = 8 kHz
$\alpha_p = 2$ dB in the passband 800 Hz $\leq f \leq$ 1000 Hz
$\alpha_s = 20$ dB in the stopband $0 \leq f \leq 400$ Hz and $2000 \leq f \leq \infty$

(Anna University, December, 2006)

Solution

$$\frac{\omega_1 T}{2} = \frac{2 \times \pi \times 400}{2 \times 8000} = \frac{\pi}{20} \qquad \left[T = \frac{1}{f_s} = \frac{1}{8000}\right]$$

$$\frac{\omega_1 T}{2} = \frac{2 \times \pi \times 800}{2 \times 8000} = \frac{\pi}{10}$$

$$\frac{\omega_u T}{2} = \frac{2\pi \times 1000}{2 \times 8000} = \frac{\pi}{8}$$

$$\frac{\omega_2 T}{2} = \frac{2\pi \times 2000}{2 \times 8000} = \frac{\pi}{4}$$

Prewarped analog frequencies are given by

$$\frac{\Omega_1 T}{2} = \tan\frac{\omega_1 T}{2} = \tan\frac{\pi}{20} = 0.1584$$

$$\frac{\Omega_l T}{2} = \tan\frac{\omega_l T}{2} = \tan\frac{\pi}{10} = 0.325$$

$$\frac{\Omega_u T}{2} = \tan\frac{\omega_u T}{2} = \tan\frac{\pi}{8} = 0.4142$$

$$\frac{\Omega_2 T}{2} = \tan\frac{\omega_2 T}{2} = \tan\frac{\pi}{4} = 1$$

First we design a prototype normalized compass filter and then use suitable transformation to obtain the transfer function of bandpass filter. To reduce computational complexity we use above values to find Ω_r and substitute $s = \frac{1-z^{-1}}{1+z^{-1}}$ for bilinear transformation ($\because$ all the above frequencies contains the term $T/2$)

$$A = \frac{-\Omega_1^2 + \Omega_l \Omega_u}{\Omega_1(\Omega_u - \Omega_l)}$$

$$= \frac{-(0.1584)^2 + (0.325)(0.4142)}{0.1584(0.4142 - 0.325)}$$

$$A = 11.303$$

$$B = \frac{\Omega_2^2 - \Omega_l\Omega_u}{\Omega_2(\Omega_u - \Omega_l)} = \frac{1-(0.4142)(0.325)}{1(0.4142-0.325)}$$

$$= \frac{1-0.1346}{0.0892} = \frac{0.865385}{0.0892}$$

$$= 9.7016$$

$$\Omega_r = \min\{|A|, |B|\} = 9.7016$$

$$N = \frac{\log_{10}\sqrt{\frac{10^2-1}{10^{0.2}-1}}}{\log_{10}(9.7016)} = \frac{\log_{10}(13.01)}{\log_{10}(9.7016)} = \frac{1.1142}{0.9868}$$

$$= 1.1290$$

$$N = 2$$

The second order normalised Butterworth lowpass filter transfer function given by

$$H(s) = \frac{1}{s^2 + 1.4142s + 1}$$

The transformation for the bandpass filter is

$$s \to \frac{s^2 + \Omega_l\Omega_u}{s(\Omega_u - \Omega_l)} = \frac{s^2 + 0.1346}{s(0.0892)}$$

$$H(s) = \left.\frac{1}{s^2 + 1.4142s + 1}\right|_{s=\frac{s^2+0.1346}{(0.0892)s}}$$

$$= \frac{1}{\left(\frac{s^2+0.1346}{(0.0892)s}\right)^2 + 1.4142\left(\frac{s^2+0.1346}{(0.0892)s}\right) + 1}$$

$$= \frac{0.0079s^2}{s^4 + 0.2692s^2 + 0.0181 + 1.4142(0.0892)s(s^2+0.1346) + 0.0079s^2}$$

$$= \frac{0.0079s^2}{s^4 + 0.2692s^2 + 0.0181 + 0.126s(s^2+0.1346) + 0.0079s^2}$$

$$= \frac{0.0079s^2}{s^4 + 0.2692s^2 + 0.0181 + 0.126s^3 + 0.0169s + 0.0079s^2}$$

$$H(s) = \frac{0.0079s^4}{s^4 + 0.126s^3 + 0.2771s^2 + 0.0169s + 0.0181}$$

$$H(z) = H(s)\Big|_{s=\frac{1-z^{-1}}{1+z^{-1}}}$$

$$= \frac{0.0079\left(\frac{1-z^{-1}}{1+z^{-1}}\right)^2}{\left(\frac{1-z^{-1}}{1+z^{-1}}\right)^4 + 0.126\left(\frac{1-z^{-1}}{1+z^{-1}}\right)^3 + 0.277\left(\frac{1-z^{-1}}{1+z^{-1}}\right)^2 + 0.169\left(\frac{1-z^{-1}}{1+z^{-1}}\right) + 0.0181}$$

$$= 0.0079(1-z^{-1})^2 \Big/ \Big[(1-z^{-1})^4 + 0.126(1-z^{-1})^3(1+z^{-1})$$

$$+ 0.2692(1-z^{-1})^2(1+z^{-1})^2 + 0.169(1-z^{-1})(1+z^{-1})^3$$

$$+ 0.0181(1+z^{-1})^4\Big]$$

$$= 0.0079(1-z^{-2})^2 \Big/ \Big[1-4z^{-1}+6z^{-2}-4z^{-3}+z^{-4}$$

$$+ 0.126(1-2z^{-1}+2z^{-3}-z^{-4}) + 0.2677(1-2z^{-2}$$

$$+z^{-4}) + 0.169(1+2z^{-1}-2z^{-3}-z^{-4}) + 0.0181(1+4z^{-1}$$

$$+6z^{-2}+4z^{-3}+z^{-4})\Big]$$

$$= \frac{0.0079(1-z^{-2})^2}{7.1871-3.8416z^{-1}+0.644z^{-2}-4.086z^{-3}+0.9908z^{-4}}$$

3.9 Design of Lowpass Digital Chebyshev Filter

3.9.1 Analog Chebyshev Filter

It is designed by approximating the ideal frequency response using error function.

The Chebyshev characteristic provides an alternative method of getting a suitable analog transfer function $H_a(s)$ from which lowpass digital filters are designed using either bilinear transformation or impulse invariance. There are two types of Chebyshev filters available as type I and type II filters. The type I filter characteristic for odd value of N is shown in Figure 3.21(a) and type II characteristic for even value of N is shown in Figure 3.21(b). The characteristic of type I filters have equal ripple in the passband and monotonic in the stopband. They are all pole filters. Type II Chebyshev filter characteristics are shown in Figures 3.22(a) and (b) for odd and even values of N. These filters have equal ripples in the stopband and monotonic in the passband. Further, they have both poles and zeros in the transfer function.

3.9.2 Determination of the Order of the Chebyshev Filter

The type I of Nth order Chebyshev filter can be expressed as,

$$|H(j\Omega)|^2 = \frac{1}{\left[1+\epsilon^2 C_N^2\left(\frac{\Omega}{\Omega_p}\right)\right]}; \quad N = 1, 2, \ldots \tag{3.53a}$$

where ϵ is a parameter which is the function of the ripple in the passband. $C_N(x)$ is the Chebyshev polynomial of order N. In the passband and stopband it is defined as,

$$C_N(x) = \cos(N\cos^{-1}x), \quad |x| \le 1$$
$$C_N(x) = \cosh(N\cosh^{-1}x), \quad |x| > 1$$

The Chebyshev polynomial is also expressed by the following recursive formula.

$$C_N(x) = 2xC_{N-1}(x) - C_{N-2}(x), \quad N > 1$$

where $C_0(x) = 1$ and $C_1(x) = x$.

Taking logarithm for equation (3.53a) we get

$$20\log|H(\Omega)| = -10\log\left[1 + \epsilon^2 C_N^2\left(\frac{\Omega}{\Omega_p}\right)\right]$$

At passband $\Omega = \Omega_p$

$$20\log|H(\Omega)| = -\alpha_p$$
$$\alpha_p = 10\log\left[1 + \epsilon^2 C_N^2\left(\frac{\Omega_p}{\Omega_p}\right)\right]$$

Using the property of $C_N(1) = 1$, we get

$$\alpha_p = 10\log(1 + \epsilon^2)$$
$$\epsilon = \sqrt{10^{0.1\alpha_p} - 1}$$

At stopband $\Omega = \Omega_s$.

$$20\log|H(j\Omega)| = -\alpha_s \log\left[1 + \epsilon^2 C_N^2\left(\frac{\Omega_s}{\Omega_p}\right)\right]$$

But $C_N = \left(\frac{\Omega_s}{\Omega_p}\right) = \cosh\left[N\cosh^{-1}\frac{\Omega_s}{\Omega_p}\right]$

$$\alpha_s = 10\log\left[1 + \epsilon^2\left\{\cosh\left(N\cosh^{-1}\left(\frac{\Omega_s}{\Omega_p}\right)\right)\right\}^2\right]$$

But

$$\cosh\left(N\cosh^{-1}\left(\frac{\Omega_s}{\Omega_p}\right)\right]^2 = \frac{10^{0.1\alpha_s} - 1}{\epsilon^2} = \frac{10^{0.1\alpha_s} - 1}{(10^{0.1\alpha_p} - 1)}$$

$$N\cosh^{-1}\left(\frac{\Omega_s}{\Omega_p}\right) = \cosh^{-1}\left[\frac{(10^{0.1\alpha_s}) - 1}{10^{0.1\alpha_p} - 1}\right]^{1/2}$$

$$N \geq \frac{\cosh^{-1}\left[\frac{10^{0.1\alpha_s}-1}{10^{0.1\alpha_p}-1}\right]^{1/2}}{\cosh^{-1}\left(\frac{\Omega_s}{\Omega_p}\right)}$$

or

$$N \geq \frac{\cosh^{-1}\left[\frac{1}{\epsilon}\left(\frac{1}{A_s^2}-1\right)^{1/2}\right]}{\cosh^{-1}\left(\frac{\Omega_s}{\Omega_p}\right)}$$

Note: $\cosh^{-1} x$ can be evaluated using the following identity:

$$\cosh^{-1} x = \ln[x + \sqrt{(x^2 - 1)}]$$

They are two types:

I. **Type-I:** The magnitude response is equiripple in the passband and monotonic in the stopband as shown in Figure 3.21.

II. **Type-II:** The magnitude response is monotonic in passband and equiripple in stopband as shown in Figure 3.22.

The magnitude response of type-I lowpass filter is given by

$$|H_a(\Omega)|^2 = \frac{1}{1 + \epsilon^2 C_N^2\left(\frac{\Omega}{\Omega_c}\right)} \tag{3.54}$$

where ϵ is attenuation constant and C_N is Chebyshev polynomial

$$\epsilon = \left[\frac{1}{A_p^2} - 1\right]^{1/2} \tag{3.55}$$

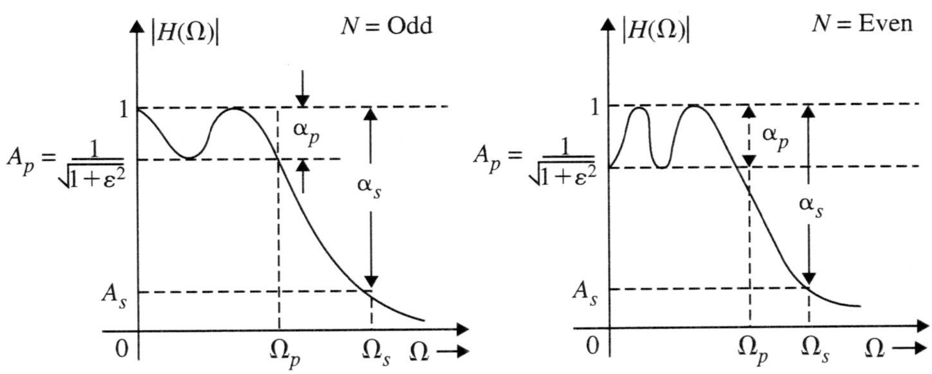

Figure 3.21 Frequency response of type-I Chebyshev filter.

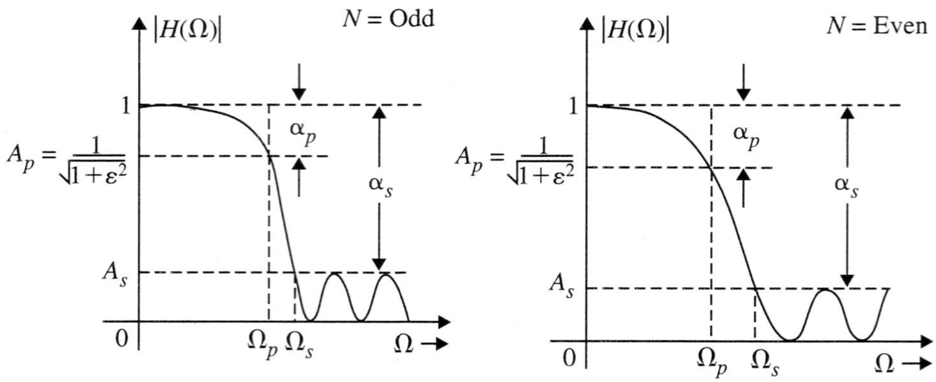

Figure 3.22 Frequency response of type-II Chebyshev filter. (*a*) N is odd and (*b*) N is even.

where $s = j\Omega$ gives $\Omega = s/j$. Substitute $\Omega = s/j$ in above equation

$$H_a(s)H_a(-s) = \frac{1}{1+\epsilon^2 C_N^2\left(\frac{s/j}{\Omega_c}\right)}$$

$$H_a(s)H_a(-s) = \frac{1}{1+\epsilon^2 C_N^2\left(-js_n\right)} \tag{3.56}$$

If N is even all poles are complex. When N is odd one of the poles is real and all other poles are complex.

3.9.3 Un-normalized Chebyshev Lowpass Filter Transfer Function

When N is even

$$H_a(s) = \prod_{k=1}^{N/2} \frac{B_k\Omega_c^2}{s^2 + b_k\Omega_c^2 s + C_k\Omega_c^2} \tag{3.57}$$

When N is odd

$$H_a(s) = \frac{B_0\Omega_c}{s + C_0\Omega_c} \prod_{k=1}^{N-1/2} \frac{B_k\Omega_c^2}{s^2 + b_k\Omega_c^2 s + C_k\Omega_c^2} \tag{3.58}$$

where

$$b_k = 2Y_N \sin\left(\frac{(2k-1)\pi}{2N}\right) \tag{3.59}$$

$$c_k = Y_N^2 + \cos^2\left(\frac{(2k-1)\pi}{2N}\right) \tag{3.60}$$

$$c_0 = Y_N \tag{3.61}$$

$$Y_N = \frac{1}{2}\left\{\left[\left(\frac{1}{\epsilon^2} - 1\right)^{1/2} + \frac{1}{\epsilon}\right]^{1/N} - \left[\left(\frac{1}{\epsilon^2} + 1\right)^{1/2} + \frac{1}{\epsilon}\right]^{-(1/N)}\right\} \tag{3.62}$$

For N is even, parameter B_k is evaluated by

$$H_a(s)\bigg|_{s=0} = \frac{1}{(1+\epsilon^2)^{1/2}} \tag{3.63}$$

for N is odd, B_k is calculated by

$$H_a(s)\bigg|_{s=0} = 1 \quad \text{and} \quad B_0 = B_1 = B_2 = \cdots = B_k \tag{3.64}$$

3.9.4 Frequency Response of Chebyshev Filter

The frequency response of Chebyshev filter is shown in Figure 3.29.

$$N \geq \frac{\cos h^{-1}\left\{\frac{1}{\epsilon}\left(\frac{1}{A_s^2}-1\right)^{1/2}\right\}}{\cos h^{-1}\left(\frac{\Omega_s}{\Omega_p}\right)} \tag{3.65}$$

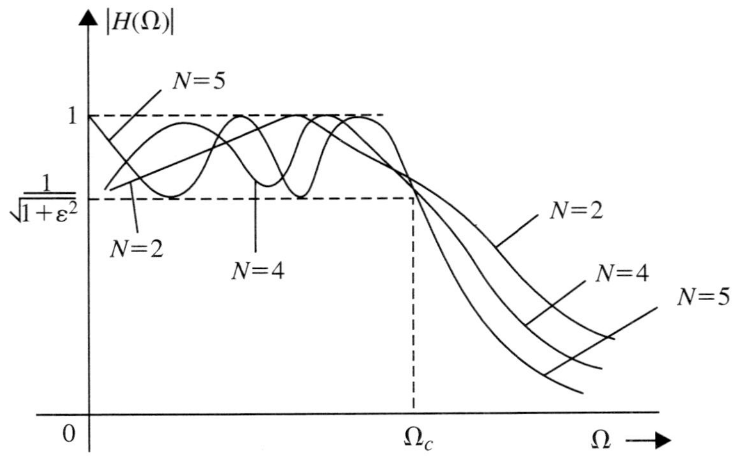

Figure 3.23 Frequency response of Chebyshev filter type-I filter.

3.9.5 Properties of Chebyshev Filter (Type I)

1. The magnitude oscillates between 1 and $\frac{1}{\sqrt{1+\epsilon^2}}$ with in passband (equiripple in the passband).
2. At cut off frequency Ω_c, the magnitude is $\frac{1}{\sqrt{1+\epsilon^2}}$.
3. Magnitude is monotonic outside the passband.
4. Chebyshev filter are all pole design.
5. As N increases, it is approaches to ideal response.

3.9.6 Design Procedures for Lowpass Digital Chebyshev IIR Filter

1. Choose either bilinear or impulse invariant transformation.
2. Calculate the attenuation constant ϵ

$$\epsilon = \left[\frac{1}{A_p^2} - 1\right]^{1/2}$$

3. Calculate the ratio Ω_s/Ω_p using the following equation which is appropriate.

$$\text{For bilinear transformation, } \frac{\Omega_s}{\Omega_p} = \frac{\tan(\omega_s/2)}{\tan(\omega_p/2)}$$

$$\text{For impulse invariant, } \frac{\Omega_s}{\Omega_p} = \frac{\omega_s}{\omega_p}$$

4. Decide the order N of the filter from

$$N \leq \frac{\cos h^{-1}\left\{\frac{1}{\epsilon}\left[\frac{1}{A_2^s} - 1\right]^{1/2}\right\}}{\cos h^{-1}\left(\frac{\Omega_s}{\Omega_p}\right)}$$

5. Calculate the analog cut off frequency Ω_c from the equations given below:

$$\text{For bilinear transformation, } \Omega_c = \frac{2}{T}\frac{\tan(\omega_p/2)}{\left[\frac{1}{A_p^2} - 1\right]^{1/2N}}$$

$$\text{For impulse invariant, } \Omega_c = \frac{(\omega_p/T)}{\left[\frac{1}{A_p^2} - 1\right]^{1/2N}}$$

6. Determine analog transfer function, when N is even

$$H_a(s) = \prod_{k=1}^{N/2} \frac{B_k\Omega_c^2}{s^2 + b_k\Omega_c s + c_k\Omega_c^2}$$

When N is odd

$$H_a(s) = \frac{B_0\Omega_c}{s + c_0\Omega_c} \prod_{k=1}^{N-1/2} \frac{B_k\Omega_c^2}{s^2 + b_k\Omega_c s + c_k\Omega_c^2}$$

where

$$b_k = 2Y_N \sin\left(\frac{(2k-1)\pi}{2N}\right)$$

$$c_k = Y_N^2 + \cos^2\left(\frac{(2k-1)\pi}{2N}\right)$$

$$c_0 = Y_N$$

$$Y_N = \frac{1}{2}\left\{\left[\left(\frac{1}{\epsilon^2}+1\right)^{1/2}+\frac{1}{\epsilon}\right]^{1/N} - \left[\left(\frac{1}{\epsilon^2}+1\right)^{1/2}+\frac{1}{\epsilon}\right]^{-(1/N)}\right\}$$

B_k can be calculated from

$$N = \text{even}; \qquad H_a(s)\Big|_{s=0} = \frac{1}{(1+\epsilon^2)^{1/2}}$$

$$N = \text{odd}; \qquad H_a(s)\Big|_{s=0} = 1$$

(The normal practice is to take $B_0 = B_1 = B_2, \ldots, B_k$).

7. Convert $H_a(s)$ into $H(z)$ using the chosen transform (Bilinear or impulse invariance).
8. Realize the digital filter transfer function by a suitable structure.

3.10 Frequency Transformation

3.10.1 Analog Frequency Transformation

The IIR lowpass analog filters are designed for the given specifications. By applying appropriate approximations, and transformations lowpass digital filters are designed. By using frequency transformations it is possible to design lowpass filters with different passband frequencies, highpass filters, bandpass filters and bandstop filters. In the frequency transformation, the variable s of normalized ($\Omega_c = 1$) lowpass filter is replaced by appropriate variable. From the normalized lowpass filter, the following filters are designed:

1. Low pass to Low pass.
2. Low pass to Highpass filter.
3. Low pass to Bandpass filter.
4. Low pass to Band elimination filter (Band stop filter).

Let Ω_p be the passband frequency of lowpass analog filter. Let Ω'_p be the edge frequency of the lowpass filter which we wish to convert. The frequency transformation to achieve this is given by

$$\boxed{s \rightarrow \frac{\Omega_p}{\Omega'_p}} \tag{3.66}$$

3.10.1.1 *Low Pass to High Pass Filter*

The transformation that is made to convert the lowpass to highpass filter is given by

$$\boxed{s \rightarrow \frac{\Omega_p \Omega'_p}{s}} \tag{3.67}$$

where Ω_p = Edge frequency of the prototype lowpass filter and Ω'_p = Edge frequency of the highpass filter.

3.10.1.2 *Low Pass to Bandpass Filter*

Let Ω_l be the lower band edge frequency of bandpass filter and Ω_u be the upper band edge frequency of the same filter. The transfer function from lowpass filter to bandpass filter is achieved by the following transformation:

$$\boxed{s \rightarrow \Omega_p \frac{(s^2 + \Omega_l \Omega_u)}{s(\Omega_u - \Omega_l)}} \tag{3.68}$$

3.10.1.3 *Low Pass to Bandstop Filter*

Let

Ω_p = Passband edge frequency of the given lowpass filter.
Ω_u = Upper band edge frequency of the bandstop filter.
Ω_l = Lower band edge frequency of the bandstop filter.

The transfer function from lowpass prototype to bandstop filter transfer function is achieved by the following transformation.

$$s \rightarrow \Omega_p \frac{s(\Omega_u - \Omega_l)}{(s^2 + \Omega_u \Omega_l)} \tag{3.69}$$

3.10.2 Digital Frequency Transformation

If we design a lowpass digital filter and wish to convert to desired lowpass filter, highpass filter, Bandpass filter and bandstop filter, the following frequency transformation may be used.

3.10.2.1 *Lowpass to Lowpass Filter*

$$\boxed{z^{-1} \rightarrow \frac{z^{-1} - \alpha}{1 - \alpha z^{-1}}} \tag{3.70}$$

where

$\alpha = \frac{\sin[(\omega_p - \omega'_p/2)]}{\sin[(\omega_p + \omega'_p)/2]}$.
ω_p = Band edge frequency of the lowpass original filter.
ω'_p = Band edge frequency of the lowpass desired filter.

3.10.2.2 *Lowpass to Highpass Filter*

$$\boxed{z^{-1} \rightarrow \frac{z^{-1} + \alpha}{1 + \alpha z^{-1}}} \tag{3.71}$$

$$\alpha = \frac{\cos[(\omega_p + \omega_p')/2]}{\cos[(\omega_p - \omega_p')/2]}$$

3.10.2.3 Lowpass to Bandpass Filter

$$\boxed{z^{-1} \rightarrow \frac{(z^{-2} - \alpha_1 z^{-1} + \alpha_2)}{(\alpha_2 z^{-2} - \alpha_1 z^{-1} + 1)}} \tag{3.72}$$

$$\alpha_1 = \frac{2\alpha k}{k+1}$$

$$\alpha_2 = \frac{(k-1)}{(k+1)}$$

$$\alpha = \frac{\cos[(\omega_u + \omega_l)/2]}{\cos[(\omega_u - \omega_l)/2]}$$

$$k = \cot\frac{(\omega_u - \omega_l)}{2}\tan\frac{\omega_p}{2}$$

3.10.2.4 Lowpass to Bandstop Filter

$$\boxed{z^{-1} \rightarrow \frac{(z^{-2} - \alpha_1 z^{-1} + \alpha_2)}{(\alpha_2 z^{-1} - \alpha_1 z^{-1} + 1)}} \tag{3.73}$$

$$\alpha_1 = \frac{2\alpha}{(k+1)}$$

$$\alpha_2 = \frac{(1-k)}{(1+k)}$$

$$\alpha = \frac{\cos[(\omega_u + \omega_l)/2]}{\cos[(\omega_u - \omega_l)/2]}$$

$$k = \tan\frac{(\omega_u - \omega_l)}{2}\tan\frac{\omega_p}{2}$$

	Filter Type	Transformation
1.	Lowpass	$s \rightarrow \frac{s}{\Omega_c}$
2.	Highpass	$s \rightarrow \frac{\Omega_c}{s}$
3.	Bandpass	$s \rightarrow \frac{Q(s^2 + \Omega_0^2)}{\Omega_0 s}$
4.	Bandstop	$s \rightarrow \frac{\Omega_0 s}{Q(s^2 + \Omega_0^2)}$

where Ω_0 is center frequency, $\Omega_0 = \sqrt{\Omega_p \Omega_s}$ where Q is quality factor, $Q = \frac{\Omega_0}{\Omega_s - \Omega_p}$.

Example 3.21

The specification of the desired lowpass filter is

$$0.8 \le |H(\omega)| \le 1.0; \qquad 0 \le \omega < 0.2\pi$$
$$|H(\omega)| \le 0.2; \qquad 0.32\pi \le \omega \le \pi$$

Design Chebyshev digital filter using bilinear transformation.

Solution Given $A_p = 0.8$ at $\omega_p = 0.2\pi$ rad/sec. and $A_s = 0.2$ at $\omega_s = 0.32\pi$ rad/sec. For bilinear transformation we get,

$$\frac{\Omega_s}{\Omega_p} = \frac{\tan(\omega_s/2)}{\tan(\omega_p/2)} = \frac{\tan(0.32\pi/2)}{\tan(0.2\pi/2)} = 1.692$$

The attenuation constant $\epsilon = \left(\frac{1}{A_p^2} - 1\right)^{1/2} = 0.75$

$$N \ge \frac{\cos h^{-1}\left\{\frac{1}{\epsilon}\left[\frac{1}{A_s^2} - 1\right]^{1/2}\right\}}{\cos h^{-1}\frac{\Omega_s}{\Omega_p}} = \frac{\cos h^{-1}\left\{\frac{1}{0.75}\left[\frac{1}{0.2^2} - 1\right]^{1/2}\right\}}{\cos h^{-1}1.692}$$

$$= \frac{\cos h^{-1}6.53}{\cos h^{-1}1.692}$$

$$\cos h^{-1}6.53 = \ln(6.53 + \sqrt{6.53^2 - 1})$$
$$= 2.56$$
$$\cos h^{-1}1.692 = \ln(1.692 + \sqrt{1.692^2 - 1})$$
$$= 1.1173$$
$$N = \frac{2.56}{1.1173}$$
$$N \ge 2.295$$
$$N = 3$$

Let $T = 1$sec. The analog cut off frequency

$$\Omega_c = \frac{2}{T}\frac{\tan(\omega_p/2)}{\left[\frac{1}{A_p^2} - 1\right]^{1/2N}}$$

$$\Omega_c = 2\frac{\tan(0.2\pi/2)}{\left[\frac{1}{(0.8)^2} - 1\right]^{1/6}}$$

$$\Omega_c = 0.715 \text{ rad/sec.}$$

For N is odd, the analog transfer function

$$H_a(s) = \frac{B_0\Omega_c}{s + c_0\Omega_c}\prod_{k=1}^{(N-1)/2}\frac{B_k\Omega_c^2}{s^2 + b_k\Omega_c s + c_k\Omega_c^2}$$
$$= \frac{B_0\Omega_c}{s + c_0\Omega_c}\frac{B_1\Omega_c^2}{s^2 + b_1\Omega_c s + c_1\Omega_c^2}$$
$$Y_N = \frac{1}{2}\left\{\left[\left(\frac{1}{\epsilon^2}+1\right)^{1/2}+\frac{1}{\epsilon}\right]^{1/N} - \left[\left(\frac{1}{\epsilon^2}+1\right)^{1/2}+\frac{1}{\epsilon}\right]^{-(1/N)}\right\}$$
$$= \frac{1}{2}\left\{\left[\left(\frac{1}{0.75^2}+1\right)^{1/2}+\frac{1}{0.75}\right]^{1/3} - \left[\left(\frac{1}{0.75^2}+1\right)^{1/2}+\frac{1}{0.75}\right]^{-(1/3)}\right\}$$
$$= 0.7211 - 0.3467 = 0.3744$$
$$c_0 = Y_N = 0.3744$$
$$c_k = Y_N^2 + \cos^2\frac{(2k-1)\pi}{2N}$$
$$c_1 = Y_N^2 + \cos^2\left(\frac{\pi}{6}\right) = 0.3744^2 + \cos^2\left(\frac{\pi}{6}\right) = 0.8902$$
$$b_k = 2Y_N \sin\left[\frac{(2k-1)\pi}{2N}\right]$$
$$b_1 = 2 \times 0.3744 \sin\left[\frac{\pi}{6}\right] = 0.3744$$
$$H_a(s) = \frac{0.715B_0}{(s + 0.3744 \times 0.715)} \times \frac{(0.715)^2 B_1}{s^2 + 0.3744 \times 0.715s + 0.8902 \times 0.715^2}$$
$$= \frac{0.3655B_0B_1}{(s + 0.2677)(s^2 + 0.2677s + 0.4551)}$$

$$H_a(s)\Big|_{s=0} = 1$$
$$\frac{0.3655B_0B_1}{0.2677 \times 0.4551} = 1$$
$$3B_0B_1 = 1$$
$$B_0B_1 = \frac{1}{3}$$
$$B_0^2 = \frac{1}{3}$$
$$B_0 = 0.577$$
$$\therefore\ B_0 = B_1 = 0.577$$

$$H_a(s) = \frac{0.3655 \times 0.577^2}{(s+0.2677)(s^2+0.2677s+0.4551)}$$
$$= \frac{0.1217}{(s+0.2677)(s^2+0.2677s+0.4551)}$$

$$H(z) = H_a(s)\Big|_{s=\frac{2(1-z^{-1})}{1+z^{-1}}} \qquad \text{(Let } T = 1 \text{ sec.)}$$

$$H(z) = \frac{0.1217}{\left(\frac{2(1-z^{-1})}{1+z^{-1}} + 0.2677\right)\left(\left(\frac{2(1-z^{-1})}{1+z^{-1}}\right)^2 + 0.2677 \times \frac{2(1-z^{-1})}{1+z^{-1}} + 0.4551\right)}$$

$$= 0.1217(1+z^{-1})^3 \Big/ (2.2677 - 1.7323z^{-1})(4 + 4z^{-2} - 8z^{-1} + 0.5354 - 0.5354z^{-2} + 0.4551 + 0.4551z^{-2} + 0.9102z^{-1})$$

$$= \frac{0.1217(1+z^{-1})^3}{(2.2677 - 1.7323z^{-1})(4.4551 - 7.089z^{-1} + 3.9197z^{-2})}$$

$$= \frac{0.012(1+z^{-1})^3}{(1-0.7639z^{-1})(1-1.5913z^{-1}+0.8798z^{-2})}$$

$$\boxed{H(z) = \frac{0.012(1+z^{-1})(1+2z^{-1}+z^{-2})}{(1-0.7639z^{-1})(1-1.5913z^{-1}+0.8792z^{-2})}}$$

The cascade form realization is shown in Figure 3.24.

Example 3.22

The specifications of the desired lowpass digital filter are:

$$0.9 \le |H(\omega)| \le 1; \qquad 0 \le \omega < 0.25\pi$$
$$|H(\omega)| \le 0.24; \qquad 0.5\pi \le \omega \le \pi$$

Design Chebyshev digital filter using impulse invariant transformation.

(Anna University, December, 2007)

Solution Given $A_p = 0.9$ at $\omega_p = 0.25\pi$ rad/sec. and $A_s = 0.24$ at $\omega_s = 0.5\pi$ rad/sec.

$$\frac{\Omega_s}{\Omega_p} = \frac{\omega_s}{\omega_p} = \frac{0.5\pi}{0.25\pi} = 2$$

$$\epsilon = \left(\frac{1}{A_p^2} - 1\right)^{1/2} = \left(\frac{1}{(0.9)^2} - 1\right)^{1/2} = 0.484$$

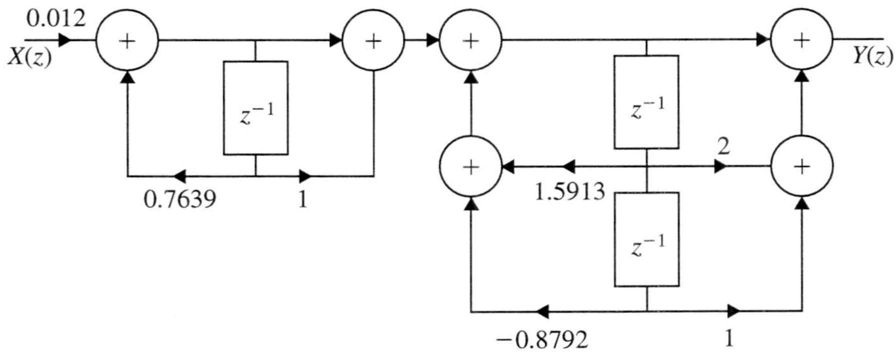

Figure 3.24 Cascade form realization of $H(z)$ for the Example 3.22.

$$N \geq \frac{\cosh^{-1}\left\{\frac{1}{\epsilon}\left[\frac{1}{A_s^2}-1\right]^{1/2}\right\}}{\cos h^{-1}\frac{\Omega_s}{\Omega_p}}$$

$$\geq \frac{\cosh^{-1}\left\{\frac{1}{0.484}\left[\frac{1}{0.24^2}-1\right]^{1/2}\right\}}{\cos h^{-1} 2}$$

$$\geq \frac{\cosh^{-1} 2.8126}{\cosh^{-1} 2}$$

$$N \geq 2.136$$

$$N = 3$$

Let $T = 1$ sec.

$$\Omega_c = \frac{\omega_p/T}{\left[\frac{1}{A_p^2}-1\right]^{1/2N}}$$

$$\Omega_c = \frac{0.25\pi}{\left[\frac{1}{(0.9)^2}-1\right]^{1/6}}$$

$$\Omega_c = 1 \text{ rad/sec.}$$

The analog transfer function for N is odd is given by

$$H_a(s) = \frac{B_0\Omega_c}{s+c_0\Omega_c}\prod_{k=1}^{(N-1)/2}\frac{B_k\Omega_c^2}{s^2+b_k\Omega_c s+c_k\Omega_c^2}$$

$$= \frac{B_0\Omega_c}{s+c_0\Omega_c}\cdot\frac{B_1\Omega_c^2}{s^2+b_1\Omega_c s+c_1\Omega_c^2}$$

$$Y_N = \frac{1}{2}\left\{\left[\left(\frac{1}{\epsilon^2}+1\right)^{1/2}+\frac{1}{\epsilon}\right]^{1/N} - \left[\left(\frac{1}{\epsilon^2}+1\right)^{1/2}+\frac{1}{\epsilon}\right]^{-(1/N)}\right\}$$

$$= \frac{1}{2}\left\{\left[\left(\frac{1}{0.484^2}+1\right)^{1/2}+\frac{1}{0.484}\right]^{1/3} - \left[\left(\frac{1}{0.484^2}+1\right)^{1/2}+\frac{1}{0.484}\right]^{-(1/3)}\right\}$$

$$= \frac{1}{2}\left\{1.6338 - \frac{1}{1.6338}\right\}$$

$$Y_N = 0.511$$

$$c_0 = Y_N = 0.511$$

$$c_k = Y_N^2 + \cos^2\frac{(2k-1)\pi}{2N}$$

$$c_1 = 0.511^2 + \cos^2\left(\frac{\pi}{6}\right) = 1.011$$

$$b_k = 2Y_N \sin\left[\frac{(2k-1)\pi}{2N}\right]$$

$$b_1 = 2 \times 0.511 \sin\left[\frac{\pi}{6}\right] = 0.511$$

$$\therefore\ H_a(s) = \frac{B_0 B_1}{(s+0.511)(s^2+0.511s+1.011)}$$

$$H_a(s)\Big|_{s=0} = 1$$

$$\frac{B_0 B_1}{0.511 \times 1.011} = 1 \qquad (\text{Let } B_0 = B_1)$$

$$B_0^2 = \frac{1}{1.939}$$

$$B_0 = 0.719$$

$$\therefore\ B_0 = B_1 = 0.719$$

$$H_a(s) = \frac{(0.719)^2}{(s+0.511)(s^2+0.511s+1.011)}$$

$$= \frac{0.517}{(s+0.511)(s^2+0.511s+1.011)}$$

$$= \frac{A}{(s+0.511)} + \frac{Bs+C}{(s^2+0.511s+1.011)}$$

$$A(s^2+0.511s+1.011) + (Bs+C)(s+0.511) = 0.517$$

Put $s = -0.511$

$$A(1.011) = 0.5166; \quad A = 0.511$$

Put $s = 0$

$$1.01A + 0.51C = 0.517; \quad C = 0$$

Equating the coefficients of s^2 we get

$$A + B = 0$$
$$B = -0.511$$

$A = 0.511, B = -0.511$ and $C = 0$

$$H_a(s) = \frac{0.511}{(s+0.511)} - \frac{0.511s}{(s^2+0.511s+1.011)}$$
$$= \frac{0.511}{(s+0.511)} - 0.511\frac{s+0.256-0.256}{(s+0.256)^2+0.972^2}$$
$$= \frac{0.511}{(s+0.511)} - 0.511\frac{s+0.256}{(s+0.256)^2+0.972^2}$$
$$+ 0.0511 \cdot \frac{0.256}{(s+0.256)^2+0.972^2}$$
$$= \frac{0.511}{(s+0.511)} - 0.511\frac{s+0.256}{(s+0.256)^2+0.972^2} + \frac{0.0511}{0.972}$$
$$\times 0.256 \cdot \frac{0.972}{(s+0.256)^2+0.972^2}$$
$$H(s) = \frac{0.511}{(s+0.511)} - 0.511\frac{s+0.256}{(s+0.256)^2+0.972^2} + 0.135$$
$$\times \frac{0.972}{(s+0.256)^2+0.972}$$
$$H(z) = \frac{0.511}{1-e^{-0.511}z^{-1}} - 0.511\frac{1-e^{-0.256}\cos(0.972)z^{-1}}{1-2e^{-0.256}(\cos 0.972)z^{-1}+e^{-2\times 0.256}z^{-2}}$$
$$+ 0.135\frac{e^{-0.256}\sin(0.972)z^{-1}}{1-2e^{-0.256}(\cos 0.972)z^{-1}+e^{-2\times 0.256}z^{-2}}$$
$$= \frac{0.511}{1-0.6z^{-1}} + \frac{-0.511+0.223z^{-1}}{1-0.873z^{-1}+0.6z^{-2}} + \frac{0.086z^{-1}}{1-0.873z^{-1}+0.6z^{-2}}$$
$$= \frac{0.511}{1-0.6z^{-1}} + \frac{-0.511+0.223z^{-1}+0.086z^{-1}}{1-0.873z^{-1}+0.6z^{-2}}$$

$$\boxed{H(z) = \frac{0.511}{1-0.6z^{-1}} + \frac{-0.511+0.309z^{-1}}{1-0.873z^{-1}+0.6z^{-2}}}$$

Example 3.23

Determine the system lowest order Chebyshev digital filter that meets the following specification:

(*a*) 1 dB ripple in the passband $0 \leq |\omega| \leq 0.3\pi$.

(*b*) Atleast 60 dB attenuation in the stopband $0.35\pi \leq |\omega| \leq \pi$. Use the bilinear transformation.

Solution

$$-20\log A_p = 1 \text{ dB}, \quad \omega_p = 0.3\pi$$

$$-20\log A_s = 60 \text{ dB}, \quad \omega_s = 0.35\pi$$

$$20\log A_p = -1,$$

$$A_p = 0.89125,$$

$$20\log A_s = -60,$$

$$A_s = 0.001$$

$$\text{The attenuation constant } \epsilon = \left(\frac{1}{A_p^2} - 1\right)^{\frac{1}{2}}$$

$$= \left(\frac{1}{(0.89)^2} - 1\right)^{\frac{1}{2}} = 0.5123$$

$$\frac{\Omega_s}{\Omega_p} = \frac{\tan\left(\frac{\omega_s}{2}\right)}{\tan\left(\frac{\omega_p}{2}\right)} = \frac{\tan\left(0.35\frac{\pi}{2}\right)}{\tan\left(0.3\frac{\pi}{2}\right)} = \frac{0.6128}{0.5045}$$

$$= 1.203$$

$$N \geq \frac{\cosh^{-1}\left\{\frac{1}{\epsilon}\left[\frac{1}{A_s^2} - 1\right]^{\frac{1}{2}}\right\}}{\cosh^{-1}\frac{\Omega_s}{\Omega_p}}$$

$$\geq \frac{\cosh^{-1}\left\{\frac{1}{0.5123}\left[\frac{1}{(0.001)^2} - 1\right]^{\frac{1}{2}}\right\}}{\cosh^{-1}(1.203)}$$

$$\geq \frac{\cosh^{-1}(1951.98)}{\cosh^{-1}(1.203)}$$

$$\geq \frac{8.2697}{0.6265}$$

$$N \geq 13.1935$$

$$\boxed{N = 14}$$

Example 3.24

Design a Chebyshev filter with a maximum passband attenuation of 2.5 dB at $\Omega_p = 20$ rad/sec and the stopband attenuation of $\Omega_s = 50$ rad/sec.

(*Anna University, May, 2007*)

Solution Given

$$-20\log A_p = 2.5, \quad \Omega_p = 20 \text{ rad/sec}$$
$$A_p = 0.749,$$
$$A_p \approx 0.75$$
$$-20\log A_s = 30, \quad \Omega_s = 50 \text{ rad/sec}$$
$$A_s = 0.0316$$

$$\text{The attenuation constant } \epsilon = \left(\frac{1}{A_p^2} - 1\right)^{\frac{1}{2}}$$
$$= \left(\frac{1}{(0.75)^2} - 1\right)^{\frac{1}{2}} = 0.8819$$
$$\frac{\Omega_s}{\Omega_p} = \frac{50}{20} = 2.5$$
$$N \geq \frac{\cosh^{-1}\left\{\frac{1}{\epsilon}\left[\frac{1}{A_s^2} - 1\right]^{\frac{1}{2}}\right\}}{\cosh^{-1}\left(\frac{\Omega_s}{\Omega_p}\right)}$$
$$\geq \frac{\cosh^{-1}\left\{\frac{1}{0.8819}\left[\frac{1}{(0.0316)^2} - 1\right]^{\frac{1}{2}}\right\}}{\cosh^{-1}(2.5)}$$
$$\geq \frac{\cosh^{-1}(35.8654)}{\cosh^{-1}(2.5)}$$
$$\geq \frac{4.2727}{1.5667}$$
$$\geq 2.72$$
$$N = 3$$

The analog cut off frequency

$$\Omega_c \approx \Omega_p = 20 \text{ rad/sec}$$

For N is odd

$$H_a(s) = \frac{B_0\Omega_c}{s+c_0\Omega_c}\prod_{k=1}^{\frac{N-1}{2}}\frac{B_k\Omega_c^2}{s^2+b_k\Omega_c s+c_k\Omega_c^2}$$

$$= \frac{B_0\times 20}{s+(c_0\times 20)}\prod_{k=1}^{\frac{3-1}{2}}\frac{B_k(20)^2}{s^2+b_k 20s+c_k(20)^2}$$

$$= \frac{20B_0}{s+20c_0}\times\frac{20B_1}{s^2+b_1 20s+(20)^2c_1}$$

$$b_k = 2Y_N\sin\left(\frac{(2k-1)\pi}{2N}\right)$$

$$Y_N = \frac{1}{2}\left\{\left[\left(\frac{1}{\epsilon^2}+1\right)^{\frac{1}{2}}+\frac{1}{\epsilon}\right]^{\frac{1}{N}}-\left[\left(\frac{1}{\epsilon^2}+1\right)^{\frac{1}{2}}+\frac{1}{\epsilon}\right]^{-\left(\frac{1}{N}\right)}\right\}$$

$$= \frac{1}{2}\left\{\left[\left(\frac{1}{(0.8819)^2}+1\right)^{\frac{1}{2}}+\frac{1}{0.8819}\right]^{\frac{1}{3}}-\left[\left(\frac{1}{(0.8819)^2}+1\right)^{\frac{1}{2}}+\frac{1}{0.8819}\right]^{-\frac{1}{3}}\right\}$$

$$= \frac{1}{2}\left\{[1.51187+1.134]^{\frac{1}{3}}-[1.51187+1.134]^{-\frac{1}{3}}\right\}$$

$$= \frac{1}{2}\{1.3831-0.723\}$$

$$Y_N = 0.33$$

$$b_1 = 2Y_N\sin\left(\frac{(2-1)\pi}{2\times 3}\right)$$

$$= 2\times 0.33\sin\left[\frac{\pi}{6}\right]$$

$$b_1 = 0.33$$

$$c_0 = Y_N = 0.33$$

$$c_k = Y_n^2+\cos^2\left(\frac{(2k-1)\pi}{2N}\right)$$

$$c_1 = (0.33)^2+\cos^2\left[\frac{(2-1)\pi}{2\times 3}\right]$$

$$= (0.33)^2+\cos^2\left[\frac{\pi}{6}\right]$$

$$= (0.33)^2+0.75$$

$$c_1 = 0.8589$$

$$H_a(s) = \frac{20B_0}{s + (20 \times 0.33)} \times \frac{20^2 B_1}{s^2 + (0.33)(20)s + ((20)^2 \times 0.8589)}$$

$$H_a(s) = \frac{20B_0}{s + 6.6} \times \frac{20^2 B_1}{s^2 + 6.6s + 343.56}$$

For $N = $ odd, B_k can be calculated from

$$H_a(s)\Big|_{s=0} = 1, \quad [B_0 = B_1 = B_2 \cdots B_N]$$

$$\frac{20B_0}{6.6} \times \frac{20^2 B_1}{343.56} = 1$$

$$\frac{8000 B_0^2}{2267.496} = 1$$

$$B_0^2 = 0.2834$$

$$B_0 = 0.532$$

$$B_0 = B_1 = 0.532$$

$$H_a(s) = \frac{20 \times 0.532}{s + 6.6} \times \frac{20^2 \times 0.532}{s^2 + 6.6s + 343.56}$$

$$= \frac{10.64}{s + 6.6} \cdot \frac{212.8}{s^2 + 6.6s + 343.56}$$

$$H_a(s) = \frac{2265.76}{(s + 6.6)(s^2 + 6.6s + 343.56)}$$

$$H(z) = H_a(s)\Big|_{s=\frac{2}{T}\frac{(z-1)}{(z+1)}}, \quad \text{Let } T = 1 \text{ sec.}$$

$$= \frac{2265.76}{\left(\frac{2(z-1)}{z+1} + 6.6\right)\left[\left(\frac{2(z-1)}{(z+1)}\right)^2 + 6.6 \times \frac{2(z-1)}{(z+1)} + 343.56\right]}$$

$$= \frac{2265.76}{\left(\frac{2(z-1)+6.6(z+1)}{(z+1)}\right)\left(\frac{4(z-1)^2+13.2(z-1)(z+1)+343.56(z+1)^2}{(z+1)^2}\right)}$$

$$= \frac{2265.76(z+1)^3}{[2(z-1) + 6.6(z+1)][4(z^2 - 2z + 1) + 13.2(z^2 - 1) + 343.56(z^2 + 2z + 1)]}$$

$$= \frac{2265.76(z+1)^2}{[8.6z + 4.6][4z^2 - 8z + 2 + 13.2z^2 - 13.2 + 343.56z^2 + 687.12z + 343.56]}$$

$$\boxed{H(z) = \frac{2265.76(z+1)^2}{(8.6z + 4.6)[360.76z^2 + 687.72z + 332.36]}}$$

Example 3.25

Design a digital Chebyshev filter to meet the constraints

$$\frac{1}{\sqrt{2}} \leq |H(\omega)| \leq 1; \quad 0 \leq \omega \leq 0.2\pi$$

$$0 \leq |H(\omega)| \leq 0.1; \quad 0.5\pi \leq \omega \leq \pi$$

by using bilinear transformation. Assume $T = 1$ sec.

(Anna University)

Solution Given

$$A_p = 0.707 \text{ at } \omega_p = 0.2\pi \text{ rad/sec}$$
$$A_s = 0.2 \text{ at } \omega_s = 0.5\pi \text{ rad/sec}$$

The attenuation constant $\epsilon = \left(\frac{1}{A_p^2} - 1\right)^{\frac{1}{2}} = (2-1)^{\frac{1}{2}}$

$$\epsilon = 1$$

$$\frac{\Omega_s}{\Omega_p} = \frac{\tan\left(\frac{\omega_s}{2}\right)}{\tan\left(\frac{\omega_p}{2}\right)} = \frac{\tan\left(\frac{0.5\pi}{2}\right)}{\tan\frac{0.2\pi}{2}} = \frac{1}{0.3249}$$

$$\frac{\Omega_s}{\Omega_p} = 3.0378$$

$$n \geq \frac{\cosh^{-1}\left\{\frac{1}{\epsilon}\left[\frac{1}{A_s^2} - 1\right]^{\frac{1}{2}}\right\}}{\cosh^{-1}\frac{\Omega_s}{\Omega_p}}$$

$$\geq \frac{\cosh^{-1}\left\{\frac{1}{1}\left[\frac{1}{0.2^2} - 1\right]^{\frac{1}{2}}\right\}}{\cosh^{-1}(3.078)}$$

$$\geq \frac{\cosh^{-1}(4.899)}{\cosh^{-1}(3.078)}$$

$$\geq \frac{2.2716}{1.7899} \geq 1.269$$

$$N = 2$$

Given T = 1 sec. The analog cut off frequency

$$\Omega_c = \frac{2}{T}\frac{\tan\left(\frac{\omega_p}{2}\right)}{\left[\frac{1}{A_p^2}-1\right]^{\frac{1}{2}N}}$$

$$\Omega_c = 2\frac{\tan\left(\frac{0.2\pi}{2}\right)}{\left[\frac{1}{(0.707)^2}-1\right]^{\frac{1}{4}}} = \frac{0.6498}{1} = 0.6498 \text{ rad/sec}$$

For N is even

$$H_a(s) = \prod_{k=1}^{\frac{N}{2}} \frac{B_k\Omega_c^2}{s^2+b_k\Omega_c s+c_k\Omega_c^2}$$

$$= \frac{B_1\Omega_c^2}{s^2+b_1\Omega_c s+c_1\Omega_c^2}$$

$$Y_N = \frac{1}{2}\left\{\left[\left(\frac{1}{\epsilon^2}+1\right)^{\frac{1}{2}}+\frac{1}{\epsilon}\right]^{\frac{1}{N}} - \left[\left(\frac{1}{\epsilon^2}+1\right)^{\frac{1}{2}}+\frac{1}{\epsilon}\right]^{-\left(\frac{1}{N}\right)}\right\}$$

$$= \frac{1}{2}\left\{\left[\left(\frac{1}{1^2}+1\right)^{\frac{1}{2}}+\frac{1}{1}\right]^{\frac{1}{2}} - \left[\left(\frac{1}{1^2}+1\right)^{\frac{1}{2}}+\frac{1}{1}\right]^{-\frac{1}{2}}\right\}$$

$$= \frac{1}{2}\left\{[4.4142+1]^{\frac{1}{2}} - [4.4142+1]^{-\frac{1}{2}}\right\}$$

$$= \frac{1}{2}\{1.554-0.6435\}$$

$$Y_N = 0.45525$$

$$b_k = 2Y_n \sin\left(\frac{(2k-1)\pi}{2N}\right)$$

$$b_1 = 2Y_N \sin\left(\frac{(2-1)\pi}{4}\right)$$

$$= 2Y_N \sin\left(\frac{\pi}{4}\right)$$

$$= 2\times 0.45525 \sin\left(\frac{\pi}{4}\right)$$

$$b_1 = 0.6438$$

$$c_k = Y_N^2 + \cos^2\left(\frac{(2k-1)\pi}{2N}\right)$$

$$c_1 = (0.45525)^2 + \cos^2\left(\frac{\pi}{4}\right)$$

$$= (0.45525)^2 + 0.5$$

$$c_1 = 0.707$$

$$H_a(s) = \frac{B_1\Omega_c^2}{s^2 + 0.6438\Omega_c s + 0.707\Omega_c^2}$$

$$= \frac{B_1(0.6498)^2}{s^2 + 0.6438 \times 0.6498s + 0.707(0.6498)^2}$$

$$H_a(s)\frac{B_1 0.4222}{s^2 + 0.4183s + 0.2985}$$

For N is even.

$$H_a(s)\Big|_{s=0} = \frac{1}{(1+\epsilon^2)^{\frac{1}{2}}}$$

$$\frac{B_1 \times 0.4222}{0.2985} = \frac{1}{(1+1^2)^{\frac{1}{2}}}$$

$$\frac{0.4222B_1}{0.2985} = 1$$

$$B_1 = \frac{0.2985}{0.4222}$$

$$B_1 = 0.707$$

$$H_a(s) = \frac{0.707 \times 0.4222}{s^2 + 0.4183s + 0.2985}$$

$$H_a(s) = \frac{0.2985}{s^2 + 0.4183s + 0.2985}$$

Using bilinear transformation we get

$$H(z) = H_a(s)\Big|_{s=\frac{2}{T}\frac{z-1}{z+1}}, \quad T = 1 \text{ sec.}$$

$$= \frac{0.2985}{\left(2\frac{Z-1}{Z+1}\right)^2 + 0.4183\left(s\frac{(Z-1)}{(Z+1)}\right)2 + 0.2985}$$

$$= \frac{0.2985(z+1)^2}{4(z-1)^2 + 0.8366(z-1)(z+1) + 0.2985(z+1)^2}$$

$$= \frac{0.2985(z^2+2z+1)}{4(z^2-2z+1) + 0.8366(z^2-1) + 0.2985(z^2+2z+1)}$$

$$= \frac{0.2985(z^2+2z+1)}{4z^2 - 8z + 4 + 0.8366z^2 - 0.8366 + 0.2985z^2 + 0.597z + 0.2985}$$

$$= \frac{0.2985(z^2+2z+1)}{5.1351z^2 - 7.403z + 3.4619}$$

$$H(z) = \frac{0.2985(z^{-2}+2z^{-1}+1)}{3.4619z^{-2} - 7.403z^{-1} + 5.1351}$$

$$= \frac{0.2985(z^{-2}+2z^{-1}+1)}{5.1351(0.674z^{-2} - 1.4416z^{-1} + 1)}$$

$$\boxed{H(z) = \frac{0.0581(z^{-2}+2z^{-1}+1)}{0.674z^{-2} - 1.4416z^{-1} + 1}}$$

Example 3.26

The transfer function of an analog LPF is

$$H(z) = \frac{1}{s+1}$$

with a bandwidth of 1 rad/sec. Use bilinear transform to design a digital filter with a bandwidth of 20 Hz at a sampling frequency of 600 Hz.

(Anna University, December, 2005)

Solution Given

$$H(z) = \frac{1}{s+1}, \quad \Omega_p = 1 \text{ rad/sec.}$$

$$f'_p = 20\text{Hz}$$

$$\Omega'_p = 2\pi f'_p$$

$$= 2\pi \times 20$$

$$= 125.66 \text{ rad/sec.}$$

Analog lowpass filter to lowpass filter transformation from equation (3.66) obtain by replacing $s \rightarrow \frac{\Omega_p}{\Omega'_p} \cdot s$

$$H(s) = \frac{1}{\frac{s}{125.66} + 1} = \frac{125.66}{s + 125.66}$$

The sampling frequency is given as $f_s = 60Hz$

$$T = \frac{1}{f_s} = \frac{1}{60} = 0.0167 \text{ sec.}$$

Using bilinear transformation we get,

$$H(z) = H(s)\Big|_{s=\frac{2}{T}\frac{(1-z^{-1})}{1+z^{-1}}}$$

$$H(z) = \frac{125.66}{s + 125.66}\Big|_{s} = \frac{2}{0.0167}\frac{1-z^{-1}}{1+z^{-1}}$$

$$= \frac{125.66}{120\frac{(1-z^{-1})}{(1+z^{-1})} + 125.66}$$

$$= \frac{125.66(1+z^{-1})}{120(1-z^{-1}) + 125.66(1+z^{-1})}$$

$$= \frac{125.66(1+z^{-1})}{120 - 120z^{-1} + 125.66 + 125.66z^{-1}}$$

$$= \frac{125.66(1+z^{-1})}{245.66 + 5.66z^{-1}}$$

$$= \frac{125.66(1+z^{-1})}{245.66(1 + 0.023z^{-1})}$$

$$\boxed{H(z) = \frac{0.512(1+z^{-1})}{1 + 0.023z^{-1}}}$$

3.11 IIR Filter Design by Approximation of Derivatives

One way of converting an analog filter into a digital filter is to approximate the differential equation governing the analog filter by an equivalent difference equation. Thus, the first order differential equation can be approximated and written as follows.

$$\left.\frac{dy(t)}{dt}\right|_{t=nT} = \frac{y(nT) - y(nT - T)}{T}$$

$$= \frac{y(n) - y(n-1)}{T}$$

where T is the sampling interval. The above equation can be written with analog system function as $H(s) = s$ and digital system function $H(z) = \frac{(1-z^{-1})}{T}$. The frequency domain equivalence is therefore written as

$$\boxed{s = \frac{(1 - z^{-1})}{T}} \tag{3.74}$$

Thus, the system function for the digital IIR filter is written as

$$\boxed{H(z) = H_a(s)\Big|_{s=\left(\frac{1-z^{-1}}{T}\right)}.} \tag{3.75}$$

The stable analog filter when converted into digital filter should also be stable. The mapping of the LHP in the s-plane to z-plane has to be investigated. Equation (3.74) can be written as

$$z = \frac{1}{(1 - sT)}$$

Substituting $s = j\Omega$ in the above equation we have

$$z = \frac{1}{1 + j\Omega T}$$

$$= \frac{1 + j\Omega T}{(1 + j\Omega T)(1 + j\Omega T)}$$

$$= \frac{1}{(1 + \Omega^2 T^2)} + \frac{j\Omega T}{(1 + \Omega^2 T^2)}$$

Let

$$z = x + jy$$

$$x = \frac{1}{(1 + \Omega^2 T^2)} \quad \text{and} \quad y = \frac{\Omega T}{(1 + \Omega^2 T^2)}$$

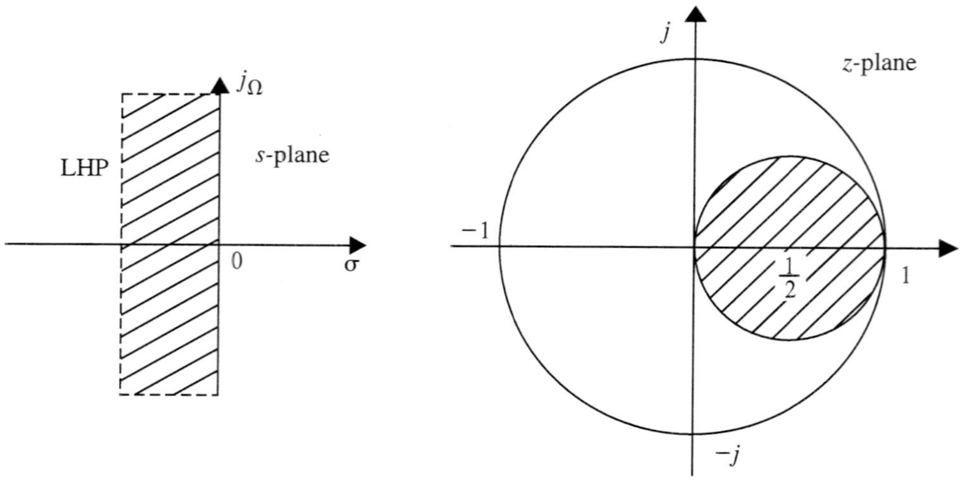

Figure 3.25 The mapping from s-plane to z-plane by approximation of derivatives.

Consider the following equation

$$\left(x-\frac{1}{2}\right)^2+y^2=\left[\frac{1}{(1+\Omega^2T^2)}-\frac{1}{2}\right]^2+\frac{\Omega^2T^2}{(1+\Omega^2T^2)}$$
$$=\left(\frac{1}{2}\right)^2.$$

This is the equation of a circle in the z-plane with centre at $z=\frac{1}{2}$ and radius $\frac{1}{2}$. Thus the mapping takes the points in LHP of the s-plane (for stable analog filter) into corresponding points inside this circle in the z-plane as shown in Figure 3.25.

From Figure 3.25 it is evident that the mapping $s=\frac{(1-z^{-1})}{T}$ takes LHP in the s-plane into points inside the circle of radius $\frac{1}{2}$ and at centre $z=\frac{1}{2}$ in the z-plane. Thus, the location of the poles of the digital filter so designed are confined to a small frequency range which means it is suitable for the design of lowpass and bandpass filters of small resonant frequencies and not suitable for highpass digital filter design. The method is illustrated by the following numerical example.

Example 3.27

Convert the analog bandpass filter with the system function

$$H_a(s)=\frac{1}{(s+0.1)^2+5}; \qquad T=0.1 \text{ sec}$$

into a digital IIR filter using the backward difference for the derivative.

Solution

$$H_a(s) = \frac{1}{(s+0.1)^2+5}$$

Substituting

$$s = \frac{(1+z^{-1})}{T} = (10+10z^{-1})$$

$$H(z) = \frac{1}{(10.10+10z^{-1})^2+5}$$

$$\boxed{H(z) = \frac{9.34\times 10^{-3}}{1-1.8877z^{-1}+0.934z^{-2}}}$$

The poles are at

$$z = 0.9438 \pm j0.209$$
$$= 0.9667\angle \pm 12.5^\circ$$

The poles are within the circle at centre $z = \frac{1}{2}$ and radius $\frac{1}{2}$. Hence, the digital filter so designed is stable.

3.12 Frequency Response from Transfer Function *H*(*z*)

The frequency response of a discrete time system can be determined from the transfer function $H(z)$. Several methods are available to achieve this. The geometric method of evaluation of frequency response is described here.

Consider the transfer function $H(z)$ expressed in terms of poles and zeros are given below:

$$H(z) = \frac{K(z-z_1)(z-z_2)\cdots(z-z_n)}{(z-p_1)(z-p_2)\cdots(z-p_n)} = \prod_{i=1}^{N}\frac{k(z-z_i)}{(z-p_i)}$$

The frequency response is obtained by substituting $z = e^{j\omega T}$ where $0 \leq \omega \leq \omega_s/2$; ω_s is sampling frequency; and T is sampling period.

The frequency response of $H(z)$ written as $H(e^{j\omega T})$ is given below:

$$H(e^{j\omega T}) = \frac{\prod_{i=1}^{N} k(e^{j\omega T}-z_i)}{\prod_{i=1}^{N}(e^{j\omega T}-p_i)}$$

For simplicity consider a system function $H(z)$ having two poles and two zeros. The pole zero diagram is shown in Figure 3.26. The zeros are located at z_1 and $-z_2$ and the poles are located at p_1 and p_2. Consider any point P on the unit circle. Draw a radial line from the origin to the point P. The line OP makes angle θ from the reference axis. θ and ωT are related as follows.

$$\theta = \omega_1 T$$

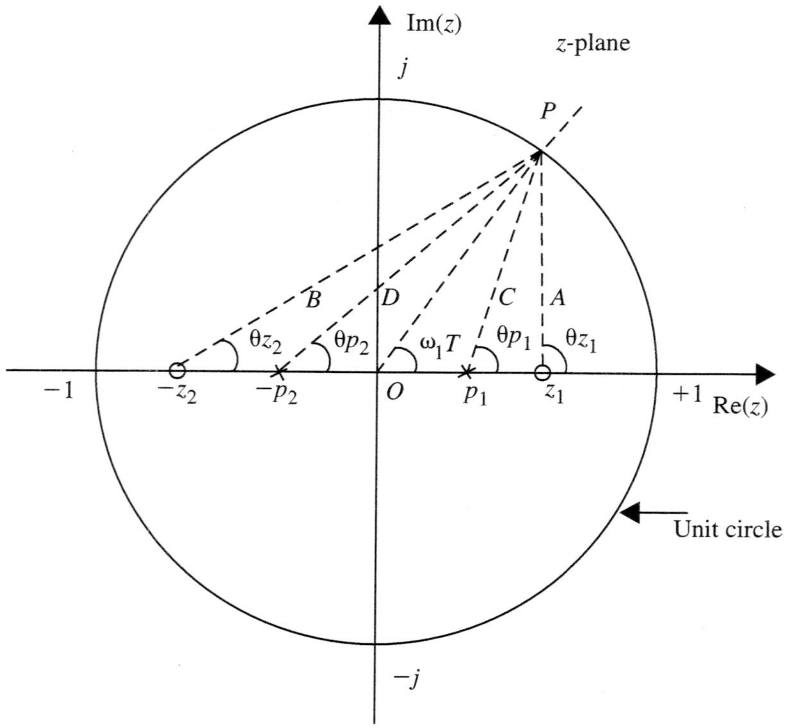

Figure 3.26 Pole-zero diagram of $H(z)$.

Knowing θ and the sampling period T, the frequency ω_1 at point P can be calculated. Draw radial lines from poles and zeros of $H(z)$ to the point P. Then

$$H(e^{j\omega T}) = K\frac{A\angle\theta_{z_1}B\angle\theta_{z_2}}{C\angle\theta_{p_1}D\angle\theta_{p_2}}$$

Knowing K, A, B, C and D, $|H(e^{j\omega T})|$ can be estimated. Similarly, knowing θ_{z_1}, θ_{z_2}, θ_{p_1} and θ_{p_2}, $\angle H(e^{j\omega T})$ can be estimated at $\omega = \omega_1$. By moving the point P on the unit circle, at $\omega = \omega_2$, the magnitude and phase of $H(e^{j\omega T})$ can be estimated. Since the frequency response gets repeated for every $\omega = \frac{\omega_s}{2}$, it is necessary to estimate the magnitude and phase of $H(e^{j\omega T})$ for the frequency interval $0 \le \omega \le \frac{\omega_s}{2}$. The following example illustrates the above procedure.

Example 3.28

Consider the following system function of a certain discrete time system:

$$H(z) = \frac{0.632z}{(z-1)(z-0.368)}$$

Draw the frequency response plot. Assume $T = 1$ sec.

Solution

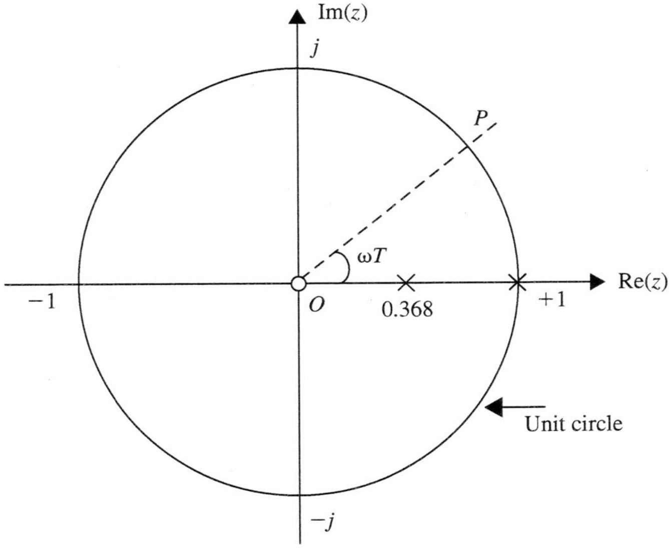

Figure 3.27 Pole-zero diagram of Example 3.28.

The poles and zeros of $H(z)$ are located in the z-plane as shown in Figure 3.27 and a unit circle is drawn. Any point P is chosen on the unit circle and radial line from the origin is drawn. From Figure 3.27 ωT is found and knowing $T = 1$, ω is estimated $|H(e^{j\omega T})|$ and $\angle H(e^{j\omega T})$ are also estimated at point P. This is repeated upto $\omega = \frac{\pi}{T} = \pi$. The values are tabulated as shown below:

ω	0	$\frac{\pi}{2}$	π	$\frac{3\pi}{2}$	2π
$\|H(e^{j\omega})\|$	∞	0.42	0.231	0.42	π
$\|H(e^{j\omega})\|$	$-90°$	$-155°$	$-180°$	$-205°$	$-270°$

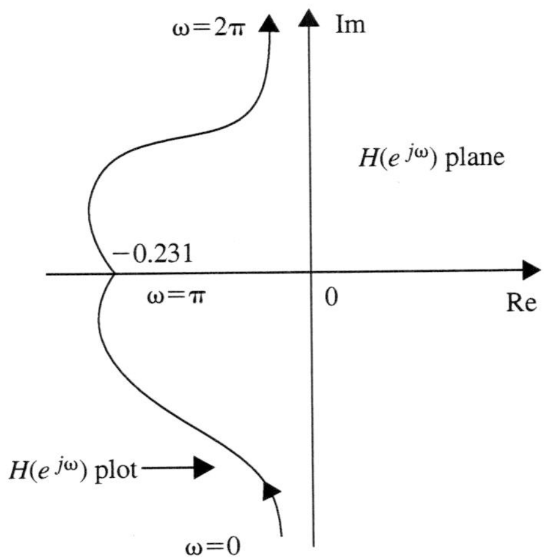

Figure 3.28 (*a*) Frequency response polar plot of discrete system.

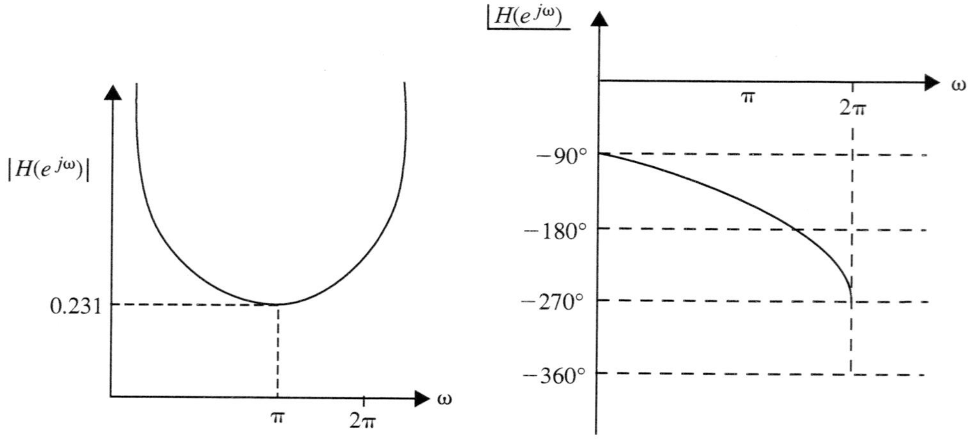

Figure 3.28 (*b*) Magnitude response. (*c*) Phase response.

The frequency response polar plot of the discrete time system is shown in Figure 3.28(*a*). The magnitude and phase responses are shown in Figures 3.28(*b*) and 3.28(*c*) respectively.

3.13 Structure Realization of IIR System

The IIR system can be described by the following difference equation.

$$y(n) = -\sum_{k=1}^{N} a_k y(n-k) + \sum_{k=0}^{M} b_k x(n-k) \tag{3.76}$$

Taking z-transform on both sides we get,

$$Y(z) = -\sum_{k=1}^{N} a_k z^{-k} Y(z) + \sum_{k=0}^{M} b_k z^{-k} X(z) \tag{3.77}$$

$$Y(z) + \sum_{k=1}^{N} a_k z^{-k} Y(z) = \sum_{k=0}^{M} b_k z^{-k} X(z)$$

$$Y(z)\left[1 + \sum_{k=1}^{N} a_k z^{-k}\right] = X(z) \sum_{k=0}^{M} b_k z^{-k}$$

$$\frac{Y(z)}{X(z)} = H(z) = \frac{\sum_{k=0}^{M} b_k z^{-k}}{1 + \sum_{k=1}^{N} a_k z^{-k}} \tag{3.78}$$

$$H(z) = \frac{b_0 + b_1 z^{-1} + b_2 z^{-2} + \cdots + b_M z^{-M}}{1 + a_1 z^{-1} + a_2 z^{-2} + \cdots + a_N z^{-N}} \tag{3.79}$$

where $H(z) \rightarrow$ transfer function of IIR system.

The different types of structures for realizing IIR Systems are:

(*i*) Direct form-I structure
(*ii*) Direct form-II structure
(*iii*) Cascade form structure
(*iv*) Parallel form structure
(*v*) Transposed direct form realization
(*vi*) Lattice structure form

3.13.1 Direct Form-I Structure

Consider the following difference equation of an IIR system.

$$y(n) = -\sum_{k=1}^{N} a_k y(n-k) + \sum_{k=0}^{M} b_k x(n-k)$$

$$\begin{aligned} y(n) &= -a_1 y(n-1) - a_2 y(n-2) - \cdots - a_N y(n-N) \\ &\quad + b_0 x(n) + b_1 x(n-1) + b_2 x(n-2) + \cdots + +b_M x(n-M) \end{aligned} \tag{3.80}$$

Taking z-transform, we get

$$\begin{aligned} Y(z) &= -a_1 z^{-1} Y(z) - a_2 z^{-2} Y(z) - \cdots - a_N z^{-N} Y(z) \\ &\quad + b_0 X(z) + b_1 z^{-1} X(z) + b_2 z^{-2} X(z) + \cdots + +b_M z^{-M} X(z) \end{aligned} \tag{3.81}$$

Equation (3.81) is represented in Figure 3.29.

This structure uses different delays (z^{-1}) for input and output. So more memory is required for realizing.

3.13.2 Direct Form-II Structure

Direct form-II structure uses less number of delays compared to Direct form-I. Consider the IIR difference equation (3.80)

$$y(n) = -\sum_{k=1}^{N} a_k y(n-k) + \sum_{k=0}^{M} b_k x(n-k)$$

$$\begin{aligned} y(n) &= -a_1 y(n-1) - a_2 y(n-2) - \cdots - a_N y(n-N) \\ &\quad + b_0 x(n) + b_1 x(n-1) + b_2 x(n-2) + \cdots + b_M x(n-M) \end{aligned}$$

Taking z-transform on both sides we get,

$$\begin{aligned} Y(z) &= -a_1 z^{-1} Y(z) - a_2 z^{-2} Y(z) - \cdots - a_N z^{-N} Y(z) \\ &\quad + b_0 X(z) + b_1 z^{-1} X(z) + b_2 z^{-2} X(z) + \cdots + b_M z^{-M} X(z) \end{aligned}$$

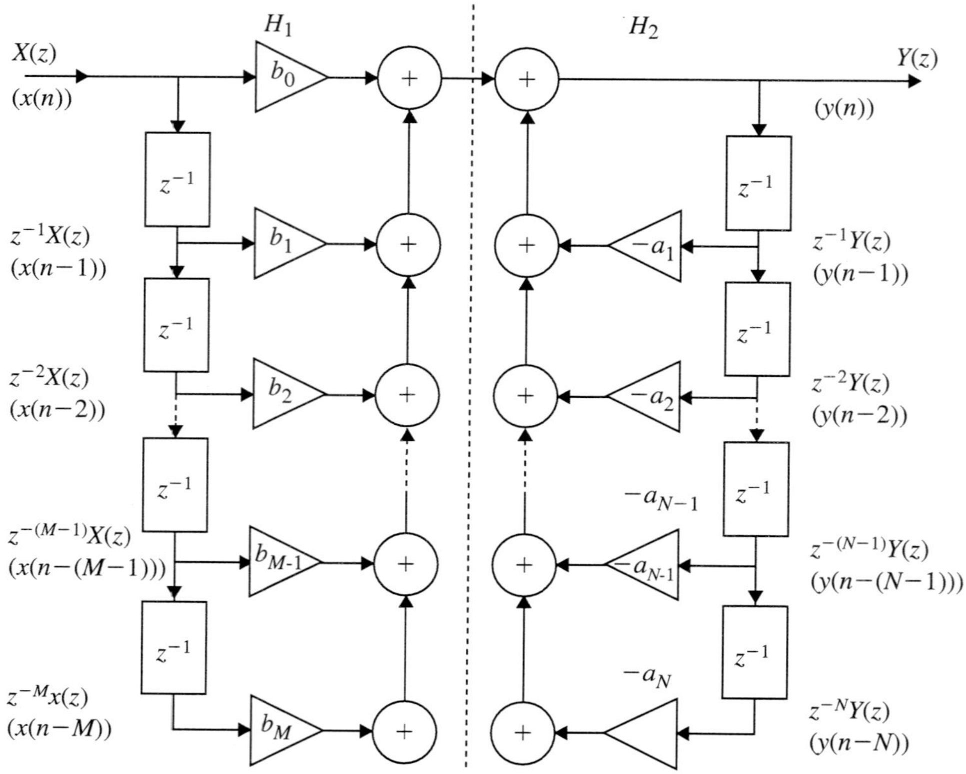

Figure 3.29 Direct form-I realization.

$$Y(z) + a_1 z^{-1} Y(z) + a_2 z^{-2} Y(z) + \cdots + a_N z^{-N} Y(z)$$
$$= b_0 X(z) + b_1 X(z) z^{-1} + b_2 z^{-2} X(z) + \cdots + b_M z^{-M} X(z)$$
$$Y(z)[1 + a_1 z^{-1} + a_2 z^{-2} + \cdots + a_N z^{-N}]$$
$$= X(z)[b_0 + b_1 z^{-1} + b_2 z^{-2} + \cdots + b_M z^{-M}]$$
$$\frac{Y(z)}{X(z)} = \frac{b_0 + b_1 z^{-1} + b_2 z^{-2} + \cdots + b_M z^{-M}}{1 + a_1 z^{-1} + a_2 z^{-2} + \cdots + a_N z^{-N}}$$

Let

$$\frac{Y(z)}{X(z)} = \frac{W(z)}{X(z)} \frac{Y(z)}{W(z)} \text{ where } \frac{W(z)}{X(z)} = \frac{1}{1 + a_1 z^{-1} + \cdots + +a_N z^{-N}} \tag{3.82}$$

$$\text{and } \frac{Y(z)}{W(z)} = b_0 + b_1 z^{-1} + b_2 z^{-2} + \cdots + b_M z^{-M} \tag{3.83}$$

Cross multiplying equation (3.82) we get,

$$W(z) + a_1 z^{-1} W(z) + a_2 z^{-2} W(z) + \cdots + a_N z^{-N} W(z) = X(z)$$
$$\therefore W(z) = X(z) - a_1 z^{-1} W(z) - a_2 z^{-2} W(z) - \cdots - a_N z^{-N} W(z) \tag{3.84}$$

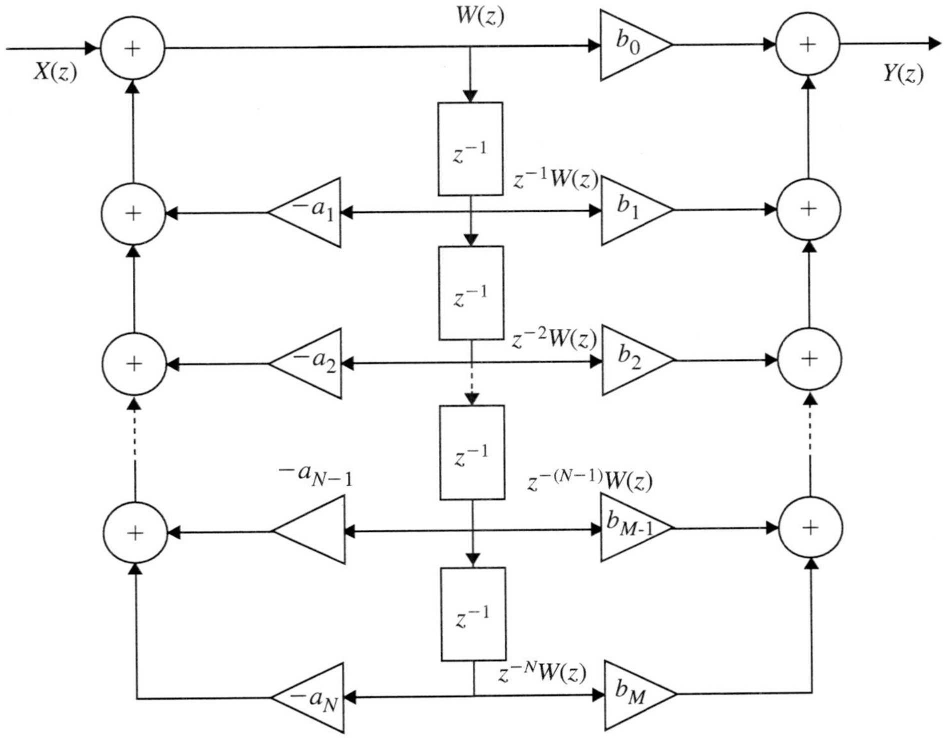

Figure 3.30 Direct form II structure of IIR system for $N = M$.

Cross multiplying equation (3.84)

$$Y(z) = b_0 W(z) + b_1 z^{-1} W(z) + b_2 z^{-2} W(z) + \cdots + b_M z^{-M} W(z) \qquad (3.85)$$

Equations (3.84) and (3.85) represent IIR system in z domain. It can be realized by direct form-II structure as shown in Figure 3.30.

3.13.2.1 Conversion of DF-I Structure to DF-II Structure

DF-I can be converted to DF-II by interchanging the order of cascading of two systems H_1 and H_2. It can be interchanged by linearity property.

Now we combine the delay elements to get a single system and the resultant structure will be DF-II structure as shown in Figure 3.31.

3.13.3 Cascade Form Realization

The transfer function $H(z)$ can be expressed as a product of a number of second order or first order sections.

$$H(z) = \frac{Y(z)}{X(z)} = \prod_{i=1}^{k} H_i(z) \qquad (3.86)$$

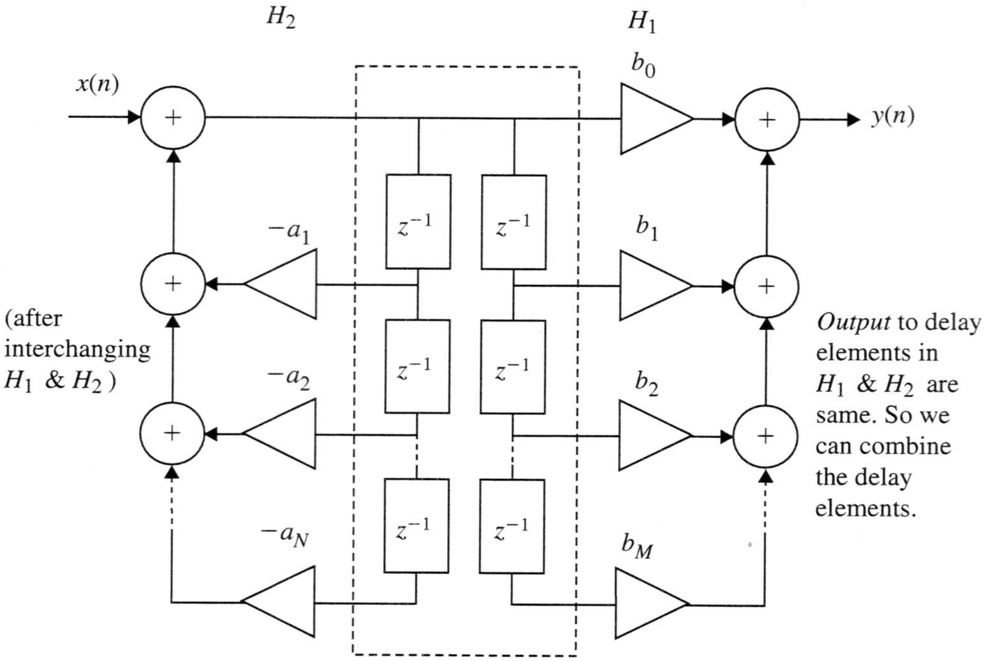

Figure 3.31 Conversion of Direct form I to Direct form II structure.

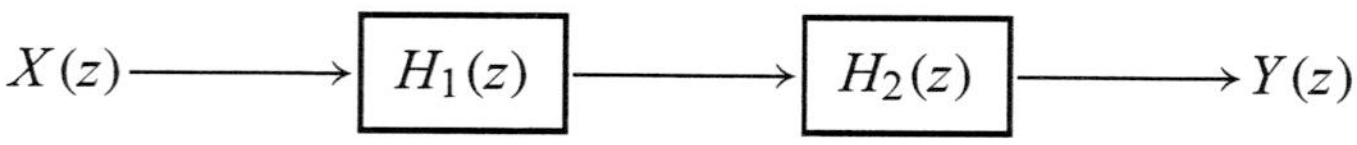

Figure 3.32 Cascade realization of IIR System.

where

$$H_i(z) = \frac{C_{0i} + C_{1i}z^{-1} + C_{2i}z^{-2}}{d_{0i} + d_{1i}z^{-1} + d_{2i}z^{-2}} \quad \text{(2nd order section)} \tag{3.87}$$

or

$$H_i(z) = \frac{C_{0i} + C_{1i}z^{-1}}{d_{0i} + d_{1i}z^{-1}} \quad \text{(1st order section)} \tag{3.88}$$

The individual second order or first order sections can be realised either in direct form-I or DF-II structures. The overall system is obtained by cascading the individual sections.

The cascade form is shown in Figure 3.32. The difficulty in realising the system in cascade form are:

(*i*) Decision of pairing poles and zeros.
(*ii*) Deciding the order of cascading the 1st and 2nd order sections.
(*iii*) Scaring multipliers should be provided between individual sections to prevent the filter variable from becoming too large or too small.

3.13.4 Parallel Form Realization

By applying partial fraction to $H(z)$, the system can be expressed as sum of 1st and 2nd order sections as given below.

$$H(z) = \frac{Y(z)}{X(z)} = C + \sum_{i=1}^{k} H_i(z) \tag{3.89}$$

where,

$$H_i(z) = \frac{C_{0i} + C_{1i}z^{-1}}{d_{0i} + d_{1i}z^{-1} + d_{2i}z^{-2}} \quad \text{(2nd order section)} \tag{3.90}$$

or

$$H_i(z) = \frac{C_{0i}}{d_{0i} + d_{1i}z^{-1}} \quad \text{(1st order section)} \tag{3.91}$$

The individual 1st and 2nd order section can be realized either in DF-I or in DF-II structure. Then the overall system is obtained by connecting the individual sections in parallel as shown in Figure 3.33.

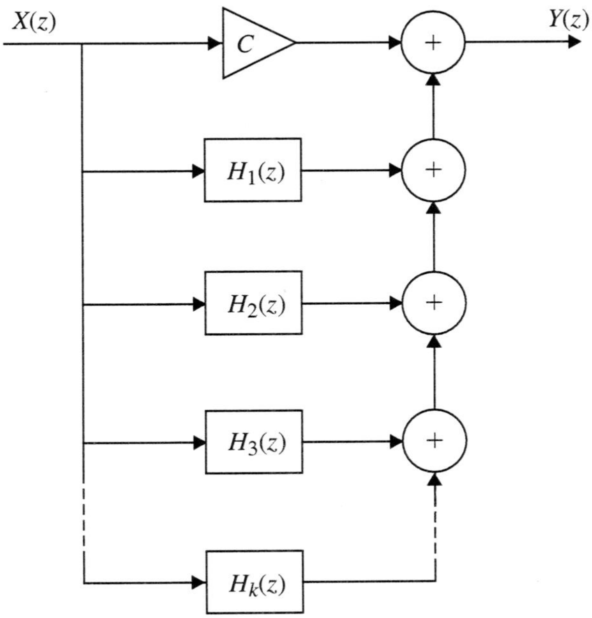

Figure 3.33 Parallel form realization of IIR filter.

3.13.5 Transposed Direct Form Realization

3.13.5.1 Signal Flow Graph

It is a graphical representation of the relationship between the variables of a set of linear difference equations. The basic elements of signal flow graph are branches and nodes.

Nodes: Represent system variables, which is equal to the sum of incoming signals from all branches connecting to the node. Nodes having two types:

Source Nodes → have only outgoing branches.
Sink Nodes → have only incoming branches.

Arrow head shows the direction of branch. The branch gain is indicated next to arrow head. The delay is indicated by the branch transmittance z^{-1}.

When branch transmittance is unity it is unlabelled. Consider the block diagram of 1st order digital filter as shown in Figure 3.34.

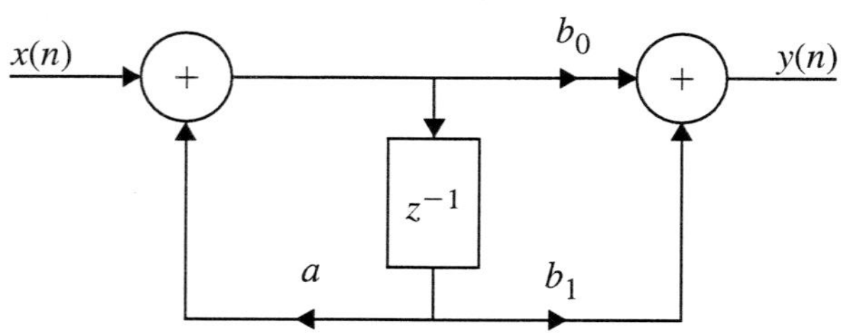

Figure 3.34 First order system.

The signal flow graph is shown in Figure 3.35.

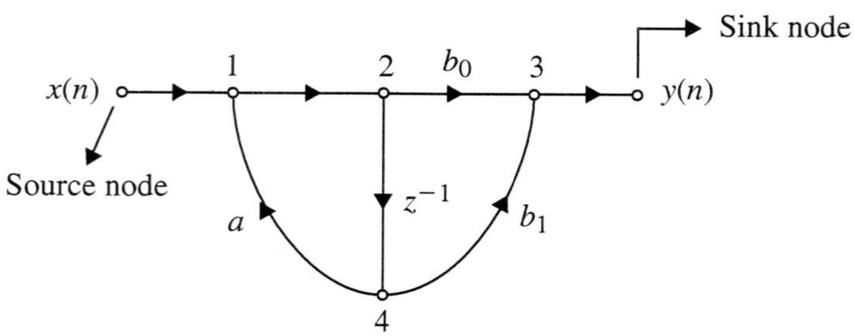

Figure 3.35 Signal flow graph of first order system.

Here we have 4 nodes out of this 2 nodes are running nodes, while other 2 are branching points. The delay is indicated by branch transmittance z^{-1}. Branch transmittance are indicated next to arrow head. The signal flow graph of first order filter is shown in Figure 3.35.

3.13.6 Transposition Theorem and Transposed Structure

The transpose of a structure is defined by the following operations:

(*i*) Reverse the direction of all branches in the signal flow graph.
(*ii*) Interchange the inputs and outputs.
(*iii*) Reverse the roles of all nodes in the flow graph.
(*vi*) Summing points become branching points.
(*v*) Branching points become running points.

According to transportation theorem, the system transfer function remains unchanged by transposition.

Example 3.29

Realise the 2nd order digital filter

$$y(n) = 2n\cos\omega_0 y(n-1) - r^2 y(n-2) + x(n) - r\cos\omega_0 x(n-1).$$

Solution Let

$$x(n) - r\cos(\omega_0)x(n-1) = \omega(n)$$

$$y(n) = 2r\cos\omega_0 y(n-1) - r^2 y(n-2) + \omega(n)$$

The realization is shown in Figure 3.36.

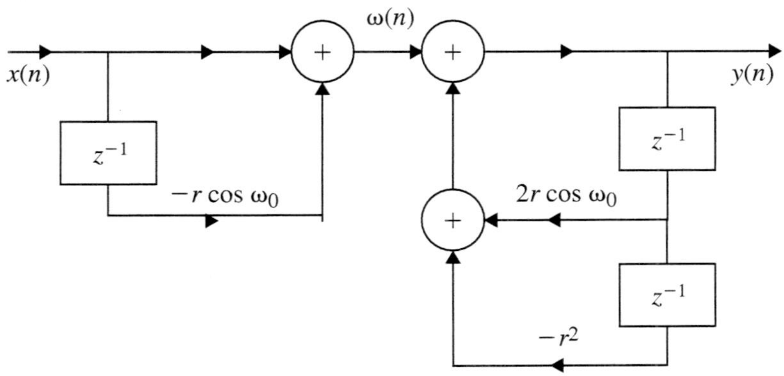

Figure 3.36 Direct form-I realization for Example 3.29.

Example 3.30

Obtain the DF-I realisation for the system described by difference equation

$$y(n) = 0.5y(n-1) - 0.25y(n-2) + x(n) + 0.4x(n-1)$$

Solution Let

$$x(n) + 0.4x(n-1) = \omega(n)$$

$$y(n) = 0.5y(n-1) - 0.25y(n-2) + \omega(n)$$

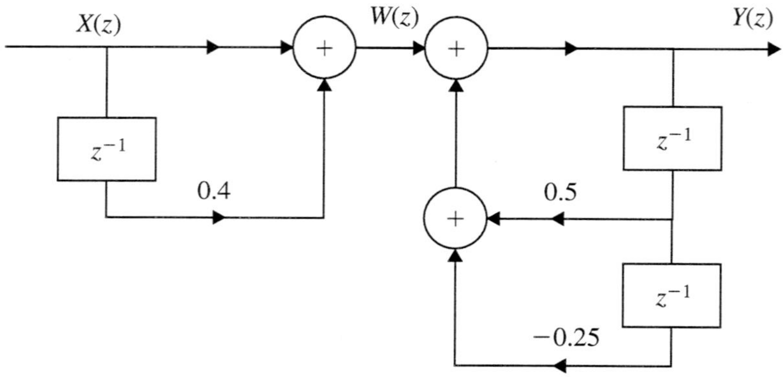

Figure 3.37 Direct form I realization for Example 3.30.

The direct form I is shown in Figure 3.37.

Example 3.31

Realise the 2nd order system $y(n) = 2r\cos\omega_0 y(n-1) - r^2 y(n-2) + x(n) - r\cos(\omega_0)x(n-1)$ in DF-II.

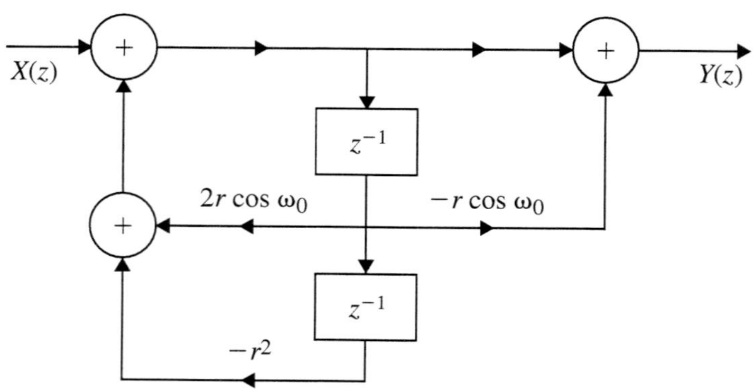

Figure 3.38 Direct form II realization for Example 3.31.

Solution

$$y(n) = 2r\cos\omega_0 y(n-1) - r^2 y(n-2) + x(n) - r\cos(\omega_0)x(n-1)$$

$$Y(z)(1 - 2r\cos\omega_0 z^{-1} + r^2 z^{-2}) = X(z)(1 - r\cos\omega_0 z^{-1})$$

$$\frac{Y(z)}{X(z)} = \frac{1 - r\cos\omega_0 z^{-1}}{1 - 2r\cos\omega_0 z^{-1} + r^2 z^{-2}}$$

The direct form II realization is shown in Figure 3.38.

Example 3.32

Determine the DF-II realization for the following system $y(n) = -0.1y(n-1) + 0.72y(n-2) + 0.7x(n) - 0.252x(n-2)$.

Solution

$$Y(z)(1 + 0.1z^{-1} - 0.72z^{-2}) = X(z)(0.7 - 0.252z^{-2})$$

$$\frac{Y(z)}{X(z)} = \frac{0.7 - 0.252z^{-2}}{1 + 0.1z^{-1} - 0.72z^{-2}}$$

Direct form II realization is shown in Figure 3.39.

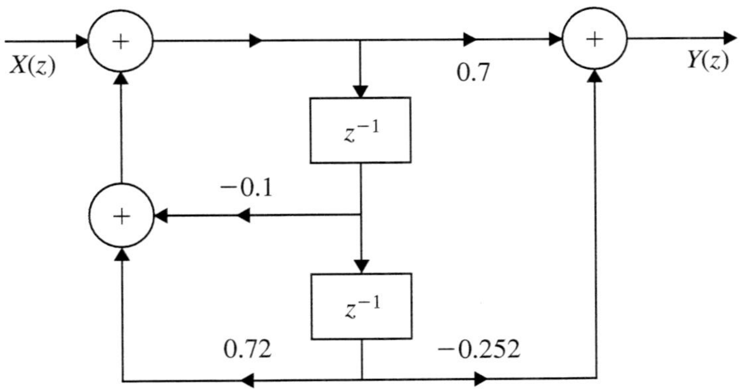

Figure 3.39 Direct form II realization for Example 3.32.

Example 3.33

Realise the system with difference equation

$$y(n) = \frac{3}{4}y(n-1) - \frac{1}{8}y(n-2) + \frac{1}{3}x(n-1) + x(n)$$

in cascade form.

Solution

$$Y(z)\left(1 - \frac{3}{4}z^{-1} + \frac{1}{8}z^{-2}\right) = X(z)\left(1 + \frac{1}{3}z^{-1}\right)$$

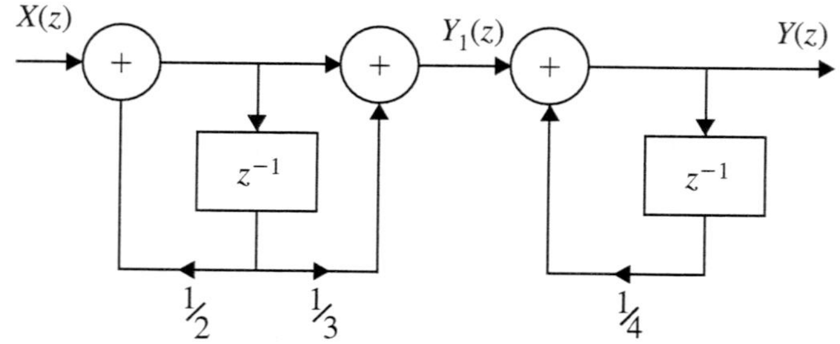

Figure 3.40 Cascade form realization for Example 3.33.

$$H(z) = \frac{Y(z)}{X(z)} = \frac{1 + \frac{1}{3}z^{-1}}{1 - \frac{3}{4}z^{-1} + \frac{1}{8}z^{-2}}$$

$$= \frac{1 + \frac{1}{3}z^{-1}}{\left(1 - \frac{1}{2}z^{-1}\right)\left(1 - \frac{1}{4}z^{-1}\right)} = H_1(z) \cdot H_2(z)$$

$$H_1(z) = \frac{1 + \frac{1}{3}z^{-1}}{1 - \frac{1}{2}z^{-2}}, \quad H_2(z) = \frac{1}{1 - \frac{1}{4}z^{-1}}$$

The cascade form realization is shown in Figure 3.40.

Example 3.34

Obtain the DF-I, DF-II, cascade and parallel form realisation for the system

$$y(n) = -0.1y(n-1) + 0.2y(n-2) + 3x(n) + 3.6x(n-1) + 0.6x(n-2)$$

DF-I

(a)

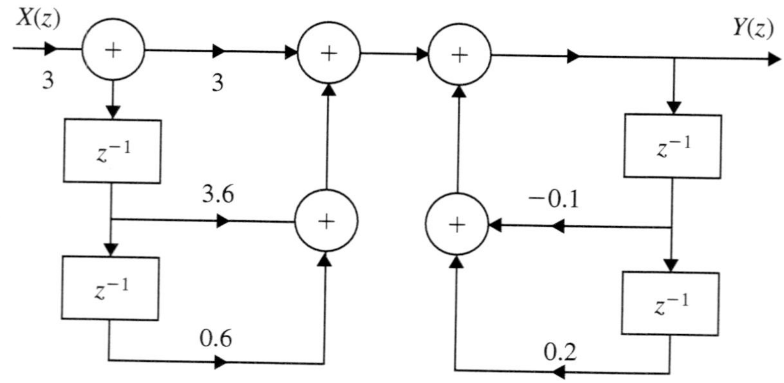

Figure 3.41 (*a*)

Solution

$$y(n) = -0.1y(n-1) + 0.2y(n-2) + 3x(n) + 3.6x(n-1) + 0.6x(n-2)$$

$$Y(z)[1 + 0.1z^{-1} - 0.2z^{-2}] = X(z)(3 + 3.6z^{-1} + 0.6z^{-2})$$

$$H(z) = \frac{Y(z)}{X(z)} = \frac{3 + 3.6z^{-1} + 0.6z^{-2}}{1 + 0.1z^{-1} - 0.2z^{-2}} = \left(\frac{3 + 3.6z^{-1} + 0.6z^{-2}}{1 + 0.1z^{-1} - 0.2z^{-2}}\right)$$

DF-II

(b)

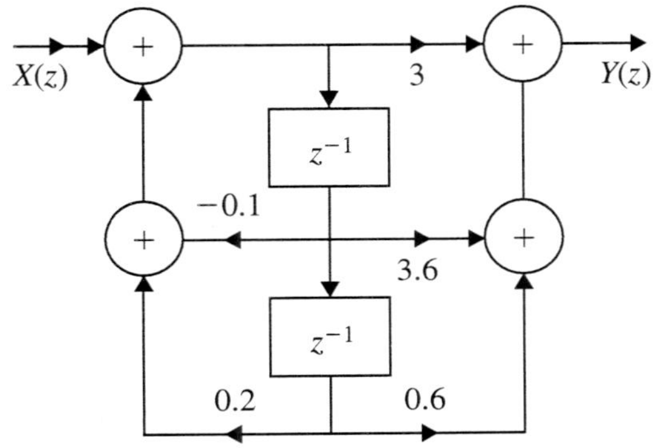

Figure 3.41 (*b*) Direct form I and II realization for Example 3.34.

Cascade Form

$$\frac{Y(z)}{X(z)} = \frac{3 + 3.6z^{-1} + 0.6z^{-2}}{1 + 0.1z^{-1} - 0.2z^{-2}}$$

$$= \frac{(3 + 0.6z^{-1})(1 + z^{-1})}{(1 + 0.5z^{-1})(1 - 0.4z^{-1})}$$

Let

$$H_1(z) = \frac{3 + 0.6z^{-1}}{1 + 0.5z^{-1}}, \quad H_2(z) = \frac{1 + z^{-1}}{1 - 0.4z^{-1}}$$

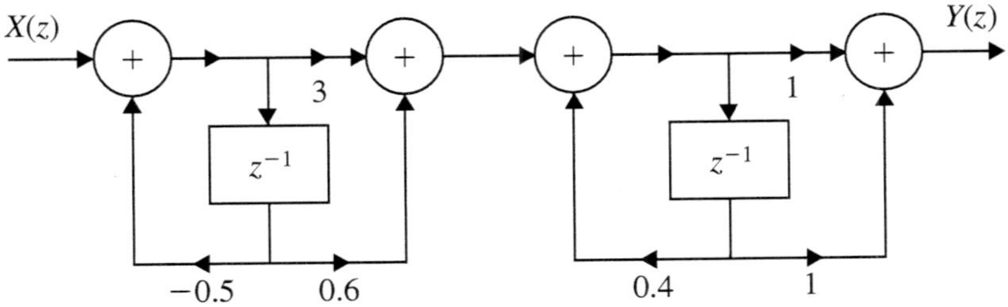

Figure 3.42 Cascade form realization for Example 3.34.

Parallel Form

$$H(z) = \frac{3 + 3.6z^{-1} + 0.6z^{-2}}{1 + 0.1z^{-1} - 0.2z^{-2}}$$

$$= -3 + \frac{3.9z^{-1} + 6}{1 + 0.1z^{-1} - 0.2z^{-2}}$$

Consider

$$\frac{3.9z^{-1} + 6}{1 + 0.1z^{-1} - 0.2z^{-2}} = \frac{3.9z^{-1} + 6}{(1 - 0.4z^{-1})(1 + 0.5z^{-1})}$$

$$= \frac{A}{1 - 0.4z^{-1}} + \frac{B}{1 + 0.5z^{-1}}$$

$$\Rightarrow A = (1 - 0.4z^{-1}) \cdot \frac{3.9z^{-1} + 6}{(1 - 0.4z^{-1})(1 + 0.5z^{-1})}\bigg|_{z^{-1}=\frac{1}{0.4}}$$

$$= 7$$

$$\Rightarrow B = (1 - 0.5z^{-1}) \cdot \frac{3.9z^{-1} + 6}{(1 - 0.4z^{-1})(1 + 0.5z^{-1})}\bigg|_{z^{-1}=\frac{-1}{0.5}}$$

$$= -1$$

$$\therefore H(z) = -3 + \frac{7}{1 - 0.4z^{-1}} - \frac{1}{1 + 0.5z^{-1}}$$

$$= C + H_1(z) + H_2(z)$$

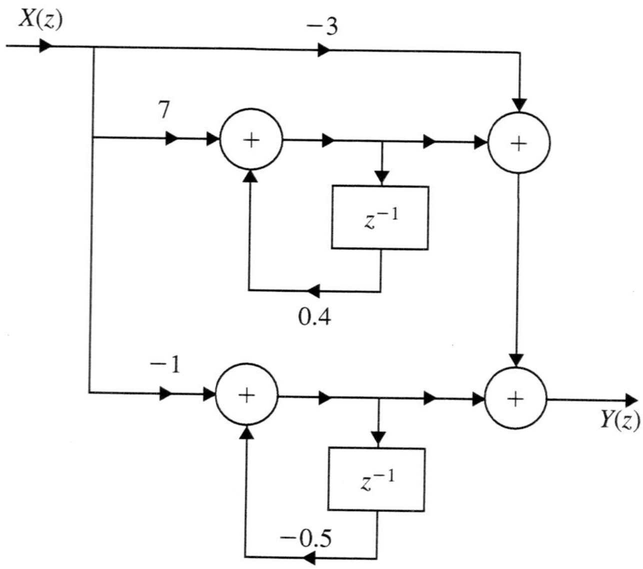

Figure 3.43 Parallel form realization for Example 3.34.

Example 3.35

Obtain the cascade realization for the following system.

$$H(z) = \frac{(1 + \frac{3}{2}z^{-1} + \frac{1}{2}z^{-2})(1 - \frac{3}{2}z^{-1} + z^{-2})}{(1 + z^{-1} + \frac{1}{4}z^{-2})(1 + \frac{1}{4}z^{-1} + \frac{1}{2}z^{-2})}$$

Solution Let $H(z) = H_1(z)H_2(z)$

$$H_1(z) = \frac{1 + \frac{3}{2}z^{-1} + \frac{1}{2}z^{-2}}{1 + z^{-1} + \frac{1}{4}z^{-2}}, \quad H_2(z) = \frac{1 - \frac{3}{2}z^{-1} + z^{-2}}{1 + \frac{1}{4}z^{-1} + \frac{1}{2}z^{-2}},$$

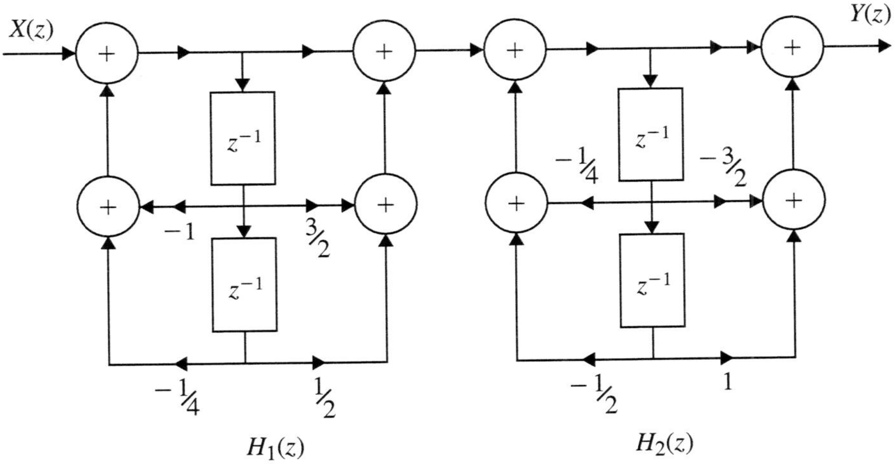

Figure 3.44 Cascade form realization for Example 3.35.

Example 3.36

Obtain the cascade realization of the system

$$H(z) = \frac{(1 - \frac{1}{2}z^{-1})(1 - \frac{1}{2}z^{-1} + \frac{1}{4}z^{-2})}{(1 + \frac{1}{4}z^{-1})(1 + z^{-1} + \frac{1}{2}z^{-2})(1 - \frac{1}{4}z^{-1} + \frac{1}{2}z^{-2})}$$

Solution Let

$$H(z) = H_1(z)H_2(z)H_3(z)$$

where

$$H_1(z) = \frac{1 - \frac{1}{2}z^{-1}}{1 + \frac{1}{4}z^{-1}}; \; H_2(z) = \frac{1 - \frac{1}{2}z^{-1} + \frac{1}{4}z^{-2}}{1 + z^{-1} + \frac{1}{2}z^{-2}}; \; H_3(z) = \frac{1}{1 - \frac{1}{4}z^{-1} + \frac{1}{2}z^{-2}}$$

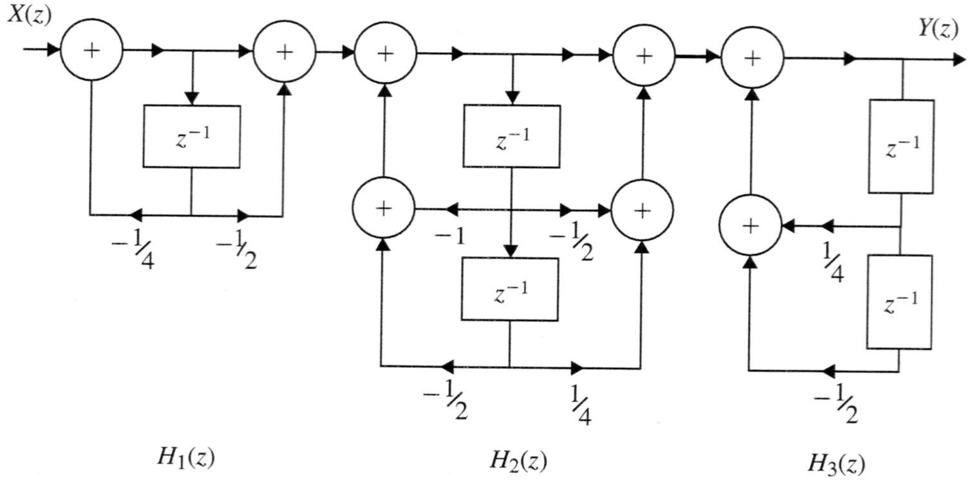

Figure 3.45 Cascade form realization for Example 3.36.

Example 3.37

Obtain the direct form I, direct form II, cascade and parallel form realization of LTI system governed by the equation

$$y(n) = -\frac{3}{8}y(n-1) + \frac{3}{32}y(n-2) + \frac{1}{64}y(n-3) + x(n) + 3x(n-1) + 2x(n-2)$$

(Anna University, April, 2004)

Solution **Direct form I**

$$y(n) = -\frac{3}{8}y(n-1) + \frac{3}{32}y(n-2) + \frac{1}{64}y(n-3) + x(n) + 3x(n-1) + 2x(n-2)$$

$$Y(z) = -\frac{3}{8}z^{-1}Y(z) + \frac{3}{32}z^{-2}Y(z) + \frac{1}{64}z^{-3}Y(z) + X(z) + 3z^{-1}X(z) + 2z^{-2}X(z)$$

Direct form II

$$H(z) = \frac{Y(z)}{X(z)} = \frac{Y(z)}{W(z)} \times \frac{W(z)}{X(z)} = \frac{1 + 3z^{-1} + 2z^{-2}}{1 + \frac{3}{8}z^{-1} - \frac{3}{32}z^{-2} - \frac{1}{64}z^{-3}}$$

where

$$\frac{W(z)}{X(z)} = \frac{1}{1 + \frac{3}{8}z^{-1} - \frac{3}{32}z^{-2} - \frac{1}{64}z^{-3}}$$

$$\frac{Y(z)}{W(z)} = 1 + 3z^{-1} + 2z^{-2}$$

$$X(z) = W(z)\left(1 + \frac{3}{8}z^{-1} - \frac{3}{32}z^{-2} - \frac{1}{64}z^{-3}\right)$$

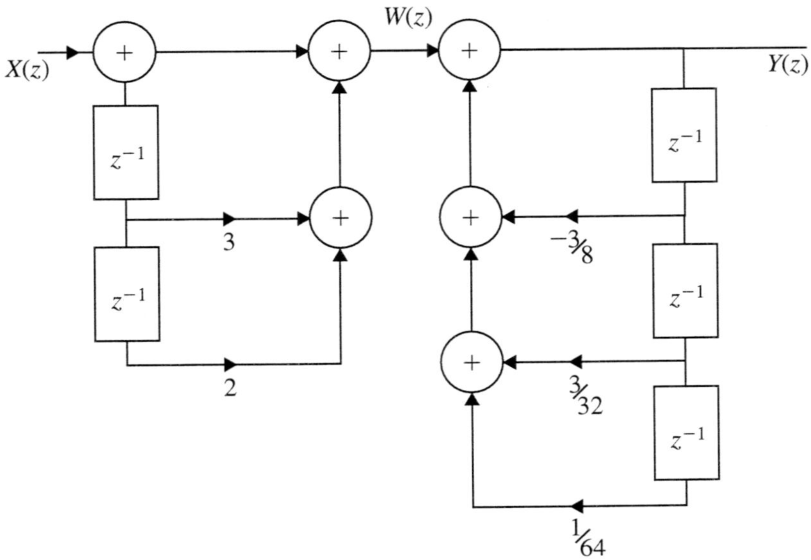

Figure 3.46 Direct form I realization of $H(z)$ for the Example 3.37.

$$W(z) = X(z) - \frac{3}{8}z^{-1}W(z) + \frac{3}{32}z^{-2}W(z) + \frac{1}{64}z^{-3}W(z)$$

$$Y(z) = W(z) + 3z^{-1}W(z) + 2z^{-2}W(z)$$

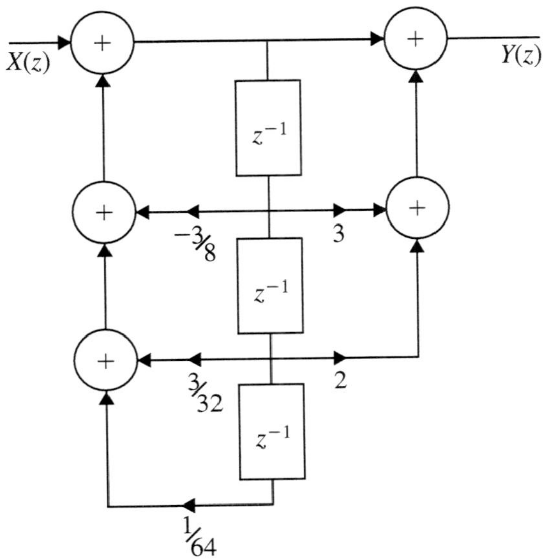

Figure 3.47 Direct form-II realization of $H(z)$ for the Example 3.37.

Cascade Form Realization

$$H(z) = \frac{1+3z^{-1}+2z^{-2}}{1+\frac{3}{8}z^{-1}-\frac{3}{32}z^{-2}-\frac{1}{64}z^{-3}}$$

$$= \frac{(1+z^{-1})(1+2z^{-1})}{\left(1+\frac{1}{8}z^{-1}\right)\left(1+\frac{1}{2}z^{-1}\right)\left(1-\frac{1}{4}z^{-1}\right)}$$

$$H(z) = H_1(z)H_2(z)H_3(z)$$

where

$$H_1(z) = \frac{1+z^{-1}}{1+\frac{1}{8}z^{-1}};\ H_2(z) = \frac{1+2z^{-1}}{1+\frac{1}{2}z^{-1}};\ H_3(z) = \frac{1}{1-\frac{1}{4}z^{-1}}$$

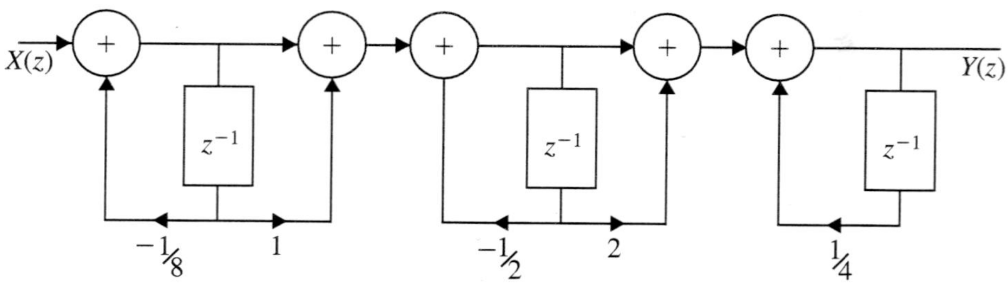

Figure 3.48 Cascade form realization of $H(z)$ for the Example 3.37.

Parallel Form

$$H(z) = \frac{(1+z^{-1})(1+2z^{-1})}{\left(1+\frac{1}{8}z^{-1}\right)\left(1+\frac{1}{2}z^{-1}\right)\left(1-\frac{1}{4}z^{-1}\right)}$$

$$= \frac{A}{1+\frac{1}{8}z^{-1}} + \frac{B}{1+\frac{1}{2}z^{-1}} + \frac{C}{1-\frac{1}{4}z^{-1}}$$

$$A = \left.\frac{(1+z^{-1})(1+2z^{-1})}{\left(1+\frac{1}{2}z^{-1}\right)\left(1-\frac{1}{4}z^{-1}\right)}\right|_{z^{-1}=-8} = -\frac{35}{3}$$

$$B = \left.\frac{(1+z^{-1})(1+2z^{-1})}{\left(1+\frac{1}{8}z^{-1}\right)\left(1-\frac{1}{4}z^{-1}\right)}\right|_{z^{-1}=-2} = \frac{8}{3}$$

$$C = \left.\frac{(1+z^{-1})(1+2z^{-1})}{\left(1+\frac{1}{8}z^{-1}\right)\left(1+\frac{1}{2}z^{-1}\right)}\right|_{z^{-1}=4} = 10$$

$$H(z) = -\frac{35}{3}\left(\frac{1}{1+\frac{1}{8}z^{-1}}\right) + \frac{8}{3}\left(\frac{1}{1+\frac{1}{2}z^{-1}}\right) + 10\left(\frac{1}{1-\frac{1}{4}z^{-1}}\right)$$

$$H(z) = H_1(z) + H_2(z) + H_3(z)$$

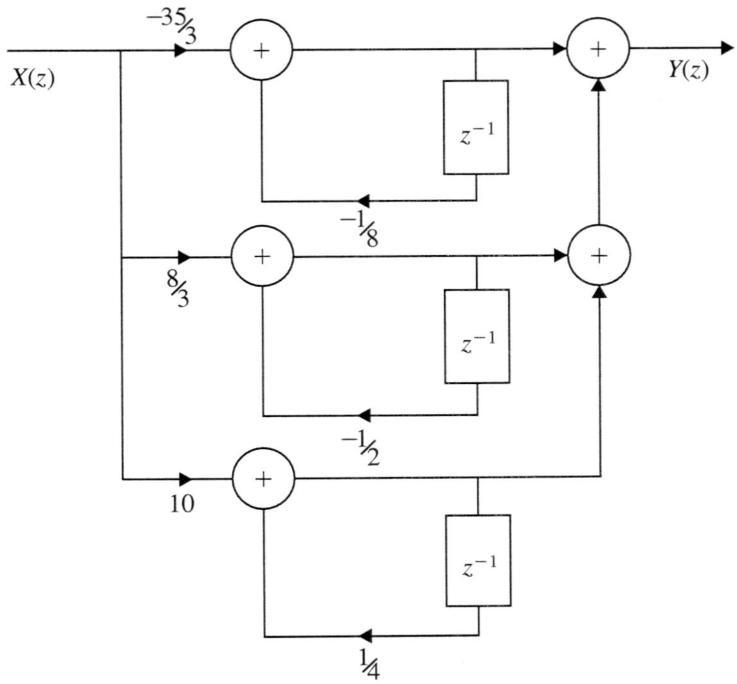

Figure 3.49 Parallel form realization of $H(z)$ for the Example 3.37.

Example 3.38

Realize the given system in cascade and parallel form

$$H(z) = \frac{1 + \frac{1}{2}z^{-1}}{\left(1 - z^{-1} + \frac{1}{4}z^{-2}\right)\left(1 - z^{-1} + \frac{1}{2}z^{-2}\right)}$$

Solution **Cascade Form Realization**

$$H(z) = \frac{1 + \frac{1}{2}z^{-1}}{\left(1 - z^{-1} + \frac{1}{4}z^{-2}\right)\left(1 - z^{-1} + \frac{1}{2}z^{-2}\right)}$$

$$= \frac{1}{1 - z^{-1} + \frac{1}{4}z^{-2}} \cdot \frac{1 + \frac{1}{2}z^{-1}}{1 - z^{-1} + \frac{1}{2}z^{-2}}$$

$$H(z) = H_1(z)H_2(z)$$

where

$$H_1(z) = \frac{1}{1 + z^{-1} + \frac{1}{4}z^{-2}}; \; H_2(z) = \frac{1 + \frac{1}{2}z^{-1}}{1 - z^{-1} + \frac{1}{2}z^{-2}}$$

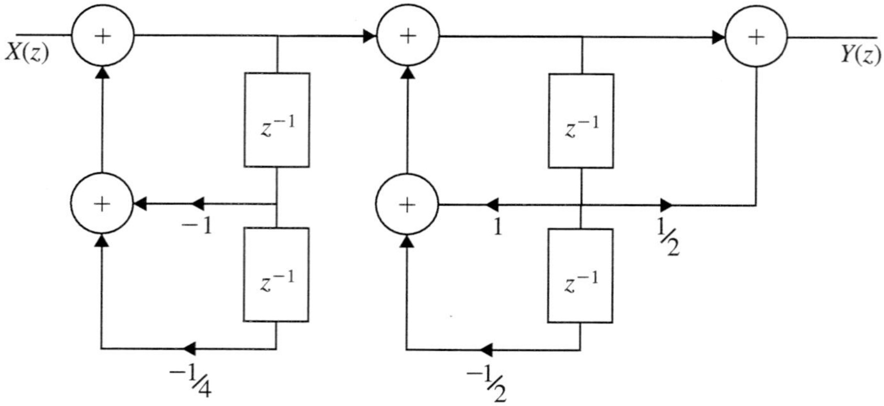

Figure 3.50 Cascade form realization of $H(z)$ for the Example 3.38.

Parallel Form Realization

$$H(z) = \frac{1 + \frac{1}{2}z^{-1}}{\left(1 - z^{-1} + \frac{1}{4}z^{-2}\right)\left(1 - z^{-1} + \frac{1}{2}z^{-2}\right)}$$

$$= \frac{z\left(z^3 + \frac{1}{2}z^2\right)}{\left(z^2 - z + \frac{1}{4}\right)\left(z^2 - z + \frac{1}{2}\right)}$$

$$\frac{H(z)}{z} = \frac{Az + B}{z^2 - z + \frac{1}{4}} + \frac{Cz + D}{z^2 - z + \frac{1}{2}}$$

$$= \frac{5z - \frac{3}{2}}{z^2 - z + \frac{1}{4}} + \frac{-4z + 3}{z^2 - z + \frac{1}{2}}$$

$$H(z) = \frac{5 - \frac{3}{2}z^{-1}}{1 - z^{-1} + \frac{1}{4}z^{-2}} + \frac{-4 + 3z^{-1}}{1 - z^{-1} + \frac{1}{4}z^{-2}}$$

$$= H_1(z)H_2(z)$$

$$H(z) = \frac{5 - \frac{3}{2}z^{-1}}{1 - z^2 + \frac{1}{4}z^{-2}} + \frac{-4 + 3z^{-1}}{1 - z^{-1} + \frac{1}{2}z^{-2}}$$

$$= \frac{5\left(1 - \frac{3}{10}z^{-1}\right)}{1 - z^{-1} + \frac{1}{4}z^{-2}} + \frac{-4\left(1 - \frac{3}{4}z^{-1}\right)}{1 - z^{-1} + \frac{1}{2}z^{-2}}$$

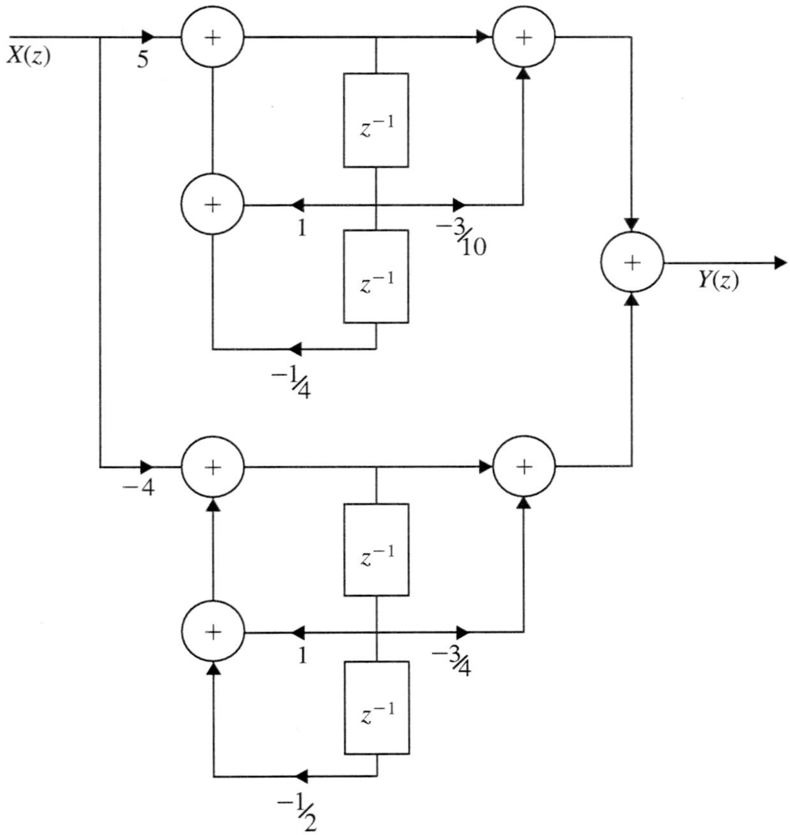

Figure 3.51 Parallel form realization of $H(z)$ for the Example 3.38.

Example 3.39

The transfer function of a system is given by

$$H(z) = \frac{(1+z^{-1})^3}{\left(1-\frac{1}{4}z^{-1}\right)\left(1-z^{-1}+\frac{1}{2}z^{-2}\right)}$$

Realize the system in cascade and parallel structures.

Solution **Cascade Form Realization**

$$H(z) = \frac{1+z^{-1}}{1-\frac{1}{4}z^{-1}} \cdot \frac{\left(1+z^{-1}\right)^2}{1-z^{-1}+\frac{1}{2}z^{-2}}$$

$$= \frac{1+z^{-1}}{1-\frac{1}{4}z^{-1}} \cdot \frac{1+2z^{-1}+z^{-2}}{1-z^{-1}+\frac{1}{2}z^{-2}}$$

$$H(z) = H_1(z)H_2(z)$$

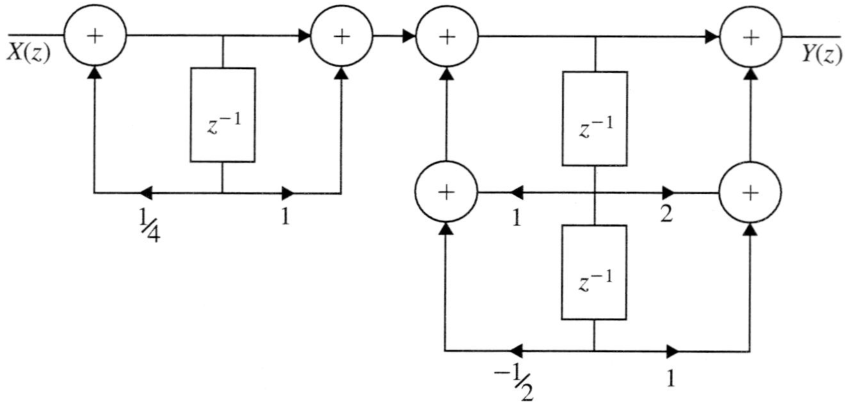

Figure 3.52 Cascade form realization of $H(z)$ for the Example 3.39.

where

$$H_1(z) = \frac{1+z^{-1}}{1-\frac{1}{4}z^{-1}} \quad \text{and} \quad H_2(z) = \frac{1+2z^{-1}+z^{-2}}{1-z^{-1}+\frac{1}{2}z^{-2}}$$

Parallel Form

$$H(z) = \frac{(1+z^{-1})^3}{\left(1-\frac{1}{4}z^{-1}\right)\left(1-z^{-1}+\frac{1}{2}z^{-2}\right)}$$

$$H(z) = \frac{1+3z^{-1}+3z^{-2}+z^{-3}}{1-\frac{5}{4}z^{-1}+\frac{3}{4}z^{-2}-\frac{1}{8}z^{-3}}$$

$$= \frac{z^3+3z^2+3z+1}{z^3-\frac{5}{4}z^{-2}+\frac{3}{4}z-\frac{1}{8}}$$

$$= 1+\frac{\frac{17}{4}z^2+\frac{9}{4}z+\frac{9}{8}}{z^3-\frac{5}{4}z^{-2}+\frac{3}{4}z-\frac{1}{8}}$$

$$= 1+\frac{\frac{17}{4}z^2+\frac{9}{4}z+\frac{9}{8}}{\left(z-\frac{1}{4}\right)\left(z^2-z+\frac{1}{2}\right)}$$

$$\frac{\frac{17}{4}z^2+\frac{9}{4}z+\frac{9}{8}}{\left(z-\frac{1}{4}\right)\left(z^2-z+\frac{1}{2}\right)} = \frac{A}{z-\frac{1}{4}}+\frac{Bz+C}{z^2-z+\frac{1}{2}}$$

$$= \frac{\frac{25}{4}}{z-\frac{1}{4}}+\frac{-2z+8}{z^2-z+\frac{1}{2}}$$

$$H(z) = 1+\frac{\frac{25}{4}z^{-1}}{1-\frac{1}{4}z^{-1}}+\frac{-2z^{-1}+8z^{-2}}{1-z^{-1}+\frac{1}{2}z^{-2}}$$

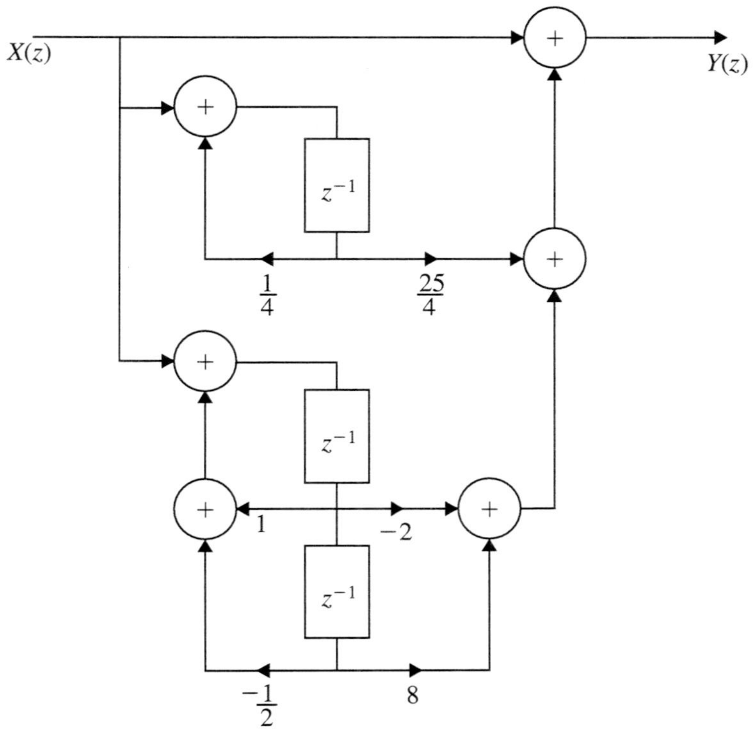

Figure 3.53 Parallel form realization of $H(z)$ for the Example 3.39.

Example 3.40

Determine the direct form II and transposed direct form II for the given system

$$y(n) = \frac{1}{2}y(n-1) - \frac{1}{4}y(n-2) + x(n) + x(n-1)$$

Solution Given

$$Y(z) = \frac{1}{2}z^{-1}Y(z) - \frac{1}{4}z^{-2}Y(z) + X(z) + z^{-1}X(z)$$

$$H(z) = \frac{Y(z)}{X(z)} = \frac{1+z^{-1}}{1-\frac{1}{2}z^{-1}+\frac{1}{4}z^{-2}}$$

Direct Form II Realization

To get transposed direct form II do the following operation:

1. Change the direction of all branches.
2. Interchange the input and output.
3. Change the summing point to branching point and *vice versa*.

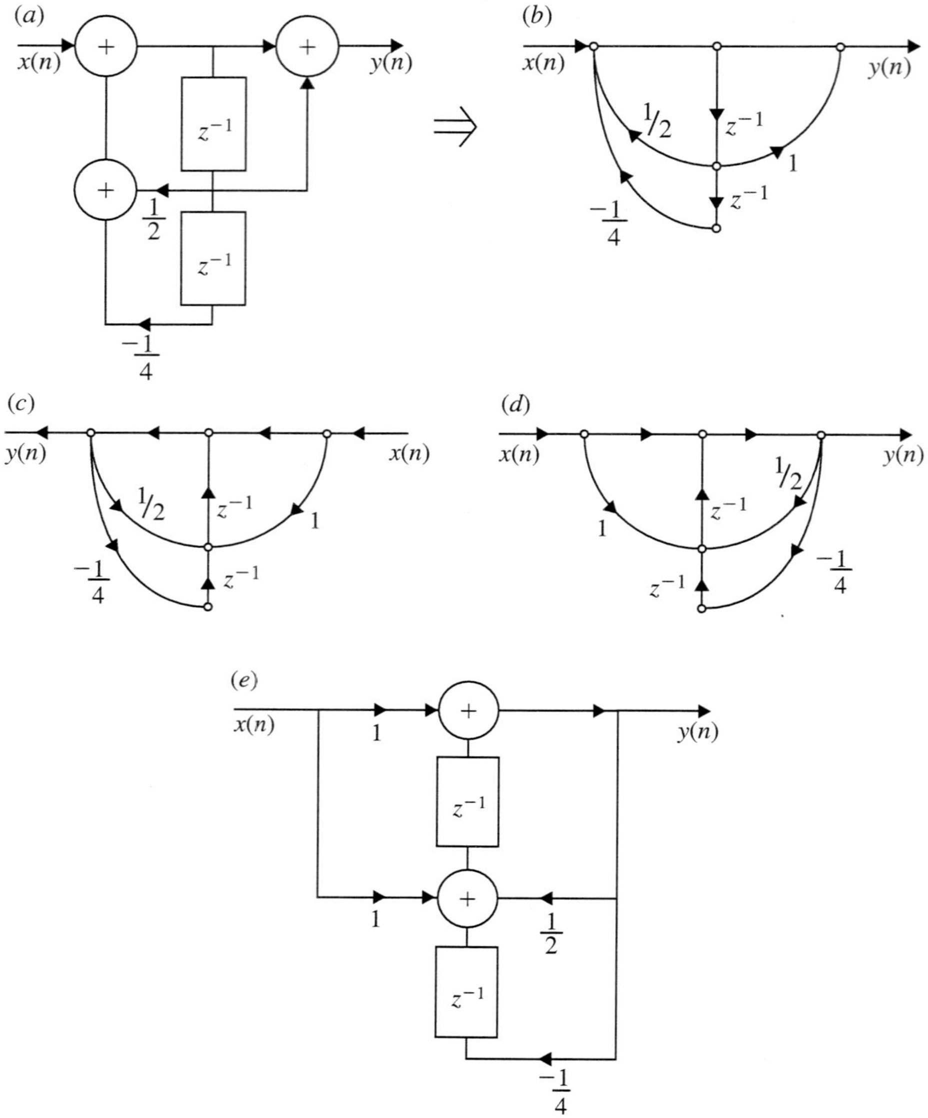

Figure 3.54 Transposed direct form II realization for the Example 3.40.

Example 3.41

Realize the system given by difference equation

$$y(n) = -0.1y(n-1) + 0.72y(n-2) + 0.7x(n) - 0.252x(n-2)$$

in parallel form.

(Anna University, May, 2007)

Solution

$$\begin{aligned}H(z) &= \frac{0.7-0.252z^{-2}}{1+0.1z^{-1}-0.72z^{-2}}\\ &= 0.35+\frac{0.35-0.035z^{-1}}{1+0.1z^{-1}-0.72z^{-2}}\\ &= 0.35+\frac{0.35-0.035z^{-1}}{(1+0.9z^{-1})(1-0.8z^{-1})}\\ &= 0.35+\frac{A}{(1+0.9z^{-1})}+\frac{B}{(1-0.8z^{-1})}\\ &= 0.35+\frac{0.206}{(1+0.9z^{-1})}+\frac{0.1444}{(1-0.8z^{-1})}\\ &= C+H_1(z)+H_2(z)\end{aligned}$$

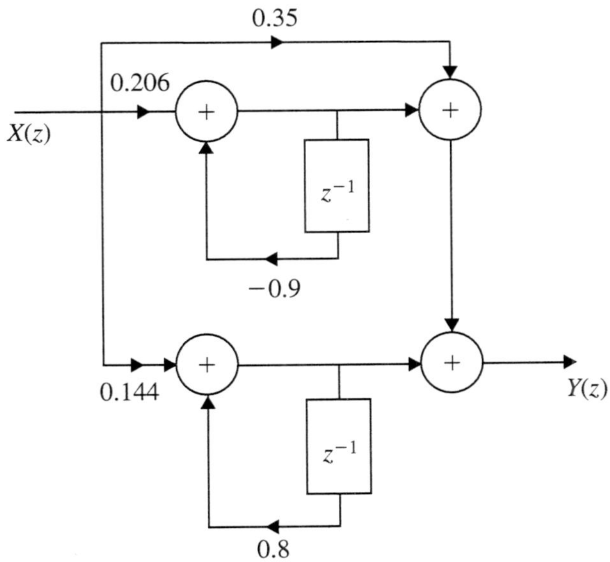

Figure 3.55 Parallel form realization of $H(z)$ for Example 3.41.

3.13.7 Lattice Structure of IIR System

Let us consider an all-pole system with system function

$$H(z)=\frac{1}{1+\sum_{k=1}^{N}a_N z^{-k}}=\frac{1}{A_N(z)} \tag{3.92}$$

The difference equation for this IIR system is derived as follows.

$$\frac{Y(z)}{X(z)}=\frac{1}{1+\sum_{k=1}^{N}a_N z^{-k}}$$

$$Y(z) + \sum_{k=1}^{N} a_N z^{-k} Y(z) = X(z)$$

$$Y(z) = -\sum_{k=1}^{N} a_N z^{-k} Y(z) + X(z)$$

$$y(n) = -\sum_{k=1}^{N} a_N(k) y(n-k) + x(n) \tag{3.93}$$

or

$$x(n) = y(n) + \sum_{k=1}^{N} a_N(k) y(n-k) \tag{3.94}$$

For $N = 1$

$$x(n) = y(n) + a_1(1) y(n-1) \tag{3.95}$$

The equation (3.95) can be realised in lattice structure as shown in Figure 3.56.

From Figure 3.56, we can obtain

$$x(n) = f_1(n) \tag{3.96}$$

$$\begin{aligned} y(n) &= f_0(n) = f_1(n) - k_1 g_0(n-1) \\ &= x(n) - k_1 y(n-1) \end{aligned} \tag{3.97}$$

$$\begin{aligned} g_1(n) &= k_1 f_0(n) + g_0(n-1) \\ &= k_1 y(n) + y(n-1) \end{aligned} \tag{3.98}$$

$$k_1 = a_1(1) \tag{3.99}$$

Now, let us consider for the case $N = 2$, then

$$x(n) = f_2(n) \tag{3.100}$$

$$y(n) = x(n) - a_1(1) y(n-1) - a_2(2) y(n-2) \tag{3.101}$$

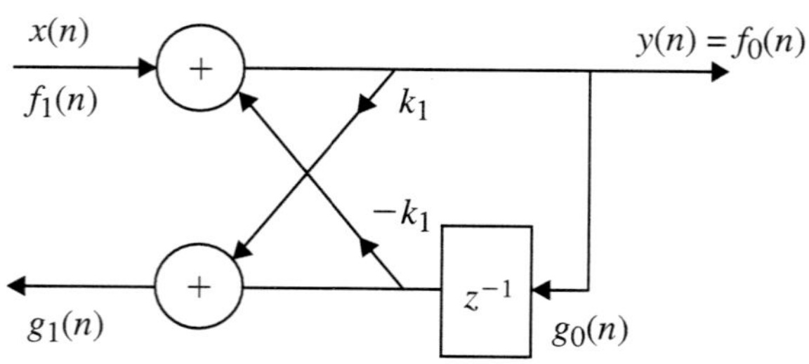

Figure 3.56 Single stage all-pole lattice structure.

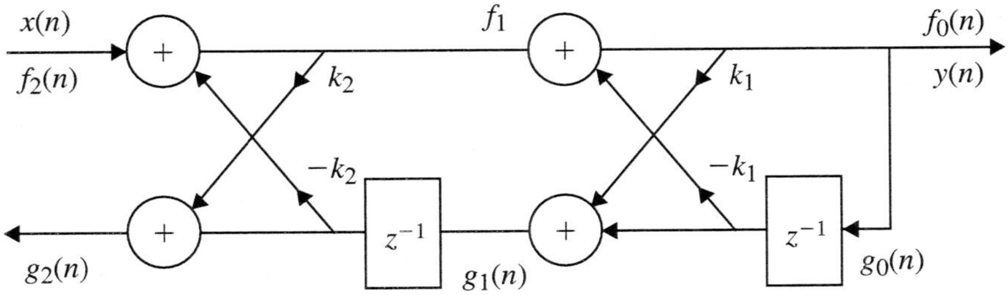

Figure 3.57 Two stage all-pole lattice filter.

This output can also be obtained from a two-stage lattice structure as shown in Figure 3.57 from which we have

$$
\begin{aligned}
f_2(n) &= x(n) && (3.102)\\
f_1(n) &= f_2(n) - k_2 g_1(n-1) && (3.103)\\
g_2(n) &= k_2 f_1(n) + g_1(n-1) && (3.104)\\
f_0(n) &= f_1(n) - k_1 g_0(n-1) && (3.105)\\
g_1(n) &= k_1 f_0(n) + g_0(n-1) && (3.106)\\
y(n) &= f_0(n) = g_0(n) && (3.107)\\
&= f_1(n) - k_1 g_0(n-1)\\
&= f_2(n) - k_2 g_1(n-1) - k_1 g_0(n-1)\\
&= f_2(n) - k_2[k_1 f_0(n-1) + g_0(n-2)] - k_1 g_0(n-1)\\
&= f_2(n) - k_1(1+k_2)y(n-1) - k_2 y(n-2) && (3.108)
\end{aligned}
$$

Similarly

$$g_2(n) = k_2 y(n) + k_1(1+k_2)y(n-1) + y(n-2) \tag{3.109}$$

Comparing equation (3.101) and equation (3.108) we get

$$a_2(0) = 1, \quad a_2(1) = k_1(1+k_2), \quad a_2(2) = k_2 \tag{3.110}$$

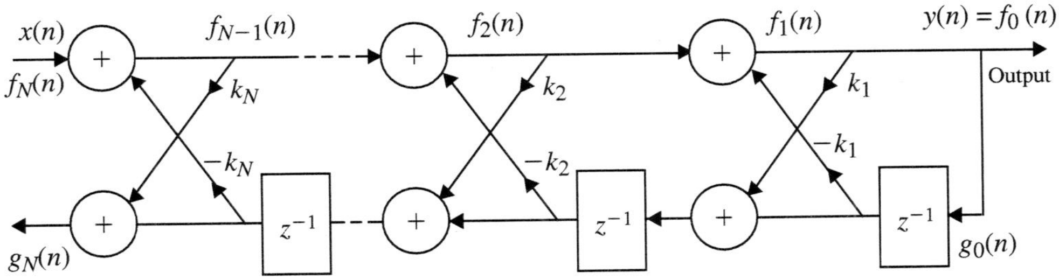

Figure 3.58 All-pole lattice filter.

For a N-stage IIR filter realised in lattice structure as shown in Figure 3.58, we get

$$f_N(n) = x(n) \tag{3.111}$$

$$f_{m-1}(n) = f_m(n) - k_m g_{m-1}(n-1), \quad m = N, N-1, \ldots, 1 \tag{3.112}$$

$$g_m(n) = k_m f_{m-1}(n) + g_{m-1}(n-1), \quad m = N, N-1, \ldots, 1 \tag{3.113}$$

$$y(n) = f_0(n) = g_0(n) \tag{3.114}$$

3.13.8 Conversion from Direct Form to Lattice Structure

For a 3-stage IIR system

$$x(n) = f_3(n) = f_2(n) + k_3 g_2(n-1) \tag{3.115}$$

$$g_3(n) = k_3 f_2(n) + g_2(n-1) \tag{3.116}$$

from which

$$g_2(n-1) = g_3(n) - k_3 f_2(n) \tag{3.117}$$

Substituting equation (3.117) in equation (3.115) we get,

$$f_3(n) = f_2(n) + k_3[g_3(n) - k_3 f_2(n)]$$

and

$$f_2(n) = \frac{f_3(n) - k_3 g_3(n)}{1 - k_3^2}$$

$$= \frac{\begin{bmatrix} y(n) + a_3(1)y(n-1) + a_3(2)y(n-2) + a_3(3)y(n-3) \\ +k_3 a_3(3)y(n) - k_3 a_3(2)y(n-2) \\ -k_3 a_3(n)y(n-1) - a_3 y(n-3) \end{bmatrix}}{1 - k_3^2}$$

$$= y(n) + \frac{a_3(1) - a_3(3)a_3(2)}{1 - a_3^2(3)} y(n-1) + \frac{a_3(2) - a_3(2)a_3(3)}{1 - a_3^2(3)} y(n-2) + \cdots \tag{3.118}$$

Comparing equation (3.118) and equation (3.101) we have

$$a_2(0) = 1, \quad a_2(1) = \frac{a_3(1) - a_3(3)a_3(2)}{a - a_3^2(3)}, \quad a_2(2) = \frac{a_3(2) - a_3(2)a_3(3)}{1 - a_3^2(3)} \tag{3.119}$$

In general

$$a_{m-1}(0) = 1$$

$$k_m = a_m(m)$$

$$\boxed{a_{m-1}(k) = \frac{a_m(k) - a_m(m)a_m(m-k)}{1 - a_m^2(m)}} \tag{3.120}$$

Equation (3.120) can be used to convert direct form to lattice structure.

3.13.9 Lattice–Ladder Structure

A general IIR filter containing both poles and zeros can be realized using an all pole lattice as the basic building block.

Consider an IIR filter with system function

$$H(z) = \frac{B_M(z)}{A_N(z)} = \frac{\sum_{k=0}^{N} b_M(k)z^{-k}}{1 + \sum_{k=1}^{N} a_N(k)z^{-k}} \tag{3.121}$$

where $N \geq M$. A lattice structure for equation (3.121) can be constructed by filter realizing an all-pole lattice coefficients, k_m, $1 \leq M \leq N$ for the denominator $A_N(z)$, and then adding a ladder part as shown in Figure 3.59 for $M = N$. The output of the ladder part can be expressed as a weighted linear combination of $\{g_m(n)\}$.

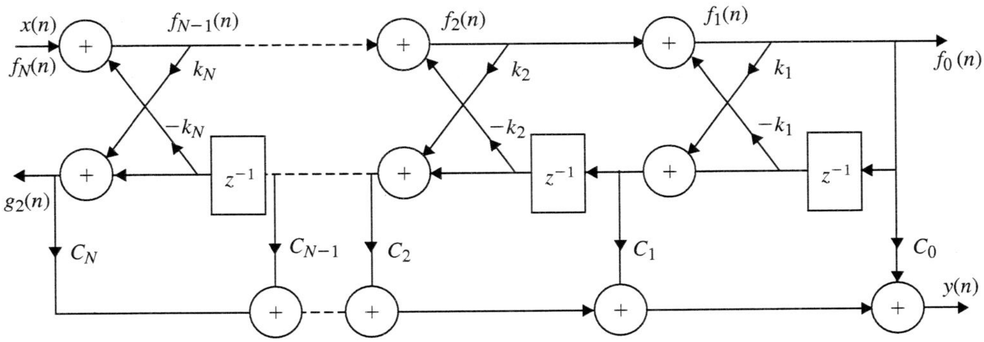

Figure 3.59 Lattice–ladder structure for realizing a pole-zero IIR filter.

Now the output is given by

$$y(n) = \sum_{m=0}^{M} C_m g_m(n) \tag{3.122}$$

where $\{c_m\}$ are called the ladder co-efficients and can be obtained using the recursive relation.

$$\boxed{C_m = b_m - \sum_{i=m+1}^{M} C_i a_i(i-m); \quad m = M, M-1, \ldots, 0} \tag{3.123}$$

Example 3.42

Realize the following system function in lattice ladder structure

$$H(z) = \frac{1 + \frac{3}{2}z^{-1} + \frac{1}{2}z^{-2}}{1 + z^{-1} + \frac{1}{4}z^{-2}}$$

Solution

$$\text{Given}\quad B_M(z) = 1 + \frac{3}{2}z^{-1} + \frac{1}{2}z^{-2}$$

$$A_N(z) = 1 + z^{-1} + \frac{1}{4}z^{-2}$$

$$a_2(0) = 1, \quad a_2(1) = 1, \quad a_2(2) = \frac{1}{4}$$

$$k_2 = a_2(2) = \frac{1}{4}$$

From equation (3.121) we have

$$a_{m-1}(k) = \frac{a_m(k) - a_m(m)a_m(m-k)}{1 - a_m^2(m)}$$

For $m = 2$ and $k = 1$

$$k_1 = a_1(1) = \frac{a_2(1) - a_2(2)a_2(1)}{a - a_2^2(2)}$$

$$= \frac{1 - \frac{1}{4} \cdot 1}{1 - \left(\frac{1}{4}\right)^2} = \frac{0.75}{0.9375} = 0.8$$

For $m = 2$ and $k = 0$

$$a_1(0) = \frac{a_2(0) - a_2(2)a_2(2)}{1 - a_2^2(2)} = \frac{1 - \left(\frac{1}{4}\right)^2}{1 - \left(\frac{1}{4}\right)^2} = 1$$

Therefore, for lattice structure

$$k_1 = 0.8, \quad k_2 = 0.25$$

For ladder structure

$$C_m = b_m - \sum_{i=m+1}^{M} C_i a_i(i-m), \quad m = M, M-1, \ldots, 0$$

$$C_2 = b_2 = \frac{1}{2}$$

$$C_1 = b_1 - c_2 a_2(0)$$

$$= \frac{3}{2} - \frac{1}{2}(1) = 1$$

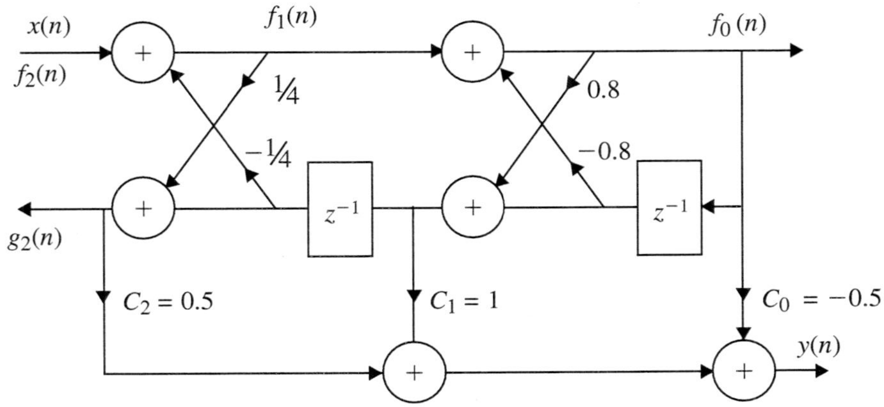

Figure 3.60 Lattice-ladder form for the Example 3.42.

$$\begin{aligned} C_0 &= b_0 - [C_1 a_1(0) + C_2 a_2(1)] \\ &= 1 - \left[1 \cdot 1 + \frac{1}{2} \cdot 1\right] \\ &= 1 - \left[1 + \frac{1}{2}\right] = -0.5 \end{aligned}$$

The lattice ladder structure for the given pole-zero is shown in Figure 3.60.

Example 3.43

Convert the following all-pole IIR filter into a lattice structure.

$$H(z) = \frac{1}{1 + \frac{13}{24}z^{-1} + \frac{5}{8}z^{-2} + \frac{1}{3}z^{-3}}$$

Solution Given

$$A_N(z) = 1 + \frac{13}{24}z^{-1} + \frac{5}{8}z^{-2} + \frac{1}{3}z^{-3}$$

$$a_3(0) = 1, \quad a_3(1) = \frac{13}{24}, \quad a_3(2) = \frac{5}{8}; \quad a_3(3) = \frac{1}{3}$$

$$K_3 = a_3(3) = \frac{1}{3}$$

From equation (3.121) we have

$$a_{m-1}(k) = \frac{a_m(k) - a_m(m)a_m(m-k)}{1 - a_m^2(m)}$$

For $m = 2$, and $k = 1$

$$a_2(1) = \frac{a_3(1) - a_3(3)a_3(2)}{1 - a_3^2(3)}$$

$$= \frac{\frac{13}{24} - \frac{1}{3}\left(\frac{5}{8}\right)}{1 - \left(\frac{2}{3}\right)^2} = \frac{3}{8}$$

For $m = 3$ and $k = 2$

$$k_2 = a_2(2) = \frac{a_3(2) - a_3(3)a_3(1)}{1 - a_3^2(3)}$$

$$= \frac{\frac{5}{8} - \frac{1}{3}\left(\frac{13}{24}\right)}{1 - \left(\frac{1}{3}\right)^2} = \frac{1}{2}$$

For $m = 2$ and $k = 1$

$$k_1 = a_1(1) = \frac{a_2(1) - a_2(2)a_2(1)}{1 - a_2^2(2)}$$

$$= \frac{\frac{3}{8} - \frac{1}{2}\left(\frac{3}{8}\right)}{1 - \left(\frac{1}{2}\right)^2} = \frac{1}{4}$$

Therefore, for lattice structure

$$k_1 = \frac{1}{4}, \quad k_2 = \frac{1}{2}, \quad k_3 = \frac{1}{3}$$

The lattice structure for the given all-pole filter is shown in Figure 3.61.

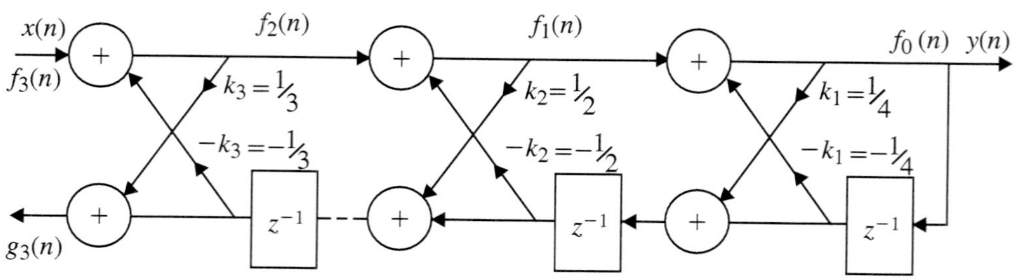

Figure 3.61 Lattice structure for the Example 3.43.

Summary

- Digital filters are broadly classified as Infinite Impulse Response (IIR) and Finite Impulse Response (FIR) filters. The design of IIR filter is presented in this chapter.
- The design methodology for analog filters is a well-developed one. By proper transformations, these analog filters can be converted to digital filters. Impulse invariant transformation and bilinear transformation are used to convert analog filters to digital filters.
- When stable analog filters are converted to digital filters, it is necessary that the poles of these digital filters lie within the unit circle in the s-plane, so that the filter is causal and stable.
- In the design of lowpass filters, when the specifications are given in the frequency domain it may not be always possible to get physically realizable stable filters. The magnitude response needs to be approximated.
- Several approximations to design low-pass filters are available in the literature. However, in this chapter, Butterworth and Chebyshev approximations and approximation of derivatives are used to design lowpass filters.
- By analog to digital frequency transformation, it is possible to convert lowpass prototype analog filter into either a bandpass, highpass or stop band filter.
- Several methods such as direct form-I, direct form-II parallel form, cascade form are available to realize the structure of the digital filter. They are described in this chapter. Finally the method of getting frequency response plot for the system function $H(z)$ is described.

Short Questions and Answers

1. What are the requirements for an analog filter to be stable and causal?

- The analog transfer function $H(s)$ should be a rational function of s and the co-efficients of s should be real, so that the system is causal.
- The poles should lie in the left half of s-plane, so that the system is stable.
- The number of zeros should be less than or equal to number of poles.

2. What are the requirements for a digital filter to be stable and causal?

- The digital transfer function $H(z)$ should be a rational function of z and the co-efficients of z should be real, so that the system is causal.
- The poles should lie inside of the unit circle in z-plane, so that the system is stable.

3. Define ripples in a filter.

The limits of tolerance in the magnitude of passband and stopband are called ripples. The tolerance in passband is denoted by δ_p and that in stopband is denoted by δ_s.

4. Mention any two techniques for digitizing the transfer function of an analog filter.

The bilinear transformation and the impulse invariant transformations are the two techniques available for digitizing the analog filter transfer function.

5. Compare the digital and analog filters.

Digital Filter	Analog Filter
1. Operates on digital samples of the signal.	Operates on analog samples of the signal.
2. It is governed by linear difference equation.	It is governed by linear differential equation.
3. It consists of adders, multipliers and delays implemented digital logic.	It consists of electrical components like resistors, capacitors and inductors.
4. In digital filters the filter co-efficients are designed to satisfy the desired frequency response.	In analog filters the approximation problem is solved to satisfy the desired frequency response.

6. What are the advantages and disadvantages of digital filters?

Advantages:

- High thermal stability due to absence of electrical components.
- The performance characteristics like accuracy, dynamic range, stability and tolerance can be enhanced by increasing the length of the registers.
- The digital filters are programmable.
- Multiplexing and adaptive filtering are possible.

Disadvantages:

- The bandwidth of the discrete signal is limited by the sampling frequency.
- The performance of digital filter depends on the hardware used to implement the filter.

7. Mention the important features of IIR filters.

- The physically realizable IIR filter does not have linear phase.
- The IIR specifications include the desired characteristics for the magnitude response only.

8. What is impulse invariant transformation?

The transformation of analog filter to digital filter without modifying the impulse response of the filter is called impulse invariant transformation *i.e.*, in this transformation the impulse response of the digital filter will be sampled version of the impulse response of analog filters.

9. What is the main objective of impulse invariant transformation?

The main objective is to develop an IIR filter transfer function whose impulse response is the sampled version of impulse response of the analog filter. Therefore, the frequency response characteristics of analog filter is preserved.

10. How analog poles are mapped to digital poles in impulse invariant/bilinear transformation?

In impulse invariant/linear transformation the mapping of analog to digital poles are as follows:

- The analog poles on the left half of s-plane are mapped into the interior of unit circle in z-plane.
- The analog poles on the imaginary axis of s-plane are mapped into the unit circle in z-plane.
- The analog poles on the right half of s-plane are mapped into the exterior of unit circle in z-plane.

11. What is the importance of poles in filter design?

The stability of a filter is related to the location of the poles. For a stable analog filter the poles should lie on the left half of the s-plane. For a stable digital filter the poles should lie inside of the unit circle of z-plane.

12. Write the impulse invariant transformation used to transform real poles with and without multiplicity.

The impulse invariant transformation used to transform real pole (at $s = -p_i$) without multiplicity is

$$\frac{1}{(s+p_i)} \xrightarrow{\text{is transformed to}} \frac{1}{1-e^{-p_iT}z^{-1}}$$

13. Write the impulse invariant transform used to transform complex conjugate poles.

$$\frac{(s+a)}{(s+a)^2+b^2} \xrightarrow{\text{is transformed to}} \frac{1-e^{-aT}(\cos bT)z^{-1}}{1-2e^{-aT}(\cos bT)z^{-1}+e^{-2aT}z^{-2}}$$

$$\frac{b}{(s+a)^2+b^2} \xrightarrow{\text{is transformed to}} \frac{1-e^{-aT}(\sin bT)z^{-1}}{1-2e^{-aT}(\cos bT)z^{-1}+e^{-2aT}z^{-2}}$$

14. What is the relation between analog and digital frequency in impulse invariant transformation?

The relation between analog and digital frequency in impulse invariant transformation is given by,

$$\text{Digital frequency, } \omega = \Omega T$$

where, Ω = analog frequency and T = sampling time period.

15. What is aliasing?

The phenomena of high frequency sinusoidal components acquiring the identity of low frequency sinusoidal components after sampling is called aliasing (*i.e.*, aliasing is higher frequencies impersonating lower frequencies). The aliasing, problem will arise if the sampling rate does not satisfy the Nyquist sampling criteria.

16. Why an impulse invariant transformation is not considered to be one-to-one?

In impulse invariant transformation any strip of width $(2\pi)/T$ in the s-plane for values of s in the range $(2k-1)\pi/T \leq \Omega \leq (2k+1)\pi/T$ (where k is an integer) is mapped into the entire z-plane. The left half portion of each strip in s-plane maps into the interior of the unit circle in z-plane, right half portion of each strip in s-plane maps into the exterior of the unit circle in z-plane and the imaginary axis of each strip in s-plane maps into the unit circle in z-plane. Hence, the impulse invariant transformation is many-to-one.

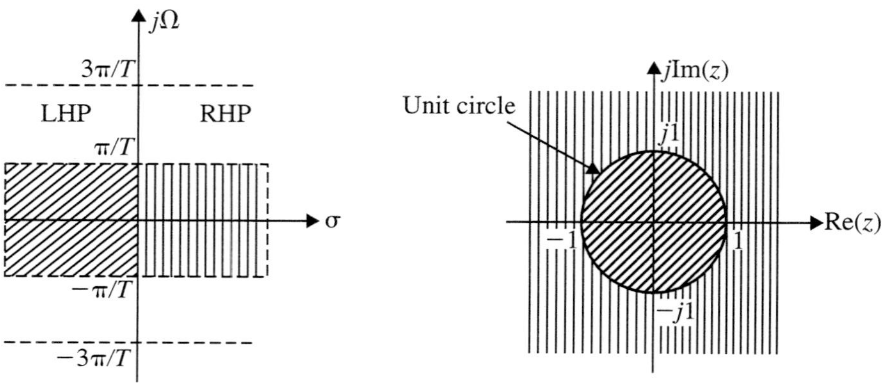

Figure 3.62 Mapping of s-plane into z-plane in impulse invariant transformation.

17. What is aliasing problem in impulse invariant method of designing digital filter? Why it is absent in bilinear transformation?

In impulse invariant mapping, the analog frequencies in the interval $(2k-1)\pi/T \leq \Omega \leq (2k+1)\pi/T$ (where k is an integer) maps into corresponding values of digital frequencies in the interval $-\pi \leq \omega \leq \pi$. Hence, the mapping of Ω to ω is many-to-one.

This will result in high frequency components acquiring the identity of the low frequency components if the analog filter is not bandlimited. This effect is called aliasing. The aliasing can be avoided in bandlimited filters by choosing very small values of sampling time. The bilinear mapping is one-to-one mapping and so there is no effect of aliasing.

18. What is bilinear transformation?

The bilinear transformation is a conformal mapping that transforms the s-plane to z-plane. In this mapping the imaginary axis of s-plane is mapped into the unit circle in z-plane, the left half of s-plane is mapped into interior of unit circle in z-plane and right half of s-plane is mapped into exterior of unit circle in z-plane. The bilinear mapping is a one-to-one mapping and it is accomplished when

$$s = \frac{2}{T}\frac{1-z^{-1}}{1+z^{-1}}$$

19. What is the relation between analog and digital frequency in bilinear transformation?

The relation between analog and digital frequency in bilinear transformation is given by,

$$\text{Digital frequency, } \omega = 2\tan^{-1}\left(\frac{\Omega T}{2}\right)$$

where, Ω = analog frequency and T = sampling time period.

20. What is frequency warping?

In bilinear transformation the relation between analog and digital frequencies is non-linear. When the s-plane is mapped into z-plane using bilinear transformation, this non-linear relationship introduces distortion in frequency axis, which is called frequency warping.

21. What is pre-warping? Why it is employed?

In IIR filter design using bilinear transformation, the conversion of the specified digital frequencies to analog frequencies is called pre-warping. The pre-warping is necessary to eliminate the effect of warping on amplitude response.

22. Explain the technique of pre-warping.

In IIR filter design using bilinear transformation the specified digital frequencies are converted to analog frequencies which are called pre-warp frequencies. Using the pre-warped frequencies, the analog filter transfer function is designed and then it is transferred to digital filter transfer function.

23. Compare the impulse invariant and bilinear transformation.

Impulse Invariant	Bilinear Transformation
1. It is many-to-one mapping.	It is one-to-one mapping.
2. The relation between analog and digital frequency is linear.	The relation between analog and digital frequency is non-linear.
3. To prevent the problem of aliasing the analog filters should be bandlimits.	There is no problem of aliasing and the filters need not be bandlimits.

24. Obtain the impulse response of digital filter to correspond to an analog filter with impulse response $h_a(t) = 0.3e^{-2t}$ and with a sampling rate of 1.0 kHz using impulse invariant method.

Given that, $h_a(t) = 0.3e^{-2t}$ and sampling frequency, $F = 1\text{kHz} = 1 \times 10^3$ Hz.

$$\therefore \text{ Sampling time, } T = \frac{1}{F} = \frac{1}{1 \times 10^3} = 10^{-3} \text{ sec.}$$

$$\text{Impulse response of digital fitter } h(n) = h_e(t)|_{t=nT} = 0.3e^{-2t}|_{t=nT} = 0.3e^{-2nT}$$

$$= 0.3(e^{-2T})^n = 0.3(e^{-2\times 10^{-3}})^n$$

$$= 0.3(0.998)^n; \quad \text{for } n \geq 0.$$

25. Given that, $H_a(s) = 1/(s+1)$. By impulse invariant method, obtain the digital filter transfer function and the difference equation of digital filter.

Given that, $H_a(s) = 1/(s+1)$. In impulse invariant transformation,

$$\frac{1}{s+p_i} \xrightarrow{\text{is transformed to}} \frac{1}{1-e^{-p_i T}z^{-1}}$$

Let $T = 1$ sec. Transfer function of digital filter

$$H(z) = \frac{1}{1-e^{-T}z^{-1}} = \frac{1}{1-e^{-1}z^{-1}} = \frac{1}{1-0.368z^{-1}}$$

We know that,

$$H(z) = \frac{Y(z)}{X(z)}$$

$$\frac{Y(z)}{X(z)} = \frac{1}{1-0.368z^{-1}}$$

On cross multiplying we get

$$Y(z) - 0.368z^{-1}Y(z) = X(z)$$

$$\therefore\ Y(z) = X(z) + 0.368z^{-1}Y(z)$$

On taking inverse z-transform we get,

$$y(n) = x(n) + 0.368y(n-1)$$

26. Sketch the mapping of s-plane to z-plane in bilinear transformation.

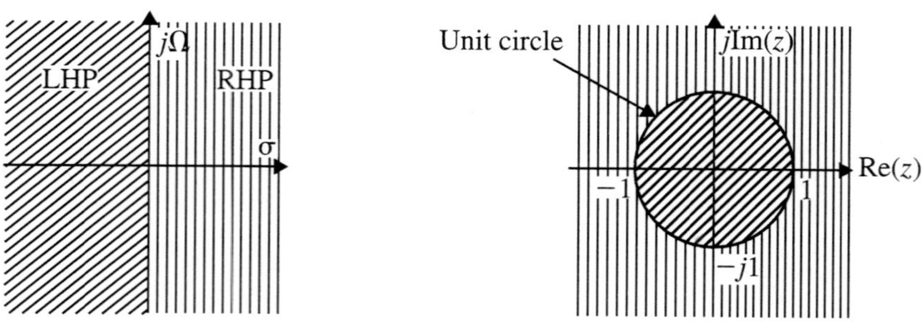

Figure 3.63 Mapping of s-plane to z-plane.

27. How does the order of the filter affect the frequency response of Butterworth filter?

The magnitude response of Butterworth filter is shown in Figure 3.64, from which it can be observed that the magnitude response approaches the ideal response as the order of the filter is increased.

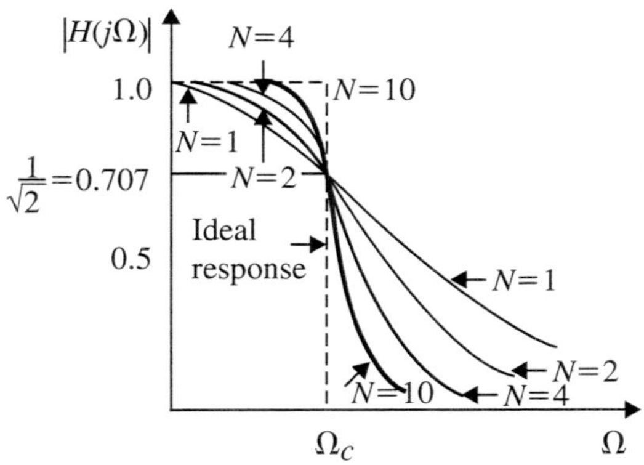

Figure 3.64 Magnitude response of Butterworth lowpass filter for various values of N.

28. Write the transfer function of un-normalized Butterworth lowpass filter.

When N is even, transfer function of analog lowpass Butterworth filter is,

$$H_a(s) = \sum_{k=1}^{N/2} \frac{\Omega_c^2}{s^2 + b_k \Omega_c s + \Omega_c^2}$$

When N is odd, transfer function of analog lowpass Butterworth filter is,

$$H_a(s) = \frac{\Omega_c}{s + \Omega_c} \sum_{k=1}^{(N-1)/2} \frac{\Omega_c^2}{s^2 + b_k \Omega_c s + \Omega_c^2}$$

where

$$b_k = 2\sin\left[\frac{(2k-1)\pi}{2N}\right]$$

N = Order of the fitter and Ω_c = Analog cutoff frequency.

29. How will you choose the order N for a Butterworth filter?

Calculate a parameter N_1 using the following equation and correct, it to nearest integer.

$$N_1 = \frac{1}{2} \frac{\log\left\{\left[\frac{1}{A_p^2} - 1\right] \Big/ \left[\frac{1}{A_s^2 - 1}\right]\right\}}{\log\left(\frac{\Omega_s}{\Omega_p}\right)}$$

Choose the order N of the filter such that $N \geq N_1$.

30. Write the properties of Butterworth filter.

(*i*) The Butterworth filters have all poles designs.

(*ii*) At the cutoff frequency Ω_c, the magnitude of normalized Butterworth filter is $1/\sqrt{2}$.

(*iii*) The filter order N, completely specifies the filter and as the value of N increases the magnitude response approaches the ideal response.

31. Find the digital transfer function $H(z)$ by using impulse invariant method for the analog T.F. $H(s) = \frac{1}{(s+2)}$. Assume $T = 0.1$ sec and 0.5 sec.

(Anna University, December, 2007)

$$H(z) = \frac{1}{(1 - 0.8187z^{-1})} \quad \text{for } T = 0.1 \text{ sec.}$$

$$H(z) = \frac{1}{(1 - 0.3679z^{-1})} \quad \text{for } T = 0.5 \text{ sec.}$$

32. Realize the following system using Direct Form II.

(Anna University, December, 2007)

$$y(n) - \frac{1}{2}y(n-1) = x(n) + \frac{1}{2}x(n-1)$$

$$H(z) = \frac{(1 + \frac{1}{2}z^{-1})}{(1 - \frac{1}{2}z^{-1})}$$

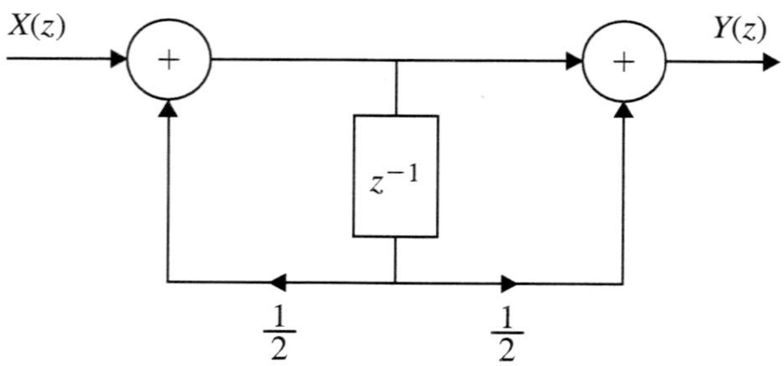

Figure 3.65 Realization of $H(z) = \frac{(1+\frac{1}{2}z^{-1})}{(1-\frac{1}{2}z^{-1})}$.

33. Transform the single pole low-pass Butterworth filter with system function $H(s) = \frac{\Omega_p}{(\frac{\Omega_p}{s}+\Omega_p)}$ into a bandpass filter with upper and lower band edge frequencies Ω_u and Ω_l respectively.

(Anna University, June, 2007)

$$H(s) = \frac{\Omega_p(s^2 + \Omega_l\Omega_u)}{\Omega_p(s^2 + \Omega_l + \Omega_u) + s(\Omega_u - \Omega_l)}$$

34. Convert the analog bandpass filter.

$$H_a(s) = \frac{1}{(s + 0.1)^2 + 9}$$

into a digital IIR filter by use of the mapping $s = \frac{1}{T}\frac{(z-1)}{(z+1)}$.

(Anna University, June, 2007)

$$H(z) = \frac{T^2(1 + 2z^{-1} + z^{-2})}{[9.01T^2 + (18.02T^2 - 2)z^{-1} + (9.01T^2 - 2T + 1)z^{-2}]}$$

35. Write the equation for frequency transformation from lowpass to bandpass filter.

(Anna University, June, 2007)

$$s \to \Omega_p \frac{(s^2 + \Omega_l \Omega_u)}{s(\Omega_u - \Omega_l)}$$

36. Find the digital filter equivalent for $H(s) = \frac{1}{(s+8)}$

(Anna University, June, 2007)

$$H(z) = \frac{1}{(1 - e^{-8T}z^{-1})}$$

37. What are the parameters (specifications) of a Chebyshev filter?

(Anna University, June, 2007)

The parameters of a Chebyshev filter are (*a*) passband ripple, (*b*) passband cutoff frequency, (*c*) stopband frequency, (*d*) attenuation beyond stopband frequency.

38. Give the location of poles of normalized Butterworth filter.

(Anna University, June, 2007)

The poles of the normalized Butterworth filter occur on a unit circle at equally spaced points in the complex s-plane. The pole locations are identified as

$$s_k = e^{j\pi/2} e^{j(2k+1)\frac{\pi}{N}}, \quad k = 0, 1, 2 \ldots (N - 1)$$

N is order of the filter. For stable filter only LHP poles are taken.

39. State two advantages of bilinear transformation

(Anna University, December, 2006)

The two advantages of bilinear transformation are:

(*a*) It avoids aliasing in frequency components.
(*b*) The transformation of stable analog filter results in a stable digital filter.

40. What is Chebyshev approximation?

In Chebyshev approximation, the error is defined as the difference between the ideal brickwall characteristic and the actual response and this is minimized over a prescribed band of frequencies. There are two types of Chebshev transfer functions. In the type 1, approximation, the magnitude characteristic is equiripple in the passband and monotonic in the stopband. In type 2 approximation, the magnitude response is monotonic in the passband and equiripple in the stopband.

41. What is Butterworth approximation?

The frequency response characteristic of the lowpass Butterworth filter is monotonic in both the passband and stopband. The response approximates to the ideal response as the order N of the filter increases. (Flat Characteristics).

42. What are the parameters that can be obtained from the Chebyshev filter specifications?

For a given set of specifications, the order N of the filter can be determined. Knowing N, the poles and zeros can be located.

43. Write down the transfer functions of a first order Butterworth normalised lowpass filter and highpass filter.

The normalised first order Butterworth normalised lowpass filter is

$$h_a(s) = \frac{1}{(s+1)}$$

The first order highpass filter normalised transfer function is

$$h_a(s) = \frac{1}{\frac{1}{s}+1} = \frac{s}{s+1}$$

44. Compare the lowpass Butterworth filter with lowpass Chebyshev filter.

(*a*) In the Butterworth filter, the frequency response decreases monotically while the magnitude response of the Chebyshev filter contains ripples in the passband and monotically decreases in the stopband.

(*b*) The poles of the Butterworth filter lie on unit circle whereas the poles of Chebyshev filter lie on ellipse.

(*c*) The transition band is more in Butterworth filter compared to Chebyshev filter.

(*d*) For the same specifications, the order of the Butterworth filter is higher than that of Chebyshev filter.

45. Why IIR filters do not have linear phase?

A linear phase filter must have a system function

$$H(z) = \pm z^{-N} H(z^{-1})$$

where z^{-N} represents a delay of N units. For this it is necessary to have a mirror image pole outside the unit circle for every pole inside the unit circle in the z-plane. This means the filter will be unstable. Hence, a causal and stable IIR filter cannot have linear phase if it is to be physically realizable.

46. What are the disadvantages of Impulse invariance method of designing filters?

If the sampling interval T is large, the IIR filter designed using impulse invariance method results in aliasing due to sampling. This method is not suitable to design highpass filter due to the spectrum aliasing which results from the sampling process.

Long Answer Type Questions

1. Explain the impulse invariance method of IIR filter design.
2. Explain bilinear transformation method of IIR filter design.
3. Draw the direct form-I and direct form-II structure of IIR system.
4. Convert the analog transfer function of the second order Butterworth filter into digital transfer function using bilinear transformation.
5. What is meant by aliasing? Explain with example.
6. Describe the procedure for the design of digital filters from analog filters and advantages and disadvantages of digital filters.
7. State and prove the conditions satisfied by a stable and causal discrete-time filter in the z-transform domain.
8. Design a Butterworth filter using impulse invariant method for the following specifications:

$$0.8 \le |H(e^{j\omega})| \le 1; \quad 0 \le \omega \le 0.2\pi$$
$$|H(e^{j\omega})| \le 0.2; \quad 0.6 \le \omega \le \pi$$

9. Mention the advantages and disadvantages of FIR and IIR filters.
10. Design a Butterworth digital filter to meet the following constraints:

$$0.9 \le |H(\omega)| \le 1; \quad 0 \le \omega \le \frac{\pi}{2}$$
$$|H(\omega)| \le 0.2; \quad \frac{3\pi}{4} \le \omega \le \pi$$

    Use bilinear transformation mapping technique. Assume $T = 1$ sec.
11. Develop impulse invariant mapping technique for designing IIR filter.
12. Realize the given transfer function using direct form-I and parallel methods

$$H(z) = \frac{(4z^2 + 11z - 2)}{(z+1)(z-3)}.$$

13. Derive the equation for calculating the order of the Butterworth filter.
14. Design and realize a digital filter using bilinear transformation for the following specifications:
    (*a*) Monotonic passband and stopband.
    (*b*) -3 dB cutoff at 0.5π rad.
    (*c*) magnitude down at least 15 dB at $\omega = 0.75\pi$ rad.
15. Using impulse invariant method find $H(z)$ at $T = 1$ sec.

$$H(s) = \frac{2}{s^2 + 8s + 15}$$

16. Enumerate the various steps involved in the design of LF digital Butterworth IIR filter.

17. Obtain direct form-II, cascade and parallel realizations of a discrete time system described by the difference equation

$$y(n) - \frac{5}{8}y(n-1) - \frac{1}{16}y(n-2) = x(n) - 3x(n-1) + 3x(n-2) - x(n-3)$$

(Anna University)

Ans: Direct Form II

$$\frac{Y(z)}{X(z)} = \frac{(1 - 3z^{-1} + 3z^{-2} - z^{-3})}{\left(1 - \frac{5}{8}z^{-1} - \frac{1}{16}z^{-2}\right)}$$

Cascade Form

$$H_1(z) = \frac{(1 - z^{-1})}{(1 - 0.7125z^{-1})}$$

$$H_2(z) = \frac{(1 - 2z^{-1} + z^{-2})}{(1 + 0.086z^{-1})}$$

Parallel Form

$$H(z) = -208 + 16z^{-1} + \frac{209 - 149z^{-1}}{\left(1 - \frac{5}{8}z^{-1} - \frac{1}{16}z^{-2}\right)}$$

18. Determine the system function $H(z)$ of the lowest order Chebyshev digital filter that meets the following specifications.

    (*a*) 1 dB ripple in the passband $0 \leq \omega \leq 0.3\pi$.
    (*b*) At least 60 dB altenuation in the stopband $0.35 \leq |\omega| \leq \pi$. Use the bilinear transformation.

(Anna University)

19. Design a Chebyshev filter with a maximum passband altenuation of 2.5 dB at $\Omega_p = 20$ rad/sec and the stopband altenuation of 30 dB at $\Omega_s = 50$ rad/sec.

(Anna University)

20. Find the direct form-I and direct form-II realization of the filter

$$H(z) = \frac{1 - 2z^{-2} + 3z^{-3}}{1 - 0.2z^{-3}}$$

(Anna University, May, 2006)

21. Obtain the direct form I, Canonic form and parallel form realization structures for the system given by the difference equation

$$y(n) = -0.1y(n-1) + 0.72y(n-2) + 0.7x(n) - 0.252x(n-2)$$

(Anna University, June, 2006)

Ans: Direct Form-I and Canonic Form

$$H(z) = \frac{(0.7 - 0.252z^{-2})}{(1 + 0.1z^{-1} - 0.72z^{-2})}$$

Parallel Form

$$H(z) = 0.35 + \frac{0.1441}{(1 - 0.8z^{-1})} + \frac{0.2058}{(1 + 0.9z^{-1})}$$

MATLAB PROGRAM

Program - 1

```
%To design a Butterworth lowpass filter for
    the specification
clear all;
alphap=.2; %Passband attenuation in dB
alphas=40; %stopband attenuation in dB
fp=300; %Passband frequency in Hz
fs=800; %stopband frequency in Hz
F=2000; %sampling frequency in Hz
omp=2*fp/F; %Passband frequency in dB
oms=2*fs/F; %stopband frequency in dB
% To find the cut-off frequency and order of the filter
[n,wn]=buttord(omp,oms,alphap,alphas);
% system function of the filter
[b,a]=butter(n,wn);
w=0:.01:pi;
[h,om]=freqz(b,a,w,'whole');
m=20*log10(abs(h));
disp('output');b,a
an=angle(h);
subplot(2,1,1);plot(om/pi,m);grid;
ylabel('gain in dB');
xlabel('normalized nfrequency');
subplot(2,1,2);plot(om/pi,an);grid;
ylabel('phase in radians');
xlabel('normalized nfrequency');
```

```
OUTPUT
b = 0.0890     0.3559     0.5339     0.3559     0.0890
a = 1.0000    -0.0674     0.4875    -0.0141     0.0178
```

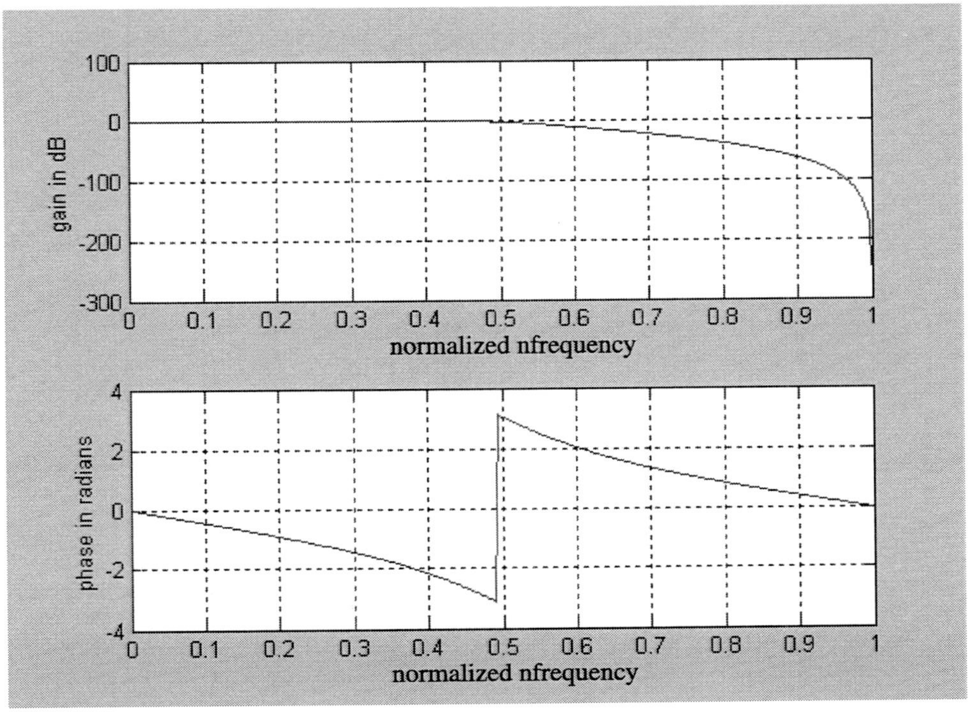

Program - 2

```
%To design a Butterworth bandpass filter
     for the specification
clear all;
alphap=2; %Passband attenuation in dB
alphas=20; %stopband attenuation in dB
wp=[.2*pi,.4*pi]; %Passband frequency in rad
ws=[.1*pi,.5*pi]; %stopband frequency in rad
% To find the cut-off frequency and order of the filter
[n,wn]=buttord(wp/pi,ws/pi,alphap,alphas);
%system function of the filter
[b,a]=butter(n,wn);
w=0:.01:pi;
[h,ph]=freqz(b,a,w);
m=20*log10(abs(h));
disp('output');b,a
an=angle(h);
subplot(2,1,1);plot(ph/pi,m);grid;
ylabel('gain in dB');
xlabel('normalized nfrequency');
subplot(2,1,2);plot(ph/pi,an);grid;
```

```
ylabel('phase in radians');
xlabel('normalized nfrequency');
```

OUTPUT

```
b = 0.0060        0 -0.0240        0  0.0359        0 -0.0240        0 0.0060
a = 1.0000 -3.8710 7.9699 -10.6417 10.0781 -6.8167 3.2579 -1.0044 0.1670
```

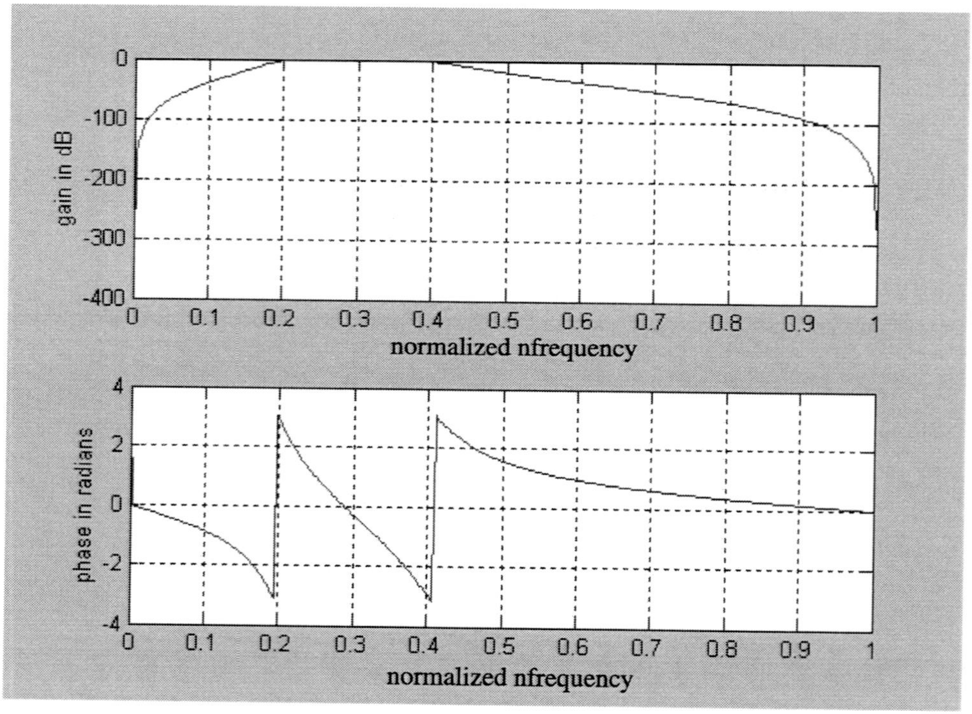

Program - 3

```
%To design a Butterworth highpass filter
    for the specification
clear all;
alphap=.5; %Passband attenuation in dB
alphas=50; %stopband attenuation in dB
fp=1200; %Passband frequency in Hz
fs=2400; %stopband frequency in Hz
F=10000; %sampling frequency in Hz
omp=2*fp/F; %Passband frequency in dB
oms=2*fs/F; %stopband frequency in dB
% To find the cut-off frequency and order of the filter
[n,wn]=buttord(omp,oms,alphap,alphas);
```

```
%system function of the filter
[b,a]=butter(n,wn,'high');
w=0:.01:pi;
[h,om]=freqz(b,a,w,'whole');
m=20*log10(abs(h));
disp('output');b,a
an=angle(h);
subplot(2,1,1);plot(om/pi,m);grid;
ylabel('gain in dB');
xlabel('normalized nfrequency');
subplot(2,1,2);plot(om/pi,an);grid;
ylabel('phase in radians');
xlabel('normalized nfrequency');
```

OUTPUT

```
b = 0.0621 -0.5592 2.2369 -5.2193 7.8290 -7.8290 5.2193 -2.2369 0.5592 -0.0621
a = 1.0000 -3.7158 6.9551 -8.1655 6.5233 -3.6339 1.4016 -0.3589 0.0551 -0.0039
```

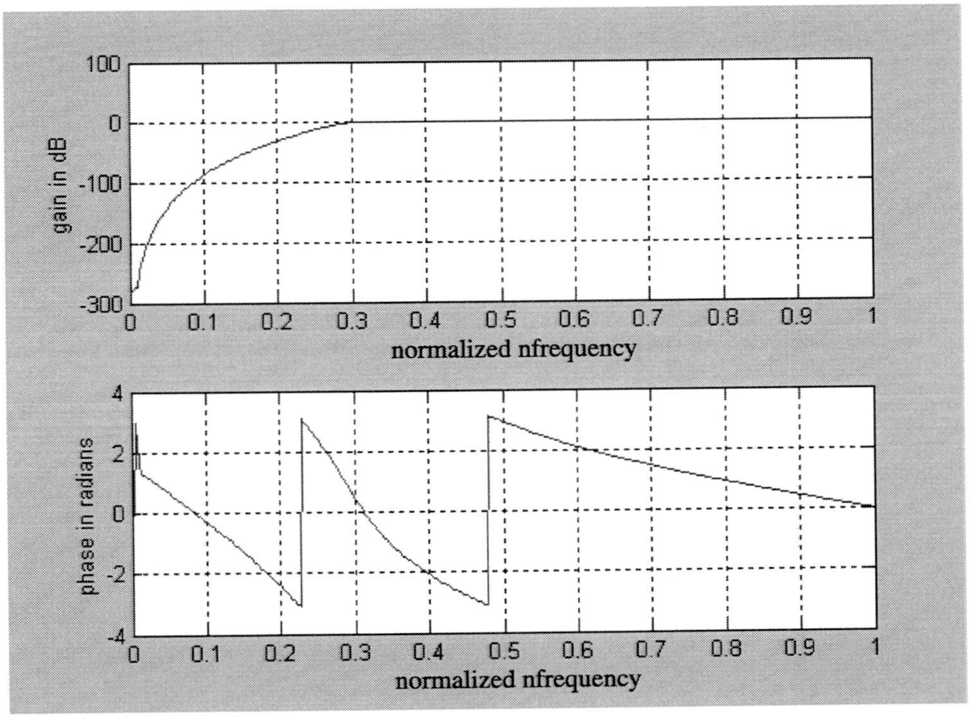

Program - 4

```
%To design a Butterworth bandstop filter
    for the specification
clear all;
alphap=2; %Passband attenuation in dB
alphas=20; %stopband attenuation in dB
wp=[.3*pi,.5*pi]; %Passband frequency in rad
ws=[.2*pi,.6*pi]; %stopband frequency in rad
% To find the cut-off frequency and order of the filter
[n,wn]=buttord(wp/pi,ws/pi,alphap,alphas);
%system function of the filter
[b,a]=butter(n,wn,'stop');
w=0:.01:pi;
[h,ph]=freqz(b,a,w);
m=20*log10(abs(h));
disp('output');b,a
an=angle(h);
subplot(2,1,1);plot(ph/pi,m);grid;
ylabel('gain in dB');
xlabel('normalized nfrequency');
subplot(2,1,2);plot(ph/pi,an);grid;
ylabel('phase in radians');
xlabel('normalized nfrequency');
```

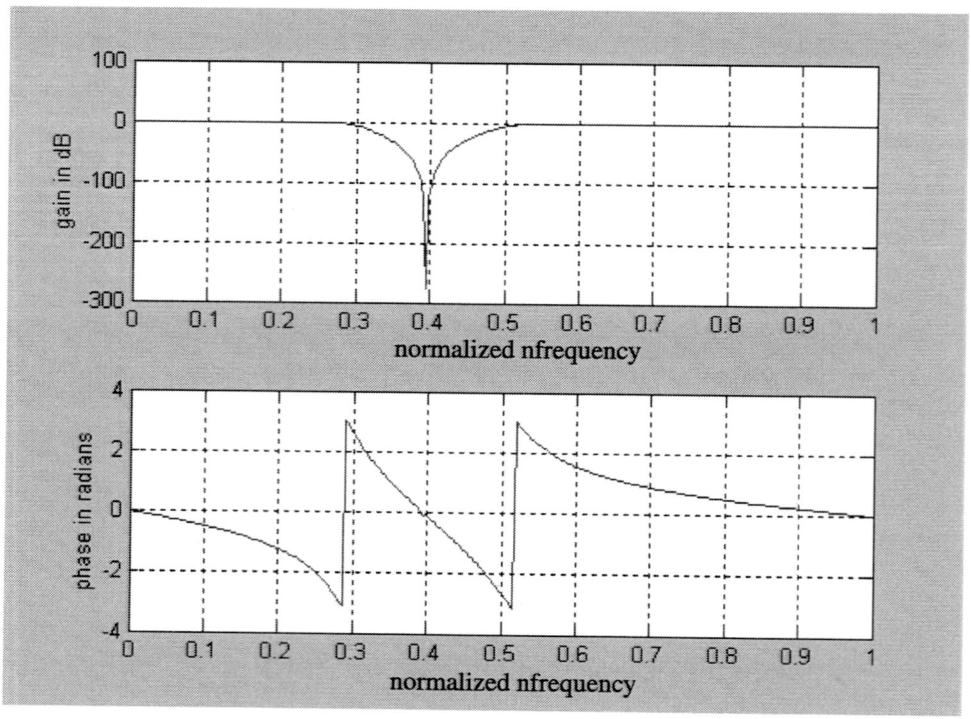

```
OUTPUT
b = 0.3817 -0.9923 2.4942 -3.3958 4.2929 -3.3958 2.4942 -0.9923 0.3817
a = 1.0000 -1.9950 3.6590 -3.8870 3.8162 -2.4275 1.4238 -0.4667 0.1458
```

Program - 5

```
%To design a Chebyshev Type-I lowpass filter
    for the specification
clear all;
alphap=.2; %Passband attenuation in dB
alphas=40; %stopband attenuation in dB
fp=300; %Passband frequency in Hz
fs=800; %stopband frequency in Hz
F=2000; %sampling frequency in Hz
omp=2*fp/F; %Passband frequency in dB
oms=2*fs/F; %stopband frequency in dB
% To find the cut-off frequency and order of the filter
[n,wn]=cheb1ord(omp,oms,alphap,alphas);
%system function of the filter
[b,a]=cheby1(n,alphap,wn);
w=0:.01:pi;
[h,om]=freqz(b,a,w,'whole');
m=20*log10(abs(h));
disp('output');b,a
an=angle(h);
subplot(2,1,1);plot(om/pi,m);grid;
ylabel('gain in dB');
xlabel('normalized nfrequency');
subplot(2,1,2);plot(om/pi,an);grid;
ylabel('phase in radians');
xlabel('normalized nfrequency');
```

```
OUTPUT
b = 0.0604    0.1812    0.1812     0.0604
a = 1.0000   -1.1238    0.8278    -0.2208
```

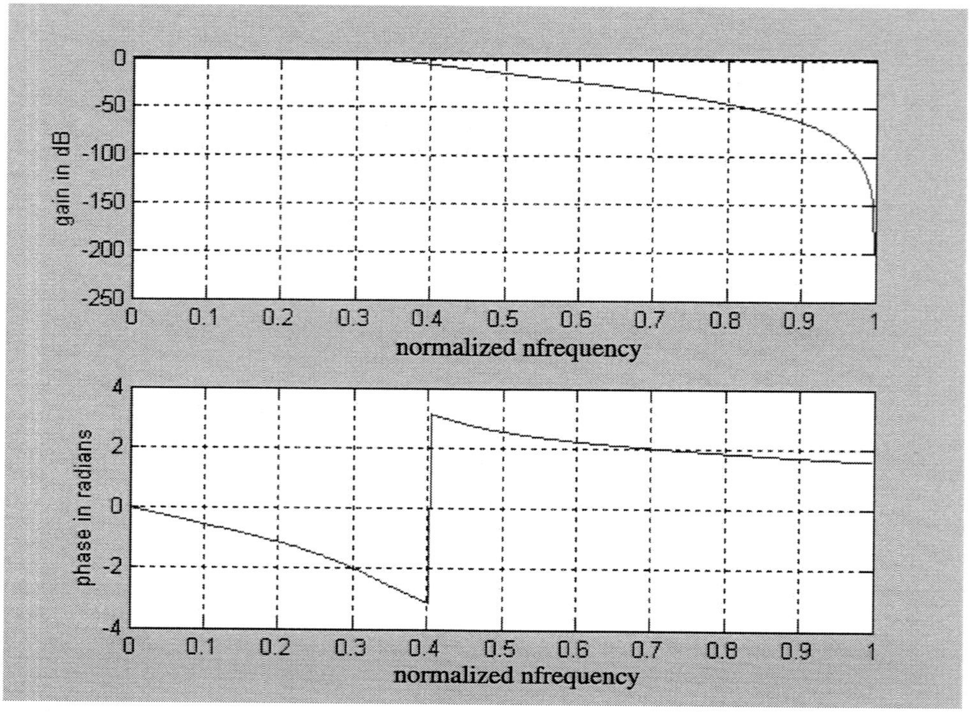

Program - 6

```
%To design a Chebyshev Type-I highpass filter
    for the specification
clear all;
alphap=.3; %Passband attenuation in dB
alphas=50; %stopband attenuation in dB
fp=1200; %Passband frequency in Hz
fs=2400; %stopband frequency in Hz
F=10000; %sampling frequency in Hz
omp=2*fp/F; %Passband frequency in dB
oms=2*fs/F; %stopband frequency in dB
% To find the cut-off frequency and order of the filter
[n,wn]=cheb1ord(omp,oms,alphap,alphas);
%system function of the filter
[b,a]=cheby1(n,alphap,wn,'high');
w=0:.01:pi;
[h,om]=freqz(b,a,w,'whole');
m=20*log10(abs(h));
disp('output');b,a
an=angle(h);
subplot(2,1,1);plot(om/pi,m);grid;
```

```
ylabel('gain in dB');
xlabel('normalized nfrequency');
subplot(2,1,2);plot(om/pi,an);grid;
ylabel('phase in radians');
xlabel('normalized nfrequency');
```

```
OUTPUT
b = 0.1555 -0.9333 2.3332 -3.1110 2.3332 -0.9333 0.1555
a = 1.0000 -2.4494 3.1820 -2.2677 1.0649 -0.2713 0.0696
```

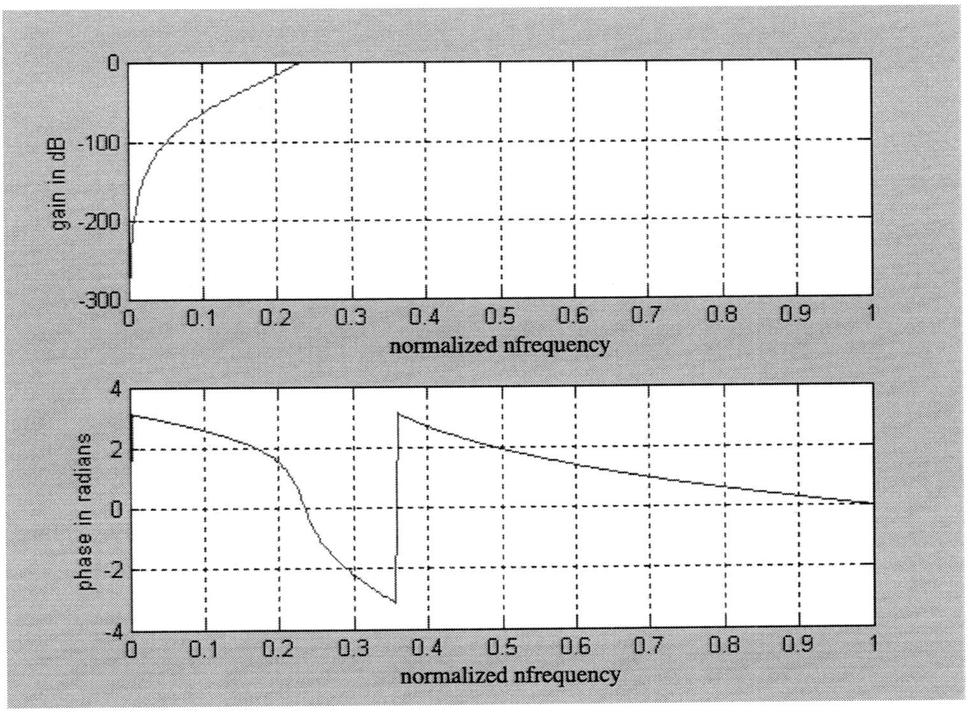

Program - 7

```
%To design a Chebyshev Type-I bandpass filter
    for the specification
clear all;
alphap=2; %Passband attenuation in dB
alphas=20; %stopband attenuation in dB
wp=[.2*pi,.4*pi]; %Passband frequency in rad
ws=[.1*pi,.5*pi]; %stopband frequency in rad
```

```
% To find the cut-off frequency and order of the filter
[n,wn]=cheb1ord(wp/pi,ws/pi,alphap,alphas);
%system function of the filter
[b,a]=cheby1(n,alphap,wn);
w=0:.01:pi;
[h,ph]=freqz(b,a,w);
m=20*log10(abs(h));
disp('output');b,a
an=angle(h);
subplot(2,1,1);plot(ph/pi,m);grid;
ylabel('gain in dB');
xlabel('normalized nfrequency');
subplot(2,1,2);plot(ph/pi,an);grid;
ylabel('phase in radians');
xlabel('normalized nfrequency');
```

```
OUTPUT
b = 0.0083        0 -0.0248        0 0.0248        0 -0.0083
a = 1.0000 -3.2632 5.9226 -6.6513 5.0802 -2.3909 0.6307
```

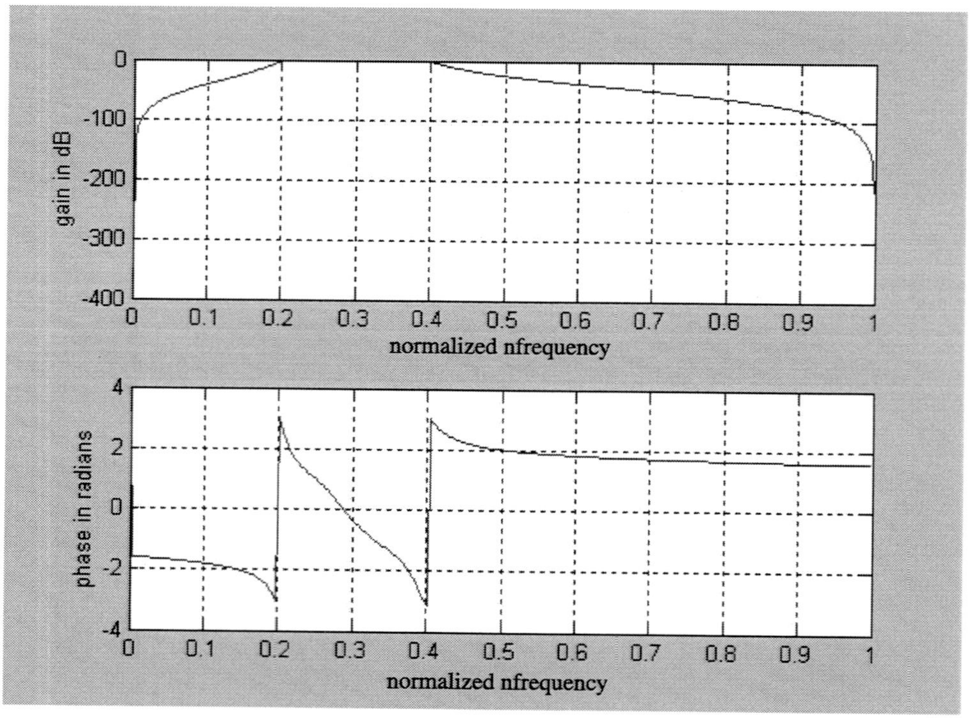

Program - 8

```
%To design a Chebyshev Type-I stopband filter
    for the specification
clear all;
alphap=2; %Passband attenuation in dB
alphas=20; %stopband attenuation in dB
wp=[.3*pi,.5*pi]; %Passband frequency in rad
ws=[.2*pi,.6*pi]; %stopband frequency in rad

% To find the cut-off frequency and order of the filter
[n,wn]=cheb1ord(wp/pi,ws/pi,alphap,alphas);
%system function of the filter
[b,a]=cheby1(n,alphap,wn,'stop');
w=0:.01:pi;
[h,ph]=freqz(b,a,w);
m=20*log10(abs(h));
disp('output');b,a
an=angle(h);
subplot(2,1,1);plot(ph/pi,m);grid;
ylabel('gain in dB');
xlabel('normalized nfrequency');
subplot(2,1,2);plot(ph/pi,an);grid;
ylabel('phase in radians');
xlabel('normalized nfrequency');
```

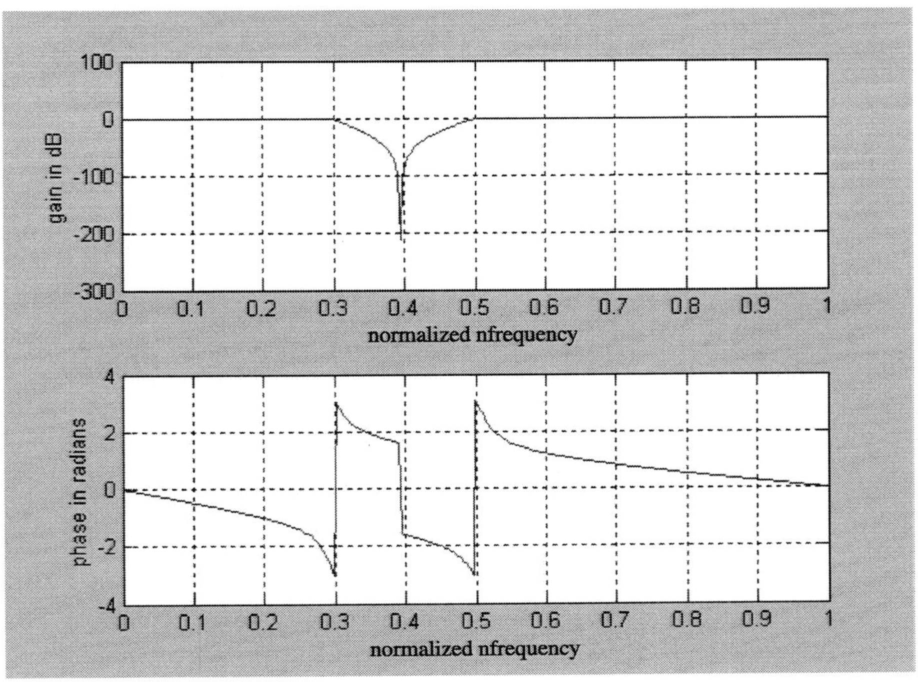

```
OUTPUT
b = 0.4239 -0.8263 1.8086 -1.7690 1.8086 -0.8263 0.4239
a = 1.0000 -1.4517 2.1867 -1.6377 1.2285 -0.3322 0.0497
```

Program - 9

```
%To design a digital Butterworth lowpass filter using
    impulse invariant transformation for
    the specification
clear all;
alphap=.2; %Passband attenuation in dB
alphas=40; %stopband attenuation in dB
fp=300; %Passband frequency in Hz
fs=800; %stopband frequency in Hz
F=2000; %sampling frequency in Hz
omp=2*fp/F; %Passband frequency in dB
oms=2*fs/F; %stopband frequency in dB
% To find the cut-off frequency and order of the filter
[n,wn]=buttord(omp,oms,alphap,alphas);
%system function of the filter
[b,a]=butter(n,wn);
w=0:.01:pi;
[h,om]=freqz(b,a,w,'whole');
m=20*log10(abs(h));
an=angle(h);
subplot(2,1,1);plot(om/pi,m);grid;
ylabel('gain in dB');
xlabel('normalized nfrequency');
subplot(2,1,2);plot(om/pi,an);grid;
ylabel('phase in radians');
xlabel('normalized nfrequency');
% To convert the analog filter into digital filter
    using impulse invariant transformation
[bz,az]=impinvar(b,a,fs);
disp('output');bz,az
```

```
OUTPUT
bz = 0.0006   -0.0018   0.0020   -0.0009   0.0001
az = 1.0000   -4.0001   6.0003   -4.0003   1.0001
```

Program - 10

```
%To design a digital Butterworth lowpass filter
    using bilinear transformation for
    the specification
clear all;
alphap=.2; %Passband attenuation in dB
alphas=40; %stopband attenuation in dB
fp=300; %Passband frequency in Hz
fs=800; %stopband frequency in Hz
F=2000; %sampling frequency in Hz
omp=2*fp/F; %Passband frequency in dB
oms=2*fs/F; %stopband frequency in dB
% To find the cut-off frequency and order of the filter
[n,wn]=buttord(omp,oms,alphap,alphas);
%system function of the filter
[b,a]=butter(n,wn);
w=0:.01:pi;
[h,om]=freqz(b,a,w,'whole');
m=20*log10(abs(h));
an=angle(h);
subplot(2,1,1);plot(om/pi,m);grid;
ylabel('gain in dB');
xlabel('normalized nfrequency');
subplot(2,1,2);plot(om/pi,an);grid;
ylabel('phase in radians');
xlabel('normalized nfrequency');
% To convert the analog filter into digital filter
    using impulse invariant transformation
[bz,az]=bilinear(b,a,fs);
disp('output');bz,az
```

```
OUTPUT
bz = 0.0892   -0.3564   0.5339   -0.3555   0.0888
az = 1.0000   -4.0001   6.0003   -4.0003   1.0001
```

4 Finite Impulse Response (FIR) Filter Design

Learning Objectives

After completing this chapter, you should be able to:

- study the characteristic of practical frequency selective digital filters.
- realize the Finite Impulse Response (FIR) filter structure.
- study the characteristics of FIR filters with linear phase.
- study different type of symmetry of the impulse response of linear phase FIR filters.
- design FIR filter by frequency sampling method.
- design linear phase FIR filters using windows.
- design FIR differentiators.

4.1 Introduction

In Chapter 3, the design of IIR filter was considered. These filters are designed by transformation from analog domain to digital domain. They are called recursive filters since feedback are used. Hence, IIR filters should be carefully designed to ensure that the system function $H(z)$ is stable. In the case of FIR filter design which is non-recursive in nature, the stability problem does not arise. Since the system function $H(z)$ is a polynomial of z^{-1} it always guarantees the stability of the filter. Further, unlike IIR filter design which has non-liner phase characteristic, the FIR digital filter has linear phase. A filter with a non-linear phase characteristic causes phase distortion in the signal which is undesirable in much practical applications such as data transmission, music, video *etc.* However, to meet the same frequency response specifications, the order of FIR filter transfer function is much higher than that of an IIR digital filter. Hence, FIR filters require more parameters more memory and has more computational complexity.

The basic approach to the design of FIR digital filter is based on direct approximation of the specified magnitude response in addition to the requirement of linear phase response. Unlike IIR filter, it does not have any connection with the analog filter. Linear phase FIR filters are designed based on whether the impulse response function $h(n)$ is positive or negative and the order of the filter is odd or even. Thus there are four types of linear phase FIR filters. FIR filters are also designed based on Fourier coefficients which have infinite length. By truncating these coefficients of infinite Fourier series, FIR filters are designed. This is called windowing. Several windowing techniques are available. FIR filter design using the above techniques are discussed in this chapter.

4.1.1 LTI System as Frequency Selective Filters

An LTI system performs a type of filtering among the various frequency components at its input. The nature of this filtering is determined by the frequency response characteristics $H(\omega)$, which in turn depends on the choice of the system parameters [a_k and b_k coefficient]. Thus, by proper selection of the coefficients we can design frequency selective filters that pass signals with frequency components in some bands while they attenuate signals that contain frequency components in other frequency bands.

In general an LTI system modifies the input spectrum $X(\omega)$ according to its frequency response $H(\omega)$ to yield an output signal with spectrum $Y(\omega) = H(\omega)X(\omega)$. $H(\omega)$ acts as a weighting function or a spectral shaping function to the different frequency components in the input signal.

Let us consider a signal $x(n)$ with frequency content in a band of frequencies $\omega_1 < \omega < \omega_2$ (*i.e.*, band limited signal)

$$X(\omega) = 0 \quad \text{for } \omega \geq \omega_2 \quad \text{and} \quad \omega \leq \omega_1 \tag{4.1}$$

If it is passed through a filter with frequency response,

$$H(\omega) = \begin{cases} Ce^{-j\omega\alpha}, & \omega_1 < \omega < \omega_2 \\ 0, & \text{otherwise, where } C \text{ and } \alpha = +\text{ve constants} \end{cases} \tag{4.2}$$

The signal at the output of the filter has the spectrum which is expressed as,

$$\begin{aligned} Y(\omega) &= X(\omega)H(\omega) \\ &= X(\omega)Ce^{-j\omega\alpha} \qquad (4.3) \\ &= CX(\omega)e^{-j\omega\alpha} \qquad (4.4) \end{aligned}$$

Using the following identity we get,

$$F[x(n-\alpha)] = X(\omega)e^{-j\omega\alpha}$$

$$\therefore\ Y(\omega) = CF[x(n-\alpha)]$$

Taking inverse Fourier transform on both sides we get,

$$y(n) = Cx(n-\alpha)$$

i.e., the filter output is simply a delayed and amplitude scaled version of the input signal. A pure delay is usually tolerable and is not considered a distortion of the signal. Likewise the amplitude scaling. The filter defined by

$$H(\omega) = \begin{cases} Ce^{-j\omega\alpha}, & \omega_1 < \omega < \omega_2 \\ 0, & \text{otherwise} \end{cases}$$

is called an ideal filter.

$$\begin{aligned} H(\omega) &= |H(\omega)| \angle H(\omega) \\ |H(\omega)| &= C, \quad \angle H(\omega) = \theta(\omega) = -\alpha\omega \\ |H(\omega)| \text{ (amplitude)} &= \text{constant} \\ |H(\omega)| \text{ (phase)} &= \text{linear function of frequency } \omega \end{aligned} \tag{4.5}$$

In general any deviation of the frequency response characteristics of a linear filter from the ideal response results in signal distortion.

(*i*) *Amplitude distortion:* If the filter has a variable magnitude frequency response characteristic in the passband then the filter has amplitude distortion.
(*ii*) *Phase distortion:* If the phase characteristic is not linear within the desired frequency band, the signal undergoes phase distortion.
(*iii*) *Signal delay:* The derivative of the phase with respect to frequency has the units of delay

$$\tau(\omega) = -\frac{d\theta(\omega)}{d\omega} = -\frac{d}{d\omega}(-\alpha\omega) = \alpha \tag{4.6}$$

Filters are classified according to their frequency response characteristics. The ideal frequency response $H(\omega)$ of four major types of filters are:

(*i*) Ideal frequency response of LPF

$$H_d(\omega) = \begin{cases} Ce^{-j\alpha\omega}, & -\omega_c \le \omega \le \omega_c \\ 0, & -\pi < \omega < -\omega_c \quad \text{and} \quad \omega_c < \omega < \pi \end{cases} \tag{4.7}$$

(*ii*) Ideal frequency response of HPF

$$H_d(\omega) = \begin{cases} Ce^{-j\alpha\omega}, & -\pi \le \omega \le -\omega_c, \ \omega_c \le \omega \le \pi, \\ 0, & -\omega_c < \omega < \omega_c \end{cases} \tag{4.8}$$

(*iii*) Ideal frequency response of BPF

$$H_d(\omega) = \begin{cases} Ce^{-j\alpha\omega}, & -\omega_{c_2} \le \omega \le -\omega_{c_1} \text{ and } \omega_{c_1} \le \omega \le \omega_{c_2} \\ 0, & -\pi \le \omega \le -\omega_{c_2} \ \& \ -\omega_{c_1} \le \omega \le \omega_{c_1} \ \& \ \omega_{c_2} \le \omega \le \pi \end{cases} \tag{4.9}$$

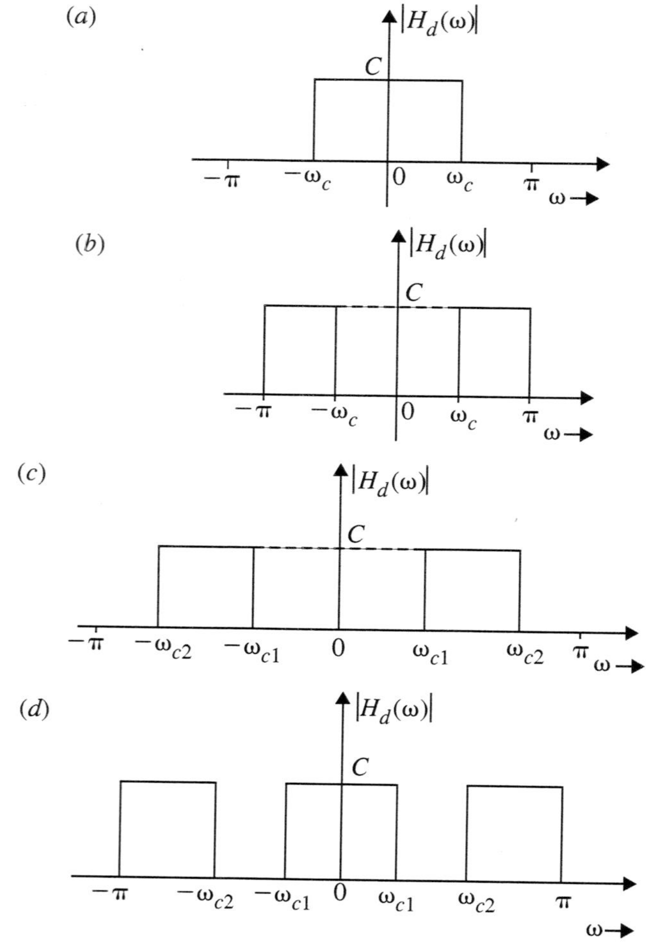

Figure 4.1 Magnitude response of ideal low pass, high pass, band pass and band stop filter.

(*iv*) Ideal frequency response of BSF

$$H_d(\omega) = \begin{cases} Ce^{-j\alpha\omega}, & -\pi \leq \omega \leq -\omega_{c_2} \;\&\; -\omega_{c_1} \leq \omega \leq \omega_{c_1} \;\&\; \omega_{c_2} \leq \omega \leq \pi \\ 0, & -\omega_{c_2} < \omega < -\omega_{c_1} \text{ and } \omega_{c_1} < \omega < \omega_{c_2} \end{cases} \tag{4.10}$$

The magnitude response of ideal lowpass, high pass, bandpass and band stop filters are shown in Figures 4.1(*a*), (*b*), (*c*) and (*d*) respectively.

4.2 Characteristic of Practical Frequency Selective Filters

Causality has very important implications is the design of frequency-selective filters. Causality implies that the frequency response characteristic $H(\omega)$ of the filter cannot be zero, except at a finite set of points in the frequency range. In addition, $H(\omega)$ cannot have an infinitely sharp cut off from passband to stopband. That is $H(\omega)$ cannot drop from unity to zero abruptly. Therefore, the ideal filters are non-causal and hence physically un-realizable for the real time signal processing applications.

The input $x(n)$ and output $y(n)$ of a LTI system is governed by the following N^{th} order difference equation.

$$y(n) = -\sum_{k=1}^{N} a_k y(n-k) + \sum_{k=0}^{M} b_k x(n-k)$$

On taking Fourier transform on both sides we get

$$Y(\omega) = -\sum_{k=1}^{N} a_k e^{-j\omega k} Y(\omega) + \sum_{k=0}^{M} b_k e^{-j\omega k} X(\omega)$$

$$Y(\omega)\left[1 + \sum_{k=1}^{N} a_k e^{-j\omega k}\right] = \sum_{k=0}^{M} b_k e^{-j\omega k} X(\omega)$$

$$H(\omega) = \frac{Y(\omega)}{X(\omega)}$$

$$= \frac{\sum_{k=0}^{M} b_k e^{-j\omega k}}{1 + \sum_{k=1}^{N} a_k e^{-j\omega k}}; \quad N \geq M \tag{4.11}$$

which are causal and physically realizable. The basic digital filter design problem is to approximate any of the ideal frequency response characteristics with a system that has frequency response $H(\omega)$ by properly selecting the coefficient $\{a_k\}$ and $\{b_k\}$.

In practice it is not necessary to insist that the magnitude $|H(\omega)|$ is constant in the entire passband of the filters. A small amount of ripple in the passband is usually tolerable. Similarly it is not necessary for the filter response $|H(\omega)|$ to be zero in the stopband. A small non-zero value or a small amount of ripple in the stopband is also tolerable. The magnitude response of a practical lowpass filter is shown in Figure 4.2.

The transition of the frequency response from passband to stopband defines the transition band or transition region of the filter. The band-edge frequency ω_p defines the edge of the passband, while the frequency ω_s denotes the beginning of the stopband. Thus the width of the transition band is $\omega_s - \omega_p$. The width of the passband is usually called the bandwidth of the filter.

In any filter design problem, one may specify

(*i*) the maximum passband ripple δ_p.
(*ii*) the maximum stopband ripple δ_s.

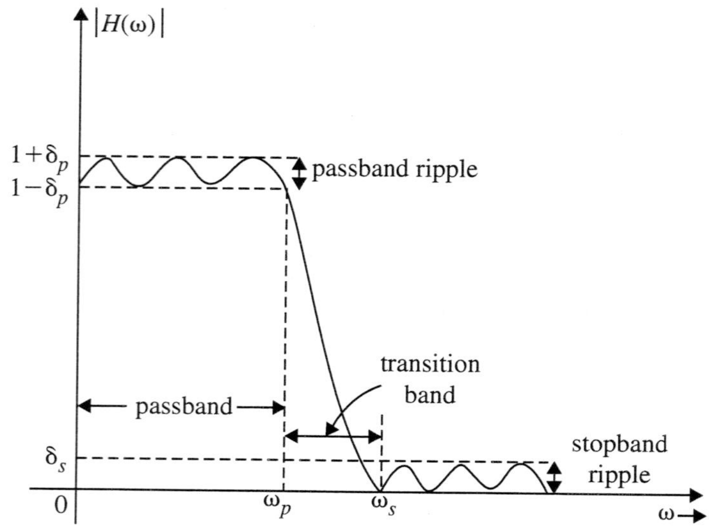

Figure 4.2 Magnitude response of a practical low pass filter.

(*iii*) passband edge frequency ω_p.
(*iv*) stopband edge frequency ω_s.

Based on these specifications, we may select the parameters a_k and b_k in the frequency response characteristic which best approximates the desired specifications.

4.3 Structures for Realization of the FIR Filter

In general an FIR system is described by the following difference equation:

$$y(n) = \sum_{k=0}^{N-1} b_k x(n-k) \tag{4.12}$$

$$Y(z) = \sum_{k=0}^{N-1} b_k z^{-k} X(z)$$

$$H(z) = \frac{Y(z)}{X(z)} = \sum_{k=0}^{N-1} b_k z^{-k} = b_0 + b_1 z^{-1} + b_2 z^{-2} + \cdots + b_{N-1} z^{-(N-1)} \tag{4.13}$$

where $H(z)$ is transfer function.

$$H(z) = Z[h(n)]$$

$$= \sum_{k=0}^{N-1} h(k) z^{-k} = h(0) + h(1)z^{-1} + h(2)z^{-2} + \cdots + h(N-1)z^{-(N-1)} \tag{4.14}$$

On comparing equations (4.13) and (4.14) we get

$$b_k = h(k) \quad \text{for} \quad k = 0, 1, 2, 3, \ldots, N-1 \tag{4.15}$$

The different types of structures for realizing FIR systems are:

1. Direct form realization.
2. Cascade form realization.
3. Linear phase realization.

4.3.1 Direct Form Realization

The direct form structure that can be obtained from the z-domains equation governing the FIR system is shown in Figure 4.3.

$$\begin{aligned} Y(z) &= \sum_{k=0}^{N-1} b_k z^{-k} X(z) \\ &= b_0 X(z) + b_1 z^{-1} X(z) + b_2 z^{-2} X(z) + \cdots + b_{N-1} z^{-(N-1)} X(z) \end{aligned} \tag{4.16}$$

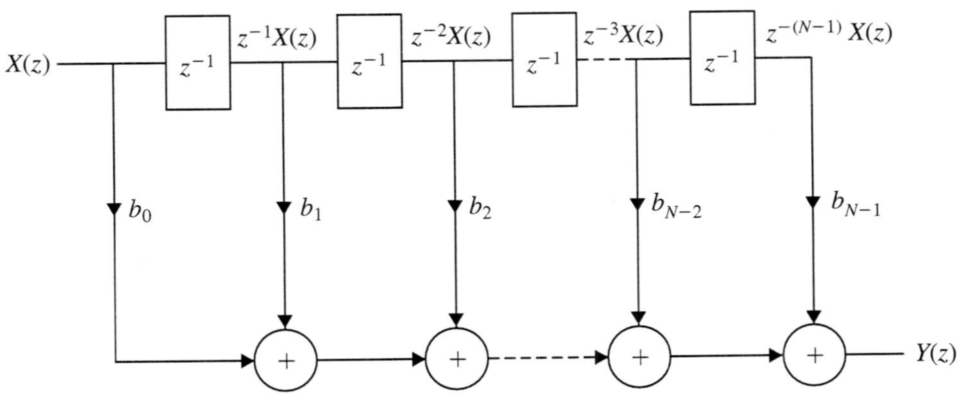

Figure 4.3 Direct form realization.

4.3.2 Cascade Form Realization

The transfer function of FIR system is $(N-1)^{\text{th}}$ order polynomial in z. This polynomial can be factorised into second order factors (when N is odd) and the transfer function can be expressed as a product of second order factors.

$$\begin{aligned} \text{When } N \text{ is odd, } H(z) &= \prod_{i=1}^{(N-1)/2} (c_{0i} + c_{1i} z^{-1} + c_{2i} z^{-2}) \\ &= H_1 H_2 \ldots H_{(N-1)/2} \end{aligned} \tag{4.17}$$

When N is even, $H(z)$ will have one first order and $(N-2)/2$ second order section.

$$\text{When } N \text{ is even, } H(z) = (c_{01} + c_{11}z^{-1}) \prod_{i=2}^{N/2} (c_{0i} + c_{1i}z^{-1} + c_{2i}z^{-2}) \qquad (4.18)$$
$$= H_1 H_2 \ldots H_{N/2}$$

4.3.3 Linear Phase Realization

In FIR systems for linear phase response, the impulse response should be symmetrical. For this,

$$h(k) = h(N-1-k) \qquad (4.19)$$

When N is Even

$$H(z) = \sum_{k=0}^{N-1} h(k)z^{-k} = \sum_{k=0}^{(N/2)-1} h(k)z^{-k} + \sum_{k=(N/2)}^{N-1} h(k)z^{-k} \qquad (4.20)$$

$$\text{Let } m = N-1-k \Longrightarrow k = N-1-m$$
$$\text{When } k = \frac{N}{2}; \Longrightarrow m = N-1-\frac{N}{2} = \frac{N}{2}-1$$
$$\text{When } k = N-1; \Longrightarrow m = N-1-(N-1) = 0$$

$$\therefore\ H(z) = \sum_{k=0}^{(N/2)-1} h(k)z^{-k} + \sum_{m=0}^{(N/2)-1} h(N-1-m)z^{-(N-1-m)}$$

On replacing m by k we get,

$$H(z) = \sum_{k=0}^{(N/2)-1} h(k)z^{-k} + \sum_{k=0}^{(N/2)-1} h(N-1-k)z^{-(N-1-k)}$$
$$= \sum_{k=0}^{(N/2)-1} h(k)z^{-k} + \sum_{k=0}^{(N/2)-1} h(k)z^{-(N-1-k)}$$
$$H(z) = \sum_{k=0}^{(N/2)-1} h(k)[z^{-k} + z^{-(N-1-k)}]$$

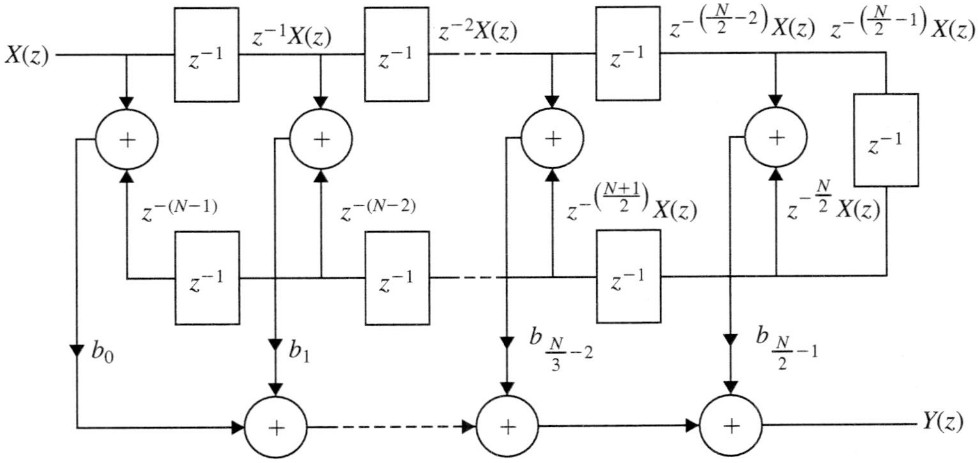

Figure 4.4 Linear phase realization when N is even.

Therefore,

$$\begin{aligned} Y(z) &= \sum_{k=0}^{(N/2)-1} h(k)[z^{-k}X(z) + z^{-(N-1-k)}X(z)] \quad \text{where } h(k) = b_k \\ &= b_0[X(z) + z^{-(N-1)}X(z)] + b_1[z^{-1}X(z) + z^{-(N-2)}X(z)] \\ &\quad + \cdots + b_{(N/2)-1}[z^{-[(N/2)-1]}X(z) + z^{-(N/2)}X(z)] \end{aligned} \tag{4.21}$$

The equation (4.21) is realized in Figure 4.4.

When N is Odd

$$H(z) = \sum_{k=0}^{N-1} h(k)z^{-k} = \sum_{k=0}^{\frac{N-3}{2}} h(k)z^{-k} + h\left(\frac{N-1}{2}\right)z^{-\left(\frac{N-1}{2}\right)} + \sum_{k=\frac{N+1}{2}}^{N-1} z^{-1} \tag{4.22}$$

$$\text{Let } m = N-1-k \Longrightarrow k = N-1-m$$
$$\text{When } k = \frac{N+1}{2}; \Longrightarrow m = \frac{N-3}{2}$$
$$\text{When } k = N-1; \Longrightarrow m = 0$$

$$\therefore\ H(z) = \sum_{k=0}^{\frac{N-3}{2}} h(k)z^{-k} + h\left(\frac{N-1}{2}\right)z^{-\left(\frac{N-1}{2}\right)} \sum_{m=0}^{\frac{N-3}{2}} h(N-1-m)z^{-(N-1-m)}$$

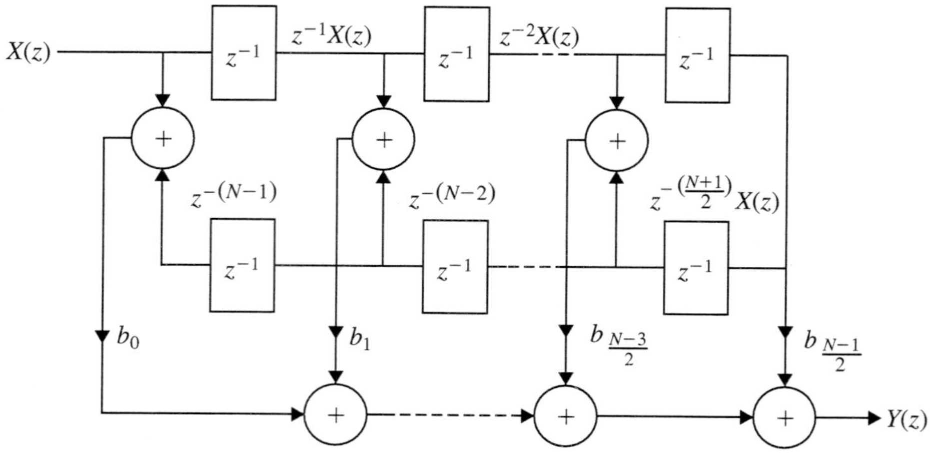

Figure 4.5 Linear phase realization when N is odd.

On replacing m by k we get

$$H(z) = \sum_{k=0}^{\frac{N-3}{2}} h(k)z^{-k} + h\left(\frac{N-1}{2}\right) z^{-\left(\frac{N-1}{2}\right)} \sum_{k=0}^{\frac{N-3}{2}} h(N-1-k)z^{-(N-1-k)}$$

$$= \sum_{k=0}^{\frac{N-3}{2}} h(k)[z^{-k} + z^{-(N-1-k)}] + h\left(\frac{N-1}{2}\right) z^{-\left(\frac{N-1}{2}\right)} \qquad \because (b_k = h(k))$$

$$Y(z) = b_{\frac{N-1}{2}} z^{-\left(\frac{N-1}{2}\right)} X(z) + \sum_{k=0}^{\frac{N-3}{2}} b_k (z^{-k}X(z)) + z^{-(N-1-k)}X(z)$$

$$\boxed{\begin{aligned} Y(z) &= b_{\frac{N-1}{2}} z^{-\left(\frac{N-1}{2}\right)} X(z) + b_0[X(z) + z^{-(N-1)}X(z)] + \cdots \\ &+ b_{\frac{N-3}{2}}\left[z^{-\left(\frac{N-3}{2}\right)} X(z) + z^{-(N+2)}X(z)\right] \end{aligned}} \tag{4.23}$$

The equation (4.23) is realised in Figure 4.5.

Example 4.1

Draw the direct form structure of the FIR system described by the following transfer function:

$$H(z) = 1 + \frac{1}{2}z^{-1} + \frac{3}{4}z^{-2} + \frac{1}{4}z^{-3} + \frac{1}{2}z^{-4} + \frac{1}{5}z^{-5}$$

Solution

$$Y(z) = X(z) + \frac{1}{2}z^{-1}X(z) + \frac{3}{4}z^{-2}X(z) + \frac{1}{4}z^{-3}X(z) + \frac{1}{2}z^{-4}X(z) + \frac{1}{5}z^{-5}X(z)$$

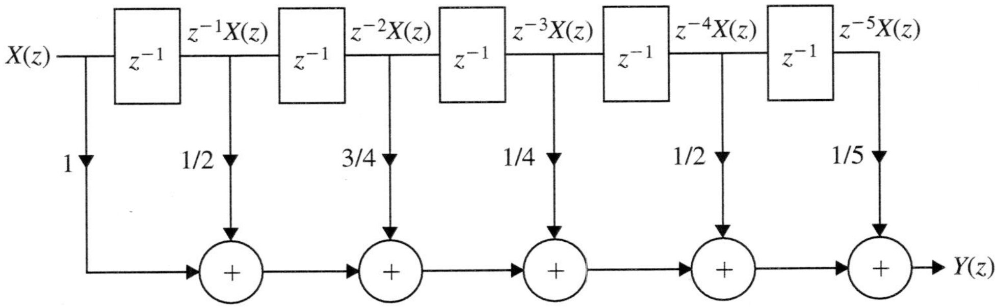

Figure 4.6 Direct form (or) transversal realization of $H(z)$ for Example 4.1.

Example 4.2

Realize the FIR system in (1) Direct form (2) Cascade form.

$$H(z) = \left(1 + \frac{1}{2}z^{-1}\right)\left(1 + \frac{1}{2}z^{-1} + \frac{1}{4}z^{-2}\right)$$

(Anna University, December, 2005)

Solution Given

$$H(z) = \left(1 + \frac{1}{2}z^{-1}\right)\left(1 + \frac{1}{2}z^{-1} + \frac{1}{4}z^{-2}\right)$$

(1) Direct form realization

$$H(z) = \frac{Y(z)}{X(z)}$$

$$= 1 + \frac{1}{2}z^{-1} + \frac{1}{4}z^{-2} + \frac{1}{2}z^{-1} + \frac{1}{4}z^{-2} + \frac{1}{8}z^{-3}$$

$$= 1 + z^{-1} + \frac{1}{2}z^{-2} + \frac{1}{8}z^{-3}$$

$$Y(z) = X(z) + z^{-1}X(z) + \frac{1}{2}z^{-2}X(z) + \frac{1}{8}z^{-3}X(z)$$

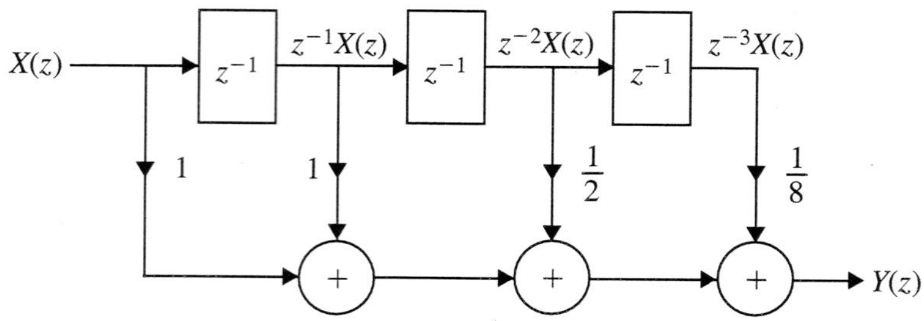

Figure 4.7 Direct form realization of FIR filter for Example 4.2.

(2) Cascade form realization

$$H(z) = \left(1 + \frac{1}{2}z^{-1}\right)\left(1 + \frac{1}{2}z^{-1} + \frac{1}{4}z^{-2}\right)$$
$$= H_1(z) \cdot H_2(z)$$

where

$$H_1(z) = 1 + \frac{1}{2}z^{-1}$$
$$H_2(z) = 1 + \frac{1}{2}z^{-1} + \frac{1}{4}z^{-2}$$
$$h_1(n) = \left\{1, \frac{1}{2}\right\}$$
$$h_2(n) = \left\{1, \frac{1}{2}, \frac{1}{4}\right\}$$

Here $h_1(n)$ and $h_2(n)$ do not satisfy the condition $h(n) \neq h(\infty - 1 - \infty)$. Therefore, both systems are realized in direct form.

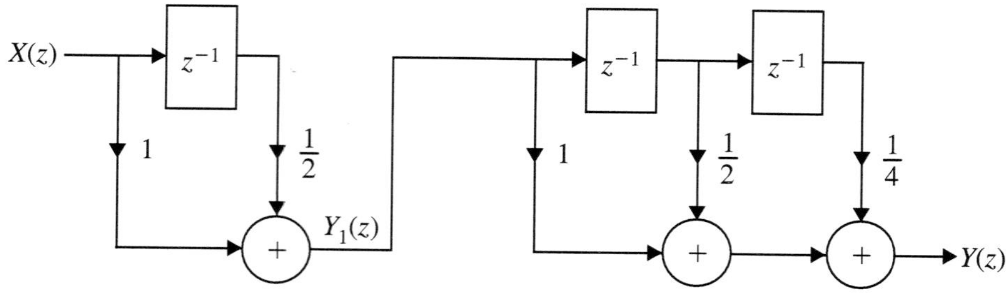

Figure 4.8 Cascade form realization of FIR filter for Example 4.2.

Example 4.3

Obtain cascade realization of linear phase FIR filter having system function

$$H(z) = \left(1 + \frac{1}{2}z^{-1} + z^{-2}\right)\left(2 + \frac{1}{4}z^{-1} + 2z^{-2}\right)$$

using minimum number of multipliers.

(*Anna University, April, 2005*)

Solution Given

$$H(z) = \left(1 + \frac{1}{2}z^{-1} + z^{-2}\right)\left(2 + \frac{1}{4}z^{-1} + z^{-2}\right)$$
$$= H_1(z)H_2(z)$$

where

$$H_1(z) = 1 + \frac{1}{2}z^{-1} + z^{-2},$$
$$H_2(z) = 2 + \frac{1}{4}z^{-1} - 2z^{-2}$$
$$h_1(n) = \left\{1 + \frac{1}{2}, 1\right\} \text{ and } N = 3,$$
$$h_2(n) = \left\{2 + \frac{1}{4}, 2\right\} \text{ and } N = 3$$

Here $h_1(n)$ and $h_2(n)$ satisfy the condition $h(n) = h(N - 1 - n)$.

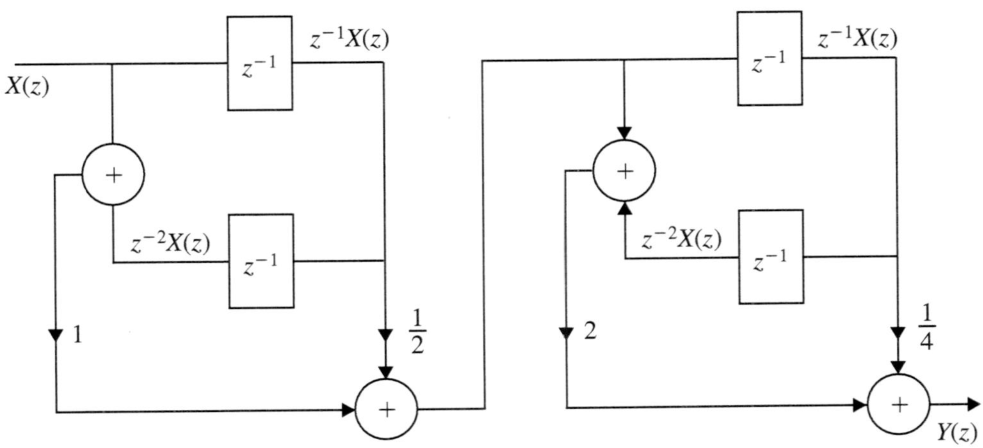

Figure 4.9 Cascade connection of linear phase FIR filter of Example 4.3.

Therefore,

$$H_1(z) = (1 + z^{-2}) + \frac{1}{2}z^{-1}$$

$$H_2(z) = 2(1 + z^{-2}) + \frac{1}{4}z^{-1}$$

Example 4.4

Realize the following system with minimum number of multipliers

$$(i) \qquad H(z) = \frac{1}{4} + \frac{1}{2}z^{-1} + \frac{3}{4}z^{-2} + \frac{1}{2}z^{-3} + \frac{1}{4}z^{-4}$$

$$(ii) \qquad H(z) = 1 + \frac{1}{2}z^{-1} + \frac{1}{2}z^{-2} + z^{-3}$$

$$(iii) \qquad H(z) = \left(1 + \frac{1}{2}z^{-1} + z^{-2}\right)\left(1 + \frac{1}{4}z^{-1} + z^{-2}\right)$$

Solution

(*i*) Given

$$H(z) = \frac{1}{4} + \frac{1}{2}z^{-1} + \frac{3}{4}z^{-2} + \frac{1}{2}z^{-3} + \frac{1}{4}z^{-4}$$

$$H(z) = \sum_{n=0}^{\infty} h(n)z^{-n} = h(0) + h(1)z^{-1} + h(2)z^{-2} + h(3)z^{-3} + \cdots$$

Comparing these two equations, we get the following impulse response:

$$h(n) = \left\{\frac{1}{4}, \frac{1}{2}, \frac{3}{4}, \frac{1}{2}, \frac{1}{4}\right\} \quad \text{and} \quad N = 5$$

Here $h(n)$ satisfies the condition $h(n) = h(N - 1 - n)$

$$\therefore\ H(z) = \frac{Y(z)}{X(z)} = \frac{1}{4} + \frac{1}{2}z^{-1} + \frac{3}{4}z^{-2} + \frac{1}{2}z^{-3} + \frac{1}{4}z^{-4}$$

$$= \frac{Y(z)}{X(z)} = \frac{1}{4}\left(1 + z^{-4}\right) + \frac{1}{2}\left(z^{-1} + z^{-3}\right) + \frac{3}{4}z^{-2}$$

$$Y(z) = \frac{1}{4}\left(X(z) + z^{-4}X(z)\right) + \frac{1}{2}\left(z^{-1}X(z) + z^{-3}X(z)\right) + \frac{3}{4}z^{-2}X(z)$$

$Y(z)$ is realized as shown in Figure 4.10.

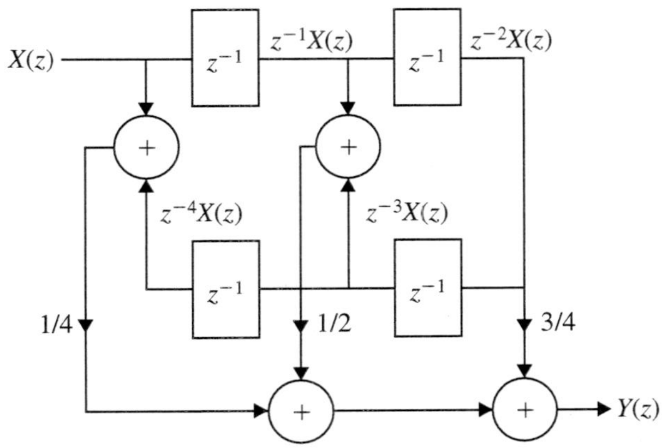

Figure 4.10 Linear phase realization of $H(z)$ for Example 4.4(*i*).

(*ii*) Given

$$H(z) = 1 + \frac{1}{2}z^{-1} + \frac{1}{2}z^{-2} + z^{-3}$$

Impulse response

$$h(n) = \left\{1, \frac{1}{2}, \frac{1}{2}, 1\right\} \quad \text{and} \quad N = 4$$

Here $h(n)$ satisfies the condition

$$h(n) = h(N - 1 - n)$$

$$\therefore \quad \frac{Y(z)}{X(z)} = [1 + z^{-3}] + \frac{1}{2}[z^{-1} + z^{-2}]$$

$$Y(z) = [X(z) + z^{-3}X(z)] + \frac{1}{2}[z^{-1}X(z) + z^{-2}X(z)]$$

$Y(z)$ is realized as shown in Figure 4.11.

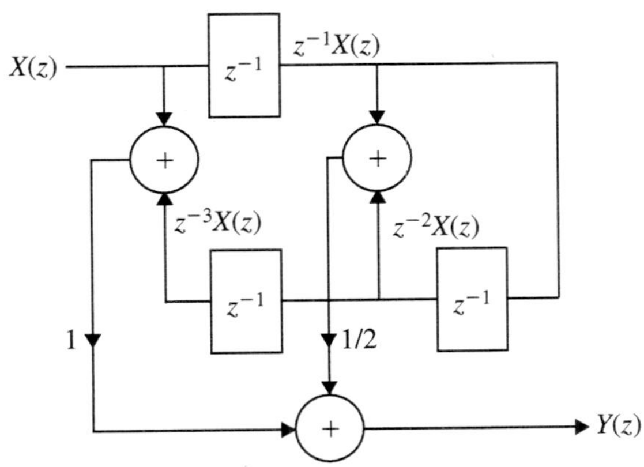

Figure 4.11 Linear phase realization of $H(z)$ for Example 4.4(*ii*).

(*iii*) Given

$$H(z) = \left(1 + \frac{1}{2}z^{-1} + z^{-2}\right)\left(1 + \frac{1}{4}z^{-1} + z^{-2}\right)$$
$$= H_1(z)H_2(z)$$

where

$$H_1(z) = 1 + \frac{1}{2}z^{-1} + z^{-2} = (1 + z^{-2}) + \frac{1}{2}z^{-1}$$
$$H_2(z) = 1 + \frac{1}{4}z^{-1} + z^{-2} = (1 + z^{-2}) + \frac{1}{4}z^{-1}$$

Consider

$$H_1(z) = \frac{Y_1(z)}{X(z)} = (1 + z^{-2}) + \left(\frac{1}{2}z^{-1}\right)$$
$$Y_1(z) = [X(z) + z^{-2}X(z)] + \frac{1}{2}z^{-1}X(z)$$

Consider

$$H_2(z) = \frac{Y(z)}{Y_1(z)} = (1 + z^{-2}) + \left(\frac{1}{4}z^{-1}\right)$$
$$Y(z) = [Y_1(z) + z^{-2}Y_1(z)] + \frac{1}{4}z^{-1}Y_1(z)$$

$Y(z)$ is realized as shown in Figure 4.12.

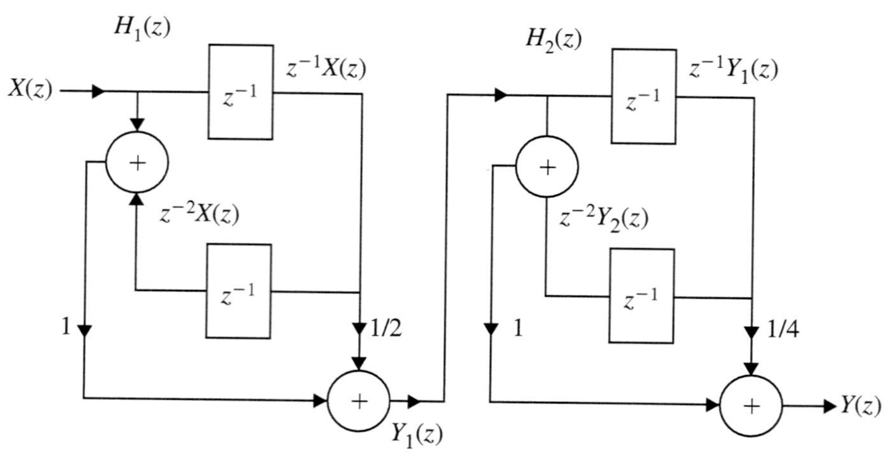

Figure 4.12 Linear phase realization of $H(z)$ for Example 4.4(*iii*).

4.3.4 Lattice Structure of an FIR Filter

Let us consider an FIR filter with system function

$$H(z) = A_m(z) = 1 + \sum_{k=1}^{m} \alpha_m(k) z^{-k}, \quad m \geq 1$$

$$\frac{Y(z)}{X(z)} = 1 + \sum_{k=1}^{m} \alpha_m(k) z^{-k}$$

$$Y(z) = X(z) + \sum_{k=1}^{m} \alpha_m(k) z^{-k} X(z)$$

Taking inverse z-transform on both sides we get

$$y(n) = x(n) + \sum_{k=1}^{m} \alpha_m(k) x(n-k) \qquad (4.24)$$

Interchanging the role of input and output in Equation (4.24) we get

$$x(n) = y(n) + \sum_{k=1}^{m} \alpha_m(k) y(n-k) \qquad (4.25)$$

We find that Equation (4.25) describes an IIR system having the system function $H(z) = \frac{1}{A_m(z)}$, while the system described by the difference equation in Equation (4.24) represents an FIR system with system function $H(z) = A_m(z)$.

Based on this, we use lattice structure system described in Chapter 3 to obtain a lattice structure for an all-zero FIR system by interchanging the role of input and output.

For an all-pole filter the input $x(n) = f_N(n)$ and the output $y(n) = f_0(n)$. For an all-zero FIR filter of order $M-1$ the input $x(n) = f_0(n)$ and the output $y(n) = f_{m-1}(n)$.

For $m = 1$ the Equation (4.24) reduces to

$$y(n) = x(n) + \alpha_1 x(n-1) \qquad (4.26)$$

This output can also be obtained from a single-stage lattice filter shown in Figure 4.13 from which we have

$$\begin{aligned} x(n) &= f_0(n) = g_0(n) \\ y(n) &= f_1(n) = f_0(n) + k_1 g_0(n-1) \\ &= x(n) + k_1 x(n-1) \end{aligned} \qquad (4.27)$$

and

$$\begin{aligned} g_1(n) &= k_1 f_0(n) + g_0(n-1) \\ &= k_1 x(n) + x(n-1) \end{aligned} \qquad (4.28)$$

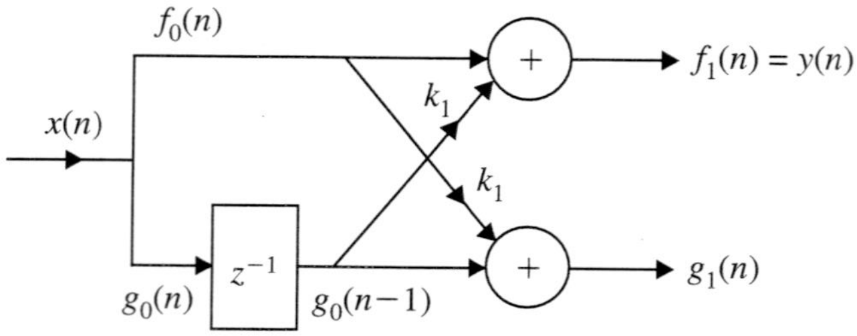

Figure 4.13 Single stage all-zero lattice structure.

Comparing Equation (4.26) with Equation (4.27) we get

$$\alpha_1(0) = 1$$
$$\alpha_1(1) = k_1$$

Now let us consider an FIR filter for which $m = 2$.

$$y(n) = x(n) + \alpha_2(1)x(n-1) + \alpha_2(2)x(n-2) \tag{4.29}$$

By cascading two lattice stage as shown in Figure 4.14 it is possible to obtain the output $y(n)$.

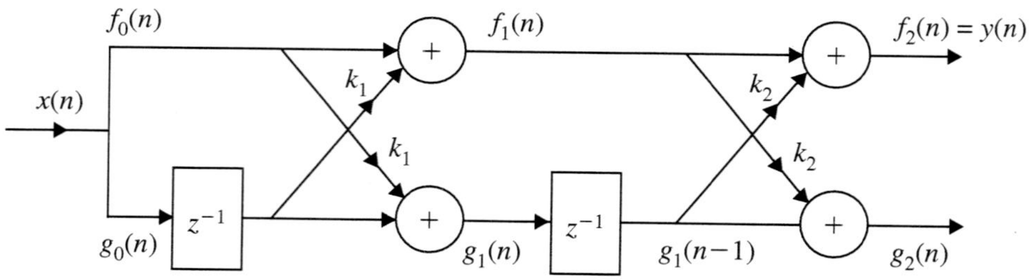

Figure 4.14 Two stage all-zero lattice structure.

From Figure 4.14 the output from second stage is obtained as,

$$\begin{aligned} y(n) = f_2(n) &= f_1(n) + k_2 g_1(n-1) \\ g_2(n) &= k_2 f_1(n) + g_1(n-1) \end{aligned} \tag{4.30}$$

Substituting for $f_1(n)$ and $g_1(n-1)$ from Equation (4.28) in Equation (4.30), we get

$$\begin{aligned} y(n) = f_2(n) &= x(n) + k_1 x(n-1) + k_2[k_1 x(n-1) + x(n-2)] \\ &= x(n) + k_1(1 + k_2)x(n-1) + k_2 x(n-2) \end{aligned} \tag{4.31}$$

Equation (4.31) is identical to Equation (4.29) from which we have

$$\begin{aligned}\alpha_2(0) &= 1,\\ \alpha_2(2) &= k_2,\\ \alpha_2(1) &= k_1(1+k_2)\\ &= \alpha_1(1)[1+\alpha_2(2)]\end{aligned} \tag{4.32}$$

Similarly

$$g_2(n) = \alpha_2 x(n) + k_1(1+k_2)x(n-1) + x(n-2) \tag{4.33}$$

From Equation (4.31) and Equation (4.33), we observe that the filter coefficients for the lattice filter that produces $f_2(n)$ are $\{1, \alpha_2(1), \alpha_2(2)\}$ while the coefficients for filter with output $g_2(n)$ are $\{\alpha_2(2),\ \alpha_2(1), 1\}$. We also note that these two sets of coefficients are in reverse order.

For a $m-1$ stage filter

$$\begin{aligned}f_0(n) &= g_0(n)\\ f_m(n) &= f_{m-1}(n) + k_m g_{m-1}(n-1)\\ g_m(n) &= k_m f_{m-1}(n) + g_{m-1}(n-1), \quad m = 1, 2, \ldots m-1\end{aligned} \tag{4.34}$$

The output of $m-1$ stage filter

$$y(n) = f_{m-1}(n)$$

4.3.4.1 Conversion of Lattice Coefficients to Direct Form Filter Coefficients

For $m = 3$ the Equation (4.24) can be written as

$$y(n) = x(n) + \alpha_3(1)x(n-1) + \alpha_3(2)x(n-2) + \alpha_3(3)x(n-3) \tag{4.35}$$

We have

$$\begin{aligned}y(n) = f_3(n) &= f_2(n) + k_3 g_2(n-1)\\ &= x(n) + \alpha_2(1)x(n-1) + \alpha_2(2)x(n-2) + k_3\alpha_2(2)x(n-1)\\ &\quad + k_3\alpha_2(1)x(n-2) + k_3x(n-3)\\ &= x(n) + [\alpha_2(1) + k_3\alpha_2(1)]x(n-1) + [\alpha_2(2) + k_3\alpha_2(1)]x(n-2)\\ &\quad + k_3x(n-3)\end{aligned} \tag{4.36}$$

Comparing Equations (4.35) and (4.36) we get

$$\begin{aligned}
\alpha_3(0) &= 1 \\
\alpha_3(1) &= \alpha_2(1) + k_3\alpha_2(1) \\
&= \alpha_2(1) + \alpha_3(3)\alpha_2(1) \\
\alpha_3(2) &= \alpha_2(2) + k_3(3)\alpha_2(1) \\
&= \alpha_2(2) + \alpha_3(3)\alpha_2(1) \\
\alpha_3(3) &= k_3
\end{aligned} \tag{4.37}$$

From Equations (4.32) and (4.37) for a general case we find that

$$\begin{aligned}
\alpha_m(0) &= 1 \\
\alpha_m(m) &= k_m \\
\alpha_m(k) &= \alpha_{m-1}(k) + k_m(m)\alpha_{m-1}(m-k)
\end{aligned} \tag{4.38}$$

The Equation (4.38) can be used to convert the lattice filter coefficients to direct form FIR filter coefficients.

Example 4.5

Consider an FIR lattice filter coefficients

$$k_1 = \frac{1}{3}, \quad k_2 = \frac{1}{4}, \quad k_3 = \frac{1}{2}$$

Determine the FIR filter coefficients for the direct form structure.

Solution From the given data and from Equation (4.38) we find that

$$\begin{aligned}
\alpha_3(0) &= 1 \\
\alpha_3(3) &= k_3 = \frac{1}{2} \\
\alpha_1(1) &= k_1 = \frac{1}{3} \\
\alpha_2(2) &= k_2 = \frac{1}{4}
\end{aligned}$$

From Equation (4.38) we write

$$\alpha_m(k) = \alpha_{m-1}(k) + k_m\alpha_{m-1}(m-k)$$

For $m = 2$ and $k = 1$

$$\begin{aligned}
\alpha_2(1) &= \alpha_1(1) + k_2\alpha_1(1) \\
&= \frac{1}{3} + \frac{1}{4}\cdot\frac{1}{3} = \frac{1}{3} + \frac{1}{12} = \frac{4+1}{12} = \frac{5}{12}
\end{aligned}$$

For $m = 3$ and $k = 1$

$$\begin{aligned}\alpha_3(1) &= \alpha_2(1) + \alpha_3(3)\alpha_2(2) \\ &= \frac{5}{12} + \frac{1}{2}\cdot\frac{1}{4} \\ &= \frac{5}{12} + \frac{1}{8} \\ &= \frac{40+12}{96} \\ &= \frac{52}{96} = \frac{13}{24}\end{aligned}$$

For $m = 2$ and $k = 2$

$$\begin{aligned}\alpha_3(2) &= \alpha_3(2) + \alpha_3(3)\alpha_2(1) \\ &= \frac{1}{4} + \frac{1}{2}\cdot\frac{5}{12} \\ &= \frac{1}{4} + \frac{5}{24} \\ &= \frac{6+5}{24} \\ &= \frac{11}{24}\end{aligned}$$

$$\boxed{\alpha_3(0) = 1, \quad \alpha_3(1) = \frac{13}{24}, \quad \alpha_3(2) = \frac{11}{2}, \quad \alpha_3(3) = \frac{1}{2}}$$

4.3.4.2 Conversion of Direct Form FIR Filter Coefficients to Lattice Coefficients

For a 3 stage direct form FIR filter

$$y(n) = x(n) + \alpha_3(1)x(n-1) + \alpha_3(2)x(n-2) + \alpha_3(3)x(n-3) \quad (4.39)$$

For a 3 stage lattice structure

$$\begin{aligned}y(n) = f_3(n) &= f_2(n) + k_3 g_2(n-1) \\ g_3(n) &= k_3 f_2(n) + g_2(n-1) \\ y(n) = f_3(n) &= f_2(n) + k_3[g_3(n) - k_3 f_2(n)] \\ y(n) = f_3(n) &= f_2(n)[1-k_3^2] + k_3 g_3(n) \\ f_2(n)[1-k_3^2] &= f_3(n) - k_3 g_3(n)\end{aligned}$$

$$f_2(n) = \frac{f_3(n) - k_3 g_3(n)}{1 - k_3^2}$$

$$= \Big[x(n) + \alpha_3(1)x(n-1) + \alpha_3(2)x(n-2) + \alpha_3(3)x(n-3)$$

$$- k_3^2 x(n) - \alpha_3(3)\alpha_3(2)x(n-1) - \alpha_3(3)\alpha_3(1)x(n-2)$$

$$- \alpha_3(3)x(n-3)\Big] \Big/ 1 - \alpha_3^2(3)$$

$$= x(n) + \frac{\alpha_3(1) - \alpha_3(2)\alpha_3(2)}{1 - \alpha_3^2(2)} x(n-1) + \frac{\alpha_3(2) - \alpha_3(3)\alpha_3(1)}{1 - \alpha_3^2(3)} x(n-2) \tag{4.40}$$

Comparing equation (4.39) and (4.40) we get

$$\alpha_2(0) = 1$$

$$\alpha_2(1) = \frac{\alpha_3(1) - \alpha_3(3)\alpha_3(2)}{1 - \alpha_3^2(3)}$$

$$\alpha_2(2) = \frac{\alpha_3(2) - \alpha_3(3)\alpha_3(1)}{1 - \alpha_3^2(3)}$$

In general for a m-stage filter

$$\boxed{\begin{array}{c} \alpha_{m-1}(0) = 1 \\ k_m = \alpha_m(m) \\ \alpha_{m-1}(k) = \dfrac{\alpha_m(k) - \alpha_m(m)\alpha_m(m-k)}{1 - \alpha_m^2(m)}, \quad 1 \le k \le m-1 \end{array}} \tag{4.41}$$

Example 4.6

An FIR filter is given by the difference equation

$$y(n) = x(n) + \frac{4}{3}x(n-1) + \frac{1}{2}x(n-2) + \frac{2}{3}x(n-3)$$

Determine its lattice form.

Solution Given

$$y(n) = x(n) + \frac{4}{3}x(n-1) + \frac{1}{2}x(n-2) + \frac{2}{3}x(n-3)$$

$$\alpha_3(0) = 1, \quad \alpha_3(1) = \frac{4}{3}, \quad \alpha_3(2) = \frac{1}{2}, \quad \alpha_3(3) = \frac{2}{3}$$

From equation (4.41) we get

$$\alpha_2(0) = 1$$

$$k_3 = \alpha_3(3) = \frac{2}{3}$$

$$\alpha_{m-1}(k) = \frac{\alpha_m(k) - \alpha_m(m)\alpha_m(m-k)}{1 - \alpha_m^2(m)}, \quad 1 \le k \le 2$$

For $m = 3$ and $k = 1$

$$\begin{aligned} \alpha_2(1) &= \frac{\alpha_3(1) - \alpha_3(3)\alpha_3(2)}{1 - \alpha_3^2(3)} \\ &= \frac{\frac{4}{3} - \frac{2}{3} \cdot \frac{1}{2}}{1 - (\frac{2}{3})^2} \\ &= \frac{\frac{4}{3} - \frac{2}{6}}{1 - \frac{4}{9}} \\ &= 1.8 \end{aligned}$$

For $m = 3$ and $k = 2$

$$\begin{aligned} k_2 = \alpha_2(2) &= \frac{\alpha_3(2) - \alpha_3(3)\alpha_3(1)}{1 - \alpha_3^2(3)} \\ &= \frac{\frac{1}{2} - \frac{2}{3} \cdot \frac{4}{3}}{1 - (\frac{2}{3})^2} \\ &= \frac{\frac{1}{2} - \frac{8}{9}}{1 - \frac{4}{9}} \\ &= -0.7 \end{aligned}$$

For $m = 2$ and $k = 1$

$$\begin{aligned} k_1 = \alpha_1(1) &= \frac{\alpha_2(1) - \alpha_2(2)\alpha_2(1)}{1 - \alpha_2^2(2)} \\ &= \frac{1.8 - (-0.7)(1.8)}{1 - (-0.7)^2} \\ &= \frac{3.06}{0.51} \\ &= 6 \end{aligned}$$

$$\boxed{k_1 = 6, \quad k_2 = -0.7, \quad k_3 = 0.6667}$$

The lattice structure is shown in Figure 4.15.

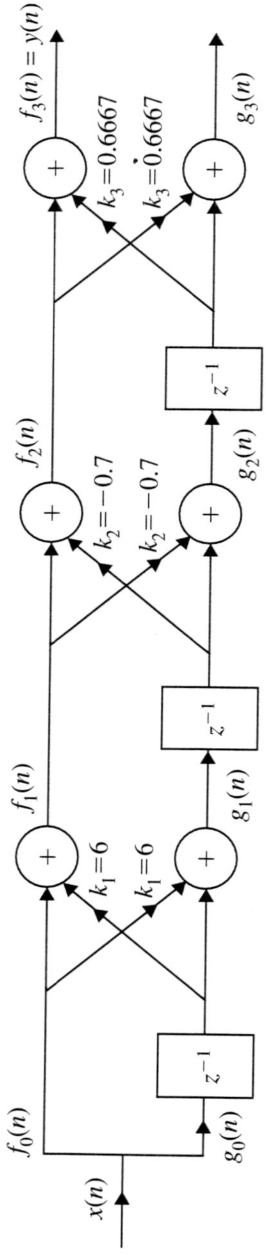

Figure 4.15 Lattice structure for the Example 4.6.

Example 4.7(a)

An FIR filter is given by the difference equation

$$y(n) = 2x(n) + \frac{4}{5}x(n-1) + \frac{3}{2}x(n-2) + \frac{2}{3}x(n-3)$$

Determine the lattice form.

(Anna University, May 2007)

Solution Given

$$\begin{aligned} y(n) &= 2x(n) + \frac{4}{5}x(n-1) + \frac{3}{2}x(n-2) + \frac{2}{3}x(n-3) \\ &= 2\left[x(n) + \frac{2}{5}x(n-1) + \frac{3}{4}x(n-2) + \frac{1}{3}x(n-3)\right] \\ &= k_0\left[1 + \sum_{k=1}^{3} \alpha_m(k)x(n-k)\right] \end{aligned}$$

where $k_0 = 2$

$$\alpha_3(0) = 1,\ \alpha_3(1) = \frac{2}{5},\ \alpha_3(2) = \frac{3}{4},\ \alpha_3(3) = \frac{1}{3}$$

From Equation (4.24), we get

$$\alpha_2(0) = 1$$

$$k_3 = \alpha_3(3) = \frac{1}{3}$$

$$\alpha_{m-1}(k) = \frac{\alpha_m(k) - \alpha_m(m)\alpha_m(m-k)}{1-\alpha_m^2(m)}, \quad 1 \le k \le 2$$

For $m = 3$ and $k = 1$

$$\begin{aligned} \alpha_2(1) &= \frac{\alpha_3(1) - \alpha_3(3)\alpha_3(2)}{1-\alpha_3^2(3)} \\ &= \frac{\frac{2}{5} - \frac{1}{3}\cdot\frac{3}{4}}{1-(\frac{1}{3})^2} \\ \alpha_2(1) &= 0.16875 \end{aligned}$$

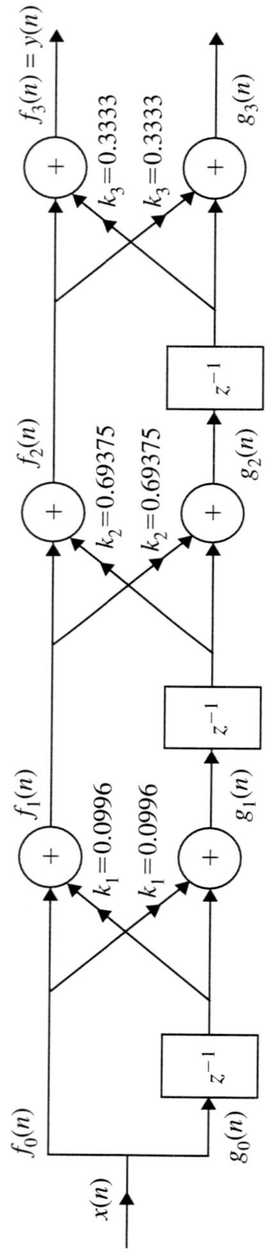

Figure 4.16 Lattice Form for the Example 4.7(*a*).

For $m = 3$ and $k = 2$

$$k_2 = \alpha_2(2) = \frac{\alpha_3(2) - \alpha_3(3)\alpha_3(1)}{1 - \alpha_3^2(3)}$$

$$= \frac{\frac{3}{4} - \frac{1}{3} \cdot \frac{2}{5}}{1 - (\frac{1}{3})^2}$$

$$= \frac{111}{160}$$

$$\boxed{k_2 = 0.69375}$$

For $m = 2$ and $k = 1$

$$k_1 = \alpha_1(1) = \frac{\alpha_2(1) - \alpha_2(2)\alpha_2(1)}{1 - \alpha_2^2(2)}$$

$$= \frac{0.16875 - (0.69375)(0.16875)}{1 - (0.69375)^2}$$

$$\boxed{k_1 = 0.0996}$$

Lattice form coefficients are,

$$k_1 = 0.0996, \quad k_2 = 0.69375, \quad k_3 = 0.3333.$$

Example 4.7(b)

Given a three stage lattice filter with coefficients $k_1 = \frac{1}{4}$ and $k_2 = \frac{1}{4}$, $k_3 = \frac{1}{3}$. Determine the FIR filter coefficients for the direct form structure?

(Anna University, May, 2007)

Solution From the given data and from Equation (4.38), we can find that

$$\alpha_3(0) = 1, \quad \alpha_3(3) = k_3 = \frac{1}{3}$$

$$\alpha_1(1) = k_1 = \frac{1}{4}, \quad \alpha_2(2) = k_2 = \frac{1}{4}$$

We know that

$$\alpha_m(k) = \alpha_{m-1}(k) + k_m\alpha_{m-1}(m - k)$$

For $m = 2$ and $k = 1$

$$\alpha_2(1) = \alpha_1(1) + k_2\alpha_1(1)$$
$$\alpha_2(1) = \frac{1}{4} + \frac{1}{4}.\frac{1}{4} = \frac{1}{4} + \frac{1}{16}$$
$$= \frac{4+1}{16} = \frac{5}{16}$$

For $m = 3$ and $k = 1$

$$\alpha_3(1) = \alpha_2(1) + \alpha_3(3)\alpha_2(2)$$
$$= \frac{5}{16} + \frac{1}{3}.\frac{1}{4} = \frac{5}{16} + \frac{1}{12}$$
$$= \frac{60+16}{192} = \frac{76}{192}$$
$$= 0.3958$$
$$= \frac{19}{48}$$

For $m = 3$ and $k = 2$

$$\alpha_3(2) = \alpha_2(2) + k_3\alpha_2(1)$$
$$= \frac{1}{4} + \frac{1}{3}.\frac{5}{16}$$
$$\alpha_3(2) = \frac{1}{4} + \frac{5}{48} = \frac{12+5}{48} = \frac{17}{48}$$

Direct form coefficients are,

$$\boxed{\alpha_3(0) = 1, \quad \alpha_3(1) = \frac{19}{48}, \quad \alpha_3(2) = \frac{17}{48}, \quad \alpha_3(3) = \frac{1}{3}}$$

4.4 FIR Filters

The filters designed by using finite number of samples of impulse response are called FIR filters. These finite number of samples are obtained from the infinite duration desired impulse response $h_d(n)$. Here $h_d(n)$ is the inverse Fourier transform of $H_d(\omega)$, where $H_d(\omega)$ is the ideal (desired) frequency response. The various methods of designing FIR filters differ only in the method of determining the samples of $h(n)$ from the samples of $h_d(n)$. They are discussed ahead.

4.4.1 Characteristics of FIR Filters with Linear Phase

Let $h(n)$ be a causal finite duration sequence defined over the interval $0 \le n \le N-1$ and the samples of $h(n)$ be real. The Fourier transform of $h(n)$ is given by

$$H(\omega) = \sum_{n=0}^{N-1} h(n)e^{-j\omega n} \tag{4.42}$$

which is periodic with period 2π. Therefore

$$H(\omega) = H(\omega + 2\pi m), \quad m = 0, \pm 1, \pm 2, \ldots \tag{4.43}$$

with the constraint that $h(n)$ is real and $H(\omega)$ is complex.

$$H(\omega) = \pm|H(\omega)|e^{j\theta(\omega)}$$

The operators '$\pm$' represents real part of $H(\omega)$ taking on both +ve and −ve values. When $h(n)$ is real then $|H(\omega)|$ is symmetric function and $\angle H(\omega)$ or $\angle\theta(\omega)$ is anti-symmetric function, *i.e.*,

$$\begin{aligned} |H(\omega)| &= |H(-\omega)| \\ \angle\theta(\omega) &= -\angle\theta(-\omega) \end{aligned} \tag{4.44}$$

For many practical FIR filters, exact linearity of phase is a desired goal.

Let us assume that the phase of $H(\omega)$ is a linear function of ω, *i.e.*,

$$\begin{aligned} &\theta(\omega) \propto \omega \\ &\theta(\omega) \propto -\alpha\omega, \qquad -\pi \le \omega \le \pi \end{aligned} \tag{4.45}$$

where α is a constant phase delay in samples. From equations (4.43) and (4.45) we get

$$H(\omega) = \pm|H(\omega)|e^{-j\alpha\omega}$$

From equation (4.24) we get

$$H(\omega) = \sum_{n=0}^{N-1} h(n)e^{-j\omega n}$$

$$\sum_{n=0}^{N-1} h(n)e^{-j\omega n} = \pm|H(\omega)|e^{-j\alpha\omega} \tag{4.46}$$

$$\sum_{n=0}^{N-1} h(n)[\cos\omega n - j\sin\omega n] = \pm|H(\omega)|[\cos\alpha\omega - j\sin\alpha\omega]$$

On equating the real and imaginary parts we get,

$$\pm|H(\omega)|\cos\alpha\omega = \sum_{n=0}^{N-1} h(n)\cos\omega n \tag{4.47}$$

$$\pm|H(\omega)|\sin\alpha\omega = \sum_{n=0}^{N-1} h(n)\sin\omega n \tag{4.48}$$

Dividing the equation (4.20) by equation (4.48), we get

$$\frac{\sin\alpha\omega}{\cos\alpha\omega} = \frac{\sum_{n=0}^{N-1} h(n)\sin\omega n}{\sum_{n=0}^{N-1} h(n)\cos\omega n} \tag{4.49}$$

$$\sin\alpha\omega\sum_{n=0}^{N-1} h(n)\cos\omega n = \cos\alpha\omega\sum_{n=0}^{N-1} h(n)\sin\omega n$$

$$\sum_{n=0}^{N-1} h(n)[\sin\alpha\omega\cos\omega n - \cos\alpha\omega\sin\omega n] = 0 \tag{4.50}$$

$$\sum_{n=0}^{N-1} h(n)\sin(\alpha - n)\omega = 0 \tag{4.51}$$

The solution of equation (4.51) exits when

$$\alpha = \frac{N-1}{2} \quad \text{and} \quad h(n) = h(N-1-n), \quad 0 \le n \le N-1 \tag{4.52}$$

From the condition, $\alpha = \frac{N-1}{2}$ we can say that for every value of N there is only one value of phase delay α for which linear phase can be obtained easily.

From the condition, $h(n) = h(N-1-n)$ we can say that for this value of α, the $h(n)$ has a special kind of symmetry. The symmetry impulse response is shown in Figure 4.17.

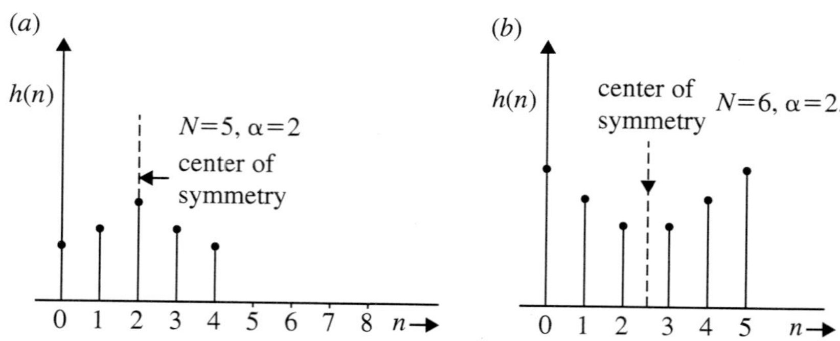

Figure 4.17 Symmetry impulse response for N = odd and N = even.

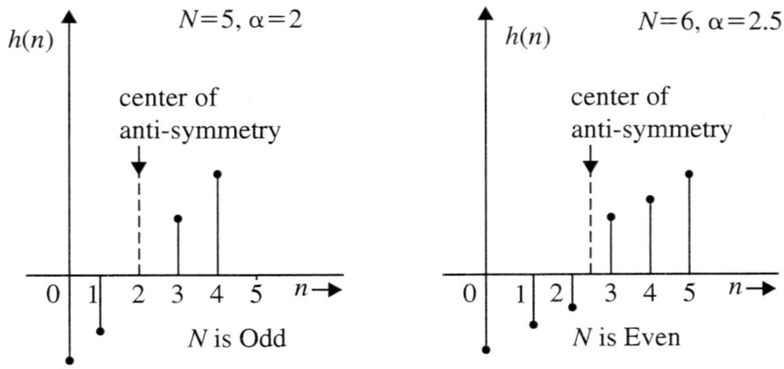

Figure 4.18 Anti-symmetry impulse response for N = odd and N = even.

The definition of linear phase filter $\theta(\omega) = -\omega\alpha$ requires to have both constant group delay and constant phase delay.

If only constant group delay is required an another type of linear phase filter exists, in which, the phase of $H(\omega)$ is a piece-wise linear function of ω. For this case $H(\omega)$ can be expressed as

$$H(\omega) = \pm|H(\omega)|e^{+j(\beta-\omega\alpha)} \tag{4.53}$$

Solution of Equation (4.53) exists only if $\alpha = \frac{N-1}{\alpha}$, $\beta = \pm\frac{\pi}{2}$ and

$$h(n) = -h(N-1-n) \quad \text{for} \quad 0 \leq n \leq -1 \tag{4.54}$$

The anti-symmetric impulse response is shown in Figure 4.18.

4.4.1.1 *Phase Delay and Group Delay*

The phase delay and group delay are the two important parameters that characterize the frequency response characteristics of a digital filter. Suppose the system is excited by the following input which is sinusoidal of frequency ω_0 and amplitude A.

$$x(n) = A\cos(\omega_0 n + \phi)$$

For the LTI system, the output may be expressed by the following equation.

$$\begin{aligned} y(n) &= A|H(e^{j\omega_0})|\cos\left(\omega_0\left(n + \frac{\theta(\omega_0)}{\omega_0}\right) + \Phi\right) \\ &= A|H(e^{j\omega_0})|\cos(\omega_0(n - \tau_p(\omega_0) + \Phi) \end{aligned}$$

where

$$\boxed{\tau_p(\omega_0) = \frac{\theta(\omega_0)}{\omega_0}}$$

τ_p is called the phase delay. Now the output is a time delayed version of the input $x(n)$.

When the input signal contains many sinusoidal components with different frequencies which are different from harmonics, each component will go through different phase delays when they are passed through a LTI discrete system and the signal delay now is determined by what is named as group delay denoted by the letter $\tau_g(\omega)$. The group delay is defined as,

$$\boxed{\tau_g(\omega) = \frac{d\theta(\omega)}{d\omega}}$$

Example 4.8

Determine the frequency response of FIR filter defined by $y(n) = 0.25x(n) + x(n-1) + 0.25x(n-2)$. Calculate the phase delay and group delay.

(Anna University, December, 2005)

Solution Given

$$y(n) = 0.25x(n) + x(n-1) + 0.25x(n-2)$$

Taking Fourier transform on both sides

$$Y(e^{j\omega}) = 0.25X(e^{j\omega}) + e^{-j\omega}X(e^{j\omega}) + 0.25e^{-j2\omega}X(e^{j\omega})$$

$$\begin{aligned}
H(e^{j\omega}) &= \frac{Y(e^{j\omega})}{X(e^{j\omega})} = 0.25 + e^{-j\omega} + 0.25e^{-2j\omega} \\
&= e^{-j\omega}(0.25e^{j\omega} + 1 + 0.25e^{-j\omega}) \\
&= e^{-j\omega}(1 + 0.5\cos\omega) \\
H(e^{j\omega}) &= e^{-j\omega}\bar{H}(e^{j\omega})
\end{aligned}$$

We know that

$$H(e^{j\omega}) = e^{j\theta(\omega)}\bar{H}(e^{j\omega})$$

Comparing these two equations, we get

$$\theta(\omega) = -\omega$$

The phase delay

$$\boxed{\tau_p = \frac{-\theta(\omega)}{\omega} = \frac{\omega}{\omega} = 1}$$

The group delay

$$\boxed{-\frac{d\theta(\omega)}{d\omega} = -\frac{d}{d\omega}(-\omega) = 1}$$

4.4.2 Frequency Response of Linear Phase FIR Filter

Depending on the value of N and the type of symmetry of the filter impulse response there are four possible types of linear phase. The following are the four cases of impulse response for the linear phase FIR filters.

Case I. Symmetric impulse response when N is odd.
Case II. Symmetric impulse response when N is even.
Case III. Anti-symmetric impulse response when N is odd.
Case IV. Anti-symmetric impulse response when N is even.

4.4.2.1 *Symmetric Impulse Response of the Linear Phase FIR Filters When N is Odd*

The Fourier transform of $h(n)$ is

$$H(\omega) = H(e^{j\omega}) = \sum_{n=-\infty}^{\infty} h(n)e^{-j\omega n}$$

Since the impulse response of FIR filter has only N samples, the limits of summation can be changed to $n = 0$ to $N - 1$

$$H(\omega) = \sum_{n=-\infty}^{N-1} h(n)e^{-j\omega n}$$

Let impulse response $h(n)$ be symmetric and it has odd number of samples. Let $N = 9$. The symmetrical impulse response is shown in Figure 4.19.

When N is an odd number, the symmetrical impulse response will have the centre of symmetry at $n = (N - 1)/2$. Hence, $H(e^{j\omega})$ can be expressed as

$$H(\omega) = \sum_{n=0}^{\frac{N-3}{2}} h(n)e^{-j\omega n} + h\left[\frac{N-1}{2}\right]e^{-j\omega\left[\frac{N-1}{2}\right]} + \sum_{n=(N+1)/2}^{N-1} h(n)e^{-j\omega n} \quad (4.55)$$

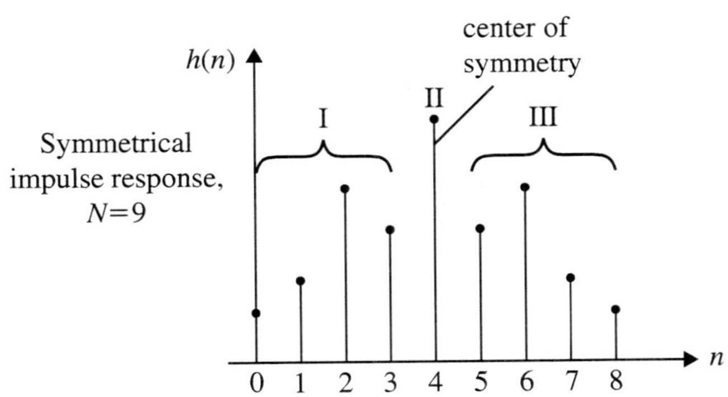

Figure 4.19 Symmetry impulse response when N = odd.

Let $m = N - 1 - n$. Therefore, $n = N - 1 - m$.

$$\text{When } n = \frac{N+1}{2}; \quad m = N - 1 - \frac{N+1}{2} = \frac{N-3}{2}$$

$$\text{When } n = N - 1; \quad m = N - 1 - (N - 1) = 0$$

$$H(\omega) = \sum_{n=0}^{\frac{N-3}{2}} h(n)e^{-j\omega n} + h\left[\frac{N-1}{2}\right]e^{-j\omega[\frac{N-1}{2}]} + \sum_{m=0}^{\frac{N-3}{2}} h(N-1-m)e^{-j\omega(N-1-m)}$$

Replacing m by n we get

$$H(\omega) = \sum_{n=0}^{\frac{N-3}{2}} h(n)e^{-j\omega n} + h\left[\frac{N-1}{2}\right]e^{-j\omega[\frac{N-1}{2}]} + \sum_{n=0}^{\frac{N-3}{2}} h(N-1-n)e^{-j\omega(N-1-n)}$$

For symmetrical impulse response $h(N-1-n) = h(n)$. Therefore

$$H(\omega) = \sum_{n=0}^{\frac{N-3}{2}} h(n)e^{-j\omega n} + h\left[\frac{N-1}{2}\right]e^{-j\omega[\frac{N-1}{2}]} + \sum_{n=0}^{\frac{N-3}{2}} h(n)e^{(-j\omega(N-1)+j\omega n)}$$

$$H(\omega) = e^{-j\omega\left[\frac{N-1}{2}\right]}\left[h\left[\frac{N-1}{2}\right] + \sum_{n=0}^{\frac{N-3}{2}} h(n)\left[e^{j\omega[\frac{N-1}{2}]-j\omega n} + e^{-j\omega[\frac{N-1}{2}]+j\omega n}\right]\right]$$

$$= e^{-j\omega\left[\frac{N-1}{2}\right]}\left[h\left[\frac{N-1}{2}\right] + \sum_{n=0}^{\frac{N-3}{2}} h(n)\left[e^{j\omega[\frac{N-1}{2}-n]} + e^{-j\omega[\frac{N-1}{2}-n]}\right]\right]$$

$$= e^{-j\omega\left[\frac{N-1}{2}\right]}\left[h\left[\frac{N-1}{2}\right] + \sum_{n=0}^{\frac{N-3}{2}} 2h(n)\cos\omega\left(\frac{N-1}{2} - n\right)\right]$$

$$\text{Let } k = \frac{N-1}{2} - n; \quad n = \frac{N-1}{2} - k$$

When $n = 0$, $k = \frac{N-1}{2}$ and

When $n = \frac{N-3}{2}$, $k = 1$

$$= e^{-j\omega\left[\frac{N-1}{2}\right]}\left[h\left[\frac{N-1}{2}\right] + \sum_{k=1}^{\frac{N-1}{2}} 2\left(\frac{N-1}{2} - k\right)\cos\omega k\right]$$

Replacing k by n we get

$$H(\omega) = e^{-j\omega\left[\frac{N-1}{2}\right]}\left[h\left[\frac{N-1}{2}\right] + 2\sum_{n=1}^{\frac{N-1}{2}} h\left(\frac{N-1}{2} - n\right)\cos\omega n\right] \quad (4.56)$$

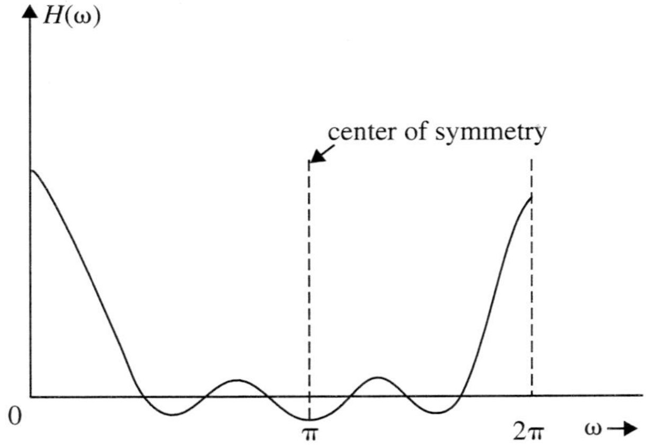

Figure 4.20 Magnitude response of $H(\omega)$.

The equation (4.56) is the frequency response of linear phase FIR filter when impulse response is symmetric and N is odd.

Magnitude function of $H(\omega)$ is given by

$$|H(\omega)| = h\left[\frac{N-1}{2}\right] + 2\sum_{n=1}^{\frac{N-1}{2}} h\left(\frac{N-1}{2} - n\right)\cos\omega n \tag{4.57}$$

Phase function of $H(\omega)$ is given by

$$\angle H(\omega) = -\omega\left[\frac{N-1}{2}\right] = -\omega\alpha \tag{4.58}$$

where $\alpha = (N-1)/2$. The magnitude response of $H(\omega)$ is shown in Figure 4.20.

The magnitude response of $H(\omega)$ is symmetric with $\omega = \pi$ when the impulse response is symmetric and N is odd.

4.4.2.2 Symmetric Impulse Response of the Linear Phase FIR Filters When N is Even

Let $h(n)$ be symmetric and impulse response, for $N = 10$ is shown in Figure 4.21.

The Fourier transform of $h(n)$ is

$$H(\omega) = \sum_{n=0}^{N-1} h(n)e^{-j\omega n}$$

$$= \sum_{n=0}^{\frac{N}{2}-1} h(n)e^{-j\omega n} + \sum_{n=\frac{N}{2}}^{N-1} h(n)e^{-j\omega n} \tag{4.59}$$

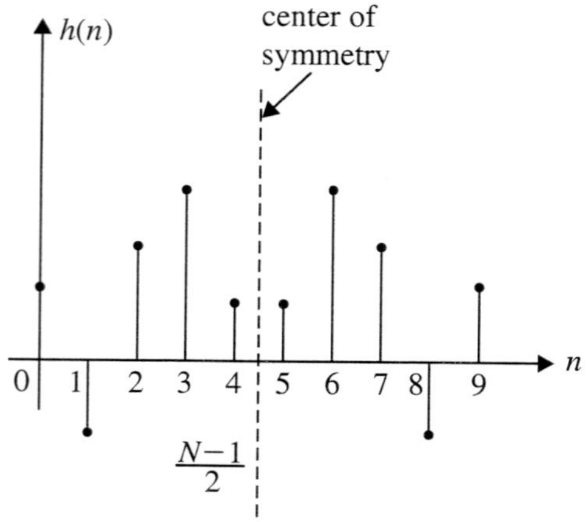

Figure 4.21 Symmetry impulse response when $N=$ even.

Let $m = N-1-n \Longrightarrow n = N-1-m$

When $n = \frac{n}{2}; \Longrightarrow m = N-1-\frac{N}{2} = \frac{N}{2}-1$

When $n = N-1; \Longrightarrow m = N-1-N+1 = 0$

$$H(\omega) = \sum_{n=0}^{\frac{N}{2}-1} h(n)e^{-j\omega n} + \sum_{m=0}^{\frac{N}{2}-1} h(N-1-m)e^{-j\omega(N-1-m)}$$

replace m by n and $h(n) = h(N-1-m)$

$$H(\omega) = \sum_{n=0}^{\frac{N}{2}-1} h(n)e^{-j\omega n} + \sum_{n=0}^{\frac{N}{2}-1} h(n)e^{-j\omega(N-1)+j\omega n}$$

$$= e^{-j\omega\left(\frac{N-1}{2}\right)}\left[\sum_{n=0}^{\frac{N}{2}-1} h(n)\left(e^{j\omega\left(\frac{N-1}{2}\right)-j\omega n} + e^{-j\omega\left(\frac{N-1}{2}\right)+j\omega n}\right)\right]$$

$$= e^{-j\omega\left(\frac{N-1}{2}\right)}\left[\sum_{n=0}^{\frac{N}{2}-1} h(n)\left(e^{j\omega\left(\frac{N-1}{2}-n\right)} + e^{-j\omega\left(\frac{N-1}{2}-n\right)}\right)\right]$$

$$= e^{-j\omega\left(\frac{N-1}{2}\right)}\left[\sum_{n=0}^{\frac{N}{2}-1} 2h(n)\cos\left(\frac{N-1}{2}-n\right)\omega\right] \quad \left(\because \cos\theta = \frac{e^{i\theta}+e^{-i\theta}}{2}\right)$$

$$= e^{-j\omega\left(\frac{N-1}{2}\right)}\left[\sum_{n=0}^{\frac{N}{2}-1} 2h(n)\cos\left(\frac{N}{2}-n-\frac{1}{2}\right)\omega\right]$$

$$\text{Let } k = \frac{N}{2} - n \Longrightarrow n = \frac{N}{2} - k$$

$$\text{When } n = 0; \Longrightarrow k = \frac{N}{2}$$

$$\text{When } n = \frac{N}{2} - 1; \Longrightarrow k = 1$$

$$H(\omega) = e^{-j\omega\left(\frac{N-1}{2}\right)}\left[\sum_{k=1}^{\frac{N}{2}} 2h\left(\frac{N}{2} - k\right)\cos\omega\left(k - \frac{1}{2}\right)\right]$$

Replacing k by n we get

$$H(\omega) = e^{-j\omega\left(\frac{N-1}{2}\right)}\left[\sum_{n=1}^{\frac{N}{2}} 2h\left(\frac{N}{2} - n\right)\cos\omega\left(n - \frac{1}{2}\right)\right] \tag{4.60}$$

The equation (4.60) is the frequency response of linear phase FIR filter when impulse response is symmetric and N is even.

Magnitude function of $H(\omega)$ is given by

$$|H(\omega)| = \sum_{n=1}^{N/2} 2h\left(\frac{N}{2} - n\right)\cos\left(n - \frac{1}{2}\right)\omega \tag{4.61}$$

Phase function of $H(\omega)$ is given by

$$\angle|H(e^{j\omega}) = -\omega\left[\frac{N-1}{2}\right] = -\omega\alpha \quad \text{where } \alpha = \frac{N-1}{2}$$

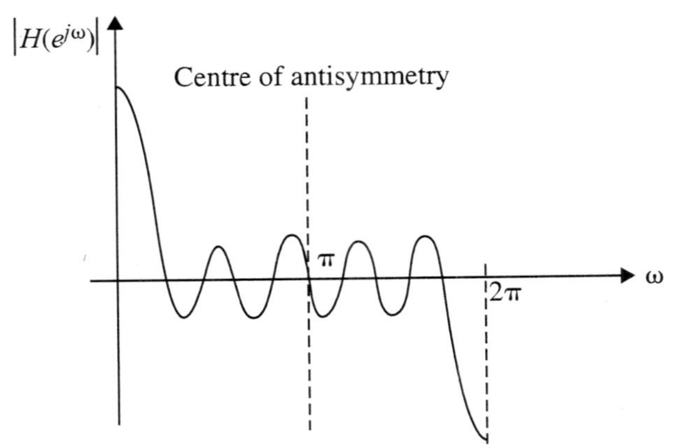

Figure 4.22 Magnitude function of $H(\omega)$.

The magnitude function of $H(\omega)$ is anti-symmetric with $\omega = \pi$, when impulse response is symmetric and N is even is shown in Figure 4.22.

4.4.2.3 Frequency Response of Linear Phase FIR Filters when Impulse Response is Anti-Symmetric When N is Odd

The Fourier transform of $h(n)$ is,

$$H(\omega) = \sum_{n=-\infty}^{\infty} h(n)e^{-j\omega n}$$

Since, the impulse response has only N samples the limit of summation can be changed from $N = 0$ to $N - 1$.

$$\therefore\ H(\omega) = \sum_{n=0}^{N-1} h(n)e^{-j\omega n}$$

The impulse response is anti-symmetric at $n = \left(\frac{N-1}{2}\right)$, and $h\left(\frac{N-1}{2}\right) = 0$. Hence $H(\omega)$ can be expressed as,

$$H(\omega) = \sum_{n=0}^{\frac{N-3}{2}} h(n)e^{-j\omega n} + h\left(\frac{N-1}{2}\right)e^{-j\omega\left(\frac{N-1}{2}\right)} + \sum_{n=\frac{N+1}{2}}^{N-1} h(n)e^{-j\omega n}$$

$$= \sum_{n=0}^{\frac{N-3}{2}} h(n)e^{-j\omega n} + \sum_{n=\frac{N+1}{2}}^{N-1} h(n)e^{-j\omega n} \tag{4.62}$$

Let $m = N - 1 - n \Longrightarrow n = N - 1 - m$

When $n = \dfrac{N+1}{2}; \Longrightarrow m = N - 1 - \left(\dfrac{N+1}{2}\right) = \dfrac{N-3}{2}$

When $n = N - 1; \Longrightarrow m = N - 1 - (N - 1) = 0$

Using the above relations, equation (4.62) can be written as

$$H(\omega) = \sum_{n=0}^{\frac{N-3}{2}} h(n)e^{-j\omega n} + \sum_{m=0}^{\frac{N-3}{2}} h(N-1-m)e^{-j\omega(N-1-m)}$$

On replacing m by n we get

$$H(\omega) = \sum_{n=0}^{\frac{N-3}{2}} h(n)e^{-j\omega n} + \sum_{n=0}^{\frac{N-3}{2}} h(N-1-m)e^{-j\omega(N-1-n)}$$

For anti-symmetric impulse response, $h(N-1-n) = -h(n)$. Therefore,

$$H(\omega) = \sum_{n=0}^{\frac{N-3}{2}} h(n)e^{-j\omega n} + \sum_{n=0}^{\frac{N-3}{2}} (-h(n))e^{-j\omega(-n)-j\omega(N-1)}$$

$$H(\omega) = \left[\sum_{n=0}^{\frac{N-3}{2}} h(n)\left[e^{-j\omega n+j\omega\left(\frac{N-1}{2}\right)} - e^{-j\omega(-n)-j\omega(N-1)+j\omega\left(\frac{N-1}{2}\right)}\right]\right] e^{-j\omega\left(\frac{N-1}{2}\right)}$$

$$= \left[\sum_{n=0}^{\frac{N-3}{2}} h(n)\left[e^{j\omega\left(\frac{N-1}{2}-n\right)} - e^{-j\omega\left(\frac{N-1}{2}-n\right)}\right]\right] e^{-j\omega\left(\frac{N-1}{2}\right)}$$

because

$$\sin\theta = \frac{e^{j\theta - e^{-j\theta}}}{2j}$$

$$H(\omega) = \left[\sum_{n=0}^{\frac{N-3}{2}} h(n)2j\sin\left[\omega\left(\frac{N-1}{2} - n\right)\right]\right] e^{-j\omega\left(\frac{N-1}{2}\right)}$$

The operator j can be written as $e^{(j\pi)/2}$

$$\therefore\ H(\omega) = \left[\sum_{n=0}^{\frac{N-3}{2}} 2h(n)e^{\frac{j\pi}{2}}\sin\left[\omega\left(\frac{N-1}{2} - n\right)\right]\right] e^{-j\omega\left(\frac{N-1}{2}\right)}$$

$$= \left[\sum_{n=0}^{\frac{N-3}{2}} 2h(n)\sin\left[\omega\left(\frac{N-1}{2} - n\right)\right]\right] e^{j\left(\frac{\pi}{2}-\omega\left(\frac{N-1}{2}\right)\right)}$$

$$\text{Let } k = \frac{N-1}{2} - n \Longrightarrow n = \frac{N-1}{2} - k$$

$$\text{When } n = 0; \Longrightarrow k = \frac{N-1}{2}$$

$$\text{When } n = \frac{N-3}{2}; \Longrightarrow k = \frac{N-1}{2} - \frac{N-3}{2} = 1$$

$$H(\omega) = \left[\sum_{k=0}^{\frac{N-1}{2}} 2h\left(\frac{N-1}{2} - k\right)\sin\omega k\right] e^{j\left(\frac{\pi}{2}-\omega\left(\frac{N-1}{2}\right)\right)}$$

On replacing k by n we get,

$$H(\omega) = \left[\sum_{k=0}^{\frac{N-1}{2}} 2h\left(\frac{N-1}{2}\right) \sin \omega n \right] e^{j\left(\frac{\pi}{2} - \omega\left(\frac{N-1}{2}\right)\right)} \tag{4.63}$$

The equation (4.63) is the frequency response of linear phase FIR filter when impulse response in anti-symmetric and N is odd. The magnitude function is given by equation (4.64). Magnitude function

$$\boxed{|H(\omega)| = \sum_{n=1}^{\frac{N-1}{2}} 2h\left(\frac{N-1}{2}\right) \sin \omega n} \tag{4.64}$$

The phase function is given by equation (4.65)

$$\boxed{\angle H(\omega) = \frac{\pi}{2} - \omega\left(\frac{N-1}{2}\right) = \beta - \alpha\omega} \tag{4.65}$$

where $\beta = \frac{\pi}{2}$ and $\alpha = \frac{N-1}{2}$.

The sketch of symmetrical impulse response when $N = 8$ and its corresponding magnitude response is shown in Figures 4.23(a) and (b) respectively.

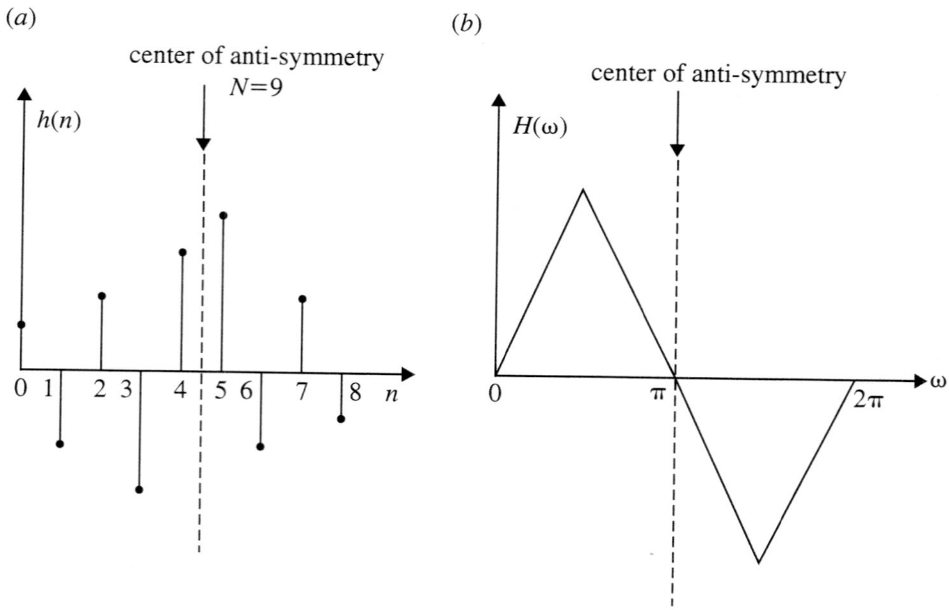

Figure 4.23 (a) Anti-symmetric impulse response for $N = 9$. (b) Magnitude function of $H(\omega)$.

4.4.2.4 Frequency Response of Linear Phase FIR Filters when Impulse Response is Anti-Symmetric When N is Even

Let impulse response anti-symmetric with N is even is shown in Figure 4.24.

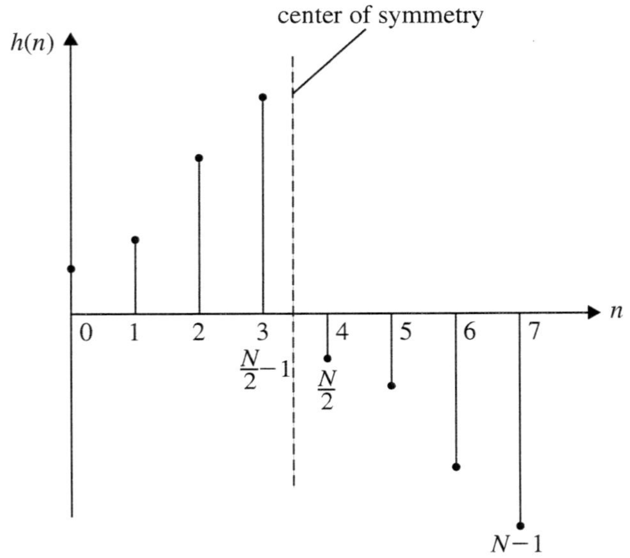

Figure 4.24 Anti-symmetric impulse response for N = even.

The Fourier transform of $h(n)$ for, impulse response of N samples

$$H(\omega) = \sum_{n=0}^{N-1} h(n)e^{-j\omega n}$$

The impulse response is asymmetric in between $n = \frac{N}{2} - 1$ and $n = \frac{N}{2}$

$$H(\omega) = \sum_{n=0}^{\frac{N}{2}-1} h(n)e^{-j\omega n} + \sum_{n=\frac{N}{2}}^{N-1} h(n)e^{-j\omega n} \tag{4.66}$$

Let $m = N - 1 - n \Longrightarrow n = N - 1 - m$

When $n = \dfrac{N}{2}; \Longrightarrow m = N - 1 - \dfrac{N}{2} = \dfrac{N}{2} - 1$

When $n = N - 1; \Longrightarrow m = N - 1 - (N - 1) = 0$

$$H(\omega) = \sum_{n=0}^{\frac{N}{2}-1} h(n)e^{-j\omega n} + \sum_{m=0}^{\frac{N}{2}-1} h(N - 1 - m)e^{-j\omega(N-1-m)}$$

On replacing m by n we get

$$H(\omega)=\sum_{n=0}^{\frac{N}{2}-1} h(n)e^{-j\omega n}+\sum_{n=0}^{\frac{N}{2}-1} h(N-1-n)e^{-j\omega(N-1-n)}$$

For anti-symmetric $h(N-1-n)=-h(n)$

$$H(\omega)=\sum_{n=0}^{\frac{N}{2}-1} h(n)e^{-j\omega n}-\sum_{n=0}^{\frac{N}{2}-1} h(n)e^{-j\omega(N-1)+j\omega n}$$

$$=e^{-j\omega\left(\frac{N-1}{2}\right)}\left[\sum_{n=0}^{\frac{N}{2}-1} h(n)e^{-j\omega\left(\frac{N-1}{2}\right)-j\omega n}-\sum_{n=0}^{\frac{N}{2}-1} h(n)e^{-j\omega\left(\frac{N-1}{2}\right)+j\omega n}\right]$$

$$=e^{-j\omega\left(\frac{N-1}{2}\right)}\left[\sum_{n=0}^{\frac{N}{2}-1} h(n)\left[e^{j\omega\left(\frac{N-1}{2}-n\right)}-e^{-j\omega\left(\frac{N-1}{2}-n\right)}\right]\right]$$

$$=e^{-j\omega\left(\frac{N-1}{2}\right)}\left[\sum_{n=0}^{\frac{N}{2}-1} h(n)\left[2j\sin\left(\frac{N-1}{2}-n\right)\omega\right]\right]$$

$$=e^{-j\omega\left(\frac{N-1}{2}\right)}e^{j\pi/2}\left[\sum_{n=0}^{\frac{N}{2}-1} 2h(n)\sin\left(\frac{N-1}{2}-n\right)\omega\right]$$

$$=e^{j\left(\frac{\pi}{2}-\omega\left(\frac{N-1}{2}\right)\right)}\left[\sum_{n=0}^{\frac{N}{2}-1} 2h(n)\sin\left(\frac{N-1}{2}-n\right)\omega\right]$$

$$=e^{j\left(\frac{\pi}{2}-\omega\left(\frac{N-1}{2}\right)\right)}\left[\sum_{n=0}^{\frac{N}{2}-1} 2h(n)\sin\left(\frac{N}{2}-n-\frac{1}{2}\right)\omega\right]$$

Substitute $k=\frac{N}{2}-n \Longrightarrow n=\frac{N}{2}-k$

$$\text{When } n=0;\Longrightarrow k=\frac{N}{2}$$

$$\text{When } n=\frac{N}{2}-1;\Longrightarrow k=\frac{N}{2}-\frac{N}{2}+1=1$$

$$H(\omega)=e^{j\left(\frac{\pi}{2}-\omega\left(\frac{N-1}{2}\right)\right)}\left[\sum_{k=1}^{\frac{N}{2}} 2h\left(\frac{N}{2}-k\right)\sin\left(k-\frac{1}{2}\right)\omega\right]$$

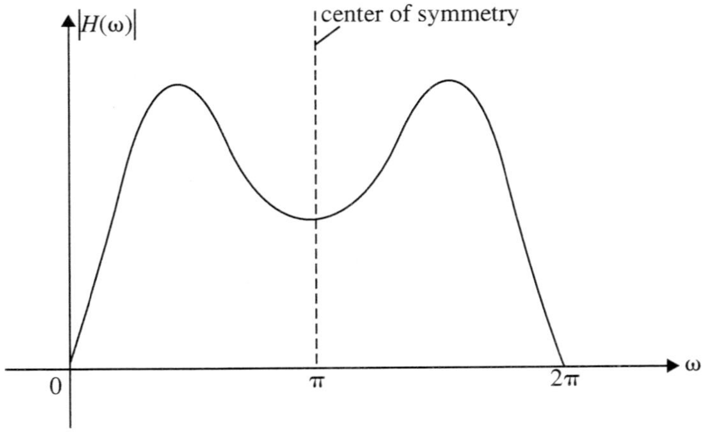

Figure 4.25 Magnitude function of $H(e^{j\omega})$.

Replacing k by n we get,

$$H(\omega) = e^{j\left(\frac{\pi}{2}-\omega\left(\frac{N-1}{2}\right)\right)} \left[\sum_{n=1}^{\frac{N}{2}} 2h\left(\frac{N}{2}-n\right)\sin\left(n-\frac{1}{2}\right)\omega\right] \tag{4.67}$$

The equation (4.67) represents frequency response of linear phase FIR filter with impulse response as anti-symmetric when N is even. The magnitude response is given by equation (4.68) and is shown in Figure 4.25.

$$\boxed{|H(e^{j\omega})| = \sum_{n=1}^{\frac{N}{2}} 2h\left(\frac{N}{2}-n\right)\sin\left(n-\frac{1}{2}\right)\omega} \tag{4.68}$$

The phase response is given by

$$\boxed{\begin{aligned} \angle H(e^{j\omega}) &= \frac{\pi}{2} - \omega\left(\frac{N-1}{2}\right) \\ \angle H(\omega) &= \beta - \omega\alpha \end{aligned}} \tag{4.69}$$

where $\alpha = \frac{N-1}{2}$ and $\beta = \frac{\pi}{2}$.

4.5 Design Techniques for Linear Phase FIR Filters

Some of the well-known method of design techniques for linear phase FIR filters are:

1. Fourier serious method
2. Window method
3. Frequency sampling method

4.5.1 Fourier Series Method of FIR Filter Design

Fourier series analysis exists only for periodic function. That is, any periodic function can be expressed as a linear combination of complex exponentials. The frequency response of a digital filter is periodic, with period equal to the sampling frequency. Therefore, the desired frequency response of an FIR digital filter can be represented by Fourier series as

$$H_d(\omega)|_{\omega=\omega T} = H_d(\omega T) = \sum_{n=-\infty}^{\infty} h_d(n)e^{-j\omega nT} \tag{4.70}$$

where the Fourier series coefficients $h_d(n)$ are the desired impulse response and are given by

$$h_d(n) = \frac{1}{\omega_s}\int_{-\omega_s/2}^{\omega_s/2} H_d(\omega T)e^{j\omega nT}\,d\omega \tag{4.71}$$

where

$$f_s = \text{sampling frequency in Hz.}$$
$$\omega_s = 2\pi f_s = \text{sampling frequency in rad/sec.}$$
$$T = \frac{1}{f_s} = \text{sampling period in sec.}$$

The impulse response $h_d(n)$ has infinite number of samples. For FIR filters, we truncate this infinite impulse response to a finite duration sequence of length N, where N is odd.

$$\therefore\ h(n) = h_d(n); \quad |n| \leq \left(\frac{N-1}{2}\right) \tag{4.72}$$

On taking z-transform of equation (4.72) we get

$$H(z) = \sum_{n=-\frac{(N-1)}{2}}^{\frac{N-1}{2}} h(n)z^{-n} \tag{4.73}$$

The transfer function of equation (4.73) represents non-causal filter. Hence, the transfer function is multiplied by $z^{-\frac{(N-1)}{2}}$. This modification does not affect the amplitude response of the filter.

$$H(z) = z^{-\left(\frac{N-1}{2}\right)} \sum_{n=-\frac{(N-1)}{2}}^{\frac{N-1}{2}} h(n)z^{-n} \tag{4.74}$$

$$= z^{-\left(\frac{N-1}{2}\right)}\left[\sum_{n=-\frac{(N-1)}{2}}^{-1} h(n)z^{-n} + h(0) + \sum_{n=1}^{\frac{N-1}{2}} h(n)z^{-n}\right]$$

$$H(z) = z^{-\left(\frac{N-1}{2}\right)} \left[\sum_{n=1}^{\frac{N-1}{2}} h(-n)z^{n} + h(0) + \sum_{n=1}^{\frac{N-1}{2}} h(n)z^{-n} \right]$$

$$H(z) = z^{-\left(\frac{N-1}{2}\right)} \left[h(0) + \sum_{n=1}^{\frac{N-1}{2}} h(n)[z^{n} + z^{-n}] \right] \quad \because h(n) = h(-n) \tag{4.75}$$

The abrupt truncation of the Fourier series results in oscillations in the passband and stopband. These oscillations are due to the slow convergence of the Fourier series at the points of discontinuity. This effect is known as "Gibbs phenomenon". This oscillation can be reduced by multiplying the desired impulse response coefficients by an appropriate window function.

The specifications of lowpass, highpass, bandpass and bandstop filters design by Fourier series are given below:

$$\text{Lowpass, } H_d(\omega) = \begin{cases} 1, & -\omega_c \le \omega \le \omega_c \\ 0, & -\frac{\omega_s}{2} \le \omega \le -\omega_c \text{ and } \omega_c < \omega \le \frac{\omega_s}{2} \end{cases} \tag{4.76}$$

$$\text{Highpass, } H_d(\omega) = \begin{cases} 1, & -\frac{\omega_s}{2} \le \omega \le -\omega_c \text{ and } \omega_c \le \omega \le \frac{\omega_s}{2} \\ 0, & -\omega_c \le \omega \le \omega_c \end{cases} \tag{4.77}$$

$$\text{Bandpass, } H_d(\omega) = \begin{cases} 1, & -\omega_{c_2} \le \omega \le -\omega_{c_1} \text{ and } \omega_{c_1} \le \omega \le \omega_{c_2} \\ 0, & -\frac{\omega_s}{2} \le \omega_c < -\omega_{c_2},\ -\omega_{c_1} \le \omega \le \omega_{c_1}, \text{ and } \omega_{c_2} < \omega \le \frac{\omega_s}{2} \end{cases} \tag{4.78}$$

$$\text{Bandstop, } H_d(\omega) = \begin{cases} 1, & -\frac{\omega_s}{2} \le \omega_c < -\omega_{c_2},\ -\omega_{c_1} \le \omega \le \omega_{c_1}, \text{ and } \omega_{c_2} \le \omega \le \frac{\omega_s}{2} \\ 0, & -\omega_{c_2} < \omega < -\omega_{c_1} \text{ and } \omega_{c_1} < \omega < \omega_{c_2} \end{cases} \tag{4.79}$$

Example 4.9

Design an ideal lowpass filter with a frequency response

$$H_d(e^{j\omega}) = \begin{cases} 1, & \text{for } -\frac{\pi}{2} \le |\omega| \le \frac{\pi}{2} \\ 0, & \text{for } \frac{\pi}{2} \le |\omega| \le \pi \end{cases}$$

Find the values of $h(n)$ for $N = 11$. Find $H(z)$.

Solution $h_d(n)$ is shown in Figure 4.26(a)

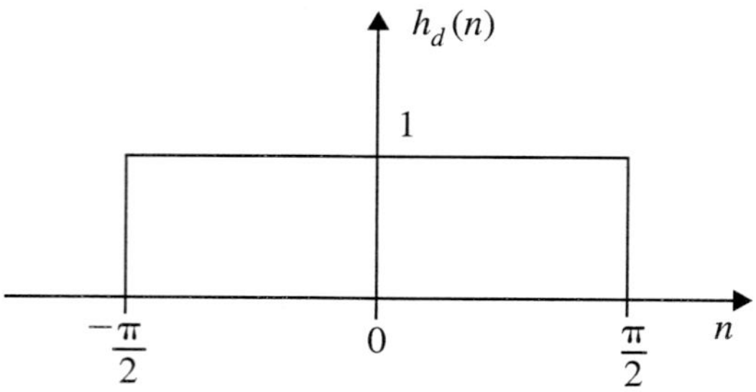

Figure 4.26 (a) Impulse response of LPF for Example 4.9.

$$h_d(n) = \frac{1}{2\pi}\int_{-\pi}^{\pi} H_d(e^{j\omega})e^{j\omega n}d\omega$$

$$= \frac{1}{2\pi}\int_{-\pi/2}^{\pi/2} e^{j\omega n}d\omega$$

$$= \frac{1}{2\pi jn}[e^{j\omega n}]_{-\pi/2}^{\pi/2}$$

$$= \frac{1}{\pi n}\left[\frac{e^{j(\pi/2)n} - e^{-j(\pi/2)n}}{2j}\right]$$

$$= \frac{\sin(\pi/2)n}{\pi n}, \qquad -\infty \le n \le 11$$

Here $n = 11$

$$\therefore\ h(n) = \begin{cases} \frac{\sin(\pi/2)n}{\pi n}, & \text{for } |n| \le 5 \\ 0, & \text{otherwise} \end{cases}$$

For $n = 0$

$$h_d(n) = \lim_{n\to 0} \frac{\sin(\pi/2)n}{\pi n}$$

$$= \frac{1}{2}\lim_{n\to 0} \frac{\sin(\pi/2)n}{(\pi/2)n} \qquad \left[\because \lim_{\theta\to 0}\frac{\sin\theta}{\theta} = 1\right]$$

$$= \frac{1}{2}$$

From the frequency response, $H_d(e^{j\omega})$ we find that $\alpha = 0$, and therefore, filter coefficients are symmetrical about $n = 0$, *i.e.*, $h(n) = h(-n)$.

For $n = 1$: $h(1) = h(-1) = \frac{\sin(\pi/2)}{\pi} = \frac{1}{\pi} = 0.3183$

For $n = 2$: $h(2) = h(-2) = \frac{\sin 2(\pi/2)}{2\pi} = 0$

$$\text{For } n = 3: \quad h(3) = h(-3) = \frac{\sin 3(\pi/2)}{3\pi} = -0.106$$

$$\text{For } n = 4: \quad h(4) = h(-4) = \frac{\sin 2\pi}{4\pi} = 0$$

$$\text{For } n = 5: \quad h(5) = h(-5) = \frac{\sin 5(\pi/2)}{5\pi} = 0.06366$$

$$H(z) = z^{-\left(\frac{N-1}{2}\right)} \left[\sum_{n=1}^{\frac{N-1}{2}} h(n)[z^n + z^{-n}] + h(0) \right]$$

$$= z^{-5} \left[h(0) + \sum_{n=1}^{5} h(n)[z^n + z^{-n}] \right]$$

$$= z^{-5} \left[0.5 + h(1)(z + z^{-1}) + h(2)(z^2 + z^{-2}) + h(3)(z^3 + z^{-3}) + h(4)(z^4 + z^{-4}) + h(5)(z^5 + z^{-5})\right]$$

$$H(z) = 0.53z^{-5} + 0.3183(z^{-4} + z^{-6}) + 0 - 0.106(z^{-2} + z^{-8}) + 0.063(z^{-10} + 1)$$

$$Y(z) = 0.5z^{-5}X(z) + 0.3183(z^{-4} + z^{-6})X(z) - 0.106[X(z)z^{-2} + X(z)z^{-8}] + 0.063[X(z)z^{-10} + X(z)]$$

The structure realization is shown in Figure 4.26(b).

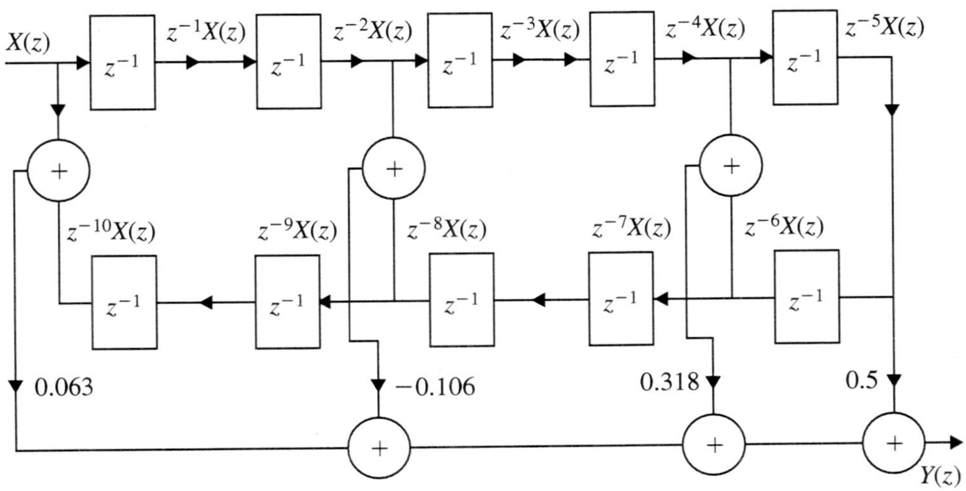

Figure 4.26 (b) Structure realization for Example 4.9.

Example 4.10

Design an ideal highpass filter with a frequency response

$$H_d(e^{j\omega}) = \begin{cases} 1, & \text{for } -\frac{\pi}{4} \le |\omega| \le \pi \\ 0, & \text{for } |\omega| < \frac{\pi}{4} \end{cases}$$

Find the values of $h(n)$ for $N = 11$. Find $H(z)$. Plot the magnitude response.

(Anna University, December, 2006)

Solution $h_d(n)$ is shown in Figure 4.27(a)

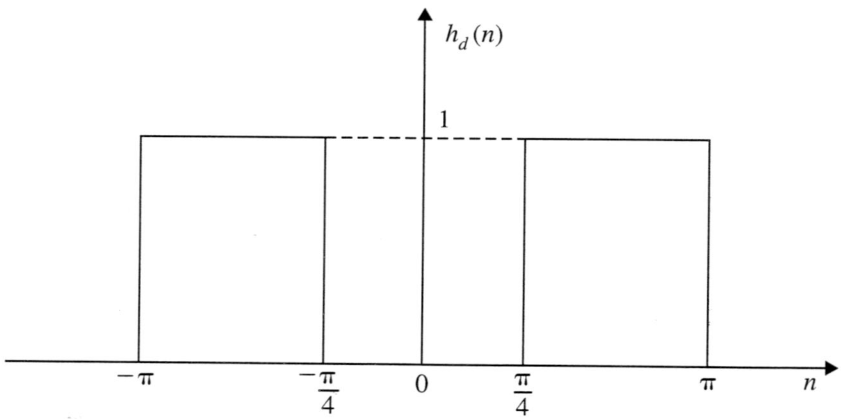

Figure 4.27 (a) Impulse response for Example 4.10.

$$h_d(n) = \frac{1}{2\pi}\int_{-\pi}^{\pi} H_d(e^{j\omega})e^{j\omega n}d\omega$$

$$= \frac{1}{2\pi}\left[\int_{-\pi}^{-\pi/4} e^{j\omega n}d\omega + \int_{\pi/4}^{\pi} e^{j\omega n}d\omega\right]$$

$$= \frac{1}{2\pi jn}\left[e^{j\omega n}\Big|_{-\pi}^{-\pi/4} + e^{j\omega n}\Big|_{\pi/4}^{\pi}\right]$$

$$= \frac{1}{\pi n(2j)}\left[e^{-j(\pi/4)n} - e^{-j\pi n} + e^{j\pi n} - e^{j(\pi/4)n}\right]$$

$$h_d(n) = \begin{cases} \frac{1}{\pi n}[\sin \pi n - \sin(\pi/4)n], & \text{for } |n| \le 5 \\ 0, & \text{otherwise} \end{cases}$$

For $n = 0$

$$h(n) = \lim_{n\to 0} \frac{\sin \pi n}{\pi n} - \lim_{n\to 0} \frac{\sin(\pi/4)n}{4(\pi n/4)}$$
$$= 1 - \frac{1}{4} = 0.75$$

For $n = 1$: $\quad h(1) = h(-1) = \dfrac{\sin \pi - \sin(\pi/4)}{\pi}$
$$= -0.225$$

For $n = 2$: $\quad h(2) = h(-2) = \dfrac{\sin 2\pi - \sin(2\pi/4)}{2\pi}$
$$= -0.159$$

For $n = 3$: $\quad h(3) = h(-3) = \dfrac{\sin 3\pi - \sin(3\pi/4)}{3\pi}$
$$= -0.075$$

For $n = 4$: $\quad h(4) = h(-4) = \dfrac{\sin 4\pi - \sin \pi}{4\pi}$
$$= 0$$

For $n = 5$: $\quad h(5) = h(-5) = \dfrac{\sin 5\pi - \sin(5\pi/4)}{5\pi}$
$$= 0.045$$

$$H(z) = z^{-5}\left[\sum_{n-1}^{N} h(n)(z^n + z^{-n}) + h(0)\right]$$

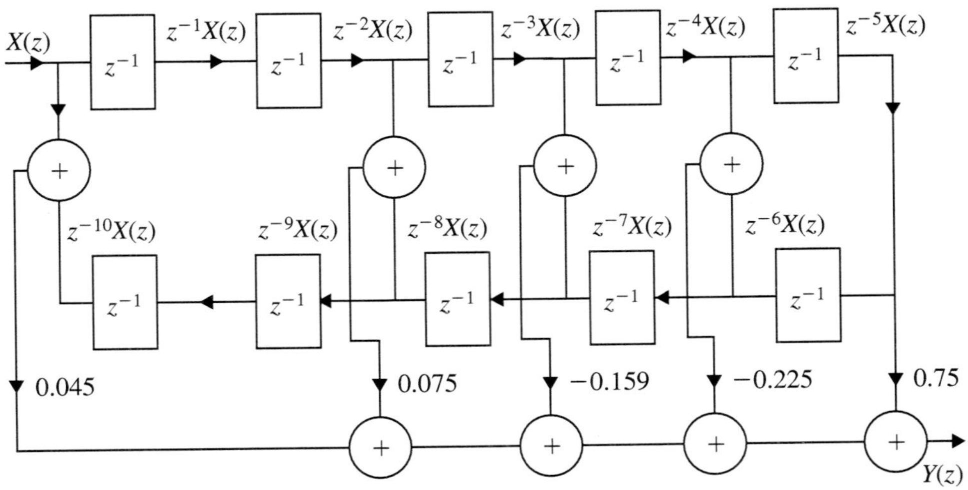

Figure 4.27 (*b*) Structure realization for Example 4.10.

$$= z^{-5}\left[h(0) + h(1)(z + z^{-1}) + h(2)(z^2 + z^{-2}) + h(3)(z^3 + z^{-3}) + h(4)(z^4 + z^{-4}) + h(5)(z^5 + z^{-5})\right]$$

$$H(z) = 0.75z^{-5} - 0.225(z^{-4} + z^{-6}) - 0.159(z^{-3} + z^{-7}) - 0.075(z^{-2} + z^{-8}) + 0.045(1 + z^{-10})$$

$$Y(z) = 0.75z^{-5}X(z) - 0.225[X(z)z^{-4} + X(z)z^{-6}] - 0.159[X(z)z^{-3} + X(z)z^{-7}] - 0.075[X(z)z^{-2} + X(z)z^{-8}] + 0.045[X(z) + X(z)z^{-10}]$$

The structure realization FIR high pass filter is shown in Figure 4.27(b).

Magnitude Response

The frequency response of FIR filter when impulse response is symmetric and N is odd.

$$H(e^{j\omega}) = \sum_{n=0}^{\frac{N-1}{2}} a(n)\cos\omega n$$

where

$$a(0) = h\left(\frac{N-1}{2}\right) = h(5) = 0.75$$

$$a(n) = 2h\left(\frac{N-1}{2} - n\right)$$

$$a(1) = 2h(5-1) = 2h(4) = -0.45$$

$$a(2) = 2h(5-2) = 2h(3) = -0.318$$

$$a(3) = 2h(5-3) = 2h(2) = -0.15$$

$$a(4) = 2h(5-4) = 2h(1) = 0$$

$$a(5) = 2h(5-5) = 2h(0) = 0.09$$

$$H(e^{j\omega}) = a(0) + a(1)\cos\omega + a(2)\cos 2\omega + a(3)\cos 3\omega + a(4)\cos 4\omega + a(5)\cos 5\omega$$

$$= 0.75 - 0.45\cos\omega - 0.318\cos 2\omega - 0.15\cos 3\omega + 0.09\cos 5\omega$$

The magnitude response is shown in Figure 4.27(c).

ω (deg/sec)	0	10	30	50	80	100	120	140	160	170
$H(e^{j\omega})$	−0.08	−0.066	0.122	0.61	1.11	0.98	0.94	1.26	1.01	0.96
$\lvert H(e^{j\omega})\rvert_{\text{dB}}$	−22	−23.62	−18.2	−4.2	0.95	−0.132	−0.537	2	0.16	−0.31

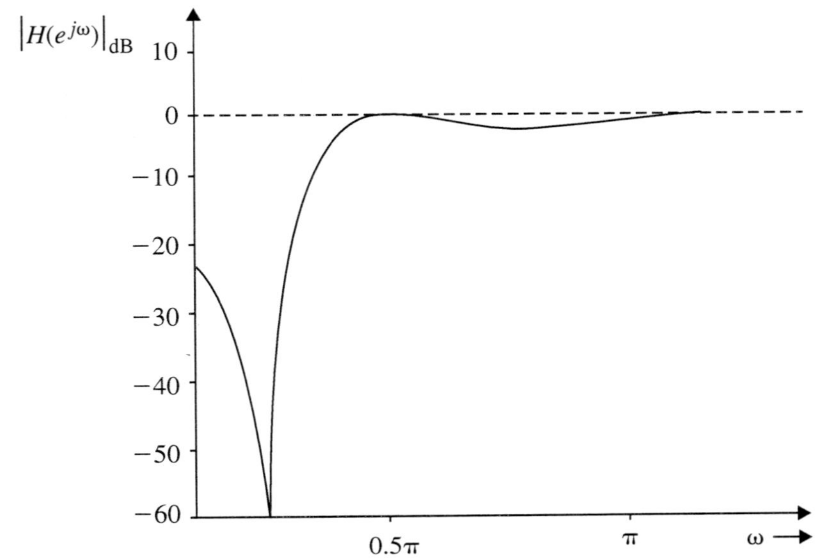

Figure 4.27 (*c*) Magnitude response for the Example 4.10.

Example 4.11

Design an ideal bandpass filter with a frequency response

$$H_d(e^{j\omega}) = \begin{cases} 1, & \text{for } \frac{\pi}{4} \le |\omega| \le \frac{3\pi}{4} \\ 0, & \text{otherwise} \end{cases}$$

Find the values of $h(n)$ for $N = 11$. Find $H(z)$ and also plot the frequency response.

(*Anna University, December, 2004 and May, 2005*)

Solution The impulse response $h_d(n)$ is shown in Figure 4.28(*a*).

$$h_d(n) = \frac{1}{2\pi}\int_{-\pi}^{\pi} H_d(e^{j\omega})e^{j\omega n}$$

$$= \frac{1}{2\pi}\left[\int_{-(3\pi/4)}^{-\pi/4} e^{j\omega n}d\omega + \int_{\pi/4}^{(3\pi)/4} e^{j\omega n}d\omega\right]$$

$$= \frac{1}{2\pi jn}\left[e^{(-j\pi n)/4} - e^{(j3\pi n)/4} + e^{(j3\pi n)/4} - e^{(j\pi n)/4}\right]$$

$$h_d(n) = \begin{cases} \frac{1}{\pi n}[\sin[(3\pi)/4]n - \sin(\pi/4)n], & \text{for } |n| \le 5 \\ 0, & \text{otherwise} \end{cases}$$

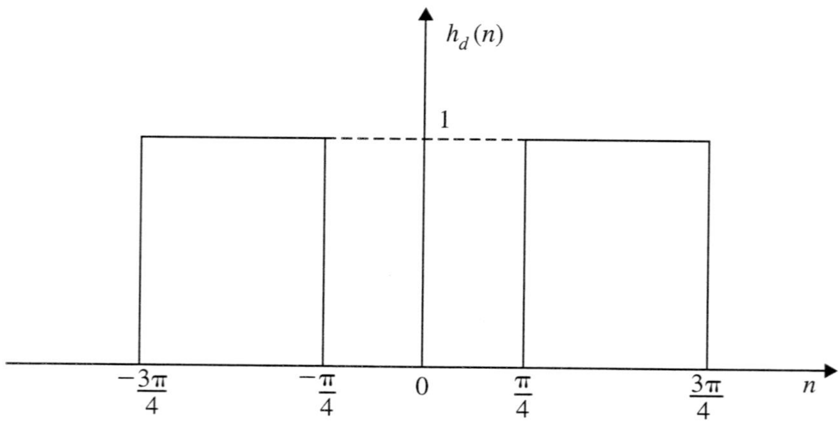

Figure 4.28 (*a*) Impulse response for the Example 4.11.

For $n = 0$

$$h_d(0) = \lim_{n\to 0} \frac{\sin(3\pi/4)n}{\frac{4}{3}\left(\frac{\pi n 3}{4}\right)} - \lim_{n\to 0} \frac{\sin(\pi/4)n}{4\left(\frac{\pi n}{4}\right)}$$

$$= \frac{3}{4} - \frac{1}{4} = 0.5$$

$$\text{For } n = 1: \quad h(1) = h(-1) = \frac{\sin\frac{3\pi}{4} - \sin\frac{\pi}{4}}{\pi} = 0$$

$$\text{For } n = 2: \quad h(2) = h(-2) = \frac{\sin\frac{3\pi}{2} - \sin\frac{\pi}{2}}{2\pi} = -\frac{2}{2\pi} = -0.3183$$

$$\text{For } n = 3: \quad h(3) = h(-3) = \frac{\sin\frac{9\pi}{4} - \sin\frac{3\pi}{4}}{3\pi} = 0$$

$$\text{For } n = 4: \quad h(4) = h(-4) = \frac{\sin 3\pi - \sin\pi}{4\pi} = 0$$

$$\text{For } n = 5: \quad h(5) = h(-5) = \frac{\sin\frac{15\pi}{4} - \sin\frac{5\pi}{4}}{5\pi} = 0$$

$$H(z) = z^{-5}\left[\sum_{n=1}^{5} h(n)(z^n + z^{-n}) + h(0)\right]$$

$$= 0.5z^{-5} - 0.3183(z^{-3} + z^{-7})$$

The filter coefficients of the causal filters are

$$h(0) = h(10) = h(1) = h(9) = h(2) = h(8) = h(4) = h(6) = 0$$

$$h(3) = h(7) = -0.3183$$

$$h(5) = 0.5$$

The filter structure is shown in Figure 4.28(b).

$$|H(e^{j\omega})| = \sum_{n=1}^{\frac{N-1}{2}} 2h\left(\frac{N-1}{2} - n\right)\cos\omega n + h\left(\frac{N-1}{2}\right)$$

$$= \sum_{n=1}^{\frac{N-1}{2}} a(n)\cos\omega n + a(0)$$

where

$$a(0) = h\left(\frac{N-1}{2}\right) = h(5) = 0.5$$

$$a(n) = 2h\left(\frac{N-1}{2} - n\right)$$

$$a(1) = 2h(5-1) = 2h(4) = 0$$

$$a(2) = 2h(5-2) = 2h(3) = -0.6366$$

$$a(3) = 2h(5-3) = 2h(2) = 0$$

$$a(4) = 2h(5-4) = 2h(1) = 0$$

$$a(5) = 2h(5-5) = 2h(0) = 0$$

$$|H(e^{j\omega})| = 0.5 - 0.6366\cos 2\omega$$

ω (deg/sec)	0	20	45	60	90	120	135	180
$H(e^{j\omega})$	−0.1366	0.012	0.5	0.818	1.1366	0.818	0.5	−0.1366
$\lvert H(e^{j\omega})\rvert_{\text{dB}}$	−17.3	−38.17	−6.02	−1.74	1.11	−1.74	−6.02	−17.32

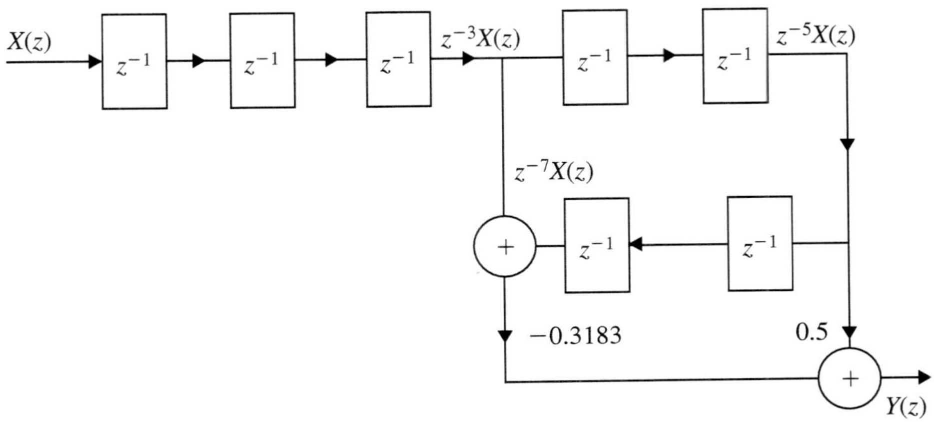

Figure 4.28 (b) Structure realization for Example 4.11.

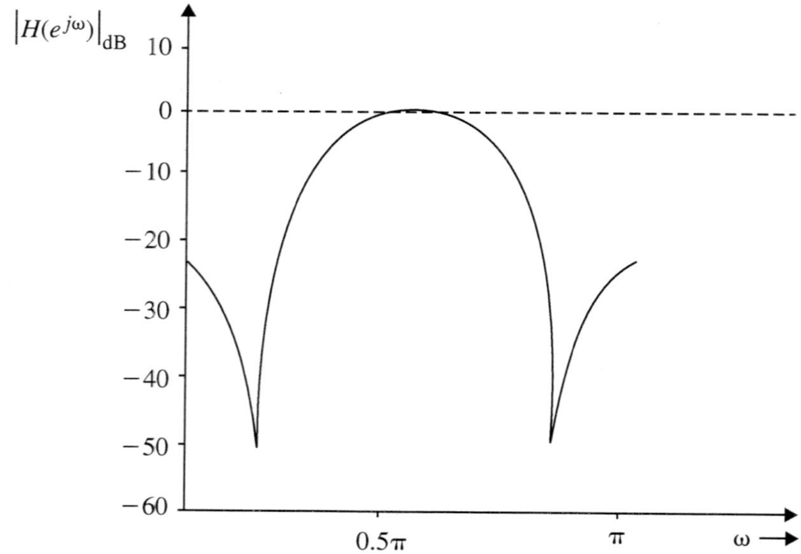

Figure 4.28 (*c*) Frequency response of bandpass filter of Example 4.11.

The magnitude response is shown in Figure 4.28(*c*).

Example 4.12

Design an ideal band reject filter with a desired frequency response

$$H_d(e^{j\omega}) = 1 \quad \text{for } |\omega| \le \frac{\pi}{3} \text{ and } |\omega| \ge \frac{2\pi}{3}$$

Find the values of $h(n)$ for $N = 11$. Find $H(z)$.

Solution The impulse response $h_d(n)$ is shown in Figure 4.29(*a*)

$$\begin{aligned} h_d(n) &= \frac{1}{2\pi}\int_{-\pi}^{\pi} H_d(e^{j\omega})e^{j\omega n}\,d\omega \\ &= \frac{1}{2\pi}\left[\int_{-\pi}^{-2\pi/3} e^{j\omega n}\,d\omega + \int_{-(\pi/3)}^{\pi/3} e^{j\omega n}\,d\omega + \int_{2\pi/3}^{\pi} e^{j\omega n}\,d\omega\right] \\ &= \frac{1}{2\pi jn}\left[e^{-j2\pi n/3} - e^{-j\pi n} + e^{j\pi n/3} - e^{-j\pi n/3} + e^{j\pi n} - e^{j2\pi n/3}\right] \end{aligned}$$

$$h_d(n) = \begin{cases} \frac{1}{\pi n}\left[\sin \pi n + \sin \frac{\pi}{3}n - \sin \frac{2\pi}{3}n\right], & |n| \le 5 \\ 0, & \text{otherwise} \end{cases}$$

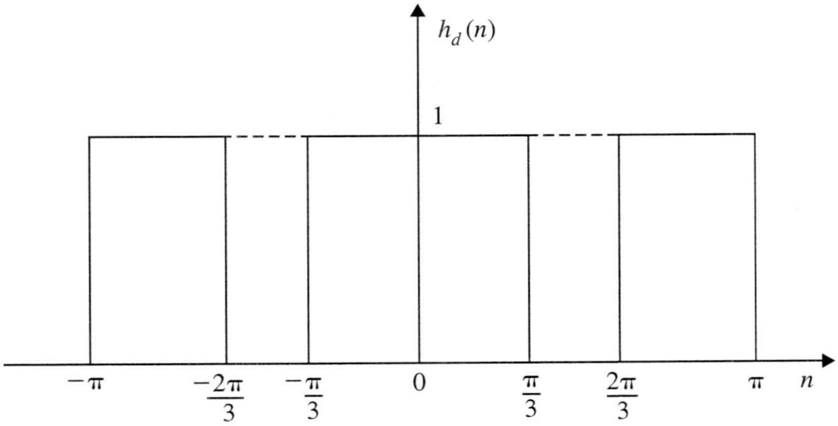

Figure 4.29 (*a*) Impulse response for Example 4.12.

The filter coefficients are symmetrical about $n = 0$ satisfying the condition $h(n) = h(-n)$. For $n = 0$

$$h_d(0) = \lim_{n\to 0}\left[\frac{\sin \pi n}{\pi n} + \frac{\sin(\pi/3)n}{\pi n} - \frac{\sin(2\pi/3)n}{\pi n}\right]$$
$$= \left[1 + \frac{1}{3} - \frac{2}{3}\right] = 0.667$$

For $n = 1$: $h(1) = h(-1) = \dfrac{\sin \pi + \sin \frac{\pi}{3} - \sin \frac{2\pi}{3}}{\pi} = 0$

For $n = 2$: $h(2) = h(-2) = \dfrac{\sin 2\pi + \sin \frac{2\pi}{3} - \sin \frac{4\pi}{3}}{2\pi} = 0.2757$

For $n = 3$: $h(3) = h(-3) = \dfrac{\sin 3\pi + \sin \pi - \sin 2\pi}{3\pi} = 0$

For $n = 4$: $h(4) = h(-4) = \dfrac{\sin 4\pi + \sin \frac{4\pi}{3} - \sin \frac{8\pi}{3}}{4\pi} = -0.1378$

For $n = 5$: $h(5) = h(-5) = \dfrac{\sin 5\pi + \sin \frac{5\pi}{3} - \sin \frac{10\pi}{3}}{5\pi} = 0$

$$H(z) = z^{-5}\left[\sum_{n=1}^{5} h(n)(z^n + z^{-n}) + h(0)\right]$$
$$= 0.667z^{-5} + 0.2757(z^{-3} + z^{-7}) - 0.1378(z^{-1} + z^{-9})$$
$$Y(z) = 0.667z^{-5}X(z) + 0.2757[X(z)z^{-3} + X(z)z^{-7}]$$
$$- 0.1378[X(z)z^{-1} + X(z)z^{-9}]$$

The structure realization is shown in Figure 4.29(*b*).

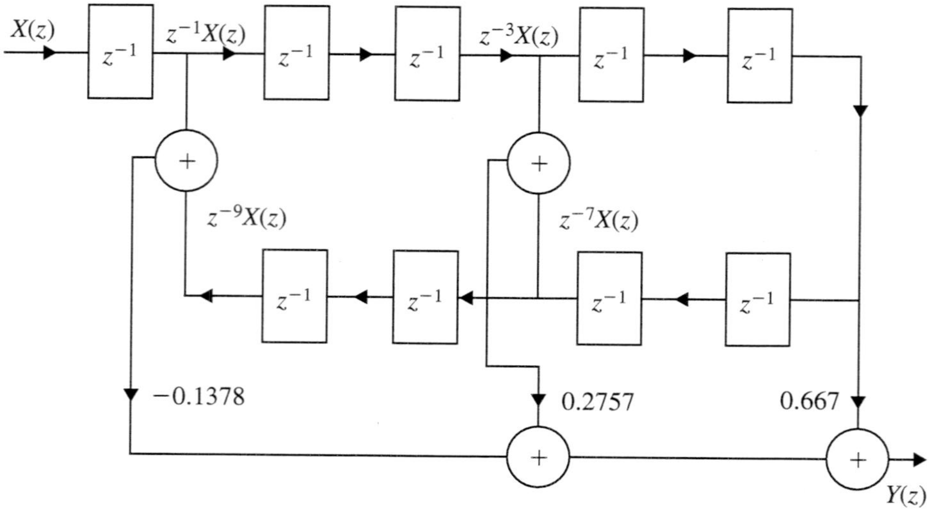

Figure 4.29 (*b*) Structure realization for Example 4.12.

4.5.2 Window Method

4.5.2.1 *Rectangular Window*

Rectangular window function,

$$W_R(n) = \begin{cases} 1; & 0 \leq n \leq N-1 \\ 0; & \text{otherwise} \end{cases} \tag{4.80}$$

(or)

$$W_R(n) = \begin{cases} 1; & -\left(\frac{N-1}{2}\right) \leq n \leq \frac{N-1}{2} \\ 0; & \text{otherwise} \end{cases} \tag{4.81}$$

The spectrum of the Rectangular window is given by

$$\begin{aligned} W_R(\omega) = \sum_{n=-((N-1)/2)}^{\frac{N-1}{2}} e^{-j\omega n} &= e^{j\omega\frac{(N-1)}{2}} + \cdots + e^{j\omega} + 1 + e^{-j\omega} \\ &+ e^{-2j\omega} + \cdots + e^{-j\omega\left(\frac{N-1}{2}\right)} \\ &= e^{j\omega\frac{(N-1)}{2}}\left[1 + e^{-j\omega} + \cdots + e^{-j\omega(N-1)}\right] \\ &= e^{j\omega\frac{(N-1)}{2}}\left[\frac{1 - e^{-j\omega N}}{1 - e^{-j\omega}}\right] \qquad \left(\because\ 1 + x + x^2 + \cdots + x^{N-1} = \frac{1 - x^N}{1 - x}\right) \end{aligned} \tag{4.82}$$

$$= \frac{e^{\frac{j\omega N}{2}}(1 - e^{-j\omega N})}{e^{\frac{j\omega}{2}}(1 - e^{-j\omega})} = \frac{e^{\frac{j\omega N}{2}} - e^{-\frac{j\omega N}{2}}}{e^{\frac{j\omega}{2}} - e^{-\frac{j\omega}{2}}}$$

$$= \frac{\sin(\omega N/2)}{\sin(\omega/2)} \tag{4.83}$$

The window spectrum for $N = 31$ is shown in Figure 4.30. The spectrum of $W_R(\omega)$ has two important features and they are:

1. Width of mainlobe $= \frac{4\pi}{N}$
2. Peak sidelobe magnitude (dB) $= -13$ dB

The magnitude response $|H(\omega)|$ of the lowpass filter designed using Rectangular window is shown in Figure 4.30. The approximated filter response differs from the ideal desired response, *i.e.*, in the passband a series of overshoots and undershoots occur. In the stopband the FIR filter has a non-zero response. This can be explained in terms of the features of the window spectrum.

The width of the transition region is related to the width of the main lobe of $W_R(\omega)$. Since the main-lobe width of $W_R(\omega)$ is equal to $\frac{4\pi}{N}$, the size of this transition region can be reduced to any desired size by increasing the size N of the window sequence. The increase in N also increases the number of computations necessary to implement the FIR filter.

In the passband the sidelobe effect of the $W_R(\omega)$ appears as both overshoots and undershoots in the desired response. In the stopband these effects appear as a non-zero response. These side-lobe effects do not diminish significantly, but remain constant as the duration of Rectangular window is increased.

It is observed that whatever be the number of elements of $h_d(n)$ included in the $h(n)$, the magnitudes of the overshoot and leakage will not change significantly. This result is known as Gibb's phenomenon. To reduce these sidelobe effects, we must consider alternate window sequences having spectrum exhibiting smaller side-lobes. We can observe that the sidelobes of the window spectrum represents the contribution of the high frequency components. For the Rectangular window, these high frequency components are due to the sharp transitions form 0 to 1 and 1 to 0 at the edges of window sequence. Hence the amplitude of these high frequency components *i.e.*, side lobe levels can be reduced by replacing these sharp transitions by more gradually ones. So we go for Raised Cosine window sequences.

Design Procedure

Step 1: Choose the desired frequency response of the filter, $H_d(\omega)$.

Step 2: Take inverse Fourier transform of $H_d(\omega)$ to obtain the desired impulse response, $h_d(n)$.

Step 3: Choose the window sequence $W(n)$ and multiply $h_d(n)$ by $W(n)$ [*i.e.*, $h(n) = W(n) \times h_d(n)$] to convert the infinite impulse response to finite impulse response.

$$W(n) = \begin{cases} 1, & 0 \le n \le N-1 \\ 0, & \text{otherwise} \end{cases}$$

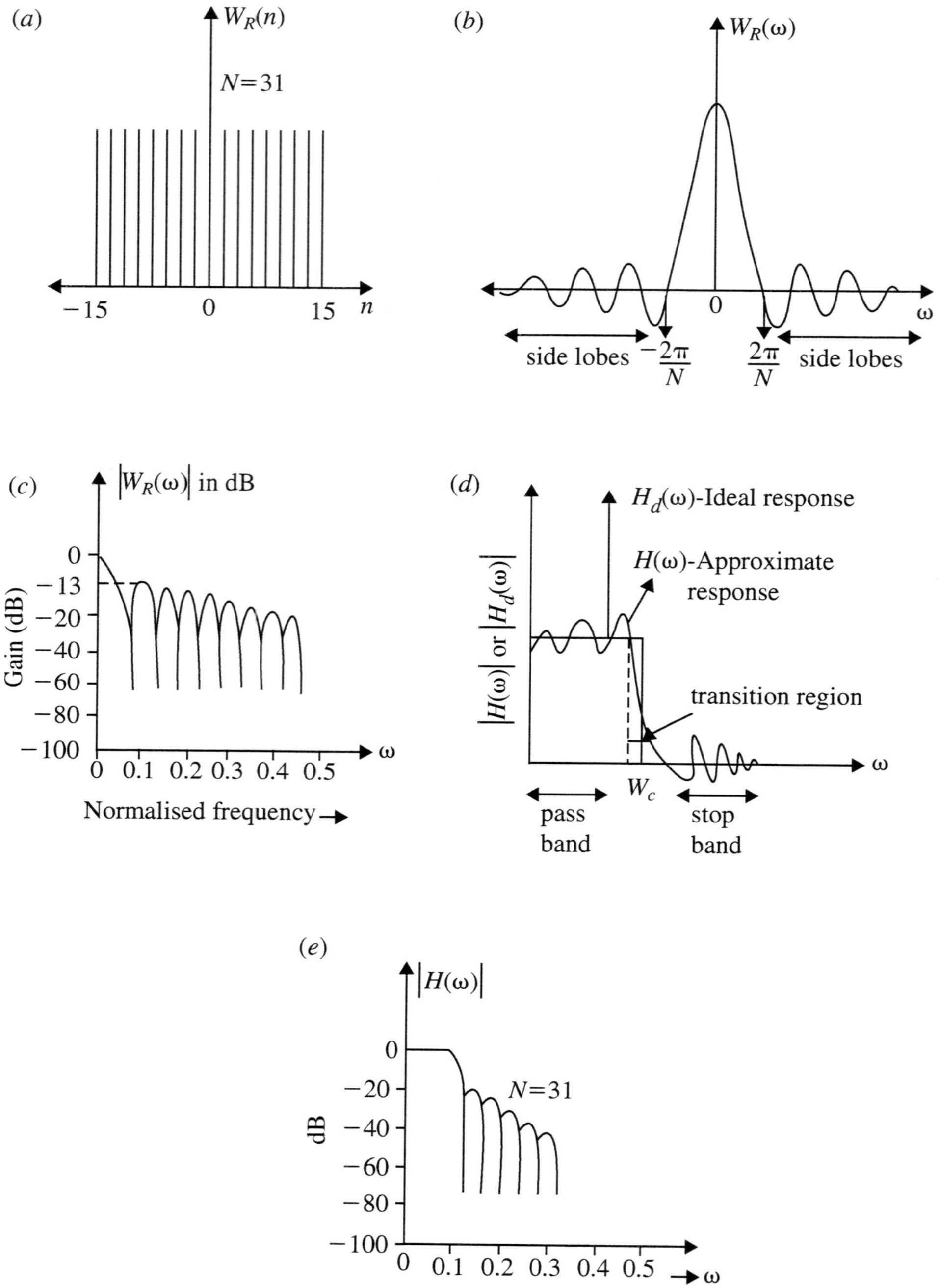

Figure 4.30 Rectangular window sequence and its frequency response. (*a*) Rectangular window sequence; (*b*) Magnitude response of Rectangular window; (*c*) Log-magnitude response of Rectangular window; (*d*) Magnitude response of LPF approximated using Rectangular window and (*e*) Log-magnitude response of FIR LPF designed using Rectangular window.

Step 4: The transfer function of the filter $H(z)$ is obtained by taking z-transform of $h(n)$.

Step 5: Realize the filter using suitable realization method (either direct form (or) linear phase realization).

Example 4.13

Design a LPF using Rectangular window by taking 9 samples of $W(n)$ and with cut-off frequency of 1.2 rad/sec.?

Solution

Step 1: Choose the Desired Frequency Response

$$H_d(\omega) = \begin{cases} e^{-j\omega\alpha}, & -\omega_c \le \omega \le \omega_c \quad \text{[for LPF]} \\ 0, & -\pi \le \omega \le -\omega_c \quad \text{and} \quad \omega_c \le \omega \le \pi \end{cases}$$

Step 2: To Find $H_d(n)$

Take inverse Fourier transform of $H_d(\omega)$. That is,

$$\begin{aligned} h_d(n) &= \frac{1}{2\pi}\int_{-\pi}^{\pi} H_d(\omega)e^{j\omega n}d\omega \\ &= \frac{1}{2\pi}\int_{-\omega_c}^{\omega_c} e^{-j\omega\alpha}e^{j\omega n}d\omega \\ &= \frac{1}{2\pi}\int_{-\omega_c}^{\omega_c} e^{j\omega(n-\alpha)}d\omega \\ &= \frac{1}{2\pi}\left[\frac{e^{j\omega(n-\alpha)}}{j(n-\alpha)}\right]_{-\omega_c}^{\omega_c} \\ &= \frac{1}{2j\pi(n-\alpha)}\left[e^{j\omega_c(n-\alpha)} - e^{-j\omega_c(n-\alpha)}\right] \\ &= \frac{1}{\pi(n-\alpha)}[\sin\omega_c(n-\alpha)] \\ \therefore\ h_d(n) &= \frac{1}{\pi(n-\alpha)}[\sin\omega_c(n-\alpha)] \end{aligned}$$

Step 3: Conversion of Infinite to Finite Sequence

$$h(n) = W(n) \times h_d(n)$$

Here, for Rectangular window,

$$W(n) = \begin{cases} 1, & \text{for} \quad 0 \le n \le (N-1) \\ 0, & \text{for} \quad \text{otherwise} \end{cases}$$

$$\therefore h(n) = \begin{cases} \frac{\sin \omega_c(n-\alpha)}{\pi(n-\alpha)}; & 0 \le n \le (N-1) \\ 0, & \text{otherwise} \end{cases}$$

where

$$\omega_c = 1.2 \text{ rad/sec.},$$
$$n = 0 \text{ to } 8 \quad [\because 9 \text{ samples}]$$
$$\alpha = \frac{N+1}{2} = \frac{9-1}{2} = 4$$

Therefore

$$h(0) = \frac{\sin 1.2(0-4)}{\pi(0-4)} = -0.079$$
$$h(1) = \frac{\sin 1.2(1-4)}{\pi(1-4)} = -0.0469$$
$$h(2) = \frac{\sin 1.2(2-4)}{\pi(2-4)} = 0.107$$
$$h(3) = \frac{\sin 1.2(3-4)}{\pi(3-4)} = 0.296$$
$$h(4) = \frac{\sin 1.2(4-4)}{\pi(4-4)} = 0$$

Apply 'L' Hospitals rule $\lim\limits_{\theta \to 0} \dfrac{\sin A\theta}{\theta} = \lim\limits_{\theta \to 0} \dfrac{\cos A\theta \cdot A}{A\theta} = A$

$$\therefore h(4) = \frac{\sin 1.2(n-4)}{\pi(n-4)} = \frac{1.2}{\pi} = 0.3819$$
$$h(5) = \frac{\sin 1.2(5-4)}{\pi(5-4)} = 0.296$$
$$h(6) = \frac{\sin 1.2(6-4)}{\pi(6-4)} = 0.107$$
$$h(7) = \frac{\sin 1.2(7-4)}{\pi(7-4)} = -0.0469$$
$$h(8) = \frac{\sin 1.2(8-4)}{\pi(8-4)} = -0.079.$$

Step 4: To Find $H(z)$

$$
\begin{aligned}
H(z) &= \sum_{n=0}^{N-1} h(n)z^{-n} \\
&= h(0) + h(1)z^{-1} + h(2)z^{-2} + h(3)z^{-3} + h(4)z^{-4} + h(5)z^{-5} \\
&\quad + h(6)z^{-6} + h(7)z^{-7} + h(8)z^{-8} \\
&= -0.079 - 0.0469z^{-1} + 0.107z^{-2} + 0.296z^{-3} + 0.3819z^{-4} \\
&\quad + 0.296z^{-5} + 0.107z^{-6} - 0.0469z^{-7} - 0.079z^{-8} \\
&= -0.079(1 + z^{-8}) - 0.0469(z^{-1} + z^{-7}) \\
&\quad + 0.107(z^{-2} + z^{-6}) + 0.296(z^{-3} + z^{-5}) + 0.3819z^{-4}
\end{aligned}
$$

Step 5: Linear Phase Realization

The structure realization is shown in Figure 4.31.

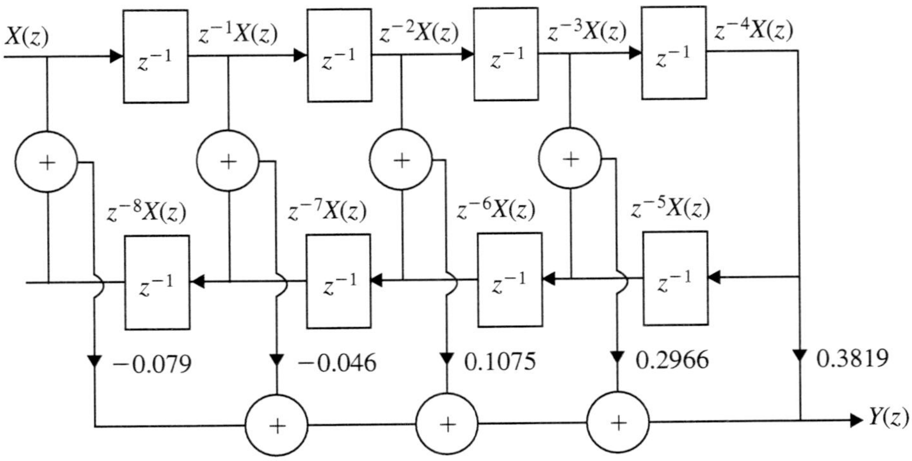

Figure 4.31 Linear phase realization of $H(z)$ for Example 4.13.

4.5.2.2 *Raised Cosine Windows*

The raised cosine windows are smoother at the ends, but closer to one at the middle. The smoother ends and the broader middle section produce less distortion of $h_d(n)$ around $n = 0$.

The window function is of the form

$$
W_\alpha(n) = \begin{cases} \alpha + (1-\alpha)\cos\left(\frac{2\pi n}{N-1}\right), & -\left(\frac{N-1}{2}\right) \le n \le \frac{N-1}{2} \\ 0, & \text{otherwise} \end{cases} \tag{4.84}
$$

If $\alpha = 0.5$, the window is called as Hanning Window. If $\alpha = 0.54$, the window is called as Hamming Window. The window spectrum for Raised Cosine window is given by

$$W_\alpha(\omega) = \sum_{n=-\left(\frac{N-1}{2}\right)}^{\frac{N-1}{2}} \left[\alpha + (1-\alpha)\cos\left(\frac{2\pi n}{N-1}\right)\right] e^{-j\omega n} \tag{4.85}$$

$$= \underbrace{\alpha \sum_{n=-\left(\frac{N-1}{2}\right)}^{\frac{N-1}{2}} e^{-j\omega n}}_{X} + \underbrace{\left(\frac{1-\alpha}{2}\right) \sum_{n=-\left(\frac{N-1}{2}\right)}^{\frac{N-1}{2}} e^{-j\left(\omega - \frac{2\pi}{N-1}\right)n}}_{Y}$$

$$+ \underbrace{\left(\frac{1-\alpha}{2}\right) \sum_{n=-\left(\frac{N-1}{2}\right)}^{\frac{N-1}{2}} e^{-j\left(\omega + \frac{2\pi}{N-1}\right)n}}_{Z} \tag{4.86}$$

$$X = \alpha\left[e^{j\omega\left(\frac{N-1}{2}\right)} + \cdots + e^{j\omega} + 1 + e^{-j\omega} + \cdots + e^{-j\omega\left(\frac{N-1}{2}\right)}\right]$$

$$= \alpha\left[\frac{1-e^{-j\omega N}}{1-e^{-j\omega}}\right] e^{j\omega\left(\frac{N-1}{2}\right)}$$

$$= \alpha\left[\frac{e^{\frac{j\omega N}{2}} - e^{-\frac{j\omega N}{2}}}{e^{\frac{j\omega}{2}} - e^{-\frac{j\omega}{2}}}\right]$$

$$X = \alpha\left[\frac{\sin\frac{\omega N}{2}}{\sin\frac{\omega}{2}}\right] \tag{4.87}$$

$$Y = \frac{1-\alpha}{2}\left[e^{j\left(\omega - \frac{2\pi}{N-1}\right)\left(\frac{N-1}{2}\right)} + \cdots + e^{j\left(\omega - \frac{2\pi}{N-1}\right)}\right.$$

$$\left. +1 + e^{-j\left(\omega - \frac{2\pi}{N-1}\right)} + \cdots + e^{-j\left(\omega - \frac{2\pi}{N-1}\right)\left(\frac{N-1}{2}\right)}\right]$$

$$= \frac{1-\alpha}{2}\left[\frac{e^{j\left(\omega - \frac{2\pi}{N-1}\right)\left(\frac{N-1}{2}\right)}\left[1 - e^{-j\left(\omega - \frac{2\pi}{N-1}\right)N}\right]}{e^{j\left(\frac{\omega}{2} - \frac{\pi}{N-1}\right)}\left[1 - e^{-j\left(\omega - \frac{2\pi}{N-1}\right)}\right]}\right]$$

$$= \frac{1-\alpha}{2}\left[\frac{e^{j\left(\frac{\omega N}{2} - \frac{\pi N}{N-1}\right)} - e^{-j\left(\frac{\omega N}{2} - \frac{\pi N}{N-1}\right)}}{e^{j\left(\frac{\omega N}{2} - \frac{\pi}{N-1}\right)} - e^{-j\left(\frac{\omega}{2} - \frac{\pi}{N-1}\right)}}\right]$$

$$= \frac{1-\alpha}{2}\left[\frac{\sin\left(\frac{\omega N}{2} - \frac{\pi N}{N-1}\right)}{\sin\left(\frac{\omega}{2} - \frac{\pi}{N-1}\right)}\right] \tag{4.88}$$

Similarly

$$z = \frac{1-\alpha}{2}\left[\frac{\sin\left(\frac{\omega N}{2}+\frac{\pi N}{N-1}\right)}{\sin\left(\frac{\omega}{2}+\frac{\pi}{N-1}\right)}\right] \tag{4.89}$$

Substituting equations (4.87) to (4.89) in equation (4.85), we get

$$W_\alpha(\omega) = \alpha\frac{\sin\frac{\omega N}{2}}{\sin\frac{\omega}{2}} + \frac{1-\alpha}{2}\left[\frac{\sin\left(\frac{\omega N}{2}-\frac{\pi N}{N-1}\right)}{\sin\left(\frac{\omega}{2}-\frac{\pi}{N-1}\right)}\right] + \frac{1-\alpha}{2}\left[\frac{\sin\left(\frac{\omega N}{2}+\frac{\pi N}{N-1}\right)}{\sin\left(\frac{\omega}{2}+\frac{\pi}{N-1}\right)}\right] \tag{4.90}$$

4.5.2.3 *Hanning Window*

The Hanning window sequence can be obtained by substituting $\alpha = 0.5$ in equation (4.84)

$$W_C(n) = \begin{cases} 0.5 + 0.5\cos\left(\frac{2\pi n}{N-1}\right); & -\left(\frac{N-1}{2}\right) \le n \le \frac{N-1}{2} \\ 0; & \text{otherwise} \end{cases} \tag{4.91}$$

(or)

$$W_C(n) = \begin{cases} 0.5 - 0.5\cos\frac{2n\pi}{N-1}; & 0 \le n \le N-1 \\ 0; & \text{otherwise} \end{cases} \tag{4.92}$$

Frequency response of the Hanning window is given by

$$W_C(\omega) = 0.5\frac{\sin\frac{\omega N}{2}}{\sin(\omega/2)} + 0.25\frac{\sin\left(\frac{\omega N}{2}-\frac{\pi N}{N-1}\right)}{\sin\left(\frac{\omega}{2}-\frac{\pi}{N-1}\right)} + 0.25\frac{\sin\left(\frac{\omega N}{2}+\frac{\pi N}{N-1}\right)}{\sin\left(\frac{\omega}{2}+\frac{\pi}{N-1}\right)} \tag{4.93}$$

$$\text{Width of mainlobe} = \frac{8\pi}{N}$$

$$\text{Peak sidelobe magnitude (dB)} = -31 \text{ dB}$$

In the log magnitude response of $W_C(\omega)$ the magnitude of the first sidelobe is -31dB, an improvement of 6dB over triangular window. Mainlobe width is same as in triangular window. But the magnitude of sidelobes is reduced, as shown in Figure 4.32. Hence the Hanning window is preferable to triangular window since the magnitude responses of lowpass filter have improved stopband characteristics.

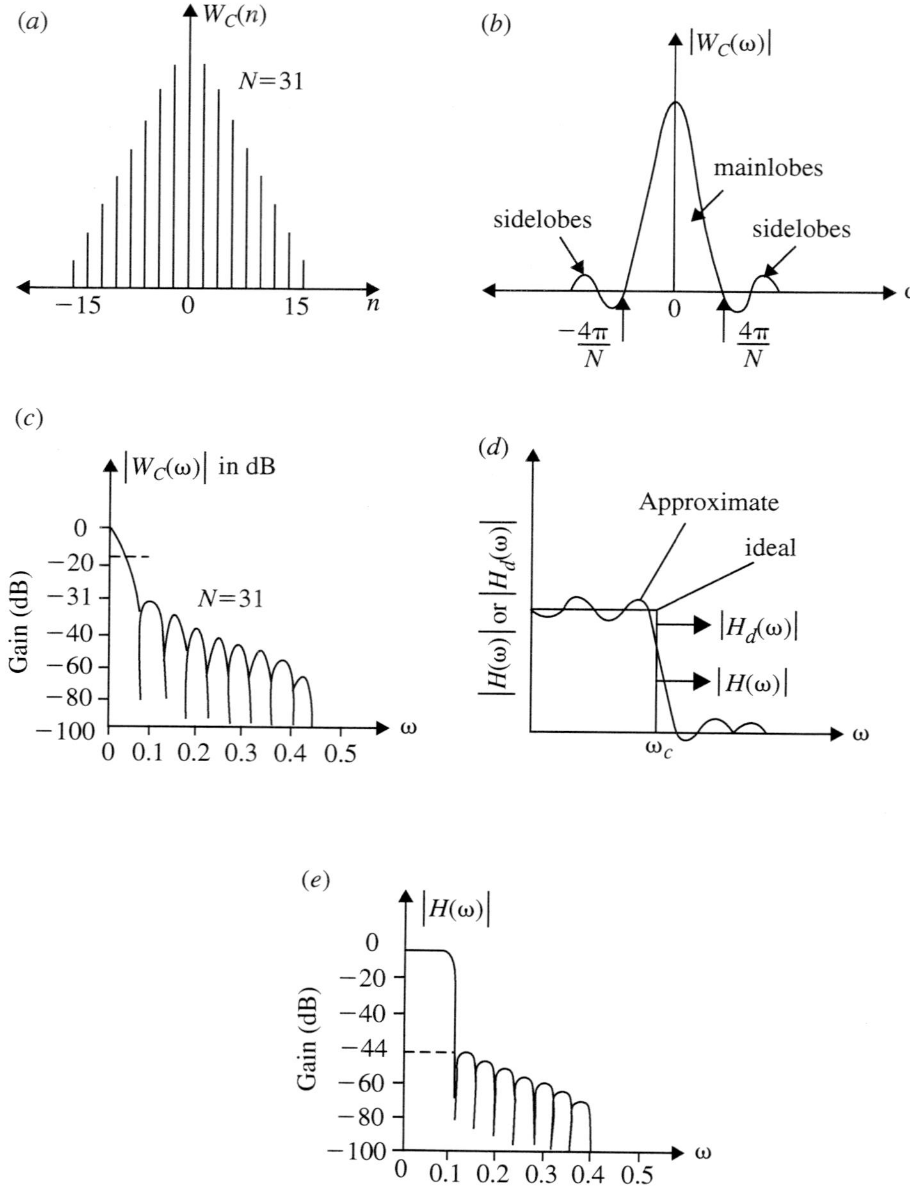

Figure 4.32 Hanning window sequence and its frequency response. (*a*) Rectangular window sequence; (*b*) Magnitude response of Hanning window; (*c*) Log-magnitude response of Hanning window; (*d*) Magnitude response of LPF approximated using Hanning window and (*e*) Log-magnitude response of FIR filter using Hanning window.

Design Procedure

Step 1: Choose the desired frequency response of the filter $[H_d(\omega)]$.

Step 2: Take inverse Fourier transform of $H_d(\omega)$ to obtain the desired impulse response $h_d(n)$.

Step 3: Choose a window sequence $W(n)$.

$$W(n) = \begin{cases} 0.5 - 0.5\cos\left(\frac{2\pi n}{N-1}\right), & 0 \le n \le N-1 \\ 0, & \text{otherwise} \end{cases}$$

Multiply $h_d(n)$ by $W(n)$ to convert the infinite impulse response to a finite impulse response $h(n)$. That is

$$h(n) = h_d(n) \times W(n)$$

Step 4: The transfer function of the filter *i.e.*, $H(z)$ is obtained by taking z-transform of $h(n)$.

Step 5: Realize the filter using suitable realization method (use Direct Form or Linear Phase).

Example 4.14

Design a BPF to pass frequencies in the range 1–2 rad/sec. using Hanning window, with $N = 5$.

Solution

Step 1: Choose $H_d(\omega)$ such that

$$H_d(\omega) = \begin{cases} e^{-j\omega\alpha}, & -\omega_{c_2} \le \omega \le -\omega_{c_1} \text{ and } \omega_{c_1} \le \omega \le \omega_{c_2} \\ 0, & \text{otherwise} \end{cases}$$

Step 2: To Find $h_d(n)$

$$h_d(n) = \frac{1}{2\pi}\left[\int_{-\omega_{c_2}}^{-\omega_{c_1}} e^{-j\omega\alpha} e^{j\omega n} d\omega + \int_{\omega_{c_1}}^{\omega_{c_2}} e^{-j\omega\alpha} e^{j\omega n} d\omega\right]$$

$$= \frac{1}{2\pi}\left[\int_{-\omega_{c_2}}^{-\omega_{c_1}} e^{j\omega(n-\alpha)} d\omega + \int_{\omega_{c_1}}^{\omega_{c_2}} e^{j\omega(n-\alpha)} d\omega\right]$$

$$= \frac{1}{2\pi}\left[\frac{e^{j\omega(n-\alpha)}}{j(n-\alpha)}\right]_{-\omega_{c_2}}^{-\omega_{c_1}} + \frac{1}{2\pi}\left[\frac{e^{j\omega(n-\alpha)}}{j(n-\alpha)}\right]_{\omega_{c_1}}^{\omega_{c_2}}$$

$$= \frac{1}{2\pi j(n-\alpha)}\left[e^{-j\omega_{c_1}(n-\alpha)} - e^{-j\omega_{c_2}(n-\alpha)} + e^{j\omega_{c_2}(n-\alpha)} - e^{j\omega_{c_1}(n-\alpha)}\right]$$

$$= \frac{1}{2\pi j(n-\alpha)}\left[\left(e^{j\omega_{c_2}(n-\alpha)} - e^{-j\omega_{c_2}(n-\alpha)}\right) - \left(e^{j\omega_{c_1}(n-\alpha)} - e^{-j\omega_{c_1}(n-\alpha)}\right)\right]$$

$$= \frac{1}{2\pi j(n-\alpha)} \times 2j\left[\sin\omega_{c_2}(n-\alpha) - \sin\omega_{c_1}(n-\alpha)\right]$$

$$= \frac{1}{\pi(n-\alpha)}\left[\sin\omega_{c_2}(n-\alpha) - \sin\omega_{c_1}(n-\alpha)\right]$$

Given that $\omega_{c_1} = 1$ rad/sec. and $\omega_{c_2} = 2$ rad/sec., $\alpha = \frac{N-1}{2} \longrightarrow \alpha = 2.$

Step 3: To Find $h(n)$

$$W(n) = 0.5 - 0.5\cos\left(\frac{2\pi n}{N-1}\right)$$

$$h(n) = h_d(n) \times W(n)$$

$$= \frac{1}{\pi(n-2)}[\sin 2(n-2) - \sin(n-2)]\left[0.5 - 0.5\cos\left(\frac{2\pi n}{4}\right)\right]$$

$h(0) = 0$

$h(1) = 0.0108$

$h(2) = 0.318$ [Applying L'Hospital's rule]

$h(3) = 0.0108$

$h(4) = 0$

Step 4: Take z-transform

$$H(z) = \sum_{n=0}^{4} h(n)z^{-n} = h(0) + h(1)z^{-1} + h(2)z^{-2} + h(3)z^{-3} + h(4)z^{-4}$$

$$\boxed{H(z) = 0.0108[z^{-1} + z^{-3}] + 0.318z^{-2}}$$

Step 5: Draw the realisation structure. This is shown in Figure 4.33.

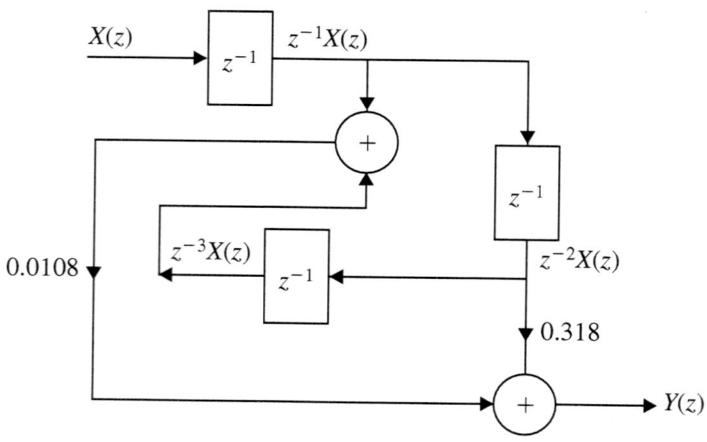

Figure 4.33 Linear phase realization of $H(z)$ for Example 4.14.

4.5.2.4 Hamming Window

The Hamming window sequence can be obtained by substituting $\alpha = 0.54$ in equation (4.84)

$$W_H(n) = \begin{cases} 0.54 + 0.46\cos\left(\frac{2\pi n}{N-1}\right); & -\left(\frac{N-1}{2}\right) \le n \le \frac{N-1}{2} \\ 0; & \text{otherwise} \end{cases} \tag{4.94}$$

(or)

$$W_H(n) = \begin{cases} 0.54 - 0.46\cos\frac{2n\pi}{N-1}; & 0 \le n \le N-1 \\ 0; & \text{otherwise} \end{cases} \tag{4.95}$$

Frequency response,

$$W_H(\omega) = 0.54\frac{\sin\frac{\omega N}{2}}{\sin(\omega/2)} + 0.23\frac{\sin\left(\frac{\omega N}{2} - \frac{\pi N}{N-1}\right)}{\sin\left(\frac{\omega}{2} - \frac{\pi}{N-1}\right)} + 0.23\frac{\sin\left(\frac{\omega N}{2} + \frac{\pi N}{N-1}\right)}{\sin\left(\frac{\omega}{2} + \frac{\pi}{N-1}\right)} \tag{4.96}$$

$$\text{Width of mainlobe} = \frac{8\pi}{N}$$

$$\text{Peak sidelobe magnitude (dB)} = -41 \text{ dB}$$

The Hamming window and its frequency response are shown in Figure 4.34. The magnitude of the first sidelobe has been reduced to −41dB, an improvement of 10dB compared to the Hanning window. But sidelobe magnitude at high frequencies, is almost constant.

Design Procedure

Step 1: Choose the desired frequency response of the filter *i.e.*, $H_d(\omega)$.

Step 2: Take the inverse Fourier transform of $H_d(\omega)$ to obtain the desired impulse response $h_d(n)$.

Step 3: Choose a window sequence (here) Hamming window sequence with

$$W(n) = \begin{cases} 0.54 - 0.46\cos\left(\frac{2\pi n}{N-1}\right); & 0 \le n \le N-1 \\ 0; & \text{otherwise} \end{cases}$$

Now multiply $h_d(n)$ and $W(n)$ to get $h(n)$

$$h(n) = h_d(n) \times W(n)$$

This step converts the infinite impulse response to finite impulse response $h(n)$.

Step 4: The transfer function of the filter, $H(z)$ is obtained by taking the z-transform of $h(n)$.

Step 5: Realise the filter using suitable realisation method (use Direct Form or Linear Phase).

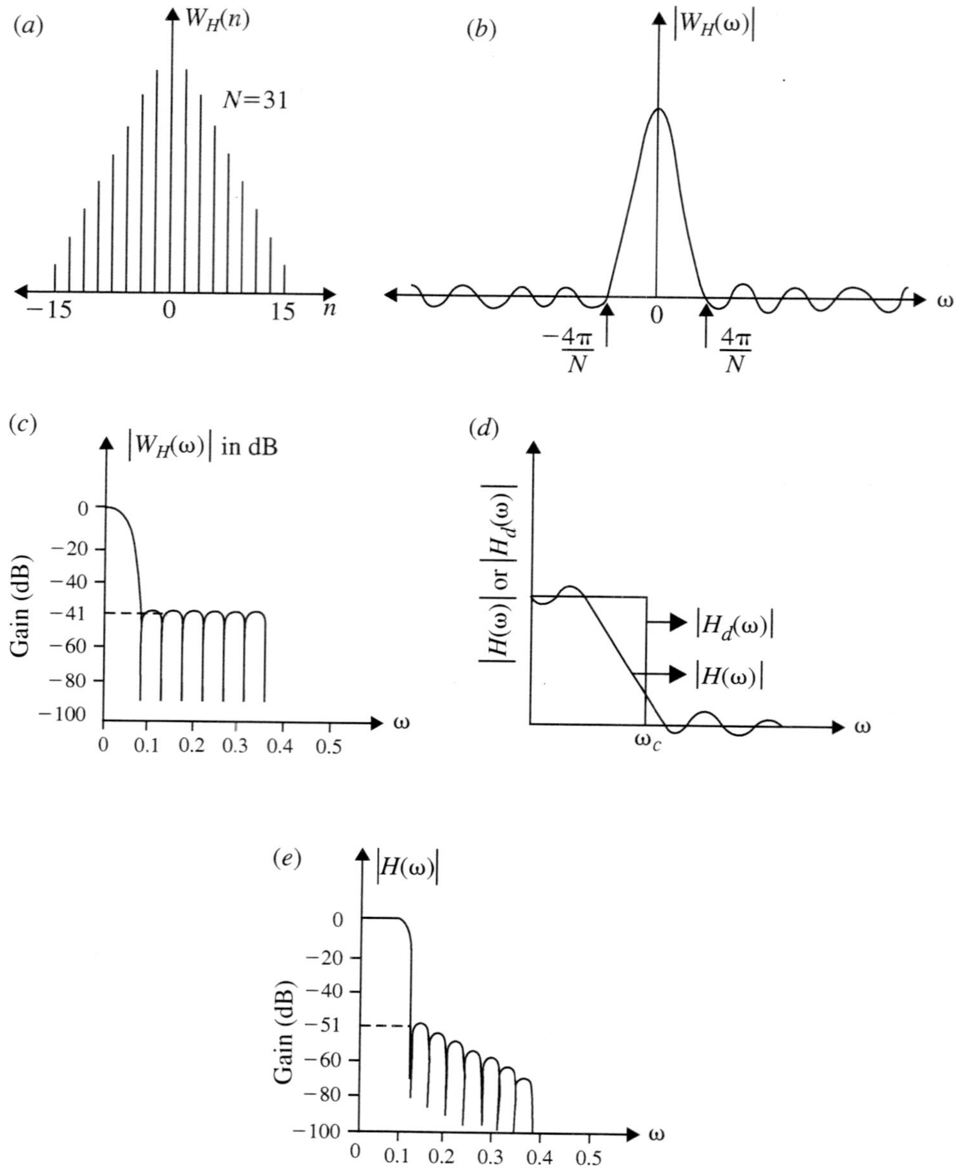

Figure 4.34 Hamming window sequence and its frequency response. (*a*) Hamming window sequence; (*b*) Magnitude response of Hamming window; (*c*) Log-magnitude response of Hamming window; (*d*) Magnitude response of LPF approximated using Hamming window and (*e*) Log-magnitude response of FIR filter using Hamming window.

Example 4.15

Design a HPF with Hamming window. The cut off frequency is 1.2 rad s^{-1} $N = 9$.

Solution

Step 1: Choose $H_d(\omega)$: The Hamming window characteristic is shown in Figure 4.35(a).

$$H(e^{j\omega}) = H_d(\omega) = \begin{cases} e^{-j\omega\alpha}; & -\pi \le \omega \le -\omega_c \quad \text{and} \quad \omega_c \le \omega \le \pi \\ 0; & \text{otherwise} \end{cases}$$

Step 2: To Find $h_d(n)$

$$\begin{aligned} h_d(n) &= \frac{1}{2\pi}\int_{-\pi}^{\pi} H_d(\omega)e^{j\omega n}d\omega \\ &= \frac{1}{2\pi}\int_{-\pi}^{-\omega_c} e^{-j\omega\alpha}e^{j\omega n}d\omega + \frac{1}{2\pi}\int_{\omega_c}^{\pi} e^{-j\omega\alpha}e^{j\omega n}d\omega \\ &= \frac{1}{2\pi}\left[\int_{-\pi}^{-\omega_c} e^{j\omega(n-\alpha)}d\omega + \int_{\omega_c}^{\pi} e^{j\omega(n-\alpha)}d\omega\right] \\ &= \frac{1}{2\pi}\left[\left[\frac{e^{j\omega(n-\alpha)}}{j(n-\alpha)}\right]_{-\pi}^{-\omega_c} + \left[\frac{e^{j\omega(n-\alpha)}}{j(n-\alpha)}\right]_{\omega_c}^{\pi}\right] \\ &= \frac{1}{j2\pi(n-\alpha)}\left[e^{-j\omega_c(n-\alpha)} - e^{-j\pi(n-\alpha)} + e^{j\pi(n-\alpha)} - e^{j\omega_c(n-\alpha)}\right] \\ &= \frac{1}{j2\pi(n-\alpha)}(2j)\left[\sin(n-\alpha)\pi - \sin\omega_c(n-\alpha)\right] \\ &= \frac{1}{\pi(n-\alpha)}\left[\sin\pi(n-\alpha) - \sin\omega_c(n-\alpha)\right] \end{aligned}$$

Step 3: To Find $h(n)$

$$\begin{aligned} W(n) &= \left[0.54 - 0.46\cos\left(\frac{2\pi n}{N-1}\right)\right] \\ h(n) &= h_d(n) \times W(n) \\ &= \frac{\left[\sin\pi(n-\alpha) - \sin\omega_c(n-\alpha)\right]}{\pi(n-\alpha)}\left[0.54 - 0.46\cos\left(\frac{2\pi n}{N-1}\right)\right] \end{aligned}$$

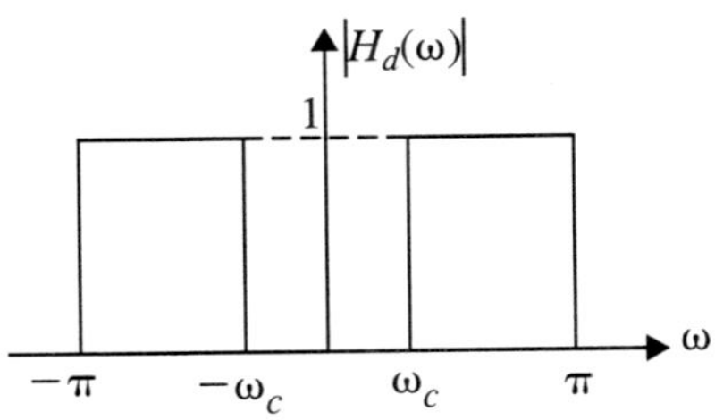

Figure 4.35 (a) Hamming window characteristic.

where $\alpha = \frac{N-1}{2} = 4$

$$h(n) = \frac{[\sin \pi(n-4) - \sin 1.2(n-4)]}{\pi(n-4)}\left[0.54 - 0.46\cos\left(\frac{n\pi}{4}\right)\right]$$

$$h(0) = 6 \times 10^{-3} = 0.0063$$
$$h(1) = 0.0101$$
$$h(2) = 0.0581$$
$$h(3) = -0.2367$$
$$h(4) = -0.6180 \qquad \text{(Applying L' Hospital rule)}$$
$$h(5) = -0.2567$$
$$h(6) = 0.0581$$
$$h(7) = 0.0101$$
$$h(8) = 6.34 \times 10^{-3}$$

Step 4: Take z-transform:

$$H(z) = \sum_{n=0}^{N-1} h(n)z^{-n}$$

$$H(z) = 0.0063[1 + z^{-8}] + 0.101[z^{-1} + z^{-7}] + 0.0581[z^{-2} + z^{-6}] - 0.2367[z^{-3} + z^{-5}] + (-0.6180)z^{-4}$$

Step 5: Draw the realisation structure. The structure is realized as shown in Figure 4.35(b).

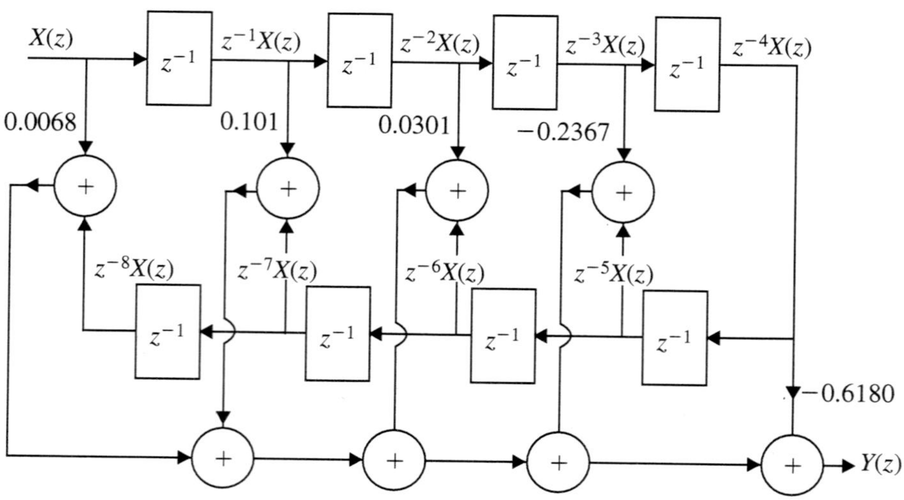

Figure 4.35 (b) Linear phase realization of $H(z)$ for Example 4.15.

4.5.2.5 Blackman Window

The Blackman window function is another type of cosine window and is given by the following equation:

$$W_B(n) = \begin{cases} 0.42 + 0.5\cos\frac{2n\pi}{N-1} + 0.08\cos\frac{4n\pi}{N-1}; & -\left(\frac{N-1}{2}\right) \le n \le \frac{N-1}{2} \\ 0; & \text{otherwise} \end{cases} \quad (4.97)$$

(or)

$$W_B(n) = \begin{cases} 0.42 - 0.5\cos\frac{2n\pi}{N-1} + 0.08\cos\frac{4n\pi}{N-1}; & 0 \le n \le N-1 \\ 0; & \text{otherwise} \end{cases} \quad (4.98)$$

$$\text{Width of mainlobe} = \frac{12\pi}{N}$$

Peak sidelobe magnitude (dB) $= -58$ dB

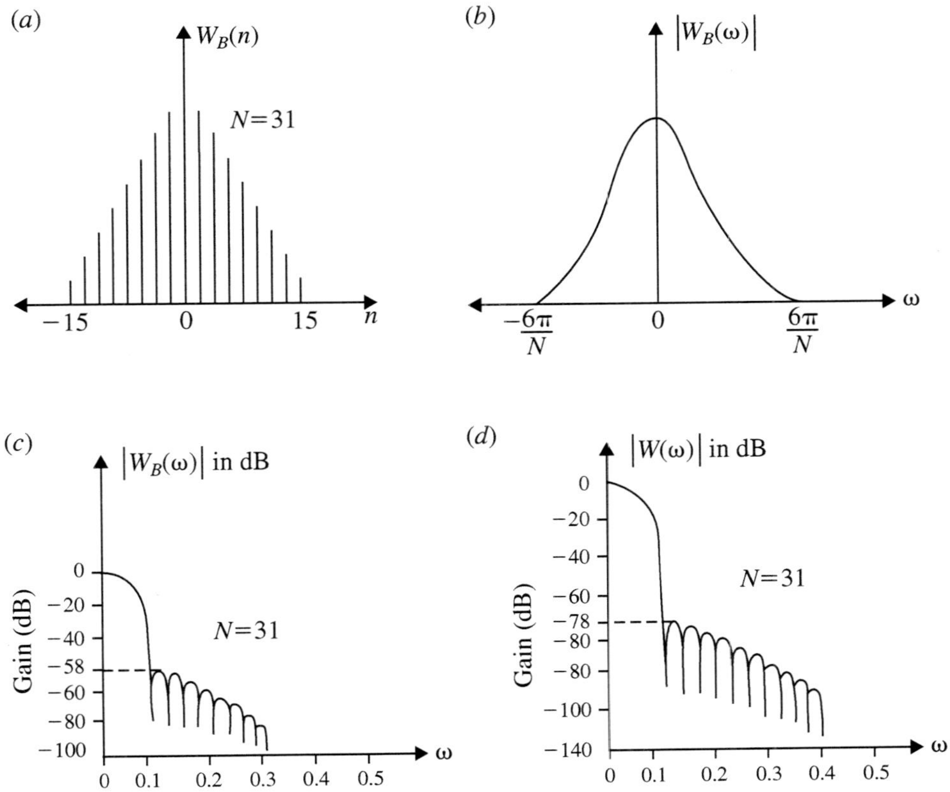

Figure 4.36 Blackman window sequence and its frequency response. (*a*) Blackman window sequence; (*b*) Magnitude response of Blackman window; (*c*) Log-magnitude response of Blackman window and (*d*) Log-magnitude response of FIR LPF approximated using Blackman window.

The frequency response and impulse response characteristics of Blackmann window are shown in Figure 4.36.

The frequency response of Blackman window is shown in Figure 4.36. The magnitude of the first sidelobe is -58dB and the sidelobe magnitude decreases with frequency. This desirable feature is achieved at the expense of increased mainlobe width.

Design Procedure

1. Choose the desired frequency response $H_d(\omega)$. Take inverse Fourier transform of $H_d(\omega)$ to obtain the desired impulse response $h_d(n)$.
2. Choose a window sequence $W(n)$ and multiply $h_d(n)$ and $W(n)$ to convert the infinite impulse response to finite impulse response $h(n)$.
3. The transfer function $H(z)$ is obtained by taking z-transform of $h(n)$.
4. Realize the filter using suitable realization method.

Example 4.16

Design an ideal band pass filter using Blackman window to pass frequencies in the range 1.2 to 1.7 rad/s with $N = 7$.

Solution

Step 1: Choose desired frequency response

$$H_d(e^{j\omega}) = \begin{cases} e^{-j\omega\alpha}, & -\omega_{c_2} \le \omega \le \omega_{c_1} \text{ and } \omega_{c_1} \le \omega \le \omega_{c_2} \\ 0, & \text{else} \end{cases}$$

$$\therefore\ H_d(e^{j\omega}) = \begin{cases} e^{-j\omega\alpha}, & -1.7 \le \omega \le -1.2 \text{ and } 1.2 \le \omega \le 1.7 \\ 0, & \text{else} \end{cases}$$

$$h_d(n) = \frac{1}{2\pi}\int_{-\pi}^{\pi} H_d(e^{j\omega})e^{j\omega n}d\omega$$

$$h_d(n) = \frac{1}{2\pi}\int_{-1.7}^{-1.2} e^{-j\omega\alpha}\cdot e^{j\omega n}d\omega + \frac{1}{2\pi}\int_{1.2}^{1.7} e^{-j\omega\alpha}\cdot e^{j\omega n}d\omega$$

$$= \frac{1}{2\pi}\left[\frac{e^{j\omega(n-\alpha)}}{j(n-\alpha)}\right]_{-1.7}^{-1.2} + \frac{1}{2\pi}\left[\frac{e^{j\omega(n-\alpha)}}{j(n-\alpha)}\right]_{1.2}^{1.7}$$

$$= \frac{1}{2\pi}\left[\frac{e^{-j1.7(n-\alpha)}}{j(n-\alpha)} - \frac{e^{-1.2j(n-\alpha)}}{j(n-\alpha)} + \frac{e^{1.7j(n-\alpha)}}{j(n-\alpha)} - \frac{e^{j1.2(n-\alpha)}}{j(n-\alpha)}\right]$$

$$= \frac{1}{2\pi}\left[\frac{2j\sin 1.7(n-\alpha) - 2j\sin 1.2(n-\alpha)}{j(n-\alpha)}\right]$$

$$= \frac{1}{\pi(n-\alpha)}[\sin 1.7(n-\alpha) - \sin 1.2(n-\alpha)]$$

where $\alpha = \frac{N-1}{2} = 3$

$$\therefore\ h_d(n) = \frac{1}{\pi(n-3)}[\sin 1.7(n-3) - \sin 1.2(n-3)]$$

$$W(n) = \begin{cases} 0.42 - 0.5\cos\left(\frac{2\pi n}{6}\right) + 0.08\cos\left(\frac{4\pi n}{6}\right); & 0 \le n \le 6 \\ 0; & \text{otherwise} \end{cases}$$

Step 2:

$$\begin{aligned} h(n) &= W(n)h_d(n) \qquad 0 \le n \le N-1 \\ &= \left[0.42 - 0.5\cos\left(\frac{2\pi n}{6}\right) + 0.08\cos\left(\frac{4\pi n}{6}\right)\right] \\ &\quad \times \frac{1}{\pi(n-3)}[\sin 1.7(n-3) - \sin 1.2(n-3)]; \quad 0 \le n \le 6 \end{aligned}$$

$$\begin{aligned} h(0) &= 0 \\ h(1) &= -0.019 \\ h(2) &= 0.0119 \\ h(3) &= \text{Apply } L\text{' Hospital's Rule} \\ h(4) &= 0.0119 \\ h(5) &= -0.019 \\ h(6) &= 0 \end{aligned}$$

$$\begin{aligned} h(3) &= \left(\left[0.42 - 0.5\sin\left(\frac{2\pi \times 3}{6}\right) - 0.08\sin\left(\frac{4\pi \times 3}{6}\right)\right]\right. \\ &\quad \times [\sin 1.7(n-3) - \sin 1.2(n-3)] \Big/ \pi(n-3) \\ &= \left[0.42 - 0.5\cos\left(\frac{2\pi \times 3}{6}\right) + 0.08\cos\left(\frac{4\pi \times 3}{6}\right)\right] \\ &\quad \left.\times \left[\frac{\sin 1.7(n-3)}{1.7(n-3)} \cdot 1 \cdot 7 - \frac{\sin 1.2(n-3)}{1.2(n-3)} \cdot 1 \cdot 2\right]\right) \Big/ \pi \\ &= \frac{1 \times (0.5)}{\pi} = 0.162 \end{aligned}$$

Step 3:

$$\begin{aligned} H(z) &= \sum_{n=0}^{N-1} h(n)z^{-n} = h(0) + h(1)z^{-1} + h(2)z^{-2} + h(3)z^{-3} + h(4)z^{-4} \\ &\quad + h(5)z^{-5} + h(6)z^{-6} \end{aligned}$$

$$\begin{aligned} H(z) &= -0.019z^{-1} + 0.0119z^{-2} + 0.162z^{-3} + 0.0119z^{-4} - 0.019z^{-5} \\ &= -0.019(z^{-1} + z^{-5}) + 0.0119(z^{-2} + z^{-4}) + 0.162z^{-3} \end{aligned}$$

Step 4: Realization Structure

The structure realization is shown in Figure 4.37.

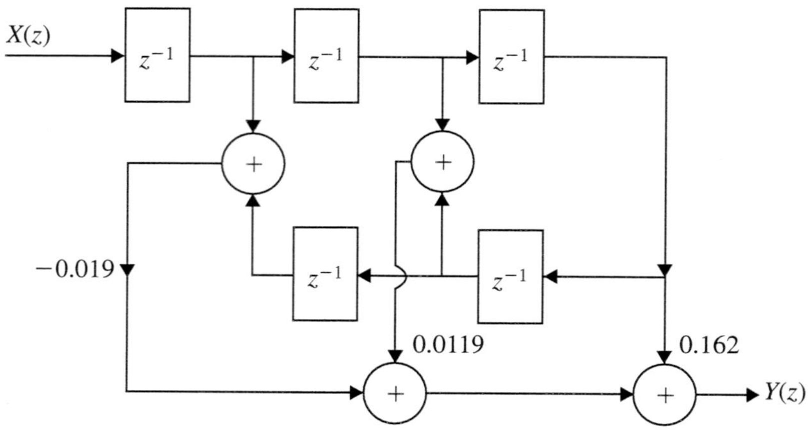

Figure 4.37 Linear phase realization of $H(z)$ for Example 4.16.

4.5.2.6 *Kaiser Window*

Kaiser window function is given in the following form:

$$W_K(n) = \begin{cases} \dfrac{I_0\left(\alpha\sqrt{1-\left(\frac{2n}{N-1}\right)^2}\right)}{I_0(\alpha)}; & -\left(\frac{N-1}{2}\right) \le n \le \frac{N-1}{2} \\ 0; & \text{otherwise} \end{cases} \tag{4.99}$$

or

$$W_K(n) = \begin{cases} \dfrac{I_0\left(\alpha\sqrt{\left(\frac{N-1}{2}\right)^2-\left(n-\frac{N-1}{2}\right)^2}\right)}{I_0(\alpha\frac{N-1}{2})}; & 0 \le n \le \frac{N-1}{2} \\ 0; & \text{otherwise} \end{cases} \tag{4.100}$$

The parameter α is an independent variable that can be varied to control the sidelobe levels with respect to the mainlobe peak. The modified Bessel function of the first kind $I_0(x)$ is given by

$$I_0(x) = 1 + \sum_{k=1}^{\infty}\left[\frac{1}{k!}\left(\frac{x}{2}\right)^k\right]^2 = 1 + \sum_{k=1}^{\infty}\left(\frac{(0.5)^2}{(k!)^2}\right)^k \tag{4.101}$$

$$= 1 + \frac{(0.25x^2)^2}{(k!)^2} = 1 + \frac{0.25x^2}{(1!)^2} + \frac{(0.25x^2)^2}{(2!)^2} + \cdots \tag{4.102}$$

This equation can be used to compute $I_0(\alpha)$ and $I_0\left(\alpha\sqrt{\left(\frac{2n}{N-1}\right)^2}\right)$. Figure 4.38 shows the Kaiser window sequence and its frequency response. The width of the mainlobe can be adjusted by varying the length N of the window sequence.

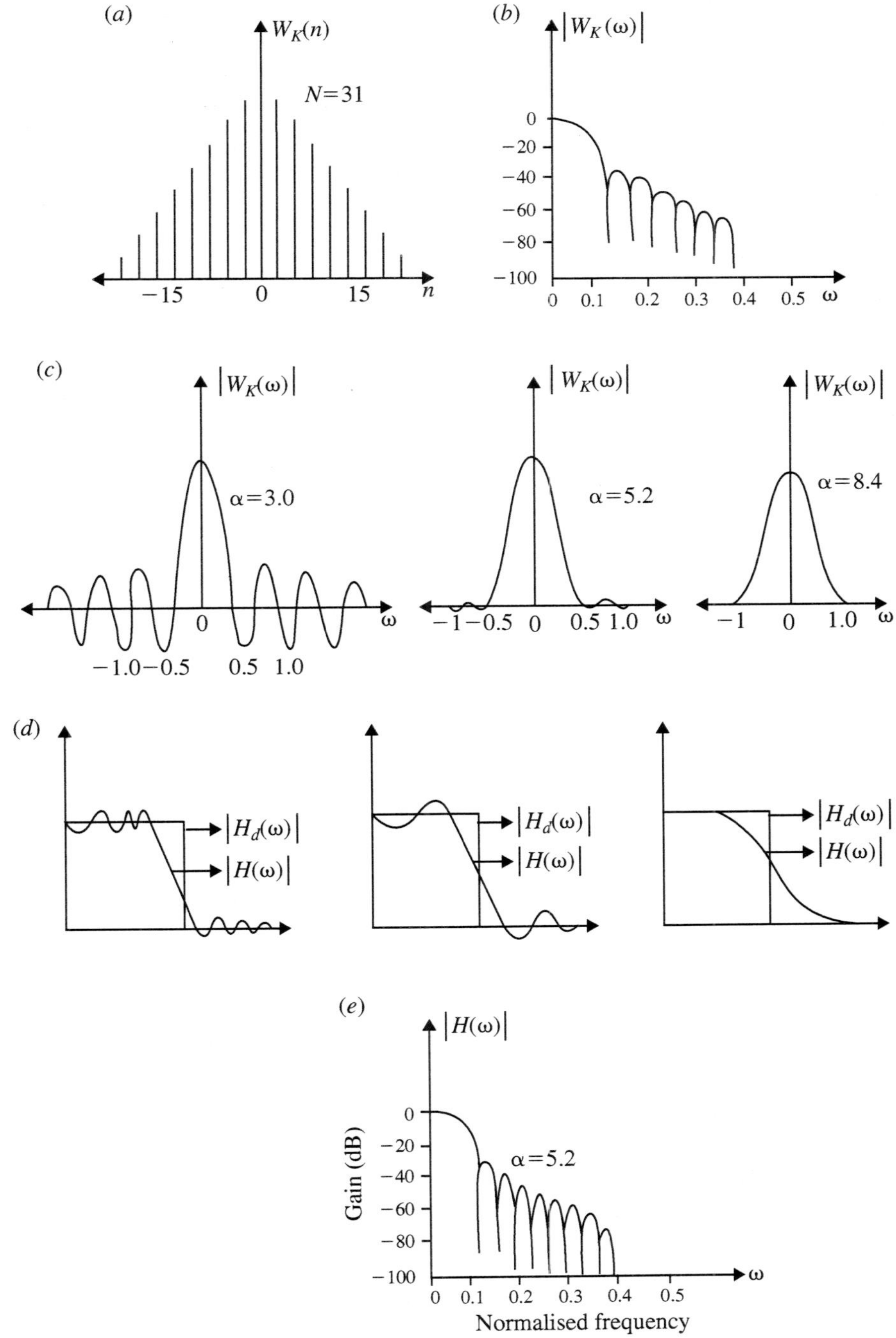

Figure 4.38 Kaiser window sequence and its frequency response. (*a*) Kaiser window sequence; (*b*) Log-magnitude response of Kaiser window; (*c*) Magnitude frequency response of Kaiser window for different values of α (when $N = 31$); (*d*) Magnitude response of Kaiser window for different values of α (when $N = 31$) and (*e*) Log-magnitude response of FIR LPF designed using Kaiser window.

Table 4.1 Comparison of window function in frequency domain characteristics

Type of Window	Approximate Width of Mainlobe	Peak Sidelobe Magnitude (dB)
Rectangular	$4\pi/N$	−13
Hanning	$8\pi/N$	−31
Hamming	$8\pi/N$	−41
Blackman	$12\pi/N$	−58

Design Procedure

(*i*) Determine 'δ' using the formula

$$\delta = \min(\delta_p, \delta_s)$$

where

$$\delta_p = \frac{10^{0.05A_p} - 1}{10^{0.05A_p} + 1}$$

$$\delta_s = 10^{-0.05A_s}$$

(*ii*) Find the actual stop band attenuation using 'δ'

$$A_s' = -20\log_{10}\delta$$

(*iii*) Determine Kaiser window design parameter using the following equation:

$$\alpha_k = \begin{cases} 0, & A_s' \le 21 \\ 0.5842(A_s' - 21)^{0.4} + 0.07886(A_s' - 21), & 21 \le A_s' \le 50 \\ 0.1102(A_s - 8.7), & A_s' > 50 \end{cases}$$

(*iv*) Determine the design parameter 'D' using the following equation:

$$D = \begin{cases} 0.9222, & A_s' \le 21 \\ \frac{A_s' - 7.95}{14.36}, & A_s' > 21 \end{cases}$$

(*v*) Determine the order of filter using the following equation:

$$N \ge \frac{FD}{\Delta_f} + 1$$

$$\Delta_f = f_s - f_p$$

where D = design parameter and F = sampling frequency.

(*vi*) Select the desired frequency response $H_d(\omega)$

$$\omega_c = \frac{2\pi f_c}{F} = \frac{2\pi(1/2)(f_p + f_s)}{F}$$

where $f_c = (1/2)(f_p + f_s)$.

(*vii*) Find $h_d(n)$ using inverse Fourier transform

$$h_d(n) = \frac{1}{2\pi}\int_{-\pi}^{\pi} H_d(\omega)e^{j\omega n}d\omega$$

(*viii*) Find the window function using $\omega(n)$ equation. Bessel function

$$I_0(x) = 1 + \frac{0.25x^2}{(1!)^2} + \frac{(0.25x^2)^2}{(2!)^2} + \frac{(0.25x^2)^3}{(3!)^2} + \frac{(0.25x^2)^4}{(4!)^2} + \frac{(0.25x^2)^5}{(5!)^2} + \frac{(0.25x^2)^6}{(6!)^2}$$

$$\omega(n) = \frac{I_0\left[\alpha_k\sqrt{\left(\frac{N-1}{2}\right)^2\left(n - \frac{N-1}{2}\right)^2}\right]}{I_0\left[\alpha_k\left(\frac{N-1}{2}\right)\right]}; \qquad 0 \le n \le N-1$$

$$\omega(n) = \frac{I_0\left[\alpha\sqrt{1 - \left(\frac{2n}{N-1}\right)^2}\right]}{I_0[\alpha]}; \; -\left(\frac{N-1}{2}\right) \le n \le \frac{N-1}{2}; \text{ and } |n| \le \frac{N-1}{2}$$

(*ix*) Find $h(n)$ using $h(n) = h_d(n)\omega(n)$.

(*x*) Find $H(z)$ using z-transform

$$H(z) = \sum_{n=0}^{N-1} h(n)z^{-n}$$

(*xi*) Draw suitable realization.

Example 4.17

Design a FIR low pass filter using Kaiser window filter the following specifications.

Passband cut-off frequency = 150 Hz

Stopband cut-off frequency = 250 Hz

Passband ripple = 0.1 dB

Stopband attenuation = 40 dB

Sampling frequency = 1000 Hz

Solution Given

$$f_p = 150 \text{ Hz}$$
$$f_s = 250 \text{ Hz}$$
$$A_p = 0.1 \text{ dB}$$
$$A_s = 40 \text{ dB}$$
$$F = 1000 \text{ Hz}$$

Step 1: Find δ using the following equation:

$$\delta_p = \frac{10^{0.05A_p} - 1}{10^{0.05A_p} + 1} = \frac{10^{0.05\times 0.1} - 1}{10^{0.05\times 0.1} + 1} = 5.76 \times 10^{-3}$$
$$= 0.00576$$
$$\delta_s = 10^{-0.05A_s} = 10^{-0.05\times 40} = 0.01$$
$$\delta = \min(\delta_p, \delta_s)$$
$$\therefore\ \delta = 0.00576$$

Step 2: Find actual stopband attenuation, A_s' using the following equation:

$$A_S' = -20\log_{10}\delta$$
$$= -20\log_{10}(0.00576)$$
$$\therefore\ A_s' = 44.8 \text{ dB}$$

Step 3: Find the Kaiser window parameter, α_k using the following equation:

$$\alpha_k = 0.5842(A_s' - 21)^{0.4} + 0.07886(A_s' - 21)$$
$$\alpha_k = 0.5842(44.8 - 21)^{0.4} + 0.07886(44.8 - 21)$$
$$\therefore\ \alpha_k = 3.953$$

Step 4: Find the design parameter 'D' (because $A_s' > 21$) using the following equation:

$$D = \frac{A_s' - 7.95}{14.36} = \frac{44.8 - 7.95}{14.36}$$
$$\therefore\ D = 2.566$$

Step 5: Find the order of the filter, N using the following equation:

$$N \geq \frac{F\cdot D}{\Delta f} + 1 = \frac{F\cdot D}{f_s - f_p} + 1$$
$$= \frac{1000 \times 2.566}{(250 - 150)} + 1$$
$$= 26.66$$
$$\therefore\ N = 27$$

Step 6: To find cut off frequency, ω_c, using the following equation is used

$$f_c = \frac{1}{2}(f_s + f_p)$$
$$= \frac{1}{2}(250 + 150) = 200 \text{ Hz}$$
$$\omega_c = \frac{2\pi f_c}{F} \qquad \text{(normalized by } F\text{)}$$
$$\omega_c = \frac{2\pi \times 200}{1000} = 1.2566$$
$$\therefore \omega_c = 1.2566$$

Step 7: To find $h_d(n)$, the following procedure is followed.

For a low pass filter, the frequency response is given by

$$H_d(e^{j\omega}) = \begin{cases} e^{-j\omega\alpha}, & -\omega_c \leq \omega \leq \omega_c \\ 0, & \text{else} \end{cases}$$
$$h_d(n) = \frac{1}{2\pi}\int_{-\pi}^{\pi} H_d(e^{j\omega})e^{j\omega n}d\omega$$
$$h_d(n) = \frac{1}{2\pi}\int_{-\omega_c}^{\omega_c} e^{-j\omega\alpha}e^{j\omega n}d\omega$$

as $\omega_c = 1.2566$ (from Step 6)

$$h_d(n) = \frac{1}{2\pi}\int_{-1.2566}^{1.2566} e^{j\omega(n-\alpha)}d\omega$$
$$h_d(n) = \frac{1}{2\pi}\frac{e^{j\omega(n-\alpha)}}{j(n-\alpha)}\bigg|_{-1.2566}^{1.2566}$$
$$h_d(n) = \frac{1}{2\pi}\left[\frac{e^{j1.2566(n-\alpha)} - e^{-j1.2566(n-\alpha)}}{j(n-\alpha)}\right]$$
$$h_d(n) = \frac{\sin 1.2566(n-\alpha)}{\pi(n-\alpha)}$$

because

$$\sin\theta = \frac{e^{i\theta} - e^{-i\theta}}{2i}$$

As $\alpha = \frac{N-1}{2} = \frac{27-1}{2} = 13$

$$h_d(n) = \frac{\sin 1.2566(n-13)}{\pi(n-13)} \qquad 0 \leq n \leq N-1 \text{ and } 0 \leq n \leq 26$$

$$h_d(0) = -0.01438 \qquad h_d(7) = 0.050$$
$$h_d(1) = 0.0156 \qquad h_d(8) = -1.1797 \times 10^{-5}$$
$$h_d(2) = 0.0275 \qquad h_d(9) = -0.075$$
$$h_d(3) = -1.1797 \times 10^{-5} \qquad h_d(10) = -0.0623$$
$$h_d(4) = -0.033 \qquad h_d(11) = 0.09355$$
$$h_d(5) = -0.0233 \qquad h_d(12) = 0.3027$$
$$h_d(6) = 0.0267 \qquad h_d(13) = \frac{1.2566}{\pi} = 0.3999$$

Step 8: To find the window function $W(n)$. As N is very large

$$W(n) = \frac{I_0\left[\alpha_k\sqrt{1-\left(\frac{2n}{N-1}\right)^2}\right]}{I_0[\alpha_k]} \qquad 0 \le n \le N-1;\ 0 \le n \le 26$$

$$W(n) = \frac{I_0\left[3.953\sqrt{1-(\frac{2n}{26})^2}\right]}{I_0[3.953]} \qquad [\because\ N = 27]$$

$$I_0[x] = 1 + \frac{0.25x^2}{(1!)^2} + \frac{(0.25x^2)^2}{(2!)^2} + \frac{(0.25x^2)^3}{(3!)^2} + \cdots + \frac{(0.25x^2)^6}{(6!)^2}$$

$$W(0) = \frac{I_0[3.953]}{I_0[3.953]} = \frac{10.824}{10.824} = 1$$
$$W(1) = \frac{I_0[3.938]}{10.824} = 0.99$$
$$W(2) = \frac{I_0[3.9]}{10.824} = 0.9582$$
$$W(3) = \frac{I_0[3.843]}{10.824} = 0.9125$$
$$W(4) = \frac{I_0[3.758]}{10.824} = 0.8485$$
$$W(5) = \frac{I_0[3.646]}{10.824} = 0.77$$
$$W(6) = \frac{I_0[3.504]}{10.824} = 0.684$$
$$W(7) = \frac{I_0[3.328]}{10.824} = 0.5905$$
$$W(8) = \frac{I_0[3.113]}{10.824} = 0.4955$$

$$W(9) = \frac{I_0[2.85]}{10.824} = 0.3998$$

$$W(10) = \frac{I_0[2.5239]}{10.824} = 0.30967$$

$$W(11) = \frac{I_0[2.105]}{10.824} = 0.22689$$

$$W(12) = \frac{I_0[1.519]}{10.824} = 0.1539$$

$$W(13) = \frac{I_0[0]}{10.824} = 0.09242$$

Step 9: To Find $h(n)$

$$h(n) = h_d(n)W(n) \qquad 0 \leq n \leq 26$$

$h(0) = -0.01438$ $\qquad$ $h(7) = 0.029526$

$h(1) = 0.015444$ $\qquad$ $h(8) = -5.8419 \times 10^{-6}$

$h(2) = 0.02635$ $\qquad$ $h(9) = -0.02998$

$h(3) = -1.0758 \times 10^{-5}$ $\qquad$ $h(10) = -0.01929$

$h(4) = -0.028$ $\qquad$ $h(11) = 0.02122$

$h(5) = -0.0179$ $\qquad$ $h(12) = 0.04658$

$h(6) = 0.01826$ $\qquad$ $h(13) = 0.036958$

Applying the linear phase condition of an FIR filter, that is, $h(n) = h(N - 1 - n)$, we get

$h(0) = h(26)$ $\qquad$ $h(7) = h(19)$

$h(1) = h(25)$ $\qquad$ $h(8) = h(18)$

$h(2) = h(24)$ $\qquad$ $h(9) = h(17)$

$h(3) = h(23)$ $\qquad$ $h(10) = h(16)$

$h(4) = h(22)$ $\qquad$ $h(11) = h(15)$

$h(5) = h(21)$ $\qquad$ $h(12) = h(14)$

$h(6) = h(20)$ $\qquad$ $h(13) = h(13)$

Step 10: To Find $H(z)$

$$\begin{aligned} H(z) = &-0.01438(1+z^{-26})+0.01544(z^{-1}+z^{-25})+0.02635(z^{-2}+z^{-24}) \\ &- 1.075 \times 10^{-5}(z^{-3} + z^{-23}) - 0.0028(z^{-4} + z^{-22}) \\ &- 0.0179(z^{-5} + z^{-21}) + 0.01826(z^{-6} + z^{-20}) \\ &+ 0.029525(z^{-7} + z^{-19}) - 5.8419 \times 10^{-6}(z^{-8} + z^{-18}) \end{aligned}$$

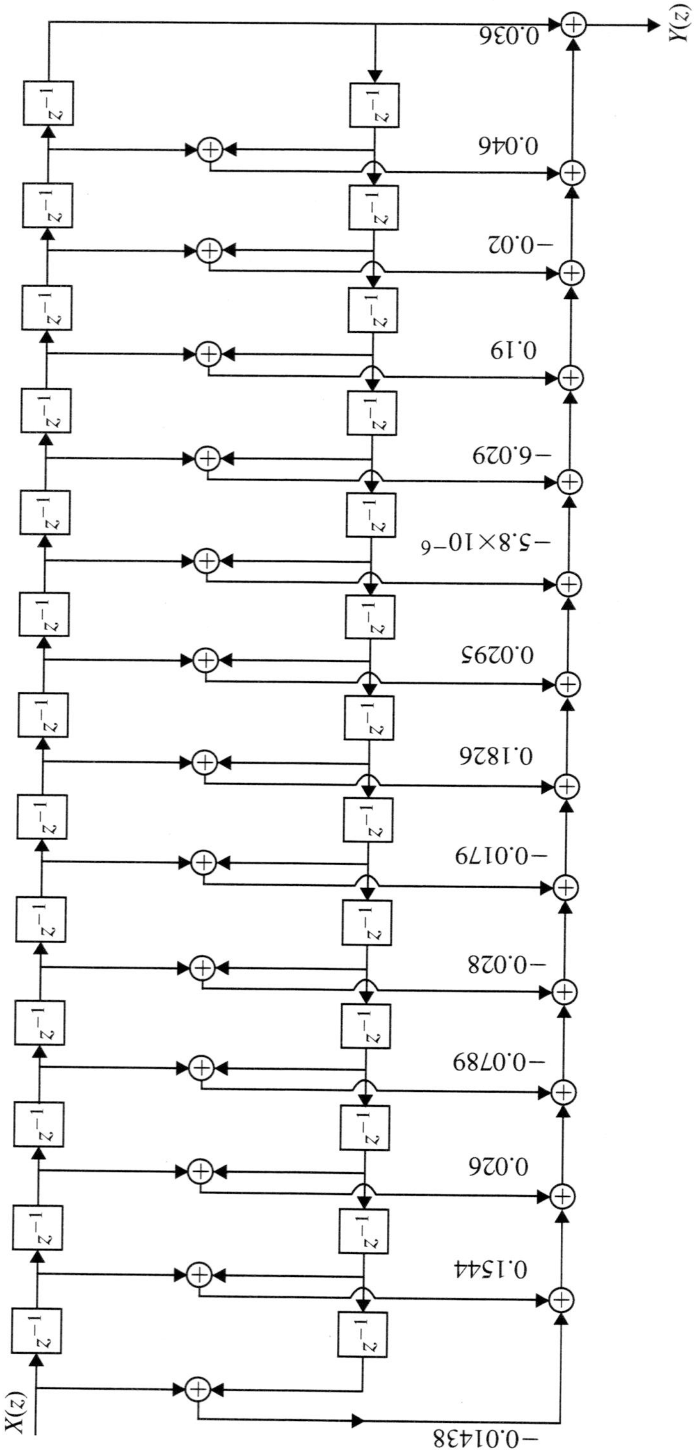

Figure 4.39 Linear phase realization of $H(z)$ for Example 4.17.

$$- 0.02998(z^{-9} + z^{-17}) - 0.01929(z^{-10} + z^{-16})$$
$$+0.02122(z^{-11}+z^{-15})+0.04658(z^{-12}+z^{-14})+0.036958(z^{-13})$$

Step 11: Draw the realisation structure. This is shown in Figure 4.39.

4.5.3 Frequency Sampling Method

In this method the ideal frequency response is sampled at sufficient number of points.

Let $h(n)$ be the filter coefficients of an FIR filter and $H(k)$ be the DFT of $h(n)$

$$H(k) = \sum_{k=0}^{N-1} h(n)e^{-j\frac{2\pi kn}{N}}, \qquad k = 0, 1, \ldots, N-1$$

$$h(n) = \frac{1}{N}\sum_{k=0}^{N-1} H(k)e^{j\frac{2\pi kn}{N}}, \qquad n = 0, 1, \ldots, N-1$$

The DFT samples $H(k)$ for an FIR sequence can be regarded as samples of the filter z-transform evaluated at N-points equally spaced around the unit circle.

$$H(k) = H(z)\Big|_{z=e^{j\frac{2\pi k}{N}}}$$

The transfer function $H(z)$ of an FIR filter is given by

$$H(z) = \sum_{n=0}^{N-1} h(n)z^{-n}$$

$$H(z) = \sum_{n=0}^{N-1}\left[\frac{1}{N}\sum_{k=0}^{N-1} H(k)e^{j\frac{2\pi kn}{N}}\right]z^{-n}$$

$$= \sum_{k=0}^{N-1}\frac{H(k)}{N}\sum_{k=0}^{N-1} H(k)\left(e^{j\frac{2\pi k}{N}}z^{-1}\right)^{n}$$

$$= \sum_{k=0}^{N-1}\frac{H(k)}{N}\frac{1-\left(e^{j\frac{2\pi k}{N}}z^{-1}\right)^{N}}{1-e^{\frac{j2\pi k}{N}}z^{-1}}$$

$$= \frac{1-z^{-N}}{N}\sum_{k=0}^{N-1}\frac{H(k)}{1-e^{\frac{j2\pi k}{N}}z^{-1}}$$

Using the following identity we get

$$H(e^{j\omega})\Big|_{\omega=\frac{2\pi k}{N}} = H(e^{j\frac{2\pi kn}{N}}) = H(k)$$

i.e., $H(k)$ is the kth DFT component obtained by sampling the frequency response $H(e^{j\omega})$. As such this approach for designing FIR filter is called the frequency sampling. There are two design procedures.

1. Type-1 design procedure.
2. Type-2 design procedure.

Type-1 Design Procedure

Step 1: Choose the desired frequency response $H_d(\omega)$.
Step 2: Sample $H_d(\omega)$ at 'N' points by taking $\omega = \frac{2\pi k}{N}$ and generate the sequence

$$\tilde{H}(k) = H_d(\omega)\big|_{\omega=\frac{2\pi k}{N}}, \qquad k = 0 \text{ to } N-1 \tag{4.103}$$

Step 3: Compute $h(n)$ using the following equations.

$$\text{When } N \text{ is odd } h(n) = \frac{1}{N}\left\{\tilde{H}(0) + 2\sum_{k=1}^{\frac{N-1}{2}} \text{Re}\left[\tilde{H}(k)e^{\frac{j2\pi kn}{N}}\right]\right\} \tag{4.104}$$

$$\text{When } N \text{ is even } h(n) = \frac{1}{N}\left\{\tilde{H}(0) + 2\sum_{k=1}^{(N/2)-1} \text{Re}\left[\tilde{H}(k)e^{\frac{j2\pi kn}{N}}\right]\right\} \tag{4.105}$$

Step 4: Take z-transform of $h(n)$

$$H(z) = \sum_{n=0}^{N-1} h(n)z^{-n} \tag{4.106}$$

Step 5: Draw the realisation structure.

Type-2 Design Procedure

Step 1: Choose the desired frequency response $H_d(\omega)$.
Step 2: Sample $H_d(\omega)$ at 'N' points by taking $\omega = \frac{\pi(2k+1)}{N}$ and generate the sequence, *i.e.*,

$$\tilde{H}(k) = H_d(\omega)\Big|_{\omega=\frac{\pi(2k+1)}{N}}, \qquad k = 0, 1, \ldots, N-1 \tag{4.107}$$

Step 3: Compute $h(n)$ using the following equations

$$\text{When } N \text{ is odd, } h(n) = \frac{2}{N}\left\{\sum_{k=0}^{\frac{N-3}{2}} \text{Re}\left[\tilde{H}(k)e^{\frac{jn\pi(2k+1)}{N}}\right]\right\} \tag{4.108}$$

$$\text{When } N \text{ is even, } h(n) = \frac{2}{N}\left\{\sum_{k=0}^{(N/2)-1} \text{Re}\left[\tilde{H}(k)e^{\frac{jn\pi(2k+1}{N}}\right]\right\} \tag{4.109}$$

Step 4: Take z-transform of $h(n)$

$$H(z) = \sum_{n=0}^{N-1} h(n) z^{-n} \tag{4.110}$$

Step 5: Draw the realisation structure.

Example 4.18

Determine the filters coefficient of a linear phase FIR filter of length $N = 15$, which has a symmetric unit sample response and a frequency response that satisfies the following conditions.

$$H_r\left(\frac{2\pi k}{15}\right) = \begin{cases} 1; & k = 0, 1, 2, 3 \\ 0.4; & k = 4 \\ 0; & k = 5, 6, 7 \end{cases}$$

(Anna University, May, 2007)

Solution

Step 1:

$$\tilde{H}(k) = H_d(\omega) \Big/ \omega = \frac{2\pi k}{15} = \begin{cases} 1e^{-j\omega\alpha}; & k = 0, 1, 2, 3 \\ 0.4e^{-j\omega\alpha}; & k = 4 \\ 0; & k = 5, 6, 7 \end{cases}$$

$$\alpha = \frac{N-1}{2} = 7$$

$$\tilde{H}(k) = \begin{cases} e^{-j\frac{2\pi k}{15}\cdot\alpha}; & k = 0, 1, 2, 3 \\ 0.4e^{-j\frac{2\pi k}{15}\alpha}; & k = 4 \\ 0; & k = 5, 6, 7 \end{cases}$$

Step 2: When

$$k = 0, \quad \tilde{H}(0) = 1$$

$$k = 1, \quad \tilde{H}(1) = e^{-j\frac{2\pi}{15}(1)\times 7} = e^{-j\frac{14\pi}{15}}$$

$$k = 2, \quad \tilde{H}(2) = e^{-j\frac{2\pi}{15}(2)\times 7} = e^{-j\frac{28\pi}{15}}$$

$$k = 3, \quad \tilde{H}(3) = e^{-j\frac{2\pi}{15}(3)\times 7} = e^{-j\frac{42\pi}{15}}$$

$$k = 4, \quad \tilde{H}(4) = 0.4e^{-j\frac{2\pi}{15}(4)\times 7} = 0.4e^{-j\frac{56\pi}{15}}$$

$$k = 5, \quad \tilde{H}(5) = 0$$

$$k = 6, \quad \tilde{H}(6) = 0$$

$$k = 7, \quad \tilde{H}(7) = 0$$

Step 3: To Find $h(n)$. Here $N = 15$ (odd)

$$\therefore\ h(n) = \frac{1}{N}\left[\tilde{H}(0) + 2\sum_{k=1}^{7}\text{Re}\left[\tilde{H}(k)e^{j\frac{2\pi kn}{N}}\right]\right]$$

$$h(n) = \frac{1}{15}\left[1 + 2\sum_{k=1}^{3}\text{Re}\left[e^{-j7\times\frac{2\pi k}{15}} \times e^{j\frac{2\pi nk}{15}}\right] + 2\text{Re}\left[0.4 \times e^{-j\frac{56\pi}{15}} \times e^{j\frac{2\pi nk}{15}}\right]\right]$$

$$= \frac{1}{15}\left[1 + 2\sum_{k=1}^{3}\cos\frac{2\pi k}{15}(n-7) + 0.8\cos\frac{8\pi}{15}(n-7)\right]$$

$$= \frac{1}{15} + \frac{2}{15}\cos\frac{2\pi}{15}(n-7) + \frac{2}{15}\cos\frac{4\pi}{15}(n-7) + \frac{2}{15}\cos\frac{6\pi}{15}(n-7) + \frac{0.8}{15}\cos\frac{8\pi}{15}(n-7)$$

$h(0) = -0.71155$

$h(1) = 0.575$

$h(2) = 0.973$

$h(3) = -0.499$

$h(4) = -1.6015$

$h(5) = 0.459$

$h(6) = 4.778$

$h(7) = 7.053$

$h(8) = 4.778$

$h(9) = 0.459$

$h(10) = -1.6015$

$h(11) = -0.499$

$h(12) = 0.973$

$h(13) = 0.575$

$h(14) = -0.71155$

Example 4.19

A lowpass filter is to be designed with the following desired frequency response

$$H_d(e^{j\omega}) = \begin{cases} e^{-j2\omega}, & -\pi/4 \le \omega \le \pi/4 \\ 0; & \pi/4 \le |\omega| \le \pi \end{cases}$$

Determine the filter coefficients $h_d(n)$ if window function

$$\omega(n) = \begin{cases} 1, & 0 \le n \le 4 \\ 0, & \text{otherwise} \end{cases}$$

(Anna University, December, 2007)

Solution Given

$$H_d(e^{j\omega}) = \begin{cases} e^{-j2\omega}, & -\pi/4 \le \omega \le \pi/4 \\ 0; & \pi/4 \le |\omega| \le \pi \end{cases}$$

$$h_d(n) = \frac{1}{2\pi}\int_{-\pi}^{\pi} H_d(e^{j\omega})e^{j\omega n}d\omega$$

$$= \frac{1}{2\pi}\int_{-\pi/4}^{\pi/4} e^{-j2\omega}.e^{j\omega n}d\omega$$

$$= \frac{1}{2\pi}\int_{-\pi/4}^{\pi/4} e^{j\omega(n-2)}d\omega$$

$$= \frac{1}{2\pi}\left[\frac{e^{j\omega(n-2)}}{j(n-2)}\right]_{-\pi/4}^{\pi/4}$$

$$= \frac{1}{2\pi}\left[\frac{e^{j(\pi/4)(n-2)} - e^{-j(\pi/4)(n-2)}}{j(n-2)}\right]$$

$$= \frac{1}{2\pi}\left[\frac{\sin(\pi/4)(n-2)}{(n-2)}\right] \qquad n \ne 2$$

From the given frequency response it is clear that

$$N - 1 = 4 \Rightarrow N = 5 \Rightarrow \alpha = \frac{N-1}{2} = 2$$

if $n = 2$. Apply L' Hospital's rule.

$$h_d(n) = \operatorname*{Lim}_{n\to 2} \frac{\cos(\pi/4)(n-2) - (\pi/4)}{\pi(-1)}$$

$$h_d(2) = 1 \cdot \frac{\pi/4}{\pi} = \frac{1}{4}$$

$$\therefore\ h_d(n) = \begin{cases} \frac{\sin(\pi/4)(n-2)}{\pi(n-2)}, & n \ne 2 \\ \frac{1}{4}, & n = 2 \end{cases}$$

To determine finite impulse response $h(n)$

$$h(n) = h_d(n)\omega(n) \qquad \left[\therefore\ \omega(n) = \begin{cases} 1, & 0 \le n \le 4 \\ 0, & \text{else} \end{cases}\right]$$

$$h(n) = \begin{cases} h_d(n), & 0 \le n \le 4 \\ 0, & \text{else} \end{cases}$$

Therefore, filter coefficients are

$$h(0) = \frac{\sin(\pi/4)(-2)}{\pi(n-2)} = 0.159$$

$$h(1) = \frac{\sin(\pi/4)(-1)}{\pi(-1)} = 0.225$$

$$h(2) = \frac{1}{4}$$

$$h(3) = \frac{\sin(\pi/4)(1)}{\pi(1)} = 0.225$$

$$h(4) = \frac{\sin(\pi/4)(2)}{\pi(2)} = 0.159$$

Example 4.20

A filter is to be designed with the following desired frequency response

$$H_d(e^{j\omega}) = \begin{cases} 0, & -\pi/4 \le \omega \le \pi/4 \\ e^{-j2\omega}; & \pi/4 \le |\omega| \le \pi \end{cases}$$

Determine the filter coefficients $h_d(n)$ using Hanning window with $N = 5$.

Solution Given

$$H_d(e^{j\omega}) = \begin{cases} 0, & -\pi/4 \le \omega \le \pi/4 \\ e^{-j2\omega}, & \pi/4 \le |\omega| \le \pi \end{cases}$$

$$h_d(n) = \frac{1}{2\pi}\int_{-\pi}^{\pi} H_d(e^{j\omega})e^{j\omega n}d\omega$$

$$= \frac{1}{2\pi}\left[\int_{-\pi}^{-\pi/4} e^{-j2\omega}\cdot e^{j\omega n}d\omega + \int_{\pi/4}^{\pi} e^{-j2\omega}\cdot e^{j\omega n}d\omega\right]$$

$$= \frac{1}{2\pi}\left[\int_{-\pi}^{-\pi/4} e^{j\omega(n-2)}d\omega + \int_{\pi/4}^{\pi} e^{j\omega(n-2)}d\omega\right]$$

$$= \frac{1}{2\pi}\left[\left[\frac{e^{j\omega(n-2)}}{j(n-2)}\right]_{-\pi}^{-(\pi/4)} + \left[\frac{e^{j\omega(n-2)}}{j(n-2)}\right]_{\pi/4}^{\pi}\right]$$

$$= \frac{1}{2\pi}\left[\frac{e^{-j(\pi/4)(n-2)} - e^{-j\pi(n-2)} + e^{j\pi(n-2)} - e^{j(\pi/4)(n-2)}}{j(n-2)}\right]$$

$$h_d(n) = \left[\frac{\sin\pi(n-2) - \sin(\pi/4)(n-2)}{\pi(n-2)}\right] \qquad n \ne 2$$

if $n = 2$. Apply L' Hospital's rule.

$$h_d(n) = \lim_{n\to 2} \frac{\cos\pi(n-2)(-\pi) - \cos(\pi/4)(n-2)[-(\pi/4)]}{\pi(-1)}$$

$$h_d(2) = \frac{\pi - (\pi/4)}{\pi} = \frac{(3\pi/4)}{4} = \frac{3}{4}$$

$$\therefore\ h_d(n) = \begin{cases} \frac{\sin\pi(n-2)-\sin(\pi/4)(n-2)}{\pi(n-2)}, & n \neq 2 \\ \frac{3}{4}, & n = 2 \end{cases}$$

To determine $h(n)$,

$$h(n) = h_d(n)\omega(n)$$

where

$$\omega_{\text{Han}}(n) = \begin{cases} 0.5 - 0.5\cos\frac{2\pi n}{N-1}, & 0 < n < N-1 \\ 0, & \text{otherwise} \end{cases}$$

Therefore

$$\omega_{\text{Han}}(n) = \begin{cases} 0.5 - 0.5\cos\frac{2\pi n}{4}, & 0 < n < 4 \\ 0, & \text{otherwise} \end{cases}$$

Therefore, the filter coefficients are,

$h_d(0) = -0.159$	$\omega(0) = 0$	$h(0) = 0$
$h_d(1) = -0.225$	$\omega(1) = 0.5$	$h(1) = -0.1125$
$h_d(2) = \frac{3}{4}$	$\omega(2) = 1$	$h(2) = \frac{3}{4}$
$h_d(3) = -0.225$	$\omega(3) = 0.5$	$h(3) = -0.1125$
$h_d(4) = -0.159$	$\omega(4) = 0$	$h(4) = 0$

Example 4.21

The desired response of a LPF is

$$H_d(e^{j\omega}) = \begin{cases} e^{-j3\omega}, & -3\pi/4 \le \omega \le 3\pi/4 \\ 0; & 3\pi/4 \le |\omega| \le \pi \end{cases}$$

Determine the frequency response of the filter for $N = 7$ using Hamming window.

(Anna University, December, 2003)

Solution Given

$$H_d(e^{j\omega}) = \begin{cases} e^{-j3\omega} & -3\pi/4 \le \omega \le 3\pi/4 \\ 0, & 3\pi/4 \le |\omega| \le \pi \end{cases}$$

$$h_d(n) = \frac{1}{2\pi}\int_{-3\pi/4}^{3\pi/4} e^{-j3\omega} e^{j\omega n} d\omega$$

$$= \frac{1}{2\pi}\left[\int_{-3\pi/4}^{3\pi/4} e^{j\omega(n-3)} d\omega\right]$$

$$= \frac{1}{2\pi}\left[\frac{e^{j\omega(n-3)}}{j(n-3)}\right]_{-3\pi/4}^{3\pi/4}$$

$$= \frac{1}{2\pi}\left[\frac{e^{j(3\pi/4)(n-3)} - e^{-j(3\pi/4)(n-3)}}{j(n-3)}\right]$$

$$h_d(n) = \left[\frac{\sin(3\pi/4)(n-3)}{\pi(n-3)}\right] \qquad n \ne 3$$

For $n = 3$, apply L' Hospital's rule.

$$h_d(n) = \operatorname*{Lim}_{n \to 3} \frac{\cos(3\pi/4)(n-3)[(3\pi/4) - 1]}{\pi(-1)}$$

$$h_d(3) = 1 \cdot \frac{(3\pi/4)}{\pi} = \frac{3}{4}$$

$$\therefore\ h_d(n) = \begin{cases} \frac{\sin(3\pi/4)(n-3)}{\pi(n-3)}, & n \ne 3 \\ \frac{3}{4}, & n = 3 \end{cases}$$

To determine $h(n)$,

$$h(n) = h_d(n)\omega(n) \quad \text{where } \omega_{\text{Ham}}(n) = \begin{cases} 0.54 - 0.46\cos\frac{2\pi n}{6}, & 0 < n < 6 \\ 0, & \text{otherwise} \end{cases}$$

Therefore, filter coefficients are

$h_d(0) = 0.0750$ $\quad \omega(0) = 0.08$ $\quad h(0) = 0.006$

$h_d(1) = -0.1592$ $\quad \omega(1) = 0.31$ $\quad h(1) = -0.0494$

$h_d(2) = 0.2251$ $\quad \omega(2) = 0.77$ $\quad h(2) = 0.1733$

$h_d(3) = 0.75$ $\quad \omega(3) = 1$ $\quad h(3) = 0.75$

$h_d(4) = 0.2251$ $\quad \omega(4) = 0.77$ $\quad h(4) = 0.1733$

$h_d(5) = -0.1592$ $\quad \omega(5) = 0.31$ $\quad h(5) = -0.0494$

$h_d(6) = 0.0750$ $\quad \omega(6) = 0.08$ $\quad h(6) = 0.006$

The transfer function of the system is,

$$H(z) = \sum_{n=0}^{N-1} h(n)z^{-n}$$

$$= h(0)z^{-0} + h(1)z^{-1} + h(2)z^{-2} + h(3)z^{-3} + h(4)z^{-4} + h(5)z^{-5} + h(6)z^{-6}$$

$$= h(0)[1 + z^{-6}] + h(1)[z^{-1} + z^{-5}] + h(2)[z^{-2} + z^{-4}] + h(3)z^{-3}$$

$$= 0.006[1 + z^{-6}] - 0.0494[z^{-1} + z^{-5}] + 0.1733[z^{-2} + z^{-4}] + 0.75z^{-3}$$

The frequency response of the filter is,

$$H(e^{j\omega}) = \left[h\left[\frac{N-1}{2}\right] + 2\sum_{n=1}^{\frac{N-1}{2}} h\left(\frac{N-1}{2} - n\right)\cos\omega n\right] e^{-j\omega\left(\frac{N-1}{2}\right)}$$

$$= \left[h(3) + 2\sum_{n=1}^{3} h(3-n)\cos\omega n\right] e^{-j3\omega}$$

$$= (h(3) + 2h(2)\cos\omega + 2h(1)\cos 2\omega + 2h(0)\cos 3\omega)e^{-j3\omega}$$

$$H(e^{j\omega}) = (0.75 + 0.3466\cos\omega - 0.0988\cos 2\omega + 0.012\cos 3\omega)e^{-j3\omega}$$

Magnitude response

$$H(e^{j\omega}) = 0.75 + 0.3466\cos\omega - 0.0988\cos 2\omega + 0.012\cos 3\omega$$

Phase response

$$\angle H(e^{j\omega}) = -3\omega$$

Example 4.22

A lowpass filter should have the frequency response given below. Find filter coefficients $h_d(n)$. Also determine τ if $h_d(n) = h_d(-n)$

$$H_d(e^{j\omega}) = \begin{cases} e^{-j\omega\tau}, & -\omega_c \le \omega \le \omega_c \\ 0; & \omega_c \le |\omega| \le \pi \end{cases}$$

Solution Given

$$H_d(e^{j\omega}) = \begin{cases} e^{-j\omega\tau} & -\omega_c \le \omega \le \omega_c \\ 0; & \omega_c \le |\omega| \le \pi \end{cases}$$

$$h_d(n) = \frac{1}{2\pi}\int_{-\omega_c}^{\omega_c} e^{-j\omega\tau} e^{j\omega n} d\omega$$

$$= \frac{1}{2\pi}\int_{-\omega_c}^{\omega_c} e^{j\omega(n-\tau)} d\omega$$

$$= \frac{1}{2\pi}\left[\frac{e^{j\omega(n-\tau)}}{j(n-\tau)}\right]_{-\omega_c}^{\omega_c}$$

$$= \frac{1}{2\pi}\left[\frac{e^{j\omega_c(n-\tau)} - e^{-j\omega_c(n-\tau)}}{j(n-\tau)}\right]$$

$$h_d(n) = \left[\frac{\sin\omega_c(n-\tau)}{\pi(n-\tau)}\right] \qquad n \neq \tau$$

if $n = \tau$; apply L' Hospital's rule

$$h_d(n) = \lim_{n\to\tau} \frac{\cos\omega_c(n-\tau)(-\omega_c)}{\pi(-1)}$$

$$h_d(\tau) = \frac{\omega_c}{\pi}$$

$$\therefore\ h_d(n) = \begin{cases} \frac{\sin\omega_c(n-\tau)}{\pi(n-\tau)}, & n \neq \tau \\ \frac{\omega_c}{\pi}, & n = \tau \end{cases}$$

To determine τ, given

$$h(n) = h_d(-n)$$

$$h_d(-n) = \frac{\sin\omega_c(n-\tau)}{\pi(n-\tau)} \Rightarrow \frac{-\sin\omega_c(n+\tau)}{-\pi(n+\tau)} = \frac{\sin\omega_c(n+\tau)}{\pi(n+\tau)}$$

$$= \frac{\sin\omega_c(n-\tau)}{\pi(n-\tau)} = \frac{\sin\omega_c(n+\tau)}{\pi(n+\tau)}$$

This exists only if

$$(n-\tau) = n+\tau$$

To achieve this τ should be 0.

$$\tau = 0$$

Example 4.23

A LPF has the desired response as given below:

$$H_d(e^{j\omega}) = \begin{cases} e^{-j3\omega}, & 0 \leq \omega \leq \pi/2 \\ 0; & \pi/2 \leq \omega \leq \pi \end{cases}$$

Determine filter coefficients $h(n)$ for $N = 7$ using type 1 frequency sampling technique.

Solution Given

$$H_d(e^{j\omega}) = \begin{cases} e^{-j3\omega}, & 0 \le \omega \le \pi/2 \\ 0, & \pi/2 \le \omega \le \pi \end{cases}$$

$$\tilde{H}(k) = H_d(\omega)\Big|_{\omega=\omega_k=\frac{2\pi k}{N}} \qquad k = 0, 1, \ldots, N-1$$

$$= H_d(\omega)\Big|_{\omega_k=\frac{2\pi k}{N}} \qquad k = 0, 1, \ldots, 6$$

The magnitude response is shown in Figure 4.40.

$$\omega_k = \frac{2\pi k}{7}$$

where $k = 0 \quad \omega_0 = 0$

$k = 1 \quad \omega_1 = \frac{2\pi}{7}$

$k = 2 \quad \omega_2 = \frac{4\pi}{7}$

$k = 3 \quad \omega_3 = \frac{6\pi}{7}$

$k = 4 \quad \omega_4 = \frac{8\pi}{7}$

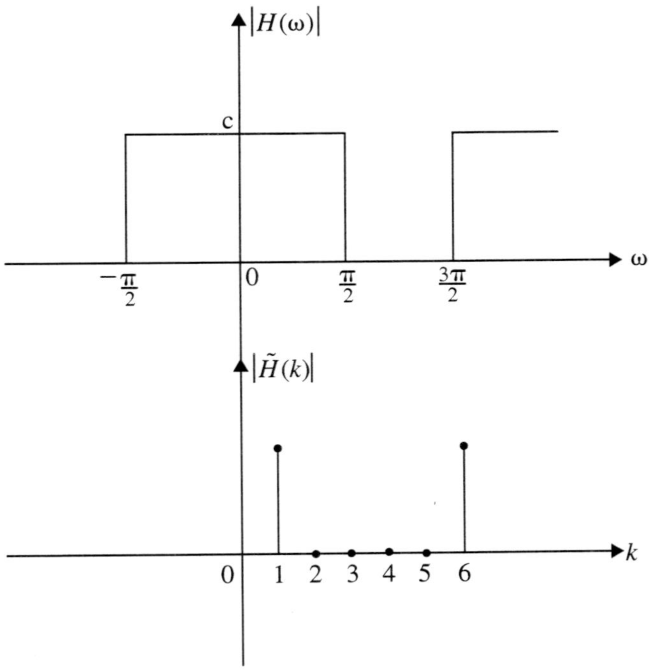

Figure 4.40 Magnitude response for Example 4.23.

$$k = 5 \qquad \omega_5 = \frac{10\pi}{7}$$

$$k = 6 \qquad \omega_6 = \frac{12\pi}{7} \rightarrow \omega_k > \frac{3\pi}{2}$$

$$\tilde{H}(k) = \begin{cases} e^{-j3\omega_k}, & k = 0, 1 \\ 0, & k = 2, 3, 4, 5 \\ e^{-j3\omega_k}, & k = 6 \end{cases}$$

$$= \begin{cases} e^{-j6\pi k/7}, & k = 0, 1 \\ 0, & k = 2, 3, 4, 5 \qquad \therefore N \text{ is odd} \\ e^{-j6\pi k/7}, & k = 6 \end{cases}$$

$$h(n) = \frac{1}{N}\left[\tilde{H}(0) + 2\sum_{k=1}^{\frac{N-1}{2}} \mathrm{Re}\left[\tilde{H}(k)e^{j\frac{2\pi kn}{N}}\right]\right]$$

$$= \frac{1}{7}\left[\tilde{H}(0) + 2\sum_{k=1}^{3} \mathrm{Re}\left[\tilde{H}(k)e^{j\frac{2\pi kn}{N}}\right]\right]$$

$$= \frac{1}{7}\left[\tilde{H}(0) + 2\sum_{k=1}^{3} \mathrm{Re}\left[e^{j\frac{-j6\pi k}{7}} \cdot e^{j\frac{2\pi kn}{7}}\right]\right]$$

$$= \frac{1}{7}\left[1 + 2\sum_{k=1} \mathrm{Re}\left[e^{j\frac{2\pi k}{7}(n-3)}\right]\right]$$

$$= \frac{1}{7}\left[1 + 2\sum_{k=1} \cos\frac{2\pi k}{7}(n-3)\right]$$

$$h(n) = \frac{1}{7}\left[1 + 2\cos\frac{2\pi}{7}(n-3)\right]$$

The filter coefficients are

$$h(0) = -0.11456$$

$$h(1) = 0.07927$$

$$h(2) = 0.321$$

$$h(3) = 0.4285$$

$$h(4) = h(2) = 0.321$$

$$h(5) = h(1) = 0.07927$$

$$h(6) = h(0) = -0.1145$$

Example 4.24

Design a high pass filter with frequency response

$$H_d(e^{j\omega}) = \begin{cases} e^{-j\omega\alpha}, & -\pi/4 \le \omega \le \pi \\ 0; & |\omega| \le \pi/4 \end{cases}$$

using (*i*) Hanning and (*ii*) Hamming window with $N = 11$.

Solution

Hanning Window

Step 1:

$$H_d(e^{j\omega}) = \begin{cases} e^{-j\omega\alpha}, & -\pi/4 \le \omega \le -\pi,\ \pi/4 \le \omega \le \pi \\ 0, & \text{otherwise} \end{cases}$$

Step 2:

$$\begin{aligned}
h_d(n) &= \frac{1}{2\pi}\left[\int_{-\pi}^{-\pi/4} e^{-j\omega\alpha}e^{j\omega n}d\omega + \int_{\pi/4}^{\pi} e^{-j\omega\alpha}e^{j\omega n}d\omega\right] \\
&= \frac{1}{2\pi}\left[\int_{-\pi}^{-\pi/4} e^{j\omega(n-\alpha)}d\omega + \int_{\pi/4}^{\pi} e^{j\omega(n-\alpha)}d\omega\right] \\
&= \frac{1}{2\pi}\left[\frac{e^{j\omega(n-\alpha)}}{j(n-\alpha)}\right]_{-\pi}^{-\pi/4} + \left[\frac{e^{j\omega(n-\alpha)}}{j(n-\alpha)}\right]_{\pi/4}^{\pi} \\
&= \frac{1}{2\pi}\left[\frac{e^{-j(\pi/4)(n-\alpha)} - e^{-j\pi(n-\alpha)} + e^{j\pi(n-\alpha)} - e^{j(\pi/4)(n-\alpha)}}{j(n-\alpha)}\right] \\
&= \frac{1}{2\pi j(n-\alpha)}2j\left[\sin\pi(n-\alpha) - \sin\frac{\pi}{4}(n-\alpha)\right]
\end{aligned}$$

$$h_d(n) = \frac{\sin\pi(n-\alpha) - \sin\frac{\pi}{4}(n-\alpha)}{\pi(n-\alpha)}, \qquad n \ne \alpha$$

When $n = \alpha$; apply L' hospital's rule.

$$\begin{aligned}
h_d(n) &= \lim_{n\to\alpha}\frac{\cos\pi(n-\alpha)\pi - \cos(\pi/4)(n-\alpha)\pi/4}{\pi} \\
&= \frac{\pi - (\pi/4)}{\pi} = 0.75
\end{aligned}$$

$$h_d(n) = \begin{cases} \frac{\sin\pi(n-\alpha) - \sin(\pi/4)(n-\alpha)}{\pi(n-\alpha)}, & n \ne \alpha \\ 0.75, & n = \alpha \end{cases}$$

Step 3:

$$h(d) = h_d(n) + \omega_H(n)$$

$$\omega_H(n) = \begin{cases} 0.5 - 0.5\cos\left(\frac{2\pi n}{N-1}\right), & 0 \le n \le N-1 \\ 0, & \text{otherwise} \end{cases}$$

$$\omega_H(n) = \begin{cases} 0.5 - 0.5\cos\left(\frac{\pi n}{5}\right), & 0 \le n \le 10 \\ 0, & \text{otherwise} \end{cases}$$

$$\omega_H(0) = 0 \qquad \omega_H(6) = 0.9045$$

$$\omega_H(1) = 0.0954 \qquad \omega_H(7) = 0.6545$$

$$\omega_H(2) = 0.3454 \qquad \omega_H(8) = 0.3454$$

$$\omega_H(3) = 0.6545 \qquad \omega_H(9) = 0.0954$$

$$\omega_H(4) = 0.9045 \qquad \omega_H(10) = 0$$

$$\omega_H(5) = 1$$

$$\alpha = \frac{N-1}{2} = 5$$

$$h_d(n) = \begin{cases} \frac{\sin\pi(n-5) - \sin(\pi/4)(n-5)}{\pi(n-5)}, & n \ne 5 \\ 0.75, & n = 5 \end{cases}$$

$$h_d(0) = \frac{\sin\pi(-5) - \sin(\pi/4)(-5)}{\pi(-5)} = 0.0450$$

$$h_d(1) = 0 \qquad h_d(6) = -0.225$$

$$h_d(2) = -0.075 \qquad h_d(6) = -0.159$$

$$h_d(3) = -0.159 \qquad h_d(6) = -0.075$$

$$h_d(4) = -0.225 \qquad h_d(6) = 0$$

$$h_d(5) = 0.75 \qquad h_d(6) = 0.0450$$

$$h(n) = h_d(n)\omega_H(n)$$

$$h(0) = 0.045 \times 0 = 0$$

$$h(1) = 0 \times 0.0954 = 0$$

$$h(2) = -0.075 \times 0.3454 = -0.0259$$

$$h(3) = -0.159 \times 0.6545 = -0.104$$

$$h(4) = -0.225 \times 0.9045 = -0.203$$

$$h(5) = 0.75 \times 1 = 0.75$$

$$h(6) = -0.225 \times 0.9045 = -0.203$$
$$h(7) = -0.159 \times 0.6545 = -0.104$$
$$h(8) = -0.075 \times 0.3454 = -0.0259$$
$$h(9) = 0 \times 0.954 = 0$$
$$h(10) = 0.045 \times 0 = 0$$

Step 4:

$$H(z) = \sum_{n=0}^{10} h(n)z^{-n}$$
$$H(z) = -0.0259[z^{-2} + z^{-8}] - 0.104[z^{-3} + z^{-7}] - 0.203[z^{-4} + z^{-6}] + 0.75z^{-5}$$

Step 5: The structure realization is shown in Figure 4.40(a).

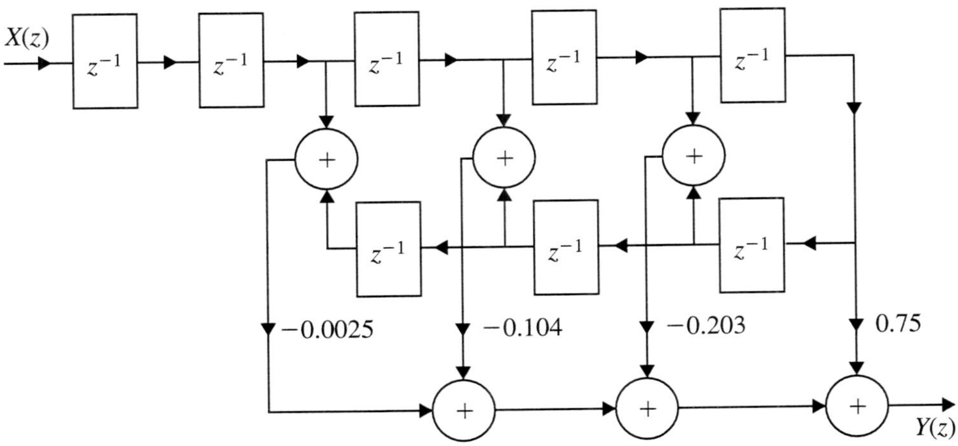

Figure 4.40 (a) Structure realization for Example 4.24.

Hamming Window

Step 1:

$$H_d(e^{j\omega}) = \begin{cases} e^{-j\omega\alpha}, & -\pi/4 \leq \omega \leq -\pi,\ \pi/4 \leq \omega \leq \pi \\ 0, & \text{otherwise} \end{cases}$$

Step 2:

$$h_d(n) = \begin{cases} \frac{\sin(n-\alpha) - \sin(\pi/4)(n-\alpha)}{\pi(n-\alpha)}, & n \neq \alpha \\ 0.75, & n = \alpha \end{cases}$$

Step 3:

$$h(d) = h_d(n)\omega_H(n)$$

$$\omega_H(n) = \begin{cases} 0.54 - 0.46\cos\left(\frac{2\pi n}{N-1}\right), & 0 \le n \le N-1 \\ 0.54 - 0.46\cos\left(\frac{\pi n}{5}\right), & 0 \le n \le 10 \end{cases}$$

$$\omega_H(0) = 0.08 \qquad \omega_H(6) = 0.9121$$
$$\omega_H(1) = 0.1678 \qquad \omega_H(7) = 0.6821$$
$$\omega_H(2) = 0.3978 \qquad \omega_H(8) = 0.3978$$
$$\omega_H(3) = 0.6821 \qquad \omega_H(9) = 0.1678$$
$$\omega_H(4) = 0.9121 \qquad \omega_H(10) = 0.08$$
$$\omega_H(5) = 1$$

$$h(n) = h_d(n)\omega_H(n) \quad [\because\ h_d(n) \text{ same as above problem}]$$

$$h(0) = 0.045 \times 0.08 = 0.0036$$
$$h(1) = 0 \times 0.1678 = 0$$
$$h(2) = -0.075 \times 0.3978 = -0.0298$$
$$h(3) = -0.159 \times 0.6821 = -0.1084$$
$$h(4) = -0.225 \times 0.9121 = -0.2052$$
$$h(5) = 0.75 \times 1 = 0.75$$
$$h(6) = -0.255 \times 0.9121 = -0.2052$$
$$h(7) = -0.159 \times 0.6821 = -0.1084$$
$$h(8) = -0.075 \times 0.3978 = -0.0298$$
$$h(9) = 0 \times 0.1678 = 0$$
$$h(10) = 0.045 \times 0.08 = 0.0036$$

Step 4:

$$H(z) = \sum_{n=0}^{N-1} h(n)z^{-n} = \sum_{n=0}^{10} h(n)z^{-n}$$

$$H(z) = 0.0036[1 + z^{-10}] - 0.0298[z^{-2} + z^{-8}] - 0.1084[z^{-3} + z^{-7}] - 0.2052[z^{-4} + z^{-6}] + 0.75z^{-5}$$

Step 5: The structure realization is shown in Figure 4.40(b).

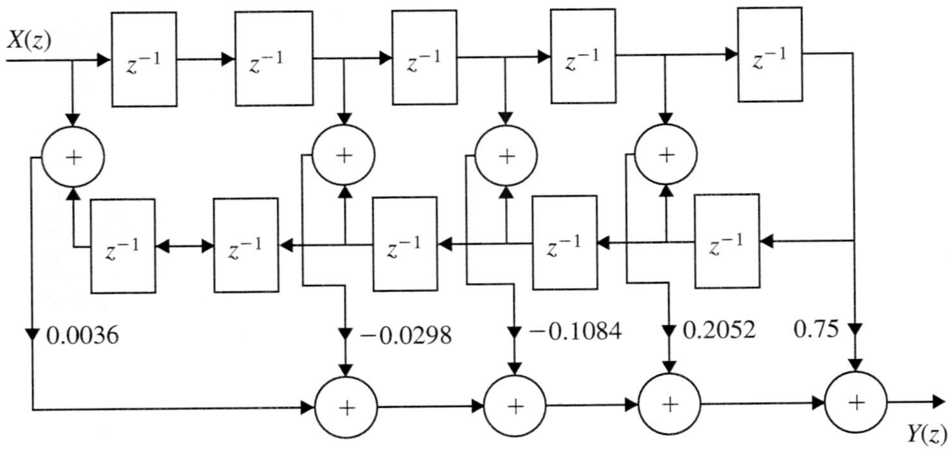

Figure 4.40 (*b*) Structure realization for Example 4.24.

Example 4.25

Design an ideal differentiator with frequency response

$$H(e^{j\omega}) = j\omega, \qquad -\pi \le \omega \le \pi$$

using (*i*) Rectangular and (*ii*) Hamming window with $N = 8$. For both cases plot magnitude response.

(*Anna University, December, 2006*)

Solution

Rectangular Window

Step 1:

$$H(e^{j\omega}) = j\omega = e^{j(\pi/2)}\omega$$
$$H(e^{j\omega}) = e^{j(\pi/2)}e^{-j\alpha\omega}H(e^{j\omega}), \quad \alpha = 0$$
$$H_d(e^{j\omega}) = j\omega e^{-j\omega\alpha} \quad \text{for } -\pi \le \omega \le \pi,\ N = 8$$

Step 2:

$$h_d(n) = \frac{1}{2\pi}\int_{-\pi}^{\pi} j\omega e^{-j\omega\alpha} e^{j\omega n} d\omega$$
$$= \frac{1}{2\pi}j\int_{-\pi}^{\pi} \omega e^{j\omega(n-\alpha)} d\omega$$
$$= \frac{1}{2\pi}\left[\frac{\omega e^{j\omega(n-\alpha)}}{j(n-\alpha)}\right]_{-\pi}^{\pi} - \left[\frac{e^{j\omega(n-\alpha)}}{[j(n-\alpha)]^2}\right]_{-\pi}^{\pi}$$

$$= \frac{1}{2\pi}\left[\frac{\omega e^{j\omega(n-\alpha)}}{j(n-\alpha)} - \frac{e^{j\omega(n-\alpha)}}{[j(n-\alpha)]^2}\right]_{-\pi}^{\pi}$$

$$= \frac{1}{2\pi}\left[\frac{\pi e^{j\pi(n-\alpha)}}{j(n-\alpha)} - \frac{e^{j\pi(n-\alpha)}}{j^2(n-\alpha)^2} - \frac{(-\pi)e^{-j\pi(n-\alpha)}}{j(n-\alpha)} + \frac{e^{-j\pi(n-\alpha)}}{j(n-\alpha)^2}\right]$$

$$= \frac{1}{2\pi}\left[\pi\frac{2\cos\pi(n-\alpha)}{j(n-\alpha)} + \frac{2j\sin\pi(n-\alpha)}{(n-\alpha)^2}\right]$$

$$h_d(n) = \frac{\cos\pi(n-\alpha)}{n-\alpha} - \frac{\sin\pi(n-\alpha)}{\pi(n-\alpha)^2} \quad \text{where } N = \text{even}$$

$$h_d(n) = \frac{-\sin\pi(n-\alpha)}{\pi(n-\alpha)^2}$$

Step 3:

$$h(n) = h_d(n)\omega_H(n)$$
$$\omega_H(n) = 1$$
$$h(n) = h_d(n)$$

$h_d(n)$ is anti-symmetry. So

$$h_d(n) = -h_d(N-1-n)$$

where

$$\alpha = (N-1)/2 = \frac{7}{2}.$$

$$h_d(0) = -h_d(7) = \frac{-\sin(-7/2)\pi}{\pi(-7/2)} = -0.026$$
$$h_d(1) = -h_d(6) = 0.0509$$
$$h_d(2) = -h_d(5) = -0.1415$$
$$h_d(3) = -h_d(4) = 1.27$$
$$h(n) = h_d(n)$$
$$h_d(0) = -h_d(7) = -0.026$$
$$h_d(1) = -h_d(6) = 0.0509$$
$$h_d(2) = -h_d(5) = -0.1415$$
$$h_d(3) = -h_d(4) = 1.27$$

Step 4:

$$H(z) = \sum_{n=0}^{7} h(n)z^{-n}$$
$$= -0.026[1 - z^{-7}] + 0.0509[z^{-1} - z^{-6}] - 0.1415[z^{-2} - z^{-5}] + 1.27[z^{-3} - z^{-4}]$$

Step 5: The structure realized as shown in Figure 4.41(a).

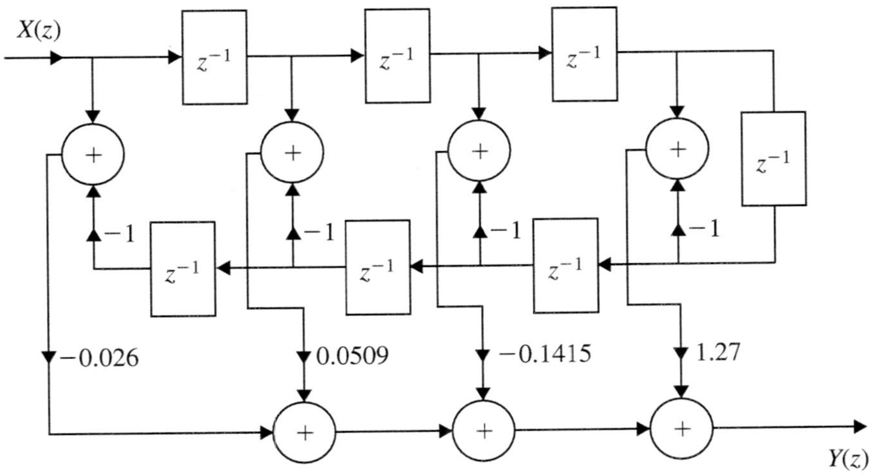

Figure 4.41 (a) Structure realization (rectangular window) for Example 4.25.

Frequency response of ideal differentiator for antisymmetric impulse response and $N =$ even is,

$$H(e^{j\omega}) = \sum_{n=1}^{\frac{N}{2}} d(n) \sin \omega \left(n - \frac{1}{2}\right)$$

where

$$d(n) = \sum_{n=1}^{\frac{N}{2}} 2h\left(\frac{N}{2} - n\right)$$

$$d(1) = 2h\left(\frac{N}{2} - 1\right) = 2h(4-1) = 2h(3) = 2.54$$
$$d(2) = 2h(4-2) = 2h(2) = -0.283$$
$$d(3) = 2h(4-3) = 2h(1) = 0.1010$$
$$d(4) = 2h(0) = -0.52$$

$$H(e^{j\omega}) = d(1)\sin\frac{\omega}{2} + d(2)\sin\frac{3\omega}{2} + d(3)\sin\frac{5\omega}{2} + d(4)\sin\frac{7\omega}{2}$$
$$= 2.54\sin\frac{\omega}{2} - 0.283\sin\frac{3\omega}{2} + 0.1010\sin\frac{5\omega}{2} - 0.52\sin\frac{7\omega}{2}$$
$$H(e^{j\omega}) = j\left(2.54\sin\frac{\omega}{2} - 0.283\sin\frac{3\omega}{2} + 0.1010\sin\frac{5\omega}{2} - 0.52\sin\frac{7\omega}{2}\right)$$

ω deg/sec	0	20	40	60	80	100	180	240	270	360
$H(e^{j\omega})$	0	$j0.5839$	$j0.3889$	$j1.2975$	$j0.5795$	$j1.9945$	$j3.444$	$j1.662$	$j1.89$	0

The frequency response plot is shown in Figure 4.41(b).

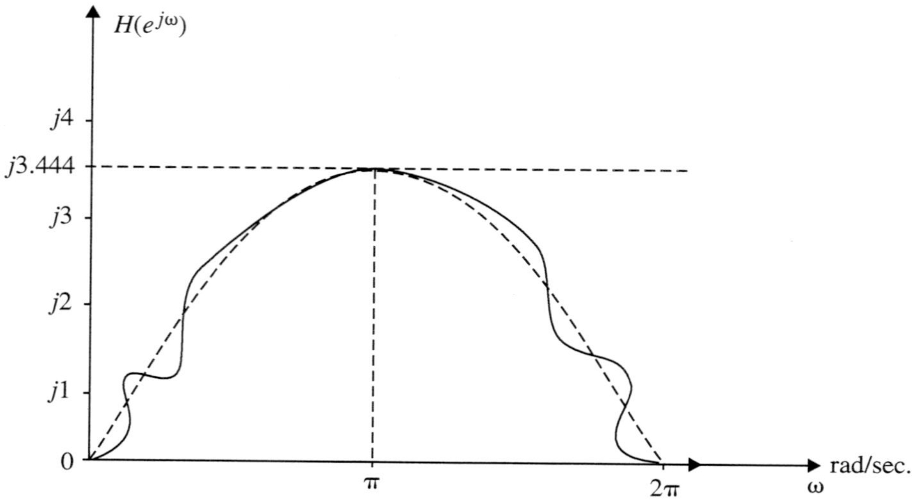

Figure 4.41 (b) Frequency response plot.

Hamming Window

Steps 1 and 2: Same as Rectangular window.
Step 3:

$$\omega_H(n) = \begin{cases} 0.54 - 0.46\cos\left(\frac{2\pi n}{N-1}\right), & 0 \le n \le N-1 \\ 0.54 - 0.46\left(\cos\frac{\pi n}{5}\right), & 0 \le n \le N \end{cases}$$

$$\omega_H(0) = \omega_H(7) = 0.08$$
$$\omega_H(1) = \omega_H(6) = 0.2532$$
$$\omega_H(2) = \omega_H(5) = 0.6424$$
$$\omega_H(3) = \omega_H(4) = 0.954$$

$h_d(n)$ same as above.

$$h(0) = -h(7) = h_d(0)\omega_H(0) = -0.0021$$
$$h(1) = -h(6) = h_d(1)\omega_H(1) = 0.0129$$
$$h(2) = -h(5) = h_d(2)\omega_H(2) = -0.0909$$
$$h(3) = -h(4) = h_d(3)\omega_H(3) = 1.2152$$

Step 4:

$$H(z) = -0.0021[1 - z^{-7}] + 0.0129[z^{-1} - z^{-6}] - 0.0909[z^{-2} - z^{-5}] + 1.2152[z^{-3} - z^{-4}]$$

Step 5: The structure realization is shown in Figure 4.41(c).

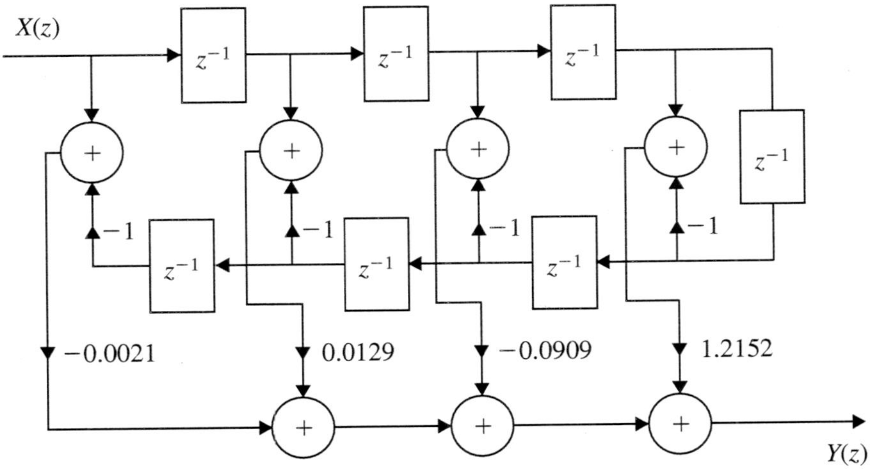

Figure 4.41 (c) Structure realization (Hamming window) for Example 4.25.

Frequency response

$$\bar{H}(e^{j\omega}) = \sum_{n=1}^{\frac{N}{2}} d(n) \sin\left(n - \frac{1}{2}\right)\omega$$

where

$$d(n) = \sum_{n=1}^{\frac{N}{2}} 2h\left(\frac{N}{2} - n\right)$$

$$= \sum_{n=1}^{4} 2h(4 - n)$$

$$d(1) = 2h(4-1) = 2h(3) = 2.4304$$

$$d(2) = 2h(4-2) = 2h(2) = -0.1818$$

$$d(3) = 2h(4-3) = 2h(1) = 0.0258$$

$$d(4) = 2h(0) = -0.0042$$

$$\bar{H}(e^{j\omega}) = d(1)\sin\frac{\omega}{2} + d(2)\sin\frac{3\omega}{2} + d(3)\sin\frac{5\omega}{2} + d(4)\sin\frac{7\omega}{2}$$

$$= 2.4304\sin\frac{\omega}{2} - 0.1818\sin\frac{3\omega}{2} + 0.0258\sin\frac{5\omega}{2} - 0.0042\sin\frac{7\omega}{2}$$

$$H(e^{j\omega}) = j\bar{H}(e^{j\omega})$$

$$= j\left(2.4304\sin\frac{\omega}{2} - 0.1818\sin\frac{3\omega}{2} + 0.0258\sin\frac{5\omega}{2} - 0.0042\sin\frac{7\omega}{2}\right)$$

ω deg/sec.	0	45	90	120	180	240	270	315	360
$\lvert H(e^{j\omega})\rvert$	0	$j0.7875$	$j1.568$	$j2.078$	$j2.6422$	$j2.078$	$j1.568$	$j0.7875$	0

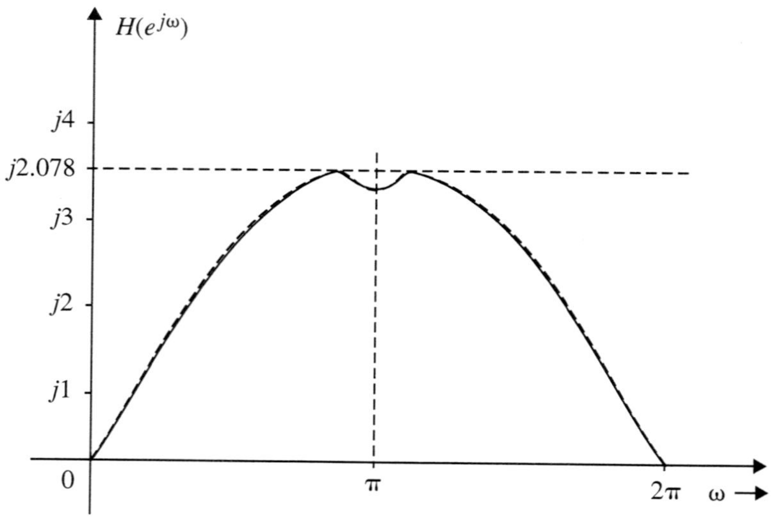

Figure 4.41 (*d*)

Example 4.26

Design an ideal Hilbert transformer having frequency response

$$H(e^{j\omega}) = \begin{cases} j, & -\pi \le \omega \le 0 \\ -j, & 0 \le \omega \le \pi \end{cases}$$

using (*i*) Rectangular window and (*ii*) Blackman window with $N = 11$.

(*Anna University, May, 2007*)

Solution

Step 1:

$$H(e^{j\omega}) = \begin{cases} j, & -\pi \leq \omega \leq 0 \\ -j, & 0 \leq \omega \leq \pi \end{cases}$$

Step 2:

$$\begin{aligned}
h_d(n) &= \frac{1}{2\pi}\left[\int_{-\pi}^{0} je^{j\omega n}d\omega + \int_{0}^{\pi} -je^{j\omega n}d\omega\right] \\
&= \frac{j}{2\pi}\left[\left[\frac{e^{j\omega n}}{jn}\right]_{-\pi}^{0} - \left[\frac{e^{j\omega n}}{jn}\right]_{0}^{\pi}\right] \\
&= \frac{j}{2\pi}\frac{1}{jn}\left[\left[e^{0} - e^{-j\pi n} - e^{j\pi n} + e^{0}\right]\right] \\
&= \frac{1}{2\pi n}\left[2 - e^{j\pi n} + e^{-j\pi n}\right] \\
&= \frac{1}{2\pi n}\left[2 - 2\cos\pi n\right] \\
&= \frac{1-\cos\pi n}{\pi n} = \begin{cases} \frac{2\sin^2(\frac{\pi n}{2})}{\pi n}, & n \neq 0 \\ 0, & n = 0 \end{cases}
\end{aligned}$$

$$h_d(n) = \frac{1-\cos\pi n}{\pi n} \quad \therefore\ h_d(n) \text{ is antisymmetry}$$

$$h_d(0) = \frac{1-\cos 0}{\pi 0} = 0$$

$$h_d(1) = \frac{1-\cos\pi}{\pi} = \frac{2}{\pi} = -h_d(-1)$$

$$h_d(2) = 0 = -h_d(-2)$$

$$h_d(3) = \frac{2}{3\pi} = -h_d(-3)$$

$$h_d(4) = 0 = -h_d(-4)$$

$$h_d(5) = \frac{2}{5\pi} = -h_d(-5)$$

Step 3:

$$h(n) = h_d(n)\omega_H(n) \quad (\text{where } \omega_h(n) = 1)$$

$$h(n) = h_d(n)$$

$$h(0) = 0$$

$$h(1) = -h(-1) = \frac{2}{\pi}$$

$$h(2) = -h(-2) = 0$$

$$h(3) = -h(-3) = \frac{2}{3\pi}$$
$$h(4) = -h(-4) = 0$$
$$h(5) = -h(-5) = \frac{2}{5\pi}$$

Step 4:

$$H(Z) = z^{-5} \sum_{n=-5}^{5} h(n) z^{-n}$$
$$= z^{-5}\left[\frac{2}{\pi}[z - z^{-1}] + \frac{2}{3\pi}[z^3 - z^{-3}] + \frac{2}{5\pi}[z^5 - z^{-5}]\right]$$
$$= \frac{2}{\pi}[z^{-4} - z^{-6}] + \frac{2}{3\pi}[z^{-2} - z^{-8}] + \frac{2}{5\pi}[1 - z^{-10}]$$

Step 5: The structure realization is shown in Figure 4.42(a)

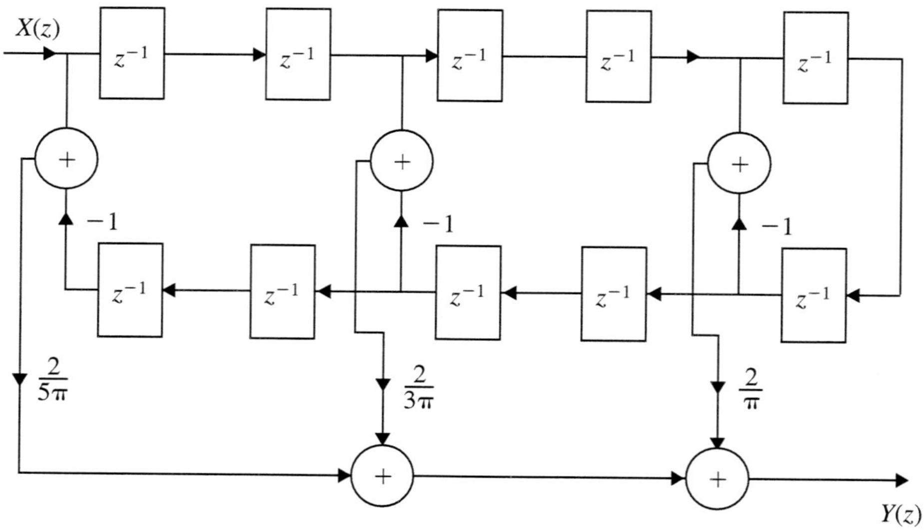

Figure 4.42 (a) Structure realization (rectangular window) for Example 4.26.

Blackman Window

Step 1 and 2: Same as Rectangular window.
Step 3:

$$\omega_B(n) = 0.42 + 0.5\cos\frac{\pi n}{5} + 0.08\cos\frac{2\pi n}{5} \qquad \text{for} -5 \le n \le 5$$
$$\omega_B(0) = 1$$
$$\omega_B(1) = \omega_B(-1) = 0.849$$

$$\omega_B(2) = \omega_B(-2) = 0.509$$
$$\omega_B(3) = \omega_B(-3) = 0.2$$
$$\omega_B(4) = \omega_B(-4) = 0.4$$
$$\omega_B(5) = \omega_B(-5) = 0$$

$$h(n) = h_d(n)\omega_B(n)$$
$$h(0) = 0$$
$$h(1) = -h(-1) = \left(\frac{2}{\pi}\right)0.849 = 0.5405$$
$$h(2) = -h(-2) = 0 = 0$$
$$h(3) = -h(-3) = \left(\frac{2}{3\pi}\right)0.2 = 0.0423$$
$$h(4) = -h(-4) = 0 = 0$$
$$h(5) = -h(-5) = \left(\frac{2}{5\pi}\right)0 = 0$$

Step 4:

$$H(z) = z^{-5}\sum_{n=-5}^{5} h(n)z^{-n}$$
$$= z^{-5}[0.54(z - z^{-1}) + 0.0424(z^3 - z^{-3})]$$
$$= 0.54[z^{-4} - z^{-6}] + 0.0424[z^{-2} - z^{-8}]$$

Step 5: The structure realization is shown in Figure 4.42(b)

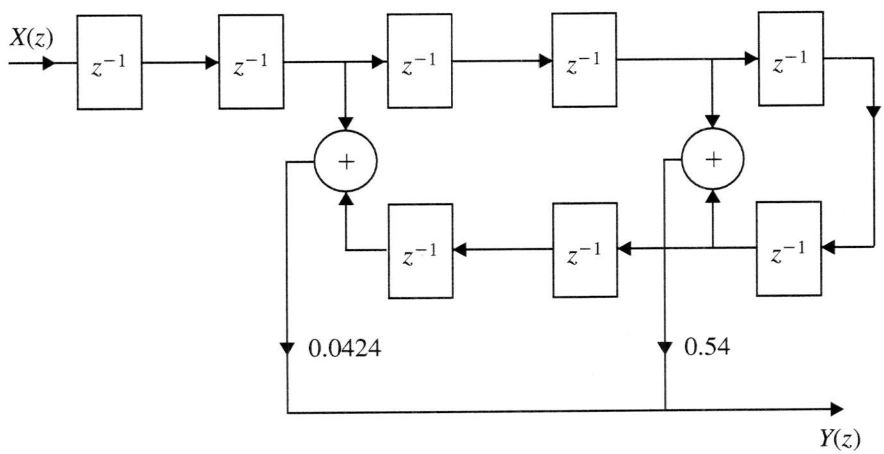

Figure 4.42 (b) Structure realization (Blackmann window) for Example 4.26.

Example 4.27

Using a rectangular window technique design a low pass filter with passband gain of unity, cut off frequency of 100 Hz and working at a sampling frequency of 5 kHz. The length of the impulse response should be 7.

(Anna University, May, 2007)

Solution Given $f_c = 1000$ Hz, $F = 5000$ Hz

$$H_d(e^{i\omega}) = \begin{cases} 1, & -\omega_c \le \omega \le \omega_c \\ 0, & -\pi \le -\omega \le -\omega_c \text{ and } \omega_c \le \omega \le \pi \end{cases}$$

where

$$\begin{aligned} \omega_c &= 2\pi f_c \\ &= 2\pi \times 1000.T \end{aligned}$$

$$\boxed{\omega_c = \frac{2000\pi}{5000} = \frac{2\pi}{5}}$$

The desired frequency response of the LPF is shown in Figure 4.43(*a*).

The filter coefficients are given by

$$\begin{aligned} h_d(n) &= \frac{1}{2\pi}\int_{-\pi}^{\pi} H_d(e^{j\omega}).e^{j\omega n} d\omega \\ &= \frac{1}{2\pi}\int_{-\omega c}^{\omega c} e^{j\omega n} d\omega \\ &= \frac{1}{2\pi}\int_{\frac{-2\pi}{5}}^{\frac{2\pi}{5}} e^{j\omega n} d\omega \end{aligned}$$

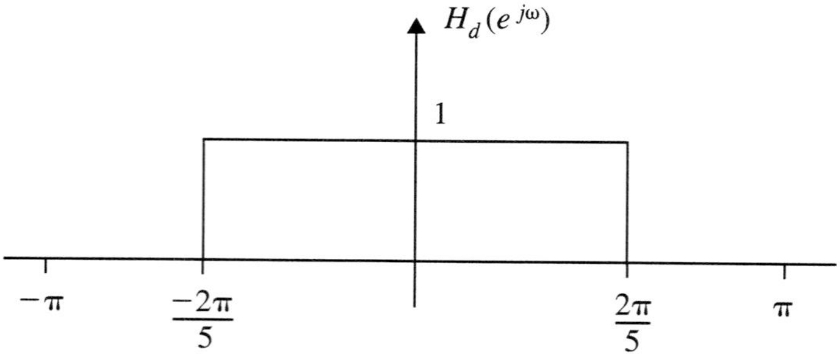

Figure 4.43 (*a*) Frequency Response of for Example 4.27.

$$= \frac{1}{2\pi}\left[\frac{e^{j\omega n}}{jn}\right]_{\frac{-2\pi}{5}}^{\frac{2\pi}{5}}$$

$$= \frac{1}{n\pi}\left[\frac{e^{\frac{j2\pi n}{5}} - e^{\frac{-j2\pi n}{5}}}{2j}\right]$$

$$h_d(n) = \frac{\sin\frac{2\pi n}{5}}{n\pi}, -\infty \le n \le \infty$$

The rectangular window for $N = 7$ is given by

$$\omega_R(n) = \begin{cases} 1, & -3 \le n \le 3 \\ 0, & \text{otherwise} \end{cases}$$

The filter coefficient

$$h(n) = h_d(n) \times \omega_R(n)$$

$$h_(n) = \begin{cases} h_d(n), & -3 \le n \le 3 \\ 0, & \text{otherwise} \end{cases}$$

For $n = 0$,

$$h(0) = h_d(0) = \lim_{n\to 0} \frac{\sin\frac{2\pi n}{5}}{n\pi}$$

$$= \lim_{n\to 0} \frac{2}{5}\frac{\sin\frac{2\pi n}{5}}{\frac{2\pi n}{5}}$$

$$= \lim_{n\to 0} \frac{2}{5}$$

$$h(0) = \frac{2}{5}$$

For $n = 1$;

$$h(1) = h(-1) = \frac{\sin\frac{2\pi}{5}}{\pi} = 0.3027$$

For $n = 2$;

$$h(2) = h(-2) = \frac{\sin\frac{4\pi}{5}}{2\pi} = 0.0935$$

For $n = 3$;

$$h(3) = h(-3) = \frac{\sin\frac{6\pi}{5}}{3\pi} = -0.06236$$

The filter coefficients of realizable filter are:

$$h(0) = h(6) = -0.06236$$
$$h(1) = h(5) = 0.0935$$
$$h(2) = h(4) = 0.3027$$
$$h(3) = 0.4$$

It is symmetric about $\alpha = \frac{N-1}{2} = \frac{7-1}{2} = 3$. The transfer function of realizable filter is

$$\begin{aligned} H(z) &= \sum_{n=0}^{N-1} h(n)z^{-n} \\ &= \sum_{n=0}^{6} h(n)z^{-n} \\ &= h(0) + h(1)z^{-1} + h(2)z^{-2} + h(3)z^{-3} \\ &\quad + h(4)z^{-4} + h(5)z^{-5} + h(6)z^{-6} \\ H(z) &= \frac{Y(z)}{X(z)} \\ &= h(0)[1 + z^{-6}] + h(1)[z^{-1} + z^{-5}] + h(2)[z^{-2} \\ &\quad + z^{-4}] + h(3)z^{-3} \\ Y(z) &= -0.06236[1 + z^{-6}]X(z) + 0.0935[z^{-1} + z^{-5}]X(z) \\ &\quad + 0.3027[z^{-2} + z^{-4}]X(z) + 0.4z^{-3}X(z) \end{aligned}$$

Linear phase realization of the filter is shown in Figure 4.43(b).

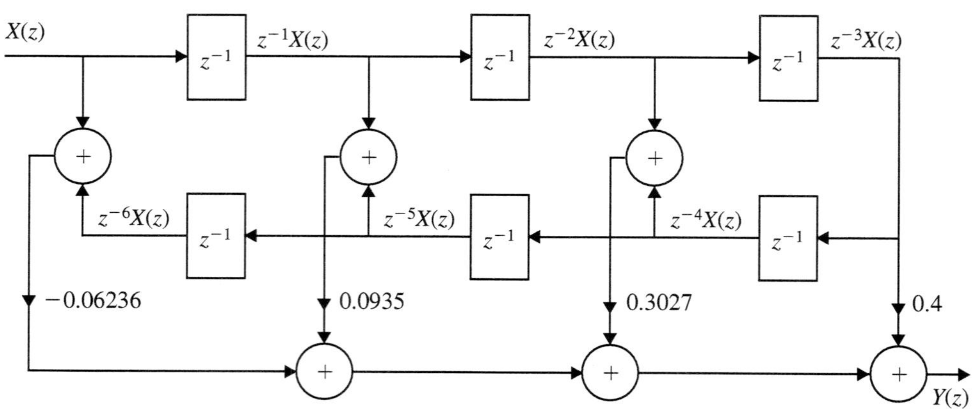

Figure 4.43 (b) Linear phase realization of FIR filter for Example 4.27.

Example 4.28

Design a bandpass filter which approximates the ideal filter with cut off frequencies at 0.2 rad/sec and 0.3 rad/sec.The filter order is $N = 7$. Use Hamming window.

(Anna University, December, 2007)

Solution Given $\omega c_1 = 0.2$ rad/sec, $\omega c_2 = 0.3$ rad/sec, $N = 7$.

Step 1: Choose $H_d(\omega)$ ideal filter such that

$$H_d(\omega) = \begin{cases} 1, & -\omega c_2 \leq \omega \leq -\omega c_1 \text{ and } \omega c_1 \leq \omega \leq -\omega c_2 \\ 0, & \text{otherwise} \end{cases}$$

Step 2: To Find $h_d(n)$

$$\begin{aligned}
h_d(n) &= \frac{1}{2\pi}\left[\int_{-\omega c_2}^{-\omega c_1} H_d(\omega)e^{j\omega n}d\omega + \int_{\omega c_1}^{\omega c_2} H_d(\omega)e^{j\omega n}d\omega\right] \\
&= \frac{1}{2\pi}\left[\int_{-0.3}^{-0.2} e^{j\omega n}d\omega + \int_{0.2}^{0.3} ej\omega nd\omega\right] \\
&= \frac{1}{2\pi}\left[\left[\frac{e^{j\omega n}}{jn}\right]_{-0.3}^{-0.2} + \left[\frac{e^{j\omega n}}{jn}\right]_{0.2}^{0.3}\right] \\
&= \frac{1}{2n\pi j}\left[e^{-j0.2n} - e^{-j0.3n} + e^{j0.3n} - e^{j0.2n}\right] \\
&= \frac{1}{n\pi}\left[\frac{e^{j0.3n} - e^{-j0.3n}}{2j} - \frac{e^{j0.2n} - e^{-j0.2n}}{2j}\right] \\
&= \frac{1}{n\pi}[\sin 0.3n - \sin 0.2n] \\
h_d(n) &= \frac{1}{n\pi}[\sin 0.3n - \sin 0.2n]
\end{aligned}$$

Step 3: To Find $h(n)$

$$h(n) = h_d(n) \times \omega_H(n)$$

Hamming window function is,

$$\omega_H(n) = \begin{cases} 0.54 + 0.46\cos(\frac{2\pi n}{N-1}) & -\frac{(N-1)}{2} \leq n \leq \frac{(N-1)}{2} \\ 0, & \text{otherwise} \end{cases}$$

$$\omega_H(0) = 0.54 + 0.46 = 1$$
$$\omega_H(1) = \omega_H(-1) = 0.54 + 0.46\cos\frac{2\pi}{6} = 0.77$$
$$\omega_H(2) = \omega_H(-2) = 0.54 + 0.46\cos\frac{4\pi}{6} = 0.31$$
$$\omega_H(3) = \omega_H(-3) = 0.54 + 0.46\cos\frac{6\pi}{6} = 0.08$$

$$h_d(n) = \frac{1}{n\pi}[\sin 0.3n - \sin 0.2n], \qquad -3 \le n \le 3$$
$$h_d(0) = \operatorname*{Lim}_{n\to 0}\frac{1}{\pi}\left[0.3\frac{\sin 0.3n}{0.3n} - 0.2\frac{\sin 0.2n}{0.2n}\right]$$
$$= \frac{0.3 - 0.2}{\pi} = 0.03183$$
$$h_d(1) = h_d(-1) = \frac{1}{\pi}[\sin 0.3 - \sin 0.2] = 0.0308$$
$$h_d(2) = h_d(-2) = \frac{1}{2\pi}[\sin 0.6 - \sin 0.4] = 0.0278$$
$$h_d(3) = h_d(-3) = \frac{1}{3\pi}[\sin 0.9 - \sin 0.6] = 0.0232$$
$$h(n) = h_d(n) \times \omega_H(n)$$
$$h(0) = h_d(0) \times \omega_H(0) = 0.03183$$
$$h(1) = h(-1) = h_d(+1) \times \omega_H(+1) = 0.02926$$
$$h(2) = h(-2) = h_d(2) \times \omega_H(2) = 0.0086$$
$$h(3) = h(-3) = h_d(3) \times \omega_H(3) = 0.01856$$

Step 4: To Find $H(z)$

$$H(z) = z^{-\left(\frac{N-1}{2}\right)}\left[\sum_{n=1}^{\frac{N-1}{2}} h(n)[z^n + z^{-n}] + h(0)\right]$$
$$= z^{-3}\left[h(0) + \sum_{n=1}^{3} h(n)[z^n + z^{-n}]\right]$$
$$= z^{-3}\left[h(0) + h(1)[z^1 + z^{-1}] + h(2)[z^2 + z^{-2}] + h(3)[z^3 + z^{-3}]\right]$$

$$\boxed{\begin{aligned} H(z) = \big[&h(0)z^{-3} + h(1)[z^{-2} + z^{-4}] + h(2)[z^{-1} + z^{-5}] \\ &+ h(3)[1 + z^{-6}]\big]\end{aligned}}$$

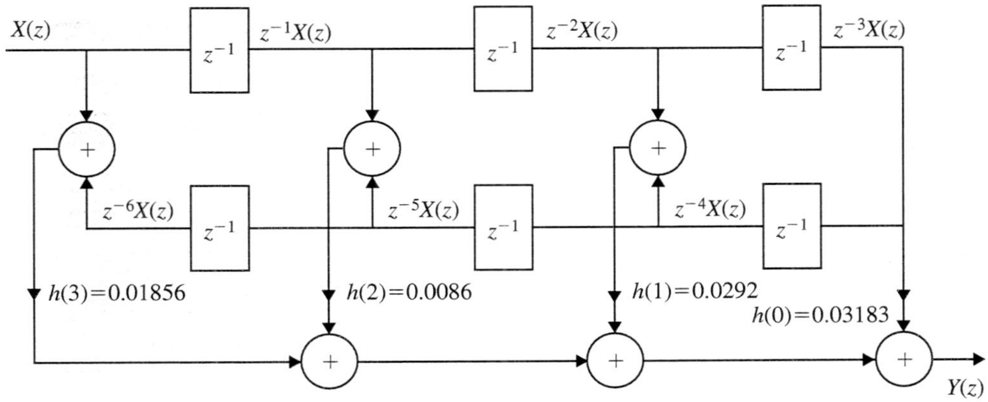

Figure 4.44 Realization of FIR filter for Example 4.28.

$$H(z) = 0.03183z^{-3} + 0.02926[z^{-2} + z^{-4}] + 0.0086[z^{-1} + z^{-5}] + 0.01856[1 + z^{-6}]$$

Step 5: Realization of the filter

$$\begin{aligned} Y(z) &= h(0)z^{-3}X(z) + h(1)[z^{-2} + z^{-4}]X(z) \\ &+ h(2)[z^{-1} + z^{-5}]X(z) \\ &+ h(3)[1 + z^{-6}]X(z) \end{aligned}$$

FIR filter is realized as shown in Figure 4.44.

Example 4.29

Obtain linear phase structure with minimum member of multipliers for the system described by the equation.

$$y(n) = x(n) + \frac{1}{2}x(n-1) - \frac{1}{4}x(n-2) + \frac{1}{2}x(n-3) + x(n-4)$$

(Anna University, December, 2007)

Solution Given

$$y(n) = x(n) + \frac{1}{2}x(n-1) - \frac{1}{4}x(n-2) + \frac{1}{2}x(n-3) + x(n-4)$$

Taking z-transform on both sides, we get

$$Y(z) = X(z) + \frac{1}{2}z^{-1}X(z) - \frac{1}{4}z^{-2}X(z) + \frac{1}{2}z^{-3}X(z) + z^{-4}X(z)$$

$$= X(z)\left[1 + \frac{1}{2}z^{-1} - \frac{1}{4}z^{-2} + \frac{1}{2}z^{-3} + z^{-4}\right]$$

$$\frac{Y(z)}{X(z)} = 1 + \frac{1}{2}z^{-1} - \frac{1}{4}z^{-2} + \frac{1}{2}z^{-3} + z^{-4}$$

$$H(z) = 1 + \frac{1}{2}z^{-1} - \frac{1}{4}z^{-2} + \frac{1}{2}z^{-3} + z^{-4}$$

$$H(z) = \sum_{n=0}^{\infty} h(n)z^{-n}$$

$$= h(0) + h(1)z^{-1} + h(2)z^{-2} + h(3)z^{-3} + h(4)z^{-4} + \cdots$$

Comparing these equations, we get impulse response.

$$h(0) = 1, \quad h(1) = \frac{1}{2}, \quad h(2) = \frac{-1}{4}, \quad h(3) = \frac{1}{2}, \quad h(4) = 1$$

$$h(n) = \{1, \frac{1}{2}, \frac{-1}{4}, \frac{1}{2}, 1\} \text{ and } N = 5$$

Here $h(n)$ satisfies the condition $h(n) = h(N - 1 - n)$

$$H(z) = \frac{Y(z)}{X(z)} = (1 + z^{-4}) + \frac{1}{2}[z^{-1} + z^{-3}] - \frac{1}{4}z^{-2}$$

$$Y(z) = [X(z) + z^{-4}X(z)] + \frac{1}{2}[z^{-1}X(z) + z^{-3}X(z)] - \frac{1}{4}z^{-2}X(z)$$

$Y(z)$ is realized as shown in Figure 4.45.

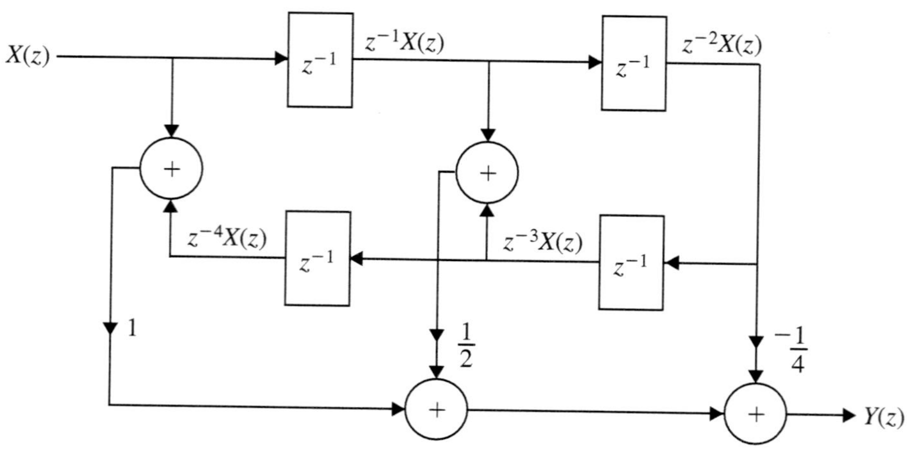

Figure 4.45 Linear Phase Realization for the Example 4.29.

Example 4.30

Design a linear phase FIR digital filter for the given specifications using Hamming window of length $M = 7$.

$$H_d(\omega) = \begin{cases} e^{-j3\omega}, & \text{for } |\omega| \le \frac{\pi}{6} \\ 0, & \text{for } \frac{\pi}{6} \le |\omega| \le \pi \end{cases}$$

(Anna University, May, 2007)

Solution Given

$$H_d(\omega) = \begin{cases} e^{-j3\omega}, & |\omega| \le \frac{\pi}{6} \\ 0, & \frac{\pi}{6} \le |\omega| \le \pi \end{cases}$$

The frequency response having a term $e^{-j\omega(\frac{N-1}{2})}$, gives $h(n)$ which is symmetrical about $\alpha = \frac{N-1}{2} = 3$, *i.e.*, We get a causal sequence.

$$\begin{aligned}
h_d(n) &= \frac{1}{2\pi}\int_{\frac{-\pi}{6}}^{\frac{\pi}{6}} e^{-j\omega n}\,d\omega \\
&= \frac{1}{2\pi}\int_{\frac{-\pi}{6}}^{\frac{\pi}{6}} e^{j(n-3)\omega}\,d\omega \\
&= \frac{1}{2\pi}\left[\frac{e^{j(n-3)\omega}}{j(n-3)}\right]_{\frac{-\pi}{6}}^{\frac{\pi}{6}} \\
&= \frac{1}{\pi(n-3)}\left[\frac{e^{j\frac{\pi}{6}(n-3)} - e^{-j\frac{\pi}{6}(n-3)}}{2j}\right] \\
h_d(n) &= \frac{\sin\frac{\pi}{6}(n-3)}{\pi(n-3)}, \qquad 0 \le n \le N-1, \quad 0 \le n \le 6 \\
h_d(0) = h_d(6) &= \frac{\sin(\frac{\pi}{2})}{3\pi} = 0.1061 \\
h_d(1) = h_d(5) &= \frac{\sin(\frac{\pi}{3})}{2\pi} = 0.1378 \\
h_d(2) = h_d(4) &= \frac{\sin(\frac{\pi}{6})}{\pi} = 0.1591 \\
h_d(3) &= \lim_{n\to 3}\frac{\sin\frac{\pi}{6}(n-3)}{6.\frac{\pi}{6}(n-3)} = \frac{1}{6} = 0.1666
\end{aligned}$$

Hamming window function is,

$$\omega_H(n) = \begin{cases} 0.54 - 0.46\cos(\frac{2\pi n}{N-1}), & 0 \le n \le N-1 \\ 0, & \text{otherwise} \end{cases}$$

$$\omega_H(n) = \begin{cases} 0.54 - 0.46\cos(\frac{2\pi n}{6}), & 0 \le n \le 6 \\ 0, & \text{otherwise} \end{cases}$$

$$\omega_H(0) = 0.54 - 0.46 = 0.08$$

$$\omega_H(1) = 0.54 - 0.46\cos\left(\frac{2\pi}{6}\right) = 0.31$$

$$\omega_H(2) = 0.54 - 0.46\cos\left(\frac{4\pi}{6}\right) = 0.77$$

$$\omega_H(3) = 0.54 - 0.46\cos\left(\frac{6\pi}{6}\right) = 1$$

$$\omega_H(4) = \omega_H(2) = 0.77$$

$$\omega_H(5) = \omega_H(1) = 0.31$$

$$\omega_H(6) = \omega_H(0) = 0.08$$

$$h(n) = h_d(n) \times \omega_H(n)$$

$$h(0) = h_d(0) \times \omega_H(0)$$

$$h(0) = 0.0048$$

$$h(6) = h(0) = 0.0048$$

$$h(1) = h(5) = h_d(1) \times \omega_H(1) = 0.04271$$

$$h(2) = h(4) = h_d(2) \times \omega_H(2) = 0.1225$$

$$h(3) = h_d(3) \times \omega_H(3) = 0.16667$$

$$H(z) = \sum_{n=0}^{N-1} h(n)z^{-n}$$

$$= h(0) + h(1)z^{-1} + h(2)z^{-2} + h(3)z^{-3} + h(4)z^{-4} + h(5)z^{-5} + h(6)z^{-6}$$

$$= h(0)[1 + z^{-6}] + h(1)[z^{-1} + z^{-5}] + h(2)[z^{-2} + z^{-4}] + h(3)z^{-3}$$

$$\boxed{\begin{aligned} H(z) = 0.0048[1 + z^{-6}] + 0.04271[z^{-1} + z^{-5}] \\ +0.1225[z^{-2} + z^{-4}] + 0.16667z^{-3} \end{aligned}}$$

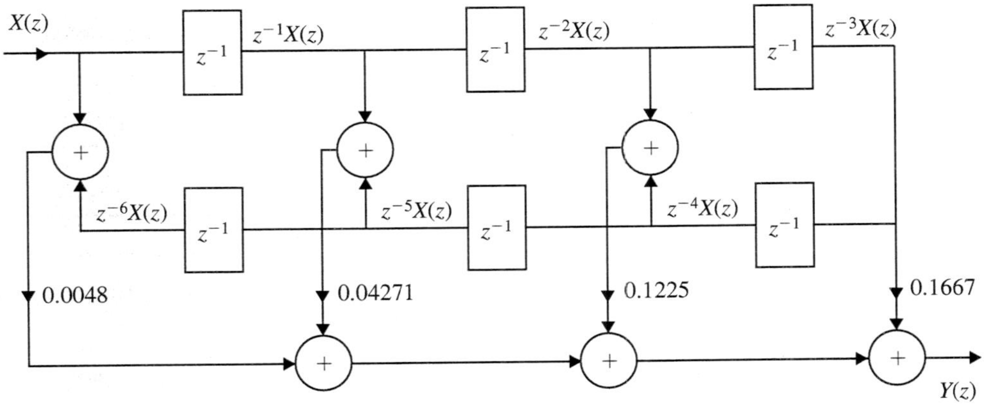

Figure 4.46 FIR filter structure Example 4.30.

Realization of the filter is

$$\begin{aligned} H(z) &= \frac{Y(z)}{X(z)} \\ &= 0.0048[1+z^{-6}] + 0.04271[z^{-1}+z^{-5}] + 0.1225[z^{-2}+z^{-4}] \\ &\quad + 0.16667z^{-3} \\ Y(z) &= 0.0048[X(z)+z^{-6}X(z)] + 0.04271[z^{-1}X(z)+z^{-5}X(z)] \\ &\quad + 0.1225[z^{-2}X(z)+z^{-4}X(z)] + 0.16667z^{-3}X(z) \end{aligned}$$

The structure of the filter is shown in Figure 4.46.

Example 4.31

Design and implement linear phase FIR filter of length $N = 15$ which has following unit sample sequence:

$$H(k) = \begin{cases} 1, & k = 0, 1, 2, 3 \\ 0, & k = 4, 5, 6, 7 \end{cases}$$

(Anna University, May 2007)

Solution Linear phase FIR filter is symmetric about

$$\alpha = \frac{N-1}{2} = \frac{15-1}{2} = 7$$

$$|H(k)| = \begin{cases} 1, & \text{for } 0 \le k \le 3 \text{ and } 11 \le k \le 14 \\ 0, & \text{for } 4 \le k \le 10 \end{cases}$$

$$H(k) = \begin{cases} e^{-j\omega\alpha}, & k = 0, 1, 2, 3 \\ 0, & k = 4, 5, 6, 7 \end{cases}$$

$$H(k) = \begin{cases} e^{\frac{-j2\pi k\alpha}{15}}, & k = 0, 1, 2, 3 \\ 0, & k = 4, 5, 6, 7 \end{cases}$$

$$H(k) = \begin{cases} e^{\frac{-j14\pi k}{15}}, & k = 0, 1, 2, 3 \\ 0, & 4 \le k \le 10 \\ e^{\frac{-j14\pi(k-15)}{15}}, & 11 \le k \le 14 \end{cases}$$

$$H(k) = \begin{cases} e^{\frac{j14\pi k}{15}}, & k = 0, 1, 2, 3 \\ 0, & k = 4, 5, 6, 7 \end{cases}$$

$$h(n) = \frac{1}{N}\left[H(0) + 2\sum_{k=1}^{\frac{N-1}{2}} Re(H(k)e^{\frac{j2\pi nk}{15}})\right]$$

$$= \frac{1}{15}\left[1 + 2\sum_{k=1}^{7} Re[e^{\frac{j14\pi k}{15}}.e^{\frac{j2\pi nk}{15}}]\right]$$

$$= \frac{1}{15}\left[1 + 2\sum_{k=1}^{3} \cos\frac{2\pi k(7-n)}{15}\right]$$

$$h(n) = \frac{1}{15}\left[1 + 2\cos\frac{2\pi(7-n)}{15} + 2\cos\frac{4\pi(7-n)}{15} + 2\cos\frac{6\pi(7-n)}{15}\right]$$

$$h(0) = h(14) = \frac{1}{15}\left[1 + 2\cos\frac{14\pi}{15} + 2\cos\frac{28\pi}{15} + 2\cos\frac{42\pi}{15}\right] = -0.05$$

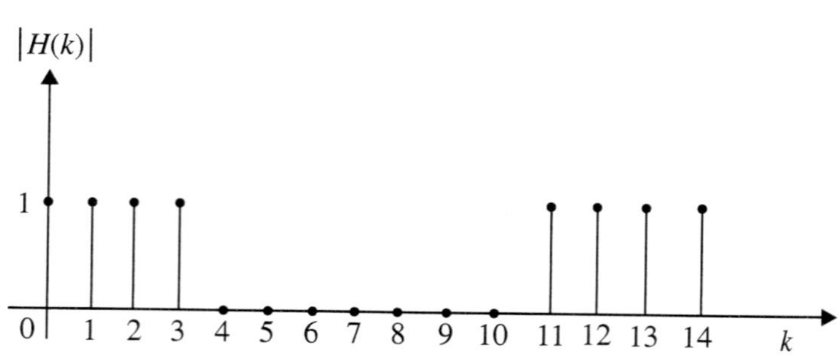

Figure 4.47 (*a*) Ideal magnitude response for Example 4.31.

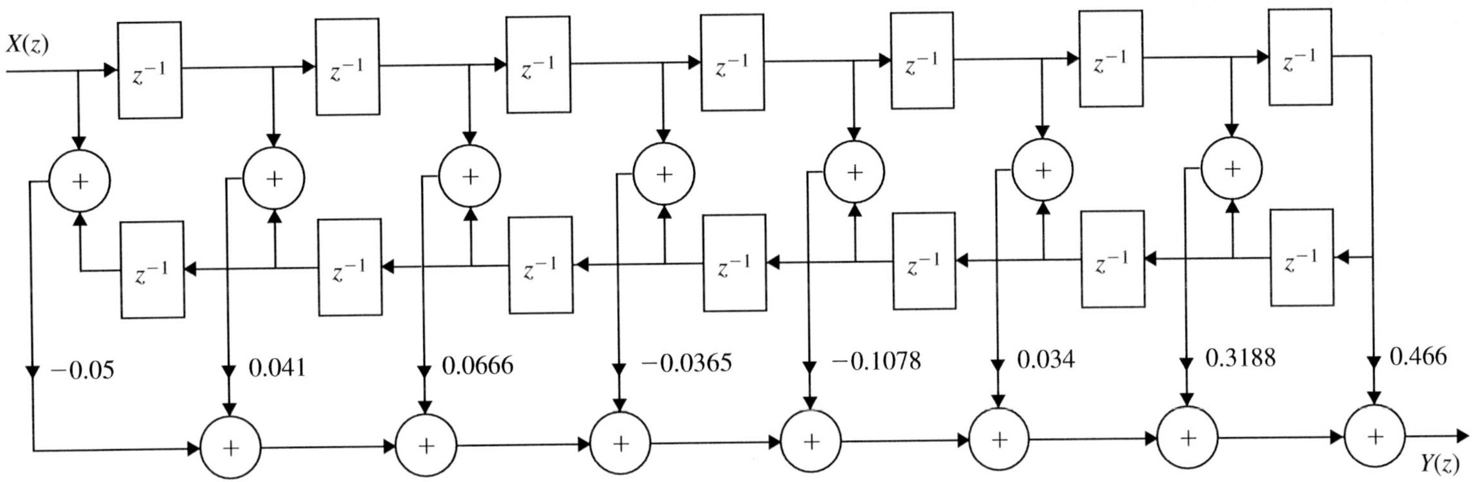

Figure 4.47 (*b*) Structure realization for Example 4.31.

$$h(1) = h(13) = \frac{1}{15}\left[1 + 2\cos\frac{12\pi}{15} + 2\cos\frac{24\pi}{15} + 2\cos\frac{36\pi}{15}\right] = 0.041$$

$$h(2) = h(12) = \frac{1}{15}\left[1 + 2\cos\frac{10\pi}{15} + 2\cos\frac{20\pi}{15} + 2\cos\frac{30\pi}{15}\right] = 0.0666$$

$$h(3) = h(11) = -0.0365$$

$$h(4) = h(10) = -0.1078$$

$$h(5) = h(9) = 0.034$$

$$h(6) = h(8) = 0.3188$$

$$h(7) = = 0.466$$

$$H(z) = \sum_{n=0}^{N-1} h(n)z^{-n}$$

$$= h(0)z^{-1} + h(1)z^{-2} + \cdots$$

$$= h(0)[1 + z^{-14}] + h(1)[z^{-1} + z^{-13}] + h(2)[z^{-2} + z^{-12}] + h(3)[z^{-3} + z^{-11}] + h(4)[z^{-4} + z^{-10}] + h(5)[z^{-5} + z^{-9}] + h(6)[z^{-6} + z^{-8}] + h(7)z^{-7}$$

$$H(z) = -0.05[1 + z^{-14}] + 0.041[z^{-1} + z^{-13}] + 0.0666[z^{-2} + z^{-12}] - 0.0365[z^{-3} + z^{-11}] - 0.1078[z^{-4} + z^{-10}] + 0.034[z^{-5} + z^{-9}] + 0.3188[z^{-6} + z^{-8}] + 0.466z^{-7}$$

The structure is shown in Figure 4.47.

Example 4.32

Design a FIR filter approximating the ideal frequency response.

$$H_d(e^{j\omega}) = \begin{cases} e^{-j\alpha\omega}, & \text{for } |\omega| \le \frac{\pi}{6} \\ 0, & \text{for } \frac{\pi}{6} \le |\omega| \le \pi \end{cases}$$

Determine the filter coefficients for $N = 13$.

(Anna University, December, 2005)

Solution We know that,

$$h_d(n) = \frac{1}{2\pi}\int_{-\pi}^{\pi} H_d(e^{j\omega})e^{j\omega n}d\omega$$

$$= \frac{1}{2\pi}\int_{\frac{-\pi}{6}}^{\frac{\pi}{6}} e^{-j\alpha\omega n}e^{j\omega n}d\omega$$

$$= \frac{1}{2\pi}\int_{\frac{-\pi}{6}}^{\frac{\pi}{6}} e^{j(n-\alpha)\omega} d\omega$$

$$= \frac{1}{2}\left[\frac{e^{j(n-\alpha)\omega}}{j(n-\alpha)}\right]_{\frac{-\pi}{6}}^{\frac{\pi}{6}}$$

$$= \frac{1}{\pi(n-\alpha)}\left[\frac{e^{j(n-\alpha)\frac{\pi}{6}}}{2j} - \frac{e^{-j(n-\alpha)\frac{\pi}{6}}}{2j}\right]$$

$$= \frac{\sin(n-\alpha)\frac{\pi}{6}}{\pi(n-\alpha)}$$

Form the frequency response we can find that the filter coefficients are symmetrical about $\alpha = \frac{N-1}{2} = 6$, satisfying $h(n) = h(N-1-n)$

$$h_n = \begin{cases} h_d(n), & \text{for } 0 \le n \le 12 \\ 0, & \text{otherwise} \end{cases}$$

$$h_n = \begin{cases} \frac{\sin\frac{\pi}{6}(n-\alpha)}{\pi(n-\alpha)}, & 0 \le n \le 12 \\ 0, & \text{otherwise} \end{cases}$$

$$h(n) = h(N-1-n)$$
$$h(n) = h(13-1-0) = h(12) = 0$$
$$h(1) = h(11) = 0.0318$$
$$h(2) = h(10) = 0.0689$$
$$h(3) = h(9) = 0.106$$
$$h(4) = h(8) = 0.1379$$
$$h(5) = h(7) = 0.159$$
$$h(6) = \underset{n\to 6}{\text{Lim}} \frac{\sin\frac{\pi}{6}(n-6)}{6\frac{\pi}{6}(n-6)} = \frac{1}{6} = 0.1667$$

$$H(z) = \sum_{n=0}^{N-1} h(n)z^{-n}$$
$$= \sum_{n=0}^{12} h(n)z^{-n}$$
$$= h(0) + h(1)z^{-1} + h(2)z^{-2} + h(3)z^{-3} + \cdots + h(12)z^{-12}$$
$$= h(0)[1 + z^{-12}] + h(1)[z^{-1} + z^{-11}] + h(2)[z^{-2} + z^{-10}]$$
$$+ h(3)[z^{-3} + z^{-9}] + h(4)[z^{-4} + z^{-8}] + h(5)[z^{-5} + z^{-7}] + h(6)z^{-6}$$

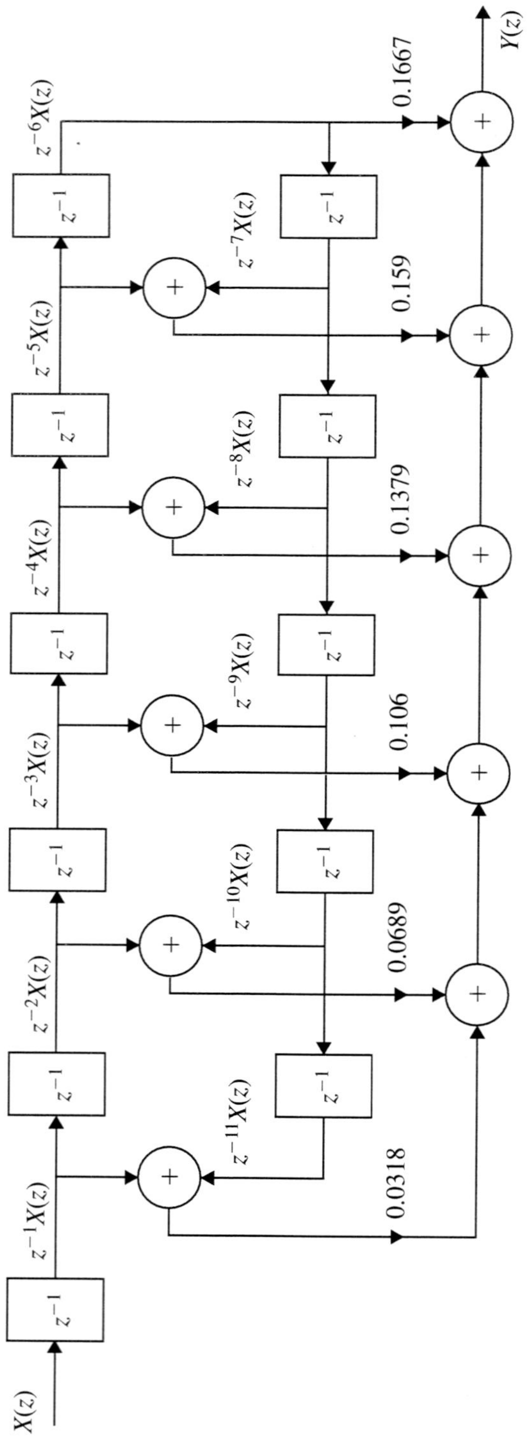

Figure 4.48 Structure realization for Example 4.32.

$$H(z) = 0.0318[z^{-1} + z^{-11}] + 0.0689[z^{-2} + z^{-10}] + 0.106[z^{-3} + z^{-9}] + 0.1379[z^{-4} + z^{-8}] + 0.159[z^{-5} + z^{-7}] + 0.1667z^{-6}$$

The structure realization is shown in Figure 4.48.

Example 4.33

Design a filter with

$$H_d(e^{-j\omega}) = \begin{cases} e^{-j3\omega}, & \frac{-\pi}{4} \le \omega \le \frac{\pi}{4} \\ 0, & \frac{\pi}{4} < |\omega| \le \pi \end{cases}$$

(Anna University, May, 2004)

Solution Given

$$H_d(e^{-j\omega}) = e^{-j3\omega}$$
$$\alpha = 3 = \frac{N-1}{2}$$
$$N = 7$$

The frequency response is having a term $e^{-j\omega(\frac{N-1}{2})}$ which gives $h(n)$ symmetrical about $n = \frac{N-1}{2} = 3$. Therefore, we get casual sequence.

$$h_d(n) = \int_{\frac{-\pi}{4}}^{\frac{\pi}{4}} e^{-j3\omega} e^{j\omega n} d\omega$$
$$= \int_{\frac{-\pi}{4}}^{\frac{\pi}{4}} e^{j(n-3)\omega} d\omega$$
$$= \int_{\frac{-\pi}{4}}^{\frac{\pi}{4}} \left[\frac{e^{j(n-3)\omega}}{j(n-3)}\right]_{\frac{-\pi}{4}}^{\frac{\pi}{4}}$$
$$h_d(n) = \frac{\sin\frac{\pi}{4}(n-3)}{\pi(n-3)}$$

For $N = 7$, the filter coefficients are,

$$h(n) = h_d(n)$$
$$h(0) = h(6) = 0.075$$
$$h(1) = h(5) = 0.159$$
$$h(2) = h(4) = 0.22$$
$$h(3) = 0.25$$

$$H(z) = \sum_{n=0}^{N-1} h(n)z^{-n} = \sum_{n=0}^{6} h(n)z^{-n}$$

$$= h(0) + h(1)z^{-1} + h(2)z^{-2} + h(3)z^{-3} + h(4)z^{-4} + h(5)z^{-5} + h(6)z^{-6}$$

$$= h(0)[1 + z^{-6}] + h(1)[z^{-1} + z^{-5}] + h(2)[z^{-2} + z^{-4}] + h(3)z^{-3}$$

$$\boxed{H(z) = 0.075[1 + z^{-6}] + 0.159[z^{-1} + z^{-5}] + 0.22[z^{-2} + z^{-4}] + 0.25z^{-3}}$$

Example 4.34

Design a filter with

$$H_d(e^{-j\omega}) = \begin{cases} e^{-j3\omega}, & \frac{-\pi}{4} \leq \omega \leq \frac{\pi}{4} \\ 0, & \frac{\pi}{4} \leq |\omega| \leq \pi \end{cases}$$

using a Hamming window with $N = 7$.

(*Anna University, December, 2004*)

Solution Given

$$H_d(e^{-j\omega}) = \begin{cases} e^{-j3\omega}, & \frac{-\pi}{4} \leq \omega \leq \frac{\pi}{4} \\ 0, & \frac{\pi}{4} \leq -|\omega| \leq \pi \end{cases}$$

$\alpha = 3$; $\frac{N-1}{2} = 3$; $N = 7$. Impulse response $h(n)$ is symmetric about $\alpha = 3$. Since the frequency response is having a term $e^{-j\omega\alpha}$

$$h_d(n) = \frac{1}{2\pi} \int_{\frac{-\pi}{4}}^{\frac{\pi}{4}} e^{-j3\omega} e^{j\omega n} d\omega$$

$$= \frac{1}{2\pi} \int_{\frac{-\pi}{4}}^{\frac{\pi}{4}} e^{j(n-3)\omega} d\omega$$

$$h_d(n) = \frac{\sin \frac{\pi}{4}(n-3)}{\pi(n-3)}$$

$$h_d(0) = h_d(6) = 0.075$$

$$h_d(1) = h_d(5) = 0.159$$

$$h_d(2) = h_d(4) = 0.22$$

$$h_d(3) = \lim_{n \to 3} \frac{\sin \frac{\pi}{4}(n-3)}{4.\frac{\pi}{4}(n-3)}$$

$$h_d(3) = \frac{1}{4} = 0.25$$

Hamming window function is,

$$\omega_H(n) = \begin{cases} 0.54 - 0.46\cos(\frac{2\pi n}{N-1}), & 0 \le n \le N-1 \\ 0, & \text{otherwise} \end{cases}$$

$$\omega_H(n) = \begin{cases} 0.54 - 0.46\cos(\frac{2\pi n}{6}), & 0 \le n \le 6 \\ 0, & \text{otherwise} \end{cases}$$

$$\begin{aligned} \omega_H(0) &= 0.08 \\ \omega_H(1) &= 0.31 \\ \omega_H(2) &= 0.77 \\ \omega_H(3) &= 1 \\ \omega_H(4) &= 0.77 \\ \omega_H(5) &= 0.31 \\ \omega_H(6) &= 0.08 \end{aligned}$$

The filter coefficients are,

$$\begin{aligned} h(n) &= h_d(n) \times \omega_H(n) \\ h(0) &= h(6) \\ &= h_d(0) \times \omega_H(0) \\ &= 0.006 \\ h(1) &= h(5) \\ &= h_d(0) \times \omega_H(1) \\ &= 0.049 \\ h(2) &= h(4) \\ &= h_d(0) \times \omega_H(2) \\ &= 0.1694 \\ h(3) &= h_d(3)\omega_H(3) \\ &= 0.25 \end{aligned}$$

The transfer function of the filter is,

$$\begin{aligned} H(z) &= \sum_{n=0}^{N-1} h(n)z^{-n} \\ &= \sum_{n=0}^{6} h(n)z^{-n} \end{aligned}$$

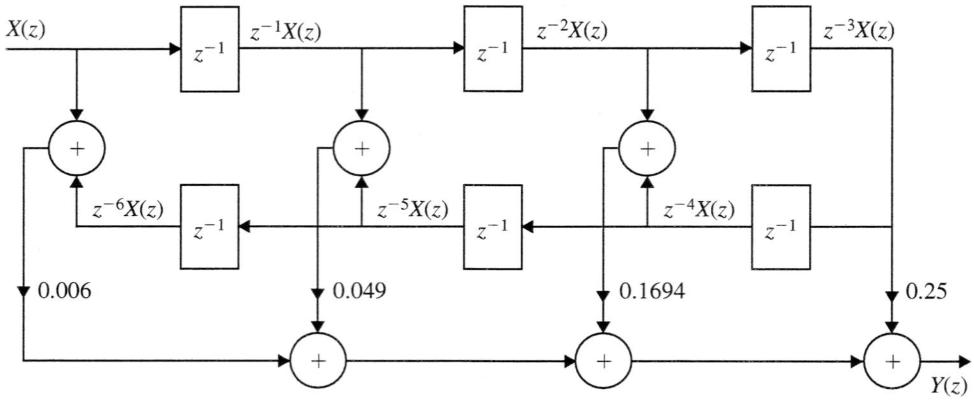

Figure 4.49 Structure realization for Example 4.34.

$$= h(0) + h(1)z^{-1} + h(2)z^{-2} + h(3)z^{-3} + h(4)z^{-4} + h(5)z^{-5} + h(6)z^{-6}$$
$$= h(0)[1 + z^{-6}] + h(1)[z^{-1} + z^{-5}] + h(2)[z^{-2} + z^{-4}] + h(3)z^{-3}$$

$$H(z) = 0.006[1 + z^{-6}] + 0.049[z^{-1} + z^{-5}] + 0.1694[z^{-2} + z^{-4}] + 0.25z^{-3}$$

The structure realized as shown in Figure 4.49.

Example 4.35

A low pass filter is required to be designed with the desired frequency response.

$$H_d(\omega) = \begin{cases} e^{-j2\omega}, & -0.25\pi \le \omega \le 0.25\pi \\ 0, & 0.25\pi \le \omega \le \pi \end{cases}$$

Obtain the filter coefficients, $h(n)$ using Hamming window function. Also fluid the frequency response $H(\omega)$ of the designed filter.

(Anna University, April, 2005)

Solution Given

$$H_d(\omega) = \begin{cases} e^{-j2\omega}, & -0.25\pi \le \omega \le 0.25\pi \\ 0, & 0.25\pi \le \omega \le \pi \end{cases}$$

$$h_d(n) = \frac{1}{2\pi}\int_{-\pi}^{\pi} H_d(\omega)e^{j\omega n}d\omega$$

$$= \frac{1}{2\pi}\int_{-0.25\pi}^{0.25\pi} e^{-j2\omega}e^{j\omega n}d\omega$$

$$= \frac{1}{2\pi}\int_{-0.25\pi}^{0.25\pi} e^{j(n-2)\omega}d\omega$$

$$= \frac{1}{2\pi}\left[\frac{e^{j(n-2)\omega}}{j(n-2)}\right]_{-0.25\pi}^{0.25\pi}$$

$$= \frac{1}{\pi(n-2)}\left[\frac{e^{j0.25\pi(n-2)} - e{-}j0.25\pi(n-2)}{2j}\right]$$

$$h_d(n) = \frac{1}{\pi(n-2)}.\sin 0.25\pi(n-2)$$

From the given frequency it is clear that

$$\frac{N-1}{2} = 2 \rightarrow N-1 = 4 \rightarrow N = 5$$

$$\alpha = \frac{N-1}{2} = 2$$

If $n = 2$,

$$h_d(n) = \lim_{n\to 2}\frac{\sin(\frac{\pi}{4})(n-2)}{4.\frac{\pi}{4}(n-2)}$$

$$= \frac{1}{4}$$

$$H_d = \begin{cases} \frac{\sin 0.25(n-2)}{\pi(n-2)} & ,n \neq 2 \\ \frac{1}{4} & ,n = 2 \end{cases}$$

$$h_d(0) = h_d(4) = \frac{\sin 0.25(-2)}{\pi(-2)} = 0.159$$

$$h_d(1) = h_d(3) = \frac{\sin 0.25(-1)}{\pi(-1)} = 0.225$$

$$h_d(2) = = \frac{1}{4} = 0.25$$

Hamming window

$$\omega_H(n) = \begin{cases} 0.54 - 0.46\cos(\frac{2\pi n}{N-1}), & 0 \le n \le N \le 1 \\ 0, & \text{otherwise} \end{cases}$$

$$= \begin{cases} 0.54 - 0.46\cos(\frac{2\pi n}{4}), & 0 \le n \le N \le 4 \\ 0, & \text{otherwise} \end{cases}$$

$$\omega_H(0) = 0.54 - 0.46 = 0.08$$

$$\omega_H(1) = 0.54$$

$$\omega_H(2) = 1$$

$$\omega_H(3) = 0.54$$

$$\omega_H(4) = 0.54 - 0.46 = 0.08$$

$$h(n) = h_d(n) \times \omega_H(n)$$

$$h(0) = h(4) = h_d(0) \times \omega_H(0) = 0.0127$$

$$h(1) = h(3) = h_d(1) \times \omega_H(1) = 0.1215$$

$$h(2) = h_d(2) \times \omega_H(2) = 0.25$$

Filter coefficients are,

$$\boxed{\begin{aligned} h(0) = h(4) &= 0.0127 \\ h(1) = h(3) &= 0.1215 \\ h(2) &= 0.25 \end{aligned}}$$

Summary

- Digital filters are classified as FIR and IIR filters. They have their own merits and demerits. The choice of the filter is made depending upon the application.
- The difference equation which describes FIR filter is non-recursive; the output response is a function only of past and present values of the input. When FIR is implemented in this form it is always stable.
- FIR filters have exactly linear phase characteristic which has unique properties and helps in the design and applications.
- The design of FIR filters are divided into five independent stages. They are:

  (*a*) Filter specifications
  (*b*) Coefficient calculation
  (*c*) Realization
  (*d*) Analysis of errors, and
  (*e*) Implementation

- FIR filters are designed usually by the following methods among others:
  - (*a*) Frequency sampling method
  - (*b*) Fourier series method
  - (*c*) Design using windows
- The following windowing techniques are generally used to design FIR filters:
  - (*a*) Rectangular window
  - (*b*) Raised cosine window
  - (*c*) Hanning window
  - (*d*) Hamming window
  - (*e*) Blackman window
  - (*f*) Kaiser window
- There are different types of structures for realizing FIR filter system. The following structures are described in this chapter:
  - (*a*) Direct from realization
  - (*b*) Cascade form realization
  - (*c*) Linear phase realization
  - (*d*) Lattice structure realization

Short Questions and Answers

1. **What are FIR Filters?**
   The specifications of the desired filter will be given in terms of ideal frequency response $H_d(\omega)$. The impulse response $h_d(n)$ of desired filter can be obtained by inverse Fourier transform of $H_d(\omega)$, which consists of infinite number of samples. The filters designed by selecting finite number of samples of impulse response are called FIR filters.
2. **What are advantages of FIR filters?**
   The advantages of FIR filters are:
   - Linear phase FIR filters can be easily designed.
   - Efficient realizations of FIR filter exist as both recursive and non-recursive structures.
   - FIR filters realized non-recursively are always stable.
   - The roundoff noise can be made small in non-recursive realization of FIR filter.
3. **What are disadvantages of FIR filters?**
   The disadvantages of FIR filters are:
   - The duration of impulse response should be large to realize sharp cutoff filters.
   - The non-integral delay can lead to problems in some signal processing applications.

4. **What are the conditions to be satisfied for constant phase delay in linear phase FIR filters?**
The conditions for constant phase delay are:

$$\text{Phase delay, } \alpha = \frac{N-1}{2} \text{ (i.e., phase delay is constant)}$$

Impulse response, $h(n) = h(N-1-n)$ (*i.e.*, impulse response is symmetric)

5. **What are the possible types of impulse response for linear phase FIR filter?**
There are four types of impulse response for linear phase FIR filter.

- Symmetric impulse response for N is odd.
- Symmetric impulse response for N is even.
- Anti-symmetric impulse response for N is odd.
- Anti-symmetric impulse response for N is even.

6. **Write the magnitude and phase function of FIR filter when impulse response is symmetric and N is odd.**

$$\text{Magnitude function, } |H(\omega)| = h\left(\frac{N-1}{2}\right) + \sum_{n=1}^{N-1} 2h\left(\frac{N-1}{2} - n\right) \cos \omega n$$

$$\text{Phase function, } \angle H(\omega) = -\alpha\omega$$

7. **Write the magnitude and phase function of FIR filter when impulse response is symmetric and N is even.**

$$\text{Magnitude function, } |H(\omega)| = \sum_{n=1}^{N/2} 2h\left(\frac{N-1}{N} - n\right) \cos\left(\omega\left(n - \frac{1}{2}\right)\right)$$

$$\text{Phase function, } \angle H(\omega) = -\alpha\omega$$

8. **Write the magnitude and phase function of FIR filter when impulse response is anti-symmetric and N is odd.**

$$\text{Magnitude function, } |H(\omega)| = \sum_{n=1}^{\frac{N-1}{2}} 2h\left(\frac{N-1}{N} - n\right) \sin \omega n$$

$$\text{Phase function, } \angle H(\omega) = \beta - \alpha\omega$$

9. **Write the magnitude and phase function of FIR filter when impulse response is anti-symmetric and N is even**

$$\text{Magnitude function, } |H(\omega)| = \sum_{n=1}^{N/2} 2h\left(\frac{N}{2} - n\right) \sin\left(\omega\left(n - \frac{1}{2}\right)\right)$$

$$\text{Phase function, } \angle H(\omega) = \beta - \alpha\omega$$

10. **List the well-known design techniques for linear phase FIR filter.**
There are three well-known methods of design techniques for linear phase FIR filters. They are:

- Fourier series method and window method.
- Frequency sampling method.
- Optimal filter design method.

11. **What is Gibb's phenomenon (or Gibb's oscillation)?**
In FIR filter design by Fourier series method (or Rectangular window method) the finite duration impulse response is truncated to finite duration impulse response. The abrupt truncation of impulse response introduces oscillations in the passband and stopband. This effect is known as Gibb's phenomenon (or Gibb's oscillation).

12. **Write the procedure for designing FIR filter using windows?**

- Choose the desired frequency response of the filter $H_d(\omega)$.
- Take inverse Fourier transform of $H_d(\omega)$ to obtain the desired impulse response $h_d(n)$.
- Choose a window sequence $\omega(n)$ and multiply $h_d(n)$ by $\omega(n)$ to convert the infinite duration impulse response $h(n)$.
- The transfer function $H(z)$ of the filter is obtained by taking z-transform of $h(n)$.

13. **Write the procedure for FIR filters designed by frequency sampling method.**

- Choose the desired frequency response $H_d(\omega)$.
- Take N-samples of $H_d(\omega)$ to generate the sequence $H(k)$.
- Take inverse DFT of $H(k)$ to get the impulse response $h(n)$.
- The transfer function $H(z)$ of the filter is obtained by taking z-transform of impulse response.

14. **What is the drawback in FIR filter design using windows and frequency sampling method? How is it overcome?**
The FIR filter designs by window and frequency sampling method do not have precise control over the critical frequencies such as ω_p, and ω_s.

This drawback can be overcome by designing FIR filter using Chebyshev approximation technique. In this technique an error function is used to approximate the ideal frequency response, in order to satisfy the desired specifications.

15. **Write the characteristics features of Rectangular window.**

- The mainlobe width is equal to $4\pi/N$.
- The maximum sidelobe magnitude is -13dB.
- The sidelobe magnitude does not decrease significantly with increasing ω.

16. **List the features of FIR filter designed using Rectangular window.**

- The width of the transition region is related to the width of the mainlobe of window spectrum.

- Gibb's oscillations are noticed in the passband and stopband.
- The attenuation in the stopband is constant and cannot be varied.

17. **How the transition width of the FIR filter can be reduced in design using windows?**
In FIR filter design using windows, the width of the transition region is related to the width of the mainlobe in window spectrum If the mainlobe width is narrow then the transition region in FIR filter will be small. In general the width of mainlobe is $x\pi/N$, where $x = 4$ or 8 or 12 and N is the length of the window sequence used for designing the filter. Hence, the width of mainlobe can be reduced by increasing the value of N, which in turn reduces the width of the transition region in the FIR filter.
18. **Why Gibb's oscillations are developed in Rectangular window and how can it be eliminated or reduced?**
The Gibb's oscillations in Rectangular window are due to sharp transition from 1 to 0 at the edges of window sequence. These oscillations can be eliminated or reduced by replacing the sharp transition by gradual transition. This is the motivation for development of triangular and cosine windows.
19. **List the characteristics of FIR filters designed using windows.**
    - The width of transition band depends on the type of window.
    - The width of transition band can be made narrow by increasing the value of N where N is the length of window sequence.
    - The attenuation in the stopband is fixed for a given window, except in case of Kaiser window where it is variable.
20. **Write the frequency response of Hanning window.**
Frequency response of Hanning window is,

$$W_C(\omega) = 0.5\frac{\sin\omega(N/2)}{\sin\omega/2} + 0.25\frac{\sin(\omega N/2 - \pi N/(N-1))}{\sin(\omega/2 - \pi/(N-1))} + 0.25\frac{\sin(\omega N/2 + \pi N/(N-1))}{\sin(\omega/2 + \pi/(N-1))}$$

21. **Write the frequency response of Hamming window.**
Frequency response of Hamming window is,

$$W_H(\omega) = 0.54\frac{\sin\omega(N/2)}{\sin\omega/2} + 0.23\frac{\sin(\omega N/2 - \pi N/(N-1))}{\sin(\omega/2 - \pi/(N-1))} + 0.23\frac{\sin(\omega N/2 + \pi N/(N-1))}{\sin(\omega/2 + \pi/(N-1))}$$

22. **Give the equation for Hanning window function.**
Hanning window function is,

$$W_C(n) = \begin{cases} 0.5 - 0.5\cos(2\pi n/(N-1)); & \text{for } 0 \le n \le (N-1) \\ 0; & \text{else} \end{cases}$$

23. **List the features of Hanning window spectrum.**

- The mainlobe width is equal to $8\pi/N$.
- The maximum sidelobe magnitude is -31 dB.
- The sidelobe magnitude decreases with increasing ω.

24. **Compare the Rectangular window and Hanning window.**

	Rectangular Window	Hanning Window
1.	The mainlobe width is equal to $4\pi/N$.	The mainlobe width is equal to $8\pi/N$.
2.	The maximum sidelobe magnitude in window spectrum is -13dB.	The maximum sidelobe magnitude in window spectrum is -31dB.
3.	In window spectrum, the sidelobe magnitude slightly decreases with increasing ω.	In window spectrum, the sidelobe magnitude decreases with increasing ω.
4.	In FIR filter designed using Rectangular window, the minimum stopband attenuation is 22dB.	In FIR filter designed using Hanning window, the minimum stopband attenuation is 44dB.

25. **Write the equation for Hamming window function.**
Hanning window function is,

$$W_H(n) = \begin{cases} 0.54 - 0.46\cos(2\pi n/(N-1)); & \text{for } 0 \le n \le (N-1) \\ 0; & \text{else} \end{cases}$$

26. **Sketch the log-magnitude spectrum of Hamming window.**

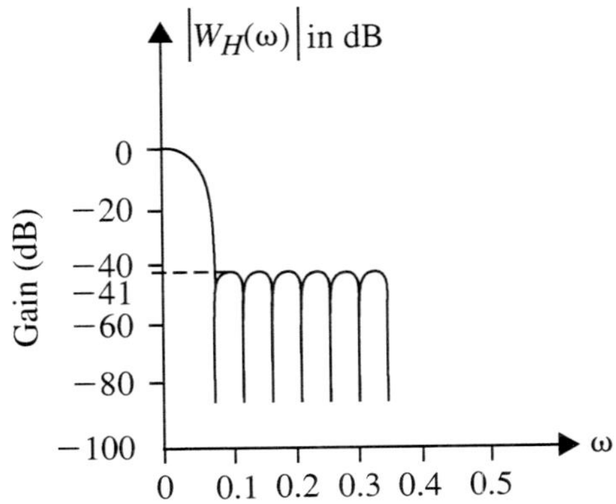

Figure 4.50 Log magnitude spectrum of Hamming window.

27. **Compare the Rectangular window and Hamming window.**

	Rectangular Window	Hamming Window
1.	The mainlobe width is equal to $4\pi/N$.	The mainlobe width is equal to $8\pi/N$.
2.	The maximum sidelobe magnitude in window spectrum is -13dB.	The maximum sidelobe magnitude in window spectrum is -41dB.
3.	In window spectrum, the sidelobe magnitude slightly decreases with increasing ω.	In window spectrum, the sidelobe magnitude remains constant.
4.	In FIR filter designed using Rectangular window, the minimum stopband attenuation is 22dB.	In FIR filter designed using Hamming window, the minimum stopband attenuation is 51dB.

28. **List the features of Hamming window spectrum.**

- The mainlobe width is equal to $8\pi/N$.
- The maximum sidelobe magnitude is -41dB.
- The sidelobe magnitude remains constant for increasing ω.

29. **Compare the Hanning window and Hamming window.**

	Hanning Window	Hamming Window
1.	The mainlobe width in window spectrum is equal to $8\pi/N$.	The mainlobe width in window spectrum is equal to $8\pi/N$.
2.	The maximum sidelobe magnitude in window spectrum is -31dB.	The maximum sidelobe magnitude in window spectrum is -41dB.
3.	In window spectrum, the sidelobe magnitude decreases with increasing ω.	In window spectrum, the sidelobe magnitude remains constant. Here, the increased sidelobe attenuation is achieved at the expense of constant attenuation at high frequencies.
4.	In FIR filter designed using Hanning window, the minimum stopband attenuation is 44dB.	In FIR filter designed using Hamming window, the minimum stopband attenuation is 51dB.

30. **Compare Hamming window and Blackman window?**

	Hamming Window	Blackman Window
1.	The mainlobe width in window spectrum is equal to $8\pi/N$.	The mainlobe width in window spectrum is equal to $12\pi/N$.
2.	The maximum sidelobe magnitude in window spectrum is -41dB.	The maximum sidelobe magnitude in window spectrum is -58dB.
3.	The higher value of sidelobe, attenuation is achieved at the expense of constant attenuation at high frequencies.	The higher value of sidelobe attenuation is achieved at the expense of increased mainlobe width.
4.	In widow spectrum, the side lobe magnitude remains constant with increasing ω.	In window spectrum, the side lobe magnitude decreases rapidly with increasing ω.
5.	In FIR filter designed using Hamming window, the minimum stopband attenuation is 51dB.	In FIR filter designed using Blackman window, the minimum stopband attenuation is 78dB.

31. **List the features of Blackman window spectrum.**

- The mainlobe width is $12\pi/N$.
- The maximum sidelobe magnitude is -58dB.
- The sidelobe magnitude decreases with increasing ω.
- The sidelobe attenuation in Blackman window is the highest among windows, which is achieved at the expense of increased mainlobe width. However, the mainlobe width can be reduced by increasing the value of N.

32. **Write the expression for Kaiser window function.**

Kaiser window function is,

$$W_k(n) = \begin{cases} \frac{I_0(\beta)}{I_0(\alpha)}; & \text{for } -(N-1)/2 \leq n \leq (N-1)/2 \\ 0; & \text{else.} \end{cases}$$

$$\text{where } \beta = \alpha\left(1 - \left(\frac{2n}{(N-1)}\right)^2\right)^{0.5}$$

$$I_0(x) = 1 + \frac{0.25x^2}{(1!)^2} + \frac{(0.25x^2)^2}{(2!)^2} + \frac{(0.25x^2)^3}{(3!)^2} + \cdots$$

The series of $I_0(x)$ is used to compute $I_0(\beta)$ and $I_0(\alpha)$ and are computed for any desired accuracy. Usually 25 terms of the series are sufficient for most practical purposes.

33. **List the desirable features of Kaiser window spectrum.**
   - The width of mainlobe and the peak sidelobe are variable.
   - The parameter α in the Kaiser window function, is an independent variable that can be varied to control the sidelobe levels with respect to mainlobe peak.
   - The width of the mainlobe in window spectrum can be varied by varying the length N of the window sequence.

34. **Compare the Hamming window and Kaiser window.**

	Hamming Window	**Kaiser Window**
1.	The width of mainlobe in window spectrum is $8\pi/N$.	The width of mainlobe in window spectrum depends on the values of α and N.
2.	The maximum sidelobe magnitude in windows spectrum is fixed at -41dB.	The maximum sidelobe magnitude with respect to peak of mainlobe is variable using the parameter α.
3.	In window spectrum, the sidelobe magnitude remains constant with increasing ω.	In window spectrum, the sidelobe magnitude decreases with increasing ω.
4.	In FIR filter designed using Hamming window, the minimum stopband attenuation is 51dB.	In FIR filter designed using Kaiser window, the minimum stopband attenuation is variable and depends on the value of α.

35. **Define an IIR filter.**
   The filter designed by considering all the infinite samples of impulse response are called IIR filter. The impulse response is obtained by taking inverse Fourier transform of ideal frequency response.

36. **Compare IIR and FIR filter.**

	IIR Filter	**FIR Filter**
1.	All infinite samples of impulse response are considered.	Only N samples of impulse response are considered.
2.	The impulse response cannot be directly converted to digital filter transfer function.	The impulse response can be directly converted to digital filter transfer function.
3.	The design involves design of analog filter and then transforming analog filter to digital filter.	The digital filter can be directly designed to achieve the desired specification.
4.	The specifications include the desired characteristics for magnitude response only.	The specifications include the desired characteristics for both magnitude and phase response.
5.	Linear phase characteristics cannot be achieved.	Linear phase filters can be easily designed.

37. **What are the properties that are maintained same in the transformation of analog to digital filters? (Or mention two properties that an analog filter should have for effective transformation).**
The analog filters should be stable and causal for effective transformation to digital filters. While transforming the analog filters to digital filters these two properties (*i.e.*, stability and causality) are maintained same, which means that the transformed digital filter should also be stable and physically realizable.

38. **What is the condition to be satisfied by linear phase FIR filter?**
(Anna University, 2007)
For an FIR filter to have linear phase, its phase response should satisfy the following equations

$$\theta(\omega) = -\alpha\omega$$

$$\theta(\omega) = \beta - \alpha\omega$$

If the first equation is satisfied, the filter will have constant group and constant phase delay responses. For this the impulse response of the filter must have positive symmetry. If the second equation is satisfied, the filter will have constant group delay. In this case, the impulse response of the filter will have negative symmetry.

39. **In the design of FIR filter, how is Kaiser window different from other windows?**
In other windows the width of the main lobe and the attenuation of the side lobes depend only upon the length N of the filter and they cannot be controlled independently whereas in Kaiser window it is possible to control the length of the filter and the transition width of the main lobe by introducing additional parameter.

40. **Show that the filter with $h(n) = \{-1, 0, 1\}$ is a linear phase filter.**

$$H(e^{j\omega}) = -e^{-j\omega}2\sin\omega$$

$$\theta(\omega) = \pi - \omega$$

Hence, it has linear phase.

41. **What is the desirable characteristic of the frequency response of window function?**
The desirable characteristics of the frequency response of window function are:

(*a*) The central lobe of the frequency response of the window should be narrow and contain maximum energy.
(*b*) The side lobes should decrease in energy as ω tends π.
(*c*) The highest side lobe level should be small.

42. **Why is linear phase is important in digital signal processing applications?**
The linear phase does not alter the shape of the signal and hence the output response is not distorted. Hence, digital filters with linear phase are designed.

43. **List out the well-known design techniques for linear phase FIR filter?**
The following techniques are used to design linear phase FIR filter.
    (*a*) Frequency sampling method
    (*b*) Windows method
    (*c*) Optimal or minimax design
44. **What are the disadvantages of FIR filter?**
The disadvantages of FIR filter are:
    (*a*) Memory requirement and execution time are very high.
    (*b*) FIR filters require narrow transition band which increases the cost as it requires large arithmetic operations and hardware components such as multipliers, adders and time delay elements.
45. **What is frequency sampling?**
The filter coefficients $h(n)$ can be obtained as the inverse DFT of the frequency samples,

$$h(n) = \frac{1}{N}\sum_{k=0}^{N-1} H(k)e^{j\left(\frac{2\pi}{N}\right)nk}$$

where, $H(k) = 0, 1, \ldots, (N-1)$ are samples of the ideal frequency response. For linear phase, with positive symmetrical impulse response, the above equation is written as

$$h(n) = \frac{1}{N}\left[\sum_{k=1}^{\frac{N}{2}-1} 2|H(k)|\cos\frac{2\pi k(n-\alpha)}{N} + H(0)\right]$$

where $\alpha = (N-1)/2$. The resulting filter will have a frequency response which is exactly same as the original response at the sampling instants. This is called frequency sampling.
46. **For what type of filters frequency sampling method is suitable?**
The frequency sampling method is very suitable for the design of non recursive FIR frequency selective filters such as low pass, high pass and band pass filters and also for filters with arbitrary frequency response.
47. **What is meant by FIR filter and why is it stable?**
Consider the following difference equation and the transfer function of a digital filter which are described as given below:

$$y(n) = \sum_{n=0}^{N-1} h(k)x(n-k)$$

$$H(z) = \sum_{n=0}^{N-1} h(k)z^{-k}$$

where $h(n)$ are the coefficients of the filter. When the digital filter is implemented in this form, it is called FIR filters. The poles of $H(z)$ all fall at the origin of the z-plane and therefore FIR filters are always stable.

48. **Find the number of delays required in a direct form I structure that realizes a second order transfer function?**
Four delay elements are required to realize a second order system in direct form-I structure.

49. **The unit sample response of an FIR filter is**

$$h(n) = a^n\{u(n) - u(n-2)\}$$

Draw the direct form realization of this system.

$$H(z) = \frac{1}{(1 + az^{-1})}$$

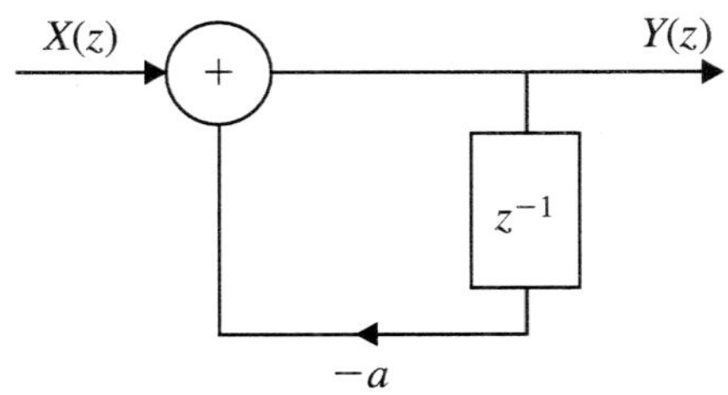

Figure 4.51 Direct form realization for Problem 49.

50. **A first order filter structure is shown in Figure 4.52. Find the transfer function?**

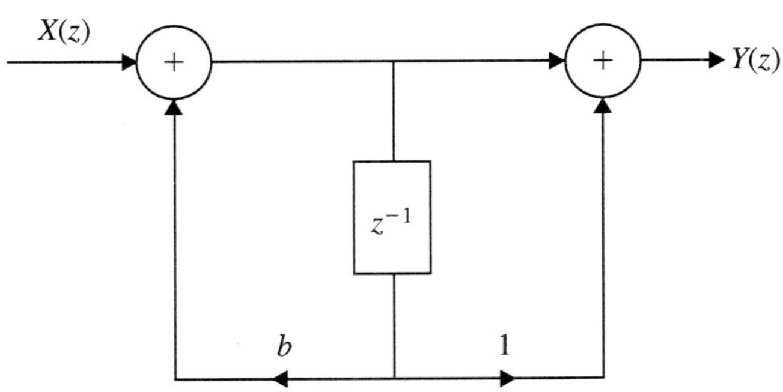

Figure 4.52 A structure for Problem 50.

$$H(z) = \frac{(1 + z^{-1})}{(1 - bz^{-1})}$$

Long Answer Type Questions

1. Describe the design of FIR filter using frequency sampling technique.
(*Anna University, December, 2007*)
2. A bandpass FIR filter of length 7 is required. It is to have lower and upper cut off frequencies of 3 kHz and 5 kHz respectively and is intended to be used with a sampling frequency of 24 kHz. Determine the filter coefficients using Hanning Window. Consider the filter to be causal.
(*Anna University June, 2007*)
3. Compare the Hamming window and Blackman window.
(*Anna University, December, 2007*)
4. Explain the polyphase decomposition for FIR filter structure.
(*Anna University, December, 2007*)
5. What is the principle of designing FIR filter using frequency sampling method?
(*Anna University, December, 2009*)
6. Design a second order band reject filter with ω_1 and ω_2 as cut off frequency and sampling interval as T.
(*Anna University, May, 2009*)
7. List the three well-known methods of design techniques for FIR filters and explain any one.
(*Anna University, December, 2006*)
8. Design an ideal low pass filter for a cut of frequency $\omega_c = 0.4$ rad using (8-tap) window design method.
(*Anna University, June, 2006*)
9. Determine the filter coefficients $h(n)$ of length $M = 15$ obtained by sampling its frequency response as

$$H\left[\left(\frac{2\pi}{15}\right)k\right] = \begin{cases} 1, & k = 0, 1, 2, 3, 4 \\ 0.4, & k = 5 \\ 0, & k = 6, 7 \end{cases}$$

using rectangular window.
(*Anna University, June, 2006*)
10. Design a digital filter with

$$H_d(e^{j\omega}) = \begin{cases} 1, & 2 \leq |\omega| \leq \pi \\ 0, & \text{otherwise} \end{cases}$$

using Hamming window with $N = 7$. Draw the frequency response.
(*Anna University, June, 2006*)
11. List the various steps in designing FIR filters.
(*Anna University, June, 2006*)
12. The desired frequency response of a desired filter is

$$H_d(\omega) = \begin{cases} e^{-j3w}, & \frac{-\pi}{4} \leq \omega \leq \frac{\pi}{4} \\ 0, & \frac{\pi}{4} \leq |\omega| \leq \pi \end{cases}$$

Determine the filter coefficients if the window function is defined as

$$\omega(x) = \begin{cases} 1, & 0 \le x \le 5 \\ 0, & \text{otherwise} \end{cases}$$

(*Anna University, June, 2006*)

13. Illustrate the steps involved in the design of linear phase FIR filter by the frequency sampling method.
14. An FIR filter is given by

$$y(n) = 2x(n) + \frac{4}{5}x(n-1) + \frac{3}{2}x(n-2) + \frac{2}{3}x(n-3)$$

Find the lattice structure coefficients.

(*Anna University, May, 2004*)

15. What are the issues in designing FIR filter using window method?

(*Anna University, May, 2004*)

16. Mention the advantages and disadvantages of FIR and IIR filters.

(*Anna University, May, 2004*)

17. Design a digital low pass FIR filter of length II with cut-off frequency of 0.5 kHz and sampling rate 2 kHz using Hamming window.

(*Anna University, May, 2004*)

18. Derive the frequency response of a linear phase FIR filter with symmetric impulse response.
19. Explain the design procedure for designing FIR filter using window function.
20. Explain the concept of optimum equiripple filter.
21. Design a Nine tap linear phase filter having the ideal response.

$$H_d(e^{j\omega}) = \begin{cases} 1, |\omega| \le \frac{\pi}{6} \\ 0, \frac{\pi}{6} \le |\omega| \le \frac{\pi}{3} \\ 1, \frac{\pi}{3} \le |\omega| \le \pi \end{cases}$$

using Hamming window and draw the realization for the same.

22. Design an FIR digital filter to approximate an ideal low pass filter with pass band gain of unity, cut-off frequency of 850 kHz and working at a sampling frequency of $f_s = 5$ kHz. The length of the impulse response should be 5. Use a rectangular window.

(*Anna University, December, 2003*)

23. The desired response of a low pass filter is,

$$H_d(e^{j\omega}) = \begin{cases} e^{-j3\omega}; & \frac{-3\pi}{4} \le \omega \le \frac{3\pi}{4} \\ 0, & \frac{3\pi}{4} \le |\omega| \le \pi \end{cases}$$

Determine the frequency response of the filter for $M = 7$ using a Hamming window.

(*Anna University, December, 2003*)

Finite Word Length Effects 5

Learning Objectives

After completing this chapter, you should be able to:

- provide an understanding of the errors that arise in practical DSP systems due to quantization and use of finite word length arithmetic.
- study the effects of errors on signal quality.
- develop the techniques to combat the errors.
- enhance the skill in the design of DSP systems.

5.1 Introduction

When digital systems are implemented either in hardware or in software, the filter coefficients are stored in binary registers. These registers can accommodate only a finite number of bits and hence, the filter coefficients have to be truncated or rounded-off in order to fit into these registers. Truncation or rounding of the data results in degradation of system performance. Also, in digital processing systems, a continuous-time input signal is sampled and quantized in order to get the digital signal. The process of quantization introduces an error in the signal which is called round off noise. This makes the system non-linear, and leads to limit cycle behaviour.

In general the effects due to finite precision representation of numbers in a digital system are commonly referred to as finite word length effects. Some of the finite word length effects in digital filters are:

1. Errors due to quantization of input data by A/D converter.
2. Errors due to quantization of filter coefficients.
3. Errors due to rounding the product in multiplication.
4. Errors due to overflow in addition.
5. Limit cycles.

The effects of these errors introduced by signal processing depend on a number of factors which include the type of arithmetic used the quality of the input signal and the DSP algorithm implemented. These are discussed in this chapter.

5.2 Representation of Numbers in Digital System

The basic operations involved in digital signal processing are multiplications, additions and delays. They are often carried out using either fixed-point or floating-point arithmetic. Block floating-point arithmetic combines the benefits of the above two operations. Fixed-point arithmetic is the most widely used arithmetic in DSP because it is very fast and less expensive when implemented. However, it is limited in the range of numbers that can be represented. Further it is susceptible to problems of overflow which may occur when the result of an addition exceeds the permissible number range. To prevent this the operands are scaled. However, this degrades the performance of DSP systems which reduces the signal to noise ratio.

Floating-point arithmetic is preferred where the magnitude of the variables or system coefficients vary widely and eliminates overflow problem. Further, floating-point processing simplifies programming. However, floating point arithmetic is more expensive and often slower. While fixed-point digital signal processors with large word lengths are extensively used in DSP techniques where wide dynamic range and high precision are required the floating point processing provides a simpler and more natural way of achieving these requirements. The applications of floating-point arithmetic include real time parameter equalization of digital audio signals, spectrum analysis in radar and sonar, seismology, biomedicine *etc.* The above two arithmetic operations are discussed below.

5.2.1 Fixed Point Representation

In fixed point representation, the bits allotted for integer part and fraction part are fixed, and so the position of binary point is also fixed.

5.2.1.1 Positive Binary Fraction Number

In fixed point representation, there is only one unique way of representing positive binary number as given by the following equation:

$$\text{Positive binary fraction number, } N_p = \sum_{i=0}^{B} d_i 2^{-i} \tag{5.1}$$

where d_i = ith digit of the number and B = number of fractional digits.

5.2.1.2 Negative Binary Fraction Number

In fixed point representation, there are three different formats for representing negative binary numbers. They are:

1. Sign magnitude format
2. One's complement format
3. Two's complement format

1. Sign Magnitude Format

Except the sign bit all other digits of the negative of a given number are same as that of its positive representation. The sign bit is 0 for positive number and 1 for negative number.

$$\text{Positive binary fraction number, } N_p = (0 \times 2^0) + \sum_{i=1}^{B} d_i 2^{-i} \tag{5.2}$$

$$\text{Negative binary fraction number, } N_n = (1 \times 2^0) + \sum_{i=1}^{B} d_i 2^{-i} \tag{5.3}$$

For example,

$$+0.125_{10} \longrightarrow 0.001_2$$
$$-0.125_{10} \longrightarrow 1.001_2$$

2. One's Complement Format

- In one's complement format, the positive number is same as that of sign-magnitude format.
- The negative of the given number is obtained by bit by bit complement of its positive representation

$$\text{Complement of } d_i = \bar{d}_i = (1 - d_i) \tag{5.4}$$

Negative binary fraction number in one's complement is,

$$N_{1c} = (1 \times 2^0) + \sum_{i=1}^{B} (1 - d_i) 2^{-i} \tag{5.5}$$

For example,

$$+0.125_{10} \longrightarrow 0.001_2$$
$$-0.125_{10} \longrightarrow 1.110_2$$

3. Two's Complement Format

- In two's complement format, the positive number is same as that of the given magnitude format.
- The negative of the given number is obtained by taking one's complement of its positive representation and then adding one to the least significant bit.

Negative binary fraction number in two's complement is,

$$N_{2c} = (1 \times 2^0) + \sum_{i=1}^{B} (1 - d_i) 2^{-i} + (1 \times 2^{-B}) \tag{5.6}$$

For example,

$$+0.125_{10} \longrightarrow 0.001_2$$
$$-0.125_{10} \longrightarrow 1.111_2$$

Disadvantage of Fixed Point Representation

It is impossible to represent too large and too small numbers by fixed point representation. Therefore, the range of numbers that can be represented in fixed point method for a given binary word size is less compared in floating point representation.

Example 5.1

Convert the decimal number 25.625 to binary form.

Solution

Integer part conversion

$$\begin{array}{r|l}
2 & 25 \\ \hline
2 & 12-1 \quad \uparrow \quad \text{(LSB)} \\ \hline
2 & 6-0 \quad \uparrow \\ \hline
2 & 3-0 \quad \uparrow \\ \hline
 & 1-1 \quad \uparrow \\
 & \rightarrow \quad \rightarrow \rightarrow \\
 & \text{(MSB)}
\end{array}$$

Fractional part conversion

	Integer	
$0.625 \times 2 = 1.25$	1	(MSB)
$0.25 \times 2 = 0.5$	0	$\downarrow$
$0.5 \times 2 = 1.0$	1	(LSB)

Therefore,

$$(25.625)_{10} = (1\ 1\ 0\ 0\ 1.1\ 0\ 1)_2$$

Example 5.2

Convert the following decimal numbers into binary. (*a*) $(20.675)_{10}$ and (*b*) $(120.75)_{10}$.

Solution

(*a*) $(20.675)_{10} \Rightarrow$ integer part conversion by successive division

$$\begin{array}{r|l}
2 & 20 \\ \hline
2 & 10-0 \quad \uparrow \quad \text{(LSB)} \\ \hline
2 & 5-0 \quad \uparrow \\ \hline
2 & 2-1 \quad \uparrow \\ \hline
 & 1-0 \quad \uparrow \\
 & \rightarrow \quad \rightarrow \rightarrow \\
 & \text{(MSB)}
\end{array}$$

$$(10100)_2$$

Fractional part conversion by successive multiplication

$$
\begin{array}{rll}
0.675 \times 2 = 1.35 & 1 & \text{(MSB)} \\
0.35 \times 2 = 0.7 & 0 & \downarrow \\
0.7 \times 2 = 1.4 & 1 & \downarrow \\
0.4 \times 2 = 0.8 & 0 & \downarrow \\
0.8 \times 2 = 1.6 & 1 & \downarrow \\
0.6 \times 2 = 1.2 & 1 & \downarrow \\
0.2 \times 2 = 0.4 & 0 & \text{(LSB)}
\end{array}
$$

$$(.1010110\ldots)_2$$

Binary equivalent of $(20.675)_{10}$ is

$$\boxed{(10100.1010110\ldots)_2}$$

(*b*) $(120.75)_{10} \Rightarrow$ integer part conversion

$$
\begin{array}{r|ll}
2 & 120 & \\ \hline
2 & 60 - 0 & \uparrow \ \text{(LSB)} \\ \hline
2 & 30 - 0 & \uparrow \\ \hline
2 & 15 - 0 & \uparrow \\ \hline
2 & 7 - 1 & \uparrow \\ \hline
2 & 3 - 1 & \uparrow \\ \hline
 & 1 - 1 & \uparrow \\
 & \rightarrow \quad \rightarrow & \rightarrow \\
 & \text{(MSB)} &
\end{array}
$$

$$(1111000)_2$$

fractional part conversion

$$
\begin{array}{rll}
0.75 \times 2 = 1.5 & 1 & \text{(MSB)} \\
 & & \downarrow \\
0.5 \times 2 = 1.0 & 1 & \text{(LSB)}
\end{array}
$$

$$(0.11)_2$$

Binary equivalent of $(120.75)_{10}$ is

$$\boxed{(1111000.11)_2}$$

Example 5.3

Represent the following number in fixed point representation.

$(a)\ +0.375_{10}$ $(b)\ -0.75_{10}$

Solution

(a) $+(0.375)_{10}$

In fixed point representation

$$+0.375_{10} = (0.011)_2$$

(b) $-(0.75)_{10}$

In fixed point representation there are three different formats for representing negative number:

(*i*) Sign-magnitude: $-(0.75)_{10} = 1.110.$
(*ii*) One's complement: $-(0.75)_{10} = 1.001.$
(*iii*) Two's complement: $-(0.75)_{10} = 1.010.$

Example 5.4

Represent the following numbers in sign magnitude form.

$(a)\ +8.25_{10}$ $(b)\ -8.25_{10}$

Solution

$$+(8.25)_{10} = \underset{\substack{\uparrow \\ \text{sign bit}}}{0}1000.010$$

$$-(8.25)_{10} = \underset{\substack{\uparrow \\ \text{sign bit}}}{1}1000.010$$

Example 5.5

Represent the following numbers in one complement form.

$(a)\ -0.375_{10}$ $(b)\ -0.0625_{10}$

Solution

(*a*) $-0.375_{10} = (1.1001111)_2$

$$0.375_{10} = (0.0110000)_2$$

Complementing each bit we get $-0.375_{10} = (1.1001111)_2$.

(*b*) $-0.0625_{10} = (1.1110111)_2$

$$0.0625_{10} = (0.0001000)_2$$

Complementing each bit we get $-0.0625_{10} = (1.1110111)_2$.

Example 5.6

Represent the following numbers in two's complement form.

(*a*) $-\ 0.125_{10}$ (*b*) $-\ 0.25_{10}$

Solution

(*a*) -0.125_{10} where $+0.125_{10} = 0.001_2$

$$\text{One's complement} \Rightarrow 1.110_2$$

$$\text{Two's complement} \Rightarrow 1.111_2$$

(*b*) -0.25_{10} where $+0.25_{10} = 0.010_2$

$$\text{One's complement} \Rightarrow 1.101_2$$

$$\text{Two's complement} \Rightarrow 1.110_2$$

5.2.2 Floating Point Representation

In floating point representation, the binary point can be shifted to desired position so that bits in the integer part and fraction part of a number can be varied. In general, the floating point number can be represented as

$$N_f = M \times 2^E \tag{5.7}$$

where M = mantissa and E = exponent.

Mantissa

- It will be in binary fraction format and in the range of $0.5 \leq M \leq 1$.
- If mantissa is characterized by 5 bits in which the left most one bit is used for representing sign and other 4 bits are used to represent a binary fraction number.

Exponent

- It is either a positive or negative integer.
- If it is characterized by 3 bits out of which the left most one bit is used to represent sign and the other two bits are used to represent a positive or negative binary integer number. The representation of floating point number is shown in Figure 5.1.

The range of number that can be represented by floating point format is from $\pm(2^{-4} \times 2^{-3})$ to $\pm((2 - 2^{-4}) \times 2^{-3})$.

Here 4 in 2^{-4} represents the 4 bits allotted for fractional binary number in mantissa and the 3 in 2^{-3} or 2^{+3} represents the maximum size of integer.

The IEEE-754 standard for 32 bit single precision floating point number is given by

$$N_f = (-1)^S \times 2^{E-127} \times M \tag{5.8}$$

where

S = 1-bit field for sign of number.
E = ε-bit field for exponent.
M = 23-bit field for Mantissa.

IEEE 754 format for 32 bit floating point number is shown in Figure 5.2.

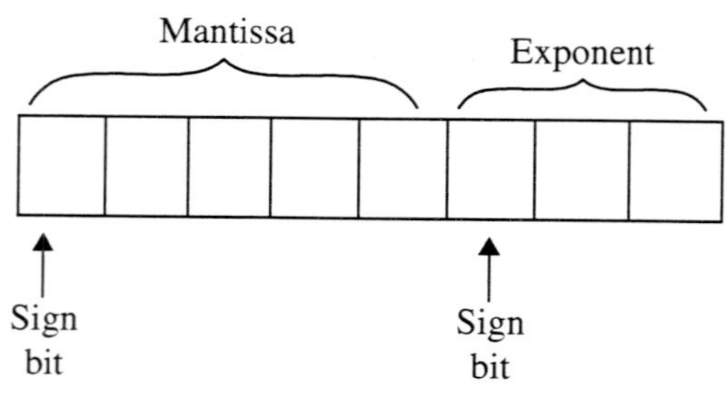

Figure 5.1 Floating point number representation.

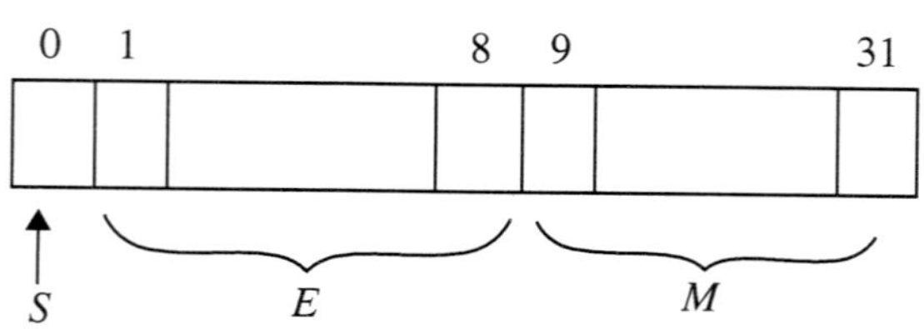

Figure 5.2 IEEE 754 format for 32 bit floating point number.

Example 5.7

Represent the following numbers in floating point representation with five bits for mantissa and three bits for exponent.

(*a*) $+7_{10}$ (*b*) $+0.25_{10}$ (*c*) -7_{10} (*d*) -0.25_{10}

Solution

(*a*)

$$+7_{10} = +111_2 = 0.1110 \times 2^{+3} = 0.1110 \times 2^{+11_2}$$

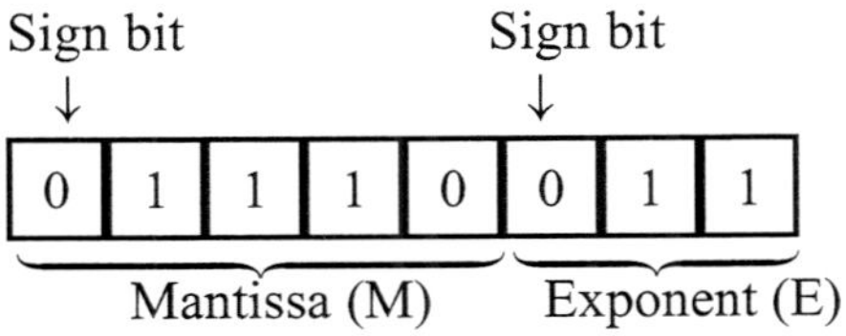

(*b*)

$$+0.25_{10} = +0.01_2 = 0.0100 \times 2^0 = 0.1000 \times 2^{-1} = 0.1000 \times 2^{-01_2}$$

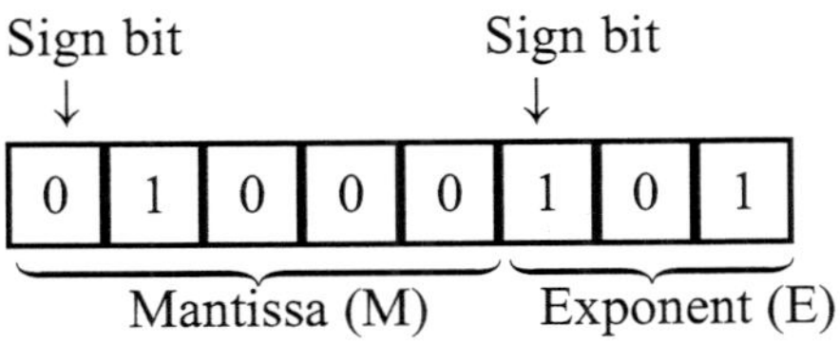

(*c*)

$$-7_{10} = -111_2 = 1.1110 \times 2^{+3} = 1.1110 \times 2^{+11_2}$$

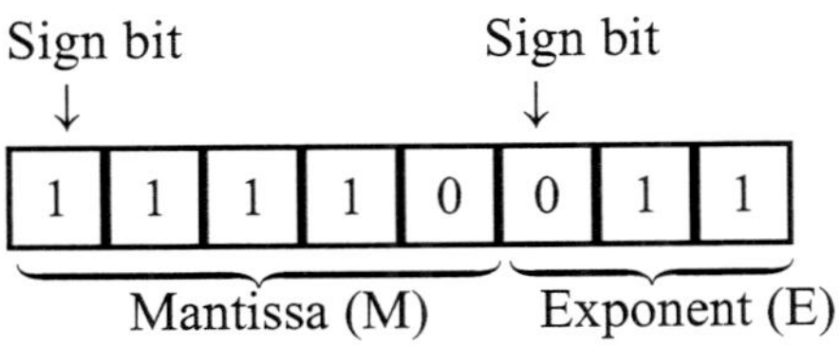

(*d*)

$$-0.25_{10} = -0.01_2 = 1.0100 \times 2^0 = 1.1000 \times 2^{-1} = 1.1000 \times 2^{-01_2}$$

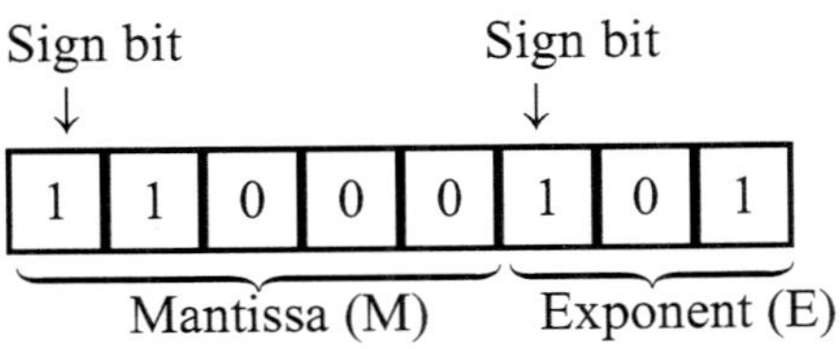

Example 5.8

Add $+0.125_{10}$ and -0.375_{10} in one's complement and two's complement form.

Solution

One's Complement Form

$$\begin{array}{rr} +0.125_{10} \Rightarrow & 0.001_2 \\ -0.375_{10} \text{ (in one's complement)} \Rightarrow & 1.100_2 \\ (+) & \overline{1.101_2} \end{array}$$

Since carry is zero the sum is negative. The sum can be converted to decimal as

$$1.101_2 \xrightarrow{\text{extract sign bit}} 0.101_2 \xrightarrow[\text{fractional part}]{\text{complement the}} -0.010_2 \xrightarrow{\text{Convert to decimal}} -0.25_{10}$$

Two's Complement Form

$$\begin{array}{rr} +0.125_{10} \Rightarrow & 0.001_2 \\ -0.375_{10} \text{ (in two's complement)} \Rightarrow & 1.101_2 \\ (+) & \overline{1.110_2} \end{array}$$

Since carry is zero the sum is negative

$$1.110_2 \xrightarrow{\text{extract sign bit}} 0.110_2 \xrightarrow{\text{2's complement}} -0.010_2 \xrightarrow{\text{Convert to decimal}} -0.25_{10}$$

Example 5.9

Add -0.125_{10} and $+0.375_{10}$ in one's complement and two's complement form.

Solution

One's Complement Form

$$\begin{array}{rr} -0.125_{10} \text{ (in one's complement)} \Rightarrow & 1.110_2 \\ +0.375_{10} \Rightarrow & 0.011_2 \\ (+) & \overline{1.001} \\ & 1 \\ & \overline{0.010} \end{array}$$

Since carry is one, the sum is positive

$$0.010_2 \xrightarrow{\text{Convert to decimal}} +.25_{10}$$

Two's Complement Form

$$\begin{aligned} -0.125_{10} \text{ (in two's complement)} &\Rightarrow 1.111_2 \\ +0.375_{10} &\Rightarrow 0.011_2 \\ (+) & \overline{10.010} \end{aligned}$$

Discard the carry, since the sum is positive.

$$0.010_2 \xrightarrow[\text{to decimal}]{\text{convert}} +0.25_{10}$$

Example 5.10

Multiply $+0.25_{10}$ and $+5_{10}$ in fixed point format.

Solution

$$+0.25_{10} = 0.010_2$$

$$+5_{10} = 101_2$$

$$\begin{array}{r} 0.010_2 \quad \times 101_2 \\ \hline 0\,0\,1\,0 \\ 0\,0\,0\,0 \\ 0\,0\,1\,0 \\ \hline 0\,0\,1.\,0\,1\,0_2 \end{array}$$

$$001.010_2 \xrightarrow{\text{convert to decimal}} 1.25_{10}$$

Example 5.11

Add $+0.125_{10}$ and $+5_{10}$ in floating point format.

Solution

$$\begin{aligned} +5_{10} = +101_2 &= 0.101000 \times 2^{+3_{10}} = 0.101000 \times 2^{11_2} \\ &= 0.101000 \times 2^{011_2} \end{aligned}$$

$$+0.125_{10} = +.001_2 = 0.100000 \times 2^{-2_{10}} \xrightarrow{\text{unnormalized}} 0.000001 \times 2^{+3_{10}}$$

$$= 0.000001 \times 2^{011_2}$$

$$+5_{10} \Rightarrow 0.101000 \times 2^{011_2}$$

$$+0.125_{10} \Rightarrow \underline{0.000001 \times 2^{011_2}}$$

$$0.101001 \times 2^{011_2}$$

$$0.101001 \times 2^{+3_2} = 101.001 \times 2^{0_2} = 101.001_2 = 5.125_{10}$$

Example 5.12

Multiply $+0.125_{10}$ and $+5_{10}$ in floating point format.

Solution

$$+0.125_{10} = 0.100000 \times 2^{-2_{10}}$$

$$+5_{10} = 0.101000 \times 2^{+3_{10}}$$

$$+0.125_{10} \times +5_{10} \Rightarrow (0.100000 \times 0.101000) \times 2^{-2+3}$$

$$\Rightarrow 0.010100 \times 2^1$$

$$0.010100 \times 2^1 \xrightarrow{\text{normalized}} 0.10100 \times 2^0 = 0.625_{10}$$

5.3 Methods of Quantization

The process of converting a discrete-time continuous amplitude signal into a digital signal by expressing each sample value as a finite number of digits is called **quantization**. The error introduced in representing the continuous valued signal by a finite set of discrete level is called "**quantization error or quantization noise**". The quantization error is a sequence which is defined as the difference between the quantized value and the actual sample value. The actual values of the samples of $x(n)$ cannot be processed by DSP or a digital computer since it is very difficult to store and manipulate all the samples. To eliminate the excess digits that occur due to quantization either discard them (truncation) or discard them by rounding the resulting number (rounding).

Thus, there are two methods of quantization employed in digital system. They are: (1) Truncation; and (2) Rounding. They are discussed below.

5.3.1 Truncation

Truncation is the process of reducing the size of binary numbers by discarding all bits less significant than the least significant bit that is retained. In the truncation of a binary numbers to b bits, all the less significant bits beyond b^{th} bit are discarded. The quantization steps are marked on y-axis and the range of unquantized numbers are marked on x-axis.

1. Any positive unquantized number in the range $0 \leq N \leq (1 \times 2^{-b})$ will be assigned the quantization step (0×2^{-b}).
2. Any positive unquantized number in the range $(1 \times 2^{-b}) \leq N \leq (2 \times 2^{-b})$ will be assigned the quantization step (1×2^{-b}) and so on.

Example 5.13

Perform the quantization of 0.875_{10} to 2 bit by truncation.

Solution

$$0.875_{10} \xrightarrow[\text{to binary}]{\text{convert}} 0.1110_2 \xrightarrow{\text{truncate to 2 bits}} 0.11_2 \xrightarrow[\text{to decimal}]{\text{convert}} 0.75_{10}$$

5.3.1.1 *Fixed Point Number System*

In fixed point number system, the effect of truncation on positive numbers are same in all the three representations. The error due to truncation of negative number depends on the type of representation of the number. Let N = unquantized fixed point binary numbers and N_t = fixed point binary number quantized by truncation. The quantization error due to truncation is

$$\text{Truncation error, } e_t = N_t - N \tag{5.9}$$

The range of errors in truncation of fixed point numbers in different types of representation are shown in Figure 5.3 and tabulated in Table 5.1.

The truncation of a positive number results in a number that is smaller than the unquantized number hence truncation error is always negative.

For the truncation of negative numbers represented in sign magnitude and one's complement format, the error is always positive because truncation basically reduces the magnitude of the numbers.

Table 5.1 Range of error in truncation of fixed point numbers

Numbers and its representation	Range of error when truncated to b bits
Positive numbers	$0 \geq e > -2^{-b}$
Sign magnitude negative number	$0 \leq e < -2^{-b}$
One's complement negative number	$0 \leq e < -2^{-b}$
Two's complement negative number	$0 \geq e > -2^{-b}$

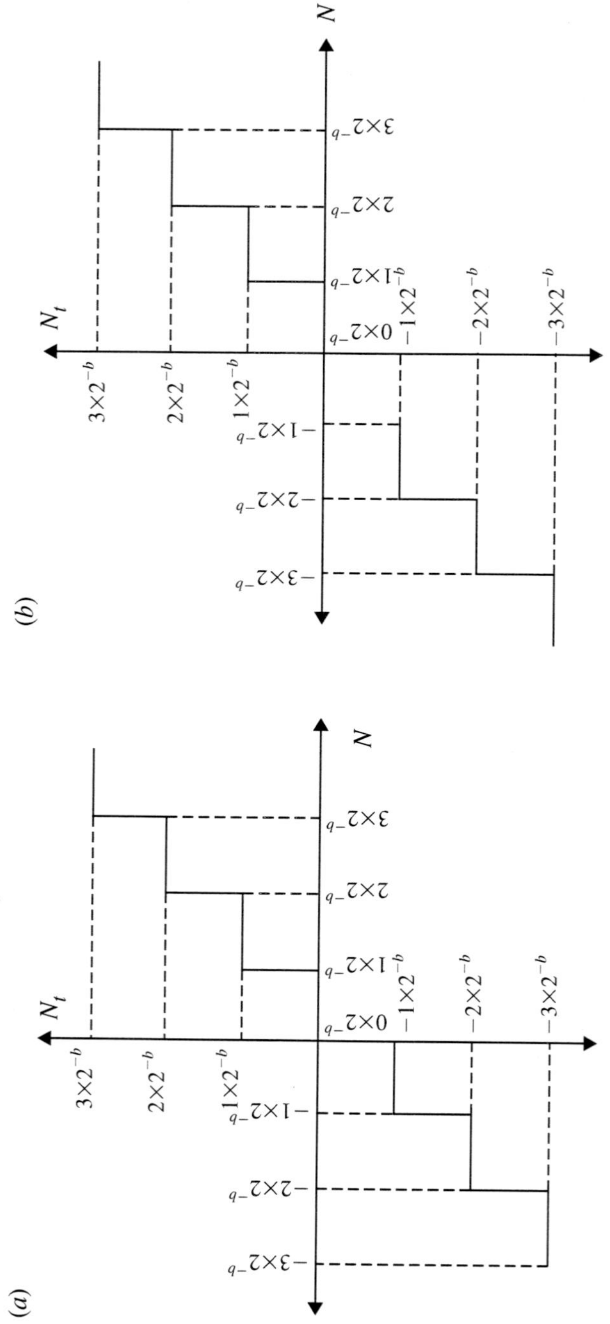

Figure 5.3 Truncation characteristics of (*a*) 2's complement, (*b*) sign magnitude and 1's complement.

In the two's complement representation the negative of a number is obtained by subtracting the corresponding positive number from 2. Therefore, the effect of truncation on a negative number is to increase the magnitude of the negative number and so the truncation error is always negative.

5.3.1.2 Floating Point Number System

In floating point representation, the mantissa of the number alone is truncated. The truncation error in a floating point number is proportional to the number being quantized.

Let N_f = unquantized floating point binary number and N_{tf} = truncated floating point binary number. Now

$$N_{tf} = N_f + N_f \varepsilon_t \tag{5.10}$$

where ε_t is the relative error due to truncation of floating point number. Relative error due to truncation is,

$$\varepsilon_t = \frac{N_{tf} - N_f}{N_f} \tag{5.11}$$

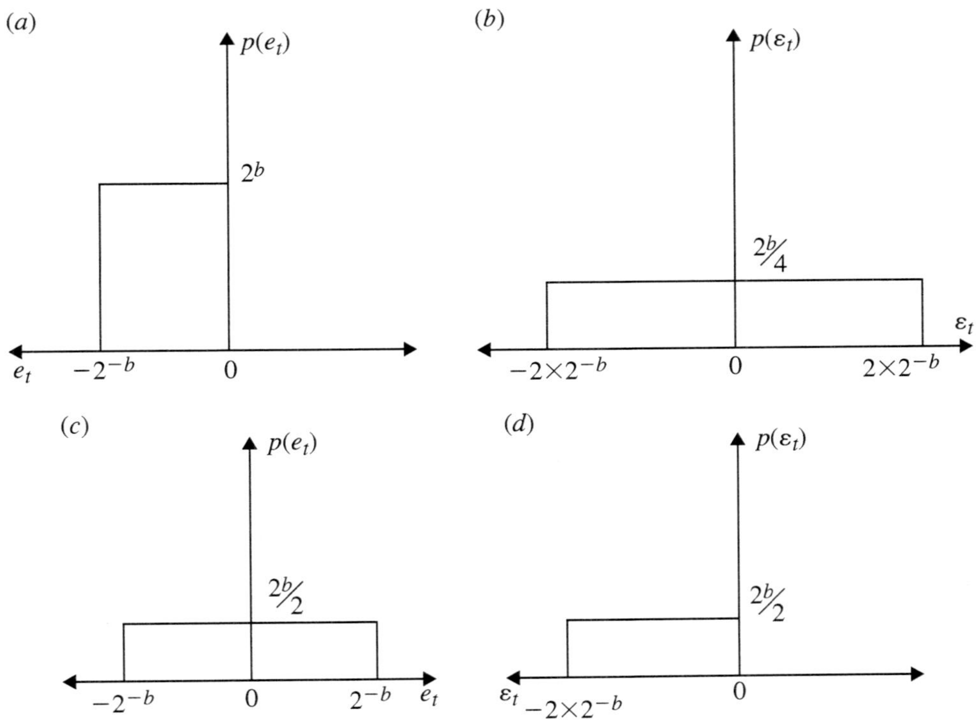

Figure 5.4 Quantization noise probability density function for truncations. (*a*) Fixed point-two complement, (*b*) Floating point when mantissa in two's complement, (*c*) Fixed point-one's complement or sign magnitude and (*d*) Floating point when mantissa is one's complement or in sign magnitude.

Table 5.2 Range of error in truncation of floating point number

Type of representation for mantissa	Range of error when mantissa is truncated to b bits
Two's complement positive mantissa	$0 \geq \varepsilon_t > -2^{-b} \times 2$
Two's complement negative mantissa	$0 \leq \varepsilon_t < 2^{-b} \times 2$
One's complement positive and negative mantissa	$0 \leq \varepsilon_t < -2 \times 2^{-b}$
Sign magnitude positive and negative mantissa	$0 \leq \varepsilon_t < -2 \times 2^{-b}$

In truncation of binary number, the range of error is known but the probability of obtaining an error within the range is not known. Hence, it is assumed that the errors occur uniformly throughout the interval. The range of error in truncation of floating point number is shown in Table 5.2 and the corresponding quantization noise probability density function is shown in Figure 5.4.

5.3.2 Rounding

Rounding is the process of reducing the size of a binary number to finite word size of b bits such that the rounded b bit number is closest to the original unquantized number. The rounding process consists of truncation and addition. In rounding of a number to b bits, first the unquantized number is truncated to b bits by retaining the most significant b bits. Then a zero or one is added to LSB of the truncated number depending on the bit that is next to the least significant bit that is retained. If the bit next to the least significant bit that is retained is zero, then zero is added to the least significant bit of the truncated number. If the bit next to the least significant bit that is retained is one, then one is added to the least significant bit of the truncated number. The input-output characteristics of the quantizer used for rounding is shown in Figure 5.5.

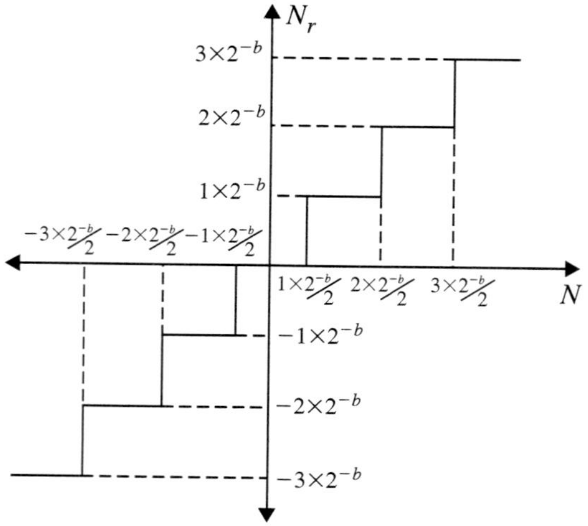

Figure 5.5 Input-output characteristics of the quantizer used for rounding.

The quantization steps are marked on y-axis and the range of unquantized numbers are marked on x-axis.

1. Any positive unquantized number in the range $1 \times \frac{2^{-b}}{2} \leq N < 2 \times \frac{2^{-b}}{2}$ will be assigned the quantization step 1×2^{-b}.
2. Any positive unquantized number in the range $2 \times \frac{2^{-b}}{2} \leq N < 3 \times \frac{3^{-b}}{2}$ will be assigned the quantization step 2×2^{-b} and so on.

Example 5.14

Perform the quantization of 0.0625_{10} to 3 bit by rounding.

Solution

$$0.0625_{10} \xrightarrow[\text{to binary}]{\text{convert}} 0.0001_2 \xrightarrow{\text{rounded to 3 bits}} 0.001_2 \xrightarrow[\text{to decimal}]{\text{convert}} 0.125_{10}$$

Fixed Point Number

Let $N =$ unquantized fixed point binary number and $N_r =$ fixed point binary number quantized by rounding. The quantization error in fixed point number due to rounding is defined as

$$\text{Rounding error, } e_r = N_r - N \tag{5.12}$$

The range of error due to rounding for all the three formats of fixed point representation is same. In fixed point representation the range of error made by rounding a number to b bits is

$$\frac{-2^{-b}}{2} \leq e_r \leq \frac{2^{-b}}{2} \tag{5.13}$$

Floating Point Number

Let $N_f =$ unquantized floating point binary number and $N_{rf} =$ rounded floating point binary number. Now

$$N_{rf} = N_f + N_f \varepsilon_r \tag{5.14}$$

where ε_r is the relative error due to rounding of a floating point number.

$$\therefore \text{Relative error due to rounding, } \varepsilon_r = \frac{N_{rf} - N_f}{N_f} \tag{5.15}$$

The range of error by rounding a number in floating point representation to b bits is,

$$-2^{-b} \leq \varepsilon_r \leq 2^{-b}. \tag{5.16}$$

The probability density function for rounding fixed point and floating numbers are shown in Figure 5.6.

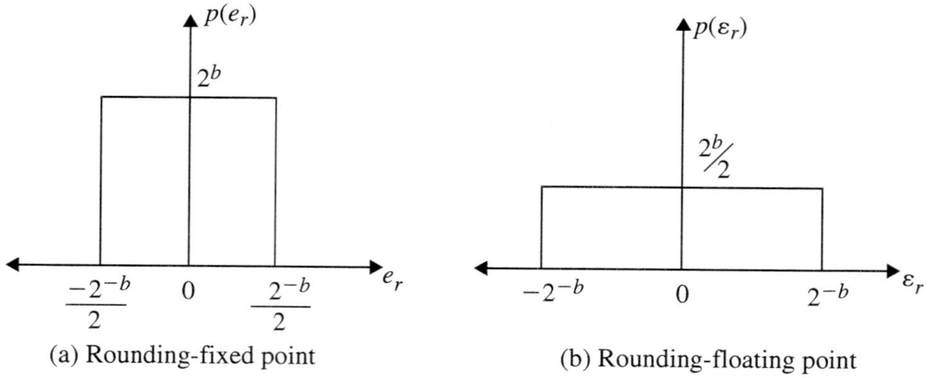

Figure 5.6 Quantization noise probability density functions for rounding.

5.4 Quantization of Input Data by Analog to Digital Converter

The process of analog to digital conversion involves: (i) sampling the continuous time signal at a rate much greater than Nyguist rate and (ii) qunatising the amplitude of the sampled signal into a set of discrete amplitude levels. The input-output characteristics of a uniform quantizers is shown in Figure 5.7. This quantizer rounds the sampled signal to the nearest quantized output level. The difference between the quantized signal amplitude $x_q(n)$ and the actual signal amplitude $x(n)$ is called the quantization error $e(n)$. That is

$$e(n) = x_q(n) - x(n)$$

Since, rounding is involved in the process of quantization the range of values for the quantization error is

$$-\frac{2^{-b}}{2} \leq e(n) \leq \frac{2^{-b}}{2} \tag{5.17}$$

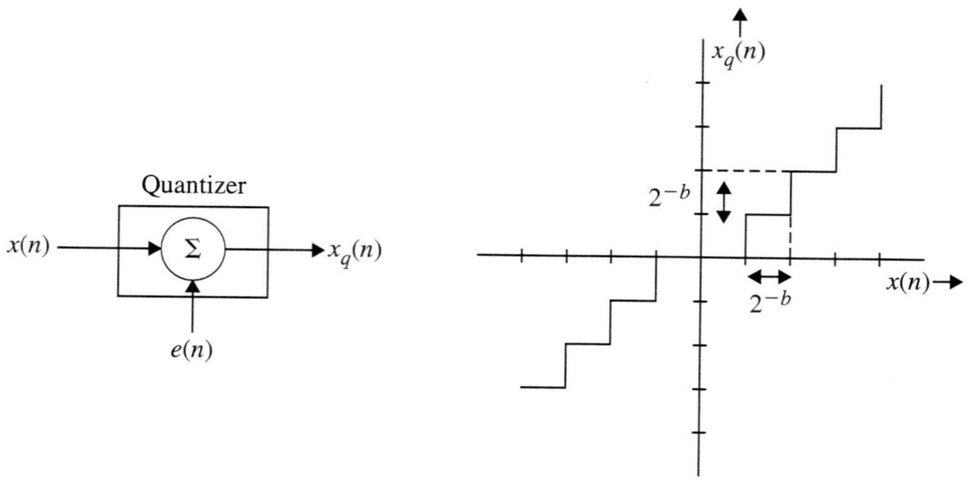

Figure 5.7 Two complement number quantization.

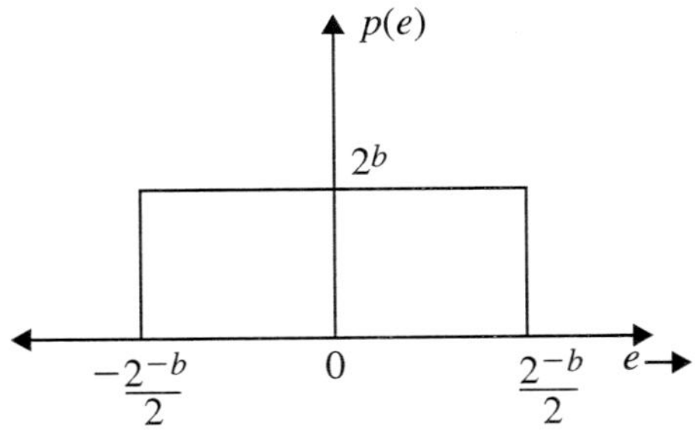

Figure 5.8 Probability density function for quantization round-off error in A/D conversion.

The quantization error is assumed to be uniformly distributed over $-\frac{2^{-b}}{2} \leq e(n) \leq \frac{2^{-b}}{2}$. It is also assumed that this quantization noise $e(n)$ is a stationary white noise sequence $x(n)$ which traverses several quantization levels between two successive samples.

In the process of quantization, the samples value is rounded off to the nearest quantization level. The probability density function for the quantization round off error in A/D conversion is shown in Figure 5.8.

It can be noted from the Figure 5.8, that the quantization error is uniformly distributed and the mean value of error in zero. The power of the quantization noise, which is nothing but variance (σ_e^2) is given by

$$\sigma_e^2 = E[e^2(n)] - E^2[e(n)] \tag{5.18}$$

$$= E[e^2(n)] \tag{5.19}$$

Therefore, mean value of error is zero, *i.e.*, $E[e(n)] = 0$.

Qualification step size is expressed as,

$$q = \frac{R}{2^b} \qquad \text{(for two's complement)} \tag{5.20}$$

where R = range of analog signal to be quantized. Usually the analog signal is scaled such that the magnitude of quantized signal is less or equal to one. In such case the range of analog signal to be quantized is -1 to 1 therefore $R = 2$.

$$\text{Quantization step size } q = \frac{2}{2^b} = 2.2^{-b} \tag{5.21}$$

The quantization error for rounding will be in the range of $-q/2$ to $+q/2$

$$\therefore \text{ Variance of error signal } \sigma_e^2 = \frac{1}{\frac{q}{2} - (-q/2)} \int_{-q/2}^{q/2} e^2 de \tag{5.22}$$

$$= \frac{1}{q}\left[\frac{e^3}{3}\right]_{-(q/2)}^{q/2} = \frac{1}{3q}\left[\frac{q^3}{8} + \frac{q^3}{8}\right]$$

$$= \frac{1}{3q} \cdot \frac{2q^3}{8} = \frac{q^2}{12} \tag{5.23}$$

$$\boxed{\sigma_e^2 = \frac{1}{12}\left(\frac{R}{2^{-b}}\right)^2} \tag{5.24}$$

The variance of error signal is also called steady state noise power due to input quantization.

5.4.1 Output Noise Power due to the Quantization Error Signal

After converting the continuous time signal into digital signal, let us assume that this quantized signal is applied as an input to a digital system with impulse response $h(n)$.

The quantized input signal of a digital system can be represented as a sum of unquantized signal $x(n)$ and error signal $e(n)$ as shown in Figure 5.9

$$y'(n) = x_q(n) * h(n) \tag{5.25}$$

$$= [x(n) + e(n)] * h(n)$$

$$y'(n) = [x(n) * h(n)] + [e(n) * h(n)] \tag{5.26}$$

$$y'(n) = y(n) + e(n) \tag{5.27}$$

where

$y(n) = x(n) * h(n)$ is the output due to input signal

$\epsilon(n) = e(n) * h(n)$ is the output due to error signal

Variance of the signal $\epsilon(n)$ is called the output noise power or steady output noise power.

Output noise power (or) steady state output noise power due to quantization errors is given by the following equation:

$$\sigma_{e0}^2 = \sigma_e^2 \sum_{n=0}^{\infty} h^2(n) \tag{5.28}$$

The summation of $h^2(n)$ can be evaluated using Parseval's theorem

$$\sigma_{e0}^2 = \sigma_e^2 \sum_{n=0}^{\infty} h^2(n) = \sigma_e^2 \frac{1}{2\pi j} \oint_c H(z)H(z^{-1})z^{-1}dz \tag{5.29}$$

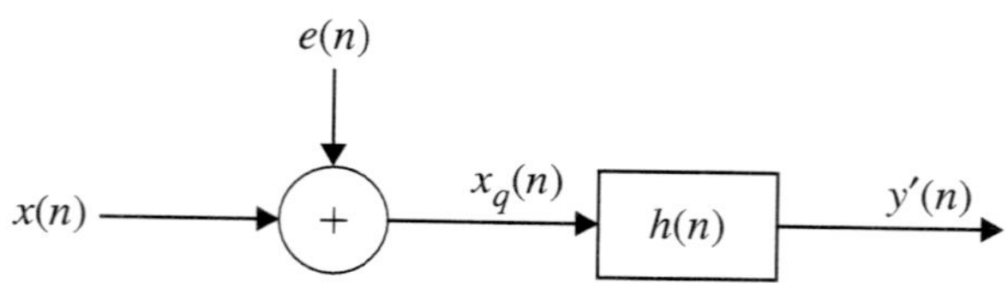

Figure 5.9 Representation of quantization noise in digital system.

The closed contour integration can be evaluated using residue theorem of z-transform

$$\sigma_{e0}^2 = \sigma_e^2 \sum_{i=1}^{N} \text{Res}[H(z)H(z^{-1})z^{-1}]|_{z=p_i} \tag{5.30}$$

where $p_1, p_2, \ldots, p_n$ are poles of $H(z)H(z^{-1})z^{-1}$. Since the closed contour integration is around the unit circle $|z| = 1$, only the residue of the poles that is inside the unit circle are considered.

Example 5.15

The output of an A/D converter is applied to a digital filter whose system function is,

$$H(z) = \frac{z(0.5)}{z - 0.5}$$

Find the output noise power from the digital filter, when the input signal is quantized to have eight bits.

Solution Given $b = 8$ (assuming sign bit is included). Let $R = 2$

$$\text{Quantization step size } q = \frac{R}{2^b} = \frac{2}{2^b} = 2^{2^{-b}} = 2 \times 2^{-8} = 2^{-7}.$$

The input quantization noise power is obtained using equation (5.23)

$$\sigma_e^2 = \frac{q^2}{12} = \frac{(2^{-7})^2}{12} = \frac{2^{-4}}{12} = 5.086 \times 10^{-6}$$

The output noise power is given by

$$\sigma_{e0}^2 = \frac{\sigma_e^2}{2\pi j} \oint_c H(z)H(z^{-1})z^{-1} dz$$

$$= \sigma_e^2 \sum_{i=1}^{N} \text{Res}[H(z)H(z^{-1})z^{-1}]|_{z=p_i}$$

$$H(z)H(z^{-1})z^{-1} = \frac{0.5z}{z-0.5} \cdot \frac{0.5z^{-1}}{z^{-1}-0.5} \cdot z^{-1}$$

$$= \frac{0.25z^{-1}}{z^{-1}(z-0.5)(1-0.5z)}$$

$$= \frac{0.25}{(z-0.5)(1-0.5z)} \qquad [\text{poles are at } z = 0.5,\ z = 2]$$

$\text{Res}[H(z)H(z^{-1})z^{-1}]$ due to pole $z = 0.5$ alone is to be considered.

$$\text{Res}[H(z)H(z^{-1})z^{-1}]|_{z=0.5} = \left.\frac{(z-0.5)0.25}{(z-0.5)(1-0.5z)}\right|_{z=0.5}$$

[$\because$ $z = 0.5$ pole lies insider the unit circle]

$$= \frac{1}{3}$$

Therefore, the output noise power is

$$\sigma_{e0}^2 = \sigma_e^2 \times \text{Res}[H(z)H(z^{-1})z^{-1}]|_{z=0.5}$$

$$= 5.086 \times 10^{-6} \times \frac{1}{3}$$

$$\boxed{\sigma_{e0}^2 = 1.6954 \times 10^{-6}.}$$

Example 5.16

For the recursive filter shown in figure, the input $x(n)$ has a peak value of 10V, represented by 6 bits. Compute the variance of output due to A/D conversion process

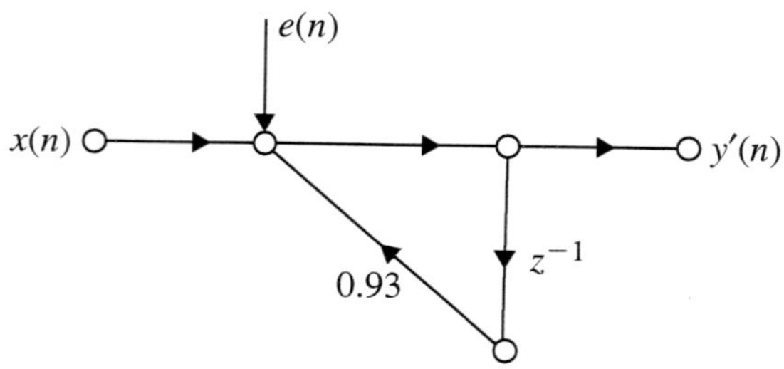

Solution Given $R = 10V$, $b = 6$ bits.

Note: If in case, R value is not mentioned in the problem assume $R = 2V$.

$$\text{Quantization step size, } q = \frac{R}{2^b}$$

$$\therefore\ q = \frac{10}{2^6} = 0.15625$$

The variance of the error signal is σ_2^2.

$$\therefore\ \sigma_e^2 = \frac{q^2}{12} = \frac{(0.15625)^2}{12} = 2.0345 \times 10^{-3}$$

The given recursive (first order) filter can be redrawn as follows:

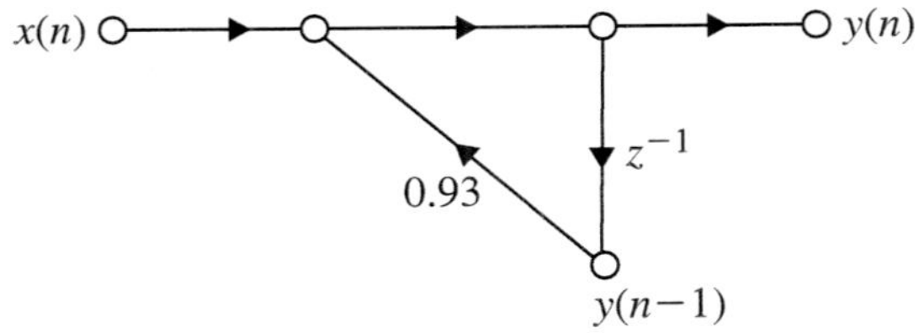

The difference equation of the system is,

$$y(n) = 0.93y(n-1) + x(n)$$

Taking z-transform for the above equation we get

$$Z\{y(n)\} = 0.93Z\{y(n-1)\} + Z\{x(n)\}$$

$$Y(z) = 0.93z^{-1}Y(z) + X(z) \qquad [\because Z\{f(n-1)\} = z^{-1}F(z)]$$

$$X(z) = Y(z)(1 - 0.93z^{-1})$$

$$\frac{Y(z)}{X(z)} = \frac{1}{(1 - 0.93z^{-1})} = H(z)$$

The steady state output noise power due to quantization is,

$$\sigma_{e0}^2 = \sigma_e^2 \sum_{i=1}^{N} \text{Res}[H(z)H(z^{-1})z^{-1}]|_{z=p_i}$$

$$H(z) = \frac{1}{1 - 0.93z^{-1}} = \frac{z}{z - 0.93}$$

$$H(z^{-1}) = \frac{z^{-1}}{z^{-1} - 0.93} \qquad [\text{Replace } z \text{ by } z^{-1} \text{ in } H(z) \text{ to get } H(z^{-1})]$$

$$\therefore\ H(z)H(z^{-1})z^{-1} = \frac{z}{z - 0.93} \times \frac{z^{-1}}{z^{-1} - 0.93} \times z^{-1}$$

$$= \frac{z^{-1}}{(z - 0.93)(z^{-1} - 0.93)}$$

$$= \frac{1}{(z - 0.93)(1 - 0.93z)}$$

Here $H(z)$ has only one pole at $p_i = 0.93$.

$$\therefore\ \sum_{i=1}^{N} \text{Res}[H(z)H(z^{-1})z^{-1}]|_{z=p_i}$$

$$= \text{Res}[H(z)H(z^{-1})z^{-1}]|_{z=0.93}$$

$$[\because \text{ if } p_i \text{ is the pole } \text{Res}[H(z)] = (s - p_i) \times H(z)_{z=p_i}]$$

$$\sum_{i=1}^{N} = \left.\frac{(z-0.93)z^{-1}}{(z-0.93)(z^{-1}-0.93)}\right|_{z=0.93}$$

$$= \frac{(0.93)^{-1}}{((0.93)^{-1}-0.93)} = 7.4019$$

Therefore, the output noise power (or variance) due to A/D conversion process is,

$$\sigma_{e0}^2 = \sigma_e^2 \sum_{i=1}^{N} \text{Res}[H(z)H(z^{-1})z^{-1}]|_{z=0.93}$$

$$= 2.0345 \times 10^{-3} \times 7.4019$$

$$\boxed{\sigma_{e0}^2 = 0.0151}$$

Example 5.17

The input to the system

$$y(n) = 0.999y(n-1) + x(n)$$

is applied to an ADC. What is the power produced by the quantization noise at the output of the filter if the input is quantized to (*a*) 8 bits and (*b*) 16 bits?

(*Anna University, May, 2007*)

Solution Given

$$y(n) = 0.999y(n-1) + x(n)$$

Taking z-transform on the both sides we get

$$Y(z) = 0.999z^{-1}Y(z) + X(z)$$

$$H(z) = \frac{Y(z)}{X(z)} = \frac{1}{1-0.999z^{-1}}$$

The quantization noise power at the output of the digital filter is

$$\sigma_{e0}^2 = \sigma_e^2 \sum_{i=1}^{N} \text{Res}[H(z)H(z^{-1})z^{-1}]|_{z=p_i}$$

$$H(z)H(z^{-1})z^{-1} = \left(\frac{1}{1-0.999z^{-1}}\right)\left(\frac{1}{1-0.999z}\right)z^{-1}$$

$$= \frac{z^{-1}}{z^{-1}(z-0.999)(1-0.999z)}$$

$$= \frac{z^{-1}}{(z-0.999)(1-0.999z)}$$

Here $H(z)$ has only one pole at $p = 0.999$ which lies inside the unit circle. Therefore

$$\sum_{i=1}^{N} \text{Res}[H(z)H(z^{-1})z^{-1}]\Big|_{z=p_i} = \text{Res}[H(z)H(z^{-1})z^{-1}]\Big|_{z=0.999}$$

$$= (z-0.999)\frac{1}{[z-0.999][1-0.999z]}\Big|_{z=0.999}$$

$$= \frac{1}{(1-0.999z)}\Big|_{z=0.999}$$

$$= \frac{1}{(1-0.999z)^2}$$

$$= 500.25$$

Therefore

$$\sigma_{e0}^2 = \sigma_e^2(500.25)$$

$$= \frac{q^2}{12}(500.25) = \frac{\left(\frac{R}{2^b}\right)^2}{12}(500.25)$$

Let $R = 2V$

(a) Given $b = 8$ bits (including sign bit)

$$\sigma_{e0}^2 = \frac{\left(\frac{2}{2^8}\right)^2}{12}[500.25]$$

$$= \frac{2^{-14}}{12}(500.25) = 2.544 \times 10^{-3}$$

(b) Given $b = 16$ bits

$$\sigma_{e0}^2 = \frac{\left(\frac{2}{2^{16}}\right)^2}{12}[500.25]$$

$$= \frac{2^{-30}}{12}(500.25) = 3.882 \times 10^{-8}$$

Example 5.18

Consider $(b+1)$-bits (including sign bit) bipolar A/D converter. Obtain an expression for signal to quantization noise ratio. State the assumption made.

(Anna University, May 2007)

Solution The quantization noise model of A/D converter is,

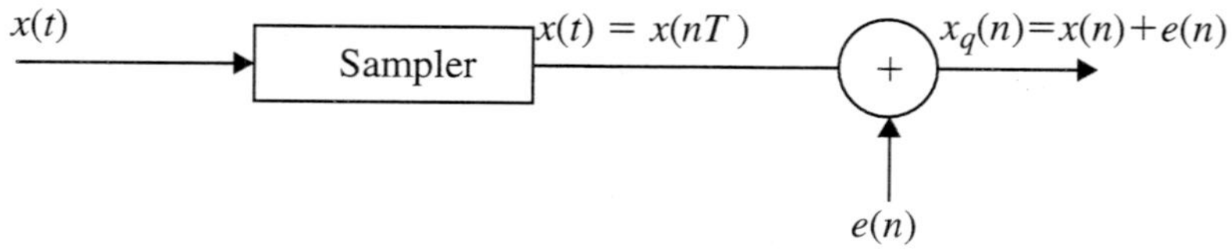

The A/D converter output is the sum of the input signal $x(n)$ and the error signal $e(n)$. If the rounding is used for quantization then the quantization error is

$$e(n) = x_q(n) - x(n) \text{ is bounded by } \frac{-q}{2} \leq e(n) \leq \frac{q}{2}$$

In most cases, we can assume that the A/D conversion error $e(n)$ has the following properties:

(*i*) The error sequence $e(n)$ is a sample sequence of a stationary random process.
(*ii*) The error signal is uncorrected with $x(n)$ and other signal in the system.
(*iii*) The error is a white noise process with uniform amplitude probability distribution over the range of quantization error.

The variance of $e(n)$ is given by

$$\sigma_e^2 = E[e^2(n)] - E^2[e(n)]$$

$$\sigma_e^2 = E[e^2(n)]$$

$$= \frac{1}{q}\int_{-q/2}^{q/2} e^2(n)de = \frac{1}{q}\left[\frac{e^3}{3}\right]_{-q/2}^{q/2}$$

$$= \frac{1}{3q} \times \left[\frac{q^3}{8} + \frac{q^3}{8}\right] = \frac{q^2}{12}$$

$$\sigma_e^2 = \frac{\left(\frac{2}{2^{b+1}}\right)^2}{12}$$

$$\boxed{\sigma_e^2 = \frac{2^{-2b}}{12}}$$

where b is number of bits (excluding sign bit). σ_e^2 is also known as the steady state noise power due to input quantization.

If the input signal is $x(n)$ and its variance is σ_x^2, then the ratio of signal power to noise power which is known as signal to noise ratio for rounding is

$$\boxed{\text{SNR} = \frac{\sigma_x^2}{\sigma_e^2} = \frac{\sigma_x^2}{\frac{2^{-2b}}{12}} = 12(2^{2b}\sigma_x^2)}$$

Signal to noise ratio in dB is expressed as

$$\text{SNR (dB)} = 10 \log_{10} \frac{\sigma_x^2}{\sigma_e^2} = 10 \log_{10}(12\ 2^{2b} \sigma_x^2)$$

$$\boxed{\text{SNR (dB)} = 6.02b + 10.79 + 10 \log_{10} \sigma_x^2}$$

SNR increases approximately by 6 dB for each bit added to register length.

5.5 Quantization of Filter Coefficients

In the design of a digital filter the coefficients are evaluated with infinite precision. But they are limited by the word length of the register used to store the coefficients. Usually the filter coefficients are quantized to the word size of the register used to store them either by truncation or by rounding.

The location of poles and zeros of the digital filters directly depends on the value of filter coefficients. The quantization of the filter coefficients will modify the value of poles and zeros and so the location of the poles and zeros will be shifted from the desired location. This will create deviation in the frequency response of the system. Hence we obtain a filter having a frequency response that is different from the frequency response of the filter with unquantized coefficients. The sensitivity of the filter frequency response characteristics to quantization of the filter coefficients is minimized by realizing the filter having a large number of poles and zeros as an interconnection of second-order section. **Therefore, the coefficient quantization has less effect in cascade realization when compared to other realizations.**

Example 5.19

For the second order IIR filter, the system function is,

$$H(z) = \frac{1}{(1 - 0.5z^{-1})(1 - 0.45z^{-1})}$$

Study the effect of shift in pole location with 3 bit coefficient representation in direct and cascade forms.

Solution

$$H(z) = \frac{1}{(1 - 0.5z^{-1})(1 - 0.45z^{-1})} = \frac{z^2}{(z - 0.5)(z - 0.45)}$$

Original poles of $H(z) \Longrightarrow p_1 = 0.5$ and $p_2 = 0.45$.

Case (*i*) Direct Form

$$H(z) = \frac{1}{(1-0.5z^{-1})(1-0.45z^{-1})} = \frac{1}{(1-0.95z^{-1}+0.225z^{-1})}$$

Quantization of coefficient by truncation

$$.95_{10} \xrightarrow{\text{Convert to binary}} .1111_2 \xrightarrow{\text{Truncate to 3 bits}} .111_2 \xrightarrow{\text{Convert to decimal}} .815_{10}$$

$$.225_{10} \xrightarrow{\text{Convert to binary}} .0011_2 \xrightarrow{\text{Truncate to 3 bits}} .001_2 \xrightarrow{\text{Convert to decimal}} .125_{10}$$

$$H(z) = \frac{1}{1-0.875z^{-1}+0.125z^{-2}}$$

$$\boxed{H(z) = \frac{1}{(1-0.695z^{-1})(1-0.179z^{-1})}}$$

The poles are at $p_1 = 0.695$ and $p_2 = 0.179$.

Case (*ii*) Cascade Form

$$H(z) = \frac{1}{(1-0.5z^{-1})(1-0.45z^{-1})}$$

Quantization by truncation

$$.5_{10} \xrightarrow{\text{Convert to binary}} .1000_2 \xrightarrow{\text{Truncate to 3 bits}} .100_2 \xrightarrow{\text{Convert to decimal}} .5_{10}$$

$$.45_{10} \xrightarrow{\text{Convert to binary}} .0111_2 \xrightarrow{\text{Truncate to 3 bits}} .011_2 \xrightarrow{\text{Convert to decimal}} .375_{10}$$

$$\boxed{H(z) = \frac{1}{1-0.52z^{-1}} \times \frac{1}{1-0.375z^{-1}}}$$

The poles are $p_1 = 0.5$ and $p_2 = 0.375$.

Conclusion:

- From direct form, we can see that the quantized poles deviate very much from the original poles.
- From cascade form, we can see that one pole is exactly the same while the other pole is very close to the original pole.

5.6 Product Quantization Error

In fixed point arithmetic the product of two b bit numbers results in number of $2b$ bits length. If the word length of the register used to store the result is b bit, then

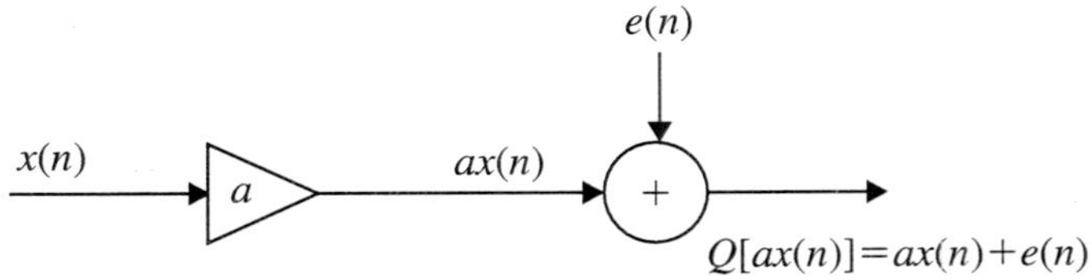

Figure 5.10 Fixed point product round off noise model.

it is necessary to quantize the product to b bits, which produce an error known as **product quantization error or product round off noise**. In realization structures of digital system, multipliers are used to multiply the signal by constants.

The model for fixed point round off noise following a multiplication is shown in Figure 5.10.

The multiplication is modelled as an infinite precision multipliers followed by an adder where round off noise is added to the product so that over all result equals some quantization level. The roundoff noise sample is a zero mean random variable with a variance $(2^{-2b}/3)$, where b is the number of bits used to represent the variables.

In general the following assumptions are made regarding the statistical independence of the various noise sources in the digital filter.

1. Any two different samples from the same noise source are uncorrelated.
2. Any two different noise source, when considered as random processes are uncorrelated.
3. Each noise source is uncorrelated with the input sequence.

The product quantization noise model for first order and second order system are shown in Figure 5.11. The product quantization noise models for IIR using cascade is shown in Figure 5.12.

In each noise model there are a number of noise sources. The output noise variance due to each source is computed separately by considering one noise source at a time. The total output noise variance is given by sum of the output noise variance at all the noise sources. For each noise source, the noise transfer function (NTF) has to be determined by treating the noise source as input and the output being the output of the system. NTF for noise sources $e_{a11}(n)$ in Figure 5.12 $= H_1(z)$ and NTF for noise sources $e_{a12}(n)$ in Figure 5.12 $= H_2(z)$.

Let $e_k(n)$ be the error signal from k^{th} noise source, $h_k(n)$ the impulse response for k^{th} noise source and $T_k(n)$ the noise transfer function (NTF) for k^{th} noise source.

$$\text{Variance of } k^{\text{th}} \text{ noise source } \sigma_{ek}^2 = \frac{q^2}{12} = \frac{2^{-2b}}{3} \qquad [\because R = 2]$$

Output noise variance due to k^{th} noise source is,

$$\sigma_{e0k}^2 = \sigma_{ek}^2 \sum_{n=0}^{\infty} h_k^2(n)$$

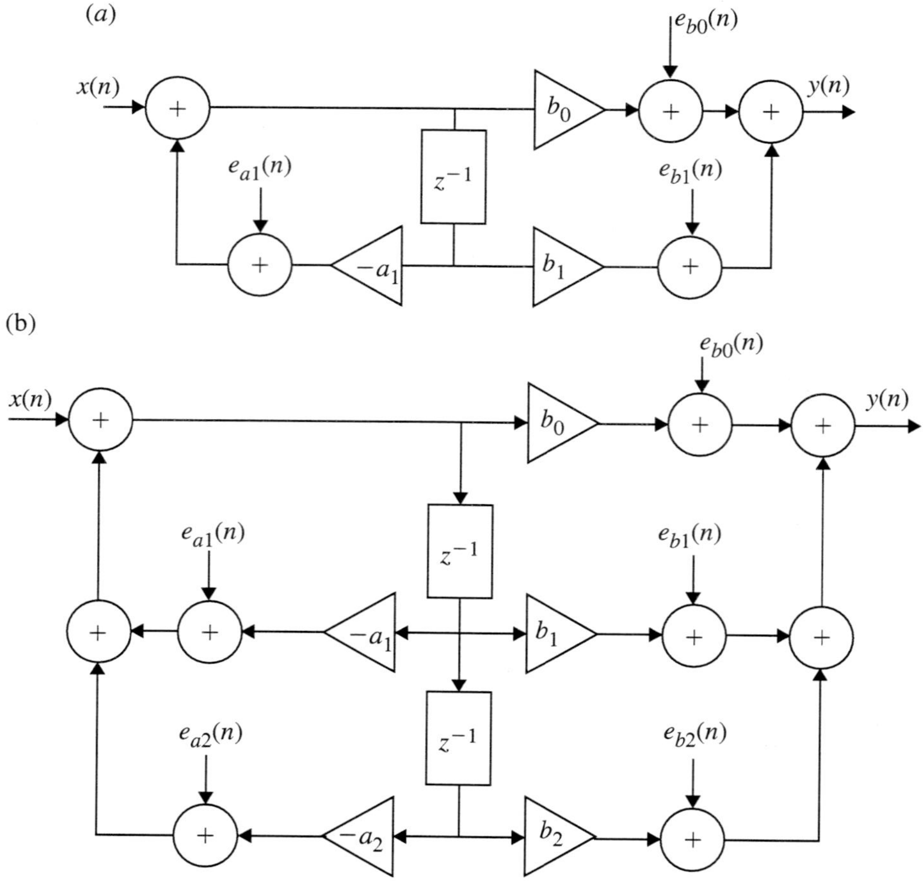

Figure 5.11 Product quantization noise models of IIR systems for direct form realization. (*a*) First order direct form-II and (*b*) Second order direct form-II.

$$\sigma_{e0k}^2 = \sigma_{ek}^2 \frac{1}{2kj} \oint T_k(z)T_k(z^{-1})z^{-1}dz$$

$$= \sigma_{ek}^2 \sum_{i=1}^{n} \text{Res}\left[T_k(z)T_k(z^-1)z^-1\right]_{z=p_i} \tag{5.31}$$

where $p_1, p_2, p_3, \ldots, p_n$ are poles of $T_k(z)T_k(z^{-1})z^{-1}$. Let the number of noise sources in digital system be M.

Therefore, total output noise variance due to product quantization error is,

$$\sigma_{e0}^2 = \sum_{k=1}^{M} \sigma_{e0k}^2 \tag{5.32}$$

$$\boxed{\sigma_{e0}^2 = \sigma_{e01}^2 + \sigma_{e02}^2 + \sigma_{e0M}^2}$$

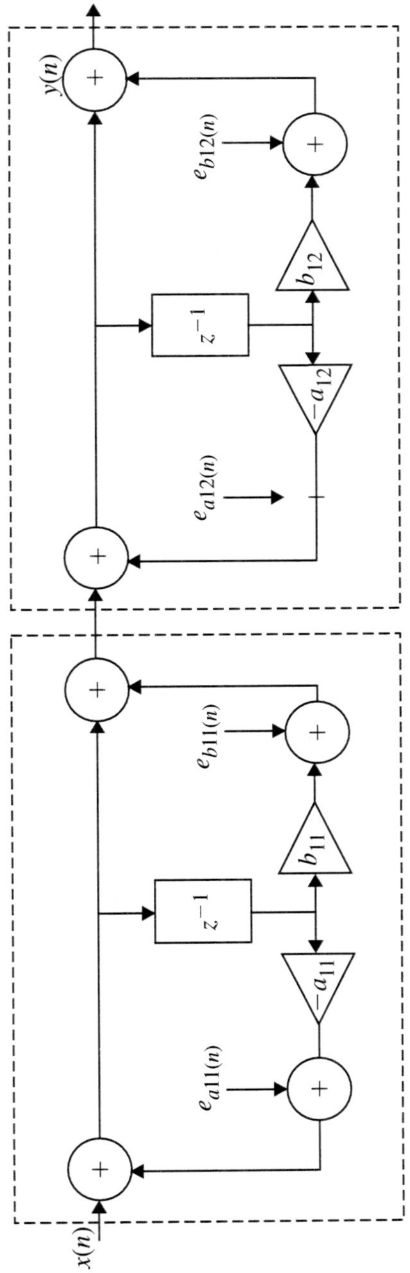

Figure 5.12 Cascading of two first order sections.

Example 5.20

In the IIR system given below the products are rounded to 4 bits (including sign bits). The system function is

$$H(z) = \frac{1}{(1 - 0.35z^{-1})(1 - 0.62z^{-1})}$$

Find the output roundoff noise power in (*a*) direct form realization and (*b*) cascade form realization.

Solution

(*a*) Direct Form Realization

$$H(z) = \frac{1}{(1 - 0.35z^{-1})(1 - 0.62z^{-1})}$$

$$H(z) = \frac{1}{(1 - 0.97z^{-1} + 0.217z^{-2})}$$

Direct form realization of $H(z)$ is shown in Figure 5.13.

The variance of the error signal is,

$$\sigma_e^2 = \frac{q^2}{12}; \qquad q = \frac{R}{2^b}$$

Here R is not given. So take $R = 2V$ and $b = 4$ bits

$$\therefore\ q = \frac{R}{2^b} = \frac{2}{2^4} = \frac{1}{2^3} = \frac{1}{8}$$

$$\sigma_e^2 = \frac{(1/8)^2}{12} = \frac{q^2}{12}$$

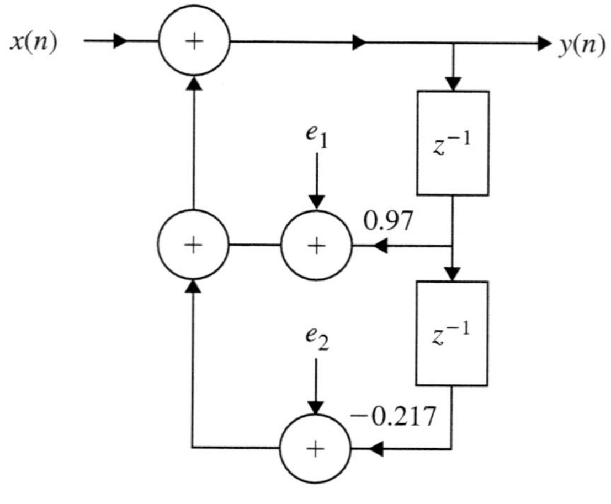

Figure 5.13 Direct form realization of $H(z)$ for Example 5.20.

$$\boxed{\sigma_e^2 = 1.3021 \times 10^{-3}}$$

Output noise power due to the noise signal $e_1(n)$ is,

$$\sigma_{e01}^2 = \sigma_e^2 \sum_{i=1}^{N} \text{Res}[T_1(z)T_1(z^{-1})z^{-1}]|_{z=p_i}$$

Here

$$T_1(z) = H(z) = \frac{z^2}{(z-0.35)(z-0.62)}$$

Therefore

$$T_1(z)T_1(z^{-1})z^{-1} = \frac{z^2}{(z-0.35)(z-0.62)} \times \frac{z^{-2}}{(z^{-1}-0.35)(z^{-1}-0.62)} \times z^{-1}$$

$$= \frac{z^{-1}}{(z-0.35)(z-0.62)(z^{-1}-0.35)(z^{-1}-0.62)}$$

The poles of $H(z)$ are $p_1 = 0.35$ and $p_2 = 0.62$.

$$\text{Res}[T(z)T(z^{-1})z^{-1}]|_{z=0.35}$$

$$= (z-0.35)\left.\frac{z^{-1}}{(z-0.35)(z-0.62)(z^{-1}-0.35)(z^{-1}-0.62)}\right|_{z=0.35}$$

$$= -1.8867$$

$$\text{Res}[T_1(z)T_1(z^{-1})z^{-1}]|_{z=0.62}$$

$$= (z-0.62)\left.\frac{z^{-1}}{(z-0.35)(z-0.62)(z^{-1}-0.35)(z^{-1}-0.62)}\right|_{z=0.62}$$

$$= 4.7640$$

$$\sum_{i=1}^{N} \text{Res}[T_1(z)T_1(z^{-1})z^{-1}]$$

$$= \text{Res}[T_1(z)T_1(z^{-1})z^{-1}]|_{z=0.35} + \text{Res}[T_1(z)T_1(z^{-1})z^{-1}]|_{z=0.62}$$

$$= -1.8867 + 4.7640$$

$$= 2.8773.$$

Therefore

$$\sigma_{e01}^2 = \sigma_e^2 \sum_{i=1}^{N} \text{Res}[T_1(z)T_1(z^{-1})z^{-1}]|_{z=p_i}$$

$$= 1.3021 \times 10^{-3} \times 2.8733$$

$$\sigma_{e01}^2 = 3.7465 \times 10^{-3}$$

Here the output noise due to error source $e_2(n)$ is same as that of $e_1(n)$, *i.e.*,

$$e_2(n)\text{'s noise power} = \text{noise power of } e_1(n)$$

$$\sigma_{e01}^2 = \sigma_{e02}^2$$

$$= 3.7465 \times 10^{-3}$$

Total output noise power due to all the noise sources is,

$$\sigma_{e0}^2 = \sigma_{e01}^2 + \sigma_{e02}^2$$

$$\boxed{\sigma_{e0}^2 = 7.493 \times 10^{-3}}$$

(*b*) Cascade Realization

Given

$$H(z) = \frac{1}{(1 - 0.35z^{-1})(1 - 0.62z^{-1})}$$

Let $H(z) = H_1(z)H_2(z)$, *i.e.*,

$$H_1(z) = \frac{1}{(1 - 0.35z^{-1})} \quad \text{and} \quad H_2(z) = \frac{1}{(1 - 0.62z^{-1})}$$

Case (*i*) $H(z) = H_1(z)H_2(z)$

The cascade form realization of $H(z)$ is shown in Figure 5.14.

The order of cascading is $H_1(z)H_2(z)$. Output noise power due to error signal $e_1(n)$ is

$$\sigma_{e01}^2 = \sigma_e^2 \sum_{i=1}^{N} \text{Res}[H(z)H(z^{-1})z^{-1}]|_{z=p_i} = 3.7465 \times 10^{-3}$$

[Refer Direct Form where $H(z) = T(z)$].

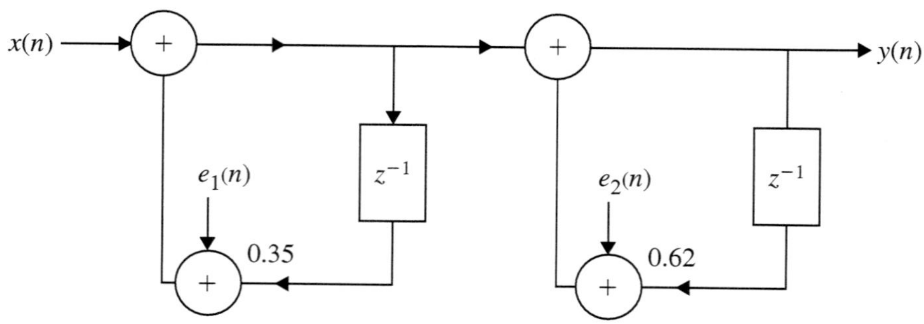

Figure 5.14 Cascade form realization of $H(z)$ for Example 5.20.

Output noise power due to the error, signal $e_2(n)$ is

$$\sigma_{e02}^2 = \sigma_e^2 \sum_{i=1}^{N} \text{Res}[T_2(z)T_2(z^{-1})z^{-1}]|_{z=p_i}$$

Here $T_2(z) = H_2(z)$

$$T_2(z)T_2(z^{-1})(z^{-1}) = \frac{z^{-1}}{(z-0.62)(z^{-1}-0.62)}$$

$$\sum_{i=1}^{N} \text{Res}[T_2(z)T_2(z^{-1})z^{-1}]|_{z=p_i} = \left.\frac{z^{-1} \times (z-0.62)}{(z-0.62)(z^{-1}-0.62)}\right|_{z=0.62}$$

$$= 1.6244$$

$$\sigma_{e02}^2 = \sigma_e^2 \times \sum_{i=1}^{N} \text{Res}[T_2(z)T_2(z^{-1})z^{-1}]$$

$$= 1.3021 \times 10^{-3} \times 1.6244$$

$$= 2.1151 \times 10^{-3}$$

Output noise power

$$\sigma_{e0}^2 = \sigma_{e01}^2 + \sigma_{e02}^2$$

$$= 3.7465 \times 10^{-3} + 2.1151 \times 10^{-3}$$

$$\boxed{\sigma_{e0}^2 = 5.8616 \times 10^{-3}}$$

Case (*ii*) The order of cascading is $H(z) = H_2(z)H_1(z)$ and is shown in Figure 5.15.

The output noise power due to error source e_1 is,

$$\sigma_{e01}^2 = 3.7465 \times 10^{-3}$$

[Same as in Direct Form because $T(z) = H(z)$].

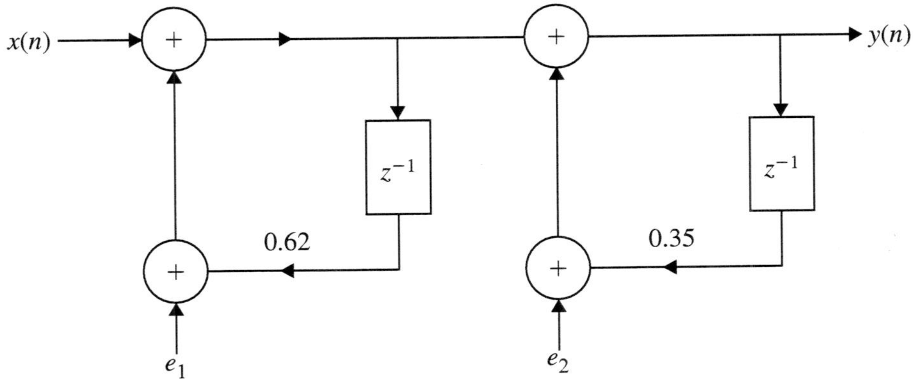

Figure 5.15 Cascade form realization of $H(z)$ for Example 5.20.

The output noise power due to error source $e_2(n)$ is,

$$\sigma_{e02}^2 = \sigma_e^2 \sum_{i=1}^{N} \text{Res}[T_3(z)T_3(z^{-1})]_{z=p_i}$$

Here $T_3(z) = H_1(z)$

$$\text{Res}[T_3(z)T_3(z^{-1})z^{-1}]|_{z=p_i} = \left.\frac{(z-0.35)z^{-1}}{(z-0.35)(z^{-1}-0.35)}\right|_{z=0.35}$$

$$= 1.1396$$

$$\sigma_{e02}^2 = 1.1396 \times 1.3021 \times 10^{-3}$$

$$= 1.4839 \times 10^{-3}$$

Total output noise power

$$\sigma_{e0}^2 = \sigma_{e01}^2 + \sigma_{e02}^2$$

$$= 3.7465 \times 10^{-3} + 1.4839 \times 10^{-3}$$

$$\boxed{\sigma_{e0}^2 = 5.2304 \times 10^{-3}}$$

Conclusion: Thus, in cascade form realization, the product noise roundoff power is less in case (*ii*) when compared to case (*i*) and also direct form realization.

5.7 Limit Cycles in Recursive System

5.7.1 Zero-Input Limit Cycles

In recursive systems, when the input is zero or some non-zero constant value, the non-linearities due to finite precision arithmetic operation may cause periodic oscillations, in the output. During periodic oscillations, the output $y(n)$ of a system will oscillate between a finite positive and negative value for increasing n or the output will become constant for increasing n. Such oscillations are called limit cycles. If the system output enters a limit cycle, it will continue to remain in limit cycle even when the input is made zero. Hence, these limit cycles are also called zero input limit cycles.

Consider the following difference equation of first order system with one pole only.

$$y(n) = ay(n-1) + x(n) \tag{5.33}$$

The system has one product $ay(n-1)$. If the product is quantized to finite word length then the response $y(n)$ will deviate from actual value. Let $y'(n)$ be the response of the system when the product is quantized.

$$y'(n) = Q\left[ay'(n-1)\right] + x(n) \tag{5.34}$$

Let $y'(n) = 0, \quad \text{for} \quad n < 0$ and $a = \frac{1}{2}$

$$x(n) = \begin{cases} 0.875, & n = 0 \\ 0, & n \neq 0 \end{cases}$$

Let the product be quantized to three bit (excluding sign bit) binary by rounding when $n = 0$,

$$\begin{aligned} y'(n) &= Q\left[ay'(n-1)\right] + x(n) \\ y'(0) &= Q\left[\frac{1}{2}y'(-1)\right] + x(0) \\ &= Q\left[\frac{1}{2} \times 0\right] + 0.875 = 0.875_{10} = \frac{7}{8} \end{aligned}$$

When $n = 1$,

$$\begin{aligned} y'(1) &= Q\left[ay'(0)\right] + x(1) \\ &= Q\left[\frac{1}{2} \times 0.875\right] + 0 \\ &= Q\left[\frac{1}{2} \times \frac{7}{8}\right] = Q\left[\frac{7}{16}\right] = Q\,[0.4375] \end{aligned}$$

$$0.4375_{10} \xrightarrow{\text{Convert to binary}} .011100_2 \xrightarrow{\text{add sign bit}} 0.011100_2 \xrightarrow{\text{round to 3 bit}} 0.100_2$$
$$\xrightarrow{\text{Extract sign bit}} 0.100_2 \xrightarrow{\text{Convert to decimal}} 0.5_{10} = \frac{1}{2}$$

When $n = 2$,

$$\begin{aligned} y'(2) &= Q\left[ay'(1)\right] + x(2) \\ &= Q\left[\frac{1}{2} \times \frac{1}{2}\right] + 0 \\ &= Q\left[\frac{1}{4}\right] = Q\,[0.25] \end{aligned}$$

$$0.25_{10} \xrightarrow{\text{Convert to binary}} 0.01000_2 \xrightarrow{\text{round to 3 bit}} 0.010_2 \xrightarrow{\text{Convert to decimal}} 0.25_{10} = \frac{1}{4}$$

When $n = 3$,

$$\begin{aligned} y'(3) &= Q\left[ay'(2)\right] + x(3) \\ &= Q\left[\frac{1}{2} \times \frac{1}{4}\right] + 0 \\ &= Q\left[\frac{1}{8}\right] = Q\,[0.125] \end{aligned}$$

Table 5.3

n	$x(n)$	$y(n-1)$	$ay(n-1)$	$Q[ay(n-1)]$	$y'(n) = Q\,[ay(n-1)] + x(n)$
0	0.875	0	0	0.000	7/8
1	0	7/8	−7/16	1.100	−1/2
2	0	−1/2	1/4	0.010	1/4
3	0	1/4	−1/8	−0.001	−1/8
4	0	−1/8	1/16	0.001	1/8
5	0	1/8	−1/16	1.001	−1/8
6	0	−1/8	1/16	0.001	1/8

$$0.125_{10} \xrightarrow{\text{Convert to binary}} 0.00100_2 \xrightarrow{\text{round to 3 bit}} 0.001_2 \xrightarrow{\text{Convert to decimal}} 0.25_{10} = \frac{1}{8}$$

When $n = 4$,

$$y'(4) = Q\left[ay'(3)\right] + x(4)$$
$$= Q\left[\frac{1}{2} \times \frac{1}{8}\right] + 0 = Q\left[\frac{1}{16}\right] = Q\,[0.0625]$$

$$0.0625_{10} \xrightarrow{\text{Convert to binary}} 0.000100_2 \xrightarrow{\text{round to 3 bit}} 0.001_2 \xrightarrow{\text{Convert to decimal}} 0.125_{10} = \frac{1}{8}$$

When $n = 5$,

$$y'(5) = Q\left[ay'(4)\right] + x(5)$$
$$= Q\left[\frac{1}{2} \times \frac{1}{8}\right] + 0 = Q\left[\frac{1}{16}\right] = 0.125 = \frac{1}{8}$$

For all values of n, where $n \geq 3$, the $y'(n) = 1/8 = 0.001$. Hence, the output becomes constant for $n \geq 3$. Also for $n \geq 3$, the input $x(n)$ is zero. Therefore, the system enters a limit cycle even though the input becomes zero for $n \geq 3$.

When $a = -1/2$ we can see from Table 5.3 that the output oscillates between $+0.125$ and -0.125.

Dead Band

In a limit cycle the amplitudes of the output are confined to a range of values, which is called the dead band of the filter.

For a first order system described by the equation, $y(n) = ay(n-1) + x(n)$, the dead band is given by

$$\text{Dead band} = \pm\frac{2^{-b}}{1-|a|} = \left[\frac{-2^{-b}}{1-|a|},\ +\frac{2^{-b}}{1-|a|}\right] \tag{5.35}$$

where b = number of bits (including sign bits) used to represent the product. For a second order system described by the difference equation $y(n) = a_1 y(n-1) + a_2 y(n-2) + x(n)$, the dead band in

$$\text{Dead band} = \pm\frac{2^{-b}}{1-|a_2|} = \left[\frac{-2^{-b}}{1-|a_2|}, +\frac{2^{-b}}{1-|a_2|}\right] \tag{5.36}$$

The following example illustrates the method if finding dead band.

Example 5.21

Explain the characteristics of a limit cycle oscillation with respect to the system described by the equation

$$y(n) = 0.95y(n-1) + x(n).$$

Determine the dead band of the filter.

(Anna University, December, 2006)

Solution Given that

$$y(n) = 0.95y(n-1) + x(n)$$

The recursive realization of the given system involves the product $0.95y(n-1)$. Let $y'(n)$ be the response of system when the product is quantized by rounding.

$$\therefore\ y'(n) = Q[0.95y(n-1)] + x(n)$$

where Q is quantization. Let us consider 5 bit sign-magnitude binary representation with 4 bit for magnitude and 1 bit for sign. Let

$$y'(n) = 0 \quad \text{for} \quad n < 0$$

and

$$x(n) = \begin{cases} 0.75, & \text{for } n = 0 \\ 0, & \text{for } n \neq 0 \end{cases}$$

When $n = 0$,

$$\begin{aligned} y'[0] &= Q[0.95y(-1)] + x[0] \\ &= Q[0.95 \times 0] + 0.75 \\ &= Q[0] + 0.75 \\ y'[0] &= 0.75_{10} = 0.1100_2 \end{aligned}$$

$$+.75 \xrightarrow{\text{Convert to binary}} .11000_2 \xrightarrow{\text{add sign bit}} 0.11000_2 \xrightarrow{\text{round to 4 bit}} 0.1100_2$$

$$+0.1100_2 \xrightarrow{\text{Convert to decimal}} +.75_{10}$$

When $n = 1$,

$$\begin{aligned} y'[n] = y'[1] &= Q[0.95y'(n-1)] + x[n] \\ &= Q[0.95y'(0)] + x[1] \\ &= Q[0.95 \times 0.75] + 0 \\ &= Q[0.7125] \\ y'[1] &= 0.6875_{10} = 0.1011_2 \end{aligned}$$

$Q[0.7125] \Longrightarrow$

$$+.7125 \xrightarrow{\text{Convert to binary}} .10110_2 \xrightarrow{\text{add sign bit}} 0.10110_2 \xrightarrow{\text{round to 4 bit}} 0.1011_2$$

$$+0.1011_2 \xrightarrow{\text{Convert to decimal}} +.6875_{10}$$

When $n = 2$,

$$\begin{aligned} y'[2] &= Q[0.95y'(1)] + x[2] \\ &= Q[0.95 \times 0.6875] + 0 \\ &= Q[0.653125] \\ y'[2] &= 0.625 \\ &= 0.01010_2 \end{aligned}$$

$Q[0.653125_{10}] \Longrightarrow$

$$.653125_{10} \xrightarrow{\text{Convert to binary}} .10100_2 \xrightarrow{\text{add sign bit}} 0.10100_2 \xrightarrow{\text{round to 4 bit}} 0.1010_2$$

$$+0.1010_2 \xrightarrow{\text{Convert to decimal}} +.625_{10}$$

When $n = 3$,

$$\begin{aligned} y'[3] &= Q[0.95y'(2)] + x[3] \\ &= Q[0.95 \times 0.625] + 0 \\ &= Q[0.59375] \\ y'[3] &= 0.625_{10} \\ &= 0.1010_2 \end{aligned}$$

$Q[0.59375] \Longrightarrow$

$$.59375 \xrightarrow{\text{Convert to binary}} .10011_2 \xrightarrow{\text{add sign bit}} 0.10011_2 \xrightarrow{\text{round to 4 bit}} 0.1010_2$$

$$+0.1010_2 \xrightarrow{\text{Convert to decimal}} +0.625_{10}$$

Thus, $y'(2) = y'(3)$, and hence for all values of $n \geq 2$, $y'(n)$ will remain as 0.625. Therefore, the system enters into the limit cycle when $n = 2$.

For the first order system with only one pole, dead band is given by

$$\text{Dead band} = \pm\frac{2^{-b}}{1-|a|}$$

where b is number of bit in binary representation and $|a| = |0.95|$

$$\begin{aligned}\text{Dead band} &= \pm\frac{2^{-5}}{1-0.95} = \pm 0.625\\ &= [-0.625, +0.625]\end{aligned}$$

Example 5.22

An IIR causal filter has the system function

$$H(z) = \frac{z}{z-0.97}$$

Assume that the input signal is zero valued and the computed output signal values are rounded to one decimal place. Show that under those stated conditions, the filter output exhibits dead band effect. What is the dead band range?

(Anna University, May, 2007)

Solution Given

$$\begin{aligned}H(z) &= \frac{z}{z-0.97}\\ H(z) &= \frac{Y(z)}{X(z)} = \frac{z}{z-0.97}\\ &= \frac{Y(z)}{X(z)} = \frac{1}{1-0.97z^{-1}}\\ X(z) &= Y(z) - 0.97z^{-1}Y(z)\end{aligned}$$

Taking inverse z-transform on both sides we get

$$\begin{aligned}y(n) - 0.97y(n-1) &= x(n)\\ y(n) &= 0.97y(n-1) + x(n)\end{aligned}$$

Let $y'(n)$ be the response of the system when the product is quantized by rounding

$$y'(n) = Q[0.97y'(n-1)] + x(n)$$

For a causal filter

$$y(n) = 0, \qquad \text{for } n < 0$$

Let

$$x(n) = \begin{cases} 11, & n = 0, \\ 0, & n \neq 0. \end{cases}$$

When $n = 0$,

$$\begin{aligned} y'(0) &= Q[0.97y'(n-1)] + x(n) \\ &= 0 + 11 = 11 \end{aligned}$$

When $n = 1$,

$$\begin{aligned} y'(1) &= Q[0.97y(0)] + x(1) \\ &= Q[0.97 \times 11] + 0 \\ &= Q[10.67] \end{aligned}$$

$Q[10.67] \Rightarrow$

$$(10.67)_{10} \xrightarrow[\text{to binary}]{\text{convert}} (1010.101)_2 \xrightarrow[\text{decimal place}]{\text{rounded to the}} (1010.1)_2 \xrightarrow[\text{to decimal}]{\text{convert}} (10.5)_{10}$$

$y'(1) = Q[10.67] = 10.5$

When $n = 2$,

$$\begin{aligned} y'(2) &= Q[0.97y'(1)] \\ &= Q[0.97 \times 10.5] \\ &= Q[10.185] \end{aligned}$$

$Q[10.185] \Rightarrow$

$$(10.185)_{10} \xrightarrow[\text{to binary}]{\text{convert}} (1010.001)_2 \xrightarrow[\text{one decimal}]{\text{rounded to the}} (1010)_2 \xrightarrow[\text{to decimal}]{\text{convert}} (10)_{10}$$

$y'(2) = Q[10.185] = 10$

When $n = 3$,

$$\begin{aligned} y'(3) &= Q[0.97y'(2)] \\ &= Q[0.97 \times 10] \\ &= Q[9.7] \end{aligned}$$

$$Q[9.7] \Rightarrow (9.7)_{10} \xrightarrow[\text{to binary}]{\text{convert}} (1001.101)_2 \xrightarrow[\text{one decimal}]{\text{rounded to}} (1001.1)_2 \xrightarrow[\text{to decimal}]{\text{convert}} (9.5)_{10}$$

$y'(3) = Q[9.7] = 9.5$

When $n = 4$,

$$\begin{aligned} y'(4) &= Q[0.97y'(3)] \\ &= Q[0.97 \times 9.5] \\ &= Q[9.215] \end{aligned}$$

$$Q[9.215] \Rightarrow (9.215)_{10} \xrightarrow[\text{to binary}]{\text{convert}} (1001.001)_2 \xrightarrow[\text{one decimal}]{\text{rounded to}} (1001)_2 \xrightarrow[\text{to decimal}]{\text{convert}} (9)_{10}$$

$y'(4) = Q[9.215] = 9$

When $n = 5$,

$$\begin{aligned} y'(5) &= Q[0.97y'(4)] \\ &= Q[0.97 \times 9] \\ &= Q[8.73] \end{aligned}$$

$Q[8.73] \Rightarrow$

$$(8.73)_{10} \xrightarrow[\text{to binary}]{\text{convert}} (1001.101)_2 \xrightarrow[\text{one decimal}]{\text{rounded to}} (1000.1)_2 \xrightarrow[\text{to decimal}]{\text{convert}} (8.5)_{10}$$

$y'(5) = Q[8.73] = 8.5$

When $n = 6$,

$$\begin{aligned} y'(6) &= Q[0.97y'(5)] \\ &= Q[0.97 \times 8.5] \\ &= Q[8.245] \end{aligned}$$

$$Q[8.245] \Rightarrow (8.245)_{10} \xrightarrow[\text{to binary}]{\text{convert}} (1000.001)_2 \xrightarrow[\text{one decimal}]{\text{rounded to}} (1000)_2 \xrightarrow[\text{to decimal}]{\text{convert}} (8)_{10}$$

$y'(6) = Q[8.245] = 8$

When $n = 7$,

$$\begin{aligned} y'(7) &= Q[0.97y'(6)] \\ &= Q[0.97 \times 8] \\ &= Q[7.76] \end{aligned}$$

$$Q[7.76] \Rightarrow (7.76)_{10} \xrightarrow[\text{to binary}]{\text{convert}} (0111.110)_2 \xrightarrow[\text{one decimal}]{\text{rounded to}} (1000)_2 \xrightarrow[\text{to decimal}]{\text{convert}} (8)_{10}$$

$y'(7) = Q[7.76] = 8$

Thus, $y'(7) = y'(6)$ and hence for all values of $n \geq 6$, $y'(n)$ will remain as 8. Therefore, the system enters into limit cycle when $n = 6$

$$\begin{aligned} \text{Dead band} &= \pm\frac{2^{-b}}{1-|\alpha|} \\ &= \pm\frac{2^{-2}}{1-0.97} \\ \text{Dead band} &= \pm 8.333 \end{aligned}$$

Thus, the dead band interval is $[-8.333, 8.333]$.

Example 5.23

A causal filter is defined by the difference equation

$$y(n) = x(n) - 0.9y(n-1)$$

The unit sample response $h(n)$ is computed such that the computed values are rounded to one decimal place. Show that the filter exhibits dead band effect. Determine the dead band range.

(Anna University, May, 2007)

Solution Given

$$y(n) = x(n) - 0.9y(n-1)$$

For causal system $y(n) = 0$, for $n < 0$. Consider the input

$$x(n) = \begin{cases} 12, & n = 0, \\ 0, & n \neq 0. \end{cases}$$

Let $y'(n)$ be the response of the filter when the product is quantized by rounding.

$$y'(n) = -Q[0.9y'(n-1)] + x(n)$$

When $n = 0$,

$$\begin{aligned} y'(0) &= -Q[0.9y'(-1)] + x(0) \\ &= 0 + 12 \\ &= 12 \end{aligned}$$

When $n = 1$,

$$\begin{aligned} y'(1) &= -Q[0.9y'(0)] + x(1) \\ &= -Q[0.9 \times 12] + 0 \\ &= -Q[10.8] \end{aligned}$$

$$Q[10.8] \Rightarrow (10.8)_{10} \xrightarrow[\text{to binary}]{\text{convert}} (1010.110)_2 \xrightarrow[\text{one decimal}]{\text{rounded to the}} (1011)_2 \xrightarrow[\text{to decimal}]{\text{convert}} (11)_{10}$$

$y'(1) = -Q[10.185] = -11$

When $n = 2$,

$$\begin{aligned} y'(2) &= -Q[0.9y'(1)] \\ &= -Q[0.9 \times (-11)] \\ &= -Q[-9.9] \end{aligned}$$

$$Q[-9.9] \Rightarrow -(9.9)_{10} \xrightarrow[\text{(2's complement)}]{\text{convert to binary}} (0110.001)_2 \xrightarrow[\text{decimal place}]{\text{rounded to one}} (0110)_2$$

$$\xrightarrow[\text{complement}]{\text{take 2's}} (1010)_2 \xrightarrow[\text{to decimal}]{\text{convert}} -(10)_{10}$$

$$y'(2) = -Q[9.9] = -(-10) = 10$$

When $n = 3$,

$$\begin{aligned} y'(3) &= -Q[0.9y'(2)] \\ &= -Q[0.9 \times 10] \\ &= -Q[9] = -9 \end{aligned}$$

When $n = 4$,

$$\begin{aligned} y'(4) &= -Q[0.9y'(3)] \\ &= -Q[0.9 \times (-9)] \\ &= -Q[-8.1] \end{aligned}$$

$$Q[-8.1] \Rightarrow -(8.1)_{10} \xrightarrow[\text{(2's complement)}]{\text{convert to binary}} (1000.000)_2 \xrightarrow[\text{one decimal}]{\text{rounded to}} (1000)_2$$

$$\xrightarrow[\text{complement}]{\text{take 2's}} -(1000)_2 \xrightarrow[\text{to decimal}]{\text{convert}} -(8)_{10}$$

$$y'(4) = -Q[-8.1] = -(-8) = 8$$

When $n = 5$,

$$\begin{aligned} y'(5) &= -Q[0.9y'(4)] \\ &= -Q[0.9 \times 8] \\ &= -Q[7.2] \end{aligned}$$

$$Q[7.2] \Rightarrow (7.2)_{10} \xrightarrow[\text{to binary}]{\text{convert}} (0111.001)_2 \xrightarrow[\text{one decimal}]{\text{rounded to}} (0111)_2 \xrightarrow[\text{to decimal}]{\text{convert}} (7)_{10}$$

$$y'(5) = -Q[7.2] = -7$$

When $n = 6$,

$$\begin{aligned} y'(6) &= -Q[0.9y'(5)] \\ &= -Q[0.9 \times (-7)] \\ &= -Q[-6.3] \end{aligned}$$

$$Q[-6.3] \Rightarrow -(6.3)_{10} \xrightarrow[\text{(2's complement)}]{\text{convert to binary}} (1001.110)_2 \xrightarrow[\text{one decimal}]{\text{rounded to}} (1010)_2$$

$$\xrightarrow[\text{complement}]{\text{take 2's}} -(0110)_2 \xrightarrow[\text{to decimal}]{\text{convert}} (-6)_{10}$$

$$y'(6) = -Q[-6.3] = -(-6) = 6$$

When $n = 7$,

$$\begin{aligned} y'(7) &= -Q[0.9y'(6)] \\ &= -Q[0.9 \times 6] \\ &= -Q[5.4] \end{aligned}$$

$$Q[5.4] \Rightarrow (5.4)_{10} \xrightarrow[\text{to binary}]{\text{convert}} (0101.011)_2 \xrightarrow[\text{one decimal}]{\text{rounded to}} (0101)_2 \xrightarrow[\text{to decimal}]{\text{convert}} (5.5)_{10}$$

$$y'(7) = -Q[5.4] = -5.5$$

When $n = 8$,

$$\begin{aligned} y'(8) &= -Q[0.9y'(7)] \\ &= -Q[0.9 \times (-5.5)] \\ &= -Q[-4.95] \end{aligned}$$

$$Q[-4.95] \Rightarrow -(4.95)_{10} \xrightarrow[\text{(2's complement)}]{\text{convert to binary}} (1011.001)_2 \xrightarrow[\text{one decimal}]{\text{rounded to}} (1011)_2$$

$$\xrightarrow[\text{complement}]{\text{take 2's}} -(0101)_2 \xrightarrow[\text{to decimal}]{\text{convert}} (-5)_{10}$$

$$y'(8) = -Q[-4.95] = -(-5) = 5$$

When $n = 9$,

$$\begin{aligned} y'(9) &= -Q[0.9y'(8)] \\ &= -Q[0.9 \times 5] \\ &= -Q[4.5] \end{aligned}$$

$$Q[4.5] \Rightarrow (4.5)_{10} \xrightarrow[\text{to binary}]{\text{convert}} (0100.10)_2 \xrightarrow[\text{one decimal}]{\text{rounded to}} (0100.1)_2 \xrightarrow[\text{to decimal}]{\text{convert}} (4.5)_{10}$$

$y'(9) = -Q[4.5] = -4.5$

When $n = 10$,

$$\begin{aligned} y'(10) &= -Q[0.9y'(9)] \\ &= -Q[0.9 \times (-4.5)] \\ &= -Q[-4.05] \end{aligned}$$

$$Q[-4.05] \Rightarrow -(4.05)_{10} \xrightarrow[\text{(2's complement)}]{\text{convert to binary}} (1100.000)_2 \xrightarrow[\text{one decimal}]{\text{rounded to}} (1100)_2$$

$$\xrightarrow[\text{complement}]{\text{take 2's}} -(0100)_2 \xrightarrow[\text{to decimal}]{\text{convert}} (-4)_{10}$$

$$y'(10) = -Q[-4.05] = -(-4) = 4$$

When $n = 11$,

$$\begin{aligned} y'(11) &= -Q[0.9y'(10)] \\ &= -Q[0.9 \times 4] \\ &= -Q[3.6] \end{aligned}$$

$$Q[3.6] \Rightarrow (3.6)_{10} \xrightarrow[\text{to binary}]{\text{convert}} (0011.100)_2 \xrightarrow[\text{one decimal}]{\text{rounded to}} (0011.1)_2 \xrightarrow[\text{to decimal}]{\text{convert}} (3.5)_{10}$$

$y'(11) = -Q[3.6] = -3.5$

When $n = 12$,

$$\begin{aligned} y'(12) &= -Q[0.9y'(11)] \\ &= -Q[0.9 \times 3.5] \\ &= -Q[-3.15] \end{aligned}$$

$$Q[-3.15] \Rightarrow -(3.15)_{10} \xrightarrow[\text{(2's complement)}]{\text{convert to binary}} (1100.111)_2 \xrightarrow[\text{one decimal}]{\text{rounded to}} (1101)_2$$

$$\xrightarrow[\text{complement}]{\text{take 2's}} -(0011)_2 \xrightarrow[\text{to decimal}]{\text{convert}} (-3)_{10}$$

$$y'(12) = -Q[-3.15] = -(-3) = 3$$

When $n = 13$,

$$\begin{aligned} y'(13) &= -Q[0.9y'(12)] \\ &= -Q[0.9 \times 3] \\ &= -Q[2.7] \end{aligned}$$

$$Q[2.7] \Rightarrow (2.7)_{10} \xrightarrow[\text{to binary}]{\text{convert}} (0010.101)_2 \xrightarrow[\text{one decimal}]{\text{rounded to}} (0010.1)_2 \xrightarrow[\text{to decimal}]{\text{convert}} (2.5)_{10}$$

$y'(13) = -Q[2.7] = -2.5$

When $n = 14$,

$$\begin{aligned} y'(14) &= -Q[0.9y'(13)] \\ &= -Q[0.9 \times (-2.5)] \\ &= -Q[-2.25] \end{aligned}$$

$$Q[-2.25] \Rightarrow -(2.25)_{10} \xrightarrow[\text{(2's complement)}]{\text{convert to binary}} (1101.10)_2 \xrightarrow[\text{one decimal}]{\text{rounded to}} (1101.1)_2$$

$$\xrightarrow[\text{complement}]{\text{take 2's}} -(0010.1)_2 \xrightarrow[\text{to decimal}]{\text{convert}} -(2.5)_{10}$$

$$y'(14) = -Q[-2.25] = -(-2.5) = 2.5$$

For all values of $n \geq 13$, $y'(n)$ will remain in the same magnitude as 2.5 with alternative sign. Therefore, the system enters into limit cycle when $n = 13$

$$\text{Dead band} = \pm\frac{2^{-b}}{1 - |\alpha|} = \pm\frac{2^{-2}}{1 - 0.9}$$

$$\begin{aligned} \text{Dead band} &= \pm\frac{0.25}{1 - 0.9} \\ &= \pm 2.5 \end{aligned}$$

Thus the dead band interval is $[-2.5, 2.5]$.

Unit Impulse Response

Given

$$y(n) = -0.9y(n-1) + x(n)$$

Taking z-transform on the both sides, we get

$$\begin{aligned} Y(z) &= -0.9z^{-1}Y(z) + X(z) \\ Y(z)[1 + 0.9z^{-1}] &= Y(z) \\ H(z) &= \frac{Y(z)}{X(z)} = \frac{1}{1 + 0.9z^{-1}} \end{aligned}$$

The unit impulse response $h(n)$ is

$$h(n) = z^{-1}[H(z)]$$

$$\boxed{h(n) = (-0.9)^n u(n)}$$

Example 5.24

A digital system is characterized by the difference equation

$$y(n) = 0.9y(n-1) + x(n)$$

Determine the dead band of the system when $x(n) = 0$ and $y(-1) = 12$.

(Anna University, May, 2004)

Solution Given

$$y(n) = -0.9y(n-1) + x(n)$$

where $x(n) = 0$, $y(-1) = 12$. Let $y'(n)$ be the response of the filter when the product is quantized.

$$y'(n) = Q[0.9y'(n-1)] + x(n)$$

When $n = 0$,

$$\begin{aligned} y'(0) &= Q[0.9y'(-1)] \\ &= Q[0.9 \times 12] \\ &= Q[10.8] \end{aligned}$$

$$Q[10.8] \Rightarrow (10.8)_{10} \xrightarrow[\text{to binary}]{\text{convert}} (1010.110)_2 \xrightarrow[\text{one decimal}]{\text{rounded to the}} (1011)_2 \xrightarrow[\text{to decimal}]{\text{convert}} (11)_{10}$$

$y'(0) = Q[10.8] = 1$

When $n = 1$,

$$\begin{aligned} y'(1) &= Q[0.9y'(0)] \\ &= Q[0.9 \times 11] \\ &= Q[9.9] \end{aligned}$$

$$Q[9.9] \Rightarrow (9.9)_{10} \xrightarrow[\text{to binary}]{\text{convert}} (1001.111)_2 \xrightarrow[\text{one decimal}]{\text{rounded to the}} (1010)_2 \xrightarrow[\text{to decimal}]{\text{convert}} (10)_{10}$$

$y'(1) = Q[9.9] = 10$

When $n = 2$,

$$\begin{aligned} y'(2) &= Q[0.9y'(1)] \\ &= Q[0.9 \times 10] \\ &= Q[9] = 9 \end{aligned}$$

When $n = 3$,

$$\begin{aligned} y'(3) &= Q[0.9y'(2)] \\ &= Q[0.9 \times 9] \\ &= Q[8.1] \end{aligned}$$

$$Q[8.1] \Rightarrow (8.1)_{10} \xrightarrow[\text{to binary}]{\text{convert}} (1000.000)_2 \xrightarrow[\text{one decimal}]{\text{rounded to the}} (1000)_2 \xrightarrow[\text{to decimal}]{\text{convert}} (8)_{10}$$

$y'(3) = Q[8.1] = 8$

When $n = 4$,

$$\begin{aligned} y'(4) &= Q[0.9y'(3)] \\ &= Q[0.9 \times 8] \\ &= Q[7.2] \end{aligned}$$

$$Q[7.2] \Rightarrow (7.2)_{10} \xrightarrow[\text{to binary}]{\text{convert}} (0111.000)_2 \xrightarrow[\text{one decimal}]{\text{rounded to}} (0111)_2 \xrightarrow[\text{to decimal}]{\text{convert}} (7)_{10}$$

$y'(4) = Q[7.2] = 7$

When $n = 5$,

$$\begin{aligned} y'(5) &= Q[0.9y'(4)] \\ &= Q[0.9 \times 7] \\ &= Q[6.3] \end{aligned}$$

$$Q[6.3] \Rightarrow (6.3)_{10} \xrightarrow[\text{to binary}]{\text{convert}} (0110.010)_2 \xrightarrow[\text{one decimal}]{\text{rounded to}} (0110.1)_2 \xrightarrow[\text{to decimal}]{\text{convert}} (6.5)_{10}$$

$y'(5) = Q[6.3] = 6.5$

When $n = 6$,

$$\begin{aligned} y'(6) &= Q[0.9y'(5)] \\ &= Q[0.9 \times 6.5] \\ &= Q[5.85] \end{aligned}$$

$$Q[5.85] \Rightarrow (5.85)_{10} \xrightarrow[\text{to binary}]{\text{convert}} (0101.110)_2 \xrightarrow[\text{one decimal}]{\text{rounded to}} (0110)_2 \xrightarrow[\text{to decimal}]{\text{convert}} (6)_{10}$$

$y'(6) = Q[5.85] = 6$

When $n = 7$,

$$\begin{aligned} y'(7) &= Q[0.9y'(6)] \\ &= Q[0.9 \times 6] \\ &= Q[5.4] \end{aligned}$$

$$Q[5.4] \Rightarrow (5.4)_{10} \xrightarrow[\text{to binary}]{\text{convert}} (0101.011)_2 \xrightarrow[\text{one decimal}]{\text{rounded to}} (0101.1)_2 \xrightarrow[\text{to decimal}]{\text{convert}} (5.5)_{10}$$

$y'(7) = Q[5.4] = 5.5$

When $n = 8$,

$$\begin{aligned} y'(8) &= Q[0.9y'(7)] \\ &= Q[0.9 \times 5.5] \\ &= Q[4.95] \end{aligned}$$

$$Q[4.95] \Rightarrow (4.95)_{10} \xrightarrow[\text{binary}]{\text{convert to}} (0100.111)_2 \xrightarrow[\text{one decimal}]{\text{rounded to}} (0101)_2 \xrightarrow[\text{to decimal}]{\text{convert}} (5)_{10}$$

$y'(8) = Q[4.95] = 5$

When $n = 9$,

$$\begin{aligned} y'(9) &= Q[0.9y'(8)] \\ &= Q[0.9 \times 5] \\ &= Q[4.5] \end{aligned}$$

$$Q[4.5] \Rightarrow (4.5)_{10} \xrightarrow[\text{to binary}]{\text{convert}} (0100.10)_2 \xrightarrow[\text{one decimal}]{\text{rounded to}} (0100.1)_2 \xrightarrow[\text{to decimal}]{\text{convert}} (4.5)_{10}$$

$y'(9) = Q[4.5] = 4.5$

When $n = 10$,

$$\begin{aligned} y'(10) &= Q[0.9y'(9)] \\ &= Q[0.9 \times 4.5] \\ &= Q[4.05] \end{aligned}$$

$$Q[4.05] \Rightarrow (4.05)_{10} \xrightarrow[\text{binary}]{\text{convert to}} (0100.000)_2 \xrightarrow[\text{one decimal}]{\text{rounded to}} (0100)_2 \xrightarrow[\text{to decimal}]{\text{convert}} (4)_{10}$$

$y'(10) = Q[4.05] = 4$

When $n = 11$,

$$\begin{aligned} y'(11) &= Q[0.9y'(10)] \\ &= Q[0.9 \times 4] \\ &= Q[3.6] \end{aligned}$$

$$Q[3.6] \Rightarrow (3.6)_{10} \xrightarrow[\text{to binary}]{\text{convert}} (0011.100)_2 \xrightarrow[\text{one decimal}]{\text{rounded to}} (0011.1)_2 \xrightarrow[\text{to decimal}]{\text{convert}} (3.5)_{10}$$

$y'(11) = Q[3.6] = 3.5$

When $n = 12$,

$$\begin{aligned} y'(12) &= Q[0.9y'(11)] \\ &= Q[0.9 \times 3.5] \\ &= Q[3.15] \end{aligned}$$

$$Q[3.15] \Rightarrow (3.15)_{10} \xrightarrow[\text{binary}]{\text{convert to}} (0011.001)_2 \xrightarrow[\text{one decimal}]{\text{rounded to}} (0011)_2 \xrightarrow[\text{to decimal}]{\text{convert}} (3)_{10}$$

$y'(12) = Q[3.15] = 3$

When $n = 13$,

$$\begin{aligned} y'(13) &= Q[0.9y'(12)] \\ &= Q[0.9 \times 3] \\ &= Q[2.7] \end{aligned}$$

$$Q[2.7] \Rightarrow (2.7)_{10} \xrightarrow[\text{to binary}]{\text{convert}} (0010.101)_2 \xrightarrow[\text{one decimal}]{\text{rounded to}} (0010.1)_2 \xrightarrow[\text{to decimal}]{\text{convert}} (2.5)_{10}$$

$y'(13) = Q[2.7] = 2.5$

When $n = 14$,

$$\begin{aligned} y'(14) &= Q[0.9y'(13)] \\ &= Q[0.9 \times 2.5] \\ &= Q[2.25] \end{aligned}$$

$$Q[2.25] \Rightarrow (2.25)_{10} \xrightarrow[\text{binary}]{\text{convert to}} (0010.010)_2 \xrightarrow[\text{one decimal}]{\text{rounded to}} (0010.1)_2 \xrightarrow[\text{to decimal}]{\text{convert}} (2.5)_{10}$$

$y'(14) = Q[2.25] = 2.5$

For all values of $n \geq 13$, $y'(n)$ will remain with the same magnitude as 2.5. Therefore, the system enters into limit cycle when $n = 13$

$$\text{Dead band} = \pm\frac{2^{-b}}{1-|\alpha|}$$

$$= \pm\frac{2^{-2}}{1-0.9}$$

$$\text{Dead band} = \pm\frac{0.25}{0.1}$$

$$= \pm 2.5$$

Thus, the dead band interval is $[-2.5, 2.5]$.

Example 5.25

Determine the dead band of the following filter if 8 bits are used for representation

$$y(n) = 0.2y(n-1) + 0.5y(n-2) + x(n)$$

(Anna University, December, 2003)

Solution Given $b = 8$ bits (including sign bit)

$$y(n) = 0.2y(n-1) + 0.5y(n-2) + x(n)$$

Consider the second order system, which is described by the following difference equation.

$$y(n) = a_1 y(n-1) + a_2 y(n-2) + x(n)$$

Comparing these two equations we get $a_1 = 0.2$ and $a_2 = 0.5$.

For the second order system, dead band is given by

$$\text{Dead band} = \pm\frac{2^{-b}}{1-|a_2|}$$

$$= \pm\frac{2^{-8}}{1-|0.5|}$$

$$\boxed{\text{Dead band} = \pm 0.0078125}$$

Thus, the dead band has the interval of $[-0.0078125, +0.0078125]$.

5.7.2 Overflow Limit Cycle Oscillation

In fixed point addition of two binary numbers the overflow occurs when the sum exceeds the finite word length of the register used to store the sum. The overflow in addition may lead to oscillation in the output which are referred to as an overflow limit cycle. An overflow in addition of two or more binary numbers occurs when the sum exceeds the dynamic range of number system. Let us consider two positive numbers n_1 and n_2 which is represented in sign magnitudes.

$$n_1 = \frac{3}{8} \rightarrow 0.011$$

$$n_2 = \frac{6}{8} \rightarrow 0.110$$

$$n_1 + n_2 = 1.001 \rightarrow -\frac{1}{8} \text{ in sign magnitude}$$

In the above example, when two positive numbers are added the sum is wrongly interpreted as a negative number. The transfer characteristics of an adder is shown in Figure 5.16, where n is the input to the adder and $y(n)$ is the corresponding output. The overflow oscillations can be eliminated if saturation arithmetic is performed.

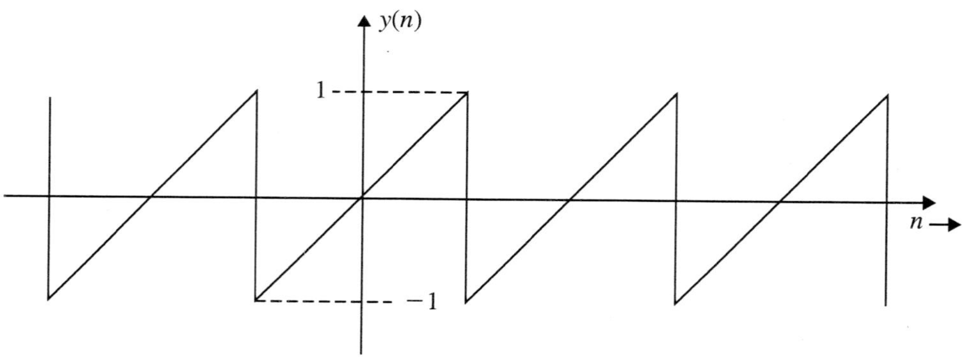

Figure 5.16 Transfer characteristics of an adder.

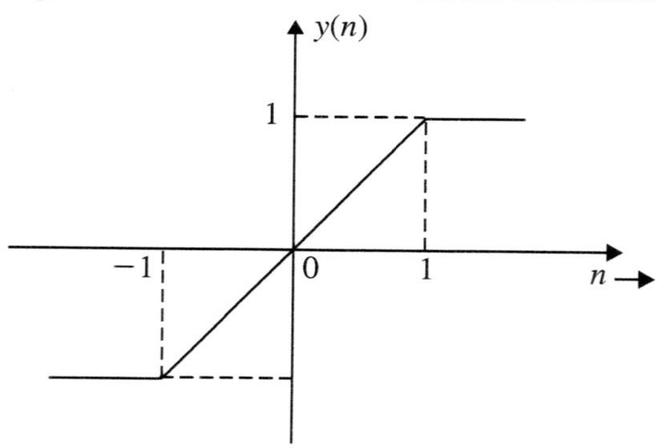

Figure 5.17 Characteristics of saturation adder.

The characteristics of saturation adder is shown in Figure 5.17. In saturation arithmetic, when an overflow is sensed, the output is set equal to maximum allowable value and when an underflow is sensed, the output (sum) is set equal to minimum allowable value. The saturation arithmetic introduces non-linearity in the adder and the signal distortion due to this non-linearity is small if the saturation occurs infrequently.

5.8 Scaling to Prevent Overflow

Saturation arithmetic eliminates limit cycle due to overflow, but it causes undesirable signal distortion due to non-linearity of the clipper. In order to limit the amount of non-linear distortion, it is important to scale the input signal to the adder such that the overflow becomes a rare event. Let

$$x(n) = \text{Input to the system}$$
$$h_m(n) = \text{Impulse response between the input and output of node } -m$$
$$y_m(n) = \text{Response of the system at node } -m$$

To scale the input signal so that

$$\sum_{n=-\infty}^{\infty} |y_m(n)|^2 \le S^2 \sum_{n=-\infty}^{\infty} |x(n)|^2$$

where S is the scaling factor, using Parseval's and residue theorems the expression for scaling factor is given by

$$S^2 = \frac{1}{\sum_{n=-\infty}^{\infty} |h_m(n)|^2} = \frac{1}{2\pi j \oint_c S(z)S(z^{-1})z^{-1}dz}$$
$$S^2 = \frac{1}{\sum_{i=1}^{N} \text{Res}[S(z)S(z^{-1})z^{-1}dz]|_{z=p_i}} \tag{5.37}$$

where $S(z)$ is the transfer function seen between the input to system and output of summing node $-m$. For example, consider the second order system which is shown in Figure 5.18.

The transfer function between the input to the system and output of adder A is given by

$$S(z) = \frac{W(z)}{X(z)}$$

The output signal of adder A is

$$W(z) = X(z) - a_1 z^{-1} W(z) - a_2 z^{-2} W(z)$$
$$X(z) = W(z) + a_1 z^{-1} W(z) + a_2 z^{-2} W(z)$$

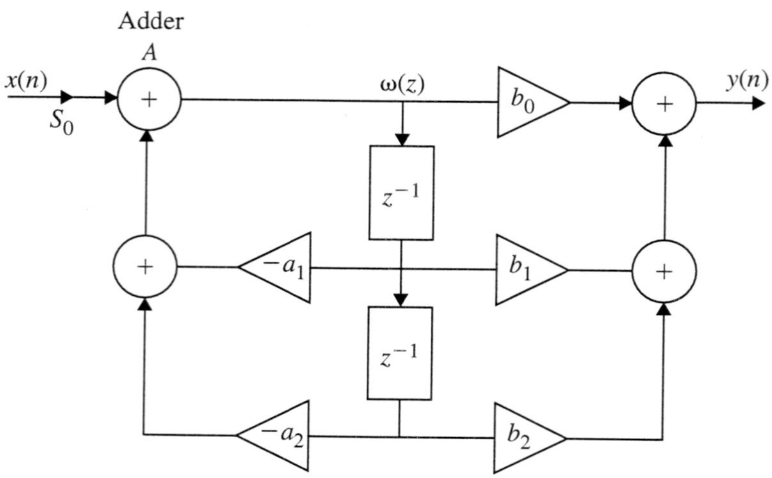

Figure 5.18 Second order system with input in sealed by S_0.

$$\therefore\ S(z) = \frac{W(z)}{X(z)} = \frac{1}{1 + a_1 z^{-1} + a_2 z^{-2}}$$

Example 5.26

For digital network shown in figure, find $H(z)$ and scale factor so to avoid overflow in register A_1.

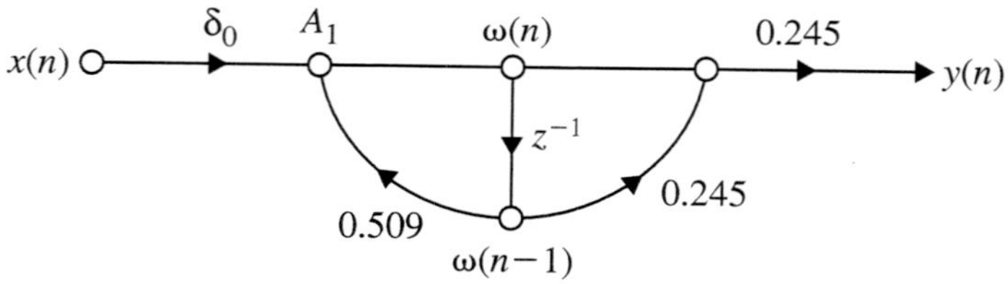

Solution In figure, the output signal at node A_1, is $\omega(n)$. At node A_1, the following equation is written.

$$\omega(n) = \delta_0 x(n) + 0.509(\omega(n-1))$$

On taking z-transform we get,

$$W(z) = \delta_0 X(z) + 0.509z^{-1}W(z)$$

$$W(z) - 0.509z^{-1}W(z) = \delta_0 X(z)$$

$$W(z)[1 - 0.509z^{-1}] = \delta_0 X(z)$$

$$\frac{W(z)}{X(z)} = \frac{\delta_0}{1 - 0.509z^{-1}}$$

At the output node the following equation is written.

$$y(n) = 0.245(\omega(n) + 0.245\omega(n-1))$$
$$y(n) = 0.245\omega(n) + 0.06\omega(n-1)$$

On taking z-transform we get,

$$Y(z) = 0.245W(z) + 0.06W(z)z^{-1}$$
$$Y(z) = (0.245 + 0.06z^{-1})W(z)$$
$$\therefore \quad \frac{Y(z)}{W(z)} = (0.245 + 0.06z^{-1})$$

The transfer function of the system $\frac{Y(z)}{X(z)}$ is obtained by multiplying $W(z)/X(z)$ and $Y(z)/W(z)$

$$\therefore \text{ Transfer function of the system } \frac{Y(z)}{X(z)} = \frac{Y(z)}{W(z)} \times \frac{W(z)}{X(z)}$$
$$= \frac{\delta_0[0.245 + 0.06z^{-1}]}{[1 - 0.509z^{-1}]}$$

The scaling factor δ_0 is given by

$$\delta_0^2 = \frac{1}{\frac{1}{2\pi j}\oint_c \delta(z)\delta(z^{-1})z^{-1}dz}$$

where $\delta(z) \rightarrow$ transfer function seen between system input and output of register A_1.

$$\delta(z) = \frac{W(z)}{X(z)}$$

When there is no scaling multiplier, we get

$$\delta(z) = \frac{1}{1 - 0.509z^{-1}} = \frac{z}{z - 0.509}$$
$$\therefore \quad \delta(z)\delta(z^{-1})z^{-1} = \frac{z^{-1}}{(z - 0.509)(z^{-1} - 0.509)}$$
$$\frac{1}{2\pi j}\oint_c \delta(z)\delta(z^{-1})z^{-1}dz = \sum_{i=1}^{N} \text{Res}[\delta(z)\delta(z^{-1})z^{-1}]_{z=p_i}$$

We have only one pole at $z = 0.509$

$$= (z - 0.509)\left.\frac{z^{-1}}{(z - 0.509)(z^{-1} - 0.509)}\right|_{z=0.509}$$
$$= \left.\frac{z^{-1}}{z^{-1} - 0.509}\right|_{z=0.509}$$

$$= \frac{0.509^{-1}}{0.509^{-1} - 0.509} = 1.3497$$

$$\therefore \ \delta_0^2 = \frac{1}{1.3497} = 0.7409$$

Scaling factor

$$\boxed{\delta_0 = \sqrt{0.7409} = 0.8608.}$$

Example 5.27

The output signal of an A/D converter is passed through a first order lowpass filter, with transfer function given by

$$H(z) = \frac{(1-a)z}{z-a}, \qquad 0 < a < 1$$

Find the steady state output noise power due to quantization at the output of the digital filter.

Solution Using Equations (5.29) and (5.30) we get,

$$\sigma_{e0}^2 = \sigma_e^2 \frac{1}{2\pi j} \oint_c H(z)H(z^{-1})z^{-1}dz$$

$$= \sigma_e^2 \sum_{i=1}^{N} [\text{Res}(H(z)H(z^{-1})z^{-1}dz)]|_{z=p_i}$$

Given,

$$H(z) = \frac{(1-a)z}{z-a}$$

$$H(z^{-1}) = \frac{(1-a)z^{-1}}{z^{-1}-a}$$

$$H(z)H(z^{-1})z^{-1} = \frac{(1-a)z(1-a)z^{-1} \cdot z^{-1}}{(z-a)(z^{-1}-a)} = \frac{(1-a)^2 z^{-1}}{(z-a)(z^{-1}-a)}$$

There are two poles at $z = a$, $z = 1/a$ out of which the pole at $z = a$ lies inside of the unit circle since $0 < a < 1$. Therefore, residue due to pole $z = a$ is given as,

$$\text{Res}[H(z)H(z^{-1})z^{-1}]|_{z=a} = (z-a)\left.\frac{(1-a)^2 z^{-1}}{(z-a)(z^{-1}-a)}\right|_{z=a}$$

$$= \frac{(1-a)^2 a^{-1}}{a^{-1}-a}$$

$$= \frac{(1-a)^2}{(1-a^2)}$$

Therefore, steady state output noise power is

$$\begin{aligned}\sigma_{e0}^2 &= \sigma_e^2 \text{Res}[H(z)H(z^{-1})z^{-1}]|_{z=a} \\ &= \sigma_e^2 \left[\frac{(1-a)^2}{1-a^2}\right] \\ &= \sigma_e^2 \left[\frac{1-a}{1+a}\right]\end{aligned}$$

where $\sigma_e^2 = (q^2/12)$, if $R = 1$

$$\boxed{\sigma_e^2 = \left(\frac{2^{-2b}}{12}\right).}$$

Example 5.28

Find the steady state variance of the noise in the output due to quantization of input for the first order filter described by the following difference equation.

$$y(n) = 0.5y(n-1) + x(n)$$

(Anna University, May, 2007)

Solution Given

$$y(n) = 0.5y(n-1) + x(n)$$

Taking z-transform on both sides we have

$$\begin{aligned}Y(z) &= 0.5z^{-1}Y(z) + X(z) \\ H(z) &= \frac{Y(z)}{X(z)} = \frac{1}{1-0.5z^{-1}} = \frac{z}{z-0.5} \\ H(z^{-1}) &= \frac{z^{-1}}{z^{-1}-0.5}\end{aligned}$$

The steady state output noise power as given by equation (5.30) is,

$$\sigma_{e0}^2 = \sigma_e^2 \sum_{i=1}^{N} \text{Res}[H(z)H(z^{-1})z^{-1}]|_{z=p_i}$$

$$\begin{aligned}H(z)H(z^{-1})z^{-1} &= \frac{z \cdot z^{-1} \cdot z^{-1}}{(z-0.5)(z^{-1}-0.5)} \\ &= \frac{z^{-1}}{(z-0.5)(z^{-1}-0.5)}\end{aligned}$$

The pole $z = 0.5$ only lies inside of the unit circle, and therefore

$$\begin{aligned}\text{Res}[H(z)H(z^{-1})z^{-1}]|_{z=0.5} &= (z-0.5)\frac{z^{-1}}{(z-0.5)(z^{-1}-0.5)}\bigg|_{z=0.5}\\ &= \frac{(0.5)^{-1}}{(0.5)^{-1}-0.5}\\ &= \frac{1}{1-(0.5)^2} = \frac{1}{1-0.25} = 1.333\end{aligned}$$

The steady state output noise variance (power) is

$$\sigma_{e0}^2 = \sigma_e^2 \text{Res}[H(z)H(z^{-1})z^{-1}]|_{z=0.5}$$

$$\boxed{\sigma_{e0}^2 = \sigma_e^2 1.333.}$$

Example 5.29

Consider the transfer function

$$H(z) = H_1(z)H_2(z)$$

where

$$H_1(z) = \frac{1}{1-0.5z^{-1}} \quad \text{and} \quad H_2(z) = \frac{1}{1-0.6z^{-1}}$$

Find the output roundoff noise power.

(Anna University, May, 2007)

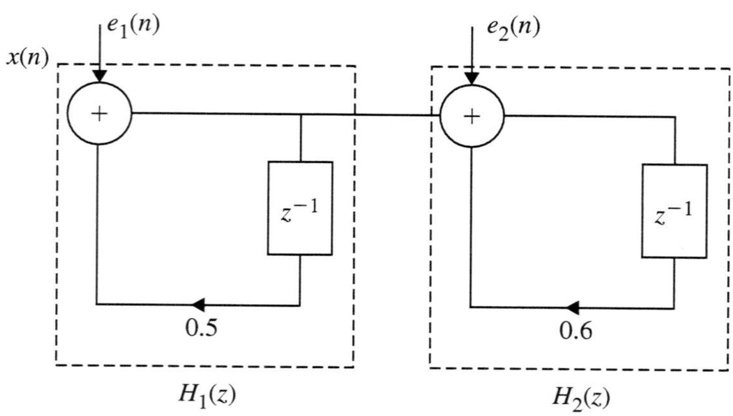

Figure 5.19 Round off noise model for Example 5.29.

Solution The roundoff noise model for $H(z) = H_1(z)H_2(z)$ is shown in Figure 5.19. From the realization, the noise transfer function seen by noise source $e_1(n)$ is written as,

$$T_1(z) = H(z) = H_1(z)H_2(z) = \frac{1}{(1-0.5z^{-1})(1-0.6z^{-1})}$$

The noise transfer function seen by $e_2(n)$ is written as,

$$T_2(z) = H_2(z) = \frac{1}{1-0.6z^{-1}}$$

The steady state output noise power due to $e_1(n)$ as given by equation (5.30) is,

$$\sigma_{e0_1}^2 = \sigma_e^2 \sum_{i=1}^{N} [\text{Res}(T_1(z)T_1(z^{-1})z^{-1})]|_{z=p_i}$$

$$= \sigma_e^2 \text{Res}\left[\frac{z^{-1}}{(1-0.5z^{-1})(1-0.6z^{-1})(1-0.5z)(1-0.6)}\right]_{z=0.5,0.6,(1/0.5),(1/0.6)}$$

Only two poles at $z = 0.5$ and $z = 0.6$ lie inside of unit circle

$$\sigma_{e0_1}^2 = \sigma_e^2 \left[\sum \text{Res}(T_1(z)T_1(z^{-1})z^{-1})\right]\Bigg|_{z=0.5 \text{ and } z=0.6}$$

$$= \sigma_e^2 \left[(z-0.5)\frac{z}{(z-0.5)(z-0.6)(1-0.5z)(1-0.6)}\Bigg|_{z=0.5} + (z-0.6)\frac{z}{(z-0.5)(z-0.6)(1-0.5z)(1-0.6)}\Bigg|_{z=0.6}\right]$$

$$= \sigma_e^2 \left[\frac{0.5}{(0.5-0.6)(1-.25)(1-0.3)} + \frac{0.6}{(0.6-0.5)(1-0.3)(1-0.36)}\right]$$

$$= \sigma_e^2 [-9.5238 + 13.3928]$$

$$\boxed{\sigma_{e0_1}^2 = \sigma_e^2 [3.8690]}$$

The steady state output noise power due to $e_2(n)$ is,

$$\sigma_{e0_2}^2 = \sigma_e^2 \sum_{i=1}^{N} \text{Res}[(T_2(z)T_2(z^{-1})z^{-1})]|_{z=p_i}$$

$$= \sigma_e^2 \sum_{i=1}^{N} \text{Res}[(H_2(z)H_2(z^{-1})z^{-1})]|_{z=p_i}$$

$$= \sigma_e^2 \sum \text{Res}\left[\frac{1}{1-0.6z^{-1}} \cdot \frac{1}{1-0.6z} \cdot z^{-1}\right]_{z=0.6 \text{ and } z=(1/0.6)}$$

The residue at pole $z = (1/0.6)$ is zero, since that pole lies outside of the unit circle

$$\sigma_{e0_2}^2 = \sigma_e^2 \text{Res}\left[\frac{1}{(z-0.6)(1-0.6z)}\right]_{z=0.6}$$

$$= \sigma_e^2 \left[(z-0.6)\frac{1}{(z-0.6)(1-0.6z)}\right]_{z=0.6}$$

$$\boxed{\sigma_{e0_2}^2 = \sigma_e^2\,[1.5626]}$$

The total steady state output noise power is,

$$\sigma_{e0}^2 = \sigma_{e0_1}^2 + \sigma_{e0_2}^2$$

$$= \sigma_e^2\,[3.8690 + 1.5626]$$

$$= \sigma_e^2\,[5.4315]$$

For example for $b = 4$ bits (including sign bit)

$$\sigma_e^2 = \frac{q^2}{12} = \frac{(R/2^b)^2}{12}$$

$$\sigma_e^2 = \frac{(2/2^4)^2}{12} = \frac{2^{-6}}{12} = 1.302 \times 10^{-3}$$

$$\sigma_{e0}^2 = 1.302 \times 10^{-3} \times 5.4315 = 7.0718 \times 10^{-3}$$

The total round-off noise power is,

$$\boxed{\sigma_{e0}^2 = 7.0718 \times 10^{-3}}$$

Example 5.30

Draw the quantization noise model for a second order system

$$H(z) = \frac{1}{1 - 2r\cos\theta z^{-1} + r^2 z^{-2}}$$

and find the steady state output noise variance.

(Anna University, May, 2005)

Solution Given

$$H(z) = \frac{1}{1 - 2r\cos\theta z^{-1} + r^2 z^{-2}}$$

The quantization noise model is shown in Figure 5.20.

$$\sigma_{e0}^2 = \sigma_{e0_1}^2 + \sigma_{e0_2}^2$$

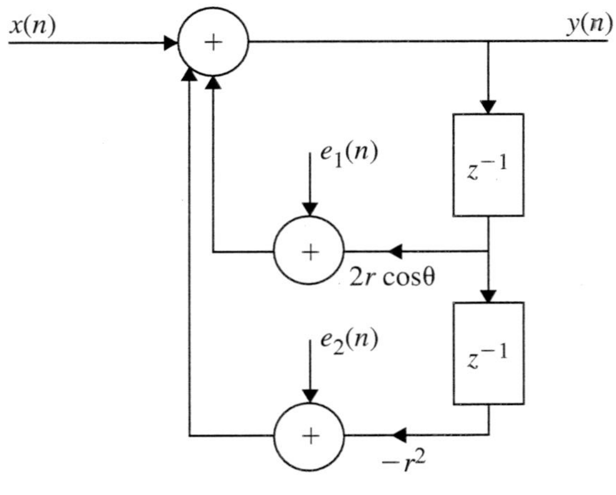

Figure 5.20 Quantization noise model for Example 5.30.

Both noise sources see the same transfer function

$$H(z) = \frac{1}{1 - 2r\cos\theta z^{-1} + r^2 z^{-2}}$$

$$\sigma_{e0_1}^2 = \sigma_{e0_2}^2$$

The impulse response of the transfer function is given by

$$h(n) = r^n \frac{\sin(n+1)\theta}{\sin\theta} u(n)$$

(Please refer z-transform table)

$$\sigma_{e0_1}^2 = \sigma_{e0_2}^2 = \sigma_e^2 \sum_{n=-\infty}^{\infty} h^2(n)$$

$$\begin{aligned}
\sigma_{e0}^2 &= 2\sigma_{e0_1}^2 \\
&= 2\sigma_e^2 \sum_{n=0}^{\infty} \frac{r^{2n}\sin^2(n+1)\theta}{\sin^2\theta} \\
&= 2\sigma_e^2 \frac{1}{2\sin^2\theta} \sum_{n=0}^{\infty} r^{2n}[1 - \cos 2(n+1)\theta] \quad [\because \cos 2\theta = 1 - 2\sin^2\theta] \\
&= 2\sigma_e^2 \frac{1}{2\sin^2\theta} \left[\sum_{n=0}^{\infty} r^{2n} - \sum_{n=0}^{\infty} r^{2n}\cos 2(n+1)\theta\right] \\
&= 2\sigma_e^2 \frac{1}{2\sin^2\theta} \left[\frac{1}{1-r^2} - \frac{1}{2}\left[\sum_{n=0}^{\infty} r^{2n} e^{j(2n+1)\theta} + \sum_{n=0}^{\infty} r^{2n} e^{-j(2n+1)\theta}\right]\right] \\
&= 2\sigma_e^2 \cdot \frac{1}{2\sin^2\theta} \left[\frac{1}{1-r^2} - \frac{1}{2}\left[\frac{e^{2j\theta}}{1 - r^2 e^{2j\theta}} + \frac{e^{-2j\theta}}{1 - r^2 e^{-2j\theta}}\right]\right]
\end{aligned}$$

$$\sigma_{e0}^2 = 2\sigma_e^2 \cdot \frac{1}{2\sin^2\theta}\left[\frac{1}{1-r^2} - \frac{\cos 2\theta - r^2}{1-2r^2\cos 2\theta + r^4}\right]$$

$$= 2\sigma_e^2 \cdot \frac{1}{2\sin^2\theta}\left[\frac{(1+r^2)(1-\cos 2\theta)}{(1-r^2)(1-2r^2\cos 2\theta + r^4)}\right]$$

$$= 2\sigma_e^2 \cdot \frac{1}{2\sin^2\theta}\left[\frac{(1+r^2)2\sin^2\theta}{(1-r^2)(1-2r^2\cos 2\theta + r^4)}\right]$$

$$\boxed{\sigma_{e0}^2 = 2\sigma_e^2\left[\frac{1+r^2}{(1-r^2)(1-2r^2\cos 2\theta + r^4)}\right]}$$

where

$$\sigma_e^2 = \left(\frac{q^2}{12}\right) = \frac{(R/2b)^2}{12}.$$

Example 5.31

Given

$$H(z) = \frac{0.5 + 0.4z^{-1}}{1 - 0.312z^{-1}}$$

is the transfer function of a digital filter. Find the scaling factor S_0 to avoid overflow in adder of the digital filter shown in Figure 5.21.

Solution From Equation (5.37), the scaling factor is written as,

$$S_0^2 = \left.\frac{1}{\sum_{i=1}^{N} \mathrm{Res}(S(z)S(z^{-1})z^{-1})}\right|_{z=p_i}$$

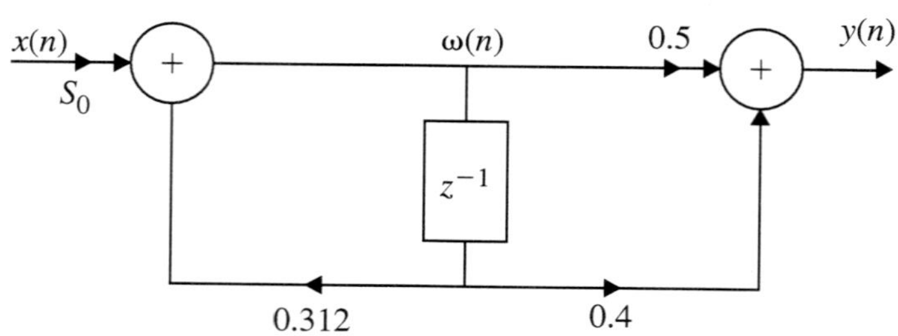

Figure 5.21 Realization of transfer function for Example 5.31.

where

$$S(z) = \frac{W(z)}{X(z)}$$

$$\omega(n) = x(n) + 0.312\omega(n-1)$$

$$W(z) = X(z) + 0.312z^{-1}W(z)$$

$$S(z) = \frac{W(z)}{X(z)} = \frac{1}{1-0.312z^{-1}}$$

$$S_0^2 = \frac{1}{\sum \text{Res}\left[\frac{z^{-1}}{(1-0.312z^{-1})(1-0.312z)}\right]}$$

$$= \frac{1}{\sum \text{Res}\left[\frac{1}{(z-0.312)(1-0.312z)}\right]}$$

$$= \frac{1}{\text{Res}\left[\frac{1}{(z-0.312)(1-0.312z)}\right]}\Bigg|_{z=0.312}$$

$$= \frac{1}{(z-0.312)\left[\frac{1}{(z-0.312)(1-0.312z)}\right]_{z=0.312}}$$

$$S_0^2 = \frac{1}{1.1078}$$

$$\boxed{S_0 = 0.9501.}$$

Summary

- The performance of a DSP system is limited by the number of bits used in the implementation. The common sources of errors are due to input quantization, coefficient quantization, product round off and addition overflow.
- The ADC quantization noise is reduced by increasing the number of ADC bits or by using multirate techniques.
- When an IIR digital filter is implemented, errors arise in representing the filter coefficients. These errors can be reduced to acceptable level by using more bits. However, this increases the cost.
- Addition of two large numbers of a similar sign may produce an overflow which results in excess of permissible word length. This occurs at the output of adders and can be prevented by scaling the inputs to the adders in such a way that the outputs are kept low. However, this reduces the signal to noise ratio and increases the cost.
- In digital filter, the product of two variables requires very long bits. For recursive filters, if it is not reduced, subsequent computations will cause the number of bits to grow without limit. Truncation or rounding is used to quantize the products to

the permissible word length. When the products are quantized, roundoff errors occur and they may lead to oscillations in the output even when there is no input. Further the signal to noise ratio is also small. The roundoff noise can be reduced or minimized by passing through subsequent sections of a cascade structure where it is alternated.

- Reduction in signal to noise ratio due to roundoff error can be offset by the use of error spectral shaping scheme. However this scheme increases the number of multiplications and additions but computationally more efficient.

Short Questions and Answers

1. **What is meant by finite word length effects in digital filters?**
The fundamental operations in digital filters are multiplication and addition. When these operations are performed in a digital system, the input data as well as the product and sum (output data) have to be represented in finite word length, which depends on the size (length) of the register used to store the data. In digital computation the input and output data (sum and product) are quantized by rounding or truncation to convert them into finite word size. This creates error (in noise) in the output or creates oscillations (limit cycles) in the output. These effects due to finite precision representation of numbers in digital system are called as finite word length effects.

2. **List some of the finite word length effects in digital filters.**

    1. Errors due to quantization of the input data.
    2. Errors due to quantization of the filter coefficients.
    3. Errors due to rounding the product in multiplications.
    4. Limit cycles due to product quantization and overflow in addition.

3. **Explain the fixed point representation of binary numbers.**
In fixed point representation of binary numbers in a given word size, the bits allotted for integer part and fraction part of the numbers are fixed and therefore the position of binary point is fixed. The most significant bit is used to represent the sign of the number. This is shown in Figure 5.22.

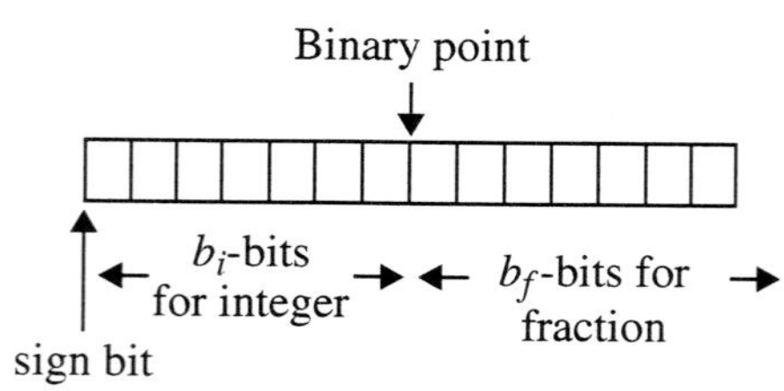

Figure 5.22

4. **What are the different formats of fixed point representation?**
   In fixed point representation, there are three different formats for representing binary numbers:

   1. Sign – magnitude format.
   2. One's – complement format.
   3. Two's – complement format.

   In all the three formats, the positive number is same but they differ only in representing negative numbers.

5. **Explain the floating point representation of binary numbers.**
   The floating numbers will have a mantissa part and exponent part. In a given word size the bits allotted for mantissa and exponent are fixed. The mantissa is used to represent a binary fraction number and the exponent is a positive or negative binary integer. The value of the exponent can be adjusted to move the position of the binary point in mantissa. Hence, this representation is called floating point. The floating point number is expressed as

$$\text{Floating point number, } N_f = M \times 2^E$$

   where M = mantissa and E = exponent.

6. **Give the IEEE-754 standard format for 32 bit floating point numbers.**
   The IEEE-754 standard for 32 bit single precision floating point number is given by floating point numbers, $N_f = (-1) \times 2^{E-127} \times M$. This is shown in Figure 5.23.

   S = 1 bit field for sign of number.
   E = 8 bit field for exponent.
   M = 23 bit field for mantissa.

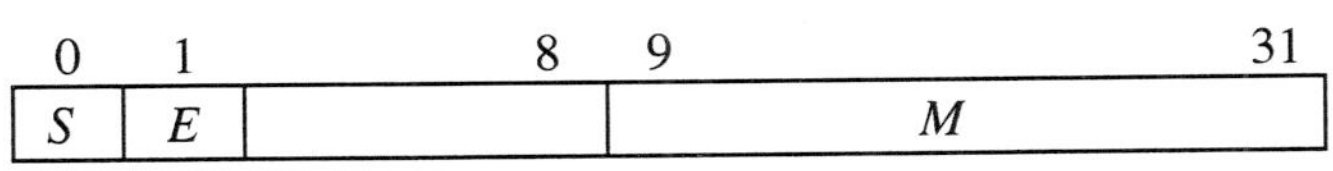

Figure 5.23

7. **What are the types of arithmetic used in digital computers?**
   The floating point arithmetic and two's complement arithmetic are the two types of arithmetic employed in digital systems.

8. **Compare the fixed point and floating point number representations.**

Fixed Point Representation	Floating Point Representation
1. In a b bit binary the range of numbers represented is less when compared to floating point representation.	In a b bit binary the range of the numbers represented is large when compared to fixed point representation.
2. The position of binary point is fixed.	The position of binary point is variable.
3. The resolution is uniform throughout the range.	The resolution is variable.

9. **Compare the fixed point and floating point arithmetic.**

Fixed Point Arithmetic	Floating Point Arithmetic
1. The accuracy of the result is less due to smaller dynamic range.	The accuracy of the result will be higher due to larger dynamic range.
2. Speed of processing is high.	Speed of processing is low.
3. Hardware implementation is cheaper.	Hardware implementation is costlier.
4. Fixed point arithmetic can be used for real time computation.	Floating point arithmetic cannot be used for real time computation.
5. Quantization error occurs only in multiplication.	Quantization error occurs in both multiplication and addition.

10. **What are the two types of quantization employed in digital system?**
The two type of quantization in digital system are truncation and rounding.

11. **What is Truncation?**
The truncation is the process of reducing the size of binary number by discarding all bits less significant than the least significant bit that is retained. (In truncation of a binary number to b bits all the less significant bits beyond b^{th} bit are discarded).

12. **Sketch the characteristics of the quantizer used for truncation.**

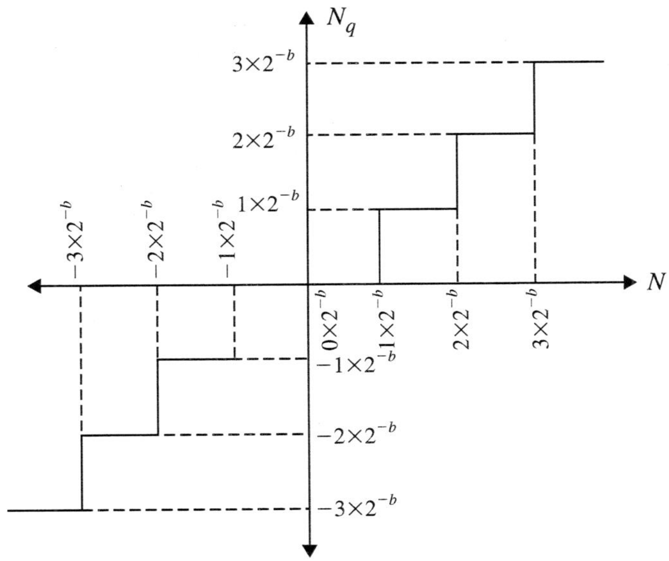

Figure 5.24

13. **What is rounding?**
Rounding is the process of reducing the size of a binary number to finite word sizes of b bits such that, the rounded b bit number is closest to the original unquantized number.
14. **Sketch the noise probability density function for rounding.**

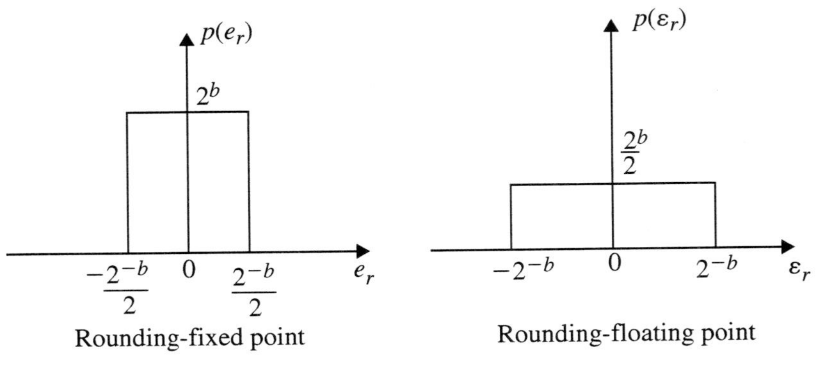

Figure 5.25

15. **What are the errors generated by A/D process?**
The A/D process generates two types of errors. They are quantization error and saturation error. The quantization error is due to representation of the sampled signal by a fixed number of digital level (quantization levels). The

saturation error occurs when the analog signal exceeds the dynamic range of A/D converter.

16. **What is quantization step size?**
    In digital systems, the numbers are represented in binary. With b bit binary we can generate 2^b different binary codes. Any range of analog value to be represented in binary should be divided into 2^b levels with equal increment. The 2^b levels are called quantization levels and the increment in each level is called quantization step size. If R is the range of analog signal then,

$$\text{Quantization step size, } q = \frac{R}{2^b}$$

17. **How the input quantization noise is represented in LTI system?**
    The quantized input signal of a digital system can be represented as a sum of unquantized signal $x(n)$ and error signal $e(n)$ as shown in Figure 5.26 below.

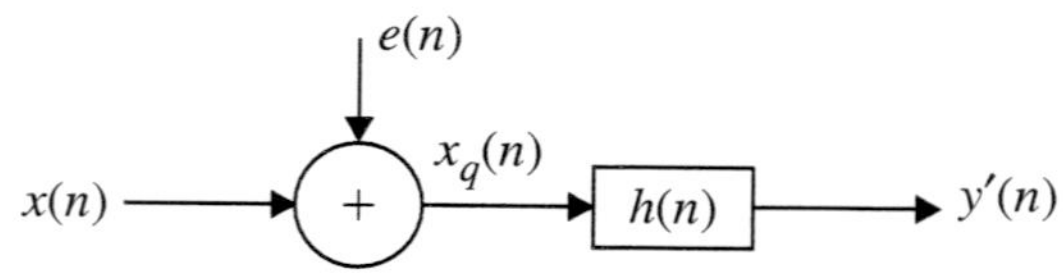

Figure 5.26

18. **What is steady state output noise due to input quantization?**
    The input signal to digital system can be considered as a sum of unquantized signal and error signal due to input quantization. The response of the system can be expressed as a summation of response due to unquantized input and error signal. The response of the system due to error signal is given by convolution of error signal and impulse response. The variance of the response of the system for error signal is called steady state output noise power.
19. **How the digital filter is affected by quantization of filter coefficients?**
    The quantization of filter coefficients will modify the values of poles and zeros and so the location of poles and zeros will be shifted from the desired location. This will create deviation in the frequency response of the system. Hence, the resultant filter will have a frequency response different from that of the filter with unquantized coefficients.
20. **What is meant by product quantization error?**
    In digital computation, the output of the multiplier *i.e.*, the products are quantized to the finite word length in order to store them in registers and to be used in subsequent calculation. The error due to the quantization of the output of multiplier is referred to as product quantization error.
21. **Why rounding is preferred for quantizing the product?**
    In digital system the product quantization is performed by rounding due to the following desirable characteristics of rounding.

(i) The rounding error is independent of the type of arithmetic.
(ii) The mean value of rounding error signal is zero.
(iii) The variance of the rounding error signal is least.

22. **Define noise transfer function (NTF).**
The noise transfer function (NTF) is defined as the transfer function from the noise source to the filter output. The NTF depends on the structure of the digital network.
23. **Draw the statistical model of the fixed point product quantization.**
The multiplier is considered as an infinite precision multiplier. Using an adder the error signal is added to the output of the multiplier so that the output of the adder is equal to the quantized product.

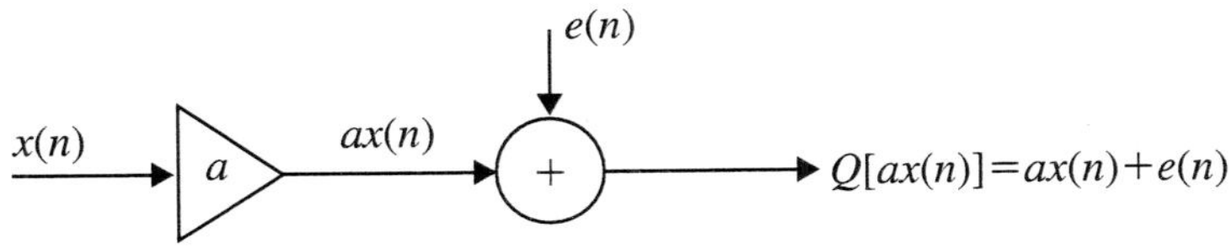

Figure 5.27

24. **Draw the product quantization noise model of second order IIR system.**

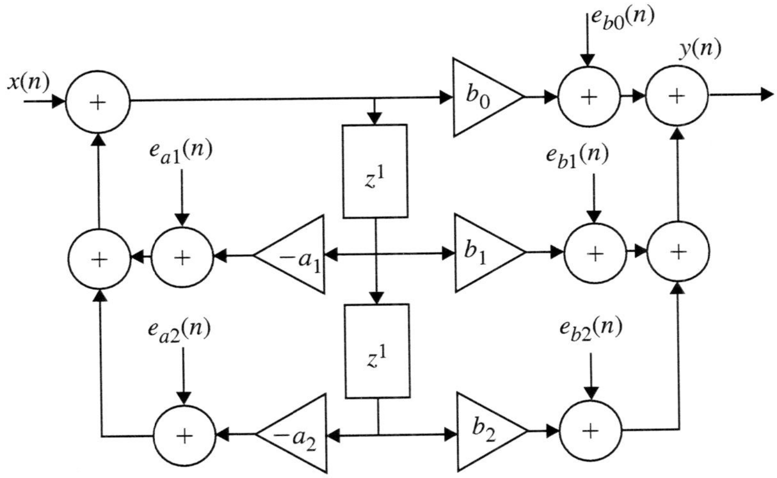

Figure 5.28

25. **Draw the product quantization noise model of second order IIR system with two first order section in cascade?**

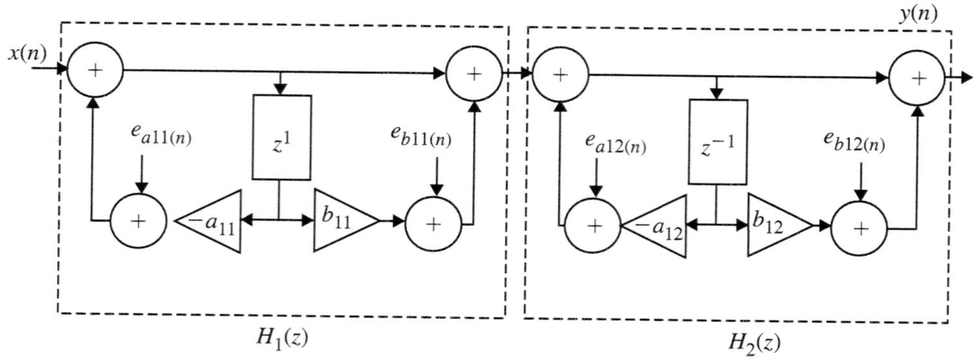

Figure 5.29

26. **What are limit cycles?**
In recursive systems when the input is zero or some non-zero constant value, the non-linearities due to finite precision arithmetic operations may cause periodic oscillations in the output. These oscillations are called limit cycles.
27. **What are two types of limit cycles?**
The two types of limit cycles are zero input limit cycle and overflow limit cycle.
28. **What is zero Input limit cycle?**
In recursive system, the product quantization may create periodic oscillations in the output. These oscillations are called limit cycles. If the system output enters a limit cycle, it will continue to remain in limit cycle even when the input is made zero. Hence, these limit cycles are also called zero input limit cycles.
29. **What is dead band?**
In a limit cycle the amplitudes of the output are confined to a range of values, which is called dead band of a filter.
30. **How the system output can be brought out of the limit cycle?**
The system output can be brought out of limit cycle by applying an input of large magnitude, which is sufficient to drive the system out of limit cycle.

31. **Draw the transfer characteristics of two's complement adder?**

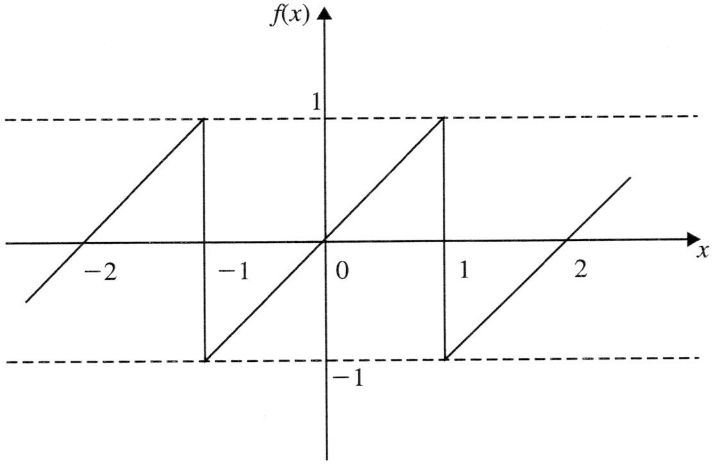

Figure 5.30

32. **What is saturation arithmetic?**
In saturation arithmetic when the result of arithmetic operations exceeds the dynamic range of number system, then the result is set to maximum or minimum possible value. If the upper limit is exceeded, then the result is set to maximum possible value. If the lower limit is exceeded, then the result is set to minimum possible value.
33. **What is overflow limit cycle?**
In fixed point addition the overflow occurs when the sum exceeds the finite word length of the register used to store the sum. The overflow in addition may lead to oscillations in the output which is called overflow limit cycle.
34. **How overflow limit cycles can be eliminated?**
The overflow limit cycles can be eliminated either by using saturation arithmetic or by scaling the input signal to the adder.
35. **What is the drawback in saturation arithmetic?**
The saturation arithmetic introduces non-linearity in the adder which leads to signal distortion.
36. **Give the rounding errors for fixed and floating print arithmetic.**

For fixed point arithmetic

$$\text{Rounding error, } e_r = N_r - N$$

where N_r is the fixed point binary number quantized by rounding and N is the unquantized fixed point binary number.

The range of error due to rounding is

$$-\frac{2^{-b}}{2} \leq e_r \leq \frac{2^{-b}}{2}$$

For floating point arithmetic

$$\text{Rounding error, } E_r = \frac{N_{rf} - N_f}{N_f}$$

where N_{rf} is rounded floating point binary number and N_f unquantized floating point binary number.

The range of error due to rounding is

$$-2^{-b} \le e_r \le 2^{-b}$$

37. **What is the steady state noise power at the output of an LTI system due to the quantization at the input to L bits?**

$$\text{Quantization step } (q) = \frac{R}{2^{-b}} = \frac{R}{2^{-L}}$$

$$\text{Steady state input noise power } \sigma_e^2 = \frac{q^2}{12} = \frac{(R/2^{-L})^2}{12}$$

$$\text{Steady state noise power at the output is } \sigma_{e0}^2 = \sigma_e^2 \sum_{i=1}^{N} \text{Re}[H(z)H(z^{-1})z^{-1}]|_{z=p_i}$$

38. **What are the three quantization errors due to finite word length, registers in digital filters?**
    1. Input quantization error.
    2. Coefficient quantization error.
    3. Product quantization error.
39. **Write the 2's complement of the following (*a*) +7 and (*b*) −7**

$$(a) + 7_{10} = (0111)_2$$
$$(b) - 7_{10} = \text{1's complement} \Rightarrow 1000$$
$$= \text{2's complement} \Rightarrow 1001$$
$$-7_{10} = (1001)_2$$

40. **What is the steady state noise power due to quantization if the number of bits is b?**

    Steady state noise power

$$\sigma_e^2 = \frac{2^{-2b}}{12}$$

where b is the number of bits excluding sign bit.

41. **Why rounding is preferred to truncation in realizing digital filter?**
Rounding is preferred to truncation due to the following desirable characteristics of rounding.
    1. The rounding error is independent of the type of arithmetic.
    2. The mean value of rounding error signal is zero.
    3. The variance of rounding error signal is least.
42. **Express the fraction $(-7/32)$ in signed magnitude and two's complement notation using 6 bits?**

$$\left(\frac{-7}{32}\right)_{10} = -(0.21875)_{10}$$

$$\text{signed magnitude: } \left(\frac{-7}{32}\right)_{10} = (1.0011)_2$$

$$\text{two's complement: } \left(\frac{-7}{32}\right)_{10} = (1.11001)_2$$

43. **Identify the various factors which degrade the performance of the digital filter implementation when finite word length is used.**
    1. Error due to quantization of the input data.
    2. Error due to quantization of the filter coefficients.
    3. Error due to rounding the product in multiplication.
    4. Limit cycles due to product quantization and overflow in addition.
44. **Express the fraction $(7/8)$ and $(-7/8)$ in sign magnitude and two's complement and 1's complement.**

$$\text{Fraction: } \left(\frac{7}{8}\right)_{10} = (0.111)_2 \text{ in sign magnitude}$$

$$= (0.111)_2 \text{ is 1's and 2's complement}$$

$$\text{Fraction: } \left(-\frac{7}{8}\right)_{10} = (1.111)_2 \text{ in sign magnitude}$$

$$= (1.000)_2 \text{ in 1's complement}$$

$$= (1.001)_2 \text{ in 2's complement}$$

45. **What are the different quantization methods?**
The common methods of quantization are (1) Truncation and (2) Rounding.

46. Plot the truncation error for sign magnitude and two's complement numbers.

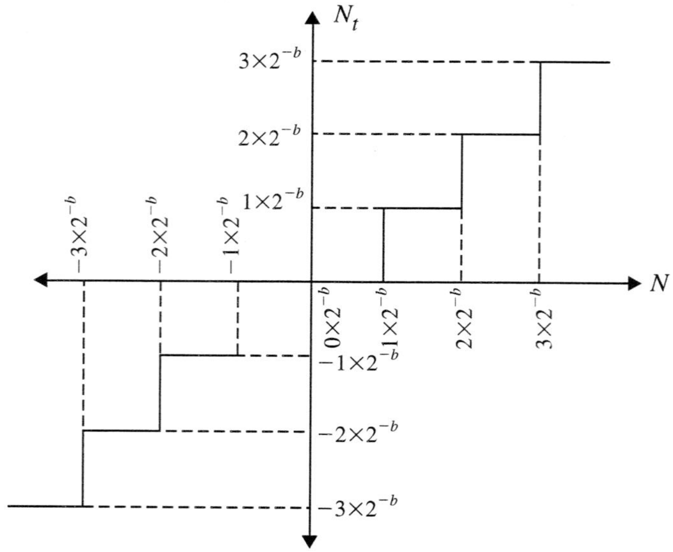

Figure 5.31 Two's complement.

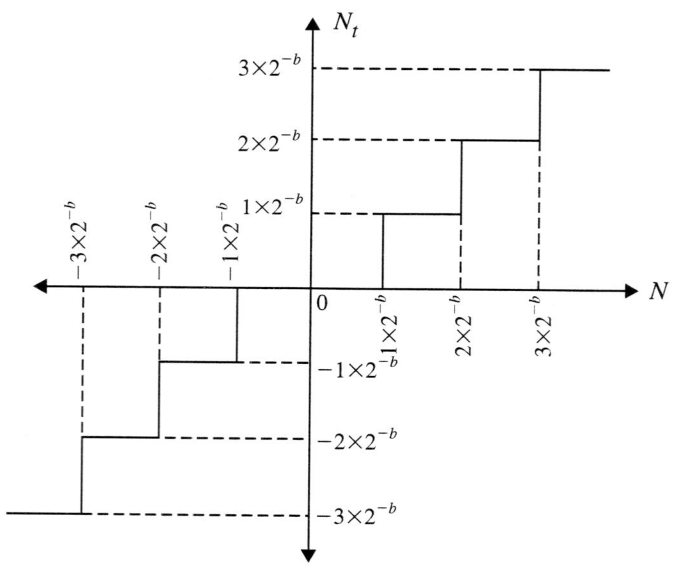

Figure 5.32 Sign complement.

47. Give the expression for signal to quantization noise ratio and calculate the improvement with an increase of 2 bits to the existing bit.

$$\text{SNR (signal to noise ratio)} = 6b - 1.24\text{dB}$$

With an increase of 2 bits, increase in SNR is approximately 12 dB.

Long Answer Type Questions

1. Explain coefficient quantization effects in direct form realization of IIR filter.
2. Explain about fixed point and floating point representations.
3. Derive the steady state noise power at the output of an LTI system due to quantization at the input.
4. Explain the aliasing effect in the down sampling process if the original spectrum is not band limited to $\omega = \pi/M$.
5. Prove that the up sampler is time varying system.
6. Illustrate the characteristics of a limit cycle oscillation of a typical first order system.
7. Enumerate with suitable examples the truncation and rounding errors.
8. The output of an A/D converter is applied to a digital filter with the system function

$$H(z) = \frac{0.53}{(z - 0.5)}$$

Find the output noise power from the digital filter when the input signal is quantized to have eight bits.
Ans:

$$\sigma_{e0}^2 = 1.675 \times 10^{-6}$$

9. What do you mean by down sampling?
10. Obtain the spectrum (expression) of the down sampled signal.
11. Plot the spectra of any signal $x(n)$ and its down sampled version.
12. Discuss on efficient transversal structure for decimator and interpolator.
13. Consider the truncation of negative fraction numbers represented in $(\beta+1)$-bit fixed point binary form including sign bit. Let $(\beta - b)$ bits be truncated. Obtain the range of truncation error for signed magnitude, 2's complements and 1's complement representations of the negative numbers.
Ans:

$$\begin{aligned} \text{Sign magnitude: } &= 0 \le e < -2^{-(\beta-b)} \\ \text{One's complement: } &= 0 \le e < -2^{-(\beta-b)} \\ \text{Two's complement: } &= 0 \ge e > -2^{-(\beta-b)} \end{aligned}$$

14. An 8-bit ADC feeds a DSP system characterized by the following transfer function

$$H(z) = \frac{1}{(z + 0.5)}$$

Estimate the steady state quantization noise power at the output of the system.

Ans:

$$\sigma_{e0}^2 = 6.7813 \times 10^{-6}$$

15. The coefficients of a system defined by

$$H(z) = \frac{1}{(1 - 0.4z^{-1})(1 - 0.55z^{-1})}$$

are represented in a number system with a sign bit and 3 data bits using signed magnitude representation and truncation. Determine the new pole locations for direct realization and for cascade realization of first order systems.
Ans:

Direct form realization = New pole locations are $z_1 = 0.695,\ z_2 = 0.1798$

Cascade form realization = New pole locations are $z_1 = 0.5,\ z_2 = 0.375$

16. Draw the product quantization noise model of second order IIR system.
17. Find the output roundoff noise power for the system having transfer function

$$H(z) = \frac{1}{(1 - 0.5z^{-1})(1 - 0.4z^{-1})}$$

Which is realized in cascade form. Assume word length is 4 bits.
Ans:

$$\sigma_{e0}^2 = 4.648 \times 10^{-3}$$

18. Explain signal scaling to prevent overflow limit cycle in the second order digital filter implementation.
19. Determine $H(z) = \frac{Y(z)}{X(z)}$ for Figure 5.33.

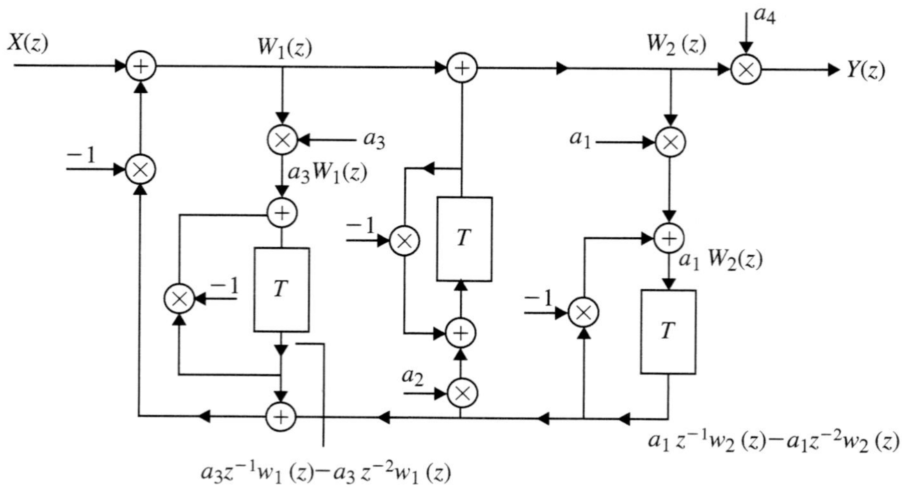

Figure 5.33

Ans:

$$H(z) = \frac{Y(z)}{X(z)}$$

$$= a_4 \Big/ \Big[1 + (a_1 + a_1a_2 + a_3)z^{-1} - (-a_1 + 2a_1a_2 + a_1a_2a_3 - a_3)z^{-2}$$

$$+(a_1a_2 - a_1a_2a_3)z^{-3} - (3a_1a_2a_3)z^{-4} + (a_1a_2a_3)z^{-5}\Big]$$

20. For the given T.F. $H(z) = H_1(z)H_2(z)$ where

$$H_1(z) = \frac{1}{(1 - 0.5z^{-1})} \quad \text{and} \quad H_2(z) = \frac{1}{(1 - 0.4z^{-1})},$$

find the output round off noise power. Calculate the value if $b = 3$ (excluding sign bit). What is the round off noise power if the system realized is in direct form?

Ans:

$$\sigma_{e0}^2 = 6.1968 \times 10^{-3}$$

21. Find the effect of coefficient quantization on pole location of the given second order IIR system when it is realized in direct form I and in cascade form. Assume a word length of 4 bits through truncation.
22. Explain the effects of word length in FIR digital filters.
23. Describe briefly about limit cycle oscillations in recursive systems.
24. Determine the variance of the round off noise at the output of the two cascade realization of the filter with system function.

$$H(z) = H_1(z)H_2(z)$$

$$H_1(z) = \frac{1}{(1 - 0.5z^{-1})}$$

$$H_2(z) = \frac{1}{(1 - 0.25z^{-1})}$$

Ans:

$$\sigma_{e0}^2 = 2.8953\sigma_e^2, \quad \sigma_e^2 = \frac{2^{-2b}}{12}$$

25. Explain in detail about finite word length effect in the digital filter design.
26. Explain fixed point representation of binary numbers.

Multi-rate Digital Signal Processing 6

Learning Objectives

After completing this chapter, you should be able to:

- understand the concept of multi-rate digital signal processing and its application.
- understand decimation by integer factors (downsampling).
- understand interpolation by integer factors (sampling rate increase-upsampling).
- represent the spectrum of down and upsampled signals.
- implement polyphase structure of decimator and interpolator.
- understand the various applications of MDSP.

6.1 INTRODUCTION

Modern digital systems require to process data at more than one sampling rate. Systems that use single sampling rate from A/D converter to D/A converter are called single rate systems. The discrete systems that process data at more than one sampling rate are known as multi-rate systems and the processing of signals by these systems is called Multi-rate Digital Signal Processing (MDSP). In many practical applications such as digital audio and video, different sampling rates are used. This is achieved using an upsampler and downsampler. In MDSP, this is achieved by interpolation and decimation. The process of decimation and interpolation are the fundamental operations in DSP. The sampling frequency is increased or decreased without any undesirable effects of errors due to quantization and aliasing.

In multi-rate signal processing, the sampling rate conversion is generally done by two methods. In the first method sampling rate conversion is achieved by D/A and A/D converters as shown in Figure 6.1(*a*).

In this method, the digital signal is passed through a D/A converter, filtered if necessary and then re-sampled at the desired sampling rate using A/D converter. In the second method, the sampling rate is achieved through interpolator and decimator depending upon the sampling rate requirement. The fundamental operations of interpolation and decimation of an MDSP are discussed in this chapter.

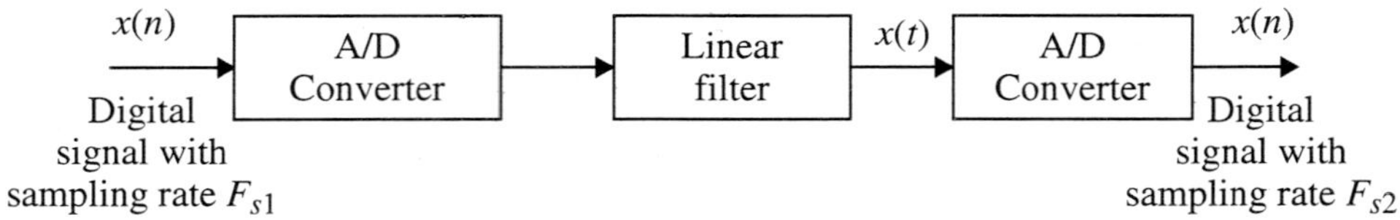

Figure 6.1 (*a*) Sampling rate conversion using D/A and A/D converters.

6.2 Advantages and Applications of Multi-rate Signal Processing

Advantages and applications of multi-rate signal processing are many. They are listed below:

1. In speech processing, the use of MDSP reduces the transmission rate of speech data. The original speech is reconstructed from the low bit rate representation.
2. In data acquisition and storage systems, signals of different bandwidths which require different sampling frequencies are efficiently handled without anti-aliasing analog filters.
3. MDSP efficiently implements DSP functions such as implementation of narrow band digital FIR filters with less computational requirements.
4. It is used in the compact disc player and simplifies the use of D/A conversion process without loss of quality of sound.
5. It is used in the acquisition of high quality data, high resolution spectral analysis and design and implementation of narrow band digital filters.
6. MDSP is widely used in antenna systems, communication systems and radar systems.

6.3 Downsampling (Decimator)

Downsampling of a signal is the process of decimating a signal $x(n)$ by an integer factor M and this is represented in Figure 6.1(*b*). The sampling rate compressor is represented by a down arrow along with the decimation factor M. The output

$$y(n) = x(Mn)$$

Here, the sampling rate reduction is achieved by discarding $(M - 1)$ samples for every M samples. Figure 6.2 shows the downsampling for $M = 3$.

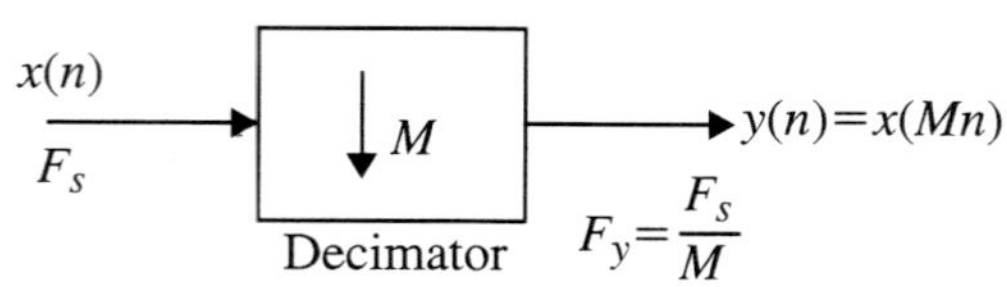

Figure 6.1 (*b*) Block diagram of a decimator.

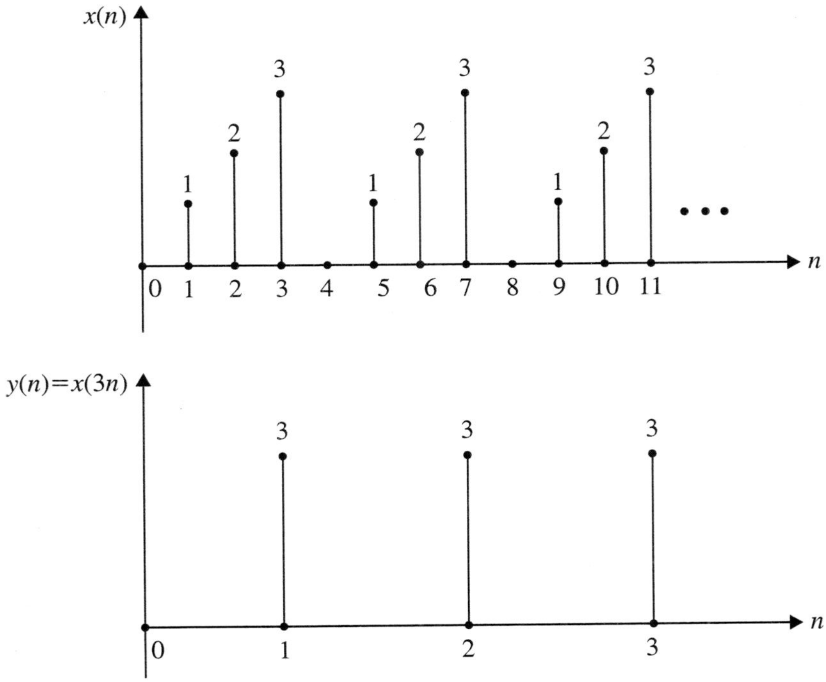

Figure 6.2 Downsampling the signal for $M = 3$, illustrated.

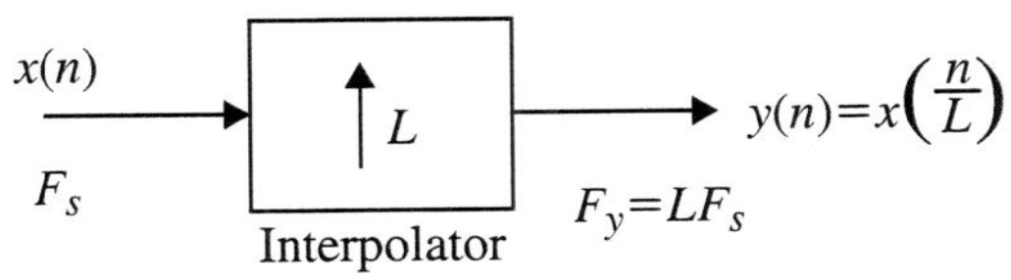

Figure 6.3 Block diagram representation of an upsampler.

6.4 Upsampling (Interpolator)

Upsampling is the process of increasing the sampling frequency of the signal. Upsampling is also called sampled rate expander or interpolator. The interpolator is represented by an upward arrow along with the interpolation factor L. While the input sampling frequency F_s is changed as F_s/M in downsampling, it is changed as F_sL by upsampling. The upsampling of $x(n)$ is illustrated in Figure 6.4 for $L = 4$.

For upsampling, for each sample of $x(n)$, the interpolator includes $(L - 1)$ zero valued samples to form the new signal at a rate of LF_S.

It is noted that for downsampling an anti-aliasing filter is to be connected before it is applied to a decimator. By this, the input $x(n)$ is bandlimited to less than $F_s/2M$. Similarly when upsampling is done, the signal $x(n)$ after passing through the interpolator (sample rate expander) it should be passed through anti-imaging filter. This is necessary to remove image frequencies created by the rate increase of L output samples.

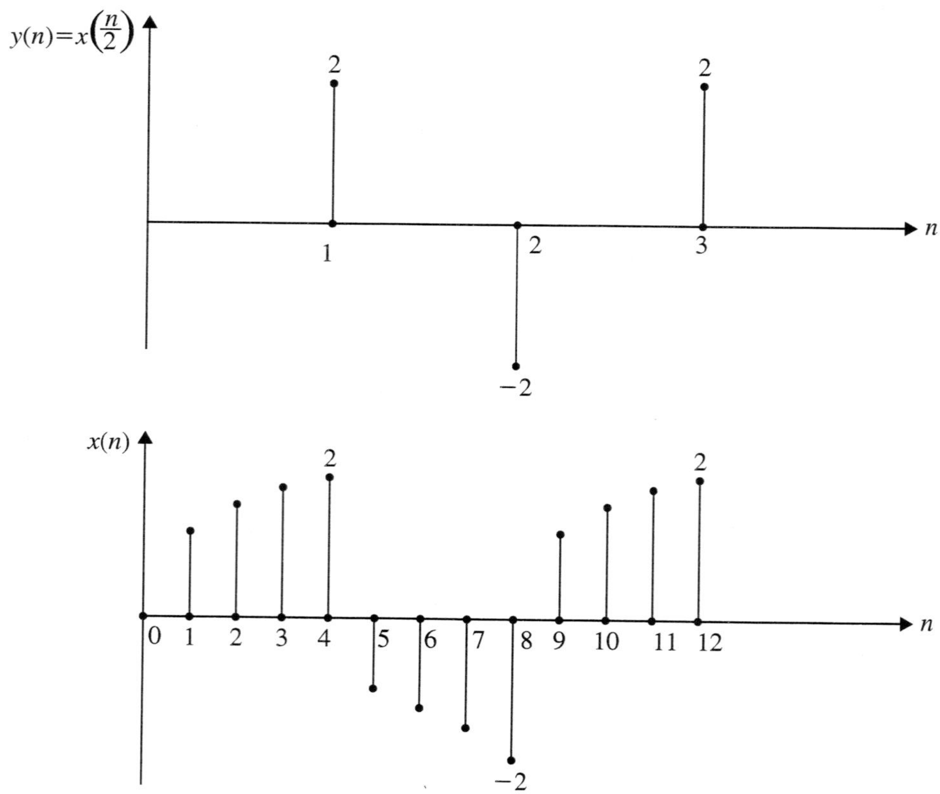

Figure 6.4 Illustration of upsampled DT signal for $L = 4$.

6.5 Sampling Rate Conversion by Non-Integer Factors Represented by Rational Number

Some applications of multi-rate digital signal processing require sampling rate by non-integer factor. When two different digital audio systems have different sampling rates, the transfer of data from one storage system to another require non-integer factor. For example, when the data from a compact disc at a rate of 44.1 kHz is transferred to a digital audio tape at 48 kHz, it requires data rate upsampling by a factor 48/44.1, which is a non-integer. However, this non-integer factor can be achieved by the rational numbers L and M which are integers. Here, the sampling frequency change is achieved by an interpolator as shown in Figure 6.5(a) with interpolation factor L. The output of the interpolator is passed through a LPF and the upsampling frequency is obtained as LF_s. This signal is passed through a downsampler with a decimation factor M. It is necessary to pass the upsampled signal to pass through the LPF before it is applied to the downsampler to avoid removal of some of the desired frequency components. Since the two LPF filters $h_0(k)$ and $h_D(k)$ which form part of the interpolator and downsampler respectively are connected in cascade and are operated at same frequency rate they can be replaced by a single LPF $h(k)$ as shown in Figure 6.5(b). Further, it should be noted

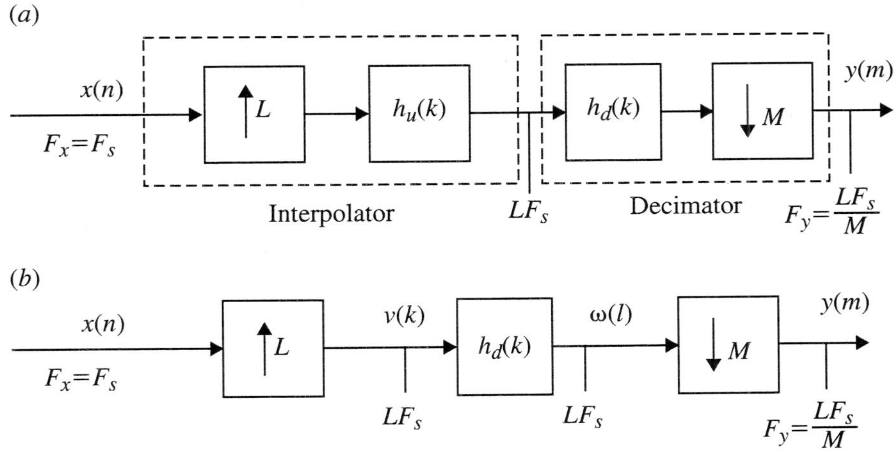

Figure 6.5 Sampling rate conversion integer factors.

that the interpolation process should precede decimation process to preserve the spectral characteristics of $x(n)$.

The sampling rate conversion by non-integer factors as applied to CD and digital audio tape can be explained as follows. Let us choose $L = 160$. The CD data rate is increased to $LF_s = 160 \times 44.1 = 7056$ Hz. By choosing the decimation factor $M = 147$, the data rate of DAT becomes $7056 \div 147 = 48$ kHz. Here, L and M are integers. Further, the ratios $\frac{L}{M} = \frac{160}{147}$ is rational. It is to be noted that, in general if $M < L$, the operation is a decimation process and $M > 1$, it is integer interpolation process. The mathematical proof of the above concept is derived as shown below:

Let $H(\omega_v)$ be the frequency response function of the low pass filter $h(k)$ which can be characterized as given below:

$$H(\omega_v) = \begin{cases} 1, & 0 \leq |\omega_v| \leq \min\left(\frac{\pi}{M}, \frac{\pi}{L}\right) \\ 0, & \text{otherwise} \end{cases} \tag{6.1}$$

The output of the upsampler is given by the following sequence:

$$V(l) = \begin{cases} x(\frac{l}{L}), & l = 0, \pm L \pm 2L : \pm \ldots \\ 0, & \text{otherwise} \end{cases} \tag{6.2}$$

The output of the LPF can be written by its convolution as

$$\omega(L) = \sum_{k=-\infty}^{\infty} h(l-k)v(k)$$

$$= \sum_{k=-\infty}^{\infty} h(l-kL)x(k) \tag{6.3}$$

In the above equation $h(k)$ is the impulse response of the LPF. The output $y(m)$ is obtained by downsampling $\omega(l)$ and the following equation is written.

$$\begin{aligned} y(m) &= \omega(mM) \\ &= \sum_{k=-\infty}^{\infty} h(mM - kL)x(k) \end{aligned} \tag{6.4}$$

Let

$$k = \left\lfloor \frac{mM}{L} \right\rfloor - n \tag{6.5}$$

Substituting equation (6.5) in (6.4) we get,

$$y(m) = \sum_{n=-\infty}^{\infty} x\left(\left\lfloor \frac{mM}{L} - n \right\rfloor\right) h\left(mM - \left[\frac{mM}{L}\right] L + nL\right) \tag{6.6}$$

Substituting the following

$$\begin{aligned} mM - \left\lfloor \frac{mM}{L} \right\rfloor L &= mM \quad \text{modulo} \quad L \\ &= (mM)_I \end{aligned}$$

in equation (6.6) we get,

$$y(m) = \sum_{n=-\infty}^{\infty} x\left(\left\lfloor \frac{mM}{L} - n \right\rfloor\right) h(nL + (mM)_I) \tag{6.7}$$

Equation (6.7) shows that the output $y(m)$ is obtained by passing through the time invariant filter with the following impulse response.

$$g(n, m) = h(nL + (mM)_I) \qquad -\infty < m, n < \infty \tag{6.8}$$

In equation (6.8) $h(k)$ is the impulse response of the time invariant LPF whose sampling rate is LF_s. Equation (6.8), for any integer k, can be written as follows:

$$\begin{aligned} g(n, m + kL) &= h(nL + (mM + kML)_I) \\ &= h(nL + (mM)_I) \\ &= g(n, m) \end{aligned} \tag{6.9}$$

This shows that $g(n, m)$ is periodic with period L. The frequency response of the LPF can be written as

$$V(\omega_v) = H(\omega_v)X(\omega_v L)$$

$$V(\omega_v) = \begin{cases} LX(\omega_v L), & 0 \le \omega_v \le \min\left(\frac{\pi}{M}, \frac{\pi}{L}\right) \\ 0, & \text{otherwise} \end{cases}$$

The spectrum of the output sequence is expressed as

$$Y(\omega_y) = \frac{1}{L}\sum_{k=0}^{M-1} V\left(\frac{\omega_y - 2\pi k}{L}\right) \tag{6.10}$$

Since the linear filter prevents aliasing, equation (6.10) is written as,

$$Y(\omega_y) = \begin{cases} \frac{L}{M}X\left(\frac{\omega_y}{M}\right), & 0 \le |\omega_y| \le \min\left(\pi, \frac{\pi M}{L}\right) \\ 0, & \text{otherwise} \end{cases} \tag{6.11}$$

From equation (6.11) it is evident that the sampling rate conversion can be achieved by a factor $\frac{L}{M}$ by first increasing the sampling rate by L accomplished by inserting $(L-1)$ zeros between successive values of the input sequence $x(n)$, followed by linear filtering of the resulting sequence to eliminate unwanted images of $X(\omega)$ and finally by downsampling the filtered signal by a factor M.

Example 6.1

A three stage decimator is used to reduce the sampling rate from 3072 kHz. The decimation factors are 16, 8 and 4. Draw the block diagram and indicate the sampling rate at the output of each stages.

Solution To retain all the desired frequency components of the signal to be downsampled, it is necessary that the signal is passed through low pass filter which is shown in Figure 6.6. for three stages.

At the end of stage 1, the sampling rate is

$$F_{s1} = \frac{3072}{16} = 192\,\text{kHz}$$

At the end of the second stage the frequency sampling rate is

$$F_{s2} = \frac{192}{8} = 24\,\text{kHz}$$

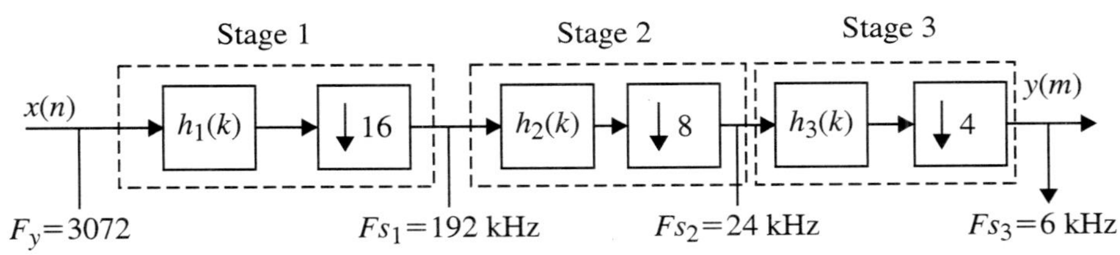

Figure 6.6 Sampling rate reduction in three stages.

At the end of the third stage the frequency sampling rate is

$$F_{s3} = \frac{24}{4} = 6\,\text{kHz}$$

6.6 Characteristics of Filter and Downsampler

As already stated while a signal is downsampled, it is necessary to have anti-aliasing filter. By this the signal is band limited before it is applied to the downsampler. The input sequence $x(n)$ is passed through a low pass filter whose impulse response is $h(n)$ and the frequency response $H_D(\omega)$ which satisfies the following condition:

$$H_D(\omega) = \begin{cases} 1, & |\omega| \leq \frac{\pi}{M} \\ 0, & \text{otherwise} \end{cases} \tag{6.12}$$

Equation (6.12) implies that the spectrum $X(\omega)$ is eliminated by the filter in the range $\frac{\pi}{M} < \omega < \pi$ and allows the components in the range $|\omega| \leq \frac{\pi}{M}$ for further processing. Now consider Figure 6.7.

The output of LPF sequence $v(n)$ is obtained using convolution as

$$v(n) = \sum_{k=0}^{\infty} h(k)x(n-k) \tag{6.13}$$

The sequence $v(n)$ is applied to the decimator and the output of the decimator is given by

$$\begin{aligned} y(m) &= v(mM) \\ &= \sum_{k=0}^{\infty} h(k)x(mM-k) \end{aligned} \tag{6.14}$$

It is well-known that the low pass filter is linear and time invariant. However, the decimator even though has linear characteristics, is time varying. This is also true in the case of an interpolator. The mathematical proof of the above statement is given in the section to follow.

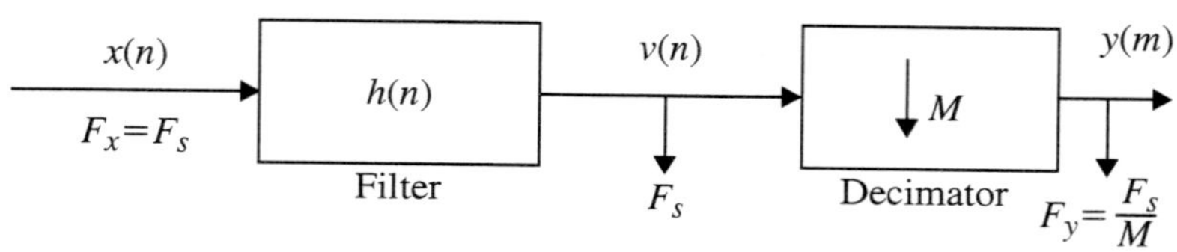

Figure 6.7 Representation of a decimator with filter.

6.7 Linearity and Time Invariancy of Decimator and Interpolator

6.7.1 Linearity of Decimator

A discrete time system is linear if the weighted sum of the output is equal to the output due to the weighted sum of the input. The input-output of a decimator is written as

$$\begin{aligned} y(m) &= x(nM) \\ y_1(m) &= x_1(nM) \\ y_2(m) &= x_2(nM) \end{aligned} \tag{6.15}$$

The weighted sum of the output is,

$$\begin{aligned} y_3(m) &= a_1 y_1(m) + a_2 y_2(m) \\ &= a_1 x_1(nm) + a_2 x_2(nm) \end{aligned}$$

The output due to the weighted sum of the input is

$$\begin{aligned} y_4(m) &= a_1 x_1(nM) + a_2 x_2(nM) \\ \therefore \quad y_3(m) &= y_4(m) \end{aligned}$$

The weighted sum of the output is equal to the output due to the weighted sum of the input. Hence, the system with a downsampler is linear.

6.7.2 Linearity of an Interpolator

The input-output of an interpolator is written as

$$\begin{aligned} y(m) &= x\left(\frac{n}{L}\right) \\ y_1(m) &= x_1\left(\frac{n}{L}\right) \\ y_2(m) &= x_2\left(\frac{n}{L}\right) \end{aligned} \tag{6.16}$$

The weighted sum of the output is

$$\begin{aligned} y_3(m) &= a_1 y_1(m) + a_2 y_2(m) \\ &= a_1 x_1\left(\frac{n}{L}\right) + a_2 x_2\left(\frac{n}{L}\right) \end{aligned}$$

The output due to the weighted sum of the input is

$$y_4(m) = a_1 x_1\left(\frac{n}{L}\right) + a_2 x_2\left(\frac{n}{L}\right)$$

The weighted sum of the output is equal to the output due to the weighted sum of the input. Hence, the system with interpolator is linear.

6.7.3 Time Invariancy of a Decimator

A discrete time system is said to be time invariant if the delayed output $y(n, n_0)$ where n_0 is the delay, is equal to the output $y(n - n_0)$ which is due to the delayed input.

Consider the decimator with the following equation:

$$y(n) = x(nM)$$

The delayed output is,

$$\begin{aligned} y(n - n_0) &= x((n - n_0)M) \\ &= x(nM - n_0M) \end{aligned}$$

The output due to the delayed input is

$$y(n, n_0) = x(nM - n_0)$$

$$y(n, n_0) \neq y(n - n_0)$$

Hence, the decimator is a time varying system. However, it can be made time invariant if the delay n_0 is made multiple of the decimation factor M.

6.7.4 Time Invariancy of an Interpolator

Let us consider the interpolator with the following equation:

$$y(n) = x\left(\frac{n}{L}\right)$$

The delayed output is

$$y(n, n_0) = x\left(\frac{n - n_0}{L}\right)$$

The output due to the delayed input is

$$y(n - n_0) = x\left(\frac{n}{L} - n_0\right)$$

$$y(n, n_0) \neq y(n - n_0)$$

Hence, the interpolator is a time varying system.

6.8 Spectrum of Downsampled Signal

Consider Figure 6.7 where the downsampler together with the LPF is connected. The frequency response of the output sequence $y(m)$ with that of the input sequence $x(n)$ is obtained as given below. The sequence $v(n)$ is defined as follows:

$$\bar{v}(n) = \begin{cases} v(n), & n = 0, \pm M, \pm 2M, \ldots \\ 0, & \text{otherwise} \end{cases} \tag{6.17}$$

$\bar{v}(n)$ is interpreted as a sequence obtained by multiplying $v(n)$ by train of impulses $p(n)$ with period M. $p(n)$ can be expressed in discrete Fourier series as

$$p(n) = \frac{1}{M}\sum_{k=0}^{M-1} e^{j2\pi kn/M} \tag{6.18}$$

Also,

$$\bar{v}(n) = v(n)p(n) \tag{6.19}$$

$$\begin{aligned} y(m) &= \bar{v}(mM) \\ &= v(mM)p(mM) \\ &= v(mM) \end{aligned} \tag{6.20}$$

The z-transform of the output sequence is,

$$\begin{aligned} Y(z) &= \sum_{m=-\infty}^{\infty} y(m)z^{-m} \\ &= \sum_{m=-\infty}^{\infty} \bar{v}(mM)z^{-m} \end{aligned} \tag{6.21}$$

Since $\bar{v}(m) = 0$ except at multiples of M, the above equation is written as:

$$Y(z) = \sum_{m=-\infty}^{\infty} \bar{v}(m)z^{\frac{-m}{M}}$$

Using equations (6.18), (6.19) and (6.21) we get,

$$\begin{aligned} Y(z) &= \sum_{m=-\infty}^{\infty} v(m)\left[\frac{1}{M}\sum_{k=0}^{M-1} e^{j2\pi mk/M}\right] z^{\frac{-m}{M}} \\ &= \frac{1}{M}\sum_{k=0}^{M-1}\sum_{m=-\infty}^{\infty} v(m)(e^{-j2\pi k/M} z^{-\frac{1}{M}})^{-m} \\ &= \frac{1}{M}\sum_{k=0}^{M-1} V(e^{-j2\pi k/M} z^{\frac{1}{M}}) \end{aligned}$$

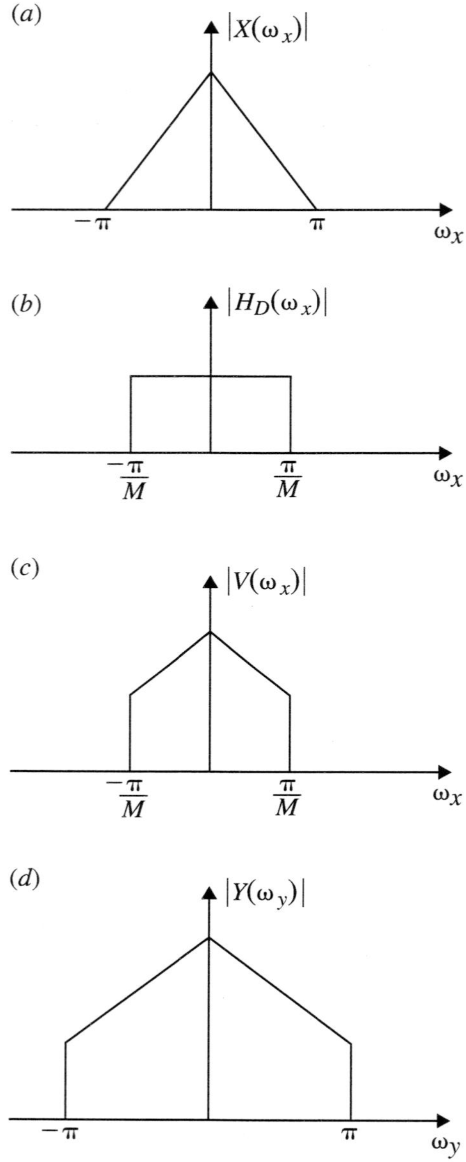

Figure 6.8 Frequency spectra of decimated signal

Making use of the property that $V(z) = H_D(z)X(z)$ the above equation is written as

$$Y(z) = \frac{1}{M}\sum_{k=0}^{M-1} H_D(e^{-j2\pi k/M}z^{\frac{1}{M}})X(e^{-j2\pi k/M}z^{\frac{1}{M}}) \tag{6.22}$$

The spectrum of the output $y(m)$ is obtained by evaluating $Y(z)$ in the unit circle. Denoting the frequency variable of $y(m)$ by ω_y, equation (6.22) becomes

$$Y(\omega_y) = \frac{1}{M}\sum_{k=0}^{M-1} H_D\frac{(\omega_y - 2\pi k)}{M}X\frac{(\omega_y - 2\pi k)}{M} \tag{6.23}$$

where ω_y is expressed in rad/sec.

Also

$$\omega_y = 2\pi F_y$$
$$\omega_y = M\omega_x$$

If aliasing is eliminated by proper design of LPF, equation (6.23) is written as:

$$Y(\omega_y) = \frac{1}{M}H_D\left(\frac{\omega_y}{M}\right)X\left(\frac{\omega_y}{M}\right) \tag{6.24}$$

For $0 \leq |\omega_y| \leq \pi$, the above equation is written as:

$$Y(\omega_y) = \frac{1}{M}X\left(\frac{\omega_y}{M}\right) \tag{6.25}$$

The spectra of $x(n)$, $h(n)$, $v(n)$and $y(m)$ are shown in Figure 6.8.

6.9 Effect of Aliasing in Downsampling

The signal $x(n)$ is passed through a low pass filter before it is passed through a decimator. The function of this anti-aliasing filter is to prevent aliasing of the sampled signal. Aliasing refers to distortion of the signal spectrum due to low sampling rate. Now consider the downsampler without the LPF in Figure 6.7. From equation (6.22), the z-transform of the output is obtained as

$$Y(z) = \frac{1}{M}\sum_{k=0}^{M-1} X(e^{-j2\pi k/M}z^{\frac{1}{M}}) \tag{6.26}$$

The frequency spectrum of the above equation is obtained by substituting $z = e^{j\omega}$

$$Y(e^{j\omega}) = \frac{1}{M}\sum_{k=0}^{M-1} X(e^{\frac{-j2\pi k}{M}}e^{\frac{j\omega}{M}}) \tag{6.27}$$

$$= \frac{1}{M}\sum_{k=0}^{M-1} X(e^{\frac{j(\omega-2\pi k)}{M}}) \tag{6.28}$$

The plots of $|X(e^{j\omega})|$ and $|Y(e^{j\omega})|$ with respect to ω_x and the plot of $|Y(e^{j\omega})|$ with respect to ω_y are shown in Figure 6.9. The spectrum of $X(e^{j\omega})$ is a periodic one

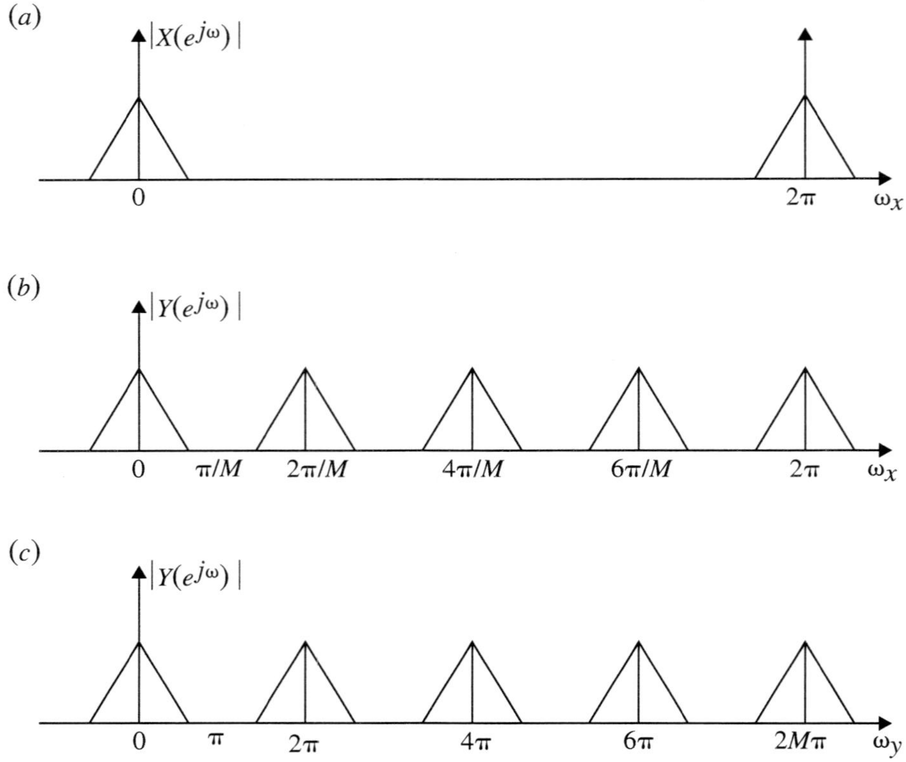

Figure 6.9 Magnitude of $X(e^{j\omega})$ and $Y(e^{j\omega})$.

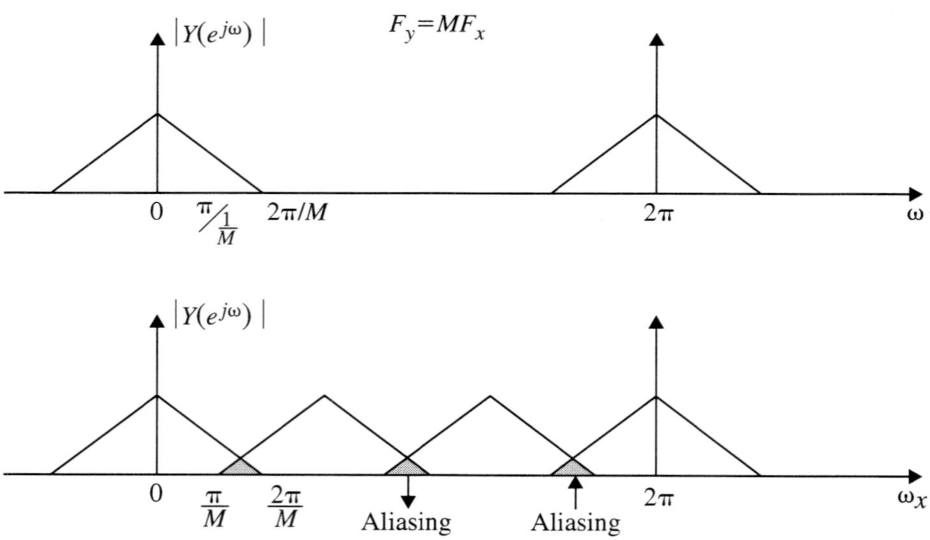

Figure 6.10 Aliasing effect in decimator.

with period 2π. The plot of $|Y(e^{j\omega})|$ with respect to ω_x is nothing but the stretched version of $|X(e^{j\omega})|$ and scaled by a factor $\frac{1}{M}$. In the interval 0 to 2π, there will be $(M-1)$ equally spaced replica of $X(e^{j\omega})$ with period $\frac{2\pi}{M}$. This is shown in Figure 6.9(b). Using the relation $F_y = MF_x$, the plot of $|Y(e^{j\omega})|$ drawn for ω_y is shown in Figure 6.9(c).

Now consider the signal $x(n)$ whose frequency is greater than $\pm\frac{\pi}{m}$. The frequency spectra of $|X(e^{j\omega})|$ and $|Y(e^{j\omega})|$ are plotted as shown in Figure 6.10(a) and 6.10(b) respectively. In Figure 6.10(b) the aliasing effect is shown. Because of aliasing signal distortion in $y(m)$ will take place and hence a low pass filter is to be connected before the signal $x(n)$ is passed through the downsampler. This will limit the input signal to the downsampler to $\pm\frac{\pi}{M}$ which avoids aliasing and hence signal distortion.

6.10 Spectrum of Upsampling Signal

The increase in sampling rate is achieved by an interpolator or an upsampler. The output of the interpolator is passed through the LPF to avoid removal of some of the desired frequency components of the sampled signal. Let $v(m)$ be the sequence obtained from the interpolator. $v(m)$ is obtained by adding $(L-1)$ zeros between successive values of $x(n)$. If F_s is the sampling rate of $x(n)$, then the sampling rate of $v(m)$ is LF_s which is same as the sampling rate of $y(m)$. The interpolator system is shown in Figure 6.11(a). $v(m)$ is characterized by the following equation:

$$v(m) = \begin{cases} x(\frac{m}{L}), & m = 0, \pm L, \pm 2L, \ldots \\ 0, & \text{otherwise} \end{cases} \tag{6.29}$$

The z-transform of the above equation is written as:

$$\begin{aligned} V(z) &= \sum_{m=-\infty}^{\infty} v(m) z^{-m} \\ &= \sum_{m=-\infty}^{\infty} x(m) z^{-mL} \\ &= X(z^L) \end{aligned} \tag{6.30}$$

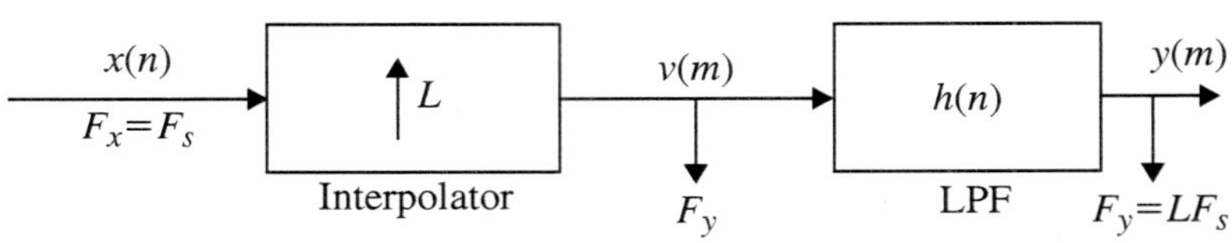

Figure 6.11 (a) Interpolator with a filter.

The frequency spectrum of $v(m)$ is obtained by evaluating $V(z)$ on the unit circle $(z = e^{j\omega})$ in the z-plane. Thus,

$$V(e^{j\omega}) = X(e^{j\omega_y L})$$
$$\text{or} \quad V(\omega_y) = X(\omega_y L) \tag{6.31}$$

where $\omega_y = 2\pi F_y$ and $L\omega_y = \omega_x$.

The spectra of $|X(\omega_x)|$, $|V(\omega_y)|$, $|H(\omega_y)|$ and $|Y(\omega_y)|$ are shown in Figure 6.11(b). From Figure 6.11(b) it is observed that $(L - 1)$ zero samples are added between successive values of $x(n)$.

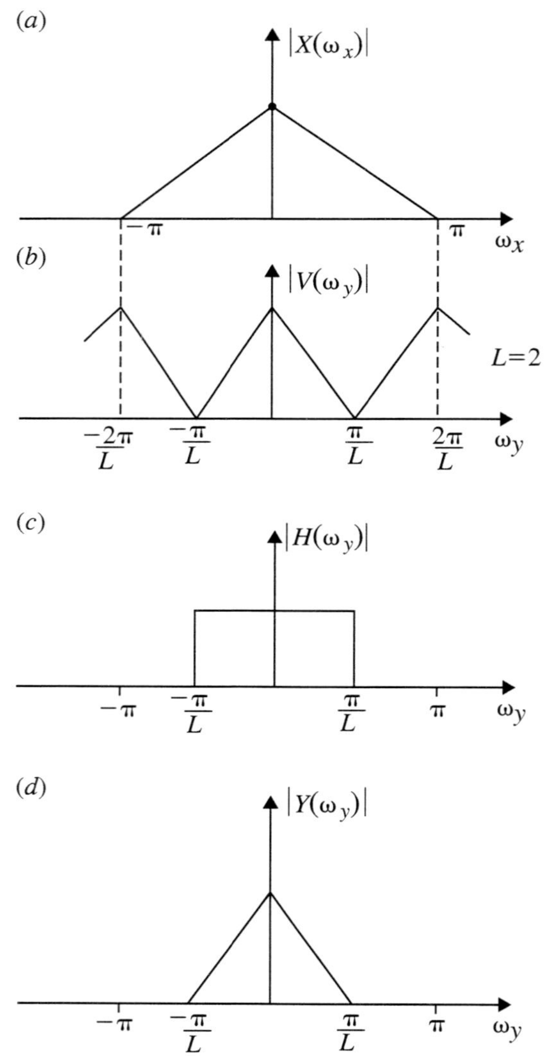

Figure 6.11 (b) Frequency spectra of $x(n)$, $v(n)$, $h(n)$ and $y(m)$.

6.10.1 Anti-Imaging Filter

In the interpolation process when the sampling rate is increased by a factor L, the sampling frequency is also increased by the same factor. For each sample of the input signal $x(n)$, the interpolator inserts $(L-1)$ zero valued samples to form the new signal $v(m)$ at the rate LF_s where F_s is the sampling frequency of $x(n)$. However $v(m)$ contains images created by the rate increase and hence it becomes necessary to remove these image frequencies by passing through the LPF and the output $y(m)$ is obtained which has a sampling rate LF_s. The insertion of $(L-1)$ zero valued samples spreads the energy of each signal sample over L output samples. This interpolation process is called anti-image filtering which is shown in Figure 6.11(a).

Example 6.2

Plot the spectra of any signal $x(n)$ and its downsampled version for a sampling rate $M=2$.

Solution From equation (6.28) the frequency response of a downsampler is given by

$$Y(e^{j\omega}) = \sum_{k=0}^{M-1} X(e^{j(\omega-2\pi k)/M})$$

For $M=2$, the above equation is written as:

$$\begin{aligned}
Y(e^{j\omega}) &= \frac{1}{2}\sum_{k=0}^{1} X(e^{j(\omega-2\pi k)/2}) \\
&= \frac{1}{2}[X(e^{j\omega/2}) + X(e^{j(\omega-2\pi)/2})] \\
&= \frac{1}{2}[X(e^{j\omega/2}) + X(e^{j\omega/2}e^{-j\pi})] \\
&= \frac{1}{2}[X(e^{j\omega/2}) + X(-e^{j\omega/2})]
\end{aligned}$$

The plots of $X(e^{j\omega})$, $X(e^{j\omega/2})$, $X(-e^{j\omega/2})$ and $Y(e^{j\omega})$ are shown in Figure 6.12.

The spectrum $|X(e^{j\omega})|$ of an arbitrary sequence $x(n)$ is shown in Figure 6.12(a). The plot of $|X(e^{j\omega/2})|$ is shown in Figure 6.12(b) whose frequency is expanded by a factor 2 and its maximum amplitude remains the same as 1. The plot of $|X(-e^{j\omega/2})|$ is nothing but the spectrum of $|X(e^{j\omega/2})|$ shifted by 2π and is shown in Figure 6.12(c). $|Y(e^{j\omega})|$ is obtained by adding Figure 6.12(b) and Figure 6.12(c) with the amplitude being divided by the factor 2 and is shown in Figure 6.12(d). It is evident from Figure 6.12(d), that if the signal is band limited to $\frac{\pi}{2}$ there is no overlapping in $Y(e^{j\omega})$ and there won't be any aliasing. If the signal frequency is greater than $\frac{\pi}{2}$, aliasing occurs. To avoid aliasing, in general, the signal before downsampled, should be band limited to $\frac{\pi}{M}$.

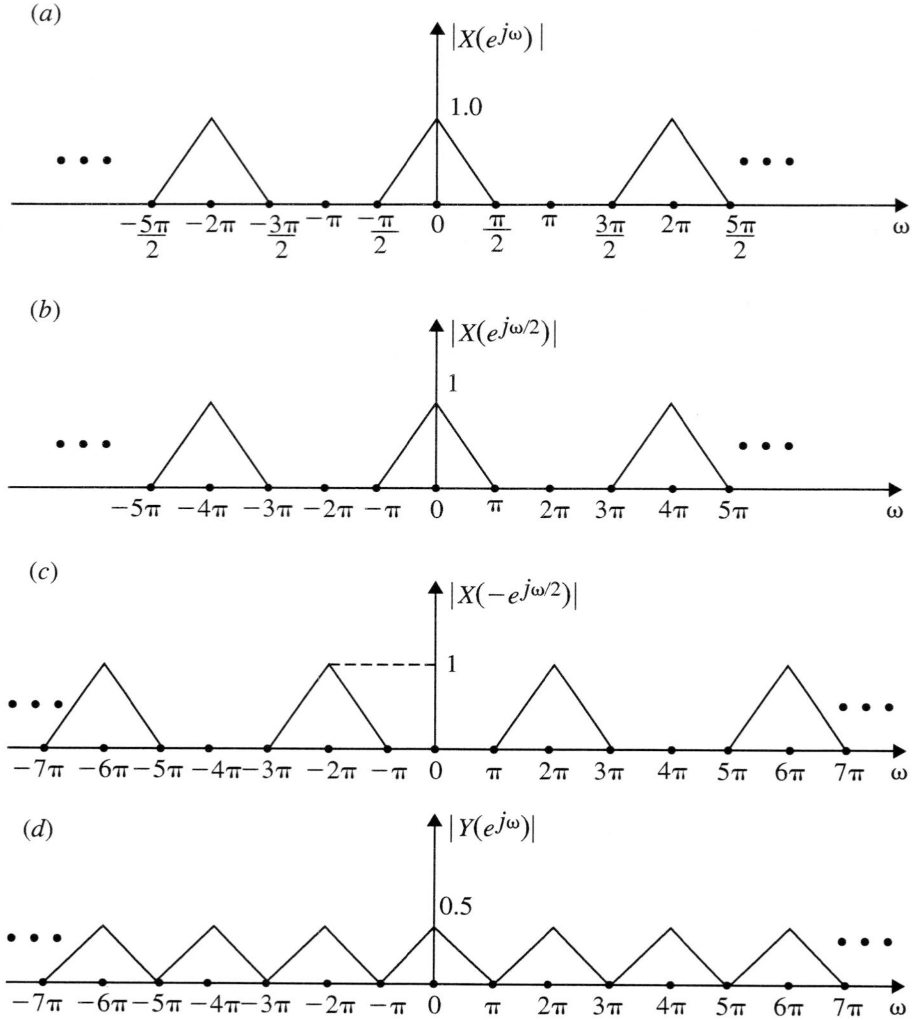

Figure 6.12 Spectrum of $x(n)$.

Example 6.3

Draw the spectra of any signal $x(n)$ and its upsampled version for a sampling rate of $L = 3$.

Solution Recall equation (6.31) which gives the frequency response for any input $x(n)$ of an upsampler.

$$Y(e^{j\omega}) = X(e^{j\omega L})$$

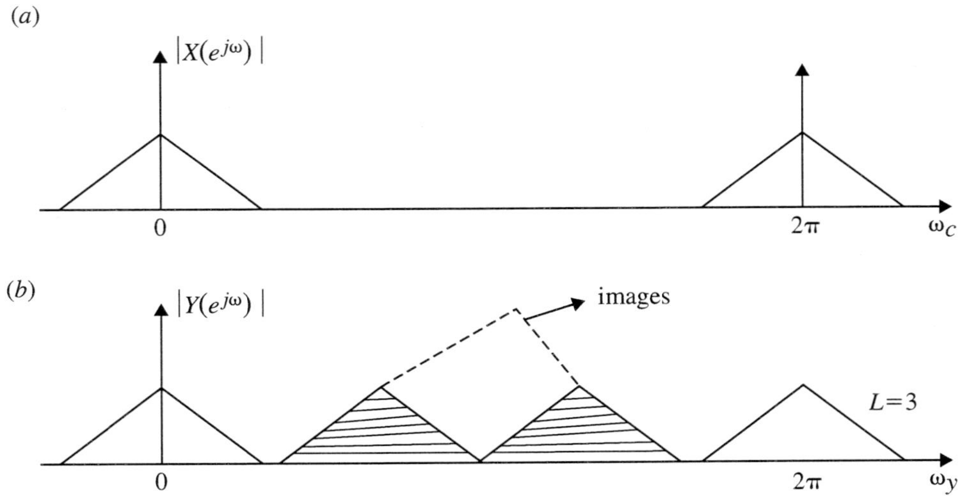

Figure 6.13 Magnitude spectrum of $X(e^{j\omega})$ and $Y(e^{j\omega})$.

For $L = 3$, the above equation is written as:

$$Y(e^{j\omega}) = X(e^{j3\omega})$$

$X(e^{j3\omega})$ implies that $X(e^{j\omega})$ is repeated 3 times. The plot of $X(e^{j\omega})$ is plotted as shown in Figure 6.13(a) for any arbitrary signal $x(n)$ which has a periodicity 2π. In the frequency interval $0 < \omega_y < 2\pi$, there should be $L - 1 = 3 - 1 = 2$ images of $X(e^{j\omega})$ which has the same spectrum as $x(n)$ with appropriate scaling factor. This is represented in Figure 6.13(b).

6.11 Efficient Transversal Structure for Decimator

The decimator consists of an anti-aliasing filter and a downsampler. The anti-aliasing filter can be realized using a direct form structure as shown in Figure 6.14. In this configuration, the filter is operating at a high sampling rate F_s while only one output out of every M output samples is required and such a decimator is inefficient. Now consider the decimator shown in Figure 6.15.

In this structure all the multiplications and additions are performed at lower sampling rate $\frac{F_s}{M}$ and works more efficiently.

6.12 Efficient Transversal Structure for Interpolator

The interpolator inserts $(L - 1)$ zeros between samples of the sequence $x(n)$ and filtered. FIR filter is normally used for filtering. The upsampler connected to the transposed direct form FIR filter is shown in Figure 6.16. If the sampling rate of $x(n)$ is F_s, the input sampling rate at the input of FIR filter is LF_s and hence filter

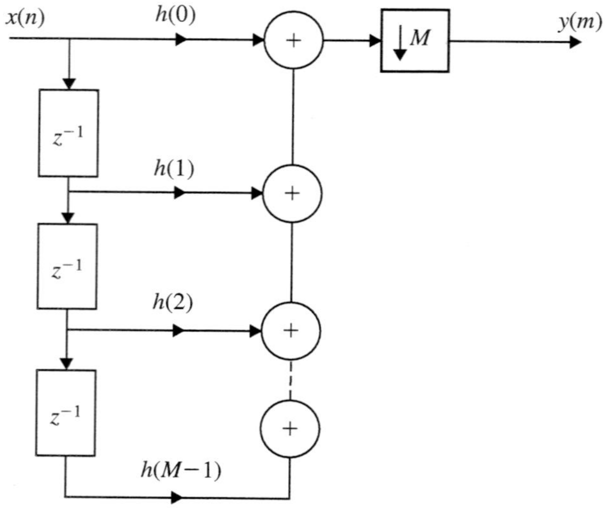

Figure 6.14 Direct form realization of decimator inefficient.

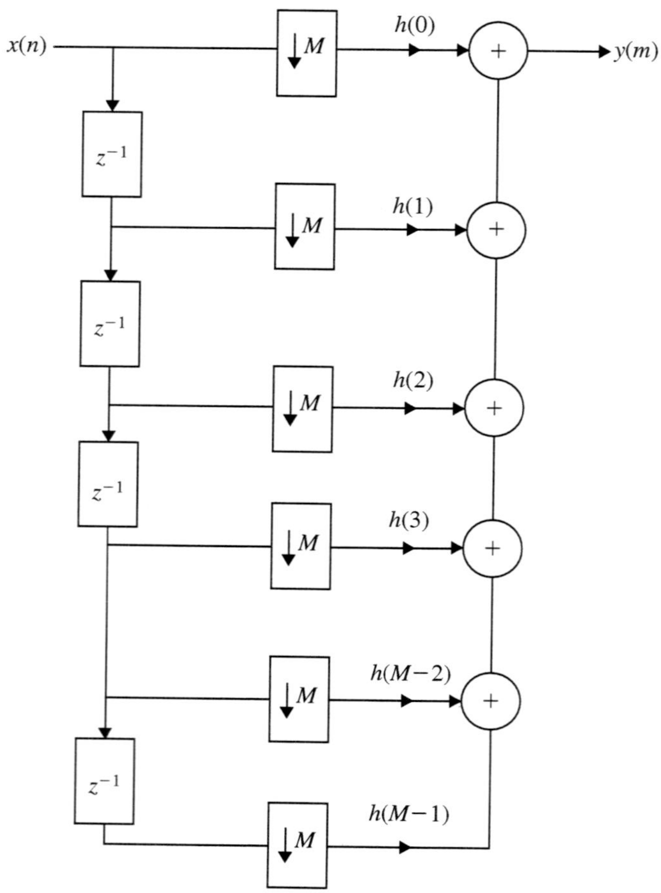

Figure 6.15 Efficient realization for decimator.

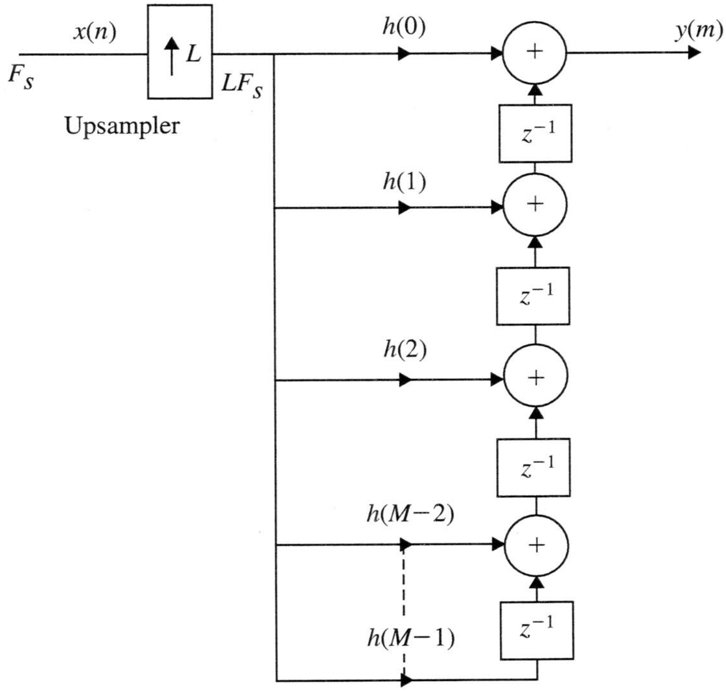

Figure 6.16 Transposed direct form realization for interpolator.

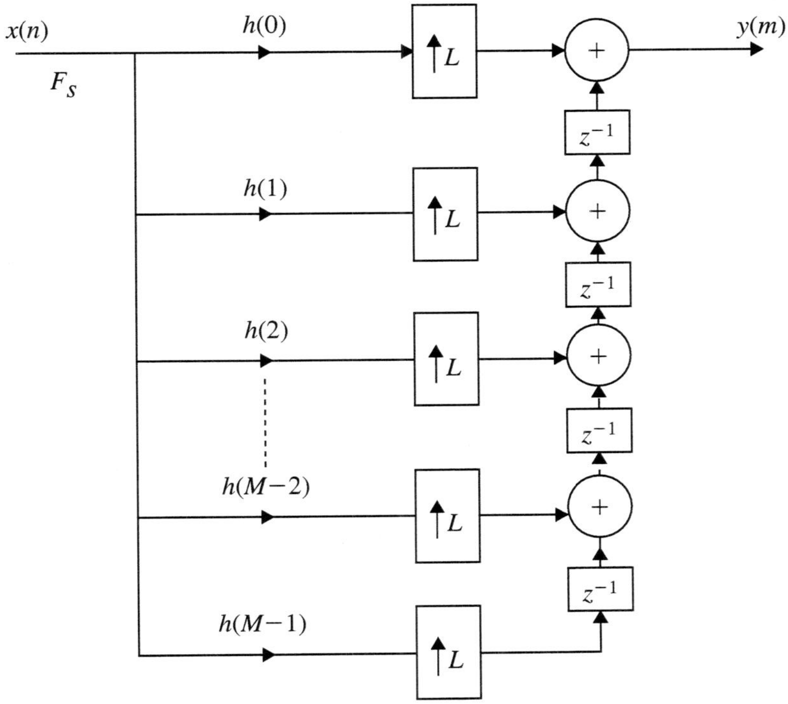

Figure 6.17 Efficient realization for interpolator.

computations are to be performed at this high sampling rate and the interpolator becomes an inefficient one. The interpolator is made more efficient by putting the upsampler within the filter as shown in Figure 6.17. This enables that all the filter multiplications and additions are performed at the low sampling rate F_s and the interpolator becomes more efficient.

6.13 Identities

The sampling rate decimation and interpolation are represented in block diagram. The block diagrams can be modified and represented in convenient form using identities. These identities (equivalence) are given below without proof in Figure 6.18.

6.14 Polyphase Filter Structure of a Decimator

Efficient implementation of sampling rate conversion was discussed in Sections 6.11 and 6.12 for upsampling and downsampling respectively in a single

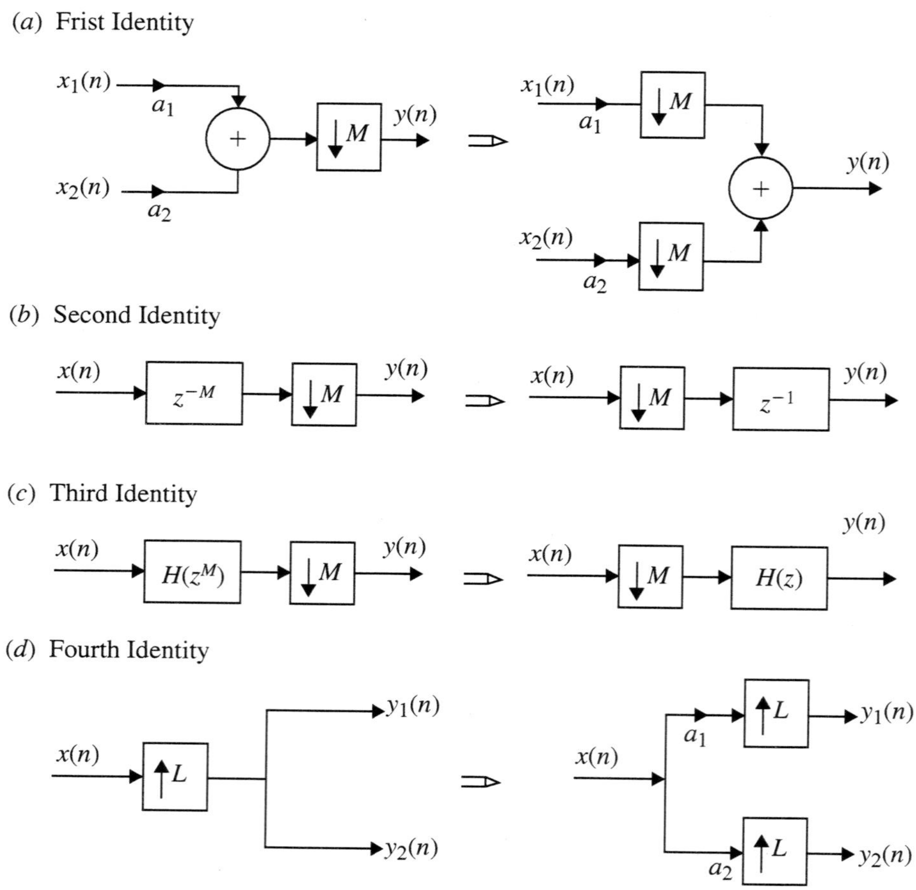

Figure 6.18 Continued.

(e) Fifth Identity

(f) Sixth Identity

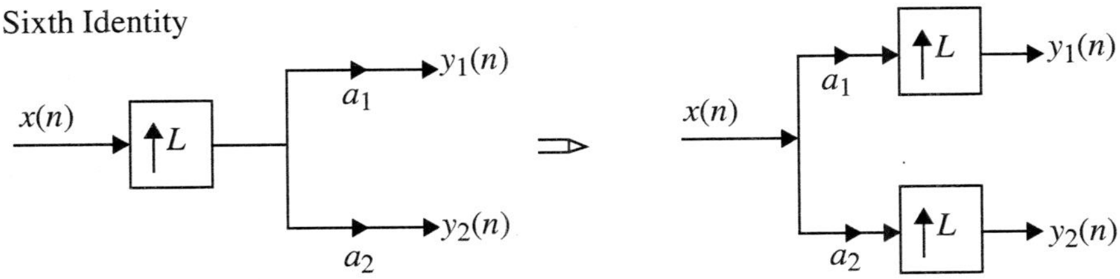

Figure 6.18 Identities of downsampling and upsampling.

stage. The computational requirements can be further decreased using multi-stage design.

Additional reduction in the computational complexity is possible by realizing the FIR filters using the polyphase decomposition which is described below:

6.14.1 The Polyphase Decomposition

Consider an FIR with an impulse response having N-coefficients. The system function is written as:

$$H(z) = \sum_{n=0}^{N-1} h(n)z^{-n} \tag{6.32}$$

For $N = 7$, the above equation is written as:

$$\begin{aligned} H(z) &= \sum_{n=0}^{6} h(n)z^{-n} \\ &= h(0) + h(1)z^{-1} + h(2)z^{-2} + h(3)z^{-3} + h(4)z^{-4} \\ &\quad + h(5)z^{-5} + h(6)z^{-6} \\ &= (h(0) + h(2)z^{-2} + h(4)z^{-4} + h(6)z^{-6}) + \\ &\quad z^{-1}(h(1) + h(3)z^{-2} + h(5)z^{-4}) \\ &= P_0(z^2) + z^{-1}P_1(z^2) \end{aligned} \tag{6.33}$$

where

$$P_0(z^2) = h(0) + +h(2)z^{-1} + h(4)z^{-2} + h(6)z^{-4}$$
$$P_1(z^2) = h(1) + h(3)z^{-1} + h(5)z^{-2}$$

The decomposition of $H(z)$ as given in equation (6.33) is known as polyphase decomposition of the system function with two branches. In general for M branches $H(z)$ can be decomposed as

$$H(z) = \sum_{m=0}^{N-1} z^{-m} P_m(z^M) \tag{6.34}$$

where

$$P_m(z^m) = \sum_{n=0}^{(N+1)/M} h(Mn+m)z^{-n} \qquad 0 \le m \le M-1$$

The z-transform of infinite duration sequence is given by

$$H(z) = \sum_{n=-\infty}^{\infty} h(n)z^{-n} \tag{6.35}$$

If $H(z)$ is decomposed into M-branches we get,

$$H(z) = \sum_{m=0}^{M-1} z^{-m} P_m(z^m) \tag{6.36}$$

where

$$P_m(z) = \sum_{l=-\infty}^{\infty} h(lM+m)z^{-l}$$

$$H(z) = \sum_{m=0}^{M-1} \sum_{l=-\infty}^{\infty} h(lM+m)z^{-Ml}$$

$$= \sum_{m=0}^{M-1} \sum_{l=-\infty}^{\infty} h(lM+m)z^{-(lM+m)}$$

Let $h(lM+m) = P_m(l)$

$$\frac{Y(z)}{X(z)} = H(z) = \sum_{m=0}^{M-1} \sum_{l=-\infty}^{\infty} P_m(l)z^{-(lM+m)}$$

$$Y(z) = \sum_{m=0}^{M-1} \sum_{l=-\infty}^{\infty} P_m(l)z^{-(lM+m)}X(z)$$

$$= \sum_{m=0}^{M-1} \sum_{l=-\infty}^{\infty} P_m(l)Z[x(n-(lM+m))]$$

Taking inverse z-transform on both sides we get,

$$y(n) = \sum_{m=0}^{m-1} \sum_{l=-\infty}^{\infty} P_m(l)x(n-(lM+m)) \tag{6.37}$$

Let $x_m(l) = x(lM - m)$

$$y(n) = \sum_{m=0}^{M-1} \sum_{l=-\infty}^{\infty} P_m(l)x(n-l)$$

$$= \sum_{m=0}^{M-1} P_m(n) * x_m(n) \tag{6.38}$$

$$= \sum_{m=0}^{M-1} y_m(n) \tag{6.39}$$

where $y_m(n) = P_m(n) * x_m(n)$ which is known as polyphase convolution. For example for $M = 2$, equation (6.38) becomes

$$y(n) = \sum_{m=0}^{1} P_m(l) * x_m(n)$$

$$y(n) = P_0(n) * x_0(n) + P_1(n) * x_1(n)$$

In equation (6.38), $x_m(n)$ is obtained first by delaying $x(n)$ by m units and desampling by a factor M. $y_m(n)$ is obtained by convolving $x_m(n)$ with $P_m(n)$. The structure of a polyphase decimator with two branches is shown in Figure 6.19(a) and the polyphase structure of a M branch decimator is shown in Figure 6.19(b).

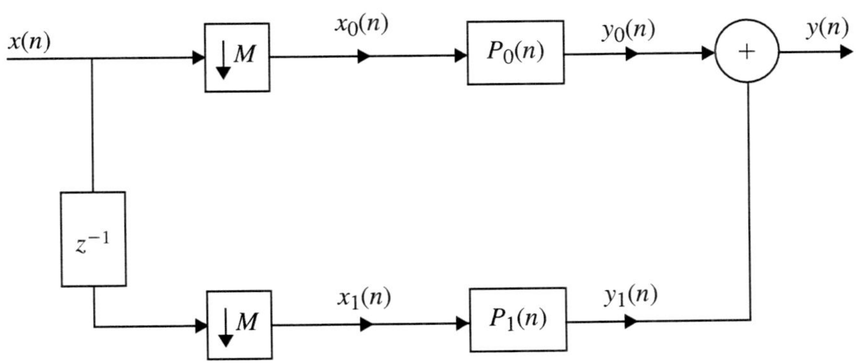

Figure 6.19 (a) Polyphase structure of a two branch decimator.

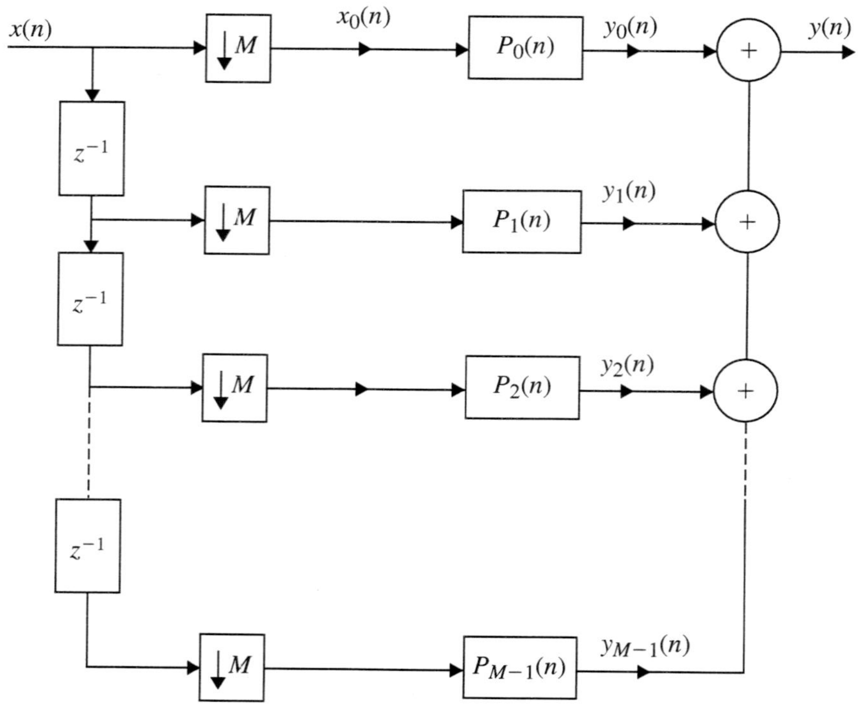

Figure 6.19 (*b*) Polyphase structure of M branch decimator.

6.14.2 Polyphase Structure of a Decimator Using *z*-Transform

Consider equation (6.36) which gives the FIR filter function.

$$H(z) = \sum_{m=0}^{N-1} z^{-m} P_m(z^M)$$

We have M sub-filters $P_0(z), P_1(z), \ldots, P_{M-1}(z)$ of FIR filters and can be represented as shown in Figure 6.20.

Using first identity Figure 6.20 can be represented as shown in Figure 6.21 and using third identity Figure 6.20 can be represented as shown in Figure 6.22.

6.14.3 Polyphase Structure of an Interpolator

The polyphase structure of an interpolator can be obtained by transposing the structure of a decimator which is shown in Figure 6.20. Here, the polyphase components of impulse responses are given by the following equation (refer to equation (6.37)).

$$P_m(l) = h(lL + m), \quad m = 0, 1, 2, \ldots (L - 1)$$

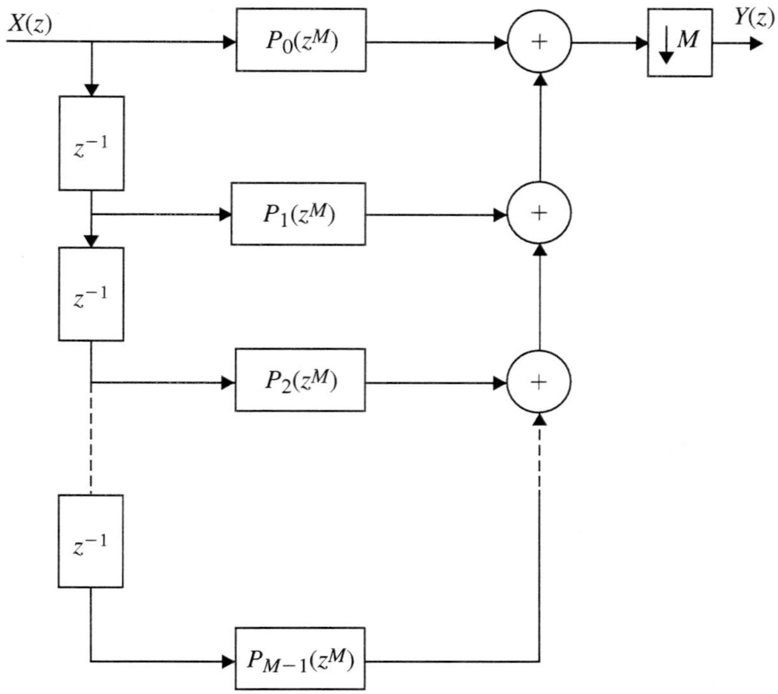

Figure 6.20 Polyphase structure of M branch decimator using z-transform.

the output of L sub-filters are represented as

$$y_m(n) = x(n) \times P_m(n)$$

The overall output of the interpolator is (refer equation (6.39))

$$y(n) = \sum_{m=0}^{(L-1)} y_m(n)$$

For $L = 3$

$$\begin{aligned} y(n) &= \sum_{m=0}^{2} y_m(n) \\ &= y_0(n) + y_1(n) + y_2(n) \\ &= x(n) \times P_0(n) + x(n) \times P_1(n) + x(n) \times P_2(n) \end{aligned}$$

The polyphase structure of an interpolator with three branch is shown in Figure 6.23. In general, when the sampling rate increases to L, the polyphase structure with L branch is shown in Figure 6.24.

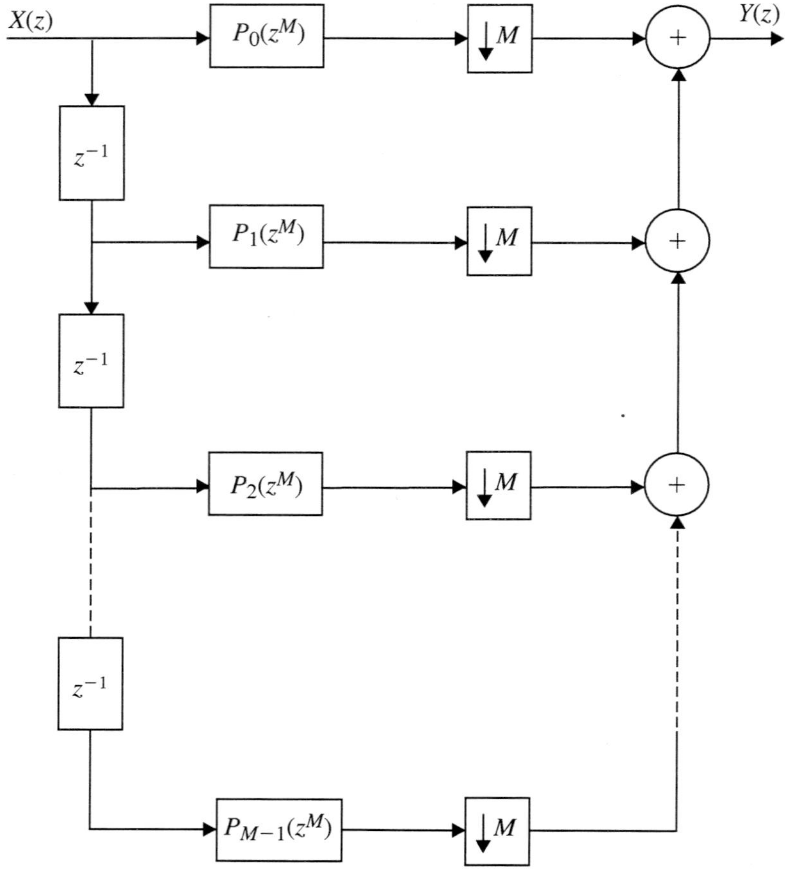

Figure 6.21 z-transform representation of polyphase decimation.

6.14.4 Polyphase Structure of an Interpolator Using *z*-transform

From equation (6.34), the transfer function of an interpolator is written by replacing M by L

$$\begin{aligned} H(z) &= \sum_{m=0}^{L-1} z^{-m} P_m(z^L) \qquad (6.40) \\ &= P_0(z) + z^{-1}P_1(z^L) + z^{-2}P_2(z^L) + \cdots \\ &\quad + z^{-(L-1)}P_{L-1}(z^L) \end{aligned}$$

The interpolator with the system function $H(z)$ is shown in Figure 6.25. Using fourth and sixth identities an efficient polyphase, structure of the interpolator is realized as shown in Figure 6.26.

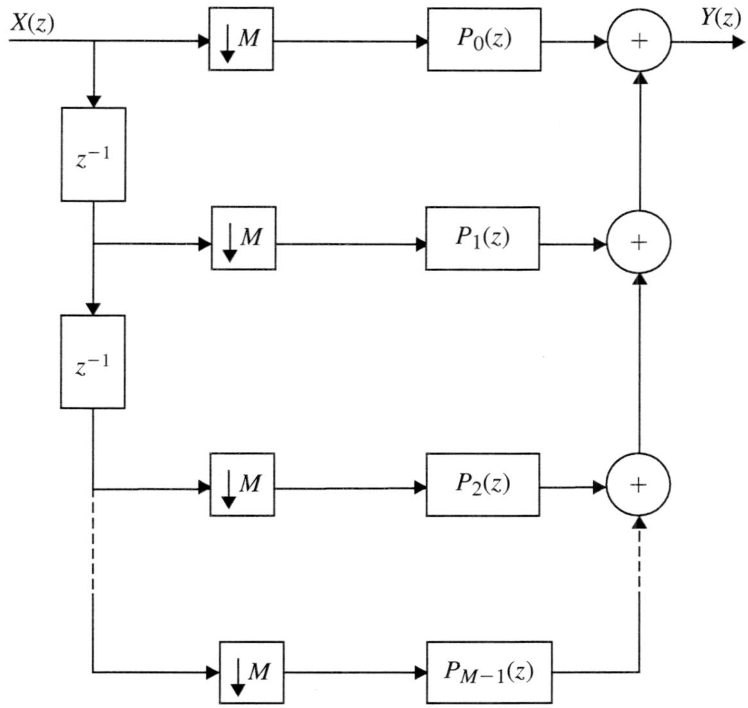

Figure 6.22 z-transform representation of polyphase decimation.

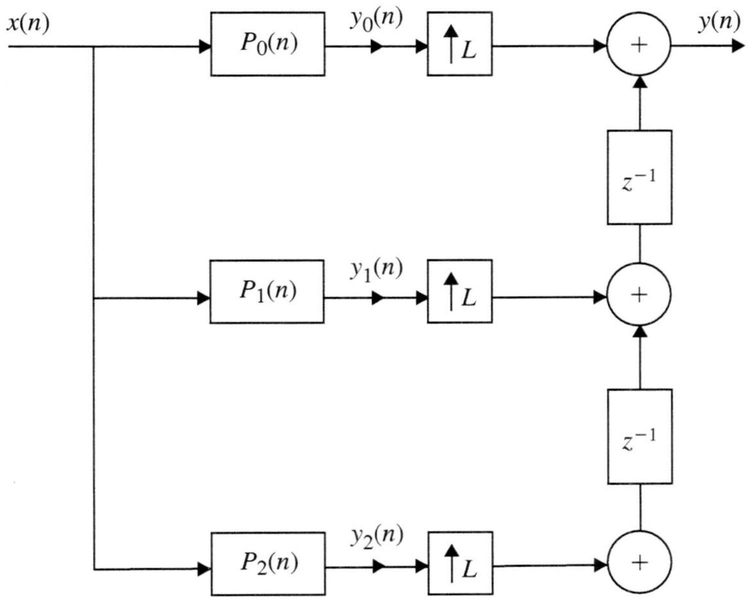

Figure 6.23 Polyphase structure of a three branch interpolator.

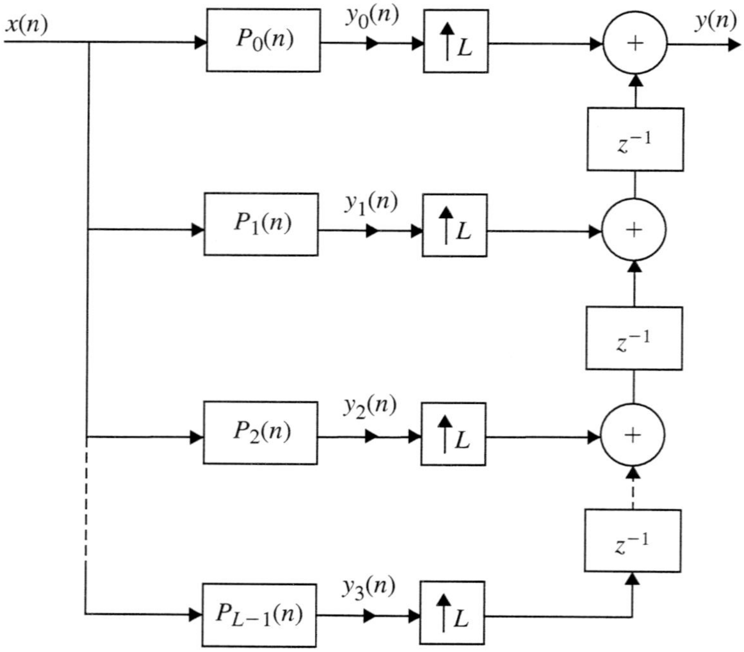

Figure 6.24 Polyphase structure of a L branch interpolator.

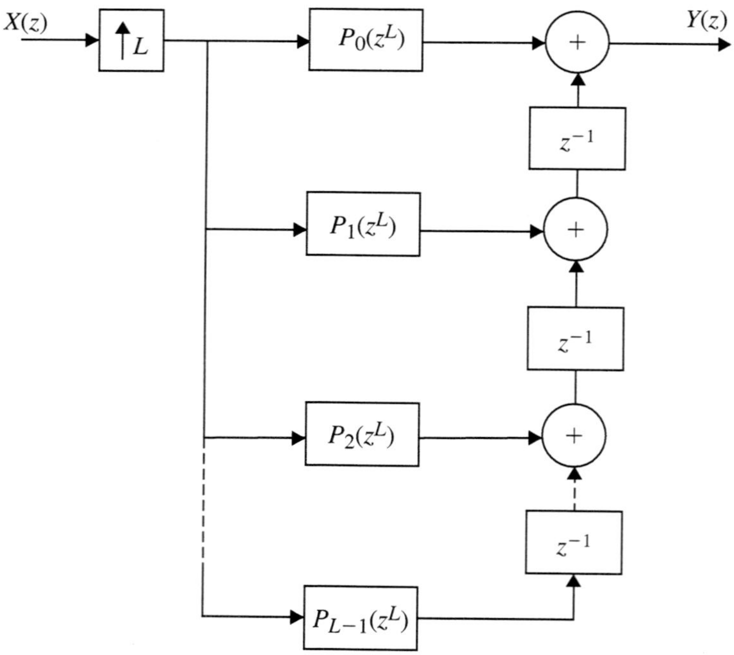

Figure 6.25 Polyphase structure of interpolator (z-transform representation).

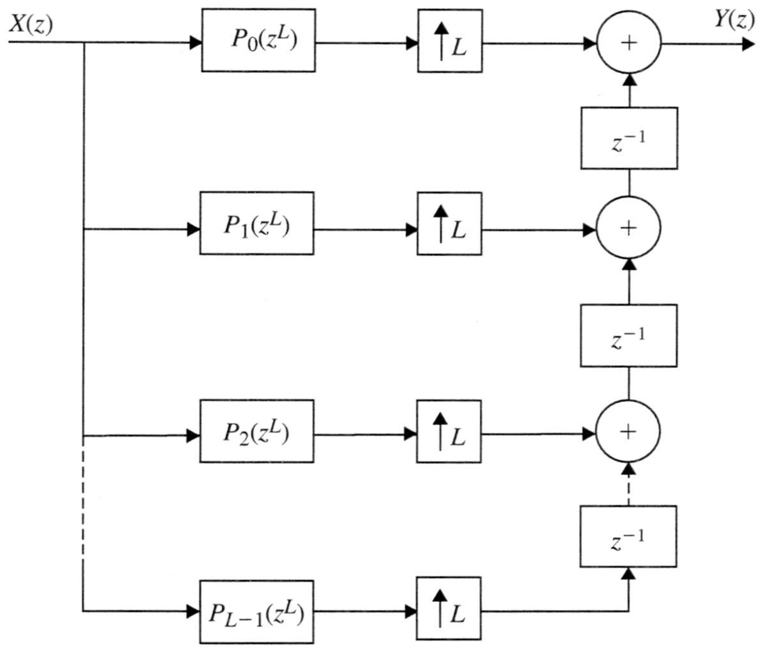

Figure 6.26 Efficient polyphase z-transform representation of interpolator.

Example 6.4

For the structure shown in figure, find the relationship between $x(n)$ and $y(n)$.

(Anna University, April, 2005)

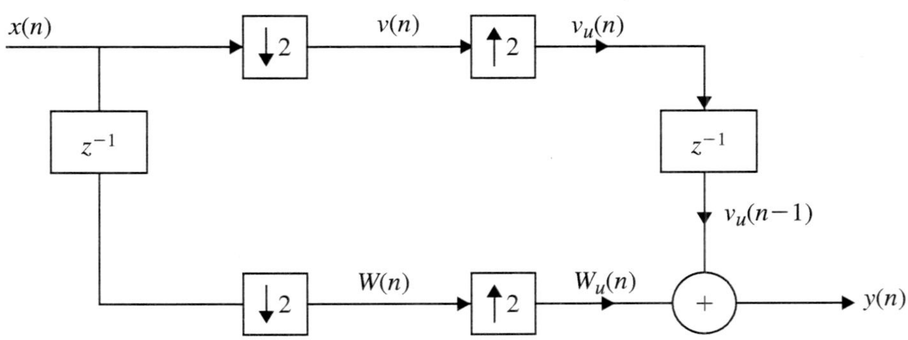

Figure 6.27 Structure for Example 6.4.

Solution The relations between various signal variables and the input are tabulated below:

n	0	1	2	3	4	5	6
$x(n)$	$x(0)$	$x(1)$	$x(2)$	$x(3)$	$x(4)$	$x(5)$	$x(6)$
$v(n)$	$x(0)$	$x(2)$	$x(4)$	$x(6)$	$x(8)$	$x(10)$	$x(12)$
$w(n)$	$x(-1)$	$x(1)$	$x(3)$	$x(5)$	$x(7)$	$x(9)$	$x(11)$
$v_u(n)$	$x(0)$	0	$x(2)$	0	$x(4)$	0	$x(6)$
$w_u(n)$	$x(-1)$	0	$x(1)$	0	$x(3)$	0	$x(5)$
$v_u(n-1)$	0	$x(0)$	0	$x(2)$	0	$x(4)$	0
$y(n)$	$x(-1)$	$x(0)$	$x(1)$	$x(2)$	$x(3)$	$x(4)$	$x(5)$

$$\begin{aligned} y(n) &= w_n(n) + v_n(n-1) \\ &= x(-1) + x(0) + x(1) + x(2) + x(3) + \cdots \end{aligned}$$

$$\boxed{y(n) = x(n-1)}$$

6.15 Polyphase Decomposition of IIR Transfer Function

The polyphase decomposition of IIR transfer function $H(z)$ is not that straight forward as that of FIR transfer function explained above. One approach is to decompose

$$H(z) = \frac{P(z)}{D(z)}$$

into $P'(z)/D'(z^M)$ by multiplying the denominator $D(z)$ and the numerator $P(z)$ by an appropriate polynomial. The M-branch polyphase decomposition is done for $P'(z)$. This is illustrated by the following example.

Example 6.5

Consider the following IIR transfer function:

$$H(z) = \frac{(1-3z^{-1})}{(1+4z^{-1})}$$

Obtain a two band decomposition with $M = 2$.

Solution

$$H(z) = \frac{(1-3z^{-1})}{(1+4z^{-1})}$$

Multiplying the numerator and the denominator by $(1 - 4z^{-1})$ we get

$$
\begin{aligned}
H(z) &= \frac{(1 - 3z^{-1})(1 - 4z^{-1})}{(1 + 4z^{-1})(1 - 4z^{-1})} \\
&= \frac{(1 - 7z^{-1} + 12z^{-2})}{(1 - 16z^{-2})} \\
&= \frac{(1 + 12z^{-2})}{(1 - 16z^{-2})} + z^{-1}\frac{(-7)}{(1 - 16z^{-2})} \\
&= E_0(z^2) + E_1(z^2)
\end{aligned}
$$

where

$$
E_0(z) = \frac{(1 + 12z^{-1})}{(1 - 16z^{-1})}
$$

$$
E_1(z) = \frac{-7}{(1 - 16z^{-1})}
$$

6.16 Cascading of Upsampler and Downsampler

The sampling rate alteration devices change the sampling rate of signal by an integer. If fractional change in the sampling rate is required, it is possible to achieve this by cascading an upsampler with downsampler without any change in the input-output relation. Consider the cascade structure shown in Figure 6.28(a). The following equations are written.

$$
V_1(z) = X(z^2) \tag{6.41}
$$

$$
Y_1(z) = \frac{1}{M}\sum_{k=0}^{M-1} V_1(z^{1/M} W_M^{-k}) \tag{6.42}
$$

where $W_M = e^{-j2\pi/M}$.

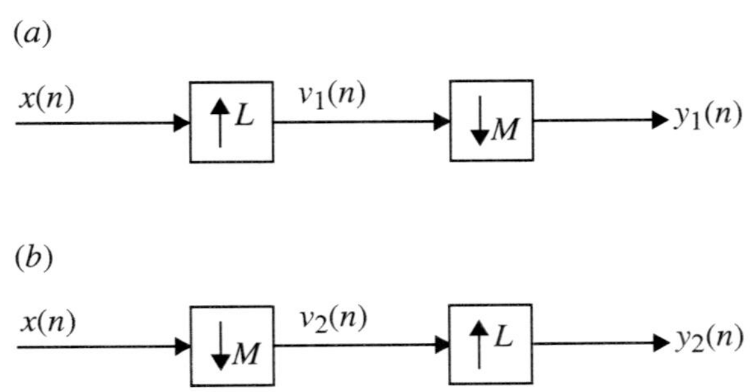

Figure 6.28 Cascading of up and downsamplers.

Combining the above two equations we get

$$Y_1(z) = \frac{1}{M} \sum_{k=0}^{M-1} X(z^{L/M} W_M^{-kL}) \tag{6.43}$$

Now consider Figure 6.28(b). The following equations are written:

$$V_2(z) = \frac{1}{M} \sum_{k=0}^{M-1} X(z^{L/M} W_M^{-k}) \tag{6.44}$$

$$Y_2(z) = V_2(z^L) \tag{6.45}$$

Combining equations (6.44) and (6.45) we get

$$Y_2(z) = \frac{1}{M} \sum_{k=0}^{M-1} X(z^{L/M} W_M^{-k}) \tag{6.46}$$

For $Y_1(z) = Y_2(z)$, the following conditions is to be satisfied.

$$\sum_{k=0}^{M-1} X(z^{L/M} W_M^{-kL}) = \sum_{k=0}^{M-1} X(z^{L/M} W_M^{-k}) \tag{6.47}$$

Equation (6.47) is valid iff M and L do not have a common factor which is an integer greater than one.

6.17 Multi-stage Rating of Sampling Rate Conversion

Single stage sampling rate conversion is inefficient if the decimation factor M or interpolation factor L are very much greater than unity. If $M \gg 1$ or $L \gg 1$, sampling rate conversion is done in multi-stage. The multi-stage conversion where $M \gg 1$ is represented in Figure 6.29. The decimation factor M is expressed as a product of positive integers as given below:

$$M = \prod_{k=1}^{N} M_k \tag{6.48}$$

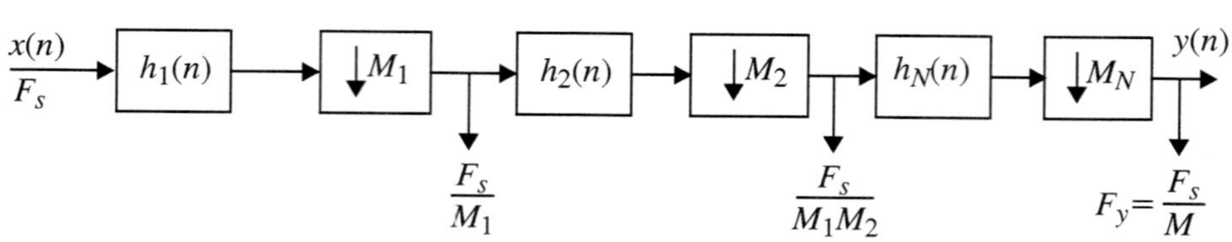

Figure 6.29 Multi-stage implementation of sampling rate conversion for $M \gg 1$.

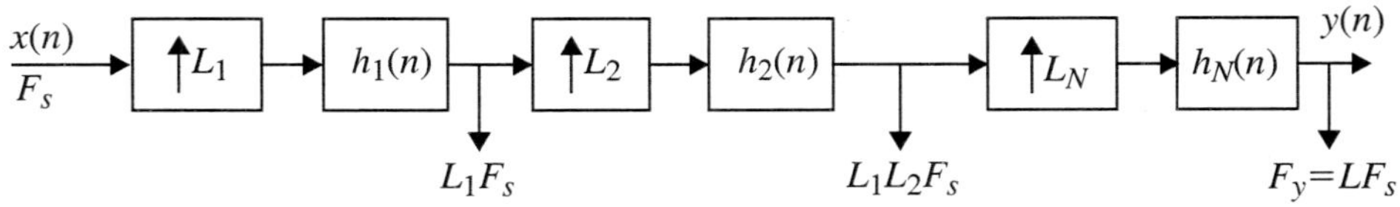

Figure 6.30 Multi-stage implementation of sampling rate conversion for $L \gg 1$.

Each decimator is implemented and cascaded to get N stages as shown in Figure 6.29. The final sampling rate achieved is

$$F_y = \frac{F_s}{M}$$

where $M = M_1 M_2 \ldots M_N$.

Similar to multi-stage downsampling multi-stage upsampling is done in N stages. Here, the final sampling rate achieved is

$$F_y = LF_s.$$

For $L \gg 1$, this is represented in Figure 6.30. The interpolation factor is expressed as

$$L = \prod_{k=1}^{N} L_k$$

6.18 Implementation of Narrow Band Low Pass Filter

A narrow band filter is identified with a narrow pass band and a narrow transition band. It requires a very large number of filter coefficients and therefore finite word length effect occurs in such a digital filter design. Further it requires more number of computations and memory locations. To overcome these problems, multi-rate signal processing is applied using decimator and interpolator, which are connected in cascade as shown in Figure 6.31. The sampling rate of the sequence $x(n)$ is reduced by a factor M and low pass filtering is preformed. The sampling rate of the output sequence $y(n)$ is increased by a factor M. Thus, the sampling rates of $x(n)$ and $y(n)$ are the same which is F_s. The filters in decimator $h_1(n)$ and interpolator $h_2(n)$ are chosen to be identical with pass band ripple $\delta_{p/2}$ and stop band ripple $\delta_{s/2}$ to get the desired specification of a narrow band LPF.

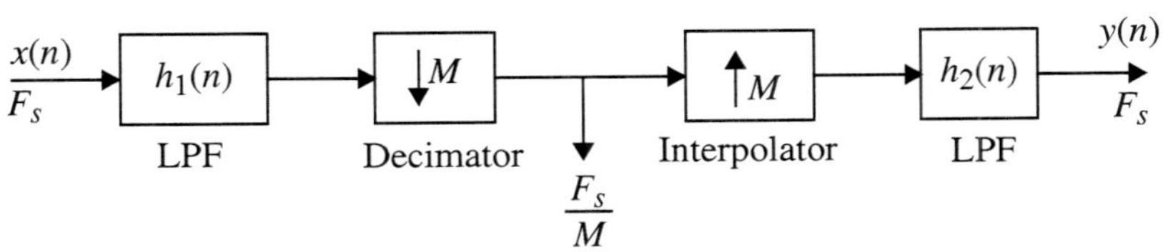

Figure 6.31 Implementation of narrow band LPF.

Example 6.6

The block diagram of a three stage decimator (Figure 6.32) which is used to reduce the sampling range from 96 kHz to 1 kHz is given. Assuming decimation factors of 8, 6, 2, indicate the sampling rate at the output of each of the three stages.

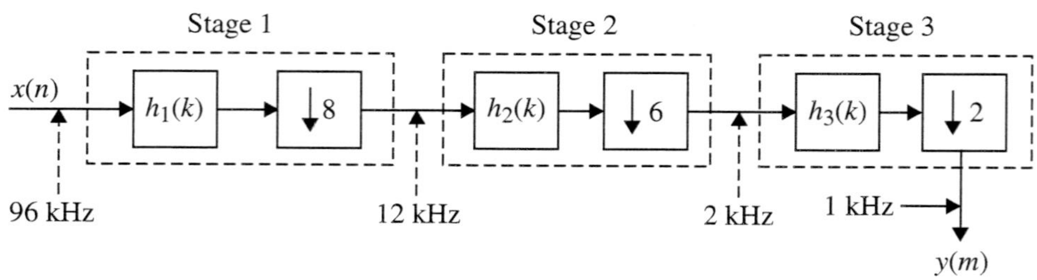

Figure 6.32 Three stage decimator for Example 6.6.

Solution

- At the first stage sampling rate is reduced by a factor of 8 from 96 kHz to 12 kHz.
- At the second stage sampling rate is further reduced by a factor of 6 from 12 kHz to 2 kHz.
- At the third stage the sampling rate is reduced by a factor of 2 from 2 kHz to 1 kHz.

Example 6.7

Assume that the decimator in Example 6.6 satisfies the following overall specifications.

$$\begin{aligned}\text{Input sampling frequency } F &= 96\,\text{kHz}\\ \text{Decimator factor } M &= 96\\ \text{Pass band ripple } &= 0.01\,\text{dB}\\ \text{Stop band ripple } &= 60\,\text{dB}\\ \text{Frequency band of interest} &= 0 - 450\,\text{kHz}\end{aligned}$$

Determine band edge frequency for the decimating filter at each stage.

Solution The pass band edge frequency of each of three decimating filters is the same (namely 455 Hz) to preserve the frequency band of interest.

The stop band edge frequencies are different to exploit the differences in the sampling rate. The band stop frequencies are given by the relation as,

$$f_{si} = F_i - \frac{F_s}{2M}, \qquad 1, 2, 3$$

Stage One:

$$\begin{aligned} f_{s_1} &= 12 - \frac{96}{2 \times 96} \\ &= 11.5\,\text{kHz} \end{aligned}$$

Thus, band edge frequencies are 0, 450 kHz, 11.5 kHz, 48 kHz.

Stage Two:

$$\begin{aligned} f_{s_2} &= 2 - \frac{96}{2 \times 96} \\ &= 1.5\,\text{kHz} \end{aligned}$$

Thus, band edge frequencies are 0, 450 kHz, 1.5 kHz, 6 kHz.

Stage Three:

$$\begin{aligned} f_{s_3} &= 1 - \frac{96}{2 \times 96} \\ &= 0.5\,\text{kHz} \end{aligned}$$

Thus, band edge frequencies are 0, 450 kHz, 0.5 kHz, 1 kHz.

Example 6.8

Assume that the input and output sampling rate of a decimator are 96 kHz and 1 kHz respectively:

(i) Write down the overall decimator factor.
(ii) Write down all the possible sets of integer decimation factor (written in descending order only) assuming two stages of decimation.
(iii) Repeat *(ii)* but assuming three stages of decimation.
(iv) Repeat *(iii)* but assuming four stages of decimation.

Solution

(i) Overall decimator factor is $96/1$ or $8 \times 6 \times 2 = 96$.
(ii)

$$48 \times 2$$

$$24 \times 4$$

$$12 \times 8$$

(iii)

$$24 \times 2 \times 2$$
$$6 \times 4 \times 4$$

(iv)

$$3 \times 2 \times 4 \times 4$$

Example 6.9

For the decimator in Example 6.6, calculate the total number of multiplications per seconds (MPs) and to storage requirement.

Solution

$$\text{MPs} = \sum_{i=1}^{I} N_i F_i$$

$$\text{TSR} = \sum_{i=1}^{I} N_i$$

where N_i is number of filter coefficients for 'i' stages.

$$\text{MPs} = N_1 \times 12 \times 10^3 + N_2 \times 2 \times 10^3 + N_3 \times 1 \times 10^3$$
$$\text{TSR} = N_1 + N_2 + N_3$$

6.19 Applications of MDSP

6.19.1 Speech Processing

The three main areas of speech processing are: (*i*) speech synthesis, (*ii*) speech recognition and (*iii*) speech coding.

(i) Speech Synthesis: In this a machine converting a piece of english text into a natural rounding text is developed.
Application: Speech output from computers, reading machine for the visually challenged, interrogating database from an ordinary telephone *etc.*

(ii) Speech Recognition: A system to recognize a speech from any speaker of a given language is developed.
Application: Telephone-banking, quality control, direct control of machines by human voice *etc.*

(iii) Speech Coding: It deals with the techniques which exploit the redundancy in the speech signal, to reduce the number of bits required to present it.
Application: Voice mail systems, telephone channel, military communications *etc.*

Speech Sounds

Speech sounds can be classified as: (*i*) voiced sounds, (*ii*) unvoiced on fricative sounds and (*iii*) plosive sounds. This is based on the mode of excitation due to which sounds are produced by vocal mechanism.

(i) Voiced Sounds: These are produced when the vocal cords vibrate in a relaxations mode. These vibrations can be obtained by forcing air through the glottis and adjusting the tension of the vocal cords and thereby producing quasi-periodic pulses of air which excite the vocal tract.

(ii) Fricative or Unvoiced Sounds: This is generated by forming a constriction at some point in the vocal tract and as air forced past it, turbulence occurs which causes a random noise excitation.

(iii) Plosive Sounds: For this sound, the vocal tract is closed at some point, the air pressure is allowed to build up and then suddenly released. The rapid release of this pressure provides a transient excitation of the vocal tract.

6.19.2 Speech Analysis

There are several methods for analysis of speech. But the following methods are commonly used:

1. Short time Fourier analysis
2. Cepstral analysis
3. Linear prediction analysis

6.19.2.1 Short Time Fourier Analysis

The short time Fourier transform of a signal $X_n(e^{j\omega})$ is expressed as,

$$X_n(e^{j\omega}) = \sum_{n=-\infty}^{\infty} x(m)\omega(n-m)e^{-j\omega n} \qquad (6.49)$$

where $X_n(e^{j\omega})$ – low pass representation of the signal in a band centered at ω_k and $\omega(n)$ – analysis window.

There are two common methods of implementing a short time spectral analysis. The first is by means of a filter bank which may be either implemented directly or the fast Fourier transform algorithm may be used. In this method the reconstructed signal is formed as

$$y(n) = \sum_{k=0}^{N-1} X_n(e^{-j\omega_k})e^{j\omega_k} \qquad (6.50)$$

In the second method, called the overlap addition method, the reconstructed signal is given by,

$$y(n) = \sum_{n=-\infty}^{\infty} \frac{1}{N} \sum_{k=0}^{N-1} Y_n(e^{-j\omega_k})(e^{j\omega_k n}) \tag{6.51}$$

where $Y_n(e^{-j\omega_k}) = X_n R(e^{j\omega_k})$ *i.e.*, windowed segments spaced by R samples in time and overlapped and added to produce the reconstructed signal.

6.19.2.2 Cepstral Analysis of Speech

Let $x(n)$ be the voiced speech signal, $e(n)$ excitation function and $h(n)$ the vocal tract impulse response. Then, the excitation function and the vocal tract impulse response are convolved to produce a speech signal which is given by,

$$x(n) = e(n) * h(n)$$

De-convolution of speech is carried out by the general non-linear filtering technique which is referred to as homomorphic filtering. In this method,the convolution operation is converted into addition giving the output known as complex cepstrum.

The system H_* in the Figure 6.33 is defined by the property that

$$\hat{X}(z) = \log X(z) \tag{6.52}$$

where $X(z) \rightarrow z$ transform of $x(n)$ and $\hat{X}(z) \rightarrow Z[\hat{x}(n)]$.

The system T is linear and the system H_*^{-1} is the inverse of the system H_*. If

$$x(n) = x_1(n) * x_2(n)$$

then

$$X(z) = X_1(z) * X_2(z)$$

Taking log on both sides we get

$$\log X(z) = \log X_1(z) + \log X_2(z)$$
$$\hat{X}(z) = \hat{X}_1(z) + \hat{X}_2(z)$$

Consequently

$$\hat{x}(n) = \hat{x}_1(n) + \hat{x}_2(n) \tag{6.53}$$

Therefore, the convolution of components are transferred to sum. The output of the system H_* is referred to as the complex cepstrum.

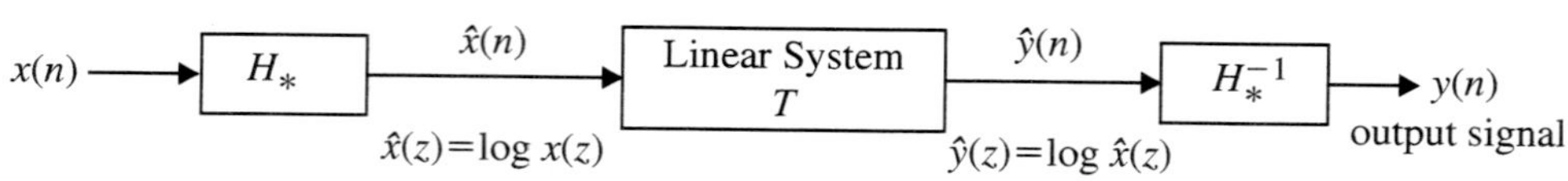

Figure 6.33 Cepstral analysis of speech signal.

6.19.2.3 Linear Prediction Analysis

It is a powerful and important speech processing technique. The basic concept is that sample values of speech, $x(n)$, can be approximated as a linear combination of the past p samples. Mathematically, it can be written as:

$$\begin{aligned}\tilde{x}(n) &= a_1x(n-1) + a_2x(n-2) + a_3x(n-3) + \cdots + a_px(n-p)\\ &= \sum_{k=1}^{p} a_kx(n-p), \quad n > 0. \end{aligned} \tag{6.54}$$

where $a_1,\ a_2, \ldots, a_p$ are prediction coefficients.

The difference between actual samples $x(n)$ and predicted sample $\tilde{x}(n)$ is known as prediction error $e(n)$ which is given by

$$\begin{aligned} e(n) &= x(n) - \tilde{x}(n), \quad n > 0\\ &= x(n) - \sum_{k=1}^{p} a_kx(n-k), \quad n > 0. \end{aligned} \tag{6.55}$$

The total mean squared error is expressed as

$$E_p = \sum_{n=1}^{N-1} e^2(n) = \sum_{n=1}^{N-1}\left[x(n) - \sum_{k=1}^{p} a_kx(n-k)\right]^2 \tag{6.56}$$

The parameter $\{a_k\}$ that minimizes E_p can be determined by partially derivating E_p with respect to each coefficient a_i, $i = 1, 2, \ldots, p$ and equating to zero. That is

$$\frac{\partial E_p}{\partial a_i} = -\alpha \sum_{n=1}^{N-1} x(n-i)\left[x(n) - \sum_{k=1}^{p} a_kx(n-k)\right] = 0 \tag{6.57}$$

Therefore,

$$\sum_{k=1}^{p} a_k \sum_{n=1}^{N-1} x(n-i)x(n-k) = \sum_{n=1}^{N-1} x(n)x(n-i)$$

where $i = 1, 2, \ldots, p$.

$$\sum_{n=1}^{N-1} a\varphi_{ik} = \varphi_{i0} \tag{6.58}$$

where $i = 1, 2, \ldots, p$.

$$\varphi_{ik} = \sum_{n=1}^{N-1} x(n-i)x(n-k) \tag{6.59}$$

and

$$\varphi_{i0} = \sum_{n=1}^{N-1} x(n)x(n-i). \tag{6.60}$$

6.19.3 Speech Coding

Speech coding is the application of data compression of digital audio signals containing speech. The two most important applications of speech coding are mobile telephony and voice over IP.

Speech coding differs from other forms of audio coding in that speech is a much simpler signal than most other audio signals and that there is a lot more statistical information about the properties of speech. As a result some auditory information which is relevant in audio coding can be unnecessary in the speech coding context. In speech coding, the most important criterion is preservation of intelligibility and pleasantness of speech with a constrained amount of transmitted data.

Different methods of speech coding techniques are:

1. Waveform coding (time domain).
2. Frequency domain coding.

6.19.3.1 Waveform Coding (Time Domain Coding)

Waveform codes attempt without using any knowledge of how the signal to be coded is generated to produce a reconstructed signal whose waveform is as close as possible to the original. That is they should be signal independent. They are low complexity codes which produce high quality speech at rates above 16K bits/s. Types of modulation used are:

(i) pulse code modulation
(ii) adaptive pulse code modulation
(iii) different pulse code modulation
(iv) adaptive differential pulse code modulation
(v) delta modulation
(vi)) adaptive delta modulation

6.19.3.2 Frequency Domain Coding

(i) Transform coding
(ii) Adaptive transform coding
(iii) Sub band coding

Transform Coding

Transform coding is a frequency domain technique. The transformation is typically lossy, resulting in a lower quality copy of original input. In transform coding knowledge of the application is used to choose information to discard thereby lowering its bandwidth.

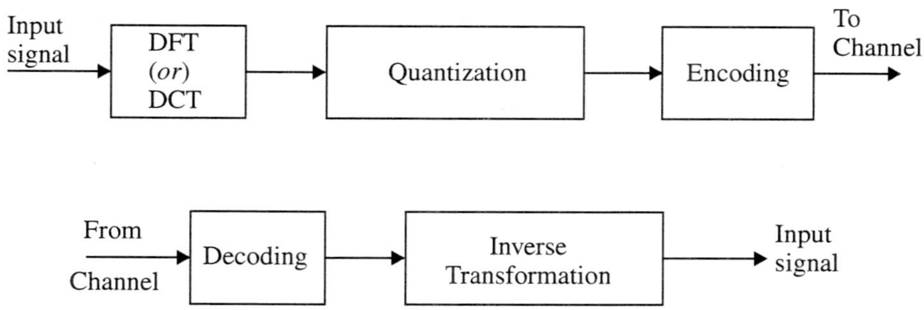

Figure 6.34 Block diagram representation of transform coding.

The block diagram representation of transform coding is shown in Figure 6.34. The input samples are taken and linearly transformed using DFT or DCT computation via a FFT algorithm. Then the transformation of the signal is efficiently coded by assigning bits to transform coefficients. At receiver, inverse transformation is used to reconstruct the speech signal. In transform coding the total no of bits available to quantize the transform coefficients remain constant to each coefficient changes from frame to frame.

This dynamic bit allocation is controlled by the time varying characteristics of speech,which has to be transmitted as side information. The side information is also used to determine the step size of the various coefficient quantizes. The number of bits assigned to each transform coefficient is proportional to its corresponding spectral energy value.

6.20 Sub-band Coding

Sub-band coding is a form of transform coding that breaks a signal into a number of different frequency bands by BPF and encodes each one independently. The basic idea of SBC is to enable a data reduction by discarding information about frequencies which are masked. The result differs from the original signal but if the discarded information is chosen carefully, the difference will not be noticeable. It can be illustrated with example – Human ears are normally sensitive to a wide range of frequencies, but when a sufficiently loud signal is present at one frequency, the ear will not hear weaker signals and we say that the louder signal mask the softer ones. The louder signal is called masker and the paint about which masking occurs is known as masking threshold. In sub-band coding the input signal is first split into member of non-overlapping frequency bands by bandpass filters and is shown in Figure 6.35.

The output of each bandpass filter is decimated or downsampled by a factor M. The output of decimator is quantized using the techniques like PCM, DPCM *etc.*, and transmitted to the receiver and decoded and then each sub-bands signal is interpolated by inverse sequence. The sub-bands are de-multiplexed and zeros are inserted to replace the samples discarded during decimation at the transmitter. The

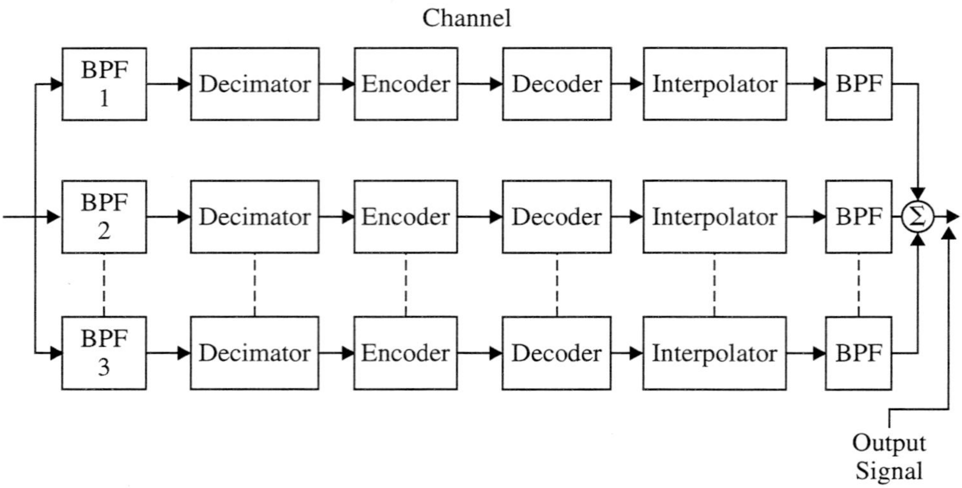

Figure 6.35 Block diagram of sub-band coding.

output of interpolator is applied to bandpass filters. All bandpass filter outputs are summed together to produce the original signal.

6.21 Vocoder

6.21.1 Channel Vocoder

$$\text{Vocoder} \rightarrow \text{Voice} + \text{Coder}$$

The channel vocoder consists of both an analyzer and a synthesizer. The analyzer consists of a number of bandpass filters with impulse response $\omega(n)\cos\omega_k n$ followed by a full wave rectifier and low pass filter. The rectifier and low pass filter serve as an envelope detector. In order to represent proper excitation for the speech signal, a channel vocoder has voiced and unvoiced detector and pitch detector. The resulting information, together with the amplitude of the signal forms the representations of the speech signal. These parameters are sampled and quantized. At the receiver a wide band excitation source is generated using voiced/unvoiced signal. The generator is used to switch in a random voice (for unvoiced speech) or a pulse generator (for voiced speech), with the fundamental frequency of the pulse generator being controlled by the pitch signal. The received channel signals are used to modulate the amplitude of the excitation signal, which excites the corresponding bandpass filter. The channel vocoder is illustrated in Figure 6.36. The bandpass filter outputs are summed to produce the speech signal.

6.21.2 Homomorphic Vocoder

In cepstral analysis of speech, the basic speech parameters are clearly displayed and isolated from one another, *i.e.*, the low frequency coefficients in the cepstrum

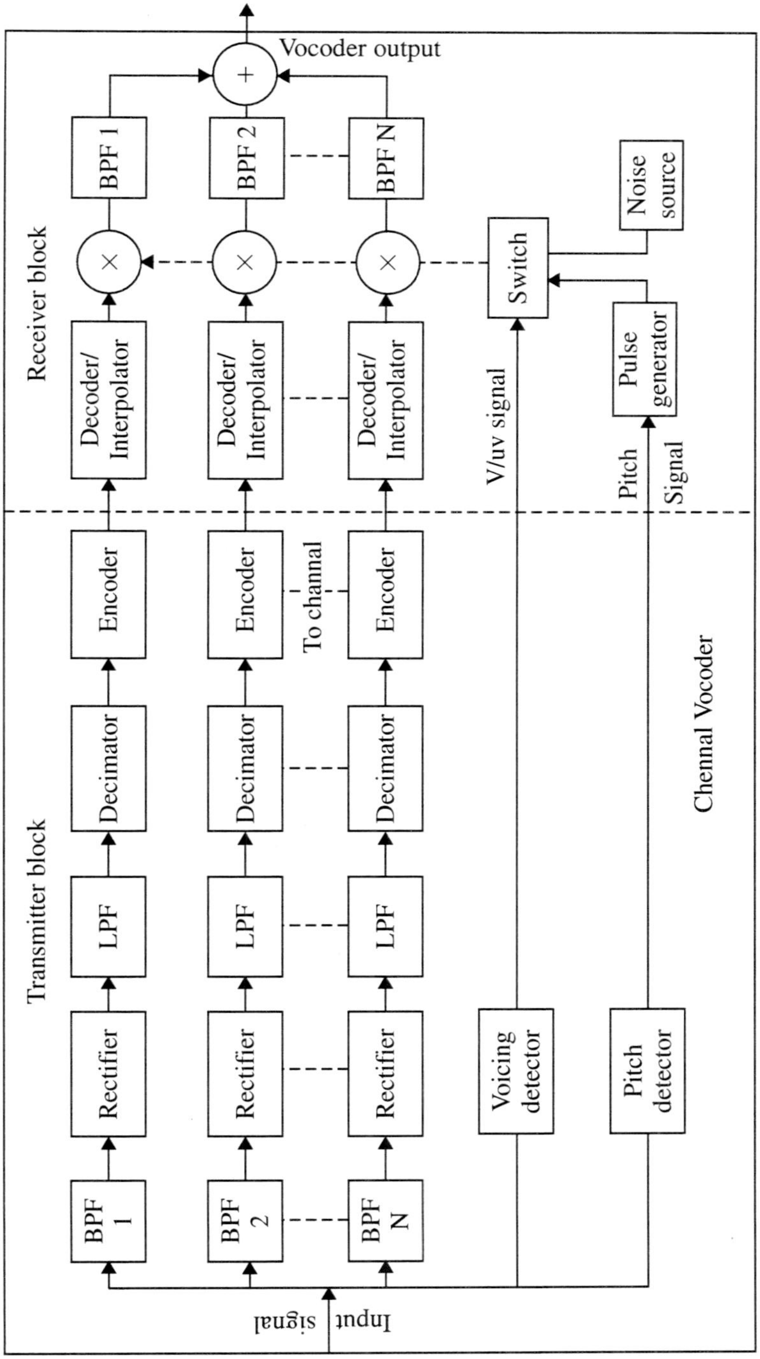

Figure 6.36 Channel vocoder.

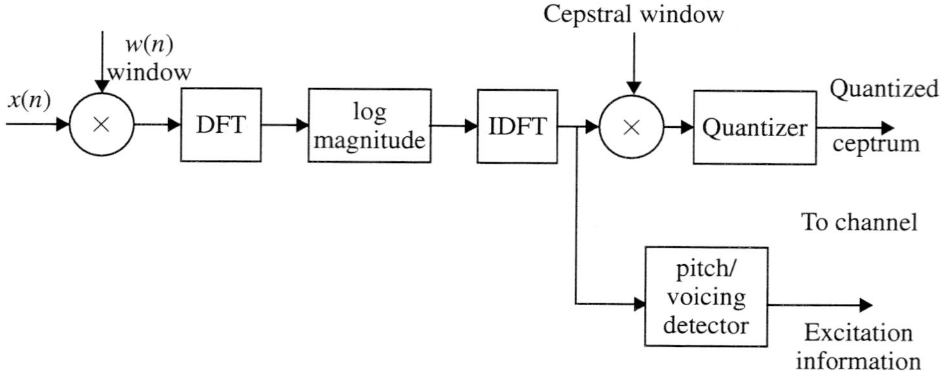

Figure 6.37 Homomorphic vocoder.

correspond to the vocal tract and the high frequency coefficients correspond to excitation information. In homomorphic vocoder, the cepstrum is computed once in every 10–20 sec. The vocal track cepstral coefficients are separated from the excitation coefficient by a linear filtering operation, which involves multiplying the cepstral coefficients by an appropriate window function. The block diagram of homomorphic vocoder is shown in Figure 6.37.

The excitation information together with the quantized cepstrum values are transmitted to the synthesizer. At synthesizer the vocal tract cepstral coefficients are Fourier transformed, exponentiated and inverse Fourier transformed to produce the vocal tract impulse response. By convolving this impulse response with a voiced/unvoiced signal the original speech is reconstructed.

6.22 Digital Signal Processing of Audio Signals

Digital signal processing has made an impact on several aspects of *audio engineering*, which encompasses the recording, storage, transmission and reception of signals. The signals include natural and electronic music, theatrical performance, natural sounds and cine songs.

6.22.1 Digital Tape Recording

The block diagram of digital tape recorder system is shown in Figure 6.38.

- Each input is applied to a low pass filter, which eliminates high frequency noise.
- The Output from the filter is sampled and converted into digital form by ADC.
- The bit streams are multiplexed. In addition, bit for timing, for correcting errors, parity checking and block scaling are introduced.
- The modulator is used to convert the composite bit streams into a series of analog pulses.
- During Reproduction the signal is decoded and distributed to each outputs.

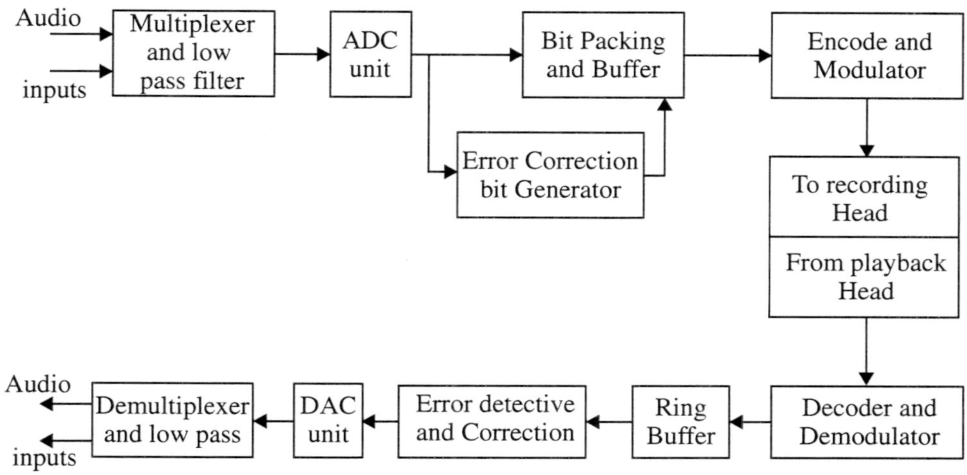

Figure 6.38 Block diagram of digital tape recorder system.

6.22.2 Advantages of Digital Recording

- High signal to noise ratio is limited only by ADC
- Absence of harmonic distortion
- No inter-channel cross talk
- Elimination of amplitude variation due to changes in magnetization of the tape

6.23 Radar Signal Processing

6.23.1 Radar

RADAR – Radio Detection And Ranging is a measuring instrument in which the echo of a pulse of microwave radiation is used to detect and locate distant objects.

RADAR Signal processing is an important application of Digital Signal Processing.

Principle

A RADAR dish/antenna sends out pulses of radio waves/microwaves. These waves bounce off any object in their path, and return to the dish, which detects them. The time it takes for the reflected waves to return to the dish enables a computer to calculate how far away the object is, its radial velocity and other characters. The basic principles involved include:

- Reflection,
- Polarization,
- Interference.

Instrumentation

A modern RADAR system which consists of a data processing system, control unit, signal generator, transmitting and receiving antenna, and matched filter is shown in Figure 6.39.

Working

- The *signal generator* provides test signal.
- This signal is converted into RF range and then amplified by the *modulator*.
- The RF signal is transmitted towards the target by the *transmitting antenna*. The reflected energy from the target can be used to measure target characteristics.
- The signal received is applied to a *demodulator* to convert it to baseband.
- The baseband signal is applied to a *signal processor* which performs *three* major signal processing functions:

  (1) *Matched Filtering* for the received waveforms.
  (2) *Thresholding* that reduces the data volume and rate to values that are appropriate for the data processing system (DPS).
  (3) *Estimation* of target position in range, angle and velocity.

- When the processing is done digitally, it is necessary to have an *analog pre-filter* and *ADC*.
- The *DPS*, a large general purpose computer co-ordinates all the activities of all parts of entire RADAR system.
- The *DPS* tells the signal generator what waveform to synthesize, position of radar antenna and specifies the signal processing algorithm to be used.
- The *control unit* decodes commands and provides the appropriate system timing.

Applications RADAR Signal Processing

- Distance measurement.
- Speed measurement.
- Reduction of radar interface effect.
- Plot and track extraction—to discard spurious and interfering signals.
- Air traffic control.
- Weather mapping.

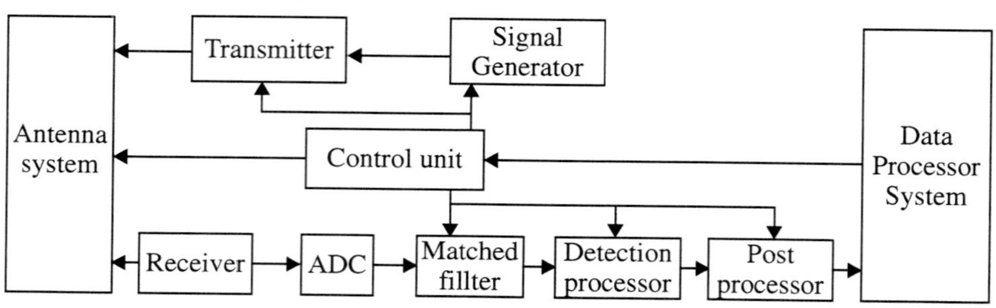

Figure 6.39 Block diagram of modern radar system.

- Ship navigation, military systems.
- Detection of speed of automobiles by police.

6.24 DSP Based Measurement Systems

The introduction of DSP techniques in modern instrumentation and measurement systems has given them the *capacity of implementing different functions on same hardware architecture.* The block diagram of DSP based measurement system is shown in Figure 6.40.

It consists of

- *Anti-aliasing filter:* It removes the possible aliasing results.
- *Amplifier:* It amplifies the output of the anti-aliasing filter.
- *A/D conversion unit:* It converts the input signals into a digital representation, with the resolution and sampling rate required by the correct execution of the measurement algorithm.
- *DSP unit:* This block performs the measurement algorithm by specified time slot.

In DSP based measurement systems, a measurement process is associated with *a dedicated algorithm* that is implemented on the *same general purpose computing system.* By changing the algorithm, the same computing system performs new measuring process.

Features of DSP Based Instruments

- They can combine information coming from many different transducers.
- They can implement complex measurement algorithms.
- They can work under strict environmental conditions and correct measurement results according to actual working conditions.
- These instruments have capability of networking, self-calibration and self-monitoring.
- High integration capability.

Merits

- Improved instrument performance.
- Cost effective.

They are highly suitable for automatic testing equipment.

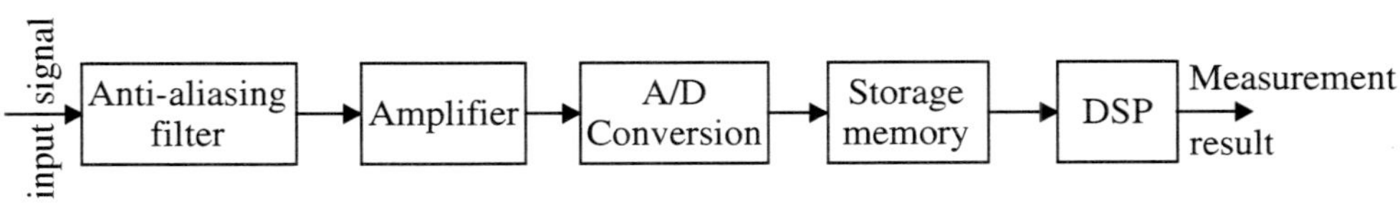

Figure 6.40 Block diagram of DSP based measurement systems.

6.25 Speech Compression

Speech compression of signals has many practical applications such as fixed or mobile digital telephony, pocket network transmitter (internet), video conferencing, radio and television and various storage applications. In digital cellular technology many users share the same frequency bandwidth. Compression allows more users to share the system than otherwise possible. For a given memory size compression allows longer messages to be stored than otherwise. Thus, the aim of speech compression is to produce a compact representation of speech sounds such that when reconstructed it is perceived to be close to the original. The two main measures of closeness are intelligibility and naturalness.

Digital speech signals were normally sampled at a rate of 8000 samples per second. Typically each sample is represented by 8 bits using mu-law. This corresponds to an uncompressed rate of 64 kbps. With current compression technique it is possible to reduce the rate to 8 kbps with almost no perceptible loss in quality. Further compression is possible at a cost of lower quality. All the current low-rate speech coders are based on the principle of linear perceptive coding (LPC). To obtain more compression with quality reproduction, specific properties of the speech signal must be modelling. The main assumption is known as the source filter model of speech production. This assumes that a source (voicing) is passed through a filter (the vocal tract response) to produce the speech. At every frame the speech is analysed to compute the filter coefficients, the energy of the excitation, a voicing decision, and a pitch value it voiced. At the decoder a regular set of pulses of voiced speech or white noise for unvoiced speech is passed through the linear filter and multiplied by the gain to produce the speech. This is a very efficient system and typically produces speech coded at 1200–2400 bps. With clever acoustic vector prediction this can be reduced to 300–600 bps. The disadvantages are a loss of naturalness over most of the speech and occasionally a loss of intelligibility.

Narrowband speech is defined as speech filtered in continuous time in the frequency band (300–3200 Hz), and then sampled at 8 kHz. Narrowband speech is usually called "speech" in the telephony band and is used in the second generation of mobile telephony. Narrowband speech coding makes it possible to obtain a reconstructed speech signal with sufficient quality for telephony. However the reconstructed signal does not have a natural consonance and may sound metallic or even synthetic. It is sometimes difficult to distinguish two fricative consonants.

Wideband speech is defined as the speech filtered in continuous time, in frequency band (5,07,000 Hz) and then sampled at 16 kHz. The interest of processing a wideband speech signal is to obtain a reconstructed signal that is clearer, more natural and intelligible than narrowband speech.

There is a great diversity of speech coding techniques. Wave form coders use Pulse Code Modulation (PCM) or Adaptive Differential PCM (ADPCM). These coders make it possible to obtain an excellent quality of the reconstructed signal but generally result in a low compression ratio. Other techniques such as those based on CELP (Code Excited Linear Prediction) use a coding scheme carrying out analysis–by–synthesis and are based on speech production and perception models. Such coders result in a reconstructed signal of good quality with a higher compression ratio.

ESPLAB has worked for a long time in software and hardware implementation of various narrowband speech coding functionalities. With the diffusion of multimedia technologies and the introduction of services for the 3rd and 4th generations of mobile telephony, wideband speech coding became a prevailing research field and ESPLAB has developed a proprietary multi-rate wideband speech coder.

6.26 Musical Sound Processing

Musical sound processing is one of the many applications of digital signal processing. All musical programmers are produced basically in two stages. First, sound from each individual instrument is recorded in an acoustically inert studio on a single track of a multi-track tape and recorder. Then the signals from each track are manipulated by the sound engineer to add special audio effects and are combined to in a mix down system to finally generate the stereo recording on a two track tape recorder. The audio effects are artificially generated using various signal processing circuits and devices, and they are increasingly being performed using digital signal processing techniques. They can be done by Time-Domain and Frequency-Domain operations.

For years musicians have been using different techniques to give their music a unique sound. Some of these techniques were found by accident, while others were found after a lot of work and experimentation. While the effects have not changed much in the past few years, the ways in which these effects are produced have. In recent years there has been a movement away from analog signal processing towards digital signal processing of music. This movement has allowed for very precise and easily reproduced effects.

Audio signals are two types. One is speech signal which is used in variety of applications such as telephony and video telephony and the other is music-quality audio which are extensively used in applications such as CD-on-demand and broadcast television. Audio signals are produced either naturally or electronically using a synthesizer. When the synthesizer is used, the audio signal is converted into digital form and stored. In the case of an analog signal it should be converted into a digital form using an audio signal encoder. To get the music or speech from a loudspeaker which is analog in nature, the digitized values must be inverted into analog form using an audio signal decoder.

The bandwidth of a typical speech signal is from 50 Hz through 10 kHz and that of the music signal from 15 Hz through to 20 kHz. The sampling rate for these signals should be in excess of the Nuquist rate. Hence, for speech signal the sampling rate should be greater than 20 ksps and for music it should be above 40 ksps. The quantization noise generated by the sampling process, the number of bits per sample for speech is chosen as 12 and for music it is chosen as 16. Further, in applications involving music stereophonic sound is used the bit rate should be doubled since two such signals are to be digitized. However in practice, in music, the sampling rate is often lowered in order to reduce the amount of memory that is required to store a particular passage of music.

6.26.1 CD-Quality Audio

The digital storage devices that are used for stereophonic music and multimedia are CD players and CD-ROMs. As stated earlier, music has an audible bandwidth of from 15 Hz through to 20 kHz and therefore requires the minimum sampling rate of 40 ksps. In practice it is chosen slightly higher to allow for imperfections in the band limiting filter used. One of the sampling rates used is 44.1 ksps for which the signal is to be sampled at 23 microsecond intervals. With 16 bits per sample, linear quantization can be used which gives 65536 equal quantization intervals. The recording of music requires two separate channels.

$$\begin{aligned}\text{Bit rate per channel} &= \text{Sampling rate} \times \text{Bits per sample}\\ &= 44.1 \times 10^3 \times 16\\ &= 705.6\,\text{kbps}\end{aligned}$$

For two channels,

$$\begin{aligned}\text{Total bit rates} &= 2.705.6\\ &= 1.411\,\text{Mbps}\end{aligned}$$

This is also the bit rate used with CD-ROMs.

6.26.2 Synthesized Audio

The digitized music signal is stored within a computer. However the memory required is very large. To reduce the storage capacity, the audio signal is synthesized and then stored in the computer. By this the amount of memory saved is between two and three orders. Further, it is much easier to edit synthesized audio and to mix several passes together.

It consists of a computer, the keyboard and a set of sound generators. The computer takes the input command from the keyboard and the output from the computer is given to the sound generators which produce sound wave forms. The key on the keyboard of the synthesizer has the same effect of the computer keyboard. From each key when pressed a message is sent indicating which key on the keyboard is pressed and the pressure applied. The control panel contains a range of switches and sliders through which additional information such as the volume of the generated output and sound effects are sent to the computer. The secondary storage interface allows the sequence of messages to be stored. It is used to mix several stored passes together. The sequencer program associated with the synthesizer ensures that the resulting sequence of messages are synchronized and given as the input to the sound generators to which speakers are attached.

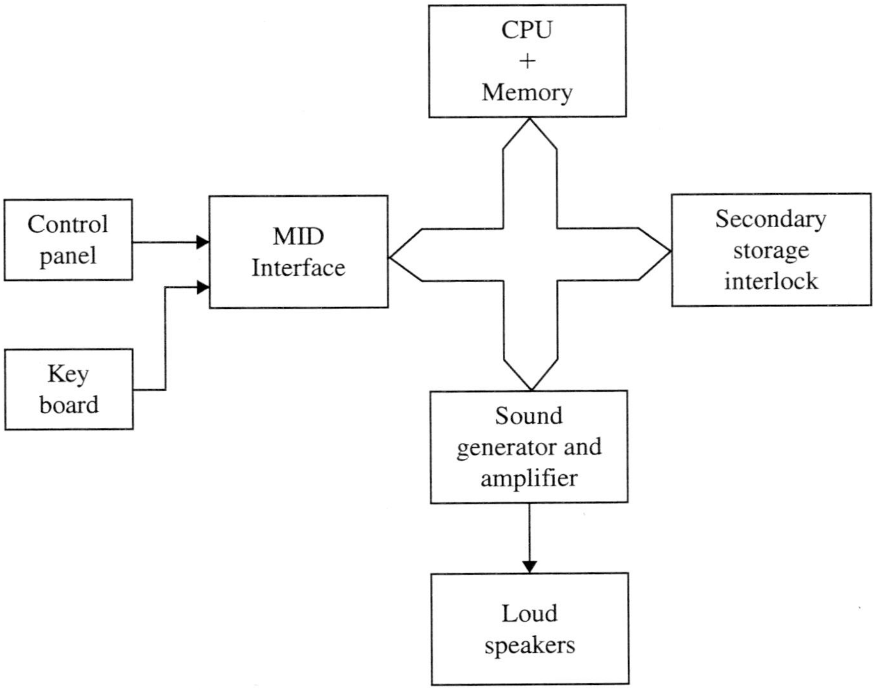

Figure 6.41 Audio/sound synthesizer.

6.27 Adaptive Filters

In Chapters 3 and 4, IIR and FIR filters design was discussed which requires the knowledge of second order statistics of the signals. However in applications such as channel equalization, echo cancellation and system modelling to mention a few these statistics cannot be specified a prior. In such applications digital filters with adjustable coefficients are designed. These filters have self-adjusting characteristics and therefore they are called as ADAPTIVE FILTERS. These filters are widely used in communication systems, control systems, adaptive antenna systems, digital communication receivers, adaptive noise cancelling technique, *etc.* An adaptive filter has the property that it automatically adjusts or modifies its frequency response characteristics according to the changes in the input signal characteristics. These filters are also used when there is spectral overlap between the signal and noise is unknown. In these cases the conventional filters would lead to distortion of the desired signal.

6.27.1 Concepts of Adaptive Filtering

An adaptive filter consists of two distinct parts and they are:

1. A digital filter with adjustable coefficients.
2. An adaptive algorithm which is used to adjust or modify the coefficients.

In almost all adaptive systems, FIR digital filter is used since it has simple structure and stability is guaranteed. Only in limited applications, IIR or lattice filter is used. Adaptive algorithms commonly used are:

1. Least Mean Square (LMS) algorithm
2. Recursive Least Square (RLS) algorithm

There are many configurations of adaptive filter. Some of them include the following:

1. Adaptive noise canceller
2. Adaptive self tuning filter
3. Adaptive line enhancer
4. System modeling
5. Linear combiner

The above configurations are described below.

6.27.2 Adaptive Noise Canceller

The block diagram of an adaptive filter as a noise canceller is shown in Figure 6.42.

The input signals x_k and y_k are simultaneously applied. x_k is the noise y_k contains the desired signal s_k polluted with noise n_k. The noise x_k is processed by the digital filter and gives out the estimate $\bar{n}_k$ of n_k. An estimate of the desired signal is obtained by subtracting the digital filter output $\bar{n}_k$ form y_k. From Figure 6.42 the following equation is written.

$$\bar{s}_k = y_k - \bar{n}_k = s_k + n_k - \bar{n}_k \tag{6.61}$$

From equation (6.61), it is evident that optimum estimate of the desired signal s_k is obtained by producing an optimum estimate of the noise in the polluted signal. This is achieved by feeding the signal estimate $\bar{s}_k$ to the adaptive filter which adjusts the digital filter coefficients. By using suitable adaptive algorithm, the noise in $\bar{s}_k$ is minimized. Thus the output signal $\bar{s}_k$ is used as an estimate of the desired signal s_k and also as an error signal which is used to adjust the filter coefficients.

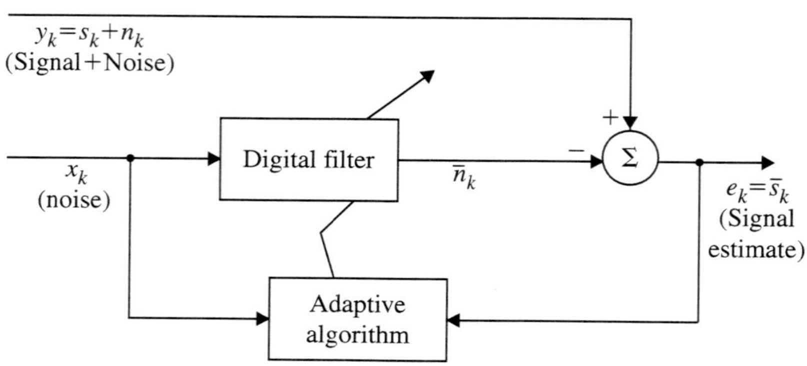

Figure 6.42 Block diagram of an adaptive filter as a noise canceller.

The configurations of adaptive self-tuning filter, adaptive line enhancer, adaptive system modelling and adaptive linear combiner are shown in Figures 6.43(*a*), (*b*), (*c*) and (*d*) respectively.

6.27.3 Main Components of the Adaptive Filter

In most of the systems, the digital filter shown in Figure 6.42 is used. The output can be obtained as

$$\bar{n}_k = \sum_{i=0}^{N-1} w_k(i)x_{k-i} \tag{6.62}$$

where $w_k(i),\ i = 0, 1 \ldots,$ are the adjustable filter coefficients or the weights, and $x_k(i)$ and $\bar{n}_k$ are the input and output of the filter. Figure 6.44 shows the single input–signal output system.

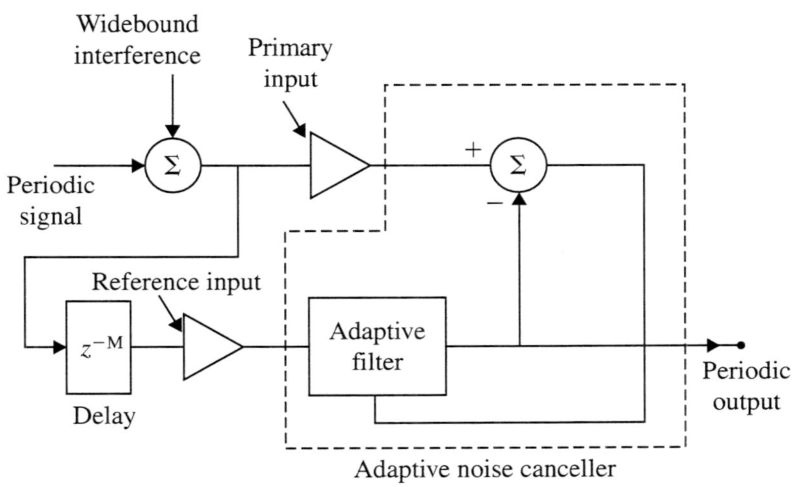

Figure 6.43 (*a*) Adaptive self-tuning filter.

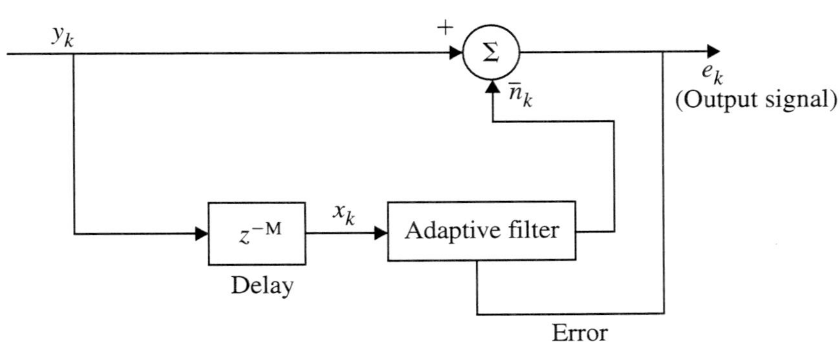

Figure 6.43 (*b*) Adaptive line enhancer.

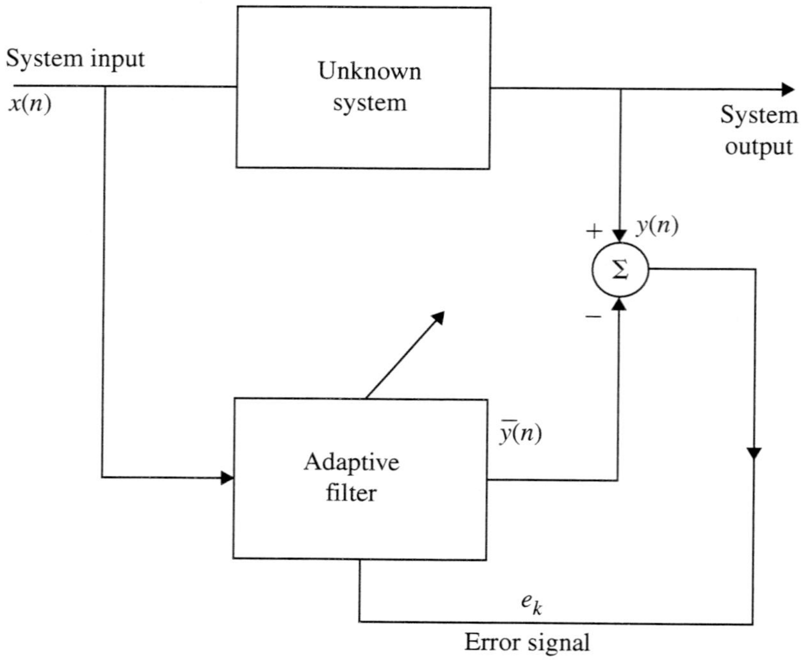

Figure 6.43 (*c*) System modelling.

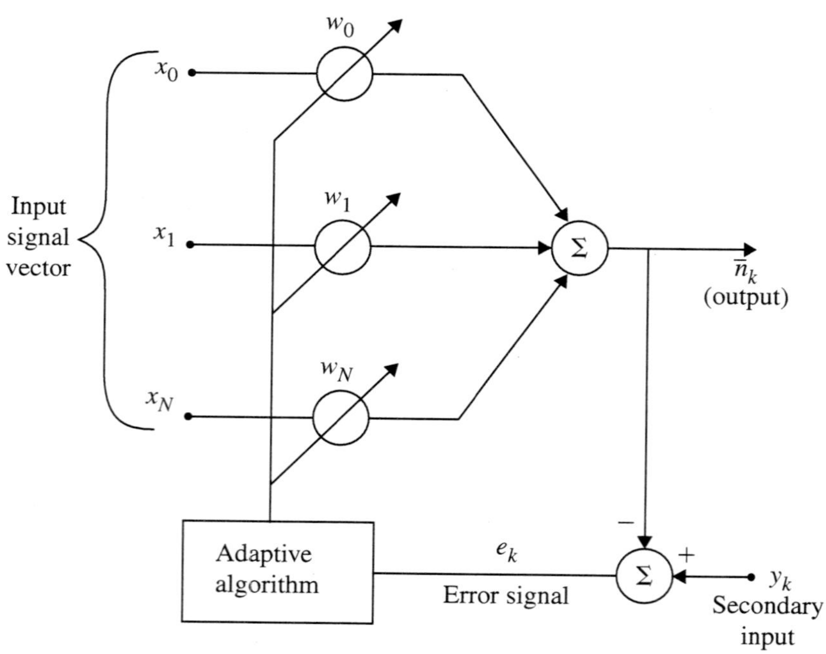

Figure 6.43 (*d*) Adaptive linear combiner.

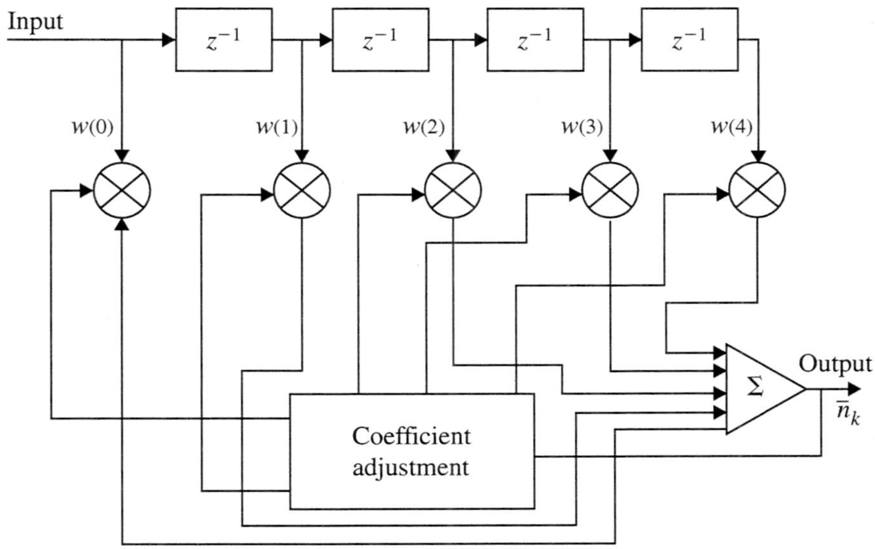

Figure 6.44 Direct form adaptive FIR filter.

6.27.4 Adaptive Algorithms

Adaptive algorithms are used to adjust or modify the coefficients of digital filter so that the error signal e_k is minimized to meet certain constraints. The most commonly used algorithms in adaptive filters are:

1. Least Mean Square (LMS) algorithm
2. Recursive Least Squares (RLS) algorithm
3. Kalman Filter algorithm

LMS algorithm is the most efficient algorithm in terms of computation and storage requirements. It also does not suffer from numerical instability problem which is inherently present in other two algorithms. However, RLS algorithm has superior convergence properties. In the section to follow LMS and RMS algorithms are described.

6.27.4.1 Least Mean Square (LMS) Algorithm

In LMS algorithm the coefficients of the digital filter are adjusted from sample to sample in such a way as to minimize the Mean Square Error (MSE). The weight vectors are updated from sample to sample as given below:

$$W_{k+1} = W_r - \mu \nabla_k \tag{6.63}$$

where W_k and ∇_k are the weights and true gradient vectors respectively at the kth instant and μ controls the stability and rate of convergence. The LMS algorithm aims at getting the digital filter weight W_k. The LMS algorithm for updating the weights from sample to sample as suggested by Widow-Hopf is given by

$$W_{k+1} = W_r + 2\mu e_k X_k \tag{6.64}$$

where

$$e_k = y_k - W_x^T x_k \tag{6.65}$$

where x_k is the input vector. The weights obtained by the LMS algorithm are only the estimates which gradually improve with time as the weights are adjusted and the filter learns the characteristics of the signals and finally the weights converge with the following condition.

$$0 < \mu < \frac{1}{\lambda_{\max}} \tag{6.66}$$

where $\lambda_{\max}$ is the maximum eighn value of the input data matrix. The computational procedure for the LMS algorithm is summarized below.

1. Initially, set each weight $w_k(i) = 0, 1, \ldots, N-1$ to an arbitrary fixed value. For subsequent sampling instant k, carry out the following steps.
2. Compute filter output
$$\bar{n}_k = \sum_{i=0}^{N-1} w_k(i) x_{k-i}$$
3. Compute the error estimate
$$e_k = y_k - \bar{n}_k$$
4. Update the next filter weights
$$w_{k+1}(i) = w_k(i) + 2\mu e_k x_{k-i}$$

The LMS algorithm requires approximately $2N + 1$ multiplications and $2N + 1$ addition for each new set of input and output samples. Modern DSPs are very much suited for direct implementation of LMS algorithm. The simplicity and ease of implementation make the LMS algorithm of first choice in many real time systems. The flow chart of LMS algorithm is given in Figure 6.45.

6.27.4.2 *Recursive Least Squares Algorithm*

The major advantage of the LMS algorithm is its simplicity in computation. However, if the eigenvalues of the auto correlation matrix has a large spread, convergence becomes very slow which is a major disadvantage of LMS algorithm. Further the algorithm has a single adjustable parameter for controlling the convergence rate. To obtain the faster convergence more than one adjustable parameters are required. In recursive least squares algorithm for each eigenvalue one parameter is chosen and convergence becomes faster. However the algorithm becomes more complex.

The RLS algorithm is based on the least squares method which is illustrated in Figure 6.46. From Figure 6.37, the following equation connecting the input and output is written:

$$y_k = \sum_{i=0}^{n-1} w(i) x_k(i) + e_k \tag{6.67}$$

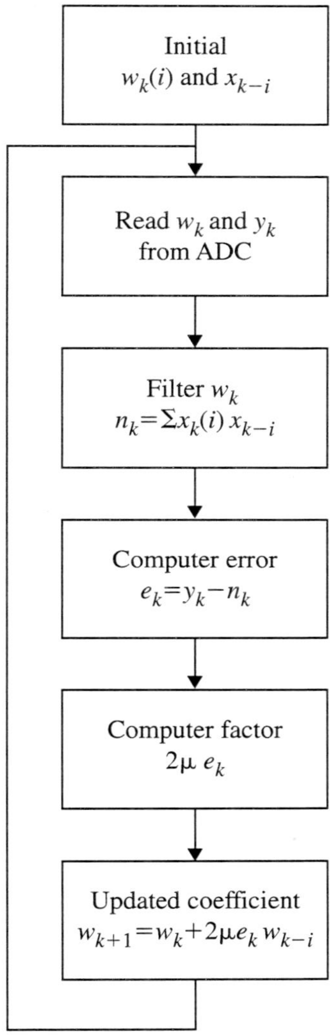

Figure 6.45 Flow chart for LMS adaptive filter.

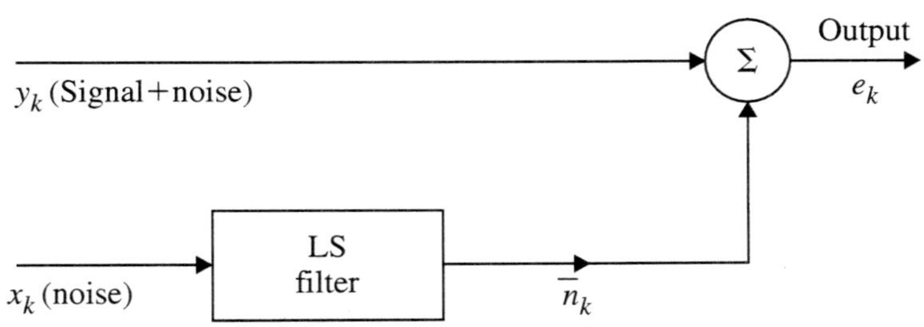

Figure 6.46 Illustrations of RLS.

where e_k is the error, $w(i)$ is the weight of the ith input and y_k is the primary signal which contains noise. In the least square method, the objective is to estimate $w(o)$ to $w(n-1)$ given $x_k(i)$ and y_k. For the filter weight $w(i)$, the optimum estimates are given as

$$W_m = [X_m^T X_M]^{-1} X_m^T Y_m \tag{6.68}$$

where W_m, X_m and Y_m are given by

$$Y_m = \begin{bmatrix} y_0 \\ y_1 \\ y_2 \\ \cdots \\ y_{m-1} \end{bmatrix}; \qquad X_m = \begin{bmatrix} X^T(0) \\ X^T(1) \\ X^T(2) \\ \cdots \\ X^T(m-1) \end{bmatrix}; \qquad W_m = \begin{bmatrix} w(0) \\ w(1) \\ w(2) \\ \cdots \\ w(n-1) \end{bmatrix}$$

The filter output is obtained as

$$\bar{n}_k = \sum_{i=0}^{n-1} \bar{w}(i) x_{k-i}, \qquad k = 1, 2, \ldots, m \tag{6.69}$$

In equation (6.55), the estimates of W_m is obtained using recursive method. Here, the estimates of W_m are updated for each new set of data acquired. A suitable RLS algorithm is obtained by exponentially weighting the data to remove gradually the effects of old data on W_m. Thus, the following equation is written:

$$W_k = W_{k-1} + G_k e_k \tag{6.70}$$

$$P_k = \frac{1}{\gamma}[P_{k-1} - G_k X^T P_{k-1}] \tag{6.71}$$

where

$$G_k = \frac{P_{k-1} X(k)}{\alpha_k} \tag{6.72}$$

$$e_k = y_k - X^T(k) W_{k-1} \tag{6.73}$$

$$\alpha_k = \gamma + X^T(k) P_{k-1} X(k) \tag{6.74}$$

In equation (6.71) P_k represents recursive way of computing $[X_k^T X_k]^{-1}$. k represents that the quantities are obtained at each sample when k is varied and gamma is called the forgetting factor.

The main limitation of RLS algorithm is its sensitivity to computer round off errors which leads to instability.

6.28 Image Enhancement

By image enhancement we mean that the appearance of the image is improved either by increasing the dominance of certain features or by decreasing the ambiguity in different regions of the image. The enhancement of certain features can be achieved by the following techniques:

1. Contrast intensification
2. Noise cleaning and smoothing
3. Edge sharpening or crispening

Image enhancement approaches are divided into two broad categories namely spatial domain methods and frequency domain methods. Spatial domain refers to the image plane itself and the approaches are based of manipulating of pixels in an image. On the other hand frequency domain processing techniques are based on modifying the Fourier transform of an image. Spatial domain refers to the aggregate of pixels composing an image. Spatial domain processes are denoted by the following expression.

$$G(x, y) = T[f(x, y)]$$

where $f(x, y)$ is the input image and $g(x, y)$ is the processed image and T is an operator on f. On the other hand, in frequency domain the operators are called filters. Filtering in the frequency domain consists of the following steps:

1. Multiply the input image by $(-1)^{x+y}$
2. Compute $F(u, v)$, the DFT of the image form (1)
3. Multiply $F(u, v)$ by a filter function $H(u, v)$
4. Compute the inverse DFT of the result in (3)
5. Obtain the real part of the result in (4)
6. Multiply the result in (5) by $(-1)^{x+y}$

If $f(x, y)$ represents the input image in step1 and $F(u, v)$ it's FT, then FT of the output image is given by

$$G(u, v) = H(u, v)F(u, v)$$

The filtered image is obtained using the following equation

$$\text{Filtered image} = F^{-1}[G(u, v)]$$

The filtering procedure is represented in Figure 6.47.

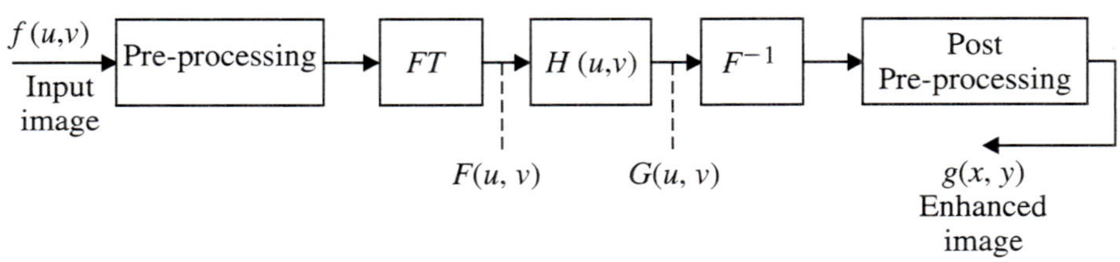

Figure 6.47 Image enhancing in frequency domain.

6.28.1 Contrast Intensification

Poor contrast is one of the common defects found in recorded image. Because of inadequate lighting, non-linear mapping and aperture size the degradation may be caused. The Contrast can be improved by scaling the gray level of each pixel. This operation is called histogram stretching. Other types of stretching used for image enhancement include linear stretching and fuzzy property modification.

The defects in the recorded image is reflected on the gray level histogram. In stretching, the transformation function is used to map the input gray level to the output gray level. In linear stretching the transformation function is used in the form of a straight line. This linear transformation function stretches the gray level range of the input image such that it occupies the entire dynamic range. The slope of the transformation function should be much greater than one for image enhancement. If the slope is one, there won't be any enhancement.

Non-linear stretching is used when the gray level histogram contains large number of pixels in the lower gray level zone of the grey scale. This portion is stretched more while the higher gray level zone is compressed. Here, logarithmic type of transformation function is used. This type of transformation is also useful when image grey level occupies a wide dynamic range. Square root, cube root or in general *n*th root non-linear transformation functions are normally used.

The technique used in Fuzzy property modification is based on the modification of pixel values in fuzzy domain. Image enhancement is obtained by decreasing the membership values which are below 0.5 and increase those which are above 0.5.

6.28.2 Histogram Specification

Image enhancement is achieved by mapping the input gray levels such that the processed gray level histogram attains a desired shape. This technique is called histogram equilibrium. From the input shape of gray level histogram the overall appearance of the image is obtained. The positively skewed gray level histogram looks brighter than an image with a negatively skewed gray level histogram since the positively skewed gray level histogram image has more number of pixels having high gray values than that in negatively skewed gray level histogram image.

6.28.3 Local Contrast Stretching

The linear and non-linear stretching and the histogram equilibrium described above are global. Here, the pixel intensities are modified by transformation function. However, the contrast over a small region is very poor and therefore image enhancement by global transformation of gray level has little scope. It is therefore necessary to stretch the contrast over a small area. This is achieved by the technique called local contrast stretching. In this method, the transformation function amplifies the difference between the gray level of the concerned pixel and the local brightness and at the same time preserving the local brightness level. Thus, the local contrast of the image is greatly increased and the smoothness of the existing regions is maintained.

6.28.4 Smoothing

Smoothing operations are used to remove the effect of noise and blur the false contours that may be present in a digital image. Detection and recording errors, transmission channel noise, digitization error or a combination of the above produce these unwanted effects. When the noise is removed using smoothing techniques, it will degrade the sharpness. Smoothing algorithm in the spatial domain is developed as given below:

$$G(x,y) = f(x,y) + \eta(x,y)$$

where $n(x,y)$ represents the additive noise. In matrix vector notation, the above equation is written as follows.

$$g = f + \eta$$

The transformation matrix T_m which is given by the following equation will reduce the unwanted noise.

$$g(x,y) = T_m[g(x,y), Q(x,y)]$$

where $Q(x,y)$ is the set of gray levels of the neighboring pixels.

6.28.5 Image Sharpening

Blurring is one thing which degrades the image. It attenuates high spatial frequency components. The decoded image can be enhanced by differentiation in spatial domain. The gray level image $\bar{g}(x,y)$ may be written as

$$\bar{g}(x,y) = \Delta^2 g(x,y)$$

where Δ^2 is Laplacian second order derivative operator. By adding gray values of the observed image with the negative of the Laplacian, the equation for the crisp end is obtained as

$$\bar{g}(x,y) = g(x,y) - \Delta^2 g(x,y).$$

From the above equation, it is clear that the sharpened image $\bar{g}(x,y)$ contains only the enhanced edges and the gray levels of all smooth regions are unaffected.

Summary

- Multi-rate signal processing has many applications in which the given sampling rate is converted into another signal with a different sampling rate.
- The two basic sampling rate alteration devices are the up-sampler and the down-sampler.
- To down-sample a signal it is essential to pass the signal through an anti-aliasing LPF to band limit the signal before it is applied to the decimator.
- If an interpolator is used to up sample a signal, it is essential that the output of the signal from the interpolator is passed through a LPF to avoid removal of some of the desired frequency components of the sampled signal.
- The up sampler and down-sampler possess the property of linearity and time variancy.

- If F_s is the sampling rate of the sequence $x(n)$, the down-sampled signal will have the sampling rate $\frac{F_s}{M}$ and the up sampled signal will have the sampling rate LF_s.
- If a signal $x(n)$ is down-sampled by a factor M and then up sampled by a factor L, then the sampling rate conversion is L/M which is a rational factor.
- Sampling rate conversion can be more efficiently done using polyphase decomposition. This reduces computational complexity.
- Some of the applications of MDSP include speech processing, vocoder, digital tape recording, radar signal processing *etc.*

Short Questions and Answers

1. **What do you understand by down-sampling?**
   Down-sampling is the process of creating an output sequence $y(n)$ from the input sequence $x(n)$ using a down-sampler with a sampling factor of M where M is a positive integer. The down-sampling operation is implemented by keeping every Mth sample of the input sequence $x(n)$ and removing $(M-1)$ in between samples. The input–output are related by the following equation

$$y(n) = x(nM)$$

2. **What do you understand by up-sampling?**
   Up-sampling is the process of sampling rate alteration in which the sampling rate of the output sequence is L times larger than that of the input sequence where L is a positive integer, which is called up-sampling factor. Here, $(L-1)$ equidistant zero valued samples between two consequential samples of the input sequence are inserted. The input–output are related by the following equation.

$$y(n) = \begin{cases} x\left(\frac{n}{L}\right), & n = 0, \pm L, \pm 2L, \cdots \\ 0, & \text{otherwise} \end{cases}$$

3. **What is a Decimator?**
   The decimator consists of two blocks. The input sequence is applied to a low pass filter followed by down-sampler. The LPF is used to avoid aliasing. When both these blocks are connected in cascade the unit is called decimator.
4. **What is an Interpolator?**
   The process of up sampling is done by an up sampler and a LPF which are connected in cascade. The LPF removes unwanted images from the signal. The up-sampler together with LPF is called an Interpolator.
5. **What is sampling rate conversion?**
   The process of converting a signal from a given sampling rate to a different sampling rate is called sampling rate conversion.

6. **What is a multi-rate systems?**
Discrete time system with unequal sampling rates at various parts of the system are called multi-rate systems.
7. **What is aliasing?**
When the signal $x(n)$ is down-sampled, the plot of the frequency response of the output $Y(e^{j\omega})$ has an overlap and the original shape of the input $X(e^{j\omega})$ is lost. This is aliasing. If $X(e^{j\omega})$ is zero for $|\omega| \geq \frac{\pi}{2}$ there is no aliasing. To avoid aliasing the signal is first sent through anti-aliasing LPF and then the band limited signal is down-sampled.
8. **What is anti-imaging filter?**
The frequency response of an up-sampled signal $y(n)$ with a factor L, contains $(L-1)$ additional images of the input spectrum. These images are due to the addition of $(L-1)$ zero samples inserted by the up sampler between successive samples of $x(n)$. To eliminate this image spectra a LPF with a cut off frequency of π/L is connected in cascade with the up sampler.
9. **How decimators and interpolators are classified in respect of linearity and time invariancy?**
Both decimators and interpolator are classified as linear and time varying.
10. **What is the necessary condition to be satisfied for connecting up-sampler and down-sampler in cascade?**
The necessary condition for connecting the up-sampler and down-sampler in cascade is that the decimation and interpolation factor M and L are relatively prime. This implies that M and L do not have a common factor that is an integer which is greater than one.
11. **Mention some of the applications of MDSP.**
The applications of MDSP include the following:

    (*a*) Speech processing
    (*b*) Wave for coding
    (*c*) Vocoder
    (*d*) Digital tape recording
    (*e*) Radar signal processing, antenna system and communication system

12. **What are the advantages of MDSP?**
The advantages of using MDSP are:

    (*a*) In general processing it reduces the transmission rate of speech data.
    (*b*) In data acquisition and storage systems signal of different bandwidth which require different sampling frequencies are efficiently handled without anti-aliasing analog filters.
    (*c*) MDSP efficiently implements DSP functions.

13. **What is sub-band coding?**
Sub-band coding is a form of transform coding that breaks a signal into a number of different frequency bands by BPF and encodes each one independently.

Long Answer Type Questions

1. Explain the need for multi-stage implementation of sampling rate conversion.
2. Explain clearly the down-sampling and up-sampling in multi-rate signal processing.
3. Explain sampling rate reduction by an integer factor M and derive input–output relationship in both time and frequency domains.
4. Explain sampling rate increase by an integer factor L and derive input–output relationship in both time and frequency domains.
5. Propose a scheme for a sampling rate conversion by a rational factor L/M where L is the up-sampling integer factor and M is the down-sampling integer factor.
6. Prove that decimator and interpolators are linear and time varying.
7. Derive the spectrum of the output of a decimator.
8. Derive the spectrum of the output of a interpolator.
9. Explain the aliasing effect in the down-sampling process if the original spectrum is not band limited to $|\omega| = \pi/M$.
10. Explain the identities used in multi-rate processing.
11. Discuss the efficient transversal structure for decimator and interpolator.
12. Explain the polyphase decomposition for FIR filter structure.
13. Explain filter design and implementation (structure) for sampling rate conversion system.
14. What is sub-band coding? Draw a block diagram of sub-band coding of speech and audio signal and explain?
15. Explain Vocoder.
16. With the help of block diagram, explain the modern radar system.
17. With the help of block diagram, explain the digital tape re-coder system.

Index